48: *American Poets, 1880-1945*, Second Series, edited by Peter Quartermain (1986)

49: *American Literary Publishing Houses, 1638-1899*, 2 parts, edited by Peter Dzwonkoski (1986)

50: *Afro-American Writers Before the Harlem Renaissance*, edited by Trudier Harris (1986)

51: *Afro-American Writers from the Harlem Renaissance to 1940*, edited by Trudier Harris (1987)

52: *American Writers for Children Since 1960: Fiction*, edited by Glenn E. Estes (1986)

53: *Canadian Writers Since 1960*, First Series, edited by W. H. New (1986)

54: *American Poets, 1880-1945*, Third Series, 2 parts, edited by Peter Quartermain (1987)

55: *Victorian Prose Writers Before 1867*, edited by William B. Thesing (1987)

56: *German Fiction Writers, 1914-1945*, edited by James Hardin (1987)

57: *Victorian Prose Writers After 1867*, edited by William B. Thesing (1987)

58: *Jacobean and Caroline Dramatists*, edited by Fredson Bowers (1987)

59: *American Literary Critics and Scholars, 1800-1850*, edited by John W. Rathbun and Monica M. Grecu (1987)

60: *Canadian Writers Since 1960*, Second Series, edited by W. H. New (1987)

61: *American Writers for Children Since 1960: Poets, Illustrators, and Nonfiction Authors*, edited by Glenn E. Estes (1987)

62: *Elizabethan Dramatists*, edited by Fredson Bowers (1987)

63: *Modern American Critics, 1920-1955*, edited by Gregory S. Jay (1988)

64: *American Literary Critics and Scholars, 1850-1880*, edited by John W. Rathbun and Monica M. Grecu (1988)

65: *French Novelists, 1900-1930*, edited by Catharine Savage Brosman (1988)

66: *German Fiction Writers, 1885-1913*, 2 parts, edited by James Hardin (1988)

67: *Modern American Critics Since 1955*, edited by Gregory S. Jay (1988)

68: *Canadian Writers, 1920-1959*, First Series, edited by W. H. New (1988)

69: *Contemporary German Fiction Writers*, First Series, edited by Wolfgang D. Elfe and James Hardin (1988)

70: *British Mystery Writers, 1860-1919*, edited by Bernard Benstock and Thomas F. Staley (1988)

Documentary Series

1: *Sherwood Anderson, Willa Cather, John Dos Passos, Theodore Dreiser, F. Scott Fitzgerald, Ernest Hemingway, Sinclair Lewis*, edited by Margaret A. Van Antwerp (1982)

2: *James Gould Cozzens, James T. Farrell, William Faulkner, John O'Hara, John Steinbeck, Thomas Wolfe, Richard Wright*, edited by Margaret A. Van Antwerp (1982)

3: *Saul Bellow, Jack Kerouac, Norman Mailer, Vladimir Nabokov, John Updike, Kurt Vonnegut*, edited by Mary Bruccoli (1983)

4: *Tennessee Williams*, edited by Margaret A. Van Antwerp and Sally Johns (1984)

5: *American Transcendentalists*, edited by Joel Myerson (1988)

Yearbooks

1980, edited by Karen L. Rood, Jean W. Ross, and Richard Ziegfeld (1981)

1981, edited by Karen L. Rood, Jean W. Ross, and Richard Ziegfeld (1982)

1982, edited by Richard Ziegfeld; associate editors: Jean W. Ross and Lynne C. Zeigler (1983)

1983, edited by Mary Bruccoli and Jean W. Ross; associate editor: Richard Ziegfeld (1984)

1984, edited by Jean W. Ross (1985)

1985, edited by Jean W. Ross (1986)

1986, edited by J. M. Brook (1987)

1987, edited by J. M. Brook (1988)

Concise Series

The New Consciousness, 1941-1968 (1987)

Colonization to the American Renaissance, 1640-1865 (1988)

Realism, Naturalism, and Local Color, 1865-1917 (1988)

Concise Dictionary of American Literary Biography

The New Consciousness, 1941-1968

Dictionary of Literary Biography

Documentary Series

Yearbooks

Concise Series

Concise Dictionary of American Literary Biography

The New Consciousness, 1941-1968

A Bruccoli Clark Layman Book
Gale Research Company • Book Tower • Detroit, Michigan 48226

Advisory Board for
CONCISE DICTIONARY
OF AMERICAN LITERARY BIOGRAPHY

Matthew J. Bruccoli and Richard Layman, *Editorial Directors*
C. E. Frazer Clark, Jr., *Managing Editor*

Manufactured by Edwards Brothers, Inc.
Ann Arbor, Michigan
Printed in the United States of America

Library of Congress Cataloging-in-Publication Data

The new consciousness, 1941-1968

(Concise dictionary of American literary biography)
(A Bruccoli Clark Layman book)
  1. American literature—20th century—History and criticism. 2. American literature—20th century—Bio-bibliography. 3. Authors, American—20th century—Biography—Dictionaries. I. Title. II. Series: Concise dictionary of American literary biography.
PS225.A44 1987 810'.9'0054 [B] 86-33657
ISBN 0-8103-1822-9

Contents

Plan of the Work

The six-volume *Concise Dictionary of American Literary Biography* was developed in response to requests from high school and junior college teachers and librarians, and from small- to medium-sized public libraries, for a compilation of entries from the standard *Dictionary of Literary Biography* chosen to meet their needs and their budgets. The *DLB*, which comprises nearly eighty volumes as of the end of 1986, is moving steadily toward its goal of providing a history of literature in all languages developed through the biographies of writers. Basic as the *DLB* is, many librarians have expressed the need for a less comprehensive reference work which in other respects retains the merits of *DLB*. The *Concise DALB* provides this resource.

This series was planned by a seven-member advisory board, consisting primarily of secondary school educators, who developed a method of organization and presentation for selected *DLB* entries suitable for high school and beginning college students. Their preliminary plan was circulated to some five thousand school librarians and English teachers, who were asked to respond to the organization of the series and the tables of contents. Those responses were incorporated into the plan described here.

Uses for the Concise DALB

Students are the primary audience for the *Concise DALB*. The stated purpose of the standard *DLB* is to make our literary heritage more accessible. *Concise DALB* has the same goal and seeks a wider audience. What the author wrote; what the facts of his life are; a description of his literary works; a discussion of the critical response to his works; and a bibliography of critical works to be consulted for further information: These are the elements of a *Concise DALB* entry.

The first step in the planning process for this series, after identifying the audience, was to contemplate its uses. The advisory board acknowledged that the integrity of *Concise DALB* as a reference book is crucial to its utility. The *Concise DALB* adheres to the scholarly standards established by the parent series. Thus, within the scope of major American literary figures, the *Concise DALB* is a ready reference source of established

value, providing reliable biographical and bibliographical information.

It is anticipated that this series will not be confined to uses within the library. Just as *DLB* has been a tool for stimulating students' literary interests in the college classroom—for comparative studies of authors, for example, and, through its ample illustrations, as a means of invigorating literary study—the *Concise DALB* is a primary resource for high school and junior college educators. The series is organized to facilitate lesson planning, and the contextual diagrams (explained below) that introduce each entry are a source of topics for classroom discussion and writing assignments.

Organization

The advisory board determined that entries from the standard *DLB* should be presented complete—without abridgment. Their feeling was that the utility of the *DLB* format has been proven, and that only minimal changes should be made.

The advisory board further decided that the organization of the *Concise DALB* should be chronological to emphasize the historical development of American literature. Each volume is devoted to a single historical period and includes the most significant literary figures from all genres who were active during that time. Thus, the volume that includes modern mainstream novelists Saul Bellow, Bernard Malamud, and John Cheever will also include poets who were active at the same time—such as Allen Ginsberg, Lawrence Ferlinghetti, and John Berryman—and dramatists who were their contemporaries—such as Tennessee Williams, Arthur Miller, and William Inge. It should be noted that the volume of the *Concise DALB* that includes these authors comprises thirty-six entries, while the volumes in the standard *DLB* covering the same period include some four hundred author biographies. The *Concise DALB* limits itself to major figures, but it provides the same coverage of those figures as the *DLB* does.

The six period volumes of the *Concise DALB* are: *Colonization to the American Renaissance, 1640-1865; Realism, Naturalism, and Local Color, 1865-1917; Literary Responses to the Jazz Age, 1917-1929; The Age of Maturity, 1929-1941; The New Consciousness, 1941-1968; Broadening Views, 1968-1987.* The sixth volume will also contain a comprehensive index by subjects and proper names to the entire *Concise DALB*. (As in the standard *DLB* series, there is a cumulative index to author entries in each *Concise DALB* volume.)

Form of Entry

The form of entry in the *Concise DALB* is substantially the same as in the standard series, with the following alterations:

1) Each entry has been updated to include a discussion of works published since the standard entry appeared and to reflect recent criticism and research of interest to the high school audience.

2) The secondary bibliography for each entry has been selected to include those books and articles of particular interest and usefulness to high school and junior college students. In addition, the secondary bibliography has been annotated to assist students in assessing whether a reference will meet their needs.

3) Each entry is preceded by a "contextual diagram"—a graphic presentation of the places, literary influences, personal relationships, literary movements, major themes, cultural and artistic influences, and social and economic forces associated with the author. This chart allows students—and teachers—to place the author in his literary and social context at a glance.

It bears repeating that the *Concise DALB* is restricted to major American literary figures. It is anticipated that users of this series will find it advantageous to consult the standard *DLB* for information about those writers omitted from the *Concise DALB* whose significance to contemporary readers may have faded but whose contribution to our cultural heritage remains meaningful.

Comments about the series and suggestions about how to improve it are earnestly invited.

A Note to Students

The purpose of the *Concise DALB* is to enrich the study of literature. In their various ways, writers react in their works to the circumstances of their lives, the events of their time, and the culture that envelops them (which are represented on the contextual diagrams that precede each *Concise DALB* entry). Writers provide a way to see and understand what they have observed and experienced. Besides being inherently interesting, biographies of writers provide a basic perspective on literature.

Concise DALB entries start with the most important facts about writers: What they wrote. We strongly recommend that you also start there. The chronological listing of an author's works is an outline for the examination of his or her career achievement. The biographies that follow set the stage for the presentation of the works. Each of the author's important works and the most respected critical evaluations of them are discussed in *Concise DALB*. If you require more information about the author or fuller critical studies of the author's works, the annotated references section at the end of the entry will guide you.

Illustrations are an integral element of *Concise DALB* entries. Photographs of the author are reminders that literature is the product of a writer's imagination; facsimiles of the author's working drafts are the best evidence available for understanding the act of composition—the author in the process of refining his work and acting as self-editor; dust jacket and advertisements demonstrate how literature comes to us through the marketplace, which sometimes serves to alter our perceptions of the works.

Literary study is a complex and immensely rewarding endeavor. Our goal is to provide you with the information you need to make that experience as rich as possible.

Acknowledgments

This book was produced by Bruccoli Clark Layman, Inc. Karen L. Rood is senior editor for the *Dictionary of Literary Biography* series. Richard Layman and Lucia Tarbox were the in-house editors.

Art supervisor is Pamela Haynes. Copyediting supervisor is Patricia Coate. Production coordinator is Kimberly Casey. Typesetting supervisor is Laura Ingram. The production staff includes Rowena Betts, David R. Bowdler, Mary S. Dye, Charles Egleston, Kathleen M. Flanagan, Joyce Fowler, Karen Fritz, Judith K. Ingle, Judith E. McCray, Janet Phelps, and Joycelyn R. Smith. Jean W. Ross is permissions editor. Joseph Caldwell, photography editor, and Joseph Matthew Bruccoli did photographic copy work for the volume.

Walter W. Ross and Rhonda Marshall did the library research with the assistance of the staff at the Thomas Cooper Library of the University of South Carolina: Lynn Barron, Daniel Boice, Connie Crider, Kathy Eckman, Michael Freeman, Gary Geer, David L. Haggard, Jens Holley, Marcia Martin, Dana Rabon, Jean Rhyne, Jan Squire, Ellen Tillett, and Virginia Weathers.

Concise Dictionary of American Literary Biography

The New Consciousness, 1941-1968

Concise Dictionary of American Literary Biography

James Agee

This entry was updated by Robert E. Burkholder (Pennsylvania State University) from his entry in DLB 2, American Novelists Since World War II.

Places	Knoxville, Tennessee Cambridge, Massa- chusetts	Sewanee, Tennessee Alabama	New York City
Influences and Relationships	Archibald MacLeish Dwight MacDonald	I. A. Richards Robert Fitzgerald	John Huston Walker Evans
Literary Movements and Forms	New Journalism Prophetic Poetry	Southern Literary Renaissance	Nonfiction Novel
Major Themes	Initiation Death Autobiography	Family Moral Courage Individualism	Search for Identity Role of First-Person Narrator
Cultural and Artistic Influences	Film	Christianity	
Social and Economic Influences	The Depression McCarthyism	Communism	Hiroshima

3

See also the Agee entry in DLB 26, American Screenwriters.

BIRTH: Knoxville, Tennessee, 27 November 1909, to Hugh James and Laura Tyler Agee.

EDUCATION: A.B., Harvard University, 1932.

MARRIAGES: 28 January 1933 to Olivia Saunders (divorced). 1939 to Alma Mailman (divorced); child: Joel. 1946 to Mia Fritsch; child: Julia Teresa.

AWARDS AND HONORS: Pulitzer Prize for *A Death in the Family,* 1958 (awarded posthumously).

DEATH: New York, New York, 16 May 1955.

BOOKS: *Permit Me Voyage* (New Haven: Yale University Press, 1934);
Let Us Now Praise Famous Men, photographs by Walker Evans (Boston: Houghton Mifflin, 1941; London: Peter Owen, 1965);

James Agee (photo by Florence Homolka)

The Morning Watch (Boston: Houghton Mifflin, 1951; London: Secker & Warburg, 1952);
A Death in the Family (New York: McDowell, Obolensky, 1957; London: Gollancz, 1958);
Agee on Film: Reviews and Comments (New York: McDowell, Obolensky, 1958; London: Peter Owen, 1963);
Agee on Film, Volume II: Five Film Scripts (New York: McDowell, Obolensky, 1960; London: Peter Owen, 1965);
The Collected Poems of James Agee, edited by Robert Fitzgerald (Boston: Houghton Mifflin, 1968; London: Calder & Boyars, 1972);
The Collected Short Prose of James Agee, edited by Fitzgerald (Boston: Houghton Mifflin, 1968; London: Calder & Boyars, 1972);
James Agee: Selected Journalism, edited by Paul Ashdown (Knoxville: University of Tennessee Press, 1985).

SCREENPLAYS: *The Quiet One,* Museum of Modern Art, 1949, narration;
The African Queen, United Artists, 1951, screenplay by Agee and John Huston;
Genghis Khan, Italian Film Exports, 1952, narration;
The Bride Comes to Yellow Sky (half of *Face to Face*), RKO, 1953, screenplay;
White Mane, Rembrandt Films and Contemporary Films, 1953, script;
The Night of the Hunter, United Artists, 1955, screenplay;
Green Magic, Italian Film Exports, 1955, script.

TELEVISION SCRIPTS: *The Blue Hotel, Omnibus,* NBC, late 1940s, script;
Abraham Lincoln, Omnibus, NBC, 1953, scripts.

OTHER: "Notes for a Moving Picture: The House," in *New Letters in America,* edited by Horace Gregory (New York: Norton, 1937), pp. 37-55.

PERIODICAL PUBLICATIONS: "Any Seventh Son," *Phillips Exeter Monthly,* 31 (June 1927): 107-109;
"Man's Fate—A Film Treatment of the Malraux Novel," *Films,* 1 (1939): 51-60;
"Dedication Day," *Politics,* 3 (April 1946): 121-125.

James Rufus Agee, novelist, poet, journalist, film critic, and screenwriter, is best known for a documentary study of three Alabama tenant-farming families in the midst of the Depression, *Let Us Now Praise Famous Men,* and an unfinished novel, *A Death in the Family.* Born in Knoxville, Tennessee, on 27 November 1909, Agee's childhood was marred by the death of his father, Hugh James Agee, in an automobile accident in May 1916, an event which Agee would draw on in both his published novels.

In 1919 Agee was enrolled at an Episcopalian boarding school, St. Andrew's, near Sewanee, Tennessee. During his five years at St. Andrew's, Agee formed a close personal friendship with one of the teachers, Father James Harold Flye. In 1924-1925 Agee attended Knoxville High School, and after a trip to Europe with Father Flye in the summer of 1925, he enrolled at Phillips Exeter Academy in Exeter, New Hampshire. It was at Phillips Exeter that Agee first became interested in writing, perhaps only because of the social distinction it afforded a poor southern boy at an exclusive northern school. One of his first role models at the school was Dwight MacDonald, who had graduated several years before Agee and gone on to Yale. Agee began a correspondence with MacDonald during these years that would last most of his lifetime, and with MacDonald's help he later secured a job at *Fortune* magazine. By the time Agee had matriculated at Harvard in 1928, he was committed to both the aesthetic and professional aspects of a literary career, writing poetry and prose and editing the *Harvard Advocate* during his career there. Agee also formed an important literary friendship at Harvard with his classmate Robert Fitzgerald, who would later become a noted translator.

In 1931 Agee fell under the influence of a visiting Harvard professor, I. A. Richards, whose theories about using language to embody physical reality greatly affected Agee's writing during the 1930s. The most important direct influence Richards's theories had upon Agee's approach to his art involves an increased role for the narrator in Agee's stories. Because he was impressed by Richards's idea that the final effect of any poetic endeavor depends upon the complex relationship between the poem, referent, and reader, Agee decided that it would increase chances for the original poetic experience to be communicated if his first-person narrators not only served as major characters in the chronological narrative, but also as aestheticians who explain the problems of perception involved in their secondary roles as intermediaries

between the experience and the audience. From the early short story "They That Sow in Sorrow Shall Reap" (which Agee was preparing for publication during his initial exposure to Richards and which appeared in the *Harvard Advocate* in May 1931), the technique of employing a first-person narrator with the dual functions of major character and aesthetician is a distinguishing feature of Agee's prose. It is also the technique upon which he would rely most heavily in attempting to re-create the physical reality of three tenant families in *Let Us Now Praise Famous Men.*

In 1932, after graduation from Harvard, Agee was hired by *Fortune* magazine. Agee, whose roots were in the soil rather than the boardroom, worked hard on his *Fortune* assignments, but to him the best aspect of his employment was the money and free time it allowed him to pursue his artistic interests. It may seem odd that Agee, who was decidedly sympathetic to communism, would work for one of the most prominent organs of capitalism, but Henry Luce of *Fortune* prided himself on hiring the best writers for his magazine, regardless of political leanings. Also, the example of Archibald MacLeish, then *Fortune*'s chief writer, convinced Agee that one could work for the magazine and still accomplish personal writing projects. The outcome of this limited freedom was a book of poetry, *Permit Me Voyage* (1934), which was published as part of the Yale Series of Younger Poets. More than any volume of Agee's work, *Permit Me Voyage* demonstrates the dramatic turn Agee's aesthetic approach took following his exposure to Richards at Harvard. It also demonstrates Agee's indebtedness to a number of prophetic poets that he himself numbered as important influences, including William Blake, Walt Whitman, and Hart Crane.

On 28 January 1933 Agee married Olivia (Via) Saunders, the daughter of a Hamilton College history professor, whom Agee had met on vacation from Harvard in 1930. When his marriage to Via went through a final break in 1939, Agee was already seeing Alma Mailman, a friend of the Saunderses, whose lower-class background seems to have appealed to Agee's sense of social justice. To Alma fell the thankless task of aiding Agee during the composition of *Let Us Now Praise Famous Men.* After that book was published, and shortly after the birth of their son, Joel, in 1940, Alma left Agee. Despite the fact that Agee seems to have found both his marriages too restrictive to his personal freedom, he needed the stability and companionship that marriage provided. Therefore, in 1946, he married Mia Fritsch, whom he had met at *Fortune.* Agee's marriage to Mia produced one child, Julia Teresa (born in November 1946), and lasted until Agee's death in 1955.

In 1936 *Fortune* asked Agee and photographer Walker Evans to go to Alabama and do a photo-story on tenant farming. When Agee finally finished the project more than three years later, he had channeled enough of his sensibility into the subject to produce one large book and projections for three more volumes about his Alabama experience (these projected studies never materialized). *Let Us Now Praise Famous Men* (1941) is now recognized as the centerpiece of Agee's career. Not quite a novel but too poetic to be nonfiction, *Famous Men* is perhaps a "non-fiction novel" or what Tom Wolfe has called the "new journalism." It is a supreme attempt at recreating the squalor and beauty of the tenant farmers' lives through use of experimental techniques, such as a shifting point of view, several narrative levels and time schemes, and a structure which combines elements of the Mass, five-act drama, and the sonata. Because of Agee's unconventional approach and subject matter far removed from the concerns of a nation preparing to enter World War II, most of the critics considered *Famous Men* a pretentious failure. When a second edition was published in 1960, the critics found it a failure still, but most were willing to grant Agee credit for an aesthetic attempt far beyond the scope of most writers.

Agee's aesthetic concerns in *Famous Men* involved his ability and the ability of his chosen medium, with all its variables, to capture the physical reality of the tenant farmers. These concerns were serious enough to make Agee consider a form of communication other than written language:

> If I could, I'd do no writing at all here. It would be photographs; the rest would be fragments of cloth, bits of cotton, lumps of earth, records of speech, pieces of wood and iron, phials of odors, plates of food and excrement.

This alternative to words is, perhaps, a much more effective way of recreating an experience in the minds of the audience, but, as Agee speculated, the American public would probably turn it into some sort of parlor game. Besides, Agee did not wish to abandon his vocation as a writer before attempting to accomplish the re-creation of reality with words. Therefore, he exploited his personal involvement in the lives of the three tenant families—the Woods, Gudgers, and Ricketts—by writing about

that involvement and by recording the difficulties of writing in the first person. What this technique achieves is the feeling that the writer is working from a sincere concern for the people with whom he has lived and labored. The lack of authorial detachment in *Famous Men* aids in reinforcing the sense that the artist is motivated by his desire to tell the truth. It follows that if the reader is able to appreciate the artist's desire for truth, the artist's job of communicating experience will be easier.

But communication of the experience is not enough. The reader must also understand its significance. In *Practical Criticism* (1929) I. A. Richards says that "we understand when the words prompt in us action or emotion appropriate to the attitude of the person who speaks them." Obviously, the best way to make the reader aware of the attitudes of the person speaking in a work as large as *Famous Men* is to make that speaker the center of the action. By doing this, Agee is able to post the reader on how his attitude changes from section to section with shifts in tone.

Another rhetorical stance which seems to pervade *Famous Men* follows Richards's dictum that "nearly all good poetry is disconcerting." Therefore, Agee was willing to go to any length to assure the reader that his story was both real and frightening, from the lists of the Rickettses' possessions and household decorations to his masterly description of his first sleepless nights in the Rickettses' insect-infested shack. Agee simply did not wish his book to be considered an objet d'art, but it is too consciously artistic to fit into the "documentary" genre beside Erskine Caldwell and Margaret Bourke-White's *You Have Seen Their Faces*. The basic problem is that Agee wanted *Famous Men* to be the sort of fury that can change man's attitude toward himself. To classify such a fury as art would mean that it has been accepted, discussed at teas and cocktail parties, and its message forgotten. As Agee says in his "Preface": "The deadliest blow the enemy of the human soul can strike is to do fury honor. Swift, Blake, Beethoven, Christ, Joyce, Kafka, name me one who has not been thus castrated." This passionate intensity, so typical of *Famous Men*, disappears in most of Agee's work after 1941.

In 1938, while still hard at work on *Famous Men*, Agee began reviewing books for *Time*. Soon he shifted to reviews of movies, and in 1942 he also began writing a weekly column on film for the *Nation*. He held both posts until 1948. The distinctive quality of Agee's film criticism is the subjectivity with which he approaches his subject, reacting to each film he considers in a personal, rather than a critical or scholarly, way and always siding with the comparatively naive movie audience. Film, in effect, was the medium for which Agee's sensibility most suited him, because it offered the artist a means of communicating a reality directly. Therefore, much of Agee's criticism suggests the potential of film as an artistic medium which, with its blending of reality and fiction, could produce works of art much more real than any other art form. As testimony to Agee's personal approach to movies, his most famous piece of criticism, "Comedy's Greatest Era" (published in *Life* magazine on 3 September 1949), actually parodies analytic criticism by grading the four stages of laughter, from titter to boffo, and then, in Agee's most evocative prose, attempts to capture the poetry of the silent comedian in brief discussions of Turpin, Sennett, Chaplin, Lloyd, Langdon, and Keaton. This evocative quality is really the essence of Agee's film criticism. His ultimate desire was to recreate the film under consideration through written language so that the audience could decide for itself.

From 1948 until his death Agee divided his interest between writing film scripts and fiction. While he wrote several adaptations and one full-length original script, Agee's Hollywood work will always be remembered for the part he had in coauthoring *The African Queen* with director John Huston. It was while working on that film in January 1951 that Agee suffered the first of many heart attacks. But Agee's original film script *Noa Noa*, based upon the journals of Paul Gauguin, was his most ambitious project for the screen (although never produced), as well as his definitive statement about the role of the artist in society.

While working at *Time*, Agee formed a number of friendships with fellow staffers, including Whittaker Chambers and T. S. Matthews. As managing editor, it was Matthews who assigned Agee the task of producing a profound lead story for the 20 August 1945 issue that was devoted to the explosion of the atomic bomb at Hiroshima on 6 August. The essay that resulted may still be one of the best descriptions of man at a critical moment in his history, as well as a revelation of Agee's own abiding concern for the individual and the individual's responsibility for the rest of mankind. "When the bomb split open the universe and revealed the prospect of the infinitely extraordinary," Agee wrote, "it also revealed the oldest, simplest, commonest, most neglected and most important of facts: that each man is eternally and above all else responsible for his own soul.... Man's fate has

Katharine Hepburn and Humphrey Bogart in The African Queen. *Agee collaborated with John Huston on this adaptation of C. S. Forester's novel.*

forever been shaped between the hands of reason and spirit, now in collaboration, again in conflict.... If either or anything is to survive, they must find a way to create an indissolvable partnership."

Probably the best way to characterize Agee after 1941 is as a man who had extended himself too far. When he accepted the job of doing movie reviews for the *Nation* in the 1940s he found that he had little time to spend on his own personal projects. For instance, in 1937 Agee had projected plans for an autobiographical novel:

> Only relatively small portions would be fiction (though techniques of fiction might be much used); and these would be subjected to non-fictional analysis. This work would contain photographs and records as well as words.

Obviously, as Agee originally planned his novel, it was intended to combine some fictional techniques with the kind proposed for *Famous Men* (records and photographs). As it turned out, Agee only published one novel during his lifetime, and it is far different from his ambitious proposal of 1937. *The Morning Watch* (first published in 1950 in the Italian journal *Botteghe Oscure* and published in America in 1951) is indeed autobiographical, but it does not employ photographs, records, or nonfictional analysis—all those things disappear from Agee's work after *Famous Men*. It is a simply wrought tale about a young boy, Richard, who undergoes an awakening during a period of five hours on a Good Friday morning. All of the traditional Christian imagery of resurrection is here, rather heavy-handedly linked to Richard's discovery of a recently vacated locust shell and a snake which has shed its skin, but the conventionalities of *The Morning Watch* are of little interest compared with its symmetrical structure. Richard is a sensitive child, an artist figure of sorts, and all his actions are motivated by his desire to be a saint. However, Richard is a student at a small, private religious academy in the South (not unlike Agee's own St. Andrew's), and his fellow students represent a world totally unlike that of the church. Throughout the novel Richard is poised between the world of the spirit and the world of experience. This symmetrical conflict is resolved when Richard is able to find a proper balance of the two worlds. This balance is achieved when Richard kills a snake, acts against a commandment, and, therefore, gives up his right to sainthood, winning the respect of his classmates, Hobe and Jimmy.

A Death in the Family (1957) is far more complex than *A Morning Watch*, and yet it seems to rely upon many of the same techniques used in the shorter novel. For instance, like *A Morning Watch*, much of the action in *A Death in the Family* is created by an exploration of tensions. In *A Death in the Family*, however, this examination of polarities takes on a new complexity. There are tensions between individuals, notably the religious differences between Jay and his wife, the different qualities of manhood displayed by Jay and his brother, Ralph, and the differences between the sensitive young Rufus and his classmates. There are also those larger tensions which seem inherent in both individuals and the society in general: such things as the difference between black and white, rich and poor, being from the country as opposed to being from the city, and, most important, the difference between life and death. But the structure of *A Death in the Family* depends largely upon the difference created between "then" and "now." "Then" is the reminiscences of the narrator which deal with times

before his father died. Nearly all of these reminiscences involve the narrator's initiation into a new fact of life (like the meaning of parental love, pregnancy, or the problems between the races). This italicized secondary narrative is woven throughout the primary narrative, the story of Jay Follet's death in a freak automobile accident and the family's reaction to it. Therefore, the reader is aware of two levels of time working concurrently in the novel. This effect is created by suggestions of one level running through another, the recapitulation of past experiences in the present.

At the center of all these tensions is young Rufus Follet, who we are led to believe is the narrator. The opening section of the novel, "Knoxville: Summer 1915," begins with these words: "We are talking now of summer evenings in Knoxville, Tennessee, in the time that I lived there so successfully disguised to myself as a child." His disguise is that of a young boy, but he is actually a fully grown and developed artist who will not be limited by speaking through an adolescent persona. Therefore, the narrator creates the sense that he sees and understands far more than a boy Rufus's age could, and at times the narrator is even omniscient. Since we are made immediately aware of the dual identity of the narrator, we might conclude that all of *A Death in the Family* is aimed at merging these two identities: through experience the boy's disguise is slowly removed, and at the end of the novel we no longer have a boy at all, but a man. Thus the removal of disguise—Agee's trappings as a reporter for *Fortune* in *Famous Men*, Richard's saintliness in *The Morning Watch*, and Rufus's childhood innocence in *A Death in the Family*—is an important theme in all of Agee's work.

Agee's health problems, originally signalled by his first heart attack in 1951, grew progressively worse. In late 1952 he was hospitalized for a recurrence of his heart trouble, but Agee found it difficult to practice the abstinence his doctors recommended, often working on several projects at the same time. By the end of 1954, after nearly a year of good health, Agee's heart attacks began again. But this time they were much more severe and frequent, occurring up to eight times a day. Another series of attacks began in March 1955. In the midst of several film projects, including a screenplay for Colonial Williamsburg, Agee suffered a series of heart attacks and died while riding in a taxicab in New York City on 16 May 1955. In 1957 McDowell and Obolensky published *A Death in the Family*, tentatively arranging Agee's unfinished, and nearly indecipherable, working draft. *A*

Agee (center) as Frank Gudger in The Bride Comes to Yellow Sky. *This movie, for which Agee wrote the screenplay, was one of two filmed short stories released under the title* Face to Face.

Death in the Family was awarded the Pulitzer Prize for fiction in 1958.

Despite Agee's comparative anonymity during his lifetime, he has received both acknowledgment and respect since the publication of *A Death in the Family*. Not only did that novel win a Pulitzer Prize, but in 1960 it was adapted for the theater by Fred Coe and Arthur Cantor, and subsequently turned into a television drama in 1961 and the movie *All the Way Home* in 1962. The popularity of *Letters of James Agee to Father Flye* and the re-evaluation of *Let Us Now Praise Famous Men* as one of the most important books of the 1930s, after its republication in 1960, have aided in advancing Agee's reputation. Finally, the publication of the two volumes of *Agee on Film* in 1958 and 1960 gave the public a new insight into the genius that motivated Agee's movie reviews and film scripts.

Agee's personality was of the iconoclastic sort which seems to draw worshipers and imitators. After his death, those closest to him tended to mythologize Agee's life in much the same way that F.

Scott Fitzgerald's has been mythologized: the incredibly gifted artist drained of talent and energy by a society unable to appreciate him. But the legend of Agee is the smallest part of his legacy.

Letters:

Letters of James Agee to Father Flye, edited by James H. Flye (New York: George Braziller, 1962; London: Peter Owen, 1964);
Agee's letters to Flye, his lifelong friend and confidant, are central to an understanding of Agee's life and work. The second edition of this book (1971) includes some letters of Flye to Agee.

Bibliographies:

Genevieve Fabre, "A Bibliography of the Works of James Agee," *Bulletin of Bibliography*, 24 (May-August 1965): 145-148, 163-166;
Bibliography of Agee's published work, including books, poetry, short stories, and criticism.

Nancy Lyman Huse, *John Hersey and James Agee: A Reference Guide* (Boston: G. K. Hall, 1978);
Lists books and articles written about Agee. Entries have long and valuable annotations.

References:

Alfred T. Barson, *A Way of Seeing: A Critical Study of James Agee* (Amherst: University of Massachusetts Press, 1972);
A study of Agee's development as an artist that focuses on aesthetic theory and practice.

Laurence Bergreen, *James Agee: A Life* (New York: Dutton, 1984);
The most thorough and revealing biography of Agee. Bergreen uses many unpublished letters and manuscripts, and his work contains solid analysis of Agee's life and work. Especially strong on *Let Us Now Praise Famous Men*.

Mark A. Doty, *Tell Me Who I Am: James Agee's Search for Selfhood* (Baton Rouge: Louisiana State University Press, 1981);
An examination of the relationship of Agee's life and art. Doty argues that Agee used autobiographical writing as a way of sorting out his own life.

Victor A. Kramer, *James Agee* (Boston: Twayne, 1975);
Blends biography with superior analysis of Agee's work. Kramer's study is the most valuable introduction to Agee's life and work.

Erling Larsen, *James Agee* (Minneapolis: University of Minnesota Press, 1971);
Brief overview of Agee's life and work.

David Madden, *Remembering James Agee* (Baton Rouge: Louisiana State University Press, 1974);
A collection of essays on Agee by those who knew him. Most are reprinted from previously published sources.

Genevieve Moreau, *The Restless Journey of James Agee* (New York: Morrow, 1977);
An accessible consideration of Agee's life and work that attempts to separate what was real from the legend that has grown up around Agee's memory.

Peter H. Ohlin, *Agee* (New York: Obolensky, 1966);
An examination of Agee's writing in light of Ohlin's belief that the "absolute commitment to the holiness of human reality" is the theme that links all his work.

Kenneth Seib, *James Agee: Promise and Fulfillment* (Pittsburgh: University of Pittsburgh Press, 1968);
An overview of Agee's career that lacks documentation and is sometimes incorrect.

Ross Spears and Jude Cassidy, eds., with narrative by Robert Coles, *Agee: His Life Remembered* (New York: Holt, Rinehart & Winston, 1985);
Based on the 1979 film, *Agee*, this volume presents pictures and reminiscences by those who knew Agee. The essay by Coles was composed specifically for this book.

Papers:

The University of Texas has a large collection of Agee's literary manuscripts and correspondence; see Victor A. Kramer, "James Agee Papers at the University of Texas," *Library Chronicle of the University of Texas*, 8, no. 2 (1966): 33-36.

Edward Albee

This entry was updated by Stephen M. Vallillo (New York, New York) from the entry by John MacNicholas (University of South Carolina) in DLB 7, *Twentieth-Century American Dramatists.*

Places	New York City
Influences and Relationships	
Literary Movements and Forms	Theatre of the Absurd
Major Themes	Dying · Identity · Relation of Art to Society · Alienation · Isolation vs. Communication · Illusion vs. Reality · Relationship between Love and Hate
Cultural and Artistic Influences	
Social and Economic Influences	Post World War II American Society

BIRTH: Virginia, 12 March 1928. Adopted by Reed and Frances Albee.

EDUCATION: Trinity College, Hartford, Connecticut, 1946-1947.

AWARDS AND HONORS: Berlin Festival Award, 1959; Vernon Rice Memorial Award, 1960; Obie Award for *The Zoo Story*, 1960; *The Death of Bessie Smith* and *The American Dream* chosen as best plays of the 1960-1961 season by the Foreign Press Association; Berlin Festival Award for *The Death of Bessie Smith*, 1961; Lola D'Annunzio Award for *The American Dream*, 1961; New York Drama Critics Circle Award, Foreign Press Association Award, American National Theatre and Academy (ANTA) award, two Tony awards and one Outer Circle Award for *Who's Afraid of Virginia Woolf?*, 1963; with Richard Barr and Clinton Wilder, the Margo Jones Award for encouraging new plays and playwrights, 1965; election to the National Institute of Arts and Letters, 1966; Pulitzer Prize for *A Delicate Balance*, 1967; D.Litt., Emerson College, 1967; Trinity College, 1974; Pulitzer Prize for *Seascape*, 1975; Gold Medal for drama from The American Academy and Institute of Arts and Letters, 1980.

Edward Albee (Billy Rose Theatre Collection, New York Public Library at Lincoln Center, Astor, Lenox and Tilden Foundations)

SELECTED BOOKS: *The Zoo Story, The Death of Bessie Smith, The Sandbox* (New York: Coward-McCann, 1960; London: Cape, 1962);
The American Dream (New York: Coward-McCann, 1961; London: French, 1962);
The American Dream, The Death of Bessie Smith, Fam and Yam (New York: Dramatists Play Service, 1962);
Who's Afraid of Virginia Woolf? (New York: Atheneum, 1962; London: Cape, 1964);
The Play The Ballad of the Sad Cafe, Carson McCullers' Novella Adapted to the Stage (Boston: Houghton Mifflin, 1963; New York: Atheneum, 1963; London: Cape, 1965);
Tiny Alice (New York: Atheneum, 1965; London: Cape, 1966);
Malcolm, Adapted by Edward Albee from the Novel by James Purdy (New York: Atheneum, 1966; London: Cape/Secker & Warburg, 1967);
A Delicate Balance (New York: Atheneum, 1966; London: Cape, 1968);
Everything in the Garden from the Play by Giles Cooper (New York: Atheneum, 1968);
Box and Quotations from Chairman Mao Tse-Tung: Two Inter-Related Plays (New York: Atheneum, 1969; London: Cape, 1970);

All Over (New York: Atheneum, 1971; London: Cape, 1972);
Seascape (New York: Atheneum, 1975; London: Cape, 1976);
Counting the Ways and Listening, Two Plays (New York: Atheneum, 1977);
The Lady from Dubuque (New York: Atheneum, 1980).

SELECTED PLAY PRODUCTIONS: *The Zoo Story*, Berlin, Schiller Theater Werkstatt, 28 September 1959; New York, Provincetown Playhouse, 14 January 1960, 582 [performances];
The Death of Bessie Smith, Berlin, Schlosspark Theater, 21 April 1960; New York, York Theatre, 28 February 1961, 328;
The Sandbox, New York, Jazz Gallery, 15 May 1960;
Fam and Yam, Westport, Conn., White Barn Theatre, 27 August 1960;
The American Dream, New York, York Theatre, 24 January 1961, 360;
Who's Afraid of Virginia Woolf?, New York, Billy Rose Theatre, 13 October 1962, 644;

The Ballad of the Sad Cafe, adapted from Carson McCullers's novella, New York, Martin Beck Theatre, 30 October 1963, 123;

Tiny Alice, New York, Billy Rose Theatre, 29 December 1964, 167;

Malcolm, adapted from James Purdy's novel, New York, Shubert Theatre, 11 January 1966, 7;

A Delicate Balance, New York, Martin Beck Theatre, 22 September 1966, 132;

Everything in the Garden, adapted from Giles Cooper's play, New York, Plymouth Theatre, 29 November 1967, 84;

Box and *Quotations from Chairman Mao Tse-Tung,* Buffalo, Studio Arena Theatre, 6 March 1968; New York, Billy Rose Theatre, 30 September 1968, 12;

All Over, New York, Martin Beck Theatre, 27 March 1971, 40;

Seascape, New York, Shubert Theatre, 26 January 1975, 63;

Listening and *Counting the Ways,* Hartford, Conn., Hartford Stage Company, 28 January 1977;

The Lady from Dubuque, New York, Morosco Theatre, 31 January 1980, 12;

Lolita, adapted from Vladimir Nabokov's novel, New York, Brooks Atkinson Theatre, 19 March 1981, 12;

The Man Who Had Three Arms, New York, Lyceum Theatre, 5 April 1983, 16;

Finding the Sun, Greeley, Colo., Frazier Theatre, 10 May 1983, limited run of 5.

OTHER: Introduction to *Three Plays by Noel Coward: Blithe Spirit, Hay Fever, Private Lives* (New York: Delta, 1965).

PERIODICAL PUBLICATION: "Which Theatre Is the Absurd One?," *New York Times Magazine,* 25 February 1962, pp. 30-31, 64, 66;
An article defending experimental theater and condemning mainstream, Broadway theater, which he calls absurd.

In the early 1960s it was customary to find the names of four young playwrights linked: Edward Albee, Jack Gelber, Arthur Kopit, and Jack Richardson. These, and certain others like them, wished to prevent theater in the United States from retreating further into a detached lethargy. These playwrights were turning to Europe for new forms to experiment with, much as Eugene O'Neill had done two generations earlier. In their hands the nature of human experience was not to be rendered either by a straightforward brand of realism

or by a merely genteel departure from it. Of these four playwrights, the most successful, prolific, and controversial is Edward Albee. The nature of the controversy surrounding his work seems little changed over the past two and a half decades. His willingness to experiment with the medium and to challenge the received ideas of theater audiences and society in general has, if anything, increased with age. His work betrays no signs of retrenchment, no evidence that he will cease being an acerbic, painstaking, vivid, lyrical, funny, and altogether serious scribe of human loss, self-delusion, and entropy.

Though he was probably born somewhere in Virginia, the place of Albee's birth is officially listed as Washington, D.C. Two weeks after his birth, Albee's natural parents gave him up for adoption to Reed and Frances Albee in the District of Columbia. Albee does not know and has been legally prohibited from seeking verification of the identities of his natural parents or his actual place of birth.

Reed Albee was the wealthy owner of part of the Keith-Albee vaudeville circuit started by his father, Edward Franklin Albee II. Reed and Frances Albee lived in Larchmont, New York, where they raised their adopted son amid the conspicuous splendor of a large Tudor house, servants, tutors, horses, pets, toys, and chauffeured limousines. Also present in the house was Mrs. Albee's mother, Grandma Cotter. Albee was frequently driven into the city for the matinee performances of shows. In addition, many show business personalities visited Albee's home over the years, even though Reed Albee retired from his business in 1928, the year of Albee's birth. Albee's mother was younger and much larger than her husband, who was a quiet man. According to Albee, his mother was "an excellent horsewoman and saddle horse judge. . . . I was riding from the time I was able to walk." Albee expresses no bitterness toward his adoptive parents; however, he has acknowledged "a deep-seated resentment against my natural parents for abandoning me." He was closely attached to his grandmother, whose generosity clearly extended far beyond the trust fund she gave Albee. The relatively modest income from the trust enabled Albee to leave home in 1950 and pursue his own interests. That he dedicated *The Sandbox* (1960) to her (she died in 1959, just as Albee's career was gathering momentum) reflects perhaps not only his grief but also an awareness of the way her life had contributed to his.

Albee's parents traveled to Florida and Arizona during the winters; consequently, the early years of his primary education suffered constant interruptions. At the age of eleven he was sent to the first of a succession of boarding schools—Lawrenceville, Valley Forge Military Academy (Albee referred to it as "Valley Forge Concentration Camp"), and Choate—in which his academic record was poor. At Choate, however, he was very happy. There was little resembling the military routine in school policies, and he found teachers who encouraged his writing. He energetically attempted every genre, pouring out numerous poems, stories, a play (*Schism*, published in the school literary magazine), and a lengthy novel entitled "The Flesh of Unbelievers." One of his poems appeared in a Texas literary magazine. His chief literary activity, in fact, was poetry until his late twenties.

In 1946 Albee attended Trinity College in Hartford, Connecticut, where he took little interest in the curriculum, although he portrayed the Emperor Franz Joseph in Maxwell Anderson's *The Masque of Kings*. He left Trinity after a year and a half, bringing his formal education to a close. Returning home, he took his first job at the WNYC radio station, where he wrote continuity (the transitional spoken parts) for its programs. He left his parents' home in 1950, settling in Greenwich Village. In the decade that followed, he lived at a variety of addresses and supplemented the income from his trust by working in various jobs: an office boy in an advertising agency, a record salesman, a book salesman, and, for three years, a messenger for Western Union—"any job so long as it had no future."

In his own art, however, he met with frustration. In 1952 he lived for nearly half a year in Italy, where he wrote a novel. In New York he met W. H. Auden, who read some of Albee's poetry and suggested that he write pornographic verse as an exercise to improve his style. In New Hampshire, Thornton Wilder advised him to turn his efforts toward drama. Composer William Flanagan, Albee's friend and roommate during these years, reports that Albee saw nearly everything of even "mild importance" in theater; Albee continued to profess a "thoroughly unfashionable admiration for the work of Tennessee Williams."

The apparent aimlessness and floundering in Albee's life after leaving home was a trial-and-error process by which he discovered his métier. By his own account, his thirtieth birthday in 1958 seemed terribly significant—it would not be casually passed. He quit his job with Western Union and

wrote *The Zoo Story* in three weeks: "I did a draft, made pencil revisions, and typed a second script, and that's the way I've been doing my plays since." Rejected by several New York producers, *The Zoo Story*'s premiere occurred on 28 September 1959 at the Schiller Theater Werkstatt in Berlin. Four months later it played on a double bill with Samuel Beckett's *Krapp's Last Tape* at the Provincetown Playhouse in Greenwich Village and was generally received as the creation of a formidable talent—winning the Vernon Rice Memorial Award in 1960.

Although the setting and conception of *The Zoo Story* are simple, the modulation of language and emotion is sophisticated. Jerry and Peter meet in Central Park. Jerry skillfully induces Peter, a "normally reticent," uninvolved observer, to listen to much of his life's story. Out of loneliness and a courageous desire to connect with something outside of himself, Jerry goads Peter into a fight and kills himself upon the knife he has given Peter. Peter cannot, therefore, dismiss Jerry as merely obstreperous or inconvenient; their actions have transcended the limits of Peter's tidy view of the world. No matter what the cost, authentic *contact* has been achieved. The exorbitant cost is, of course, Albee's point.

In the course of Jerry's outpouring of himself, he raises, with varying emphasis, issues that have often recurred in Albee's work: the connections between love and aggression ("I had tried to love, and I had tried to kill, and both had been unsuccessful by themselves"); loss and isolation ("I have gained solitary free passage, if that much further loss can be said to be gain"); the concept of God ("God who is a colored queen"); the relationship between fantasy and experience ("when you're a kid you use the [pornographic] cards as a substitute for the real experience, and when you're older you use real experience as a substitute for the fantasy"; moreover, Jerry's lustful landlady "believes and relives what never happened" between them); the danger of unexamined preconceptions of reality ("*was* trying to feed the dog [poisoned meat] an act of love? And, perhaps, was the dog's attempt to bite me *not* an act of love? If we can so misunderstand, well then, why have we invented the word love in the first place?"); the paradox of reality and art ("fact is better left to fiction"); and even evolution, as Jerry speculates on the size of his landlady's brain, and at the end of the play assures Peter that he, Peter, is not a vegetable but an animal.

Albee's ability to use the incongruity of little-child talk for dramatic effect first appears in *The Zoo Story*. When Jerry attempts to usurp the bench,

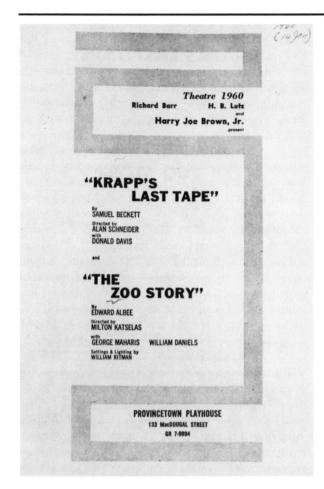

Playbill (Billy Rose Theatre Collection, New York Public Library at Lincoln Center, Astor, Lenox and Tilden Foundations)

Peter exclaims "I'm a GROWNUP." This follows Jerry's promise to tell Peter, "as if to a child," what happened at the zoo. The little-child diction becomes even more of a satiric weapon in *The Sandbox, The American Dream* (1961), and *Who's Afraid of Virginia Woolf?* (1962). The concluding scene of Jerry recumbent upon the bench and bleeding to death alone has more than a casual resemblance to the final tableau of Julian's death in *Tiny Alice* (1964). Although the plays differ radically, both Jerry and Julian have died in an attempt to find transcendent meaning, and each play asserts that to search for such meaning is a spiritual necessity.

The apathy which *The Zoo Story* attacks is both individual and social. Jerry accuses Peter of trying to pigeonhole him (Peter incorrectly guesses that Jerry lives in Greenwich Village), but Jerry himself rather expertly sums up Peter's life and attitudes toward income, class structure, and marriage, as well as the threatening, ugly elements of his own world, such as the landlady, her dog, and the other

tenants in her brownstone rooming house on the upper West Side near Columbus Avenue. Jerry's picture of his world is both intensely personal and societal, and Peter's unwillingness to look at the picture precipitates the final action of the play: "I don't want to hear any more." His refusal to permit the contact and understanding which Jerry has sought with desperate articulateness causes Jerry to realize, rather wearily, that the barriers in Peter's world will dissolve in nothing less than blood. Since Jerry is not himself a killer, the blood must be his and not Peter's. Jerry is no psychotic: the dialectic of the play strongly implies that Jerry is all too sane.

The Zoo Story, although not written out of a formalized credo, was the result of certain convictions Albee had consistently held. Some of these convictions were set forth in two quite different pieces of writing: the play *Fam and Yam,* produced in 1960, and Albee's essay two years later on the theater of the absurd. *Fam and Yam* is a brief sketch in which a *Fam*ous *Am*erican Writer is interviewed by a *Y*oung *Am*erican Writer. Fam is about fifty years old and looks like "a faintly foppish Professor of History." He drinks much sherry and does not take very seriously anything that Yam ("an intense, bony young man, whose crew cut is in need of a trim") has to say—until it is too late. Fam is associated with Arthur Miller, Tennessee Williams, Thornton Wilder, and William Inge. Fam fears that the younger playwrights—Richardson, Gelber, Kopit, and Yam himself—are going to displace his own generation. Yam says that his interview will indict the entire commercial theater industry: theater owners, producers, unions, critics, even playwrights who are merely out to grab as much loot as possible—"everybody's culpable." Fam, getting drunk, thinks Yam's diatribe is uproariously funny, until he suspects that Yam means exactly what he says. And Yam does.

In February 1962 the *New York Times Magazine* published Albee's article "Which Theatre Is the Absurd One?," containing an even more succinct criticism of the commercial theater than *Fam and Yam.* In it Albee claims that when he first heard the phrase "theatre of the absurd" applied to his own recently published plays (*The Zoo Story, The American Dream, The Sandbox*), he was deeply offended, assuming that "theatre of the absurd" referred to usual Broadway fare: "What (I was reasoning to myself) could be more absurd than a theater in which the esthetic criterion is something like this: A 'good' play is one which makes money; a 'bad' play (in the sense of 'Naughty! Naughty!' I guess) is one which does not; a theater in which perform-

15

ers have plays rewritten to correspond to the public relations image of themselves; a theater in which playwrights are encouraged (what a funny word!) to think of themselves as little cogs in a great big wheel; a theater in which imitation has given way to imitation of imitation; a theater in which London 'hits' are, willy-nilly, in a kind of reverse chauvinism, greeted in a manner not unlike a colony's obeisance to the Crown; a theater in which real estate owners and theater party managements predetermine the success of unknown quantities; a theater in which everybody scratches and bites for billing as though it meant access to the last bomb shelter on earth; a theater in which, in a given season, there was not a single performance of a play by Beckett, Brecht, Chekhov, Genet, Ibsen, O'Casey, Pirandello, Shaw, Strindberg—or Shakespeare? What, indeed, I thought, could be more absurd than that?" This idealism can be perceived in all of Albee's work, much of which dramatizes his belief that "the health of a nation, a society, can be determined by the art it demands."

Albee's next three plays (*The Sandbox, The American Dream,* and *The Death of Bessie Smith,* all produced in 1960-1961) attack certain features in American society. Commissioned by the Spoleto Festival of the Two Worlds in Italy, *The Sandbox* was first performed in New York. *The Sandbox* and *The American Dream* (a longer play from which the materials of *The Sandbox* were excerpted) are identical in subject matter and technique; both attack indifference to love, pity, and compassion. In both plays the characters of Mommy and Daddy live in a kind of moral narcosis. Much of the humor in each derives from Albee's attack upon trite, insincere chatter and upon theatrical clichés. Grandma in both is the foil to a pervasive vacuity. Her acute and funny perceptions deflate the conventionalized responses of Mommy and Daddy. Left on the beach (the sandbox) to die, Grandma wields her toy shovel, as if burying herself: "I don't know how I'm supposed to do anything with this goddamn toy shovel." When Grandma has apparently "died," Mommy says, "she looks . . . so happy. It pays to do things well." After Mommy and Daddy leave her there, a muscle-flexing young man, the Angel of Death, haltingly tells Grandma, "I am . . . uh . . . I am come for you." The use of the offstage rumble, music, and tears on cue satirize stale methods of sentimental theater. ("It was an off-stage rumble," says Mommy, beginning to weep, "and you know what *that* means. . . .") However, the second death of Grandma, when the Angel of Death puts his hands on hers, has more poignancy. It does not evoke laughter but a pause.

Albee's attack upon false values in family life was even more pointed in the longer one-act play *The American Dream,* set in a rather stuffy apartment. The subservient Daddy, whom Mommy married only for his wealth and nothing more, has a larger role in *The American Dream.* Human relationships are valued strictly in commercial terms: Mommy and Daddy bought a baby; Mommy sold sex to Daddy; the young man, who has no emotions, will "do almost anything for money." Sterility of spirit is mirrored by sterility of the body. Daddy and Mommy's purchased "bumble of joy" suffers a series of losses until it is finally deprived of eyes, heart, sexual organs, hands—virtually all means of making contact. When it dies, they demand their money back because their purchase did not give them "satisfaction." As in *The Sandbox,* Grandma constantly exposes the hollowness around her.

The implications in Albee's play, which he characterizes as "an attack on the substitution of artificial for real values in our society," are indeed quite frightening, because the prospects for renewal in a culture that promotes emasculation are quite dim. The comedy of *The American Dream* poses its issues with clarity: "you got to have a sense of dignity," says Grandma, "even if you don't care, 'cause, if you don't have that, civilization's doomed."

The Death of Bessie Smith also premiered in Berlin, opening in April of 1960. It, too, attacks certain forces that alienate people from each other, but it lacks the mesmerizing intensity of *The Zoo Story.* Albee has indicated that the idea for *The Death of Bessie Smith* occurred to him as he was reading the notes on a record album by the black singer. Bessie Smith was injured in an automobile accident, and after being refused entrance into a white hospital she bled to death on 26 September 1937 in Memphis, Tennessee. Albee uses these facts to establish the situation and setting of his play. However, *The Death of Bessie Smith* is not a narrow protest play. The title character never appears on stage; instead, the action focuses primarily upon a confused, frightened, bigoted, and sadistic nurse. In the course of the play, she interacts with three men: her father, whom she detests; an intern, whose lust for her is a force by which she manipulates him; and a black orderly who, defenseless against her degradation of him, learns to assume her methods against another black (Bessie's companion, Jack). The play is unified by the nurse's character, for in each of these relationships the point of Albee's attack is not to castigate racism per se; rather, it is to show how a fearful personality utilizes power to destroy and not to heal. The play's central assumption, that racism is only one exponent of primal fear, makes its philosophical stance wider than that of a typical protest play, and the play's imagery, both verbal and visual, suggests that the inevitable result of protracted inhumanity is holocaust.

The construction of *The Death of Bessie Smith* is sufficient to sustain pathos and anguish but not apocalypse. Critical reaction to *The Death of Bessie Smith* has been decidedly cool, and it is regarded as inferior to Albee's other early works.

Many still regard Albee's first full-length play, *Who's Afraid of Virginia Woolf?*, as his finest work. It has certainly proved to be his most popular, with a run of 644 performances on Broadway firmly establishing Albee as a major playwright. During a late-night party in their living room, George, a history professor, and his wife, Martha, whose father is president of the college, interact with their two somewhat younger guests, Nick and Honey. Within these seemingly narrow confines Albee gives extended treatment to several concerns raised in his shorter plays: the nature of marital and family structures; the sterility of American culture; the latent fascism in American mythology; and the nec-

essary blend of truth and illusion in human consciousness.

The mode of *Who's Afraid of Virginia Woolf?* is basically realistic, but the play wields a constant and merciless sense of humor. George and Martha's humor, particularly, extends from grotesque savagery to childlike delight, governing the tone of the entire play by interweaving the stuff of tragedy with the stuff of ordinary life. Their combative minds, whether experiencing pain, confusion, defeat, embarrassment, or delight, clash unpredictably, nearly always moving toward deflationary or purgative laughter. In its vigor, precision, and range of emotion, the humor of *Who's Afraid of Virginia Woolf?* is extraordinary. No other comic work in the American tradition has so effectively rendered both the conciliatory and destructive appetites in the human soul.

As in *The American Dream*, the conflict in *Who's Afraid of Virginia Woolf?* proceeds from a distinct, though reduced, difference in age. George and Martha, aged forty-six and fifty-two respectively, are childless, and out of this painful void they have invented an entire private fantasy: a son, whom they have raised for twenty-one years. This fantasy son is, therefore, not much younger than Nick and Honey (aged twenty-eight and twenty-six), whom George and Martha repeatedly refer to as the "kids." Nick and Honey are "making their way" in New Carthage, Nick just having been appointed to the biology faculty. Superimposed upon this difference in age is a radical difference in values. Albee has acknowledged that it is not accidental (nor of great importance, either) that the principals of this play have the same given names as George and Martha Washington. The ironic overtone is that the Revolutionary values that once gave birth to a nation seem to have been forgotten or betrayed— "good, better, best, bested." The voracious totalitarianism whose threat George senses is represented by Nick, and is insinuated also in the similarity between his name and the Russian leader's, Nikita Khrushchev. These are recessed cues, however, and to regard them as a direct allegory is to ignore the depth of characterization of the entire play.

Whatever their failures, Albee's George and Martha are substantial individuals. George is fascinated by the unpredictability of history, by the capacity of human events to surprise and mystify. Nick, on the other hand, is a scientist whose duty it is to avoid surprise and to establish predictable order. But a completely predictable universe is a passionless universe. Nick actually admits that pas-

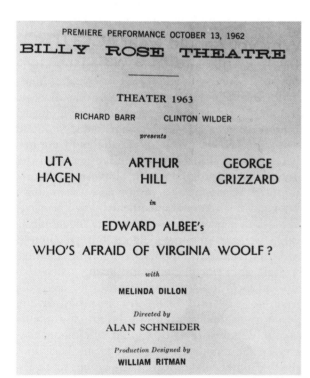

PREMIERE PERFORMANCE OCTOBER 13, 1962

BILLY ROSE THEATRE

THEATER 1963

RICHARD BARR   CLINTON WILDER

presents

| UTA HAGEN | ARTHUR HILL | GEORGE GRIZZARD |

in

EDWARD ALBEE's

WHO'S AFRAID OF VIRGINIA WOOLF?

with

MELINDA DILLON

Directed by
ALAN SCHNEIDER

Production Designed by
WILLIAM RITMAN

Playbill (Billy Rose Theatre Collection, New York Public Library at Lincoln Center, Astor, Lenox and Tilden Foundations)

sion did not animate his marriage to Honey, not "even at the beginning." In retrospect it becomes apparent that Nick is a close dramatic cousin of the Young Man in *The American Dream,* a cousin made over in a realistic environment, but one who nonetheless shares the Young Man's emotional emptiness, his midwestern origins (Nick is from Kansas), his youth, good looks, body type, and most crucially, his willingness to prostitute himself for professional advancement. Martha, like Mommy in *The American Dream,* sidles up to Nick, but the result of their sexual encounter is impotency.

Unlike the Young Man, Nick has a sharp, if limited, intelligence. One of the main conflicts in the play arises from George's fantasy that Nick's type will assume control of the world by a fascistic program of eugenics. As George farcically insists upon his fantasy, Nick, perhaps as much from amazement as from a desire to maintain decorum, makes little more than token denials. George's grisly Orwellian vision of genetic engineering, which will scientifically eliminate human "imbalances" by enforced sterilization of "the ugly, the stupid . . . the . . . unfit" and which will produce a cultureless race of men physically resembling Nick, is—the play seems to imply—the logical conclusion of a peculiarly American faith in technology, with its control of, rather than respect for, nature, and in the tendency of a more powerful race to dominate a weaker race.

Quite understandably, Nick regards George's assertions as silly, but the events of the evening prove that George's mythic fantasy is not wild guesswork. Nick and George do engage in something like a duel. When George reveals that Nick and Honey's marriage was prompted by a false or hysterical pregnancy, Nick vows revenge. Nick and Honey are also childless, and George resents Honey's refusal to have children. Martha, wishing to humiliate George for his game of "Get the Guests" (among other reasons), takes Nick upstairs to bed. While they are upstairs, George reads from a book that "the west, encumbered by crippling alliances, and burdened with a morality too rigid to accommodate itself to the swing of events, must . . . inevitably . . . fall." In great anger he hurls the book against the doorbell chimes, whose sound announces the concluding stroke of act two—namely, the telegram bringing news of the death of George and Martha's fantasy son.

At the heart of *Who's Afraid of Virginia Woolf?* is Albee's insistence that cultures are like individuals: they are born, may thrive, have consciences, make errors, maintain illusions at great cost, suffer paralysis, defeat, insanity, or death. George tries to warn Nick of how easy it is to lose sight of one's principles; Nick responds with harsh sarcasm: "Up yours." George ponders, among other things, how mankind constructs a civilization in which "you make government and art, and realize that they are, must be, both the same." Then civilization reaches the "saddest of all points . . . the point where there *is* something to lose." Through all of this—George says to Nick—comes the Day of Judgment: "What does the trumpet sound? Up yours." The point of George's speech is more than a cheap retort. To keep a mature civilization from lapsing into smugness and apathy is far more difficult and, Albee seems to imply, far more noble than to destroy it and start anew. Government and art are the same in that they are constructs of the human imagination which make justice, law, beauty, and religion possible. In this sense *Who's Afraid of Virginia Woolf?* is a radically political play. Albee's commitment to the connection between art and politics is quite genuine. It sets *Who's Afraid of Virginia Woolf?* apart from the utterly nihilistic visions found in much of Beckett's or Ionesco's work.

The cruelty of George and Martha's "fun and games" is not gratuitous, being borne out of thwarted passion and remorse. However, Martha and George have inventive minds; what is left of their wits is more than most people ever have. They admire each other's mental agility. There is a genuine and loving bond between them, which persists even in their assaults: "you're going bald," Martha tells George; "so are you," he replies, after which they pause and "both laugh." George berates Martha for leaving her half-filled glasses everywhere in the house, and claims he "even found one in the freezer." Martha objects, of course, but is "amused in spite of herself." To label Martha and George's marriage as nothing but a repulsive sickness is to ignore a strong undercurrent of mutual and undisguised affection. The prototype of their marriage may be found in Shakespeare's *The Taming of the Shrew,* a play which has some fairly strong physical as well as emotional violence, but which ends in reconciliation with the husband having the final say. Likewise, Martha thinks the boxing match that she and George had many years earlier has "colored our whole life." Like Petruchio arbitrarily insisting upon the alterations of the sun and moon, George declares in act three that "the moon may very well have gone down . . . but it came back up." Martha, unlike Shakespeare's Kate, is not yet ready to accede to her husband's notions of reality. Only after George kills the fantasy child does Martha accept George's view of themselves and their connection to each other. Then, and only then, can she admit fear.

The subtitle of act three, "The Exorcism" (which was the working title of the whole play), implies that the expulsion of this fantasy is healthy, for the word itself connotes possession by an alien spirit. The twin themes of illusion versus reality and insanity versus sanity are bound together in the pun of the actual title of the play. To live in a fantasy is to remain defenseless before the wolf. Their heavy drinking indicates not insanity but a reluctance to reappraise the basis of their lives. Although they never forget that their son is a fantasy, a private solace, George and Martha's recriminations for the void in their lives have made their marriage a hell.

Although the play ends on an indefinite note, the basis for reconciliation is readily apparent. When Martha talks about how she raised their "son," Honey involuntarily blurts out that she, too, wants a child. Later, as Nick realizes that Martha and George's son is a fantasy, he asks George: "you couldn't have . . . any?" If Martha is barren, then George could use this opportunity for revenge; yet he says, "*We* couldn't." The same opportunity for revenge is available to Martha if George is infertile, yet she, too, asserts, "*We* couldn't." Since they have ruthlessly exposed other equally humiliating facts of their lives during the long evening, their closing ranks and sharing the loss in this final moment provides an exquisite succor. It is sadness mutually claimed and mutually supported; it therefore stands starkly opposed to the attack-and-destroy games of the evening. In the quiet, slow, gentle, and monosyllabic conclusion of the play, this sense of shared sorrow establishes the intimacy which George and Martha have both feared and sought all evening. Admission of fear suggests that some kind of revaluation is possible. "It was time to do it," George says simply.

Who's Afraid of Virginia Woolf? received the New York Drama Critics Circle Award as well as two Antoinette Perry (Tony) and one Outer Circle awards. John Gassner and John Mason Brown resigned in protest their memberships on the Pulitzer jury when it refused to award the Pulitzer Prize to Albee. In 1966 Warner Brothers released its film of *Who's Afraid of Virginia Woolf?* directed by Mike Nichols, which is generally regarded as a successful rendering of the play.

Following such conspicuous success, Albee's next play, an adaptation of Carson McCullers's *The Ballad of the Sad Cafe* (1963), may necessarily have suffered in its reception. Albee has stated that one of his reasons for writing adaptations (he has done four so far) is to determine whether they can be done successfully. Most modern adaptations, he asserts, involve an uncompensated reduction of the original's form and vigor. Albee's own adaptations, however, have not been as well received as his original plays.

Albee's adaptation certainly shows a faithfulness to McCullers's favorite theme of the destructive potential of romantic love. Moreover, Albee invented a narrator to preserve much of the richly cadenced prose in the novella. The action is quite unified and direct: a physically strong, independent, shrewd, nearly asexual woman, Amelia Evans, runs a general store and operates a still. She is a jack-of-all-trades in a small Georgia cotton-mill community. She takes in a small hunchbacked dwarf, Lyman Willis, who claims to be related to her. Cousin Lyman's presence effects a strange and wonderful change in Miss Amelia: before his arrival she was a gritty and hard, no-nonsense woman, but Lyman makes her softer, happier, even joyful. This change, moreover, is contagious, affecting the entire community. Her store becomes a meeting place where people enjoy a respite from the dull and oppressive routine of their lives in the cotton mill. She permits them to drink on her premises, and this simple decision ends the isolation people ordinarily suffer. It is evident that Cousin Lyman's strange, almost childlike personality has been instrumental in the founding of the cafe.

Because of the cafe, the spirit of the whole town flourishes until Amelia's former husband, Marvin Macy, returns. Years earlier, for reasons known only to herself, Miss Amelia had married him, a union which lasted only "ten unholy days which became a legend, a whispered legend in the town." When he had tried to consummate their marriage, she struck his jaw, breaking one of his teeth, but inflicting a more severe wound upon his pride. Humiliated, he left town. Rumors circulated over the years that he had reverted to his earlier and wilder days, landing in the penitentiary. When Macy returns, Miss Amelia orders him to leave, but Cousin Lyman inexplicably abandons the woman who has befriended and loved him, siding with Macy against Miss Amelia. The play quickly builds to the same climax as the novella: Miss Amelia and Macy battle each other physically, Amelia appearing to win until Cousin Lyman jumps upon her back. Taking advantage of her surprise and humiliation, Macy "beats her senseless, furiously, excessively, as the crowd gasps, yells." Macy and

Lyman completely vandalize the cafe; then they leave town together, having formed a strange bond. Amelia Evans, devastated, retreats irrevocably into exile and solitude, her "terrible dim face . . . like the faces known in dreams" occasionally looking down through the shutters upon the dreary town. The cafe never reopens, and so the whole town, according to the narrator, comes to "silence."

The central theme of both adaptation and novella is poetically represented in the narrator's discourse on love: "Therefore, the quality and value of any love is determined solely by the lover himself. It is for this reason that most of us would rather love than be loved; and the curt truth is that, in a deep secret way, the state of being beloved is intolerable to many; for the lover craves any possible relation with the beloved, even if this experience can cause them both only pain." The triangle formed by Miss Amelia, Cousin Lyman, and Marvin Macy results in a stalemate and contains the seed of tragedy. Both the novella and Albee's adaptation present the tragedy without its causes. Cousin Lyman's motives for betraying Miss Amelia are not dramatized, nor are Miss Amelia's for marrying a man toward whom she feels not the slightest sexual attraction. These paradoxes of behavior, wrapped in the poetic texture of McCullers's prose, appeared to many viewers as purely arbitrary on stage, even though Albee was adhering very closely to his source. This impression is reinforced by the fact that the central characters are extreme individuals, grotesques. Several critics objected to Albee's decision to use a black actor to play the narrator, incorrectly assuming that he was injecting into the play an extraneous element. In an interview Albee stated that his intent was to have the narrator as removed from the townspeople as possible so that his voice and perspective would be objective. Albee's adaptation, although it received mixed reviews, was generally regarded as faithful to the spirit of the novella.

Albee argued in 1968 that audiences, critics and "everybody in general, including playwrights, [should] get rid of this whole notion of the conscious symbolism in realistic or symbolic plays and begin to understand that the use of the unconscious in the 20th Century theatre is its most interesting development." His comment was made with reference to *Box* and *Quotations from Chairman Mao Tse-Tung* (1968), but it could apply as well to several of his other plays, especially to the ambitious and challenging *Tiny Alice* produced in 1964. Even in *Who's Afraid of Virginia Woolf?* one finds elements out of place in a strictly realistic environment. The

origin of Albee's characters, especially in a play like *Tiny Alice*, may be traced to a deep concern with the unconscious. This connection is manifested, at least in part, by Albee's habit of not giving his characters surnames. No character in his original plays has one.

Tiny Alice inquires deeply into the basis of religious thought and feeling. It depicts the struggle of a lay brother, Julian, who confronts the limits of his faith and sanity as he is maneuvered by a Machiavellian scheme into the position of a martyr. During the play's run on Broadway, Albee summarized the central action of the play and suggested how an audience might approach it: "A lay brother, a man who would have become a priest except that he could not reconcile his idea of God with the God which men create in their own image, is sent by his superior to tie up loose ends of a business matter between the church and a wealthy woman. The lay brother becomes enmeshed in an environment which, at its core and shifting surface, contains all the elements which have confused and bothered him throughout his life; the relationship between sexual hysteria and religious ecstasy; the conflict between the selflessness of service and the conspicuous splendor of martyrdom. The lay brother is brought to the point, finally, of having to accept what he had insisted he wanted: union with the abstraction, rather than man-made image of it, its substitution. He is left with pure abstraction—whatever it be called: God, or Alice—and in the end, according to your faith, one of two things happens. Either the abstraction personifies itself, is proved real, or the dying man, in the last necessary effort of self-delusion creates and believes in what he knows does not exist.

"It is, you see, a perfectly straightforward story, dealt with in terms of reality and illusion, symbol and actuality. It is the very simplicity of the play, I think, that has confused so many. It is, of course, neither a straight psychological study nor a philosophical tract, but something of a metaphysical dream play which must be entered into and experienced without preconception, without predetermination of how a play is supposed to go. One must let the play happen to one; one must let the mind loose to respond as it will, to receive impressions without immediately categorizing them, to sense rather than know, to gather rather than immediately understand. The play is full of symbols and allusions, naturally, but they are to be taken as echoes in a cave, things overheard, not fully understood at first. If the play is approached this way, the experience of it will be quite simple.

If, on the other hand, one is instructed to follow the allegory as it moves, to count and relate the symbols, then, of course, the result is confusion, opacity, difficulty."

Most of the action of *Tiny Alice* occurs in a huge castle presumably belonging to Miss Alice. The "business matter" is a gift of two billion dollars Miss Alice wishes to confer upon the church. The gift is being arranged by a lawyer and a cardinal, two men who loathe each other. Gradually it becomes apparent that the cardinal's personal secretary, the lay brother Julian, is to be sacrificed in return for the enormous gift—or more precisely, his soul is to be exchanged for it. This exchange is mediated by Miss Alice, an attractive woman who will marry Julian.

The first of two crucial elements dramatizing this exchange is the interrelation between the huge castle and a detailed miniature or "doll's house" of the castle, kept in the library. In the first act, the butler makes what appears to be a mild joke, suggesting that he and Julian might themselves be represented within the miniature, which, like a Chinese box, contains a miniature of the miniature. When Julian notices a fire in the model, the butler urgently demands to know in which room the fire is burning. When he finds that it is in the chapel, he runs to the castle's chapel and demands that Julian follow to help extinguish the fire. Miss Alice is also frightened, sending the lawyer after them. Alone, Miss Alice both prays and talks to the model. She makes no attempt to extinguish the fire in the model. Later, Julian returns, saying that the chapel was indeed on fire, and that they have put it out. He notices that the miniature chapel is no longer on fire.

The second and related thematic element is Julian's desire not to worship the symbols of God in the place of God Himself: "men make God in their own image," Julian is quoted as saying, enabling them to reduce God's essence, using God merely as an "older brother, scout leader." Refusing to accept this view of God, Julian put himself in an asylum for six years, because he believes he suffers from a loss of faith: "I did not go there to *look* for my faith, but because *it* had left me." During the asylum period Julian had several hallucinations; at least one of them was explicitly sexual. Both he and Miss Alice raise the question of whether the six years in the asylum were not a period of *sanity*. That the hallucinations may have indeed been a true apprehension of reality is posed as a possibility which Julian does not lightly dismiss. Albee's method in *Tiny Alice* is to undermine ex-

pectancy: Is the miniature copied from the castle, or is the miniature the primary construct of which the castle is the replica? Likewise, were Julian's hallucinations the result of true faith, the only one he has known, or were they lapses in a mind made defenseless by sundered faith? The issue is central to Julian's life, and hence to the play itself. He says simply, "my faith and my sanity . . . they are one and the same."

The dramatic progression to Julian's martyrdom is made menacing by the completely unsympathetic characters of the cardinal, butler, and above all, the lawyer, in whose jealous grasp Miss Alice seems helpless, a mere puppet. At the end of act two, Miss Alice and Julian decide to marry. She strongly implies that his marriage is a kind of sacrifice: "come to Alice, Julian, in your sacrifice." The division between Miss Alice, the character, and Alice, the mysterious and God-like abstraction, becomes more apparent.

In act three, Miss Alice, the lawyer, and the butler prepare to leave a confused and horrified Julian alone with Alice, who inhabits the model. The lawyer says, "We are surrogates; our task is done now." Julian insists that he has indeed married a woman. Miss Alice demurs: "no, Julian; you have married her . . . through me." They urge him to remain with the model; *his* task will be to sacrifice himself to that reality as an act of faith: "I am the . . . illusion," Miss Alice insists. But Julian objects: "there is nothing there! There is nothing there!" The cardinal, obeying the lawyer, then orders Julian to remain with the model. In wonder and panic Julian asks himself again whether that time in the asylum was a period of sanity. He decides to go back to the asylum rather than accept Alice, whereupon the lawyer calmly shoots him, and a few seconds later hands the briefcase to the distraught cardinal: "All legal now, the total grant: two billion, kid, twenty years of grace for no work at all; no labor, at least not yours." They leave Julian alone to die.

In the concluding moments he either gives himself completely to Alice, uniting his soul with what is ultimately real, with pure abstraction, or his imagination desperately seizes upon something that his intellect perceives as nonexistent. These perceptions are dramatized in the final seconds of the play by the sound of a heartbeat, which increases in volume from barely audible to nearly deafening, and by the appearance of a shadow that "fills the stage; it is the shadow of a great presence filling the room." The technical achievement of *Tiny Alice* is that Albee has succeeded in representing on the stage a spiritual force as reality. The mystery and force of the central symbol of the play—the miniature model of the castle—derive from a skillful integration of the model with the spiritual struggle between Julian and the other characters.

The critical furor over the virtues, or lack of them, in *Tiny Alice* may now be set aside. "It is indecent to fault a work for being difficult," Albee argued. "Are we to assume that audiences can grasp nothing more complex than simple addition or subtraction?" Certain problems in interpretation do, of course, lie in the work itself. The mystery that is shared by the conspirators but not by the audience for two long acts becomes, in effect, an alienating force. Moreover, if a play has greater clarity in the reading than in the viewing (as Albee claimed *Tiny Alice* did), what conception does the playwright have of the form of the play? Albee's argument here is that there are some plays whose density of construction warrants more than one viewing.

Albee's next production was an adaptation of James Purdy's satiric novel *Malcolm*. Generally regarded as a fiasco, the play closed after the seventh performance. Albee's *Malcolm* (1966) is distinctly inferior to his first adaptation. Why he would have responded to Purdy's novel is readily apparent. The story traces the adventures of a fifteen-year-old boy who has no contact with his parents. The play, like the novel, has a picaresque insouciance. Malcolm is introduced to various bizarre people: Kermit, who claims to be 192 years old; Professor Cox, an astrologer who starts Malcolm on his metaphorical journey; the fabulously wealthy Girards, who try to adopt him; a couple of artists, the Braces; and Melba, a sexually insatiable rock singer, who asks a friend, Gus, to supply Malcolm with some experience—"mature him up a little." Gus takes Malcolm to a cheap brothel, thus preparing him for Melba, whom he marries. The prostitution of basic human values is the governing theme of the play. Through Melba's debauchery Malcolm expires, before the age of twenty, from "acute alcoholism and sexual hyperesthesia," which the doctor defines as "a violent protracted excess of sexual intercourse." Professor Cox declares simply that Malcolm "didn't have the stuff . . . that's all." In the final tableau Malcolm goes to heaven on his golden bench.

Malcolm's journey is a parody of certain American myths, chiefly that wealth and appearances are valuable; human relationships and innocence, however, are but inconvenient hindrances best discarded as quickly as possible. Malcolm has no identity, save that which he absorbs from his companions, none of whom respect anything but indulgence and material gratification. Although these themes may be apparent in the novel, they were not convincing in the production. Many reviewers felt that *Malcolm* was simply a failure in which Albee came closer to self-parody than to the spirit of Purdy's novel.

A Delicate Balance (1966), Albee's next play and winner of his first Pulitzer Prize (1967), demonstrates that traditional terms such as realism, surrealism, absurdism, and naturalism have limited value in describing his mature work. The set—a "living room of a large and well-appointed suburban house"—could well be the physical environment for an Ibsen play, but the two couples (one "normal," the other "deranged"), the controlled modulation of the dialogue (the play concludes with a rather lengthy monologue which Albee compares to an aria), and the perception of a systemic yet undefined crisis invading the lives of all the characters separate *A Delicate Balance* from conventional realism.

Agnes and Tobias, in their late fifties, are well-to-do educated people whose regulated lives suffer a series of jolts between a Friday night and Sunday morning. Living with them is Claire, Agnes's younger sister and an alcoholic (or, as she thinks of it, a willfully heavy drinker). Their thirty-six-year-old daughter Julia returns home, having just broken up with her fourth husband. Finally, Harry and Edna, lifelong friends of Agnes and Tobias, unexpectedly drop in. After several awkward moments it becomes clear that Harry and Edna are suffering from a completely unexplained although quite genuine fear. They have come to Agnes and Tobias—"our best friends in the world"—because they are scared, terrified: "it was like being lost: very young again, with the dark, lost." Slowly Agnes and Tobias realize that Harry and Edna do not intend to return home, except briefly to retrieve some clothes. These events produce a crisis for all six people in the play. Julia predictably has the strongest reaction. She retreats into the hysteria of a little girl dispossessed of her room. Claire remains the dart-tongued bystander. Therefore the unavoidable task of resolving the crisis falls on Agnes and Tobias.

A Delicate Balance concerns itself with loss: not loss which occurs in one swift traumatic stroke, but that which evolves slowly in increments of gentle and lethal acquiescence. Tobias and Agnes have been drifting for some time, of course, but one of the definitive moments of "unmooring" can be traced to the death of their very young son many years earlier. In a complex response of guilt, anger, and refusal to have another child, Tobias moved into another bedroom shortly after his son's death. Agnes suffered this break silently as she went through menopause: "we *could* have had another son; we could have tried," she now tells him. And now Julia, too, is nearing the age of menopause. Agnes is distressed that she may never have any grandchildren. Part of Julia's role in the play is to mirror in an intense fashion her parents' habit of avoiding the consequences of decisions they have made.

However, the appearance of Harry and Edna instigates Tobias's return to Agnes's bed: "it was nice to have you there," she tells him. Agnes contrasts her experience to Proust's: "*Le temps perdu.* I've never understood that; *perdu* means lost, not merely . . . past." This is the central theme of the play. There is a great sense of loss in Agnes's understanding that "everything becomes . . . too late, finally." The time during which basic choices can be made is not everlasting, though one might conduct his life as though it were. *A Delicate Balance,* therefore, examines the passage of time in a crisis, and how the crisis affects one's perception of time.

Much of the criticism of the play attacks Albee for being repetitive: two couples in a living room engaged in a crisis; the death of a child; the sterility of settling down; the failures of educated, intelligent, well-intentioned, and altogether decent people. Such criticism ignores the development of the play. If Tobias is something of an older Peter (from *The Zoo Story*), then it must also be acknowledged that *A Delicate Balance* dramatizes the consequences of the crisis with which *The Zoo Story* ends. Agnes refuses to knit the myriad strands of this new chaos; Tobias must decide what to do with Harry and Edna. It is a major change for them both, because Agnes has trained herself to run her husband's life. The delicate balance of the title, therefore, refers to the precariousness of most people's routine patterns. The surfaces are ordered and neat; the undercurrents are unperceived, or at least unacknowledged—hence dangerous.

A second change is registered in Tobias's climactic outburst in act three. Harry acknowledges that he and Edna would not have taken in Agnes and Tobias in similar circumstances. Tobias reacts finally, horrified at the admission of bankruptcy after forty years of conventionalized friendship: "I DON'T WANT YOU HERE! YOU ASKED?! NO! I DON'T BUT BY CHRIST YOU'RE GOING TO STAY HERE! YOU'VE GOT THE RIGHT!" It is probably the first time Tobias has ever spoken a threatening truth to his friend. The noxious delicate balance has for once been upset, and he has felt the terror beneath. It is a liberating moment, although Agnes smugly predicts that they will soon brush it aside, forget that it happened.

Albee's third adaptation, *Everything in the Garden* (1967), is drawn from a play by the same title written by the late English dramatist Giles Cooper. It is a satire attacking a hollow, materialistic suburban society, and it follows its parent play fairly closely in theme and incident, but differs markedly in tone and characterization. Richard and Jenny are stereotypical suburbanites who, desiring to live beyond their modestly affluent means, have become callous to each other and to their son. They bicker about not buying new clothes; not having a maid; not going on weekend trips; paying for a house, car, their son's private school, and taxes; and finally, about not having a greenhouse. Richard's and Jenny's feelings of self-esteem are determined solely by exterior standards. They consider the price of everything and the value of nothing.

Into their lives comes Mrs. Toothe, an English procuress who offers Jenny afternoon employment in her bordello staffed by middle-class housewives. By degrees Jenny is surprised, horrified, indignant, fascinated, and acquiescent. Without Richard's knowledge she begins her new career as a whore and brings home lots of money. Richard and Jenny's friend, Jack, an alcoholic heir to millions who amuses himself by painting ("God, the ambition you have to have to overcome good fortune. I haven't *got* it," he sardonically moans), witness the arrival of a package of $5,000 in cash which Jenny has anonymously sent to Richard. Albee has Jack step outside the action and directly address the audience throughout the play, the only character to do so. Giles Cooper's Jack is neither wealthy nor does he separate from the action of the play. Albee's Jack is equipped with a delightful sense of humor and a genial disposition. He tells the audience he has decided to leave all his money to Richard and Jenny, since he likes them and has no other connections.

After Jack leaves the house, Richard discovers the origin of the money. He reviles his wife, then weeps at the end of act one as she makes out a liquor list for a party to which she has invited their suburban neighbors. The party scene, which immediately follows in act two, reveals that Richard and Jenny's friends are very much like themselves, obsessed with money and class. Quite unexpectedly, Mrs. Toothe arrives. Jenny panics, but Mrs. Toothe, always cool and firm, refuses to leave. As Jenny's guests wander in from the backyard (Richard has been showing them where the greenhouse will be), Jenny discovers that they, too, are employees of Mrs. Toothe, who now faces a crisis: the police have ordered her out of her establishment. Either the husbands of her staff find her a new place, or she takes the business out of the vicinity. Richard is the only husband who has but recently discovered that his wife is a whore; all the others have known for some time. They elect Richard chairman of the meeting and, to Richard's amazement, calmly settle upon a new location.

Jack arrives from the club, quite drunk. He suddenly recalls Mrs. Toothe's being in the same business many years ago in London. In a fit of laughter, he realizes that the wives of his club friends are all prostitutes. Mrs. Toothe simply says, as Jack is about to leave, "He'll talk. You must make him be quiet." The men suffocate Jack with a sofa pillow. They bury him in a trench in Richard's backyard where Richard has been looking for the cesspool line. The others calmly return to their party. Later Jack steps forward and addresses the audience. Since the authorities can assume only that he has disappeared, it will be seven years before he can be declared legally dead. Richard and Jenny must wait for Jack's money, unaware that Jack had made them his heirs.

The satirical attack of *Everything in the Garden* lacks the force and range of Albee's original plays. It is weakened by a series of belabored coincidences: Jenny's friends worked for Mrs. Toothe without Jenny's knowledge; Jack did not recognize Mrs. Toothe in the first act but could do so in the second; Mrs. Toothe visits Jenny in the second act just as Jenny's party gets under way; and Jenny apparently has no friend who is not employed by Mrs. Toothe. Even though Jack's ability to address the audience directly relieves the playwright from observing realistic conventions, the savagery of Jack's death and the pain and anger in Richard's recognition at the end of act one are authentic. *Everything in the Garden* has an uncertain center of gravity; the objects of its satirical attack are straw men by comparison to those in Albee's other plays.

Albee presented his next two plays, *Box* and *Quotations from Chairman Mao Tse-Tung,* as one interrelated whole. His introductory comment in the published text describes their kinship: although the two plays "are separate works, were conceived at different though not distant moments, stand by themselves, and can be played one without the company of the other, I feel that they are more effective performed enmeshed.... I have attempted, in these two related plays, several experiments having to do—in the main—with the application of musical form to dramatic structure, and the use of *Box* as a parenthesis around *Mao* is part of that experiment."

The structure of both plays represents a radical departure in form. *Box* has no characters, no movement, no narrative. The audience sees only a large cube on stage; through the open side facing the audience one can see the other five sides. A very bright light remains constantly on the cube while a woman's voice can be heard coming not from the cube but from the back or sides of the theater. In a lyrical, supplicating tone this voice ruminates on various images and themes: the beauty of the box, the death of seven hundred million babies, the nature of artistic accomplishment and the pain of its corruption, the sea, nature, a swarm of blackbirds skimming across the ocean, and, above all, loss ("we give up something for something"). The faint sounds of buoys and sea gulls are heard in the background in the conclusion. These thoughts are repeated elegiacally by the voice, none more insistently than that the corruption of humanity is complete "when art hurts," when "the beauty of it reminds us of *loss.* Instead of the attainable. When it tells us what we cannot have . . . well, then . . . it no longer relates . . . *does* it? That is the thing about music. That is why we cannot listen any more. (*Pause*) Because we cry."

The stark immobility of the box on the stage frustrates the audience's natural inclination to look for action, narrative, and explanations. *Box* makes no direct appeal to the intellect. "Whatever symbolic content there may be in *Box* and *Quotations from Chairman Mao Tse-Tung,*" Albee stated in an interview, "both plays deal with the unconscious, primarily. That's where it is, and it must not be pigeonholed, examined, and specified." The simplicity and changelessness of the box on the stage force the audience to receive the voice as a prose poem which explores the relation between art and society. The voice suggests not an individual conflict but summation of the human conscience, of the consequences of man's self-enslavement to method and machinery: "System as conclusion, in the sense of method as an end, the dice so big you can hardly throw them any more. Seven hundred million babies dead in the time it takes, took, to knead the dough to make a proper loaf." *Box* implies that survival of the arts and survival of humanity are absolutely inseparable. The most lethal symptom of a dying society is not war but apathy. The apathy *Box* is concerned with might be defined as an indifference to precision in thought or feeling; an unwillingness to listen or to question; a mammoth passivity; a surrender to the ceaselessly vended baubles of technology.

The distinction between death and dying is vividly drawn in the companion piece, *Quotations from Chairman Mao Tse-Tung*. The second play has four characters: Chairman Mao (who should physically resemble the Chinese leader), the long-winded lady, an old woman, and a minister. However, they speak independently of one another. (The minister nods in and out of sleep and has no lines.) There is no interconnected conflict. The two plays are unified visually by the set of *Box* appearing within the set of *Quotations from Chairman Mao Tse-Tung*, which is the deck of an ocean liner. Moreover, the woman's voice repeats passages from *Box* at various intervals in *Quotations from Chairman Mao Tse-Tung*.

Mao's speeches, taken from the historical leader's writings, consist mostly of bromides which extol communism and attack American capitalism. Individualism is necessarily an anathema in Mao's world. Mao preaches, rather chillingly, the necessity of war as a cathartic virtue, purging poison and filth from the world. "His tone is always reasonable," Albee notes, putting great tension between the manner and matter of his words.

Juxtaposed to Mao are the old woman, who repeats a doggerel poem, "Over the Hill to the Poor-House," and the long-winded lady, whose articulate memory is akin to Agnes's in *A Delicate Balance*. The old woman's poem tells a melodramatic story of a woman who worked hard, was a good wife, and raised her six children, only to be put in the poorhouse after her husband's death and subsequent rejection by her children. The long-winded lady's husband has died too, and she makes the point that he only had to suffer his dying whereas she had to survive both his dying and his death. "Death? You stop about death, finally, seriously, when you're on to *dying*. . . . Death is nothing; there . . . there *is* no death. There is only life and dying."

The concluding part of *Box*, which is subtitled "Reprise," recapitulates the themes of loss and corruption of art; for when art begins to hurt, "it's time to look around. Yes it is." Together the two plays present death, revolution, war, societal decline and its corollary of artistic falsification (the mendacity of mere craft) as consequences of self-destroying apathy. Dying (as opposed to death) is not a matter of chronology; rather, it is the im-mediate result of becoming careless, indifferent, content with blandishments. Both works insist that the opposite of dying is not to be functional but to be vigilant. Each play is designed to appeal to the intuitive rather than to the rational mind, to that sector of the imagination which draws directly upon the unconscious.

All Over (1971), Albee's next work, is his most developed statement about death and dying. Set in a large paneled bedroom/sitting room, the play examines how the family members of a famous, powerful, and dying man attempt to understand their own lives. A large four-poster bed occupies the back of the room. The audience never sees or hears the dying man, who is obscured by a hospital screen around the bed. The family and the press have gathered to witness his final hours.

In the room are his wife (age seventy-one), son (fifty-two), daughter (forty-five), and mistress (sixty-one); also his best friend (seventy-three), his doctor (eighty-six), and nurse (sixty-five). No character is given a name. Except for the son and daughter, who leave the room only for brief periods, these characters remain on the stage for the entire play.

All Over is almost entirely devoid of incident. Sentimentality never threatens the tone of the play. Since the dying man is only a presence, Albee avoids disproportionate pathos. Instead, seven intimately related people wrestle with loneliness, the failure to love, the vulnerability of being loved, loss, and the irrevocability of the past. The structure of the play could hardly be more uncluttered: they simply wait for a man to die. The only incident is the brief intrusion and violent expulsion of two photographers and a reporter. The man's death at the play's conclusion is almost superfluous. The physical fact of death is hardly more than the closing of a parenthesis since the substance of dying is the major concern. The mistress, wife, and best friend all remark on the "closing down" of some portion of the self. That, and not the formal name of disease, is the cause of death: "it can be anything, or nearly nothing," the mistress says, "except that it moves you back into yourself a little, the knowledge that all your sharing has been . . . willful, and that nothing has been inevitable . . . or even necessary. When the eyes close down; go out."

All Over strongly implies that the opposite of love is not hate but dying. The physical processes of dying are a response to the will of the soul. At the conclusion of the first act, the daughter asks if she is loved by anyone. The mother rejoins: "Do *you* love anyone?" After the daughter angrily leaves the room, the wife recalls how the same exchange had occurred many years earlier between herself and her aunt, whereupon the aunt slapped her. This memory is the basis for the climax in act two. The wife realizes that she cannot resent the mistress's usurpation "because I no longer had what you up and took." Then the wife tells the mistress, "I don't love you. I don't love *anyone.* (*Pause*) Any more." Contrary to the view of love expressed in *The Ballad of the Sad Cafe,* the wife believes that "we love to *be* loved, and when it's taken away . . . then why not rage . . . or pule."

Like *A Delicate Balance, All Over* ends with an elegiac recognition reached by the central character (here it is the wife). Confronting the foundation of her life, she has the courage to acknowledge its hollowness, its unhappiness. The verbal texture of *All Over,* however, seems closer to that of *Box* and *Quotations from Chairman Mao Tse-Tung,* particularly in the way its speeches overlap rather than interconnect.

The battle against settling in in middle age receives a startlingly different treatment in *Seascape,* which appeared four years after *All Over,* in 1975. *Seascape* places this issue distinctly within the context of evolution. Albee's familiar psychological territory—two couples confronting themselves as they confront each other—is altered by a rather extraordinary feature: two green sea creatures who have the gift of speech are one of the couples. *Seascape* is extremely witty in its treatment of fundamental losses: loss of purpose in life, racial differences, child rearing, the problems of mutual understanding.

At the opening of *Seascape,* Nancy and Charlie are finishing a picnic lunch on a bright sand dune near the ocean. Having raised three children, they seem to have no major activity now. Nancy spins a charming daydream of their becoming "seaside nomads," traveling all about the world visiting beaches: "There's nothing binding us; you *hate* the city." Nancy is still adventurous; Charlie is the opposite. They debate the state of their marriage, the position their lives have come to, and the play's energy and sympathy clearly fall on Nancy's side.

Two large sea creatures which resemble lizards raise their heads over the dunes. They each have four legs, a long tail, and scales, but they behave in most respects like humans. Charlie's immediate response to the lizards is fear and defense; Nancy's is enthusiastic wonder. As act one concludes, Charlie and Nancy roll over on their backs, draw their legs up, and smile broadly in imitation

of a submissive posture which Nancy recalls having seen in a book long ago.

In act two, the audience learns that the sea creatures, named Leslie and Sarah (who have not spoken in the first act), are intelligent creatures. After some uneasy moments, they begin talking with the humans about their different environments and manners: Sarah has laid about seven thousand eggs, but Nancy has had only three children ("What did I tell you?!" Leslie explodes at Sarah; "They don't even lay eggs!"); Nancy shows her breasts to Sarah (Charlie objects when Leslie starts to have a look), and Sarah realizes that Nancy's body must be similar in some way to a whale's; and more dangerously, Nancy and Charlie try to explain the emotions: "Fear. Hatred. Apprehension. Loss. Love." Leslie and Sarah become more and more confused. Much of the humor of *Seascape* arises from the dilemma that the sea creatures are just as rational and intelligent as Charlie and Nancy and have the same problems as humans (Leslie is a bigot when it comes to fish: fish are dirty and stupid); but they are, of course, alien to Western civilization. They have come out of the ocean because "we had a sense of not belonging any more." Charlie talks about evolutionary change, the opting for alteration and the continuance of life with new forms. Species unable to alter themselves are doomed. And not just species, the play asserts, but civilizations and individuals are treading a death march if they turn their backs upon the phenomenon Charlie calls "flux." The flux was produced out of the "primordial soup? the glop? That heartbreaking second when it all got together, the sugars and the acids and the ultraviolets, and the next thing you knew there were tangerines and string quartets."

The pertinence of these remarks is obvious: the sea creatures have decided to make a fundamental change in their lives rather than shrivel in complacent superannuation. They are the foils to Charlie and Nancy's problems presented in act one: will the humans make changes and remain vital, or settle in and go back to sleep?

This choice reaches a crisis as Charlie evokes, rather than defines, an emotion for the sea creatures. He asks Sarah what she would do "if Leslie went away . . . and if you knew he was never coming back? What about that?" Sarah begins to cry; "I want to go back [to the ocean]. I don't want to stay here any more." It is the first time Sarah has ever cried, ever felt loss or mortality. Leslie attacks Charlie, hitting and choking him. The women prevail upon Leslie, and he releases Charlie. Dejected, the sea creatures start retreating to the ocean. Nancy says they can't return there: "you don't have any choice. Don't you know that? You'll have to come back up." Then she offers to help them in their new environment, and so does Charlie. The play concludes with Leslie's response: "All right. Begin." This challenge suggests that Charlie and Nancy have little choice but to alter their lives as well. *Seascape*, which won the Pulitzer Prize in 1975, is a distinguished work. Its originality, its wit, theme, reversals, its steady eye on that which lives or perishes, and Albee's characteristically precise ear for dialogue are combined with unusual control.

Listening and *Counting the Ways* were composed separately but presented together on 28 January 1977 at the Hartford Stage Company. *Listening,* subtitled "A Chamber Play," was commissioned as a radio play and broadcast in 1976. Its characters are a man and a woman, both about fifty years old, a "thin, fragile, pretty" girl about twenty-five, and a recorded voice. *Listening* is largely concerned with mental illness and remorse.

The unifying stylistic device is the woman's seemingly omnipotent control over the younger girl. When the woman snaps her fingers, the girl springs animatedly into conversation, and the recorded voice counts the beat. There are twenty beats or scenes in the play, and the voice has the curtain word "End" as the girl commits (reenacts?) her suicide by slitting her wrists. *Listening* explores how the mind succumbs to habit, draws false pictures for itself rather than attend carefully to what is being said. The girl's reiterated gambit each time the woman snaps her fingers is: "You don't listen. . . . Pay attention, rather, is what you don't do." This gambit is reversed just before her suicide when the woman speaks these lines to the hesitant and fearful girl. Not to listen is not to validate another's existence. *Listening* presents remorse as the most certain, perhaps the most irreducible element in a threatened mind: "I cried when my parents died," the woman says, "I cried when *I* . . . died."

Counting the Ways, subtitled "A Vaudeville," is a variation on the related theme of how one verifies (or refuses to verify) another's love. Divided into twenty-one scenes, most of them quite brief, this one-act piece presents two characters permuting a single question: "Do you love me?" But the play constantly deflates sentimental notions about love. Part of Albee's method is to give one character a long "straight" speech and the other the "gag" lines, as in the vaudeville skits he no doubt saw in his adoptive father's theaters. The play's poignancy arises out of its carefully insinuated assumption: to

love is to be vulnerable to loss; and to be loved is to have one's identity subject to the support of another.

In his next play, *The Lady from Dubuque*, produced on Broadway at the Morosco Theatre on 31 January 1980, Albee returned to the same ground he covered in *All Over:* the process of dying. *The Lady from Dubuque* is a mysterious intruder who arrives to comfort Jo, suffering from a painful, fatal disease, and to help her die. The unidentified woman, who claims to be Jo's mother, provides the relief that Jo's husband and neighbors cannot.

The play begins in familiar Albee territory. Three couples spend the first act playing games and sniping at each other. The play begins with the question "Who am I?" (the characters are playing Twenty Questions), which is repeated throughout the evening. Unfortunately, the characters are uninteresting types rather than actual people, and the "closed-circuit bitchery," as John Simon described it, repeats what Albee had done in his earlier plays.

At the end of the first act, after the neighbors have traded insults and departed, Jo has another attack and her husband Sam carries her upstairs to bed. Elizabeth, the mysterious visitor, and Oscar, her elegant, middle-aged black companion, arrive as the curtain falls. In the second act, when Sam awakens, he confronts the pair downstairs and demands to know their identities. He is outraged when Elizabeth says she is Jo's mother from Dubuque. After trying in vain to get rid of the two, Sam finally agrees to bring Jo down, hoping that when she doesn't recognize them, they will leave. When he goes to get Jo, the guests from the previous night arrive. They are confused by Elizabeth and Oscar, but they soon accept Elizabeth's explanation of their presence. When Jo appears, she blindly goes to Elizabeth, who promises to hold and comfort her. In despair, Sam tries to drag Jo from Elizabeth's arms, but he is immobilized by Oscar, a karate expert. Sam's friends berate him and support Elizabeth. After they leave, Jo's condition worsens, and Sam tries to rouse her, but she asks him to just let her die. Obliging her, Oscar, dressed in Sam's robe, carries her up to her room. When he returns, the pair leaves as the curtain falls.

Critics almost unanimously saw Elizabeth as the Angel of Death and Oscar as her Messenger in an echo of *The Sandbox*. Albee himself denied that interpretation. In a *New York Times* interview, 27 January 1980, he said, "Angel of Death? I'd hate to say that. We have whatever Jo needs. . . . The play is about her moving into her own plane of reality so she can die, and it's about her husband Sam's loss, the fact that he has lost contact with her. If anybody wants to see Elizabeth and Oscar as the Angel of Death, I don't suppose there's anything I can do to stop them."

The critical reaction was mainly negative and the production ran for only twelve performances. Critics noted that the characters seemed artificial and that the two acts seemed to come from separate plays. They also faulted Albee's device of allowing the characters to address the audience directly, calling it a purposeless distraction. However, Otis Guernsey did select the play as one of *The Best Plays of 1979-1980*.

Albee's next Broadway production was another adaptation. This time he tackled Vladimir Nabokov's *Lolita*, produced at the Brooks Atkinson Theatre on 19 March 1981. The play was embroiled in controversy before rehearsals even started due to the decision by the playwright and the producer to cast a young teenage girl in the title role. The casting calls were protested by Women Against Pornography, who later picketed the finished production as well, and the production team finally decided to cast twenty-three-year-old Blanche Baker as Lolita when they couldn't find a younger actress with the qualities they were seeking.

Despite problems with the script and the performers during tryouts in Boston, performances were sold out, but the play opened to negative reviews in New York. In general the critics noted that instead of showing Humbert Humbert's obsession with the nymphet Lolita, Albee's adaptation concentrated on the seamier side of their relationship. To preserve some of Nabokov's prose, Albee created a narrator, called a Certain Gentleman, who summarized action and conversed with Humbert. Most viewers felt that this character was unsuccessful. John Simon went so far as to write that Albee's adaptation was "not only not heterosexual, but it exudes homosexual camp." While Simon may have overstated his case, questions about homosexual attitudes in Albee's work had been raised throughout the 1970s and 1980s. After twelve performances, *Lolita* left Broadway.

The Man Who Had Three Arms, presented at the Lyceum Theatre on 5 April 1983, is Albee's most recent Broadway production. Commissioned by the New World Festival, the play was first produced at the Players State Theatre in Miami and presented at Chicago's Goodman Theatre in October 1982 before it reached New York.

Most critics agreed with Frank Rich who thought *The Man Who Had Three Arms* wasn't a play, but a "temper tantrum in two acts." The protagonist, known simply as Himself, is the substitute speaker at a lecture series (the scheduled speaker has just died), and his address is the entire play. Two other performers introduce the speaker and act out a few scenes illustrating Himself's past as he speaks. In his speech, he describes the fame he received when a third arm suddenly grew out of his back and the bitterness he feels when his celebrity vanished as soon as the extra arm did. He complains that the money, fame, and sex to which he helped himself freely have been withdrawn and announces that they were empty. He insults the audience while comparing his experience to martyrdom, and he admits an inability to distinguish between self-disgust and his disgust with others. Finally working himself into a rage, he falls to his knees yelling at the audience to leave and begging it to stay as the curtain falls.

While Albee may have written the play as an indictment of the material values that have come to dominate American society, many viewers saw it as an autobiographical rant. They felt that the unsympathetic hero, who complains about the shallow perquisites of his fame that he had greedily embraced, was a substitute for the playwright himself, lamenting the deterioration of his talents and his failure to fill the role of Great American Playwright ordained for him after the success of *Who's Afraid of Virginia Woolf?*

The play was also faulted for its misogyny. During his attacks on the audience and the people in his past, Himself especially targeted women. According to Frank Rich, "baggage" was perhaps the nicest phrase used to describe women. By 1983 critics had come to see these misogynistic attacks as characteristic of Albee's style. The play, which Albee also directed, ran for only sixteen performances.

Albee's latest play, *Finding the Sun*, was commissioned by the University of Northern Colorado and presented 10-14 May 1983 at the Frazier Theatre, Greeley, Colorado. Albee, in residence at the university, staged the one-act drama himself. The play, which he described as "pointillist in manner," presented the relationship between three married couples and a mother and son in twenty-two scenes. Albee plans to revise the work, and it may eventually be produced professionally.

Although Albee's popularity has declined in the past decade, his plays still provoke much interest and discussion. His greatest achievements

Patricia Kilgarriff as The Woman, Robert Drivas as Himself, and William Prince as The Man in a scene from The Man with Three Arms. *The play ran on Broadway for sixteen days (photo by Martha Swope).*

have been his ability to explore various dramatic traditions and forms, his capacity for experimentation, and his continual challenging of his audiences. His plays of the 1960s assure him a prominent place in American dramatic history.

Interviews:

Digby Diehl, "Edward Albee Interviewed," *Transatlantic Review*, 13 (Summer 1963): 57-72;
An interview discussing Albee's dissatisfaction with American society.

R. S. Stewart, "John Gielgud and Edward Albee Talk About the Theatre," *Atlantic*, 215 (April 1965): 61-68;
Discussions about the production of *Tiny Alice*,

mentioning Albee's theories of playwriting and the responsibilities of the writer.

Michael E. Rutenberg, "Two Interviews with Edward Albee," in his *Edward Albee, Playwright in Protest* (New York: DBS Publishers, 1970), pp. 229-260;
The first interview, 17 March 1965, discusses structure, characterization, staging, and interpretation of plays from *The Zoo Story* through *Tiny Alice*. The second interview, 7 August 1968, discusses later plays, screenwriting, the title and idea of *Tiny Alice*, and the homosexual implications of *Virginia Woolf*.

Bibliographies:

Richard E. Amacher and Margaret Rule, *Edward*

Albee at Home and Abroad (New York: AMS Press, 1973);

Charles Lee Green, *Edward Albee: An Annotated Bibliography 1968-1977* (New York: AMS Press, 1980).

References:

Linda Ben-Zvi, Review of *Finding the Sun, Theatre Journal*, 36 (March 1984): 102-103;
One of the few reviews of this Albee play produced in Colorado.

C. W. E. Bigsby, *Albee* (Edinburgh: Oliver & Boyd, 1969);
This book gives Albee's biography to 1958 and analyzes the plays up to *A Delicate Balance*.

Robert Brustein, *Seasons of Discontent* (New York: Simon & Schuster, 1965), pp. 26-29, 46-49, 145-148, 155-158, 304-311;
Reviews of Albee's productions.

Brustein, *The Theatre of Revolt: An Approach to Modern Drama* (Boston: Little, Brown, 1964);
This book on experimental theater relates Albee to existential revolt and the Pirandellian theme of conflict between illusion and reality.

Martin Esslin, *The Theatre of the Absurd* (Garden City: Doubleday, 1969), pp. 266-270;
This valuable overview of the experimental theater discusses Albee and his contemporaries.

John Gassner, "Edward Albee: An American Dream?," in *Dramatic Soundings* (New York: Crown, 1968), pp. 591-607;
Discussion of Albee's plays.

Mel Gussow, "Albee, Odd Man in on Broadway," *Newsweek*, 61 (4 February 1963): 49-52;
An interview with Albee relating him to the other American absurdist dramatists.

Barbara La Fontant, "Triple Threat On, Off and Off-Off Broadway," *New York Times*, 25 February 1968, pp. 36-37, 39, 40, 42, 44, 46;
An extensive article on Albee as a person and on the Albee-Barr-Wilder producing team and their encouragement of young writers.

Anne Paolucci, *From Tension to Tonic: The Plays of Edward Albee* (Carbondale: Southern Illinois University Press, 1972);
Discusses Albee's work as existential and considers him the first important writer since O'Neill to break away from message plays.

Michael E. Rutenberg, *Edward Albee: Playwright in Protest* (New York: DBS Publishers, 1970);
A general analysis of Albee's plays up to *Box* and *Chairman Mao Tse-Tung*. Includes two important interviews with Albee.

Nelson Algren

This entry was updated by Kenneth G. McCollum (Lisbonfalls, Maine) from his entry in
DLB 9, American Novelists, 1910-1945.

Places	Chicago France	New Orleans University of Iowa	Patterson, New Jersey University of Florida
Influences and Relationships	Richard Wright Simone de Beauvoir	Jack Conroy Willard Motley Charles-Pierre Baudelaire	Studs Terkel Ernest Hemingway
Literary Movements and Forms	Naturalism	Proletarian Fiction	
Major Themes	Social Protest Poverty and Failure Racial and Ethnic Prejudice	Slum Dwelling Derrogation of Women Environmental Entrapment	Social Injustice Drug Addiction American Dream Gone Wrong
Cultural and Artistic Influences	Boxing	Horse Racing	
Social and Economic Influences	The Army Urban Poverty	Socialism Judicial System	The Depression

See the Algren entries in DLB Yearbook 1981, 1982.

BIRTH: Detroit, Michigan, 28 March 1909.

EDUCATION: B.A., University of Illinois, 1931.

MARRIAGES: 1936 to Amanda Kontowicz (divorced). 1965 to Betty Ann Jones (divorced).

AWARDS AND HONORS: National Book Award for *The Man with the Golden Arm,* 1950; elected to American Academy, National Institute of Arts and Letters, 1981.

DEATH: Sag Harbor, Long Island, 9 May 1981.

BOOKS: *Somebody in Boots* (New York: Vanguard, 1935; London: Constable, 1937);
Never Come Morning (New York & London: Harper, 1942; London: Spearman, 1958);
The Neon Wilderness (Garden City: Doubleday, 1947; London: Deutsch, 1965);
The Man with the Golden Arm (Garden City: Doubleday, 1949; London: Spearman, 1959);
Chicago: City on the Make (Garden City: Doubleday, 1951);
A Walk on the Wild Side (New York: Farrar, Straus & Cudahy, 1956; London: Spearman, 1957);
Who Lost an American? (London: Deutsch, 1963; New York: Macmillan, 1963);
Notes From a Sea Diary: Hemingway All the Way (New York: Putnam's, 1965; London: Deutsch, 1966);
The Last Carousel (New York: Putnam's, 1973);
Calhoun [German translation] (Frankfurt: Zweitausendeins, 1982); republished in English as *The Devil's Stocking* (New York: Arbor House, 1983).

OTHER: *Nelson Algren's Own Book of Lonesome Monsters,* edited, with a preface, by Algren (New York: Lancer, 1962; London: Hamilton, 1964).

Nelson Algren can be categorized, first of all, as a journalist. For forty-eight years he recorded life in the back alleys of America's cities and the problems of isolated people with no skills who are victims of hostile environments with which they are in constant combat. Born Nelson Ahlgren Abraham in Detroit, Michigan, he spent most of his early years in Chicago and was awarded a degree in journalism from the University of Illinois in 1931, dur-

Nelson Algren

ing the depths of the Depression. Unable to find employment, he left Chicago and drifted to New Orleans and later to the Southwest, riding boxcars and taking odd jobs when he could find them.

In 1933 an Algren short story, "So Help Me," was accepted and published by *Story* magazine. This tale of the Southwest, based on Algren's experience, was noticed by Vanguard publishers, who gave him a small advance to work on a novel that appeared in 1935. *Somebody in Boots* is the picaresque story of Cass McKay, an illiterate youth from a Texas border town "where even children drank and smoked." Driven from home by a violent father, Cass becomes the prototypical wandering hobo of the early 1930s.

Originally titled "Native Son," *Somebody in Boots,* dedicated to "Those innumerable thousands: The Homeless Boys of America," is a proletarian novel by an author disillusioned with the American Dream and the standard concept of success. Algren was aligned with the Communist party when he wrote the novel, although he was not a member. He continued to support the party line advanced in the Soviet Union by the Russian Association of Proletarian Writers until the late 1930s, when the Federal Writers Project gave him a job and a chance to write. Of *Somebody in Boots*, Algren says in a 1973 letter, "It was dead-serious. It was dead-serious because the author was dead-serious. . . . No room for laughs. Survival was the story and revolution the theme. The Proletariat was about to rise and build the New Jerusalem on the ashes of Capitalist Imperialism. The book was originally intended as a trumpet-call to arms."

Somebody in Boots has an erratic style, ranging from tender romance to didactic Marxism. The story is often loose and rambling, partly because the lives of the characters portrayed are uncertain and disconnected. There are, however, certain Algren characteristics in this first book that recur in his later novels: a preoccupation with the nearness of death; the choice of poverty-stricken, illiterate characters; and a rich, lyrical prose style that employs poetic techniques. Algren relies heavily on images of light and darkness for effect in *Somebody in Boots*. Particularly evident are yellow and black, "the colors of sun and blood, the hue of life and the shade of death." When Cass McKay meets Norah Egan in Chicago, he experiences "Such a sudden coming into the sun, after the night that had been so long. . . . His head had been clogged with darkness, and now it was clear."

Cass is always conscious of the nearness of death, and death at its most grotesque haunts him constantly. His brother Bryan kills a cat by wrenching off its head. After Cass has been beaten and thrown in an alley in New Orleans, he awakens to see a dog's head with ants in its eyes. Finally, after seeing a Mexican girl beheaded by a train, Cass wonders, "Was this all that poor people did? Did everything—cats and hawks and men and women—did all these live only to eat, fight, and die?"

There is also an intense concentration on the biological needs of the characters in *Somebody in Boots* and defiance of any Judeo-Christian significance or principles. Cass McKay's sister, in pondering her circumstances, says, "Mebbe we been sinnin' an' he are punishin'," but Cass replies, "Reckon the wrongest sin we done, sister, was just bein' bo'n hungry in a pesthole in Texas." It is not surprising that such French Existentialists as Simone de Beauvoir and Jean-Paul Sartre were attracted later to Algren's work. Without conscious philosophical design, Algren deals with man in a world of chance in a universe that is indifferent or even hostile to his sense of himself. Algren's works

abound with manifestations of such existential terms as *dread, anxiety, despair, nothingness, alienation,* and *the absurd.*

There is a sharp contrast between the clean, pampered American women of the bourgeoisie and Algren's women. Because they have no skills, the women in *Somebody in Boots* resort to prostitution and are doomed to poverty, disease, and mistreatment by men. Further, blacks and Mexicans are treated by society as subhumans who have no rights. For these iniquities, Algren warns capitalists, "Get all you can while yet you may. For the red day will come for your kind, be assured."

Algren's panoramic onslaught also engaged American journalism, which he accuses of misleading the public, specifically regarding the Chicago World's Fair of 1934. He observes that the "good Christian editors" put out "star-spangled spew that they termed 'editorials.' They were proud of their souls, for their souls were clean; and proud of their churches, for their churches were large; and proud of their schools, for their schools taught conformity; but proudest by far were they of their Fair, their great Century-of-Progress slut stretched out on a six-mile bed along the lake. . . ."

These attacks contrast the standard American interpretation of success with what Algren had seen of poverty and failure. For his effort, he was generally accepted by the Marxists in the proletarian movement, as evidenced by an excerpt from *Somebody in Boots* in *Masses*, a radical magazine published in Toronto during the early 1930s. However, the *New Republic* found that "*Somebody in Boots* deals with matters that can't help being interesting for themselves when authentic; but it would make a fair book only if its author had thrown it out and used what he has apparently learned to write another." James T. Farrell said much later that *Somebody in Boots* is "A powerful work . . . one of the books of the thirties which is likely to outlive its own time."

Disappointed with the reception of *Somebody in Boots*, Algren did not attempt another novel until 1940, when he began writing *Never Come Morning*. Between 1935 and 1940 he wrote for the WPA, published a few poems, and, with Jack Conroy, edited the *New Anvil*, a small leftist magazine. In 1936 Algren married Amanda Kontowicz, to whom he later dedicated *The Man with the Golden Arm* (1949). In 1939 their marriage ended in divorce as did his marriage to Betty Ann Jones from 1965 to 1967.

Never Come Morning (1942) received favorable comments from the critics, although the subject matter and some of the themes Algren developed in the 1930s continue in this novel and his subsequent novels written after World War II. Richard Wright, in the introduction, suggests the intent of the book: "To the greater understanding of our times, *Never Come Morning* portrays what actually exists in the nerve, brain, and blood of our boys on the street, be they black, white, or foreign born."

Never Come Morning avoids the melodrama and sentimentality of *Somebody in Boots* but evidences the same tone of naturalism, or that type of realism, as Philip Rahv says, "in which the individual is portrayed not merely as subordinate to his background but wholly determined by it—that type of realism, in other words, in which the environment displaces its inhabitants in the role of the hero."

The story is set in a Polish community of the Chicago slums in the WPA days of the late 1930s. The author establishes his position in this setting with an epigraph taken from Walt Whitman's "You Felons on Trial in Courts" in *Autumn Rivulets:*

I feel I am of them—
I belong to those convicts and prostitutes myself—
And henceforth I will not deny them—
For how can I deny myself?

At the time, Algren was living in a section of Chicago's Cottage Grove Avenue. The neighborhood was called Rat Alley for its large rats that, according to Jack Conroy, "Nelson fought tooth and nail. . . . Even flattened tin cans over their holes."

The protagonist of *Never Come Morning*, Bruno Bicek, is a tough street kid who wants to be a champion fighter. Unlike the typical American hero, Bruno lies, steals, drinks, turns pimp, and even commits a murder. His girl, Steffi Rostenkowski, like the women in *Somebody in Boots*, is a two-dimensional accessory in Algren's plot. She is an innocent resident of the slums and is seduced by Bruno, who even permits his gang to rape her in the shadows of the El. Bruno's physical conquest of Steffi smacks of lower-animal sexuality. There is no love on Bruno's part—only conquest, symbolic of the differences between Algren's perception and the middle-class idea of what was going on in America. To Algren, niceness, purity, and fairness were part of a myth that disguised the strong taking from the weak.

Steffi, very similar to Maggie in Stephen Crane's *Maggie: A Girl of the Streets* (1893), is driven to prostitution. Her obsession with money is the strongest Marxist statement in the book, although

by now Algren had become an independent radical without any specific political affiliation. Steffi assumes bitterly that money to pay the police is the only way out of her troubles and the only salvation for Bruno. To be without money is certain destruction.

Algren continues his effective use of light and dark in *Never Come Morning,* as Bruno "remembered the sun as a hostile thing coming between the El ties; remembered sunlight as others recall it seen first through trees or climbing vines. . . . His preference for shadows remained." Indeed, all of the Algren characters have a preference for shadows. Sunlight and daytime are "hostile things." The Algren people exist by night, as the title of this second novel indicates.

Never Come Morning reaches a climax when Bruno wins a fight with Honeyboy Tucker and becomes a contender for the championship. After being betrayed by two members of his gang, however, Bruno is arrested for a murder he has committed. His environment has caught up with him, and there is little hope for him or Steffi.

Algren entered the army as a private in 1942 and remained a private until his discharge in 1945. While there, he found more material for his writing, some of which went into *The Neon Wilderness* (1947), called by Maxwell Geismar "an excellent collection of short stories, perhaps one of the best we had in the 1940's." Some of his army experience also found its way into the novel for which Algren is best known, *The Man with the Golden Arm* (1949), winner of the first National Book Award.

In *The Man with the Golden Arm*, Algren brings together all the sympathy he felt for the people of the street with the stronger characterization he had begun to develop in *Never Come Morning*. The setting is again the Chicago slums, where Frankie Machine (Francis Majcinek), an ex-GI, deals cards in a local gambling house. Frankie, a morphine addict, is haunted by his guilt over causing an auto accident that crippled his wife Zosh. Zosh uses her infirmity to bind Frankie to her, as her fear of losing him becomes a psychotic obsession.

Appropriately for an Algren novel, *The Man with the Golden Arm* begins in a local precinct jail. The "leaden station-house twilight," the "smoke-colored rain," the "twenty-watt bulbs," and a dark "oversized roach twirling its feelers . . . from beneath a radiator" establish Algren's characteristic low-light mood for the novel. The characters never emerge from this darkness, which is reinforced by the psychological darkness in the quotation from F. Scott Fitzgerald's *The Crack-Up* (1945) beginning

Dust jacket for Algren's 1947 collection of stories about the dispossessed

part two of the novel, "In the real dark night of the soul it is always three o'clock in the morning day after day."

Algren uses several techniques in *The Man with the Golden Arm* that he had not developed fully in his previous novels. The personal interactions of the characters have more impact on the progression of the plot than does the effect of total environment. The romantic sexual love Frankie and his mistress, Molly Novotny, feel for each other not only contributes to a more unified story, but also adds to the book's popular appeal.

The characterization of women in *The Man with the Golden Arm* is decidedly stronger, as Algren brings to fruition in Molly Novotny the type of character he had tried to develop with the good-hearted prostitutes Norah and Steffi in his first two novels. Frankie even tells her, "you got the good kind of heart, the kind that melts a guy." Molly, however, is not a prostitute, although she hustles drinks at a local bar. She is married to a drunk who constantly abuses her, but she remains psychologically virginal, as Algren indicates symbolically. The first night that Frankie makes love to Molly, she greets him at the door in a fresh white dress. Furthermore, "she kept the window's single curtain fresh, to hang as white and limply as a curtain overlooking a country lawn." Molly is perceptive enough to understand Frankie's needs but represents simple, uncomplicated sexual love. She alone provides true relief for Frankie's despair.

Frankie is finally pursued for the murder of Nifty Louie, his pusher, and goes on the run. In his confusion and desolation, he takes his own life. However, the personal tragedy of Frankie Machine is not death, but loneliness and isolation in an environment where everybody hustles and everybody is on the take. Frankie has found "It was just so damned hard to fight alone . . . with so little to fight for."

Algren had reached maturity as a writer by the time of *The Man with the Golden Arm*. *Time* magazine found that the novel "shows up a rotted piece of U.S. life without indulging in a paragraph of preaching," and *Saturday Review* proclaimed that "Nelson Algren seems to be about the only one willing and capable enough to carry on a tradition that passed through mutations given it by Sherwood Anderson, Ben Hecht, Carl Sandburg, and James T. Farrell." A film version of *The Man with the Golden Arm* was produced by Otto Preminger. The movie was received well, although Algren was appalled by the selection of Frank Sinatra as Frankie Machine. Algren eventually filed a lawsuit against Preminger concerning the movie rights, but he lost the case.

French novelist Simone de Beauvoir came to America in 1947 while Algren was working on *The Man with the Golden Arm*. She had heard from friends that there were people with the *Partisan Review* who would help her see New York. Her contacts there steered her to Algren in Chicago,

Dust jacket for Algren's 1949 novel about Frankie Machine, a doomed dope addict in Chicago's Division Street. Algren was dismayed by the decision to cast Frank Sinatra as Machine in the movie adaptation.

after finding that she had a natural attraction for typical Algren haunts. The two soon became friends and traveling companions, touring the United States and parts of Latin America during her first visit. Later she wrote, "To explore an unfamiliar country is work, but to possess it through the love of an appealing foreigner is a miracle." In 1949 Algren joined de Beauvoir in Paris, where she introduced him to such members of her circle as Jean-Paul Sartre and Juliette Greco. They also visited Marseilles, a city with which Algren had fallen in love during World War II.

In the summer of 1950 Algren and de Beauvoir shared a cottage on Lake Michigan, but during this time his affection for her waned. A break in the affair came in the fall of 1951 when de Beauvoir joined Algren in Miller, Indiana, after having been in Paris for a year. In 1960, however, they met in Seville and traveled to Istanbul, Crete, Athens, and Paris. De Beauvoir wrote of her experiences with Algren in her diary, *America Day by Day* (1948), in her semi-autobiographical novel, *The Mandarins* (1954), and in her autobiography, *Force of Circumstance* (1963). Algren found these exposés repulsive, and he lashed out in *Harper's* with a review of *Force of Circumstance* titled "The Question of Simone de Beauvoir." He even attacked her writing style: "While other writers reproach the reader gently, she flattens his nose against the blackboard,

gooses him with a twelve-inch ruler, and warns him if he doesn't start acting grown-up, she's going to hold her breath until he does."

Algren's next significant publication after *The Man with the Golden Arm* was a book-length essay, *Chicago: City on the Make* (1951). This prose poem, dedicated to Carl Sandburg, is a biting, yet compassionate, verbal journey through Chicago's back streets, ball parks, and bars. Algren said that the book immediately went "under the counters" because of an editor too timid to stand by his own thinking. It was largely ignored for ten years until Jean-Paul Sartre translated it into French and had it published in Europe, where it gained wide popularity. *Chicago: City on the Make* was revived in 1961 in the United States for three additional printings.

One of Algren's characteristics as an author is repetition of phrases, such as "lion-colored hills" of Africa, "right-hander's wind," "paper moon," and "all the alleyways of home," which appear in several works. Steffi in *Never Come Morning* and Zosh in *The Man with the Golden Arm* both utter, in their deepest despair, "God has forgotten us all." However, perhaps the greatest reuse of material is his rewriting of *Somebody in Boots* into what some consider his best novel, *A Walk on the Wild Side* (1956), a book that Algren said was not written until long after it had been walked. He was referring, of course, to the time he spent in New Orleans in the summer of 1931, although he returned to New Orleans in the 1950s to write the book.

The *Nation* heralded *A Walk on the Wild Side* as part of an underground movement against conformity and regimentation of the mind, two prime targets of intellectualism in the 1950s. *Nation* also saw the novel as not merely the "result" of our social order but of that social order growing wild, where Algren swept up all the old orthodoxies and dumped them into the garbage can. *Saturday Review* saw the story as so true that, to complete the effect, "one could only ask for Toulouse-Lautrec illustrations and Louis Armstrong music." The book was also highly praised by James T. Farrell in the *New Republic*. Critics Leslie Fiedler and Norman Podhoretz, however, were far less kind.

A Walk on the Wild Side is the story of a poor-white illiterate, Dove Linkhorn (Cass McKay revived), who drifts from Texas to New Orleans and becomes involved with a host of prostitutes, pimps, and derelicts in the old French Quarter. Dove goes from jobs as a door-to-door con man to a performer in a perverted peep-show sex routine in a house of prostitution. He is finally beaten and blinded by a legless man from whom he has stolen a mulatto girl. The book ends with Dove as an isolated figure

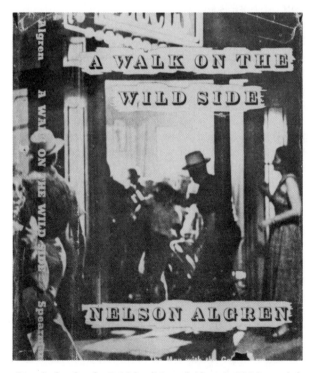

Dust jacket for the British edition of Algren's 1956 novel described by a reviewer in the Nation *as part of an underground movement against conformity and regimentation of the mind*

with little hope, a blind man with no skills.

A Walk on the Wild Side, like Algren's previous novels, is a tough, masculine work. However, in this novel Algren's mode is black humor, as bitter, ironic comedy becomes dominant. The narrative goes from tenderness to sad burlesque, and the ominous sense of death that permeates Algren's other novels is absent. Dove Linkhorn is unaware that he is being defeated by a hostile environment. His optimism is purely blind hope, which he, as a blind man at the end of the story, clearly symbolizes. Dove's fate is far from the expectations he voices at the beginning of the story when he surmises, "I don't know what kind of great I'm bound to be, . . . all I know for certain is I'm a born world-shaker." Also absent in *A Walk on the Wild Side* is the innocence of the female characters, previously typified by Cass McKay's sister in *Somebody in Boots*, Steffi in *Never Come Morning*, and Molly in *The Man with the Golden Arm*. A film version of *A Walk on the Wild Side* was produced with Charles Levine. Again Algren was not happy with the selection of the actors and said that he had never seen the film.

Following *A Walk on the Wild Side* came Algren's most productive, and least noteworthy, period. A book of short stories called *Nelson Algren's Own Book of Lonesome Monsters* was published in 1962. Only the preface and one story were by Algren—the rest were stories by others selected by his agent. A travel book, *Who Lost an American?*, came out in 1963, followed by a book-length interview, called *Conversations with Nelson Algren*, in 1964. Another travelogue, *Notes From a Sea Diary: Hemingway All the Way*, was published in 1965, followed in 1973 by a collection of Algren stories, *The Last Carousel*. None of these recent works received much critical notice or popular success.

In addition, Algren covered events in Vietnam in the 1960s and also produced a regular column for the *Chicago Free Press* in 1970. He once owned a racehorse called Jealous Widow, renamed by associates "Algren's Folly." He taught creative writing at the University of Iowa and the University of Florida and was much in demand for lectures and book reviews. He had a novel left in him, though.

A discussion of Algren's last novel should be prefaced by his statement, "I consider myself a free-lance journalist. But I can occasionally get into something more lasting than just day-to-day journalism." Published in Germany in 1982 as *Calhoun* and in the United States in 1983 as *The Devil's Stocking*, the novel concludes things its author had wanted to accomplish for many years. In the mid

1960s Algren said in an interview that he wanted to write a boxing novel: "I'd like to do that kind of book because it would be about more than just boxing. . . . [It] would be just a reporting job. I wouldn't do more than discuss details and get the speech down. . . ." He also said he would be interested in "showing an operation of how the courts work, of the whole comedy. . . ."

In 1975 the opportunity came when *Esquire* magazine asked him to write an article about Ruben "Hurricane" Carter, a former middleweight contender, who was given three consecutive life sentences for a triple murder in a Paterson, New Jersey, bar in the 1960s. Algren was interested in the case and moved to Paterson to be close to the scene of the crime, to the records, and to Carter. He actually tried to rent a room above the bar where the shootings occurred.

Esquire did not use the article, but Algren had come to believe in Carter's innocence and produced a book of investigative journalism, which had much promise in light of Carter's new trial granted in 1976. When asked if Carter had seen the book, Algren replied, "He saw half the book. He's not too pleased. It's all right; he's not easy to please. He wanted something more, maybe a declaration of his innocence. I do know he got a bad trial."

When the second trial, which Algren attended, again found Carter guilty, Algren could not find a publisher for his documentary and began work on a novel based on the Carter story. Algren's street people are depicted, as in his previous novels, in a hostile, low-light, this time racially torn, environment which provided little escape. In fact, the racial hostility in Paterson was so bad while he was investigating the Carter story that Algren moved to Hackensack.

In the novel, Algren begins by describing Ruby Calhoun's Jersey City background, where he grew up learning to fight and steal. Ruby was charged with atrocious assault at fourteen and sent to a home for boys. His friend Red Haloways, a mulatto, was "locked" with him for a mugging conviction. Ruby escaped at age sixteen and with his mother's help got into the army where he started boxing. At nineteen he was honorably discharged, as army light-welterweight champion, but he was arrested and given a nine-month prison term for his previous escape from the detention home. Upon release, he was soon arrested for felonious assault and sentenced to four years.

Ruby enters the fight game when he is freed and becomes a middleweight contender. He marries his manager's daughter and has an affair with

Red Haloways's mistress. His future is looking bright when there is a neighborhood shooting in which Red Haloways's father is killed by a white man. Shortly thereafter, a black man enters a white bar and kills three people. Revenge appears to be the motive, and Ruby was seen earlier at the bar. Algren implies that the shootings were done by Red Haloways.

Witnesses at the trial, because of police pressure, commit perjury for the reward and reduced sentences to their own crimes, and Ruby is given the same sentence as Ruben Carter.

Algren devotes considerable space to the mockery of the first trial and the second, which Calhoun also loses. In crisp journalistic style, Algren explores police corruption, incompetency of judges, manipulation of witnesses, and the deplorable shortcoming of the prison system. Calhoun states, "When the prisoner gets back on the street he's been destroyed morally—which is what the prison system is aiming at. It's easier for a man to become a shadow in prison, and to believe that shadow to be real, than it is to become a responsible human being." He continues, "The farther you remove a man from the real world, the more dangerous he becomes."

Of "country boy" prison guards, the Prison Commission's chief psychiatrist states, "If the prison's purpose is simply to keep men off the streets, and to keep them from killing one another inside the walls, these men can do the job. But for anything more than custody, they are not fitted." After a prison riot, an officer explains, "The confrontation was forced upon us by inmates already confined for heinous crimes against society." Algren writes, "For the most heinous crime, that of demanding that men be broken to dogs, committed by society against the criminal, no mention was made."

Interwoven in Calhoun's story are Algren's prostitutes, pimps, petty thieves, and worn-out fighters. The descriptions of the brothels and the dialogue of the prostitutes are almost identical to those in earlier Algren novels, particularly *Never Come Morning* and *A Walk on the Wild Side*. A statement from boxer Tony Zale was also lifted from a previous Algren work, as was a scene describing a near-blind fighter, Salazar, who judged the location of his opponents by listening to their feet shuffle.

The Devil's Stocking lacks most of the sentiment of Algren's previous novels and much of the humor, although there is still some burlesque in the brothel scenes and in the parodies of a local TV talk show. But there are still flashes of vintage Algren. After the stunning verdict in the second trial, the courtroom becomes suddenly quiet. "Then a small crippled wind, like a wind off some old half-sunken grave, began limping soundlessly about the courtroom." When Calhoun, who refused to testify in his own behalf, is asked by a state investigator if he would respond in the same way again, Calhoun replies, "Lord, I don't ask you to move mountains. Just give me the strength to climb this one." There is one small flicker of optimism that Calhoun might file an appeal, but he has no money to support such a fight.

After many years, the state investigator returns to the scene of the shooting for which Calhoun was convicted. The neighborhood has changed, and blacks now own the bar. The investigator asks the black female bartender if this wasn't the place that made the news some years back.

> "Maybe it is. Then again maybe it isn't," she replied, concealing her hostility beneath the guise of courtesy. "We don't know anything about this place when it was a white bar."

Algren concludes, "All, all is changed. And everything remains the same."

Nelson Algren died on 9 May 1981 in Sag Harbor, Long Island. He was found in his home by a guest arriving to celebrate Algren's recent election into the American Academy, National Institute of Arts and Letters.

Bibliographies:

Kenneth G. McCollum, *Nelson Algren: A Checklist* (Detroit: Gale, 1973);

Introduction by Studs Terkel. Includes facsimiles of letters, inscriptions, and a revised Algren typescript done in the 1930s.

Matthew J. Bruccoli, *Nelson Algren: A Descriptive Bibliography* (Pittsburgh: University of Pittsburgh Press, 1985);
The most extensive primary bibliography of Algren's work.

References:

George Bluestone, "Nelson Algren," *Western Review*, 22 (Autumn 1957): 22-44;
A critical review of Algren's work through *A Walk on the Wild Side*.

Martha H. Cox and Wayne Chatterton, *Nelson Algren* (Boston: Twayne, 1975);
A biography and a critical review of Algren's work through *A Walk on the Wild Side*.

H. E. F. Donohue, *Conversations with Nelson Algren* (New York: Hill & Wang, 1964);
An interview with Algren covering his family background, writing, Hollywood experience, travels, and ideology.

Maxwell Geismar, "Nelson Algren: The Iron Sanctuary," in *American Moderns, From Rebellion to Conformity* (New York: Hill & Wang, 1968), pp. 187-194;
Critical review of Algren's work through *A Walk on the Wild Side*.

James Baldwin

This entry was updated by Fred L. Standley (Florida State University) from his entries in DLB 2, American Novelists Since World War II, *and* DLB 7, Twentieth-Century American Dramatists, *and from the entry by John W. Roberts (University of Pennsylvania) in* DLB 33, Afro-American Fiction Writers After 1955.

Places	New York City Istanbul	Paris	Atlanta
Influences and Relationships	Harriet Beecher Stowe Countee Cullen Nikki Giovanni Fyodor Dostoyevski	Charles Dickens Richard Wright Ralph Ellison	Henry James Norman Mailer William Styron
Literary Movements and Forms	Realism Meditative Poetry	Literature as Social Criticism	Personal Essay
Major Themes	Love and Power in Society Misplaced Emphasis in American Value System Need for Sexual and Psychological Identity White Society's Conception of God	Homosexuality Indivisibility of Private and Public Life Responsibility of the Artist in Society	The Roots of Racism History and Potential of the Racial Crisis Dominance of White Society
Cultural and Artistic Influences	Music: Blues, Jazz, and Gospel	Religion	Theater
Social and Economic Influences	Civil Rights Movement Public Schools	White Racism Black Anti-Semitism	The Church Street Culture

BIRTH: New York City, 2 August 1924, to Emma Berdis Jones.

AWARDS AND HONORS: Eugene F. Saxton Fellowship, 1945; Rosenwald Fellowship, 1948; Guggenheim Fellowship, 1954; *Partisan Review* Fellowship, 1956; National Institute of Arts and Letters grant, 1956; Ford Foundation grant, 1959; National Conference of Christians and Jews Brotherhood Award, 1962; George Polk Award, 1963; Foreign Drama Critics Award, 1964; elected to National Institute of Arts and Letters, 1964; Hon. Litt.D., Morehouse College, 1976.

BOOKS: *Go Tell It on the Mountain* (New York: Knopf, 1953; London: Joseph, 1954);
Notes of a Native Son (Boston: Beacon, 1955; London: Mayflower, 1958);
Giovanni's Room (New York: Dial, 1956; London: Joseph, 1957);
Nobody Knows My Name (New York: Dial, 1961; London: Joseph, 1964);
Another Country (New York: Dial, 1962; London: Joseph, 1963);
The Fire Next Time (New York: Dial, 1963; London: Joseph, 1963);
Nothing Personal, with photographs by Richard Avedon (New York: Atheneum, 1964; Harmondsworth, U.K.: Penguin, 1964);
Blues for Mister Charlie (New York: Dial, 1964; London: Joseph, 1965);
Going to Meet the Man (New York: Dial, 1965; London: Joseph, 1965);
The Amen Corner (New York: Dial, 1968; London: Joseph, 1969);
Tell Me How Long the Train's Been Gone (New York: Dial, 1968; London: Joseph, 1968);
A Rap on Race, by Baldwin and Margaret Mead (Philadelphia & New York: Lippincott, 1971; London: Joseph, 1971);
One Day When I Was Lost: A Scenario Based on 'The Autobiography of Malcolm X' (London: Joseph, 1972; New York: Dial, 1973);
No Name in the Street (New York: Dial, 1972; London: Joseph, 1972);
A Dialogue, with Nikki Giovanni (Philadelphia & New York: Lippincott, 1973; London: Joseph, 1975);
If Beale Street Could Talk (London: Joseph, 1974; New York: Dial, 1974);
The Devil Finds Work (New York: Dial, 1976; London: Joseph, 1976);

James Baldwin (Granger Collection)

Little Man, Little Man: A Story of Childhood, by Baldwin and Yoran Cazac (London: Joseph, 1976; New York: Dial, 1976);
Just Above My Head (New York: Dial, 1979; London: Joseph, 1979);
The Evidence of Things Not Seen (New York: Holt, Rinehart & Winston, 1985);
Jimmy's Blues: Selected Poems (New York: St. Martin's, 1985; London: Joseph, 1985);
The Price of the Ticket: Collected Non-Fiction 1948-1985 (New York: St. Martin's, 1985).

PLAY PRODUCTIONS: *The Amen Corner,* Washington, D.C., Howard University, 1955; New York, Ethel Barrymore Theatre, 5 April 1965;
Giovanni's Room, New York, Actors' Studio, 1957;
Blues for Mister Charlie, New York, ANTA Theatre, 23 April 1964;
A Deed from the King of Spain, New York, American Center for Stanislavski Theatre Art, 24 January 1974.

OTHER: "Mass Culture and the Creative Artist: Some Personal Notes," in *Culture for the Millions* (Princeton: Van Nostrand, 1959);

"In Search of a Basis for Mutual Understanding and Racial Harmony," in *The Nature of a Humane Society*, edited by H. Ober Hesse (Philadelphia: Fortress, 1976-1977).

PERIODICAL PUBLICATIONS: "The Negro Writer in America: A Symposium," *Negro Digest*, 12 (June 1963): 54-65;
"The Creative Dilemma: 'The War of an Artist With His Society Is a Lover's War,'" *Saturday Review*, 47 (8 February 1964): 14-15, 18;
"Theatre: The Negro In and Out," *Negro Digest*, 15 (October 1966): 37-44;
"Sidney Poitier," *Look*, 32 (23 July 1968): 50-58;
"White Racism or World Community?," *Ecumenical Review*, 20 (October 1968): 371-376;
"*Roots:* The Saga of an American Family," *Unique*, 1 (1976): 31-32.

James Baldwin's eminence as a man of letters is now well established; indeed, his books, essays, and numerous other pieces attest to the truth of Benjamin DeMott's statement that "this author retains a place in an extremely select group: that comprised of the few genuinely indispensable American writers." As novelist, essayist, dramatist, and social critic, Baldwin's writings demonstrate not only a sustained productivity but also a consistent and sensitive human perspective. At times alternately praised and damned by blacks and whites alike, he has never lacked an audience. While the rationale for this public interest in his work obviously consists of multiple factors, the principal points would surely include his prophetic tone, moral concern, existential analysis, perceptive relevance, intense language, and poignant sincerity.

From the age of twelve, when he published a short story on the Spanish Revolution in a church newspaper, and a short time later, when he received a letter of congratulations from New York Mayor La Guardia for one of his poems, Baldwin has nurtured a passionate devotion to writing: "I consider that I have many responsibilities but none greater than this: to last, as Hemingway says, and get my work done. I want to be an honest man and a good writer." To fulfill that ambition he recognizes that "the artist . . . cannot allow any consideration to supercede his responsibility to reveal all that he can possibly discover concerning the mystery of the human being"; and for Baldwin this means that the role of the artist is to express the existential knowledge of experience: "The states of birth, suffering, love and death . . . extreme

states—extreme, universal, and inescapable. . . . The artist is present to correct the delusions to which we fall prey in our attempts to avoid this knowledge." An adequate perspective of man for our technological era is possible, in Baldwin's view, only when the artist analyzes man as not "merely a member of a society or group or a deplorable conundrum to be explained by Science . . . but something resolutely indefinable, unpredictable." Thus, in the effort to confront and reveal "the disquieting complexity of ourselves," the only real concern for the artist is "to recreate out of the disorder of life that order which is art" and "to describe things which other people are too busy to describe." Baldwin is unequivocal in declaring this to be "a special function" and that "people who do it cannot by that token do many other things."

Additionally, Baldwin advocates explicitly a conception of literary art involving both personal and social responsibility. Personal responsibility implies a duty to avoid self-delusion by the "attempt to look on himself and the world as they are"; however, the writer is also "responsible to and for—the social order" by developing an ethical vision and historical orientation. Thus, in his essay "The Creative Dilemma," Baldwin views the artist as "the incorrigible disturber of the peace" who "cannot and must not take anything for granted" in the society but "must drive to the heart of every answer and expose that question the answer hides." He believes that every society and culture, especially in the United States, will determinedly endeavor to restrict the artist's vision of human experience "in which one discovers that life is tragic, and therefore unutterably beautiful." This perspective of experience presumes the validity of paradox as a mode of explanation and exploration; however, America is "a country devoted to the death of paradox." For Baldwin, then, the artist's inherent duty produces a condition of warring with his society; nevertheless, "the war of an artist with his society is a lover's war, and he does, at his best, what lovers do, which is to reveal the beloved to himself and, with that revelation, to make freedom real." That purpose was hauntingly reiterated in an interview with Baldwin entitled "Looking Toward the Eighties" in which he said that the author's "function is very particular and so is his responsibility. After all, to write, if taken seriously, is to be subversive. To disturb the peace." As an artist who has examined a multitude of subjects and themes throughout his career, Baldwin states forthrightly his conviction that only two options are available to all "writers—black or white—to be immoral and uphold the *sta-*

tus quo or to be moral and try to change the world."

Within this context Baldwin's works have passionately and perceptively explored a broad spectrum of thematic concerns: the misplaced emphasis in the value systems of America; the indivisibility of the private life and the public life; the intertwining of love and power in the universal scheme of existence and in society's structures; the past historical significance and the potential explosiveness of the present racial crisis; the essential need to develop sexual and psychological consciousness and identity; and the responsibility of the artist to promote the evolution of the individual and society. In the development of this view about the vocation of writing, Baldwin's own childhood and adolescence were especially influential. In fact his evolution as a writer constitutes a narrative nearly as dramatic and compelling as much of his fiction.

"My childhood was awful," Baldwin once said. He was born in Harlem in 1924, the son of Emma Berdis Jones, who was unmarried at the time of his birth. In 1927 when he was almost three years old, his mother married David Baldwin, a disillusioned and embittered New Orleans preacher who had recently migrated to Harlem. Although Baldwin once described his stepfather as the only man he ever hated, he has admitted on several occasions that he both loved and hated, respected and despised this man whose unabashed love he was never able to win. Nevertheless, Baldwin's ambivalent relationship with his stepfather served as a constant source of tension during his formative years and informs some of his most mature works. For example, David Baldwin became a model for Gabriel Grimes, a central character in *Go Tell It on the Mountain* (1953), and his death and funeral are vividly described in the essay "Notes of A Native Son."

The marriage between David Baldwin and Emma Jones produced eight children whose care fell primarily to young Jimmy. The demands of caring for younger siblings and his stepfather's repressive religious convictions in large part helped to shield him from the harsh realities of Harlem street life during the 1930s. White racism and mistreatment, drugs, alcohol, and social and economic exploitation were real dangers endemic to the environment of the Baldwin family. The family's personal situation, of course, was complicated by the general misfortune of the Depression years. Baldwin was nevertheless able to expand his own world through reading, an activity he found compatible with his babysitting chores. Reading also became his insulation from his stepfather's frequent tirades against white racism and sin. Baldwin claims that

by age thirteen he had read most of the books in the two Harlem libraries. He then began going downtown to the main branch of the New York Public Library on Forty-second Street, where he discovered worlds removed from his own. As he cared for a succession of younger brothers and sisters, Baldwin first became acquainted with Harriet Beecher Stowe's *Uncle Tom's Cabin*, developed a passion for Charles Dickens's novels, and dreamed and discovered the path to riches with the heroes of Horatio Alger.

His passion for reading naturally led him to try his hand at writing. "For me writing was an act of love. It was an attempt—not to get the world's attention—it was an attempt to be loved. It seemed a way to save myself and to save my family. It came out of despair. And it seemed the only way to another world." His love of writing became a refuge from both the hate he believed his stepfather felt for him and the ridicule that he received in school. His superior intellectual abilities as a student and his unattractive appearance made him a natural target for the insults of other children at school. He found both support and sanctuary in the school's literary club guided by renowned poet Countee Cullen. In recognition of his writing ability, Baldwin was made editor of the *Douglass Pilot*, the school newspaper at P.S. 139.

Despite these activities, Baldwin had become convinced of his depravity by age fourteen. Everything he experienced during the summer of his fourteenth birthday, especially the changes in his own body, led him toward religious conversion. Through the influence of an older friend, Arthur Moore, and partly in defiance of his stepfather, Baldwin underwent a dramatic religious conversion and became a member of Mount Calvary of the Pentecostal Faith Church. He eventually reached the level of junior minister.

Shortly after his conversion, young Baldwin's religious devotion received a challenge. He was accepted at De Witt Clinton High School, a predominantly white school in the Bronx. For the first time he came into contact with white students his own age, many of whom were Jewish. The intellectual stimulation offered by his new environment was, however, soured by his stepfather's insistence that he was now flirting with the enemy. In addition, the sharp contrast between the religious convictions of his fellow students and his own fundamentalist beliefs caused young Baldwin to examine critically his religious stance. Moreover, his academic and social problems at De Witt Clinton stemmed from the realization that "when the school day was over,

I went back into a condition which they could not imagine, and I knew, no matter what anybody said, that the future I faced was not the future they faced."

In part, Baldwin's feelings of guilt and inadequacy severely hampered his academic performance in high school. He did not graduate with his class. He did, however, receive his diploma six months later in 1942. He also established several important and lasting friendships at De Witt Clinton. One of the most significant was with Richard Avedon, with whom he shared editorial duties on the *Magpie*, the school's literary magazine. He was later to collaborate with Avedon on a picture book of America entitled *Nothing Personal* (1964).

Thus by the time of his high school graduation, Baldwin had served as editor of the literary magazine, spent three years as a Holy Roller preacher, and been indelibly influenced by the fiction he had read. Twenty years later, as Fern Eckman has shown, "*Uncle Tom's Cabin* was to be ranked by Baldwin—along with Dostoevsky's *The Possessed*, *Crime and Punishment*, and *The Brothers Karamazov*, Henry James's *The Princess Casamassima* and *The Portrait of a Lady*, Dickens' *A Tale of Two Cities*, Ralph Ellison's *Invisible Man*, Richard Wright's *Black Boy* and Charles Wright's *The Messenger*—among the ten books that had helped him break out of the ghetto."

In the meantime Baldwin's stepfather had been forced to give up work because of his deteriorating mental condition. To help support the family, Baldwin took a job in Belle Mead, New Jersey, arranged by another high school friend, Emile Capouya. In New Jersey Baldwin worked on the construction of the Army Quartermaster Depot. Discrimination made the entire experience a personal hell for him. He was fired twice and rehired after Capouya intervened on his behalf. All the while he worked, Baldwin lived frugally and sent most of his money home to his mother. By the summer of 1943, Baldwin's stepfather was near death, and his mother was about to give birth to her eighth child. After being fired a third time, Baldwin returned to Harlem, where he was coerced by an aunt into visiting his stepfather, now confined to a mental institution on Long Island. Several days before Baldwin's nineteenth birthday, his stepfather died and his mother gave birth to a baby girl whom James named Paula Maria.

Baldwin realized that the financial strain on the family following his stepfather's death could destroy his ambition of becoming a writer if he allowed it to happen. Consequently, he tried a long shot: "The long shot was simply that I would turn into a writer before my mother died and before the children were all put into jail—or became junkies or whores. I had to leave Harlem. I had to leave because I understood very well, in some part of myself, that I would never be able to fit in anywhere unless I jumped. I knew I had to jump then." He moved to Greenwich Village, where he worked at a variety of jobs and began working seriously on his first novel, which he had originally titled "Crying Holy." He changed the title to "In My Father's House" and began working diligently to complete it. He would work at his job all day, sleep three to four hours a night, and write the rest of the time. It was also during this period that he first met Richard Wright. At Wright's request, Baldwin later mailed him the first sixty pages of "In My Father's House," which Wright liked enough to arrange a Eugene F. Saxton Memorial Trust Award for Baldwin. Despite his furious efforts to finish the novel, Baldwin was not able to complete it during the tenure of the fellowship. Disappointed with himself, he began reassessing himself as a writer and turned to other types of writing projects which he felt would sharpen his skills.

Success of sorts finally came in 1946 at age twenty-two when he sold his first book review (on Maxim Gorki) to the *Nation*. This review was followed by another. He also did reviews for the *New Leader* on the Negro problem. His abilities as an essayist were recognized by Robert Warshow, editor of *Commentary*, the publication of the American Jewish Committee, who asked him to do an article on Harlem. The article, entitled "The Harlem Ghetto," dealt with black anti-Semitism. Since his high school days Baldwin had been wrestling with this question because his experiences with Jews at De Witt Clinton had not paralleled those narrated by most blacks in Harlem. Although it caused controversy in both the black and Jewish communities, the article nevertheless launched Baldwin's career as a writer. He received numerous offers to do articles for other magazines.

Following his early successes, Baldwin began work on a second novel, "Ignorant Armies," which he never completed. That novel was based on the case of Wayne Lonergin, a homosexual who was accused of killing his wife in a disagreement over extramarital affairs. Baldwin's failure to complete the novel stems from his inability to come to terms with his own sexuality at the time. "I was dealing with—it was a very halting attempt to deal with some element in myself, which I had not, at that point in my life, really come to grips with at *all*.

The whole *sexual* element. . . . Well, the whole—what I was grappling with *really*, without knowing it, was the—all the implications in this society of being *bisexual*." The issue of bisexuality would not be explored in his fiction until 1956 with the publication of *Giovanni's Room*.

Baldwin's abandonment of "Ignorant Armies" allowed him to explore other subjects equally as important to his development as a writer. He worked with Theodore Pelalowski on a documentary about storefront churches. Although the documentary was never published, the project won for him a Rosenwald Foundation Fellowship. He then completed his first short story, "Previous Condition," which was published in *Commentary* in October 1948.

"I wrote it in a white heat," Baldwin once said of "Previous Condition," and the story seems a thinly veiled version of Baldwin's condition in 1948. Images suggestive of torture and restraint introduce the reader to Peter, the black unemployed actor and narrator of the story. He woke up "to find the sheet was gray and twisted like a rope. I breathed like I had been running. I couldn't move for the longest while. I just lay on my back, spread eagled. . . ." The room in which Peter is living had been rented for him by his white Jewish friend, Jules, and Peter fully expects to be kicked out when discovered by the landlady. When he is evicted, Peter simply resigns himself to it despite urgings to fight back from Jules and his Irish female friend, Ida. Finally, he goes uptown seeking the comfort of familiar surroundings in a bar in Harlem. It is at this point that the reader begins to realize that Peter's dispossession has broader implications. His dispossession of his living quarters is simply a metaphor for his dispossession within American society. The whites reject him because he is black, and he, as black artist, finds himself alienated from his own people because of his sensibilities. At the bar in Harlem Peter is approached by an older woman who asks him, "What's your story?" He replies, "I got no story, Ma." Peter has no story because he has no identity, a theme that will repeatedly recur in Baldwin's fiction.

The feelings of dispossession experienced by Peter in "Previous Condition" are representative of Baldwin during this period. Although he had achieved a modicum of success as a writer, he had yet to produce a major work. His village life-style and experiences were also taking their toll. In a desperate effort to save himself, Baldwin made the decision to use his last Rosenwald Foundation Fellowship check to book passage to France. On 11 November 1948 he left New York for Paris.

As with many other American writers, Paris did not greet Baldwin with open arms. After a brief reunion with Richard Wright, Baldwin found himself in dire financial straits. He had arrived in Paris with only about fifty dollars in his pocket; shortly afterwards he was broke, locked out of his hotel room for lack of payment, and forced to sell his clothes and typewriter to live. He fell ill and was nursed back to health by a Corsican woman who had taken a liking to him. He eventually ended up in jail for stealing a bedsheet, a charge of which he was innocent. Nevertheless he found respite in Paris from those pressures that had hampered his growth as a writer in the States. He discovered that even in jail he was an American first and a black man second. "I got over—and a lot beyond—the terms of—all the terms in which Americans identified me—in my own mind."

Six months after arriving in Paris, Baldwin wrote one of his best known and most influential essays, "Everybody's Protest Novel." The essay was to be Baldwin's personal emancipation proclamation from the stereotypical writings expected of black writers in America. This essay is best known, however, for its attack on protest fiction, especially that of Richard Wright. The essay traces protest fiction from Harriet Beecher Stowe's *Uncle Tom's Cabin* to Richard Wright's *Native Son*. Baldwin denounces protest fiction because it robs black men of their humanity and has the effect of reinforcing the very stereotypes that it is intended to destroy. Although Baldwin naively hoped that Wright would praise his essay, Wright felt betrayed by his younger protégé. The rift between the two was never truly overcome, though efforts to do so were made.

Alternating between loneliness and starvation in Paris, he became acquainted with other American writers, including James Jones, Philip Roth, William Styron, and Norman Mailer. It was there also that, influenced by Henry James, he began to evolve a clean conception of literary form and technique, especially what Charles Newman has described as the "dialectical art," which views the world in terms of primary conflicts and a "symmetry" based on the inherent drama of these polar conflicts.

After having outlined the principles on which future Afro-American literature should be based in "Everybody's Protest Novel," Baldwin was still laboring to finish "In My Father's House" in 1951. When he had almost decided to abandon the book, it suddenly began falling into place. He moved to a chalet owned by the parents of his friend Lucien Happersberger. Living in virtual isolation, Baldwin completed the manuscript in three months. On 26 February 1952 he mailed the final draft to Helen Strauss of the William Morris Agency, who had agreed earlier to serve as his literary agent. Baldwin then moved back to Paris, where Ms. Strauss notified him that Knopf was interested in publishing the novel. To put added pressure on Knopf, Baldwin decided to return to New York after an absence of four years.

"In My Father's House," retitled *Go Tell It on the Mountain,* was finally published in 1953 to excellent reviews. Baldwin's ten-year struggle with his stepfather's legacy was temporarily abated, if not over. "In one sense I wrote to redeem my father," Baldwin once said of the novel. "I had to understand the forces, the experience, the life that shaped him before I could grow up myself, before I could become a writer." *Go Tell It on the Mountain* proved that James Baldwin had become a writer of enormous power and skill.

Baldwin's first novel focuses on the religious conversion of John Grimes. It is set in Harlem's storefront Temple of the Fire Baptised, on the fourteenth birthday of Grimes, whose experiences closely resemble those of the author's youth. The novel is divided into three parts.

Part one, "The Seventh Day," provides an introduction to the Grimes family in Harlem in 1935. John feels constricted and frustrated by the repressive, hate-suffused, hell's fire sermons of his father, Gabriel, who is the leader of the Temple of the Fire Baptised. John struggles with guilt about sex, ambivalent emotions toward his parents, and latent hatred of whites.

Part two, "The Prayers of the Saints," is a complex artistic rendering by the use of flashbacks of the Grimes's familial background centering upon three prayers: Aunt Florence, Gabriel, and Elizabeth, John's mother. Florence's prayer reminisces about the times of her and Gabriel's mother and their expectations of black family life being dominated by the male; her fleeing from the South about 1900, after having been asked by a white employer to become his "concubine"; her relationship with Frank, whose caramel color eventually led to the end of their marriage because of her disdain for his "common nigger" friends and her continued use of "them old skin-whitners," while he remarked "that black's a mighty pretty color." Florence's prayer ends "with terror and rage" as she asks God why "he preferred her mother and her brother, the old, black woman, and the low,

black man, while she, who had sought only to walk upright, was come to die, alone and in poverty, in a dirty, furnished room?" Gabriel's prayer section recapitulates twenty years of his life—his earlier marriage with Deborah, "a holy fool"; the affair with Esther and the birth and death of their son, Royal; his own distaste for the "big, comfortable, ordained" evangelists at the Twenty-Four Elders Revival Meeting; his internal struggle between pietism and lust; and his ambivalence of feeling toward Elizabeth's bastard son, John. Elizabeth's prayer recounts what various experiences of love have meant to her: the "furious affectation of maternal concern" toward her; the enforced "separation of herself from her father" by the aunt; her life with Richard in New York and his ultimate suicide after being humiliated by the police; and her marriage to Gabriel after the birth of John. Elizabeth "hated it all—the white city, the white world" and finds her relief in the thought that "Only God could establish order in this chaos; to Him the soul must turn to be delivered."

Part three, "The Threshing Floor," emphasizes John's conversion on the floor before the altar surrounded by Mother Washington, Elisha, and other "saints," his mind tortured by guilt, fear, and hatred. Finally, "in the silence something died in John, and something came alive," and at dawn he emerges from the Temple, smiling and confident about the future.

In spite of the novel's numerous scriptural references and allusions, its use of biblical names for characters, its seeming preoccupation with church practices, *Go Tell It on the Mountain* is not primarily a religious novel; rather it is a novel embodying a major cultural concept of which religion is only one element. Dr. Johnetta Cole's pervasive exploration of life-styles in "nigger culture" as being comprised of the Street, Downhome, Militant, and Upward-bound provides a significant point of entry for interpreting the novel. While "the street" or urban setting appears to be dominant, it is really the "down-home" life-style that pervades the book and occurs repetitively in the text, "indicating one's point of origin, down south, or the simple, decent way of life . . . basically rural and Southern" and centering in "the kitchens . . . the church halls . . . and the fraternal orders." Within that context, this is a sociopolitical novel that harshly indicts a white-controlled society for radically delimiting the lives and hopes of blacks. For those whose skin color offers no hope better than "the back door, and the dark stairs, and the kitchen or basement," the alternatives seem to be escapism through drugs, drink, and sex or through the church. John Grimes must learn to accept the reality of the experiences recited in the lives of Florence, Gabriel, and Elizabeth; the options open to him on the threshing floor are to leave the community of the faithful and court disaster or to remain in the group and reduce his range of possibilities by embracing a hopeless otherworldliness divorced from reality. Thus the novel indicts not only the white society's racism but also the black's reliance upon a religious mode of behavior that is illusory and irrelevant to his daily existence.

The primary literary technique for exhibiting the dual points of sociopolitical condemnation is irony. Despite his "religious" conversion, nothing is really changed for John Grimes at the end of this novel; "whom the son sets free is free indeed" is a scriptural illusion here. The ethical norm of the book is established and enforced by the community of saints, especially in their effort to be in the world but not of the world; yet each of the principal saints has his or her own secret code of behavior at variance with the so-called norm. Elizabeth's favorite scriptural passage is "everything works together for good for them that love the Lord," but loving the Lord has made no real change in the pain, suffering and victimization of her family in the past or present. Gabriel's favorite biblical text is "set this house in order," yet all of the households connected with him have been in disorder and his fanatical belief structure is a rationalization for evading responsibility; the words of Gabriel as "God's messenger" are of despair, deceit, destruction, and disorder.

Go Tell It on the Mountain, then, is a prefiguration of themes and motifs that Baldwin pursues further in subsequent writing. Baldwin derides and derogates those who would oversimplify an authentic and effective mode of response to the white society's dominance over the black's existence; and he reveals that refuge in an otherworldly religion, rationalized by a conception of God borrowed from the white world, is an illusion and, therefore, damnation not salvation.

After the publication of *Go Tell It on the Mountain*, Baldwin returned to Europe and began to work on his first play, *The Amen Corner*. Unable to complete the play, he returned to New York during the summer of 1954. From that summer to the spring of 1955, he virtually completed *Giovanni's Room*, a second novel; *The Amen Corner*, his first play; and *Notes of a Native Son*, a book of essays. During the spring of 1955, Howard University decided to produce *The Amen Corner* under the di-

rection of Owen Dodson. Baldwin went to Washington, rewrote many of the speeches while the play was still in the rehearsal stage, remained for the performance, and was pleased at the reception the play received.

Like Baldwin's first novel, *Go Tell It on the Mountain* (1953), the play draws heavily upon his earlier religious experience, especially his role as a young preacher in the Fireside Pentecostal Assembly and his experiences at Harlem's Mount Calvary of the Pentecostal Faith Church, presided over by Mother Horn, "a tall, dynamic woman, the leader of a large flock, in her own way as opinionated and domineering as David Baldwin." Darwin Turner argues that *The Amen Corner* is a "Black Arts" drama that ignores the relationship between blacks and whites, stresses the necessity for love in the black family and community, and rejects any doctrine of the church that emphasizes only a God of Wrath. This final point is a recognition that Baldwin expresses in the play, a basic idea also expressed in *The Fire Next Time* (1963): "If the concept of God has any validity or use, it can only be to make us larger, freer, and more loving. If God cannot do this, then it is time we got rid of Him."

In act three of *The Amen Corner* Sister Margaret Alexander, pastor of a Harlem church, finally grasps the complete significance inherent in the realization that "it's an awful thing to think about, the way love never dies!" Having given up her rigid and legalistic religious discipline in the process of agonizingly accepting the return of her estranged, dying husband; the departure of her maturing, independent son; and the rejection by her rebellious congregation, Sister Margaret acquires compassion: "To love the Lord is to love all his children— all of them, everyone!—and suffer with them and rejoice with them and never count the cost."

In *Notes of a Native Son* (1955) Baldwin collected ten essays that had previously appeared in *Commentary*, *Partisan Review*, and other magazines. This volume marked his formal entry into the literary tradition of the personal essay. These essays, primarily autobiographical and impressionistic, offer penetrating and intense comments on a variety of subjects: the novel of protest from Stowe to Wright; ghetto experiences in Harlem; black-white encounters in Europe; the film *Carmen Jones;* and other subjects that frequently overlap with the material treated in his fiction. "Stranger in the Village" has since been much anthologized. It not only reveals the author's unique experience of being the first black man encountered by a small Swiss village, but it also becomes the instrument of expressing forcefully the basic premise of the racial revolution of the twentieth century: "the people who shut their eyes to reality simply invite their own destruction. . . . The world is white no longer, and it will never be white again." For Baldwin it is the business of the writer to embark on "this journey toward a more vast reality which must take precedence over all other claims." Consequently a significant stress in this book is on the revelation of what it means to be black, especially in America, i.e., to be regarded as inferior and thus "to live in a constant state of rage." Langston Hughes contended that these essays were "thought-provoking, tantalizing, irritating, abusing and amusing" and that "few American writers handle words more effectively in the essay form than James Baldwin."

During this same period Baldwin was having difficulty in finding a publisher for *Giovanni's Room,* to which publishers reacted negatively because of the novel's explicit homosexual theme. Although the details of its final acceptance are conflicting, Dial Press did sign Baldwin and accept *Giovanni's Room* in 1956. After the novel was accepted, Baldwin returned to Paris, where he put the finishing touches on it and mailed it to his agent in April 1956.

At first glance *Giovanni's Room* would appear to be a rather complete departure from Baldwin's prior books. Indeed, as Fern Eckman points out, the work "concerns itself entirely with the white world. Not a single Negro enters its radically segregated pages." The narrative focuses on David, a tall, blond, white American, who fluctuates between his fiancée, Hella, and his male Italian lover, Giovanni, until Hella discovers that David's body is "the incarnation of a mystery" manifesting itself in love for another man. Nevertheless, the principal concerns of the novel are similar to those of previous books—the search for sexual awareness and psychological identity; the complexity of the father-son relationship; the paradox of the relation between freedom and attachment; the painful and baffling complexity of relations among male and female, male and male. Critical responses have been mixed to this endeavor to treat the physical and psychological aspects of male love: Anthony West acknowledged the solemnity of the story but advocated that it "described a *passade,* a riffle in the surface of life, that completely lacks the validity of actual experience"; on the other hand, David Karp insisted that Baldwin had taken "a very special theme" and treated it with "great artistry and restraint," and Stanley Macebuh praised the work as "one of the few novels in America in which the homosexual sensibility is treated with some measure of creative seriousness."

Artistically, *Giovanni's Room* is one of Baldwin's finest creations. The failure of the novel, or at least the one that has been most often pointed out, involves the conceptualization of David as protagonist. David and homosexuality are rendered negatively, mainly because David fails to resolve his sexual conflict. In reality, Baldwin does not attempt to resolve the conflict, and if he had, the ending would necessarily have been contrived. The point that Baldwin attempts to make is that David cannot move beyond simply experiencing conflict because Western society has provided him with no other means of viewing his situation. Because Baldwin sees in the plight of the homosexual a parallel to that of the black American, his predicament, at this point in history, can only be exposed, not resolved. The homosexual, like the black American, has no place in Western society, and if he is to have a place he must make it for himself. If he allows the culture to define him, his fate is reflective of David's— confusion, disorientation, and frustration with self and society.

After the publication of *Giovanni's Room,* Baldwin was still convinced that the theme broached in the novel had not been fully developed and its potential for illuminating American racial and sexual attitudes had not been exhausted. While still in Paris, he began working on a third novel, *Another Country,* in which he would leave no room for confusion as to what he saw as the parallel. It was also during the summer of 1956 that Baldwin first established his well-publicized friendship with Norman Mailer. Their personalities, however, made for frequent arguments and exasperating stalemates. "Norman and I are alike in this," Baldwin observes, "that we both tend to suspect others of putting us down, and we strike before we're struck." This tendency to respond to supposed insults resulted in their now infamous conflict in 1962. Baldwin and Mailer were both covering the Liston-Patterson heavyweight fight in Chicago. Mailer was representing *Esquire* and Baldwin was covering the event for *Nugget,* a less well-known magazine. Baldwin indirectly accused Mailer of being a liberal, a badge that Mailer refuses to wear since he considers himself a radical. Mailer retaliated by suggesting that Baldwin did not know the difference between a radical and a liberal, and a heated argument ensued.

At summer's end in 1956, Baldwin was still wrestling with *Another Country.* He decided to return to New York for inspiration. He arrived in an

America on the verge of revolution. The 1954 Supreme Court decision on school desegregation had brought with it a new atmosphere of unrest among blacks. The revolution, however, was not occurring in the North; New York had not changed. Consequently, Baldwin wanted to be a part of this action, so he temporarily abandoned the novel and made his first trip to the South, a part of his own country that he had always feared. He was impressed by the courage and determination that he sensed in the people, especially the children who were bearing the brunt of the hostility of those opposed to school integration. He was fortified by the bravery and stamina of those who faced the storms of insults hurled at them each day and could continue knowing "that it was all to be gone through again."

By the time of his return to New York, *Giovanni's Room* had been accepted by the reading public and had been optioned as a Broadway play. Baldwin was besieged by a number of would-be Giovannis. He was not impressed with any of them until he met Engin Cezzar, a Turk. When Cezzar read the script for the Broadway production, however, he lost his enthusiasm for doing the part. He suggested that Baldwin write the play himself, which Baldwin eventually did. Although the play was never produced on Broadway, it was dramatized in 1957 by the Actors' Studio Workshop with Cezzar playing the lead.

Baldwin's work on the play left him with a desire to work in the theater. He apprenticed himself as a kind of playwright-in-training to director Elia Kazan. He acted as Kazan's assistant during the rehearsals of Archibald MacLeish's *J.B.* and Tennessee Williams's *Sweet Bird of Youth*. It was during this time that Baldwin began nursing an idea for a second play which he enthusiastically discussed with Kazan. He wanted to write a play based on the case of Emmett Till, a black youth murdered in Mississippi in 1955 for flirting with a white woman. Kazan frustrated Baldwin's efforts to begin work on the play by suggesting that it would make a better movie. Baldwin had no desire to write a movie script and put the idea aside.

Meanwhile Baldwin had written several pieces for periodicals, and in 1961 came the publication of *Nobody Knows My Name*, with the subtitle of *More Notes of a Native Son*, a collection of thirteen essays predominantly concerned with "the question of color" and the functions and problems of the artist in "the bottomless confusion which is both public and private of the American republic." Combining personal honesty with touches of irreverent and extravagant opinion, Baldwin commented on Harlem, the South, William Faulkner, Norman Mailer, André Gide, Ingmar Bergman, and other interests. "East River Downtown" exploded the naive notion that Communists inspired the Negro riots at the United Nations following the death of Patrice Lumumba and asserted that any effort "to keep the Negro in his 'place' can only have the most extreme and unlucky repercussions." The frequently reprinted *apologia* entitled "The Discovery of What It Means to be an American" posits that a foreign sojourn can help the American writer to gain "a new sense of life's possibilities" and "unprecedented opportunities" in his own society because "there are no untroubled countries in this fearfully troubled world."

Moving between New York and France, Baldwin had been unable to complete *Another Country;* thus, ready to resume work, he moved into the guest cottage of William Styron and his wife. Plagued by interruptions from family and friends, he again dashed off to France with his youngest sister, Paula Maria. After only a couple of weeks, he left Paula Maria in Paris and flew to Istanbul, where he finally completed *Another Country.*

Another Country (1962) represents the author's magnum opus in fiction, though the novel has evoked considerable disapprobation. Robert Bone called the novel "a failure on the grand scale," with a plot that is "little more than a series of occasions for talk and fornication"; Howard Harper, Jr., described it as "a long playing record of frantic embraces and frantic questions"; and Eugenia Collier contended that it is "a lurid tale . . . seasoned with violence and obscenity," with "something offensive for everyone." In spite of such detractors, a small number of essays have insisted on serious critical treatment of the novel. Granville Hicks argued that it was "shaped with rigorous care" and explored the complexities of love and hate; Norman Podhoretz defended it as a "maltreated bestseller" and lauded "the militancy and cruelty of its vision of life," its "remorseless insistence on a truth," and its "element of sweet spiritual generosity."

Another Country deserves to be read as a competent and compelling book—structurally, symbolically, and thematically. Structurally there are three sections: (1) "Easy Rider"; (2) "Any Day Now"; and (3) "Toward Bethlehem." The plot is composed of four narrative strands involving two main characters in each strand: (1) Rufus Scott and Leona (black man, white woman); (2) Ida Scott and Vivaldo Moore (black woman, white man); (3) Richard and Cass Silenski (white man and woman); (4)

Eric Jones and Yves (white homosexual, white male lover). These narrative accounts converge and intertwine at various points in a kind of phantasmagoria of interracial and intersexual relations among friends and strangers in New York City. The novel seems basically the story of Ida and Vivaldo; their strand is central to the movement of the work, and the conclusion focuses on their emergence as the principal norm of value, with the new mode of life for Eric and Yves embodying a subsidiary value.

Symbolically the novel is richly suggestive in setting and title. The former is vividly described in imagery suggesting the danger, brutality, disease, lust, indifference, and despair of those who experience the ache of estrangement: "in New York, one had, still, to fight very hard in order not to perish of loneliness." The "strange climate of the city" mirrors the spiritual condition of the people in a kind of Dantesque hell of entrapment and isolation, a wasteland in which the characters struggle to live and relate to each other in order to justify self-awareness and renew the sense of being human. The title is reminiscent of Hemingway's story "In Another Country," set in the conflict of warfare and correlating the physical locale with the psychic terrain of the characters. Geographically, the title symbolizes: (1) New York, the other "country" within American society; (2) Harlem, the "other country" within a city, "which no white man can ever comprehend"; and (3) other countries, for example, France, where a black and a white can live with less guilt and dread and more possibility of joy. Ethically and philosophically, "another country" is the place wherein the values of the white majority lead to spiritual destruction because they are success oriented and where the sense of American escapism denies the need of learning to confront the tragic—that pain, suffering, and death which belong to the essence of "the blues" that pulsate as a background in the novel. Psychologically the title reflects the enormity of the mystery of sexual experience; to be out of touch with or to fear sensual reality is to deny the human, whether that sexual reality be expressed heterosexually, homosexually, or bisexually. It is only through the expressiveness of sexual encounter that one can overcome estrangement and experience the reality of another in that compassion and tenderness which are the essence of love. To enter "another country" is to enter that mystery in the wilderness of the love experience which is both terrifying and joyful: as Baldwin said in an earlier essay, "love takes off the masks that we fear we cannot live without and know we cannot live within. . . . Love . . . not in the infantile American sense of being made happy but in the tough and universal sense of quest and daring and growth."

Thematically, *Another Country* embodies the variety of subjects that are reiterated and modulated in the author's other works: the search for personal identity; the intensity of the emotions; the racial skirmishing of blacks and whites, involving both overt patterns of behavior and subtle psychological conditions; the need for recognition of the profound terror and joy in sexual encounter; the reality of pain, misery, and suffering in making human life tragic; and the indictment of the American dream. Within the novel, the human personality in all of its baffling mystery, its enigmatic perplexity, its web of tangled desire and frustration, is presented with force and pungency. Baldwin later confessed: "What I was trying to do was create for the first time my own apprehension of the country and the world. I understood that if I could discharge venom, I could discharge love (they frighten me equally). When I was a little boy, I hated all white people, but in this book I got beyond the hate. I faced my life by that book and it's a good book. It's as honest as I can be." From the early pages the leitmotif of aloneness and the necessity for love is explicitly expressed: "He stood there, wide legged, humping the air . . . screaming through the horn, Do you love me? Do you love me? Do you love me? . . . and yet the question was terrible and real."

In *Another Country* Baldwin explores the possibilities of the Afro-American blues tradition to deal with the chaos of twentieth-century life. The novel is literally filled with lyrics from blues songs, and the characters, in one sense, are evaluated in terms of their relationship to the blues aesthetic. The blues is a form of expression that allows man to bring order to his chaotic world on a personal level and through the shared experience of the audience transforms its chaos as well. The blues is not the exclusive possession of black Americans; it is just that they have been able to use it more effectively than whites because they have a greater and more immediate sense of their suffering. And when whites are forced to recognize their suffering, they find that the world in which they have so much faith is incapable of supplying a definition for them. At this point they too can become acquainted with the power of the blues. They learn that the power to deal with suffering comes from within.

From this perspective the novel becomes what Stanley Edgar Hyman calls "a parable of reconciliation, sin and forgiveness" through the central narrative strand of Vivaldo and Ida and the chief subsidiary strand of Eric and Yves. While the major characters discover ugly truths about themselves and each other, the novel concludes on a note of reconciliation; "another country" is the country of love which takes off the masks and makes reconciliation a possibility even among those of different races or of the same sex. Thus Baldwin has been audacious enough, prior to most other artists, to grapple candidly with the usually taboo subjects of American society and culture: interracial sexual intercourse, homosexuality as a normal experience, and bisexuality as a real phenomenon. This novel is an excursion into those areas of human relations about which insight is lacking and experience limited. The writer has given both in a novel that fulfills his own credo for the artistic function: "Real writers question their age. They demand Yes and No answers. Typers collaborate. You collaborate or you question."

In the intensification of the Civil Rights Movement during the early 1960s Baldwin became an active participant. As various groups struggled to end racial discrimination and segregation, Baldwin became an increasingly ardent spokesman, enunciating in essays and speeches the agony of being black in America. While the role was not new for him, the activities of the 1960s were undertaken because of his reputation. Whether with Medgar Evers or James Meredith in Mississippi, at a session with Robert Kennedy in New York, on a speaking tour for the Congress of Racial Equality, or helping in the voter registration drive in Selma, Alabama, Baldwin was committed "to end the racial nightmare of our country and change the history of the world." The culmination of his literary effort in this era was the publication of *The Fire Next Time* (1963), a treatise which very likely helped "in restoring the personal essay to its place as a form of creative literature," as John Henrik Clarke has asserted.

The Fire Next Time consists of two essays in the form of letters, with the first as prefatory to the beliefs and concepts presented in the second. "My Dungeon Shook" contains advice to a young black male who is the author's nephew and is about to enter the domain of racial conflict on the anniversary of the proclamation that is supposed to have set him free. It is a forthright assault upon the "impertinent assumption . . . that black men are inferior to white men" and an assertion of the black's inherent "unassailable and monumental dignity."

The second essay, "Down at the Cross," is an autobiographical account in three sections: recollections of growing up in Harlem, an evaluation of the Black Muslims, and the statement of a personal credo. The Harlem section analyzes the psychological condition of learning to be black and "fighting the man" in a "white country, an Anglo-Teutonic, anti-sexual country," of experiencing the principles of "Blindness, Loneliness, and Terror" in the Christian church, and of recognizing that "if the concept of God has any validity or any use, it can only be to make us larger, freer, and loving." The Black Muslim portion evaluates Elijah Muhammad as a charismatic and disciplined leader who "refuses to accept the white world's definitions" and therefore threatens its power. The "personal credo" posits a series of ideas relevant to contemporary America: the fact that "life is tragic"; the need "to apprehend the nature of change, to be able and willing to change"; the importance of discarding "that collection of myths to which white Americans cling"; the reality that blacks may not rise to power "but they are very well placed indeed to precipitate chaos and ring down the curtain on the American dream." Finally, in a note of compelling alarm, Baldwin prophesies that "the relatively conscious" whites and blacks may be able "to end the racial nightmare, and achieve our country, and change the history of the world"; otherwise, "no more water the fire next time."

Although this book did not offer any easy solutions to the political, social, and psychological conditions of being black in America, it did suggest democracy as a means of promoting change and set forth what could be expected if such change were not forthcoming. Perhaps the greatest value of the essay's rhetorical flourishes of confession, anguish, quest, and warning was its dramatization of emotional conditions with the underlying design of evoking the emotional response of empathy.

In 1964 Baldwin completed *Blues for Mister Charlie*, his third play, and remained in New York to oversee its opening on 23 April. *Blues for Mister Charlie* obviously reflects the author's participation in the Civil Rights Movement, for the play is based on the 1955 murder of Emmett Till that had interested Baldwin since the days of his apprenticeship to Elia Kazan. Two white men were acquitted of the crime by an all-white jury, though one of them subsequently bragged about the murder and recounted the details. While some critics have dismissed the play as propagandistic, bombastic, and melodramatic, others have praised the manner in which it reveals the myths and stereotypes relating

12

Juanita

No matter what Parnell may be thinking at the bottom of his heart,
he keeps right on running down to that court-house and raising
money - I don't know how he does it, he must have something on
everybody in this town - to get the kids out of jail, and he
keeps on raising hell in his newspaper. I think it's hard on
him. Things are changing, everything is changing, and that's
always hard, even when they're changes you know should happen
and that you've worked to bring about. I'm with Mother Henry,
here. I don't think we should be hard on Parnell. He suffers.

Lorenzo

Only, he's not used to it.

> Pete: And, beside, he's got his eyes for Juanita.
> Juanita: OK, Pete, stop it. That's just Parnell's way.
> It ain't that ~~blacker~~ emancipated.

Mother Henry

There are lots of ways to suffer. And nobody ever gets used to it.

Jimmy

I wonder if they'll convict him.

Juanita

Convict him. Convict him. Youre asking for heaven on earth. I
tell you, they haven't even arrested him yet. And, anyway -
why **should** they convict him, after all? Why **him**? He's **no** worse
than all the others. He's **only** done what they do all the time -
he's an honorable tribesman and he's defended, with blood, the
honor of his tribe!

~~Lights up on~~ Whitetown. LYLE holds his infant son up
above his head, laughing.

Lyle

You hear me, sir? I expect you to control your bladder, like a
gentleman, whenever your Papa's got you on his knee.

JO enters.

He got a mighty big bladder, too, for such a little fellow.

Blues for Mr. Charlie *revised typescript (Billy Rose Theatre Collection, New York Public Library at Lincoln Center, Astor, Lenox and Tilden Foundations)* to black-white relations, a thematic emphasis Baldwin had explored poignantly a year earlier in *The Fire Next Time.*

Blues for Mister Charlie is a complex drama that uses its dual settings of Whitetown (the courthouse) and Blacktown (the church) to present several stories and to explore several ideas simultaneously. Whereas Richard Henry, the young black entertainer who has returned home from New York after being hooked on dope, and the black student Juanita, who is friendly with the local white liberal newspaper editor, and Lyle Britten, the white store owner who kills Richard, play central roles in the unfolding story, the two major characters are Parnell James, the editor, and Rev. Meridian Henry, local minister and father of Richard. These latter two figures embody the persistent motif of Baldwin's work at that point in his literary career: namely, the need for "the relatively conscious whites and the relatively conscious blacks, who must, like lovers, insist on, or create, the consciousness of the others." Unfortunately, and rather tragically, *Blues for Mister Charlie* concludes with Parnell James, the white liberal, lacking the courage to testify at the trial that Jo Britten has lied about Richard, and with Meridian Henry, the embodiment of black moderation and nonviolence, conjoining "the Bible and the gun" in the pulpit "like the pilgrims of old." Darwin Turner has suggested in his essay "Visions of Love and Manliness in a Blackening World" that *Blues for Mister Charlie* was written for a white audience and belongs in the general category of that "traditional drama" which stresses the similarities between blacks and whites, examines the dilemma of middle-class blacks, and uses black characters who challenge whites verbally but passively reject physical confrontation.

In *Blues for Mister Charlie* and *The Amen Corner,* as in his other literary works, Baldwin explores a variety of thematic concerns: the historical significance and the potential explosiveness in black-white relations; the necessity for developing a sexual and psychological consciousness and identity; the intertwining of love and power in the universal scheme of existence as well as in the structures of society; the misplaced priorities in the value systems in America; and the responsibility of the artist to promote the evolution of the individual and the society. The extent of Baldwin's success as a man of letters in the genre of drama remains, however, a moot question. On the one side some critics contend, as does Gerald Weales, that "despite the incidental virtues of both plays, they indicate that the dramatic form is not a congenial one for Baldwin."

In contrast Carlton Molette advocates in "James Baldwin as Playwright" that the author, essentially a novelist and essayist, has demonstrated as dramatist his trust of and reliance upon many other artists; that "the ability to accomplish that collaborative working relationship may very well be the reason for Baldwin's success as a playwright where so many other novelists have failed"; and that "given the present system of producing plays professionally in the United States, we are lucky indeed to get one play per decade from the likes of James Baldwin." Significantly, Baldwin is one of the few black playwrights who has had more than one production on Broadway.

Two years elapsed between *The Fire Next Time* and the author's collection of eight short stories called *Going to Meet the Man* (1965). However, in those years the drama *Blues for Mister Charlie* (1964) and the collaborative volume of photographs and text, *Nothing Personal* (1964, with Richard Avedon), were published. The short stories indicate clearly the influence of Henry James, and each "shows a sure sense of the short story form, a moment of illumination that has significance for the total life of the character," as George Kent phrases it. Furthermore, the stories reflect the range of Baldwin's early thematic interests and demonstrate a realistic sense of personal experiences.

The first two stories, "The Rockpile" and "The Outing," present the concern with family antagonisms and the memories of the church and thereby strongly resemble *Go Tell It on the Mountain.* "The Man Child" is a kind of horror story involving murder and illustrating Baldwin's contention in an essay on Wright that "no American Negro exists who does not have his private Bigger Thomas living in the skull." "Previous Condition" initiates a subject later treated more fully in *Tell Me How Long the Train's Been Gone* (1968) and *If Beale Street Could Talk* (1974)—the struggle for survival by the black artist and especially his ambivalent relations with whites. "Sonny's Blues" is the record of a young man's search for identity and self-expression through drugs, words, and music, and "through the almost ritualistic repetition of feeling, emotion and mood the blues singer achieves," wrote Stanley Macebuh. "This Morning, This Evening, So Soon" deals with a seemingly successful black actor in a similar situation. "Come Out the Wilderness" concerns a young black woman from the South seeking love and success in the city and living with a white man, and an ambitious but lonely black actor from the South. "Going to Meet the Man" concludes the volume and coalesces the elements of history, the

*Dust jacket for Baldwin's last novel of the 1960s, his fictional examination of how
celebrity affects the black artist*

South, sex, violence, blacks, and whites in a narrative that explores the moral, psychological, and sociological roots of racism by analyzing the causes for impotency and violence in a white deputy sheriff. In this volume, as John Rees Moore says, the "people are lonely, frustrated, fearful, often angry, and above all lovelorn.... Most of them have a vision of a better land, a better life, but their moments of happiness are always precarious."

During this period, though continuing to reside in Europe with periodic treks to the United States, Baldwin maintained an unflagging interest in the implications and effects of the Civil Rights Movement within American society and culture. He also received several awards during this period. In 1959 he received a Ford Foundation fellowship. He was awarded a National Conference of Christians and Jews Brotherhood Award in 1962, a George Polk Award in 1963, an honorary doctor of letters degree from the University of British Columbia in 1964, and the Foreign Drama Critics Award in 1964; and he was made a member of the National Institute of Arts and Letters in that same year.

Tell Me How Long the Train's Been Gone (1968) was Baldwin's last novel of the 1960s. Critics were quick to point out its flaws—flat characters, vulgarity for its own sake, and polemicism. While these criticisms have some merit, the apparent flaws in the novel stem more from what Baldwin is attempting than from any lack of ability, as some critics suggested. The novel deals indirectly with the Civil Rights Movement and the role of the black artist/celebrity in that movement.

Tell Me How Long the Train's Been Gone (1968) has been denigrated as "a work of self-indulgence" and "drearily irrelevant" but commended as a realistic account of "one black man's struggle to overcome the definition of himself handed down by his white countrymen." It is the life story of a thirty-nine-year-old famous American black actor, Leo Proudhammer, who suffers a heart attack at the pinnacle of his career. During the period of his convalescence, a series of complicated flashbacks presents the momentous and significant events of his past: a childhood in Harlem; a hero-worship of his older, militant brother, Caleb; a long affair with a white actress, Barbara; police and prison guard brutality; and an attachment to a young and male black revolutionary, Christopher. The book repeats the homosexual and heterosexual, interracial lovemaking of earlier works as well as the assertive renunciation of religion and God as capable means of effective social change in the racial struggle. However, there are also distinctive changes in this novel compared to those preceding it; as Stanley Macebuh has persuasively argued, Baldwin creates for the first time a "Black Christopher" committed to "the politics of active confrontation" as an affirmation of "the essential worth of man" and makes homosexuality an intrinsic part of the revolutionary commitment so as "to present the homosexual as an authentic instrument of change in society." Thus, there appears in the novel a shift from reliance upon stressing the fictional protagonist's essential privacy as an individual to an emphasis upon the development of a "confident, proud, determined" black man devoted to public action.

Tell Me How Long the Train's Been Gone reflects Baldwin's internal struggle with his role as artist/celebrity and civil rights spokesman during the 1960s. The black celebrity has two choices: he can become a "fatcat," as Leo is labeled at one point, and withdraw into the protective shell of his success, or he can use his status as a symbol for the black community. The first situation demands no recognition of roots. But the second choice requires a conscious recognition and acceptance of roots. *Tell Me How Long the Train's Been Gone* is not so much about the making of a revolutionary as it is about the making of a celebrity/spokesman, an image that plagued Baldwin throughout the 1960s.

The decade of the 1970s proved to be less active politically for Baldwin but quite productive in a literary sense. In 1971 his conversations with anthropologist Margaret Mead on world racism were published as *A Rap on Race*. Another improvised dialogue was published in 1973, this time with black poet-activist Nikki Giovanni, as simply *A Dialogue*. Two books of essays also appeared during the 1970s: *No Name in the Street* (1972), his most militant statement to date; and *The Devil Finds Work* (1976), a history of blacks in film. *One Day When I Was Lost* (1972), a movie scenario based on Alex Haley's *Autobiography of Malcolm X*, was published but not produced because Baldwin refused to compromise with Columbia Pictures on his perceptions of Malcolm X's life. A little-known fictional work, *Little Man, Little Man: A Story of Childhood*, a children's book written in black dialect and with a ghetto setting, also appeared in 1976, the year Baldwin received an honorary doctor of letters de-

gree from Morehouse College. He also published two novels: *If Beale Street Could Talk* (1974), a best-seller; and *Just Above My Head* (1979).

If Beale Street Could Talk contributed to the familiar pattern of critical response, for it too evoked not only such caustic epithets as "an almost total disaster" and "a vehemently sentimental love story" but also such complimentary descriptions as this from Joyce Carol Oates—"a quite moving and very traditional celebration of love." The story focuses upon the adversities of a young black couple: Fonny, the twenty-two-year-old sculptor; and his nineteen-year-old, pregnant fiancée, Tish. Fonny is arrested and charged for a rape he did not commit, and he is capable of being freed before trial only if the bail money is raised.

In one sense, the antagonist in the novel is the American judicial system. Tish says at one point that "The calendars were full—it would take about a thousand years to try all the people in the American prisons, but the Americans are optimistic, and still hope for time—and sympathetic or merely intelligent judges are as rare as snowstorms in the tropics." Also, it is because of the white policeman Bell, a representative of that system, that Fonny is in jail. Bell frames Fonny because he is made to look foolish when a white witness clears Fonny of blame in a street fight over Tish. Moreover, that Fonny's case is not affected when the chief witness against him, the rape victim, flees to San Juan and will probably not return, is another indication of the unfairness of the system.

In a less threatening way, the Hunt women, Fonny's mother and sisters, act as obstacles to Fonny's release. They are devoutly religious. Their religion, however, simply serves as a way of achieving social respectability within the community and has nothing to do with Christian charity. When Fonny is put in jail, the Hunt women refuse to have anything to do with him because their acknowledgment of a known criminal would severely compromise their social standing, even though the criminal is son and brother. The confrontations between the Hunt women and the Rivers women are brutal and somewhat comic as the religious Hunts always come off looking absurd. The religious position, as in *Tell Me How Long the Train's Been Gone*, once again appears ineffectual and outright destructive in light of the realities of Fonny's and Tish's situation.

The novel ends on a note of uncertainty, much like the lives of the characters. In the end, Fonny is working on a piece of sculpture and the baby is heard crying in the background. Whether this is a fantasy created out of labor pains or whether Fonny is really out of jail is unclear. The novel presents the familial bond of sacrifice and love within the context of a society in which the black minority stands perpetually accused and trying to make bail for freedom. The major shift in this novel as compared to earlier works is that Baldwin concentrates for the first time on the question of what it means to be an artist in the society; previous works of fiction revealed persons of artistic sensibility, but Fonny is the closest that Baldwin has come in dealing with the common topic that nearly every twentieth-century fiction writer of stature has treated at one time or another.

Just Above My Head is perhaps Baldwin's most ambitious work of fiction to date. Critical responses to the novel were mixed. Richard Gilman referred to "the disagreeable work of reviewing" the book and found it "a melancholy piece of creation," an "apologia for homosexuality," that alternates in dialogue between jive and street talk on the one hand and literary hyperbole on the other. Paul Darcy Boles, however, argued that "the power of love redeems the dead as well as the living" in this work which "continually discards outworn and shallow visions of existence" and rejects all pat religious or political answers to difficult human problems.

This novel is long (nearly 600 pages) and complex. Baldwin uses gospel music for purposes of structural organization, character development, and thematic emphasis; and common to those three uses is the aesthetic concept of music and its accompanying lyrics as "the verbalization of deeply felt feelings," feelings which in their totality of expression offer a poignant statement about the meaning of being human. In the early essay "Many Thousands Gone," Baldwin had asserted that "it is only in his music, which Americans are able to admire because a protective sentimentality limits their understanding of it, that the Negro in America has been able to tell his story." Later, in *The Fire Next Time,* he was to attest that "there is no music like that music . . . and all those voices coming together and crying holy unto the Lord. . . . I have never seen anything equal to the fire and excitement that sometimes, without warning, fills a church, causing the church, as Leadbelly and so many others have testified, to 'rock.'" Again, in the same essay he described the crucial relationship between music, including gospel songs, and the concepts of freedom and survival: "In spite of everything there was in the life I fled a zest and a joy and a capacity for facing and surviving disaster that are very moving and very rare. . . . We sometimes achieved with

each other a freedom that was close to love. . . . This is the freedom that one hears in some gospel songs, for example, and in jazz. In all jazz, and especially in the blues, there is something tart and ironic, authoritative and double-edged."

This long novel with its nearly 100 references to gospel music (and its two dozen references to the blues) is divided into five sections. Each section has a subtitle and an epigraph grounded in the gospel music tradition.

Book I	Have Mercy
Epigraph:	Work, for the night is coming.

Book II	Twelve Gates to the City
Epigraph:	Come on in the Lord's house: It's going to rain.

Book III	The Gospel Singer
Epigraph:	Work, for the night is coming.

Book IV	Stepchild
Epigraph:	Lead me to the rock That is higher than I.

Book V	The Gates of Hell
Epigraph:	It's me, it's me, It's me, oh, Lord, Standing in the need of prayer.
	I know my robe's going to fit me well I tried it on at the gates of hell.

Through its central focus on gospel music in the lives of brothers Hall and Arthur Montana, this novel explores such themes as the Civil Rights Movement, the Korean War and the draft, the storefront church and religious passion, childhood preaching, incest, white racism, homosexuality, and the family.

The plot of the novel is complex, and the narrator is forty-eight-year-old Hall Montana, who organizes the narrative by means of differing locales—New York, Atlanta, Birmingham, London—and time shifts during basically the 1950s, 1960s, and early 1970s. Ruminating and reflecting on events from the Korean War to the post-Civil Rights Movement, Hall Montana moves back in time to pick up relevant threads of action prior to the 1950s, especially about his early family life.

In what he describes as "a love song to my brother . . . an attempt to face both love and death," Hall is presumably telling the story of his younger brother, Arthur, a famous gospel singer known both in the States and abroad as "The Soul Emperor." Arthur had died at age thirty-nine, two years before the present action of the book, probably of a stroke, in a London pub. Hall, in trying to re-create the story of his brother, is also trying to make sense of his own life. Thus, both men are revealed through Hall's myriad reflections and reminiscences. The narrator is on a quest for meaning and value; the boundaries of his consciousness are stretched as he struggles with freedom, responsibility, and the significance of history.

Arthur Montana is not a fully developed character in the book, though Hall also gives the views of others about his brother. Hall reveals Arthur's temperament, tenderness, vulnerability, and artistry as well as his private life as a homosexual. As the story unfolds, the obvious biblical question is posed: "Am I my brother's keeper?" That question about the brotherhood of man assumes special poignancy within the framework of gospel music, as Hall explains: "Niggers can sing gospel as no other people can because they aren't singing gospel. . . . When a nigger quotes the Gospel, he is not quoting: he is telling you what happened to him today, and what is certainly going to happen to you tomorrow. . . . Our suffering is our bridge to one another."

Baldwin's view of himself as literary artist has remained unchanged throughout his career. In his early essay "The Creative Dilemma," he described the artist as "the incorrigible disturber of the peace" with whom "all societies have battled"; after all, "the war of an artist with his society is a lover's war, and he does at his best what lovers do, which is to reveal the beloved to himself and, with that revelation, to make freedom real." In an interview after the appearance of his last novel, Baldwin commented that "what I've really been feeling is that I've come full circle. From *Go Tell It on the Mountain* to *Just Above My Head* sums up something of my experience—it's difficult to articulate—that sets me free to go someplace else."

Most recently Baldwin has, indeed, gone on to "someplace else." The year 1985 saw the release of three more books, each of a very different kind. While *The Price of the Ticket: Collected Non-Fiction 1948-1985* is a compilation of fifty-one essays previously published, several of them have never been collected in book form and are therefore frequently

difficult to locate for the ordinary reader; also, the book contains an insightful autobiographical introduction that is both revelatory and confessional of the artist's life.

The Evidence of Things Not Seen is something of a polemic and meditation motivated by the infamous series of Atlanta child-murders in late 1979 and the early 1980s; it was written on commission for *Playboy* magazine. Using the arrest of Wayne Williams and the series of murders as primary subject matter, Baldwin ranged over a variety of other topics pertaining to the general conditions of American society in the 1980s, with special emphasis on an issue that had long been a major concern for the writer: the problem of being black in predominantly white America. This extended essay uses facts and documentary evidence both for analytical thought and speculative judgments. The most serious indictment is that directed toward the coveted concept of the American Dream (an old theme of Baldwin) as "the final manifestation of the European/Western/Christian dominance."

Jimmy's Blues: Selected Poems is a slender volume of nineteen poems, the author's only published book of verse. Numerous moods are expressed in these verses which range over a variety of thematic emphases that are generally already known to readers familiar with the earlier works of Baldwin, in particular what it means to be black in white America. The diction of the poems is deceptively simple, for it embodies emotions that are acute and intense and clothed in irony as well as direct statement:

> I always wonder
> what they think the niggers are doing
> while they, the pink and alabaster pragmatists,
> are containing
> Russia
> and defining and re-defining and re-aligning
> China . . . [.]

An excursion through the poetry discovers both the commitment and the toughness of Baldwin's earlier fiction, drama, and essays.

James Baldwin's career as an American man of letters has spanned nearly four decades. By the quantity and quality of his efforts, his place is now secure in the mainstream of American literature. As Louis Pratt argues so cogently, Baldwin has analyzed "the black experience for its universal dimensions" and has used "that experience as a means of joining hands with humanity, with the universal brotherhood of mankind, and this effort may prove to be his ultimate triumph and distinction."

Interviews:

"The Negro in American Culture," *Cross Currents*, 11 (Summer 1961): 205-224;

E. Auchincloss and N. Lynch, "Disturber of the Peace," *Mademoiselle* (May 1963): 174-175, 199-207;

"At a Crucial Time a Negro Talks Tough: 'There's a bill due that has to be paid,' " *Life*, 54 (24 May 1963): 81-86A;

Kenneth B. Clark, "A Conversation with James Baldwin," *Freedomways*, 3 (Summer 1963): 361-368;

William F. Buckley, Jr., "The American Dream and the American Negro," *New York Times Magazine*, 7 March 1965, pp. 32-33, 87-89;

"James Baldwin Breaks His Silence: An Interview," *Atlas*, 13 (March 1967): 47-49;

Dan Georgakas, "James Baldwin . . . in Conversation," in *Black Voices: An Anthology of Afro-American Literature*, edited by Abraham Chapman (New York: New American Library, 1968), pp. 660-668;

"How Can We Get the Black People To Cool It? An Interview with James Baldwin," *Esquire*, 66 (July 1968): 49-53, 116;

Karen Wild, " 'We Are All the Viet Cong!': An Interview with James Baldwin," *Nickel Review*, 4 (27 February 1970): 5;

David Frost, "Are We on the Edge of Civil War?," in his *The Americans* (New York: Stein & Day, 1970), pp. 145-150;

Herbert R. Lottman, "It's Hard to Be James Baldwin," *Intellectual Digest*, 2 (July 1972): 67-68;

"Why I Left America. Conversation: Ida Lewis and James Baldwin," in *New Black Voices*, edited by Chapman (New York: New American Library, 1972), pp. 409-419;

Joe Walker, "Exclusive Interview with James Baldwin," *Muhammad Speaks*, 8 September 1973, pp. 13-14; 15 September 1973, p. 29; 29 September 1973, pp. 29-30; 6 October 1973, pp. 30-31;

"The Black Scholar Interviews: James Baldwin," *Black Scholar*, 5 (December 1973-January 1974): 33-42;

Jewell Hardy Gresham, "James Baldwin Comes Home," *Essence*, 7 (June 1976): 54-55, 80, 82, 85;

Mel Watkins, "James Baldwin Writing and Talking," *New York Times Book Review*, 23 September 1979, pp. 35-36;

Kalamu ya Salaam, "James Baldwin: Looking Towards the Eighties," *Black Collegian* (December/January 1980): 105-110.

Bibliographies:

M. Thomas Inge and others, eds., *Black American Writers. Bibliographical Essays. Vol. II. Richard Wright, Ralph Ellison, James Baldwin, and Amiri Baraka* (New York: St. Martin's, 1978);

    A selective, annotated listing of primary works (books, essays, short stories, interviews, discussions, etc.) and secondary works (books and essays).

Fred L. and Nancy V. Standley, *James Baldwin: A Reference Guide* (Boston: G. K. Hall, 1981);

    The most comprehensive, annotated, secondary bibliography published to date; arranged chronologically and indexed by author and title. It includes, also, a bibliographical listing of Baldwin's primary works.

References:

Fern Marja Eckman, *The Furious Passage of James Baldwin* (New York: Evans, 1966);

    The most important single source of autobiographical and biographical information about the author, based on taped interviews and revealing dimensions and facets of the writer's personality and thought not available in other sources.

Trudier Harris, *Black Women in the Fiction of James Baldwin* (Knoxville: University of Tennessee Press, 1985);

    Analysis of works of fiction written over a thirty-year period to reveal how Baldwin's development of female characters progresses through time from those dominated by religious influences to those who became caring and contented outside the church.

Keneth Kinnamon, ed., *James Baldwin. A Collection of Critical Essays* (Englewood Cliffs, N.J.: Prentice-Hall, 1974);

    Anthology of previously published essays by several authors to show the diversity of opinions about Baldwin; also includes chronology, bibliography, and introduction that emphasizes themes of the works.

Stanley Macebuh, *James Baldwin: A Critical Study* (New York: Third Press, 1973);

    Contains a detailed analysis of the works, particularly the novels, and places Baldwin in the black tradition by showing the links between politics and literature and the meaning of black aesthetic.

Therman B. O'Daniel, ed., *James Baldwin: A Critical Evaluation* (Washington: Howard University Press, 1977);
Anthology of secondary sources by numerous persons covering all dimensions of Baldwin's work: fiction, drama, essays, dialogues; also has a bibliography.

Louis Pratt, *James Baldwin* (Boston: Twayne, 1978);
Interprets the literary art in order to delineate the broader concerns of the author in contrast to the "white versus black" problem.

Fred L. Standley and Nancy V. Burt, eds., *Critical Essays on James Baldwin* (Boston: G. K. Hall, 1987);

A collection of essays and reviews, both reprinted and original, treating the fiction and nonfiction as well as general themes of the works.

Carolyn W. Sylvander, *James Baldwin* (New York: Ungar, 1980);
An exposition of the meaning of Baldwin's works as shaped by the age in which he has lived, showing him as a man of conviction, passion, and honesty.

W. J. Weatherby, *Squaring Off: Mailer vs. Baldwin* (New York: Mason/Charter, 1977);
Presents his own personal experiences with Norman Mailer and Baldwin via discussions, dinners, interviews, etc., as "representative figures of the sixties, when blacks and whites were struggling creatively to understand each other."

Amiri Baraka
(LeRoi Jones)

This entry was updated by James A. Miller (Trinity College) from his entry in DLB 16,
The Beats: Literary Bohemians in Postwar America.

Places	Newark, New Jersey New York's Lower East Side	Washington, D.C. / Howard University	Harlem
Influences and Relationships	Charles Olson Larry Neal Ezra Pound	Allen Ginsberg Langston Hughes Diane DiPrima	Frank O'Hara William Carlos Williams Maulana Ron Karenga
Literary Movements and Forms	The Black Mountain Poets The Black Arts Movement	The "New York" Poets The Beats	The Black Arts Repertory Theatre
Major Themes	Cultural Alienation Interracial Conflict Action vs. Contemplation Afro-American Cultural Traditions	Critique of Western Values and Society Necessity for Revolutionary Change	Search for Identity The Divided Self The Victim Quest for Unified Consciousness
Cultural and Artistic Influences	Afro-American Music Zen Buddhism The Congress of the African Peoples	Islam Phenomenology Abstract Expression- ist Art	Yoruba Religion The *Kawaida* Doctrine
Social and Economic Influences	Civil Rights Movement Pan-Africanism	Cuban Revolution Maoism	Black Nationalism Marxism-Leninism

See also the Baraka entries in DLB 5, American Poets Since World War II, DLB 7, Twentieth-Century American Dramatists, *and* DLB 38, Afro-American Writers After 1955: Dramatists and Prose Writers.

BIRTH: Newark, New Jersey, 7 October 1934, to Coyette LeRoy and Anna Lois Russ Jones.

EDUCATION: Rutgers University, 1951-1952; Howard University, 1952-1954.

MARRIAGES: 13 October 1958 to Hettie Cohen (divorced); children: Kellie, Lisa. August 1967 to Sylvia Robinson (Amina); children: Obalaji, Ras Jua, Shani, Amiri, Ahi.

AWARDS AND HONORS: John Hay Whitney Fellowship, 1960-1961; Longview Award for *Cuba Libre,* 1961; Obie Award for *Dutchman,* 1964; Guggenheim Fellowship, 1965-1966; Second Prize, First World Festival of Negro Arts, Dakar, Senegal, for *The Slave,* 1966; Doctorate of Humane Letters, Malcolm X College, Chicago, 1977.

SELECTED BOOKS: *Cuba Libre,* as LeRoi Jones (New York: Fair Play for Cuba Committee, 1961);
Preface To A Twenty Volume Suicide Note. . . . , as LeRoi Jones (New York: Totem Press/Corinth Books, 1961);
Blues People. . . . Negro Music in White America, as LeRoi Jones (New York: Morrow, 1963; London: MacGibbon & Kee, 1965);
Dutchman and The Slave, as LeRoi Jones (New York: Morrow, 1964; London: Faber & Faber, 1965);
The Dead Lecturer, as LeRoi Jones (New York: Grove, 1964);
The System of Dante's Hell, as LeRoi Jones (New York: Grove, 1965; London: MacGibbon & Kee, 1966);
Home: Social Essays, as LeRoi Jones (New York: Morrow, 1966; London: MacGibbon & Kee, 1968);
Black Art, as LeRoi Jones (Newark, N.J.: Jihad, 1966);
Slave Ship, as LeRoi Jones (Newark, N.J.: Jihad, 1967);
The Baptism and The Toilet, as LeRoi Jones (New York: Grove, 1967);
Arm Yourself, or Harm Yourself! A One Act Play, as LeRoi Jones (Newark, N.J.: Jihad, 1967);

Amiri Baraka (photo by Layle Silbert)

Tales, as LeRoi Jones (New York: Grove, 1967; London: MacGibbon & Kee, 1969);
Black Music, as LeRoi Jones (New York: Morrow, 1967; London: MacGibbon & Kee, 1969);
Black Magic: Sabotage; Target Study; Black Art; Collected Poetry 1961-1967, as LeRoi Jones (Indianapolis & New York: Bobbs-Merrill, 1969; London: MacGibbon & Kee, 1969);
Four Black Revolutionary Plays, as LeRoi Jones (Indianapolis & New York: Bobbs-Merrill, 1969; London: Calder & Boyars, 1971)—includes *Experimental Death Unit #1, A Black Mass, Great Goodness of Life (A Coon Show),* and *Madheart;*
A Black Value System (Newark, N.J.: Jihad, 1970);
J-E-L-L-O (Chicago: Third World Press, 1970);
It's Nation Time (Chicago: Third World Press, 1970);
In Our Terribleness (Some Elements and Meaning in Black Style), by Baraka and Fundi (Billy Abernathy) (Indianapolis & New York: Bobbs-Merrill, 1970);
Raise Race Rays Raze: Essays Since 1965 (New York: Random House, 1971);

Strategy and Tactics of a Pan-African Nationalist Party (Newark, N.J.: Jihad, 1971);

Kawaida Studies: The New Nationalism (Chicago: Third World Press, 1972);

Spirit Reach (Newark, N.J.: Jihad, 1972);

Crisis in Boston (Newark, N.J.: Vita Wa Watu—People's War Publishing, 1974);

Hard Facts (Newark, N.J.: People's War Publishing, 1975);

The Motion of History and Other Plays (New York: Morrow, 1978)—includes *The Motion of History, Slave Ship,* and *S-1;*

The Sidney Poet Heroical (Berkeley: Reed & Cannon, 1979);

Selected Plays and Prose of Amiri Baraka/LeRoi Jones (New York: Morrow, 1979);

Selected Poetry of Amiri Baraka/LeRoi Jones (New York: Morrow, 1979);

Reggae or Not (New York: Contact Two, 1981);

Daggers and Javelins, Essays, 1974-1979 (New York: Morrow, 1984);

The Autobiography of LeRoi Jones (New York: Freundlich Books, 1984).

PLAY PRODUCTIONS: *A Good Girl Is Hard To Find,* Montclair, N.J., Sterington House, 28 August 1958;

Dante, New York, Off Bowery Theatre, October 1961; produced again as *The Eighth Ditch,* New York, New Bowery Theatre, 1964;

Dutchman, New York, Village South Theatre, 12 January 1964; New York, Cherry Lane Theatre, 24 March 1964;

The Baptism, New York, Writers' Stage Theatre, 1 May 1964;

The Slave and *The Toilet,* New York, St. Mark's Playhouse, 16 December 1964;

J-E-L-L-O, New York, Black Arts Repertory Theatre, 1965;

Experimental Death Unit #1, New York, St. Mark's Playhouse, 1 March 1965;

A Black Mass, Newark, N.J., Proctor's Theatre, May 1966;

Slave Ship: A Historical Pageant, Newark, N.J., Spirit House, March 1967;

Madheart, San Francisco, San Francisco State College, May 1967;

Arm Yourself, or Harm Yourself!, Newark, N.J., Spirit House, 1967;

Great Goodness of Life (A Coon Show), Newark, N.J., Spirit House, November 1967;

Home on the Range, Newark, N.J., Spirit House, March 1968;

Resurrection in Life, Harlem, N.Y., 24 August 1969;

Junkies Are Full of (SHH. . .) and *Bloodrites,* New York, Henry Street Playhouse, 21 November 1970;

A Recent Killing, New York, New Federal Theatre, 26 January 1973;

The New Ark's a moverin, Newark, N.J., February 1974;

Sidnee Poet Heroical or If in Danger of Suit, The Kid Poet Heroical, New York, New Federal Theatre, 15 May 1975;

S-1, New York, Afro-American Studios, 23 July 1976;

The Motion of History, New York, New York City Theatre Ensemble, 27 May 1977;

What Was the Relationship of the Lone Ranger to the Means of Production?, New York, Ladies Fort, May 1979.

SCREENPLAYS: *Dutchman,* Gene Persson Enterprises, February 1967;

Black Spring, Jihad Productions, Spring 1967;

A Fable, based on Jones's play *The Slave,* MFR Productions, 1971.

OTHER: *Four Young Lady Poets,* edited by Jones (New York: Corinth Books, 1962);

The Moderns: An Anthology of New Writing in America, edited, with an introduction, by Jones (New York: Corinth Books, 1963);

David Henderson, *Felix of the Silent Forest,* introduction by Jones (New York: Poets Press, 1967);

Black Fire: An Anthology of Afro-American Writing, edited, with contributions, by Jones and Larry Neal (New York: Morrow, 1968);

Larry Neal, *Black Boogaloo (Notes on Black Liberation),* preface by Jones (San Francisco: Journal of Black Poetry Press, 1969);

African Congress: A Documentary of the First Modern Pan-African Congress, edited, with an introduction, by Baraka (New York: Morrow, 1972);

Confirmation: An Anthology of African American Women, edited by Amiri and Amina Baraka (New York: Morrow, 1983).

An influential figure among the literary avant-garde of Greenwich Village and the Lower East Side during the late 1950s and early 1960s, Amiri Baraka (known as LeRoi Jones until 1968) has been a seminal force in the development of contemporary Afro-American literature. Poet, music critic, essayist, dramatist, novelist, and political activist, Baraka's extraordinary talent and literary innovations have established him as a major writer. His prominence rests not only on his substantial literary achievement but also on the durability of his public personality, one whose extraliterary escapades and political activities have engaged the attention of his public for over two decades. Beginning in 1964, when the success of his play *Dutchman* established him as an outspoken commentator on American racial relations, Baraka has lived his artistic and political life in public view.

A protean personality, fond of manifestos and vehement repudiations, he has shifted guises and discarded identities with such astonishing rapidity that critics have often been frustrated, suspended in the act of defining a man who is no longer there, while his admirers have been left abandoned or challenged to readjust themselves to his new posture. In "The Liar," an early poem written while he still called himself Jones, he commented on this aspect of his personality, almost as if he anticipated his various guises and the direction his writing would take in the future:

> Though I am a man
> who is loud
> on the birth
> of his ways. Publicly redefining
> each change in my soul, as if I had predicted
> them,
>> and profited, biblically, even tho
>> their chanting weight,
>>> erased familiarity
>>> from my face.

Baraka's life and work resist easy classification or simplistic judgments; yet, beneath the often violent shifts and turns of his artistic and political views, it is possible to view his work in distinct stages as an evolving spiritual autobiography shaped by the imperatives of an intensely self-conscious sensibility. If there is any single preoccupation which runs through Baraka's work, it is the theme of change itself, the endless quest for appropriate vehicles of expression and action in a world which is itself constantly changing. Nevertheless there are significant and sometimes subtle lines of continuity between phases of his career. From this point of view his initial involvement with the New York literary avant-garde provides important clues to the aesthetic and ideological underpinnings of his subsequent artistic and political activity.

Like many artists and intellectuals drawn to the cultural and intellectual ferment of Greenwich Village during the late 1950s, Jones's early odyssey was shaped by a posture of sharply defined and somewhat exaggerated alienation from his own social background. Born Everett LeRoi Jones to Coyette Leroy Jones, a postal worker, and Anna Lois Russ Jones, a social worker, Jones was raised with his younger sister, Sandra Elaine, in a family which was middle class in outlook, if not in economic status. Jones's autobiographical allusions in his early works often depict him as a highly sensitive, introspective character, isolated by social class and sensibility from his environment. At the same time, guided by E. Franklin Frazier's penetrating critique of black middle-class values, *Black Bourgeoisie* (1957), Jones mercilessly satirizes the values and "false consciousness" of his parents' generation.

A product of the Newark public school system, Jones attended Central Avenue School and was one of the few black students to attend Barringer High School—a fact which probably heightened his sense of personal and cultural dislocation. Graduating from high school in 1951, Jones attended Rutgers University on a science scholarship in the fall of that year. As he later wryly observed: "I had to go to Rutgers before I found people who thought grits were meant to be eaten with milk and sugar, instead of gravy and pork sausage . . . and that's one of the reasons I left." Jones transferred to Howard University in 1952, where his interests shifted to philosophy, religion, German, and English literature. He would later single out Howard University as the symbolic capstone of the black bourgeoisie, observing in one of his essays: "Howard University shocked me into realizing how desperately sick the Negro could be, how he could be led into self-destruction and how he would not realize that it was the society that had forced him into a great sickness. . . ." Nevertheless Jones clearly derived both social and intellectual benefits from attending Howard, studying with such prominent American scholars and teachers as E. Franklin Frazier, Nathan A. Scott, Jr., who taught a course on Dante, and Sterling A. Brown, widely regarded as the patriarch of Afro-American literary critics. Sterling Brown's influence was particularly important for Jones because Brown also conducted informal classes on black music. Jones and A. B. Spellman, one of the few black poets whose works later appeared in the pages of Jones's avant-garde literary magazine *Yūgen*, both attended these gatherings regularly.

Jones enlisted in the U.S. Air Force in October 1954. After basic training in South Carolina, he was assigned as a weatherman and gunner on a B-36 in Puerto Rico. Although biographical sketches about Jones sometimes report that he traveled extensively in Europe, Africa, and the Middle East during this period, he spent most of his time stationed at the Strategic Air Command post in Puerto Rico, with his overseas travel limited almost exclusively to Germany.

Jones's return to civilian life in January 1957 coincided with an auspicious moment in American cultural and political life, a period of intellectual ferment, radical experimentation in the arts, and incipient social conflict. Allen Ginsberg's sensational reading of *Howl* at the Six Gallery in San Francisco in 1955 had attracted widespread public attention and announced the emergence of the Beat Generation. Another significant expression of rebellion against the dominant practices of poetry and criticism appeared in the pages of *Black Mountain Review*, organized by Charles Olson and Robert Creeley at North Carolina's experimental Black Mountain College. Published between 1954 and 1957, the *Black Mountain Review* featured the works of many poets whom Jones would later claim as his contemporaries and close associates. When the decision was made to shut down Black Mountain College in 1956, the community dispersed, some to California, others to New York's Greenwich Village. The Cedar Street Tavern, a bar made popular by internationally known abstractionist painters Jackson Pollock, Franz Kline, Willem de Kooning, and other New York School artists, soon became the gathering spot for Ginsberg, Gregory Corso, some of the Black Mountain poets, and other artists and intellectuals. At the same time the opening of the Thelonious Monk Quartet at the Five Spot in 1957 (with John Coltrane, tenor saxophone; Wilbur Ware, bass; and Shadow Wilson, drums) signaled the arrival of what Jones was later to dub the "new music"—an important dimension of the cultural ambience of Greenwich Village. All of these diverse literary and cultural influences shaped the direction of Jones's life and art.

After returning to Newark briefly, Jones moved to Greenwich Village in 1957. While employed as a clerk at the *Record Changer* magazine, he met Hettie Roberta Cohen, a young Jewish woman who shared many of his interests in music and literature. Their relationship deepened and they were married on 13 October 1958. By that time Hettie Cohen had become the advertising and business manager of *Partisan Review*, and it was in this journal that Jones issued one of his first published statements, a defense of the Beat Generation. For the Summer 1958 issue Jones wrote a sharp response to critic Norman Podhoretz's arti-

cle, "The Know-Nothing Bohemians." Declaring his aesthetic allegiance to Beat literature, Jones aligned himself with the literary innovations of Jack Kerouac and Allen Ginsberg, while attacking Podhoretz as an example of the entrenched cultural and literary values the Beats were challenging. Beat literature, he declared, was "less a movement than a reaction against . . . fifteen years of sterile unreadable magazine poetry. . . ." Jones maintained that writers of his generation "must resort to violence in literature, a kind of violence that has in such a short time begun to shake us out of the woeful literary sterility which characterized the 40's. . . ." Turning to Podhoretz's contention that "Bohemianism . . . is for the Negro a means of entry into the world of whites. . . ," Jones argued: "Harlem is today the veritable capital city of the Black Bourgeoisie. The Negro Bohemian's flight from Harlem is not a flight from the world of color but the flight of any would-be Bohemian from what Mr. Podhoretz himself calls 'the provinciality, philistinism, and moral hypocrisy of American life.' "

Jones's attack on Podhoretz suggested some of the social attitudes and aesthetic strategies characteristic of his early work. He typically defined literary and cultural movements in both personal and generational terms, revealing an iconoclastic and irreverent disdain for the past. More specifically, he sought to locate himself within an aesthetic tradition defined by the poetic practices of his contemporaries, the "new" poets of the 1950s, many of whom claimed Ezra Pound and William Carlos Williams as their literary ancestors. As Jones wrote in "How You Sound?," a personal statement included in Donald M. Allen's *The New American Poetry: 1945-1960:* "For me, Lorca, Williams, Pound and Charles Olson have had the greatest influence. Eliot, earlier (rhetoric can be so lovely, for a time . . . but only remains so for the rhetorician). And there are so many young wizards around now doing great things that everybody calling himself poet can learn from . . . Whalen, Snyder, McClure, O'Hara, Loewinsohn, Wieners, Creeley, Ginsberg &cc. &cc. &cc." Of all of the poets Jones cited, Ginsberg was the most influential. Struck by the power of *Howl*, a poem Jones later described as "the single most important poetic influence of the period," he wrote Ginsberg a letter on a piece of toilet paper and sent it to him in Paris. Ginsberg responded, including some of his poetry for *Yūgen*, which Jones and his wife were organizing, as well as work from Philip Whalen, Gregory Corso, Gary Snyder, Jack Kerouac, Frank O'Hara, and many other poets. Ginsberg also encouraged Jones's efforts by circulating his name throughout the literary community. Jones and Ginsberg met in Greenwich Village in 1958. He recalled the experience in a recent article for the *Village Voice:* "Ginsberg began introducing me to a score of other people. But more important, he explained to me what he was doing poetically and ran down an oral history of Western poetry from Chris Smart and Blake, through Whitman and William C. Williams, to the present. We talked endlessly about poetry, about prosody, about literature and it is clear to me that my poetry would not have evolved as it has without AG's ideas. He let me in on poetry as a living phenomenon, a world of human concern, and literature as a breathing force in one's life, the task of a lifetime. I absorbed and grew because of these ideas, and even in resisting some of Ginsberg's other ideas, I still grew and developed because of contact with them." During the same period he met Langston Hughes, the "poet laureate" of Afro-American life, after Hughes read his poetry accompanied by the music of Charlie Mingus at the Five Spot. Hughes encouraged Jones to continue to write and included two of his poems in his anthology, *New Negro Poets: U.S.A.* (1964).

In March 1958 Jones and his wife published the first issue of *Yūgen*, which ran eight issues before it ceased publication in December 1962. One of the first journals on the New York literary scene to devote itself to the "new" poetry, *Yūgen* featured contributions from Ginsberg, Corso, Diane DiPrima, Gary Snyder, Bob Hamilton, William Burroughs, Joel Oppenheimer, Charles Olson, and many others. As editor, Jones accepted works by friends and associates from the Beats, the Black Mountain School, and the New York School—all of whom shared a loose affinity with the "New American Poetry."

In 1958 Jones established Totem Press. During 1958 and 1959 he edited and published Charles Olson's *Projective Verse*, Michael McClure's *For Artaud*, Diane DiPrima's *This Kind of Bird Flies Backward*, and Ron Loewinsohn's *Watermelons*, and other literary broadsides. Beginning in 1960 Totem Press, in conjunction with Ted Wilentz's Corinth Books, published a number of books of contemporary poetry, including Kerouac's *The Script of the Golden Eternity*, Frank O'Hara's *Second Avenue*, Gary Snyder's *Myths and Texts*, and Ginsberg's *Empty Mirror*. Jones's first volume of poetry, *Preface To A Twenty Volume Suicide Note. . . .* (1961), was also published by Totem Press/Corinth Books. Jones's efforts on behalf of *Yūgen* and Totem Press quickly established him as a leading figure on the

New York literary scene. In his reminiscences of life in the Greenwich Village literary community during the 1950s and 1960s, Gilbert Sorrentino recalled Jones as a dynamic presence in the village: "LeRoi Jones had a magnetic and powerful personality, and his magazine immediately began to flourish—so much so, in fact, that the poets and writers who contributed to it and who were drawn to Jones's apartment (first on West 20th Street in Chelsea and later on East 14th Street) became known as the '*Yūgen* crowd.' Jones had informal gatherings in his apartment for readings, discussions, talk, and drinking, and often these gatherings would turn into all-night parties. A not at all atypical party at Jones' would include Selby, Rumaker, Kerouac, Ginsberg, Bremser, Corso, Rosenthal, Oppenheimer, Finstein, and when they were in New York, Wieners, George Stanley, Dorn, and Burroughs. There was often music played by Ornette Coleman, Archie Shepp, Wilbur Ware, and Don Cherry. About 1960 or so, Frank O'Hara, Koch, Bill Berkson and other people of the New York School also began to frequent Jones' place. It assumed the character of a freewheeling and noisy salon." During the same period Jones began to write prolifically, contributing poetry, book reviews, and jazz criticism to such little magazines as *Yūgen, Naked Ear, Quicksilver, Hearse, Odyssey, Penny Poems, White Dove Review, Mutiny, Jazz Review,* and *Metronome.*

Among his literary ancestors Jones cited William Carlos Williams as an important guide, pointing out during an interview that Williams taught him "how to write in my own language—how to write the way I *speak* rather than the way I *think* a poem ought to be written—to write just the way it comes to me, in my own speech, utilizing the rhythms of speech rather than any kind of metrical concept. To talk verse. Spoken verse."

At the same time Jones acknowledged an important debt to Kerouac. In 1959 he wrote a letter to *Evergreen Review* praising Kerouac's essay "Essentials of Spontaneous Prose." In his essay Kerouac invoked the popular Beat image of the poet as jazz musician to define the act of literary creation as an "undisturbed flow from the mind of personal secret idea-words, *blowing* (as per jazz musician) on subject of image." Pursuing the musical analogy, Kerouac called for the dismantling of conventional poetic and metrical structures, describing instead a system of composition based on breath pauses: "No periods separating sentence-structures already arbitrarily riddled by false colons and timid usually needless commas—but the vigorous space dash separating rhetorical breathing (as jazz musician drawing breath between outblown phrases)." Jones's intimate acquaintance with black music and with the "new" black music springing up in Greenwich Village and the Lower East Side made him unusually alert to the implications of music for his own poetry. He seized upon Kerouac's essay as an important aesthetic statement and later included it in his anthology of contemporary writing, *The Moderns: An Anthology of New Writing in America* (1963).

Another important personal and literary influence was Charles Olson, a leading figure in contemporary American poetry. In his capacity as editor of *Yūgen*, Jones wrote to Olson in 1958, initiating a correspondence and personal friendship that continued through the mid 1960s. Olson's definition of a poem as a "high-energy construct," an "OPEN" field in which "ONE PERCEPTION MUST IMMEDIATELY AND DIRECTLY LEAD TO A FURTHER PERCEPTION," was an important influence on Jones's poetic practice. Olson's ideas about open poetry, poetic energy, speech-force, and the manipulation of typographical space to correspond to breath pauses were all ideas Jones appropriated for his own use.

Although Jones closely identified himself with many aesthetic strategies of his contemporaries, he nevertheless emerged as a distinctive poet in his own right. His first collection of poetry, *Preface To A Twenty Volume Suicide Note. . . .*, introduced the range of his early aesthetic concerns as well as his thematic preoccupations. The title of the collection is ironic. In William C. Fischer's words: "To bring so much heavy apparatus to bear—prefaces and volumes—on a mere note is to mock the ostensible value of the poems themselves." But the title also defines the posture of the narrator/poet, who is variously wry and sardonic, gentle and lyrical, or fiercely satiric, but always isolated and solipsistic, unable or unwilling to establish meaningful contact with the world. The title poem, for example, establishes a sharp contrast between the narrator's nihilism and his daughter's religious faith:

And then last night, I tiptoed up
To my daughter's room and heard her
Talking to someone, and when I opened
The door, there was no one there. . . .
Only she on her knees, peeking into

Her own clasped hands.

The narrator's awareness of his own spiritual malaise initiates what Lee Jacobus calls the "quest

for moral order," one of the underlying themes of *Preface To A Twenty Volume Suicide Note. . . .* At the same time the narrator reveals a sense of ironic detachment, of playfulness and wit—often at his own expense. One of the best poems in *Preface To A Twenty Volume Suicide Note. . . .*, "Hymn For Lanie Poo," ridicules the behavior of the black bourgeoisie but also reserves some of its sharpest satiric thrusts for the figure of the black bohemian. One of the few poems in the collection to suggest the emergence of a distinctively Afro-American voice, "Hymn For Lanie Poo" presents a subtle tension between the narrative voice and the values and symbols of a stifling, predominantly white, American culture, represented in the poem by:

the huge & loveless
white anglo-sun/of
benevolent step
mother America.

Another group of poems is concerned with the narrator's "maudlin nostalgia" for the popular culture and superheroes of his youth. On the one hand these poems suggest a tension between adulthood and childhood, an attempt to recover the lost innocence of youth. On the other hand Jones often uses popular culture as a means of inverting and assaulting the values of American society. His choice of popular heroes reveals a strong preference for characters who don disguises, who lead secret and adventurous lives beneath the placid surface of daily existence. Jones's ironic awareness of himself as a black poet often breaks in and inverts some of the meanings associated with these popular figures:

My silver bullets all gone
My black mask trampled in the dust

& Tonto way off in the hills
moaning like Bessie Smith.

Yet another group of poems treats the literary context of the poet himself. "To a Publisher . . . cut-out" begins by attacking publishers for their commercialism and concludes with commentary on the act of writing poetry. Poems like "One Night Stand" and "Way Out West," addressed to Ginsberg and Gary Snyder respectively, suggest some discomfort with the literary preoccupations of his contemporaries, a mood which culminates in "The Bridge." Jones's pun on musical terminology (the "bridge" refers to that passage of a jazz composition which leads players back to the main melody) suggests something of the journey Jones's narrator feels compelled to make: a journey back to his own cultural antecedents, particularly as they are symbolized by black music. The poem begins on a note of spiritual dislocation ("I have forgotten the head/ of where I am. . . ."), moves to an actual crossing ("I can't see the bridge now, I've past/it. . . ."), and ends with an uncertain resolution. Some of the poems in *Preface To A Twenty Volume Suicide Note. . . .* do suggest the possibility of a regenerative process, the stirring of a new, dark energy. Poems like "The Turncoat," "The Clearing," "Theory of Art," and "The New Sheriff" begin a movement away from the self-preoccupation of the earlier poems. This movement is heralded by "Betancourt," dedicated to Rubi Betancourt whom Jones met during his trip to Cuba in 1960. "Betancourt" suggests the struggle of the narrator to achieve a new basis for his art, one which will require him to disengage himself from the stifling influences of his immediate artistic and social environment:

> (I mean I think
> I know now
> what a poem
> is) A
> turning away . . .
> from what
> it was
> had moved
> us . . .
>   A
> madness.

The final poem of *Preface To A Twenty Volume Suicide Note. . . .*, "Notes For A Speech," addresses the question of alienation in specifically racial and cultural terms: "African blues/does not know me/ . . . . Does/not feel/what I am." While the poet recognizes his cultural estrangement, he is unable to resolve it, and the poem concludes on a note of resignation: "You are/as any other sad man here/ american."

Preface To A Twenty Volume Suicide Note. . . . established Jones as a distinctive voice among the "new" American poets. Nevertheless critical reception was mixed. Gilbert Sorrentino, a friend and literary associate, offered probably the most trenchant criticism of Jones's early poetry: "Thinks too fast for the words, too many typographical tricks, too many ocular distractions, parentheses, the words speed on, the thought struggles to catch up. . . . Too much junk in shape of side remarks, off the cuff comments on what has taken place in

the narrative itself. . . . A feeling that you're being, somehow, tricked. . . . However a pro, should be fine if he gets tight, and cuts out what is prettiest."

Sorrentino's comments point to some of the difficulties of Jones's early poetry. Because it is the expression of an alienated and narcissistic self—one for whom reality is simply an extension of the narrator's subjective consciousness—it is often oblique, dependent on deeply personal references and symbols which do not convey single meanings.

Preface To A Twenty Volume Suicide Note. . . . also attracted the attention of poet Denise Levertov. In a review of the work of Jones and several of his contemporaries, Levertov praised Jones's poetic talent. While acknowledging some of the obvious literary influences on his work, Levertov also pointed to several qualities which made Jones's poetry unique: the influence of jazz rhythms, for example, and a natural inclination for the incantatory. While she praised several of his poems, she also cautioned her readers that Jones's concern with public issues made it difficult to classify him as a predominantly lyric poet. Levertov's observation about the social and political impulses at work in Jones's early poetry was remarkably perceptive and prophetic. Jones was, in fact, beginning to move toward the heightened social awareness and political activism characteristic of his later career.

To a great extent the cultural milieu Jones and his literary and artistic contemporaries inhabited was a self-contained universe, one with its own intellectual climate and life-style. Nevertheless events on the periphery of Greenwich Village and the Lower East Side began to have a significant impact on Jones's outlook. He became increasingly absorbed in the development of the Civil Rights Movement during the late 1950s, even though he was highly critical of its nonviolent tactics. Even more central to his political development was his trip to Cuba in July 1960.

At the invitation of the New York chapter of the Fair Play for Cuba Committee, Jones, along with John Henrik Clarke, Julian Mayfield, Sarah Wright, Harold Cruse, Robert Williams, and other black artists and intellectuals, traveled to Cuba to participate in the annual July 26th celebration of Fidel Castro's first, unsuccessful attempt to launch the Cuban revolution by attacking the Moncada barracks. *Cuba Libre* (1961), Jones's accounts of his encounters with more politically active foreign writers who attended the celebration, is a remarkably honest document, one which signals his growing discomfort with his own aesthetic and social stance as well as with that of his fellow artists in Greenwich

Dust jacket for Baraka's 1984 autobiography

Village. In typical fashion, Jones quickly establishes a sharp distinction between his own sensibility and that of the majority of his traveling companions, describing some members of his group in mocking, satiric terms: "One embarrassingly dull (white) communist, his professional Negro (i.e. unstraightened hair, 1930s bohemian peasant blouses, etc., militant integrationist, etc.) wife who wrote embarrassingly inept social comment-type poems, usually about one or sometimes a group of Negroes being mistreated in general (usually in Alabama, etc.). Two middle-class young Negro ladies from Philadelphia. . . . One 1920's 'New Negro' type African scholar (one of those terrible examples of what the 'Harlem Renaissance' was at its worst). . . ."

Jones would later appropriate many of the values he so freely mocked, but in 1960 he approached politics with the distrust of ideology characteristic of his contemporaries. As the essay proceeds, however, Jones's view of himself and of the world comes under increasingly sharp scrutiny and attack from many of the delegates he meets, a process he charts with a remarkable degree of detachment. Challenged by Rubi Betancourt and other young Latin American writers about his po-

litical naiveté, Jones can only respond defensively: "Look, why jump on me? . . . I'm a poet . . . what can I do? I write, that's all, I'm not even interested in politics."

Although he was jolted by sharp exchanges with the Latin American writers and intellectuals he met in Cuba, Jones did not immediately formulate a new aesthetic code or political direction. While he sensed the limitations of his own social and political views, he was unable to propose meaningful alternatives to them, and *Cuba Libre* moves toward a pessimistic conclusion: "The rebels among us have become merely people like myself who grow beards and will not participate in politics. . . . But name an alternative here. Something not inextricably bound up in a lie. Something not part of liberal stupidity or the actual filth of vested interest. There is none. It's much too late. We are an *old* people already. Even the vitality of our art is like bright flowers growing up through a rotting carcass."

Jones nevertheless returned from Cuba with a heightened sense of his own social and political mission, becoming increasingly involved in radical politics. Back in Greenwich Village he formed the

Organization of Young Men, a group of black artists and intellectuals including Alvin Simon, A. B. Spellman, Bob Thompson, and Bill White. At the same time Jones was beginning to venture from the Village to Harlem, taking the first steps in a symbolic journey "home to Harlem" which would culminate with his involvement in the Black Arts Repertory Theatre/School during the mid 1960s. Harold Cruse, a perceptive social critic and a veteran observer of the Harlem political scene, recalled meeting Jones periodically during these years: "At the time, Jones appeared very quiet, unassuming, reticent, even meek—although curious about everything. But thinking back, one wonders if perhaps his inner personality had not been grossly misinterpreted."

Jones helped organize an interracial Harlem group, the On Guard For Freedom Committee, in 1961. Organized to address themselves to national and international issues, members of the On Guard For Freedom Committee participated in the violent demonstrations at the United Nations after the murder of Congo prime minister Patrice Lumumba in February 1961. They also supported Robert F. Williams, an NAACP leader in Monroe, North Carolina, who had gained national attention for advocating armed self-defense for the black community in Monroe. Jones also worked with the Monroe Defense Committee (formed after Williams fled the South to avoid false charges of kidnapping and assault) and was elected president of the New York chapter of the Fair Play for Cuba Committee in late 1961.

During these early years Jones's outlook was far removed from the militant antiwhite stance he would assume in the mid 1960s. According to Harold Cruse, Jones disagreed with black nationalists in the On Guard For Freedom Committee who objected to the presence of whites at their meetings. Further, Jones argued, he could not understand why blacks in Harlem should hate whites.

At this stage in his career, Jones seemed to define his social role as a mediator between the black and white communities. He was becoming increasingly responsive to the cultural and political dynamics of the black community while attempting to bridge the gulf between Harlem and Greenwich Village at the same time.

Jones's increased political involvement during this period did not detract from his prolific literary activity. In the spring of 1960 he became a contributing editor of *Kulchur*, an important little magazine devoted to commentary and criticism of literature, art, dance, film, politics, and popular culture. In early 1961 Jones and Diane DiPrima founded the *Floating Bear*, an underground newsletter which circulated works by aspiring writers among established members of New York's literary community. At approximately the same time Jones, DiPrima, and several of their associates organized the American Theatre For Poets. Jones's involvement with the *Floating Bear* and the American Theatre For Poets soon led to his first clash with legal authorities, one of many which have marked his public career.

The June 1961 issue of the *Floating Bear* included *The Eighth Ditch*, a short play published under the title of *Dante* in Jones's experimental work, *The System of Dante's Hell* (1965). Distributed by mail, one copy of this issue was sent to an imprisoned poet at Rahway (New Jersey) State Prison, where it was intercepted by the prison authorities. Nothing further happened until the American Theatre For Poets scheduled its first performance of *The Eighth Ditch*. On 26 October 1961 Jones's apartment was raided by federal authorities and he was arrested, charged with sending obscenity through the mails. Diane DiPrima voluntarily surrendered later in the day, and the coeditors of the *Floating Bear* were released on their own recognizance. The American Theatre For Poets was also drawn into the affair and fined twenty-five dollars for failing to obtain the proper license for special entertainment and sporting events. Jones successfully defended himself against the obscenity charge, however, and the case was dismissed.

The Eighth Ditch is an extension, in dramatic form, of Jones's early poetic themes and preoccupations. Set in a black boy-scout camp in 1947, the play revolves around the dramatic encounter between two characters identified as 46 and 64. The protagonist of the play, 46, is typical of Jones's early personae: passive and self-preoccupied. The antagonist, 64, an "underprivileged" black youth, is both 46's foil and an unrecognized aspect of his consciousness—46's secret self. The play establishes a sharp contrast between these two characters, with black music functioning as an index of consciousness and awareness. For example, 46 identifies with the music of Flip Phillips and Nat King Cole, while 64 is closely associated with rhythm and blues. The central scene of the play is a graphic seduction scene in which 64 seeks to merge his consciousness with 46's: "I want you to remember me . . . so you can narrate the sorrow of my life. (laughs) My inadequacies . . . an yr own. I want to sit inside yr head & scream obscenities into your speech. I want my life forever wrought up with yours."

An early dramatic experiment, *The Eighth Ditch* is more an exploration of states of consciousness than a full-fledged play. Nevertheless, in its exploration of the theme of the divided self and in its use of the blues as a recurring motif, *The Eighth Ditch* anticipates the direction Jones's dramatic work would take in the future.

The persistent allusions to the blues in *The Eighth Ditch* reveal the extent to which Jones, at an early stage in his career, was beginning to explore the aesthetic and cultural implications of black music for his own work. As a jazz promoter, he sponsored concerts in halls and lofts in Greenwich Village and the Lower East Side, featuring many of the promising musicians who had become identified with what Jones later called the "new black music." And his jazz reviews and critical essays for *Kulchur* and other publications launched a critical assault upon the established canons of jazz criticism while paving the way for greater acceptance of the music of his black contemporaries.

Two important articles, both published in *Metronome* during 1961, suggest the direction Jones's art and politics would take during the early 1960s. "Blues, Black and White America" outlined the ideas which were fully developed in Jones's later path-blazing study of black music, *Blues People. . . . Negro Music in White America* (1963). In "The Jazz Avant Garde," he attempted to define the boundaries of contemporary black music. Arguing that there is a fundamental tension between African/Afro-American and Western/European-American music, Jones insisted that the ideas behind the music shaped the musician's characteristic approach as opposed to the emphasis of some formalist critics on technical mastery. Although Jones's argument is not as fully developed as it would become in *Blues People. . . . Negro Music in White America*, these two articles reveal a growing commitment to a cultural frame of reference defined by black music and the black musician. It was this dedication that led to Jones's conclusion that black music was the primary expressive language in Afro-American culture, as he stated in "The Myth of a Negro Literature" (collected in the 1966 work *Home: Social Essays*): "It is impossible to mention the achievements of the Negro in any area of artistic endeavor with as much significance as in spirituals, blues and jazz. There has never been an equivalent to Duke Ellington or Louis Armstrong in Negro writing, and even the best of contemporary literature written by Negroes cannot be compared to the fantastic beauty of the music of Charlie Parker."

Consistent with his own antimainstream, antibourgeois outlook, Jones celebrated precisely those values in Afro-American music, rooted in jazz and bebop, which remained most resistant to Western ideals and musical styles. This posture led Jones toward conclusions which had important implications for his perspective on Afro-American culture as well as for his own writing. It explains why, for example, allusions to black music are often so central to his work and why the figure of the black musician as a healer and shaper of consciousness appears with such frequency, particularly during the period when Jones emerged as a major cultural spokesman for black nationalism. Black music not only epitomized meaningful alternatives to the mainstream values of American society; it also pointed toward solutions to the problem of divided consciousness.

While Jones argued that Afro-American music symbolized the depths of the estrangement of the black community from American society, he was not yet prepared to translate this awareness into a specific political vision. His public statements about race and culture during the years 1962 and 1963 often seemed ambivalent because they reflected Jones's own uncertainty at the time.

In "Black Is a Country" (collected in *Home: Social Essays*) the nationalist struggles in Asia, Africa, and Latin America were examples that blacks should follow in their own struggle for independence in the United States. Nevertheless Jones derided the idea of a separate black society, insisting that "America is as much a black country as a white one. The lives and destinies of the white American are bound up inextricably with those of the black American. . . ." In "City of Harlem" (also collected in *Home: Social Essays*) he celebrated Harlem as the capital of black America, a "community of nonconformists." In view of his attack on Harlem as the capital of the black bourgeoisie four years earlier, this article signaled an important ideological shift in his writing.

Many of the ideas Jones was grappling with during this period converged in *Blues People. . . .*, an analysis of the historical and cultural implications of Afro-American music. Polemical in tone, *Blues People* is not a scholarly work; rather, it is Jones's exploration of Afro-American music and an attempt to define its tradition in a meaningful way. In *Blues People. . . .* Jones argues that Afro-American music is "essentially the expression of an attitude, or a collection of attitudes, about the world," a "socio-cultural philosophy" emerging out of the historical realities of black life in the United States. Viewing black music as the record of the emotional history of black people in America, Jones charts its progress from its African origins to the emergence of the jazz avant-garde.

Although Jones insists upon recognizing the nationalist impulses at work in the black music he most admired, he nevertheless emphasizes the reciprocity of values which linked the jazz avant-garde to developments within American bohemia. In the conclusion to *Blues People. . . .* Jones celebrates Greenwich Village as "traditionally a breeding ground of American art and the open-air fraternity house of a kind of American Bohemianism," pointing to Charlie Parker as a model of the black artist who moved in bohemian society with relative ease. In Greenwich Village, he observes, "young Negro musicians now live as integral parts of that anonymous society to which the artist generally aspires. Their music, along with the products of other young American artists seriously involved with the revelation of contemporary truths, will help define that society, and, by contrast, the nature of the American society out of which those Americans have removed themselves." Jones thus concludes *Blues People. . . .* by stressing the common kinships, the aesthetic analogies, the similar stances which linked the community of artists and social rebels in the Village—a position he was to repudiate violently within two years.

Blues People. . . . was published to a very favorable critical reception. Widely regarded as a path-blazing work, it was soon published in British, Japanese, Mexican, French, and German editions. Two critics in particular made negative but perceptive observations about the ideological impulses at work in *Blues People. . . .* that provide deeper insight into the values underlying Jones's aesthetic judgments and cultural stance. Ralph Ellison complained that Jones's political views often interfered with his aesthetic judgments, suggesting that Jones's attempt to establish a strict correlation between race, socioeconomic class, and musical preference was muddled and oversimplified. Charles Keil praised Jones's work but attacked the "wild speculations, inconsistencies, misinformation, and absurd arguments that run through his early chapters in blues prehistory," pointing out Jones's tendency to shape his material to suit his argument.

Both Ellison and Keil exposed significant areas of tension, ambivalence, and confusion in Jones's cultural views. Although Jones continued to function within the intellectual milieu of Green-

wich Village, by 1963 his work was beginning to reflect more strongly his conflicting feelings toward his environment. This tension is expressed in his second volume of poetry, *The Dead Lecturer*, published in 1964.

The thematic continuity between *Preface To A Twenty Volume Suicide Note. . . .* and *The Dead Lecturer* is suggested by the titles themselves, hinting that the narrator still has not resolved his fundamental predicament. He still has not formulated the new identity he seeks. Nevertheless a significant development has occurred. *The Dead Lecturer* lacks the playfulness and spontaneous humor of *Preface;* the tone of the poems is sharper, more urgent, and the narrator/poet is less self-preoccupied, more prepared to explore the outside world than the narrator of *Preface*. While the poems of *Preface* moved toward a mood of alienation and despair, those of *The Dead Lecturer* re-create the struggle for new life. At one level this struggle is expressed in terms of the narrator's attempt to free himself of language and poetic forms which no longer have any use for him, as in "Rhythm and Blues":

> I am deaf and blind and lost and will not again
>   sing your quiet
> verse. I have lost
> even the act of poetry. . . .

On the other hand, the struggle for rebirth is revealed in terms of a life-and-death battle raging within the narrator's consciousness, a struggle between two sharply defined and opposing selves, as in "An Agony. As Now":

> I am inside someone
> who hates me. I look
> out from his eyes. Smell
> what fouled tunes come in
> to his breath. Love his
> wretched women.

Many of the poems in *The Dead Lecturer* explicitly criticize the artistic orientation of Jones's literary circle, challenging the fashionable view that art was superior to life. "Short Speech To My Friends" criticizes the apolitical stance of Jones's associates, while "The Green Lantern's Solo" derides those self-oriented poets who write only for themselves and their contemporaries, refusing to make any meaningful connections between their egos and the world:

> What we have created, is ourselves
> as heroes, as lovers, as disgustingly

evil. As Dialogues with the soul, with
the self. Selves, screaming furiously
to each other. As the same fingers
touch the same faces, as the same
mouths close on each other. . . .

"The Politics of Rich Painters" attacks the cultural
pretenses of a smug, self-contained world of artists
whose false egalitarianism conceals their real ties
to Western cultural and economic hegemony.

While many of the poems in *The Dead Lecturer*
are clearly indebted to the literary influences of his
contemporaries, Jones struggles against these influences at the same time. This tension is resolved
by the emergence of a distinctive Afro-American
voice. Works like "A Poem For Willie Best" move
toward systems of meaning shaped by aesthetic and
cultural references to Afro-American life. "A Poem
For Willie Best" looks beneath the stereotypic image of the Hollywood actor, probing the contradiction between Best's shuffling, happy-go-lucky
screen image and his taut inner life. The solution
to Best's dilemma, the poet suggests, can occur only
through violent release of the secret self, that self
that has been repressed to accommodate American
social and cultural values.

"Rhythm and Blues," dedicated to Robert F.
Williams—then in exile in Cuba—is an important
statement about black music as a social and political
force. In his despairing posture the poet often alludes to silence as a symbol of his spiritual predicament. But in "Rhythm and Blues" he begins to
articulate an Afro-American alternative to silence:
the scream. In *The Dead Lecturer* screaming and
shouting alternatively emerge as deeply felt Afro-
American responses to life. The shout also represents the beginning of a new role for the poet.
Unlike the individual statements of the isolated
poet, his need to shout implies a communal context,
one shaped by the ritual of call-and-response.

All of these developments converge in the
most important poem in the collection, "Black Dada
Nihilismus." Here Jones indicts the moral and spiritual bankruptcy of Western civilization, calling for
rape, murder, and the irrational release of violence
to overthrow the existing order. To legitimize his
incantation of violence and racial revenge, he invokes the memory of nonwhite civilizations destroyed by the West and recites the names of figures
from black history and his own past (including his
grandfather, Tom Russ) as well as entertainers and
popular heroes—all of whom, he suggests, were
"secret murderers," figures who skillfully concealed their desire to lash out violently at white

society. The poem concludes with an invocation of
the African god Damballah, who functions in the
poem as a vengeful black father with the will and
the strength to destroy Western civilization.

The shifts in the attitude of the poet in *The
Dead Lecturer* do not occur in an orderly or se-
quential fashion. The collection as a whole reveals
Jones's conscious effort to redefine the cultural and
aesthetic referents of his poetry, a deliberate quest
for a poetic idiom more consonant with his social
and political outlook. The process of disengagement from his literary milieu is underscored by the
final poem in *The Dead Lecturer*, "The Liar":

> When they say, "It is Roi
> who is dead?" I wonder
> who will they mean?

The critical reception of *The Dead Lecturer* was
generally unfavorable. While Richard Elman acknowledged Jones's talent, he called many of the
poems artificial because of the many masquerades
Jones adopted. Dismissing Jones's negritude as
"posturing," Elman reserved his sharpest criticism
for Jones's poetic technique, calling his cadences
"leaden" and castigating his apparent inability to
sustain a thought or mood. Some of these comments were echoed by Richard Howard, who failed
to see any formal principles underlying the poems
in *The Dead Lecturer*, "beyond the decorum of the
page and, perhaps, a pattern of breathing." Howard saw Jones as a poet "much surer of his voice"
than he was in *Preface To A Twenty Volume Suicide
Note*. . . . , but also as a writer who was inclined to
exaggerate the "desperation and fragmentation" of
his narrator. Clarence Major's general consideration of Jones's poetry offered an interesting contrast to Elman's and Howard's views. Major
maintained that Jones was primarily a literary poet,
not the jazz poet or "race" poet some critics had
taken him to be. Calling him a spiritual and romantic poet, Major praised Jones for his humorous
protest poems, but suggested that angry social protest "is not his forte." Coming at a time when Jones
was struggling to redefine his relationship to the
white literary and cultural avant-garde and to locate his work in a specifically Afro-American frame
of reference, Major's article suggested the extent
of the journey Jones would have to make before
the transition was complete.

Jones's explorations in drama during this pe-
riod closely parallel the thematic concerns of *The
Dead Lecturer*, ranging from the iconoclasm of *The
Baptism* to the drama of divided impulses in *The*

Toilet to the unrestrained fury of *Dutchman*.

The Baptism, produced in 1964, deals with the chance encounter of a fifteen-year-old boy, a homosexual, and a hypocritical minister in a "well-to-do arrogant Protestant church." Clearly indebted to the works of French playwright Jean Genet and the theater of the absurd, the play excoriates Christianity for its hypocrisy, commercialism, and sexual repression. The play lacks a clear dramatic focus and is heavily dependent upon the shock value of irreverent attitudes for its effects.

The Toilet is a much more specific and coherent play than *The Baptism* and returns to a recurring theme of Jones's early work: the drama of the sensitive, isolated individual pitted against the social codes of his community. Set in a latrine at the end of the day in an urban high school, the play concerns a gang of black youths who assemble in anticipation of a fight between their leader, Ray Foots, and a white boy, Jimmy Karolis. Foots is supposedly seeking revenge for a love note Karolis has sent him, but, when the two characters meet, it is unclear who made the first advance. In their encounter Ray tries to avoid fighting Karolis, who had already been beaten by some of the gang members, but Karolis forces the issue. When Karolis gains the advantage over Ray, the gang jumps Karolis and beats him into unconsciousness. After the gang leaves, Ray recovers, then cradles Karolis's head in his arms, weeping as the play ends.

The sentimental conclusion of *The Toilet* again reveals some of the ambivalent and contradictory impulses at work in Jones during this period. On the one hand, the dialogue of the play shows his increasing commitment to the literary possibilities of Afro-American urban speech. On the other hand, Ray Foots, Jones's sensitive and culturally divided protagonist, is portrayed as victimized by the world—as is the white boy, Jimmy Karolis. To the extent that *The Toilet* embodies a social statement, it indicts the brutal society—symbolized by the gang—that will not allow love to exist.

Early critics of the play praised it for its understated treatment of the theme of racial conflict, pointing out that the racial dimension of the play was merely incidental to the central dramatic conflict between Ray Foots and Jimmy Karolis. The central conflict of *The Toilet*, however, rests within the divided consciousness of the protagonist. Torn between his identity as Foots, the black gang leader, and Ray, the sensitive individual, the protagonist of *The Toilet* seemed to mirror the conflict within Jones himself.

Set designed by artist Larry Rivers for the first production of The Toilet *(photo by Bert Andrews)*

73

Jones's early plays paved the way for his most well-known and highly praised play, *Dutchman*. When *Dutchman* opened at the Village South Theatre on 12 January 1964, it was immediately hailed as an overwhelming success. The first full-length play to integrate the themes and motifs of Jones's earlier dramatic efforts successfully, *Dutchman* merges private themes, mythical allusions, surrealistic techniques, and social statement into a play of astonishing power and resonance. In recognition of its excellence *Dutchman* won the Obie Award for the best American play of the 1963-1964 season.

Dutchman revolves round an apparently casual encounter between a young, middle-class Negro and a white, bohemian woman on a New York subway. The woman, Lula, begins to flirt with the young man, Clay, and in the presence of other subway passengers her gestures become sexually suggestive, her taunts harsher. Goaded into anger by her unrelenting verbal attacks, Clay drops his middle-class facade and unleashes a violent verbal tirade against Lula. At the end of the play Lula calmly murders Clay and awaits her next victim, another black man who has just entered the subway.

Initially Clay represents those aspects of black life Jones mercilessly criticized elsewhere in his writing. "Buttoned down," sexually and socially repressed, Clay has concealed his true identity for the sake of conformity. Lula criticizes Clay's values from her bohemian standpoint, challenging him to drop his mask and to break through the veil of false consciousness. Up until the point that Clay verbally asserts himself, Lula functions as the central figure in the play. When Clay finally drops the masquerade, he emerges as the focal point, expressing ideas which reflect Jones's own thinking about identity, art, and liberation from social oppression. In his three-page tirade—the most often cited passage of *Dutchman*—Clay reveals the secret heart of black life, an inner life of repressed murderous impulses held in check by various masquerades and sublimated into artistic expression. Ironically it is Clay's reluctance to act which leads to his death. As he reaches for his books, Lula stabs him to death.

The play draws on mythic associations throughout literature: from ironic inversions of biblical imagery to recurring motifs in Afro-American literature. Clay is at various points in the play identified with Christ, Uncle Tom, and Bigger Thomas; Lula, the apple-eating Eve, is associated with furies and vampires. She is portrayed as a white temptress who destroys black men, a common

figure in Afro-American literature. The title of the play implies both the cyclical and repetitive nature of myth, suggested by the legend of the *Flying Dutchman*, as well as the historical legend of slavery—for it was a Dutch ship which first brought slaves to the New World.

Appearing, as it did, on the eve of widespread racial conflict in the United States, *Dutchman* immediately took on social and political overtones, suggesting in symbolic terms the vast gulf between black and white America. Significantly Jones resisted political interpretations of *Dutchman*, commenting in an article in the *New York Herald Tribune*: "I showed one white girl and one Negro boy in that play, just them, singularly, in what I hope was a revelation of private and shared anguish, which because I dealt with it specifically would somehow convey an emotional force from where I got it— the discovery of America—on over to any viewer. But for the feebleminded, black and white are always the most important aspects of anything, not what a thing really is, but how it can be made to seem, if it is to accommodate the silly version of the world they are stuck with."

Critics emphasized the sociopolitical dimensions of *Dutchman*, however, and hailed Jones as a "fierce and blazing talent." The success of *Dutchman* propelled him into the public arena, establishing him as a nationally and internationally acclaimed writer and spokesman.

Celebrated by *Playboy* magazine as "the most discussed—and admired—Negro writer since James Baldwin," Jones plunged into a whirlwind of lectures, poetry readings, and panel discussions. He continued to teach courses on contemporary American poetry and creative writing at the New School for Social Research, where he had begun teaching in 1963. Through Charles Olson's influence he secured a teaching position at the State University of New York at Buffalo during the summer of 1964 and offered a course on contemporary poetry. During the same year he taught at Columbia University.

At the same time Jones was becoming more conscious of his role as a social critic and political spokesman, as he noted in a reminiscence of his years in Greenwich Village: "I began to recognize that if I said things, people would listen much more than before. The feeling of responsibility shook me and I pledged that I would say those things that most needed saying by a whole people, not remain a flippant hipster juggling through life on the Lower East Side in integrated liberalism."

Jones's new "feeling of responsibility" took the form of a series of well-publicized verbal assaults upon his Greenwich Village associates, white liberals, and the white community in general. In June 1964 Jones and other members of Artists For Freedom, Inc., a group of black artists and intellectuals, debated several leading white liberals at New York City's town hall on the theme of "The Black Revolution and the White Backlash." While the debate itself was inconclusive, the acrimony expressed during the meeting symbolized the growing rift between black and white intellectuals over the significance and direction of the Civil Rights Movement and the black revolution in the United States. Jones's angry attack on white liberals clearly startled many members of the town hall audience, but his stance signaled an increasingly frenetic attempt to extricate himself from a community whose cultural and political values he had repudiated.

In literary terms, Jones's attempt to exorcise his earlier beliefs is revealed in his play *The Slave*, a companion piece to *Dutchman* with which it was published in 1964. Set in the future, the dramatic action of *The Slave* occurs against the background of a racial war, where blacks are clearly close to victory. Walker Vessels, the leader of the black revolutionary army, returns to the home of his former wife, Grace, presumably to reclaim his two daughters and also to stage a final confrontation with his former friends. Grace is now married to a liberal college professor, Bradford Easley. In a long and rambling conversation, these three characters discuss their past lives and debate literature, politics, and human values. The confrontation ends when Easley attacks Walker, who has become drunk and somewhat incoherent as the play progresses. Walker kills Easley and, shortly after, Grace is mortally wounded by a falling rafter. Before she dies, Walker tells her that their children are dead, but, as the play ends, the sound of a screaming child is heard.

Walker Vessels, poet and revolutionary leader, is depicted as a figure of sharply divided impulses. As the leader of the black liberation struggle, he has engulfed the entire society in a racial war, yet his social and political philosophy is essentially a nihilistic one, one which he admits will lead only to a "change in the complexion of tyranny." Moreover, he has no respect for his troops, "who have never read any book in their lives." Vessels emerges as a character trapped between his self-proclaimed public role and his private beliefs, locked into an adversary relationship with a white world against which he violently attempts to assert

himself. Beneath the revolutionary rhetoric of the play, Jones suggests that Walker Vessels's vision is self-defeating and enslaving, for Vessels changes into the character of the old slave who begins and ends the play.

Described by a *Time* magazine critic as "essentially a Greenwich Village talkfest," *The Slave* is a much more conventional and politically explicit play than *Dutchman*. It is also less effective, marred by Vessels's frequent lapses into sentimentality and self-pity. Nevertheless *The Slave* was an accurate dramatic re-creation of the debates on art and politics Jones was staging at various locations in Greenwich Village during late 1964 and early 1965. It won second prize at the First World Festival of Negro Arts held in Dakar, Senegal, in 1966.

In February 1965 Jones and jazz musician Archie Shepp staged a bitter antiwhite tirade at the Village Vanguard club, a highly publicized event which seemed to mark a fundamental turning point in Jones's relationship with his Greenwich Village associates. Inspired by the message of Malcolm X, Jones transformed his earlier antibourgeois posture into a militant black nationalist stance, one which insisted that the fundamental contradiction in American society was rooted in biological and ontological racial differences. At one point in his indictment of the predominantly white Village Vanguard audience, Jones paused and remarked, "I should not be speaking here. . . . I should be speaking to Black people."

Ironically Jones's antiwhite attacks propelled him further into the limelight of public attention. As Stephen Schneck observed: "The blasé New York culture scene was titillated by his maledictions. He was invited to all the enchanted-circle beautiful-people parties, literary, show business orgies, and hip gatherings. The more he attacked white society, the more white society patronized him. Who'd have suspected that there was so much money to be made from flagellation? Whitey seemed insatiable; the masochistic vein was a source of hitherto untapped appeal, big box office stuff, and LeRoi Jones was one of the very first to exploit it." Nevertheless, at the height of his renown as a literary celebrity, Jones, the "King of the East Village," defiantly turned his back on the promise of fame and fortune in the American literary community.

By late 1965 he had ended his marriage to Hettie Cohen, broken most of his ties with the white literary community, and moved uptown from Greenwich Village to Harlem, where he and other black associates had organized the Black Arts Repertory Theatre/School during the previous year. During this period Jones turned his attention to the study of Islam (inspired by the example of Malcolm X) and to Yoruba religion, embracing aspects of both of these religions as an alternative to Western values and as a spiritual basis for mobilizing the black community. With other young black intellectuals such as Larry Neal and Askia Muhammed Touré, Baraka debated the meaning of black cultural nationalism, establishing the foundation for the debates about the Black Aesthetic which occurred later during the 1960s.

Of all the psychological imperatives and political events which prompted Jones to repudiate the interracial world of Greenwich Village, the political message of Malcolm X had perhaps the decisive impact on the direction of his life and work. As he later wrote about Malcolm X's assassination: "Malcolm's death took me further. Surely this meant that white people, with all the broadness the abstraction conveys, must be responsible, and that our revolution, if it was to be successful, must be aimed at *them*. It was the quantitative buildup of new Black nationalist ideas, some anti-white, some anti-Semitic, some revolutionary, some not. Now there could be absolutely no ties with whites, and certainly not any intimate ones. These in themselves, we reasoned, would make us traitors. . . ."

With "The Legacy of Malcolm X, and The Coming of the Black Nation" (published in *Home: Social Essays*, 1966), Jones emerged in his new role as the spiritual heir of Malcolm X, underscoring the finality with which he had repudiated his past identity: "Black People are a race, a culture, a nation. The legacy of Malcolm X is that we know we can move from where we are."

In a sense Jones's autobiographical novel, *The System of Dante's Hell* (1965), is an epilogue to his Greenwich Village days. A recapitulation of many of the themes of Jones's early work, *The System of Dante's Hell* charts the journey of an isolated, introspective self toward spiritual wholeness and clarity. Unfolding in fragmentary, highly lyrical episodes, the narrative coalesces into meaningful patterns as it proceeds, concluding with "The Heretics," the central episode in the novel. Here the psychically divided narrator, an "imitation white boy," descends to "The Bottom," a southern black community, and achieves a partial reconciliation with the realities of black life. Although the quest for spiritual wholeness and a unified consciousness is not fully realized within the novel, a mature narrative voice comments upon the sources of the spiritual conflicts in *The System of Dante's Hell* and

suggests that they have been resolved in his own life: "The flame of social dichotomy. Split open down the center, which is the early legacy of the black man unfocused on blackness. The dichotomy of what is seen and taught and desired opposed to what is felt. Finally, God, is simply a white man, a white 'idea,' in this society, unless we have made some other image which is stronger, and can deliver us from the salvation of our enemies."

Since 1965, when Jones emerged as a leading figure in the black arts movement, his life and work have continued to undergo a series of metamorphoses. Although the Black Arts Repertory Theatre/School was a short-lived project, it revolutionized black theater in the United States by performing contemporary dramatic works shaped by black nationalist beliefs. It served also as an inspirational model which was quickly adopted in black communities throughout the country. Financed with federal funds, the Black Arts Repertory Theatre/School was raided and closed in 1966 by police, who maintained that an arms cache had been found

Joan Bailey, Barbara Landers, and Marilyn Berry in a 1972 production of Madheart *(photo by Bill Doll)*

in the building. By that time, however, Jones had returned to Newark. In August of the following year he married his present wife, Sylvia Robinson (Amina).

In his hometown Jones quickly organized a multifunctional black cultural center, Spirit House, complete with a theater and a group of actors. He also established a publishing house, Jihad (Arabic: "Holy War"), a cooperative book and record store, and an African free school, designed for young people in the community, who studied the works of Jones, Maulana Karenga, and other black thinkers. Inspired by the ideas of Maulana Ron Karenga, a Los Angeles-based theoretician of black cultural nationalism, Jones became deeply involved in local and national politics. He organized the Committee For a Unified Newark, a local political coalition which included the United Brothers, a group dedicated to increasing black participation in community government. During the height of the racial disturbances in Newark in 1967, Jones was arrested, beaten by police, and charged with unlawfully carrying firearms. Bruised and bandaged, Jones spoke at a press conference held during the National Black Power Conference—a meeting scheduled in Newark before the riots occurred. His case immediately became a cause célèbre. His subsequent trial, where the judge read Jones's famous poem "Black People" to the court, aroused a storm of protest from black intellectuals and political leaders as well as from many of his former white literary associates. Sentenced to from two and a half to three years in jail without parole, Jones later won a retrial motion and was acquitted.

Jones continued to write prolifically. *Home: Social Essays*, a collection of essays spanning the years from 1960 to 1965, was published in 1966, as was *Black Art*, the first collection of poetry to bear the imprint of Jihad Productions. These were followed by *Slave Ship* (1967), a powerful evocation of the horrors of the Middle Passage; *Arm Yourself, or Harm Yourself! A One Act Play* (1967), a short, agit-prop sketch about the necessity of self-defense; and *Tales* (1967), a collection of mostly autobiographical short stories, ranging in theme from the preoccupations of his years in Greenwich Village to explorations of black nationalist ideas.

In 1968 Jones assumed the name Ameer (later Amiri) Baraka, given him by Heshaam Jaaber, an orthodox Muslim and the man who buried Malcolm X. Ameer ("prince") Baraka ("the blessed one") also adopted the title *Imamu* (literally, one who has read the Koran, a spiritual leader), given him by Maulana Ron Karenga. In his role as a spiritual leader, Baraka worked toward defining a theological and theoretical scaffolding for his black cultural nationalist views. During this period Baraka produced *Black Music* (1967), a collection of essays and reviews on Afro-American music; *Black Fire* (1968), an anthology of contemporary black literature, which he edited with Larry Neal; *Black Magic* (1969), a collection of poetry charting his spiritual journey toward blackness; *Four Black Revolutionary Plays* (1969); *A Black Value System* (1970); *J-E-L-L-O* (1970), a satirical play assaulting the Jack Benny Show; the verse collection *It's Nation Time* (1970); and *In Our Terribleness (Some Elements and Meaning in Black Style)* (1970), a book of essays and photographs, produced with Fundi (Billy Abernathy).

A leading spokesman of black cultural nationalism during the late 1960s and early 1970s, Baraka played an important role in the organization of the Congress of African Peoples in 1970. During the same year he also campaigned vigorously for Kenneth Gibson (a political endorsement he later repudiated), who was elected the first black mayor of Newark. He played a key role in the organization of the National Black Political Assembly in 1972.

Baraka increasingly turned toward the essay during this period, probably because this literary form lent itself most readily to a direct exposition of his political views. One slender volume of poetry, *Spirit Reach* (1972), marked the culmination of his development as a self-consciously spiritual poet/leader.

In 1974 Baraka dropped the title *Imamu*, signaling another shift in his cultural and political views. Abandoning his emphasis on black cultural nationalism and Pan-Africanism, Baraka proclaimed himself an adherent of Marxist-Leninist-Maoist thought. As in the case of his decision to depart from Greenwich Village, this transformation was neither abrupt nor dramatic; it was the culmination of a series of developments within his own life, shaped by his responses to both national and international debates about the future of the black liberation struggle. An avowed Communist, Baraka, who is a member of the Revolutionary Communist League and the Anti-Imperialist Cultural Union, now emphasizes a Marxist analysis of the forces shaping American society and the black community.

Baraka's poetry and drama since 1974 reflect his new political commitments. *Hard Facts* (1975) is a collection of poetry which, in Baraka's words, "directly describes the situation of the people and tells us how we change it." Both *S-1* and *The Motion of History* (produced in 1976 and 1977 respectively and published in 1978) are reminiscent of the agitprop dramas of the 1930s, particularly in their appeals to working-class solidarity and in their suggestion that working-class revolution is society's only hope.

Selected Poetry is less self-conscious in its polemical stance, and, in his most recent work, Baraka continues to balance his political commitments with his deep allegiance to the affirmation of Afro-American culture. "Wise/Whys"—an epic poem-in-progress based on Afro-American history before and after slavery—skillfully blends Afro-American musical and verbal forms with political statements.

As has always been the case throughout Baraka's career, the act of performance remains central to his art. His recent poetry springs to life during oral performance, which underscores its dazzling verbal effects. Nevertheless, at this point in his career Baraka has clearly put politics in command of his art and continues the struggle to merge the realms of art and life, literature and politics, the struggle that has been so central to his work.

Baraka's life and art have covered an impressive range of territory over the past two decades. Although he has often expressed disdain for the literary establishment, his work has clearly defined him as a major intellectual presence in contemporary American literature and culture.

Interviews:

David Ossman, "LeRoi Jones," in his *The Sullen Art: Interviews With Modern American Poets* (New York: Corinth Books, 1963), pp. 77-81;

Saul Gottlieb, "They Think You're An Airplane And You're Really A Bird! An Interview With LeRoi Jones," *Evergreen Review*, 12 (December 1967): 51-53, 96-97;

Marvin X, Faruk, and Askia Muhammed Touré, "Islam and Black Art: An Interview With Ameer Baraka (LeRoi Jones)," *Journal of Black Poetry*, 1 (Fall 1968): 2-14;

"Conversation: Ida Lewis and LeRoi Jones," *Essence* (September 1970): 20-25;

Michael Coleman, "What is Black Theatre? Michael Coleman Questions Imamu Amiri Baraka," *Black World*, 20 (April 1971): 32-38;

"Interview: Imamu Amiri Baraka," *Black Collegian*, 3 (March-April 1973): 30-33;

Tish Dace, "LeRoi Jones/Amiri Baraka: From Muse to Malcolm To Mao," *Village Voice*, 1 August 1977, pp. 12-24;

Kimberly W. Benston, "Amiri Baraka: An Interview," *Boundary 2*, 6 (Winter 1978): 303-316.

Bibliography:

Letitia Dace, *LeRoi Jones (Imamu Amiri Baraka): A Checklist of Works By and About Him* (London: Nether Press, 1971);
A comprehensive bibliography of primary and secondary sources on Baraka's career through 1970.

References:

Kimberly W. Benston, *Baraka: The Renegade and the Mask* (New Haven: Yale University Press, 1976);
An examination of Baraka's poetry, prose, and drama through 1972, with an emphasis on his plays.

Benston, ed., *Imamu Amiri Baraka: A Collection of Critical Essays* (Englewood Cliffs, N.J.: Prentice-Hall, 1978);
An excellent collection of essays on Baraka's multifaceted life and career.

Lloyd W. Brown, *Amiri Baraka* (Boston: Twayne, 1980);
A good overview of Baraka's life and work through the late 1970s.

William C. Fischer, "The Pre-Revolutionary Writings of Imamu Amiri Baraka," *Massachusetts Review*, 14 (Spring 1973): 259-305;
An excellent discussion of Baraka's early works and of the impact of black music on his writing.

William J. Harris, *The Poetry and Poetics of Amiri Baraka: The Jazz Aesthetic* (Columbia: University of Missouri Press, 1985);
A study of the impact of the literary and jazz avant-garde on Baraka's works; includes an interview with Baraka as well as excerpts from his most recent poem, "Wise/Whys."

Theodore R. Hudson, *From LeRoi Jones to Amiri Baraka: The Literary Works* (Durham, N.C.: Duke University Press, 1973);
The first full-length study of Baraka, it includes useful biographical information.

Henry C. Lacey, *To Raise, Destroy and Create: The Poetry, Drama and Fiction of Imamu Amiri Baraka (LeRoi Jones)* (Troy, N.Y.: Whitston Publish-

ing Company, 1981);
A study of the poetry, drama, and fiction produced by Baraka from 1960 to 1970.

Werner Sollers, *Amiri Baraka/LeRoi Jones: The Quest for a "Populist Modernism"* (New York: Colum-

bia University Press, 1978);
A study of Baraka's attempts to merge populist politics and modernist literature throughout his career; includes an interview with Baraka and a bibliography of his unpublished works through 1976.

Saul Bellow

This entry was updated by Keith M. Opdahl (DePauw University) from his entry in DLB
28, Twentieth-Century American-Jewish Fiction Writers, *and*
DLB Yearbook: 1982.

Places	New York Africa	Mexico The Berkshires	Chicago (Humboldt Park, especially)
Influences and Relationships	Fyodor Dostoyevski Ernest Hemingway Marcel Proust	Mark Twain Joseph Conrad William Blake	Robert Penn Warren Theodore Dreiser Walt Whitman
Literary Movements and Forms	Realism Romanticism	Naturalism	Existentialism

Major Themes	The Jew in America
	Love and Will
	The Isolated Self
	Human Emotion
		Individual and Society
		The Personal Past
		Human Malice
		Fathers and Sons
			Existence of a
			   Transcendent Reality
			The Intellectual
			   in America

Cultural and Artistic Influences	Wilhelm Reich
	The American University
	   and Its Intellectuals
		Anthrosophism
		Jewish Religion
		   and Culture
			Existentialism
			The Emptiness of Ameri-
			   can Popular Culture

Social and Economic Influences	American Immigrant
	   Society
	The Holocaust
		Socialism and
		   Capitalism
			The Decay of
			   the Cities

See also the Bellow entries in DLB 2, American Novelists Since World War II, *and* DLB: Documentary Series 3.

BIRTH: Lachine, Quebec, Canada, 10 June 1915, to Abraham and Liza Gordon Bellows.

EDUCATION: University of Chicago, 1933-1935; B.S., Northwestern University, 1937; University of Wisconsin, 1937.

MARRIAGES: 31 December 1937 to Anita Goshkin (divorced); child: Gregory. 1 February 1956 to Alexandra Tschacbosov (divorced); child: Adam. 10 December 1961 to Susan Glassman (divorced); child: Daniel. 1974 to Alexandra Ionescu Tulcea.

AWARDS: Guggenheim Fellowship, 1948-1949; National Institute of Arts and Letters grant, 1952; Creative Writing Fellowship, Princeton University, 1952-1953; National Book Award for *The Adventures of Augie March*, 1954; Guggenheim Fellowship, 1955-1956; Ford Foundation grant, 1959-1960; Friends of Literature Fiction Award, 1960; National Book Award for *Herzog*, 1965; International Literature Prize, 1965; Jewish Heritage Award from B'nai B'rith, 1968; Croix de Chevalier des Arts et Lettres, 1968; National Book Award for *Mr. Sammler's Planet*, 1971; Pulitzer Prize for *Humboldt's Gift*, 1975; Nobel Prize for Literature, 1976.

BOOKS: *Dangling Man* (New York: Vanguard, 1944; London: Lehmann, 1946);
The Victim (New York: Vanguard, 1947; London: Lehmann, 1948);
The Adventures of Augie March (New York: Viking, 1953; London: Weidenfeld & Nicolson, 1954);
Seize the Day (New York: Viking, 1956; London: Weidenfeld & Nicolson, 1957);
Henderson the Rain King (New York: Viking, 1959; London: Weidenfeld & Nicolson, 1959);
Herzog (New York: Viking, 1964; London: Weidenfeld & Nicolson, 1965);
The Last Analysis (New York: Viking, 1965; London: Weidenfeld & Nicolson, 1966);
Mosby's Memoirs and Other Stories (New York: Viking, 1968; London: Weidenfeld & Nicolson, 1969);
Mr. Sammler's Planet (New York: Viking, 1970; London: Weidenfeld & Nicolson, 1970);
The Portable Saul Bellow (New York: Viking, 1974);

Saul Bellow, 1950s

Humboldt's Gift (New York: Viking, 1975; London: Secker & Warburg, 1975);
To Jerusalem and Back: A Personal Account (New York: Viking, 1976; London: Secker & Warburg, 1976);
Nobel Lecture (New York: Targ Editions, 1976);
The Dean's December (New York: Harper & Row, 1982; London: Secker & Warburg, 1982);
Him with His Foot in His Mouth and Other Stories (New York: Harper & Row, 1984; London: Secker & Warburg, 1984).

PLAY PRODUCTIONS: *The Last Analysis*, New York, Belasco Theatre, 1 October 1964;
Under the Weather (A Wen, Orange Soufflé, Out From Under), London, 7 June 1966; Spoleto, Italy, Festival of Two Worlds, 14 July 1966; New York, Cort Theatre, 27 October 1966.

OTHER: Isaac Bashevis Singer, "Gimpel the Fool," translated by Bellow, *Partisan Review*, 20 (May-June 1953): 300-313;
"Distractions of a Fiction Writer," in *The Living Novel*, edited by Granville Hicks (New York: Macmillan, 1957), pp. 1-20;

Great Jewish Short Stories, edited, with an introduction, by Bellow (New York: Dell, 1963);

"Literature," in *The Great Ideas Today,* edited by Mortimer Adler and Robert M. Hutchins (Chicago: *Encyclopaedia Britannica,* 1963), pp. 135-179;

"Zetland: By A Character Witness," in *Modern Occasions,* edited by Philip Rahv (Port Washington, N.Y.: Kennikat, 1974), pp. 9-30.

SELECTED PERIODICAL PUBLICATIONS:
FICTION

"Two Morning Monologues," *Partisan Review,* 8 (May-June 1941): 230-236;

"A Sermon by Dr. Pep," *Partisan Review,* 16 (May-June 1949): 455-462;

"The Trip to Galena," *Partisan Review,* 17 (November-December 1950): 769-794;

"Address by Gooley MacDowell to the Hasbeens Club of Chicago," *Hudson Review,* 4 (Summer 1951): 222-227;

A Wen, Esquire, 63 (January 1965): 72-74ff.;

Orange Soufflé, Esquire, 64 (October 1965): 130-136;

"Silver Dish," *New Yorker,* 54 (25 September 1978): 40-62;

"Him with His Foot in His Mouth," *Atlantic,* 250 (November 1982): 115-144.

NONFICTION

"The Jewish Writer and the English Literary Tradition," *Commentary,* 8 (October 1949): 366-367;

"Dreiser and the Triumph of Art," *Commentary,* 11 (May 1951): 502-503;

"Man Underground," *Commentary,* 13 (June 1952): 608-610;

"Laughter in the Ghetto," *Saturday Review of Literature,* 36 (30 May 1953): 15;

"How I Wrote Augie March's Story," *New York Times Book Review,* 31 January 1954, pp. 3, 17;

"Deep Readers of the World, Beware!," *New York Times Book Review,* 15 February 1959, pp. 1, 34;

"Where Do We Go From Here: The Future of Fiction," *Michigan Quarterly Review,* 1 (Winter 1962): 27-33.

Saul Bellow is now recognized as one of the most important writers in American literature. As one of two living American Nobel Prize-winners in literature, he inherits the mantle of Hemingway and Faulkner, even though he himself has not become a culture hero. Nor has he, like Borges or Márquez, become a cult figure; when in 1979 the *New York Times Book Review* asked twenty leading intellectuals which books since 1945 would count among the hundred important books in Western civilization, Bellow was not mentioned. He *is* mentioned elsewhere, however, and with the highest praise possible. Who are "the great inventors of narrative detail and masters of narrative voice and perspective" according to Philip Roth? "James, Conrad, Dostoevski and Bellow."

Bellow has in fact always enjoyed the kind of reputation that is won by solid and accomplished work. He is a private person, and in his public appearances he is sometimes distant or moody, without those manufactured public outlines (sportsman, southern gentleman) that give easy popular identification. But he is also our preeminent public spokesman, the writer who catches and articulates the sometimes hidden feelings of our era. Bellow puts flesh on those abstract and cliché-ridden bones, showing what alienation actually is on a winter afternoon, say, or precisely how our culture crushes a mediocre man. Does America mean opportunity? Bellow's fiction takes a larky young man about the country, exploring exactly what opportunities await him. Is life a mixture of the sublime and the vulgar? Bellow in his last novel before winning the Nobel Prize shows just what that mix can look like.

Bellow was born in Lachine, Quebec, just two years after his parents, Abraham and Liza Gordon Bellows, had emigrated from St. Petersburg, Russia. His father was a daring and not always successful businessman who in Russia had imported Egyptian onions (Bellow describes him as a "sharpie circa 1905") and in the New World attempted several often unconventional businesses. A family portrait in 1922 shows the father to be a stocky, erect man with the touchy look one would expect from Bellow's fictionalized accounts of him. Bellow's mother in the same picture is handsome, with large gentle eyes and a broad forehead. Bellow himself— the seven-year-old Solomon Bellows—is alert and knowing, the baby among two sisters and a brother, staring down the camera with something of his father's insouciance.

The Bellowses lived in a slum on St. Dominique Street "between a market and a hospital," Bellow has said. "I was generally preoccupied with what went on in it and watched from the stairs and windows." His father, who blamed himself for the family's poverty, worried that Solly would see too much; and the boy did see violence and sexuality, saying later that the raw reality of St. Dominique Street made all else in his life seem strange and foreign. "Little since then has worked upon me with such force," Bellow has written, as he has returned to the scene in *Dangling Man* and *Herzog*. He lived amid the color and spirituality of an earlier era, for Lachine was "a medieval ghetto . . . ; my childhood was in ancient times which was true of all orthodox Jews." By the age of four he knew the book of Genesis in Hebrew. "You never got to distinguish between that and the outer world."

Lachine was also a verbal environment, teaching young Bellow Hebrew, Yiddish, French, and English. He spent a year in the Royal Hospital (in the TB ward, he says, though he didn't have TB) with nothing to do but read. But by the time his family had moved to Humboldt Park in Chicago, when he was nine, he was healthy enough for sports as well as his many intellectual projects. Humboldt Park was a neighborhood of immigrants, filled with the cultural and intellectual activity of sidewalk orators, branch libraries, and mission houses that would provide a debating club a meeting room. By the time he attended Tuley High School, Bellow had such pals as Isaac Rosenfeld, Sydney J. Harris, who would become the newspaper columnist Oscar Tarkov, and David Peltz, his good friend to this day, who remembers that "Solly Bellows was the most precocious of the lot—a good runner on the track team, a fair swimmer, middling tennis player, but a remarkable writer even then. . . ." The boys were leftist in politics, and at one time crazy about surrealism.

But at home all was not well, for the father—by all accounts an impetuous, pretentious man—continued to have financial problems, and a fatal accident involving his uninsured coal truck made the family labor for years to pay off the debt. Bellow's mother died when he was fifteen, and when he was seventeen he and Sydney Harris ran away to New York for a few weeks to peddle (unsuccessfully) their first novels.

If Chicago had been a shock to the young Canadian, he had persevered. He attended the University of Chicago, where he felt the dense cultural atmosphere to be suffocating, and transferred to Northwestern, where he founded a socialists' club and graduated in 1937 with honors in sociology and anthropology. He reportedly wished to study literature but was advised that anti-Semitism would thwart his career, and so he accepted a scholarship to study anthropology at the University of Wisconsin, where his professor told him he wrote anthropology like a good novelist. In Chicago on New Year's Eve, 1937, Bellow married Anita Goshkin, a social worker, and abandoned his graduate

work. "In my innocence," he has said, "I had decided to become a writer."

It was a bold decision at that time, and such boldness has characterized Bellow's work ever since. His greatest strength as a novelist is his style, which is fluid and rich, picking up the rhythms and energy of Yiddish and the plain speech (and sharply observed detail) of the Middle West. His style is precise and lucid and gives off an air of absolute integrity—an integrity that has at times gotten Bellow into trouble, for as a writer he is as stiff-necked as his father looks. Again and again over his career, Bellow has followed his imagination wherever it may lead. In an era of experimentalism he has been a realist, claiming that "the development of realism in the nineteenth century is still the major event of modern literature." During the 1940s, in a time of deep social concern, Bellow dramatized a sense of the transcendent. When alienation was popular, Bellow celebrated accommodation. He reacted to the popularity of the Jewish novel by turning to a WASP protagonist (in *Henderson the Rain King*, 1959), and he met America's new youth culture head-on with the creation of a seventy-year-old protagonist (in *Mr. Sammler's Planet*, 1970). And yet in most of these ventures he was successful, largely because of his fertile imagination and clarity of mind.

Bellow's greatest difficulty as a writer lies in plot. He has confessed this difficulty, and many critics believe his novels to be formless. If Bellow's characters are colorful and his situations telling, he characteristically gives too much, too many ideas for us to know the central one and too many characters, too many memorable details, for us to discern a simple story. No doubt Bellow is not as formless as he seems, since his point is often the subtle insight of the realist, so easily lost among his comic characters and rich descriptions, and he himself is the most diligent of craftsmen, working through draft after draft. But the fact remains that his art is one of clearing and solidifying an abundance of materials, and when he has finished with the process the reader too has a way to go.

Indeed, one of Bellow's central themes is precisely this density of life. So too is the malice or nastiness of his protagonist and those around him. Another theme is the experience of transcendence and the fact that the issues that confront us are ultimately metaphysical or religious, an element that provides one of the keys to Bellow's style as the sense of a special meaning or significance just out of reach adds another dimension to his precisely detailed physical world. A society that can invent the inner life but give it no nourishment, a universe that requires one to twist himself to survive within its force, a protagonist seeking most of all to cure himself of some unknown malady—all of these are typical Bellow themes.

And so too is the theme of his Jewishness, but in a special and rather independent way. Although Bellow's mother wished him to become a Talmudic scholar like many others in her family, Bellow himself has insisted that he is not that exotic creature, the Jew who writes in English, but an American writer—a Western writer who happens to be Jewish. "I did not go to the public library to read the Talmud," Bellow says of his Chicago days, "but the novels and poems of Sherwood Anderson, Theodore Dreiser, Edgar Lee Masters, and Vachel Lindsay." Bellow nevertheless is singled out by Allen Guttmann in *The Jewish Writer in America* (1971) as portraying the full range of American Jewish experience. Bellow's comedy, intellectualism, moral preoccupation and alienation, his concern with the family and with rough Eastern European immigrants, his obsession with the past and with the dangers of an alien world, his emphasis on purity, his sense, as Alfred Kazin says, "of the unreality of this world as opposed to God's"—all of these elements bespeak his deep Jewish concern.

Certainly the fact that he is Jewish added a special tension to his decision to be a writer, for he entered a world dominated not only by WASPs but by WASPs from New England. He worked for the Work Projects Administration doing biographical sketches of midwestern writers and then taught at the Pestalozzi-Froebel Teacher's College. He went to Mexico in 1940, writing the never-published novel "Acatla," and lived, he says, a bohemian life. But these years were not all gaiety: "I sat at a bridge table in a back bedroom of the apartment while all rational, serious, dutiful people were at their jobs or trying to find jobs, writing something." After lunch with his mother-in-law, in whose apartment he lived, he would walk the city streets. "If I had been a dog I would have howled," he has written. He managed in 1941 to place a short story about a young man waiting for the draft in the *Partisan Review;* the next year another, about the Trotsky assassinations, appeared. And in 1943 *Partisan Review* published part of his new novel in progress.

Perhaps the most memorable quality of this first novel, published in 1944 as *Dangling Man,* is the tone of voice: modeled after that of Rilke's *Journal of My Other Self,* the voice is frank and honest, compensating for its self-pity by the depth and precision of its observation. Taking on Ernest Hem-

ingway, the most famous writer just then, the protagonist Joseph jibes at the hard-boiled: "If you have difficulties, grapple with them silently, goes one of their commandments. To hell with that! I intend to talk about mine, and if I had as many mouths as Siva has arms and kept them going all the time, I still could not do myself justice."

Like Bellow himself, Joseph has been kept dangling by his draft board, bound in the red tape surrounding his Canadian birth. His ostensibly formless journal is actually shaped by his increasing lack of self-control, as he records the failure of his attempts to write or prepare himself spiritually for the army, and then his disappointment with his friends and his wife, his in-laws and his mistress. Wanting to forge a self that would be "a member of the Army, but not a *part* of it," he must watch himself become overwhelmed by a hundred trivial details, as his self-control leaves him and the nasty bad temper he has remarked in others comes to dominate. When he strikes his landlord and realizes that his sense of the strangeness and impermanence of the world has grown, he, like Dostoyevski's Underground Man, throws in the towel, crying "Long live regimentation."

One critic thought Joseph was a "stinker," but other reviewers gave the book a remarkably affirmative judgment. Even the names of the reviewers tell us a great deal, for Edmund Wilson, Peter DeVries, Diana Trilling, and Delmore Schwartz all felt this first novel worthy of their attention. Edmund Wilson called it "one of the most honest pieces of testimony on the psychology of a whole generation," and George Mayberry proclaimed the creation of a complex character like Joseph "an event that is rare and wonderful in modern American writing." Subsequent critics have found the book narrow and Bellow's attitude toward Joseph uncertain. To some, Joseph at the end rejoins society and thus is not ironic; to others, he is totally defeated, surrendering his individuality, a reading the echo from Dostoyevski's "Notes from Underground" would support. Bellow's novel is a lively and even memorable work, with many striking figures, even if the author himself has confessed that he cannot bear to reread it.

Bellow's own dangling was ended by the army for medical reasons, and in 1943 he began to work for Mortimer Adler's "Great Books" project for the *Encyclopaedia Britannica,* reading he says some 60 of the 443 works indexed. He joined the merchant marine, which stationed him in New York, and then worked for the Maritime Commission onshore. After the war Bellow decided to stay in New

York, tasting, he has said, the intellectual life of the Village and enjoying the pleasures of fatherhood with the birth of his son Gregory. He reviewed books, edited, wrote reports for the founder of Penguin books, and, in a clash that served him well, spent two days as movie reviewer for *Time*, until Whittaker Chambers reportedly picked a quarrel and fired him on the spot—an event he would include in his next novel, *The Victim* (1947).

Joseph in *Dangling Man* had complained that upon awakening he went "in the body from nakedness to clothing and in the mind from relative purity to pollution" when he read the newspaper and admitted the world. To Joseph the world is a war that can kill him, but it is also the physical universe itself. In *The Victim* this impurity pursues the protagonist Asa Leventhal as Kirby Allbee comes one hot summer night to accuse the solitary and anxious Leventhal of causing his ruin. Leventhal had quarreled with Allbee's boss, prompting Allbee's loss of his job, he claims, and thus his drinking and the loss of his wife. Following Dostoyevski's *The Eternal Husband*, Bellow explores the intense and ambivalent relation between the two men, as Allbee presses deeper and deeper into Leventhal's life, taking money, a bed in his apartment, liberties with his mail, and finally a whore in Leventhal's own bed—an impurity that is still not the final one, since Allbee slips into the apartment late at night to attempt suicide in Leventhal's kitchen.

Was Asa Leventhal responsible? A parallel plot suggests he was not, for he mistakenly assumes the blame in a death for which he had no responsibility at all. Both Leventhal and Allbee are victims of an oppressively dense world—one of the finest creations in the novel, as Bellow catches the summer heat of New York—and of their inability to discern a clear order in it. Each argues for a version of reality that the other cannot accept. Allbee cannot bear the notion of an impersonal universe in which he might be harmed for no reason at all. He must find an agent—a Jew. To Leventhal, on the other hand, such a "human" universe is ominous, frightening, a world in which he could be ruined overnight. Allbee appears inexplicably, emerging from a crowd in a park as an embodiment of the city streets, which Leventhal, like his immigrant forebears, considers full of impurity and danger: "He really did not know what went on about him," Leventhal thinks, "what strange things, savage things."

The Victim is a remarkable advance over *Dangling Man*, for though it is dense and claustrophobic it is also rich and full of an absolutely honest life.

It raised some eyebrows, coming as it did only two years after the death camps had been opened, for to critics such as Theodore Ross in the *Chicago Jewish Forum* Allbee and Leventhal are too much alike. Was this the time to show that the psychology of Jew and bigot can be similar? Bellow had insisted on paying the Jew the same tribute he would pay all human beings, neither more nor less, and in Allbee he captured the unconscious subtleties of Jewish self-hatred, making him a messenger from not just a destructive world but Leventhal's own psyche. Leventhal's alienation is that of modern man, moreover, for by showing Jew and Gentile to be alike Bellow shows that at this time we are all Jews.

Although *The Victim* was not praised as much as it deserves (critics now judge it to be one of Bellow's best works), it was sufficiently recognized to win Bellow a Guggenheim Fellowship for 1948, freeing him from teaching at the University of Minnesota, where he had been in 1946 and 1947. In France on his fellowship he began a third novel in the same serious vein as his first two, but found he needed a relief. He took to writing a "memoir" of Chicago—which in France had become exotic to him, he says—and by 1949 had turned to it almost exclusively. "Augie was my favorite fantasy," he has said of the Chicago book. "Every time I was depressed while writing the grim one I'd treat myself to a fantasy holiday." He wrote *The Adventures of Augie March* (1953) while on the move—in trains and cafés in Paris and Rome; in Minneapolis where he returned to teach in 1949; in a cold-water flat in New York where he lectured at New York University; at Princeton where he was a Creative Writing Fellow; and even in the editorial offices at Viking Press. At some point he felt such revulsion with the "grim" work he had begun that he slid some 100,000 words down an incinerator.

Thus *The Adventures of Augie March* begins as the opposite of Bellow's serious concerns, best defined perhaps in terms of Asa Leventhal's fear of the streets. Bellow had known a lad like Augie: "He came of just such a family as I described. I hadn't seen him in 25 years, so the novel was a speculative biography." And what was particularly speculative was Bellow's definition of the young man as an enthusiast who is swept up by the people he loves, sometimes in a sexual swoon and at others as an admiring disciple. Can a young man in a harsh world of force survive without weapons other than affection and tolerance and a lack of calculation? The answer lies in the adults who surround Augie and are as large and threatening as they would appear to a child. They exist with a Balzacian vigor and importance that testifies to human worth as they act upon their environment, but they also overwhelm the passive young Augie, who becomes another Bellow hero oppressed by the world.

Augie manages to survive at first, proving Bellow's point. Augie's childhood is dominated by the wonderful Grandma Lausch, whose world is every bit as dramatic and cynical as the czar's court, and whom Bellow describes as the equal of the great politicians of the world. The crippled Einhorn is great too, even if his kingdom is a West Side neighborhood and his courtier (and male nurse) the young Augie. Augie serves the North Shore matron Mrs. Renling (until she wishes to adopt him) and acts as an aide-de-camp to his ambitious brother Simon, who marries into a wealthy family. In each case, Augie observes not only that "it wasn't so necessary to lie," as he says in the first chapter, rejecting Machiavellian cynicism, but also that these egotists finally do themselves in. Grandma Lausch's children treat her with the same impersonality she had tried to teach Augie. Simon is tormented by his position, and Einhorn outsmarts himself. Only Augie, larky, impetuous, sensual, accepting—the very opposite really of Bellow's usual protagonist and thus a true fantasy for Bellow—only Augie, it seems, is escaping a harsh and destructive world.

Yet Augie doesn't escape either. Bellow's insistence that these Chicago-neighborhood characters are of the same caliber as mythic and historic greats can work both ways. His references and allusions enrich and elevate the story, but they also darken it, reminding us of the terror at the heart of our myths and legends. Or to put it another way, Augie's style is Whitmanian in the way it picks up everything, relishing its energetic catalogues; but at the same time and in much the same way as Whitman, it contains a belying strain, a shrillness. Augie March is the Jew accepting all of America, Norman Podhoretz has said, and accepted in return, except for his "quality of willed and empty affirmation."

The truth is that Augie is hit again and again, and we can measure the novel's progress by noting his responses. In the first chapter Augie is beaten up by neighborhood punks (including Augie's good friend) for being a Jew: "But I never had any special grief from it," Augie says, "or brooded, being by and large too larky and boisterous to take it to heart. . . ." By the middle of the novel, when Augie is beaten up in a labor strike, he flees full of rage and terror. He goes to Mexico with his lover Thea, another Machiavellian who plans to hunt iguanas with a trained eagle, and suffers a concussion that makes him spend depressing weeks on the mend. When he cheats on Thea, she tells him he is not a man of love at all, but isolate or indifferent, a fact that Einhorn had earlier described as Augie's "opposition." "Me, love's servant?," Augie wails. "I wasn't at all!"

Bellow's fantasy has turned into his old nightmare, and the book becomes the memoir of a rather scarred and saddened middle-aged man who defines himself as one singing in the middle of a desolate and frozen farm field. Like the novel after which it was modeled, *Adventures of Huckleberry Finn, The Adventures of Augie March* is unable to sustain its original serenity.

Reviewers in 1953 took Bellow's intention for the deed, however, praising the novel for its energy and acceptance and stylistic fireworks. Even though it won a National Book Award in 1954, Bellow himself today has reservations, commenting that "I got stuck in a Sherwood Anderson ingenue vein: here are all these people and isn't life wonderful! By the last third of the book I wasn't feeling that way anymore." The novel had emancipated Bellow from grim labor, at any rate, but what seems notable today is not so much the sweep and energy of the work, particularly in the large numbers of characters, as the warm tone of its voice and the precision of its details. Augie promises to tell the truth, to close in on his experience, which makes the book not so much a picaresque novel skating on the surface as a deeper, closer investigation of what a life actually is. Bellow had grown up on the naturalistic work of Dreiser, Dos Passos, and Farrell, and he transforms it here into something less mechanical, less deterministic or external, focusing more on the perception and history and feeling of the inner protagonist—who finds a triumph, finally, in consciousness if not in love.

Bellow taught at Bard College in 1953-1954 and at the University of Minnesota the next year. He won a second Guggenheim Fellowship which permitted him to spend 1955 in Nevada and California, and then, having terminated his troubled marriage, he was free to marry Alexandra Tschacbosov and settle down—after almost two decades of moving about—in Dutchess County, New York, near Tivoli. It was during these same five years that he wrote the short works that would make up his next book, *Seize the Day* (1956): "Looking for Mr. Green" (1951), "A Father to Be" (1955), "The Gonzaga Manuscripts" (1956), the title novella, and a one-act play, *The Wrecker* (1954). The novella "Seize the Day" reflects the important fact that Bellow's

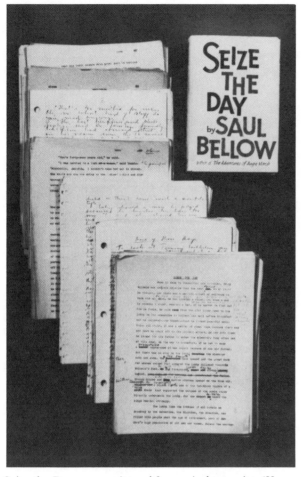

Seize the Day: *manuscript and four revised typescripts (Harry Ransom Humanities Research Center, University of Texas at Austin)*

novels are usually written over a period of years and thus do not belong to the year or even the decade in which they see publication. A friend of Bellow's reports seeing *The Victim* in two different versions by 1945, which means its composition may well have overlapped that of *Dangling Man*. When an interviewer grouped "Seize the Day" with Bellow's work in the 1940s, Bellow didn't argue with him, saying only that he had written it over a period of years. The fact remains, however, that the novella reflects a pattern of variety in Bellow's work, as each novel seems to contrast in tone with its predecessor. *The Adventures of Augie March* sprawls and attacks the world with energy; it made Bellow well known in the world of letters. "Seize the Day" is tight and sets an elegiac tone; it may well be the work that insures Bellow's position in the world of important writers.

The story recounts a day in the life of a failing middle-aged American, Tommy Wilhelm, who has made a series of poor decisions that land him jobless in his early forties at the Hotel Ansonia, where his father lives in retirement. Tommy wants his father's help—and is denied. He wants his substitute father's help too, and this father, the sometime psychologist Tamkin, is the character Bellow now finds most interesting in the tale, for "like most phony phonies, he is always somewhere near the truth. . . . But Tamkin's truths aren't really true." As he treats patients over the phone and spouts existential clichés, Tamkin promises to cure all of Tommy's troubles. He will make him strong, teaching him to "seize the day"—the very vagueness of which is Bellow's point—and he will make him financially comfortable, too, using his money to speculate on the grain market. Bellow begins the novella with Tommy emerging from his room, assuming a bold front. He gives over the first three sections to Tommy's past and his breakfast with his father, and the second three to his relations with Tamkin. In the last, climactic section, Tommy's disgusted father disowns him and Dr. Tamkin, having lost Tommy's remaining savings, disappears.

Tommy's defeat makes many readers uncomfortable, and several reviewers termed "Seize the Day" an interim work, filling the time after *The Adventures of Augie March*. Since 1956 the novella's reputation has grown steadily, however, until, as Alfred Kazin puts it, "none of his work is so widely and genuinely admired as this short novel." The reason lies in the calm and solidity of Bellow's art. The tone is almost Olympian in its treatment of Tommy's sloppy sentimentality, and Tommy himself is a significant creation. He is at once the ultimate antihero (Herbert Gold called "Seize the Day" "one of the central stories of our day") and yet a worthwhile man, and likable, with "a large, shaky, patient dignity." He is cheerful and without malice. He cares for his loved ones. More important, he is intelligently aware, undergoing his experience with depth and sensitivity.

But the finest accomplishment of the story is the novella's climactic scene. Tommy at one moment is on the New York streets, desperately looking for Tamkin and feeling the pressure of the crowd, "the inexhaustible current of millions of every race and kind pouring out, pressing round, of every age, of every genius, possessors of every secret," and at the next inside a funeral parlor, where it is suddenly "dark and cool" and where "men in formal clothes and black homburgs strode softly back and forth on the cork floor, up and down the center aisle."

In a few moments he stands before the corpse, a man he had never known, and begins to cry. He sobs at first for the man, "another human creature," he thinks, but soon he cries for himself and for all his troubles. "Soon he was past words, past reason, coherence," Bellow writes. "The source of all tears had suddenly sprung open within him, black, deep. . . ." The other guests envy the dead man, to have such mourning, but Tommy does not stop. His grief becomes a definitive and strangely triumphant moment, as the flowers and lights and music fuse within him, pouring "into him where he had hidden himself in the center of a crowd by the great and happy oblivion of tears. He heard it and sank deeper than sorrow, through torn sobs and cries toward the consummation of his heart's ultimate need."

In the first version of this concluding paragraph, as originally published in the *Partisan Review*, Bellow included "and by the way that can be found only through the midst of sorrow," implying what the prose rhythms suggest—that the humiliating moment is some kind of victory. Critics disagree about Bellow's final meaning, puzzled, as Brendan Gill puts it, by the sense that Tommy is "sobbing his heart out over his plight and yet feeling rather better than usual," but almost all readers sense the authority of the scene. As Alfred Kazin says of the whole novella, "It has a quite remarkable intensity of effect without ever seeming to force one."

More specifically the circumstance of Tommy finding his way to a stranger's funeral crystallizes Tommy's situation and needs. For he needs a father and has been denied, seeking help from people "dead" to him. He has sought all day to hide his failure, to put up a front, and here he is publicly reduced to truthfulness. Bellow himself has said that he wanted to dramatize the way New Yorkers fulfill intimate emotional needs through strangers, and so Tommy turns from his psychologist (the professional stranger) to an alien corpse—where he finally finds fulfillment. The scene gathers together other themes as well, for Tommy all day has been sinking in his tears and here drowns; he had rejected his Jewish heritage, anglicizing his name, and here grieves before the Star of David; Tommy has been a masochist too, seeking pain in a classic case of Reichian pathology, as Eusebio Rodriquez has shown, and here he finally lets go, dissolving his destructive rigidity to permit a healthy venting of emotion. Since Tommy has had mystical

promptings that his suffering somehow has a transcendent purpose, Bellow's point is also that Tommy sinks to a truer, more spiritual level of being accessible only when he is stripped of worldly pretensions.

Henderson the Rain King (1959) did not receive effusive praise when it was published, but it did not diminish Bellow's reputation either. Bellow wrote it in 1957 in Tivoli, New York, the period during which his second son, Adam, was born, and in 1958 at the University of Minnesota (an anchor for Bellow in these years and the place where he was friends with John Berryman), and then the next year in Europe, having won a two-year Ford Foundation grant.

This book about a WASP millionaire's trip to a dreamlike Africa illustrates the fertility and variety in Bellow's imagination and his desire, as he said later, to develop "a fiction that can accommodate the full tumult, the zaniness and crazed quality of modern experience." Henderson is a gigantic man in body and emotion, six feet four inches tall with "an enormous head, rugged, with hair like Persian lambs' fur. Suspicious eyes, usually narrowed. Blustering way. A great nose. . . ." He is an heir to a fortune, a hard drinker, a bully, a fighter, a man fleeing death. When the comedy of Henderson's brawling is done, his character re-

"Bigger, wilder and even better than The Adventures of Augie March (his 1954 National Book Award Winner). Henderson is a picaresque hero in the great tradition, full of a bizarre vitality with affinities both to Odysseus and Don Quixote."

Just published!

"The most brilliantly written novel to have come along in years....He has confirmed beyond any quibble his position as the great master of narrative prose in this period."

"As exciting a novel as has appeared in a long time....It is a book that should be read again and again."

"A literary event. A remarkable novel."

THE VIKING PRESS 625 Madison Ave., N.Y. 22

New York Times Book Review, *8 March 1959*

mains formed in malice. He is nasty to his wives, torments the neighbors, breaks glass on tourist beaches. His rages finally scare the family cook to death, making him seek a salvation in Africa where, he says, "the world which I thought so mighty an oppressor has removed its wrath from me." Henderson (whose initials and taste in guns are the same as Hemingway's) is the militant, insecure American who attempts to prove his manhood by killing. He is also the intelligent and sensitive man who suffers from his knowledge of human limitation. Confessing that he is most like the character Henderson, "the absurd seeker of high qualities," Bellow comments that "what Henderson is really seeking is a remedy to the anxiety over death. What he can't endure is this continuing anxiety . . . which he is foolhardy enough to resist."

In Africa Henderson encounters a harsh desert environment with a fierce white light—in essence, the inhuman physical universe. Although the novel has many realistic touches, it is essentially a fantasy, a trip deep within the Africa of Henderson's mind. For in this wasteland, reminiscent of the sheer raw power of the naturalistic world, Henderson discovers first the Arnewi, a tribe which reacts to its environment with a soft, worshiping attitude, loving its cows and its dimpled and smiling old queen, and then (after he has harmed the gentle Arnewi irremediably by blowing up their water supply) a fierce and willful and manipulative tribe that beats its gods and threatens to kill its king. Part of Bellow's point is Henderson's desire to serve a community even though it involves often bizarre and dangerous conditions, as in the case of the marvelously relaxed Wairi King Dahfu, who studies Emerson, William James, and Wilhelm Reich and who will be unceremoniously strangled if he fails to satisfy any one of his forty wives. To make the anxious Henderson equally serene, Dahfu takes him into a lion's den, where he teaches him to emulate the lion. Dahfu's tribe believes that he is not completely king until he captures the soul of his dead father . . . in a live lion. Although educated in the Western empirical tradition, which would scoff at such a view, Dahfu accepts these conditions and is killed by a lion as a result.

When Henderson then feels himself cured or freed from the world's wrath, he stumbles in explaining the cause, for he claims it was not the lion's cruel indifference that freed him but the love of the Arnewi—a statement that grows more out of Bellow's desire than the novel's events. The truth seems to be that Bellow's imagination drives (as in *The Victim* and "Seize the Day") to a final scene of violence or death which once experienced leaves the protagonist relieved and joyful. Bellow's burden as the maker of plots is to justify not just the death but the joy. When he fails to do so, as in *Henderson the Rain King*, critics complain about a murky ending.

Henderson the Rain King is an amusing novel and a good introduction to Bellow's work. Henderson is a truly comic character, and Dahfu's theories are good intellectual fun. Bellow is bolder than he had been in his previous work (it is from *Henderson* that he dates his maturity as a writer), for he here openly makes a connection between the force of the universe, particularized in the sun, say, or in an octopus's eye, and a human or spiritual principle. But Bellow once again sought variety, turning in the hectic next five years to a realistic work. He spent much of 1959 in Europe and the next year at his country home in Dutchess County. With Keith Botsford and Aaron Asher he edited the periodical the *Noble Savage*, which published writers such as Ralph Ellison, Thomas Pynchon, Josephine Herbst, and John Hawkes. He taught at the University of Puerto Rico and then settled down to his third marriage, with Susan Glassman, whom he wed in December 1961. Much sought after as a leading novelist, he taught a course in 1962 on "The Modern Novel and its Heroes" at the University of Chicago. The next year, with a new child on the way (Daniel, born in 1963) and a desire to return to his roots, Bellow left New York for Chicago, where he accepted a permanent position at the University of Chicago on the Committee on Social Thought.

In Chicago Bellow sought a greater freedom to work, a desire which bore fruit the next year with the publication of *Herzog* and the production of *The Last Analysis*. The play was a lighthearted episodic farce Bellow hoped would survive because of its entertaining qualities. The novel was more serious, embodying the theory he had announced in 1961 that a novelist must be permitted to deal with ideas. The play flopped, and the novel was a best-seller for six months. "I received two or three thousand letters from people pouring out their souls to me, saying 'This is my life, this is what it's been like for me,' " Bellow said after the publication of *Herzog*. "And then I understood that for some reason these themes were visited upon me, that I didn't always pick them, they picked me." Since the novel covered events similar to those of Bellow's life, portraying an intellectual professor devastated by the betrayal of wife and friends, some of the interest in the novel was that of a roman à clef. But most of the people who bought it were not in on the gossip; the novel articulated their own anger, their own frustration—precisely that frame of mind that characterized the late 1960s as tempers flared (and letters flew) over the issues of free speech, racial injustice, and war. Writing as early as 1960, Bellow anticipated the mood of the coming decade.

The story consists of Moses Herzog's memories as he putters alone about his country home. Herzog remembers himself in New York, where he had stayed a few days after teaching a course, and then in Chicago, where he had lurked outside his estranged wife's apartment before suffering a minor auto accident and a brief incarceration, from which the police freed him to go back to his country home in western Massachusetts.

If the geography is simple, however, the story is not. Since Herzog writes letters to all kinds of people and remembers all kinds of earlier events, the novel seems disorganized. Critics divide largely into those who forgive this disorganization (since it reflects Herzog's mind) and those who do not. And once again the protagonist at the end feels somewhat better, but the reader is not certain why. And yet the truth is that the book, which Bellow rewrote at least thirteen times, is indeed well formed. Moses Herzog had decided early in the story to shift from an emotional, "personal" life, such as the one in which his wife Madeleine abused him, to a more rational, civil, moderate one—he will shift, as he says in a letter to Eisenhower, from Tolstoy to Hegel. And much of the novel flows from this decision: he leaves Martha's Vineyard in part two because to him it represents the emotional or personal life, since he had come there seeking comfort from a friend. He reviews his intimate family and friends in part three because they too sought salvation in the personal. He carps about Ramona (who gives him gourmet dinners and what she thinks is gourmet sex) because she would cure him by means of the "personal life." Resolved to do something, he awaits his lawyer in a courtroom that portrays the horrors of the personal or sexual life and shows how the impersonal machinery of the court may give true justice.

In part six he flies to Chicago, contemplating murder of his ex-wife and her lover in order to protect his daughter Junie, reportedly locked crying in an auto outside Madeleine's apartment; but he decides once more (as the novel catches the realistic zigzags of a man trying on a new mode) that he is being extreme and indulging in personal "drama."

Thus each of the novel's sections (there are nine in all) dramatizes Bellow's theme. After he is caught the next day with the gun in his pocket, Herzog finds himself standing before a police sergeant, next to Madeleine, who in pure hatred seeks to have him imprisoned. "Her voice went up sharply, and as she spoke, Herzog saw the sergeant take a new look at her, as if he were beginning to make out her haughty peculiarities at last. . . . 'One of those was for me, wasn't it!' she says of the bullets. 'You think so? I wonder where you get such ideas? And who was the other one for?' He was quite cool as he said this, his tone was level. He was doing all he could to bring out the hidden Madeleine, the Madeleine he knew."

When the sergeant lets him go, Herzog receives a symbolic justice. The friends and relatives and even doctors who had witnessed his divorce had all failed him, but the civil authority had not. And having gotten justice he feels better. One of the problems with the novel, however, is that he feels an ecstatic joy that goes far beyond fair treatment. The truth seems to be that this novel too must be viewed as not so much a thematic statement as an experience. Herzog in Chicago undergoes a purgation, first in the pondered murder and then in being jailed. Madeleine's lover Gersbach, whom Herzog had stalked with a gun in his pocket, becomes the parallel to Allbee, Dahfu, and Tommy's dead stranger—and so too, in the cell that means ruin and death, does Herzog himself.

Herzog is notable for the controversy it caused. Bellow's second National Book Award winner, it was both praised and criticized. Alfred Kazin called it Bellow's "most brilliant" novel; Brendan Gill termed it "faultless." Other critics worried that Herzog pondered only himself, making the novel solipsistic. The key question is whether or not Herzog succeeds in making a character of himself as he looks back. Does Herzog get out of his own mind? His ability to see himself from the outside and with precise detail suggests that he might. Bellow's theme at any rate is something very much like solipsism, as Herzog is imprisoned in the "private" life.

But however one evaluates the structure of the book, *Herzog* is most notable for the style, which represents Bellow at his very best. Herzog's double remove permits Bellow to dote on detail, to slow the action when necessary to make the scenes live. And since Herzog does a great deal of observing, the novel finds its center in its descriptions. The prose is charged, rich, full of the specifics and precisely defined impressions that create the feel of mid-1960s American life. Herzog's pain seems to intensify his perception, but in many ways the novel is almost a culmination of the realistic movement, defining just that moment before the ripeness turned. Because Herzog is deflected from his course not by any insight or charged drama but by the sight of kindly Gersbach giving little Junie a bath, *Herzog* is a defense of the realistic mode, holding that the significant levels of life are often the common, whether in the home or outside in society—a view Herzog himself embraces (rejecting the fashionable existentialism) and then in his life dramatizes.

But once again Bellow was not content to work in a single key. *Herzog* joins *The Victim* and the novella "Seize the Day" to define Bellow's realistic work (a mode which more than one critic feels to be Bellow's best), but Bellow in 1964 also wrote a wilder, more fantastic piece in the play *The Last Analysis,* which he saw performed in fall 1964 and which climaxed a long interest in the theater.

Dust jacket for Bellow's second National Book Award-winning novel

One of his early essays had been about the season's Broadway plays, and in 1952 he had seen *The Victim* as adapted for the stage by Leonard Lesley. He had collaborated on a dramatization of "Seize the Day" and had included a one-act play, *The Wrecker,* among the pieces in the collection *Seize the Day.* Bellow also seems to have been motivated financially, for his novels had not made him a great deal of money, and his coming book—about a professor who writes letters to famous intellectuals—did not promise to be a best-seller. Zero Mostel would play the lead in "Humanitis," as *The Last Analysis* was originally entitled, and the play, Bellow thought, would be easy to write. He saw the theater as a form of freedom, since the footlights required a more direct, less subtle approach. He would supply the skeleton, as it were, and string some vaudevillelike bits together on it—a play with energy and emotion and sprawl not too unlike some of the work in the Yiddish theater.

By 1964, though, Bellow complained that he was writing himself into his grave. Mostel backed out, to be replaced by Sam Levene, and Bellow found playwriting more demanding than he had imagined. He persevered, however, presenting a comedian who has slipped in his career because of his seriousness and who now, in his New York warehouse studio, seeks to combine laughter and home-style psychoanalysis. The protagonist, Bummidge, seeks a cure for "humanitis," and his technique, he says, is to act out "the main events of my life, dragging repressed material into the open by sheer force of drama." In the first act he struggles to get enough money to go on closed-circuit television before a gathering of psychoanalysts and talks about his performance with his associates and relatives—his agent Winkleman, his mistress Pamela, his sexy but platonic secretary Imogen, his sister, his wife, his son—many of whom resent the money he is squandering. He rehearses his method, and then in the second and final act gives his lecture-demonstration, taking himself through the birth trauma, conflicts with his father, sexual adolescence, marriage, and then death, the experience of the last triggering an ecstatic state in which he disposes of all those who had obstructed him and determines to proceed with an institute to advance his new therapy.

So goes the published version of the play, which Bellow tells us is a substantial rewrite of the original, much tightened and simplified—abandoning the vaudevillian looseness for form and stressing the mental comedy of Bummy's method. The Broadway version flopped after twenty-eight performances, receiving poor reviews even though journalists such as John Simon tried gallantly to save it, arguing that it was the most substantial piece of comic drama produced that season. And such, at least in Bellow's rewrite, it seems to be. Bellow plays with ideas, providing a protagonist who seeks to discover what is wrong with himself by exploring the past. Bellow finds a way to visualize the internal. He combines a comedy of ideas—having fun not only with Freud but also with the intellectual's search for health—and a physical stage comedy reminiscent of vaudeville.

Bellow's second effort in the theater did no better. For in the production *Under the Weather*, Bellow combined three one-act plays, two of which have been published: *A Wen*, a delightful comedy about a scientist who has found the experience of winning the Nobel Prize less intense than the glimpse of a birthmark on a woman's thigh (a glimpse he seeks to duplicate, in middle age, with the same surprised lady) and a somewhat darker comedy, *Orange Soufflé*, about a Polish whore who wants to move in with her elderly and wealthy WASP customer. *Under the Weather* was produced in London, Spoleto, and New York, but failed to catch on.

In the novel *Herzog* Bellow attempted something like the comedy of serious thought, while in the play *The Last Analysis* he presented a clown reaching for serious ideas. Both works define a mode that would dominate Bellow's fiction for the next eighteen years, and that is the reliving of the past. *The Adventures of Augie March*, of course, was a memoir, and Henderson attempts to reach his dead parents. In *The Last Analysis* and *Herzog*, however, Bellow discovered a new center, as the protagonist relives his memories. The result was not only the creation of a special richness and color, always contrasting past and present, but a special style, one with the leisure to look and replay and sort and arrange and explore the past. "I think of myself as horribly deprived of people whom I loved and who are dead," Bellow confessed recently. "These memories serve to resurrect feelings which, at the time, I didn't want to have. . . . Now I realize how much emotion was invested in them, and I bring them back."

Bellow continued to teach in Chicago in the years following *Herzog*, although he took time out in 1967 to cover the Six-Day War for *Newsday* and in 1968 to receive the Croix de Chevalier des Arts et Lettres from France. He had begun the novel that was to become *Humboldt's Gift* (1975), but upon hearing an anecdote about an old man witnessing

a pickpocket at work, shifted to the manuscript that would become *Mr. Sammler's Planet* (1970). He had also found time to write two short stories, "Mosby's Memoirs" (1968) and "The Old System" (1967), to which he added "Leaving the Yellow House" (1957) and several tales already published in *Seize the Day* for *Mosby's Memoirs and Other Stories* (1968), a more or less "made" book designed to keep Bellow's name before the public and perhaps to capitalize on the great success of *Herzog*.

The best story of the group is "The Old System," in which the well-known scientist Samuel Braun, transparently Bellow himself, indulges in what became a characteristic Bellow posture in the late 1960s and 1970s: the middle-aged man remembering his Jewish relatives, losing himself in a colorful and exotic past. The characters are mysterious to Braun, who loves them. He ponders their reality, their evolution, the strangeness of their being. They are in one sense crude and grasping immigrants from Eastern Europe who would embarrass a third-generation Jew. But they are also vital and proud and fierce. They seem to Braun to be more intensely alive, or at least more passionate, than his modern colleagues. And indeed they are, for the remarkable story begins when Braun's fierce and fat cousin Tina, having reneged on a business deal with her brother Isaac, misses out on the fortune Isaac proceeds to make. The disappointment makes her claim Isaac cheated her, and she refuses to see him even though Isaac, as an old-fashioned believer in family, is scandalized. He spends years trying to see her, but it is only on her deathbed that she sends Isaac a message: he may visit if he pays her $20,000. To Braun remembering all this, the issue is why he is so moved now, why the event seems so precious to him. As he looks at the stars which make the episode and all else seem insignificant, he still glories in the magnificence of Tina's will and of her capriciousness—as she refuses the money when it is offered—and of her sassing the fate that gave her a fat body and the death that will soon come. He glories too in the integrity of Isaac and the old system to which he clung.

And thus it seems ironic that Bellow's next novel be marred by a lack of caring. *Mr. Sammler's Planet* was well but somewhat absentmindedly received, as though the reviewers praised Bellow by rote; a few years later it was attacked by radical young critics for political reasons, in part because Bellow had declared his independence from the liberal establishment in 1965 by attending the

White House dinner that Robert Lowell, protesting Vietnam, had boycotted.

A stubborn and difficult writer, Bellow had written about an elderly man in a decade obsessed with American youth. In this novel, as in *Herzog*, Bellow seemed to test both his readers and his own powers. Artur Sammler is an old Polish Jew who, having lived in London in the 1930s where he knew many of the Bloomsbury group, and having survived Nazi atrocities, has the civilized tastes of the intellectual English and the wisdom of the survivor. Around him he finds a host of modern young nieces, nephews, and acquaintances who reject all limits on their desire. They know no sexual bounds, no moral imperatives, no common civility. Sammler alone in New York quietly pursues something like duty. When his crazed daughter Shula steals a manuscript to help her father with his study of H. G. Wells, he doggedly seeks to return the manuscript. When his friend and benefactor Elya Gruner lies mortally ill in a hospital, Sammler alone pays homage.

The plot, which Bellow seems to have formed with a Wellsian casualness, consists largely of the young interfering with these two tasks and is typified in the running story of Sammler's relations with the black pickpocket, whose crimes he has witnessed on a bus and who follows Sammler to his apartment foyer to threaten the old man by exposing himself. Sammler mentions the incident to his opportunistic friend Feffer, only to discover later (in too much of a coincidence) the black wrestling with Feffer because he had taken pictures of the crime. And when Sammler asks his ex-son-in-law to intervene, the younger man hits to kill. In contrast to such madness, Sammler at the end praises his friend Elya Gruner, who (though sometimes an abortionist for the mob) had known how to be kind. And to do his duty. Moderation, limits, rationality—all we have, Sammler suggests, is simple human decency. Gruner had met "the terms of his contract," Sammler concludes, "the terms of which, in his inmost heart, each man knows. As I know mine. As all know. For that is the truth of it—that we all know, God, that we know, that we know, we know, we know."

Mr. Sammler's Planet is vintage Bellow, full of the precise detail and lively ideas and honest feeling that provide Bellow his strengths. If it is true, as several critics have charged, that Mr. Sammler is too right and the city too wrong, it may well be that this is the best novel the reader could hope for, written as it was so close in time to the controversial period it takes as its subject. And certainly the char-

New York Times Book Review, *25 January 1970*

acter of Sammler, who has survived the Holocaust, waking from a pile of corpses to kill fascists in his escape, is an excellent point of view from which to examine and judge American culture. Bellow captures better than anyone the feel of American society in the late 1960s, with its blend of social rebellion, sexuality, racial unrest, and personal aggrandizement.

Those who criticize the book have a point, too, although it is not a political one. Sammler's rational conservatism is totally responsible, whether we agree with it or not, for it is the result of a calm choice. "Without limits you have monstrosity, always," he says. "Within limits? Well, within limits monsters also appear. But not inevitably." What does mar the novel, finally, is Sammler's basic feeling of revulsion toward the world, both in its social form, which is cheap and distracting—Gruner's daughter worries about her sex life as her father dies—and in terms of all matter. Like Yeats sailing to Byzantium, Mr. Sammler has no use for the natural physical world, or what he calls "creatureliness. . . . Its low tricks, its doggish hind-sniffing charm." Sammler yearns to be "a soul released from Nature, from impressions, and from everyday life."

Herzog had balanced precariously between a sense of the world's beauty and its ugliness. In *Mr. Sammler's Planet* the balance is tipped, and the result is not only a book that turns sour but also one that tolerates a certain contrivance of plot, as though corny or mechanical events were a true parallel to a corny or mechanical world. Sammler on the move, fending off the crazed youth, is unconvincing. Sammler alone with his thoughts and memories, in what is now Bellow's most typical mode, is mellow and believable.

Mr. Sammler's Planet won a National Book Award in 1971. While continuing to teach at the University of Chicago (where he had become chairman of the Committee on Social Thought) and coping with the public and bitter dissolution of his third marriage, Bellow worked on two novels, segments of which were published in 1974. One of these was *Humboldt's Gift*, which in 1975 became his seventh novel and which immediately preceded his 1976 Nobel Prize for Literature.

Many reviewers praised the book, and *Newsweek* did a cover story on America's leading writer, but other critics were disappointed. "The book is not very real," Alfred Kazin confessed, although large pieces of it were. Part of the trouble seemed to be the combination of the realistic and manic: Bellow attempted to work grotesque gangsters into

a finely detailed world, and it did not work. And then the plot creaked, even though Bellow had been true to his vision once again, for if the world of affairs is contrived and vulgar, what kind of plot must a realist provide? Bellow had defined his basic intention in this novel in 1963, discussing "Literature" for *Encyclopaedia Britannica:* few modern novelists, he noted, dramatize a spiritual experience. If they feel they are important, writers "ought to show us the actualities of a religious life." *Humboldt's Gift* is a fascinating book because it does precisely that.

The story is told from the point of view of Charles Citrine, a well-known dramatist who reminisces about his friendship with Humboldt, a poet who combines qualities of John Berryman, with whom Bellow had been close friends at Minnesota, and Delmore Schwartz, whom Bellow had known in New York. It was in fact shortly after Schwartz died in 1966 that Bellow began the novel, much of which consists of Citrine trying to hang on to his memories of Humboldt and do a little anthroposophical meditation while being harassed by gangsters, lawyers, bimbos, and creeps—some funny and some not. All of them are typified by Cantabile, to whom Citrine owes money and who has Citrine's car smashed in by baseball bats and later forces the playwright to watch him defecate. An ex-wife is suing Citrine, and a mistress—the sensual Renata, an uninhibited woman who makes one think of a witty and tough Ramona—is attempting to lead him to the altar. But during all these events, Citrine moves inward in memory and meditation, seeking the images that Rudolf Steiner had promised would give spiritual salvation.

What is interesting thematically in *Humboldt's Gift* is the equation within Citrine's inner life of his meditation of spirit and his memories of his friend. Both of these exist in saving opposition to the world, although Humboldt's actual gift combines the sublime and the vulgar, for it consists first of a movie scenario on which they had collaborated and which proceeds to earn Citrine a small fortune, and then of a scribbled sentence at the end of a farewell letter: "We are not natural beings but supernatural beings."

The chief critical issue in the novel, aside from Bellow's struggle to mesh his transcendental philosophy with commercial America, is how Bellow in the same book can write both brilliantly and ineptly. Bellow moves from passages such as

> She threw a very good pass—a hard, accurate spiral. Her voice trailed as she ran

barelegged and made the catch on her breast. The ball in flight wagged like a duck's tail. It flew under the maples over the clothesline.

to passages such as this:

> I met Kathleen at a cafe and showed her the clippings. There was more in the same vein. I said, "Thraxter has a terrible weakness for making major statements. I think I might just ask for the three guns to be applied to the back of my head and the triggers pulled rather than sit through those seminars."
> "Don't be too hard on him. The man is saving his life," she said.
> "Also it's a fascinating thing, really. Where does he make the ransom pitch?"
> "Here. . . ."

Bellow at his worst sounds like an amateur playwright providing background information as he moves his characters on and offstage. Thus the later parts of the novel fall off, becoming talky and cranky, as though (as reportedly is the case) Bellow took to taking his novel to a stenographer, like the later Henry James, or as though his troubled personal life had taken its toll. The truly fine early parts of the book were written not too long after *Herzog,* while the later parts, developing some of the disenchantment with the real world Bellow expressed in *Mr. Sammler's Planet,* came after 1969.

Critics have not really done justice to the fact that good writing seems to exist in a delicate balance that the reader can sometimes see come and go. One thinks of Mark Twain, and then, perhaps, the Bellow of *Humboldt's Gift,* for this novel contains writing as good as any that Bellow has done and also the very worst that he has done. Perhaps Bellow said what he had to say in *Herzog* and now marks time. Certainly *Mr. Sammler's Planet* is very much like a brilliant piece of journalism, in which a highly intelligent man ponders our civil disruption.

And yet Bellow has always surprised his readers, and wise advocates of his work would expect to be surprised again. Bellow's 1976 book is the journalistic *To Jerusalem and Back: A Personal Account,* published after Bellow had accompanied his new wife, Alexandra, professor of mathematics at Northwestern University, to Israel. There he had adopted a fascinating premise: what could a practitioner of the humanities add to the politics and propaganda and terror of the Israeli-Arab conflict?

Could he penetrate the confusion to find some kind of order? Bellow had contemplated a book on Chicago and had served as a journalist during the Six-Day War. Could he now make some kind of contribution to solving Israel's troubles? The book describes Bellow's travels, his interviews with Israeli and American leaders, and his dinner conversations with the powerful and the humble, and then—and not least important—his reading and research into the problem.

Bellow's writing is lucid and detailed, and not without humor, as a Hasidim, for example, is offended by Bellow's eating habits and offers to send him money each month if he will return to orthodoxy. But at the end the rational and well-meaning Bellow is forced to conclude that the situation is even more dangerous than he had supposed, for he finds that nations (and their leaders) do not act consistently with even their own self-interest. If only they recognized their goals and sought them ruthlessly, Bellow suggests, the struggle would have some order. But both Arab and Jew act irrationally, creating a dangerous and unpredictable mix. That bystanders such as Jean-Paul Sartre or the United States will make use of the conflict for their own purposes—again inconsistently and irrationally defined—only makes the issue worse.

Since he won the Nobel Prize for Literature in 1976, Saul Bellow has led a quiet life. His long and public court battle with his third wife is settled. His marriage to Alexandra Ionescu Tulcea is, by all accounts, successful. He lives in a large apartment overlooking Lake Michigan, and three times a week he travels the Outer Drive to the University of Chicago, where he teaches as a member of the Committee on Social Thought.

A serene life for a sixty-seven-year-old novelist enjoying the fruits of his long labor? Not at all—Bellow has used his honored and orderly life as a podium from which to challenge and scold his country. His latest novel, *The Dean's December* (1982), is nothing less than an indictment of American society—on all levels. The blacks in our cities are in truth doomed, Bellow says; the whites show only a cruel indifference. Public officials are guilty of hypocrisy, and those unofficial public figures who have the opportunity to study the problem, our journalists and experts and professors, are guilty of jargon and cant. "Many American writers cross the bar in their 60's and 70's," Bellow has said, "and become Grand Old Men, gurus or bonzes of the Robert Frost variety. This is how society eases us out." Bellow's concern for America is deep, but his tone is anything but grandfatherly.

Dust jacket for Bellow's 1982 novel contrasting life in a Communist society with life in the United States

The novelist delivers his views in a book that seems at first to be vintage Bellow. His pages spring to life with the precision that is his finest talent. The face of a corpse, Bellow writes, "had the only-just-subtracted expression" of the dead. Winter dusk in Rumania is notable for the light: "Brown darkness took over the pavements, and then came back again from the pavements more thickly and isolated the street lamps. They were feebly yellow in the impure melancholy winter effluence. Air-sadness, Corde called this." Such description takes place in a context that is now Bellow's most characteristic mode, as an intelligent (but fumbling) protagonist has the leisure to reflect upon a shocking event in the past, providing not only the drama of a mind in action but a fascinating exercise in perspective.

Bellow's intention is ambitious and his story promising. Albert Corde, a dean of students at a Chicago college, has accompanied his sensible astronomer wife, Minna, to Bucharest, where her mother lies ill in a hospital. There petty Communist officials make it difficult for Minna to visit the dying woman, a Communist official now fallen from grace, and finally permit her only one visit—she

must choose the time. Corde's wife must suffer the ordeal of her mother dying alone, without her daughter at her bedside.

As Minna hurries about the city seeking help, Albert Corde passes the time in a chilly apartment remembering the problems he had left behind in Chicago. He had published a set of articles in *Harper's* on the black underclass of the city and had insisted upon the prosecution of two blacks for the murder of a white student. In both instances he has rocked the boat in a way administrators dare not do. He has alienated whites by reminding them of the millions of people they have abandoned. He has alienated the blacks by insisting that however victimized they may be, they must be responsible for their actions. The blacks are "startled souls," Bellow told an interviewer. "They cannot be reasoned with or talked to about anything."

To the liberal, Corde sounds suspiciously racist. To the conservative, he stirs up muddy waters. And to his provost in the university, Corde has violated academic decorum: how dare he wade into a messy social issue? Doesn't he realize that he is an officer of the university? To everyone else Corde is an aesthete, arguing that the problem is one of perception, since people have learned to evade the truth, shutting off experience. Like the nineteenth-century realistic novelists, to whom Bellow has confessed a debt, Corde believes that facing the truth can be a rare (and perhaps heroic) accomplishment. His articles (like the novel itself) are meant "to recover the world that is buried under the debris of false description or nonexperience."

What Bellow manages to do is provide several different sources of narrative interest. As the reader awaits the outcome of Minna's struggle to visit her mother, he also awaits the outcome of the trial in Chicago (Had the white student sought kinky sex? Had he asked for trouble?) and the effect of his articles on Corde's career. His job hangs by a thread. The novel moves from Rumania to Chicago, sometimes in Corde's memory and at other times in his articles or letters sent him from America. In the two cities, the style of administrators, the ways of death, and the kinds of parties (a Rumanian tea and a high-rise celebration of a dog's birthday), the dome of the crematorium and that of the telescope at Mount Palomar, California—in all these ways the novel sets contrasts that reveal and dramatize each society. The Communist society is cold and harsh, as dreary administrators parcel out pain. The capitalistic society is hot and chaotic, as the slums whirl out of control. In both countries good people struggle to be decent. Rumanian women support one another, remembering the old European culture, while black heroes such as Rufus Ridpath, a prison warden, and Toby Winthrop, the founder of a drug rehabilitation center, struggle to stop the people from brutalizing themselves and one another. And lest these issues flag, Corde's articles in *Harper's* (which Bellow excerpts in the novel) provide riveting accounts of the underclass and the officials who work with it.

And yet, much as one appreciates Bellow's fine style and excellent ideas, the novel is a disappointment to read—or so many reviewers felt, as they wrote their mixed reviews. Those who called the book a success confessed that it was a near thing. Everything depends on the protagonist, said Robert Towers in the *New York Times Book Review;* does Corde work as a character? Yes. "Sentence by sentence, page by page, Saul Bellow is simply the best writer that we have." Other reviewers objected that Corde does not have the independent existence of Bellow's other protagonists—he is clearly a spokesman for Bellow. Many critics gave Bellow high marks for struggling with this difficult but crucial subject. Some readers, most notably David Evanier in the *National Review,* were put off by Bellow's

subject. Didn't he realize it was stale? Hadn't he read the book of Job, asked another: didn't he realize that suffering we will always have with us? Others complained with more justice that the book is too grim (to read it is like hitting yourself over the head with a hammer, said one) or too talky or too full of scolding. Those who praised it were exhilarated: "He gives Corde's thoughts such palpable immediacy, such convincing shifts in tone," wrote Dean Flower in the *Hudson Review,* "that sometimes one can only revel in Bellow's gifts."

It seems true that Bellow is somewhat careless in his writing. He creates wooden dialogue at times, forgetting that a literal transcription of talk does not work in fiction. His characters can be thin and his plot does creak. All of this is true, on occasion, and so is the sparseness of Corde's character and the large amount of talk in the book. Bellow doesn't make his fiction any more attractive, moreover, by including a host of creeps and bullies he himself does not like.

One may appreciate the novel for the language, or for the play of ideas, as Corde spars with the public defenders and scientists concerned over lead poisoning. One may appreciate Bellow's moral seriousness and his instinct for what is crucial to the future of our society. But *The Dean's December* is interesting, too, in terms of its aesthetic, for while it is true that Bellow drops certain niceties for the sake of his content, it is also true that he finds a way to write about a very difficult subject: How can a wealthy and cultured white get into the experience of a desolate people? He has always been affected by a vision of suffering masses and a murderous humanity—the social reality here matches an intense, imaginative one. To place Corde in his stocking feet 6,000 miles from Chicago, surrounded by women attempting to minister to the dying, gave Bellow a personal and domestic perspective from which to view Chicago. What many reviewers found to be defects, in other words, are actually Bellow's means of providing distance: Corde's articles, the shifting from scene to scene, the use of Corde's memory and his conversations all permit Bellow to move close in, looking hard at prisons and public housing and the county hospital, and yet these devices permit him to pull back too, to avoid outrage and fear. Corde in Chicago became a partisan, entering the fray. He had to. In Rumania, indulging in a great deal of talk, he can wonder about larger causes and attempt to do justice to all parties. How do people solve problems if not by talk? In this novel the reader gets both a close look at the reality and a distant look from which to seek the larger solution. Bellow invents a form that permits him to move from one scale to the other at will.

Him with His Foot in His Mouth and Other Stories (1984) turns from the public realm to the private or personal one. It is essentially Bellow's third book of stories, following *Seize the Day* and *Mosby's Memoirs,* and, like those volumes, is a loose collection of short stories made significant by Bellow's style. Although he returns to many of his old themes (which now appear to be obsessive), he manages to make them fresh or immediate. The title story is a letter of apology from Professor Shawmut to Miss Rose, a librarian Shawmut had insulted thirty-five years previously. Shawmut is now old and sick. He hasn't done well, he confesses to his ancient victim. His impetuous tongue has insulted many people. But he too has been a victim, having innocently trusted a strong-willed, amoral character—his brother, who cheated him. Thus Bellow once again portrays an innocent or gentle character in conflict with a robust Machiavellian. In "What Kind of Day Did You Have?," the weakest of the five stories, an attractive young matron is used by a famous and powerful art critic; in "Zetland: By a Character Witness" (originally published in 1974 as part of a novel in progress), the title character marries in defiance of his angry, brooding father. In the best story of the volume, "A Silver Dish," Woody Selbst remembers his father stealing from the Christian woman who had befriended Woody, a crime that costs Woody his place in the seminary and so a career as a Christian minister—a fact his Jewish father foresaw. And in the last story, Ijah Metzger is surrounded by equally willful and amoral "Cousins," all of whom want something from him.

These characters all review the past, suffer guilt, cling to their families, and appear to be isolated. We even recognize several figures we have met under different names in Bellow's previous fiction. But in each story Bellow offers a unique tone and an individual world, making the tale fresh. "Cousins" catches the Chicago of today, investigating the bonds that hold together an extended family. "The Silver Dish" explores Chicago in the Depression, portraying the intense relationship between father and son as well as the issues of Jewish identity and assimilation. "What Kind of Day Did You Have?" places Katrina Goliger and Victor Wulpy in an American airport, where they are snowed in (and where Wulpy pulls strings to get them back to Chicago). "Zetland" reminisces lovingly about growing up in Humboldt Park, Chicago, in the 1920s.

Thus these stories, which were well received by reviewers, are solid additions to the body of Bellow's work. Bellow's characteristic weakness may be found here—the dialogue in "What Kind of Day Did You Have?" is wooden and the events somewhat contrived, for instance—but Bellow's strengths may be found as well. One who wishes to know what it is like to ride a Chicago trolley need only read "A Silver Dish." As John Updike wrote in the *New Yorker* of *The Dean's December*, Bellow "is not just a very good writer, he is one of the rare writers who when we read them feel to be taking mimesis a layer or two deeper than it has gone before. His lavish, rippling notations of persons, furniture, habiliments, and vistas awaken us to what is truly there."

Bellow's interest in the transcendent may be found in these stories (one character believes that "The Divine Spirit . . . has withdrawn in our time from the outer, visible world") and so may Bellow's characteristic blaze of colorful theory, at least in "What Kind of Day Did You Have?" But perhaps the most notable point about this volume is Bellow's concern with emotion. More than anything else, these stories are studies of human feeling, exploring the danger of emotion as well as its strength. It is Shawmut's love of his brother that causes him to give the businessman all his money, just as it is Katrina's love of Wulpy that makes her leave her children for a day to join the traveler. Woody's love of his father makes him trusting, while Ijah's deep feeling for his cousins (or at least their parents) makes him a soft touch. Again and again Bellow portrays characters bound by their emotions and vulnerable before people who do not feel. "Pop never had these groveling emotions," Woody thinks in "A Silver Dish." "There was his whole superiority. Pop had no such feelings."

Bellow believes that such emotion is also salvation, however. The emotional characters are sustained by their love, rising above petty concerns. They learn to control their feelings, when that is appropriate, and also to trust them. Ijah in "Cousins" reads the philosopher Heidegger on emotion and perception. Even hate, Ijah notes, "increases lucidity, it opens a man up; it makes him reach out and concentrates his being so that he is able to grasp himself." To another character (in the title story) "redemption from *mere* nature is the work of feeling and of the awakened eye of the Spirit." Bellow's characters think about emotion and Bellow's stories dramatize the force of emotion in their lives. Thus, Bellow's fiction finds its way to the center of human experience. But Bellow—still strong at seventy-

Bellow, 1980s (photo by Layle Silbert)

one—also creates emotion within his reader: in this volume Bellow not only explores the nature of a human life but provides the reader with vivid representation of it.

Will Bellow's work last? Even as fads come and go, even as Ph.D.'s study Bellow's difficulty with plot and others study Bellow's great success in style, Bellow's fiction gives evidence of lasting. Perhaps the most accurate testimony to Bellow's strength is given by his friend Richard Stern, when he asks, "How many American writers have published first-rate imaginative books over a thirty year period? Perhaps three, Henry James, Faulkner and now Bellow."

Interviews:

Gordon Lloyd Harper, "Saul Bellow: An Interview," in *Writers at Work: The "Paris Review" Interviews*, third series (New York: Viking, 1967), pp. 175-196;

Joseph Epstein, "A Talk with Saul Bellow," *New York Times Book Review*, 5 December 1976, pp. 3, 92-93.

Bibliographies:

B. A. Sokoloff and Mark Posner, *Saul Bellow: A Comprehensive Bibliography* (Folcroft, Pa.: Folcroft Library Editions, 1972);
Primary bibliography of Bellow's publications.

Marianne Nault, *Saul Bellow: His Works and His Critics* (New York: Garland Publishing, 1977);
An exhaustive compilation of Bellow's written pieces, with valuable summaries. It also summarizes articles and books about Bellow.

Robert G. Noreen, *Saul Bellow: A Reference Guide* (Boston: G. K. Hall, 1978);
Annotated secondary bibliography.

References:

Malcolm Bradbury, *Saul Bellow* (New York: Methuen, 1982);
Places Bellow's fiction within the contemporary cultural scene, examining each of the novels.

Jeanne Braham, *A Sort of Columbus: The American Voyages of Saul Bellow's Fiction* (Athens: Uni-

versity of Georgia Press, 1984);
Places Bellow within the American tradition, tracing themes: perception, withdrawal and return, meaning, the influence of Hemingway, and technique.

John J. Clayton, *Saul Bellow: In Defense of Man* (Bloomington: Indiana University Press, 1968);
Interprets the novels according to the resolution of psychological conflict.

Sarah Blacher Cohen, *Saul Bellow's Enigmatic Laughter* (Urbana: University of Illinois Press, 1974);
Examines the nature and role of comedy in Bellow's fiction.

Robert Detweiler, *Saul Bellow: A Critical Essay* (Grand Rapids, Mich.: Eerdmans, 1967);
Uses a Christian perspective to evaluate Bellow's fiction.

Daniel Fuchs, *Saul Bellow: Vision and Revision* (Durham, N.C.: Duke University Press, 1984);
This is a valuable look at Bellow's many revisions of his manuscripts.

David D. Galloway, *The Absurd Hero in American Fiction: Updike, Styron, Bellow, Salinger* (Austin: University of Texas Press, 1966; revised, 1970);
Bellow's characters react to the absurdity of life.

Leila Goldman, *Saul Bellow's Moral Vision: A Critical Study of Jewish Experience* (New York: Irvington, 1983);
Argues that Bellow's education as a Jew plays a dominant role in his writing.

Irving Malin, *Saul Bellow's Fiction* (Carbondale: Southern Illinois University Press, 1969);
Malin examines Bellow's themes, characters, images, styles, and best novel, *Herzog*.

Malin, ed., *Saul Bellow and the Critics* (New York: New York University Press, 1967);
This is a collection of representative essays.

Judie Newman, *Saul Bellow and History* (New York: St. Martin's Press, 1983);
Bellow is preoccupied with history, or the influence of social forces and time upon the self.

Keith Opdahl, *The Novels of Saul Bellow: An Introduction* (University Park: Pennsylvania State University Press, 1967);
Bellow's ultimate concern is a religious issue, often involving the perception of spirit.

G. I. Porter, *Whence the Power?* (Columbia: University of Missouri Press, 1974);
A close examination of each of the novels.

Eusebio Rodrigues, *Quest for the Human: An Exploration of Saul Bellow's Fiction* (Lewisburg, Pa.: Bucknell University Press, 1981);
Each of Bellow's protagonists struggles to be human.

Earl Rovit, *Saul Bellow* (Minneapolis: University of Minnesota Press, 1967);
A good, short overview of Bellow's work.

Rovit, ed., *Saul Bellow: A Collection of Critical Essays* (Englewood Cliffs, N.J.: Prentice-Hall, 1975);
A helpful compilation of critical works.

Saul Bellow Journal (1981-   );
This biannual contains a wealth of insight and information.

Brigitte Scheer-Schaetzler, *Saul Bellow* (New York: Ungar, 1972);
Stresses Bellow's compassion, arguing the novels lack resolution.

Edmond Shraepen, *Saul Bellow and His Work* (Brussels: Vrije Universitet Brussel, 1978);
Offers a group of essays growing from a conference on Bellow.

Tony Tanner, *Saul Bellow* (Edinburgh & London: Oliver & Boyd, 1965; New York: Barnes & Noble, 1965);
This is the first study of Bellow's language, themes, and conflicts.

Stanley Trachtenberg, ed., *Critical Essays on Saul Bellow* (Boston: G. K. Hall, 1979);
Contains a valuable interview with Bellow by Jo Brans, reviews of the novels, and several critical essays.

Papers:
Bellow's manuscripts are at Regenstein Library of the University of Chicago. This is an extensive col-

lection, including manuscripts from most of the novels, many different working drafts, letters, and memorabilia. Several manuscripts of *Seize the Day* are at the Humanities Research Center, University of Texas, Austin.

John Berryman

This entry was revised by John Haffenden (University of Sheffield) from his entry in DLB
48, American Poets, 1880-1945.

Places	Columbia University Cambridge University	Harvard University	Minneapolis
Influences and Relationships	Mark Van Doren R. P. Blackmur	Dylan Thomas Robert Lowell	Delmore Schwartz Saul Bellow
Literary Movements and Forms	The Middle Generation	Confessional Poetry	
Major Themes	Chaos of Modern Life Illicit Love	Dream Analysis Guilt	"Individual Human Soul Under Stress"
Cultural and Artistic Influences	Freudian Psychology		
Social and Economic Influences	The Holocaust		

BIRTH: McAlester, Oklahoma, 25 October 1914, to Martha Little and John Allyn Smith.

EDUCATION: B.A., Columbia University, 1936; B.A., Clare College, Cambridge, 1938.

MARRIAGES: 24 October 1942 to Eileen Patricia Mulligan (divorced). 1956 to Elizabeth Ann Levine (divorced); child: Paul. 1 September 1961 to Kathleen Donahue; children: Martha, Sarah Rebecca.

AWARDS AND HONORS: Euretta J. Kellett Fellowship, 1936; Charles Oldham Shakespeare Scholarship, 1937; Rockefeller Foundation research fellowship, 1944, 1945; *Kenyon Review*—Doubleday short-story prize for "The Imaginary Jew," 1945; Guarantors Prize (*Poetry*), 1949; Shelley Memorial Award (Poetry Society of America), 1949; Levinson Prize (*Poetry*), 1950; Guggenheim Fellowship, 1952, renewed 1953; Rockefeller Fellowship in poetry, 1956; Harriet Monroe Poetry Award, 1957; Brandeis University Creative Arts Citation, 1960; Ingram Merrill Foundation award, 1963; Russell Loines Award (National Institute of Arts and Letters), 1964; Pulitzer Prize for *77 Dream Songs*, 1965; Guggenheim Fellowship, 1966; Academy of American Poets Fellowship, 1966; National Endowment for the Arts Grant, 1967; National Book Award for *His Toy, His Dream, His Rest*, 1969; Bollingen Prize in Poetry, 1969; D.Litt., Drake University, 1969; Regents' Professor of Humanities, University of Minnesota, 1969; Senior Fellowship, National Endowment for the Humanities, 1971.

DEATH: Minneapolis, Minnesota, 7 January 1972.

BOOKS: *Poems* (Norfolk, Conn.: New Directions, 1942);
The Dispossessed (New York: William Sloane, 1948);
Stephen Crane (New York: William Sloane, 1950; London: Methuen, 1950; with additional material, Cleveland & New York: World, 1962);
Homage to Mistress Bradstreet (New York: Farrar, Straus & Cudahy, 1956);
His Thought Made Pockets & the Plane Buckt (Pawlet, Vt.: Claude Fredericks, 1958);
Homage to Mistress Bradstreet and Other Poems (London: Faber & Faber, 1959; New York: Farrar, Straus & Giroux, 1968);
The Arts of Reading, by Berryman, Ralph Ross, and Allen Tate (New York: Crowell, 1960);
77 Dream Songs (New York: Farrar, Straus, 1964; London: Faber & Faber, 1964);

John Berryman (courtesy of Eileen Simpson)

Berryman's Sonnets (New York: Farrar, Straus & Giroux, 1967; London: Faber & Faber, 1968);
Short Poems (New York: Farrar, Straus & Giroux, 1967);
His Toy, His Dream, His Rest (New York: Farrar, Straus & Giroux, 1968; London: Faber & Faber, 1969);
The Dream Songs (New York: Farrar, Straus & Giroux, 1969);
Love & Fame (New York: Farrar, Straus & Giroux, 1970; revised edition, London: Faber & Faber, 1971);
Delusions, Etc. (New York: Farrar, Straus & Giroux, 1972; London: Faber & Faber, 1972);
Selected Poems 1938-1968 (London: Faber & Faber, 1972);
Recovery (New York: Farrar, Straus & Giroux, 1973; London: Faber & Faber, 1973);
The Freedom of the Poet (New York: Farrar, Straus & Giroux, 1976);
Henry's Fate & Other Poems 1967-1972, edited by John Haffenden (New York: Farrar, Straus & Giroux, 1977; London: Faber & Faber, 1978).

OTHER: "Twenty Poems," in *Five Young American Poets* (Norfolk, Conn.: New Directions, 1940);
Answers to "The State of American Writing, 1948: Seven Questions," *Partisan Review,* 15 (August 1948): 856-860;
"Three and a half years at Columbia," in *University on the Heights,* edited by Wesley First (Garden City: Doubleday, 1969), pp. 51-60.

John Berryman is associated with a group of poets who have become known as the "Middle Generation," a group that includes Delmore Schwartz, Randall Jarrell, Theodore Roethke, and Robert Lowell. It is a critical convenience to label much of the work of Berryman and Lowell, along with that of Sylvia Plath, as "confessional," but the tag is certainly belittling. It suggests a poetry which indulges in vulgar self-exposure, and neglects to note, for example, that Berryman's poems—even in *The Dream Songs* (1969) and *Love & Fame* (1970), which are supposedly his most confessional volumes—are in fact the products of sustained imagination and craft. Berryman and his contemporaries certainly had highly disturbed lives, with elements of self-victimization, but the poems should not be mistaken for the lives. Literary historians must eventually evaluate those lives from the perspectives both of individual psychology and of cultural context. Robert Lowell worried the question in an 18 March 1963 letter to Berryman: "What queer lives we've had even for poets! There seems something generic about it, and determined beyond anything we could do." In view of the fact that this generation reached adulthood just before World War II, they had also to wonder, as Lowell later put it, "Were we uncomfortable epigoni of Frost, Pound, Eliot, Marianne Moore, etc? This bitter possibility came to us at the moment of our *arrival.*"

Faced with such great antecedents, Berryman had to serve a long apprenticeship as a poet, burdened by influence, which lasted until the late 1940s. "Berryman's earlier work," Kenneth Connelly has observed, "is often that of a very self-conscious, sometimes too respectful scholar sweating in the poet's academy, with results, as Dudley Fitts noted long ago, which were marred by 'an aura of contrivance' " (*Yale Review,* Spring 1969). But the apprenticeship paid off, for his major works, *Homage to Mistress Bradstreet* (1956) and *The Dream Songs,* are sui generis, unprecedented long poems of humane interest and high literary art, not of unmediated expressiveness or merely confessional interest. As Denis Donoghue observed of *The Dream Songs,* "the poem is all perception, surrounded by feeling. The feeling is not on show, on parade; it comes into the lines only because it attends upon perceptions which could not appear without that favour." Berryman's life is at the center of his best poetry, and his poetry is a function of his obsessions. He in fact experienced the whole gamut of obsessions—emotional, psychological, philosophical, religious—which a modern man might endure, but he managed to stand outside himself in his poems by means of personae. "His poems are so close to a sense of life, an imparting of truth complete with the bias of technique and personality, that they have the true flavour of fiction," Douglas Dunn has written. "An enormously comprehensive and unsentimental pathos slips out of his work, complicated and perplexing. We realize that although it may all be about ordinary Berryman, it generalizes itself, it has compass."

Berryman suffered from mismatched parents. His father, John Allyn Smith, had migrated from the family home in Minnesota and worked in the banking business in Oklahoma, where he met and married a young schoolmistress, Martha Little. It is evident that honor came before passion in their marriage, for Martha soon realized her incompatibility with her husband; she was snobbish, capable, and ambitious, while Smith seems to have been a decent but unstriving character. After ten years in Oklahoma, Smith resigned from the bank, and the family, including a second son, Robert Jefferson (born in 1917), moved to Florida to try their business prospects. But the Florida boom collapsed in the mid 1920s; Smith's professional hopes foundered and he became depressed and withdrawn. In addition, perhaps because he had come to feel emotionally dispossessed by his wife's strong, exclusive love for the children, Smith showed every sign of being dangerously unstable and fickle in his behavior. He committed suicide by shooting himself on 26 June 1926.

Berryman often regarded that event, which took place in his twelfth year, as the trauma of his life, and in later years he was obsessed with grief, self-identity, and psychological dislocation, as well as with questions of temporal and religious destiny, all of which infused his major poetry. His cast of mind construed affliction as a creative stimulant. Burdened by his mother's influence and dominance, he continually worried the neurotic conflict he believed his father's suicide had triggered. From time to time, in an effort to rationalize the tribulations which fed his poetry, he quizzed his mother for the truth about his father, but most of what she told him characterized Smith as a man deeply alien-nated, at a point of existential crisis, and irreme-diably selfish. Although Berryman often reckoned with the fact that his mother must have contributed to the sense of rejection Smith experienced, he mostly suppressed his own feeling of disaffection for her and so perpetuated the self-divisions which charged his best poetry. While self-dramatization galvanized his mature creative output—as late as 1970, he claimed that he retained "enough feel-ings" about his father to "dominate" *The Dream Songs*—he struggled through his personal life in a state of continual disequilibrium, rage and re-morse, relieved only by periods of exultation.

In Florida the Smiths had been befriended by a man named John Angus McAlpin Berryman. Late in 1926 he married Martha Smith, and the family presently moved to New York City. Young John, who duly adopted his stepfather's surname, attended the newly founded "jock" school, South Kent School in Connecticut, where he boarded for four years from 1928. At that time the school set the highest value on excellence in competitive sports, much more than on academic accomplish-ments, and it is clear that Berryman, who had all too little aptitude for the playing field, was griev-ously misplaced. He was subjected to an emotion-ally confusing existence which forced him to separate his natural abilities from his pretended ambitions and interests. Although he attained high academic success he had to do so while affecting self-disparagement and in the face of what amounted to the school's depreciation. He suffered from a certain amount of bullying, which provoked him to one suicide attempt on 7 March 1931, but his studiousness and cleverness, much encouraged by his mother, at last worked to his good: he was the first boy in the history of the school to bypass the sixth form and to go straight from the fifth into college.

At Columbia College of Columbia University in New York, he spent two years compensating to himself by becoming a great social success and a lion among the coeds, but his failure in one ex-amination shocked him so much that he soon made steadier academic progress. His mother played an enormously influential part in fostering his intel-lectual and creative talents, but it was the example and guidance of Mark Van Doren, who became a fatherly mentor, which finally fixed his ambitions. Berryman credited Van Doren as being "the pre-siding genius of all my work until my second year, when I fell under the influence of W. B. Yeats," and characterized his teaching as "strongly struc-

tured, lit with wit, leaving ample play for grace and charm. . . . It stuck steadily to its subject and was highly disciplined. . . . If during my stay at Colum-bia I had met only Mark Van Doren and his work, it would have been worth the trouble. It was the force of his example, for instance, that made me a poet." For his part, Van Doren remembered Ber-ryman as "first and last a literary youth: all of his thought sank into poetry, which he studied and wrote as if there were no other exercise for the human brain. Slender, abstracted, courteous, he lived one life alone, and walked with verse as in a trance." Berryman published several poems and reviews in the *Columbia Review,* and studied so hard that the dean of Columbia College eventually con-sidered him "conspicuously qualified . . . for aca-demic distinction."

He finally won the distinction of becoming Kellett Fellow, which enabled him to study for two years (1936-1938) at Clare College, Cambridge, where he worked under George Rylands and won the prestigious Oldham Shakespeare Scholarship in his second year. He met W. H. Auden in En-gland, befriended Dylan Thomas, whom he "half-adored" for "his intricate booms & indecent tales/ almost entirely untrue" (*Delusions, Etc.,* 1972), and received an audience with his hero W. B. Yeats, who left him, as he recorded at the time, with "an impression of tremendous but querulous force, a wandering intensely personal mind which resists natural bent (formal metaphysics by intuition, re-sponsible vision) to its own exhaustion." Also in England, he became engaged to a young woman, who visited him in New York when he returned there for the academic year 1938-1939, but the relationship could not last when she decided to stay in England for the duration of World War II.

While in England Berryman had determined to become a teacher, but he failed to gain a job on returning to New York and spent one year in a state of considerable nervous stress, writing poems (some of them were published in *Southern Review*), abortive plays, and book reviews for *New York Her-ald Tribune Books*. In 1939 he became for one year part-time poetry editor of the *Nation,* and took up an appointment as instructor in English at Wayne University in Detroit (now Wayne State University), where he lived and worked with a charismatic young friend, Bhain Campbell. A poet and Marxist, Campbell strove to inject some social and political consciousness into Berryman's apprentice poetry, but Berryman's early work manifests a concern with the craft of poetry—the dynamics of style, form, metrics—to the extent of neglecting content.

105

The strain of his year at Wayne caused Berryman to suffer from exhaustion and from attacks which were diagnosed as petit mal epilepsy. Furthermore, Bhain Campbell contracted cancer and died late in 1940, an event which caused Berryman a profound grief which he associated with the death of his father. In 1940 he began work as an instructor in English at Harvard University, and in 1942 he married his first wife, Eileen Patricia Mulligan, whose love and moral support for his work and whose sufferance of his increasingly bizarre neurotic drives kept them together for a period of more than ten years.

Berryman's earliest poems were first brought together, along with poems by Mary Barnard, Randall Jarrell, W. R. Moses, and George Marion O'Donnell, in *Five Young American Poets* (1940), and then in a slim volume of his own, *Poems* (1942). Most of the items in those first collections were written in 1939, and have been well characterized by Joel Conarroe as "ominous, flat, social, indistinctly allusive, exhausted . . . an echo chamber."

Eileen Mulligan, 1942 (courtesy of Eileen Simpson)

Well schooled and crafted, infused with a sense of loss and unlocated portentousness, they mostly fail to synthesize personal feeling and reflection, and have pretensions to the meditative poise Berryman valued in the poetry of Yeats's middle period. Too much in them is labored and realized only through rhetoric, so that even poems which figure sociopolitical subjects (prompted by Berryman's association with Bhain Campbell) bury the contemporary ills and evils they treat in specious gestures and solemn style. Conrad Aiken, R. P. Blackmur, Allen Tate, Oscar Williams, and John Crowe Ransom spotted the promise of Berryman and of Randall Jarrell in the group volume of 1940, and indeed certain poems, such as Berryman's "Winter Landscape," deserve their reward as anthology pieces. However, Berryman recognized at an early stage that he had been beguiled by literary influences, Yeats, Auden, and Delmore Schwartz being chief among them, and that both the forms and attitudes of his first published poems derived as much from works of literature as from subjects of real personal concern. "Desires of Men and Women," for example, might have been entitled "Variation on a Theme by Delmore Schwartz"; Berryman once pointed out that "the first line is a variant of his 'Tired and unhappy, you think of houses.' " (Likewise, what really interested Berryman about "The Animal Trainer," a poem in two parts completed by March 1940 but published four years later, was that its form derived from poems by Conrad Aiken and Bhain Campbell.) Berryman struggled to find his own voice throughout the 1940s, trying all the while to break away from the dominant influence of Yeats on what he called "the compositional base" of his poems. Since he protractedly worried the claims of literature over life—he once wondered "what day of mere living presents so rich & complicated an experience" as the life of literature—it is ironic that his greatest achievements as a poet finally came from fashioning the literature of life.

In 1943 he started teaching as an instructor in English at Princeton University, where he worked under another of his heroes, Richard Blackmur, and numbered among his talented students W. S. Merwin, Frederick Buechner, and William Arrowsmith. Berryman showed great respect and affection for Blackmur, Frederick Buechner recalls: "Blackmur seemed an old gull drying his wise wings in the sun, Berryman a sandpiper skittering along the edge of the tide." Princeton was Berryman's home for the next decade, and his circle of friends expanded markedly during that time. After his initial period of teaching, in 1944 he un-

The sun rushed up the sky, the taxi flew.
There was a kind of fever on the clock
That morning. We arrived at Waterloo
With time to spare and couldn't find my track.

The bitter coffee in a small café
Gave us our conversation. When the train
Began to move I saw you turn away
And vanish, and the vessels in my brain

Burst, the train roared, the other travellers
In flames leapt, burning on the tilted air
Cut si cruccia. I heard the devils curse
And shriek with joy in that place beyond prayer.

Fair copy of "Parting as Descent," Five Young American Poets, *published by New Directions in 1940 (from* Homage to Mistress Bradstreet and Other Poems, *copyright © 1968 by John Berryman; reprinted by permission of Farrar, Straus & Giroux, Inc.; courtesy of Thomas Cooper Library, University of South Carolina)* dertook a two-and-a-half-year stretch of independent research in Shakespearean textual criticism (supported by a Rockefeller Foundation research fellowship, he virtually completed an edition of *King Lear* which has never been published) before he was again appointed to the teaching faculty in 1946. He was successively associate in creative writing, resident fellow in creative writing, and Alfred Hodder Fellow and became a conspicuously successful teacher with a charisma that awed his students. Those students and other friends who were closest to him nonetheless discerned the psychological pressure and pain under which he labored, a restlessness of the spirit coupled with a deep despair of himself. At Harvard University from 1940 to 1943 he had suffered a more oppressive intellectual climate, from much of which (unlike his colleague Delmore Schwartz) he had shielded himself, only to indulge in increasingly morbid and paralyzing self-appraisal. At Princeton long hours of isolated study caused him to brood more and more. His tolerance for personal and professional setbacks became lower than ever, and by the late 1940s he assumed a sort of second nature, a guise in which to face what he believed to be the overwhelming demands of his work and society. Many of his acquaintances saw his public role as that of an eccentric, a combination of braggart, womanizer, unpredictable drinker, and formidable—sometimes savagely assertive or dismissive—intellectual. In fact, whether intimidating or endearing, his behavior was often just the superficial aspect of a temperament that was all too often tormented by acute insecurity, self-recrimination, and self-exaction. To a degree, after 1947, Berryman came to hide his fears in drink. His diaries from the 1940s give the impression of a man stricken by neurosis and self-analysis, paradoxically sustaining himself by greater demands on the self, and too little evidence of the many happy times he enjoyed with his wife.

In 1948 William Sloane Associates published *The Dispossessed*, a volume of rhymed stanzaic poems burdened by feelings of hopelessness and confusion, wielding abstruse images and torturing syntax in an unrewarding fashion. It was characteristic of Berryman's desolated attitude during the early and mid 1940s that he should have followed in some verses the example and tone of Louis Aragon, especially as in *Le Crève-Coeur* (1941; Berryman later complained that he had been "conned" by Aragon), where a bitter sentimentality and sense of personal defeatism vis-à-vis World War II harmonized with Berryman's sense of affairs. He tended to see his

own inner conflicts mirrored in the European holocaust. Some of the poems of *The Dispossessed*, milling with inflated sentiment and opaque image, are virtually incomprehensible in whole or in part. The title poem, for instance, begins with a quotation from Luigi Pirandello and leads into a surrealistic assemblage of images; it is easy to miss the point that the poem actually concerns the dropping of the atomic bomb on Hiroshima—"an evil sky (where the umbrella bloomed)/twirled its mustaches." Joel Conarroe properly comments: "The humorless, abstract, often bloodless quality of much of the early work, inhibited even in an age of arid art, gives evidence of the price Berryman paid for rejecting the validity of his own sensory experience. . . . Berryman succeeds less well with the social-ironic speculative poem, by way of Auden, than with the personal lyric . . . that has its source in his own feelings." Contemporary reviewers understandably felt they could find little to praise in the collection, though a number of them expressed hopes for Berryman's future. While Randall Jarrell reasonably discovered "raw or overdone lines side by side with imaginative and satisfying ones" (*Nation*, 17 July 1948), Yvor Winters taxed Berryman's "disinclination to understand and discipline his emotions. Most of his poems appear to deal with a single all-inclusive topic: the desperate chaos, social, religious, philosophical, and psychological, of modern life, and the corresponding chaos and desperation of John Berryman" (*Hudson Review*, Fall 1948). However, one group of nine dramatic monologues, "The Nervous Songs" (which are to some extent influenced by Rainer Maria Rilke), stand out as psychologically vibrant dramas which prefigure Berryman's mature work. As Conarroe has written, "In its form, the three six-line stanzas with flexible rhyme schemes, and in its mood of intense auto-revelation, the sequence is an important forerunner of *The Dream Songs*."

The year 1947, however, had finally brought contingent reality directly into the center of Berryman's creative life. He had an illicit affair with a woman to whom he gave the pseudonym Lise and wrote a running commentary on its progress in the form of a sequence of sonnets which were published only twenty years later as *Berryman's Sonnets* (1967). The sonnets use a Petrarchan rhyme scheme, much archaic or antic diction, and dislocated syntax (which at best reflects the turbulence of the poet's moods and at worst draws attention to itself as factitious and gauche). The sequence in some ways corresponds to a traditional and perhaps artificial scheme—moving from hope and anxiety through dangerous and guilty fulfillment to withdrawal and reproach—but that paradigmatic design was in fact fortuitous, for the sequence at all stages logs the actuality of the affair. *Berryman's Sonnets* provides an inventory of the poet's being, mind, and moods, at stages on a blind road. Berryman quickly assumed the role of a spectator of his own drama, and the sonnets served appetite as much as satisfaction. He became at once obsessively "in love" with his mistress and self-consciously withdrawn, exercising a double consciousness which left a discrete gap between the man who experienced and suffered and the writer who evaluated and composed emotion into a literary artifact.

Since circumstances kept Berryman and Lise apart for much of the summer, he was often compelled to fashion an image of her, a myth, drawing on imaginative invention and on literary analogues. Accordingly, the sonnets sometimes fall short of what Roy Pascal has called a "correlative in the outer world" (*Design and Truth in Autobiography,* 1960). Berryman leaned toward literature to find models of his love, sometimes with a consequent excess of self-regard. In sonnet 75, he compares himself to Petrarch, in 29 to Honoré de Balzac, in 21 to David in relation with Bathsheba; sonnet 16 was suggested by Philip Sidney's second sonnet to Stella. In other words, by comparing himself to well-known precursors in the role of adulterer or sonneteer, he was drawn to behold himself in the role of poet and to diminish attention to the lady. His literary self-consciousness is marked even in the first sonnet of the sequence—"I wished, all the mild days of middle March/ . . . your blond good-nature might/(Lady) admit . . ./Me to your story"—which alludes to Stéphane Mallarmé's poem "M'introduire dans ton histoire"; the first four lines of sonnet 102 (a poem, Berryman recorded in his journal, written on "15 August in the morning after my worst nightmare for months: a killer, mad") are a loose imitation of the first four lines of Tristan Corbière's poem "Heures"; sonnet 105 is a virtuoso performance prompted by a reading of the Grimms' tale "The Duration of Life." Likewise, the final line of sonnet 52 includes a slightly mistranscribed quotation from the last line—"Da ist meiner Liebsten Haus"—of Wilhelm Müller's "Wasserflut" ("The Water's Flow"), set to music, as part of *Winterreise,* by Franz Schubert: it is one of many private references in the sequence, for Berryman and Lise loved playing recordings of Schubert's song cycle together. A good deal of the obscurity and inscrutability of the sonnets may be attributed, not only to

the necessity of subterfuge and secrecy, but to the fact that much of their content and thematic linkage was the product of the poet's isolation from his love, compelling him to be self-conscious and literary. Many of the sonnets, he knew, were authentic in impulse but made insincere by artistic devices.

On the other hand, perhaps just as many were written in direct response to the lover, and they include the best of all the sonnets, which are fully charged with personal emotion, anguish, and poignancy, and communicate it to the reader. They served, like Jonathan Swift's *Journal to Stella* or Laurence Sterne's *Journal to Eliza,* as a way of imparting his feelings to Lise. In that sense the most accomplished sonnets were a form of homage, poems about as well as to his love. Berryman's journal entry for 16 July 1947, for instance, includes the sincere comments: "(. . . she is my *conscience* as well as my inspiration); four new sonnets, and even better (what I couldn't get peace for earlier) four old ones perfected—still I die of longing: if I hadn't faith in her I don't know what I would do." Milton Gilman points to the cold surface texture of many of the allusive sonnets, and perceptively argues that Lise "is, in a sense, the creative agent of every poem, the source of tone, rhythm, image, and theme." She is "a provisional deity. . . . The real center of interest is the increasingly complex psychological state of the speaker. . . . the *illicit* nature of the affair is so important in the Sonnets, providing an opportunity to release all kinds of feeling: lust, longing, scorn, guilt, pity, fatigue, despair, fear, impatience, joy."

Reviewers of *Berryman's Sonnets,* when they at last appeared in 1967, highlighted the importance of their style as laying the ground for Berryman's use of disrupted syntax in his major works, *Homage to Mistress Bradstreet* and *The Dream Songs,* where style—what Anthony Thwaite called in a review for the *New Statesman* (17 May 1968) the "awful spasmodics" of *Berryman's Sonnets*—is integrated with subject, functional and not gratuitous. But what is perhaps equally important about the achievement of *Berryman's Sonnets* is that they showed him the way to marry his creative gift to his life. The essence of Berryman's art and his literary success lay in his ability to tap and impart the deepest reaches of the human personality and consciousness.

Berryman's desire and guilt over the affair of 1947, and over other illicit affairs in the late 1940s, immediately charged the theme and form of his first major work, *Homage to Mistress Bradstreet,* which he began in 1948 and finished in 1953. A long poem of fifty-seven stanzas, with a complex metric and sophisticated rhyme scheme, it succeeds both as lyric and as drama, and has been called by Edmund Wilson "the most distinguished long poem by an American since *The Waste Land*." Berryman himself declared that he "set up the *Bradstreet* poem as an attack on *The Waste Land*: personality, and plot—no anthropology, no Tarot pack, no Wagner." He deplored Eliot's notion of the impersonality of the poet, and rather professed the "passionate sense of identification" he found in Walt Whitman.

Homage to Mistress Bradstreet employs an apparently objective scheme of two voices—the voice of Anne Bradstreet, the first poet of New England, and that of the "poet" who both conjures up the heroine and appears to be conjured up by her (since the poem largely follows the putative experiences of her life). Berryman's Bradstreet is rendered as an alienated, creative woman, rebellious against husband, father, and God. She registers a sense of spiritual and domestic displacement, bears a child, momentarily succumbs to the seductive blandishments of the "poet" who figures as a sort of demon lover, but then withdraws from him and moves forward into her declining years and death. The poem ends with a sense of historical quietus and fatalism. Much of the poem draws on the facts of the life of the real Anne Bradstreet, some of which are distorted, even perverted, for imaginative purposes which justifiably serve the work's major themes—religious apostasy, adulterous inclination, creative stultification, guilt, retribution, remorse—all of which match Berryman's personal obsessions. Berryman's own marriage and adulteries are sublimated in the poem, so that its fictive form actually speaks directly for the poet's passionate concerns. In depicting a relationship beyond space and time, Berryman deploys a conceptual device which transcends and encompasses subjective utterance and accordingly succeeds on a multiplicity of structural and thematic levels. In a sense *Homage to Mistress Bradstreet* does offer a personal confession and an exploration of its subject, but in a form which transfigures self-exhibition through art.

It may be fair, as John Frederick Nims wrote in a 1958 review, to judge that the poem stresses "a sort of depressing propaganda for the view that the flesh is evil," but it needs to be said that the poem is stylistically far more flexible (moving swiftly, for example, between moments of tenderness, triumph, hysteria, and pathos) than the limits Nims sets: "In Berryman's stanza everything is tense, numb, shivering, painful. . . . Throughout the poem I find this alternation of strength, gravity, even nobility with a shrill hectic fury, a whipped-up excitement, a maudlin violence of *mal protesi nervi*." (Berryman himself reasonably explained, "I was taking chances at the time of my poem. I had to get a language that was not hers, but not mine, but would *not be pastiche*, like Ben Jonson's projection of Spenser.") Nims's comments are as just as those by any other adverse critic of the poem (compare, for instance, the severely critical long essay "The Life of the Modern Poet," in the 23 February 1973 issue of the *Times Literary Supplement*), where the anonymous reviewer perceptively argues that "purportedly concerned with Anne Bradstreet, [Berryman's] poem is really about 'the poet' himself, his romantic and exacerbated personality, his sense of loneliness, his need for a mistress, confidante, confessor"; but his conclusion that Berryman "has too little human reality to sustain his myth" may be disputed by emphasizing the transcendent imaginative richness of the achievement.

Homage to Mistress Bradstreet, as one or two critics have pointed out, has some likeness to Robert Lowell's poem *Lord Weary's Castle* (1946), but any comparison necessarily fails in essentials: Berryman's poem is peculiar to himself in both style and concerns. He was undoubtedly correct when he observed, "In the Bradstreet poem, as I seized inspiration from [Saul Bellow's novel *The Adventures of Augie March* 1953], I sort of seized inspiration, I think, from Lowell, rather than imitated him." Berryman had befriended Lowell as early as 1944, and enthusiastically reviewed *Lord Weary's Castle* in 1947.

Lowell himself recalled that Berryman "was humorous, thrustingly vehement in liking . . . more adolescent than boyish. . . . Hyperenthusiasms made him a hot friend, and could also make him wearing to friends—one of his dearest, Delmore Schwartz, used to say that no one had John's loyalty, but you liked him to live in another city. . . . John could quote with vibrance to all lengths, even prose, even late Shakespeare, to show me what could be done with disrupted and mended syntax. This was the start of his real style."

There is no doubt that Berryman managed to be both fiercely loving and very competitive toward Lowell and other poets, but he invariably gave his love and kept the rivalry to himself. On the whole, he felt that his own achievements as a poet came second to Lowell's, as he wrote in an undated, not necessarily disingenuous letter to his mother shortly after Robert Frost's death in 1963: "Frost's going puts—as you wouldn't think it would—a

problem to me. I have never wanted to be king. . . .
I've been comfortable since 1946 with the feeling
that Lowell is far my superior. . . ."

Berryman's obsessional self-inquisition and
his growing dependence on alcohol (he first began
to drink heavily in 1947) put undue strains on his
private life, but it enabled him to develop a strong
sense of identification with what he discovered to
be (in a sometimes willful and not always strictly
scholarly way) the psychological problems of Stephen Crane. Reviewers received *Stephen Crane*
(1950), his critical biography, respectfully but on
the whole skeptically, for a number shared Graham
Greene's criticism of the book's "tortured prose"
and of Berryman's dubious use of depth psychology as a mode of literary criticism. Morgan Blum,
on the other hand, considered it a "flawed but distinguished book"—distinguished in its treatment of
the intersections between Crane's life and work.

Berryman's bravura teaching continued to
flourish: he taught at the University of Washington
in early 1950, and spent a most successful semester
as Elliston Professor of Poetry at the University of
Cincinnati in spring 1952. His endeavors as a
Shakespearean scholar (which at many stages of his
life he valued as highly as his work in poetry) and
his poetry writing were equally rewarded with a
Guggenheim Fellowship for critical study and for
creative writing, which enabled him to complete
Homage to Mistress Bradstreet. But his psychological
disturbances compelled him to seek the help of a
psychiatrist, whom he consulted at length in the
late 1940s and early 1950s, and he also spent some
time in group therapy. Moreover, the stresses of
his drinking, his anguished disposition, and his increasingly wayward conduct caused his first wife to
leave him at the end of a hectic summer in Europe
in 1953. Eileen Berryman Simpson has published
two books of her own, a worthy novel, *The Maze*
(1975), which is, according to one reviewer, "quite
transparently the story of the marriage's
breakup. . . . less satisfying as fiction than as biography," and a memoir, *Poets in Their Youth* (1982).

Berryman then taught in the Writers' Workshop at the University of Iowa in spring 1954 and
at Harvard University during that summer. ("He
taught by exemplitude," Edward Hoagland, who
studied under him at Harvard, has recalled. "He
talked mostly about books he had loved with a fever
that amounted to a kind of courage.") He returned
to the University of Iowa that fall, but he was
obliged to resign after a drunken altercation with
his landlord which resulted in a night's imprisonment. (His students in the Writers' Workshop in-

cluded W. D. Snodgrass, Donald Justice, William
Dickey, and Jane Cooper.) Allen Tate, whom he
had regarded as a master since they first met at
Columbia in 1935, saved the situation by inviting
him to Minneapolis ("Site without history!" Berryman ironically invoked the city in one of his late
poems, "Mpls, Mother"), where he started teaching
courses in humanities in 1955. It was in Minneapolis that Berryman became fast friends with Saul
Bellow, whom he always looked to as a model of
literary style and energy. In 1956 he married Elizabeth Ann Levine, who bore him a son, Paul, the
following year, but the relationship fared badly and
ended in divorce in 1959.

Berryman's sense of personal dereliction led
him to undertake a long period of dream analysis
on his arrival in Minneapolis, and to embark upon
the greatest work of his career, *The Dream Songs*,
first published in two parts, *77 Dream Songs* (1964)
and *His Toy, His Dream, His Rest* (1968).

"I set up *The Dream Songs* as hostile to every
visible tendency in both American and English poetry," Berryman later declared. "The aim was . . .
the reproduction or invention of the motions of a
human personality, free and determined. . . ." *The
Dream Songs* is a long poem of 385 sections, each
(with small exceptions) being composed of three
six-line stanzas, which deal with the multitudinous
preoccupations and adventures, notions, and emotions, of a persona named Henry (alias Henry Pussycat, Henry House, Mr. Bones). Henry is now and
then challenged and ineffectually corrected by an
unidentified friend, his interlocutor. It is neither a
narrative nor a philosophical poem, but a poem to
which Berryman opened his entire mind and being,
acts and eventualities, high thoughts and dark obsessions. Berryman once announced that poetry
aims "at the reformation of the poet, as prayer
does. In the grand cases—as, in our century—Yeats
and Eliot—it enables the poet gradually, again and
again, to become almost another man. . . ." He
therefore declared that Henry was not himself, the
poet, but "a white American in early middle age
sometimes in blackface, who has suffered an irreversible loss and talks about himself sometimes in
the first person, sometimes in the third, and sometimes even in the second." The shifting pronominal
identification of Henry (who *is* obviously, to all in-
tents and purposes, Berryman himself) became a
function of Berryman's self-exploration, an ironic
device which throws character and attitude free of
solipsism or egotism. Berryman told Jane Howard
that "the various parts of [Henry's] identity are
fluid. They slide, and the reader is made to guess

who is talking to whom. Out of this ambiguity arises richness. The reader becomes more aware, is forced to enter into himself."

The device of splitting facets of himself into dramatis personae owed much to Freud's analysis of ego and id, and to the classical opposition of alazon and eiron (the egoistic and pretentious man confronted by an ironic man who staggers self-possession), but also to an insight which Berryman independently perceived but later found rehearsed by W. H. Auden in "Balaam and His Ass" (*The Dyer's Hand,* 1963): "To present artistically a human personality in its full depth, its inner dialectic, its self-disclosure and self-concealment, through the medium of a single character is almost impossible."

In an interview dating from 1963, Berryman said, "I have an anti-hero in [*The Dream Songs*] who's a character the world gives a hard time to." The poem is often obscure and abstruse, especially in *77 Dream Songs,* with private references and arcane allusions; it also uses daring and lively syntax, and a mixed diction including what the poet himself called "coon talk." Such a motley style owes much

Elizabeth Ann, John, and Paul Berryman, 1957 (courtesy of Princeton University Library)

to a tradition which reaches back through the ethos, rhythms, and attitudes of the blues to the minstrel tradition. Berryman himself pinpointed one source of his inspiration in the figure of Thomas Dartmouth Rice, a white actor of the early-nineteenth century who mimicked a black—"Jim Crow"—so finely that he managed to transform painful dispossession into art. Berryman identified with the social and spiritual underdog, and his Henry in a black mask expresses his own pain and pathos in a mode which extends beyond egotism and embraces other outcasts. Minstrelsy, as William Wasserstrom has written, "represents the climactic and synoptic solution to the poet's 'long, often back-breaking search for an inclusive style, a style that could use his erudition,' Robert Lowell says, and 'catch the high, even frenetic, intensity of his experience, disgusts and enthusiasm.' "

The Dream Songs, which Berryman called an epic, is a poem as ambitious as Walt Whitman's *Song of Myself,* William Carlos Williams's *Paterson,* or Hart Crane's *The Bridge,* but unlike *Song of Myself,* for instance, it proposes no system. It contains and bodies forth a personality, and philosophical and theological notions, but it is above all a pragmatic poem, essaying ideas and emotions, love, lust, lament, grief. Several of the finest poems are elegies for fellow poets—Delmore Schwartz, Randall Jarrell, Theodore Roethke, Sylvia Plath—and certain key songs compass Berryman's ambivalent feelings for his dead father. "Always," Kenneth Connelly has written, "Henry stands above his 'father's grave with rage,' resentful, compassionate, jealous, accusing, finally gaining the courage to spit upon it. (The mystery of a careless earthly father modulates inevitably into Henry's analogous broodings over the Heavenly Father and his family, provoking some of the most brilliant religious poems of our time.)" Through the persona of Henry, Berryman, as Wasserstrom expresses it, "synthesizes all fragments of the self [and] helps the self to mediate, accommodate, comply and in this way avoid all menace of extinction."

Berryman believed that feelings might be imaginatively controlled in the order of art, and hoped that *The Dream Songs* might be as useful to the reader as to himself. "These Songs are not meant to be understood, you understand./They are only meant to terrify & comfort." He felt that Whitman's *Song of Myself* was a poem that "will do good to us," and the same may be true of *The Dream Songs,* which is by turns highly comic and savagely painful. It also has inevitable weaknesses and faults, one of which is perhaps not unlike the fault Berryman found in *Song of Myself* when he described it as "too idiosyncratic, like *Paradise Lost,* to rank with the very best poems. . . ." A number of critics have objected to Berryman's "abuse" of syntax, the whirligig of his demotic and literary diction (Robert Lowell found himself "rattled" by "mannerisms"), and what Denis Donoghue has called his "hotspur materials." However, a larger area of unrest, which Berryman always shared, concerns the shape and structure of *The Dream Songs,* epic or otherwise. Berryman continually attempted to model his poem on traditional epic structures, including Dante's *Divine Comedy,* the liturgy of the Bible, and the *Iliad,* and included a group of poems in which the hero dies and visits the underworld (book four, the opus posthumous sequence which occupies the middle section of the poem, many critics consider to be among the finest of the songs; Robert Lowell told Berryman he considered book four "the crown of your wonderful work, witty, heartbreaking, all of a piece. . . . one of the lovely things in our literature"), but the nature of the songs entirely depended on the plotless fortunes of Berryman's own life during the thirteen years of writing. The "individual human soul under stress" to which he referred in a 1970 conversation with Richard Kostelanetz is that of Berryman as Henry; Berryman could no more map the poem to a prefigured narrative or philosophical conclusion than he could forecast the luck of his own life, as he virtually acknowledged in an interview for the *Paris Review:* "I was what you might call open-ended. That is to say, Henry to some extent was in the situation that we are all in in actual life—namely, he didn't know and I didn't know what the bloody fucking hell was going to happen next. Whatever it was he had to confront it and get through."

Song 311 gives us both the poet's predicament and his procedure:

Hunger was constitutional with him,
women, cigarettes, liquor, need need need
until he went to pieces.
The pieces sat up & wrote. They did not heed
their piecedom but kept very quietly on
among the chaos.

The dissociated "pieces," as Denis Donoghue has explained, go to make up the whole of the man and his work: "This is not Whitman's way. Whitman's aesthetic implies that the self is the sum of its experiences, not the sum of its dissociated fragments. . . ." In a 29 April 1962 letter to Robert Lowell, Berryman worried that the songs "are partly

independent but only if . . . the reader is familiar with Henry's tone, personality, friend, activities; otherwise, in small numbers, they seem simply crazy . . . ," but many good critics have demonstrated not only the folly of accusing the poem of confessional self-indulgence and disorder but also that what Berryman thought a weakness is actually a strength. Adrienne Rich, for instance (in a review Berryman called "the most serious study any large area of my work's ever had"), observed, "first of all, the presence through the book of an effective unifying identity, and second, the power of that identity to define its surroundings so accurately. . . . a truly original work, in the sense in which Berryman has made one, is superior in inner necessity and by the force of a unique human character."

Berryman fought hard to finish *The Dream Songs,* and incorporated into it all the adventures, observations, and vicissitudes of his life. In 1957, for instance, he undertook a successful but exhausting lecture tour of India, which gave him acute insights into a foreign culture. At home in Minneapolis the disestablishment of the department of interdisciplinary studies in 1958 sustained his sense that his professional life would always be hapless and harrowing. He nonetheless fully committed himself (for the rest of his life, as it turned out) to teaching in the humanities program at the University of Minnesota, and developed a spectacular pedagogical style, ardent and terrified, and accentuated by the problems of alcoholism. The *Minneapolis Star* reported after his death: "In the classroom, Berryman was electrifying. . . . When he was wrapped up in a lecture—and he usually was, whatever the specific topic—he would stalk from one side of the room to the other, now whispering, now bellowing, invariably trembling with emotion and perspiring freely." His academic career reached a peak in 1969, when he was appointed Regents' Professor of Humanities, a distinction which left him far more humbled than conceited, and Drake University conferred on him an honorary doctorate. He also became a formidably successful performer in the role of public bard, and in his last decade he gave many campus readings at which his voice was by turns thick with drink, engagingly bombastic, and even menacing. His audiences found him thrilling, alarming, exhilarating, ripe with quips and asides. Jane Howard's profile of the poet (*Life,* 21 July 1967) served as much as any other report of the 1960s to sell Berryman in an image reminiscent of Dylan Thomas; she perfectly reflected the eccentric style—sensa-

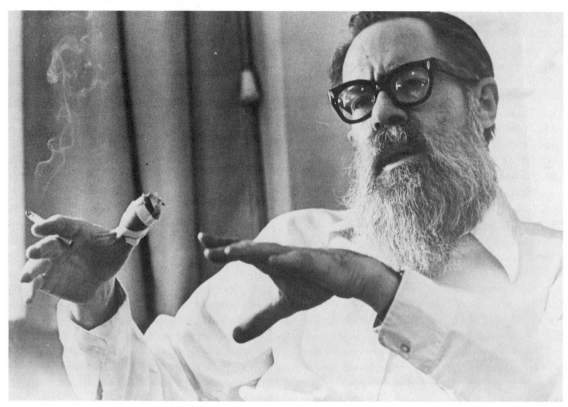

John Berryman (photograph by Michael Chikiris)

tional, temperamental, learned—he had encouraged in his conduct. William Heyen, Berryman's host at a visit to the Brockport Writers Forum in 1970, likewise described him as "Charming, disputatious, dominating, brilliant." Like Samuel Johnson, however, Berryman always felt the anxieties of fame, and sustained himself with equal parts of arrogance, self-irony, and terror.

He gained much happiness and a focus for his personal life when he married his third and last wife, Kathleen (Kate) Donahue, in 1961. Three years later they managed to buy a modest house, the first and last home Berryman ever owned, on Arthur Avenue in Minneapolis. The couple had two children, Martha in 1962 and Sarah Rebecca in 1971. In 1966-1967 the family lived on a Guggenheim Fellowship in Dublin, where Berryman passed long hours drinking but finally assembled *The Dream Songs.* The conclusion of that poem after thirteen years of work could not be but a great loss to him, for reasons he might have known when he recalled (in "A Tribute," *Agenda*, 4, 1965) how he had once pressed T. S. Eliot to urge Ezra Pound to finish *The Cantos:* " 'Oh no,' Eliot said gravely, 'I could never do that. That would be the end of him. He would have nothing to do.' I did not then like

this attitude but it was right and I was wrong."

The consensus of critical opinion on Berryman's next volume of poetry, *Love & Fame* (1970), is that it marks a falling off in inspiration and technique, an unfortunate return to the lyric form. Wistful for the ambition and scope of his major works, even Berryman registered the inevitable limits of his latest venture: "if I keep on writing lyric poems, that's all I'll be doing, I'm going to run out sooner or later." Half of *Love & Fame* consists of autobiographical poems, which Robert Lowell considered "profane and often in bad taste, the license of John's old college dates recollected at fifty." Quite apart from the question of "bad taste" (which several reviewers impugned), the lyrics are in fact compellingly accessible, witty, and often ironic. The volume acquired a fortuitously ironic structure when Berryman ended it with "Eleven Addresses to the Lord," a group of lyrics which reaffirm a querulous and ambiguous religious faith—"I only as far as gratitude & awe/confidently & absolutely go"—and require the reader to measure the secular and lubricious poems which precede them only in the context of the book as a whole. One reviewer, Walter Clemons, gave this perceptive and generous construction of *Love &*

Fame: "Some of those poems are very hard to take. Behind a coarse jocularity, a desperate man was trying to cheer himself up, I thought when I first read and disliked them. I now think he was deliberately caricaturing, in bold poster colors, the bumptious, lost eagerness of his youth." However, no reader can afford to overlook the cautionary irony of Robert Lowell's comment that Berryman may have found his autobiographical excursions "too inspiring and less a breaking of new ground than he knew."

As with all Berryman's major works, the writing of *Love & Fame* ran in tandem with the experience of his life. He recovered his faith in Christ while undergoing treatment for alcoholism in 1970. He had suffered from alcoholism for more than twenty years, and first took steps to recover in 1969. The lessons he learned during two courses of treatment at St. Mary's Hospital, Minneapolis, in 1970, which included his conviction that a "God of rescue" had interceded in his life, established him as a recovering alcoholic but also left him feeling perilously self-exposed. He tried hard to take a stable view of his anguished sensibility and of his disturbed career (which he too often insisted on dating back to his father's suicide), but years of sickness and waste of spirit had taken their toll. Berryman's "late conversion," Douglas Dunn has saliently written, "proves the honesty of his anguish at the cruelty of the world, the competition without kindness. Yet it derives from fatigue."

Berryman drafted an autobiographical novel about the process of becoming a recovering alcoholic, but most critics have judged that the unfinished *Recovery* (1973) stands as an extraordinary and readable document about Berryman himself rather than as a fully realized work of literary art. He also completed a last book of poems, *Delusions, Etc.* (1972), but it fails on the whole to embody the passionate intensity of his best work, despite the undoubted success of certain poems—the idiosyncratic relish, for example, of "Beethoven Triumphant" and "Scholars at the Orchid Pavilion," the fierce identification of "Drugs Alcohol Little Sister" and "Tampa Stomp," and the poignant lament of "He Resigns." As the anonymous author of "The Life of the Modern Poet" (*Times Literary Supplement,* 23 February 1973) has written, "The last books have an intense but narrowly documentary appeal," and represent "the brave valediction of a man who chose his own way to die." In 1971 Berryman won a Senior Fellowship from the National Endowment for the Humanities in order to complete a critical biography, "Shakespeare's Reality,"

but he would not live to do so. He found that he no longer had the patience or energy for persevering with his writing, and ultimately that his capacity had failed; he committed suicide by jumping from the Washington Avenue Bridge in Minneapolis on 7 January 1972.

Berryman spent himself in his dedication to the work of poetry, as Daniel Hughes, who witnessed him at his desk in the early 1960s, observes: "I have never seen before or since such concentration. . . . I felt the presences of his terrible cost and commitment, and I loved him." When an interviewer asked him in 1965 to state the most important elements of good poetry, he replied, "Imagination, love, intellect—and pain. Yes, you've got to know pain." In at least one other interview Berryman seemed to find self-gratification in his "overdevelopment of sensibility"—"It's the price we pay," he announced. But whatever strain of misplaced and painfully ironic complacency that observation contains need not condition our reading of his best creative work, in which he found a dynamic form and style to make art of his life and obsessions. *Homage to Mistress Bradstreet* offers a remarkably imagined and densely achieved drama, with conceptual vigor and intricate execution, and deserves the praise it received from Edmund Wilson, Conrad Aiken, and Robert Lowell. That poem and *The Dream Songs* survive as the supreme achievements of a poet who believed that the essence of poetry is "the expression of emotion in action," and that "Art is created out of ordeal and crisis." Despite its vaunted difficulty and occasional weakness—local incoherence, word thickness, stylistic obscurity—*The Dream Songs* is a richly imagined and moving work. Berryman also merits attention as one of the most notable religious poets of recent years. In addition, what many of his last poems do fulfill is Berryman's own prescription that "Some of the best writing is really transparent. . . . The artist just says what he thinks, or says how he feels. . . . The art comes just in placing, pure syntax."

It is worth emphasizing the word *heroic* in Robert Lowell's claim that *The Dream Songs* is "the single most heroic work in English poetry since the War, since Ezra Pound's *Pisan Cantos*." Any discussion of literary history since World War II will also need to take account of the fact that *The Dream Songs* manifestly inspired Lowell to emulate Berryman's achievement with his own *Notebook* (1969), a work he subsequently refashioned and (according to some critics) weakened by imposing on it an overtly chronological and possibly lame form in its revised version, *History* (1973).

Interviews:

Jonathan Sisson, "My Whiskers Fly: An Interview with John Berryman," *Ivory Tower,* 14 (3 October 1966): 14-18, 34-35;

Jane Howard, "Whiskey and Ink, Whiskey and Ink," *Life,* 63 (21 July 1967): 67-68, 70, 73-76;

Elizabeth Nussbaum, "Berryman and Tate: Poets Extraordinaire," *Minnesota Daily,* 9 November 1967, pp. 7, 10;

John Plotz and others, "An Interview with John Berryman," *Harvard Advocate,* 103 (Spring 1969): 4-9;

Richard Kostelanetz, "Conversation with John Berryman," *Massachusetts Review,* 11 (Spring 1970): 340-347;

Martin Berg, "A Truly Gentle Man Tightens and Paces: An Interview with John Berryman," *Minnesota Daily* (University of Minnesota), 20 January 1971, pp. 9, 10, 14-15, 17;

Peter A. Stitt, "The Art of Poetry XVI: John Berryman 1914-1972," *Paris Review,* 14 (Winter 1972): 176-207;

William Heyen, "John Berryman: A Memoir and an Interview," *Ohio Review,* 15 (Winter 1974): 46-65.

Bibliographies:

Richard J. Kelly, *John Berryman: A Checklist* (Metuchen, N.J.: Scarecrow Press, 1972);
Contains a chronology and lists of works by and about Berryman. Preface includes a brief memoir of the author.

Ernest C. Stefanik, Jr., *John Berryman: A Descriptive Bibliography* (Pittsburgh: University of Pittsburgh Press, 1974);
Extensive list of works by Berryman. This detailed publication has two appendices and has no listing of works about Berryman.

Gary Q. Arpin, *John Berryman: A Reference Guide* (Boston, Mass.: G. K. Hall, 1976);
Includes works by and about the author and annotations are detailed.

Biographies:

John Haffenden, *The Life of John Berryman* (London & Boston: Routledge & Kegan Paul, 1982);

Eileen Simpson, *Poets in Their Youth* (New York: Random House, 1982; London: Faber & Faber, 1982).

References:

Conrad Aiken, "A Letter," *Harvard Advocate,* 103 (Spring 1969): 23;
Includes praise for *His Toy, His Dream, His Rest* and describes *The Dream Songs.*

John Bayley, "John Berryman: A Question of Imperial Sway," in *Contemporary Poetry in America,* edited by Robert Boyers (New York: Schocken, 1974), pp. 59-77;
Describes the relationship between Berryman and Henry in *The Dream Songs.*

Edward Butscher, "John Berryman: In Memorial Perspective," *Georgia Review,* 27 (Winter 1973): 518-525;
Focuses on *The Dream Songs* and discusses the poem's view of America's international role.

Walter Clemons, "Man on a Tightrope," review of *Delusions, Etc., Newsweek,* 79 (1 May 1972): 113-114;
Describes Berryman's career and concentrates on his last poems.

Joel Conarroe, "After Mr. Bones: John Berryman's Last Poems," review of *Delusions, Etc., Hollins Critic,* 13 (October 1976): 1-12;
Discusses the characteristics of Berryman's later work.

Conarroe, *John Berryman: An Introduction to the Poetry* (New York: Columbia University Press, 1977);
An overview of the poet's work.

Kenneth Connelly, "Henry Pussycat, He Come Home Good," review of *His Toy, His Dream, His Rest, Yale Review,* 58 (Spring 1969): 419-427;
Credits Joyce with influencing Berryman in this review of *His Day, His Dream, His Rest.*

Martin Dodsworth, "John Berryman: An Introduction," in *The Survival of Poetry,* edited by Dodsworth (London: Faber & Faber, 1970), pp. 100-132;
Describes the author's work as being a part of the Symbolist movement. Discusses *The Dream*

Songs as an acceptance of the state of the world.

Denis Donoghue, "Berryman's Long Dream," review of *The Dream Songs, Art International,* 13 (20 March 1969): 61-64;
Discusses Berryman's oneness with the character Henry and describes Dream Song 385, in which Berryman is separate from him.

Douglas Dunn, "Gaiety & Lamentation: The Defeat of John Berryman," *Encounter,* 43 (August 1974): 72-77;
Describes the poet's career, specifically *The Dream Songs.*

Milton Gilman, "Berryman and the Sonnets," review of *Berryman's Sonnets, Chelsea,* 22/23 (June 1968): 158-169;
Discusses *Berryman's Sonnets* in terms of the poet's growth during his involvement with a mistress.

John Haffenden, *John Berryman: A Critical Commentary* (London: Macmillan, 1980; New York: New York University Press, 1980);
A detailed description of the poet's work.

Alan Holder, "Anne Bradstreet Resurrected," *Concerning Poetry,* 2 (Spring 1969): 11-18;
An article on *Homage to Mistress Bradstreet* which claims a lack of historical accuracy.

Randall Jarrell, "Verse Chronicle," *Nation,* 168 (17 July 1948): 80-81;
Reviews *The Dispossessed* and praises Berryman's evolution as a poet.

"The Life of the Modern Poet," *Times Literary Supplement,* 23 February 1973, pp. 193-195;
Discusses Berryman's career and reviews *Delusions, Etc.*

J. M. Linebarger, "A Commentary on *Berryman's Sonnets,*" *John Berryman Studies,* 1 (January 1975): 13-24;
Discusses each sonnet individually and identifies their cultural allusions.

Linebarger, *John Berryman* (New York: Twayne, 1974);
A full-length study of Berryman's poetry—its development and major themes.

Robert Lowell, "For John Berryman," *New York Review of Books,* 6 April 1972, pp. 3-4;
Memoir which discusses the poet and his experiences with Lowell.

Lowell, "The Poetry of John Berryman," *New York Review of Books,* 28 May 1964, pp. 2-3;
Reviews *77 Dream Songs* and discusses the strengths and weaknesses of Berryman's style.

William J. Martz, *John Berryman* (Minneapolis: University of Minnesota Press, 1969);
A monograph which is divided chronologically into two parts—before and after the syntactic shifts of *Homage to Mistress Bradstreet.*

Edward Mendelson, "How to Read Berryman's *Dream Songs,*" in *American Poetry Since 1960,* edited by Robert B. Shaw (Cheadle Hulme, Cheshire: Carcanet Press, 1973), pp. 29-43;
Discusses the successes and failures of *The Dream Songs.*

John Frederick Nims, "Homage in Measure to Mr. Berryman," review of *Homage to Mistress Bradstreet, Prairie Schooner,* 32 (Spring 1958): 1-7;
Describes the themes, accomplishments, and problems of *Homage to Mistress Bradstreet.*

Sergio Perosa, "A Commentary on *Homage to Mistress Bradstreet,*" *John Berryman Studies,* 2 (Winter 1976): 4-25;
A detailed discussion of the poem.

Adrienne Rich, "Mr. Bones, He Lives," review of *77 Dream Songs, Nation,* 198 (25 May 1964): 538, 540;
Describes the character of Henry and praises the poet's lyrical voice.

Ernest C. Stefanik, "A Cursing Glory: John Berryman's *Love & Fame,*" *Renascence,* 25 (Summer 1973): 115-127;
Claims that fuller meaning may be given to the poems when they are read individually, rather than as a collection.

William Wasserstrom, "Cagey John: Berryman as Medicine Man," review of *His Toy, His Dream, His Rest, Centennial Review,* 12 (Summer 1968): 334-354;
Compares Crane's Henrys with Berryman's Henry and discusses the themes and structure of *77 Dream Songs.*

Yvor Winters, "Three Poets," *Hudson Review,* 1 (Autumn 1948): 404-405;
　Reviews *The Dispossessed* and urges Berryman to develop his talent for language.

Papers:
The John Berryman Papers are owned by University of Minnesota Libraries.

Gwendolyn Brooks

*This entry was updated by Charles Israel (Columbia College) from his entry in DLB 5,
American Poets Since World War II.*

Places	Chicago	Africa	
Influences and Relationships	Don Lee Langston Hughes	Malcolm X LeRoi Jones (Amiri Baraka)	Robert Frost Walt Whitman
Literary Movements and Forms	Black Protest Literature	Realism	
Major Themes	Lives of American Blacks Family Life	War Social Injustice	Racism Black Ghettos
Cultural and Artistic Influences	Civil Rights Movement	Black Power Movement	
Social and Economic Influences	Poverty Family Life	Racism	War

119

BIRTH: Topeka, Kansas, 7 June 1917, to Keziah Corinne Wims and David Anderson Brooks.

EDUCATION: Associate of Literature and Arts, Wilson Junior College, 1936.

MARRIAGE: 17 September 1939 to Henry L. Blakely (divorced); children: Henry L., Nora.

AWARDS: Guggenheim Fellowships, 1946, 1947; National Institute of Arts and Letters Award, 1946; Eunice Tietjens Memorial Prize (*Poetry* magazine), 1949; Pulitzer Prize for *Annie Allen,* 1950; Robert F. Ferguson Memorial Award (Friends of Literature) for *Selected Poems,* 1964; L.H.D., Columbia College, 1964; D.Litt., Lake Forest College, 1965; Anisfield-Wolf Award for *In The Mecca,* 1968; Poet Laureate of Illinois, 1969-   ; D.Litt., Brown University, 1974; Shelley Memorial Award, 1976.

SELECTED BOOKS: *A Street in Bronzeville* (New York: Harper, 1945);
Annie Allen (New York: Harper, 1949);
Maud Martha (New York: Harper, 1953);
Bronzeville Boys and Girls (New York: Harper, 1956);
The Bean Eaters (New York: Harper, 1960);
Selected Poems (New York: Harper & Row, 1963);
In The Mecca: Poems (New York: Harper & Row, 1968);
Riot (Detroit: Broadside Press, 1969);
Family Pictures (Detroit: Broadside Press, 1970);
Aloneness (Detroit: Broadside Press, 1971);
The World of Gwendolyn Brooks (New York: Harper & Row, 1971);
Report from Part One (Detroit: Broadside Press, 1972);
The Tiger Who Wore White Gloves (Chicago: Third World Press, 1974);
Beckonings (Detroit: Broadside Press, 1975);
Primer for Blacks (Chicago: Black Position Press, 1980);
To Disembark (Chicago: Third World Press, 1981).

OTHER: *A Broadside Treasury,* edited by Brooks (Detroit: Broadside Press, 1971);
Jump Bad: A New Chicago Anthology, edited by Brooks (Detroit: Broadside Press, 1971);
A Capsule Course in Black Poetry Writing, includes an essay by Brooks (Detroit: Broadside Press, 1975).

According to her autobiography, *Report from Part One* (1972), Gwendolyn Brooks was a shy and

(photo by Layle Silbert)

Gwen Brooks

sensitive schoolgirl who, while yearning for the glamour and popularity of some girls around her, spent her time in reading, in participating in a close family life, and in writing verse: "My mother says I began rhyming at seven. . . . *Of course* I would be a poet! *Was* a poet! Didn't I write a poem every day? Sometimes *two* poems?"

During the 1930s, Brooks served as publicity director for the NAACP Youth Council in Chicago. Since that time she has gone through school, marriage, the births of two children, divorce, and increasing renown to become a major voice in contemporary American poetry. She has had a varied and successful teaching career at Northeastern Illinois University, University of Wisconsin at Madison, Columbia College in Chicago, Elmhurst College in Elmhurst, Illinois, and City College, City University of New York, where she was Distinguished Professor of the Arts. She has also edited the *Black Position* magazine.

Brooks's first book of poetry, *A Street in Bronzeville,* was published in 1945. The first section contains vignettes of people like Pearl May Lee, De Witt Williams, and Satin-Legs Smith, ordinary citizens of the Bronzeville section of Chicago. These are people who live in dreams and frustration and who suffer poverty, deprivation, and the oppression of racism. She describes some of them:

> We are things of dry hours and the involuntary plan,
> Grayed in, and gray. "Dream" makes a giddy sound,
> > not strong
> Like "rent," "feeding a wife," "satisfying a man."

Here are street scenes, meetings at the beauty parlor, the sights of lonely old people forgotten and forgetting, whores on the prowl, cleaning women who resent their employers and employers who resent their cleaning women, funerals, abortions, wife beatings, rapes. The first section is a realistic portrait of life around the poet-observer, who is herself a part of the life she describes.

The second section of *A Street in Bronzeville* is composed of twelve off-rhyme sonnets under the general title of "Gay Chaps at the Bar." These poems are concerned with World War II and its impact on the nation. In "the white troops had their orders but the Negroes looked like men," Brooks writes of the irony of a race-divided nation forced to unify itself for war. The white troops have been told "to devise/A type of cold, a type of hooded gaze" in dealing with black soldiers, but

> These Negroes looked like men. Besides, it taxed
> Time and the temper to remember those
> Congenital iniquities that cause
> Disfavor of the darkness.

A Street in Bronzeville initiates the themes that would occupy Brooks for two decades: the search for dignity and happiness, the twin oppressions of racism and poverty, life in the American family, and the shock of war. Here can be found also the poetic forms that dominate her early work: the ballad, the sonnet, blank verse, quatrains, and free verse.

The influence of older American literature echoes throughout *A Street in Bronzeville*. In an interview with George Stavros, Brooks has called attention to the impact of Ralph Waldo Emerson, Robert Frost, T. S. Eliot, and Emily Dickinson on her early poetry. Walt Whitman's influence has been the strongest and most pervasive; Brooks frequently assumes the role of the "democratic" bard and takes up the post of spokesman for large groups of Americans.

Two Guggenheim fellowships and a grant from the National Institute of Arts and Letters allowed Brooks leisure to work on the poems for her second book, *Annie Allen* (1949). After a short memorial poem to Edward Bland, killed in World War II, the book moves to "Notes from the Childhood and Girlhood" of Annie Allen. The reader learns of Annie's parents, their establishment of order and certainty at home, of the death of an old relative, and of the moral and ethical lessons of Annie's youth. This information is followed by "The Anniad," a long mock-heroic poem in rhymed, seven-line stanzas. "The Anniad" tells of the maturation of "sweet and chocolate" Annie, of her loves and losses. This section of the book ends with a *sonnet-ballad*, a form of Brooks's invention that combines a colloquial love complaint and the formality of the Shakespearean sonnet.

"The Anniad" is followed by a section entitled "The Womanhood," which contains poems similar to many of the Bronzeville poems of everyday life. Brooks recognizes the apparent flimsiness of poetry when it is pitted against the ugly realities of poverty and neglect:

> What shall I give my children? Who are poor,
> Who are adjudged the leastwise of the land.
> Who are my sweetest lepers, who demand
> No velvet and no velvety velour;
>
> My hand is stuffed with mode, design, device.
> But I lack access to my proper stone.

She knows that the creation of poetry is satisfying, but she also realizes that there is a chasm between art and social problems, a chasm she later tries to bridge with a new kind of poetry.

In "Beverly Hills, Chicago," the "leastwise of the land" are set against wealthy suburbanites who "walk their golden gardens." The speaker of the poem is riding by the houses of the rich:

> Nobody is furious. Nobody hates these people.
> At least, nobody driving by in this car.
> It is only natural, however, that it should occur to us
> How much more fortunate they are than we are.
>
> We do not want them to have less.
> But it is only natural that we should think
> > we have not enough.
> We drive on, we drive on.
> When we speak to each other our voices are a little
> > gruff.

In *Annie Allen*, Brooks sees poverty as both sign and symbol of racism and injustice. She shows that poor people frequently conduct egocentric and fruitless searches for identity and certitude.

Annie Allen ends on a note of social protest, but it takes the form of a quiet request:

> Rise.
> Let us combine. There are no magics or elves
> Or timely godmothers to guide us. We are lost, must
> Wizard a track through our own screaming weed.

Brooks's next book of poetry for adults was *The Bean Eaters* (1960). The major theme of this book is that of the ghetto dwellers' quests for purpose and relief from aimlessness. Brooks catalogues the many ways her characters seek security: through identification with the heroes of western movies, through wearing flashy clothes, through religion, through integration of the races, and through careless and profligate living. Pursued to excess, these misdirected forays, these escapes, have one thing in common—failure. They are activities used momentarily to mask frightful uncertainty and insecurity. Brooks writes of these machinations with compassion mixed with heavy irony. The most famous of the quest poems from *The Bean Eaters* is "We Real Cool," subtitled "The Pool Players. Seven at the Golden Shovel," which ends:

> We
>
> Sing sin. We
> Thin gin. We
>
> Jazz June. We
> Die soon.

Brooks has said of these pool players: "They are supposedly dropouts. . . . These are people who are essentially saying, 'Kilroy is here. We *are*.' But they're a little uncertain of the strength of their identity. . . . I want to represent their basic uncertainty. . . ."

Another quest poem in this volume is "The Ballad of Rudolph Reed," the story of a black man who moves his family out of the ghetto (where he has heard "roaches/Falling like fat rain") to a white suburb "Where every room of many rooms/Will be full of room." Rudolph Reed and his family are "oaken," tough, insistent, malleable. Their white neighbors react to the "intrusion" of the black family, and on the third night of the Reeds' tenancy, a rock is thrown through the window of their house, wounding Rudolph's daughter Mabel. Rudolph is infuriated, and he runs from his house with a pistol and knife in his hands. He wounds

four white men before he is killed. The poem ends with this quatrain:

> Small Mabel whimpered all night long,
> For calling herself the cause.
> Her oak-eyed mother did no thing
> But change the bloody gauze.

Brooks has said that this melodramatic ballad tells of "the great yearning of man-in-misery for betterment, and his eventual irresistible reach for it."

Freedom is one of the final goals of the quest. In a world of alienation, war, fragmentation, and incertitude, Brooks makes the melancholy suggestion that often freedom is to be found only in death. The dedicatory poem of *The Bean Eaters*, written upon the death of her father, contains these lines:

> Now out upon the wide clean air
> My father's soul revives,
> All innocent of self-interest
> And the fear that strikes and strives.

Dust jacket for Brooks's 1963 collection of poems about social issues, reflecting her views about the civil rights movement

He who was Goodness, Gentleness,
And Dignity is free.

One of Brooks's main contentions at this point in her career is that political and social freedom for black people will tear down the walls between the races, that such freedom will bring relief from demeaning poverty and ignorance. It must be added, however, that in the most pessimistic moments in her early poetry, she suggests that freedom for black people is impossible in American society.

In an interview, George Stavros asked Brooks if her poetry was becoming more "socially aware." Her answer: "Many people hated *The Bean Eaters;* such people as would accuse me of forsaking lyricism for polemics despised *The Bean Eaters* because they said it was 'getting too social. Watch it, Miss Brooks!'"

Her next book, *Selected Poems* (1963), contains new poems that are primarily concerned with social issues and social protest. These poems reflect the burgeoning civil rights movement. "Riders to the Blood-Red Wrath" celebrates the Freedom Riders and others who worked for voter registration and other civil rights for blacks. Here, for the first time in Brooks's poetry, is the contrast between the "Old Freedom" of Africa and the slavery and injustice of America. "Still," she writes, "the terrors, the sufferings of my past have honed me into a better human being. Democracy and Christianity will rebegin with *me*." She envisions blacks and whites working together for racial justice; she calls this cooperation "the struggle which is in the interests of love in the largest sense . . .":

I,
My fellows, and those canny consorts of
Our spread hands in this contretemps-for-love
Ride into wrath, wraith and menagerie

To fail, to flourish, to wither or to win.
We lurch, distribute, we extend, begin.

Also included in the new poems are two noteworthy dedicatory poems to Robert Frost and Langston Hughes. Of Frost, Brooks writes,

There is a little lightning in his eyes.
Iron at the mouth.
His brows ride neither too far up nor down.
He is splendid. With a place to stand.

Some glowing in the common blood.

Some specialness within.

In the poem to Hughes, she defines the importance of his work:

In the breath
Of the holocaust he
Is helmsman, hatchet, headlight.
See
One restless in the exotic time! and ever,
Till the air is cured of its fever.

In The Mecca (1968) begins with the long title poem, a discursive story within a larger story, written mostly in free verse. The connecting narrative is the tale of Mrs. Sallie Smith's search for her lost daughter Pepita. The Smiths live in The Mecca, a dilapidated Chicago apartment building one square block in size. The larger story is composed of character studies of the denizens of The Mecca and is reminiscent of *A Street in Bronzeville* in its ironic portraits of urban lives. In her desperate search for Pepita, Sallie Smith encounters her neighbors and finds them selfishly locked into their own obsessions: here are the fraudulent "Prophet" who escapes life by fostering a crazy religion; the young woman who tries to escape The Mecca by dating a "Gentile boy" who eventually jilts her; "Way-out Morgan," who collects guns for some far-distant black revolution. These people have been so debased by poverty and oppression that they have lost even the most rudimentary human concern for others. They simply do not care what has happened to Pepita.

Sallie Smith's search ends in horror. Pepita has been raped and murdered. Brooks concludes the story in a controlled tone:

The murder of Pepita
looks at the Law unlovably. Jamaican
Edward denies and thrice denies a dealing
of any dimension with Mrs. Sallie's daughter
    Beneath his cot
a little woman lies in dust with roaches.
She never went to kindergarten.
She never learned that black is not beloved.
Was royalty when poised,
sly, at the A and P's fly-open door.
Will be royalty no more.
"I touch"—she said once—"petals of a rose.
A silky feeling through me goes!"
Her mother will try for roses.

"In The Mecca" shows a turning away from the "Democracy and Christianity" of "Riders to the

Blood-Red Wrath" and a deepening of Brooks's concern with social problems. The poem contains none of the smiling irony that informs so much of the earlier poetry but features instead a tone of impatience and determination.

"In The Mecca" also mentions an important new influence on Brooks's poetry and political thought:

> Don Lee wants
> not a various America.
> Don Lee wants
> a new nation
> under nothing;
> a physical light that waxes; he does not want to
> be exorcised, adjoining and revered
> ....
> wants
> new art and anthem; will
> want a new music screaming in the sun.

The last line is a prophecy of things to come in Brooks's poetry, a "new music" of the black revolution.

"In The Mecca" is followed by fourteen short poems, including an elegy for Malcolm X and "Two Dedications." The elegy ends:

> And in a soft and fundamental hour
> a sorcery devout and vertical
> beguiled the world.
>
> He opened us—
> Who was a key,
>
> Who was a man.

This poem points the new direction. The "sorcery," the beguiling force of Malcolm X, hints of the building of the black mystique that is the overriding theme of her later poetry.

"Two Dedications" tells of two kinds of Chicago life and two kinds of art. The first dedication is that of the Picasso statue in Chicago, unveiled on 15 August 1967, before a crowd of 50,000 people. "The Chicago Picasso," an occasional poem written at the request of Mayor Daley, emphasizes the cold reception given the statue: "Does man love Art? Man visits Art, but squirms./Art hurts."

By contrast, the Picasso poem's companion piece is "The Wall." The occasion for this poem is the unveiling of a mural, depicting "black dignity," painted on a "typical slum building." Brooks spoke at the 27 August 1967 dedication, as she reports in the poem:

> I mount the rattling wood. Walter
> says, "She is good." Says, "She
> our Sister is." In front of me
> hundreds of faces, red-brown, brown, black, ivory,
> yield to me hot trust, their yea and their Announce-
>   ment
> that they are ready to rile the high-flung ground.
> behind me, Paint.
> Heroes.
> No child has defiled
> the Heroes of this Wall this serious Appointment
> this still Wing
> this Scald this Flute this heavy Light this Hinge.

The crowd yells "Black Power" with upraised fists, and "All/worship the Wall." The fervor of the crowd and the heroic painting on the wall offer telling contrast to the sterility of the Picasso dedication.

The penultimate poem in *In The Mecca* is "The Sermon on the Warpland," prefaced by a quote from Ron Karenga: "The fact that we are black is

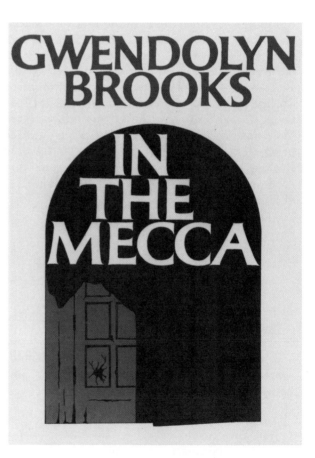

Dust jacket for Brooks's 1968 collection of poetry. The Mecca is a one-square-block apartment building that houses the subjects of her poem.

our ultimate reality." This aphorism may be taken as a solid announcement of the change in Brooks's attitudes toward her poetry and her life. *In The Mecca* is the last of her books published by Harper, ending a twenty-three-year association between poet and publisher. (In 1971 Harper published a miscellany, *The World of Gwendolyn Brooks*.) Her next book was published by a black-owned publishing firm, Broadside Press of Detroit. Of the change, she said, "I've been telling everybody who's black, 'You ought to have a black publisher,' and of course that was easy for me to say. I have left Harper not because of any difficulty therewith, but simply because my first duty is to the estimable, developing black publishing companies."

Two important events in Brooks's life are related to these changes in attitude and artistic direction. One was the Second Black Writers' Conference at Fisk University in 1967. Brooks writes,

> there I found what has stimulated my life these last three years: young people full of a new spirit. They seemed stronger and taller, ready to take on the challenges. Margaret Danner was there, another poet of my years, and she and I were both amazed to see what was happening. I was still saying "Negro," for instance. LeRoi Jones arrived during our double offering. He came in, and I said, "Ah, there's LeRoi Jones," and everybody just went mad. The audience wasn't quite aware yet that he was the new messiah, but he was very much adored. We walked around all that day, looking at these new tokens and feeling so excited.

The other event was the beginning of Brooks's association with the Blackstone Rangers, a large gang of teenaged blacks in Chicago. In the late 1960s she held a poetry workshop for the Rangers. Here she began a continuing intense interest in fostering the talents of young black poets. In one way, these new interests are not divorced from her earlier credo. Since 1967 she has directed her democratic mission, however, almost exclusively toward black people, and she has turned her missionary fervor toward black youngsters such as the Blackstone Rangers.

Brooks's commitment to black solidarity, community, and humane living, in her life and writings, was recognized by black writers in a public tribute on 28 December 1969, at the Afro-Arts Theater, on Chicago's South Side. From this celebration came a book, *To Gwen With Love* (1971), composed of testimonials (poems, stories, essays) by local black writers and those of note from all across the country.

Her trip to East Africa in 1971 cemented her commitment to both her African heritage and the Third World. The trip furnished her with an elaborate symbol for the disparity between life in America and life in Africa. In her autobiography, *Report from Part One*, she tells of her discovery. The scene is set in a Tanzanian game park:

> I experience Part One and Part Two. Part One: the animals are behind fencing; lions, the chimpanzee, monkeys, the baboon, deer; the wart hog—who looks at me so appealingly, with such tender, communicating eyes, and whose feelings must be hurt when a British-woman pushes her baby past him *fast*, rushing the buggy as if in terror, and screaming "OH, SO UGLY! What an UGLY face. Look at that UGLY *face*!" Part Two. No bars. No fencing. Animals living freely, "in their natural habitat." Lions, leopards, deer, graceful and majestic, walk in front of the Land Rover, taking their time, glancing at us or not, as they choose—but at no time afraid of us. Then lions, then deer, then *all* the animals, Sky, and hushing grass are harmony.

By implication, life for the black people of America is that of the cage, the fence, the enslavement, the chaining, while life for the African, Brooks suggests, is that of freedom, naturalness, and zest in living. In this mood of contrast, she concludes her African journal with this statement: "THE AFRICANS! They insist on calling themselves Africans and their little travelling brothers and sisters 'Afro-Americans' no matter *how* much we want them to recognize our kinship."

In 1969 Broadside Press published Brooks's thin book *Riot*, a stern declaration of her change of mind. In the title poem, a white protagonist, significantly named John Cabot, is forced to forsake the "good life" of ease and affluence when he is confronted by a race riot:

> "Don't let it touch me! the blackness! Lord!" he
> 　　　　　　　　　　　　　　　whispered
> 　　to any handy angel in the sky.
> John Cabot went down in the smoke and fire
> and broken glass and blood, and he cried "Lord!
> Forgive these nigguhs that know not what they do."

Riot dramatizes the "fire this time" and serves not as a warning but as a reminder of reality. It also depicts Brooks in her new role as spokesman for the revolution that will not wait. Her sympathies are with the rioters and the murdered looters, especially with a black woman looter dead in the riot, no longer a mother and lover. She has explained her new role: "I want to write poetry that will appeal to many, many blacks, not just the blacks who go to college but also those who have their customary habitat in taverns and the street. . . . anything I write is going to issue from a concern with and interest in blackness and its progress." The tools she chooses for the new mission are those of "ordinariness of language" and "story poems" and "loose rhythms."

In 1970 Brooks published *Family Pictures*. The first poem in the collection, "The Life of Lincoln West," is a free-verse ballad employing ordinary language and "loose rhythms." It tells the story of a young boy who is judged by a white man to be "Black, ugly, and odd." In one scene, a white man points out Lincoln as

> "One of the best
> examples of the specie. Not like
> those diluted Negroes you see so much of on
> the streets these days, but the
> real thing.
>
> Black, ugly, and odd. You
> can see the savagery. The blunt
> blankness. That is the real
> thing."

At the end of the poem Lincoln West turns the man's opprobrium into an asset:

> He told himself
> "After all, I'm the real thing."
>
> It comforted him.

In "To Keorapetse Kgositsile (Willie)," Brooks expresses a paranoiac fear of genocide, and she mentions a militant reaction to the threat:

> He teaches dolls and dynamite,
> Because he knows
> there is a scientific thinning of our ranks.
> Not merely Medgar Malcolm Martin and Black,
>   Panthers.
> but Susie. Cecil Williams. Azzie Jane.
> He teaches
> strategy and the straight aim;
> black volume;
> might of mind, black flare—

volcanoing merit, black
herohood.

In 1975 Brooks wrote an essay for Broadside Press's *A Capsule Course in Black Poetry Writing* in which she advises young black writers: "black literature is literature BY blacks, ABOUT blacks, directed TO blacks: ESSENTIAL black literature is the distillation of black life. Black life is different from white life. Different in nuance, different in 'nitty-gritty.' Different *from* birth. Different *at* death."

Also published in 1975, *Beckonings* contains thirteen new poems, some of which had been published in *Ebony*, *Broadside Series*, and *Black Scholar*. *Beckonings* could have been titled "Advice for Those Who Follow," for the tone of many of the poems is much like that of the essay in *A Capsule Course in Black Poetry Writing*. " 'When Handed a Lemon, Make Lemonade' " contains an ominous imperative.

> Do you know what to do with
> trouble, children?
> Make lemonade. Make lemonade.
> "Handed a lemon, make lemonade."

In "Boys. Black," Brooks chastises and implores:

> It is too easy to cry "ATTICA"
> and shock thy street,
> and purse thy mouth,
> and go home to thy "Gunsmoke."
> . . . .
> I tell you
> I love you
> and I trust You.
> Take my Faith.
> Make of my Faith an engine.
> Make of my Faith
> a Black Star. I am Beckoning.

The echo from Whitman in this poem is important because it defines Brooks's relationship to America. She takes the post of seer, but only in a limited sense; she proposes to be a seer for black people, a "Black Star."

Brooks's 1971 interview with Ida Lewis of *Essence* magazine helps explain her position: "I have certainly changed from where I was back in only 1967. I knew there were injustices, and I wrote about them, but I didn't know what was behind them. I didn't know what kind of society we live in. I didn't know it was all organized." She also speaks of her pre-1967 audience: "It was whites who were reading and listening to us [black writers], salving their consciences—our accusations didn't hurt too much." She concludes, "Whites are not going to understand what is happening in black literature today. Even those who want to sympathize with it still are not equipped to be proper critics." The point is that Brooks has turned away from the careful portraiture of early work to pursue a more emotional and personal type of polemic poetry. She explained that she is experimenting with new poetic forms and new attitudes to express her commitment to the cause of black unity.

In 1981 Brooks published a book of poems, *To Disembark,* composed of versions of the previously published poems "Riot," "Family Pictures," "To the Diaspora," and "Reckonings." Taken together, the poems serve as a continuing call for blacks to disengage from all that represents the oppressive atmosphere of white America. Brooks suggests in "Riot," as well as in the other poems, that this disengagement may require violent destruction and anarchy. The bitter, militant tone of this book caused one critic to label it a "distressing celebration of violence."

Bibliographies:

Jon N. Loff, "Gwendolyn Brooks: A Bibliography," *College Language Association Journal,* 17 (September 1973): 21-32;

Heidi L. Mahoney, "Selected Checklist of Material by and about Gwendolyn Brooks," *Negro American Literature Forum,* 8 (Summer 1974): 210-211.

References:

Houston A. Baker, Jr., *Singers of Daybreak: Studies in Black American Literature* (Washington, D.C.: Howard University Press, 1974), pp. 43-51;
The chapter on Brooks discusses her portrayal of the lives of "lower-echelon urban dwellers," with emphasis on her poems of social protest.

G. Leonard Bird, "Gwendolyn Brooks: Educator Extraordinaire," *Discourse,* 12 (Spring 1969): 158-166;
This essay is an extensive examination of the themes of *In The Mecca.*

Arthur P. Davis, "Gwendolyn Brooks: Poet of the Unheroic," *College Language Association Journal,* 7 (December 1963): 114-125;
An essay that argues that Brooks "appraises" rather than "condemns" the unheroic people she writes about.

William H. Hansell, "Gwendolyn Brooks's 'In the Mecca': A Rebirth into Blackness," *Negro American Literature Forum,* 8 (Summer 1974): 199-207;
Hansell sees *In The Mecca* as representative of Brooks's new interest in communal experiences.

Hansell, "The Role of Violence in Recent Poems of Gwendolyn Brooks," *Studies in Black Literature,* 5 (Spring 1974): 21-27;
This essay traces Brooks's increasing use of images of violence in her poetry.

George Kent, "The Poetry of Gwendolyn Brooks," *Black World,* 20 (September 1971): 30-48, 68-71;
A survey of the major themes and subjects of Brooks's poetry.

Patricia H. Lattin and Vernon E. Lattin, "Dual Vision in Gwendolyn Brooks's *Maud Martha,*" *Critique: Studies in Modern Fiction,* 25 (Summer 1984): 180-188;
An essay that examines Brooks's autobiographical novel as a "quest for beauty, love, and meaning" in a conflicted society.

Harry F. Shaw, *Gwendolyn Brooks* (Boston: Twayne, 1980);
This, the first full-length study of Brooks's life and work, is shallow in its judgments and incomplete in scope.

George Stavros, "An Interview with Gwendolyn Brooks," *Contemporary Literature,* 11 (Winter 1970): 1-20;
A thorough and revelatory explanation from Brooks about her alignment with black power and black awareness movements.

Truman Capote

This entry was updated by Craig Goad (Northwest Missouri State University) from his entry in DLB 2, American Novelists Since World War II.

Places	New York City New Orleans	Western Kansas Southern California	Rural South
Influences and Relationships	Harper Lee Donald Windham Gustave Flaubert	Willa Cather Jack Dunphy Marcel Proust	Christopher Isherwood Guy de Maupassant Charles Dickens
Literary Movements and Forms	Southern Gothic	New Journalism/ Nonfiction Novel	Romanticism
Major Themes	Crime and Punishment The Double	Search for a Father Betrayal of Self/Others Breakdown of the Family	Isolation Homosexuality
Cultural and Artistic Influences	The "Jet Set"/ "Beautiful People" Phenomenon	Gay Liberation	Pop Art
Social and Economic Influences	Death Penalty Controversy Prison Reform Movement	Age of the Media Celebrity The Depression	Kennedy Era "Camelot"

See also the entries on Truman Capote in DLB Year-book 1982 *and* 1984.

BIRTH: Born Truman Streckfus Persons, New Orleans, Louisiana, 30 September 1924, to Archulus and Lillie Mae Faulk Persons; adopted by Joseph G. Capote.

AWARDS AND HONORS: O. Henry Award for "The House of Flowers," 1948 and for "Shut a Final Door," 1951; Mystery Writers of America Edgar Award for *In Cold Blood,* 1967; Emmy Award for television adaptation of "A Christmas Memory," 1967.

DEATH: Los Angeles, California, 25 August 1984.

BOOKS: *Other Voices, Other Rooms* (New York: Random House, 1948; London: Heinemann, 1948);
A Tree of Night and Other Stories (New York: Random House, 1949; London: Heinemann, 1950);
Local Color (New York: Random House, 1950);
The Grass Harp (New York: Random House, 1951; London: Heinemann, 1952);
The Grass Harp (Play) (New York: Random House, 1952);
The Muses Are Heard (New York: Random House, 1956; London: Heinemann, 1957);
Breakfast at Tiffany's (New York: Random House, 1958; London: Hamilton, 1958);
Observations (New York: Simon & Schuster, 1959; London: Weidenfeld & Nicolson, 1959);
Selected Writings (New York: Random House, 1963; London: Hamilton, 1963);
In Cold Blood (New York: Random House, 1965; London: Hamilton, 1966);
A Christmas Memory (New York: Random House, 1966);
House of Flowers, by Capote and Harold Arlen (New York: Random House, 1968);
The Thanksgiving Visitor (New York: Random House, 1968; London: Hamilton, 1969);
Trilogy: An Experiment of Multimedia, by Capote with Eleanor and Frank Perry (New York: Macmillan, 1969);
The Dogs Bark: Public People and Private Places (New York: Random House, 1973; London: Weidenfeld & Nicolson, 1974);
Music for Chameleons (New York: Random House, 1980; London: Hamilton, 1981);
One Christmas (New York: Random House, 1983).

Truman Capote (Gale International Portrait Gallery)

When he died just over a month short of his sixtieth birthday, Truman Capote left behind a substantial fortune, a legacy of literary success and controversy, and a sense of incompleteness, of promise unfulfilled. Having literally made his name a household word in the late 1960s with the massive success of *In Cold Blood,* with the "party of the decade," and with frequent TV talk-show appearances, Capote produced little in the final two decades of his life—at least little that had been released. He published only two significant volumes in the years between 1966 and his death. *The Dogs Bark* appeared in 1973 and *Music for Chameleons* in 1980, but the former chiefly reprinted earlier work, some of it dating back to the beginning of his career. Only *Music for Chameleons* gave indications of what Capote had been up to in the post-*In Cold Blood* years and made any substantial claim that Capote still should be considered a significant contemporary writer. His name appeared most often in print in connection with a "near-fatal" automobile accident, with hospitalization for cancer surgery and for drug and alcohol rehabilitation, and with incidents of public breakdown. The long-promised, much-awaited major novel *Answered Prayers,* the book that Capote perceived as the culmination of his career and the final proof of his literary greatness, remained unpublished, perhaps unfinished, perhaps unfinishable. In the days after his death, Capote's friends gathered to memorialize and praise him, and the *New York Times* editorialized about him, but the fact remained that, unless *Answered Prayers* should be published and should live up to Capote's claims for it, the latter third of Truman Capote's career represented a falling off from the high standard of literary success and significance that had characterized his life since his early twenties.

Truman Capote was born Truman Streckfus Persons in New Orleans on 30 September 1924. His parents divorced when he was four, and his mother married a well-to-do businessman named Capote, whose surname his stepson chose to adopt. In the interim of several years, the child lived a life of alternating instability and warm security as he was handed from one set of relatives to another in the rural South. Capote made up stories to help deal with his loneliness and his separation from both parents, and by age ten, or thereabouts, he had decided to become a professional writer. This determination led him to ignore formal schooling, although following his mother's second marriage he attended the Trinity School at St. John's Academy in New York and the public schools of Greenwich, Connecticut. Capote said that all through his adolescence he was working steadily toward becoming a writer, and that by his midteens he was a technically accomplished stylist. Capote would claim in later years to have read all of Twain and Dickens in childhood, and very early on he fell under the sway of French writers. Near the end of Capote's life the novelist John Fowles called Flaubert, Maupassant, and Proust Capote's three masters.

Capote's formal schooling ended when he was seventeen and apparently without his earning even a high school diploma. He obtained a job at the *New Yorker* magazine, where, although little more than an errand boy, he attracted attention with his mannerisms and eccentric style of dress. It was during these years that Capote met—by chance, according to his version of events—Willa Cather, whose work he had long admired. He was also introduced to Christopher Isherwood and Donald Windham, both of whom remained his lifelong friends. In the early years of World War II, Capote's central interest continued to be in his own writing. The June 1945 appearance of his short story "Miriam" in *Mademoiselle* brought him the widespread attention that his earlier publications had not attracted and led to his signing a contract

for a first novel. Selected for the O. Henry Memorial Award volume of 1946, "Miriam" typifies the early Capote manner. It is a story of isolation, dread, and psychological breakdown told in rich, precisely managed prose. There is little technical or thematic experimentation in "Miriam" and the other Capote stories that appeared regularly in the postwar years. The shadow of Edgar Allan Poe floats over the surface of these stories, and their chief aim often seems to be only to produce a mild shudder. There is, however, enough psychological insight and vividness of characterization to suggest that Capote might be capable of something more than Gothicism.

Capote's first novel, *Other Voices, Other Rooms* (1948), demonstrated that he was capable of important work, although much of the book's initial notoriety stemmed less from its display of prose virtuosity than from the book's then-shocking homosexual theme and from the photograph of Capote on the dust jacket. The photo, which Capote later said was chosen more or less by accident and without any intent to shock, showed him reclining on an antique settee, looking as if he were dreamily contemplating some outrage against conventional morality. Many readers assumed that Capote should be identified with the novel's protagonist and that *Other Voices, Other Rooms* constituted a confession of sexual deviance. The resulting publicity helped to make the book a best-seller and made Capote, then only twenty-three, one of the most famous of young writers.

The identification of Capote with his protagonist was, in fact, an accurate way to approach *Other Voices, Other Rooms,* but not in the simplistic way that some readers made the identification in 1948. The central character, Joel Knox, is clearly a projection of the insecurities of Capote's childhood, and the main action of the book concerns a search for a father and then, that search having failed, an attempt to come to terms with a frightening world. Joel's options are progressively closed off, so that finally he can only turn to Randolph, the grotesque transvestite who has presided over his rejection of the "normal" world. The implication is clear that *an* identity, of whatever sexual orientation, is better than *no* identity. Joel's decision to stay with Randolph seemed to many critics a horrifying one, but at least Joel is able to continue to function, in contrast to most of the characters in Capote's short stories of the same period, who usually end in a moral and psychological paralysis that is a symbolic death. Despite the qualified optimism of Joel's resolution, many critics dealt with Capote only in terms of the novel's southern setting and its general atmosphere of decay and fear. *Time* found the book immature and its theme "calculated to make the flesh crawl." John W. Aldridge assigned Capote to permanent insignificance because of his failure to engage the problems of the real world. In his *After the Lost Generation*, Aldridge dismissed *Other Voices, Other Rooms* in language typical of Capote's detractors. The novel's characters, he said, "belong eternally to the special illusion Capote has created; outside it, they do nothing and are nothing. . . . The real world should, by rights, be part of the illusion; but it is not and cannot be." More than a quarter of a century after *Other Voices, Other Rooms* was published, Cynthia Ozick, writing in *New Republic*, saw the book as symbolic of an attitude of retreat from reality which ultimately rendered the novel and others like it hollow and worthless.

Other critics, however, defended the novel and Capote's artistic significance. In an article in *American Scholar*, Carvel Collins constructed an elaborate reading of *Other Voices, Other Rooms* as a working out of the quest for the Holy Grail, showing that the novel contained elements analogous to those identified with the Grail Quest myths by Jes-

sie L. Weston and others. Frank Baldanza, writing in *Georgia Review*, found in Capote's work elements of Platonic thought. According to Baldanza, the world of *Other Voices, Other Rooms* is not divorced from reality but rather is "a microcosm, symbolizing man's ordinary spiritual state." Baldanza went on to argue that throughout *Other Voices, Other Rooms* "Platonic elements dominate most of the characterization, the incident, and the style."

Perhaps the most perceptive reader of *Other Voices, Other Rooms* was Ihab Hassan. In *Radical Innocence* Hassan took into account the objections of critics like Aldridge and then argued that *Other Voices, Other Rooms* could best be understood as a "novel-romance" and that it was an attempt "to engage reality without being realistic." The realization that Capote was creating *romance*, in the sense that Hawthorne used that term in his preface to *The House of the Seven Gables*, was of considerable importance in establishing Capote's seriousness and literary worth. Such perception came, however, well after Capote's reputation as a decadent writer was fixed in the public mind, and he did not escape the southern-Gothic typecasting for many years.

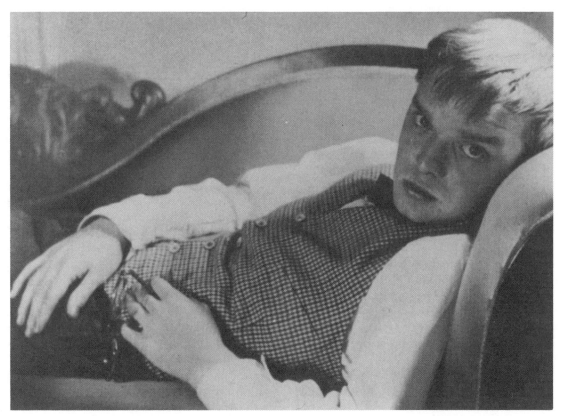

Pose struck by Capote for the dust jacket photo on his first book, Other Voices, Other Rooms

A Tree of Night and Other Stories (1949) suggested little likelihood that Capote would break away from the haunted world of his first novel. The collection included "Miriam" and the first prize winner in the 1948 O. Henry awards, "Shut a Final Door." These stories, "The Headless Hawk," "Master Misery," and the title story, all center on psychological terror, and their epiphanies show the realization of character after character that his life is empty, narcissistic, meaningless. These stories are technically accomplished, but like *Other Voices, Other Rooms,* they are conservative in style, with omniscient narration and straightforward chronological order. Although the portrayals of the empty self confronting the fact of its emptiness are vivid, the stories, for the most part, ring the same note repeatedly. Milton Crane, writing in *Saturday Review,* found these dark stories the most promising aspect of Capote's talent and predicted a successful future for Capote so long as he wrote in this "Grand Guignol" style. Crane dismissed the lighter side of Capote's talent, that revealed by "Jug of Silver" and "Children on Their Birthdays," calling the latter "derivative and pretentious."

Looked at in retrospect, however, it is clear that "Jug of Silver" and "Children on Their Birthdays" signaled an important new direction in Capote's career. The stories are light, at times almost farcical, treatments of children with the power to affect the societies in which they move. The stories are told through first-person narrators and suggest mythic dimensions for their child-protagonists. The sharp division between the haunted, nocturnal world of stories like "Shut a Final Door" and the sunlit world of the essentially comic stories was soon noted by Capote's more perceptive critics and was articulated by Mark Schorer in his important essay "McCullers and Capote: Basic Patterns." Schorer wrote: "Capote's sensibility moves in two different directions—into the most subjective drama of all, the psychic drama far below the level of reason, on the one hand, and, on the other, into objective social drama, often fanciful. . . ." Different as the two modes are in subject matter and tone, there are links between the nocturnal and sunlit worlds of Capote's early fiction. As Hassan argued in *Radical Innocence,* in both worlds the role of the unconscious is crucial. In the dark stories the unconscious breaks through to reveal the horror of the empty personality and often manifests itself as a seemingly supernatural phenomenon. In the light stories the unconscious becomes, as Hassan put it, "the source of our uniqueness, our insight and creativity." Throughout the 1950s the majority of Capote's

work came from the sunlit side of this fictional dichotomy.

Capote sailed for Europe at almost the same time *A Tree of Night and Other Stories* was published, beginning what was to be a long exile, although an exile broken by returns to the United States. In Europe, Capote continued to write fiction as well as the nonfiction that had begun to attract increasing attention. His travel pieces, the best of them collected as *Local Color* (1950), confirm Capote's engagement with the world of society and demonstrate his eye for the precision of detail and his ear for exactness of phrase. At his best, in pieces like "To Europe" and "A Ride Through Spain," Capote showed that he could take real events and shape them into something like fiction. During these European years Capote also demonstrated his capacity for meeting and charming famous people. Capote has written of his meetings with and impressions of artists as notable and diverse as Colette, André Gide, Jean Cocteau, Isak Dinesen, and Cecil Beaton.

Capote settled in Sicily for two years and, as exiles often do, returned imaginatively to his native ground, writing *The Grass Harp* (1951), a novel which draws on his boyhood experiences. The book recounts an idyllic withdrawal from society by a group of gentle rebels and the beneficial effect this Edenic interlude has on all of them. The novel is parablelike in its simplicity and is held together by its elegiac tone and by the central symbol of the harp of grass which grows in the cemetery and sings what Hassan called a "mythicized" elegy, an affirmation of human continuity. *The Grass Harp* represents a movement away from the subjectivity of *Other Voices, Other Rooms,* as William Nance noted in *The Worlds of Truman Capote.* The withdrawal into the magical, green world of romance cannot be a permanent one, and the characters must return, however regretfully, to the world of society and objective reality. The similarities between *The Grass Harp* and "Jug of Silver" and "Children on Their Birthdays" are numerous: odd characters opposing stiffly conventional societies, the mixing of slapstick comedy with pathos, the employment of a first-person narrator.

Capote's European years also marked the beginnings of his work for the theater and films. He wrote a dramatization of *The Grass Harp* which opened on Broadway in March 1952 to mixed reviews; it was not a financial success. A musical adaptation of another O. Henry Award-winning story, "The House of Flowers," opened on Broadway in December 1954. With a book by Capote and music by Harold Arlen, *House of Flowers* pleased some critics and ran for 165 performances, but it was not financially successful. Capote's first important film work, his collaboration with John Huston on *Beat the Devil* (1954), led to a financially unsuccessful film but one which is well regarded by many critics and has achieved the status of an offbeat classic.

Although Capote spent much time on theatrical and cinematic work in the early 1950s, his thinking centered on the role nonfiction could have in his career and in literature in general. He began evolving a theory about the potential of nonfiction as the art of the future, and in late 1955 he began his first extensive experiment along these lines. He accompanied the touring company of *Porgy and Bess* on its historic Russian tour and reported the goings-on in two long pieces for the *New Yorker*. Combined into a book, *The Muses Are Heard* (1956), these reports show Capote's ability to control the reader's responses to characters and events by carefully selecting and organizing details. Without losing his apparent objectivity, Capote converts real events into something like a comic novel. The same seeming objectivity characterizes Capote's 1957 interview with Marlon Brando, "The Duke in His Domain." This extended interview, an experiment in raising the celebrity profile to the level of art, gave Capote the chance to practice the techniques he believed he would need in order to write a "nonfiction novel."

Following his return to the United States, Capote produced one extended piece of fiction before he began the six-years-long work on *In Cold Blood.* That was *Breakfast at Tiffany's*, published first in *Esquire* (November 1958) and then in book form along with three short stories. Like *The Grass Harp*, "Jug of Silver," and "Children on Their Birthdays," *Breakfast at Tiffany's* employs a first-person narrator and deals with the world of real life, not the haunted isolation of *Other Voices, Other Rooms*. The central character, Holly Golightly, the demiprostitute who retains a fundamental innocence even as she accepts fifty dollars "powder room change" from her "dates," is one of Capote's most appealing characters. More than one critic compared Holly to Christopher Isherwood's Sally Bowles, and there is no doubt that the two characters have many similarities. Although the novelette ends with Holly's flight into an uncertain and dangerous future, it clearly belongs to the lighter side of Capote's work, for Holly is another catalytic figure, able to affect the society in which she finds herself and to go on being influential in the lives of those she has

touched after she is gone. Stylistically, *Breakfast at Tiffany's* is one of Capote's most perfect works, and even so severe a critic as Norman Mailer said (in *Advertisements for Myself*) that he would not change two words of it.

By late 1959 Capote was seriously searching for a subject for his proposed nonfictional novel. On 16 November of that year he read a dozen paragraphs in the *New York Times* about a multiple murder in Kansas. Within a few days he, accompanied by his childhood friend, novelist Harper Lee, was in Holcomb, Kansas, where a wealthy farmer, Herbert W. Clutter, and three members of his family had been murdered, apparently without motive and for almost no profit. Capote chose this crime as his subject, and for the next six years devoted nearly all his energies to investigating and writing about it. The finished product, published in four long articles in the *New Yorker* in late 1965 and in book form in January 1966, was *In Cold Blood,* a work which earned Capote more money than all his previous works combined and created as much controversy as any book published in the 1960s. Critics debated endlessly Capote's claim that he had invented a new literary form, questioned the propriety of making millions of dollars from a work that hinged on the deaths of six people (the four Clutters and their subsequently executed murderers), and deplored Capote's apparently endless promotion of his work ("A boy has to hustle his book," Capote said).

Much of the negative response to *In Cold Blood* could be explained by reference to nonliterary matters or to personal malice. Yet beyond such petty considerations serious artistic questions remained. For some, *In Cold Blood* could never achieve the status of literary art because it was a work of fact, not of the imagination. Writing in *The Spectator*, Tony Tanner credited Capote with creating "a stark image of the deep doubleness in American life," yet concluded that *In Cold Blood* suffered by comparison with other works which took their inspiration from reports of actual crimes but developed into true works of the imagination. Diana Trilling treated *In Cold Blood* even more harshly in her *Partisan Review* essay on it. She found Capote's prose "flaccid, often downright inept" and his narrative "overmanipulated." Further, she contended that the objectivity which Capote retained throughout the book served not to produce truth but to protect Capote from the need to take a stand on the issues his work raised. Robert Langbaum's *American Scholar* review found much to praise in *In Cold Blood,* but described it as finally unsuccessful, chiefly because Capote had failed to bring to bear the irony a novelist could attain and because his portraits of the murdered Clutter family were shallow and incomplete in comparison with those of the murderers, Hickock and Smith. Langbaum concluded that "*In Cold Blood* is first-rate entertainment that at moments gives illusory promise of being something more than that."

The defenders of *In Cold Blood* were as numerous and vocal as its detractors. Rebecca West, writing in *Harper's*, called *In Cold Blood* a "formidable statement about reality" and concluded that it was a "grave and reverend book." In the *New York Review of Books*, F. W. Dupee drew comparisons between *In Cold Blood* and works by Cervantes, Hawthorne, and Henry James. The most extended analysis of *In Cold Blood* and its place in Capote's literary career came in George Garrett's *Hollins Critic* essay "Crime and Punishment in Kansas." The comparison invited by the use of Dostoyevsky's title suggested Garrett's high regard for *In Cold Blood*, which he described as "a frank bid for greatness." Garrett detailed the development of *In Cold Blood* out of the tendencies of Capote's earlier work and showed that it contained elements of both the dark and light world that commentators like Hassan and Schorer had identified.

The controversy about the nature and literary status of *In Cold Blood* can never be wholly resolved, for it hinges on the definition of art that the individual reader accepts, but there is little doubt that the book creates a vivid portrait of western Kansas and captures the manners and speech of the people who live there. It investigates the criminal world which exists on the edges of normal society and sometimes collides with that society with disastrous results. It probes the workings of the criminal justice system and shows the difficulty that system has in dealing with sociopathic personalities. It explores the irony of the fact that the murder of the Clutters, apparently exactly the sort of crime that a prosecuting attorney can describe as being committed "in cold blood," was essentially a crime of passion, a brief explosion of repressed rage and hate, while the executions of Hickock and Smith were carried out cold-bloodedly after years of legal wrangling. Finally, and perhaps most importantly, *In Cold Blood* contains the detailed portraits of Hickock and Smith which continue to fascinate not only those with literary interests, but students of criminal psychology as well. Seldom has a writer of real ability become so involved with the mind of a murderer as Capote became with the mind of Perry Smith, and the record of Capote's long study of that distorted mind may be unique in modern literature. In a time when homicidal figures seem to hide in every shadow, the insight Capote has provided cannot be dismissed lightly.

Capote rested from his labors for a time after the success of *In Cold Blood* was assured. A televised version of Capote's 1956 short story, the autobiographical "A Christmas Memory," earned critical praise in 1967, as did the film version of *In Cold Blood* that same year. Capote became a familiar figure on the late-night television talk shows, and his views on crime, prisons, and capital punishment, backed by the expertise he had gained in the years of working on *In Cold Blood*, were frequently heard. He published hardcover versions of *A Christmas Memory* (1966) and *The Thanksgiving Visitor* (1968), another work drawn from his childhood experiences in the rural South. In 1969 Capote prepared an autobiographical introduction for a reprinting of *Other Voices, Other Rooms*; and he continued to publish nonfiction pieces and to have earlier work produced for television and on the stage. It was not until 1973, with the publication of *The Dogs Bark*, that Capote-watchers had a chance to see a new selection of Capote's work. Like the earlier *Selected Writings of Truman Capote* (1963), however, *The Dogs Bark* was made up of previously published material, some of it written as early as 1946. The volume gave readers an opportunity to see the range of Capote's interests and his skills in various kinds of nonfictional prose writing, but it offered nothing of a long-promised novel, *Answered Prayers*. except Capote's statements in "Self-Portrait," the final selection in *The Dogs Bark*, that he was working on *Answered Prayers* and that it would be far longer and more technically elaborate than any of his previous fiction.

As succeeding events would show, *The Dogs Bark* was essentially a holding action, a work that would let the world know that Capote remained a figure to be reckoned with in the literary world. But in fact Capote was in serious difficulty both personally and professionally. He had accepted a large advance for *Answered Prayers*—reportedly $750,000—in 1966 and now found himself unable to finish the book. He struggled with what he called "obsessive perfectionism" and with a growing dependence on alcohol and tranquilizers, and he made what seems in retrospect the one really bad decision in a career previously marked by daring but correct choices. He decided to publish pieces of *Answered Prayers* in *Esquire* magazine. In the June 1975 issue the first section, "Mojave," appeared, causing relatively little stir, for it seemed merely a

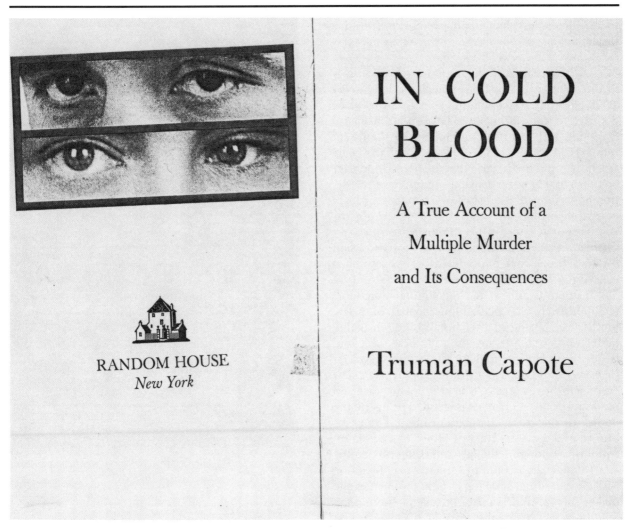

Title page spread for Capote's best-known book, a fictional account of the Clutter family murder in Kansas

conventional short story, obviously written by one familiar with the doings of the rich and powerful, but containing nothing that the average reader could identify with any specific rich and powerful person. But in the November 1975 *Esquire* "La Cote Basque, 1965" appeared, and for Capote, as Anne Taylor Fleming put it in her revealing two-part article in the *New York Times Magazine* in 1978, the publication of that story "quite simply changed his life." It named names; it made what had been the private gossip of a privileged few the common property of anyone who chanced to open that issue of *Esquire;* and it caused many of Capote's most cherished friends to turn on him, to stop talking to him, to treat him as a pariah. "I might just as well have killed the Lindbergh baby," Capote said. Two more *Answered Prayers* fragments appeared in

Esquire in 1976, "Unspoiled Monsters" in May and "Kate McCloud" in December, but neither created the kind of stir that "La Cote Basque, 1965" had produced. Neither did they suggest that the much-touted *Answered Prayers* would revolutionize fictional technique. Instead of spurring Capote on to finish *Answered Prayers,* the publication of the fragments had been a personal and professional disaster for him. And other problems assaulted him. Myrtle Bennett, his Palm Springs housekeeper and a trusted friend, died, as did his paternal grandmother. Gore Vidal sued him over an unflattering story in *Playgirl.* A four-year relationship with a married man ended. The May 1976 automobile accident that Capote described as "near-fatal" was merely one of a succession of disasters. He saw a series of psychiatrists, committed himself to an alcoholic rehabilitation center, suffered a public collapse at Towson State University in Maryland.

At this point Capote might have been utterly finished; he might, as his mother had done many years before, have committed suicide. Instead, he got back to work, bringing to bear on his problems the same sort of artistic discipline that had kept him grinding at *In Cold Blood* through all the years when he could not be sure that the book could ever be finished. He began learning again how to write, now attempting to use all he knew about every form of writing within any single piece of writing. As Capote put it later, in his "Preface" to *Music for Chameleons*, "I eventually developed a style. I had found a framework into which I could assimilate everything I knew about writing."

Capote's faith in his revolutionary fictional technique may have helped him through his crisis, but little he produced after his mid-life relearning of his craft suggests any radically new direction, either for fiction generally or for Capote. *Music for Chameleons*, the apparent product of Capote's new craftsmanship, appeared in 1980 and received modest reviews. There was good writing in the book: an insightful if too-sentimental remembrance of a day with Marilyn Monroe; a comic recounting of dodging the law and being rescued by Pearl Bailey; an account of Capote's tagging along with a pious, dope-smoking cleaning woman as she makes her rounds, a self-interview containing, among other things, the story of his chance first meeting with Willa Cather. But nothing in the volume suggested other than continued maturation of Capote's talent. The style throughout is skillful, but so was the style throughout *Selected Writings of Truman Capote,* published seventeen years earlier. Even "Handcarved Coffins," the putative pièce de résistance of the volume—the screen rights sold for a reported $300,000—displays nothing new save the story itself, and it is a story of such seeming implausibility that many readers wondered if Capote really expected his audience to believe that it was, as its subtitle asserted, "A Nonfiction Account of an American Crime." In all, *Music for Chameleons* was a book most other writers would have been glad to claim as their own, but it was not the epoch-making book Capote had been promising since 1966.

In the nearly four years that remained to him between the publication of *Music for Chameleons* and his death, Capote published only one more even marginally significant piece of writing. In 1983 Random House issued *One Christmas,* a remem-

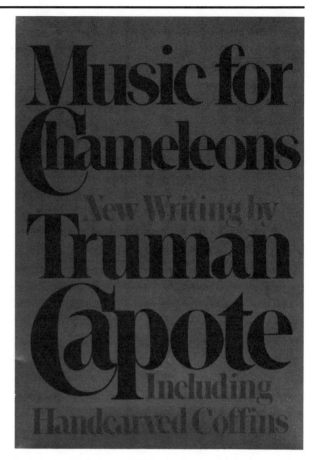

Dust jacket for Capote's 1980 collection of short works written after 1975

brance of the sort "A Christmas Memory" had been, describing a childhood Christmas when Capote had been forced to leave the security of his life with his mother's relatives and spend the holiday with his father in New Orleans. It is an unremarkable piece of writing; writing of it in the *New York Times Book Review,* Anna Shapiro spoke of "the disingenuously gooey message" and called it a "cynical Christmas card." Another reviewer described it as a "tiny, overpriced book." It adds a bit to what the world knows about Capote's childhood, but it was hardly the book any writer would choose as his final statement.

Yet *One Christmas* was the last thing Capote would publish in his lifetime. On 25 August 1984 Capote died at the Southern California home of Joanne Carson (former wife of TV host Johnny Carson), a friend who had not deserted him. An autopsy revealed that a liver ailment had caused his death, and that he had suffered as well from phlebitis and emphysema. Although rumors circulated that Capote had died of a drug overdose, the autopsy showed that while the combination of barbituates, Valium, antiseizure drugs, and pain-killers he had been taking might have worsened his health, all were properly prescribed medications. Capote's will, made public in September, left an estate valued at more than $600,000 to his companion of more than twenty-five years, Jack Dunphy, to be used as Dunphy chose during his lifetime, and, at his death, to be used to fund a literary prize, the Truman Capote Award for Literary Criticism.

In "Nocturnal Turnings," Capote's interview with himself that is the final section of *Music for Chameleons*, he spoke of a desire to be reincarnated as a buzzard because, he said, "A buzzard doesn't have to bother about his appearance or ability to beguile and please; he doesn't have to put on airs. Nobody's going to like him anyway; he is ugly, unwanted, unwelcome everywhere." Later in the same interview, Capote's thoughts turned to Flaubert's story "The Legend of St. Julian the Hospitaler," in which the once arrogant central character, having become "a pariah and a penitent," redeems himself and wins sainthood by embracing and kissing a leper. Both transformations, from man to buzzard, from pariah to saint, speak eloquently of Capote's emotional state in the last years of his life, of a sense of being an outcast who need not try to redeem himself and who yet hopes for redemption, even canonization. Probably no writer's worst fears or greatest hopes are realized, and literary history will not record Capote as either a graceless buzzard or a saint. Instead he will be recalled, barring the publication of some version of *Answered Prayers* that lives up to Capote's hopes for it, as a gifted prose stylist, as a good novelist, short story writer, and writer of reportage, and as the author of *In Cold Blood*. George Garrett's assertion that *In Cold Blood* represented "a frank bid for greatness" turns out to have been prophetic in ways that might not have been expected in 1966. Clearly *In Cold Blood* is Capote's best work, as well as his most famous. It still has the power to hold the interest of a class of college students and to speak to them about the nature of life in America. Equally clearly Capote intended to top himself, to make an even stronger bid for greatness with *Answered Prayers*. That did not happen in his lifetime and may not happen after his death. Truman Capote was a physically small man with large ambitions, and if he did not accomplish all he hoped, neither was he insignificant. He spoke with a unique voice, one that will not die out.

Bibliographies:

Jackson R. Bryer, "Truman Capote: A Bibliography," in *Truman Capote's "In Cold Blood": A Critical Handbook*, edited by Irving Malin (Belmont, Cal.: Wadsworth, 1968), pp. 239-269;
Thorough listing through 1966; especially useful for reviews of Broadway productions.

Kenneth Starosciak, *Truman Capote: A Checklist* (New Brighton, Minn.: Kenneth Starosciak, 1974);
Annotated list of editions of books through 1971, periodical publications by and about Capote, 1943-1972, extensive listing of foreign sources.

Robert J. Stanton, *Truman Capote: A Primary and Secondary Bibliography* (Boston: G. K. Hall, 1980);
Extensive listing of works by and about Capote; the crucial bibliography for serious study.

Robert A. Wilson, "Truman Capote: A Bibliographical Checklist," *American Book Collector*, 1 (July/August 1980): 8-15;
An excellent checklist of books and book appearances by Capote.

References:

John W. Aldridge, *After the Lost Generation* (New York: McGraw-Hill, 1951), pp. 194-230;
Early and generally unfavorable reading of Capote's fiction.

Frank Baldanza, "Plato in Dixie," *Georgia Review*, 12 (Summer 1958): 151-167;
Sees Platonic conceptions of reality in early work by Capote; useful in light of later importance of questions of "reality" in *In Cold Blood* and Capote's other nonfiction.

John Malcolm Brinnin, *Sextet: T. S. Eliot, Truman Capote and Others* (New York: Delacorte, 1981);
Long (nearly one-third of the volume) portrait of Capote by a fellow writer.

Anne Taylor Fleming, "The Private World of Truman Capote," *New York Times Magazine*, 9 July 1978, pp. 22-25; 16 July 1978, pp. 12-13, 15, 44;
Based on interviews with Capote and many who knew him; one of the most insightful and revealing biographical pieces on Capote.

George Garrett, "Crime and Punishment in Kansas: Truman Capote's *In Cold Blood*," *Hollins Critic*, 3 (February 1966): 1-12;
Pioneering study of connection of *In Cold Blood* to Capote's earlier fiction; more than just a review of *In Cold Blood*.

Helen S. Garson, *Truman Capote* (New York: Ungar, 1980);
Brief biography, methodical descriptions of works; useful bibliography but limited critical insight.

Lawrence Grobel, *Conversations with Capote* (New York: New American Library, 1985);
Series of interviews with Capote from 1982 to just before his death; anecdotes about famous people rather than much serious literary discussion, but still valuable.

Ihab Hassan, *Radical Innocence: Studies in the Contemporary American Novel* (Princeton, N.J.: Princeton University Press, 1961), pp. 230-258;
Excellent analysis of the fiction through *Breakfast at Tiffany's*; one of the best and most sympathetic early studies of Capote's work.

Pati Hill, "The Art of Fiction XVII: TC," *Paris Review*, 16 (Spring/Summer 1957): 34-51;
Extended interview with Capote in which he talks about his artistic methods and ambitions; a very useful source.

John Hollowell, *Fact and Fiction: The New Journalism and the Nonfiction Novel* (Chapel Hill: University of North Carolina Press, 1977), pp. 63-86;
Considers *In Cold Blood* as part of the "new journalism" of the 1960s and 1970s; shows development of Capote's nonfiction techniques in his earlier works.

Alfred Kazin, *Bright Book of Life: American Novelists and Storytellers from Hemingway to Mailer* (Boston: Little, Brown, 1971), pp. 209-219;
Discusses *In Cold Blood* as a nonfiction novel and in relation to Capote's career as a novelist.

Jack Kroll, "*In Cold Blood* . . . An American Tragedy," *Newsweek*, 24 (January 1966): 59-63;
Good background on the Clutter family murders and Capote's approach to writing (and promoting) *In Cold Blood*.

Paul Levine, "Truman Capote: The Revelation of the Broken Image," *Virginia Quarterly Review*, 34 (Autumn 1958): 600-617;
An extended interpretive reading of Capote's early fiction; an intelligent and useful source.

Irving Malin, ed., *Truman Capote's "In Cold Blood": A Critical Handbook* (Belmont, Cal.: Wadsworth, 1968);
Contains essays by Melvin Friedman, Robert K. Morris, David Galloway, and Paul Levine, ten reviews of *In Cold Blood* (including George Garrett's *Hollins Critic* essay-review), the *Paris Review* interview with Capote by Pati Hill, bibliography by Jackson R. Bryer; although centered on *In Cold Blood*, it remains the best single resource for Capote study generally.

William L. Nance, *The Worlds of Truman Capote* (New York: Stein & Day, 1970);
First book-length study of Capote; makes use of Nance's interviews with Capote for insight into the works.

Eric Norden, "*Playboy* Interview: Truman Capote," *Playboy*, 15 (March 1968): 51-62, 160-170;
Extended interview done in the aftermath of the mammoth success of *In Cold Blood;* a portrait of Capote at his most famous.

George Plimpton, "The Story Behind a Nonfiction Novel," *New York Times Book Review*, 16 January 1966, pp. 2-3, 38-43;
Useful background on the writing of *In Cold Blood*, Capote's aims and attitudes in that book.

Kenneth T. Reed, *Truman Capote* (Boston: Twayne, 1981);
Brief but generally insightful readings of Capote's work; divides works into categories and discusses the relationship of fiction to nonfiction in helpful ways.

Mark Schorer, "McCullers and Capote: Basic Patterns," in *The Creative Present: Notes on Contemporary American Fiction*, edited by Nona Balakian and Charles Simmons (Garden City: Doubleday, 1963), pp. 83-107;

One of the best early studies, with emphasis on Capote as a prose stylist.

Robert Siegle, "Capote's *Handcarved Coffins* and the Nonfiction Novel," *Contemporary Literature*, 25 (Winter 1984): 437-451;

Considers the question of relationship of fact and fiction, the nature of reality in a "nonfiction" novel, the role played by the narrator in such work; a complex and quite theoretical article.

John Cheever

This entry was updated by Robert A. Morace (Daemen College) from his entry in DLB
2, American Novelists Since World War II.

Places	Westchester County, New York	Ossining, New York	Quincy, Massachusetts
	Italy	Eastern Europe	New York

Influences and Relationships	Saul Bellow	John Updike

Literary Movements and Forms	Realism	The Grotesque	*New Yorker* School
	Novel of Manners		

Major Themes	Spiritual Strivings	Estrangement	Loss of Self-Esteem
	Middle-Class Values	Sexuality	Spiritual Dis-ease

Cultural and Artistic Influences	Film	Television

Social and Economic Influences	Suburbia	Cold War	The Depression
	"Athenian Twilight" (Decline of Culture Associated with Boston and its Environs)		

See also the entries on John Cheever in DLB Yearbook *1980 and* 1982.

BIRTH: Quincy, Massachusetts, 27 May 1912, to Frederick and Mary Liley Cheever.

MARRIAGE: 22 March 1941 to Mary Winternitz; children: Susan, Benjamin Hale, Federico.

AWARDS AND HONORS: O. Henry Award for "I'm Going to Asia," 1941; O. Henry Award for "The Pot of Gold," 1951; Guggenheim Fellowship, 1951; Benjamin Franklin Award for "The Five-Forty-Eight," 1954; O. Henry Award for "The Country Husband," 1956; National Institute of Arts and Letters grant, 1956; National Book Award for *The Wapshot Chronicle*, 1958; O. Henry Award for "The Embarkment for Cythera," 1964; American Academy of Arts and Letters Howells Medal for *The Wapshot Scandal*, 1965; Pulitzer Prize and National Book Critics Circle Award for *The Stories of John Cheever*, 1979; American Book Award for *The Stories of John Cheever*, 1981.

DEATH: Ossining, New York, 18 June 1982.

BOOKS: *The Way Some People Live* (New York: Random House, 1943);
The Enormous Radio and Other Stories (New York: Funk & Wagnalls, 1953; London: Gollancz, 1953);
The Wapshot Chronicle (New York: Harper, 1957; London: Gollancz, 1957);
The Housebreaker of Shady Hill and Other Stories (New York: Harper, 1958; London: Gollancz, 1958);
Some People, Places, and Things That Will Not Appear in My Next Novel (New York: Harper & Row, 1961; London: Gollancz, 1961);
The Wapshot Scandal (New York: Harper & Row, 1964; London: Gollancz, 1964);
The Brigadier and the Golf Widow (New York: Harper & Row, 1964; London: Gollancz, 1965);
Bullet Park (New York: Knopf, 1969; London: Cape, 1969);
The World of Apples (New York: Knopf, 1973; London: Cape, 1974);
Falconer (New York: Knopf, 1977; London: Cape, 1977);
The Stories of John Cheever (New York: Knopf, 1978; London: Cape, 1979);
Oh What a Paradise It Seems (New York: Knopf, 1982; London: Cape, 1982).

John Cheever (Gale International Portrait Gallery)

Although some critics have dismissed Cheever as a writer of the *"New Yorker* school," a chronicler of suburbia, or a clever satirist, his impressive achievements in both the short story and the novel belie these claims and attest to his importance in American letters. Cheever, unlike many contemporary American writers, is neither stylistically flamboyant nor philosophically pessimistic. Although he has experimented with various narrative techniques, his art is essentially that of the storyteller, and while he clearly recognizes those aspects of modern life which might lead to pessimism, his comic vision remains basically optimistic. His characters all face a similar problem: how to live in a world which, in spite of its middle-class comforts and assurances, suddenly appears inhospitable, even dangerous. Many of his characters go down in defeat, usually by their own hand. Those who survive, in mind as well as body, discover the personal and social virtue of compromise. Having learned of their own and their world's limitations, they can, paradoxically, learn to celebrate the wonder and possibility of life.

John Cheever, the second son of Frederick and Mary Liley Cheever, was born in Quincy, Massachusetts, on 27 May 1912 and grew up during what he has called "the Athenian twilight" of New England culture. His father, a self-made man, rose to become owner of a Lynn shoe factory only to lose his business in the 1929 stock market crash. His mother used the loss to assert her own independence, a decision which had a disastrous effect on her husband who, with his pride irreparably damaged, attempted suicide. Cheever was deeply disturbed by the strained family relationship from which he escaped when he was seventeen.

His story-telling gift, which his parents did little to encourage, evidenced itself early. At eight he improvised tales with which to entertain his classmates and two years later began to commit his stories to paper. His formal education ended at seventeen when Cheever, having gotten behind in his studies, was dismissed from Thayer Academy for smoking. The next year his first published work, "Expelled," appeared in *New Republic*. Although Cheever has referred to the story slightingly as "the reminiscences of a sorehead," his story is neither plaintive nor amateurish and in many ways anticipates the style that has since become Cheever's hallmark. The opening paragraph lures the reader into a story which, like many of the later works, is a series of sketches rather than a linear narrative. The narrator, who remains detached even while recounting his own expulsion, focuses on apparently disparate events which, taken together, create a single impression of what life at a prep school is like. Thematically, "Expelled" also anticipates Cheever's later work. There is the conflict between the decorum required by the school and the fervent longing for life felt by the individual. Cheever symbolizes this conflict in the school's decision to build a tower—an outward and visible sign—rather than to use the money to buy books for the library. The narrator is the first in a long line of displaced persons who make up Cheever's fiction. The displaced narrator can, at least temporarily, find his place in nature if not in society, but since he cannot live both completely and alone, he must return to the society which has cast him off and which he has just satirized.

Following his dismissal from Thayer, Cheever and his older brother Fred went to Boston and then Germany, where they spent the last of their money on a walking tour. Once back in the United States Cheever took up residence in New York City, where he lived during most of the 1930s, part of the time subsisting on bread and buttermilk in a squalid room on Hudson Street. Occasionally he visited the Yaddo writers' colony at Saratoga Springs, New York, where he did all-purpose help to pay for his board. Although there was little financial reward for him during this period, Cheever did gain the friendships of John Dos Passos, E. E. Cummings, James Agee, Paul Goodman, and James Farrell, and, more importantly, he began his relationship with the *New Yorker* magazine.

On 22 March 1941 Cheever married Mary Winternitz, who was then working for his literary agent, Maxim Lieber. Two years later, Cheever, halfway through his four-year army hitch, had his first book published. The thirty stories collected in *The Way Some People Live* (1943) had originally appeared in the *New Yorker*, *Story*, *Yale Review*, *Harper's Bazaar*, and *Read*. Most are either sketches or highly compressed short stories. The longer ones, such as "Of Love: A Testimony" or "The Brothers," are of interest solely as Cheever's earliest attempts at writing stories structured on a prose equivalent of incremental repetition, a form he would later perfect in "The Swimmer." The "people" whose ways of living are sketched in this collection are, except for their socioeconomic class, essentially the same Upper-East-Side and suburban residents who are found in the later fiction: those who live on the memory of past greatness in order to escape the present (the fallen aristocrats); those who try to relive their youth in order to deny their mortality (the athletes and adulterers); those who for so long have repressed their desires that their attempts to break out of the lonely world they have made for themselves are pathetically futile; those whose lives have come to nothing and who absurdly cling to a material object or to the dream of material wealth to assuage their feelings of emptiness; and those who have been jilted either by a lover or by their dreams and look for compensation in self-pity and drinking. Only a few of the stories are noteworthy—"The Cat," for example, or "Forever Hold Your Peace." The stories dealing with the war and based on Cheever's experiences as a recruit are the collection's weakest pieces. Despite the volume's shortcomings, reviewers reacted to it favorably, sensing that here was something more than just a good first book. The most perceptive was Struthers Burt, who tempered his praise with a warning: to succeed, Cheever must avoid "a hardening into an especial style that might become an affectation, and a deliberate casualness and simplicity that might become the same." Later critics have continued to debate these very points, and Cheever's literary stature depends, to some extent, on how successful he has been in avoiding these pitfalls.

Cheever's second collection, *The Enormous Radio and Other Stories* (1953), comprises fourteen stories, all of which originally appeared in the *New Yorker*. Most are set in New York City, some in the kind of Sutton Place apartment house where the Cheevers lived after the war. Many of the stories deal with naifs who have arrived in the city with boundless optimism and little else. The stories are well executed, but invariably follow the same formula and infrequently rise above the sentimental irony of an O. Henry story or the *Life With Father* television scripts Cheever was then writing. Fortunately, not all of the fourteen can be dismissed as simply the products of "a clever short-story manufacturer." In "Torch Song," for example, Jack Lorey discovers that it is not Joan Harris who has been victimized by her string of physically and spiritually infirm lovers but quite the other way around; she has used them to satisfy her bizarre vampirish craving for eternal youth. Realizing this saves Jack from falling prey to her deadly love, but whether it will also save Jack from himself—by this time he has become an alcoholic and has been twice divorced—is left unresolved.

The finest story in the collection, "The Enormous Radio," is a nearly flawless working out of one of Cheever's most prevalent themes: that beneath the surface of quotidian human life is a grotesque and destructive element that decorum (society's chief defense) can usually mask but cannot fully control. Jim and Irene Westcott are the average American couple, temperate in all things except their above-average fondness for music—that is to say, for harmony and order. But the new radio Jim buys brings disharmony rather than pleasure into their lives. Irene is dismayed by all its knobs and switches and repulsed by its ugly gumwood cabinet; when she turns it on, the radio plays not music but the cacophonous sounds of her neighbors' hidden lives. What she hears appalls her, but fascinates her too. Her hidden life is her voyeurism which she masks beneath a priggish saintliness. She soon fears that her own secret sins will become known to her neighbors. She becomes so apprehensive of the radio's power to know and tell all that she finally drives her husband to an angry outburst in which he does what she had feared the radio would do—expose her for what she is. Her sudden knowledge of the evil in the world—the world, that is, of her apartment house—causes her to adopt a false Manichean position and to then commit the worst of sins: to break, in Nathaniel Hawthorne's phrase, "the electric chain of humanity." Although the radio is de-

scribed so as to suggest evil, particularly the evil of modern technology, the association between the radio and evil is all in Irene's puritan mind. Evil, in Cheever's world, is a distinctly human trait.

Cheever continued to explore the relationship between the individual and his society in the eight stories collected in *The Housebreaker of Shady Hill and Other Stories* (1958). Although the characters are no longer the city dwellers of *The Enormous Radio* but instead the residents of Shady Hill (an affluent suburb modeled on Cheever's own experiences in the suburbs of New York City), they still are insecure and quietly desperate despite their outward conformity to Shady Hill's code or veneer of respectability. More pronounced in these stories is Cheever's comedy—his witty and ironic portrayal of the individual and the community—and his belief that the individual who separates himself from his family and community must learn to reintegrate himself in the group. As Cheever said shortly after the collection appeared, "There's been too much criticism of the middle-class way of life. Life can be as good and rich there as any place else. I am not out to be a social critic, however, nor a defender of suburbia." As in "The Enormous Radio," Cheever first explodes the society's hypocrisy and then turns on the person who, like Irene Westcott, loses his own humanity when he turns away from his fellow men.

The fears which plague these suburbanites are certainly real enough—unfaithful spouses, manic lovers, lost children, lost jobs—and because they are real, Cheever treats his suffering characters with compassion. Yet the ways in which they try to resolve their problems are so extreme and absurd as to force the reader to question, if not the validity of their plaints, then at least the degree to which they allow themselves to suffer. In the title story, Johnny Hake tells how after losing his job he turned to burgling his neighbors, an act which transforms Hake into a thief and his world into a world of thieves. Francis Weed (whose name suggests his position as an outsider) in "The Country Husband" discovers that neither his neighbors nor his family have any interest in his narrow escape from death in a plane wreck. Out of spite and longing he turns from all of them and falls in love with his children's babysitter. Hake, Weed, and the husband in "The Trouble with Marcie Flint" are driven by their fantasies of self-realization into escaping their plush, suburban cul-de-sacs. Not until they realize that their fantasies are narcissistic and therefore self-destructive can they return, rejuvenated, triumphant, yet paradoxically humbled, to their family obligations.

For some, the realization does not come so easily. Charlie Blake in "The Five-Forty-Eight" is humbled at the point of a gun, not in a moment of vision. In "O Youth and Beauty!" (which anticipates "The Swimmer" and echoes Hemingway's "The Short Happy Life of Francis Macomber"), Cash Bentley experiences no moment of regenerative humiliation. His race leads not to a goal that lies ahead but rather to one that is ironically already behind in his lost youth, and it ends when his wife fires the starter's pistol, accidentally shooting him "in midair." The desperation which drives Cash Bentley underlies life in Shady Hill, and it is precisely this underlying desperation that the community pretends does not exist. Just before the shooting, Cash's wife had been "upstairs, cutting out of a current copy of *Life* those scenes of mayhem, disaster, and violent death that she felt might corrupt her children. She always did this."

Only two of the eight stories, "The Sorrows of Gin" and "The Worm in the Apple," suffer from the sentimentality that marred the earlier collections. Otherwise *The Housebreaker of Shady Hill* evidences a significant advance in Cheever's art. Language and structure are more precise; the approaches to the material more flexible, less "slick"; the irony less pat, less a matter of formula than of vision. Moreover, Cheever has created a well-defined mythic world within which his characters— frustrated housewives and grotesques in gray flannel suits—act out the drama of American middle-class life.

Two changes occurred during the mid 1950s which radically affected Cheever's work. The decade had begun, so Cheever told fellow writer Herbert Gold, full of promise, but halfway through it, "something went terribly wrong . . . the forceful absurdities of life today find me unprepared." In order to make sense of a world that suddenly appeared absurd, Cheever began to turn his attention from the short story to the novel. "I'm still interested in the short story form," he said in 1958. "Certain situations lend themselves only to the short story. But generally it's a better form for young writers, who are more intense, whose perceptions are more fragmentary." When his first novel, *The Wapshot Chronicle* (1957), appeared, reviewers objected to the book's episodic structure and bewildering number of characters and settings—evidence, they felt, of a short story writer's inability to adapt himself to the distinctive form of the novel. To some extent the plotlessness is inten-

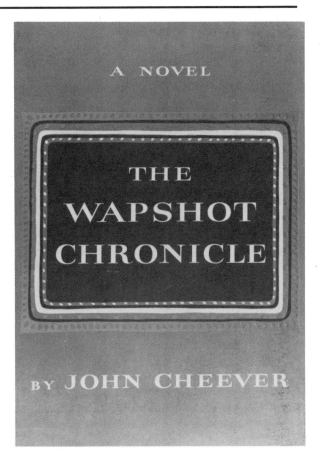

Dust jacket for Cheever's first novel (1957), winner of the National Book Award

tional: "I don't work with plot. I work with intuition, apprehension, dreams, concepts." Furthermore, Cheever felt that plot is incompatible with moral conviction and masks the chaotic nature of contemporary life.

Based upon the author's own "profoundly troubled adolescence" and especially "the harm my mother's working did to my father's self-esteem," *The Wapshot Chronicle* is autobiographical but never simply a personal memoir or confession. Part one records the breakdown of the Wapshot family and focuses on the displacement and consequent loss of self-esteem suffered by the father, Leander, at the hands of his eccentric sister Honora and his strong-willed wife Sarah. Paralleling this is the larger breakdown of the old traditions and culture of St. Botolphs (Cheever's boyhood home of Quincy) before the forces of the modern world. Parts two and three trace the comic misadventures of Leander's sons, Moses (Cheever's brother Fred) and the "ministerial" Coverly (Cheever himself), who discover how poorly the moribund and provincial St. Botolphs has prepared them for survival in Washington and New York. In part four, Moses and Coverly, scarred but alive, have themselves brought forth sons, thereby ensuring the continuance of the Wapshot line.

The novel's central figure is Leander, whose triumph is the triumph of the imagination's power to transform the world. Honora and Sarah, who represent the sexless force of decorum, speak through wills and painted signs. Leander, who represents the regenerative force of the imagination—and of life itself, speaks through his journal. As Cheever has said of his own journal-keeping (a family tradition), it is a way "to preserve the keenness of small daily sensations." The journal enables Leander to triumph over the loss of his self-esteem and the descent into self-pity that afflicts so many of Cheever's characters. It also transforms him into a writer, and writing is, Cheever has said, "the only coherent expression of man's struggle to be illustrious," an attempt on the writer's part "to make sense of [his] life." Leander dies, but his written words continue to turn up. At the novel's end, Coverly discovers his father's "Advice to my sons" in a copy of Shakespeare: "Bathe in cold water every morning. Painful but exhilarating.... Stand up straight. Admire the world. Relish the love of a gentle woman. Trust in the Lord."

The Wapshot Chronicle fully embodies Cheever's comic vision. That vision is optimistic but not, at least in this book, sentimental. Nor is *The Wapshot Chronicle* nostalgic in the pejorative sense of the word; as Cheever defines it, nostalgia means "Not regret for the past, but a keen sense of the present, saying, How splendid it was! But spoken without regret." St. Botolphs is part of "an irrecapturable past"; the images of decay in the opening chapters and Leander's death make clear that it is a world in ruins, a world that in fact never was an Eden: "if we accept the quaintness of St. Botolphs we must also accept the fact that it was a country of spite fences and internecine quarrels...." Cheever satirizes man's foibles and his tendency to wallow in his limitations; he also suggests the possibility of man's transcending his bounds, as Leander does, through a ritual celebration of life.

After completing *The Wapshot Chronicle*, Cheever used the money he had received as winner of a National Institute of Arts and Letters grant in 1956 to help finance a year-long trip to Italy. There he remained serenely unaware of how his first novel was being reviewed. Despite those reviews which sharply criticized the book's flawed structure, *The Wapshot Chronicle* won the National Book Award in 1958, thereby further establishing Cheever's place in American letters.

Prior to *The Wapshot Chronicle*, Cheever had done little experimenting with narrative points of view in his stories. Even the most successful of these, Johnny Hake's monologue in "The Housebreaker of Shady Hill," is hardly a daring innovation. Cheever became much more inventive in his first novel, where the third-person narrative is interrupted by direct assaults upon the reader ("You come, as Moses did. . ." and "Or you wake—like Coverly. . .") and entire chapters composed of Leander's journal entries. Cheever continued to experiment in his next book, *Some People, Places, and Things That Will Not Appear in My Next Novel* (1961). The collection's eight stories (there is also one "miscellany") are evenly divided between first- and third-person narration, and in one the author interrupts the story told by an American "Boy in Rome" to insert his own aside: "But I am not a boy in Rome but a grown man in the old prison and river town of Ossining. . . ." Throughout the collection, the reader can sense Cheever's uncertainty with his methods and characters. Even in the best story, "The Death of Justina," the narrator, an advertising writer, takes time out from writing copy and arranging for the burial of his wife's cousin to deliver this line for his author: "Fiction is art and art is the triumph over chaos (no less) and we can accomplish this only by the most vigilant exercise of choice, but in a world that changes more swiftly than we can perceive there is always the danger that our powers of selection will be mistaken and that the vision we serve will come to nothing."

For Cheever there were two formidable problems of selection to confront and resolve. One involves the exorcising of old characters and situations in order to move on to fresh ground. In "The Death of Justina," for example, Moses and Justina are partly drawn from *The Wapshot Chronicle* and the situation is simply a variation of the Remsden Park scenes in the book. On the other hand, the three stories set in Italy evidence a willingness to work with new material. The more complex problem concerns the conflict between Cheever's comic vision, which is often criticized as facile and middle-class in its values, and the nay-saying, antibourgeois role expected of the serious contemporary American writer. Cheever fictionalized his dilemma in "The Golden Age." The main character, the writer of a popular situation comedy, "The Best Family," is so ashamed of his success that he flees to Italy "because he wants to lead a more illustrious life." His escape to Italy and withdrawal to a lonely castle tower are in vain. The natives watch the debut of his show on Italian television and love it; the mayor tells him, "Oh, we thought, *Signore,* that you were merely a poet." Cheever's intention is "to celebrate a world that lies spread out around us like a bewildering and stupendous dream," and to accomplish this end he lists "A Miscellany of Characters That Will Not Appear" in his work: "The pretty girl at the Princeton-Dartmouth rugby game"; "all parts for Marlon Brando"; "All scornful descriptions of American landscapes . . . for these are not, as they might appear to be, the ruins of our civilization but are the temporary encampments and outposts of the civilization that we—you and I—"shall build"; "explicit scenes of sexual commerce"; "all lushes"; "all those homosexuals who have taken such a dominating position in recent fiction." What he proposes, in short, is nothing less than a complete break with that contemporary American fiction which thrives on despair and estrangement.

Cheever spent four difficult years in the writing of his second novel, *The Wapshot Scandal* (1964), a rather surprising fact considering the similarity between this and his first novel. Point of view remains much the same, only slightly more intimate in the sequel, especially in the Thackerayan second chapter. The four parts of *The Wapshot Chronicle* are compressed into three parts in *The Wapshot Scandal,* which still retains a loosely jointed, three-stranded narrative structure: Honora's ineffectual escape to Italy in order to avoid persecution for income tax evasion; Coverly and Betsey's life in Talifer, a homogeneous middle-class community; and Moses and Melissa's life in Proxmire Manor, a well-to-do suburb. Fewer characters and settings (as compared to the *Chronicle*), the frame structure of Christmas past and Christmas present, and the thematic movement tracing Honora's and Coverly's returns to St. Botolphs work together to unify the diffuse elements of *The Wapshot Scandal.* The essential difference between the two Wapshot novels is this: while both celebrate life, the sequel portrays a world in which it has become harder to see that there is anything worth celebrating. Even Coverly has turned pessimistic; when he imagines that his father's ghost has returned to St. Botolphs, he can only wonder, "Father, Father, why have you come back." The burden of the novel is to prove to Coverly and the reader that it is possible to withstand the world's poisons and to withstand one's own poisons as well. The individual can survive, even if he cannot prevail, and he can celebrate his salvation with others.

Missiles, bombs, mad scientists, and pederasts make the modern world—the world of Talifer and Proxmire Manor—a dangerous place, but no more dangerous than the ocean where previous generations of Wapshot men were tested. Coverly survives, but Moses, broken by his wife's infidelity, turns in shame to alcohol and aimless wandering. Melissa, his wife, is the Emma Bovary of Proxmire Manor. She abandons her husband for a narcissistic teenager who in turn abandons her to drink and obscene promiscuity. Honora, one of the innocents abroad, finally returns to St. Botolphs and promptly drinks herself to death. Coverly's survival, which is both physical and spiritual, derives from the three elements of his character: his father's lusty and irrepressible vitality, his aunt's sense of decorum, and his own ability to adapt himself to the modern world. Working as a "taper," Coverly translates human language into computer language. Rather than deadening his sense of beauty as such work might do, Coverly's taping is turned to aesthetic advantage: he feeds Shelley's poetry into a computer and out come new poems. Similarly, Coverly translates his "scandalous" times and his own survival as a man, a husband, a father, and a Wapshot into a Christmas dinner celebration for himself, his family, and his aunt's eight blind guests, "the raw material of human kindness."

The Brigadier and the Golf Widow (1964), Cheever's fifth short-story collection, was issued shortly after *The Wapshot Scandal.* Although it lacks the unity of *The Housebreaker of Shady Hill,* it displays a broader thematic range, greater inventiveness of style, and the perfection of Cheever's ability to invest even the most implausible, cartoonlike situation with the semblance of everyday life. In general, the collection's fourteen stories explore the contrast which exists in upper-middle-class America between the visible signs of economic security and the repressed frustrations and anxieties deriving from emotional insecurity. As Cheever has noted, "People actually sidestep the pain of death and despair by the thought of purchasing things." In these stories, Cheever forces his readers to confront "death and despair" as they observe his characters either "sidestep" that painful situation or boldly and sometimes comically meet it head on. "The Ocean," a Poe-like monologue by a mad narrator, begins, "I am keeping this journal because I believe myself to be in some danger and because I have no other way of recording my fears. I cannot report them to the police, as you will see, and I cannot confide in my friends. The losses I have suffered in self-esteem, reasonableness, and clarity are conspicuous, but there is always some painful ambiguity about who is to blame. I might be [tempted] to blame myself." In the title story, a fallout shelter symbolizes the individual's desire for physical safety in a hostile world and his desire for material proof of his economic status in an equally hostile world of downward and upward mobility. Moreover, the fallout shelter also symbolizes something the characters can feel but not understand—the frantic search for emotional security that was masked by the outwardly free-and-easy Eisenhower years. Not until a character can exorcise the fear, can he begin to live the kind of life Cheever advocates. Mrs. Pastern does this when she leaves her husband and his fallout shelter. Although there is more madness and desperation in this collection than in Cheever's previous two books, Cheever holds steadfastly to his comic vision. "The plight of man alone," he writes in "Marito in Citta," is "essentially a comic situation such as getting tangled up in a trout line."

"Clementina," one of this volume's two best stories, presents the familiar Cheever theme of the displaced person and the naif seduced by the city, but here they are given a new twist. Clementina, an Italian servant, readily adapts to American ways and eventually becomes thoroughly Americanized in her appearance. Although she is superstitious, she is not so naive as her American employer, whose ideas concerning marriage she finds boyish. His marriage, based on love, ends in divorce, while hers, to a much older man and based on practical need, is successful. Cheever's own views on marriage are neither those of the romantic employer nor those of the fatalistic Clementina, who believes that wonders are no more. When an interviewer asked Cheever for "an example of a preposterous lie that tells a great deal about life," he responded, "the vows of Holy Matrimony." The human relationship between a married couple is an entirely different matter, and Cheever has called his own marriage "a splendid example of the richness and diversity of human nature."

The collection's best story is "The Swimmer." Cheever began with the myth of Narcissus and then compiled 150 pages of notes for a story that is only fifteen pages long. Contemplating the "imponderables" made this "a terribly difficult story to write." Structurally it is his finest achievement. The story follows Neddy Merrill on his eight-mile pool-to-pool swim across Westchester. His decision to make the swim is impulsive, and the first half of the trip moves along rapidly: four miles in four pages. Then the pace becomes gradually slower, the pools

farther apart, and Neddy's swimming less exhilarating, more compulsive. The final four miles take up eleven pages of text. Contemplation replaces motion, and every time Neddy climbs out of a pool the ordeal becomes greater both for him and for the reader who already knows what Neddy refuses to face: that his life is as empty as the boarded-up house he returns to at the end of his swim. The image of the athlete who returns to his past, who tries to recapture his lost youth, recurs throughout Cheever's fiction. As Cheever has said, "The point is to finish and go on to the next thing. I also feel, not as strongly as I used to, that if I looked over my shoulder I would die." Cheever was pleased with "The Swimmer," though not with the film version made by Frank and Eleanor Perry in 1968. His belief that the fiction writer must "avoid those experiences which can be handled most expertly on film" undoubtedly accounts for some of his dissatisfaction with the Perrys' work and perhaps also explains why although film rights for *The House-breaker of Shady Hill* and the Wapshot novels were sold, no films were produced.

After spending six weeks in Russia in 1964 as part of a cultural exchange program, Cheever returned to his home in Ossining. In 1965 the American Academy of Arts and Letters awarded him the Howells Medal for *The Wapshot Scandal,* and four years later his third novel was published. *Bullet Park* (1969) pleased him greatly: "I'd done precisely what I'd wanted: a cast of three characters, a simple and resonant prose style and a scene where a man saves his beloved son from death by fire." The pleasure ended when Benjamin DeMott's review appeared in the 27 April 1969 issue of the *New York Times Book Review* and, in Cheever's estimation, turned the critical tide against his novel. DeMott cited poor characterization, "lax composition," and "perfunctoriness" among its weaknesses; more important, it was "broken-backed" and evidenced "the problem of story style vs. novel style."

Bullet Park does, at first glance, seem to be little more than two stories glued together at the end. Part one chronicles several weeks in the life of Eliot Nailles, who like his creator is a suburbanite, loves his dog and cutting wood with a chainsaw, is a writer (of mouthwash advertisements), belongs to a New York club, and has visited Italy. What Nailles gradually discovers is that he has lost control over his life. His mother has had a stroke. Neighbors come in the night to dump garbage on his property. His wife Nellie, "the raw material for a nightclub act" about the suburban housewife, seems to him no more human than a cartoon character. His son Tony is failing at school and is dropped from the football team (he is "not indispensable"). When Tony brings home the older woman he has just spent the night with, Nailles construes this as a threat to his sexual supremacy. Then Tony tells his father that he does not want to grow up in Nailles's seemingly one-dimensional image, which so provokes Nailles that he attacks his son with a golf club, precipitating Tony's Bartleby-like withdrawal from life. Outside of his home, Nailles fares no better. While waiting for a train, a man is sucked under an express and killed; the body is not found and the only evidence of his having lived at all is a shoe. Commuting to work becomes an ordeal for Nailles who begins to depend on drugs as much as the railroad to get him from Bullet Park to Manhattan. Tony is finally cured—by a guru, not drugs or modern science—and part one ends on a faintly hopeful note.

Part two traces the life of Paul Hammer, the illegitimate son of a wealthy, irresponsible capitalist and his secretary, a kleptomaniac from Indiana. Alone in the world, Hammer begins searching for a room with yellow walls where, he believes, his "illustrious" life will begin. After much melancholy drinking and wandering, Hammer gets his room, but not his dream. This loss, coupled with his marriage to an emasculating wife, drives Hammer insane. A combination of envy and righteousness motivates Hammer to follow the messianic plan of his virulently anti-American, expatriate mother: move to a typical American suburb, lead an inconspicuous life, find a man who is "a good example of a life lived without any genuine emotion or value" and then "crucify him," for "nothing less than a crucifixion will wake that world."

Hammer and Nailles are, Cheever has said, simply "two men with their own risks," not "psychiatric or social metaphors" or, as some reviewers have thought, allegorical personifications of good and evil. The risks they run form what Cheever has called the "perilous moral journey" that every American must face. Unlike Coverly Wapshot, Hammer and Nailles do not survive. The obsessive and extreme views they adopt in order to make sense of their lives ultimately blind them to the very reality they purport to see. Obsessions manifest themselves in action, but Cheever's concern is more with character. The strength of *Bullet Park* lies in the successful adaptation of style to character in each of its three parts. Part one is related in the third person, but the point of view is close to that of Nailles, and the confusing chronology of this section accurately reflects the confused state of

Nailles's mind as he attempts to order the chaos his life has become. Part two, related by Hammer, is a monologue in which a madman rationally recounts all of the events which led to his crime. In part three, the point of view alternates between Hammer and Nailles, remaining with the latter during and after the climactic scene in which Nailles—with some help from the guru and his chainsaw—saves Tony from a fire. Just before this, Nailles has resumed his sexual relationship with Nellie, an indication that he is beginning to come out of his drugged state. When he rescues his son, he is again asserting the value of life over the power of death; he saves Tony from Hammer and himself from the death-in-life state into which he has fallen. Unfortunately, his desire to celebrate life is not as strong as his desire to avoid whatever is unpleasant. "Nailles thought of pain and suffering as a principality, lying somewhere beyond the legitimate borders of western Europe," a not unreasonable idea considering the American addiction to painkillers and the Manichean mentality fostered in the cold war. Although Tony is saved, Hammer's cry in the suburban wilderness goes unheeded, and Hammer himself is hidden away in a state hospital. "Tony went back to school on Monday and Nailles—drugged—went off to work and everything was as wonderful, wonderful, wonderful, wonderful as it had been." This sentence, the final one in the novel, echoes the last paragraph of part one, thus underscoring the ironic fact that perhaps not even a crucifixion will awaken Bullet Park, which prefers the soporific blandishments of Lawrence Welk ("wonderful, wonderful") to the risks and the true wonder of life. All of Cheever's books have been critical of our modern society, but *Bullet Park*, which Wilfrid Sheed has called "a brutal vivisection of American life," is by far the most caustic and the least optimistic.

The watershed in Cheever's career is 1964, the year *The Brigadier and the Golf Widow* and *The Wapshot Scandal* appeared and, based on the few stories he has published since then, the year he completed the shift from short-story writer to novelist. His next collection of stories did not appear for nearly a decade and even then included several pre-1964 pieces. *The World of Apples* (1973) still evidences Cheever's mastery of the short story and his continuing interest in narrative experimentation. "The Jewels of the Cabots," for example, is told as if by free association, and in another story the narrator is the belly of Lawrence Farnsworth. Although this last may seem typical of the archness which characterizes contemporary American fiction, *The World of Apples* is quite distinct from most recent work by other American writers. It is, John Wain has explained, "a book by a gifted and established writer which doesn't, for once, seem to come out of negativism, alienation, despair of the human condition and frantic self-gratification. . . ." In one story, Cheever goes so far as to explicitly disassociate himself from the kind of fiction Wain describes. In another, "Mene, Mene, Tekel, Upharsin," an American returning home after a long stay in Europe discovers this odd reversal: lavatory walls scribbled over with long, floridly written stories and book racks filled with scatological and pornographic writings.

The protagonist in the title story, Asa Bascomb, is a New England poet living in Italy who suddenly finds it impossible to write anything but obscene limericks, which he burns. Only after a Christian pilgrimage and a pagan immersion in a cold forest pool is he able to begin his "long poem on the inalienable dignity of light and air that, while it would not get the Nobel Prize, would grace the last months of his life." Celebrating life frees Bascomb from his brief but artistically deadly nightmare vision of the world as an obscenity. Equally important, it frees him from the death-fear which Americans commonly ascribe to their writers who, once they have accepted the fear, find their "esteem," their "usefulness," and finally their lives destroyed.

Few of the characters in these stories are as fortunate as Asa Bascomb. Many of them are the grotesques we expect to find in Cheever's fiction: a cigar-smoking aunt who calls herself Percy; or "Artemis, the Honest Well Digger," whose father had chosen his name thinking it referred to artesian wells and whose search for pure water is as futile as his "looking for a girl as pure and fresh as the girl on the oleomargarine package." Their freakishness is matched by the absurdity of the situations they face and the extremes to which they go in order to make sense of their seemingly inexplicable worlds. The husband in "The Fourth Alarm" sees his wife metamorphose from lover to mother to dowdy social studies teacher to actress in a nude play; he takes to early morning gin drinking. Other characters resort to eccentric behavior, a veneer of social respectability, imaginary lovers, even murder and the application of Euclidean geometry to human emotions. For them, as for Hammer and Nailles, there is no redemption and no celebration as there is for Coverly Wapshot and Asa Bascomb.

The antecedents for Cheever's next book, the highly acclaimed novel *Falconer* (1977), reach far back into his life and writings: his parents, his ambivalent relationship with his brother Fred whose murder he once contemplated, *The Wapshot Chronicle*, "The Cat," and his stories about derelict fathers. Cheever has said that *Falconer* "was not written out of a singular experience" but, rather, represents "the sum of my living." The novel's immediate foreground begins with the two years Cheever spent teaching writing at Sing Sing prison in the early 1970s. Having gone there as a "do-gooder," he soon became depressed by what he saw. He continued his teaching, however, even during the Attica riot in September 1971 ("It was very exciting. When you went in you weren't always sure you were going to get out") until a series of heart attacks forced him to stop. After a brief convalescence, he returned to a task he never much liked—academic teaching. He had taught writing at Barnard College in 1956-1957 and now went first to the University of Iowa and then in 1974-1975 to Boston University, where he was visiting professor of creative writing. In Boston his depression returned and led to alcoholism and a month at the Smithers Rehabilitation Center in New York City where "the dreadfulness of the place was therapeutic."

In the novel, Sing Sing, Boston, and Smithers are all fictionalized as Falconer Prison. Cheever, who eschewed the documentary realist's use of circumstantial detail, created Falconer less as a specific prison than as a state of mind, as one of the many symbols of confinement to be found in his work— St. Botolphs, Bullet Park, and marriage, among others. *Falconer* is, therefore, not a novel about prison life but, as Cheever explained it, "the pervading sense of confinement in all apparently free behavior." This is one of the first lessons learned by Ezekiel Farragut, a forty-eight-year-old college professor and convicted fratricide, during the little more than a year he spends at Falconer. Farragut is a typical Cheever protagonist: a naif suffering the pangs of displacement. Moreover, although he has good cause to suffer—uncaring parents, a murder-minded brother, a narcissistic wife, a sadistic prison official—much of his misery is self-inflicted and derives from his own uncorrected weaknesses, particularly his drug addiction. Like Eliot Nailles in *Bullet Park*, Farragut uses drugs in order to forget a painful past and to deaden his senses to all future pain; but, also like Nailles, he has a strong desire to recall the pleasures of the past and to quicken his senses to the pleasures around him. Before Farragut can affirm life, however, he must

The day was shit. He would put visibility at five
hundred feet. Could it be exploited for an escape? He didn't think
so. The chance of escape reminded him of Jody, a remembrance that
had remained light-hearted since he had and Jody has pasionately
kissed goodbye. DiMatteo, the chaplain's dude, had brought him the
facts on Jody no more than six weeks after Jody's flight. They
had met in the tunnel on a dark night when Farragut was leaving
The Valley. DiMatteo showed him a newspaper photograph of Jody.
that he had been sent in the mail. It was Jody on his wedding day—
Ody at his most beautiful and triumphant. His brightness shone
through the letter-press of a small town paper. His bride was a
demure and a pretty young Oriental and the caption said that
H. Keith Morgan had, that day, married Sally Chou Lai, the youngest
daughter of Ling Chow Lai, President of the Viaduct Wire Company
where he groom was employed. There was nothing more and nothing
more was needed. Farragut laughed, but not DiMatteo who said
angrily, "He promised to wait for me. I saved his life and he
promised to wait for me. He loved me. Oh God, how he loved me.
He gave me his golden cross." DiMatteo lifted the cross out of
the curls on his chest and showed it to Farragut. Farragut's
knowledge of the cross were intimate and his memories of his
lover were Keen but not at all sad. "He must have married her for
her money," said BiMatteo, "she must be rich. He promised to wait
for me."

From typescript of Falconer, *"which seems to illustrate the fact that I use yellow paper and that, on good days, I seldom make revisions"* reject the separation of mind and body theorized by Descartes, his favorite writer, and, like the biblical Ezekiel, learn the importance of personal responsibility and the possibility of rebirth.

Farragut's journey to personal responsibility and rebirth involves four stages. The first involves his naive and selfish belief in justice and redress. He demands the right to be heard, the right to be given his daily dose of methadone, the antisacrament which precludes the celebration of life. In the second stage Farragut turns from the abstract to the physical. His homosexual relationship with the youthful Jody (Farragut's first) evidences his willingness to experience life, but it also forces him to question whether his desire for Jody is really love or a subconscious longing for death. Jody's escape from Falconer, a "miracle" made possible by his inverting sexuality, Christianity, and the American success ethic for his own ends, sends Farragut even deeper into his deadly self-love. Farragut has failed to learn Jody's lesson: one must transform the

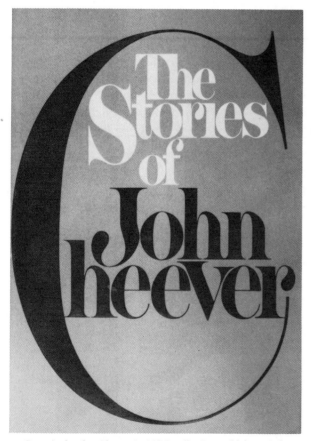

Dust jacket for Cheever's 1978 collection, which won the Pulitzer Prize, the American Book Award, the National Book Critics Circle Award, and the McDowell medal

world in order to make both it and oneself useful. Having tried to love one man, Farragut now tries to love all mankind. His vision of social change, stimulated by the Amana (Attica) uprising, leads him to one of his first constructive, and therefore risky, acts, the building of a contraband radio. Since Cheever, however, believes that individual reform must precede social reform, Farragut's grand design necessarily fails. Although Farragut perceives how the prison administration (society) sanctions and even promotes the drugged state in order to preserve the status quo, he overestimates the prisoners' desire for freedom. In the fourth stage, Farragut learns that he is free of his addiction (ironically, with the state's help). This knowledge frees him to confess the full story of his fratricide to a dying inmate who represents the final result of narcissism—loneliness—just as his beautiful wife Marcia represents its cause. The inmate's death frees Farragut from the last traces of self-love, and Farragut's escape, a parody of Edmund Dantes's escape from the Chateau d'If in *The Count of Monte Cristo,* is appropriately described in terms of the birth process. Farragut emerges from Falconer psychologically whole, free of those fears which had led him to withdraw into the prison of self. Spiritually renewed, he can, with Leander Wapshot and Asa Bascomb, face his world and "Rejoice, he thought, rejoice."

Cheever's own sense of renewal was no less dramatic. After leaving Smithers, Cheever, an Episcopalian, resumed his regular practice of going to church "to make my thanksgivings" and in just ten months wrote *Falconer,* finishing it, appropriately, on Maundy Thursday. He had overcome his depression and, considering the novel's highly favorable reviews, any lingering problem with novelistic structure.

Twelve years before the publication of *Falconer,* John Aldridge called Cheever "one of the most grievously underdiscussed important writers we have at the present." This state of affairs, which has not yet been sufficiently corrected, derived, Aldridge felt, from three chief causes: Cheever's "unfortunate" association with the *New Yorker,* his failure to explore the darker implications of his work ("he does not yet disturb us enough"), and the feeling that there is "still little to convince one that Cheever is moving on." Until *Falconer,* Cheever's fiction, although it had been widely reviewed, generated only a scant amount of academic criticism, a situation for which Cheever was himself partly responsible. An intensely private writer, he avoided literary competitiveness, disassociated himself from literary schools, and even denied having any desire for posthumous fame. Believing in "the transcendent relationship between the writer and the reader," he preferred the public's acceptance of his books to what he dismissed as "academic vivisection." His stories, although often just as slick and hopeful as any *New Yorker* fiction, are generally conceded to have a significance not generally accorded to the fiction found in this magazine; "I never wrote *for* the *New Yorker*," Cheever has stated; "they bought my stories." His comic vision precludes his saying "No! In Thunder," the sine qua non of modern American fiction established by Leslie Fiedler, but this does not mean that Cheever's stories are "coy" and "cloying" as Aldridge suggested. Even before *Bullet Park*, Cheever had explored the darker side of middle-class existence, and at *Esquire*'s third annual "Writing in America Today" symposium, he had said that because "life in the United States in 1960 is hell" the "only position for a writer now is negation." As a satirist, however, Cheever negates only as the precondition for the building of a better world. Although he believes in the inherent innovativeness of all fiction, his concern for the moral basis of literature puts him at odds with today's fabulators whose stylistic pyrotechnics he rejects: "experimentation, particularly that spinoff of innovation in which license is taken in using words in a nonverbal and inchoate sense . . . seems to be generally unsuccessful." Not surprisingly, his favorite among recent novels was *Humboldt's Gift* by Saul Bellow, a writer who shares many of Cheever's concerns.

The hard-won affirmations of *Falconer* brought Cheever a new measure of popular and critical success and made possible both the publication of a sorely needed retrospective volume of his short fiction and an intelligent reassessment of his work. As if in response to this sudden acclamation, Cheever chose to become a more accessible writer—making public appearances, giving readings, granting interviews, and accepting an honorary degree from Harvard and a Pulitzer Prize for *The Stories of John Cheever*. Adaptations of three stories were shown on public television in 1979, which also aired Cheever's original screenplay, *The Shady Hill Kidnapping*, on 12 January 1982. Six months later Cheever was dead. Even during his struggle with cancer, Cheever wrote, completing a pared-down version of the "bulky novel" he had originally conceived. *Oh What a Paradise It Seems* is a remarkable work and not simply because of the history of its composition. Brief as this short novel, or long story (100 pages), is, it sums up not only

Cheever's career but more especially the stage he eventually achieved as a writer who managed to be at once conventional and contemporary. *Oh What a Paradise It Seems* is a narrative which flirts with its own fictiveness yet which avoids the cynicism, or skepticism, usually associated with self-reflexive fiction. As much premodern as postmodern, the novel is double in other ways as well, for the story of protagonist Lemuel Sears's efforts to save Beasley Pond from chemical contamination parallels his striving to save himself from spiritual contamination. The metaphorical wedding of the physical and spiritual realms is reflected in the intertwined lives of two other characters, environmentalist Horace Chisholm and housewife Betsy Logan, who, like Sears, confront their own longings and loneliness. The novel's comic surface and decorous, self-assured style transcend the seeming waywardness of Cheever's characteristically wayward plot and provide an alternative to that sense of "spiritual ungainliness" that the characters share with their author. As Susan Cheever makes abundantly clear in her biographical memoir, *Home Before Dark*, Cheever suffered throughout his life the same feelings of displacement and psychological vertigo that afflict his characters. As the stories and novels make equally clear, however, Cheever thought of the writing of fiction not as a means for recording his own dis-ease but, instead, as in *Oh What a Paradise It Seems*, as a way of conjuring a transcendent alternative to it. And the success of his conjuring trick—of his art—readers and critics are only beginning to understand and appreciate.

Bibliographies:

Dennis Coates, "John Cheever: A Checklist, 1930-1978," *Bulletin of Bibliography*, 36 (January-March 1979): 1-13, 49;
Indispensable for its listing of Cheever's shorter works; see also Coates's supplement in the *Critical Essays* volume cited below.

Francis J. Bosha, *John Cheever: A Reference Guide* (Boston: G. K. Hall, 1981);
The annotated listing of reviews and other works about Cheever is especially helpful.

Robert A. Morace, "John Cheever," in *Contemporary Authors Bibliographical Series: American Novelists*, edited by James Martine (Detroit: Gale Research, 1986);
A descriptive and evaluative discussion of the available commentary on Cheever and his fiction.

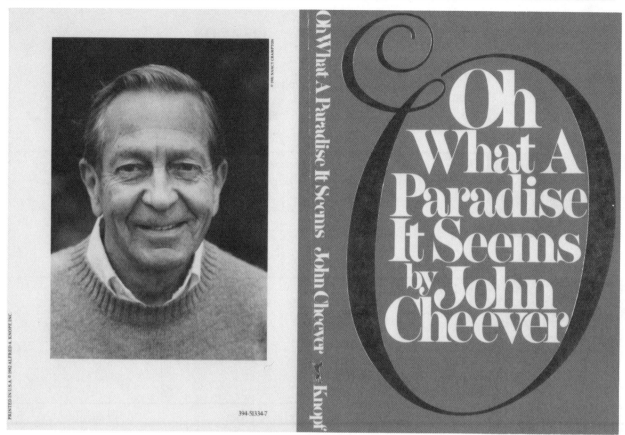

Dust jacket for Cheever's last novel

References:

Susan Cheever, *Home Before Dark* (Boston: Houghton Mifflin, 1984);

Useful both as a daughter's memoir and as a synthesis of biographical information otherwise available only in widely scattered interviews.

Samuel Coale, *John Cheever* (New York: Frederick Ungar, 1977);

An introduction to Cheever and his work.

R. G. Collins, ed., *Critical Essays on John Cheever* (Boston: G. K. Hall, 1982);

Especially valuable for its reprinting of important reviews, interviews, and critical articles about Cheever, for the editor's introduction, and for the essay by Samuel Coale.

George Hunt, *John Cheever: The Hobgoblin Company of Love* (Grand Rapids, Mich.: William B. Eerdman's, 1983);

The most extensive analysis of Cheever's style and the formal integrity of his novels yet published.

Lynne Waldeland, *John Cheever* (Boston: Twayne, 1979);

A second introduction to Cheever's fiction, more exhaustive than Coale's though less incisive.

Papers:

Brandeis University has the typescripts of many of Cheever's short stories and books, including *The Wapshot Chronicle*.

James Gould Cozzens

This entry was updated by Leland H. Cox, Jr. (Columbia, South Carolina) from his entry
in DLB 9, American Novelists, 1910-1945.

Places	Kent School (Kent, Connecticut) Cuba	Lambertville, New Jersey	Williamstown, Massachusetts
Influences and Relationships	Bernice Baumgarten		
Literary Movements and Forms	Determinism	Social Realism	Novel of Manners
Major Themes	Ethics of Duty The Professors (Law) Chain of Causation	Reason vs. Passion Limits of Free Will Youth vs. Age	Social Satisfaction and Subordination
Cultural and Artistic Influences	William Shakespeare	18th-Century English Literature	
Social and Economic Influences	World War II (Air Force)		

See also the Cozzens entry in DLB Yearbook 1984 *and* DLB Documentary Series, volume two.

BIRTH: Chicago, Illinois, 19 August 1903, to Henry William and Bertha Wood Cozzens.

EDUCATION: Harvard University, 1922-1924.

MARRIAGE: 31 December 1927 to Sylvia Bernice Baumgarten.

AWARDS AND HONORS: Pulitzer Prize for *Guard of Honor*, 1949; Litt.D., Harvard University, 1952; William Dean Howells Medal of the American Academy of Arts and Letters for *By Love Possessed*, 1960.

DEATH: Stuart, Florida, 9 August 1978.

BOOKS: *Confusion* (Boston: Brimmer, 1924);
Michael Scarlett (New York: Boni, 1925; London: Holden, 1927);
Cock Pit (New York: Morrow, 1928);
The Son of Perdition (New York: Morrow, 1929; London: Longmans, Green, 1929);
S.S. San Pedro (New York: Harcourt, Brace, 1931; London: Longmans, Green, 1931);
The Last Adam (New York: Harcourt, Brace, 1933); republished as *A Cure of Flesh* (London: Longmans, Green, 1933);
Castaway (London: Longmans, Green, 1934; New York: Random House, 1934);
Men and Brethren (New York: Harcourt, Brace, 1936; London: Longmans, Green, 1936);
Ask Me Tomorrow (New York: Harcourt, Brace, 1940; London: Longmans, Green, 1940);
The Just and the Unjust (New York: Harcourt, Brace, 1942; London: Cape, 1943);
Guard of Honor (New York: Harcourt, Brace, 1948; London: Longmans, Green, 1949);
By Love Possessed (New York: Harcourt, Brace, 1957; London: Longmans, Green, 1958);
Children and Others (New York: Harcourt, Brace & World, 1964; London: Longmans, Green, 1965);
Morning Noon and Night (New York: Harcourt, Brace & World, 1968; London: Longmans, Green, 1968);
A Flower in Her Hair (Bloomfield Hills, Mich. & Columbia, S.C.: Bruccoli Clark, 1974);
A Rope for Dr. Webster (Bloomfield Hills, Mich. & Columbia, S.C.: Bruccoli Clark, 1976);

James Gould Cozzens

Just Representations: A James Gould Cozzens Reader, edited by Matthew J. Bruccoli (Carbondale & Edwardsville: Southern Illinois University Press/New York & London: Harcourt Brace Jovanovich, 1978);
A Time of War: Air Force Diaries and Pentagon Memos, edited by Matthew J. Bruccoli (Columbia, S.C. & Bloomfield Hills, Mich.: Bruccoli Clark, 1984);
Selected Notebooks: 1960-1967, edited by Matthew J. Bruccoli (Columbia, S.C. & Bloomfield Hills, Mich.: Bruccoli Clark, 1984).

James Gould Cozzens was a private man and (as a writer) a professional who believed that his time was best spent in writing, in the perfecting and mastering of his craft. Once launched on his career as a novelist at the age of twenty-one, Cozzens did very little else; and in this sense the story of his life is the story of his art.

James Gould Cozzens was born on 19 August 1903 in Chicago, Illinois, where his parents, both New Englanders, were temporarily residing. Taking an executive position with a New York printing machinery company in 1906, Cozzens's father moved the family to Staten Island, which was still a rural locale. Cozzens later recalled that there were "wide second-growth woodlands" between villages and farms where people, "as they had for a hundred and fifty years, grew vegetables, harvested hay, raised chickens, and maintained small dairy herds."

Cozzens's formal education began at Staten Island Academy, and his first publication—a poem entitled "The Andes"—appeared in the *Quill,* the academy's magazine, in 1915. In 1916 he entered the Kent School, an Episcopal preparatory school in Connecticut. Cozzens continued to write, and several of his prose compositions were published in the *Kent Quarterly,* of which he became editor in his sixth-form year. While at Kent, as he would acknowledge later, Cozzens was strongly influenced by the school's headmaster, Father Frederick Herbert Sill, not directly in literary terms but in terms of moral precepts, discipline, and a sense of responsibility. Though Cozzens was something of a rebel at the school, he wrote for the March 1920 issue of the *Atlantic Monthly* an essay entitled "A Democratic School," which was a defense of Kent.

In 1922 Cozzens entered Harvard and began writing *Confusion,* his first novel. By his own record he completed it on 24 February 1923, and the novel was published in Boston by B. J. Brimmer on 3 April 1924. During the two years he was at Harvard, Cozzens also contributed several pieces of verse and prose to the *Harvard Advocate.* Partly because of class-cutting difficulties, Cozzens left Harvard in 1924. He turned to the writing of his second novel, *Michael Scarlett,* which was written in Nova Scotia in 1924-1925 on a small advance from Brimmer. The work was published on 2 November 1925.

From this point on, Cozzens was a professional novelist, even though he was not yet able to support himself as a writer. Other jobs were temporary, giving him a source of modest income while he continued his writing and often providing him with background material for his fiction. In 1925 and 1926 Cozzens was in Cuba, where he worked as a tutor for the children of American employees at the Czarnikow-Rionda Central Tuinucu sugar mill. Cozzens's Cuban experience gave him the basic materials for his third and fourth novels, *Cock Pit* (1928) and *The Son of Perdition* (1929). In 1927 he worked as a tutor for an American boy in Europe, and much of this experience was put to fictional purposes in *Ask Me Tomorrow* (1940), Coz-

zens's ninth novel. After returning to America in 1927, Cozzens was employed as the librarian for the New York Athletic Club, and on 31 December he was married to Bernice Baumgarten, a New York literary agent. With her husband as one of her clients, she continued her career with Brandt and Brandt.

Becoming ever more protective of his privacy, Cozzens and his wife moved to Lambertville, New Jersey, in 1933. Cozzens was now a professional author both in the sense that he was following unswervingly his chosen career and that he was earning his living from it, though his wife was providing a steady income. Cozzens's feelings about the style of life he preferred and his basic philosophy of writing are well expressed in a 1936 letter he wrote to Fred B. Millett for *Contemporary American Authors* (1940): "I do all I can by living in the country and staying there, to keep my life placid and comfortable. So far I have succeeded pretty well. I like to grow vegetables and have been trying for some years to raise an edible artichoke. I have long been interested in the Civil War and was much disappointed to see it worn out as a book subject before I was ready to write on it. . . . I am also interested in theology, either Roman or Anglican. I am very fond of beer. I have no theories about literature and other people's irk me. With great difficulty and uncertainty and much lost motion I write whatever I find that I can. The view I have of writing is that a writer does well to write in a clear and unobtrusive way, trying not to be dull, and being careful to avoid obvious untruths and general nonsense."

Cozzens also earned money from the sale of short stories during the 1920s and 1930s, and in 1938 he worked for a year as a guest editor at *Fortune* magazine. From 1942 to 1945 Cozzens served in the United States Army Air Force. Rising to the rank of major by the time of his discharge, Cozzens was first assigned to the School of Applied Tactics at Orlando, Florida, was for a brief time in New York City, and was finally assigned to a staff position at the Pentagon. His air force diaries and Pentagon memos have been posthumously published as *A Time of War* (1984). Cozzens drew on his World War II experience for *Guard of Honor* (1948), one of the major works in his canon. From Lambertville, Cozzens and his wife moved three times more during their lives: to Belle Haven, Virginia, in 1957, then to Williamstown, Massachusetts, in 1958, and to Stuart, Florida, in 1973. James Gould Cozzens died in Florida on 9 August 1978, ten days before his seventy-fifth birthday.

The simple but nonetheless high professional aims expressed by Cozzens in his letter to Millett are not easy to recognize in *Confusion* and *Michael Scarlett*. *Confusion* is a romantic novel whose central character, Cerise D'Atrée, a young French woman of noble blood, becomes increasingly disillusioned with the kind of life she finds in America and dies because she is unable to apply her aspirations to the life she experiences in a foreign culture. The novel is in effect a kind of travelogue that follows Cerise as she moves through the upper levels of society in Europe and America. In this regard Cozzens at least succeeds in presenting a realistic picture of different social structures, which he would do with increasing skill in his later fiction. In *Confusion*, however, society is described by the narrator rather than delineated through the words and deeds of the characters. Cerise's travels ultimately bring her into contact with Blair Boughton, a dashing figure who seems finally to match her romantic ideal. Cerise agrees to elope with him; but while the two are driving together in Blair's automobile there is a wreck and Blair is killed. Though Cerise survives the accident, when she learns of Blair's death, she decides that life is not worth living. She lingers for a few days and then dies from despair and heartbreak.

Michael Scarlett is a romantic adventure story set in Elizabethan England, and like *Confusion* it features a youth who is at odds with society. Michael Scarlett is also a young person of noble blood. The novel begins with a scene set on the Yorkshire coast, where Michael rescues two survivors from the Spanish Armada. One is a noble youth, much like Michael himself; Michael treats this prisoner of war courteously and according to a mutually understood code of chivalry. But when he turns his prisoners over to the Queen's men, they are killed. Thus the opening scene of the novel illustrates Michael's central weakness: he is unable to reconcile his chivalrous idealism to the realities of an unchivalrous world. His infatuation with Lady Ann Shelton results in unrequited love because, when she is forced to marry for political reasons, he does not have the maturity to understand the necessity for political marriages. And as Michael moves from Yorkshire to Cambridge and to London, he is not able to gain any wisdom from his experiences in the world. At Cambridge he has made the acquaintance of Thomas Nashe and Christopher Marlowe; and in London he comes into contact with Ben Jonson, John Donne, and William Shakespeare. Life at the Golden Asse, the inn where Michael resides in London, is riotous and dissolute;

and though he has sworn to uphold the Queen's law, he dies when he impetuously enters a fight to defend Thomas Nashe from arrest by the Queen's men. As Cozzens presents it, this is not an adequate reason for dying. Because Michael's sacrifice is spontaneous and emotional and serves no higher purpose than a purely personal one, his death is seen to be all the more tragic.

Though Cozzens's first two novels were technically flawed, it is also true, as Matthew J. Bruccoli has pointed out, that both works reveal glimpses of some of the hallmarks of Cozzens's mature fiction: "*Confusion* introduced the search for values or standards of conduct that would characterize all of Cozzens's work; and *Michael Scarlett* showed Cozzens's ability to treat a subject with authority, for the novel manifests a knowledge of Elizabethan literature and society remarkable in a twenty-two-year-old Harvard drop-out." Cozzens did not think highly of his first four novels; he considered his fifth, *S.S. San Pedro* (1931), as the first effort worthy of recognition. One might agree with his judgment regarding *Confusion* and *Michael Scarlett*, but there are grounds for arguing that *Cock Pit* and *The Son of Perdition* are worthy of inclusion in the canon. They are much less concerned with romantic idealism than Cozzens's first two novels; and, more important, the two works are based directly on experiences and observations from the time that Cozzens was living in Cuba. As Cozzens's later, major works would concentrate on different professions—medicine, the ministry, law, the military—and the characters and social orders associated with them, so *Cock Pit* and *The Son of Perdition* gave realistic pictures of the workings of the sugar industry in Cuba and the types of people that are involved in it.

Confusion and *Michael Scarlett* deal with characters who are essentially fatherless, who lack the firm and reassuring guidance of a parental hand. *Cock Pit* is a novel whose central characters form a father-and-daughter team; and the willingness of Lancy Micks and his daughter Ruth to accept responsibility is depicted in terms of their bravery, integrity, and self-reliance. Lancy Micks is a prototype of Cozzens's later heroes: he is a mature, competent professional, capable of dispassionate judgment, and his personal values are fixed strongly to his professional values. Unlike Cozzens's later novels, professional ability is shared by the sexes; Ruth is one of the few female characters in Cozzens's fiction who is able to operate effectively in a man's world. It is she, for example, who effects the defeat of Don Miguel Bautizo—a sugar magnate who is more interested in manipulating markets than in running an honest enterprise—to save her father from being assassinated. This is the only instance in Cozzens's fiction where a professional man has to be extricated from his difficulties by a woman.

The novel focuses on two aspects of the operations of the sugar company. First, and not surprisingly, the principles upon which the sugar cane mills operate are purely economic. The chief article of faith is succinctly expressed: "The company expects every pig to boost the pen"; and in their subservience to the larger corporate unit the workers in the mills are pictured as little more than a class of wage-earning slaves. That portion of the company's activities which is concerned with cultivating and harvesting the crop is presented in a more positive light. The operative principle here is that "One does not wear one's life out . . . learning the sacred meaning of that word 'crop' and disregard its traditions and obligations so easily." In this way the essence of conflict in the novel is cast in terms of a clash between industrial and traditional values. Thus, since virtually everyone in the novel is dependent on the company for a livelihood, a great deal of character judgment can be based on which of the two value systems an individual responds to.

Lancy Micks—who, as the company's field supervisor, is associated with traditional values pertaining to the crop and demands extremely high levels of performance from himself and others— is the most thoroughgoing professional man in the novel. The belief that maturity and ability go hand-in-hand is axiomatic with Micks. College graduates thinking of themselves as competent engineers are found wanting by Micks, who has "no use for youth" and who gives it "no more quarter than life itself did." Micks's professional attitude toward the proper running of things is understood by his daughter. Her father is upset about a bridge that Don Miguel Bautizo has had constructed and which is later sabotaged. The bridge itself has nothing to do with Micks's responsibilities as field supervisor or, directly, with the raising of cane; still, Ruth realizes that "it mattered to him. Of course, he knew a bridge was just a bridge. . . . But he had some natural sense of simple beauty, ultimate art, of the right thing unostentatiously, inevitably, in the right place." Micks is vocal not only in his criticism of the bridge but also in those instances where he believes company politics are interfering with the cultivating, harvesting, and milling of the crop. Finally, when the sabotaged bridge collapses, Mick rejects a bribe of $10,000 that is offered to him as

the price for his silence. The defeat of Don Miguel and the reassuring triumph of good over evil are the stuff of romance; but the values that Micks and his daughter represent foreshadow a growing concern in Cozzens's art with the proper relationship between the professional man, his work, and his social surroundings.

In *The Son of Perdition* Cozzens penetrates more deeply still into the operations of the Cuban sugar industry. The shadow cast by the United Sugar Company is huge and ominous, overwhelming the individuals who are subservient to it. Cozzens gives the impression that the map of Cuba is itself but a company chart; and for Pepe Rijo, the puppet mayor of Dosfuegos, "the United Sugar Company materialized like one of its great oil-burning locomotives, tall as ten horses, rushing down on him. . . . It was the ultimate horror. . . . His mind raced up and down and everywhere a wall marked U.S.C. confronted him." On almost every level the company is presented as an unfeeling titan, dehumanizing all that it touches. The ethics the company practices are so cold that the only means of preserving one's self-respect is to defy the company's power. To make this point, Cozzens works with a central grouping of three characters: Oliver Findley, Joel B. Stellow, and Vidal Monaga. Together the words and actions of these three men form a web of commentary on the concepts of aristocracy, professional competence, and individual integrity.

Oliver Findley can be considered an aristocrat by birth. Though his background is never given in detail, Cozzens presents him as a man of upper-class origins who, after many years in Cuba, has degenerated into a bum. Stone, a young engineer from Harvard, recognizes in Findley "the remnants of a caste, a training and a background which seemed to Stone natural and right." But remnants are all that remain; and Findley is less of a character in the novel than he is a malignant force, a symbol of negativity who is frequently associated with the devil.

Joel Stellow, the administrator general for the company, offers an ironic contrast to Findley. He is a master technician in the wielding of organized power, but he lacks the background that Findley has repudiated. As a professional administrator he is first-rate, and he controls the world in which he works with absolute self-assurance; but, because there is in Stellow's past no source of tradition that he can use as a model for responsible moral behavior, it is difficult for him to be more than an expediter of company policy. Thus, while he can recognize objectively that Oliver Findley is a threat to orderly procedure, and while he can act dispassionately (and quickly) to remove him from all contact with the company's operations, Stellow does not recognize the evil for which Findley is the agent and can therefore do nothing about it. Dr. Palacios, who is himself a bitter cynic, provides the reader with important information about Stellow that points to the basic flaw in his character: as a young man in Havana Stellow once came to Palacios seeking a cure for venereal disease. The doctor judged him immediately as "a person of no family or breeding," but also as one in whom there was "the strong impersonality and intelligent ruthlessness of which all great men are made." Palacios takes an interest in Stellow and molds Stellow's personality, teaching him "the morality of ruthless good sense." The point is clear: the gaining of maturity through experience goes for nothing if tradition has not also inculcated a sense of responsibility for moral action.

The title of the novel, as is indicated by Cozzens's choice of an epigraph from St. John, is a biblical allusion, a portion of a prayer Christ offers to God in the Garden of Gethsemane: "While I was with [the disciples] in the world, I kept them in Thy name; those that thou gavest me I have kept, and none of them is lost, but the son of perdition; that the scripture might be fulfilled." The one to whom Christ refers is Judas Iscariot, whose closest counterpart in the novel is Oliver Findley. The man who is most affected by "the son of perdition" is Vidal Monaga, who is the character with the highest sense of moral responsibility. There is no allegory here, though Findley can be said to operate as effectively as Judas in the sense that he makes the sacrifice of Vidal's only son, Osmundo, a matter of necessity. Osmundo and his sister Nida have an incestuous relationship; and when the brother learns that Findley has spent a night in Nida's bed, he flies into a jealous rage. When it dawns on Monaga that his son has committed incest, there is but one course of action to follow. He and Osmundo take their fishing boat out to sea, Vidal throws bait into the water to attract barracuda, and then he pushes his son overboard. In the context of the novel Monaga's action is a moral one. He is a natural aristocrat who understands the essential fitness of things, and he is willing to act unhesitantly for the preservation of the natural order and family pride. As he explains to Stellow, "Other people may do things which are not my business, but with which I will not have myself, my house, my name, when it is borne by a man, dirtied." When Monaga realizes that Osmundo does not understand or appreciate

these values, he decides that "he would be better dead." And he rejects Stellow's efforts to have the murder ruled an accidental death. Stellow's power derives from the industrial might of the sugar company; thus, Monaga's rejection of his help is a rejection of "the machine's inhuman beauty, the reason and might of the machine, confounded so inevitably by the rooted folly, the poor stubborn pride of man." There is then a romantic turn to the end of the novel, a small triumph of man over machine. It is by insisting on a principle of personal responsibility that Monaga counters Stellow's power to manipulate individual lives in the name of the company.

With *S.S. San Pedro*—published first in *Scribner's* magazine in 1930 and based on the actual sinking of the *Vestris*—Cozzens puts all traces of the romantic behind him. In this novel there is a clear-cut distinction between the profession of seamanship (and the code on which it is based) and the exercise of independent reason. The novel addresses a simple question: what course of action is necessary for the survival of the *San Pedro*? The code of seamanship provides an equally simple answer: maintain a strict hierarchy in the chain of command, and make certain that each individual is responsible for and capable of performing the duties that have been assigned to him. Unfortunately for those on board, this code cannot keep the ship afloat. Instead it is directly responsible for the breakdown of order which in turn leads to the sinking of the vessel.

When the *San Pedro* leaves its pier in Hoboken, New Jersey, bound for South America, almost everyone on board is aware that the ship has a list to port. The first person to notice the list is Doctor Percival, who functions in the novel as a symbol of death and whose presence on the ship is an omen of disaster. Cozzens's first description of him is given in terms of a death's-head image: "Doctor Percival's tight face was fleshless and almost gray. His lips sank in, rounded over his teeth. They were lips so scanty that you could see the line of teeth meeting. His eyes, red-rimmed, lay limp in their sockets, appearing to have no color at all." Though Percival goes ashore before the ship puts out to sea, there are brief references to him throughout the text. Marilee Mills, one of the passengers, is afraid he has remained on board. Concerning the effect Percival has on her she says, "I don't like to meet corpses walking around. It means something awful is going to happen to me." Percival is symbolically, if not physically, present on the ship. At the end of the novel the senior second officer, Anthony Bradell, lying half conscious in a lifeboat, has a vision of Percival: "At his side, in a shabby black overcoat, he saw the horrid author of that low voice, insistent, plucking at him: '*But you do not float.*'"

It is not enough to say that the *San Pedro* is destroyed simply because Doctor Percival manages to make his presence felt on the ship. His symbolic presence represents a condition that stands in need of correction—a warning that something vital to the ship's well-being is in a flawed state—not an irreversible judgment of fate. Responsibility for the disaster rests primarily on the shoulders of two men, Captain Clendening and Anthony Bradell. Clendening, who stands at the top of the chain of command, is a sick man; and as the voyage lengthens he becomes less and less able to control the ship. Bradell, who is the most capable of the ship's officers, is an almost constant witness to his captain's decline, yet he will not violate the chain of command to save the ship. In the conflict between duty (which is a function of discipline) and reason, duty wins; but duty, once divorced from reason, becomes an empty concept. And discipline without the exercise of reason degenerates into mindless habit.

When the ship becomes caught in a storm, its condition becomes more and more serious. MacGillivray, the *San Pedro*'s chief engineer, knows that the captain has lost control of the situation and urges Bradell to take command. When Bradell refuses, MacGillivray criticizes him for paying such rigid lip service to discipline and at the same time ignoring Clendening's incompetence. He tells Bradell, "if I was a sailor, I'd rather be drowned than have to tell people afterward what I was doing all morning." It is in this manner that the professional seaman, the man with abilities that are to be admired, fails to meet the highest of his responsibilities, the ones for which he is answerable not to an employer or a superior officer, but to the passengers and crew. Bradell fails not because he is a professional but because his professionalism has not yet been tempered by mature reason.

The Last Adam (1933) is the first of Cozzens's novels to examine closely and critically a single profession (in this case, medicine) and to contrast professional and community standards of conduct. Though Cozzens preferred "Bodies Terrestrial" or *A Cure of Flesh* (which was the title for the British edition) as titles for the work, *The Last Adam* was finally selected as the title for the American edition. It was the first of Cozzens's novels to be selected for the Book-of-the-Month Club. Colin S. Cass,

considering the biblical source for "Bodies Terrestrial" and *The Last Adam,* sees the novel as an ironic treatment of the Old Testament Garden of Eden myth and the New Testament's promise for spiritual immortality. Cass says that the novel does not lament "man's loss of Eden and innocence; rather, it denies that mankind had either one to lose," and regarding the New Testament's promise of immortality, the novel presents "a naturalist's version of the salvation of man. It does not entail the transcendence of any individual's mortality. But passed on from first man to last, the vitality celebrated in George Bull makes mankind what it is. . . ." The action of the novel centers on a typhoid epidemic that ravages the town of New Winton, Connecticut; *The Last Adam* is certainly not, as one inattentive critic has asserted, "a cheerful, sprawling novel of the life of an old-fashioned country doctor." It is instead a novel that holds the town of New Winton up to the mirror of reality, and in doing so it presents a picture of a tightly structured community that also has flaws. Bull himself is shown to be a man with serious shortcomings.

Ideas explored in Cozzens's earlier fiction appear in *The Last Adam* on a new level of complexity. The importance of one's background and the degree to which that background should impart a sense of responsibility toward one's profession and one's community is one of the overriding themes of the novel. Cozzens suggests that such responsibility resides primarily with the town's aristocracy. The novel gives a very clear picture of the town's various social strata, and New Winton is a place where the presence of a distinct social hierarchy is recognized explicitly. The implication is that those at the top of the social order should be most responsible for the stability of the community. With position comes responsibility; and, though both groups are native to the community, there is a sharp distinction drawn between New Winton's moneyed and nonmoneyed aristocracy.

The moneyed aristocracy of New Winton is represented by the Banning family. Though Herbert Banning has ancestral roots in the community, he does not make a strong claim to an active role in the life of the town. He is kind, well-intentioned, but weak, and he withdraws from direct contact with other people. His wife's sense of responsibility is limited for the most part to the restoration of the town's few remaining eighteenth-century homes: she is more concerned with things than with people. She becomes more involved than her husband in the life of the community insofar as she is one of those determined to have George Bull removed as county health officer on the grounds that he has been incompetent in handling the typhoid epidemic. This attempt, which is unsuccessful and culminates in a chaotic town meeting, is the primary subplot of the novel and is the means Cozzens uses to reveal the social structure of the community.

The nonmoneyed aristocracy of New Winton is represented by George Bull and Janet Cardmaker, both of whom lead private, independent lives. Janet Cardmaker, who runs a dairy farm inherited from her father, attaches little significance to family tradition, and has no qualms about the piecemeal selling of the various architectural features of her ancestral home. Though George Bull grew up in Michigan, New Winton is his family seat; yet in the years that have followed his arrival, Bull has made no effort to adapt himself to the community or to become a constructive force in it. Bull's patients receive perfunctory and sometimes belligerent treatment, and his fundamental attitudes as a doctor leave much to be desired. Speaking of the typhoid epidemic that threatens the town, and that is identified for Bull by his ninety-year-old aunt, he tells Janet Cardmaker that "eighty out of a hundred typhoid cases will get well without any treatment. . . . At least fifteen will die anyway. That means you might have five to fool with. If you don't happen to kill them, perhaps you'll cure them."

What Janet Cardmaker admires in George Bull is a "good, greedy vitality, surely the very vitality of the world and the flesh, it survived all blunders and injuries, all attacks and misfortunes, never quite fed full." At the same time, unfettered vitality can be carried to extremes and can become a matter of mindless appetite. More important, a community of individuals who seek only to satisfy the whims of their passions is no community at all. It has no center or cohesiveness. Janet is right. The "last man" will "twitch," as she says, with something of the vitality that George Bull commands. Bull, who is sixty-seven years old, has been having an affair with Janet for some twenty-eight years, since the early spring of 1903 when Janet was eighteen. Bull's attitude, which is shared by Janet, is that "if New Winton . . . noticed the improper conduct of the two, by birth of their own small number; why, let them notice! Let them notice until they burst!" There is much to be admired in the sexual vitality and fierce individualism represented by Bull and Cardmaker. Cass is correct when he says that "Bull commemorates independent men and also comments on the social types replacing them." However, a community made up of George Bulls would not be much of a community at all; and in his later

fiction—especially *The Just and the Unjust* (1942), *Guard of Honor,* and *By Love Possessed* (1957)—Cozzens's central characters emerge as men who view reason as the necessary means to counterbalance and sometimes suppress passion (or feeling) which, if left unfettered, is a threat to social stability.

Cozzens's next novel, *Castaway* (1934), is a brief tour de force. Far from being an allegory depicting the decadence of capitalist society (as one critic has argued), the novel is a psychological story of suspense, a clever and sometimes humorous inversion of the Robinson Crusoe story. At the beginning of the novel, Mr. Lecky, the central and only "real" character, finds himself alone in a large, modern department store. Filled with an unnamed dread, he arms himself with a knife and begins to climb the stairs. There is an ironic turn to almost everything Lecky does. He is utterly illogical and unreasonable; yet, in his illogic, he is consistent. Though mechanically inept, he places unquestioning trust in machines. Believing, for example, that his knife does not give him adequate protection, he thinks he should "possess himself of the best possible weapons. By the term Mr. Lecky understood some sort of firearm. The fact that he was totally unacquainted with the use of guns assisted him in the illusion that, given a revolver, he would instantly become formidable. Trusting machines, as he did, he regarded a revolver as a small killing machine."

Though he has at his disposal almost all of the material things that twentieth-century man might want or need, Lecky continues to bungle his way inexorably toward self-destruction. Unlike Robinson Crusoe, he does not have to hunt to secure food; Lecky simply goes to the sixth-floor gourmet-food department. There he eats some sardines and then takes a ham back up to the eighth floor where he found the guns. To provide himself with a sleeping place, Lecky makes a "tree house" by taking fitting-room doors off their hinges and laying them across the tops of the compartments. The next day he fortifies a lavatory. The Man Friday parallel in the novel is an "idiot"—actually Lecky's own alter ego—who Mr. Lecky seeks to destroy, first shooting and then partially decapitating this double, and in so doing destroys a part of himself.

Technically, *Castaway* is a novel in which Cozzens experiments with the compression of time and action. Soon after Mr. Lecky has fortified himself against whatever dangers might be lurking in the store, he notices that his watch has stopped at a quarter past five. When it begins running again at the end of the novel, Lecky notices that it still indicates quarter past five. Thus, all of the intervening action—the discovery, pursuit, and execution of the idiot—might be said to take place in a frozen moment of time. This technique, the occurrence of many things in a limited amount of time, reaches its highest development in *Guard of Honor* and *By Love Possessed*.

In *Men and Brethren* (1936), the compression of time and action is carried further. By limiting the action of the novel to two days in the life of Ernest Cudlipp, an Episcopal clergyman, and focusing on the multitude of people and problems he has to deal with, Cozzens examines what is referred to in *Ask Me Tomorrow* as "the dramatic inner meaning that lies in the simultaneous occurrence of diverse things." *Men and Brethren* is also a novel in which character and profession become almost indistinguishable; and the question raised by the biblical epigraph ("Men and brethren, what shall we do?") is central to the meaning of the entire work. It asks what is necessary for salvation and calls for some source of positive direction. A second, implied question has to do with the assumption of responsibility. When faced with an event whose consequences are most often impossible to foresee, but whose results may be potentially dangerous, how is one to cope, to shoulder the burden?

In seeking answers to these questions, Cozzens offers no simple solutions, but he does suggest a wide range of possibilities. It is in this way that *Men and Brethren* differs most sharply from *S.S. San Pedro* and *The Last Adam*. In these earlier novels Cozzens was most concerned with the inward processes that cause highly complex systems to fall apart. In *Men and Brethren* he presents a central character who generates positive action and who supports the values of the system in which he works by the mature acceptance of professional responsibilities. However, Ernest Cudlipp is no messianic hero; he is, in fact, a man who has unlikable qualities. He frequently lacks tact in his dealings with others, is given to snap judgments, enjoys the exercise of power, and is something of a snob. Cudlipp states the heart of his personal creed to Wilbur Quinn, a young and very idealistic assistant at Cudlipp's church, when he tells Quinn that "Realists are the only people who get things done. A realist does the best he can with things as they are. Don't waste your time trying to change things so you can do something. Do something." As a realist and as a Christian, Cudlipp will work to maintain the status quo of the Church, but not to the extent where professional fealty becomes unintelligent or non-

productive. When family and community needs are in conflict with religious dogma, Cudlipp is able to put professional ethics aside; and in doing so he shows himself to be a man who has an acute sense of balance and proportion and a strong measure of moral courage. Performance counts, and Cudlipp is a doer who prevents things from falling apart. In answer to the novel's central question, Cudlipp's actions suggest that one must do whatever is perceived as morally correct and that lies within the limits of the possible.

In addition to dealing with Wilbur Quinn—whose liberal idealism causes him to embrace communism—Cudlipp must cope with an assortment of other characters: Alice Breen, who is experiencing a marital crisis; John Wade, a young poet, and Geraldine Binney, a married woman whom Wade has gotten pregnant; and Carl Willever, a clergyman who has left the Church under the suspicion of homosexuality. And in confronting the problems raised by these individuals, Cudlipp must deal with the political hierarchy (and power) of the Church itself, the institution upon which he depends for a livelihood. Though each problem must be handled differently, the principles that determine his actions are consistent. When Cudlipp realizes that Geraldine Binney is on the verge of suicide, he arranges for her to have an abortion and advises her that the only sensible course of action is to return to her husband and children. The meaning is clear: whenever professional ethics or religious dogma do not supply practical and useful solutions to serious problems, Ernest will forge his own solutions and accept the risks.

Thus, in a period of roughly twenty-four hours, Cudlipp is beleaguered by difficulties caused by other people; and his powers of sympathy and understanding are taxed to the limit. A few of the problems have satisfactory conclusions, at least one ends tragically, and others remain unsolved. Despite his frustrations, and in some cases his self-doubts, Cudlipp consistently pursues positive and realistic courses of action. Here as in no previous book the profession and the professional man are kept at the center of the reader's consciousness. They are constant factors upon which all other actions impinge, and they provide a complex range of ethical and moral concepts against which the actions of the novel's characters can be judged.

Based in part on Cozzens's experiences in Europe in 1927 (the novel is set in the mid 1920s), *Ask Me Tomorrow* (1940) is a Bildungsroman that chronicles the maturation of Francis Ellery, a young writer with two novels to his credit. The chief

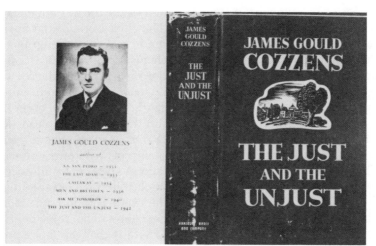

Dust jacket for Cozzens's tenth novel, which has often been called the best American novel about the legal profession

flaw in Ellery's character is pride which has not yet been tempered by maturity and reason. Ellery has been hired to tutor Walter Cunningham, who has been partially crippled by infantile paralysis. Walter's mother, Helen Cunningham, is a widow; she is also a strong and intelligent woman who perceives many of the weaknesses of Francis's character. The job is not one that Francis would normally have sought, but he is forced to take it out of economic necessity. More on his mind is the fact that, once in Montreux with Walter and his mother, he will be separated by a considerable distance from Lorna Higham, who is in Paris and with whom Francis has fallen in love. How to arrange to see Lorna is a problem around which the surface plot of the novel is constructed.

In addition to being basically selfish, Francis is overly concerned with the image he projects to the world. In college, for example, "he had heard a great deal of music" because "love of it is a mark of superior culture"; and though he professes literary ambition, his drive is not strong enough for him "to make wholesale sacrifices of his comfort and convenience." Learning from Lorna that she is going to the Riviera to visit her aunt, Francis begins to think of ways to persuade Mrs. Cunningham to go there too, without at the same time appearing to be manipulating her. He does not prove to be a very good manipulator and in his concern for his own interests gives Mrs. Cunningham reason to doubt his dependability. Francis feels "contempt for the whole monkey house of Europe and Europe's mostly undersized, jabbering, mostly not-quite-clean inhabitants. In his view, all was lumped together, a year's accumulation of

passing annoyances and small disgusts—the shoddy posturing bombast of the new Italy. . . . La Belle France with its savage avarice and all-pervasive smell of urine; the belching, blockheaded Germans—why should anyone have any patience with any of them? The only demonstrable good reason for their existing was to satisfy the curiosity or serve the convenience of traveling Americans." Mrs. Cunningham decides, quite independently from Francis's designs, to go to the Riviera. Once there, Francis's desire to be with Lorna obscures his primary responsibility. On the point of firing him, Mrs. Cunningham tells Francis, "Unless you can put yourself in the place of the person to whom you feel responsible, I don't think you can be very successful in satisfying that person." For his part, Francis at least is able to learn from his mistakes, though his vanity sometimes makes his lessons more difficult than they need be. Near the end of the novel, during a skiing trip, Walter Cunningham suffers a severe asthmatic attack. Francis does what is necessary until a doctor arrives. Francis Ellery, as a writer and as a person, shows himself to be capable of becoming an intelligent, responsible adult; and by the end of the novel he at least has arrived at a higher plateau of maturity.

Cozzens himself said that he was still learning his craft when he wrote *Ask Me Tomorrow;* and it is possible to see some autobiographical significance in his portrait of the artist as a young man. In this respect, it is significant that the novel contains a strong statement on the subject of sentimentality, of which there are no traces in Cozzens's mature fiction. Reflecting on Walter Cunningham's condition, Francis notes that the feelings called up "all thrust toward the bowels of his compassion. They were bowels not particularly easy to get at; but, on close inspection, were they any different or any more decent than the man of sensibility's bellyful? Eviscerated, gushing freely out all bowels looked alike." Ellery does not like to talk about his writing because his own artistic purposes are not fully formed, and the "Confused, fragmentary things he could say served only to reduce whatever idea he had in mind to its essential banality and the more he explained what he was planning to write, the sillier it seemed to bother to write it." Ellery wants to be able to express "the dramatic inner meaning that lies in the simultaneous occurrence of diverse things," as Cozzens himself had been trying to do, in various ways, in his previous fiction.

Cozzens succeeded in uncovering a great deal of diversity in *The Just and the Unjust* (1942), which at the time of its publication proved to be the most successful (critically and financially) of Cozzens's novels. The primary action of the novel is based on a murder trial; and in his delineation of courtroom procedures as well as in his general presentation of the law and lawyers, Cozzens is meticulously accurate. In his comments on *The Just and the Unjust* in the *Harvard Law Review*, Zechariah Chafee stated that the novel should be required reading for all young lawyers.

The novel covers three-and-a-half days during which Abner Coates, a young assistant district attorney, and district attorney Martin Bunting try two criminals—Robert Basso and Stanley Howell—for the kidnapping and murder of Frederick Zollicoffer. Roy Leming, another participant in the crime, has turned state's evidence. The trial attracts considerable attention in the small community of Childerstown because it is the first murder trial there in over ten years. Morally the trial is not a simple one, for Zollicoffer was a dope dealer and cannot be considered much of a loss to society. Therefore, the trial raises questions of law and justice, not of moral right versus moral wrong. *Dispassionate* is the word that best describes the controlling point of view throughout the novel. Certainly the criminal life is neither glorified nor romanticized. While examining Roy Leming, Abner Coates reflects silently that the world of professional crime "did not differ as much as the imagination might suggest from the everyday world of those who were not professional criminals. . . . The rank and file could count on little but drudgery and economic insecurity; and for the same reason that most men in lawful pursuits could count on little else. They had no natural abilities,

and lacked the will and intelligence to develop any." The chief irony of the novel is that, after the defense has only strengthened the case against its clients, the jury returns a verdict of guilty of murder in the second degree rather than in the first degree. The maximum punishment to which they can be sentenced is twenty years apiece; whereas Roy Leming, who pleaded guilty to the original charge in turning state's evidence, faces the possibility of life imprisonment. The theme of limitations—personal and social as well as legal—is implicit in the epigraph to the novel: "Certainty is the Mother of Repose; therefore the law aims at Certainty." The ironic point, as John Ward has observed, is that the novel proceeds to demonstrate that "there can be no certainty in anything man has a hand in by dramatizing the distance between Olympian justice and its human embodiment."

In addition to the trial, Abner Coates must cope with other situations and problems that are numerous and diverse. His father, a judge, has suffered a stroke that has left him partially paralyzed. He must also deal with county justices of the peace (one of whom is flagrantly incompetent), reach some decisions concerning his own law practice, and come to some understanding with Bonnie Drummond, his fiancée. Other business of the district attorney's office occupies Abner's time as well: a case involving a young driver who crashes into the rear of an automobile and kills the occupant, and a potentially scandalous case involving a high school teacher who has been persuading teenage girls to pose for suggestive photographs. In addition to handling the proceedings against the teacher, Abner agrees to represent the school's principal, Oliver Rawle, whose job is placed in jeopardy because of the incident.

However, aside from the murder trial, the biggest decision that Abner faces is whether or not he should run for district attorney. The job would make it more feasible for him to support a wife and is one that he believes he would be good at, an opinion that is shared by Bunting and Abner's other colleagues. But some of his idealistic notions make him balk at entering politics, particularly because he suspects the integrity of Jesse Gearhart, head of the county's Republican party and the man who asks him if he will run. Dispassionately, Abner realizes that his "grounds for disliking Jesse were not good nor reasonable." Reason, though, does not help Abner to like politics or Jesse. "In theory," Abner realizes, "the people could . . . enounce the nominations at the primaries; but in practice what they did at the primaries was accept the men Jesse

Dust jacket for Cozzens's eleventh novel, which he said "pleads the army's case." It did not sell well on publication but won the Pulitzer Prize for Fiction in 1949.

designated." As presented in the novel, this condition is neither good nor bad; it is the way it is. Perceiving Abner's concern over the appearances of things, Jesse Gearhart tells him, "You wouldn't worry so much about what people were thinking of you, if you'd just remember that most of the time they're not." Judge Coates gives Abner advice in the form of a realistic assessment: "If you want to get away from [politicians], you'll have to get away from human society. There wouldn't be any society without them. It's attempted every now and then. Some so-called reform movement made up of people who aren't politicians sometimes wins an election. Either they learn how to be politicians pretty quick, or they don't last." As the novel presents Abner Coates trying to come to terms with his own sense of idealism and integrity, it also presents a comprehensive picture of Childerstown and explores the limits within which a society—if it is to be stable—and its citizens must operate. Certainty is something that Abner Coates (or any other person) will have to learn to live without.

Abner matures considerably by the end of the novel. He is more willing to take life as he finds it and to do the best he can with things as they are. In the final scene with his father, though Abner is generally willing to accept the limitations that uncertainty places on his private as well as his professional life, he is still not sure just what is expected of him. Judge Coates tells him, "There is the present to think of, and as long as you live there always will be. In the present, every day is a miracle. The world gets up in the morning and is fed and goes

to work, and in the evening it comes home and is fed again and perhaps has a little amusement and goes to sleep. To make that possible, so much has to be done by so many people that, on the face of it, it is impossible." In this way the novel underscores the view that the apparently undramatic routine of daily life is the most essential thing in which people engage. Not just Abner Coates but all members of society have the responsibility for daily life thrust upon them whether they like it or not. All that is expected of Abner Coates and his fellowmen is that they keep doing the impossible.

Guard of Honor (1948) has been frequently praised as the best American novel of World War II, and it is considered by many critics to be Cozzens's best work. (He received the Pulitzer Prize for the novel in 1949.) *Guard of Honor* is not a novel of combat. It is set at an army air force base in Ocanara, Florida, and covers a period of three days. The action is centered on Bus Beal, a young and highly regarded general who, because of a racial situation involving a black bomber crew, as well as uncertainties about his professional abilities, has to meet the most severe test of his career. The other major character in the novel is Col. Norman Ross, a peacetime judge who is serving as the air inspector on General Beal's staff. A man of reason, Colonel Ross is one of Cozzens's mature heroes. Ross gives General Beal the benefit of his judgment and experience, and because his staff position involves him so centrally in the administration of the base, a great deal of what transpires in the novel—frequently not involving General Beal at all—is filtered through Colonel Ross's intelligence.

The first chapter takes place on a Thursday, as General Beal is flying back to Ocanara Air Base in a plane he had picked up earlier at Sellers Field in Mississippi. With him is his copilot, Lt. Col. Benny Carricker, who has served as a fighter pilot with him overseas; Colonel Ross; Capt. Nathaniel Hicks, a peacetime magazine editor; 2nd Lt. Amanda Turck; Sgt. Dominic Pellerino, General Beal's crew chief; and T5g. Mortimer McIntyre, a black enlisted man who is returning from leave. In different ways all of these characters—with the exception of McIntyre—play important fictional roles throughout the novel; and though McIntyre is not a central character, his presence signals racial problems on which the novel's main actions turn.

In the early, hard days of the war General Beal had been stationed in the Philippines and had proved himself to be an extraordinary pilot. When faced with the necessity of choosing a pilot to try to fly to Australia with important papers, he makes the correct (professional) choice by selecting himself. Those left behind are certain to become prisoners of war. His abilities confirmed by subsequent performance as a combat commander, he is rapidly promoted and becomes the youngest major general in the air force. The experience in the Philippines may weigh on Beal's conscience, but it is only one of several factors that ultimately produce a crisis of confidence. Another contributing factor is Beal's frustration at not being assigned to a combat theater. The first indication that something is wrong occurs near the end of the first chapter, as the plane approaches the landing field at Ocanara. A bomber manned by a black crew unexpectedly lands in front of General Beal's plane, and there is almost a collision. The general's reactions are not quick enough, and it is Benny Carricker who saves them. Once on the ground, Carricker assaults the black pilot—not because he is black but because he almost caused a catastrophe—who has to be treated at the base hospital. Thus is set in motion a chain of events that is not resolved until Saturday.

The production of complicated effects from simple causes is reflected on by Colonel Ross before the near accident takes place. Thinking of the incompetence of Colonel Mowbray, Ocanara's executive officer, Colonel Ross reasons that it is best not to press for his removal as a younger man might, and "let the chips fall where they may": "Colonel Ross was not sure whether today's different attitude came from being twenty years wiser or just twenty years older. He had, of course, more knowledge of

what happens in the long run, of complicated effects from simple causes, of one thing stubbornly leading to another. Experience had been busy that much longer rooting out the vestiges of youth's dear and heady hope . . . that the end will at last justify any means that might have seemed dubious when the decision to resort to them was so wisely made. Unfortunately, when you got to your end, you found all the means to it inherent there. In short, the first exhilaration of hewing to the line waned when you had to clean up that mess of chips." Benny Carricker's action at the end of the first chapter is a simple cause that sets in motion a chain of complex events that result in quite a large "mess of chips"; and paralleling this main action are other sequences of causes and effects, some of which are entirely self-contained, while others impinge in unanticipated ways on the main plot line.

The black bomber crew that almost collides with General Beal's airplane is part of a larger group of blacks being trained for combat; Carricker's attack on the black pilot, although not racially motivated, foments a racial situation that threatens to assume larger proportions. With the arrival of a black bomber group at Ocanara, it has been decided to place the officers' club off limits to avoid any potential problems with white officers—especially southerners. Carricker's attack on the black pilot complicates what is already an explosive issue. At the beginning of the second chapter (Friday) Colonel Ross does not think Carricker's action the previous night was very serious; he refers to it as a "tiresome little difficulty." He is more concerned about difficulties with Colonel Mowbray—whose suspicion of all things not military creates bad public relations with important people in the civilian population—and with information leaks to the *Ocanara Morning Sun*. These problems are intensified by the arrival of General Nichols, the deputy chief of air staff, who has come to present General Beal with the Distinguished Service Medal. Thus the various events are unfolding before the public eye as well as the official eye of air force headquarters.

In dramatizing the development of the racial situation, Cozzens presents characters with widely differing viewpoints, ranging from outright prejudice to egotistical liberalism. Colonel Ross reasons correctly that the organization of the military hierarchy will have an intimidating effect and can therefore contain the protest of a small group of blacks. And by going to visit the injured pilot with General Nichols, who presents him with the Distinguished Flying Cross in the presence of the young man's father, he helps to defuse the racial problem. General Nichols reasons that the pilot will not trade command of "a medium bomber group— at least three promotions, his name in the papers"—to push his complaint of unjust treatment. It is also General Nichols, in conversation with Colonel Ross, who comments on the theme of professional and human limitations, and the importance of operating within the limits of the possible, both of which are central to the novel itself. Discussing certain elements of the Quebec conference, General Nichols reflects, "The top echelon rides the whirlwind, all right, but sometimes the storm seems to do the directing. . . . Certain things that it might be wise to do can't be done. . . . You can't order a man to flap his wings and fly; but you can always order as many qualified pilots as you have to take as many planes as you have and fly the wrong way to the wrong place at the wrong time."

The various pressures that are placed on General Beal have a debilitating effect. By Saturday Colonel Ross cannot help but notice "that some grave change had taken place in General Beal. Something had gone out of him; some distinguishing inner mettle, a sustained tension of nerves, a spirit wound up to act." About all that Ross can do is handle things, with a fine appreciation of the irony of the situation, until General Beal comes around. Contrasting the present events at Ocanara—none of which is combat related or will likely have any direct effect on the outcome of the war— Colonel Ross speculates that "now, at this very moment, if the weather had been at all possible, Eighth Air Force bombers were turning, a certain number of them damaged with engines out and dead and wounded on board, to try to make their English bases," and at the same moment still, perhaps, "Fifth Air Force fighters were dropping belly tanks as the Zeros came climbing at them over some formerly unimportant Indonesian harbor." General Beal does recover himself, in a contest of flying nerve with Benny Carricker; but *Guard of Honor* is not so simplistic as to suggest that there will be smooth sailing from now on. During a parachute jump that is performed as part of General Beal's birthday celebration, a group of paratroopers comes down in Lake Lalage and drowns. Though upset by the incident, General Beal remains in control. He realizes his importance to the war effort, and he tells Colonel Ross at the end of the novel, "Even Jo-Jo [Nichols] knows they could do without him before they could do without me. . . . Jo-Jo can talk to Mr. Churchill; but the war, that's for us.

Without me—without us, he wouldn't have a whole hell of a lot to talk about, would he?"

The cast of characters in *Guard of Honor* is quite large. As Cozzens explained to his English publisher, he intended to dramatize the "immensity and immense complexity" of the human events: "I wanted to show that real . . . meaning of the whole business, the peculiar effects of the interaction of innumerable individuals functioning in ways at once determined by and determining the functioning of innumerable others—all in the common and in every case nearly hopeless involvement in what had ceased to be just an 'organization' . . . and became if not an organism with life and purpose of its own, at least an entity, like a crowd. . . ." The compression of time in the novel reinforces this aim. The chapters are organized as units of time— Thursday, Friday, Saturday—and the numbered sections within the chapters represent smaller units of time. Cozzens uses these sections both to show the inexorable progression of linear time—the sheer accumulation of events—and to counterpoint for ironic purposes one section or event against another. Developments within these sections relate to the theme of personal and professional limitations because irony is used to show how events often depend on the capriciousness of luck for their outcome.

By Love Possessed (1957), in popular terms and in its critical reception, was Cozzens's most successful and controversial novel. It was a Book-of-the-Month Club selection; paperback rights brought a record price; and motion picture rights were sold for $250,000. In 1960 the novel was awarded the William Dean Howells Medal of the American Academy of Arts and Letters for the most distinguished work of American fiction published during the preceding five years. John Fischer of *Harper's* declared that the novel was of Nobel Prize quality, and of Cozzens's general achievements he said, "If your great-grandchild should ever want to find out how Americans behaved and thought and felt in the mid-years of this century, Cozzens's major novels probably would be his most revealing source." The strong, positive reception of *By Love Possessed* was soon followed by a backlash of hostile criticism that charged Cozzens with using the novel as a forum for his own social and political views, which were held to be bigoted and reactionary. As a result of the critical attention given to *By Love Possessed*, Cozzens's picture appeared on the cover of *Time* magazine, and in the accompanying article ("The Hermit of Lambertville") some of Cozzens's views were misrepresented and mis-

B 1.

i.

Arthur Winner, awakening, heard the sound of wind and rain. A chilly raw wind blew from the open window into the bedroom whose darkness seemed no different than that of the middle of the night. Confused, Arthur Winner regarded the darkness doubtfully. Repossessed of his faculties, he remembered that he was going to get up early, that he wanted to be at his office by eight. He told Mrs Duffy that he would like breakfast at half past seven. Then, before he fell asleep, he told himself to wake up at quarter to seven. Turning his head, saw the luminous dial of the clock on the small table between the beds. It quarter to seven The dark would be the natural dark of an early morning in November and of a rainy day.

That he could do this --tell himself when to wake and be obeyed without fail, literally to the minute, was a matter of satisfaction to Arthur Winner. The interesting capacity discovered more than thirty years ago when he was at Law School, ... austere, really punishing regimen that struck neither him nor anyone else as excessive . As often as not he would work until the library closed at midnight, go to his room, ... at five on even four to work again. It was certainly tough; it was hard, it was even painful; but of course it was also, in its austere way, very satisfying. There was a definite exhilaration in the atmosphere; the mind, essaying its prodigies of application and concentration felt fine, taut, efficient, well managed, most frivolous matters disciplined

---

G 1.

i.

Shaken awake Arthur Winner reached mechanically for the alarm clock whose dial glowed on the table between the beds and ended its ringing. He identified the sound of steady rain outside the open window. The clock meanwhile glowed in a darkness no different from that of the middle of the night. It seemed impossible that it could be morning and in thick confusion he could not be sure whether the alarm clock actually had rung and had been shut off by him an instant ago, or whether it was dreaming. This doubt was too much for that part of his mind which, brought to consciousness, perceived that he dreamed and that the dream was bad. Another part, working to hold the phantasmagoria together, to continue him in it, now submerged him in sleep, so that he was still attempting, or attempting again, to reason; in impotent dismay putting it to himself: Now, just keep calm. Go slow. Think it out...

This difficulty, the sense of exhausting involvement ..., was what he wanted to conceal from Dunky. While he worked to remember where this was, how he came to be here, he looked fixedly at Dunky, saying nothing. In fact, he must not speak until he remembered what they were talking about. Coldly staring he saw that Dunky could not have been to bed, for he was fully dressed. Dunky of course one or the other of what two suits, practically indistinguishable -- both black, both threadbare, both, in their mean-

---

THE DREAM-MRS PRATT

i.

The night had been disturbed by dreams and Arthur Winner now struggled to leave them. He was confusedly aware that the alarm clock had rung and that he had shut it off. He had identified the sound of rain and felt the breath of wind from the open window; but in the bedroom the deep darkness of early morning in November, the delayed dawn of a rainy day, was no different from that of the middle of the night lay in doubt, wishing to awake, to have done with ... that was part of the dream; and yet the dream would not release him. The half-awakened mind sank, submerged in it with a sarcasm of annoyance: "As it happens, Dunklemann, the lady you saw is my wife. There's nothing wrong about it."

In irritable contempt, he found himself studying Dunky --the pale pasty face, the prominent Adam's apple working in the scraggly, dirty-looking throat, the air of uncertain, vainly attempted authority. Dunky wore of course one or the other of what everyone had decided must be two suits. They were hardly to be distinguished --both black, both threadbare, both in their meanness of cut and material, European, years ago bought cheap in a poor shop in a poor quarter of some German university town. Arthur Winner felt anger; the fact that Dunklemann was defenceless wretch made it hard to answer him as he ought to be answered. The resulting cruel wounds would disgust you with yourself as well as him. "Oh, go away!" he said. He gave Dunky a light push;

645.

C25 i

From the peace of sleep, Arthur Winner (he could understand) must just have stirred; even, started. To himself, with deep inquietude, with tense anxiety, he was actively repeating: I must keep calm; I must reason this out....The admonition clearly had to do with the progress of a dream which this coming to consciousness now suspended, left broken into only; not broken up. Though the waking mind clutched at its relief of recognizing the dream as such --not really real, not really happening, not really requiring such an anguished effort to grasp and to explain, the dreaming mind with desperate hypnagogic attachment would not let go, leave off. A running engine of phantasmogenesis, powerfully engaged again, pressed him to dream on; and, little as life, Dunky (could that man be still alive?) angrily, excitedly, confronted him.

Dunky was, of course, wearing one of his two funny-looking, European-made suits. He was as cadaverous as ever; his extraordinarily prominent adam's apple moving up and down in his skinny throat. Dunky was saying: This is unheard of, Winner; this is impossible....His voice was reduced to a hissing whisper. He kept rolling his eyes apprehensively as though to see behind him in case someone was coming up the ill-lit bare brick hall (this place was known perfectly to Arthur Winner; but where, but when?); in case any of the long range of doors opened. He hissed on: I am

Four drafts of Part Three, Chapter One, By Love Possessed *(courtesy of Princeton University Library).*
Top: versions "B" and "G"; bottom: version ["H"] and final draft.

quoted. Taking responsibility for not insisting that he be allowed to read proofs of the article, Cozzens later wrote in a letter to *Fact* magazine that the *Time* story "was so full of inaccuracies, of nonsense evident to anyone who knew me, that it would have amounted to a joke if much of the misinformation hadn't been phrased in a way that seemed to make me deride and despise, individually or collectively, quite a lot of people. Put into my mouth was a series of pronouncements, some asinine, some gratuitously unkind, that I'd be about the last writer in the world to make." It was not Cozzens's habit to make pronouncements on social issues, and he never used his fiction to advance his own views on any political issue. Commenting on this subject, he had written to one of his readers in 1934: "I simply put down, when I write, what the things I have seen and known look like to me. I try not to intrude what I think. It is my idea that an author's talent for writing, if he is lucky enough to have one, is the only thing of any interest or importance about him." The same point was stated even more succinctly in 1965 in Cozzens's response to a questionnaire from *Contemporary Authors:* "I don't defend anything; I don't eagerly assert anything."

By Love Possessed continued to explore the themes that Cozzens had been exploring throughout most of his writing career. The description of the clock at the beginning of the novel suggests the two major themes that are developed in the following pages: "Love conquers all. . . . said the gold scroll in a curve beneath the dial of the old French gilt clock. To the dial's right, a nymph, her head on her arm, drowsed, largely undraped, at the mouth of a gold grotto where perhaps she lived. To the dial's left, a youth, by his crook and the pair of lambs with him, a shepherd, had taken cover. Parting fronds of gold vegetation, he peeped at the sleeping beauty. On top of the dial, and all unnoticed by the youth, a smiling cupid perched, bow bent, about to loose an arrow at the peeper's heart." The themes of love—in all of its forms and ramifications—and time are at the heart of the novel. The action of the novel covers forty-nine hours in the life of Arthur Winner, Jr., a lawyer in his fifties, who models himself on his now dead father, whom he refers to as the "Man of Reason." The action of the novel is set in Brocton, a small northeastern community, and the array of characters that Cozzens presents dramatizes the various levels of love and the tensions that arise from conflicts of passion and reason, the pleas of the heart and the admonishments of the head. Lives dominated by either passion or reason are shown to be incomplete. A

heart, struck by cupid's arrow, will not act according to rules of logic; and a person like Arthur Winner, who views himself as a man of reason, will sometimes act irrationally.

Generally the novel develops along two lines of action. The first is Arthur Winner's defense of eighteen-year-old Ralph Detweiler. He is the brother of Helen Detweiler, who works as a secretary in the law firm whose principal members are Noah Tuttle (the senior partner, who, now in his eighties, is viewed by the community as a man of unquestionable probity), Arthur Winner, and Julius Penrose. Helen and Ralph Detweiler lost their parents when Ralph was a child and Helen took complete responsibility for rearing her brother. In her concern for her brother's welfare, Helen is ruled by her feelings and consequently does nothing to correct Ralph's faults, which are apparent even to her. Ralph is charged with the rape of Veronica Kovacs. Though Ralph is innocent of the charge, matters are complicated by the fact that he is also involved with Joan Moore, whom he has gotten pregnant. It appears fairly certain—at least to Arthur Winner—that the rape charge against Ralph will be dropped, but the possibility of having to face a trial and the problem posed by Joan Moore's pregnancy are too much for Ralph. He jumps bail and steals a hundred dollars. Helen, seeing all of her carefully laid out plans for Ralph's future falling apart and humiliated by her brother's actions, commits suicide. The second and more subtle line of action has to do with consequences resulting from the financial failure of the Brocton Rapid Transit Company and Noah Tuttle's misappropriation of trust funds to protect investors from complete financial ruin.

By Love Possessed is also concerned with sequences of cause and effect. Judge Fred Dealey observes at an early point, "Whatever happens, happens because a lot of other things have happened already. When it gets to where you come in—well, it's bound to be pretty late in the day. Things have been fixing for whatever this is for a long time. . . ." In such a scheme of things, primary causes are almost impossible to determine. In this sense, *By Love Possessed* is, as Bruccoli describes it, "Cozzens's most thorough examination of moral complexity. . . . there are choices in which emotion, experience, and imperfect reason respond to circumstances determined by chance and by what has already happened." Frequently the way things appear to be is not at all the way things are. Though Arthur Winner is viewed primarily as a man of reason, he is not himself immune to passion. It is revealed gradually that following the death of his first wife, Winner had a brief but intense affair with Julius Penrose's wife, Marjorie. Unknown to Arthur—until the end of the novel—Julius has known of the affair. He tells Arthur, "If you knew something that you believed I didn't know, and that you thought it better I shouldn't know, I'm persuaded you'd . . . try every way to keep it from me. . . . I'm persuaded, Arthur, that you *have* done as much for me. And, if unknown to you, I've always thanked you for it." This attitude greatly enhances the quality of Julius's love for his friend, and is one of the ways in which Julius displays a keener awareness of moral complexity than is found in Arthur Winner.

Julius has also known for some twelve years that Noah Tuttle has misappropriated the Orcutt trust. It is he who persuades Arthur that Noah be allowed to continue his practice of repaying the original shifting of funds from the Orcutt account; and that if Noah should die before completing the task that he and Arthur must carry through on it. Noah, as Julius seems to realize, acted out of feelings of love as well as self-esteem: "He would betray himself, sacrifice himself, before he let down, sacrificed, those who had put faith in him." Awareness of Noah's deed and the problem of what to do about it are the ultimate moral questions addressed in the novel. It is Julius who must persuade Arthur that strict honesty—turning Noah in—is simply the easiest, not the best, policy to follow. The most responsible thing they can do, given the events that have led to the present time, is to do what they can to make Noah's plan succeed; they, like Noah, must do what is necessary to hold the fabric of their society together.

Beginning with *Guard of Honor*, and especially with *By Love Possessed* and *Morning Noon and Night*, Cozzens's writing style went through some marked changes, becoming more parenthetical, making greater use of subordination and periodic sentences, and demonstrating a greater tendency to employ uncommon (usually Latinate) words. Before *Guard of Honor*, Cozzens's style was noteworthy for its unembellished clarity; the word selection, sentence structure, and general narrative were straightforward, designed to tell a story and to impart basic observations about human nature in as direct and economical a manner as possible. Though some critics have argued that Cozzens's later style amounts to willful obscurity, the shift represents no change in Cozzens's artistic goals or standards. Bruccoli has pointed out that the "increasing dignity of style enforces Cozzens's objec-

tivity" and that the occasional "use of uncommon words achieves exactness of statement." That Cozzens never bothered to explain the purpose of his style is not surprising. As he wrote in 1934, "To attempt to instruct . . . readers is a piece of impertinence since they are either too stupid for instruction, or quite intelligent enough to instruct themselves. . . ." Later, regarding the complexity of *Guard of Honor*, Cozzens wrote to his English publisher, "I saw that . . . I would just have to write off as readers everyone who could not or would not meet heavy demands on his attention and intelligence. . . ." The purpose of Cozzens's style—which is certainly not willfully obscure—should be evident to the careful reader. It is at once reflective and introspective; and parenthetical statements and periodic sentences help to qualify cause-and-effect relationships and the *apparent* motivations of characters. Unusual words are used not only for precision but also for ironic effect, to show the distance between the thing described and the word used to describe it.

Cozzens's next book was a collection of short stories, *Children and Others* (1964). Cozzens's stories, which were written for ready money, nevertheless exhibit the qualities of craftsmanship and deal with the themes that are found in the novels. Two of the seventeen stories in the volume—"Farewell to Cuba" and "Total Stranger"—had won O. Henry Awards, in 1931 and 1936. Cozzens's interest in Civil War materials is represented by two other stories, "Men Running" and "One Hundred Ladies." The Durham School stories in the volume—"Someday You'll Be Sorry," "We'll Recall It with Affection," "The Guns of the Enemy," and "*Candida* by Bernard Shaw"—draw on Cozzens's own experiences at Kent School. The Durham headmaster, Doctor Holt, is modeled on Kent headmaster Father Sill.

Cozzens's final novel, *Morning Noon and Night* (1968), begins with a statement and an implied question: "I have been young and now am old. Like the Psalmist long before me I find myself feeling on occasion that what I have to say about life deserves attention. We have, he and I, lived. We must have learned." The narrator here is Henry Dodd Worthington, the president of a management consulting firm, and the implied question lies in Worthington's uncertainty that he has learned anything at all. In this sense, *Morning Noon and Night* is an epistemological novel; one that asks how it is possible to know anything, and what principles can be adduced from what experience teaches.

Morning Noon and Night is the only one of Cozzens's novels to be narrated from the first-person point of view. The plot takes the form of Worthington's memoirs. At first glance it appears disjointed; but Worthington is trying to discover what his life has meant, and a straight chronology might reveal little. As Worthington explains near the end of the novel: "Reviewing my passages of writing I am obliged to see I offer little more than a disordered compilation of rough notes, exhibiting frustration rather than accomplished purpose. Perhaps my mistake was in choosing to avoid consecutive narration. I made the choice because I for long have felt that setting out courses of events in the natural, seemingly straightforward way can, oddly enough, distort truth and obscure meaning, at least in the sense of limiting or lessening for a reader his possible new acquist of true experience, since he will not have been told beforehand what he has to know if he is to grasp the real significance in many reported happenings." Worthington is not certain of what he has learned. Since at one time in his life Worthington aspired to be a writer, some of his most interesting comments are on writers and writing. Not surprisingly, his views reflect those artistic values and beliefs that are embodied in Cozzens's own fiction. Following a chain of associations rather than an ordered sequence of events, Worthington views his past self in various roles: as young boy and man, student, lover, husband, father, military man, and professional man; and he speculates on the forces that have influenced the lives of other members of his family.

Approaching old age, Worthington is troubled by feelings of uncertainty. "Opinions of mine, once quite settled, tend more and more of them to become unsettled. . . . When, as must happen from time to time, I am halted, held at one of those moments of blank surmise, confounded by new (or old, old) aspects of the nature of things, I must expect nowadays to find I simply don't know what I think." Worthington is able to acknowledge, without feeling defeated, that life is uncertain; that momentous events can and frequently do occur as the result of apparently insignificant causes; that success—however defined—depends as much on luck as on ability; that the individual must be able to cope with life as he finds it. These are the necessary articles of faith that are embraced by all of Cozzens's mature heroes.

Over the course of his career, there were several projects which Cozzens began but either did not complete or did not publish. After *Men and Brethren* was published in 1936, Cozzens began

work on a Civil War novel but did not complete the task because, as he later explained to Bruccoli, "I wasn't there: I never saw it for myself." Referring to another work in progress that he was calling "A Skyborn Music," Cozzens explained in a 1963 letter that it was to have been a novel "about a kid," but that "I had to quit when I finally let myself see that, just like everyone else writing on the subject, I was faking it."

Among those holding Cozzens's work in the highest regard are other writers. George Garrett, for example, points out that while much of American literature is "populated by criminals, anti-heroes, wise children, schizophrenic clowns . . . professors and artists," Cozzens has dealt for the most part with characters who are "mature men of various ages who believe in their disciplines and who are, in fact, the men whose work has the power to shape and direct the quality of life in this country." It is on this level that his achievement has its strongest appeal. James Gould Cozzens was a master craftsman who consistently set for himself demanding professional standards, who wrote about what he could observe and know, who valued order and discipline, and whose subject matter—far from being narrow—derived from the institutions that determine and reflect the nature of community life in twentieth-century America.

Interview:

Robert Van Gelder, "James Gould Cozzens at Work," *New York Times Book Review,* 23 June 1940, p. 14.

Biography:

Matthew J. Bruccoli, *James Gould Cozzens: A Life Apart* (San Diego & New York: Harcourt Brace Jovanovich, 1983).

Bibliographies:

Pierre Michel, *James Gould Cozzens: An Annotated Checklist* (Kent, Ohio: Kent State University Press/Brussels: Center for American Studies, 1971);

James B. Meriwether, *James Gould Cozzens: A Checklist* (Detroit: Bruccoli Clark/Gale Research, 1972)—includes an introduction by Cozzens;

Matthew J. Bruccoli, *James Gould Cozzens: A Descriptive Bibliography* (Pittsburgh: University of Pittsburgh Press, 1981).

References:

Frederick Bracher, *The Novels of James Gould Cozzens* (New York: Harcourt, Brace, 1959);

First book-length critical study; examines techniques and themes through *By Love Possessed.*

Matthew J. Bruccoli, ed., *James Gould Cozzens: New Acquist of True Experience* (Carbondale & Edwardsville: Southern Illinois University Press/ London & Amsterdam: Feffer & Simmons, 1979);
Reprints essays by Louis Coxe, John William Ward, Robert Scholes, and others.

Critique: Studies in Modern Fiction, special Cozzens issue, 1 (Winter 1958);
Critical appraisals by Frederick Bracher, George Garrett, John Lydenberg, and others.

"The Hermit of Lambertville," *Time,* 70 (2 September 1957): 72-74, 76-77;
Cover article marking the publication of *By Love Possessed;* this presentation of Cozzens triggered attacks on the author.

Granville Hicks, *James Gould Cozzens* (Minneapolis: University of Minnesota Press, 1966);
Pamphlet that concentrates on Cozzens's use of traditional material.

Dwight Macdonald, "By Cozzens Possessed," *Commentary,* 25 (January 1958): 36-47;
Attacks *By Love Possessed* and Cozzens.

D. E. S. Maxwell, *Cozzens* (Edinburgh & London: Oliver & Boyd, 1964);
Concise, well-written overview; especially good on Cozzens's narrative techniques.

Pierre Michel, *James Gould Cozzens* (New York: Twayne, 1974);
Survey of the entire canon by a Belgian scholar; critical of *By Love Possessed* and *Morning Noon and Night.*

Harry J. Mooney, Jr., *James Gould Cozzens: Novelist of Intellect* (Pittsburgh: University of Pittsburgh Press, 1963);
Focuses on Cozzens as man of reason; ignores books before *S.S. San Pedro.*

Papers:
Cozzens's manuscripts and other papers are in the Princeton University Library.

Richard Eberhart

This entry was updated from the entry by Joel Roache (University of Maryland, Eastern Shore) in DLB 48, American Poets, 1880-1945.

Places	Minnesota	Dartmouth College Cambridge University	Harvard
Influences and Relationships	I. A. Richards G. L. Kittredge W. H. Auden	F. R. Leavis Frederic Prokosch William Carlos Williams	Irving Babbitt Kenneth Rexroth
Literary Movements and Forms	Poet's Theater	Modern Romanticism	
Major Themes	Dichotomy: Mind & Body Man & Nature	Life & Death Innocence & Experience	Concreteness & Transcendence
Cultural and Artistic Influences	Theater		
Social and Economic Influences	World War II		

BIRTH: Austin, Minnesota, 5 April 1904, to Alpha
LaRue and Lena Lowenstein Eberhart.

EDUCATION: University of Minnesota, 1922-
1923; B.A., Dartmouth College, 1926; B.A., 1929,
M.A., 1933, St. John's College, Cambridge; Harvard University, 1932-1933.

MARRIAGE: 29 August 1941 to Helen Elizabeth
Butcher; children: Richard, Gretchen.

AWARDS AND HONORS: Harriet Monroe Memorial Prize, 1950; New England Poetry Club
Award, 1950; Shelley Memorial Award, 1952; Harriet Monroe Poetry Award, 1955; National Institute of Arts and Letters grant in literature, 1955;
appointment as Consultant in Poetry at the Library
of Congress, 1959-1961; Bollingen Prize in Poetry
(shared with John Hall Wheelock), Yale University,
1962; Pulitzer Prize for *Selected Poems, 1930-1965*,
1966; Academy of American Poets fellowship,
1969; National Book Award for *Collected Poems,
1930-1976*, 1977; President's Medallion, University
of Florida, 1977; Poet Laureate of the state of New
Hampshire, 1979; election to the American Academy of Arts and Letters, 1982; Poetry Society of
America's Robert Frost Medal, 1986.

BOOKS: *A Bravery of Earth* (London: Cape, 1930;
   New York: Cape & Smith, 1930);
Reading the Spirit (London: Chatto & Windus, 1936;
   New York: Oxford University Press, 1937);
Song and Idea (London: Chatto & Windus, 1940;
   New York: Oxford University Press, 1942);
A World-View (Medford, Mass.: Tufts College Press,
   1941);
Poems, New and Selected (Norfolk, Conn.: New Di-
   rections, 1945);
Burr Oaks (London: Chatto & Windus, 1947; New
   York: Oxford University Press, 1947);
Brotherhood of Men (Pawlet, Vt.: Banyan Press,
   1949);
An Herb Basket (Cummington, Mass.: Cummington
   Press, 1950);
Selected Poems (London: Chatto & Windus, 1951;
   New York: Oxford University Press, 1951);
Poetry as a Creative Principle (Norton, Mass.: Whea-
   ton College, 1952);
Undercliff: Poems 1946-1953 (London: Chatto &
   Windus, 1953; New York: Oxford University
   Press, 1953);
Great Praises (London: Chatto & Windus, 1957;
   New York: Oxford University Press, 1957);

*Richard Eberhart at Dartmouth College (courtesy of the Richard
Eberhart Collection, Baker Library, Dartmouth College)*

The Oak: A Poem (Hanover, N.H.: Pine Tree Press,
   1957);
Collected Poems: 1930-1960 (London: Chatto & Win-
   dus, 1960; New York: Oxford University
   Press, 1960);
Collected Verse Plays (Chapel Hill: University of
   North Carolina Press, 1962; London: Oxford
   University Press, 1963);
The Quarry: New Poems (New York: Oxford Uni-
   versity Press, 1964; London: Chatto & Win-
   dus, 1964);
Selected Poems, 1930-1965 (New York: New Direc-
   tions, 1965);
Thirty-One Sonnets (New York: Eakins Press, 1967);
Shifts of Being (New York: Oxford University Press,
   1968; London: Chatto & Windus, 1968);
The Achievement of Richard Eberhart, edited, with an
   introduction, by Bernard Engel (Glenview,
   Ill.: Scott, Foresman, 1968);

Three Poems (Cambridge, Mass.: Pym-Randall, 1968);

Fields of Grace (New York: Oxford University Press, 1972; London: Chatto & Windus, 1972);

Two Poems (Westchester, Pa.: Aralia Press, 1975);

Poems to Poets (Lincoln, Mass.: Penmaen Press, 1976);

Collected Poems, 1930-1976 (New York: Oxford University Press, 1976; London: Chatto & Windus, 1976);

Hour, Gnats: New Poems (Davis, Cal.: Putah Creek Press, 1977);

Of Poetry and Poets (Urbana: University of Illinois Press, 1979);

Survivors (Northport, N.Y.: Boa Editions, 1979);

Four Poems (Winston-Salem, N.C.: Palaemon Press, 1980);

New Hampshire: Nine Poems (Rosedale, Mass.: Pym-Randall Press, 1980);

Ways of Light: Poems, 1972-1980 (New York: Oxford University Press, 1980);

Chocorua (New York: Nadja Press, 1981);

Florida Poems (Gulfport, Fla.: Konglomerati Press, 1981);

The Long Reach: New and Uncollected Poems, 1948-1984 (New York: New Directions, 1984).

PLAY PRODUCTIONS: *The Visionary Farms*, Cambridge, Mass., Poets' Theatre, 1952; Seattle, Wash., 1953;

Triptych, Chicago, 1955;

Devils and Angels, Cambridge, Mass., Poets' Theatre, 1956;

The Mad Musician and *Devils and Angels*, Cambridge, Mass., 1962;

The Bride of Mantua, adapted by Eberhart, Hanover, N.H., Dartmouth College, 1964.

OTHER: *The Arts Anthology: Dartmouth Verse 1925*, includes poems by Eberhart (Portland, Maine: Mosher Press, 1925);

Cambridge Poetry, 1929, includes poems by Eberhart (London: Hogarth Press, 1929);

Michael Roberts, ed., *New Signatures*, includes poems by Eberhart (London: Hogarth Press, 1932);

War and the Poet, edited by Eberhart and Selden Rodman (New York: Devin-Adair, 1945);

Forty Dartmouth Poems, edited by Eberhart (Hanover, N.H.: Dartmouth Publications, 1962);

To Eberhart from Ginsberg: A Letter About Howl *1956*, edited by Eberhart (Lincoln, Mass.: Penmaen Press, 1976).

It is tempting to search in a poet's life for the themes of his poetry. Such an exercise is both easy and dangerous. It is easy because the most important themes are universal to both life and poetry. It is dangerous because the examination of such universals is rarely a promising method of discovering the unique, of revealing the special character of either poet or poetry.

Richard Eberhart, however, is perhaps a special case, for the conflicts central to his verse, the tensions between spirit and matter, order and chaos, are mirrored in the vicissitudes of his life, especially through its first four decades. First, an almost idyllic childhood and early youth were shattered by sudden and inexorable tragedy. Then, after a period of personal restructuring and maturation, he faced years of struggle to maintain the integrity of his talent and vision before achieving substantial recognition of his work.

The son of Alpha LaRue and Lena Lowenstein Eberhart, Richard Ghormley Eberhart was one of three children born to a prominent, close-knit, and quite well-to-do Austin, Minnesota, family. His father was a self-made man who became vice-president at the Hormel Meat Packing Company; his mother was devoted to her children and encouraged the literary inclinations that emerged very early in her son's life, inclinations which produced volumes of high school essays, short stories, and poems, at least one of which, "Indian Pipe," made its way into his published work years later, in *Undercliff: Poems 1946-1953* (1953). The poem projects the reader from the present into the past, into history, through a simple image, and shows Eberhart's characteristic sharp eye for the concrete image and his tendency to moralize upon it. Writing was not his only interest, however. As an adolescent he was also a five-letter athlete, served as an officer in his high school fraternity, and participated in a variety of other activities.

It was an enviable life, a kind of American idyll, portrayed with considerable accuracy in Eberhart's verse play *The Visionary Farms* (in *Collected Verse Plays*, 1962). The play also chronicles the collapse of the idyll, beginning with the decline of the family's fortunes, in 1921. When Hormel lost $1.25 million to an embezzler, his father's stock plummeted in value, and in January 1922 he left the company after a disagreement. The company bought the stock at its then depressed value, and the family, though never poor, were thereafter in somewhat straitened circumstances. In the summer of 1921, too, Mrs. Eberhart began to waste away in what was to be a long drawn-out and painful death from lung cancer, and Richard, just graduated from high school, watched, waited, and cared for her. Eighteen years later Eberhart would record something of the trauma of that experience in the rather melodramatic "Orchard," published in *Song and Idea* (1940). His mother died on 22 June 1922, when the young poet was eighteen. Eberhart himself has said that the death of his mother made him a poet, and some critics have suggested that this experience helps to account for what they consider his dominant preoccupation with death, but it is probably more important that his mother's death, coupled as it was with the decline in the family's income and standard of living, completed his traumatic separation from an environment which had constantly validated his identity, from a sense of belonging that he would not feel again for some time.

The separation was confirmed with his matriculation at the University of Minnesota in 1922 and then, in 1923, at Dartmouth College. He became less the assertive, all-round student he had been in high school, finding it necessary to devote a great deal of time just to keeping up his grades. His major extracurricular activities were literary, and he had by this time come to think of himself as a poet. He published poems in both of the college's undergraduate periodicals, and his work was included in *The Arts Anthology: Dartmouth Verse 1925*, which contained an introduction by Robert Frost, who was thus the first important literary figure to comment on his work.

Upon receiving his B.A. in 1926, he descended abruptly from this rarified Ivy League atmosphere: following his father's wish that he go into business, he took a job as a basement floorwalker (he also wrote a few advertisements for ladies' underwear) at Marshall Field and Company's department store in Chicago. He did some writing in his spare time and had a few poems accepted by Harriet Monroe (whom he met in Chicago) for *Poetry: A Magazine of Verse*, but after a few months, in May 1927, he left for San Francisco, en route the long way round for Cambridge University. He worked his way around the world on a succession of tramp steamers, with stops in Shanghai, Manila, Sumatra, Port Said, and many other lesser-known ports. It was not an easy journey, and on one leg of the trip, even though the captain of a German freighter, the *Etha Rickmers*, had agreed to carry him as a nonpaying passenger, he found himself set to work painting the ceiling of the engine room, at 120°F. He jumped ship at Port Said and finished

his journey in comfort as a paying passenger on the S.S. *Rajputana*.

Finally, on 14 October 1927, a week late for the start of the term, he entered St. John's College, Cambridge, beginning what he would later call "a dream of life as it ought to be." It was a life permeated with intellect and with literary values, often of the highest order. He attended debates featuring George Bernard Shaw and G. K. Chesterton, and his teachers and tutors included Arthur Quiller-Couch, Gilbert Murray, F. L. Lucas, and F. R. Leavis. He also formed a lifelong friendship with I. A. Richards, who regularly and actively encouraged and criticized his poetry, and sometimes—as in *Cambridge Poetry, 1929* (1929)—helped get it published.

At Cambridge, the lines between curricular and extracurricular were easily blurred and at tea parties he met such people as C. P. Snow and William Empson. The cultural life of London and the Continent was in easy reach. On one tour of Ireland, Eberhart spent an evening with William Butler Yeats, AE (George Russell), and Oliver St. John Gogarty, and other vacation trips took him to the cathedrals of France and as far as Majorca.

Eberhart spent slightly less than two years at Cambridge, graduating in 1929 with his second B.A. (in due course, after the payment of the proper fee, he received his M.A. in 1933). His performance as a student was characteristically respectable, if not distinguished, and, by the time he left, his reputation as a poet was established. Harriet Monroe had already, in November 1927, published eight of his poems in *Poetry,* and several more were published in British periodicals such as the *London Mercury* and *Experiment*, which in November 1929 published "For a Lamb," a poem whose almost Whitmanesque sense of death as a fusion with life anticipates the later and much more celebrated "The Groundhog":

> I saw on a slant hill a putrid lamb,
> Propped with daisies. The sleep looked deep,
> The face nudged in the green pillow
> But the guts were out for crows to eat.
>
> Where's the lamb? whose tender plaint
> Said for all the mute breeze.
> Say he's in the wind somewhere,
> Say, there's a lamb in the daisies.

A similar and decidedly romantic impulse seems to leap from the opening lines of his first book, *A Bravery of Earth* (1930): "This fevers me, this sun on green,/On grass glowing, this young spring." It is a current that persists into the late work, too, as in, say, "Ichetucknee," in *Ways of Light* (1980):

It is the continuous welling up from the earth
We must remember. Dawn comes, and the waters
Spring fresh, clear, vital from the earth.
Night comes, they well unabated from the dark.

Some of his poems were included in *Cambridge Poetry, 1929,* and he and Empson were the only poets there to be singled out for comment in a review by F. R. Leavis.

While at Cambridge he completed *A Bravery of Earth,* which he had begun during a vacation bicycle trip in the spring of 1928. A long, philosophical, and autobiographical narrative poem, it consumed much of his creative energy during 1929, as he completed it under the criticism of I. A. Richards. Another Cambridge don put him in touch with a publisher, and the book came out in both England and America in 1930.

A Bravery of Earth, now out of print for more than half a century, has been uniformly ignored by critics, and only a few passages have been in-

cluded in Eberhart's collected works. Nonetheless, the book merits study, for it establishes the dialectic, pervasive in his later work, between a sensuous enthusiasm for life and a brooding consciousness of death. In *A Bravery of Earth* he begins his lifelong exploration of the parallel dichotomy between the human being's life-seeking, order-creating spirit, and the death-dealing chaos of the exterior, "objective" world, a dichotomy that finds its only, albeit temporary, resolution in art.

The years at Dartmouth and Cambridge, intellectually and socially rewarding, stimulating, and productive in terms of poetry, restored to Eberhart something of the idyllic quality of his earliest years by providing him with a sense of community, a community which on the one hand upheld the primacy of the imagination and the reality of the intellect, and on the other confirmed his own sense of himself as primarily a poet. Despite the collapse of his childhood idyll, he kept a certain but perhaps intermittent level of intuitive optimism intact, though it was tempered by a sense of tragedy. Optimism and tragedy were both responses to the material world, and his experiences at Dartmouth and Cambridge equipped him to attempt the reconcil-

The Eberhart family in Washington, D.C., 1960 (courtesy of the Richard Eberhart Collection, Baker Library, Dartmouth College)

iation of that world, and the world of feeling, with the world of intellect. The need for such synthesis provided his major themes, and the locus of that synthesis became art, poetry itself, wherein Eberhart found an identity that he would maintain thereafter. It was, however, a decidedly abstract identity, and the 1930s were a period when it was in conflict with an irresistibly concrete world. The years at Dartmouth and Cambridge, perhaps, also left him ill-prepared to deal practically with the Great Depression; Eberhart would not, indeed, feel that he was in his true milieu as a poet until, at the age of forty-eight, he received his first academic appointment.

Upon his return to America in late August 1929 Eberhart worked for three months in a New York slaughterhouse, getting to work at 4:30 in the morning, at first making production tests on the killing floor in Manhattan and, later, checking hams in and out of cold storage in Brooklyn. He once called the slaughterhouse "a vision of hell actual." In his spare time he wrote book reviews for Edmund Wilson, associate editor at the *New Republic*, and evaluated manuscripts for Bobbs-Merrill. In December he got a job in Florida as tutor to two daughters of Mr. and Mrs. Rodney Procter (of Procter and Gamble), and in the fall of 1930 he took a job as tutor to the adopted son of the King of Siam. Eberhart recorded his distaste for the job in his comic-satiric poem "The Rape of the Cataract" (published in *Reading the Spirit*, 1936), in which, when "the veil" was "drawn off the ancient East," instead of reflecting Oriental wisdom, King Prajadhipok keeps the President of the United States waiting so that he can make "timid, deft essays with a model airplane/Its little rubber bands expanding./As with a gentle whirr it takes the air." With his savings from these jobs, Eberhart spent most of a year in Germany, returning in 1932 in time to enter graduate school at Harvard, where he studied under Irving Babbitt and G. L. Kittredge and met T. S. Eliot, who on several occasions consented to discuss his own poems with the young poet. Although his grades were uneven but quite creditable, he was uncomfortable with an academic system that was much more highly structured than England's, and early in 1933, short of funds, he began to look for a teaching position; he joined the staff at St. Mark's School, in Southboro, Massachusetts, where he remained for seven years.

He was a conscientious teacher and took an active part in the life of the school. The work itself, however, was scarcely what he had envisioned for himself, though it had its bright spots. Robert Lowell was among his students and began bringing Eberhart poems for comment and criticism in 1935, beginning an enduring friendship. A few years later in 1938, Eberhart was able to arrange with the headmaster that W. H. Auden, recently arrived from England, should teach at the school for a month, a visit that considerably enlivened the intellectual and literary atmosphere of the school.

His position at St. Mark's kept him within range of New England social and cultural life. He met Ford Madox Ford and R. P. Blackmur and attended lectures and readings by a number of poets and critics, including Wallace Stevens. If his situation was not ideal, it was often congenial, and he was at least protected from the ravages of the Depression that gripped the nation. Then, in December 1940, the Depression caught up with him. As a result of declining enrollments, St. Mark's had to let him go, and it was eighteen months before he found another position, this time at the Cambridge School, in Kendal Green, Massachusetts.

These eighteen months marked an important transitional moment in Eberhart's life. His long search for a new position, a livelihood, underscored the sharpness of his struggle throughout the 1930s to continue writing and to gain some degree of literary recognition. He had had his successes, to be sure. In 1932 some of his poems were included in a British anthology, *New Signatures*, whose editor, Michael Roberts, hoped to promote work less obscure and less remote from contemporary life than currently fashionable poetry. *New Signatures* also included work by Auden, Stephen Spender, and C. Day Lewis, whose names came to be associated (quite arbitrarily) with Eberhart's for many years. Then, on 22 August 1934, the BBC's weekly *Listener* published "The Groundhog," which came to be his best-known poem. It made the first of its many anthology appearances in England in 1936. It later appeared in *A Book of Modern Verse* (published in England in 1940) and in the United States in 1941 in Oscar Williams's annual, *New Poems: 1940*. In later years Eberhart recalled a meeting of the poets' discussion group, at which he had "enjoyed the rigorous criticism" of "The Groundhog," which some members felt should end with the narrative part, deleting the last nine lines: "If I had left them off I am sure the poem would have never got into one anthology."

In the summer of 1930, between his two jobs as tutor, Eberhart had stayed by himself as guest of his friends the Fosters in Phoenixville, Pennsylvania, at a farmhouse called Walden. "I look out on the earth for the first time," he wrote. "Every cell seems fresh to act." And it was there that he "surveyed" the corpse of a shot groundhog, lying on a plank "flat to the open sun." The animal "had lost all its form," he wrote, "all that we call grace and trimness; it was a seething mass of maggots; the shock of the sea-like motion and swirl of these was at first so great as to give the illusion of the viscera pulsing and moving. One looks at one's face in the glass, and wonders on the eternal question of consciousness. . . . It takes calm reason to stave off revulsion at decay. I think we must come to love that reality of decay, a symbol again of the very force of life. Life is the animating principle, and we are nothing but its nurslings."

In elaborating these reflections into his poem, Eberhart moved beyond the ideas he had enunciated in "For a Lamb," for the focus of the poem is not on the dead animal itself, but on the poet's reaction to it, on the intellect:

> In June, amid the golden fields,
> I saw a groundhog lying dead.
> Dead lay he; my senses shook,
> And mind outshot our naked frailty.

The mind takes its materials from the concrete and particular and seeks to transcend them; it turns to a dead groundhog, then back to itself; it conceives of death, then of life-in-death. Through reflection it creates a "wall of wisdom" that can "quell the passion of the blood" and allow the poet enough tranquility to move, at the end of the poem, outward in time and space in a vision of the struggle of the human spirit with intractable reality, in a vision of time and humanity (represented by the soldier, the scholar, and the saint) controlled by the same forces that work in the decaying groundhog:

> I stood there in the whirling summer,
> My hand capped a withered heart,
> And thought of China and of Greece,
> Of Alexander in his tent;
> Of Montaigne in his tower,
> Of Saint Theresa in her wild lament.

The themes of the poem, life and death, man and nature, mortality and immortality, mind and body, concreteness and transcendence, recur throughout Eberhart's career, and they draw upon the central dilemma of his work, a dilemma summed up in "If I could only live at the Pitch that is near Madness" (*Poetry*, January 1938, collected in *Song and Idea*, 1940), which he wrote while he was, in his own words, "a struggling poet and had . . . no status," teaching at St. Mark's School. In this poem the sense of struggle between the natural and the spiritual is couched in terms of the contrast between the innocence of childhood, when everything is "Violent, vivid, and of infinite possibility," and the adult world of experience, limitation, and disillusion:

> I gave the moral answer and I died
> And into a realm of complexity came
> Where nothing is possible but necessity
> And the truth wailing there like a red babe.

The grimness of these closing lines reflects the grim necessities that Eberhart saw surrounding him, for despite such occasional successes as "The Groundhog," the 1930s were for Eberhart-the-poet a bleak landscape. Although he made a fairly reasonable income (he managed to save $1600 in his first year teaching at St. Mark's), he was strangely depressed about money. "I would give much," he said, "for security, enough money, the possibility of a family." Friends such as Frederick Prokosch rebuked him for his continual brooding, and Elizabeth Foster told him, "You think too much about money and relate too many things to it." What Eberhart wanted, of course, was recognition as a poet. But instead he met rejection. Harriet Monroe, for instance, declined to print his work in *Poetry* during this period, calling one group of poems (including "The Rape of the Cataract") "incredibly crude. I can't understand how you could pass such stumbling halting lines. You must know better." He fared better with *Poetry* after Monroe's death in September 1936, but most periodicals, including the *Criterion* and *Scrutiny*, refused his work. What poems he did publish each year attracted little or no attention: *Reading the Spirit* was rejected by several American publishers on economic grounds (thus perhaps reinforcing his obsession with money) before the American edition finally came out at the end of 1937 to mixed reviews. He was very much alone with his art throughout the decade, sustained almost exclusively by the conviction—nourished at Dartmouth, emphatically reinforced in his years at Cambridge, but hardly confirmed at all by his publishing record—that he was a poet by calling and that his poetry was important. What he saw as undue neglect reinforced his sense of desolation and perhaps of isolation.

But October 1940 brought a radical change, for he then met Helen Elizabeth Butcher, a teacher at the Buckingham School at Cambridge. Shortly before he took up his position in the Cambridge School at Kendal Green, on 29 August 1941, Rich-

Richard Eberhart, Philip Booth, Daniel Hoffman, and Robert Lowell in Maine, 1965 (courtesy of the Richard Eberhart Collection, Baker Library, Dartmouth College)

ard and Elizabeth were married, and the future looked reasonably bright. But the Japanese attack on Pearl Harbor in December changed that future, too, and by the end of the summer of 1942 Eberhart was a naval officer teaching aerial gunnery. During the next four years he served in various training and administrative capacities at naval stations in Hollywood, Florida (until May 1943); Dam Neck, Virginia (until November 1944); Wildwood, New Jersey (until August 1945); and Alameda, California, where he served as personnel officer, at the rank of lieutenant commander, until his discharge in the spring of 1946. In California the Eberharts met and became good friends with Kenneth and Marie Rexroth, and Richard Eberhart gave poetry readings at Mills College and (at the invitation of Josephine Miles) at the University of California, Berkeley. Despite their nomadic character, these years were apparently comfortable: "I have enjoyed my Navy Career to date," he wrote to W. H. Auden from New Jersey; "a complete refreshment from the stuffiness of literary people, literary attitudes." They were also productive years: he wrote

some of his best-known poems, including "Dam Neck, Virginia" and "The Fury of Aerial Bombardment," both published in Oscar Williams's annual, *New Poems: 1944,* and collected in *Poems, New and Selected,* published in January 1945 by James Laughlin's New Directions, and he edited, with Selden Rodman, the anthology *War and the Poet* (1945). The period was also crowned, in October 1946, by the birth of a son, Richard.

By this time, Eberhart had accepted a position in his wife's family business, the Butcher Polish Company in Boston, and returned to the fertile cultural milieu of Cambridge and Boston, enjoying the company of such people as John Malcolm Brinnin, Howard Moss, Richard Wilbur, Wallace Stevens, T. S. Eliot, I. A. Richards, William Carlos Williams, Robert Frost, and many others. Eberhart stayed with the Butcher Polish Company until 1952. These years were remarkably energetic and productive: in addition to taking part in the general intellectual and social life around Harvard, he belonged to a group of poets who met, at John Ciardi's suggestion, irregularly from 1948 until 1950, for "reading and strict criticism of poems, no holds barred. And the pleasure of any consideration of poetry" (Ciardi's words). Members of the group included Ciardi, Eberhart, John Holmes, May Sarton, Richard Wilbur, Archibald MacLeish, and Robert Lowell. In June 1950 he joined William Lyon Phelps and Molly Howe in founding the Poets' Theatre in Cambridge, and the month he spent at Yaddo, the artist's colony near Saratoga Springs, New York, beginning on 5 July, was indeed fortunate. Working in a studio next to one occupied by William Carlos Williams, vitalized by the possibility of a poet's theater, in three weeks he wrote about a hundred pages of verse drama. The enforced and uninterrupted eight-hour writing day gave Eberhart the encouragement and impetus he and the others needed to make the Poets' Theatre a success. By the spring of 1952, when Eberhart left Boston, the company had produced twenty plays, including Eberhart's *The Visionary Farms* on 21 May 1952 (the Poets' Theatre would produce another of his plays, *Devils and Angels,* in January 1956). At Yaddo, too, he began to put together the selection of poems that became *Undercliff* (1953).

Between 1946 and 1952, while he was working for the family business, Eberhart's poems were appearing regularly in various periodicals: he gave numerous public readings, and in addition to a few pamphlets published two books, *Burr Oaks* (1947) and *Selected Poems* (1951). The war had given Eberhart a strong sense of liberation: while the world was at its most coercive, he came to terms with the "necessity" he had struggled with in the 1930s. "Peace has come with war," he wrote in "An Airman Considers His Power" (*Furioso,* Fall 1946, collected in *Burr Oaks*). From 1946 on Eberhart published voluminously. Sustained in part by the emotional security of his new family and his unambiguously defined social role, he projected more clearly than ever before his role as poet, as in "The Horse Chestnut Tree" (collected in *Undercliff*), where he recollects chasing young boys away from the tree in his yard. "Still I moralize upon the day," the poem ends,

> And see that we, outlaws on God's property,
> Fling out imagination beyond the skies,
> Wishing a tangible good from the unknown.
>
> And likewise death will drive us from the scene
> With the great flowering world unbroken yet,
> Which we held in idea, a little handful.

Under different historical circumstances, he might have continued indefinitely after the war as a corporate executive, while seeking out his "little handful" (much as did his friend, insurance-executive Wallace Stevens), letting his life and his art run their parallel but separate courses. But postwar prosperity brought with it the lecture circuit, the visiting writer, and the writer-in-residence. In addition Eberhart had, while tenaciously pursuing his art throughout the previous two decades, built up a reputation among professional *literati,* and that reputation won him, finally, the kind of synthesis of the personal and the professional that had been his goal since Cambridge.

Autumn 1952 found Eberhart in Seattle— with his wife, son, and one-year-old daughter, Gretchen—on a one-year teaching appointment (as poet-in-residence) at the University of Washington. It was an active year which saw Eberhart teaching one course in modern poetry and another in creative writing, giving public readings, watching rehearsals (and then performances) of some of his verse plays, and—perhaps because he found life rather slow after Cambridge—developing a system of "trying to snatch everybody within range" (as Robert Heilman, chairman of the English department, put it): he arranged for visits and readings by Oscar Williams, Caroline Gordon, Richard Wilbur, Kenneth Rexroth, and others.

Though he did not know it at the time, he was finished with the polish business forever: the appointment at Seattle was the first of a series of visiting professorships, fellowships, and the like. Eberhart had at last reached the position where his writing was the reason for his employment. After his year at Washington he taught at the University of Connecticut at Storrs, replacing R. W. Stallman for 1953-1954, and then at Wheaton College (1954-1955). Awarded a fellowship from the National Institute of Arts and Letters in 1955, he delivered the Christian Gauss Lectures and served as resident fellow at Princeton University during 1955-1956, and in the fall of 1956 he was appointed professor and poet-in-residence at his alma mater Dartmouth College, beginning an association with that institution that lasted until 1980: in 1968 he became Class of 1925 Professor at Dartmouth, a position which he held until 1971 when, officially retired, he continued to teach as professor emeritus. But he also had duties elsewhere: in 1959-1961 he served as consultant in poetry at the Library of Congress; in 1967 and in 1972 he returned to Seattle as a visiting professor; in the spring of 1975 he was adjunct professor at Columbia University, following this appointment with a regents' professorship at the University of California, Davis, that fall. Since 1974 he has taught classes both as distinguished visiting professor at the University of Florida and as professor emeritus at Dartmouth, spending his summers at Undercliff, the family's vacation home near Cape Rosier, Maine.

His university positions have allowed Eberhart ample time to write, and his teaching life, primarily devoted to poetry, has enabled him, for a period of more than thirty years, to live for poetry as writer, teacher, and catalyst. The writing has been prolific, and it has brought Eberhart recognition and honor: besides the appointment to the Library of Congress, the most prestigious of the long list of awards and honors includes a 1962 Bollingen Prize, which he shared with John Hall Wheelock; a 1966 Pulitzer Prize for *Selected Poems, 1930-1965* (1965); a 1977 National Book Award for *Collected Poems, 1930-1976* (1976); and election to one of the fifty chairs of the American Academy of Arts and Letters (1982).

The years since his appointment at Seattle at the age of forty-eight may be seen as a long, felicitous resolution to the complex and strenuous dialectic between self and world that has informed the whole of his poetic career, and although a certain serenity of tone is characteristic of much of his later work, which shows a greater clarity and a firmer mastery of his medium, the bulk of his work is more remarkable for its consistency in theme and approach than for its developmental patterns. The sense of struggle between the natural and the spiritual, visible in "If I could only live at the Pitch that is new Madness" (1938), is equally present in the breathtaking moment of suicide in "On Returning to a Lake in Spring" (collected in *Shifts of Being*, 1968); the momentary epiphany, the imaginative interpenetration of abstract vision and observed reality, commonplace in the late poetry, is nevertheless nowhere more fully embodied than in the very early "The Groundhog" (1934).

The remarkable consistency and coherence of the work enable one to discuss the early work alongside the later to advantage and thus see the persistence of Eberhart's characteristic themes, concerns, and techniques. His vision has always been rooted in the ancient confrontation between innocence and experience, between the drive for order and the awareness of reality, a confrontation that seems unresolvable in the actual world. On the side of order and innocence (a label frequently applied by earlier reviewers) are the images and motifs and tonalities that critics have called

"romantic"—they are, like Emerson's, concerned with the true, the ideal, the transcendent. On the other side, there is temporality, imperfection, the ephemeral, and the disorderly: the poet's much-remarked preoccupation with death. Thus, on the side of innocence, from "Incidence of Flight" (*Collected Poems, 1930-1976*):

> I spring joy out of my rib cage
> Like a flash of pigeons flying North
> ....
> Joy uncages man to love.

and in "The Poem as Trajectory" (1976):

> I ask questions about the poem
> Because it deals with reality,
>
> An intractable substance, which, if hit,
> May favor timelessness.

Yet, as Emerson put it, "Nature, as we know her, is no saint." "A name may be glorious," Eberhart wrote in "I Walked over the Grave of Henry James" (*Burr Oaks*, 1947), "but death is death," and we find the almost identical thought in "Loss," published in 1960 (*Massachusetts Review*, collected in *The Quarry*, 1964):

> I do not know how to say no
> To time that goes on in any case.

The balance between innocence and experience, the tension between ideality and necessity, in which virtually all his work is firmly grounded, finds perhaps its clearest expression in "The Secret Heart" (*Fields of Grace*, 1972), which asserts that we are all "Gripped by nature as was the first man/ . . . / We are compelled in this great adversity."

There is a distinctly modernist ring, tempering the romantic view, in the poem's reflection that "Eventually all ideas go underground,/The only triumph is some elegance of style."

Whereas the inspiration of the original romantics was the discovery of an eternal, natural (and/or divine) order, the heightened awareness of the modernist allows merely the creation of an order that is temporary, artificial, an "elegance of style." Transcendental is a temporary achievement at best, and is, as he writes in the first two stanzas of "Meditation Two" (*The Quarry*), a matter of style:

> Style is the perfection of a point of view,
> Nowise absolute, but held in a balance of opposites

So that for a moment the passage of time is stopped
And man is enhanced in a moment of harmony.

There are few imitations of immortality, whether in concrete reality or in abstract art. The "moment of harmony" after all lasts but "for a moment." Eberhart continues to struggle with death without ever falling into the illusion that he has won. More than the work of many of his contemporaries, his work is permeated with the realization that the best to be said of "the only triumph" is that it is the best that we can do.

Eberhart's, then, is a romantic sensibility enclosed within a modernist mentality. It is a sensibility that demands transcendence, that "cannot believe that man is here to die," that insists instinctively on a noumenal reality. And it is a mentality that insists with equal vigor upon a recognition of the finality of death, and the inevitability of the cruelty and chaos in life. He stands poised between a Whitmanesque affirmation of life-in-death and

an aestheticist construction of an imaginative armor against death-in-life, awestruck by the irrevocable reality and the pathetic inadequacy of both, in wonderment at the irresolution, the mystery, the very absence of synthesis.

It is the achievement of his poetry to dwell at the still center of the mystery, and it is not a position accessible to strictly "rational" analysis. Instead, he tells in *Of Poetry and Poets* (1979), "the poet's mind is a filament informed with the irrational vitality" of what he calls "extraordinary states of being" that "come upon one unannounced" while "in an elevated state of mind. . . ." The immediacy which results from such a method is that the significance attributed to reality seems to have been discovered, not invented or created. The poet becomes something akin to Emerson's naked eyeball, unaided either by a limiting theory or a transcendent faith. And yet the vision brings us as close to transcendence as the contemporary mind is likely to come.

Watching (in *Collected Poems: 1930-1960*, 1960)

> a half-blind, burly, old
> Man, half bent to earth
> Who once on the Princeton campus
> Spears stray papers with a nail-
> Ended stick. . . .

we claim the old man's burdens as our own

> As time bends us to earth
> And we pick up what gems and scraps
> There are from magnificence.

The thought is close to that concluding "The Groundhog" in its vision of space and time, in its view of the spirit locked in the temporal and struggling against it. In "Ospreys in Cry" (from the same book), watching an osprey catch a fish, the poet identifies with the duality, the whole process, of nature:

> I felt a staggering sense
> Of the victor and of the doomed,
> Of being the one and the other,
> Of being both at one time,
> I was the seer
> And I was revealed.

If critics have persisted in calling Eberhart romantic or religious, they have done so perhaps because he rages, in Dylan Thomas's phrase, "against the dying of the light," against irresistible fatality; at the same time, his realization that con-

Cover for the New Directions collection of Eberhart's poems written between the ages of forty-four and eighty

sciousness is finite allows us to identify with such infinite continuities as the ongoing processes of nature, the essential presentness of all time, the stubborn persistence in our species of the demand for meaning, and even for justice, where none seems to exist. Eberhart's is finally a kind of innocence that finds essences in experience, and thus seeks to convey an essential wisdom of experience, that makes tragedy not remote but accessible.

In April 1986 he received the Poetry Society of America's Robert Frost Medal.

References:

R. P. Blackmur, Review of *Reading the Spirit, Partisan Review*, 5 (February 1938): 52-56;
A review which praises the universal symbols and themes in *Reading the Spirit*.

Philip Booth, "The Varieties of Poetic Experience," *Shenandoah*, 15 (Summer 1964): 62-69;
A review of *The Quarry* which claims that Eberhart proposes simple solutions for this complex world.

Denis Donoghue, *The Third Voice* (Princeton: Princeton University Press, 1964), pp. 194-195, 223-235;
Discusses the various devices used in *The Visionary Farms* and criticizes the play's lack of originality.

Bernard F. Engel, *Richard Eberhart* (Boston: Twayne, 1972);
A thorough study of Eberhart's work. Includes chronology and selected bibliography.

Engel, "Richard Eberhart—Reader of the Spirit," in *The Achievement of Richard Eberhart* (New York: Scott, Foresman, 1968), pp. 1-21;
Praises Eberhart's poetry and discusses its diversity.

Donald Hall, "Method in Poetic Composition," *Paris Review*, 1 (Autumn 1953): 113-119;
Contrasts the opposite methods of Richard Eberhart and Richard Wright.

Daniel Hoffman, "Hunting the Master Image, the Poetry of Richard Eberhart," *Hollins Critic*, 1 (October 1964): 1-12;
Discusses Eberhart's originality and praises the lasting quality of some of his poems.

Ralph J. Mills, Jr., "Richard Eberhart," in his *Contemporary American Poetry* (New York: Random House, 1965), pp. 9-31;
A study of Eberhart's opposing themes. Claims that the poet still maintains a certain unity.

Mills, *Richard Eberhart* (Minneapolis: University of Minnesota Press, 1966);
Discusses Eberhart's avoidance of labels and studies his place in the postmodern generation.

Joel Roache, *Richard Eberhart: The Progress of an American Poet* (New York: Oxford University Press, 1971);
Provides a great deal of information about Eberhart and discusses his gradual acceptance of his society.

Peter Thorslev, "The Poetry of Richard Eberhart," *Northwestern Tri-Quarterly*, 2 (Winter 1960): 26-32; revised and republished in *Poets in Progress*, edited by Edward Hungerford (Evanston: Northwestern University Press, 1962), pp. 73-91;
Discusses Eberhart's strengths—his intelligence, his compassion, and his influence.

Papers:
Eberhart's papers are in the Richard Eberhart Collection at the Baker Library, Dartmouth College.

Ralph Waldo Ellison

This entry was revised by Leonard J. Deutsch (Marshall University) from his entry in
DLB 2, American Novelists Since World War II.

Places	Oklahoma	Tuskegee Institute	New York University
Influences and Relationships	Ralph Waldo Emerson Langston Hughes	Richard Wright	Alain Locke
Literary Movements and Forms	Surrealism	Literary and Social Criticism	
Major Themes	Racial Exploitation Social Mobility for Blacks	Duplicity Individual Responsibility	Racial Traditions
Cultural and Artistic Influences	Classical Music Sculpture	Jazz Freudian Psychology	Blues
Social and Economic Influences	Socialism	Federal Writers' Project	

BIRTH: Oklahoma City, Oklahoma, 1 March 1914, to Lewis Alfred and Ida Millsap Ellison.

EDUCATION: Tuskegee Institute, 1933-1936.

MARRIAGES: Information on first marriage unknown. 26 August 1946, to Fanny McConnell.

AWARDS AND HONORS: Rosenwald grant, 1945; National Book Award for *Invisible Man*, 1953; Russwurm Award for *Invisible Man*, 1953; Certificate of Award (*Chicago Defender*), 1953; American Academy of Arts and Letters Fellowship to Rome, 1955-1957; Medal of Freedom, 1969; Chevalier de l'Ordre des Artes and Lettres, 1970; honorary doctorates, Tuskegee, 1963; Rutgers, 1966; University of Michigan, 1967; Grinnell, 1967; Williams College, 1970; Adelphi, 1971; Long Island University, 1971; College of William and Mary, 1972; Wake Forest, 1974; University of Maryland, 1974; Harvard, 1974; Bard College, 1978; Wesleyan University, 1980; Brown University, 1980.

BOOKS: *Invisible Man* (New York: Random House, 1952; London: Gollancz, 1953);
Shadow and Act (New York: Random House, 1964; London: Secker & Warburg, 1967);
Going to the Territory (New York: Random House, 1986).

Ralph Ellison (photo by Chris Corpus)

Though his reputation rests on a single novel, many critics consider Ralph Ellison to be the preeminent Afro-American writer, and others have argued that *Invisible Man* ranks with the most significant American literary works of this century. In the thirty-five years since *Invisible Man* was published, Ellison has been largely silent, publishing only a handful of essays and stories and, between 1960 and 1977, excerpts from his novel-in-progress. Nevertheless, the accomplishment of his masterpiece is sufficient to insure his literary stature.

Ellison's parents were southerners. Ida Millsap, originally from White Oak, Georgia, met and married Lewis Ellison, an ice cream parlor owner who later entered the construction business in Abbeville, South Carolina, and moved to Oklahoma with him a few years after statehood was attained in 1907. A political activist, Ida Ellison— or "Brownie," as she was commonly called—canvassed Negro voters for Eugene Debs's Socialist party during the gubernatorial campaign in 1914, the same year her son Ralph was born. Later, she

went to jail for violating undemocratic zoning ordinances during the 1930s.

When Ralph was three and his only surviving sibling, Herbert, was four months old, their father died in an accident. Mrs. Ellison worked as a domestic in white homes and served as an apartment-house custodian, but Ralph Ellison never considered himself deprived.

Among those who inspired the young Ellison—besides his determined mother—were the men who frequented the local drugstore and barbershop, swapping tales, and believing in "the spirit of the law, if not in its application." There were also the jazz musicians who "stumbled upon the freedom lying within the restrictions of their musical tradition." Later in his career, Ellison would write essays about some of these jazzmen, including blues singer Jimmy Rushing, who at one time worked for Lewis Ellison as an ice carrier, and guitarist Charlie Christian, who was a classmate of Ellison's younger brother in elementary school.

Perhaps "aware of the suggestive power of names and the magic involved in naming," Lewis

Ellison named his son "Ralph Waldo" in honor of Emerson, the great American philosopher-poet. In school Ellison disguised his middle name by using the initial *W*, and he avoided Emerson's works "like the plague," he recalls. Only later did he come to terms with his name and with the moral obligations that Emerson assigned to American writers.

Even if he vowed to avoid Emerson, Ellison was an avid reader in his youth. He was also an ardent musician. The trumpet was his forte although he was able to play several brass instruments and the soprano saxophone as well. In an academic world alive with music-theory classes and extracurricular musical activities, Ellison chose to learn more about music by taking private lessons from Ludwig Hebestreit, conductor of the Oklahoma City Orchestra. Ellison "paid" for these lessons by mowing the maestro's lawn. To help out at home he sold newspapers, operated an elevator, worked as a soda jerk, and took other odd jobs.

Ellison left Oklahoma in 1933, at the age of nineteen, under honorable but financially strained circumstances: he had been awarded a scholarship by the state of Oklahoma, "supposedly on merit," he reports, "but the scholarship program itself was a device through which the state hoped to circumvent applications by Negro students for enrollment in the state universities of Oklahoma." Ellison chose to attend Tuskegee Institute in Macon County, Alabama, but he did not have enough money to travel in style so, like many others during the Great Depression, he hopped a freight train. While he was hoboing, two white railroad detectives carrying .45 revolvers forced him off the train in Decatur, Alabama, the town where the Scottsboro boys were being tried at that time for crimes allegedly committed while hoboing. Ellison recalls: "I had no idea of what the detectives intended to do with me, but given the atmosphere of the town I feared that it would be most unpleasant and brutal." He never found out what they had in mind, however, because when some of his traveling companions began running for their lives, so did he and he did not stop until he was safe.

Tuskegee, founded by Booker T. Washington in 1881 as a technical institute, had evolved into a liberal arts college under Presidents Robert M. Moton and Frederick Douglass Patterson. Here Ellison, majoring in music and music theory, expected to become a professional musician. As he studied under the composer William L. Dawson he aspired to write a symphony by the time he was twenty-six equal to anything Richard Wagner had written by that age, but he continued to explore other interests as well, including starring in the school play as a sophomore and reading widely.

Unlike the protagonist of his novel, *Invisible Man*, Ellison was not expelled from Tuskegee; experiencing some financial difficulties at the end of his junior year, he went to New York in the summer of 1936 to earn money, fully expecting to return for his senior year, although he never did. Arriving in New York with only seventy-five dollars he stayed at the Harlem YMCA where he got a job behind the food counter. On his second day in New York, he happened to meet Alain Locke, whom Ellison had heard speak at Tuskegee. Accompanying Locke was Langston Hughes, who subsequently would go to Harlem's Apollo Theater with Ellison on numerous occasions. At this meeting Hughes asked Ellison if he would deliver two books to a friend—André Malraux's *Man's Fate* and *Days of Wrath*—indicating that he could read them first if he wanted to. As Ellison's essays demonstrate, he not only read *Man's Fate* but it had a profound impact upon him.

Initially, Ellison expected a career in music or sculpture. A Tuskegee teacher gave him a letter of introduction to Harlem sculptor Augusta Savage, but when she could not accept any new students, Ellison studied under Richmond Barthé for about a year.

To support himself during the late Depression years he free-lanced as a photographer, worked as a file clerk-receptionist for a psychiatrist, and later built and sold hi-fi systems. When he was out of work he slept in the park below City College. His job in the psychiatrist's office inspired him to reread Freud on dream symbolism, providing knowledge he was to put to use in his fiction. The challenge to attempt fiction was issued by Richard Wright, whom Ellison had met through their mutual friend, Langston Hughes. Ellison began his literary career by writing a review of Waters E. Turpin's *These Low Grounds* for the autumn 1937 issue of *New Challenge* edited by Wright. Ellison contributed a short story, "Heine's Bull," to the winter issue but the magazine folded and the story never got beyond the galleys.

Ellison joined the Federal Writers' Project in 1938 and received $103.50 per month. With Sterling A. Brown serving as editor of Negro affairs, the project offered Ellison a number of assignments which required research and writing. While working with the Living Lore Unit—"a group consisting of twenty-seven writers who were to document New York's Urban and industrial folklore"—Ellison collected many tales including the story of

Sweet-the-Monkey, who could make himself invisible and perform all sorts of devilish acts. Besides acquiring information that would later serve as source material, Ellison was developing a greater appreciation for the function of folklore. As one critic puts it, in Ellison's fiction "lore is more than local color; it is ritualistic and reflective of a whole lifestyle."

As Ellison moved toward a literary career by submitting reviews and essays for publication, he was surrounded by friends and acquaintances who shared his left-leaning political point of view but, unlike some of them, he never joined the Communist party and he always insisted that art should never be subverted by the dictates of partisan politics. Even in his earliest critical commentaries he expected the artist to exemplify a dauntless integrity and independence and to master the techniques of his or her craft. To acquire such a background for himself he systematically scrutinized the prefaces of Henry James and Joseph Conrad, studied Faulkner, Joyce, Hemingway, Twain, and Dostoyevski, and held long conversations with Richard Wright.

His first two published short stories are clearly apprentice pieces. "Slick Gonna Learn," which appeared in the September 1939 issue of *Direction*, is an excerpt from a novel Ellison conceived but never wrote. "The Birthmark," appeared in *New Masses* on 2 July 1940. Both stories protest police brutality in a rather direct manner. His next three stories, however, are built on dialogues between two young boys, Buster and Riley, and deal with the aspirations of those whose spirits remain irrepressible despite a repressive environment. In "Afternoon" (*American Writing*, 1940); "Mister Toussan" (*New Masses*, 4 November 1941); and "That I Had the Wings" (*Common Ground*, Summer 1943), Buster and Riley seek and find positive role models within their own folklore and ethnic history.

After serving as managing editor of *The Negro Quarterly* in 1942 under editor Angelo Herndon Ellison returned to story writing and produced his two most famous, successful, and widely anthologized stories before *Invisible Man:* "Flying Home"(*Cross Section*, 1944) and "King of the Bingo Game" (*Tomorrow*, November 1944). The protagonist of "Flying Home," an aviator named Todd, learns to gain strength from his folk roots when he reconciles himself to Jefferson, the humanistic old black peasant who befriends him in his hour of need. "King of the Bingo Game" seems a rehearsal for *Invisible Man* in that it features a nameless character who, despite the absurdity of his situation,

tries desperately to manipulate his fate and forge his own identity. In this story Ellison masters surrealistic techniques and utilizes a great deal of symbolism.

In 1944 Ellison met Fanny McConnell. Born in Louisville, Kentucky, and raised in Pueblo, Colorado, and Chicago, McConnell had served as secretary to James Weldon Johnson when she attended Fisk University in Nashville, Tennessee, and she graduated from the University of Iowa where she studied drama and speech. She met Ellison in New York, and married him in 1946. It was his second marriage. Details of his first marriage are unknown.

During World War II Ellison produced one patriotic story, "In a Strange Country" (*Tomorrow*, July 1944), and served as a cook in the Merchant Marine. When he returned to the United States in 1945 exhausted from his Atlantic voyages, he accepted an invitation to recuperate on a farm in Vermont. He dismissed the notion of continuing a war novel he had begun but in Vermont the idea for *Invisible Man* began to germinate in his mind. About the same time that he was reading Lord Raglan's *The Hero* and "speculating on the nature of Negro leadership in the United States," he reveals, "I wrote the first paragraph of *Invisible Man*." With the assistance of a 1945 Rosenwald grant, he continued working on the book until its publication in 1952 although chapter 1 (England's *Horizon*, October 1947, and America's *'48*) and the prologue (*Partisan Review*, January-February 1952) appeared in earlier installments. An abortive short novel—to which he had devoted a year—was jettisoned during this period.

Invisible Man begins with the prologue, the penultimate stage in the main character's development. He has been on the run; now he is in his underground hole. Faced with his enforced hibernation, his impulses at first are vindictive: he siphons electricity from the Monopolated Light & Power Company, and he ascends to ground level where he engages in an act of personal terrorism. Repelled by his violent behavior he returns to his warm underground shelter, gets high, and listens to jazz records and Louis Armstrong's "What Did I Do to Be So Black and Blue?" As he begins a mental descent through layers of consciousness, he encounters images from his racial past: a sermon on the "Blackness of Blackness" and a dialogue between a slave woman and her mulatto children. Into his dream state also enters the image of Ras the Destroyer from whom he had fled until he plunged into his dark sanctuary. Returning to waking consciousness, the invisible man believes that the music he has been listening to demands action and "I believe in nothing if not in action."

Before he can act in a meaningful way, however, the invisible man must confront and come to terms with his identity and his life. The best way to order the chaos of his experience, he reasons, is to tell the tale of how he got into the hole in the first place. His narrative then proceeds on two levels: on the first, episodes from his life are reconstructed so readers can share them as the naive boy experienced them; simultaneously, on the second level, the voice of the older, wiser, and judgmental narrator can be heard as he interjects his satirical asides. This dual perspective, in part, accounts for the novel's complexity.

Another source of the novel's complexity is its symbolism. Ellison has remarked that during the years he wrote *Invisible Man* "the symbols and their connections were known to me. I began . . . with a chart of the three-part division. It was a conceptual frame with most of the ideas and some incidents indicated." The symbolic patterns are so dense and the symbols are so ubiquitous that literary scholars continue to produce endless explications of the work.

Some of the primary symbols in the novel are introduced in the first chapter, the battle royal scene, which one critic labels "a 'representative anecdote,' that is, an episode in which the entire novel is implicit." The battle royal consists of a group of blindfolded black youths fighting before a crowd of rich white men who pay the combatants by throwing what appear to be gold coins, but are in fact only brass slugs, on an electrified rug that shocks the youths when they touch it. The battle is itself an initiation ritual which symbolizes many aspects of race relations in a socially segregated society including white sadism and the hostile black reaction that is channeled into intraracial violence. The young protagonist allows himself to be blindfolded, symbolic of his moral myopia (blindness becomes a major motif of the novel), for he naively expects the rich white men in the smoker to give him something of great value for his efforts. What they *do* give him as a reward for his accommodationist speech that precedes the battle is a briefcase. Emblematic of his middle-class aspirations, this briefcase will eventually contain a number of symbolic documents—such as his high school diploma, his scholarship to a state college for Negroes, letters of reference, and a sambo doll—some of which the narrator will later burn in a symbolic gesture of repudiation. That night in a dream about his grandfather he sees a circus (symbolic of absurd reality), clowns (symbolic of the role assigned to blacks as entertainers), and a series of envelopes that represent years in the invisible man's life; the last envelope contains a prophetic and symbolic message: "To Whom It May Concern, Keep This Nigger-Boy Running."

The next series of events occurs at the state college campus, which is a symbolic wasteland although the naive youth prefers to see it as an Edenic paradise. The whitewashed buildings represent the socialization process which has been designed to whitewash the minds of the college's black students. Down the road is the black powerhouse, "with its engines droning earth-shaking rhythms in the dark, its windows red from the glow of the furnace." Like most of the other images employed in the novel, the powerhouse functions as a symbol—here representing, among other things, the demonic, machinelike college president, Dr. Bledsoe (whose name suggests the deracinated quality of his racial allegiance). The main character inadvertently crosses Dr. Bledsoe by allowing the white philanthropist, Mr. Norton (whose face, "pink like St. Nicholas'," ironically hints of Santa Claus, another mythical gift giver), to meet Jim Trueblood (whose name suggests his function as symbolic foil to blood-drained Bledsoe). When Trueblood relates a dream that accompanied his commission of incest with his daughter, Freudian symbols—doors, hills, rooms, and grandfather clocks—present themselves in an unrestrained tumult. Norton is unsettled by the revelation he experiences after listening to his black counterpart's story, and while he collapses, some children, appropriately enough, sing "London Bridge's Falling Down"—a tune which also suggests the dissolution of the invisible man's Edenic world.

Like the first two chapters, the other twenty-three chapters are awash with symbols and symbolic dates, scenes, episodes, and characters. There are, in fact, very few if any passages devoid of symbolic overtones. One of the novel's most overtly symbolic encounters occurs in chapter eleven when the invisible man undergoes a lobotomylike operation in the factory hospital. The contraption he is strapped into—more sophisticated than the electrified rug in chapter 1 but similar in its emasculating function—is designed to neutralize the hero, transform him into an "amiable fellow." The shock therapy does not work as the white "doctors" intend it to, however, because in peeling away surface veneers of superficial experience the invisible man returns to a more basic identity. The device he is entombed in turns out to be an ironic womb: "A huge iridescent bubble seemed to enfold me. . . . I was laved with warm liquids. . . . The sterile and weightless texture of a sheet enfolded me. I felt myself bounce, sail off like a ball thrown over the roof into the mist, striking a hidden wall beyond a pile of broken machinery and sailing back." When he emerges from this amniotic sac, his umbilical cord is severed—"I felt a tug at my belly and looked down to see one of the physicians pull the cord which was attached to the stomach node, jerking me forward"—and he is reborn. Lest the reader overlook the symbolism of this incident, Ellison has his protagonist focusing "upon the teetering scene with wild, infant's eyes" at the beginning of the next chapter.

The rest of the hero's adventures—with Lucius Brockway, Tod Clifton, Rinehart, Brother Jack, Sybil, and numerous others—culminates in the surrealistically rendered race riot. In the last chapter the invisible man takes refuge in a dark hole. The narrator's tale is now told except for the epilogue. In this final section of the novel the protagonist meditates upon the meaning of his experiences. He has, in Ellison's borrowed terms, moved from purpose to passion (or conflict) to perception. The hero's perception, or insightful self-understanding, is symbolized by the 1,369 light bulbs that illuminate his underground home. Devoid of any illusions, he still has much to affirm because as shaping artist of his tale he sees more clearly the relationship between personal responsibility and individual identity. A new sense of self emerges from this assessment of his experiences and, having transformed himself from ranter to writer, he is prepared to engage with American society on a new footing. In the epilogue, the novel's fictional narrator seems finally to comprehend what Ellison the man had known all along: that the Constitution, embodying "sacred" democratic principles, is a "vital covenant" offering unlimited possibilities for "individual self-realization."

Although Ellison's art transcends any simplistic cultural pigeonholes, one may discern the way the author draws upon a variety of literary traditions including over a century of Afro-American lore and literature. The reader unacquainted with Frederick Douglass, Booker T. Washington, W. E. B. Du Bois, James Weldon Johnson, Alain Locke, Marcus Garvey, Richard Wright, and Negro folklore may miss a dimension of the novel's art, for all contribute to the meaning of the invisible man's quest and all enrich the rhetorical texture of the work.

The youth's desire to become another Booker T. Washington testifies to his misguided ambitions early in the novel. Indeed, the speech he delivers after the battle royal—his valedictorian speech—is lifted *verbatim* from Washington's 1895 Atlanta Exposition address, an address Du Bois contemptuously dubbed "the Atlanta Compromise." "Cast down your bucket where you are," Washington had frequently advised; later in the novel two characters literally cast down their kerosene-filled buckets during a race riot and set some buildings ablaze. During the college campus chapters, the novel takes satirical swipes at the Founder (based on Washington) and his disciple, Dr. Bledsoe, whom the students surreptitiously call "Old Buckethead." The bronze statue of the "cold father symbol" puzzles the narrator who cannot decide whether the founder is lifting the veil of ignorance from the kneeling slave or lowering it more firmly in place. Such a statue of Booker T. Washington still stands on the grounds of Tuskegee University.

Standing in stark opposition to a deceptive, opportunistic, kowtowing Booker T. Washington figure is the image of Frederick Douglass, a heroic paragon whose spirit hovers in the background throughout the novel. The racial organization, The Brotherhood, welcomes the protagonist as the new Booker T. Washington but it would not be likely to tolerate a Frederick Douglass in its midst. Douglass was committed to the Constitution and never lost faith in the promise of American democracy; he personifies manly assertiveness and unobtrusive self-esteem. The narrator's grandfather and Douglass are linked together as crafty, dignified, rebellious, and fiercely independent men. Near the end of chapter 7 when Brother Tarp, who is also associated with these figures, gives the invisible man a portrait of Douglass, the hero contemplates the life of the man he would choose, at that point in his career, to emulate:

> Sometimes I sat watching the watery play of light upon Douglass' portrait, thinking how magical it was that he talked his way from slavery to a government ministry, and so swiftly. Perhaps, I thought, something of the kind is happening to me. Douglass came north to escape and find work in the shipyards; a big fellow in a sailor's suit who, like me, had taken another name. What had his true name been? [Frederick Bailey.] Whatever it was, it was as *Douglass* that he became himself, defined himself.

There are numerous ironies here, not the least of which is that it took a long time for Douglass to be appointed to a government ministry—he was over fifty years old at the time; that the invisible man triumphs as an introspective author quietly meditating upon the meaning of his experiences rather than as a crowd-rousing orator; and that Douglass chose his own name while the invisible man's "identity" is conferred on him by the Brotherhood. Perhaps the crowning irony is that the invisible man has much further to go before he approaches Douglass's standard of forthright independence, for the fugitive slave refused to accept a subordinate position in anyone else's organization—he was always his own man.

Du Bois is never explicitly mentioned in *Invisible Man* but his presence, nevertheless, makes itself felt. Both Du Bois and Ellison's narrator were troubled by a sense of double consciousness. The invisible man becomes aware that "there were two of me: the old self that . . . dreamed sometimes of my grandfather and Bledsoe and Brockway and Mary, the self that flew without wings and plunged from great heights; and the new public self that spoke for the Brotherhood . . . I seemed to run a foot race against myself." Similarly, Du Bois experienced a "peculiar sensation": "one ever feels his twoness—an American, a Negro; two souls, two thoughts, two unreconciled strivings; two warring ideals in one dark body, whose dogged strength alone keeps it from being torn asunder." Despite this sense of dichotomy, however, both Du Bois and the invisible man ultimately achieve a unified vision, the one strong enough to merge the dual selves. In discussing the Negro's relationship to America, the invisible man at one point reflects, "we . . . [are] snarled inextricably within its veins and sinews"; at another, he says, "America is woven of many strands," both of which metaphorical expressions recall Du Bois's assertion: "we have woven ourselves with the very warp and woof of this nation" in the "Of the Sorrow Songs" section of *The Souls of Black Folks*. "I am," Ellison once agreed, "a man who shares a dual culture." Du Bois asks the rhetorical question that haunts much of Ellison's writing: "Would America have been America without her Negro people?" Ellison's reply, like Du Bois's, is that such a premise is inconceivable: there simply wouldn't *be* a recognizable America or an "American" culture under such circumstances.

A literary critic who has studied the relationship between James Weldon Johnson's *The Autobiography of an Ex-Coloured Man* and *Invisible Man* calls the former a prototype of the latter. His governing thesis is that "the cultural situation that produced *The Autobiography of an Ex-Coloured Man*, the manner in which the story is set forth, and the antecedent works that influenced its author lead one easily to the informing sensibility and significant patterns of action in *Invisible Man*." The anonymous narrators of both novels offer retrospective accounts of their lives "from a position of impunity." Other parallels abound. Both novels recapitulate the various stages of Afro-American history from slave days, to Reconstruction, to the migration north to, finally, the disillusioning experiences in an urban milieu. In both works the narrators are caught in patterns of circular movement: they are haunted by a sense of déjà vu because they keep running into the same demeaning situations—no matter how different the surface circumstances of those situations may seem. Finally, both works are predicated upon a shared perception: that the "achievements of the folk cannot be minimized" in reaching the goal of freedom.

Ellison first read Alain Locke's *The New Negro* while he was still in high school. At Tuskegee he met Locke and then, on his second day in Harlem, renewed his acquaintance. Although Ellison eventually became critical of the New Negro movement, parts of *Invisible Man* seem a gloss upon Locke's famous essay, "The New Negro." Locke believed that in the process of being "transplanted" from the South to the North, the Negro was becoming transformed, that is, psychologically liberated from the strictures of the past. Locke expected many advantageous developments to follow from the improved condition of the Negro. However premature his prognosis, Locke's views still have many points of correspondence with *Invisible Man*. Both works praise the initiative of the common folk, acting as individuals en masse, while sneering at the feeble efforts of the putative leaders. Both works portray blacks as reluctant rebels. Locke says "the Negro is radical on race matters, conservative on others, in other words, a 'forced radical,' a social protestant rather than a genuine radical." The invisible man admits to a similar disposition when he yearns for "peace and quiet, tranquillity, but was too much aboil inside." He, too, is not a rebel by nature. Most important of all, Locke believed the Negro should develop a more positive self-concept which would permit him to take full responsibility for his actions and his mental life: "he must know himself and be known for precisely what he is. . . . we rejoice and pray to be delivered both from self-pity and condescension." This is precisely the con-

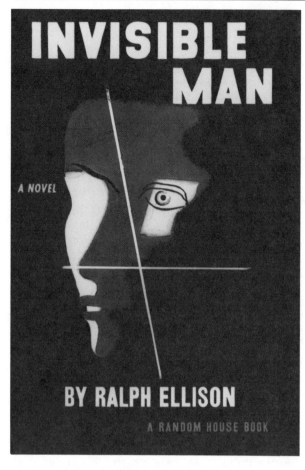

Dust jacket for Ralph Ellison's only novel

clusion Ellison's narrator comes to when he assumes responsibility for what has happened to him, and he says: "my problem was that I always tried to go in everyone's way but my own." The political solution for both the New Negro and the invisible man is to exploit what Locke calls the "new democracy in American culture," for "the Negro mind reaches out as yet to nothing but American wants, American ideas." The same glorification of cultural pluralism and political liberalism is found in the work of both authors.

Locke had little patience with "quixotic radicalisms" and so he denounced Garveyism—the militant politics and the separatist philosophy of Marcus Garvey. Although Garvey was the original spearhead of the New Negro movement, when he was sent to jail for alleged mail fraud in 1925 (the same year Locke's essay appeared), he and his radical approach to racial problems were discredited. Garvey was a flamboyant figure who wore colorful military regalia—braids, plumes, and all—when he appeared in public. Among the three most prom-

inent ideas he espoused were that black is beautiful, that black people in America should return to Mother Africa, and that they should be willing to die for their beliefs. The character Ras in *Invisible Man* (whose name pointedly resembles "race") is clearly based upon Garvey. Ellison draws upon the diction and cadences of Garvey's speech when he has Ras address Tod Clifton with: "You *my* brother, mahn. Brothers are the same color; how the hell you call these white men *brother*? . . . Brothers the same color. We sons of Mama Africa, you done forgot? You black, BLACK! . . . You African, AFRICAN!" Both in image and substance Ras the black nationalist is a latter-day Garvey.

Ellison at one time was a close friend of Richard Wright's and, arguably, *Invisible Man* incorporates more biographical incidents from Wright's life than from Ellison's own. Like the invisible man, Wright was from the South and lived for a while with his Uncle Clark in Greenwood, Mississippi; at the smoker the invisible man is introduced as "the smartest boy we've got out there in Greenwood." Wright once worked at an optical factory; the invisible man helps to make Optic White when he works at the Liberty Paints factory. While Ellison was never involved in a battle royal, in *Black Boy* Wright recounts his fight with a black acquaintance, Harrison, for five dollars (the same sum awarded the invisible man after his bout with Tatlock):

> The white men were smoking and yelling obscenities at us. . . . The fight was on, was on against our will. I felt trapped and ashamed. . . . We fought . . . slugging, grunting, spitting, cursing, crying, bleeding. The shame and anger we felt for having allowed ourselves to be duped crept into our blows and blood ran into our eyes, half blinding us. The hate we felt for the [white audience] went into the blows we threw at each other.

Wright's description is strongly echoed in *Invisible Man*.

Despairing of justice in the South, Wright pinned his hopes on going north where he joined the Communist party. Just as the Brotherhood's desire to mold the invisible man into a new Booker T. Washington prompts him to ask, "What was I, a man or a natural resource?," Wright recalls a similar episode in *American Hunger*, the second half of his autobiography. Wright reports he was told in an interview with a comrade in the late 1930s: "Look, we want to make you a mass leader," to which Wright replied: "But suppose I'm not that kind of material?" He realized that the comrade had not seriously considered anything he had said: "Our talk was a game; he was trying to outwit me. The feelings of others meant nothing to him." Wright came to distrust the authoritarian operations of the party. He especially objected to their efforts at mind control: "I had fled men who did not like the color of my skin, and now I was among men who did not like the tone of my thoughts." His run-ins with his comrades frequently sound like the invisible man's skirmishes with Brother Jack and Brother Wrestrum. Eventually, Wright felt betrayed by the party; in return he denounced it as "the god that failed." The invisible man in time comes to a similar conclusion.

Both Wright and Ellison dealt with the concept of invisibility. "The White South said that it knew 'niggers,' and I was what the White South called a 'nigger,'" Wright relates in *Black Boy*. "Well, the White South had never known *me*—never known what *I* thought, what *I* felt." Bigger Thomas, in *Native Son*, complains that he, too, feels "naked, transparent." An added ironic dimension to the narrator's invisibility in *Invisible Man* is that for a long time he had been blind to his own true nature—he had been invisible to himself. A novella by Wright, *The Man Who Lived Underground*, which appeared in 1944, one year before Ellison began writing his novel, provides numerous similarities to *Invisible Man*. Both main characters choose to be underground men and they live surrealistic lives in symbol-laden surroundings.

While all of these literary sources play an important role, no Afro-American source is so pervasively infused into *Invisible Man* as Negro music, folklore, and folk culture. These folk elements affect the very structure and texture of Ellison's book. As Ellison has observed, "Great literature is erected upon [a] humble base of folk forms." He had already used folkloric and mythic materials in his early stories such as "Mister Toussan" (with its references to black history) and "Flying Home" (with its title from a Lionel Hampton composition, and its manipulation of Jim Crow imagery), but *Invisible Man* is a veritable compendium of folk tales, folk songs, spirituals, the blues, bebop, jive (and other elements of jazz), sermons, jokes, boasts, riddles, street rap, conundrums, aphorisms, eulogies, political oratory, and the dozens.

From the beginning of the novel when, in the prologue, the invisible man listens to Louis Armstrong's "What Did I Do to Be So Black and Blue" and in a hallucinatory state imagines a slave woman's tale about miscegenation until the end of the

novel when, in the epilogue, the narrator ponders whether to "Open the window and let the foul air out" or say "It was good green corn before the harvest," black music, and especially the blues, continually informs and confirms the novel's meaning. ("Open the window and let the foul air out" comes from "Buddy Bolden's Blues," which was frequently performed by Armstrong who was nicknamed "Bad Air"; "It was good green corn before the harvest" derives from a Leadbelly song.)

Among the greatest legacies of the folk culture are the folktales, many of which originated in the slave era. Often these tales took the form of animal fables that pitted Brer Rabbit against Brer Bear. To complicate matters, Ellison seems to assign his hero the role of Brer Rabbit at certain times while assigning him the role of Brer Bear at others. The invisible man, for example, is identified with the Bear when he hibernates in his underground home ("Bear with me," he puns) and when he runs afoul of the Brer Rabbit characters—Bledsoe, Brother (i.e. Brer) Jack, Brockway (also referred to as Tar Baby)—who constantly try to trick and trap him. Concomitantly, he becomes identified with Brer Rabbit when he scampers from misadventure to misadventure but manages to make the world his briar patch all the same. He does this, for example, in the hospital scene when he realizes that "somehow I was Buckeye the Rabbit." He is the trickster figure who, at the very moment the "doctors" think they have neutralized him, wins a significant moral victory over them; he has regressed to an old folk-based identity which liberates him from his fear of all slave drivers and oppressive father figures: "Knowing now that there was nothing which I could expect from them, there was no reason to be afraid." The outcome proves to be ironic because the hero is not the mindless automaton they intended him to be but a stronger and far more dangerous individual than they realize. Beethoven's Fifth Symphony (used as the Victory-Day theme during World War II), which has been playing in the background during this ordeal, provides an appropriate accompaniment to the hero's victory.

By the end of his tale, the narrator becomes both Brer Rabbit in his warren (who cunningly enjoys his private joke by stealing electricity from the power company) and Brer Bear in his den (hibernating before his inevitable reemergence in the spring)—signifying his ability, finally, to manipulate roles rather than be manipulated by them.

As to the novel's structural principle—how it encapsulates so many ideas and events—numerous critics have looked to Afro-American music. More specifically, they have called *Invisible Man* a "literary extension of the blues." One critic claims: "It was as if Ellison had taken an everyday twelve bar blues tune (by a man from down South sitting in a manhold up North singing and signifying how he got there) and scored it for full orchestra." Another critic sees the invisible man as having achieved the perspective of a blues singer who "recounts his story with style, irony, and a sense of absurdity" as he views "his trials and glories in terms of adventure and romance." The tensions that are captured in the novel may be compared to the "antagonistic cooperation" which Ellison says characterizes the way jazz musicians combine individual and communal impulses.

Ellison has expertly grafted the vernacular style—utilizing all the energy, insight and poetry of an oral folk tradition—onto the body and into the substance of his work. *Invisible Man* continues the Afro-American literary tradition by selecting from it, synthesizing the enduring aspects of it, and expanding it to new parameters. In devising a new epic form supple enough to contain a remarkably diverse set of materials, Ellison has made an unprecedented use of black culture as a literary source.

At the same time, Ellison insists that as an American writer he works out of a tradition too complex to restrict itself solely to Afro-American sources. In fact it is not even possible to isolate an Afro-American tradition that exists independently of the other traditions which help shape the American character. Talking about a distinct "White culture" and "Black culture" is glib, he argues, "because the truth of the matter is that between the two racial groups there has always been a constant exchange of cultural, of stylistic elements. Whether in the arts, in education, in athletics, or in certain conceptions and misconceptions of democratic justice, interchange, appropriation, and integration—not segregation—have been the constants of our developing nation." The "concord of sensibilities"—cultivated in churches, in sports stadiums, on radio stations, on dance floors, and in the very home itself—is too intricately knotted for it ever to be disentangled.

The reviews of *Invisible Man* were overwhelmingly laudatory—the book was commonly hailed as a masterpiece—but there were voices of dissent. Communists, naturally, were incensed by Ellison's "reactionary" portrait of the Brotherhood; school boards banned the book for being too candid in its depiction of sexual and racial reality; and black

nationalists attacked Ellison for being too obsessed with the writer's craft and too devoid of revolutionary fervor. Descriptive terms—such as "existential," "transcends race," "complex," "ambiguous," and "universal"—used by certain critics to praise the novel were inverted by detractors to condemn it, for, to the degree *Invisible Man* could be read as the picaresque odyssey of everyman, these critics charged, Ellison was abandoning the protest tradition and shirking his proper racial commitments as a writer. Such critics were not impressed when Ellison was favorably compared to Bellow and Salinger, writers who also emphasized the primacy of personal integrity in an existentially absurd universe.

Ellison fed the polemical fires by fighting back. He rejected Wright's naturalism, he said, because naturalism deals with "everything except the nature of man." He argued that naturalism "conditions the reader to accept the less worthy values of society, and it serves to justify and absolve our sins of social irresponsibility." Those who want to write sociology, he admonished, should not write novels. His affinity for the great nineteenth-century American authors is based upon what Ellison perceives to be their willingness to confront significant moral issues, including the issue of black humanity, without sacrificing style or compromising craft. For these reasons he considered Richard Wright a "relative" rather than a literary "ancestor," explaining: "while one can do nothing about choosing one's relatives, one can, as artist, choose one's 'ancestors.'" Authors he consciously sought out and chose to learn from did not include naturalists or propagandists.

After *Invisible Man*, two more pieces showcasing the character Mary Rambo appeared: "Did You Ever Dream Lucky?" (*New World Writing*, April 1954) and "Out of the Hospital and under the Bar" (*Soon One Morning*, 1963), the second of which had originally been intended to be part of *Invisible Man*. In 1956 Ellison published one of his best stories, "A Coupla Scalped Indians" (*New World Writing*) which, in the vein of the earlier Buster and Riley stories, centers on two boys, one of whom is explicitly referred to as Buster. Determined to become Indian Scouts (not mere Cub Scouts), they work on their tests (in swimming, endurance running, and cooking) independent of any troop—despite the fact that they bear the additional burden of having recently been "scalped," that is, circumcised. The familiar Ellisonian theme, initiation into manhood, plays itself out against an encounter with the sphinxlike Aunt Mackie, portrayed alternately as appealing and repugnant, young and old, angel and devil, seductress and seduced—in short, a symbol of human experience. The story achieves a perfect and self-contained expression of its theme.

Shadow and Act (1964) collects essays and interviews written over a twenty-two-year period. Taking his title from lines in T. S. Eliot's "The Hollow Men," Ellison sets out to probe the meaning of experience, to understand what lies below the surface of the act. He arranges his materials according to three general themes: the first third of the book investigates literature and folklore; the second third deals with Negro music and the blues and jazz artists who have created it; and the last third offers a cultural and political examination of the relationship of the Negro subculture to the rest of the nation. *Shadow and Act* is essential reading for anyone who wishes to plumb the depths of the author and his work, for it is filled with precisely argued statements concerning Ellison's own literary theories and practice, and with his evaluation of other writers. In the course of the book Ellison deflates the definitions and assessments of American life which he considers inadequate; he also engages in public debate with Irving Howe (over the nature of the black experience in America), with his friend Stanley Edgar Hyman (about the nature of Negro folklore), and with LeRoi Jones (whom he castigates for misreading the nature of the blues). In addition to presenting his reformulation of what the novel is and what it should attempt to do, and offering a celebrated definition of the blues, Ellison argues for the interrelatedness of all experience and proclaims that, at least on the level of the imagination, integration has been achieved in the United States.

Many accolades and honors followed in the wake of *Invisible Man* and *Shadow and Act*. Ellison received the National Book Award, the Russwurm Award, and a Certificate of Award from the *Chicago Defender*, all in 1953; the American Academy of Arts and Letters Fellowship to Rome for 1955-1957; the Medal of Freedom in 1969; and the Chevalier de l'Ordre des Artes et Lettres from André Malraux, French Minister of Cultural Affairs, in 1970. He lent prestige to many academic institutions by accepting posts at Bard (where he taught Russian and American Literature, 1958-1961), Rutgers (where he taught Creative Writing and Comparative Literature, 1962-1969), the University of Chicago (where he was Alexander White Visiting Professor, winter of 1961), and New York University (where he served as Albert Schweitzer

Professor in the Humanities, 1970-1979, and is now professor emeritus). He has also lectured at Columbia University, at Yale (where he is an honorary fellow), at the Salzburg Seminar in Austria (where he spoke on American Literature and Negro Folklore in 1954), and at dozens of schools including Amherst, Antioch, Carnegie Mellon, Fisk, and Princeton. Honorary doctorates came at a rapid and regular pace to the college dropout: from Tuskegee (1963), Rutgers (1966), University of Michigan (1967), Grinnell (1967), Williams College (1970), Adelphi (1971), Long Island University (1971), College of William and Mary (1972), Wake Forest (1974), University of Maryland (1974), Harvard (1974), Bard College (1978), Wesleyan University (1980), and Brown (1980).

Ellison was invited to become a resident member of the Century Club and in 1974, was elected by the membership of the Modern Language Association to be an Honorary Fellow. He was elected vice-president of both P.E.N. (in 1964) and the National Institute of Arts and Letters (in 1967) and served on the Institute of Jazz Studies' board of advisors. His other affiliations include the following memberships: the National Council on the Arts (1965-1967), the Carnegie Commission on Educational Television (1966-1967), the Editorial Board of *American Scholar* (1966-1969), Honorary Consultant in American Letters, Library of Congress (1966-1972), American Academy of Arts and Sciences (1965 to the present), National Advisory Council, Hampshire College (1966 to the present), National Portrait Gallery Commission (1972-1974), Board of Advisors, Ossabaw Island Project (1972 to the present), Board of Visitors, Wake Forest University (1972 to the present), and American Academy of Arts and Letters (1975 to the present). He has also held the following trusteeships: John F. Kennedy Center for the Performing Arts (1967-1977), Educational Broadcasting Corporation (1968-1979), the New School for Social Research (1969 to the present), Bennington College (1970-1975), the Museum of the City of New York (1970 to the present), and the Colonial Williamsburg Foundation (1971 to the present).

It would seem that with all these accomplishments Ralph Ellison has achieved his childhood ambition of becoming a Renaissance man. In addition to being a world-renowned writer—*Invisible Man* has been translated into fourteen languages and both books have remained in print continuously since publication—and a respected presence in American intellectual circles, Ellison is a gourmet cook, a photographer, a musician, an art collector, a builder of hi-fi sets, and a designer of his own furniture—a jack-of-all-trades, a "thinker-tinker."

Off and on since 1955 Ellison has been working on a second novel. Sections of this new opus have appeared as excerpts from his novel-in-progress: "And Hickman Arrives" (1960), "The Roof, the Steeple and the People" (1960), "It Always Breaks Out" (1963), "Juneteenth" (1969), "Night-Talk" (1969), "A Song of Innocence" (1970), "Cadillac Flambé" (1973), and "Backwacking: A Plea to the Senator" (1977). By 1966 Ellison reportedly had written over one thousand pages of the new novel, enough to fill four bound volumes of typescript. Then, in 1967, a fire struck the Ellison's recently acquired summer home in Plainfield, Massachusetts, destroying about 350 pages which contained almost a year's worth of revisions. The political assassinations of 1968 may further have dampened the comic spirit that imbued the new work. Still, restoration of the text had progressed to such an extent by 1970 that Ellison was pondering how best to handle his gigantic manuscript and was considering whether to publish it as a trilogy.

The excerpts indicate that the novel will involve Reverend Alonzo Zuber Hickman; Bliss, his adopted son, who renounces Hickman and becomes a Negro-baiting senator known by his alias: Sunraider; Severen, the black assassin who shoots Sunraider; Cliofus, friend of Severen and an aspiring writer; Minifees, a black musician who burns his white Cadillac on Sunraider's lawn; and McIntyre, a white reporter. In a headnote to one of the excerpts—the one in which Hickman is at Sunraider's bedside following the assassination attempt on the senator's life—Ellison describes the scene as "an anguished attempt to arrive at the true shape and substance of a sundered past and its meaning." One is tempted to speculate that this may be one of the major themes of the entire novel-in-progress.

In addition to this work of fiction, Ellison completed *Going to the Territory* (1986), a collection of sixteen speeches, reviews, and essays written since 1957, all of them previously published in newspapers and magazines except two. Most of these pieces were written during the 1960s; only one, an essay commemorating Erskine Caldwell on his eightieth birthday, was written as late as 1983. The subjects range from literature to sociology, from the responsibilities of the artist to homages for Duke Ellington, Richard Wright, and Romare Bearden. While the collection demonstrates Ellison's insight as a social and literary critic, it offers

weak testimony to the author's achievement in the eighteen years since his last book.

Ellison's reputation has undergone a remarkable metamorphosis over the years. His liberalism was considered out of step with the times by the New Left and Third World spokespersons of the late 1960s and early 1970s. He incurred their displeasure in 1965 when he participated in President Johnson's White House Art Festival—a function which Robert Lowell conspicuously boycotted. The selection of *Invisible Man* that same year as the single most distinguished work published since World War II in a Book Week poll of two hundred (predominantly white) authors, critics, and editors was taken as further evidence that Ellison was "on the wrong side." By contrast, a *Negro Digest* poll in 1968 of black writers indicated that Richard Wright was *their* number one choice; Ellison came in a distant fifth. As black militancy grew in the 1960s, LeRoi Jones assailed Ellison in "Philistinism and the Negro Writer" for silently "fidgeting away in some college" while the ghettoes burned. The editors of *The Militant Black Writer* (1969) pointed out that "black self-consciousness has traveled [since *Invisible Man*'s publication] from self-knowledge to self-determination." Perhaps the most virulent diatribe was launched by Ernest Kaiser who charged: " Ellison has become an Establishment writer, an Uncle Tom, an attacker of the sociological formulations of the civil rights movement, a defender of the criminal Vietnam War of extermination against Asian (and American Negro) people, a denigrator of the great tradition of Negro protest writing and, worst of all for himself as a creative artist, a writer of weak and ineffectual fiction and essays mostly about himself and how he became an artist." Even though Langston Hughes, James Baldwin, and James Farmer (of CORE) continued to speak well of his work, Ellison was often the scapegoat of the black militant's rage.

As times change, so do attitudes. A number of young black writers who had distanced themselves from Ellison earlier have come full circle. Larry Neal, for example, who with LeRoi Jones edited *Black Fire*, a 1968 anthology of Afro-American writing (from which they excluded Ellison), subsequently admitted to "wincing" when he re-read his comments about Ellison in the afterword to *Black Fire*. Refusing to be co-opted by white critics who analyzed *Invisible Man* in formalistic terms, black critics increasingly marvel at Ellison's treatment of Afro-American life; they find his monumental novel a profound examination of the richness and beauty and heroism of the black experience. According to John Wright, by the late 1970s, in reaction to the black arts movement, Ellison had become "reluctant father figure to the new generation of black writers." The 1980 *Carleton Miscellany* entitled "A Ralph Ellison Festival" contains only glowing tributes from fellow black writers and critics.

Very few literary events have aroused greater anticipation than the long awaited appearance of Ellison's second novel. But even if Ellison never publishes another word, his *Invisible Man* is secure as a classic of literature for it not only evinces an extraordinary command of language but it contains both literal and symbolic truths about black people in particular and human beings in general.

References:

Bernard Benoit and Michel Fabre, "A Bibliography of Ralph Ellison's Published Writings," *Studies in Black Literature* (Autumn 1971);
One of the earliest attempts to supply bibliographical information, it has been superseded by more recent studies.

Black World, 20 (December 1970), special issue: "Ralph Ellison: His Literary Works and Status";
Generally an appreciative analysis by black critics, but it does contain one of the most acerbic attacks on Ellison and his work. Eight articles plus bibliography.

Carleton Miscellany, 18 (Winter 1980), special issue: "A Ralph Ellison Festival";
Based on the Ralph Ellison festival at Brown University, over a dozen erudite essays and poems in tribute to Ellison. Includes two pieces by Ellison later collected in *Going to the Territory.*

CLA Journal, 13 (March 1970), "Special Ralph Ellison Number";
Contains several illuminating essays.

Jacqueline Covo, *The Blinking Eye: Ralph Waldo Ellison and His American, French, German and Italian Critics, 1952-1971: Bibliographic Essays and a Checklist* (Metuchen, N.J.: Scarecrow Press, 1974);
Although dated, it remains the most thorough research tool; excellent for suggesting the international appeal of *Invisible Man.*

Ronald Gottesman, ed., *Studies in Invisible Man* (Columbus, Ohio: Charles E. Merrill, 1971);
A generous sampling of some of the most frequently cited criticism.

John Hershey, ed., *Ralph Ellison: A Collection of Essays* (Englewood Cliffs, N.J.: Prentice-Hall, 1974);
A helpful gathering of standard criticism.

Robert G. O'Mealley, *The Craft of Ralph Ellison* (Cambridge: Harvard University Press, 1980);
A major critical study of Ellison's artistic career.

John M. Reilly, ed., *Twentieth Century Interpretations of Invisible Man* (Englewood Cliffs, N.J.: Prentice-Hall, 1970);
A judicious selection of respected scholarship, plus a chronology of important dates.

Joseph A. Trimmer, ed., *A Casebook on Ralph Ellison's Invisible Man* (New York: Crowell, 1972);
An excellent introduction; provides some of the background texts necessary for a full appreciation of *Invisible Man.*

Joe Weixlmann and John O'Banion, "A Checklist of Ellison Criticism, 1972-1978," *Black American Literature Forum,* 12 (Summer 1978): 51-55.
A useful update for the period it covers.

Lawrence Ferlinghetti

This entry was updated by Larry Smith (Bowling Green State University, Firelands College)
from his entry in DLB 16: The Beats: Literary Bohemians in Postwar America.

Places	San Francisco Big Sur Albert Hall, London	New York City Spoleto, Italy Chapel Hill, North Carolina	Paris Cuba
Influences and Relationships	Walt Whitman Jack Kerouac Kenneth Patchen Nancy George Peters	Henry David Thoreau Thomas Wolfe Guillaume Apollinaire	Allen Ginsberg Kenneth Rexroth Jacques Prevert

Literary Movements and Forms	The Beat Movement
	San Francisco
	  Poetry Renaissance
	Absurdist Theater
		Romantic Movement
		Poetry-and-
		  Jazz Movement
		Existentialism
			Oral Street Poetry
			Confessional Poetry
			Expressionist Theater
			Surrealism

Major Themes	Personal Freedom Search for Self Moral Responsibility of the Artist	Alienation Civil Liberties The Authentic Self	Oneness with Nature Social Corruption Death
Cultural and Artistic Influences	Existentialism Civil Liberties Drugs	Engaged Art Film Jazz	Surrealistic Art Abstract Expressionist Art
Social and Economic Influences	World War II Obscenity Laws Peace Movement	Adoption Social Injustice U. S. Intervention in Central America	Threat of Nuclear War Ecology Movement Prolabor Movement

See also the Ferlinghetti entry in DLB 5, American Poets Since World War II.

BIRTH: Yonkers, New York, 24 March 1919, to Charles and Clemence Mendes-Monsanto Ferling.

EDUCATION: B.A., University of North Carolina, 1941; M.A., Columbia University, 1947; doctorate, University of Paris, Sorbonne, 1949.

MARRIAGE: 10 April 1951 to Selden Kirby-Smith (divorced); children: Lorenzo, Julie.

SELECTED BOOKS: *Pictures of the Gone World* (San Francisco: City Lights Books, 1955);
A Coney Island of the Mind (Norfolk, Conn.: New Directions, 1958; enlarged edition, London: Hutchinson, 1959; enlarged again, New York: New Directions, 1968);
Her (Norfolk, Conn.: New Directions, 1960; London: MacGibbon & Kee, 1966);
Starting from San Francisco (Norfolk, Conn.: New Directions, 1961; enlarged edition, New York: New Directions, 1967);
Unfair Arguments with Existence (New York: New Directions, 1963);
Routines (New York: New Directions, 1964);
An Eye on the World: Selected Poems (London: MacGibbon & Kee, 1967);
The Secret Meaning of Things (New York: New Directions, 1969);
Tyrannus Nix? (New York: New Directions, 1969; revised edition, New York: New Directions, 1973);
The Mexican Night (New York: New Directions, 1970);
Back Roads to Far Places (New York: New Directions, 1971);
Open Eye, bound with *Open Head* by Allen Ginsberg (Melbourne, Australia: Sun Books, 1972);
Open Eye, Open Heart (New York: New Directions, 1973);
Who Are We Now? (New York: New Directions, 1976);
Northwest Ecolog (San Francisco: City Lights Books, 1978);
Landscapes of Living and Dying (New York: New Directions, 1979);
Literary San Francisco: A Pictorial History from its Beginnings to the Present Day, by Ferlinghetti and Nancy Joyce Peters (San Francisco: City Lights Books/Harper & Row, 1980);

Lawrence Ferlinghetti in 1975 (photo by Pamela Mosher)

A Trip to Italy and France (New York: New Directions, 1980);
Endless Life: Selected Poems (New York: New Directions, 1981);
The Populist Manifestos (San Francisco: Grey Fox Press, 1983);
Over All the Obscene Boundaries: European Poems and Transitions (New York: New Directions, 1984);
Seven Days in Nicaragua Libre (San Francisco: City Lights Books, 1984);
Leaves of Life: Fifty Drawings from the Model (San Francisco: City Lights Books, 1985).

RECORDINGS: *Poetry Reading in "The Cellar,"* by Ferlinghetti and Kenneth Rexroth, Fantasy Records, 1958;
Tentative Description of a Dinner Given to Promote the Impeachment of President Eisenhower & Other Poems, Fantasy Records, 1959;
The World's Great Poets, volume 1, by Ferlinghetti, Allen Ginsberg, and Gregory Corso at the

1965 Spoleto Festival, CMS, 1971;
Tyrannus Nix? & Assassination Raga, Fantasy Records, 1971;
Contemporary American Poets Read Their Works: Lawrence Ferlinghetti, Everett/Edwards, 1972.

OTHER: Jacques Prévert, *Selections from Paroles,* translated by Ferlinghetti (San Francisco: City Lights Books, 1958);
Penguin Modern Poets 5, includes poems by Ferlinghetti (Harmondsworth, U.K.: Penguin, 1963);
"Genesis of *After the Cries of the Birds,*" in *The Poetics of the New American Poetry,* edited by Donald Allen and Warren Tallman (New York: Grove, 1973);
City Lights Anthology, edited by Ferlinghetti (San Francisco: City Lights Books, 1974).

PERIODICAL PUBLICATIONS: "Lawrence Ferlinghetti: Horn on 'HOWL,'" *Evergreen Review,* 1, no. 4 (1957): 145-158;
"Notes on Poetry in San Francisco," *Chicago Review,* 12 (Spring 1958): 3-5.

In discarding accepted notions of conformity in art as well as life, the Beats looked around for brothers of rebellion. Breaking the dam of cultural convention they stood on new and fertile ground and recognized as their predecessors other innovators: the romantics, the symbolists, the surrealists, the rebels of Greenwich Village and San Francisco, writers like William Blake, Arthur Rimbaud, Walt Whitman, Guillaume Apollinaire, Blaise Cendrars, Antonin Artaud, Ezra Pound, William Carlos Williams, E. E. Cummings, and Thomas Wolfe. Then they looked closer at older peers, writers like Kenneth Patchen, Kenneth Rexroth, Henry Miller, and one particular beacon light standing at land's end in San Francisco—Lawrence Ferlinghetti. No one better represents the various currents that emerged into the Beat movement in San Francisco's mid 1950s than this very hip Homer of the streets. Described by some as the most truly "beat" of the Beats, Ferlinghetti's life and writing stand as models of the existentially authentic and engaged life. When the Beats emerged on America's West Coast, they found this fellow poet-prophet in the world already protesting the madness and proclaiming the potential wonder:

and I am waiting
for the discovery
of a new symbolic western frontier

and I am waiting
for the American Eagle
to really spread its wings
and straighten up and fly right
and I am waiting
for the Age of Anxiety
to drop dead
and I am waiting
for the war to be fought
which will make the world safe
for anarchy.

In this early poem, "I Am Waiting," Ferlinghetti makes clear the values upon which the rebellion rests. He had followed some of the same Beat paths to this point of rebirth in a new and vital art:

and I am waiting
for some strains of unpremeditated art
to shake my typewriter
and I am waiting to write
the great indelible poem . . .
and I am waiting
perpetually and forever
a renaissance of wonder.

In this basic romantic call to action, Ferlinghetti voiced his shared goals and methods with the Beats.

This thirty-six-year-old poet, translator, editor, publisher, and bookstore owner of 1955 San Francisco had already traveled a long road to this meeting ground. Born 24 March 1919 in Yonkers, the last of five sons of an Italian immigrant auctioneer and a Portuguese-Jewish mother, he began his life in the midst of crisis and loss. His father had died before he was born, and his mother was soon institutionalized at the state hospital in Poughkeepsie, New York, as the family sank further into poverty. In his "True Confessional" poem he recalls:

I lawrence ferlinghetti
wrought from the dark in my mother long
                                            ago
born in a small back bedroom—
. . . .
Someone squeezed my heart
to make it go
I cried and sprang up
Open eye open heart where
do I wander
I cried and ran off
into the heart of the world.

This mythic search for self is one of the sustaining characteristics uniting Ferlinghetti's life and art, and it sets forth a basic pattern for the Beat quest for the sense of the self in the world.

It was his mother's aunt Emily Mendes-Monsanto who rescued him from his American tragedy and whisked him off to France for the first five years of his life. When the aunt returned to her estranged husband in New York, Ferlinghetti suffered a second loss. After Emily broke with her husband for the final time, she was forced to put young Lawrence into a Chappaqua, New York, orphanage where he stayed for seven months until she could rescue him once more. This time she took him with her when she went to serve as tutor to the wealthy Bronxville family of Presley and Anna Bisland. When Emily left the following year, this painful parallel to a Shirley Temple movie plot seemed happily complete. Here was young Lawrence in a home where all would be provided, yet his inner sense of loss was only deepened as he found himself alone again in an elderly family that could love but without affection. As he recalls in "True Confessional,"

> And I began to go
> through my number
> I was a wind-up toy
> someone had dropped wound-up
> into a world already
> running down.

Only when he was placed with the Zilla Larned Wilson family in downtown Bronxville, to attend public schools, did he begin to connect himself with a sense of family and street reality. During this adolescent period he enjoyed such mixed adventures as those he recounts in his early Beat "Autobiography" poem from *A Coney Island of the Mind* (1958):

> I still can hear the paper thump
> on lost porches . . .
> I got caught stealing pencils
> from the Five and Ten Cent Store
> the same month I made Eagle Scout.

As a corrective for his days with a street gang, the Parkway Road Pirates, he spent his high school years (1933-1937) in the austere Mount Hermon private school in Massachusetts. It was here, however, that his interest in reading flourished, fostered by the large Bisland library and challenging teachers. In particular, he made connection with the American romantics of two centuries—Henry David Thoreau and Thomas Wolfe.

He followed Wolfe's path to the University of North Carolina at Chapel Hill, studying there from 1937 to 1941 with a major in English and journalism. Under the tutelage of Prof. Phillips Russell, he was introduced to John Dos Passos, Ernest Hemingway, William Faulkner, and, most important, to such populist writers as Carl Sandburg, Edgar Lee Masters, and Vachel Lindsay. He also made an early 1939 road trip by freight train and hitchhiking to Mexico, a country that would have a permanent attraction for him as well as for other Beat movement writers.

Like most young men in the early 1940s, he launched himself into the military, serving as a lieutenant commander in the United States Navy from 1941 to 1945. Unlike most, he also began a cultural-political education at this time through visits to Greenwich Village and with Swarthmore College friend Laura Lou Lyon whose liberal friends exposed him to radical pacifist thought. He soon located in the postwar Greenwich Village scene where writers like E. E. Cummings, Henry Miller, and Kenneth Patchen added color to the place. Ironically, at about the same time that the Beat coterie of Jack Kerouac, Allen Ginsberg, and William S. Burroughs existed around Columbia University, Ferlinghetti was quietly working for his master's degree in literature there and reading such moderns as James Joyce, Gertrude Stein, T. S. Eliot, Ezra Pound, and William Butler Yeats.

Unlike the younger Beats, Ferlinghetti made the break with this country by following his yearning for an international education to Paris and the Sorbonne from 1947 to 1949. It is Ferlinghetti more than any other, with the possible exception of the Beat's pater familias Kenneth Rexroth, who gave the Beat movement an international character and perspective. His doctoral dissertation, written at the Sorbonne on "The City as Symbol in Modern Poetry: In Search of a Metropolitan Tradition," might serve to define one of the main currents of the whole Beat movement. Having attained the highest academic degree, Ferlinghetti's ultimate rejection of the pretense of academia had more character than the slurs issued from the rebel outsiders. His work at the Sorbonne did bring him close to the international avant-garde and the work of such writers as Federico Garcia Lorca, Vladimir Mayakovsky, the French surrealists, René Char, Jacques Prévert, and Emile Verhaeren. Here he completed his apprentice Thomas Wolfe novel, "The Way of Dispossession," began his semisurrealistic novel *Her* (1960), and started his "Palimpsest" poem series.

After returning to the United States in 1950 and marrying Selden Kirby-Smith ("Kirby") in April of the next year, he looked about for the best place to continue his artistic growth. Following a train ride across the States, he discovered the cosmopolitan atmosphere of San Francisco. The story of Ferlinghetti's rebirth on San Francisco shores reveals the atmosphere and character of the San Francisco Beat outpouring of the mid 1950s. Casting around for his own artistic direction and financial survival, Ferlinghetti began a series of jobs. He taught a night course in French literature at San Francisco State College and worked as an art critic for *Art Digest* and as a book reviewer for the *San Francisco Chronicle*. He worked on his painting in his waterfront studio, reworked his novel *Her*, and refined his poetry and the translations of Jacques Prévert and Guillaume Apollinaire. He began attending the literary-anarchist soiree sessions at Kenneth Rexroth's Scott Street apartment. In San Francisco he came into contact with schools of abstract-expressionist painters and the Berkeley poets (Thomas Parkinson, Philip Lamantia, Robert Duncan, William Everson). He attended the San Francisco Poetry Center's readings and reviewed such poets as Kenneth Patchen, Theodore Roethke, and Dylan Thomas. He also became attuned to the anarchist-pacifist political thought that was and is a characteristic of that city.

In 1953 he met Peter Martin, a San Francisco State College instructor and editor of *City Lights* magazine, the man who had published Ferlinghetti's early Prévert translations, and the currents came together. As is now literary history, the two men then launched the country's first all-paperback bookstore at 261 Columbus Avenue, where it flourishes still. City Lights Bookshop filled a cultural gap—featuring books of literature, political thought, and popular culture as well as offering a meeting ground for artists and writers—and it filled Ferlinghetti's personal and financial needs. When Martin left for New York in 1954, Ferlinghetti hired Shigeyoshi Murao (Shig) as the bookshop's manager (and eventual co-owner) and fulfilled his own ambition of launching a publishing house and publishing his own first book of poems, *Pictures of the Gone World,* as number one in the Pocket Poets Series in 1955. In *Pictures of the Gone World* Ferlinghetti declared his open-form poetics, akin to the practices of abstract-expressionist art, a renewed dedication to the union of life and art. In poem number twenty-six, for example, the poet shows that it is the weight of common humanity which must direct his drive:

Reading Yeats I do not think
                              of Arcady
and of its woods which Yeats thought dead
                              I think instead
of all the gone faces
        getting off at midtown places
              with their hats and their jobs

Ferlinghetti thus marks himself as a vital poet of the people, all the strange "gone faces" which demanded a stronger, more vital and caring art. He soon published two admired poets and friends as numbers two and three in the Pocket Poets Series—Kenneth Rexroth's translation *Thirty Spanish Poems of Love and Exile* and Kenneth Patchen's collection of *Poems of Humor and Protest*. City Lights Books and bookshop were off to a successful start, adding impetus to the rising tide of the whole San Francisco renaissance in poetry. Yet around the corner or down the hill was the wave that would launch an entire movement.

In 1955 a young Allen Ginsberg walked into City Lights Bookshop. Introducing himself to Ferlinghetti with a manuscript of poems, Ginsberg told him of another longer poem which more than any other captured the spirit of the times. Ferlinghetti was interested but lacked funds for a new book. However, a lasting friendship and a literary alliance began that day as Ferlinghetti and Ginsberg shared their interest in Whitman, Williams, Rexroth, and Patchen. The San Francisco Poetry Renaissance and the Beat movement merged in Ferlinghetti and Ginsberg. It was Ferlinghetti who soon afterward drove poets Gary Snyder, Philip Whalen, Michael McClure, and Philip Lamantia to the historic Six Gallery reading in which Ginsberg delivered his masterpiece *Howl* with feverish intensity. And it was Ferlinghetti who sent an Emersonian telegram to Ginsberg that night declaring, "I greet you at the beginning of a great career. When do I get the manuscript?" The story of *Howl and Other Poems,* Pocket Poets Series number four, thus began and with it the national emergence of two writers and a whole movement.

The first printing of *Howl and Other Poems* was published early in 1957, and 1,500 copies found their way to an alert and literate public. It was the second printing of 3,000 copies that ran into trouble with the U.S. Customs office in San Francisco. Five hundred copies printed by Villiers of Great Britain were seized on 25 March 1957 by Chester McPhee, who declared, "The words and the sense of the writing is obscene. You wouldn't want your children to come across it." Thus began one of the most celebrated cases of censorship in the United States since the 1933 trial of the ban on James Joyce's *Ulysses*; it was a case that would establish a legal precedent affecting the free publication of D. H. Lawrence's *Lady Chatterley's Lover* and Henry Miller's *Tropic of Cancer* in the next decade. In anticipation of such censorship problems, Ferlinghetti had already submitted a copy of *Howl and Other Poems* to the American Civil Liberties Union (ACLU), which promptly began to fight the seizure. Ferlinghetti met the publishing delay with a photo-offset edition of *Howl* prepared in San Francisco. This struggle with censorship proved to be the focus of international attention and the book's greatest test.

On 19 May in the pages of the *San Francisco Chronicle*, Ferlinghetti made a public declaration in which he claimed *Howl* was "the most significant single long poem to be published in this country since World War II, perhaps since T. S. Eliot's *Four Quartets*." Challenging critics to name another work of such significance to the contemporary time and place, Ferlinghetti boldly suggested that Chester McPhee be awarded a medal for rendering the book famous. He went on to focus clearly on the book's motive: "It is not the poet but what he observes which is revealed as obscene. The great obscene wastes of *Howl* are the sad wastes of the mechanized world, lost among atom bombs and insane nationalisms." Released by customs on 29 May, the book moved on to the second round of confrontation.

During the first week of June, Ferlinghetti and Shigeyoshi Murao were arrested and booked by the San Francisco Police Department. The ACLU posted bail and the summer-long court case began. The prosecuting deputy attorney, Ralph McIntosh, was met by some of the ablest defense attorneys the ACLU could provide—Jake Ehrlich, Lawrence Speiser, and Albert Bendrich. Other critical support poured in from editors, poets, educators, and critics, including Henry Rago (editor of *Poetry*), Ruth Witt-Diamant and Robert Duncan of the San Francisco Poetry Center, Thomas Parkinson, James Laughlin of New Directions, Kenneth Patchen, and others. Ferlinghetti attended but did not testify at the trial, and Ginsberg was not in the country. It was, nevertheless, a period of intense public attention which Ferlinghetti as a young publisher and spokesman for art and free speech accepted as a personal test. Ferlinghetti's defense was based on the expert testimony of witnesses such as Walter Van Tilburg Clark, Kenneth Rexroth, Vin-

cent McHugh, and Leo Lowenthal. The strongest defense came from critic-educator Mark Schorer, who, as the first witness, aptly summed up the work's intent and method. His explanation of the book's thematic structure around the elements of materialism, conformity, mechanization, and war and his support of the language of rebellion were dramatic. His declaration that "Each person had to determine his or her own language—from the level of their own mind and their own body" has been the lasting approach of Ferlinghetti and City Lights: language is a functional and vital reflection of the times and the personal consciousness. When the conservative Judge Clayton Horn delivered his verdict that "I do not believe that *Howl* is without even the slightest redeeming social importance," Ferlinghetti was relieved. "It ends in a plea for holy living. *Honni soit qui mal y pense* (evil to him who thinks evil)," was the judge's conclusion.

The importance of this court case to the life and career of Ferlinghetti as well as to the whole blossoming of the San Francisco renaissance in poetry and the West Coast Beat movement is difficult to overestimate. Ferlinghetti and Ginsberg became national as well as international public figures leading a revolution in thinking as well as writing. The case solidified the writing into a movement with definite principles yet an openness of form and approach. Poetry had become a public matter. By the end of the trial, 10,000 copies of *Howl and Other Poems* had been printed. City Lights Books also set a precedent for other radical small presses such as White Rabbit, Jargon, Auerhahn, and Totem. As David Kherdian observed, "An explosion of little magazines followed both in New York and in San Francisco—'Beatitude,' 'Origin,' 'Ark II-Moby I,' 'Yugen,' 'Kulchur,' 'Floating Bear,' 'Now,' 'Evergreen Review,' 'Foot,' and 'Measure.' " In the dramatic act of defiance and declaration of principles symbolized by the publication and defense of *Howl*, the rich tradition of freedom and experimentation with ideas and expression on the West Coast joined with the existential energy of the East Coast Beat movement. Ferlinghetti's role was extremely vital, as he found his inner struggle for confirmation fulfilled in this outer direction. He was truly *there*, where his new prominence demanded an authentic response.

In another arena Ferlinghetti became a public figure during these years of the late 1950s. He and Kenneth Rexroth had taken their experimenting with brother arts—poetry and jazz—to the public theater of the Cellar Club where they performed nightly. Ferlinghetti was explicit as to his motives:

"The poets today are talking to themselves, they have no other audience. The competition with the mass media is too much. . . . We're trying to capture an audience. . . . The jazz comes in as part of an attempt to get the audience back." This sentiment from the cover notes of the recording *Poetry Reading in "The Cellar"* (released by Fantasy Records at Berkeley in 1958) was shared by Kenneth Rexroth as both worked for a new synthesis of form that would widen the audience for both arts. The Beat affinity with jazz which Jack Kerouac and Neal Cassady expressed repeatedly can perhaps best be understood by the common method and motivation of both poets and musicians. Setting themselves up as cultural outsiders who blew an intense response—"hot" or "cool," emotional or cerebral— back at the world, the Beat writer, like the jazzman, was measured by the authenticity of his response. He was judged immediately by his peers who demanded above all a spontaneity and heartfelt truth. In the sessions at the Cellar Club, Ferlinghetti developed his own spontaneous form in the "Oral Messages" poems of *A Coney Island of the Mind*. Particularly the fugue-type poem "Autobiography" demonstrates that the oral poet was developing a more vital and popular form of poetry. Not only had the jazz stance emboldened him, but the lyric and vocal form helped him to release his own poetic realism. A section from "Autobiography" demonstrates Ferlinghetti's aural and verbal directness:

> I have seen the Eternal Distributor
> from a White Hill
> in South San Francisco
> and the Laughing Woman at Loona Park
> outside the Fun House
> in a great rainstorm
> still laughing
> . . . .
> I have travelled.
> I have seen goof city.
> I have seen the mass mess.
> I have heard a Kid Ory cry.
> I have heard a trombone preach.
> I have heard Debussy
> strained thru a sheet
> . . . .
> and I have read somewhere
> the Meaning of Existence
> yet have forgotten
> just exactly where.
> But I am the man
> And I'll be there.
> And I may cause the lips
> of those who are asleep
> to speak.

Like a contemporary Whitman with his own sense of humor, Ferlinghetti delivers his comic-sad ode to the rhythm of an energetic jazz flow. The lines are tight and tough and truly echo themselves in an ongoing improvisation. The poet goes public through his oral stream of consciousness. Though Ferlinghetti would abandon the poetry-and-jazz form in the rush of cheap imitations that flooded the 1960s, he has continued to seek a larger audience for poetry through its combination with music. He has worked with raga music, with his own Autoharp accompaniment, and even with the rock groups the Jefferson Airplane and The Band.

By 1958 Ferlinghetti's poems had been given prominence in the issues of *Evergreen Review* and the *Chicago Review* featuring San Francisco writers. New Directions publisher and poet James Laughlin, whose writing is much like Ferlinghetti's direct and lyric social realism, took a liking to Ferlinghetti and published his second book, *A Coney Island of the Mind*, in 1958. It is a broad collection including

Front cover for Ferlinghetti's second book of poetry

his open-form work from *Pictures of the Gone World,* the seven poems that came out of the poetry-and-jazz work as "Oral Messages," and the lyric and American surrealistic writing of the "Coney Island" poems. Though the book goes beyond it in range, this collection is one of the key works of the Beat period and one of the most popular books of contemporary poetry outselling even Ginsberg's *Howl and Other Poems.* It launched Ferlinghetti as a poet of humor and satire, who achieves an open-form expressionism and a personal lyricism. Like Ginsberg's *Howl,* and in line with Pound's edicts, it made of poetry a vital and popular art.

In what comes close to a personal manifesto, as well as a Beat statement of world view, Ferlinghetti's poem "Dog" defines his basic stance toward life and art. Personifying the dog as the poet of the streets, what emerges is a Beat portrait of the artist as a young dog:

> The dog trots freely in the street
> and sees reality
> and the things he sees
> are bigger than himself
> and the things he sees
> are his reality
> Drunks in doorways
> Moons on trees

Cataloguing in objective detail the images of common life—"Fish on newsprint/Ants in holes/Chickens in Chinatown windows/their heads a block away"—the young dog-poet also registers a consciousness of what he records. What he sees and hears affects him, becomes him:

> Although what he hears is very discouraging
> very depressing
> very absurd
> to a sad young dog like himself
> to a serious dog like himself

Refusing to be muzzled by repressive institutions like the corner policeman or Congressman Doyle of the House Un-American Activities Committee, this very existential dog is there to record and reflect reality:

> touching and tasting and testing everything
> investigating everything
> without benefit of perjury
> a real realist
> . . . .
> with something to say
>   about ontology
> something to say

> about reality
>   and how to see it
>   and how to hear it

Ultimately poised in the symbolic and existential stance which Ferlinghetti has always had, the dog becomes "a living questionmark" looking into the "great gramophone/of puzzling existence." The poem is full of colloquial crispness, direct commitment, and that dangerous lucidity which so marks Ferlinghetti's writing. He is the open and public realist who dares to speak common truths. For the Beats, Ferlinghetti had proved himself to be a verbally adept human repository of values. His poetry achieved an extreme open form yet revealed an accessibility and directness intensified by his re-creation of an oral tradition for contemporary poetry. Critic M. L. Rosenthal greeted Ferlinghetti's *A Coney Island of the Mind* with praise for his "wonderful eye for meaning in the commonplace" and described him as "a deft, rapid-paced, whirling performer." He was quickly placed in the innovative tradition of Walt Whitman, William Carlos Williams, and E. E. Cummings. He was a brave presence to the Beats and offered them a modernist connection.

A look at Ferlinghetti's Pocket Poets Series during the years of the Beat period is, in itself, a Beat chronicle. And yet it also reveals Ferlinghetti's own international perspective and his determination to extend the Beat alliance:

1955: Lawrence Ferlinghetti, *Pictures of the Gone World,* no. 1 in the series;
Thirty Spanish Poems of Love and Exile, translated by Kenneth Rexroth, no. 2;
Kenneth Patchen, *Poems of Humor and Protest,* no. 3

1956: Allen Ginsberg, *Howl and Other Poems,* no. 4;
Marie Ponsot, *True Minds,* no. 5

1957: Denise Levertov, *Here and Now,* no. 6;
William Carlos Williams, *Kora in Hell,* no. 7

1958: Gregory Corso, *Gasoline,* no. 8;
Jacques Prévert, *Selections from Paroles,* translated by Lawrence Ferlinghetti, no. 9

1960: Nicanor Parra, *Anti-Poems,* no. 12;
Kenneth Patchen, *Love Poems,* no. 13

1961: Allen Ginsberg, *Kaddish,* no. 14;
Jack Kerouac, *Book of Dreams,* no. 15

1962: Yevtushenko, Voznesensky, Kirsanov, *Red Cats: Poems of the Soviet Thaw*, translated by Anself Hollo, no. 16;
Malcolm Lowry, *Selected Poems*, no. 17

1963: Allen Ginsberg, *Reality Sandwiches*, no. 18

1964: Frank O'Hara, *Lunch Poems*, no. 19

1967: Philip Lamantia, *Selected Poems*, no. 20;
Bob Kaufman, *The Golden Sardines*, no. 21

1968: Janine Pommy-Vega, *Poems to Fernando*, no. 22;
Allen Ginsberg, *Planet News*, no. 23;
Charles Upton, *Panic Grass*, no. 24;
Pablo Picasso, *Hunk of Skin*, translated by Paul Blackburn, no. 25

1970: Robert Bly, *The Teeth Mother Naked at Last*, no. 26

1971: Diane DiPrima, *Revolutionary Letters*, no. 27;
Jack Kerouac, *Scattered Poems*, no. 28.

During this prolific period of publication Ferlinghetti also published the works of prose writers, including Norman Mailer's controversial portrait of the Beat hipster *The White Negro* (1957), Lord Buckley's hilarious *Hiporama of the Classics* (1960), Paul Bowles's experimental *A Hundred Camels in the Courtyard* (1962), *The Yage Letters* (1963), the epistolary novel pruned from the correspondence of William S. Burroughs and Allen Ginsberg concerning their experience with the yage drug, Charles Olson's *Call Me Ishmael*, a study of Melville (first published in 1947, republished by City Lights Books in 1966), Carl Solomon's *Mishaps, Perhaps* (1966), and Timothy Leary's prison writings *Eagle Brief* (1970). The press was at the forefront of the literary and cultural revolution, seeking to extend it. It should be mentioned as part of Ferlinghetti's publishing alliance with the Beats that he turned down two classic Beat novels—Kerouac's *On the Road* and Burroughs's *Naked Lunch*. His reasons for this decision were multiple and prudent. First and foremost, City Lights Books was simply not equipped to handle a big, best-selling novel; then also Ferlinghetti was afraid of being typecast as a Beat publisher at this particular time, which would have harmed both the press and its publications; and, finally, Ferlinghetti simply doubted the merits of the writing.

Ferlinghetti's relationship with Jack Kerouac is a revealing story in itself. It was a demanding relationship for Ferlinghetti both as a publisher and as a friend. Kerouac and Ferlinghetti were at opposite poles politically. Eventually, Kerouac would label Ferlinghetti and Gregory Corso Communists, and Ferlinghetti would term Kerouac a rightist reactionary. Yet, in the summer of 1960, Ferlinghetti generously offered Kerouac the use of his Bixby Canyon cabin as a place to dry out, pull himself together, and write. Ferlinghetti literally led Kerouac to the cabin with provisions and left him in solitude hoping that Kerouac would find the inner strength in isolation to complete his *Book of Dreams* (1961). Not in a solitary mood, Kerouac found the month at Bixby Canyon a nightmare. The episode was fictionalized in his novel *Big Sur* (1962), which portrayed Ferlinghetti as Lorenzo Monsanto, a cordial businessman. Ferlinghetti did not appreciate the capitalist portrait, yet they remained on friendly terms, Kerouac nicknaming Ferlinghetti "The Smiler," and Ferlinghetti maintaining his support of Kerouac's writing genius. In a recent prose-poem portrait, "Look Homeward, Jack: Two Correspondences," Ferlinghetti draws the parallel between Kerouac and Thomas Wolfe as mythic writers of America: "Wolfe's place, said Maxwell Perkins, was all America—So with Jack—Kerouac's vision a car vision, seen from the windows of old autos speeding cross-country . . . Wolfe and Jack writing together now in eternity . . . omnivorous insatiable consumers of life, which consumed them both too early."

Ferlinghetti also performed the great task of editing and publishing the manuscript of Beat hero Neal Cassady's autobiographical *The First Third & Other Writings* in 1971. Ferlinghetti's portrait of this chief Beat prototype in his *Literary San Francisco* (1980) is evidence of their personal attachment. There he recalls that Cassady was "a prototype for a certain kind of great western hero lost among machines, racing his hotrod rather than his horse (not John Wayne but Paul Newman—Cassady, in fact, looked and moved like a young Newman in *The Hustler*). Cassady was a great nonstop talker, and he rapped as he ran. It was only when he sat down silent to write it all out in his autobiography, *The First Third*, that he became a bit tongue-tied. . . ."

At the end of the 1950s a revealing and crucial development occurred in Ferlinghetti's writing, prompted by his growing involvement in social and political concerns. It is particularly his taking his writing into this realm that created a split within the Beat movement. The division was between the "engaged" and the "disengaged," a basic existential split between the aloof "coolness" of the Beat hipster and the heated activist protest of the rebel spokesman whose social consciousness still burned to transform the world. It all came to focus for Ferlinghetti in his long political poem modeled after Prévert, *Tentative Description of a Dinner Given to Promote the Impeachment of President Eisenhower* (collected in *Starting from San Francisco*, 1961). In the cover notes of his recording of that poem he documents how the poem was not accepted at its early readings at the Poets' Follies of 1958 at Berkeley and later at a convention of the American Library Association. What troubled him most was that the Beat San Francisco natives dismissed him for being "committed." His response was a fiery proclamation of engaged writing "Because Jean-Paul Sartre cares and has always hollered that the writer especially should be committed. *Engagement* is one of his favorite dirty words. He would give the horse laugh to the idea of Disengagement and the Art of the Beat Generation. Me too. And that Abominable Snowman of modern poetry, Allen Ginsberg, would probably say the same. Only the dead are disengaged. And the wiggy nihilism of the Beat hipster, if carried to its natural conclusion, actually means the death of the creative artist himself." It was a difficult and necessary assertion for Ferlinghetti to make, and it and the various protest pieces on the album *Tentative Description of a Dinner Given to Promote the Impeachment of President Eisenhower & Other Poems* (Fantasy Records, 1959) gave other Beat artists of engagement a firmer basis for an art of dissent. An examination of the works of Kerouac, Ginsberg, Gary Snyder, Philip Whalen, and William Everson will show the same commitment underlying their art.

Though most of Ferlinghetti's initial political statements were tied to the civil liberties movement of the Joseph McCarthy era, the poet had another political experience—a 1959 trip to Chile which he, his wife, and Allen Ginsberg made to the writers' conference at the University of Concepción. Surprised that the directorship of the conference was so controlled by members of the Communist party, Ferlinghetti and Ginsberg were, nevertheless, brought face to face with world poverty and social injustices. The tour through South and Central Americas for Ferlinghetti only deepened his commitment to a humanitarian socialist government. It is perhaps not surprising to learn that he and Ginsberg became the focus of an FBI investigation at this time. This was also the period in which Fer-

linghetti became involved with the unpopular Fair Play for Cuba Committee. Having visited Cuba in 1960, Ferlinghetti provided reports of Fidel Castro's regime and delivered the sympathetic poem "One Thousand Fearful Words for Fidel Castro" (in *Starting from San Francisco*) at a San Francisco rally:

> I was sitting in Mike's place, Fidel
> waiting for someone else to act
> like a good Liberal
> I hadn't quite finished reading Camus' *Rebel*
> so I couldn't quite recognize you, Fidel
> walking up and down your island
> when they came for you, Fidel.

Addressing Castro and daring to compare him with Abraham Lincoln, "one of your boyhood heroes," Ferlinghetti forecast the attempts on Castro's life and called for humane communication with his revolutionary government. In the 1980s Ferlinghetti has toured Nicaragua with poet-priest Ernesto Cardenal and called for open talks between our two governments.

Three magazines emerged in the early 1960s that supported the best of Beat writing as well as international avant-garde work. The first was *Beatitude*, founded in 1960 and coedited by Ferlinghetti, Bob Kaufman, John Kelley, William S. Margolis, and Allen Ginsberg. The following year Ferlinghetti joined forces with David Meltzer and Michael McClure in editing the *Journal for the Protection of All Beings*. Finally, there was Ferlinghetti's own *City Lights Journal*, whose first issue in 1963 set a pattern of featuring the best avant-garde work of the East and West Coasts: Kerouac, Burroughs, Ed Sanders, Ted Joans, many others. Each issue also featured an international group of writers.

What emerges from the historical panorama of Ferlinghetti's involvement is a pattern of social engagement and literary experimentation as he sought to expand the goals of the Beat movement and San Francisco Poetry Renaissance. While conformity was anathema to the Beats, what does emerge from this collection of rebel American artists is the sense of an existential confrontation with life, the form of the work being characterized chiefly by its desire to capture more fully the range of experience in a spontaneous and vital form. Thus Ferlinghetti's writing is in keeping with the Beat perspective as he produced a wide range of experimental forms. Foremost in his experimentation is the antinovel *Her*, which appeared in 1960. It is an avant-garde work that pits character and author in a battle with the subjective relativity of experience in a quest for ideals; a surrealistic encounter with the subconscious—filled with phallic symbols and prophetic visions of desire. At once existential, absurd, symbolic, expressionistic, cinematic, and surrealistic in vision and form, *Her* is controlled, as all Ferlinghetti's work is, by a drive toward expanded consciousness. One section in particular on the Poetry Police relates directly to the Beat movement. It was a section added to the book in the late 1950s and first published in Paul Carroll's *Big Table* magazine, which published many early Beat writings. The section is a symbolic portrait of the Beat spirit. The narrator, speaking in "the fourth person singular," reports a "wailing wild ragged band of American poets from the Rue Git-le-Coeur" who rush into the boulevards singing and shouting of the coming deliverance from status and convention by the rebel Poetry Police who greet them "in parachutes made from the pages of obscene dictionaries" and take to the streets of major cities to "clean up the mass mess." Ferlinghetti is at his vaudevillian best as he pictures these poetic saviors climbing aboard the backs of fellow citizens from whose necks they hang, "shouting true profound wiggy formulas for eternal mad salvation." The Poetry Police capture "all libraries, newspapers, printing presses, and automats, and force their proprietors at pen's point to print nothing henceforth but headlines of pure poetry and menus of pure love." The book is truly a spirited, though somewhat self-mocking, projection of the optimistic goals of the Beat and San Francisco poetry movements placed on a grand imaginative scale, a "Poetry Revolution" for peace and love. Ferlinghetti's experimental novel was well received abroad and acclaimed by French critic Pierre Lepape as a "laby-rêve" (labyrinth-dream) with "incredible verbal virtuosity," yet it has only recently received serious critical treatment in the United States. *Her* serves as a prime example of the academically and critically neglected works of this period.

The 1960s also witnessed Ferlinghetti's work with experimental theater. In his two collections, *Unfair Arguments with Existence* (1963) and *Routines* (1964), Ferlinghetti presents in symbolic-expressionistic-surrealistic-absurdist form his essential existential confrontation with life. Both collections present a mixture of revolutionary theater, absurd happenings, and symbolic events in which Ferlinghetti seeks to create a "Third Stream Theatre" with a declared goal: "And all to make you think of life." Following models of Artaud, Samuel Beck-

ett, Jean Genet, and Eugene Ionesco, he employed the gamut of theatrical devices—clowning, filmic gestures, mime, verbal nonsense, black comedy, dream and fantasy scenes—all in a spectacle of assault on the audience. Again the basic goal was a very Beat confrontation with existence. His brief "routines" are defined as "a song & dance, a little rout, a routing-out, a run-around, a 'round of business or amusement'" with "life itself a blackout routine, an experimental madness somewhere between dotage and megalomania, lost in the vibration of wreckage." Clearly they are metaphysical plays, symbolic acts of life, a modern hall of mirrors in which the author and his audience find themselves. Most of these plays were written in the tiny and noisy Cafe Trieste of San Francisco's North Beach district. Although they have received mostly amateur production and little critical attention, the plays remain a revealing and vital phase of Ferlinghetti's varied career. Critic Richard Duerden accurately praises Ferlinghetti as "clearly a good playwright. The form is proper to him." Though Clive Barnes finds the drama reduced at times to "windy allegories," he also recognizes that Ferlinghetti's "themes are vast and gutsy, and they talk . . . about the decay and dissolution of our civilization." Drama is a form that is natural to this outspoken and philosophical social critic.

Two books of poetry also appeared in the 1960s—*Starting from San Francisco* (1961) and *The Secret Meaning of Things* (1969). Both books reflect Ferlinghetti's increased social involvements and expanded consciousness as he journeyed outward and inward through Europe, Zen, drugs, and sociopolitical issues. *Starting from San Francisco* carries Whitman's geographic self-quest forward: "These poems represent to me a kind of a halfway house in the ascent of a mountain I hardly knew existed until I stopped and looked back at the flatlands below. Like a Zen fool lost in the woods who laughs and lies face down on the earth to find his way." Thus Ferlinghetti's search for his place in the world underlies his Whitmanesque quest for involvement and synthesis of experience into a cosmic consciousness. Predominantly in the style of oral poetry (a recording of the poet reading the key poems was included in a pocket of the original edition), the works manifest a heartfelt mixture of radical innocence and a deeply ironic voice. "Berlin" and "Situation in the West" are good examples of Ferlinghetti's basic method of composition by confrontation, of revealing experience by recording it in the total consciousness. The emphasis is on assimilation of experience and release of inner energy. Time and again what Ferlinghetti is doing in his work is singing and swinging as he seeks to "dig" life. Norman Mailer's description of what it means to "swing" from his essay *The White Negro* is a pointed revelation of Ferlinghetti's stance and that of the Beats: "For to swing is to communicate, is to convey the rhythms of one's own being to a lover, a friend, or an audience, and—equally necessary— be able to feel the rhythms of their response. To swing with the rhythms of another is to enrich one-self. . . ." All the Beats were especially adept at this, and Ferlinghetti is perhaps the best at tuning into the rhythms of places, whether Mexico, New York, San Francisco, Moscow, Berlin, or Harvard's Bick-ford Cafeteria. He manages to be "there" and to reveal as he details the surroundings. From the 1969 collection *The Secret Meaning of Things,* he gives us "Bickford's Buddha":

> Some days I'm afflicted
> with Observation Fever
> omniverous perception of phenomena
> not just visual
> like today in Bickford's Harvard Square
> sitting still seeing everything
> watching a lot of beautiful animals
> walk by
> turning & turning in their courses
> ....
> digging everything
> seeing just how much I could take in
> without missing anything
> Any thing
> Eyeballs faces lips alack
> And a threeyearoldgirl on a sidewalk
> licking the chocolate spreckles off
> a gooey ice-cream cone
> peering through the open backdoor
> of a drycleaningshop
> ....

The poem that was "Writ on the back of a map of Harvard College" goes on to catalogue and register in a stream of consciousness what Ferlinghetti perceives as the reality of the place. The poet is the ontological dog who seeks to know his world simply and fully. The poems from this fourth collection are more cosmic in perspective, yet no less provocative, and oral in style and form. In such apocalyptic statements as "Assassination Raga," "After the Cries of the Birds," and "Moscow in the Wilderness/Segovia in the Snow," the vision is both expansive and personal, dark and hopeful. Most of the poems from *Starting from San Francisco* and *The Secret Meaning of Things* were first published as

broadsides in the tradition of printing political and lyric poems on sheets to be posted for the public. This pattern of broadside publishing has since become a main feature of small-press publication. For Ferlinghetti it was a means of allowing his personal confrontations with the world to become a public matter. Seeking a regenerative vision, he becomes a poet whose art is characterized by its authentic search and its existential stance, making him at once one of America's most public and personal poets.

Ferlinghetti's contribution to the Beat movement then goes far beyond his publishing their work. Besides molding an image of the poet in the world, he created a poetic form that is at once rhetorically functional and socially vital. Chief among his developments is the oral poetry he fashioned, which in fact re-created an oral tradition in contemporary poetry. Using colloquial bluntness, mocking alliteration, internal and multiple rhyme, puns, incongruent diction, and comic allusions, he

Cover for the book in which Ferlinghetti returns to the scenes of his youth

has created an engaging vehicle for satire and sentiment. Ferlinghetti has also developed, after E. E. Cummings, a poetry of sight and sound in the open form. Fusing the principles of abstract-expressionist art and oral delivery, he creates an audiovisual page that engenders its own energy and life.

His early "Junkman's Obbligato" demonstrates his ease with the oral tradition as he adopts a clowning guise and accents it with a nearly vaudevillian wordplay. In the "Hurry up, it's time" atmosphere of Eliot's *The Wasteland,* he urges readers out into the reality of the street, where "Your missus will not miss us," where we meet the "flowery bowery" with refrains of "My country tears of thee." Such obvious multiple rhyming and punning punctuate Ferlinghetti's ironic vision effectively, yet it is not a detached vision that he projects, for he also exposes the reality of those who "Stagger befuddled into East River sunsets/Sleep in phone booths/Puke in pawnshops/wailing for a winter overcoat." His alliterative devices are also capable of poetic blues singing, as Ferlinghetti's spokesman seeks to speak his consciousness through "our tin-can cries and garbage voices." His junkman assures us: "Another flood is coming/though not the kind you think./There is still time to sink/and think." In goodbyes to Emily Post, Lowell Thomas, Broadway, and Herald Square, the whole gamut of American culture echoes through the words of this junkman, who, like Ferlinghetti, is capable of turning the satiric voice into a lyrical singing as he closes with a regenerative vision:

> Let us arise and go now
> to the Isle of Manisfree
> and live the true blue simple life
> of wisdom and wonderment
> where all things grow
> straight up
> aslant and singing
> in the yellow sun.

All the echoing devices of alliteration, internal rhyme, punning, allusion, juxtaposition of formal diction and oral phrasing lead the voice to accentuate and authenticate an act of transformation which critic Ihab Hassan noted in Ferlinghetti's oral style: "Putting aside the clownish guise, he can burst into sudden anger at sham or injustice, burst with the authentic power of poetry. Like E. E. Cummings or Kenneth Patchen before him, he can convert extravagant wit or protest into some human perception of wonder and generosity."

Ferlinghetti's creation of cinematic scenes runs throughout his poetic career. These epiphanies are finely rendered moments drawn from the common experience of a locale, such as his repeated portraits of San Francisco's Washington Square represented by poem number six in *A Coney Island of the Mind* and by "The Old Italians Dying" in the 1979 collection, *Landscapes of Living and Dying.* A sample from the latter suggests his method:

> toward ten in the morning the slow bell tolls
> in the towers of Peter & Paul
> and the old men who are still alive
> sit sunning themselves in a row
> on the wood benches in the park
> and watch the processions in and out
> funerals in the morning
> weddings in the afternoon
> ....
> You have seen them
> the ones who feed the pigeons
>   cutting the stale bread
>   with their thumbs & penknives
> the ones with old pocketwatches
> the old ones with gnarled hands
>   and wild eyebrows
> the ones with the baggy pants
>   with both belt & suspenders
> the grappa drinkers with teeth like corn

Into the midst of this cast of mythic and real characters comes a slow-moving mafioso funeral, a priest scurrying about, the sights and sounds of the park, as the poet brings to a fine closeup the aged-fisherman faces of these old Italians in San Francisco. The poem was made into a short experimental film recently by Herman Berlandt with Ferlinghetti reading. Particularly meaningful is the fact that this is a very Beat poem—existential and beatific in its feeling toward life—and that it was written in the late 1970s. A vivid, autobiographic, and lyric realism still motivates Ferlinghetti's art.

In the 1970s Ferlinghetti produced some solid volumes of poetry: the expansive *Open Eye, Open Heart* (1973), *Who Are We Now?* (1976), and *Landscapes of Living and Dying* (1979). He also, through a series of three "Populist Manifesto" poems, perpetuated the essential connection between populist, Beat, and engaged art. The manifestos, which were issued from a wide range of publications (newspapers and magazines) as well as from the radio, strike a familiar chord in an age where poetry tends toward the esoteric and hermetic. In the "First Populist Manifesto," collected in *Who Are We Now?*, Ferlinghetti declares:

> Poets, come out of your closets,
> Open your windows, open your doors,
> You have been holed-up too long
> in your closed worlds
> ....
> Where are Whitman's wild children
> where the great voices speaking out
> with a sense of sweetness and sublimity
> ....
> Poets, descend
> to the streets of the world once more
> and open your minds & eyes
> ....
> Stop mumbling and speak out
> with a new wide-open poetry
> with a new commonsensual "public surface"
> with other subjective levels
> or other subversive levels

This poem aptly characterizes both Ferlinghetti's own writing and the engaged Beat writing which he represented and encouraged. Calling for a return to poetry as a vital communication with a wide audience, he asserts,

> Poetry the common carrier
> for the transportation of the public
> to higher places
> ....
> Whitman's wild children still sleeping there,
> Awake and walk in the open air.

His work exists as a vital challenge and a living presence to the contemporary artist, as an embodiment of the strong, anticool, compassionate commitment to life in an absurd time.

His 1980s publication of *Factory* by the young Milwaukee poet Antler, *Volcan: Poems from Central America,* and the journal *Free Spirits: Annals of the Insurgent Imagination* testifies to his continuing commitment to engaged writing. In his recent *Endless Life: Selected Poems* (1981) Ferlinghetti, in his sixties, is still engaged and affirming, as he declares in the title poem:

> Endless the splendid life of the world
> Endless its lovely living and breathing
> its lovely sentient beings
> seeing and hearing feeling and thinking
> laughing and dancing sighing and crying
> through endless afternoons endless nights.

The vision behind the art and life remains this beatific sense of life's potential wonder. He is forever the romantic realist, the poet journalist, with a real tale to tell and a vital style in which to tell it. Critic Karl Malkoff presents the developing critical appreciation of Ferlinghetti's work: "It is evident that he has for himself replaced his meaningless surroundings with what is for him a living tradition, drawing from it the energy to create and possibly to revitalize his world. . . ." His work deserves the critical attention it is now winning, because it is essential to assimilate his achievement into the American literary tradition.

Having become the good, gray poet of the 1970s and 1980s, Ferlinghetti, as a poet and publisher, as a catalyst of cultural and literary innovation for several generations, is one of the key forces of contemporary writing. He extends the significance of the Beat perspective by the engaged stance of his life and work and by the powerful and popular art he has wrought.

Interviews:

Thaddeus Vane, "Lawrence Ferlinghetti: A Candid Conversation with the Man Who Founded the Beat Generation," *Penthouse,* 1 (August 1965): 24, 26, 71-73;
An interesting though dated interview of the culture and climate of North Beach, San Francisco, and the personalities who started the Beat movement.

David Meltzer, "Lawrence Ferlinghetti," in his *The San Francisco Poets* (New York: Ballantine, 1971); revised as *Golden Gate* (Berkeley: Wingbow, 1976), pp. 134-187;
A long interview in which Ferlinghetti discusses the San Francisco Poetry Renaissance and the Beat movement; includes several poems.

Jean-Jacques Lebel, "Interview," in Lawrence Ferlinghetti's *The Populist Manifestos* (San Francisco: Grey Fox Press, 1983);
This reprint of a French interview focuses on Ferlinghetti as an international writer and a social critic; provides the French perspective on Ferlinghetti as poet.

Larry Smith, "An Interview with Lawrence Ferlinghetti," *Pig Iron: The New Surrealists,* 11 (1983): 6-16;
A recent interview in which the poet speaks

of the changes in America, contemporary poetry, and his life.

Bibliographies:

David Kherdian, *Six Poets of the San Francisco Renaissance: Portraits and Checklists* (Fresno, Cal.: Caligia Press, 1967);
Dated and incomplete, yet an interesting portrait of the author with photos.

Bill Morgan, *Lawrence Ferlinghetti: A Descriptive Bibliography* (New York: Garland Publications, 1981);
An authoritative and extensive record of almost all of Ferlinghetti's published works—large and small presses.

References:

Ann Charters, *Kerouac: A Biography* (San Francisco: Straight Arrow Books, 1973);
A fine biography of novelist Jack Kerouac and the Beat movement, in which Ferlinghetti recurs as a friend and catalyst.

Samuel Charters, *Some Poems/Poets: Studies in American Underground Poetry Since 1945* (Berkeley: Oyez, 1971);
Charters focuses on San Francisco poets and provides an early analysis of the form and method of Ferlinghetti's poetry and stance.

Neeli Cherkovski, *Ferlinghetti: A Biography* (Garden City: Doubleday, 1979);
An essential starting place for biographical facts, though lacking in analysis of the works.

J. W. Ehrlich, *Howl of the Censor* (San Carlos, Cal.: Nourse Books, 1961);
A record of the celebrated censorship trial of Allen Ginsberg's *Howl* by one of the leading defense attorneys for Ferlinghetti.

William Everson, *Archetype West: The Pacific Coast as a Literary Region* (Berkeley: Oyez, 1976);
An essential book for understanding West Coast writing and the whole San Francisco Poetry Renaissance; contains a fair analysis and evaluation of Ferlinghetti's place in the larger picture.

Louis A. Haselmayer, "Beat Prophet and Beat Wit," *Iowa English Yearbook*, 6 (Fall 1961): 9-13;
An early profile of Ferlinghetti and the emerging West Coast Beat movement.

Crale D. Hopkins, "The Poetry of Lawrence Ferlinghetti: A Reconsideration," *Italian Americana* (1974): 59-76;
Excellent critical appraisal and appreciation of Ferlinghetti's writing at midcareer.

L. A. Ianni, "Lawrence Ferlinghetti's Fourth Person Singular and the Theory of Relativity," *Wisconsin Studies in Contemporary Literature*, 8 (Summer 1967): 392-406;
A critical analysis of Ferlinghetti's antinovel *Her*; scholarly and philosophical.

Alain Jouffroy, "Lawrence Ferlinghetti," *Les Temps Modernes*, no. 223 (December 1964): 990-995;
The French critical evaluation of Ferlinghetti.

Gerald D. McDonald, "Lawrence Ferlinghetti: A Coney Island of the Mind," *Library Journal* (15 June 1958);
One of the first reviews of Ferlinghetti's work; reveals the 1950s critical perspective as much as Ferlinghetti's most popular book of poetry, *A Coney Island of the Mind*.

Thomas Parkinson, "Phenomenon or Generation," in his *A Casebook on the Beat* (New York: Crowell, 1961), pp. 276-290;
One of the first books on the Beat movement, offers a fair representation of the early development of values and literature forms, by one who was intimate with the West Coast writers.

Kenneth Rexroth, *American Poetry in the Twentieth Century* (New York: Herder & Herder, 1971);
A fair appraisal of Ferlinghetti as writer and cultural influence by a longtime friend.

Rexroth, *Assays* (Norfolk, Conn.: New Directions, 1961);
An early appraisal of the Beat movement and its best San Francisco representatives.

M. L. Rosenthal, "The Naked and the Clad," *Nation* (11 October 1958): 214-215;
An early evaluation of the motives and methods of the Beat writers.

Michael Skau, "Toward Underivative Creation: Lawrence Ferlinghetti's *Her*," *Critique: Studies in Modern Fiction*, 19, no. 3 (1978);
Though somewhat scholarly, one of the rare

critical analyses of Ferlinghetti's antinovel *Her.*

Larry Smith, *Lawrence Ferlinghetti: Poet-at-Large* (Carbondale & Edwardsville: Southern Illinois University Press, 1983);
The only critical book on Ferlinghetti; contains detailed chronology, biography, and analysis of major works in each of these art forms; scholarly yet readable.

Smith, "The Poetry-and-Jazz Movement in the United States," *Itinerary*, 7 (Fall 1977): 89-104;

A revealing study of the poetry-and-jazz movement in its chief practitioners: Lawrence Ferlinghetti, Kenneth Rexroth, Kenneth Patchen.

John Tytell, *Naked Angels: The Lives & Literature of the Beat Generation* (New York: McGraw-Hill, 1976);
A revealing study of the Beat movement and its chief writers including Ginsberg, Kerouac, Burroughs, and others.

Allen Ginsberg

This entry was updated by Paul Christensen (Texas A&M University) from his entry in
DLB 16, The Beats: Literary Bohemians in Postwar America, *and incorporated
portions of the entry by John Ower (University of South Carolina) from* DLB 5, American
Poets Since World War II.

Places	Paterson, New Jersey Harlem India	San Francisco Greenwich Village Morocco	Boulder, Colorado Mexico Western Europe
Influences and Relationships	William Carlos Williams William Burroughs Gary Snyder Charles Olson	Jack Kerouac Carl Solomon Lawrence Ferlinghetti	Neal Cassady Kenneth Rexroth Gregory Corso

Literary Movements and Forms	The Beat Movement
	Antiwar Movement
	Postmodern Long
	    Poems (Postmodern-
	    ism)
		Antiwar Movement
		Improvisational Art
		Projectivism (Black
		    Mountain School)
			Performance Poetry
			San Francisco Renaissance
			Naropa School (Kerouac
			    School of Disembodied
			    Poetics)

Major Themes	Alienation Corporate Power Ideology Youth Movements	Spirituality Bohemianism Innovative Poetics	Pacifism Hallucenogenic Drugs Social Control

Cultural and Artistic Influences	Peace Demonstration
	Mid Century Jazz
	    and Folk Music
		Drug Culture
		Bohemian Inner-
		    City Culture
			Political Protests
			Gay Rights
			Hippies

Social and Economic Influences	World War II
	The Beat Movement
	Federal Surveillance
	    and Investigation
	American Jewish Traditions
		Vietnam War
		1960s Culture
		1968 Democratic
		    Convention
			Cold War
			Buddhism
			Postmodernist
			    Literature

BIRTH: Newark, New Jersey, 3 June 1926, to Louis and Naomi Levy Ginsberg.

EDUCATION: A.B., Columbia University, 1948.

AWARDS AND HONORS: Guggenheim Fellowship, 1965; National Endowment for the Arts Grant, 1966; National Institute of Arts and Letters Award, 1969; National Book Award for *The Fall of America,* 1974; Membership in the American Institute of Arts and Letters, 1974; National Arts Club Gold Medal, 1979.

SELECTED BOOKS: *Howl and Other Poems* (San Francisco: City Lights Books, 1956);

Empty Mirror: Early Poems (New York: Totem Press/ Corinth Books, 1961);

Kaddish and Other Poems: 1958-1960 (San Francisco: City Lights Books, 1961);

Reality Sandwiches: 1953-1960 (San Francisco: City Lights Books, 1963);

The Yage Letters, by Ginsberg and William S. Burroughs (San Francisco: City Lights Books, 1963);

T.V. Baby Poems (London: Cape Goliard, 1967; New York: Grossman, 1968);

Planet News: 1961-1967 (San Francisco: City Lights Books, 1968);

Ankor Wat (London: Fulcrum Press, 1968);

Airplane Dreams: Compositions from Journals (Toronto: House of Anansi Press, 1968; San Francisco: City Lights Books, 1969);

Notes After an Evening with William Carlos Williams (New York: Samuel Charters, 1970);

Indian Journals: March 1962-May 1963 (San Francisco: Dave Haselwood, 1970);

Ginsberg's Improvised Poetics, edited by Mark Robison (Buffalo: Anonym Press, 1971);

The Fall of America: Poems of These States 1965-1971 (San Francisco: City Lights Books, 1972);

The Gates of Wrath: Rhymed Poems, 1948-1952 (Bolinas, Cal.: Grey Fox Press, 1972);

Iron Horse (Toronto: Coach House, 1972; San Francisco: City Lights Books, 1974);

Allen Verbatim: Lectures on Poetry, Politics, Consciousness, edited by Gordon Ball (New York: McGraw-Hill, 1974);

The Visions of the Great Rememberer (Amherst, Mass.: Mulch Press, 1974);

Sad Dust Glories: Poems During Summer in Woods (Berkeley, Cal.: Workingmans Press, 1975);

Chicago Trial Testimony (San Francisco: City Lights Books, 1975);

Allen Ginsberg, 1981 (photo by Chris Felver)

First Blues: Rags, Ballads & Harmonium Songs 1971- 74 (New York: Full Court Press, 1975);

Journals: Early Fifties-Early Sixties, edited by Ball (New York: Grove, 1977);

Poems All Over the Place: Mostly Seventies (Cherry Valley, N.Y.: Cherry Valley Editions, 1978);

Mind Breaths: Poems 1972-1977 (San Francisco: City Lights Books, 1978);

Composed on the Tongue, edited by Donald Allen (Bolinas, Cal.: Grey Fox Press, 1980);

Plutonian Ode (San Francisco: City Lights Books, 1982);

Collected Poems: 1947-1980 (New York: Harper & Row, 1984);

White Shroud: Poems 1980-1985 (New York: Harper & Row, 1986).

PLAY PRODUCTION: *Kaddish,* Brooklyn, New York, Brooklyn Academy of Music, 10 February 1972.

OTHER: Donald Allen and Warren Tallman, eds., *Poetics of the New American Poetry,* includes critical essays by Ginsberg (New York: Grove, 1973).

Allen Ginsberg's reputation as a major poet is now secure; he has outlived the other major poets of mid century with whom he is frequently compared, such as Charles Olson, Robert Lowell, and Frank O'Hara, who with Ginsberg make up a core of writers that revolutionized the writing of American verse in the 1950s. Their collective achievement was to make for poetry the final break with European and English standards of versification that sent American poetry in pursuit of its own rhythms and forms, a direction it continues to explore with verve and astonishing variety. Each of these major writers gave to the main currents of verse his own unique voice and intelligence, but it was Ginsberg especially who seems to have awakened America's youth to the powers of poetry to make stirring prophecies and to reinvigorate the spheres of politics and ideology. Perhaps more than any other poet of his time or since, Ginsberg is the bard of disaffected youth in America, the single most potent lyric voice discoursing on national crises in ways that arouse and stimulate the young to take part in the political process. Now in his sixties, he is the venerated bard of resistance; his presence at poetry readings is serene and messianic; his podium is at once a pulpit of Buddhist wisdom and a clearinghouse of reformist priorities. From his earliest writings, he has been the champion of individual freedom, and his lifelong adversary has been social control in its myriad forms and strategies, whether of government or business or in the intangible realms of taste, customs, psychological conditioning, parental guidance, and the like. His poetry is calculated to blast the controlling opposition with spell-binding celebrations of personal freedom and spiritual liberty. As might be expected of a large canon of such work, some of it now begins to fade with its fractious rhetoric and its passing topical importance, but there remains an imperishable core of major testaments to the ideals of self-fulfillment and communal well-being that assure Ginsberg his major status among modern writers.

Although Ginsberg's image now may be that of a poet who has freed himself from all inhibitions and who thrives upon expressing his complete self from base instinct to religious exaltation, the young Ginsberg was, if anything, the opposite in nature: cautious, careful, with a reverence for poetic convention and the European verse tradition. Ginsberg was born 3 June 1926 in Newark, New Jersey,

whose landscape would later figure in his depictions of America's tarnished Eden. His father, Louis Ginsberg, was a high-school English teacher in nearby Paterson and a lyric poet of some reputation: national magazines often printed his work and three volumes of poems were published during his lifetime. But there is little in his writing to distinguish it from other prewar verse, most of which followed the Fugitive and New Critical retrenchments to English versification. As a parent, Louis Ginsberg was an apostle of order, moderation, and restraint, and if he emphasized these virtues unduly to his son, it was perhaps to counterbalance the example of his wife, Naomi Levy Ginsberg, who had dedicated her life to the cause of international communism and who was an active member in the Party as well as in other associations of the radical Left. Naomi Ginsberg's paranoid delusions of persecution by government and even by her own family led finally to her incarceration in an asylum when Ginsberg was still a child; the youth was profoundly influenced by his mother's suffering, which he must have interpreted as the price of her political beliefs. Years later the poet envisioned her as the martyr of a cause now enveloping the son, and to whom he must pay verse homage after her many lonely years spent at Pilgrim State Hospital, where she died in 1956, the year Ginsberg's first book, *Howl and Other Poems*, was published. Three years later the poet exorcised the troubling ghost of his mother in a furious and painful elegy entitled *Kaddish*, in which we may glimpse the depth of her influence upon him as well as the confused passions she evoked in him. During his childhood Ginsberg frequently missed school to nurse his mother through her periods of deep depression, and it is likely that at this time he grew to distrust the female sex as a whole from what he discovered in his own mother's illness. His early journal entries and letters to friends are filled with a mixture of longings to know women and his disgust with their frailties and manipulations. It is likely that he discovered his homosexuality while in high school, since, as John Tytell reports, he chose to enroll at Columbia University in order to follow a student he was enamored of while at Paterson High School.

Ginsberg's youth was already, then, a lesson in extremes: his father was the measure of bourgeois stolidity, his mother the ragged edge of madness and political passion, while he himself trespassed (in thought at least) the taboo against homosexuality as an adolescent, for which he was to feel the deepest guilt and consternation during the next several years at Columbia.

Ginsberg was seventeen when he enrolled at Columbia in 1943, too young to be drafted into the service. Like other universities during wartime, Columbia had rushed students through to graduation with short courses, and its enrollments had fallen sharply for incoming students. Columbia was a bastion of the new conservatism in literature, with such staunch traditionalists of culture as Mark Van Doren and Lionel Trilling on its faculty; both professors would become close friends and occasionally champions of their sometimes wayward star pupil, Ginsberg. A fellow student at the time was the poet John Hollander, with whom Ginsberg frequently compared himself then and after, when it seemed his own star was setting while Hollander became a widely published writer. Ginsberg had much to resent in his friend Hollander whose poems were wrought in strict accord with traditional verse conventions. Even though the young Ginsberg was no rogue in verse forms, he thought of himself as a rebel and outsider chafing against the limits of verse method then taught at Columbia. All the same he was a frequent contributor to the college reviews, with poems such as "Songs for the Tender Hearted Liberal," one of his first lyrics to be published, and "Do Not Despair, O Lonely Heart." The poems were clever but uninspired. His sharpest dilemma of these years was his homosexuality, which he carefully concealed from the other students. It seemed to him at the time a grotesque dimension of his psyche, something welling up from his depths which he could not control and which made him feel like an outcast. This outcast version of himself came to him in a dream and suggested one of the significant images of his early poetry, the figure of a lonely and desperate man, a monster of instinctual desire who has been rejected by society. Ginsberg at once called the figure his "shroudy stranger" and told his friend Neal Cassady some years later that it was "the same man who shrieked on the heath with King Lear, the Fool . . . and also Old Tom the Lunatic of late Yeats." Ginsberg also associated him with characters he found in seventeenth-century songs, which he felt he had reinvented in his own efforts to dramatize the shrouded stranger. As it happens, many of the poems of *The Gates of Wrath* (1972), written from 1948 to 1952, deal with versions and permutations of this haunting figure, and the poet could soothe his own distress through empathy with this desolate figure, a person who had trespassed beyond the last taboo of his civilization.

The first two years at Columbia were otherwise uneventful years of student life; Ginsberg must have contented himself that he was fulfilling his father's wishes by attending an Ivy League university; and as a pre-law major he felt he was preparing himself for a career in which he could defend the poor and weak of a capitalist democracy, thereby pleasing his mother as well. But these soothing ambitions came to a halt when Ginsberg was reported to the dean of students for a few obscene scrawls he had made in the dust of his dorm window. The dean burst upon his room, found him in bed with his new friend Jack Kerouac, who was a former student of Columbia then living near the campus, and expelled Ginsberg for the year. Ginsberg promptly moved in with William S. Burroughs, later the author of one of the most notorious satires of American life, *Naked Lunch* (1959), and there immersed himself in the New York underworld of drugs, crime, and the sexual fringe of Forty-second Street bars and gay hangouts. Kerouac, four years Ginsberg's senior, was already dedicated to becoming a writer and soon became Ginsberg's literary mentor. Burroughs, considerably older, was their guide to the subterranean world of Manhattan, who shared a broad and sophisticated knowledge of the literature of rebellion in works of Céline, Doestoyevski, Spengler, Kafka, Korzybski, Rimbaud, and others. Burroughs's apartment became a center for not only Kerouac and Ginsberg but also their friends John Clellon Holmes, Lucien Carr, and Neal Cassady, the essential figures of the "Beat Generation," Kerouac's half-joking name for the friends of his circle.

Once out on the streets of New York, Ginsberg began to recognize the narrowness of his literary education; his professors were unaware of the broad range of experimental literature Burroughs had recommended to their circle, and rather than teaching an American tradition of poetry, the literary curriculum at Columbia concentrated almost exclusively on selective English texts: American writing was still being relegated to a second-class status as late as the 1940s. Poetry as written at the time seemed utterly removed from anything the young poet now saw happening in the streets and nightlife of the city. Poets had withdrawn from the reality of the moment in order to perfect various techniques of meter and line within the closed forms of English verse. Literary education was then under the theoretical spell of T. S. Eliot, who had been advocating the study of seventeenth-century English verse as the proper source for the rejuvenation of poetry; the Fugitive poets, disenchanted with socialist criticism and political poetry, helped spread the Eliot doctrine of a return to older methods of verse art. Ginsberg discovered that the academy had taken its own political stand on art and now offered what seemed to him a censored and distorted view of the modern literary tradition.

Ginsberg's year away from college (1945-1946) ended almost too abruptly when in June 1945 he received his draft notice; by declaring homosexuality, however, he was released and sent to a merchant marine training school for the duration of the summer. In August the war had ended only to have the atomic age begin. After a year under the drug and sexual tutelage of William Burroughs, Ginsberg returned to Columbia in the fall but continued his experiments with various hallucinogenic drugs. He now wrote frequently and had his first piece of critical prose published in his hometown Paterson newspaper, a glowing review of the first book of William Carlos Williams's long poem *Paterson*. In January 1947 Ginsberg met Neal Cassady, who had already become a close friend of Kerouac. Cassady was a phenomenon of his age; he seems to have embodied in his high energy, his richly lyrical talk, his good looks, and his prodigious sexual appetite, the whole of his generation's frustrations and yearnings. He was more than a new friend of the Beat group: he was their muse. His life suggested to Kerouac, John Clellon Holmes, and Ginsberg an endless series of metaphoric acts and symbolic escapades which they noted down and later wrote books about. Kerouac spent the better part of his writing career attempting to put down in words the curious, almost inimitable spontaneity and verbal magic of this young idol. Cassady had grown up in various Denver reform schools; his father was an alcoholic derelict with whom he sometimes lived; but in spite of his long conviction record for stealing cars and engaging in other mischief, he was happy, intense, strikingly assertive, and the first truly Western blood to enter the very Eastern sensibilities of the New York Beats. Holmes celebrated the Cassady style in his novel *Go* (1952), which would propel the Beat scene to media fame. But it was Ginsberg who fell in love with Cassady and became his sexual partner, making this the first serious love affair of the young poet. The verses about Cassady poured from Ginsberg's pen, as they would for the next several decades; but Cassady himself was not in love with Ginsberg, and the affair ended bitterly, confirming Ginsberg's fears that he was fated to live a lonely, emotionally unrequited life. When Cassady died in 1968, Ginsberg dedicated his collection *Planet News: 1961-1967* (1968) to him, and he has continued to write moving lyric elegies to Cassady's memory since.

But Cassady's principal effect on the other Beat writers transcended friendship and momentary affairs: his talk was incessant, a spontaneous flow of words and ideas that accumulated in impressive and often astonishing structures. He spellbound his friends with his verbal facility, with his inexhaustible humor and detailed observation. His chatter was unlike anything they had ever heard. Only Cassady among the group had not been to college, but like the others, he began receiving literary education during long nights at the West End Cafe at the edge of the Columbia campus and in the apartments of Burroughs, Kerouac, and others of the widening group. Cassady talked with effortless artistry; he was almost the equivalent in monologues of the bop music then coming into vogue. Cassady could spin out a structure of words as subtle and demanding to the listener as were the solos of Charlie "Bird" Parker. Cassady, in other words, taught his friends the gift of spontaneity; he was the measure of the uncalculated use of energy that in and of itself magically took form and meaning. The more Cassady talked, while eating, drinking, taking drugs, driving on his legendary trips across country at speeds of 110 miles per hour, the more he undermined the strict and premeditated conventions of the writing arts for his friends. Only Cassady had lived his life on the street, talking his art, without any preconceptions of how he was to channel or direct his energies. He sought the education of his friends and implored them to give him reading lists, ideas, advice on writing. But he was at once the master of the spontaneous mode and the victim of it. As Ginsberg tutored him and offered the rather ordinary advice he had himself picked up from the classroom, Cassady could only report back his frustrations at trying to write. Kerouac attempted to teach Cassady the art of fiction. The irony of this situation is that the two writers admired the great geysering energies of Cassady the talker, who in turn admired their more studied forms of written art. In the end, both Kerouac and Ginsberg learned from Cassady the mode of high-speed spontaneous composition that would characterize Beat writing. Cassady is the source for a technique of expression that fundamentally subverted calculated choice and revision of words, a technique which the Beats saw as a means of opposing a calculating and regimented society. In creating an unrevised and spontaneous art, they believed that one declared his personal freedom in the very forms and structures he chose.

Ginsberg spent the year at Columbia, but Cassady had returned to his native Denver by March 1947, and that summer Kerouac and Ginsberg joined him. But already the relationship between Ginsberg and Cassady had foundered, and in frustration Ginsberg dropped out of Columbia once more and took a merchant ship to Africa and back. He spent the rest of the fall working at various jobs in Paterson, none of which he could satisfy for more than a few weeks. By winter he had moved to an apartment in East Harlem, where he lingered for several harrowing lonely months, almost succumbing to breakdown from the anxieties of his wayward career, the deepening mental illness of his mother, and the dead end he had reached in his emotional life. Cassady wrote in April that he was married and about to be a parent; Ginsberg felt himself pushed to his edge. Over the next few months he worked part-time as a file clerk and spent the rest of his time alone, reading Blake and St. John of the Cross. On one such afternoon, while reading "Songs of Experience" by Blake and masturbating, Ginsberg experienced his first vision, a feeling that a voice spoke from outside his window and recited first Blake's "Ah, Sunflower" and then "The Sick Rose." Ginsberg could see himself in

both poems, but the voice seemed to suggest that he was not alone in his misery, that it was the condition of life itself. The vision excited him; it affirmed the reality of a spiritual life and made him feel that he was now part of the visionary tradition. That fall he read widely in mysticism and the occult, religious history—anything pertaining to the phenomena of vision—and jubilantly harangued his friends with the mystical lore he was gathering. For Ginsberg there was something deliciously bizarre about visions and he was ecstatic to have had his own experience of one. It was an important experience for the poet because it allowed him a glimpse into realms beyond the material world; it expanded the range of his thinking and gave his poetry a new vantage from which to criticize the status quo as a heathen age and hold up to it the notion of real spiritual comfort. Although Kerouac found his friend frenzied and hysterical and feared at times for his sanity in these nights of raging and preaching, he was himself experiencing a kind of spiritual conversion similar to Ginsberg's. Both writers had come to the realization that rebellion took many forms, but religious rebellion was perhaps the profoundest gesture of the artist. In the next several years Ginsberg and Kerouac embraced Buddhism as their faith and so turned their backs on Western gods as a final rejection of the state of their culture.

After many months of brooding on the meaning of his vision in East Harlem, Ginsberg finally interpreted it as a lesson in pity. The vision had occurred at a time when he felt empty, hopeless, unable to pity himself. The two poems the voice recited depicted a world of mortality in which each life throbbed with pain and died but then moved into another realm, larger, immortal, good. Ginsberg decided that because he had worn out his own self-pity, the voice interceded to enlarge his vision to an empathy for the pains of all life, including his own. Once his self-pity had ended, Ginsberg felt part of a large immortal harmony of the spirit. The isolation he had suffered came largely from feelings of rejection as a confessed homosexual and as a Jew. In later life, Kerouac's mother, Gabrielle, would ban Ginsberg from her household for these very reasons, often keeping her son from him for months at a time. Ginsberg particularly felt the pain of these separations, but the vision now showed him the sterility of mere personal anguish. He was liberated from the mental torture of his situation and felt himself partner with the visionary poets he had studied for the past several years.

Jack Kerouac, Allen Ginsberg, Peter Orlovsky, Gregory Corso, and Lafcadio Orlovsky in Mexico City, 1956 (courtesy of Allen Ginsberg)

He concluded that the pain of one's own ego was not, finally, the subject for true poetry, which, rather, must surrender the merely personal to a vision of self with others. In the classroom, however, poetry was presented as the lyric of individual subjectivity, a language of complaint and self-analysis. One could indeed write a poetry of suffering and disgust, making one's self the litmus of pain, but the visionary poets had achieved a religious transcendence from their individual plights and found a language that incorporated the suffering and redemption of the many; it was this lyric empathy that raised their language to the level of exalted poetry. The self was still the source of the poem, but the self as emblem of the larger human reality politicized the poem and created an adversary relationship with whatever force or system ran counter to the unity of this self and its company. In these ways the poem became much more than

a vehicle for revealing the isolation of the individual in the modern world. In this new form of poem Ginsberg could still express his own pathos but raise the argument to its ethical plane and seek redress of much broader human grievance: the poem could serve both as his own lyric deliverance and as the testament of the plight of others. When this balance of elements cohered finally in his imagination, Ginsberg could then draft one of the most resonant and revitalizing lyric poems of the century, *Howl.* But before that could happen, several other lessons were required to be learned, with pain and considerable courage.

In 1949 Ginsberg left the isolation of his East Harlem apartment and moved to downtown Manhattan, living on a meager salary from part-time jobs. Some of Burroughs's old friends of the drug trade began sharing Ginsberg's apartment, particularly Herbert Huncke, who first coined the term

Allen Ginsberg, Berkeley Hills, California, 1956 (photo by Peter Orlovsky)

"beat" and who had impressed Ginsberg as the New York street version of Neal Cassady: utterly outside the pale of middle-class life, a junkie, burglar, con man, he survived in the same world as others but shared none of their values or beliefs. Ginsberg befriended him and began writing poems that, in John Tytell's estimation, mythologized his life as much as Kerouac and Holmes had made myths of Cassady's. Huncke was a version of Ginsberg's shrouded stranger, one who had passed beyond the final barriers of the moral realm. Huncke and his friends began using Ginsberg's apartment as a cache for stolen property, which soon led to a police bust. Not even the deans of Columbia could save Ginsberg from this scrape, but one did intervene to gain him a plea of mental distress and he was sent to the New York State Psychiatric Institute for "rehabilitation." There he met Carl Solomon, to whom he dedicated *Howl* and who challenged Ginsberg's remaining academic assumptions about poetry from the start of their friendship. Solomon deepened Ginsberg's understanding of the political resistance inherent in the contemporary poem and cited many writers of both fiction and verse who had become the exiled prophets and seers of their nations. Solomon made their trespasses against the social order virtues of their experimental writings. The context of their dialogues reinforced Solomon's words: they convened in the dayrooms of an asylum, two writers who had stepped one foot beyond the social fringe and who now found themselves incarcerated under the euphemism of rehabilitation. After eight months of incarceration Ginsberg was released and returned to Paterson, where he wrote and held a variety of part-time menial jobs. With his reeducation almost complete, he could draft a letter to his esteemed neighbor, William Carlos Williams, with a measure of confidence, and he enclosed several of the poems he had written since 1948. This letter, the nine poems he enclosed, and several other verses form the text of *The Gates of Wrath*, misplaced for many years and published only after Bob Dylan discovered it among his papers in 1968.

The Gates of Wrath (1972) is an accurate summation of Ginsberg's experience and poetic technique up to 1952 and shows him struggling through his emotional disappointments; his painful desire for Neal Cassady (expressed in the separately entitled "Earlier Poems," where, as he says in his afterword, he kept the gender of his lover "secret"); his search for ways to describe his dark other, the shrouded stranger, as well as the visions he was experiencing from 1948 on. But this very

brief book is nonetheless a romantic encyclopedia of youthful passions, all pitched into orthodox meters and rhymes acquired from such popular classroom texts as Sir Herbert J. C. Grierson's *Metaphysical Lyrics and Poems of the Seventeenth Century*. Ginsberg's ear was so delicately tuned to the conversational rhythms of American speech that he was unable to sustain the syncopation of British meters; his lines moved jerkily between the rhythms of British and American dialects. When Williams examined the poems, he responded delicately by saying, "In this mode perfection is basic." Williams might well have despaired for Ginsberg, thinking the young poet's orthodoxy followed Eliot's return to tradition. Ginsberg immediately relaxed his style into the more spontaneous mode Kerouac had been teaching him, which Ginsberg called "speedworthy," to suggest both the rapidity of composition and the fact that the poems were composed under the accelerating influence of the drug Benzedrine, or speed. The new texts would make up his second published book of poems, *Empty Mirror*, which appeared in 1961.

The basic themes of *The Gates of Wrath* are passionate love and the divided self. Ginsberg is the bard of experience, to use Blake's psychology, and offers us revelations of the fallen world beyond Eden. Love, especially the love Cassady promised him, is the lost innocence suffered in poems scattered through the book, such as "A Western Ballad" and "Dakar Doldrums"; another sort of love, equally passionate and innocent, is felt for Jack Kerouac, who stimulates the first "bop" versifying in these poems, particularly the happy nonsense of "Bop Lyrics," "Fie My Fum," and "Pull My Daisy." These poems inspired by Kerouac mirror satirically the much esteemed well-wrought poem by offering as tight a composition of rhyme and meter but a language that deflates sense or overturns it altogether, as in "Pull My Daisy":

> Pull my daisy
> tip my cup
> all my doors are open
> Cut my thoughts
> for coconuts
> all my eggs are broken
> Jack my Arden
> gate my shades
> woe my road is spoken
> Silk my garden
> rose my days
> now my prayers awaken

Ginsberg's revised typescripts for the first page of the first and fifth drafts of Howl *(by permission of Allen Ginsberg)*

1

```
                          HOWL
                           for
                       Carl Solomon
```

I saw the best minds of my generation destroyed by mad-
        ness, starving hysterical naked,
dragging themselves through the negro streets at dawn
        looking for an angry fix,
angelheaded hipsters burning for the ancient heavenly
        connection to the starry dynamo in the machinery
        of night,
who poverty and tatters and hollow-eyed and high sat up
        smoking in the supernatural darkness of cold-
        water flats floating across the tops of cities
        contemplating jazz,
who bared their brains to heaven under the El and saw
        Mohammedan angels staggering on tenement roofs
        illuminated,
who ~~appeared~~ Covered in unshaven rooms in underwear burning
        their money in wastebaskets amid the rubbish
        of memorable Berkeley manifestoes listening to
        the Terror through the wall,
who got busted in their pubic beards returning through Laredo
        with a belt of marijuana for New York,

The meter here is of nursery rhymes, evocative of innocence as well as of harsh adult irony; the technique was lifted from jazz to bop solos, where melodic puns on familiar tunes were woven into complex tonal collages. The effortless spontaneity is essential to the effect of these bop poems; the casual wit is in mockery of the set form. Bob Dylan would later master a more subtle use of "spontaneous" song in the mid 1960s, creating in "Subterranean Homesick Blues" a classic of the form.

The theme of the divided self takes up most of the poems of the volume: they begin with the rueful lyric "Sweet Levinsky," the name Kerouac gave to Ginsberg in his first novel, *The Town & the City* (1950). After reading the manuscript of the novel, Ginsberg was exhilarated to find his portrait there but disappointed that he fell far short of the heroic poet thus depicted. He felt he had made little progress in his life compared to the work of his friends. "Sweet Levinsky" gently chides the figure of Kerouac's creation, who is addressed as though a puppet or caricature, not the poet himself. The divisions of self widen in the youthfully morbid "Complaint of the Skeleton to Time," derivative of English graveyard songs and laments. Self-pity of this kind abounds in the volume, but there is more to the poems that build up the image of the shrouded stranger. In "Please Open the Window and Let Me In," an early version of the theme, the hooded other self begs to be admitted to shelter from his graveyard realm. He is the buried Reichian inner self, haunting the bedrooms of the sleeping like Hamlet's ghost, crying for his just revenge. ("Who is the hungry mocker of the maze, And haggard hate-ghost, hanging by the door"). The ethos of the 1950s had so denied the inner life of instinct and emotions, the poet suggests, it had moldered in a grave of social inhibitions. Now a figure much like the bandaged mummies of contemporary horror movies slouched its way to the waking world to demand love. There follows the only metrically perfected poem of the book, "The Shrouded Stranger," with its taunting invitation to make love to this embodiment of all that society rejects. Ginsberg happens here upon one of his most effective devices: the abrupt juxtaposition of pastoral and industrial images in language that flows despite its freight of contrasts. Against the poisoned industrial landscape a cry of love erupts; the tender emotion of love devolves to sex ("I give my body to an old gas tank") as images of innocence are perverted by a contagion of fumes and smokestacks, waste and neglect. The technique is again managed in "Ode to the Setting Sun," another graveyard poem in which the industrial New Jersey landscape figures importantly; it is an interesting forerunner to the lyric masterpiece "Sunflower Sutra" (collected in *Howl and Other Poems*), in which Ginsberg finally answers the voice at his East Harlem window of 1948 and gives back a poem as exquisite as Blake's simple lament.

In sum, *The Gates of Wrath* is an interesting commentary on the poet's education in America at the mid century. It is ironic that his apprenticeship should exclude any example of the American tradition in his imitations. The poems are faithful copies of sixteenth- and seventeenth-century English lyric models, with considerable attention paid to John Donne and Andrew Marvell. Orthodox versification could do Ginsberg no harm, but the difficulty of acquiring an American verse style lay ahead of him, and he advanced to it with painful digression and many anxious years of trial and failure. In an excellent essay on Ginsberg's career entitled "Bound Each to Each," Diane Middlebrook comments that *The Gates of Wrath* represents "the stage of poetic slavery. Dependence in Ginsberg's early poetry is not merely dependence on older poets, but dependence on a few talismanic words which he often gives the emphasis of rhyme position in a stanza." But she adds that Ginsberg describes his technique of writing now (1974) "as a complete abandonment of the sense of structure which dominates *The Gates of Wrath*."

In the introduction to the Totem/Corinth edition of *Empty Mirror* (1961), William Carlos Williams remarked that "This young Jewish boy, already not so young anymore, has recognized something that has escaped most of the modern age, he has found that man is lost in the world of his own head." It is remarkable praise from a poet who wrote an epic with the idea of exploring "the resemblance between the mind of modern man and a city," as Williams wrote in his preface to *Paterson*. Williams was jubilant over Ginsberg's book, in which he found evidence that his own ideas about poetry were in good hands with the next generation of poets. "The lines," he said of Ginsberg's poetry, "have an infinite variety, perfectly regular, they are all alike and yet none is like the other." One of the most interesting poems of the book is "Hymn," not so much for its sentiment, which is sophomoric gloom and doom, but rhythmically and typographically it is the precise model of *Howl*, even to its paragraphs of indented language heaved out as single gasps of breath. The language itself, however, is muddy and vague, the images too entangled to affect the reader. It is remarkable how well dis-

Front cover for Ginsberg's first book, which has remained one of the best-selling volumes of American verse since its publication in 1956

ciplined the poet is in writing his long masterpiece *Howl* when compared to the amateurish lyricism of "Hymn." Many of the poems of *Empty Mirror* are imagistic miniatures and are conscious imitations of Williams's early style. But they all advance the theme of a young man's alienation in society and of his efforts to escape the pain of loneliness through drugs, sex, and art. Typical of the pervasive morbidity is this brief poem "Sunset":

> The whole blear world
> of smoke and twisted steel
> around my head in a railroad
> car, and my mind wandering
> past the rust into futurity:
> I saw the sun go down
> in a carnal and primeval
> world, leaving darkness
> to cover my railroad train
> because the other side of the
> world was waiting for dawn.

Ginsberg seems to struggle with the imagist framework; it was too restrictive for the range of language he wanted to use. These short poems do not seem to contain themselves as firmly as did Williams's poems but read instead like canceled sections of a longer ongoing work. These are flashes from a continuum of lyric speech, not the well-crafted cameo lyric that stood completely on its own. "A Poem on America" is a fragment of imagistic language that is possibly the earliest version of Ginsberg's longer, celebrated satire "America," collected in *Howl and Other Poems*. Another early poem, "Paterson," written in 1949, shows distinct signs of poetic maturity and is cast in the long sinuous lines of his later long poems. It rages in the tone of *Howl* against his lonely life in Paterson after release from the psychiatric hospital and erupts with all the key words of the Beat vocabulary: "mad," "Marijuana," "Peyote," "suffering," "screaming and dancing," "blood," "ecstasy," and so on. The final poem of *Empty Mirror* is a second version of the earlier masterpiece in *Gates of Wrath* and is also titled "The Shrouded Stranger," written in four parts and in a short measure of two stresses per line, with heavy alliteration. Commenting on Ginsberg in his book *Out of the Vietnam Vortex: A Study of Poets and Poetry Against the War* (1974), James Messman observed that *The Empty Mirror* "is the volume in which [Ginsberg] is busy discovering the enemy. It is the one volume of Ginsberg's poems that is not 'anti-war.' "

The entire volume is fraught with the terrifying visions and dreams Ginsberg was having in his apartment in East Harlem. "The Trembling of the Veil" is addressed to the window where his first vision occurred, from which he now gazes at trees that "seemed like/organisms on the moon." They wriggle "Like a green/hairy protuberance." A dream poem of 1948, "A Meaningless Institution," shows the poet brooding on his mother's incarceration in the asylum and here envisions himself in another dreaded hospital where all the socially unfit are kept. It is, as Marianne Moore complained in a review, a very morbid book, and yet it is unmistakably the work of a great poet early in his career. Crude as the poems may be, the articulation of emotion is sure and aggressive, never flat or incompetent. The intelligence behind these slight lyrics is strong and consistent in its attention to facts, details, little surprising perceptions that would mature into the basic themes of Ginsberg's major work.

In 1952 Ginsberg experienced his first encouragement from the publishing world: *New Directions,* James Laughlin's prestigious annual anthology of contemporary writing, accepted several of his prose poems for publication a year later.

The poems bore the unmistakable influence of Kerouac, who was now in his most prolific period (1951-1956) and who preached a method of high-speed composition from undirected thought processes. Ginsberg had broken out of his old tightly measured forms and had begun experimenting with the wide-open techniques of his friend. Kerouac had become so adept at his own style of unpremeditated composition that he began using rolls of paper on his typewriter to eliminate having to insert individual sheets. Ginsberg's poetic was still tentative, but the new method allowed him more room for spontaneous verbal experiments and more daring with words and paralogical systems of imagery. By now Williams could write to him with enthusiastic support, and on several occasions the older poet made efforts to have Ginsberg's manuscripts published. But publishers routinely refused his work; the reign of orthodoxy forced Ginsberg to look for experimental magazines and finally goaded him to open rebellion by even more extreme experiments with verse language and open form. As a signal of his support, Williams inserted two of Ginsberg's letters into the fourth book of *Paterson*, published in 1951. But by 1953 Ginsberg had had only three poems published in a commercial journal. He was fictionalized in several of Kerouac's published books, was a major figure in his friend John Clellon Holmes's novel *Go*, knew the experimental writers of his day on the most intimate terms, but poetry editors seemed the last to give in to the literary revolution afoot. Over the next two years, only three more poems appeared in print, in *Variegation* and *Voices*, obscure journals with little circulation.

The dreary life of part-time jobs continued throughout 1952 and into 1953, and Ginsberg felt all the more desolate since both Cassady and Kerouac were on the West Coast for much of that time. Ginsberg seems not to have written much new material, but when Kerouac returned to New York he brought with him his contagious literary energy and their old fellowship was resumed. On 14 May 1953, Ginsberg wrote a very long letter to Cassady in California telling him of his latest interest: Chinese painting. He had begun spending his free time at the New York Public Library looking over volumes of Asiatic art and was now branching out to "reading a little about their mystique and religions which I never did from a realistic standpoint before. Most of that Buddhist writing you see is not interesting, vague, etc because it has no context for us—but if you begin to get a clear idea of the various religions, the various dynasties and epochs

of art and messianism and spiritual waves of hippness, so to speak, you begin to see the vastitude and intelligence of the yellow men, and you understand a lot of new mind and eyeball kicks, I am working eastward from Japan and have begun to familiarize myself with Zen Buddhism thru a book (Philosophical Library Pub.) by one D. T. Suzuki. . . ." Curiously enough, Kerouac himself had begun reading by chance *The Life of the Buddha* by Ashuagosa and discovered his own deep affinity for Zen religion. Both writers had separately happened upon a new religion that excited them because of its very non-Western principles, and because it seemed rooted in a realm beyond war and aggression, cause and effect, greed and regimentation. It was a religion that seemed to encourage the very sorts of mental play they practiced in their art, but which now offered spiritual justification for it as well.

For the next several months Ginsberg's letters to Cassady allude to his expanding interest in Zen literature, and on 23 June 1953, he suddenly announces he has completed a new poem entitled "The Green Automobile," in which, he says, he is "beginning to explore some of the uncharted verbal rhetorical seas that Jack (& yrself) sail in." After *Empty Mirror*, with its imagistic reductions of language to "bare bones," he tells Cassady he is now attempting "to build up a modern contemporary metaphorical yak-poem, using the kind of weaving original rhythms that Jack does in his prose, and the lush imagery. I been dry too long." The poem expresses Ginsberg's desire to escape New York and to visit Cassady and his family, which they had been entreating him to do for the past several years. The green automobile, itself a brilliant synthesis of pastoral and industrial symbols, is his "vehicle," he says in the poem, for the imagination, an image on which to build a wobbly structure of fantasy, assertion, narrative, digressive argument all meant to convey as whimsically as possible the need to travel and join old friends. The metaphor of the automobile is perfectly conceived, at once the central symbol of restless postwar Americans traveling on their vacations and equally the symbol of technology, prosperity, and free will. The poet treats his metaphor with complex humor and irony but never mocks his invention or deflates its importance. It is the first time that Ginsberg springs out of self-conscious artistry and makes his language seem effortlessly brilliant commentary. The easy grandiloquence and slang are the legacies from Kerouac, but the form, a series of thirty-four staggered four-line stanzas, is taken directly from the late poems of Williams. The stanzas give the poem its visual "beat" or tempo, but the language seems to rush in and out of its lattice work like a solo variation. The poem may lack the extreme verve and daring to be found in *Howl* and *Kaddish*, but "The Green Automobile" expresses profound imaginative pleasure in elevating a common object to a momentary symbol of flight and satisfaction only to restore it to the plain sight of ordinary reality:

We will go riding
over the Rockies,
we'll go on riding
all night long until
dawn,

then back to your railroad, the SP
your house and your children
and broken leg destiny
you'll ride down the
plains

in the morning: and back
to my visions, my office
and eastern apartment
I'll return to New
York.

The poem was published six years later in *Mattachine Review* and included in *Reality Sandwiches: 1953-1960*, published in 1963.

By the summer of 1953 New York had become an unbearably lonely city for Ginsberg. The urban life-style had worn thin; his isolation was complete after his friend Holmes departed for Connecticut; only Kerouac remained of the original circle of friends. Ginsberg had already decided he would leave for California by December of the year, and Kerouac planned to join him the following January. Ginsberg's letters to Carolyn and Neal Cassady became more and more hectic with anticipation of travel. Although he had taken a ship to Africa and in 1951 traveled to western Mexico briefly, he had not really ventured out on his own yet. Another old Columbia friend of Kerouac and Ginsberg, Lucien Carr, had long before instructed him in the necessity of keeping notebooks, which he then began using, but not with the fanatic regularity of Kerouac. Ginsberg's notebooks, later edited and published as *Journals: Early Fifties-Early Sixties* (1977) and *Indian Journals: March 1962-May 1963* (1970), were less ordered and complete than his friend's, and even during the high excitement of his sojourn in the Yucatán, his entries are rather flat or fragmentary. The letters he wrote to Kerouac and to Cassady (collected in the 1977 volume *As Ever: The Collected Correspondence of Allen Ginsberg & Neal Cassady*) during the same trip, by contrast, are marvelous and intricate commentaries on his adventures: it seems clear that unless he was composing drafts of poems, Ginsberg chafed at the time-consuming task of filling up logs with his daily activities.

The trip to California by way of Cuba and Mexico would provide the final lessons in the making of a poet. The painful solitude of the city changed into a solitude of self-knowing as he lingered on for many weeks at the cocoa plantation of his friend Karena Shields, an actress who once played Jane in the Tarzan movies, who was now an accomplished archaeologist writing about the Mayan ruins at Palenque. After a brief stay in Havana, Ginsberg wandered through Mérida and then to the jungles of Chiapas, where Shields invited him to stay at her finca at Palenque as long as he wished. Ginsberg's letters are filled with the paradisal details of his tropical adventure. He idled away his afternoons playing hollow log drums or fished out of the nearby streams; he helped the local *indios* wash cocoa berries in long vats. At one point, he advanced deeper into the jungles of Chiapas to investigate reports of a volcanic eruption and earthquakes. Posing as a reporter in Yajalón, he organized a party to climb Mt. Acavalna to determine if an eruption were in progress. At the top, he had the *indios* swear out a report of safe condition and returned to the village a hero. The next morning, a new group assembled at his house and requested that he accompany them to locate a legendary cave on the side of the mountain, which he promptly did. The letters to Cassady and Kerouac are filled with the mock heroics of his adventure: Ginsberg walking ceremoniously behind the *indios* in their white tunics and pants as they slashed away the underbrush to make him a path. After sighting the cave, which Ginsberg later described as being as large as St. James Cathedral, he reported that he believed he was the first white man ever to enter it. After exploring it, he returned a second time a hero, bearing evidence of a cave that had long ago become a legend. He returned to the finca once more, each week putting off his trip to California. It was a time of pleasurable meditation, of blissful and creative solitude, and he enriched himself on his new surroundings. He seemed to enjoy life best in a foreign country. Kerouac was a domestic migrant, a freeway gypsy most of his life; but Ginsberg became a world traveler who could later make his residence in the Arctic nearly as well as he did in Japan, or India, or Morocco. He thrived on the rootlessness of foreign residence; he was at leisure in those long sojourns around the world, and they inspired him to write longer and longer verse narratives and commentaries based upon his experiences. Travel gave plot to his art, just as it did on his first long voyage out in Mexico.

Reality Sandwiches starts with the poems of this travel, including "Havana, 1953" and his first real masterpiece, the leisurely diaristic poem "Siesta in Xbalba," written in 1954, which recounts events from the several months of his stay at Shields's finca. It departs from all that he had written before, for the attention now ranges beyond the self to take in his surroundings, the thinking processes they evoke, accounts of his journeys and of Chiapas life, all in the freely changing meter of conversation and in a vocabulary that is balanced between verse precision and the leisured generality of meditation. Ginsberg inches a step or two beyond the rolling measure of his friend Williams, who had labored several decades to perfect the usable metric, a "variable foot," as he called it. Ginsberg writes as fluidly as his master, and there emerges from the language the emblem of an artist reaching beyond his culture for sustenance and renewal. The tropical jungles were his first glimpse at life prior to an industrial age: he had fallen back many centuries into a pastoral and primal age, and it awoke in him levels of awareness he had only vaguely felt in his readings of Zen literature, as "Siesta in Xbalba" suggests:

> ---One could pass valuable months
> and years perhaps a lifetime
> doing nothing but lying in a hammock
> reading prose with the white doves
>   copulating underneath
> and monkeys barking in the interior
>   of the mountain
> and I have succumbed to this
>   temptation---

Suddenly this America seemed as old as Greece, but even more mysterious; the Mayan past was as inscrutable and profound as the deep pasts of China and Japan, and he murmured the names of the ancient Mayan cities as though they were mantras. Here is the old America, lying beneath the landscape of towers to the north;

> Pale Uxmal,
>   unhistoric, like a dream,
> Tuluum shimmering on the coast in ruins;

> Chichen Itza naked
>   constructed on a plain;
> Palenque, broken chapels in the green
>   basement of a mount;
> lone Kabah by the highway;
>   Piedras Negras buried again
> by dark archaeologists;
>   Yaxchilan
> resurrected in the wild,
> and all the limbo of Xbalba still unknown--

>   floors under the roofcomb of
>   branch,

> foundation to ornament
>   tumbled to the flowers,
> pyramids and stairways
>   raced with vine,
> limestone corbels
>   down in the river of trees,
> pillars and corridors
>   sunken under the flood of
> years;

> Time's slow wall overtopping
>   all that firmament of mind,
> as if a shining waterfall of leaves and rain
> were built down solid from the endless sky
>   through which no thought can
>   pass.

The adventure up the mountain to find the cave is cast in the language of verse; a casual event precipitates a mythic atmosphere for this poet only weeks away from his barren routines in New York:

> I alone know the great crystal door
>   to the House of Night,
> a legend of centuries
>   I and a few Indians.

> And had I mules and money I could find
>   the Cave of Amber
> and the Cave of Gold
>   rumored of the cliffs of Tumbala.

The irony of "Siesta in Xbalba" is that it is a celebration in the mode of Whitman, but not of neo-America. Here a poet reaches to the Indian past that is the root of America; he feels here the goad to seek out other gods of the ancient world, other versions of the primordial Buddha. Here is a true "Passage to India," the India of America's origins, which the poet has now bound himself to.

Mere travel has been transformed into religious pilgrimage in "Siesta in Xbalba":

> There is a god
> dying in America
> already created
> in the imagination of men
> made palpable
> for adoration;
> there is an inner
> anterior image
> of divinity
> beckoning me out
> to pilgrimage.
>
> O future, unimaginable God.

While Ginsberg lingered in Chiapas, Kerouac arrived at the Cassady household and preached his newfound Buddhism; Neal Cassady countered with visions received from the writings of the Virginia mystic Edgar Cayce. By then the evenings were filled with talk of new religious alternatives, new faiths that offered relief and escape from the materialism of the age. By April 1954, however, Kerouac tired of such domesticity and left to write in North Carolina, just days before Ginsberg arrived at the Cassadys' home in San Francisco. Ginsberg came only to find his former lover now a patriarch with wife, children, bills, and worries; the bohemian edge of his life seemed worn away by his domestic concerns. Ginsberg rekindled Cassady's affection, but the arrangement ended abruptly when Cassady's wife, Carolyn, evicted Ginsberg and forced him back on his own in San Francisco. Relying on his earlier experiences, he found a lucrative job in marketing research, acquired a girl friend, kept a small apartment in Berkeley, and settled down for a year of domestic comfort himself. By then all the Beats had dispersed to the corners of the nation to take up their own quiet lives. The nation seemed to molder in desperate fear of a communist conspiracy within the most powerful ranks of government and business; the McCarthy hearings were televised in spring 1954 and presented to the nation an orgy of confessions and painful disclosures of "un-American" acts. The stability of the Western way of life seemed threatened by great forces then beginning to reveal the depths of what appeared to be demonic motives and powers: the atomic age had unleashed the grim specter of world destruction; the cold war intensified the tension and world terror that gave the 1950s its often gloomy, colorless character; the disclosures of Nazi atrocities then filling the press and

books on the best-seller lists deepened the feeling that the West had perhaps suffered a general breakdown of beliefs and was now held together by a collective will to conform and regiment itself. To be beat then was only to be tired; the anger would erupt, however, within a year and draw the artistic forces of San Francisco into a clear coherence of rage, rebellion, and hunger for alternatives from the gray regime of the 1950s.

Ginsberg had felt isolated in New York; but in San Francisco the makings of artistic ferment were abundant. He was now part of a wide circle of writers all sharing his own feelings of frustration and sense of imminent breakthrough. The elder statesman of the writers was Kenneth Rexroth, who was the force drawing them together into a movement. A year of marketing research was all Ginsberg could take; he quit and lived for another six months on unemployment checks. During that summer, Kerouac was living in Mexico City in William Burroughs's former apartment house, writing his own free-form poetic sequence *Mexico City Blues* (1959), perhaps the most extreme instance of spontaneous, unrevised verse in American poetry. Before returning to San Francisco, he received from Ginsberg a long poem of his own, the best Kerouac had seen of Ginsberg's work, the clearest evidence that his friend had finally mastered the spontaneous method Kerouac had been preaching to him the last several years. Kerouac promptly titled it *Howl*, because it seemed to let out from some primal level of human consciousness the pent-up rage and frustrations of the inner being; the poem's lyric energy flowed from a primordial base as wild as the wolf's cry. *Howl* also struck Kerouac as the signal that a movement or literary epoch had now begun in San Francisco, with his friend at the very core of it. In October Ginsberg organized a poetry reading, the first of his career, at Six Gallery, where he and five other poets, Michael McClure, Gary Snyder, Kenneth Rexroth (acting the host), Philip Whalen, and Philip Lamantia, read before a capacity audience. When Ginsberg finished reciting *Howl*, literary history had been made. The audience felt itself transformed into an enclave, a new community within the drab masses of mid-century America. Ginsberg had leapt free of himself and become the voice of the artists and rebels of a generation and spoke for them until their plight and identity had been unforgettably illuminated. The Beat Generation had finally spoken its anger and contempt; the phenomenon of mild rebellion and bohemian fashion exploited by the media now vanished to reveal a significant literary revolution in the making. The literary movement was something more than a change in the methods of writing: it seemed to crack the twentieth century into halves: the Ur-America of the pre-World War II era and the streamlined, fully circuited complex of industrial America, with a generation now in bitter confusion over its own values and desires. Where other poets seemed capable of confessing only their most personal dilemmas, Ginsberg could voice the inner doubts of a broad spectrum of the young in the sinewy, roaming metric of Whitman, with a language sharply detailed and concrete and yet charged with abstract mappings of much complex history. The performance Ginsberg gave was uncanny, and the poem itself established his reputation as a major voice of the era.

At twenty-nine, and with only a few of his poems in print, he was now the author of a classic poem. Martha Rexroth, wife of the poet, immediately gathered together Ginsberg's available pieces and published them as *Howl for Carl Solomon* in a mimeographed and stapled edition of about fifty copies, given out to friends. This edition led to the larger selection of poems published in October 1956 by Lawrence Ferlinghetti, owner of the new City Lights Books and publisher of the Pocket Poets, a series of small paperback books of poems. *Howl and Other Poems* was only the fourth title of the series and was immediately a controversial success. The U.S. Customs and the San Francisco police seized the edition almost immediately and banned its further sale; a long court battle ensued with many testimonials taken on the merits of the work. It was then released and has since remained one of the best-selling books of poems in American literary history.

From the start of his writing career, Ginsberg had been going backward in tradition, not forward, to find the master who could galvanize his style and give him the root sense of his expression. From his academic contemporaries he seemed to learn only that they had retreated falsely into an English past; from Kerouac, he could perceive the necessity of freedom from all past conventions in order to make something new; he studied William Carlos Williams, Arthur Rimbaud, Herman Melville, William Blake, and finally found the source of his poetics in the boisterous, jubilant measure of Walt Whitman. *Howl* is written from margin to margin in the poetic of the long line, with all the verbiage heaped up against a constant rhythm of breath and racing pulse; it is a measure grounded in the rhythm of the poet's own body, not the mechanisms of a mathematical prosody. The intense compressions of language within the lines themselves are jointly the order of haiku language, which links thought almost by butting it together in elliptical chains, and the orderings of volume Ginsberg discovered in the paintings of Cézanne, where geometrical figures overlap to create a powerful sense of depth in the visual field. Whole series of interconnections between phrase elements are simply left out to cause powerful junctures to occur at a jolting pace. Almost the entire collection of *Howl and Other Poems* is given over to this new Whitmanesque measure; the print is spread wide through all but the last poems, which are earlier homages to Williams's more sculpted line. Williams wrote high praise of the poet's technique in his introduction to the volume. Ginsberg makes the reader sure of his poetic allegiance when he quotes Whitman at its outset: "Unscrew the locks from the doors!/Unscrew the doors themselves from their jambs!" And he dedicated the work to the three principal influences on his writing: to Kerouac, the "new Buddha of American prose"; to William Burroughs, whose peculiar surrealist satire of America appealed deeply to Ginsberg; and to Neal Cassady, the artist of high-speed talk, the master of casual, unstudied spoken meditation. Finally there was Carl Solomon, who showed Ginsberg how the new arts were the imaginative manifestos of artists and prophets, not performances of merely aesthetic sensibilities. The book is a composite of tradition as refashioned from old and new sources in order to force it forward into the second half of the century.

The opposite of "Siesta in Xbalba," *Howl* is the antitribute to America: it is a lamentation in long solemn exhalations. The typography of the poem scores how it is to be read: each margin line begins with a full breath which is then let out to its end in a string of conjoined phrases, series of apposites, interlocked prepositional phrases, densities of language that spring from the drawn breath out to a breathless end. It is the form of one who has come to his limits to say these things: they defy interruption, they demand absolute attention since these are a series of indictments. Part I begins by honoring the fallen, the victims of a conspiracy of forces that took down the best and brightest and threw them into the exile of urban America, to drugs, breakdown, social ostracism, who were turned into drifters, addicts, suicides. The victims are the very youth honored and celebrated by Whitman in "Song of Myself," the working young, the fresh new idealists of the nation, now persecuted and destroyed

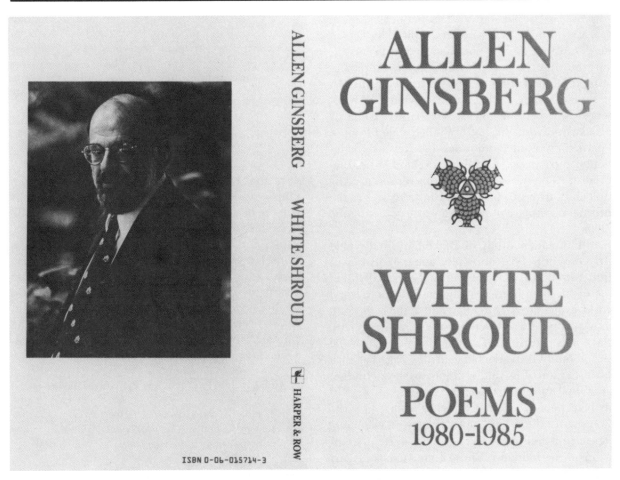

Dust jacket for Ginsberg's first collection of poems to be published by a major trade publisher

who bit detectives in the neck and shrieked
                    with delight in
policecars for committing no crime but
                    their own wild
cooking pederasty and intoxication . . .

The fallen are all the men and women Ginsberg
had known in the New York years, their lives cited
in tragic fragments of the poem, until by sheer
numbers they suggest the life of a whole generation
of Americans. The catalogue of details is factual,
accurate biography; even the Beats could not escape the confessional orgy that had taken over the
1950s, in which a thousand forms of guilt needed
to be vomited out in public forums, whether at the
House Un-American Activities Committee hearings, in the humor of Lenny Bruce, in the poetry
of Robert Lowell, Sylvia Plath, and others, or in
Beat writing: all these voices sought to escape intolerable knowledge they bore alone. *Howl* is a central document of the nation's need to confess: it

seeks to confess the sins of everyone, from the weak
who destroyed themselves to the strong who persecuted them. No one is simply and virtuously heroic in the opening part of the poem; all are
indictable in their various ways; all are sinners and
sinned against. The poem is a profound catharsis
of the conscience, in which all that is loathsome is
exposed: the image of this America that Ginsberg
creates is, as Williams promised in his introduction,
a hell, a modern pit of crushed souls and forlorn
citizens.

In Part II, written while under the influence
of peyote, he names the cause of this national victimization. It is no longer a segment of the population, or a system of ideas, necessarily; it is the
mind itself, the isolated rational functions of mind
that have made the American Eden a sulfurous hell
of industry, bureaucracy, and class structure.
America worshiped a demonic god of the dynamo,
here identified as the old Canaanite god Moloch to
whom children were regularly sacrificed, as they

were now in the postwar era. Ginsberg's symbolism was, according to Jane Kramer, inspired by "a peyote vision that . . . the poet had in San Francisco, staring . . . at the . . . Sir Francis Drake Hotel and being reminded of Moloch by the tower's grinning, mask-like facade." The sinister divinity of Ginsberg's vision becomes in Part II of "Howl" primarily a Blakean mythic image for a fallen state of mind. This is compounded of loveless indifference, judgmental puritanism, worldly pride, and brute materialism. The spiritual perversions represented by Moloch in turn produce what Ginsberg sees as the infernal nightmare of American society during the 1950s.

The patient study of Blake had finally paid off: Ginsberg could now fully understand his affinity with Blake, who had lived at the deep dividing line of Western history, at the end of the pastoral world stretching back to Eden and at the beginning of a new world created by the Enlightenment. Blake was the prophet of the doom world to be forged out of the rational faculty: he raged against the lost vision of mythic intuition, mystical glimpse, emotional fusion of thought. Ginsberg surveys in his own poem of human wreckage caused by the monism of rationalistic governance, with its merely logical functions of intellect as the sole resource of order in the human realm. All the victims of Part I suffered and died for their very expressions of the things in them that lay beyond the merely rational: their joy, sexual appetites, faith, hunger, despair caused them to be expelled from the republic of mere logic:

Moloch, whose mind is pure machinery! Mo-
                    loch whose blood is
        running money Moloch whose fingers
                            are ten armies!
        Moloch whose breast is a cannibal dy-
                    namo! Moloch whose
        ear is a smoking bomb!
Moloch whose eyes are a thousand blind win-
                    dows! Moloch whose
        skyscrapers stand in the long streets
                    like endless Jehovahs!
        Moloch whose factories dream and
                    croak in the fog!
        Moloch whose smokestacks and anten-
                    nae crown the cities!
Moloch whose love is endless oil and stone!
                    Moloch whose soul is
        electricity and banks! Moloch whose
                    fate is a cloud of sexless
        hydrogen! Moloch whose name is the

                        Mind!
. . . .
Moloch who entered my soul early! Mo-
                    loch in whom I am a
        consciousness without a body! Moloch
                    who frightened me
        out of my natural ecstasy! Moloch
                    whom I abandon!
        Wake up in Moloch! Light streaming
                    out of the sky!

Part III is an ecstatic tribute to Carl Solomon, Ginsberg's most immediate muse in the making of the poem and in the awareness necessary to write it. Solomon is hailed as the apostle of the victims' cause, the illuminator of their hidden ideology, himself a victim of the rational regime in America, discoursing in his cell on the underworld of art and the forms of its rebellion against this mad new god of the modern age. The fourth part, "Footnote to Howl," is a litany celebrating reintegration of the human being: its repetition of the word holy reverberates with its homonym, wholly:

Holy! Holy! Holy! Holy! Holy! Holy! Holy!
                    Holy! Holy!
    Holy! Holy! Holy! Holy! Holy! Holy!
    The world is holy! The soul is holy! The skin
                    is holy! . . .

All the disparate elements of the world sundered by the view of the cosmos as purely rational are here knit together again into sacred union; the tribute goes on to widen its reintegrating field to everything the poet's mind can name. The fourth seeks in vision to repair the damage catalogued in Part I, thus rounding to a close the whole four-part meditation.

The remaining poems of *Howl*, except for the brief last section of earlier poems, are permutations of the theme of innocent victimization and of the poet's epic sympathies for the forsaken realm of nature and man. "A Supermarket in California" is a jaunty salute to the poets of Ginsberg's selective tradition, a wry tribute to their Rabelaisian humanity and affectionate genius, set within the regimental metaphor of a supermarket with its surplus of uniform goods. Here too the Whitmanesque long line is indispensable in knitting together by connectives of grammar the endless data of the poet's opened sensibilities. He means to show by grammatical means the very ideology of community he envisions in meditation: the poetic heaps up language just as the argument advocates immersion into the life around the poet. Less inventive but of the same confident tone is "Transcription of Organ Music," which radiates well-being and pleasure in his art. The other masterpieces of the volume are his answer to Blake's lament for a sunflower, "Sunflower Sutra," and his satiric excoriation of Moloch, "America." "Sunflower Sutra" glimpses in the scraggly stalk beside the railroad track an emblem of all mortality, all nature cast adrift in the industrial age:

> Unholy battered old thing you were, my
>   sunflower O my soul,
>   I loved you then!
> The grime was no man's grime but death and
>   human
>   locomotives,
> all that dress of dust, that veil of darkened
>   railroad skin, that
> smog of cheek, that eyelid of black
> mis'ry, that sooty hand or phallus or
> protuberance of artificial worse-than-
>   dirt—
> industrial—modern—all that civ-
> ilization spotting your crazy gold-
>   en crown—

"America" is a dark parody of the patriotic testimonials heard often in the 1950s, in which the speaker inverts all the usual praise into blame. The poem is funny, barbed, precise in its jabs at current prejudices and nationalistic hubris; it is the very obverse of the ruling sentiment of his time and jibes well with the humor of such other iconoclasts as Lenny Bruce and William Burroughs. "In the Baggage Room at Greyhound" rounds out the collection with its sensitive record of weary travelers departing from a dreary bus station into the America Kerouac and Cassady rushed across with frantic emotions. The baggage room is a heap of soulless possessions destined for meaningless cities. All the travel seems without purport or pilgrimage: mere movement, displacement, transfer as part of the general drift of the age.

Howl and Other Poems was Ginsberg's first book and, ironically, also his best: it leaps to the mastery of a poetic for that moment's history: the catalogues, the revived Whitmanesque measure, the bleeding sensibility of the poet, the magnitude of his sympathies that far exceed any symbolized by the Statue of Liberty, give the book its yolk of content. Ginsberg's power to address the ills of the 1950s was such as to move many of his audience to take seriously their own rebellious emotions. The volume seems one of the very few in American literature to convey such a fervor of moral anger

that it could leap the bounds of literature and affect history. Although the United States has been accused often by its writers of being a nation of sheep, *Howl and Other Poems* is a singular instance of the American talking back to his country in strident language that left wounds on the national psyche. Critical response to *Howl and Other Poems* ranged from praise to vilification. In looking back at it in 1961, James Dickey observed irritably that "*Howl* is the skin of Rimbaud's *Une Saison en Enfer* thrown over the conventional maunderings of one style of American adolescent." In his book *The Poem in Its Skin,* published in 1968, Paul Carroll called *Howl and Other Poems* "one of the milestones of the generation." In *The Beat Generation,* Bruce Cook remarked that "The poet of 'Howl' and 'Kaddish' was not just a new hero to the young, but a new *kind* of hero [writing] the very antithesis of the dry, precise, and calculated verse of the academic poets."

From the moment its first audience heard the chief poem of the book *Howl* in Six Gallery to now, Ginsberg has maintained the almost messianic charisma of a poet-politician, whose only congress consists of readers of contemporary poetry, a decidedly young, college-educated segment of the population, but a powerful constituency containing a large proportion of the professional and educational elite in the nation. Ginsberg's complaints voiced the depths of anger and confusion of the young middle class, just as Robert Lowell had spoken for an older middle class equally bewildered by the postwar era; Frank O'Hara and Charles Olson seemed most potent to smaller, more sophisticated sects of artists and thinkers. Ginsberg's language was the most direct of these major voices and reached the broadest, most diversified audience. Part of its appeal is the fact that it was the subject of a landmark obscenity trial. In 1957 its publisher, Lawrence Ferlinghetti, was charged under a California statute with disseminating "indecent writings." Ferlinghetti was defended gratis in the case by J. W. Ehrlich, San Francisco's most celebrated criminal lawyer. The trial centered upon the use in "Howl" of supposedly obscene words and images. Among witnesses for the defense were Mark Schorer, Walter Van Tilburg Clark, and Kenneth Rexroth, the latter testifying that "Howl" "is probably the most remarkable single poem published by a young man since the second war." Finally presiding judge Clayton W. Horn ruled that Ginsberg's poem was not obscene, stating that true freedom of speech and of the press depended upon an individual author's right to "express his thoughts . . . in his own words."

The frequency of Ginsberg's publications picked up drastically after 1956, but some five years would pass before his second major book, *Kaddish and Other Poems: 1958-1960* (1961), would be published. Following publication of *Howl*, Ginsberg had enrolled briefly to study Buddhism at the University of California at Berkeley but quit shortly after and resumed his Beat life-style with the other San Francisco writers. The San Francisco Poetry Renaissance was in full swing and had generated its own special style of poetry reading, with dramatic recitation by the poet often to the accompaniment of jazz music in an attempt to declare the affinities of poetry with the other innovative arts of the mid century: with jazz, with abstract-expressionist painting, and with improvised theater. The San Francisco Beat life-style aimed at being the exact reverse of normal middle-class life: it was nocturnal, hedonistic, spiritually exotic, integrated with blacks, sympathetic to open marriage and given at times to sexual orgies, fonder of drugs than alcohol (although the last Beat preference was certainly fraught with exceptions, especially in the life of Kerouac). Ginsberg experimented widely with drugs during the late 1950s and early 1960s, which he writes about in the later poems of *Kaddish*, but justified the experiences as efforts to widen the dangerously narrow and confined consciousness of the times. This was the next step in the evolution of Ginsberg's poetry: to explore the outer reaches of awareness by means of hallucinogens, particularly the newly discovered lysergic acid diethylamide, as well as peyote, mescaline, psilocybin, and the patent drugs used in pyschotherapy. The mind was an inner space to be explored as vigorously as the outer space of rocket science, then blooming into an industry under Eisenhower's administration. *Kaddish* continues the tone of lamentation and rage of *Howl* but advances to a theme of exploration of that part of mind ruled off and forgotten by mass culture.

But the key experience on which Ginsberg brooded was the death of his mother in 1956. With maturity and confidence, he had come to see her as the central martyr of America's demonic regime. The poem *Kaddish* reverses the Christ myth, for here a son laments the crucifixion of his mother. He had doubted her mind and passions in his youth, but now he believed in her visions and saw in her lonely, miserable life the slow death by persecution for believing in forbidden dreams, alternative ideologies, working-class utopias. It was a profound shock to his imagination to find that he had howled in grief for all the dying young of

America, when in fact his own mother should die at the very moment of his lamentation, the prime example of political persecution. Now he must exorcise her ghost from his pained conscience and celebrate his harried mother who had feared the state had wired her brain and monitored her every breath and motion. *Kaddish* is a howl for the most innocent victim; it no longer generalizes grief for the many but concentrates its dirge on one death in which the poet can see the struggle of all the rest. No kaddish, the Jewish burial rites, had been spoken over her death; the poet thus makes up his own to lay her spirit to rest.

Kaddish is twice as long as *Howl* and a more mature achievement. The fact, perhaps, that it came second to *Howl* diminished its reception, although it is a deeper and richer work. Ginsberg reached his technical limits in this long complex elegy, a form in which many American poets have found their genius and mastery of poetics. It is diversely structured, with the second part springing so far out of the normal bounds of verse structure as to merge verse into the genre of prose. Part IV is a visual creation of language, a typographical mosaic of desperate pity that swells and shrinks with pinpoint accuracy according to the emotion felt. The poet's mental process is fully recreated in the verse text, showing the fluidities of his grief, the mercurial identities of mother and son, the throb of memories surging up through his grief.

The poem opens with the poet announcing his preparations to write an elegy: he has listened to Ray Charles's blues-singing, read Shelley's elegy to Keats entitled *Adonais*, read the kaddish, after which he subtly begins the process of the elegy by first describing a walk through New York streets and in that rhythm allows memories and visions of his mother to take over the speaking voice. Part II has a fablelike plot of the son (twelve years old) attempting to rescue his mother from the fallen world she dreads so deeply, only to leave her at a friend's house and to return fearing he had abandoned her:

> Would she hide in her room and come
> out cheerful for breakfast? Or lock her door
> and stare thru the window for side-street
> spies? Listen at keyholes for Hitlerian invis-
> ible gas? Dream in a chair—or mock me,
> by—in front of a mirror, alone?

> 12 riding the bus at nite thru New
> Jersey, have left Naomi to Parcae in Lake-
> wood's haunted house—left to my own fate
> but—sunk in a seat—all violins broken—my

heart sore in my ribs—mind was empty—
Would she were safe in her coffin—

These autobiographic details recall other such memories, as in Edward Dahlberg's tale of a son and his mother, in *Bottom Dogs* (1930) and *From Flushing to Calvary* (1932), and the bitter, lonely lives of many American youths, lives as recorded by Thomas Wolfe and James T. Farrell, Sherwood Anderson, William Faulkner, Robert Frost, Edward Arlington Robinson, Mark Twain, Walt Whitman. Somehow for Ginsberg and these writers the family in America seemed to have disintegrated from the acidity of lives and circumstances, the forces that overpowered consciousness and wrought too much pain and sadness to allow them to know or even love each other. The poem goes on to narrate nights and weeks of terror for the child, who is losing his mother to madness:

> "Don't be afraid of me because I'm just coming back home from the mental hospital—I'm your mother."
> Poor love, lost—a fear—I lay there—Said, "I love you, Naomi,"—stiff, next to her arm. I would have cried, was this the comfortless lone union?—Nervous, and she got up soon.

The dinginess of their breakups and reunions is oppressive, a long unrelieved experience that is the goad of the Beat to find joy in any extreme, any edge away from the gray centers of an empty domesticity. Part II seems to record for all the Beats the terms by which they were made to rebel against their parents' way of life, against the ordained middle way of their social class. Kerouac knew much the same drab home life; Gregory Corso, uniquely, had been abandoned at birth and had lived much of his life in jail or on the streets and so felt freer of his past than did the others. The "Hymmnn" is a benediction spoken over the dead, but equally a benediction of the living as they pursue their forbidden pleasures, their deviations from the norm, their efforts to enlarge or enrich their lives. Part III establishes complete empathy with his mother's solitary hospital life, her visions, and her last hours. The grief is finally burst by anger in Part IV, where the poet confounds his sorrow with rage; the language weaves together the son's grief at abandonment with his rage against her illness and separation from him and in a seizure of details seems to recapitulate in flashes the images he had accumulated of her from childhood to maturity,

the whole of it rendered with surrealistic distortion, in which we can gauge the suffering of the poet as he remembers and transfigures her. Part V concerns the burial service, with crows flying over the Long Island skyline, the day cold, the sunlight dry and harsh, the service mocked by the cawing of scavenger birds. After witnessing a dramatization of *Kaddish* at a New York theater, the critic Catherine Hughes wrote in April 1972, "Allen Ginsberg's *Kaddish* is a cry of pain, a cry of remembrance, a cry of love, perhaps the finest poem of the Beat Generation." *Kaddish* was started in San Francisco, but Part IV of the poem was composed in Paris in 1958, the remainder in New York, where Ginsberg resumed residence in 1959. The bulk of it was composed under various hallucinogenic drugs—amphetamine injections, morphine, and Dexedrine—and Parts I and II were completed from one morning to the following evening. (Such was the frantic, drug-induced pace at which Kerouac composed most of his novels.) Paris was the setting of a number of the poems in the volume, and a new name, that of Peter Orlovsky—Ginsberg's lover whom he met and began living with in 1954—is frequently mentioned. Orlovsky filled the void left by Cassady; he and Ginsberg have lived together ever since 1954 in a relationship that can justifiably be called a marriage. The trip to Europe was planned as a long wayward excursion to Tangier, where William Burroughs was living. Jack Kerouac had gone ahead to the destination where he met Ginsberg and Orlovsky, and all shared the new manuscript of Burroughs's *Naked Lunch*, another of the essential Beat works, which Kerouac had titled. Kerouac left by April 1958 to tour Europe, and Ginsberg stayed on visiting the Mediterranean countries, finally ending up in Paris.

Europe was the older edge of the Western world, and it could only generate images of its inner conflicts and steady self-destruction, as in "Europe! Europe!," "At Apollinaire's Grave," "Death to Van Gogh's Ear." All are elegies and comport thematically with the collection's chief poem, *Kaddish*, for they bid adieu or pay graveside homage to spirits that are the emblems of noble suffering and stubborn struggle to make art. But these long poems are composed of much looser language; the poetics of *Howl* and *Kaddish* seems to have sagged to an almost haranguing pace; less exact images come to the poet's mind as he discourses roundly on his subject. He is entertaining, but there is more of the charm of a personality than of a mind burning to denounce his enemies or to raise the ghosts of heroes. The news of Sputnik's launching in 1958 spurred his "Rocket Poem" (written in Amsterdam at the end of his journey), which offers a satire on Western religion in a mocking space travelogue. Even here the ingenuity of his puns and fantasies on rocketing through the galaxy seems to creak a little from too conscious an effort. Once back in New York in 1959, Ginsberg found himself at the hub of the New York Greenwich Village scene, during the beginning of an age of heavy drug use when the Beat rebellion seems to have crested. "Laughing Gas," "Mescaline," "Lysergic Acid," also included in *Kaddish*, are all hasty verse records of altered awareness; they are efforts to pursue the stages of each drug's effects in fragmentary verse strophes. The poet's awareness seems patchy and reduced to particles of memory or weak flashes of events; the core of his logic and his categorical data are thoroughly upset by the drugs' strong effects; his scattered senses report back an almost bland irreality, indicating perhaps the difficulty of fully recreating in language the bizarre sensations of the drug experience. The last four short poems of the volume are records of his experience with yage, or ayahuasca, a strong hallucinogen taken by Peruvian Indians. Burroughs had experimented with the drug in 1953; Ginsberg went to Peru in 1960 and also took yage. Their letters about the experience were published in 1963 as *The Yage Letters,* which gives fuller record of the terrors and potency of the drug than do these brief lyric spasms. On one occasion with yage, Ginsberg was terrified at what seemed a confrontation with a death god, a destroyer who was the opposite of the benevolent spirit of his Harlem vision of 1948. It deeply disturbed him, and these four poems are efforts to communicate with and understand the god who erupted from his drugged consciousness. This dark god, whom he called the Vomiter, finishes out the volume's broad theme of death, with its constellation of elegies to his mother and fellow poets, and now these direct confrontations with the devouring god himself.

Reality Sandwiches, published in 1963, overlaps the biography of *Kaddish* and is a general collection of poems written from 1953 to 1960. Composed almost as a verse journal, it lacks the brilliant editing and shaping of the earlier volumes but contains the early classics "The Green Automobile" and "Siesta in Xbalba." The other poems of the volume do not measure up to the technical originality of these works, but now Ginsberg has begun to consolidate his own poetics and to use it as a means of chronicling his foreign travel and maturing criticism of the American way of life. The

book describes the years of his San Francisco sojourn (1955-1956), travel to the Arctic, the long African-European tour, his return to New York, ending with his trip to Peru in 1960. The tone of these poems is less hostile and expresses an almost boyish vigor and enthusiasm for the new cultures he has discovered in these years of roaming. Success has mellowed the raw anger of the poet into a more contemplative skepticism; the devastating tirades of earlier poems have softened into skillful monologues combining humor with shrewd criticism. With the lyrics "My Sad Self," "I Beg You Come Back and Be Cheerful," "To An Old Poet In Peru," we have the beginnings of a sagelike persona who will evolve over the 1960s into the image of the venerable prophet, culminating in the poetic testament *The Fall of America* (1972).

The final poem in *Reality Sandwiches,* "Aether," is another record of a drug experience—the taking of ether—which again requires the use of fragmentary, meandering strophes to express the curious shifts of his thought as he pursues the outer reaches of his conscious processes. But there is a feeling of frustration with those sediments of mind that the drug stirs up: they seem to yield only monstrous visions or visions of an infinite emptiness unshaped by spirit, "Yet the experiments must continue!" The volume, given over to these "reality sandwiches"—the strata of unconsciousness made knowable through travel, emotional crisis, or drugged expansion—concludes in weary exasperation in this ragged lyric. Ginsberg confesses his fatigue with the monotonous ambiguity of his mental contents under hallucinogens:

> I know I am a poet—in this universe—
> but what good does that do—when in another, without these mechanical aids, I might
> be doomed to be a poor Disneyan Shoe Store
> Clerk—This consciousness an *accident* of one
> of the Ether-possible worlds, not the Final
> World[.]

"Aether" was composed while in Lima, Peru, in 1960, on the return trip home after his yage visions; it signals a coming end to the experiments with hallucinogens, announced in "The Change" (written three years later and collected in *Planet News*), in which a new vision of waking reality replaces all the prior ones of a demonic universe.

Reality Sandwiches is a valuable text as a record of Ginsberg's middle life, spanning the early New York years, residence in San Francisco, and closing with the frayed visions contained in "Aether." In his biographical study of Ginsberg, *Allen Ginsberg* (1969), Thomas Merrill comments that "It is very difficult to assess *Reality Sandwiches* as a whole because the book, which spans seven years of poetic development, modestly claims to be merely 'scribbled secret note books.' The poems are amateurish, pretentious, clumsy, and, at times, downright dull." The book is a reality sandwich enclosing the turbulent and fertile writing of the poet's ripening maturity. He describes most often his solitude, yearnings, the pains of his changing nature. It is a testament of the end of his youth, which he seems reluctant to acknowledge, and yet he clearly realizes he has used up those emotions in his poetry and hungers for a new content.

Planet News: 1961-1967, published in 1968, is a verse journal of much wider travel throughout Asia, the Indian subcontinent, and Eastern Europe, in which Ginsberg develops an increasingly wide attention to other cultures and a verse form that engages in richly detailed political commentary. The forced ecstasy of his earlier drug visions gives way to a more contemplative and sympathetic analysis of Western life; travel abroad during the early Vietnam War years allowed him to perceive his own country from the perspective of Third World nations, where the militaristic and economic foreign policy of the U.S. could be felt and observed as the powerful tentacles of an American empire. Once more Ginsberg was put into the creative emergency of having to reveal social misery within America that he could sense his reader did not or could not know. His verse resumed its most fertile function of exploring a depth of suffering and injustice in long incantatory strophes. The bearings of his verse had shifted long ago from the urge to confess the persecution of a single generation and of his own personal sufferings to revelations of national and international exploitation of masses of human beings. Hence the title, *Planet News*.

"Journal Night Thoughts," which opens the volume, is a long catalogue of nights at his East Village Apartment in New York, notable for the frequency of drugged evenings with Kerouac and others, LSD experiments with Timothy Leary—in short, a coda of the hallucinatory events recorded in his earlier books. From its opening position, the poem is intended to suggest a point of departure toward new and different realms of experience. The long prose poem that follows, "Television Was A Baby Crawling Toward That Deathchamber," returns to the measure of *Howl*, with its densely interconnected breath-shaped strophes, in which the television itself is seen as the workings of a

drugged consciousness, purveying illusions and sordid fantasies of American life. The poet's widened awareness penetrates this new televised mythology to find in it a carefully orchestrated propaganda of commercials, political distortions, melodramatic exaggerations calculated to conceal reality. Running throughout the poem is the thread of cold war symbols, a new American-styled Manichaeanism of free world versus the Soviets; nothing is in proportion, all is caricatured in the electronic nightmare of the broadcasts. Behind the myriad distorted images of the tube are the steady preparations for war in Vietnam, which the poet discovers like random puzzle pieces amid the clutter of noise and images.

With the poem "Sunset S.S. Azemour," Ginsberg begins his new journal of travel, first to Tangier, then to Jerusalem (a portion of the journey recalled in "Galilee Shore"), where he met the philosopher Martin Buber and compared visionary experiences, and to India, described in "Stotras to Kali Destroyer of Illusions." During his long residence in India, Ginsberg repeatedly sought the advice of gurus on his further pursuit of visionary consciousness but was told each time that his own physical organism was the only source of awareness. "Stotras to Kali Destroyer of Illusions" is an effort to reconcile himself with his own physical being and to achieve a new recognition of his identity without leaping to other dimensions of reality. Ginsberg first repudiates any patriotic elements of his identity as an American, which he finds symbolized in the Statue of Liberty, a goddess of illusions, a metaphor of the gross materialism seizing the whole of the West. America is foundering in what the Hindus call the Kali Yuga, an age of materialistic decadence to be followed by a cleansed order of humanity. "Describe: The Rain on Dasaswamedh," an account of an Indian street scene, is a masterful instance of Ginsberg's genius for lyric detail. The poem is crafted from the sketch techniques of Kerouac, who taught him this method of graphic construct. The poem contrasts the simple street life of India with the coarse, gaudy American style derided in the previous poem. Hindu life goaded the poet to reform his own habits, which he vows to amend in his farewell to India, "Last Night in Calcutta." On a train in Japan, traveling from Kyoto to Tokyo, after visiting Gary Snyder, then studying at a Zen monastery, Ginsberg was seized with a vision of reversal: a desire to liberate himself from his own frenzied, drug-exhausted emotions, to leap free of the morbidity and terror drugs induced in him. In "The Change," a central poem of his canon, the poet weeps at the joy of freeing himself from the demons of his hallucinations. He seems to have accepted the wisdom of the Indian gurus, allowing his own direct emotions to become his vision:

> Close the portals to the festival?
> Open the portals to what Is.

Remembering with remorse the countless evenings of drugged terror, he shudders and closes off his past to put himself once more into the waking realm of actual human reality, with which he renews his sympathy in the moving second section of the poem. With each short strophe, he seems to pass spiritually out of his own self-centered concerns into a more generalized persona who can now share the pains of the rest of humanity, particularly of those who have fallen, who are the woeful victims of his own culture. Now the sun becomes his spiritual guide, a star of consciousness, whom he invokes in the close of his poem:

> And the Sun the sun the
> > Sun my visible father
> > making by body visible
> > thru my eyes!

With "The Change" Ginsberg seems to bid farewell to the Beat age itself; its rebelliousness spent, its diffident stance reduced to posture, the retreat from a fallen Eden has led to self-destruction through drug abuse. What was best of the Beat attitude he retains and purifies in his subsequent poetry: the rage against tyranny, the hatred of a sterile and depleted rational order, the emptiness of a materialistic ethos, the exploitation of the common citizen, the systematic social control by institutions. But the Beat years were over, and the friendships of the original circle of writers in New York are memorialized in his later elegies concentrating on memories of their innocence, the generous fellowship, the devotion to a life of art and spiritual redemption. If the drug and alcohol years were the dregs of the Beat rebellion, now renounced in "The Change," Ginsberg later came to see the world of drug peddling as a means of tranquilizing the oppressed. In the late 1960s he became an ardent foe of the illegal drug industry in America, which he argued was under the aegis of federal agencies such as the CIA. Although the adversaries of his vision have changed identity many times in his career, at bottom is his conviction that the innocents, common humanity, have always been persecuted by the corporate and federal elite. His poetry has been not only an indictment of such tyranny but a petition of common cause, hence the increasingly political role he was to play during the war years of the later 1960s. While in Czechoslovakia in 1965, he was crowned Kral Majales (King of the May) by Czech students in Prague, which precipitated his deportation from the country as a dangerous pied piper of youth. In January 1967, he participated in the "Gathering of the Tribes for a Human Be-In," a "life festival" of mantra-chanting, rock music, and poetry readings that was held in San Francisco. Then, during July 1967, he took part with Paul Goodman, Stokely Carmichael, and Herbert Marcuse in a symposium entitled "Dialectics of Liberation." The poet also involved himself with protests against the Vietnam War. He directed in absentia the exorcism of the Pentagon on 21 October 1967 by the Yippies (a hip radical group who effectively furthered their political protests through an offbeat, absurdist humor and through a shrewd sense of theater) and was later arrested with Dr. Benjamin Spock for obstructing the entrance to an induction center. Ginsberg likewise aided the Yippies in their attempts to arrange at the 1968 Democratic presidential convention in Chicago a "Festival of Life" similar to the San Francisco Be-In. During some of the disturbances that accompanied the Democratic convention, the poet attempted to induce calm by mantra-chanting. While in Chicago, he also accompanied William Burroughs and Jean Genêt on a peace march led by David Dellinger. Subsequently, on 11-12 December 1969, Ginsberg testified as a witness for the defense at the conspiracy trial of the Chicago Seven. He maintained that, to the best of his knowledge, the intentions of Abbie Hoffman, Jerry Rubin, and David Dellinger had been nonviolent.

In essence "The Change" is a poem that marks by brief lyric notation a profound reorientation of his art, which had now freed him from a monotonous but unconscious clinging to his past. Such a shift seems to be symbolized in the first part of "The Change" by making love to a woman, who represents the physicality that Ginsberg is now able to embrace and affirm. He now became the bard of liberation to a whole new generation of disaffected youth who were young enough to be his children. Ginsberg continued to be a central voice of political alternatives for the young through the 1970s, a poet of astonishing durability and flexibility, whose supple lyric voice was able to adapt itself to the moment's causes and perceive in them the lasting patterns of the drama of exploitation and oppression in American life.

The second half of *Planet News* is all of a piece: lyrics of his new attitude toward the daylight world of his own day-to-day living ("Morning," "Waking in New York"); verses detailing the uncomfortable exigencies of being famous ("I Am A Victim of Telephone," "Today"); and the continuing chronicle of his political activism and role as bard along the college reading circuit—the last especially well rendered in a long, exquisitely detailed meditation entitled "Wichita Vortex Sutra," which describes an odyssey into Middle America where he read his poems. Against the background of the unchanging pastoral landscape of Kansas and Nebraska, Ginsberg thrusts up images of international tension and war in Asia and perceives in the young he reads to both their dread of combat and their innocent patriotism. The language is subtle, the thinking effortlessly brilliant in its weave of global and village events; Ginsberg's voice is mellower, older, in possession of itself, beyond rage or shrill rhetoric. Written as he was traveling in a car, the very context of the poem is an ironic reversal of his Beat past: the bold and brilliant talk on the road has now become the mature wisdom of lyric silently recorded as he is brought to various colleges to read, a famous writer, a guru of the nation. Writing a review of *Planet News* in the *New York Times* (31 August 1969), Helen Vendler observed that "Ginsberg evangelizes America, exerting pure will power, casting himself as the descendant of Blake, Christopher Smart, Whitman and Williams. For his contemporaries, he is the biographer of his time— its high schools, its streets, its drugs, its cops, its cities, its freeways, and most of all its short-cut language." In general, however, *Planet News* did not provoke the critical controversies of *Howl and Other Poems* or of *The Fall of America*.

The Fall of America (1972) and *Mind Breaths: Poems 1972-1977* (1978) further consolidate his mature image as a bard of youth. *The Fall of America* continues the theme of the nation foundering in the Hindu Kali Yuga, in which the poet can only warn his audience to believe in the old immutable values of love and fellowship in such contemplative lyrics as "A Vow":

I will haunt these States
    with beard bald head
    eyes staring out plane window,
    hair hanging in Greyhound bus
                    midnight
leaning over taxicab seat to admonish

    an angry cursing driver
      hand lifted to calm
        his outraged vehicle
that I pass with the Green Light of common
                      law.

Common sense, Common law, common tenderness & common tranquility
our means in America to control the money
    munching war machine, bright lit industry
                    dustry
everywhere digesting forests & excreting soft
    pyramids of newsprint

The entire volume is dedicated to his continuing odyssey through America, as he treats the broad themes of the devastation of the landscape by industry, the spiritual pollution of war in Asia, and his own hard-earned wisdom of simple values learned along the Hindu path of meditation and healthful asceticism that he acquired from his Indian sojourn. *Mind Breaths* is a text of even more refined lyrics in which the meditative life is not only advocated but also rigorously practiced by the poet: by then he had helped to organize the Jack Kerouac School of Disembodied Poetics at the Naropa Institute in Denver, under the supervision of the Tibetan Guru, Chogyam Trungpa. But against the quietism expressed in these lyrics, there continues the other and constant theme of his adversity with the management of America's social life, which he expresses in his antiwar poems, his political attacks, and especially by his raw, baldly stated accounts of homosexual love, which seem calculated to dismiss the myth of such love as deviant or abnormal and to show pure human passion and physical pleasure.

Upon the appearance of *The Fall of America*, perhaps Ginsberg's most ambitious and sustained sequence of poems, critics were divided in their assessment of its worth and significance. Writing for the *New York Times*, Helen Vendler complained that "The trouble with it is that the minute particulars of mankind seem to be vanishing from Ginsberg's latest verse in favor of the minute particulars of geography. *The Fall of America* [marks] the disappearance or exhaustion of long-term human relations." She goes on to remark that "the elegiac side of Ginsberg still remains to me the winning one, but it may be that in the sparseness of middle age Ginsberg needs the plurality of notation and enumeration accumulation to fill these pages." Writing for the defense, the poet Ed Sanders claimed that "Ginsberg has pointed out a wonderful new direction for poetry to take—the vehicle for the description of truth." To absorb this new direction, Sanders tells us, "you have to be willing to jump into the Ginsbergian brain-stream where the ride is gentle, comradely, and brilliant. He has become a master at the description of nature, and he has tied up and captured the horror and gore of the world within the frame of anarcho-buddhist Sky-Art."

In *The Fall of America* (as John Tytell indicates), the personal, national, and metaphysical planes are all linked with one another in communicating Ginsberg's outlook and in establishing the tone of his volume. The poet's rather grim vision is indicated on the personal level by his awareness of his aging, by the injuries that he sustained during a car crash in 1968, and by the tragic deaths of Cassady (in 1968) and Kerouac (in 1969). Such individual manifestations of mortal suffering and transiency are at once correlatives to the decay of Ginsberg's country and illustrations of the radically fallen nature of physical existence. The first of these correspondences is established in *The Fall of America* especially through the implicit belief that Kerouac and Cassady were actual contemporary embodiments of what R. W. B. Lewis has termed the American Adam. That is, Ginsberg's friends really exemplified the myth (prevalent in the United States during the nineteenth century) of the capacity of a New World culture for a heroic innocence and creativity. Seen in these terms, the deaths of Kerouac and Cassady become symbols of the loss by America of the Edenic and epic potentials celebrated by Whitman. This lapse is suggested especially through recurring autumn and winter images, a symbolic analogy clinched by the pun contained in the title of *The Fall of America*.

The title *Mind Breaths* is meant to suggest the oneness of body and mind in these meditations: in Zen meditation, the mind is directed to imagine itself poised at the nostrils like air that, when exhaled, continues to expand until the meditator requires a fresh breath. Here is the rhythm of the thinking process given the meter of the breathing body: the thought expands on waves of air from the lungs and then contracts. Midway through *Mind Breaths*, the style changes quite abruptly to a blues measure; gone are the wavy and abstract paragraphings of verse language, replaced by a more symmetrical order of song. Many of these blues poems are accompanied by score sheets indicating the melody line. The poems were sung at Ginsberg's concerts, and many of the other chants of this volume were accompanied on a small hand-operated harmonium or pump-organ, an instrument which then became a constant of his public

readings. A number of the spontaneously composed blues songs were performed in the fall of 1975 with Bob Dylan in a cross country musical tour known as the "Rolling Thunder Review," after one of the poems of this title in the volume. *Mind Breaths* is a collection evincing some of the major tendencies of his most recent verse, including poems of chanted meditation and blues poems with their basic rhythms and simply worded messages of spiritual reform. A final long sequence, "Contest of Bards," is a labored narrative of the passing of wisdom between one order of rebellious bards to a younger group, the latter possessing the vision more or less articulated throughout Ginsberg's canon. As an allegory showing the role of poetry in cultural change, the poem borrows heavily from romantic narrative, but meanders and dulls from lack of the potent compressions of speech he lavished upon *Howl, Kaddish*, "Sunflower Sutra," "Wichita Vortex Sutra," and many other of his best poems.

The careers of all the Beat writers began in controversy and critical rejection of their work. Ginsberg, like Kerouac, suffered his initial years without publication or support, except from his own circle of friends. Even in his maturity, however, the critical audience of his work has remained divided between a camp of academic critics and magazine reviewers like Diana Trilling, Norman Podhoretz, and John Ciardi, among many, who feel he has abandoned the necessary norms of verse craft, and a second camp of writers who have encouraged the avant-garde through the last three decades and found in Ginsberg a major and continuously developing voice. But even among these more receptive critics, Ginsberg's reception continues to be mixed: some writers prefer the earlier work of *Howl* and *Kaddish* to the later volumes, which seem to them less compact and climactic. Others have argued that Ginsberg's spontaneous composition has often lent itself to dull commentary and sentimental moralizing. Ginsberg's advocates, John Tytell, Gordon Ball, Thomas Parkinson, Kenneth Rexroth, Thomas Merrill, and others regard his entire work as the creative evolution of a great artist. But the controversy will continue as long as the canon is added to.

The Beat writer was so intimately a part of the times that many were caught up in the image and could not change. Kerouac's life ended in sour and abysmal retreat long before his death in 1969; Neal Cassady had become an antic performer with Ken Kesey's Merry Pranksters and died from drug abuse in Mexico in 1968; others fell into obscurity after the 1950s. Only Gary Snyder and Ginsberg of that original circle remain potent forces in the national culture today, and both write with inexhaustible energy about their times. If the poetics of Ginsberg has mellowed to a conventional meter in which daily life is too amply recorded, the thread of his moral conscience born in the fury of *Howl* and *Kaddish* still shapes and enlivens his most recent work.

In the last several years, he has turned more to the writing of simple, unembellished verse ballads and blues lyrics fit to a spare melodic accompaniment. A collection of these were published as *First Blues: Rags, Ballads & Harmonium Songs 1971-74* (1975). It is not surprising that Ginsberg pointed himself back to a poetics of concise language and elemental themes. In the annals of American literature, few poets have been able to sustain a political ideal throughout their canons; apart from the rant and dross of his enormous output, Ginsberg's unique achievement has been to voice the despair and anxiety of several generations of Americans as the nation transformed itself into a superpower. His work is one of the essential records of that profound and disturbing experience and will endure.

In 1984 Ginsberg brought together in a single volume his life's work, published by Harper and Row, the first trade publisher he permitted to publish his work, under the title *Collected Poems: 1947-1980*. The critical reception to the work was mixed. The old critical polarities have vanished since the 1950s, and the new audience for his art is not squaring up against the boundary of tradition versus innovation any longer. Rather the test imposed this time is one of reflectivity, of a capacity to capture the maelstroms of history over the last few decades. The assessment has been harsh, though no one is prepared to say that Ginsberg's genius is not in some way expressed in the book's 837 pages. Rather the classic poems seem to many to be lodged among the detritus and fragments, the harangues and incantations that will perish. This makes for a degree of confusion among those who would like to describe Ginsberg critically. Though many have tried to penetrate the figure of Ginsberg as artist and public figure, like Blake he is elusive and of many faces and modes, a phenomenon in which the critic reveals himself more than he does his subject. Much that is Ginsberg will pass with the times; but as the chronicler of a certain slant of truth at mid century, he will be cherished and remembered for many years to come. He set down things that others would have thought irrelevant,

or merely too untidy to include, and yet those very skirmishes and melees of a culture are the substance of an era, the texture and flavor of human experience. The shapeless bulk of his writings are there to test a crucial issue posed by Beat literature: whether the mind is of itself an orderly house of nature, of a condition requiring only transcription without premeditation or revision, or whether it is a chaos to be ordered through strict procedures of composition. His work stands on its ear the faction that would hold that human nature is, like the rest of nature, a thing to be set in order. For Ginsberg descends from an opposing tradition that has always held the conviction that the world is sufficient as it is, an Eden composed by nature itself, requiring no further assistance to improve it. At the heart of all of Ginsberg's complaints is the firm belief that the world is the handiwork of the gods, and that only human folly is responsible for its tragedies and mishaps. The weight of all his spontaneous writing is a testament to that faith—that nothing can improve one's human nature beyond what it already is. The Beat mode of simply taking down consciousness as it emerges is a profoundly spiritual statement in itself—and belongs to the religions of the world that have declined the virtues or promises of rationality over those of intuition. Ginsberg is that rare voice of contemporary culture that revitalizes the Gnostic imagination, with its conviction that through art man communicates with his creator, especially when his expression transcends mere logic and unfolds a larger consciousness.

Letters:

To Eberhart From Ginsberg: A Letter About Howl 1956 (Lincoln, Mass.: Penmaen Press, 1976);

As Ever: The Collected Correspondence of Allen Ginsberg & Neal Cassady, edited by Barry Gifford (Berkeley: Creative Arts, 1977);

William Burroughs, *Letters to Allen Ginsberg 1953-1957* (New York: Full Court Press, 1982).

Interviews:

David Ossman, *The Sullen Art* (New York: Corinth Books, 1963), pp. 87-95;

Edward Lucie-Smith, *Mystery of the Universe: Notes on an Interview with Allen Ginsberg* (London: Turret Books, 1965);

Thomas Clark, "Allen Ginsberg: An Interview," *Writers at Work: The Paris Review Interviews*, third series (New York: Viking, 1967), pp. 279-320;

Paul Carroll, "Playboy Interview: Allen Ginsberg," *Playboy*, 16 (April 1969): 81-82, 84-86, 88, 90, 92, 236-238, 240, 242, 244;

Alison Colbert, "A Talk with Allen Ginsberg," *Partisan Review*, 38, no. 3 (1971): 289-309;

John Tytell, "A Conversation with Allen Ginsberg," *Partisan Review*, 41, no. 2 (1974): 255-309;

William Packard, ed., *The Craft of Poetry: Interviews from The New York Quarterly* (Garden City: Doubleday, 1974), pp. 53-78;

Paul Geneson, "A Conversation with Allen Ginsberg," *Chicago Review*, 27 (Summer 1975): 27-35;

Paul Portugés, "An Interview with Allen Ginsberg," *Boston University Journal*, 25, no. 1 (1977): 47-59.

Bibliographies:

Edward Z. Menkin, "Allen Ginsberg: A Bibliography and Biographical Sketch," *Thoth*, 8 (Winter 1967): 35-44;

George Dowden, *A Bibliography of Works by Allen Ginsberg* (San Francisco: City Lights Books, 1971);

Michelle P. Kraus, *Allen Ginsberg: An Annotated Bibliography 1969-1977* (Metuchen, N.J.: Scarecrow Press, 1980).
Primary and secondary. Prepared with Ginsberg's assistance.

References:

James Breslin, "Allen Ginsberg: The Origins of 'Howl' and 'Kaddish,' " *Iowa Review*, 8 (Spring 1977): 82-108;
Discusses the personal sources of Ginsberg's best-known poems.

Anne Charters, *Kerouac: A Biography* (San Francisco: Straight Arrow Books, 1973);
The first full biography of Kerouac. Includes information about his relationship with Ginsberg throughout.

Charters, ed., *Scenes Along the Road* (New York: Gotham Book Mart, 1971);
A collection of photographs and his friends, including Ginsberg.

Bruce Cook, *The Beat Generation* (New York: Scribners, 1971), pp. 102-116;
A general history of the Beats that includes lengthy discussions of major figures. Not entirely reliable.

J. W. Ehrlich, *Howl of the Censor* (San Carlos, Cal.: Nourse, 1961);
Courtroom transcripts of the trial in which Lawrence Ferlinghetti was accused of publishing and selling obscene materials—namely *Howl*.

Allen Ginsberg, *Howl* (anniversary edition), *Original Draft Facsimile, Transcript & Variant Versions, Fully Annotated by Author, With Contemporaneous Correspondence, Account of First Public Reading, Legal Skirmishes, Precursor Texts & Bibliography*, edited by Barry Miles (New York: Harper & Row, 1986);
Includes annotations and useful background information about the poem.

Stephen Hahn, "The Prophetic Voice of Allen Ginsberg," *Prospects: An Annual of American Cultural Studies*, 2 (1976): 527-567;
A literary and cultural examination of Ginsberg's work, discussing the poet as a social prophet.

James A. Heffernan, "Politics and Freedom: Refractions of Blake in Joyce Cary and Allen Ginsberg," in *Romantic and Modern: Revaluations of Literary Tradition*, edited by George Bornstein (Pittsburgh: University of Pittsburgh Press, 1977), pp. 177-195;
A study in literary traditions.

John Clellon Holmes, *Nothing More to Declare* (New York: Dutton, 1967), pp. 53-67;
Memoirs of a leading Beat writer and friend of Ginsberg's.

Richard Howard, *Alone with America: Essays on the Art of Poetry in the United States Since 1950* (New York: Atheneum, 1969), pp. 145-152;
Uses Ginsberg's public statements to elucidate his poetry. Discusses the relationship between Ginsberg's public personality and his work.

Jane Kramer, *Allen Ginsberg in America* (New York: Random House, 1968); republished as *Paterfamilias: Allen Ginsberg in America* (London: Gollancz, 1970);
A verse account of Ginsberg's life, concentrating on events of the 1960s.

Lawrence Lipton, *The Holy Barbarians* (New York: Messner, 1959);

A highly respected sociological study of the Beats.

George W. Lyon, Jr., "Allen Ginsberg: Angel Headed Hipster," *Journal of Popular Culture*, 3 (Winter 1969): 391-403;
Discusses the mythology and mysticism of Ginsberg's vision of the world.

Dennis McNally, *Desolate Angel: Jack Kerouac, the Beat Generation, and America* (New York: Random House, 1979);
Biographical study of Kerouac and his circle.

Thomas F. Merrill, *Allen Ginsberg* (New York: Twayne, 1969);
Overview of Ginsberg's life and work in the standard Twayne format.

Fred Moramarco, "Moloch's Poet: A Retrospective Look at Allen Ginsberg's Poetry," *American Poetry Review*, 11 (September-October 1982): 10-18;
Discusses Ginsberg's treatment of experiences and the influence of Ezra Pound.

Eric Mottram, *Allen Ginsberg in the Sixties* (Seattle, Wash./Brighton, U.K.: Unicorn Bookshop, 1972);
A monograph that carefully examines Ginsberg's poetic development during the 1960s.

Gerald Nicosia, *Memory Babe: A Critical Biography of Jack Kerouac* (New York: Grove, 1983);
The best biography of Kerouac, with a discussion throughout of his relationship with Ginsberg.

Paul Portugés, *The Visionary Poetics of Allen Ginsberg* (Santa Barbara: Ross-Erikson, 1978);
A critical discussion of Ginsberg's poetry.

M. L. Rosenthal, *The New Poets: American and British Poetry Since World War II* (New York: Oxford University Press, 1967);
General discussion of Ginsberg in the context of post-World War II poetry.

Mark Shechner, "The Survival of Allen Ginsberg," *Partisan Review*, 46, no. 1 (1979): 105-112;
Generally favorable review of three volumes of Ginsberg's journals, providing insights into the poet's views on homosexuality, political hatreds, personal philosophy, and Buddhism.

Louis Simpson, *A Revolution in Taste* (New York: Macmillan/London: Collier Macmillan, 1978), pp. 45-82;
Overview by a respected poet of Ginsberg's career, linking him with his poetic tradition.

John Tytell, *Naked Angels: The Lives & Literature of the Beat Generation* (New York: McGraw-Hill, 1976), pp. 79-107, 212-257;
Excellent study of the origins and development of the Beat Generation.

unspeakable visions of the individual, nos. 1-9 (1971-1979);
Journal devoted to studies of the Beats.

Papers:
Columbia University and the Humanities Research Center, University of Texas, Austin, have collections of Ginsberg's papers.

Lorraine Hansberry

This entry was updated by Steven R. Carter (University of Puerto Rico) from his entry in DLB 38, Afro-American Writers After 1955: Dramatists and Prose Writers, and from the entry by Michael Adams (Louisiana State University) in DLB 7, Twentieth-Century American Dramatists.

Places	Chicago
	Croton-on-Hudson,
	  New York
		Mexico
		University of
		  Wisconsin
			New York
			Montevideo,
			  Uruguay

Influences and Relationships	Sean O'Casey James Baldwin Richard Wright Mary Wollstonecraft	W. E. B. Du Bois Langston Hughes Arthur Miller	William Shakespeare Ralph Ellison Simone De Beauvoir
Literary Movements and Forms	Afro-American Literature	Realism	Protest Literature

Major Themes	Pan-Africanism
	Effects of Materialism
	Aftermath of
	  Nuclear War
	Diversity vs. Conformity
		Effects of Slavery
		Roles of Women
		Black Resistance
		  to Oppression
			Effects of Colonialism
			Effects of Poverty
			Humanism vs.
			  Chritianity

Cultural and Artistic Influences	Existentialism
	Television
	Black Theater
	  Movement
		Black Music
		Movies
		Greek Tragedy
		Theater of the Absurd
			Painting
			Journalism
			Shakespearean
			  Tragedy

Social and Economic Influences	Chicago's Restrictive
	  Covenants
	Cuban Missile
	  Crisis
	World War II
	Civil Rights Movement
		Mussolini's Invasion
		  of Ethiopia
		Student Non-Violent
		  Coordinating
		  Committee
		Feminism
			African Liberation
			  Movements
			House Un-American
			  Activities Committee
			Marxism

244

BIRTH: Chicago, Illinois, 19 May 1930, to Carl A. and Nanny Perry Hansberry.

EDUCATION: University of Wisconsin, 1948-1950.

MARRIAGE: 20 June 1953 to Robert Nemiroff (divorced).

AWARDS AND HONORS: New York Drama Critics Circle Award for *A Raisin in the Sun*, 1959; Cannes Film Festival special award for screenplay *A Raisin in the Sun*, 1961; Screenwriters Guild nomination for screenplay *A Raisin in the Sun*, 1961.

DEATH: New York, New York, 12 January 1965.

BOOKS: *A Raisin in the Sun* (New York: Random House, 1959; London: Methuen, 1960);
The Movement: Documentary of a Struggle for Equality (New York: Simon & Schuster, 1964); retitled *A Matter of Colour: Documentary of the Struggles for Racial Equality in the USA* (London: Penguin, 1965);
The Sign in Sidney Brustein's Window (New York: Random House, 1965); in *Three Negro Plays* (London: Penguin, 1969);
To Be Young, Gifted and Black: Lorraine Hansberry in Her Own Words, adapted by Robert Nemiroff (Englewood Cliffs, N.J.: Prentice-Hall, 1969);
Les Blancs: The Collected Last Plays of Lorraine Hansberry, edited by Nemiroff (New York: Random House, 1972)—includes *Les Blancs, The Drinking Gourd*, and *What Use Are Flowers?*

PLAY PRODUCTIONS: *A Raisin in the Sun*, New York, Ethel Barrymore Theatre, 11 March 1959;
The Sign in Sidney Brustein's Window, New York, Longacre Theatre, 15 October 1964;
To Be Young, Gifted and Black, adapted by Robert Nemiroff, New York, Cherry Lane Theatre, 2 January 1969;
Les Blancs, adapted by Nemiroff, New York, Longacre Theatre, 15 November 1970.

SCREENPLAY: *A Raisin in the Sun*, Columbia Pictures, 1961.

TELEVISION SCRIPT: *To Be Young, Gifted and Black*, adapted from Robert Nemiroff's play based on Hansberry's writings by Robert M. Fresco, NET, January 1972.

Lorraine Hansberry (photo by David Attie, courtesy of Robert Nemiroff)

RECORDING: *Lorraine Hansberry Speaks Out: Art and Black Revolution*, selected and edited by Robert Nemiroff, Caedmon (TC 1352), 1972.

OTHER: "A Challenge to Artists," in *Voice of Black America: Major Speeches by Negroes in The United States 1797-1971*, edited by Philip S. Foner (New York: Simon & Schuster, 1972), pp. 954-959.

PERIODICAL PUBLICATIONS: "Willy Loman, Walter Lee Younger and He Who Must Live," *Village Voice*, 4 (12 August 1959): 7, 8;
"On Summer," *Playbill* (27 June 1960): 3, 25-27;

"This Complex of Womanhood," *Ebony*, 15 (August 1960): 40;

"Images and Essences: 1961 Dialogue with an Uncolored Egghead Containing Wholesome Intentions and Some Sass," *Urbanite*, 1 (May 1961): 10, 11, 36;

"Genet, Mailer and the New Paternalism," *Village Voice*, 1 (1 June 1961): 10, 15;

"A Challenge to Artists," *Freedomways*, 3 (Winter 1963): 33-35;

"The Black Revolution and the White Backlash (Transcript of Town Hall Forum)," *National Guardian* (4 July 1964): 5-9;

"The Nation Needs Your Gifts," *Negro Digest*, 13 (August 1964): 26-29;

"The Legacy of W. E. B. DuBois," *Freedomways*, 5 (Winter 1965): 19-20;

"Original Prospectus for the John Brown Memorial Theatre of Harlem," *Black Scholar*, 10 (July/ August 1979): 14-15;

"The Negro Writer and His Roots: Toward a New Romanticism," *Black Scholar*, 12 (March/April 1981): 2-12;

"All the Dark and Beautiful Warriors," *Village Voice*, 28 (16 August 1983): 1, 11-16, 18-19;

"From *All the Dark and Beautiful Warriors*," *Tri-Quarterly*, 60 (Spring/Summer 1984): 35-60;

"The Buck Williams Tennessee Memorial Association," *Southern Exposure* (September/October 1984): 28-31. (This is a portion of *All the Dark and Beautiful Warriors).*

Although her life was brutally curtailed by cancer at only thirty-four, Lorraine Hansberry's contribution to Afro-American culture was considerable, much richer and more varied than most people realize. Her first staged drama, *A Raisin in the Sun* (produced in 1959), remains her best-known work, and its popular appeal has long been acknowledged. Through it, Hansberry gained historical importance as the first black woman to have a play on Broadway, the first black and youngest American to win the New York Drama Critics Circle Award, and a trailblazer whose success enabled other blacks to get their plays produced. Having exhilarated audiences for over twenty-five years by its profound affirmation of black life in all its diversity and creativity and of black strength through generations of struggle, this play seems assured of becoming a classic. Her second drama, *The Sign in Sidney Brustein's Window* (produced in 1964), achieved far less commercial success, possibly because it had to be seen twice to be justly appreciated, possibly because it challenged too many precon-

ceptions about what subjects were appropriate for Afro-American writers. Refusing to confine her brilliant, probing, ever-curious mind to the cultural ghetto of emotional protest against black social conditions (though never denying the necessity and usefulness of such protest), she depicted a Greenwich Village Jewish intellectual in the full complexity of his personality and cultural knowledge, allowing him to refer pointedly and accurately to *Walden, Lord of the Flies, Rashomon,* and other works unknown to many in her audience. In spite of its difficulty, it should be considered a major work for its fascinating characters, witty dialogue, and superb portrayal of the social and intellectual currents of its time. That she never intended to overlook black concerns is shown by her third major drama, *Les Blancs* (produced in 1970), which painfully and forcefully set forth the African struggle against European colonialism, and her fine television script, *The Drinking Gourd* (1972), which stingingly, yet objectively, analyzed how the system of slavery made the Civil War necessary.

Her last published play, *What Use Are Flowers?* (1972), revealed again the range of her awareness since it dealt with the meaning of civilization in the context of its capacity for self-destruction through nuclear warfare. This range was further demonstrated by the two versions of *To Be Young, Gifted and Black,* the play (produced in 1969) and the much more extensive informal biography (published in 1969), that her former husband and literary executor, Robert Nemiroff, put together after her death from segments of her plays, essays, speeches, and poems. In addition to this wide range of work, the semiknown portion of her legacy, she left two splendid screenplays for *A Raisin in the Sun,* which boldly reimagined the characters and situations of the play in cinematic terms but which were never used because Columbia Pictures considered them too racially controversial. She also left fragments of several plays and a novel, as well as a finely crafted screenplay based on the Afro-Haitian novelist Jacques Roumain's *Masters of the Dew* and a playlet entitled *The Arrival of Mr. Todog,* which gleefully and mercilessly satirized Samuel Beckett's absurdist drama *Waiting for Godot.* None of these has yet been published. In addition, she was a master prose stylist and finished a wealth of published and unpublished essays on black history, black art, black feminism, the Cuban missile crisis, the House Un-American Activities Committee, existentialism, the Civil Rights Movement, world literature, her own work, and the many other topics that interested her. As dramatist, film and television scriptwriter, novelist, poet, and essayist, she was among the greatest celebrators of the black spirit as well as one of the sharpest intellects and keenest observers of her time.

Lorraine Vivian Hansberry was born in Chicago, Illinois, in 1930, to Carl A. Hansberry and Nanny Perry Hansberry and was the youngest of four children. Throughout her childhood, thanks to her family's deep involvement in the black community, she was surrounded by black politics, culture, and economics. Her father, a realtor, was very active in the NAACP and Urban League and donated large amounts of money to various causes. In addition, he served as a U.S. Marshal and ran for Congress as a Republican since it was the party of Lincoln. Her mother, a former schoolteacher, was a ward committeewoman and was also dedicated to striving for social and political change. Her uncle, William Leo Hansberry, a professor at Howard University, was so noted a scholar of African history that a college was named in his honor at the University of Nigeria, and on his visits to Chicago he frequently brought along African students and exiles, many of whom were trying to oust their colonial governments and some of whom became leaders in the liberated countries. Also into her Chicago home came such important and representative figures of the black community as Paul Robeson, Duke Ellington, Walter White, Joe Louis, and Jesse Owens. Partly because of her parents' attitudes, partly because of these visitors, Hansberry never felt in awe of the famous and, while in high school, wrote letters to congressmen, senators, and even the president concerning civic issues of importance to her.

Hansberry learned another lesson in pride and resistance in 1938 when her father, risking jail, challenged Chicago's real estate covenants, which legally upheld housing discrimination, by moving his own family into a white neighborhood. While her father was in court, a mob gathered in front of the house and began shouting and throwing bricks. A bodyguard broke it up by showing a loaded gun, but not before a large concrete slab just barely passed by the eight-year-old Hansberry's head. In spite of this reception, she and her family remained in the house until a lower court ordered them to leave. With the help of the NAACP, her father fought the case all the way to the United States Supreme Court which struck down the restrictive covenants in the famous Hansberry vs. Lee decision in 1940. Unfortunately, the practice of restrictive covenants continued in Chicago, though the law no longer supported them.

In addition to his disillusionment over the outcome of this legal battle, Carl Hansberry was soon disturbed by the segregation of blacks in the U.S. Army during World War II. One of his sons, Carl, Jr., served in a segregated unit and the other, Perry, contested his draft because he refused to serve in an army that discriminated against blacks. Carl Hansberry's embitterment over continuing American racial injustice eventually led him to purchase a house in Mexico City where he planned to relocate his family permanently. However, he died on 17 March 1946, before he could complete preparations for the move, and the family remained in Chicago. Lorraine Hansberry said that he died "of a cerebral hemorrhage, supposedly, but American racism helped kill him."

In 1948, violating a family tradition of attending Howard University, Hansberry chose to go to the University of Wisconsin. There she saw a production of Sean O'Casey's *Juno and the Paycock* which eventually sparked in her the desire to write "the melody as *I* knew it—in a different key," a desire that she fulfilled in *A Raisin in the Sun*. Unhappy with many of her courses, Hansberry left the university in 1950 "to seek an education of a different kind" in New York. As part of this new education, she started to work for Paul Robeson's radical black newspaper, *Freedom,* for which she wrote such articles as "Cry for Colonial Freedom Jolts Phony Youth Meet," "Noted Lawyer Goes to Jail: Says Negroes' Fight for Rights Menaced," "Harlem Children Face Mass Ignorance in Old, Overcrowded, Understaffed Schools," "Women Voice Demands in Capital Sojourn," and "Songs of Clarence Williams Inspire Today's Musicians." She also reviewed books and dramas by blacks, and, in 1952, she became an associate editor.

Another part of her education came through her involvement in peace and freedom movements which led to her marching on picket lines, speaking on Harlem street corners, and taking part in delegations to try to save persons whom she considered to be unjustly convicted of crimes. Moreover, when Paul Robeson was unable to travel to the Intercontinental Peace Congress in Montevideo, Uruguay, in 1952 because the State Department denied him a passport, she went as his representative. To get there, Hansberry had to pass unnoticed by officials and take a flight so bumpy and perilous that her plane barely made it to the airport, and the plane ahead of hers crashed. Even though she was so shaken by this experience in the air that she refused to fly again, she was excited by the Congress which covered a large number of inter-American problems, including the arms race, poverty, dictatorship, torture, and U.S. interference in Latin America. It also gave her the invaluable opportunity to meet a large number of women from other countries and to compare notes on the circumstances of their lives. She later commented on what she learned from these women in her unpublished essay "Simone de Beauvoir and *The Second Sex:* An American Commentary, 1957."

In 1953 she married Robert Nemiroff, an aspiring writer and graduate student in English and history at New York University. Given her interests, it was appropriate that she became acquainted with him in a picket line protesting discrimination. The strength of their mutual commitment to social justice was shown by the fact that on the night before their wedding they took part in a demonstration to save the Rosenbergs from execution for treason. This commitment never lessened, although Hansberry came to believe that the best contribution she could make to the causes she believed in was through writing. For this reason, she resigned from full-time work at *Freedom* in 1953 to concentrate on her creative efforts. From 1953 to 1956, she had three plays in progress while holding down a series of jobs—as a "tag-putter-inner-and-outer" in the garment fur industry, a typist, a production assistant in a theatrical firm, a staff member of *Sing Out* magazine, and a recreation leader at the Federation for the Handicapped. She thought being a recreation leader was "a rewarding experience," but the job as production assistant disappointed both her feminist sensibility and theatrical aspirations since her primary duty was to serve coffee, and she soon quit. During this time, her husband was also doing part-time work as a typist and copywriter while continuing his studies, and after his graduation he became promotions director for Avon Books. Then in 1956 he and Burt D'Lugoff wrote the hit song "Cindy, Oh Cindy," and shortly afterwards he went to work running a music publishing firm for their friend Philip Rose. Their financial situation improved enough that Hansberry could concentrate full-time on her writing.

For a while she worked simultaneously on a novel, several plays, and an opera, but she turned increasingly to one play which she originally called "The Crystal Stair" from a line in Langston Hughes's poem "Mother to Son." In this poem, a black mother, asserting that "life for me ain't been no crystal stair," described her struggle to provide a better life for her family and encouraged her son to continue the struggle. Although this title remained apt, since the play involved a similar

mother-son relationship and a similar message, Hansberry later changed it to *A Raisin in the Sun* from a line in Hughes's poem "Harlem," which warned that a dream deferred might "dry up/like a raisin in the sun"—or explode. This new title pointed up the bitterness of the social conditions that forcibly and continuously deferred the aspirations of the black family in the play.

Hansberry completed the play in 1957 and, after an enthusiastic response from her husband, read it to their friends Burt D'Lugoff and Philip Rose. To her astonishment, Rose announced the next morning that he would like to produce it on Broadway. Although he had never produced a play before, Rose had many contacts in the theater who could give him information and advice. He hoped that some well-known Broadway producers might join him in the production, but everyone he approached turned him down on the grounds that the play was too unlike the typical Broadway play and that theater audiences would have little interest in a black family. It was, therefore, ironic that several critics later argued that the play was a guaranteed money-maker because it resembled so many other Broadway successes with only the blackness of the characters to give it the necessary spice of the new. Undiscouraged by the producers' refusals, Rose found a large number of people willing to invest small sums in the play and sent a copy of the script to Sidney Poitier, who had appeared in several films and seemed right for the important role of the son, Walter Lee Younger. Poitier agreed to take the part and suggested his former teacher, Lloyd Richards, as director. Richards too accepted, thereby becoming the first black director on Broadway. Then Rose assembled the rest of the cast, opening a door for such outstanding yet hitherto little-known black performers and writers as Claudia McNeil, Ruby Dee, Diana Sands, Louis Gossett, Ivan Dixon, Glynn Turman, Douglas Turner Ward, Lonnie Elder III, and later, as Poitier's replacement, Ossie Davis.

Because he had trouble booking a theater on Broadway, Rose decided to take the show out of town for tryouts, first in New Haven, Connecticut, and then in Philadelphia, Pennsylvania. This gamble paid off since the out-of-town reviews were positive enough to encourage the Shubert chain of theaters to offer him a Broadway theater that would become empty in March. Since that left more than a month after the tryout in Philadelphia, Rose opted to put on the play in Chicago during the interim. Despite the fears of Hansberry's two brothers and her sister Mamie, who were running the family real estate business in their father's tradition and facing as much opposition as he had, the play received an enthusiastic response from the Chicago critics and Hansberry was welcomed as a hometown girl who had made good.

When it finally opened at the Ethel Barrymore Theatre on 11 March 1959, Hansberry's drama drew favorable reviews from all seven of the crucially influential New York newspaper critics and began a highly successful run of 538 performances. Its critical success was confirmed in May when the New York Drama Critics Circle voted it best play of the year over Tennessee Williams's *Sweet Bird of Youth*, Archibald MacLeish's *JB*, and Eugene O'Neill's *A Touch of the Poet*.

Not all the critics, then or now, agreed with the generally positive assessment. Tom F. Driver of the *New Republic* argued that *A Raisin in the Sun* "is old-fashioned," adhering to the "over-worked formulas . . . of the 'domestic play.' " He also contended that "much of its success is due to our sentimentality over the 'Negro question' " and that "it may have been Miss Hansberry's objective to show that the stage stereotypes will fit Negroes as well as white people." The novelist Nelson Algren claimed that "*Raisin* does not assert the hardbought values the Negro has won, but expresses only an eagerness to have a sports car in order to get to the psychoanalyst as fast as white folks do. Dramatically, *Raisin* does for the Negro people what hair straightener and skin-lightener have done for the Negro cosmetics trade." And social critic Harold Cruse termed it "the most cleverly written piece of glorified soap opera I, personally, have ever seen on a stage."

One of the most contested points is whether *A Raisin in the Sun* is truly a black play. Henry Hewes of the *Saturday Review*, reflecting the view of many critics, felt that the fact that the central characters "are colored people, with all the special problems of their race, seems less important than that they are people with exactly the same problems everyone else has." Taking this positive (though misconceived) interpretation and turning it on its head, Harold Cruse declared that "if this play— which is so 'American' that many whites did *not* consider it a 'Negro play'—had ever been staged by *white actors* it would be judged second-rate." In contrast, Doris Abramson, author of *Negro Playwrights in the American Theatre: 1925-1959*, observed that "members of the Negro community supported this Broadway production of a Negro play as they had supported no other," adding that "this particular Broadway play, then, was not performed for

the usual white middle-class audience." Like Abramson, James Baldwin noted at the Philadelphia tryout "that I had never in my life seen so many black people in the theater" and concluded that the reason for this "was that never before, in the entire history of the American theater, had so much of the truth of black people's lives been seen on the stage." Julius Lester similarly affirmed that "it goes right to the core of practically every black family in the ghettos of Chicago, New York, Los Angeles and elsewhere." However, the best indication of its meaning for blacks came in 1975 when Woodie King, Jr., began to prepare a documentary on the black theater. He decided to call his film "The Black Theater Movement: *A Raisin in the Sun* to the Present" because he found that of the more than sixty people he interviewed "over forty . . . said that, at one time or another, they had been influenced or aided, or both, by Lorraine Hansberry and her work."

Hansberry herself felt, "it's definitely a Negro play before it's anything else." She never made the well-known quotation that Nan Robertson erroneously attributed to her in a *New York Times* interview: "I told them this wasn't a 'Negro play.' It was a play about honest-to-God, believable, many-sided people who happened to be Negroes." This "quotation" so distorted her true views that it infuriated her, yet in spite of her many attempts to correct the record, the quotation followed her around for the rest of her life, as did a subsequent false attribution derived from it: "I'm not a Negro writer—but a writer who *happens* to be a Negro."

Her real views were expressed in a 1959 interview with Eleanor Fisher in which she acknowledged that "it is impossible to divorce the racial fact from any American Negro" since "part of his daily experience is that of being a unique person in American culture who is a Negro." Concerning the protagonists of *A Raisin in the Sun*, the Youngers, she further observed to Fisher:

> From the moment the first curtain goes up until they make their decision at the end, the fact of racial oppression, unspoken and unalluded to, other than the fact of how they live, is through the play. It's inescapable. The reason these people are in a ghetto in America is because they are Negroes. They are discriminated against brutally and horribly, so that in that sense it's always there, and the basis of many things that they feel—and which they feel are just perfectly ordinary human things between members of a family—are always predicated, are always resting

Sidney Poitier, Claudia McNeil, Ruby Dee, Glynn Turman, and Diana Sands in a scene from A Raisin in the Sun *(photo by Friedman-Abeles, courtesy of Robert Nemiroff)*

on the fact that they live ghettoized lives. . . . but overtly it isn't introduced until they are asked by the author to act on the problem which is the decision to move or not to move out of this area.

At the beginning of *A Raisin in the Sun*, the head of the Younger household, Big Walter, has just died from overwork and strain, prompted in part by his grief over the death of his third child given up "to poverty" years before. This points up the high infant mortality rate in the ghetto and its devastating effects on families. Knowing that he was pushing himself dangerously hard and always placing his children first, he had taken out a ten-thousand-dollar insurance policy, his only means of providing his family with hope for the future. The drama centers on the conflicts among family members about the best use to make of Big Walter's legacy—or, rather, how best to overcome the most restrictive and humiliating pressures that white society has placed on each of them. His son, Walter Lee, wants to use all the money to buy a liquor

store, both to free himself from his degrading position as chauffeur, a reflection of the limited job opportunities for blacks, and to provide a rich, secure, and satisfying life for the rest of his family, which he wildly imagines may eventually include pearls for his wife, Ruth, and the best university in the country for his son, Travis. Ruth, realizing that she has no right to even a penny of the money, tries to stifle any expression of her wishes, but it is clear that she would like to free herself and her son from the overcrowded, rat and cockroach infested apartment where they live. Walter Lee's sister, Beneatha, challenging both racist and male chauvinist assumptions, wants to use the money to put herself through medical school. And Walter Lee's mother, Lena (often called Mama), would like to balance all their demands but finds that they far exceed the amount of the insurance, just as the damage done to blacks in America virtually defies reparation.

Having been left control over the money, Lena makes two decisions that precipitate the climax. First, she makes a down payment on a house in a white neighborhood, having discovered that similar houses in black neighborhoods cost twice as much. Second, seeing her son start drinking heavily out of bitter frustration, she gives him the remainder of the money, asking only that he put some of it in the bank for Beneatha's education. When Walter Lee then loses all of this money to the con man who encouraged him to invest in a liquor store, he forces the family to face the most crucial choice in the play—whether to accept the money offered by a white group intent on keeping them from moving into the house Lena bought or to retain their dignity at the cost of confronting white hostility and violence. Upbeat as the ending may seem when Walter Lee chooses racial and familial pride over the insulting offer of money, Hansberry was well aware of what would happen to the family in the new neighborhood and had originally written another act in which the family was attacked by whites and Lena was forced to prowl the house at night with a loaded shotgun, just as her own mother had. At the same time, the ending reflected Hansberry's conviction that black people were too strong to be kept down forever, that all the generations of blacks in America had demonstrated an incredible measure of endurance and heroism as well as an intense drive toward change. She was not worried about the ultimate fate of the Youngers since she agreed with their refusal to accept social conditions not of their own making, even if this refusal led to all of their deaths. Like the later *Roots, A Raisin in the Sun* is finally less a work of protest than a celebration of the multigenerational black struggle for progress.

Hansberry carefully tied the Afro-American fight for self-determination to the black African liberation movement through Beneatha's African suitor, Joseph Asagai. Asagai, who was inspired by the many African students Hansberry met through her Uncle Leo, is totally dedicated to driving out the colonial government in his country and is drawn to Beneatha by her similar idealism. His presence and his social observations give the play a subtheme of Pan-Africanism that was extraordinary for the American stage in its time, though it may have been influenced by both her uncle's thinking and her training under W. E. B. Du Bois at the Jefferson School for Social Science in 1953.

Clearly, Hansberry's emphasis on black social conditions, black strength, black struggle, and Pan-Africanism make *A Raisin in the Sun* a drama first and foremost about the black experience. This does not rule out universal dimensions to the play, however. As Hansberry herself noted in a 1959 interview with Studs Terkel:

> I believe that one of the most sound ideas in dramatic writing is that, in order to create the universal, you must pay very great attention to the specific. In other words, I've told people that not only is this a Negro family, or a Southern Negro family. It is specifically about the South Side of Chicago, that kind of care, that kind of attention to the detail of reference, and so forth. In other words, I think people, to the extent they accept them and believe them as who they're supposed to be, to that extent they can become everybody's.

Her play does indeed contain many generally acknowledged universal themes—that is, themes that critics have claimed are universal because they occur in many works by white writers. Among these themes are marital and generational discord, conformity versus respect for diversity, the struggle for women's rights, idealism versus cynicism, the dangers of misdirected ambition, and religion versus atheistic humanism. However, these themes are also inextricably linked to a black perspective. Take, for example, the conflict between conformity and respect for diversity. The representative for the white neighborhood, Karl Lindner, is the one who urges conformity, arguing that people get along better "when they share a common background." This is his excuse for excluding the Youngers from his community, allowing him to assert hypocritically that racism has nothing to do with his desire to keep them out. In contrast, the differences among the members of the Younger family imply the extent of diversity among Afro-Americans; all cultures have the need to accept and even foster a range of approaches to living since this is the only way that progress can be made without excessive pain. Lena, like Big Walter, is a devout member of a black church and, as such, has believed in striving for change while leaning on God for support in her struggles; Beneatha is an atheistic humanist, believing that men and women alone can bring about progress and should give themselves full credit for their achievements. Walter Lee finds jazz comforting, his mother leans on the spirituals, Ruth likes good blues, and Beneatha dismisses all of these as "assimilationist junk," preferring—at least for the moment since she flits from one mode of expression to another—African drum music. Walter Lee believes in black capitalism; Beneatha wants to become a self-sacrificing doctor in Africa. Yet, at the end of the play, the Youngers remain united as a family and as opponents of white oppression, while continuing to argue with each other over their various differences. They thus offer an example of respect for diversity that many whites can appreciate and even identify with, but they offer it in black terms, thereby demanding a new, complex conception of universality.

Hansberry's masterful orchestration of a variety of complex themes, her skillful portrayal of black American—and African—life-styles and patterns of speech, her wit, wisdom, and powerful dramatic flare all help to place *A Raisin in the Sun* among the finest dramas of this century and make it the cornerstone of the black theater movement. Though Hansberry's characterization occasionally falters in credibility, especially in relation to Beneatha's outrageously irresponsible spending of money given to her by Walter and Ruth, and Ruth's equally outrageous tolerance of this, Hansberry's first work is an extraordinarily well-crafted and insightful accomplishment, continually offering new psychological, social, and philosophical perceptions to readers and audiences who return to it with open eyes.

When her play's success made Hansberry an overnight sensation, she found that she loved being a celebrity. She appeared on an almost endless stream of radio and television talk shows and tried to answer every letter that people from all over the country wrote to her. These activities appealed not only to her pride but also to the fun-loving side of her character, the side that led her to collect clown knickknacks, play the guitar, tussle with her dog, and write rollickingly humorous scenes. However, although she responded whimsically to questions, she never ducked a serious issue and often discomforted even hardened interviewers such as Mike Wallace, to whom she said that one should not "equalize the oppressed with the oppressor" and contended that the primary guilt for the violence from both black revolutionaries and white colonialists in Kenya lay with the whites.

She sold the movie rights to *A Raisin in the Sun* to Columbia Pictures in 1959 and in 1960 wrote two screenplays that greatly differed from the stage version, adding new dimensions to her characters and seeking to provide a panoramic—and devastating—view of the ghetto they live in and the city that surrounds it. In the first of the new scenes, Lena explains to her reluctantly comprehending white ex-employer that she is pleased to be leaving this job since her work as a servant began when she

was only a girl and lasted too long, ending now only because Big Walter's insurance has freed her. She also describes how she and Big Walter tried to become riveters during World War II, her sadness at her failure in this, and her pride at his success. In another scene, Lena expresses outrage at being ripped off at a ghetto market and tells the white clerk that she will never return, even though this means that she will be forced to take a long bus ride to another part of the city to do her shopping. A subsequent scene shows Lena in the bus, literally and symbolically being driven past the house of her dreams. This scene is juxtaposed with one of Walter Lee in another bus moving past the liquor store of his dreams.

Following this, Walter Lee seeks advice about running a business from a white liquor store owner named Herman and is outraged when Herman tells him to forget it, insisting that a man with a nine-to-five job is better off than a small-time proprietor. According to Hansberry's commentary, Herman is only expressing a typical store owner's complaint, lamenting his long hours, high overhead, and high taxes, but Walter mistakenly takes his remarks as racist, reflecting a belief that blacks are unfit for business. It is clear, however, that Herman is totally insensitive to Walter's needs; he is only talking about himself and cannot see what Walter wants.

In the most provocative of the new scenes, a black nationalist speaker on a ladder harangues a street crowd that includes Walter Lee and Asagai, though the two men are unaware of each other since they have never met. After describing the typical fate of the black from the South coming to the "Promised Land" of Chicago, for example being handed a broom when he asks for meaningful work, the speaker lauds the insurgency of African blacks and demands to know when American blacks are going to follow their example. Asagai's presence in the crowd, of course, adds potency to this point. The speaker then concludes by denouncing the disinheritance of blacks and asking where the black man's lands are and where his businesses are, the very queries that are the source of Walter's agony.

Columbia Pictures allowed none of these scenes or other new material to appear and produced a film that was basically a shortened version of the play. Given the prevailing tendency of film companies to ignore blacks or, on the rare occasions they paid attention, to present an exotic and distorted image of them, even this was a considerable triumph and Hansberry was grateful for it. The final product was good enough to earn a nomination for best screenplay of the year from the Screenwriters Guild and a special award at the Cannes Film Festival, both in 1961. Nevertheless, as Hansberry knew well, the film was far less than it might have been. Although it retained much of the force of the original story and characterizations, many of her philosophical statements were taken out, the direction was often static and unimaginative, performances perfectly suited for the stage occasionally seemed overblown on the screen, and an uninspired musical score helped to create a sense of melodrama. It is hard to know how much better the other two screenplays might have worked, particularly if they had been given to the same neophyte director on the same low budget, but they do convey a more direct sense of an entire community being pushed to the edge of a precipice and ready to flail back rather than fall off. However, they are not only readable but fascinating, and hopefully they will be published in the near future so that people may gain some idea of their quality and imagine the films that could have been made. Though they are only drafts and somewhat flawed—the first screenplay contains many references that can only be understood by referring to the play since the connections were left out—they are, in their own different ways, almost as complex and satisfying as the play.

The year 1960 also brought Hansberry into another bout with censorship. Producer-director Dore Schary commissioned her to write a drama on slavery for NBC to be the first of a series of five television dramas by leading playwrights to commemorate the centennial of the Civil War. When asked how frank it could be, Schary responded, "As frank as it needs to be." However, when Schary told the top brass at NBC that he had asked a black playwright to create the drama on slavery, he was stunned since one of them obtusely queried what her attitude was toward it. Upon learning that this question was not a joke, he felt certain that the project had no chance to survive, and in fact the entire series was eventually canceled. Fortunately, Hansberry completed the play which she called *The Drinking Gourd* and it was published in 1972, after her death, though it has yet to be produced in its entirety on television. Scenes taken from it were included in the play *To Be Young, Gifted and Black* and have generally received a warm response from audiences, including television audiences.

The Drinking Gourd may have been inspired in part by stories which her mother and grandmother told Hansberry about the slavery period, including how her grandfather ran away from his master and

Self-portrait by Hansberry (courtesy of Robert Nemiroff)

hid in the Kentucky hills and how his mother managed to bring food for him. It was certainly influenced by the immense amount of reading which she did on slavery both before and after being asked to write the play. Yet it stands finally neither as fleshed out memory nor patched together history, but as a carefully conceived, strongly unified, and deeply disturbing drama about sympathetic, believable characters at three social levels—slave owner, poor white, black slave—caught in a dehumanizing social system that has maimed and threatens to destroy all of them.

The most obvious victims of the system, of course, are the slaves—Hannibal, his mother Rissa, and his sweetheart Sarah. All of them have been deliberately kept in a state of ignorance by their master, Hiram Sweet, and have been compelled to do hard, totally unrewarded labor. Under such conditions, Hannibal, who is far from being lazy by inclination, believes that the only way he can take pride in his manhood is by malingering, doing no more than half the work his master wishes from him in the cotton fields. He also defiantly coaxes his master's younger son, Tommy, a child yet to be schooled in the prohibitions of his society, to teach him to read. Rissa, who has been with Hiram Sweet since he was just starting the plantation, wants to use her position as cook and quasi confidante to pressure Sweet into taking her son out of the fields since she fears not only the effects of hard labor on him but also the potentially fatal consequences of his continuing defiance. However, she knows too well that the life of a house slave is also no joy. Both she and Sarah are always weary from the long hours and menial tasks at the house, and Sarah lives in perpetual terror of authority and punishment. Their situation then worsens to the point that all three—Hannibal, Rissa, and even Sarah—come to recognize the intolerability of the system and the necessity of flight at whatever risk.

The situation of the poor white, Zed Dudley, is little better. With only a small farm and no slaves, he cannot compete with the large plantations and must decide either to leave the South and take a chance on the rugged and perilous West or seek a job as an overseer to keep his children from dying of starvation. After becoming an overseer for the Sweets, though, he finds that to keep his new position he must do things that horrify and brutalize him, such as putting out the eyes of Hannibal for having learned to read.

Hiram Sweet too finds that, even though he has achieved a place at the top, his participation in the slavery system forces him to do things that he would prefer not to do and that are severely damaging to him, both spiritually and physically. He has thought of himself as a "humane" master because he has made his slaves work only nine and a half hours in the fields every day, but declining market prices and a diminishing yield necessitate that he consider working them longer and harder—overwork that will probably kill some of the slaves—or else he risks losing his plantation. He has also seen that competition between the North and the South is leading inevitably toward a war that Southerners cannot win since they cannot simultaneously attack Northerners and keep the horde of discontented slaves from fleeing and then returning as soldiers to fight against them. In addition, these worries have so worsened his health that he can no longer run his plantation and must turn over control to his ruthless elder son, Everett, whom he rightly expects to undermine everything he has done. It is Everett who makes the decision to blind Hannibal, but it is his father who pays for this act since, as Rissa's "master," a man who claims to have total control, Hiram is held accountable by her and she refuses her desperately needed help when he collapses from tension. Clearly he is not the master over people and life that he thought he was.

The drama is effectively framed by the speeches on economy and history of a narrator who could be from any part of the country, but who reveals at the end that he has decided to fight for the North since, although "it is possible that slavery might destroy itself . . . it is more possible that it would destroy these United States first" and "it has already cost us, as a nation, too much of our soul." The events of the play leave no doubt about the correctness of his decision and imply that any system so harmful must be changed at any price.

Making a similar judgment on the America of her time, Hansberry argued in a later speech that "the basic fabric of our society . . . is the thing which must be changed to really solve the problem" of black oppression—and other problems. To this end, she devoted considerable time to interviews, lectures, speeches at demonstrations, and essays on issues that she felt must be addressed to move her country toward its vitally needed transformation. However, she also wanted time and isolation to continue her creative efforts which she regarded as her most important contribution to the struggle for change. Therefore, in 1961 she and her husband moved from the Greenwich Village apartment, where they had been living since their marriage, to a house in a tranquil, wooded area in Croton-on-Hudson, New York, which was within commuting distance of New York City. From this peaceful and secluded place, she maintained the necessary balance between her public and private commitments. In 1962 she mobilized support for the Student Non-Violent Coordinating Committee (SNCC) in its struggle against southern segregation; she spoke out against the House Un-American Activities Committee and the Cuban missile crisis that nearly precipitated a nuclear war; and she wrote her postatomic war play, *What Use Are Flowers?* (1972). At the end of the play some of the few children who survive a nuclear holocaust have learned the meaning of beauty from a dying hermit, and one of them is patiently reconstructing his newly invented wheel that another had broken; Hansberry remained hopeful about man's durability and potential for slow, painful, hard-won progress, despite her full awareness of man's all-too-frequent folly and viciousness.

In 1963 she was hospitalized for tests, with the results suggesting cancer. Nevertheless, she persisted in her various commitments. A scene from her work-in-progress, *Les Blancs*, was staged at the Actors Studio Writers Workshop with Roscoe Lee Browne and Arthur Hill in the major roles. Then, on 24 May, at the request of James Baldwin, she joined a meeting of several prominent blacks and a few whites with Attorney General Robert Kennedy to discuss the racial crisis. The meeting was charged with emotion since Kennedy at that time seemed unable to comprehend or respond to the urgency of the blacks and was outraged when a young civil rights activist, Jerome Smith, told him there that he would never take up arms to defend America. Hansberry hotly defended Smith and disturbed Kennedy further by informing him that she was not worried about the fate of brutally beleagured black people "who have done splendidly . . . all things considered," but about "the state of the civilization which produced that photograph of the white cop standing on that Negro woman's neck in Birmingham." On 19 June she chaired a meeting in Croton-on-Hudson to raise money for SNCC. Only five days later she was operated on unsuccessfully in New York. After a second operation in Boston on 2 August, she recovered her strength for a while, but from this point on she would be in and out of the hospital until her death from cancer a year and a half later.

Nineteen sixty-four saw the publication of *The Movement: Documentary of a Struggle for Equality*, a book prepared by SNCC with distressing and even horrifying photos of lynchings, sagging and de-

pleted buildings, savagely beaten demonstrators, and other distressing aspects of the black experience coupled with a sharply worded text by Hansberry. It also saw Hansberry's marriage end in divorce on 10 March, but her creative collaboration with Nemiroff continued, and the two of them continued to see each other daily until her death. From April to October she underwent an extensive series of radiation treatments and chemotherapy at a hospital while continuing work on a variety of projects, including *Les Blancs, The Sign in Sidney Brustein's Window*, and a play about the eighteenth-century feminist Mary Wollstonecraft for which she was doing research. On 1 May she was released from the hospital to deliver a speech to winners of the United Negro College Fund writing contest for which she coined the phrase "To be young, gifted and Black," and on 15 June she again left her sickbed to participate in the well-publicized Town Hall debate between militant black artists and white liberals on "The Black Revolution and the White Backlash."

A scene from Hansberry's The Sign in Sidney Brustein's Window *(photo by Friedman-Abeles, courtesy of Robert Nemiroff). Sidney (Gabriel Dell), a Jewish intellectual, is flanked by his half-Greek, half Irish-Cherokee wife (Rita Moreno), and banjo-playing Alton Scales (Ben Aliza).*

255

In early October Hansberry moved to the Hotel Victoria in New York to be near rehearsals of *The Sign in Sidney Brustein's Window*, which was being produced by Nemiroff and Burton D'Lugoff, and she attended its opening at the Longacre Theatre on 15 October. The play received mixed reviews, ranging from British novelist John Braine's acclamation of it as "a great play" to *Newsweek* critic Richard Gilman's denunciation of its "borrowed bitchery" and its distortion of "taste, intelligence, craft." Normally, mixed reviews would have meant the instant death of a play on Broadway, but a large number of people, deeply respectful of both the author and the work, contributed time, money, and publicity to keep it running for 101 performances, an extraordinary number under the circumstances. As Michael Adams noted in *DLB 7*, "the people involved in the production so believed in *The Sign in Sidney Brustein's Window* that they tried everything possible to keep it going; one gave eighty-five hundred dollars, her entire savings, so that it could run a second week. Eventually the play became a cause, a symbol of the kind of work Broadway and American Theatre in general have to support in order to survive. Many prominent people in show business and other fields began making donations, buying advertising, holding meetings, campaigning to keep it going. When these efforts seemed exhausted and the play was scheduled to close, the 'final' audience took up a five-thousand-dollar collection to give it another week. Similar miracles kept occurring until it finally closed when Hansberry died" on 12 January 1965.

Many critics were dismayed that Hansberry chose to center her second Broadway play around a group of white characters living in Greenwich Village, even though she had lived in the area for ten years and was well acquainted with the types of intellectuals, artists, would-be actresses, and others that she created for it. They were also surprised that the primary topics in the play were ones that they wrongly associated only with whites, such as existentialism, the theater of the absurd, male chauvinism, homosexuality, abstract art, bohemianism, middle-class values, and so on. However, Hansberry, like Richard Wright, James Baldwin, Edgar White, and other black writers, refused to accept arbitrary and irrational limits on her intellect and interests. Among the projects she had already planned, researched, or begun working on were an opera about the Haitian revolutionary Toussaint L'Ouverture; a musical based on *Laughing Boy*, Oliver La Farge's novel about the Navajos; and a drama about the ancient Egyptian ruler Akhnaton.

Nevertheless, she did not leave out explicitly black concerns in *The Sign in Sidney Brustein's Window*, though they were clearly secondary. A minor character, Alton Scales, is a black ex-Communist who, like most of the white characters in the play, is simultaneously a victim and an oppressor. Though acutely aware of the irrationality of white hostility toward blacks, he fails to observe the equal illogicality and viciousness of his own attitude toward homosexuals. Also, at the same time that he is explaining to his friend, Sidney Brustein, about the psychological wounds that society inflicted on his father for being black, he is planning to inflict as deep a wound on a formerly beloved woman whose past as a prostitute is unforgivable for him solely because she is white. These scenes with Alton further the play's general warning against making facile and fashionable judgments on groups and individuals and its imperative to root out the inhumanity in all of us. As in many of the other scenes, and nearly all of Hansberry's other works, they also point up the necessity for totally overhauling the system that fosters so many forms of inhumanity.

During the last year and a half of her life, Hansberry spent considerable time working on her African play, *Les Blancs,* both in the hospital and out. She completed several drafts, but none of them satisfied her, so she made copious notes and held long discussions about it with Robert Nemiroff to enable him to continue her work if she could not. Though the basic plotting, characterization, thematic development, and the majority of the speeches were Hansberry's, much work remained for Nemiroff, and the final product should be considered a collaborative effort.

Though some of the shifts between scenes are abrupt and the ending is a bit foreshortened, its published and produced form is a finished, clearly focused, and profoundly thoughtful and moving depiction of the radicalizing of a white reporter, Charlie Morris, and a black intellectual, Tshembe Matoseh. Charlie Morris has come to the mythical, but representative, African country of Zatembe to meet the Albert Schweitzer-like figure, Reverend Torvald Neilsen. However, witnessing the repressiveness of the white colonial government and its refusal to negotiate, and learning that Reverend Neilsen's benevolence is that of a Great White Father caring for what he regards as irresponsible black children, Morris comes to see that nothing less than a violent revolution destroying many innocent whites and blacks, including babies, can alter the appalling degradation and stripping of an entire people. Matoseh, who returns to Zatembe for his father's funeral, would like to go back to his white wife and their son in London but finds that he is called by the spirit of a woman warrior representing his people to follow the lead of his father who had organized the resistance to colonial exploitation. He discovers the pain of revolution through being forced to kill his own brother, Abioseh, who had placed himself on the side of the oppressors, and through inadvertently causing the death of Madame Neilsen, the Reverend's wife, a white woman who had been like a second mother to him. However, it is clear that he will persist in the struggle to liberate his country.

Les Blancs opened at the Longacre Theatre on 15 November 1970 and, having received violently mixed reviews, closed after forty-seven performances, but it is an immensely powerful drama both for readers and audiences. Although Hansberry, of course, could not see this production, her spirit lived in it and will continue to live.

Another posthumous work which will undoubtedly help it to live is the uncompleted novel *All the Dark and Beautiful Warriors*, currently being edited for publication by Robert Nemiroff. Judging from the three portions that have been published in the *Village Voice, Tri-Quarterly,* and *Southern Exposure* and from the excerpts in *To Be Young, Gifted and Black*, this will be a major work, even in its unfinished state. *Tri-Quarterly* describes it as "a panoramic work spanning some thirty years, with many locales, characters and levels of society." Similarly, Thulani Davis, in the introduction to the portion published in the *Village Voice*, claims that "it gives us a broader spectrum of Hansberry's America than previously published work, and, at the same time, it observes in rich detail the shaping of a black woman's internal life." The novel focuses on the intertwining stories of Candace Braithwaite, a young woman from a socially prominent, upper-middle-class black family in Chicago, and Denmark Vesey Williams (frequently called Son), a young man from a far-less-well-off farming family in Tennessee. The two are first shown separately in their very different childhoods. Though both display a similar mixture of rebellion and conformity, their first meeting is painfully awkward and unsatisfying to both. This meeting in Chicago was arranged by Candace's mother, who is from Denmark's hometown, and was not sought by either. Eventually, however, both are transformed by separate radicalizing experiences and meet again in New York where they become involved with each other and in the Civil Rights Movement, the latter prompting

them to head south together. Although the published sections occasionally display the influence of Richard Wright and Ralph Ellison, Thulani Davis seems right in asserting that the novel "shows clearly that Hansberry was not concerned simply with the ideas propounded by the largely male protest literature of the '50s, but had much to say about the separate, intimate, and often enraging rites of passage for black women."

The publication of the finished portion of the novel can only add to Hansberry's stature. Both for the artistry and intelligence of her major plays, screenplays, novel, and essays and for her example of a deeply committed life, Hansberry is sure to be remembered by future generations as one of the most important Afro-American writers.

Bibliography:

Ernest Kaiser and Robert Nemiroff, "A Lorraine Hansberry Bibliography," *Freedomways,* 19 (Fourth Quarter 1979): 285-304.

Biography:

Catherine Scheader, *They Found a Way: Lorraine Hansberry* (Chicago: Children's Press, 1978).

References:

Doris E. Abramson, *Negro Playwrights in the American Theatre: 1925-1959* (New York: Columbia University Press, 1969);
An early, valuable study of *A Raisin in the Sun* in relation to the developing tradition of black drama, though it is weak on the ending of the play.

C. W. E. Bigsby, *Confrontation and Commitment: A Study of Contemporary American Drama, 1959-1966* (London: MacGibbon & Kee, 1967; Columbia: University of Missouri Press, 1968);
A fine study of *The Sign in Sidney Brustein's Window* coupled with a less satisfactory examination of *A Raisin in the Sun.*

Lloyd W. Brown, "Lorraine Hansberry as Ironist," *Journal of Black Studies,* 4 (March 1974): 237-247;
An excellent study of the structure and artistry of *A Raisin in the Sun,* with emphasis on Hansberry's use of irony, particularly in her ending.

Steven R. Carter, "Commitment Amid Complexity: Lorraine Hansberry's Life-in-Action," *MELUS,* 7 (Fall 1980): 39-53;

A study of Hansberry's social and philosophical ideas preceded by a chronology.

Harold Cruse, *The Crisis of the Negro Intellectual* (New York: William Morrow, 1967);
A biased and venomous attack on Hansberry but important for the influence it has exerted on other critics.

Freedomways, Lorraine Hansberry Issue, 19 (Fourth Quarter 1979);
The best general introduction to Hansberry's life and work, including articles on her dramatic goals, prose style, feminism, political stands, and place in black theatrical and American history.

Loyle Hairston, "Lorraine Hansberry: Portrait of an Angry Young Writer," *Crisis*, 86 (April 1979): 123-124, 126, 128;
A reappraisal of Hansberry's life and work, emphasizing her radicalism before it became generally recognized.

Harold R. Isaacs, *The New World of Negro Americans* (New York: John Day, 1963);
An examination of Hansberry's view of Africa based on an interview with her.

David E. Ness, "*The Sign in Sidney Brustein's Window: A Black Playwright Looks at White America,*" *Freedomways*, 11 (Fourth Quarter 1971): 359-366;
One of the best studies of *A Sign in Sidney Brustein's Window* based on the chapter in his excellent dissertation on Hansberry.

Studs Terkel, "An Interview With Lorraine Hansberry," *WFMT Chicago Five Arts Guide*, 10 (April 1961): 8-14;
The best interview with Hansberry about her life and *A Raisin in the Sun*.

Papers:
The Hansberry papers are all held by Robert B. Nemiroff as literary executor, but they will eventually be placed at a major library or university.

Robert Hayden

This entry was updated by Fred M. Fetrow (United States Naval Academy) from the entry by James Mann (Columbia, South Carolina) in DLB 5, American Poets Since World War II.

Places	Detroit (Paradise Valley) Mexico	Nashville (Fisk University) Washington, D.C.	Ann Arbor (University of Michigan) Library of Congress
Influences and Relationships	W. H. Auden Stephen Vincent Benét Countee Cullen Margaret Walker	Langston Hughes Elinor Wylie Arna Bontemps	W. B. Yeats Michael S. Harper Gwendolyn Brooks
Literary Movements and Forms	Harlem Renaissance Postmodernist Period The Black Aesthetic	Modernist Period Romanticism	Symbolist Movement Transcendentalism
Major Themes	Place Religion/Faith (Baha'i) Family/Ancestry	Black History Search for Identity Appearance/Reality	People/Human Brotherhood Art/Aesthetics Alienation
Cultural and Artistic Influences	Baha'i Faith Blues and Gospel Music	Drama and Theater Other "Modern" Painters	Impressionist Painters
Social and Economic Influences	Slave Trade Era Works Progress Administration/ Federal Writers' Project	Abolition Movement Harlem Renaissance Civil Rights Movement Great Depression	Civil War Vietnam War American Bicentennial

259

BIRTH: Detroit, Michigan, 4 August 1913, to Asa and Ruth Sheffey. Foster son of Sue Ellen Westerfield and William Hayden.

EDUCATION: B.A., Wayne State University, 1936; M.A., University of Michigan, 1944.

MARRIAGE: 15 June 1940 to Erma Morris; child: Maia.

AWARDS AND HONORS: Hopwood Poetry Award, 1938, 1942; Julius Rosenwald Fellowship, 1947; Ford Foundation grant, 1954-1955; World Festival of Negro Arts Grand Prize for *A Ballad of Remembrance*, 1966; Russell Loines Award, National Institute of Arts and Letters, 1970; Consultantship in Poetry (Library of Congress), 1976-1978; Litt.D., Brown University; Grand Valley State College, 1976; Litt.D., Wayne State University; Benedict College, 1977; fellowship, Academy of American Poets, 1977; Michigan Arts Foundation award, 1977.

DEATH: Ann Arbor, Michigan, 25 February 1980.

BOOKS: *Heart-Shape in the Dust* (Detroit: Falcon Press, 1940);
The Lion and the Archer, by Hayden and Myron O'Higgins (Nashville: Hemphill Press, 1948);
Figure of Time: Poems (Nashville: Hemphill Press, 1955);
A Ballad of Remembrance (London: Paul Breman, 1962);
Selected Poems (New York: October House, 1966);
Words in the Mourning Time (New York: October House, 1970);
The Night-Blooming Cereus (London: Paul Breman, 1972);
Angle of Ascent: New and Selected Poems (New York: Liveright, 1975);
American Journal (Taunton, Mass.: Effendi Press, 1978; enlarged edition, New York: Liveright, 1982);
The Collected Prose, edited by Frederick Glaysher (Ann Arbor: University of Michigan Press, 1984);
Robert Hayden: Collected Poems, edited by Glaysher (New York: Liveright, 1985).

OTHER: *Kaleidoscope: Poems by American Negro Poets*, edited with an introduction by Hayden (New York: Harcourt, Brace & World, 1967);

Robert Hayden (photo by Timothy D. Franklin)

Alain Locke, *The New Negro*, preface by Hayden (New York: Atheneum, 1970);
Afro-American Literature: An Introduction, edited by Hayden and others (New York: Harcourt Brace Jovanovich, 1971);
The United States in Literature, edited by Hayden and others (Glenview, Ill.: Scott Foresman, 1973).

PERIODICAL PUBLICATIONS: "A Portfolio of Recent American Poems," *World Order*, 5 (Spring 1971): 33;
"Recent American Poetry—Portfolio II," *World Order*, 9 (Summer 1975): 44-45.

Even though Robert Hayden himself considered it a secondary consideration for the evaluation of his work, he is still known primarily as a black poet, and the subjects of many of his poems make use of his heritage and experience as a black American. But he stands out among poets of his race for his staunch avowal that the work of black writers must be judged wholly in the context of the literary tradition in English, rather than within the confines of the ethnocentrism sometimes found in contemporary literature written by blacks. In a 1968 interview in *Negro Digest*, for example, he asserts that a so-called black aesthetic would only be possible in a predominantly black culture, but that even black African writers do not subscribe to such an aesthetic, and he finally dismisses it as "protest and racist propaganda in a new guise." Hayden's work has a distinctly more literary flavor than is evident in the poetry of many younger blacks, and his concern for art to the exclusion of politics and sociology has brought him frequent fire from members of his own race.

After two decades of obscurity he began to emerge for the general literary public as a noteworthy practitioner of the craft of poetry with the publication of his *Selected Poems* in 1966, and his reputation has been steadily growing ever since. Ten years later he became the first black to hold the Consultantship in Poetry at the Library of Congress, an honor befitting his preeminent stature among contemporary black poets and the general respect accorded him in the literary world at large.

Robert Earl Hayden was originally named Asa Bundy Sheffey shortly after his birth in Detroit, Michigan. His natural parents went their separate ways while he was still an infant, leaving him in the care and custody of William and Sue Ellen Hayden, who gave the child their name and raised him as their own. The poet's foster father was especially instrumental in encouraging young Robert's education, and the boy took an early liking to the arts in general and to literature in particular. In a 1977 interview Hayden talked extensively and frankly about his life both as a writer and as a man. A precocious child, Hayden learned to read before going to public school, and he began to write poems, stories, and plays while still in grammar school. By the time he reached high school he had committed himself to poetry, spending most of his time reading and writing it. Reading George Eliot's novel *Romola* (1863), curiously enough, instilled in him a fascination with words (like *loggia*) and the names of things (Ponte Vecchio) so vividly that he says he lived in the book's world as if it were his own, and he had similar experiences with Nathaniel Hawthorne's *The Marble Faun* (1860) and Edward George Bulwer-Lytton's *The Last Days of Pompeii* (1834): "I loved those books, partly because they took me completely out of the environment I lived in, and they appealed to my imagination, partly because they were full of strange and wonderful things that I'd had no direct experience with."

With his penchant for literature already formed, Hayden could not afford to go to college after his graduation from high school in 1931. He educated himself through his discovery of the Harlem Renaissance poets, happening upon them in the now-famous anthology *The New Negro* (1925), edited by Alain Locke (Hayden wrote an introduction for the 1970 edition), and becoming particularly fond of Orrick Johns and Countee Cullen, whom he admired greatly. But he also read many other anthologies and made himself thoroughly familiar with the contemporary poetry of the 1920s, having as especial favorites Carl Sandburg, Sara Teasdale, Stephen Vincent Benét, Edna St. Vincent Millay, and Elinor Wylie. Of the traditional English poets he liked Chaucer, Burns, Shelley, Wordsworth, Byron, and Keats, whose poem "The Eve of St. Agnes" enchanted him. Aside from poetry he grew passionately attached to the work of Eugene O'Neill, and he recalls not having had the money to see productions of *Strange Interlude* (1928) and *Mourning Becomes Electra* (1931) when they came to Detroit.

Thus propelled by his own eclectic taste, he entered Detroit City College (now Wayne State University) on a scholarship, where he majored in foreign languages, particularly Spanish, with a minor in English. He says that although he continued to write poetry, he lacked faith in himself as a poet. While in college, however, he had a crucial experience: meeting the famous black poet Langston Hughes, who had come to Detroit to see a production of one of his plays that Hayden happened to be acting in. The young man showed Hughes some of his poems, receiving the judgment that they were imitative and derivative and that he needed to find an individual voice. Somewhat crestfallen, he was nevertheless excited by the encounter, and Hughes's example inspired him to pursue his own literary ambitions.

Upon finishing college, Hayden worked on the Federal Writers' Project in Detroit from 1936 to 1938, in charge of research into local black history and folklore. Leaving this job, he went on to another WPA project, the Historical Record Survey, while also doing part-time work as drama and music critic for the *Michigan Chronicle*, a local black newspaper. At the same time he was trying very hard to be a writer, writing a play (unpublished) about the pre-Civil War network of intrigue by which slaves escaped to the North, the so-called Underground Railroad, entitling the work "Go Down, Moses." In 1940 his first book of poems, *Heart-Shape in the Dust,* was published in Detroit, and in the same year he married. His wife was a pianist, and in 1941 he moved briefly with her to New York while she studied at Julliard School of Music. It was at this time that he met Countee Cullen. Hayden's wife's uncle had been in college with the renowned Harlem poet, who had read Hayden's book and become interested in him, and the Haydens were invited for an evening at Cullen's house that left a lasting impression on the younger man. Upon returning to Detroit, he resolved to pursue a master's degree at the University of Michigan and matriculated there in 1941.

At Michigan he soon had what has unquestionably been a central experience for him: he enrolled in a course in the analysis of poetry taught by W. H. Auden, recently expatriated from England. Hayden found Auden "awe-inspiring" and "absolutely brilliant": "he stimulated us to learn more about poetry and even to search ourselves. He made us aware of other literatures, and aware of poetry in a way that we never would have been. . . ." Auden found some of Hayden's poetry to his liking, some of it not, and instilled in Hayden critical and creative principles that have had a permanent influence on his former student's ways of practicing the art of poetry. Many years later in 1969, the two poets gave a joint reading at Columbia University, but they had not maintained ties in the interim. Theirs had been a master-apprentice relationship, one that had a crucial place in Hayden's development as a poet. In 1938 and 1942 Hayden won the Hopwood Award for poetry, and upon completing his master's degree at the University of Michigan, he became a teaching fellow there, a job he held from 1944 to 1946. Also during this period at Michigan, both Hayden and his wife became members of the Baha'i faith, which was especially supportive for him throughout his life, partly because it teaches that the work of the artist is considered a form of worship.

By 1946 one of his most famous poems of Afro-Americana had already been printed: "Middle Passage," about the slave trade, appeared in *Phylon* in 1945, and a revised version was later reproduced for Edwin Seaver's annual anthology, *Cross Section* (1946). The innovative sonnet "Frederick Douglass" found its way to a reading public through the *Atlantic Monthly* in February 1948. Hayden was also now launched on the teaching career that he followed all his life, exemplifying a pattern that has become a predominant one for poets in the United States since World War II. Like many teaching poets, he often found the conflict between his academic chores and his own creative life to have greatly limited the amount of effort he was able to devote to the latter, with the result that his four decades as a publishing poet produced a relatively slender canon. Hayden's career is a perfect illustration of the mixed blessing that the

American university has bestowed on its country's poets by welcoming them into its fold. In an interview in *World Order,* a magazine of the Baha'i faith, of which he was poetry editor, Hayden said, "I am a poet who teaches in order to earn a living so that he can write a poem or two now and then."

In 1946 Hayden accepted a position as professor of English literature at Fisk University in Nashville, Tennessee, and he held this position for more than two decades until 1969. Although long, his association with Fisk, a prominent black university, was not altogether happy, and he came to consider it a stronghold of bourgeois mediocrity by the time he eventually left to teach again at the University of Michigan. He taught literature courses of all descriptions at Fisk, including creative writing, but the constant fifteen hours per semester teaching load was a severe hindrance to the amount of his own poetry he was able to produce. Nevertheless, in the Counterpoise series, a small poetry-publishing venture that he, together with faculty colleagues, supportive friends, and university students, founded to encourage Afro-American writing of a nonpropagandistic, non-protest sort, he published his next two books in Nashville: *The Lion and the Archer* (1948) and *Figure of Time: Poems* (1955). In 1962 his fourth book, *A Ballad of Remembrance,* was published in London by a small publisher who instituted the Heritage series of books by black American poets. Perhaps mainly because his first four books were published by small presses with little distribution (although his work was published in an important anthology edited by Langston Hughes and Arna Bontemps), Hayden remained largely unknown to the American literary public until the publication in New York of his *Selected Poems* in 1966.

Moving to Nashville from Detroit was a considerable shock to Hayden psychologically because he had to confront for the first time the blatant racial segregation of buses, schools, drinking fountains, and public rest rooms. He has said that for years he would not go to a movie in Nashville because blacks had to enter the theater through an alley and then sit in a segregated balcony. For a while, Hayden's wife lived in New York so that their daughter would not have to start her education under segregated conditions, and then he himself took a year's leave from Fisk to be with them—at the end of which, however, they returned to Nashville and his daughter entered regular public school. By necessity the Haydens taught themselves to live with segregation, though never to adjust to it, and they formed relationships with unprejudiced people of goodwill who had similar interests in the arts. Hayden's concern for the art of poetry prevented him from writing in a polemic way about his experiences during these two decades, although he did employ it as subject matter. He wanted to approach it "as an artist and not as a propagandist," being as concerned with technique as he was with the material he was trying to forge into durable artistic form. Hayden elaborates on this general concern in "Recent American Poetry—Portfolio II" in *World Order,* when he attacks verse that is "amorphous in structure, trivial in substance, and pretentious. . . . informed by crass naturalism and linguistic violence which delude those responsible for it into believing they are 'telling it like it is.' . . . But the truly revolutionary poets are always those who are committed to some integrative vision of art and life. Theirs is an essentially spiritual vision. . . ."

Trying as they were, Hayden's years at Fisk were not without their rewards. In 1947 he was awarded a Rosenwald Fellowship, and in 1954 he received a Ford Foundation grant for travel and writing in Mexico, out of which came his sequence of poems " 'An Inference of Mexico.' " And finally, in 1966, he gained widespread recognition by winning, with the fervent advocacy of Langston Hughes, the Grand Prize for Poetry at the First World Festival of Negro Arts in Dakar, Senegal, for his book *A Ballad of Remembrance,* which had been published four years earlier. From that time honors accumulated at an increasing rate. In 1968 he was invited to be a visiting professor at the University of Michigan, and in the following year became a professor of English there, a position he held until his death in 1980. In 1970 his sixth book of poetry, *Words in the Mourning Time,* was nominated for a National Book Award, and in the same year he was presented the Russell Loines Award by the National Institute of Arts and Letters. In 1972 London publisher Paul Bremen brought out Hayden's small book *The Night-Blooming Cereus.*

After 1968 Hayden was increasingly in demand as a visiting poet-professor, and he held guest positions at a number of different universities, including the University of Louisville, the University of Washington, the University of Connecticut, and Denison University in Granville, Ohio. He was also a staff member at the Bread Loaf Writers' Conference in Middlebury, Vermont. In 1975 he was elected a fellow of the Academy of American Poets for "distinguished poetic achievement," and in 1976 his lifetime's accomplishment in poetry was recognized by his appoint-

ment to the Consultantship in Poetry at the Library of Congress, a position he held until 1978 while on leave from the University of Michigan. Prior to this appointment, a book that summed up his career as a poet, *Angle of Ascent: New and Selected Poems,* was published in 1975 and received widespread critical attention.

Hayden's tenure at the Library of Congress brought him great notoriety and a raft of honors. In 1977 he received a fellowship from the Academy of American Poets and an award from the Michigan Arts Foundation. He was awarded the degree of Doctor of Humane Letters in 1976 from Brown University and from Grand Valley State College, Allendale, Michigan; and in 1977 he received like degrees from his alma mater, Wayne State University, and from Benedict College in Columbia, South Carolina. *American Journal* was published by Effendi Press in 1978, and an enlarged edition was published by Liveright in 1982. Hayden found that his sudden fame made inordinate demands on his time, and he busily continued his work as a poet and teacher while trying to reconcile it with the pressures of life as a public figure.

From the beginning Hayden's poetry has always looked elegant on the page: it is usually arranged into symmetrical stanzas whose lines, although metrically fairly loose, tend to arrange themselves in consistent patterns. The stanza structures themselves are often original, even when they are individual adaptations of traditional forms, as they frequently are. Thus the poet manages to strike a kind of middle road between free verse and traditional form, a practice he may have learned from the example of his teacher W. H. Auden. Only rarely does he allow his verse to expand into freer kinds of arrangements, notably in "Middle Passage" and "Runagate, Runagate," yet even in these poems the "freedom" is tightly controlled and artistically functional. Another principal feature of Hayden's verse is that he eschews full rhyme entirely, substituting assonance or consonance for it occasionally but with no consistency. He tends to favor three-, four-, and five-line stanzas in more or less equal numbers, although often enough he will use longer ones. A few poems are arranged in two-line strophes.

Overall Hayden's poetry gives the impression of being formal in a nontraditional, original way, firm but not straitjacketed. It is obviously the product of an imagination that is exercising itself scrupulously through the architectonic faculty, yet that is not constrained or hindered by such stricture but rather channeled by it into a hard-edged precision of line that molds what the imagination wants to release in visually fine-chiseled fragmental stanzas that fit flush together with the rightness of a picture puzzle; the reader beholds in admiration the cutting and paring that create such a careful finish. The visual rightness of the design is the quality that one notices first, and last, about the work. One has no doubt that a delicate, discriminating hand has been at work on these poems in an almost physical way. Whether he is manipulating the small haiku-like numbered stanzas of a short poem like the twelve-line "Approximations," or assembling the large, obliquely dovetailed, divergent planes of his longest poem, the modernist "Middle Passage," Hayden's constructive order is sure, his modeling deft. His poems are obviously the product of a painstaking, deliberate, loving sense of form.

Hayden's verbal technique is perhaps superior even to his structural ingenuity, and it is worthy of careful scrutiny. Hayden writes mostly in a fairly straightforward descriptive or narrative style remarkable mainly for its restraint. When he does aspire to poetic effect, the results are striking, as in these lines from a relatively early poem called "Theme and Variation":

> I sense, he said, the lurking rush, the sly
> transience flickering at the edge of things.
> ....
> There is, there is, he said, an imminence
> that turns to curiosa all I know....

Here fairly strict pentameter is expertly disguised by a convincingly conversational movement, yet the language is not at all colloquial or prosaic. In a poem about the changing nature of reality as one perceives it—a "changing permanence," Hayden calls it—the use of the word "transience" is entirely predictable, but to modify it with "sly" and "flickering" is to add a metaphorical quickness to the observation that raises it to the level of fine poetry. And further to characterize this quality with the oxymoron "lurking rush" lends reality's posited fleeting presence both an evasiveness and an immediacy that are suggestive with a mysterious rightness that brings to the reader a perception he could not have without Hayden's poem: this is a mark of true poetry. The conjunction of "imminence," "curiosa," and knowledge in the next stanza further vivifies the presentation of the world as both ephemeral and yet unignorable: there is an insistent emerging that continually occurs, and its very "imminence" implies constant change so that knowledge of the world can be possessed only as a

series of recollected curiosities or "curiosa." While there is nothing philosophically new about this idea, here it is found in the hands of a poet whose word choices give it a life it could not otherwise have. "Theme and Variation" shows Hayden at his lyric best.

Hayden can also make nonmetaphorical language take on a surprisingly heightened significance. In "Belsen, Day of Liberation," from *A Ballad of Remembrance,* a young girl watches through barred windows the foreign soldiers entering Bergen-Belsen, the concentration camp where she has been a prisoner and where her parents have died:

> the golden strangers who
>
> Were Father, Brother, and her dream
>   of God. Afterwards
> she said, "They were so beautiful,
>   and they were not afraid."

Here "golden strangers" has a visionary oddness that must truly reflect the transport of wonder that the girl would have felt. But it is the last two lines of the poem that are really stunning: the girl calls the men beautiful and unafraid, selecting these two properties from all others and juxtaposing them with the childlike, unassuming presumption that they quite naturally belong together. And of course here they do, with an appropriateness that suggests an almost angelic liberation from earthly bonds.

Such verbal aptness, sometimes called *felicity,* the bedrock of poetry, appears with abrupt and startling effect in Hayden's work. In these lines from "Electrical Storm," the choice of "warring" condenses a great deal of accurate, imaginatively descriptive implication about the storm's clash in the clouds, its effectiveness doubled by its alliteration with the word it modifies: "Last night we drove/through suddenly warring weather." And in "The Ballad of Sue Ellen Westerfield," the protagonist, a plantation-owner's daughter, a free mulatto who worked as a maid on Mississippi riverboats, is rendered with great vividness and extraordinary economy in one sentence that presents and suggests her personality, appearance, and even her unique sexual power, enhanced by her social position:

> Rivermen reviled her for the rankling cold
> sardonic pride
> that gave a knife-edge to her comeliness.

With the exception of a missing initial unstressed syllable, the running meter of the whole sentence is perfectly iambic, although it loses its insistence in the last three words. The unremitting meter, the alliteration in the first line, the superbly chosen triple modifiers of the noun "pride," and the highly successful metaphor of "knife-edged" good looks: all these combine to give a remarkably full portrait with very few words.

Moreover Hayden can combine this verbal sharpness with an equally sharp wit that is one of his distinguishing characteristics: sometimes ironic, sometimes comic, always ready to enter a poem for a calculated purpose. "On Lookout Mountain" is a meditation upon the scene of an important Civil War battle, a reflection on the doubtfully useful, omnipresent fact of war and its inconsequence "here where Sunday alpinists/pick views and souvenirs." The last resigned stanza combines rather lively wit with several well-chosen words—particularly "gadget," which through its connotations of superfluity achieves especial mocking power, but "trivia" and "stuffed" are also fine strokes:

> Have done, have done. Behold how bright
> upon the mountain the gadget feet
> of trivia shine.
> Oh, hear the stuffed gold eagle sing.

Such passages show Hayden at his best.

Hayden's subject matter evolved consistently over four decades, and he constantly sought stylistic perfection during that interim. Up to and including *A Ballad of Remembrance*, his principal material has to do with the black experience in America, and it takes two forms: scenes from contemporary life and evocations of the historical past, usually through the eyes of some historical personage. Of the latter type the most outstanding poems are "Frederick Douglass," "Runagate, Runagate" (about the Underground Railroad), "The Ballad of Nat Turner," "The Ballad of Sue Ellen Westerfield," and "Middle Passage," Hayden's modernist set piece on the slave trade, which appears much influenced in its structure and manner by experimental poetry written in the 1920s, particularly T. S. Eliot's *The Waste Land* (1922) and Hart Crane's *The Bridge* (1930). Hayden's line "those are altar lights that were his eyes," for example, alludes to Shakespeare's *The Tempest* in the style of T. S. Eliot, and indeed Eliot himself quotes Shakespeare's line exactly in *The Waste Land:* "Those are pearls that were his eyes." In "Middle Passage" Hayden incorporates quotations from ships' logs and from diaries in the experimental 1920s manner and applies such diverse materials toward a transcendent,

universalizing moral theme. Hayden says in *How I Write* (1972) that he was inspired to deal with such subjects by Stephen Vincent Benét's *John Brown's Body* (1928), desiring to approach slavery and the Civil War "from the black man's point of view."

Hayden's poems about more contemporary black experience present a cultural, rather than historical, view of human behavior. "Witch Doctor," which Auden admired, is a most successful example of these poems: it is a comical, satirical, psychological profile of a black evangelist and his methods. "A Ballad of Remembrance" offers a bizarre, grotesque presentation of what is apparently a black nightlife district in New Orleans, an unlikely place indeed for the poet to rendezvous with Mark Van Doren, as he does at the end of the poem. Life in the ghetto is represented by "Mourning Poem for the Queen of Sunday" and " 'Summertime and the Living. . . .,' " and black popular culture is present in "Homage to the Empress of the Blues." Hayden is not obsessed with racial conflict, and it makes only an occasional appearance in his work: with the Ku Klux Klan in "Night, Death, Mississippi," and in "Tour 5," in which the speaker stops in a southern town to "buy gas and ask directions of a raw-boned man/whose eyes revile us as the enemy."

By 1962 Hayden's interests had expanded naturally to a more inclusive view of other cultures and topics. First of all, there is in *A Ballad of Remembrance* the sequence of eight poems about Mexican life, " 'An Inference of Mexico,' " and in addition there are a number of lyric poems on miscellaneous subjects, like "The Diver," "Full Moon," "Electrical Storm," "Snow," and "Perseus." These poems foretell the basic shift in all of Hayden's later work from predominantly black situations to a more extroverted opening up to the world at large and to a wider range of subjects, and this movement pretty well describes his development until his death. He wrote about works of art, travel, nature, animals, flowers, family, friends, assassinations, stars, mythology, the Baha'i religion: his poetry, in short, broadened its scope in his later books, although his experimental modality remains a consistent thread. He never lost sight of black experience, however, and *American Journal*, contains a sequence of poems about such matters called "Elegies for Paradise Valley"; a poem about visiting the grave of Paul Laurence Dunbar, the turn-of-the-century black poet; and "A Letter from Phillis Wheatley," the eighteenth-century slave who was brought to Boston from Senegal as a child and who, after being educated and freed by her owner, became a renowned poetess before her early death in 1784.

One of the most heartening aspects of Hayden's career was his steadfast refusal to accept literature written by blacks as separate or exempt from the same high critical standards by which works written in English must always be judged. For this defense of art itself, he was exposed to a good deal of irresponsible criticism from some blacks. No black poet has written more thoroughly, searchingly, intelligently, sincerely, or faithfully about the black experience in America, and yet at a black writers' conference at Fisk University in 1966, Hayden was attacked, vilified, and ostracized by students, colleagues, and fellow writers for his unflinching insistence that the standards of art are the only meaningful, useful, or valid criteria to apply to any literary work. Julius Lester recalls his saying at the time that there is "no such thing as black literature. There's good literature and there's bad. And that's all!" Hayden says in his introduction to *Kaleidoscope* (1967):

> bad poetry is another matter, and there is no denying that a great deal of "race poetry" is poor, because its content seems ready-made and art is displaced by argument.... There are Negro poets who believe that any poet's most clearly defined task is to create with honesty and sincerity poems that will illuminate human experience—not exclusively "Negro experience." They reject the idea of poetry as racial propaganda, of poetry that functions as a kind of sociology.

Hayden obviously considered himself among their number, and he says of himself in his biographical note in the same volume: "Opposed to the chauvinistic and the doctrinaire, he sees no reason why a Negro poet should be limited to 'racial utterance' or to having his writing judged by standards different from those applied to the work of other poets."

Nothing is so impressive about Hayden as his qualities as a man, the nobility with which he confronted his life as it came to him: the terrible pain of racial discrimination; the long period of virtually total obscurity as a writer; the excessively burdensome long hours of teaching; thoughtless and unfair criticism by members of his own race; and finally the years of honors and fame, borne with humility and grace. Having experienced extremes of fortune, he endured with dignity and with the highest principles; it is fitting that he at last gained his well-deserved recognition.

Hayden's Baha'i faith contributed to the strength that enabled him to prevail as a man and as a poet in American society. In an interview in *World Order,* he sheds significant light on his view of his place as a poet in twentieth-century America, a function that his faith taught him is one of spiritual value and service:

> The Baha'i Teachings assure us that America will be an instrument for peace in the future. I think that maybe America is being prepared for that as a result of having all the races, cultures, and nationalities of the world ... in the country.... I am interested in American history, and I have written on historical themes. This does not mean that ... I do not find much to deplore ... in our society. Thus I have written poems which lament or criticize aspects of America. I am not interested in any form of cultural nationalism, clearly. American life is a point of departure for me into awareness of the universal.

In a 1977 interview, he sums up his life as a poet, and he speaks of the high seriousness with which he sees his purpose:

> I believe in the essential oneness of all people and I believe in the basic unity of all religions. I don't believe that races are important; I think that people are important. I'm very suspicious of any form of ethnicity or nationalism; I think that these things are very crippling and are very divisive. These are all Baha'i points of view, and my work grows out of this vision. I have the feeling that by holding on to these beliefs and giving them expression in my work ... I'm doing something to prepare, maybe, for a new time, for a new world.

Hayden's poetry evinces a peacefulness, an emotional equilibrium, which, however, he labored to achieve under untoward circumstances and earned through his faith and his own personal strength and resolve. Wilburn Williams says of his verse: "Hayden's characteristically soft-spoken and fluid voice derives much of its power from the evident contrast between the maelstrom of anguish out of which it originates and the quiet reflecting pool of talk into which it is inevitably channeled." Hayden's public is still being formed, and he will be increasingly admired as a man and read as a poet.

Dust jacket for the posthumously published collection of Hayden's poems

Robert Hayden died in 1980 at the age of sixty-six, having enjoyed during the last years of his life the recognition that most critics now agree had been his due for nearly a quarter of a century. In 1984, his collected prose was published by the University of Michigan Press, and the following year Liveright published *Robert Hayden: Collected Poems*.

Interviews:

"Black Writers' Views on Literary Lions and Values," *Negro Digest*, 17 (January 1968): 33, 84-85;

How I Write / 1 (New York: Harcourt Brace Jovanovich, 1972);

John O'Brien, *Interviews with Black Writers* (New York: Liveright, 1973), pp. 109-123;

"Conversations with Americans," *World Order*, 10 (Winter 1975-1976): 46-53;

Richard Layman, "Robert Hayden," in *Conversations with Writers*, 1 (Detroit: Bruccoli Clark/ Gale Research, 1977), pp. 156-179.

Bibliography:

Nicholas Xavier, "Robert Hayden: A Bibliography," *Obsidian*, 7 (Spring 1981): 109-127; 8 (Spring 1981): 207-210;

These two articles include a full listing of Hayden's poetry volumes, his poems printed or since reprinted in journals, his poetry collected in anthologies, and his printed prose statements. Also contains an extensive examination of published criticism.

Biographies:

Robert M. Greenberg, "Robert Hayden 1913-1980," in *American Writers: A Collection of Literary Biographies,* edited by Walton Litz (New York: Scribners, 1981);

Contains a comprehensive biographical segment and adequate analytical commentary.

Pontheolla T. Williams, "Robert Hayden: A Life Upon These Shores," *World Order*, 16 (Fall 1981): 11-34;

An essay which is well detailed and comprehensive, yet tends to diminish as the account approaches the present.

References:

Arthur P. Davis, "Robert Hayden," in *From the Dark Tower: Afro-American Writers 1900-1960* (Washington, D.C.: Howard University Press, 1974), pp. 174-180;
This treatment gives a brief synopsis of Hayden's life and surveys his major publications, in addition to discussing the poet's work and philosophy.

Charles T. Davis, "Robert Hayden's Use of History," in *Modern Black Poets,* edited by Donald B. Gibson (Englewood Cliffs, N.J.: Prentice-Hall, 1973), pp. 96-111;
One of the earliest critical essays on Hayden's poetry, emphasizing the poet's interest in history in general and black history in particular.

Howard Faulkner, " 'Transformed by Steeps of Flight': The Poetry of Robert Hayden," *CLA Journal,* 21 (June 1978): 282-291;
As a discussion of *Angle of Ascent,* this article asserts that the poet's dominant theme is transformation and deals with his frequent use of oxymoron and paradox.

Fred M. Fetrow, " 'Middle Passage': Robert Hayden's Anti Epic," *CLA Journal,* 22 (June 1979): 304-318;
A substantial critical study of "Middle Passage," a poem, it is asserted that Hayden designed as a variation on the epic structure.

Fetrow, *Robert Hayden* (Boston: Twayne, 1984);
Progressing chronologically, this study treats poems according to subject, theme, and technique, and is designed to trace the poet's evolution.

Fetrow, "Robert Hayden's 'Frederick Douglass': Form and Meaning in a Modern Sonnet," *CLA Journal,* 17 (September 1973): 79-84;
A brief article which illustrates the poet's innovative approach to the traditional sonnet form.

Fetrow, "Robert Hayden's 'The Rag Man' and the Metaphysics of the Mundane," *Research Studies,* 47 (September 1979): 188-190;
An interesting exercise in psychoanalytical criticism, which approaches Hayden's "The Rag Man" as a case study in psychological projection.

Michael S. Harper, "Remembering Robert Hayden," *Michigan Quarterly Review,* 21 (Winter 1982): 182-186;
A brief memorial tribute to Hayden from a fellow poet. Praises Hayden's willingness to submerge himself into art.

John Hatcher, *From the Auroral Darkness: The Life and Poetry of Robert Hayden* (Oxford: George Ronald, 1984);
A valuable contribution to Hayden studies, this volume provides comprehensive coverage of all phases of the poet's life and work.

Julius Lester, "In Memorium: In Gratitude for Robert Hayden," *World Order,* 16 (Fall 1981): 50-55;
This eulogy by a former student praises Hayden both as a man and as an artist.

Michael P. Novak, "Meditative, Ironic, Richly Human: The Poetry of Robert Hayden," *Midwest Quarterly,* 15 (Spring 1974): 276-285;
Discusses Hayden's biographical background, career pattern, and basic philosophical views. Is occasionally superficial in treating specific poems.

Obsidian, special issue on Hayden, 8 (Spring 1981);
An extensive collection of many brief yet poignant remembrances, tributes, and portraits of Hayden.

Maurice J. O'Sullivan, Jr., "The Mask of Allusion in Robert Hayden's 'The Diver,' " *CLA Journal,* 17 (September 1973): 85-92;
A discussion of "The Diver" which rejects the poem's universal themes and focuses on its racial implications.

Gerald Parks, "The Baha'i Muse: Religion in Robert Hayden's Poetry," *World Order,* 16 (Fall 1981): 37-48;
An examination of the poet's religious convictions and of the doctrines of the Baha'i faith.

Rosey E. Pool, "Robert Hayden: Poet Laureate (An Assessment)," *Negro Digest,* 15 (June 1966): 164-175;
The first published response to the body of Hayden's work. Discusses many of his poems but lacks analytical objectivity.

Constance J. Post, "Image and Idea in the Poetry of Robert Hayden," *CLA Journal,* 20 (December 1976): 164-175;
A discussion of Hayden's recurring star imagery and dominant theme of struggle. Mistakenly reduces a complex poet to a single image and theme.

Vilma R. Potter, "A Remembrance for Robert Hayden, 1913-1980," *MELUS,* 8 (Spring 1980): 51-55;
Discusses Hayden's work as a metamorphic vision of black American experience. So narrow in scope, the article tends to oversimplify both characters and themes.

Lewis Turco, "*Angle of Ascent:* The Poetry of Robert Hayden," *Michigan Quarterly Review,* 16 (Spring 1977): 199-219;
An examination of Hayden's style and a defense of him as a black poet.

Wilburn Williams, Jr., "Covenant of Timelessness and Time: Symbolism and History in Robert Hayden's *Angle of Ascent,*" in *Chant of Saints: A Gathering of Afro-American Literature, Art, and Scholarship,* edited by Michael S. Harper and Robert B. Stepto (Urbana: University of Illinois Press, 1979), pp. 66-84;
A discussion of Hayden as a combination of symbolist and historian.

World Order, special issue on Hayden, 16 (Fall 1981);
Memorial issue of the Baha'i faith quarterly journal. Contains several essays and a few poems in tribute to Hayden.

William Inge

This entry was updated by Ralph F. Voss (University of Alabama) from his entry in DLB 7, Twentieth-Century American Dramatists.

Places	American Midwest	Kansas	
Influences and Relationships	Tennessee Williams	Elia Kazan	Joshua Logan
Literary Movements and Forms	Postwar Dramatic Realism	"Revolt from the Village"	

Major Themes	Family
	Loneliness
	Failure of
	    Love Relationships
		Frustration
		Oedipal Conflict
		Philosophical
		    Acceptance of Life
			Small Town Life
			Sexual Repression
			Restrictive Social
			    and Moral Codes

Cultural and Artistic Influences	Freudianism Alcoholism Teachers' Roles	Family Homosexuality	Psychoanalysis Discrimination
Social and Economic Influences	Great Depression	Sexual/Racial/Religious Discrimination	Small Town Codes

BIRTH: Independence, Kansas, 3 May 1913, to Luther Clayton and Maude Sarah Gibson Inge.

EDUCATION: B.A., University of Kansas, 1935; M.A., George Peabody College, Nashville, Tennessee, 1938.

AWARDS AND HONORS: George Jean Nathan Award and Theatre Time Award for *Come Back, Little Sheba*, 1950; Pulitzer Prize, New York Drama Critics Circle Award, and Donaldson Award for *Picnic*, 1953; Academy Award for Best Original Story and Screenplay for *Splendor in the Grass*, 1961.

DEATH: Los Angeles, California, 10 June 1973.

BOOKS: *Come Back, Little Sheba* (New York: Random House, 1950);
Picnic (New York: Random House, 1953);
Bus Stop (New York: Random House, 1955);
The Dark at the Top of the Stairs (New York: Random House, 1958);
Four Plays by William Inge (New York: Random House, 1958; London: Heinemann, 1960)—includes *Come Back, Little Sheba, Picnic, Bus Stop*, and *The Dark at the Top of the Stairs*;
A Loss of Roses (New York: Random House, 1960);
Splendor in the Grass (New York: Bantam, 1961);
Summer Brave and Eleven Short Plays (New York: Random House, 1962)—includes *Summer Brave, The Boy in the Basement, Bus Riley's Back in Town, An Incident at the Standish Arms, The Mall, Memory of Summer, People in the Wind, The Rainy Afternoon, A Social Event, The Strains of Triumph, The Tiny Closet*, and *To Bobolink, for Her Spirit*;
Natural Affection (New York: Random House, 1963);
Where's Daddy? (New York: Random House, 1966);
Two Short Plays (New York: Dramatists Play Service, 1968)—includes *The Call* and *A Murder*;
Good Luck, Miss Wyckoff (Boston & Toronto: Atlantic/Little, Brown, 1970; London: Deutsch, 1971);
My Son Is a Splendid Driver (Boston & Toronto: Atlantic/Little, Brown, 1971).

PLAY PRODUCTIONS: *Farther Off from Heaven*, Dallas, Margo Jones's Theatre 47, 1947;
Come Back, Little Sheba, New York, Booth Theatre, 15 February 1950, 190 [performances];
Picnic, New York, Music Box Theatre, 19 February 1953, 477;

William Inge

Bus Stop, New York, Music Box Theatre, 2 March 1955, 478;
The Dark at the Top of the Stairs, New York, Music Box Theatre, 5 December 1957, 468;
A Loss of Roses, New York, Eugene O'Neill Theatre, 28 November 1959, 25;
Natural Affection, New York, Booth Theatre, 31 January 1963, 36;
Where's Daddy?, New York, Billy Rose Theatre, 2 March 1966, 21;
Overnight, Los Angeles, University of California, 31 January 1969;
Summer Brave, New York, Master Theatre, 5 April 1973, 12.

SCREENPLAY: *Splendor in the Grass*, Warner Bros., 1961.

OTHER: *Glory in the Flower*, in *24 Favorite One-Act Plays*, edited by Bennett Cerf and Van H. Cartmell (Garden City: Doubleday, 1958), pp. 35-50;
"A Statement," in *Celebrities on the Couch: Personal Adventures of Famous People in Psychoanalysis*,

edited by Lucy Freeman (Los Angeles: Price, Sloane & Ravenna, 1970), pp. 173-174.

William Motter Inge was one of America's most successful playwrights during the 1950s. No American writer of serious drama has matched his unbroken series of critical and popular successes during that decade. *Come Back, Little Sheba* (1950), *Picnic* (1953), *Bus Stop* (1955), and *The Dark at the Top of the Stairs* (1957) all portray lonely, frustrated people who struggle to find lasting love and happiness in small towns in Inge's native midwestern America. Despite similarities of character, theme, and setting in these plays, each one was eminently successful; moreover, each was made into a popular film, further enhancing the reputation of the former schoolteacher who was nearly thirty-seven years old when *Come Back, Little Sheba* premiered. As Robert Shuman noted about this stage of Inge's career, "Critics could do little but marvel at the success of a man who wrote modest plays about the most prosaic of people, but who had never experienced a box office failure." However, Inge never again experienced critical or popular success in the New York theater after 1958, and his four midwestern plays of the 1950s remain his best and most enduring, though he wrote several more plays, screenplays, and novels before the end of his life.

Born in Independence, Kansas, William Inge was the fifth and youngest child of Maude Sarah Gibson Inge and Luther Clayton Inge. Mr. Inge was a traveling salesman who was often absent, and young William was raised in a mother-dominated home that significantly influenced his personality and his art. The young Inge was a "momma's boy" who displayed an early flair for recitation and performance, much like Sonny Flood in *The Dark at the Top of the Stairs*. Also like Sonny, Inge was teased by other boys as a sissy, but his neurasthenic mother sheltered and encouraged him. During Inge's high-school years, his performing talents expanded to acting and cheerleading, and though he was popular, he seldom dated. These formative experiences contributed to the homosexuality Inge never publicly admitted but hinted at in some of his later writing.

After his high school graduation in 1930, Inge enrolled at the University of Kansas. On campus Inge studied drama and continued acting; he also wrote dialogue for musical comedies that were produced annually. He spent undergraduate summers playing juvenile roles in a touring vaudeville show. At this point in his life, Inge fully intended to become a professional actor.

When he graduated in 1935, however, Inge decided against pursuing an acting career. His touring experience had taught him about the uncertainties inherent in acting, and he did not want a life in small-time show business. The alternative, to go to New York in hopes of being discovered, was an even more tenuous proposition. "I feared going to New York," he later said; "I had no money and no acquaintances there." He also knew he could not return to Independence; not only was employment hard to find there during the Depression, but he also felt a need to live apart from his mother. Reluctantly, he accepted a scholarship to work on a master's degree at George Peabody College in Nashville, Tennessee, in preparation for a career in "the security of teaching."

Inge was a reasonably successful graduate student but often regretted his decision against an acting career. According to Jean Gould, Inge tried to accept teaching as his profession, but " 'developed a sickness of mood and temper' which compelled him to leave for home two weeks before he was to get his degree." Back in Kansas, doubting now his fitness either for acting or teaching, Inge floundered. He worked as a laborer on a highway crew, then as a scriptwriter and announcer for a Wichita radio station. Whatever subsistence these jobs provided, they offered little satisfaction for Inge. He apparently had few friends and no romantic interests. In the fall of 1937, he began teaching English in the Columbus, Kansas, high school. The experience proved positive enough so that in the summer of 1938 he returned to Peabody, where his thesis was accepted. With master's degree in hand, Inge began an instructorship in English and drama at Stephens College in Columbia, Missouri.

At Stephens, Inge worked closely with Maude Adams, an actress who had retired from the stage. His teaching was undistinguished, but his interest in drama was renewed, though his personal life remained generally unhappy and he began to drink heavily. After suffering a brief emotional breakdown, he began to write for his own pleasure and the release of tensions. None of this writing was published, but he developed sufficient confidence in his writing so that in 1943 he eagerly accepted the opportunity to become a drama critic for the *St. Louis Star-Times*, replacing a friend who left to serve in World War II. For Inge, and ultimately for American drama, this hiatus from teaching proved fortuitous.

Just before the success of *The Glass Menagerie*, Tennessee Williams visited Saint Louis in late 1944. Inge sought Williams out for an interview, and a lifelong friendship between the two men was born. Inge told Williams that he wanted to write plays, and Williams encouraged Inge to pursue that ambition. Heartened, Inge began to write seriously. Before 1945 was over he wrote his first play, *Farther Off from Heaven*, which he later reworked into *The Dark at the Top of the Stairs*. In 1946 Inge had to relinquish the job at the *St. Louis Star-Times* when the regular critic returned from the war, and he reluctantly accepted a teaching position at Washington University of Saint Louis. "I hated it, but it was a job," Inge later said. Though he had returned to teaching out of necessity, he continued to pursue playwriting.

Through Williams, Inge met Margo Jones, a pioneer of theater in Dallas. When Jones read *Farther Off from Heaven*, she chose it for an amateur production in Dallas in 1947. Though it was limited to a few performances, it was well enough received so that both Inge and Jones were encouraged. From 1946 to 1949 Inge continued to teach while writing plays. He drank so heavily during these years that he turned to Alcoholics Anonymous in 1948, gaining a perspective on alcoholism that contributed to his characterization of Doc Delaney in *Come Back, Little Sheba*, but failing to overcome the addiction himself. In 1949 Inge sent *Come Back, Little Sheba* to Audrey Wood, a New York agent he had met through Williams. Wood brought *Come Back, Little Sheba* to the attention of New York's Theatre Guild, and by the end of the year the play had been accepted for production. Inge took a leave from Washington University to see *Come Back, Little Sheba* through production. He would never again have to teach for his livelihood.

The decade of critical and popular success that followed brought Inge the fame and fortune he had long desired. After *Come Back, Little Sheba*, the *New York Times* hailed Inge as Broadway's "most promising" playwright. Two years later, *Picnic*'s success brought him a Pulitzer Prize, a New York Drama Critics Circle Award, and a tie with Arthur Miller's *The Crucible* for the Donaldson Award. Then came *Bus Stop* and *The Dark at the Top of the Stairs*, neither of which won awards but both of which helped establish his reputation. By some estimates, he realized close to a million dollars from his plays and the films that were made from them.

But Inge still suffered depression and alcoholism. In the foreword to *Four Plays by William Inge*, published in 1958, he wrote: "Anticipating success (of any degree), I had always expected to feel hilarious, but I didn't." He had begun regular psychoanalysis in 1949 and continued through the

1950s, gaining insights readily apparent in his plays but also gaining an understanding of himself that ultimately was difficult to accept. Psychoanalysis could explain Inge's homosexuality, but it was one thing to have an explanation and another thing to accept it. Analysis no doubt helped Inge cope with his life, but over the years his public remarks about the value of psychoanalysis range from praise to disapproval. Though many of his works urge an acceptance of life's traumas, Inge himself was never fully able to do so, even during the years of his most conspicuous success. In a tribute written after Inge committed suicide, Robert Alan Aurthur commented that "Bill carefully disguised his homosexuality. To a Midwestern boy faggotry was at the very least a terrible embarrassment." Unlike his friend Tennessee Williams, Inge could not acknowledge his homosexuality, let alone overcome its troubling effects. When the string of successes ended and he lost much of his money backing his first Broadway failure, *A Loss of Roses* (1959), Inge took the harsh reviews personally. Shy, hurt, unhappy, and rejected, he ended his decade in New York by turning his attention to Hollywood.

The success of film versions of his plays made Inge feel more welcome in California. A sympathetic friend, Elia Kazan, who had directed *The Dark at the Top of the Stairs* in New York, encouraged Inge to write for the screen. Inge produced a script about the unfulfilled love of a young couple in a little Kansas town, and Warner Bros. agreed to film it with Kazan directing. The film, *Splendor in the Grass*, won Inge an Academy Award as the best original screenplay of 1961. For Inge, who played a cameo role as a minister in the film, *Splendor in the Grass* was a heartening success. It was the last he would know in his lifetime. He considered making his home in California but returned to New York where a new play, *Natural Affection*, premiered in 1963.

In *Natural Affection* Inge abandoned for the first time the rural midwestern settings that had so importantly distinguished his previous work, but he retained his concern with intense, intrafamilial tensions. *Natural Affection* met scathing reviews, however, and soon closed. Again, Inge was deeply hurt by what he felt was the personal viciousness of critics. Back in Hollywood, he worked on adapting screenplays for *That Hill Girl* and *All Fall Down*. He became convinced that his best opportunities now lay in California, so he sold his New York apartment and made a permanent move to Los Angeles in 1964. It did not prove to be a good move for his career. A final screenplay, *Bus Riley's Back in Town,* was based on his one-act play by the same name; but he had his name expunged from the 1965 film's credits because the final version bore little resemblance to his original work. He had unhappily learned that an original writer in Hollywood filmmaking had very little clout; the success of *Splendor in the Grass* had been quickly forgotten. Meanwhile, he wrote *Where's Daddy?,* his final play to appear on Broadway. Although *Where's Daddy?* (1966) is concerned with family relationships, it is unlike Inge's earlier plays, being a weak vehicle for criticism of society in general and contemporary theater in particular. Opening 2 March 1966, it closed soon afterward, shredded by critics and shunned by audiences. Less than ten years after his decade of phenomenal success, Inge suffered three consecutive Broadway failures and was never to try again in New York.

The last years of Inge's life were spent in California, where he continued to write and also participated as a teacher and adviser in theater workshops and classes at UCLA and the University of California at Irvine. Two plays, *The Last Pad* and *Overnight,* and a one-act play, *Caesarian Operations,* were performed on the West Coast, but they have not yet been published. Inge sought his widest audience at this time with two novels, *Good Luck, Miss Wyckoff,* published in 1970, and the revealing autobiographical work, *My Son Is a Splendid Driver,* published in 1971. Neither novel was widely reviewed, the first being disliked and the second praised by the few critics who read it. Neither sold enough copies for subsequent printings.

Inge lived his final years with his widowed sister, Helene Inge Connell, who eventually gave most of his private papers and manuscripts to the William Inge Collection at Independence Community College in his hometown. She frequently sought to shield Inge from critics and interviewers, but a reporter named Lloyd Steele was granted what proved to be Inge's last interview. Steele found Inge unresponsive, effective only in nostalgic reminiscence, and decided against printing the piece out of respect for the playwright. A few days later, Inge committed suicide, and Steele printed the interview because, in the light of Inge's death, it was infinitely more revealing and "unutterably more sad." Inge told Steele that life had always been very ugly to him and that if he had only one more play to write, it would be about loneliness and ineffectuality. More than anything else, the playwright said, he hoped that following generations would find "some value" in his work. That final hope, at least, is sure to be realized.

Inge was, in Robert Brustein's phrase, "Broadway's first authentic Midwestern playwright." Six of his seven major plays are set in the Midwest, five specifically in small towns. In terms of attitude toward locale, Inge's kinship lies with such "revolt-from-the-village" writers as Sherwood Anderson, Sinclair Lewis, Willa Cather, and E. W. Howe. The stereotypical view of the midwestern small town as a thoroughly wholesome environment is implicitly rejected in Inge's work, which, according to Brustein, "restored to Midwesterners their privilege to be as traumatized by life as any other Americans represented on Broadway." Inge's small town is a "burg" where everyone seems to know—and mind—everyone else's business, where prevailing mores force his characters to repress their deepest feelings, causing them to become emotionally distraught and often causing them to commit defiant acts. Unquestionably, Inge's own background in small-town Kansas provided inspiration and understanding for the settings of his major works. Inge was also deeply concerned with family relationships, particularly role responsibilities. "The American family does concern me," Inge said in an interview; "And I do have my own childhood memories to draw upon. One might say that our greatest problems stem from the family."

In Inge's work, the greatest problems are those related to finding an elusive happiness and satisfaction in life, transcending ineffectuality, frustration, and loneliness. In almost all his plays, his characters fail to find sustaining happiness and struggle for a spiritual equilibrium based upon recognizing, accepting, and coping with circumstances. Nowhere is this more evident than in Inge's first Broadway success, *Come Back, Little Sheba.*

Come Back, Little Sheba is a play about a childless married couple, Doc and Lola Delaney, who battle loss of youth, promise, and ambitions with alcohol (Doc) and fantasies (Lola). They do not find solace but come to an acceptance of reality that, at play's end, augurs hope for relative happiness through mutual dependence. Doc and Lola's marriage was forced by her father when she became pregnant, but both the child and Lola's ability to have children were lost when to avoid local gossip the couple went to a midwife for her delivery. Doc had to drop out of medical school and become a chiropractor to support Lola. At the beginning of the play, the once-beautiful Lola has become fat and slovenly. She neglects her housework to chatter nostalgically with anyone who will listen. She searches for vicarious escape by going to the mov-

Burt Lancaster, Shirley Booth, Richard Jaeckel, and Terry Moore in the film production
of Come Back, Little Sheba

ies, listening to a radio show named "Taboo," and minding the affair that Marie, a young boarder, is having with Turk, a college javelin thrower. Lola's lost youthful beauty is symbolized by the lost dog, Little Sheba, that she calls frequently in the play. Sheba, like Lola's youth, has "vanished into thin air," a phrase she often repeats. Disappointed over the losses of their child, his medical career, and Lola's beauty, Doc became a serious drinker, then an alcoholic. To avoid painful drying-out sessions and salvage his marriage and practice, Doc joined Alcoholics Anonymous. At the beginning of the play, he has been "dry" for a year, sustaining himself with the alcoholic's daily prayer, which also serves as a thematic statement for the play: "God grant me the serenity to accept the things I cannot change, courage to change the things I can, and wisdom always to tell the difference."

Marie, the young boarder, is the catalyst for the dramatic action in the play. Lola condones, even encourages, Marie's affair with Turk even though she knows that Marie is engaged to someone else. Doc, on the other hand, dotes on Marie as a surrogate daughter, considering her beautiful and pure—as Lola no longer is. Obsessed with propriety, Doc does not want to believe that Marie is

doing anything wrong. He is suspicious and jealous of Turk, whose javelin is an obvious phallic symbol for the kind of character he is (Turk is the first of a line of one-dimensional, priapic males in Inge's plays). When Doc learns that Marie and Turk slept together in the Delaney house the night before Marie's fiancé is to arrive, his fragile equilibrium is shattered. Disgusted with Marie and Lola, who has cleaned the house for the first time in years and planned a sumptuous dinner, Doc takes the quart bottle of liquor he has kept on hand as a reminder and test and goes on a binge.

When Doc returns, he is in a drunken rage. He calls Lola and Marie "a couple of sluts" and grabs a hatchet when Lola calls Alcoholics Anonymous. He threatens to "hack off" all of Lola's fat, "then wait for Marie and chop off those pretty ankles she's always dancing around on . . . then start lookin' for Turk and fix him too." Doc's drunken scene, perhaps the most intense in all of Inge's work, is the climax of the play, the purgation of all his frustrations. The threats to maim the women and castrate Turk are psychologically well motivated, but Doc passes out before he can try to accomplish them. After Doc is taken to the drunk tank, Lola calls home to see if her parents will let her return, but her father forbids it, having never forgiven her for having to marry Doc. Marie elopes with her fiancé, leaving Lola totally alone. While Doc is gone she realizes she needs him and that it is pointless to escape in fantasies.

When Doc returns he begs Lola, "Please don't ever leave me. If you do they'd have to keep me down at that place all the time." "You're all I ever had," Lola replies. Lola then recounts to Doc a dream she had in which her father, refereeing a track meet, disqualifies Turk from throwing the javelin. Doc then throws the javelin "clear up into the sky," and it never comes down. Later, still in the dream, Lola finds Little Sheba dead, but Doc refuses to allow Lola to stay and cry over Sheba. "We can't stay here, honey," he says; "We gotta go on." Lola's dream provides an obvious symbolic resolution for the play that some critics have considered all too pat, but certainly it provides a basis for Lola's declaration: "I don't think Little Sheba's ever coming back, Doc. I'm not going to call her anymore." The ending of *Come Back, Little Sheba* is hopeful, but Inge gives his audience no strong reason to expect that Doc and Lola's lasting happiness is assured. Theirs is a desperate mutual dependence rather than a renewed love.

When *Come Back, Little Sheba* was revived in New York in 1974, John Simon wrote that it was probably Inge's best play despite its casual resemblance to soap opera, because "it is much too honest and down-to-earth a work, far too concerned with existential truth, to be glibly downgraded." Simon called the character of Doc one of the most convincing portrayals of alcoholic addiction in American theater. Inge's second Broadway success, *Picnic*, is far less dramatic than *Come Back, Little Sheba*, involving several more characters and using Inge's small-town background more obviously. Though not his best play, it remains the best known.

Picnic is the story of how one sexually attractive man, an outsider to the community, affects a group of lonely, frustrated women in a Kansas town. None of the women in *Picnic*—Flo Owens and her two daughters, Madge and Millie; Rosemary Sydney, a schoolteacher who lives in the Owens home; and Helen Potts, who lives next door—has a strong relationship with a man. Flo is a widow in her forties who is mistrustful of all but the most docile and well-mannered men. Millie is an intellectual tomboy of sixteen. Helen is nearly sixty and was wed, but her parents had the marriage annulled. Rosemary is about Flo's age and has never married, but she dates Howard Bevans, a businessman of fifty. Madge, the most beautiful girl in town, has never dated anyone but the wealthy and incredibly shy Alan Seymour, who is so awed by Madge's beauty that he hardly believes she is real. Flo hopes Madge and Alan will marry, but Madge is vaguely dissatisfied with her life and with Alan as well; she questions the value of her beauty and dreams of adventure while going through the dull routine of working at the dime store and having chaste dates with Alan. Neither Madge nor Alan is sexually aggressive enough to challenge the moral climate they live in.

The handsome stranger is Hal Carter, a virile drifter who failed at everything he tried to do after his college days as a football hero. Hal was a college friend of Alan's and comes to the town hoping that Alan can offer him a job. When he first arrives, Hal does yard work for Helen in exchange for a meal. Working shirtless in Helen's yard, Hal immediately draws the notice of all the women, including the wary Flo. When Alan and Hal are reunited, Flo must reluctantly accept Hal as Alan's friend, but she senses trouble when Helen suggests that Hal be Millie's date at the upcoming Labor Day picnic.

Hal is an insecure character who affects a surface braggadocio. He enjoys the attention he gets but confesses to Alan, "I won't know how to act around all these *women*." His boasting hides his self-doubt until a climactic scene in act two, just as everyone is about to leave for the picnic. As this scene progresses and the characters drink from Howard's liquor bottle, Hal abandons the tomboy Millie for the voluptuous Madge and fails to avert the desperate attentions of the aging schoolteacher Rosemary. Rosemary and Millie get drunk, and Millie flees, feeling humiliated and rejected. Rosemary angrily condemns Hal: "You'll end your life in the gutter and it'll serve you right 'cause the gutter's where you came from and the gutter's where you belong." While Hal stands stunned by Rosemary's attack, Flo enters to forbid more drinking, declare that Millie will not go to the picnic with Hal, and order Madge to go change her provocative dress. Then Flo, Helen, Millie, and Alan leave to secure a site at the picnic—a departure that strains credibility after what has occurred—leaving Madge to come to the picnic with Rosemary and Howard after she changes. Rosemary, however, is by now very upset. The alcohol and Hal's rejection have made her conscious of her own desperation, and she tells Howard she wants "to drive into the sunset" instead of going to the picnic. When Rosemary and Howard leave, Madge and Hal are left alone.

Madge senses Hal's chagrin and tries to console him. Hal confesses his insecurities, saying that Rosemary was right. Madge, pleased that Hal has confided in her, kisses him—and the moment overwhelms them. Picking Madge up in his arms, Hal says, "We're not goin' on no goddamn picnic."

Late that night, Howard and Rosemary return, and Inge makes it clear that they have had sex instead of going to the picnic. Rosemary tells Howard he must marry her because she cannot bear to return to teaching and letting the years pass. When Howard tries to avoid commitment, she sinks to her knees and begs him. He promises only to return in the morning. After Rosemary goes inside, Hal and Madge return, and it is clear that they, too, have made love. Madge is ashamed, and they both admit that they forgot all about Alan and Flo. They have no idea how they will explain their absence, and when they kiss again, Madge tears herself away and runs into the house, crying.

Early the next morning, Rosemary tells everyone that Howard is coming to marry her, making it impossible for him to refuse when he arrives. Flo is furious about Hal and lies to Helen that nothing happened between Madge and Hal. Amid the general congratulations of Rosemary and Howard as they leave the house, Hal appears. He talks with Madge when everyone else goes offstage to see Rosemary and Howard to their car. Alan and Flo find Hal and Madge together, and Alan tries to fight Hal but is easily subdued. Hal must catch a train to Tulsa because Alan has reported him to the law. Hal and Madge admit they love each other, and Hal asks Madge to come with him. She cries that she cannot, and Hal flees. A short while later, however, Madge packs and follows Hal over Flo's objections. Flo is nonplussed over these events, but Helen admits that she liked Hal and thinks Madge did the right thing.

Robert Brustein was only partially correct when he termed *Picnic* "a satyr play glorifying the phallic male." Although Hal is very important, the play's force is generated by the women, particularly Madge and Rosemary. Inge was adept at the portrayal of female frustration; indeed his women characters are generally more compelling and memorable than his male characters. In Madge, Inge captured well the frustrations peculiar to those so beautiful that no one believes they have problems. Rosemary nearly steals dramatic focus from the other characters. A forced marriage, like that of Rosemary and Howard, is a major theme in Inge's work; seldom does he depict such love as free and happy. Madge's following Hal was not

Inge's idea; it was insisted upon by the play's director, Joshua Logan. Logan and Inge were friends at the time of *Picnic*'s original production but later became antagonists. *Summer Brave*, according to its title page the "rewritten and final version" of *Picnic*, was published in 1962. *Summer Brave* has few changes from *Picnic*, but Madge does not follow Hal in the later version. *Picnic* is the play most commonly associated with Inge, still often presented by professional and amateur groups throughout the country.

If *Picnic* is in many ways Inge's most typical play, his next New York play, *Bus Stop*, is his least typical, even though it is set in a small Kansas town. *Bus Stop* is his only play that can accurately be called a romantic comedy, and it is his only play that is not directly concerned with family relationships. Inge developed *Bus Stop* from his one-act play entitled *People in the Wind*. The earlier play provided the situation—travelers stranded at a bus stop in a blizzard—and several of the characters, but for *Bus Stop* Inge brought two of these characters, Bo Decker and Cherie, into central focus. Bo is a naive, brash, bragging cowboy from Montana who has just won many awards in a Kansas City rodeo. He met Cherie when she was performing at a nightclub, and though he had never before had a sexual experience, he spent the night with her and coaxed her into leaving for Montana with him and Virgil Blessing, his fellow cowboy and surrogate father. At the bus stop, Cherie claims she has been abducted and vows not to continue with Bo. She admits to being charmed by his innocence and good looks but resents his rough possessiveness. The central action of the play is the progress of Bo and Cherie's relationship. After Bo is humiliated in a fight with Will Masters, the local sheriff, over Cherie's right to remain at the bus stop, he apologizes to everyone—including Cherie—and she eventually gets back on the bus for Montana with him.

The extremely humorous treatment of the Bo-Cherie love relationship with its happy ending is atypical of Inge. Audiences of the mid 1950s enjoyed the characters and the happy ending, but Bo is a shallow, farcical character, a stereotypical sexy male like Turk and Hal, without the sympathy that the latter evokes. Cherie's characterization is only slightly less farcical than Bo's, but her frustration at being treated as an object makes her more sympathetic.

The minor characters of *Bus Stop* provide a somber background for the main conflict. Grace, the operator of the bus stop, is lonely but rejects the idea of trying to find a husband. She has a brief

Betty Field, Cliff Robertson, Verna Felton, Kim Novak, William Holden, Rosalind Russell, Arthur O'Connell, and Susan Strasberg in the film version of Inge's play Picnic

affair with Carl, the bus driver, but does not consider it important. "Makin' love is *one* thing," she tells Elma, the young girl who works for her, "and bein' lonesome is another." Virgil Blessing has spent many years as friend and adviser to Bo, and his good manners and mediation do much to gain tolerance of Bo by the others. However, when Cherie goes with Bo, Virgil stays behind. As Grace closes the bus stop after the bus departs, she tells Virgil he is "just left out in the cold." "That's what happens to some people," he replies. Dr. Lyman is a drunken ex-professor who rides the bus aimlessly, devoid of self-respect. He is disgusted with academia, caustic about his three failed marriages, and convinced that life is too complex to allow meaningful human love. Grace, Virgil, and Dr. Lyman are also "people in the wind," completing the composite picture of humanity that Inge claimed he was striving for in the play; but *Bus Stop*'s focus on Bo and Cherie diminishes the other characters.

Inge's final Broadway success, *The Dark at the Top of the Stairs*, returns to his more familiar serious psychological drama of family relationships. It is Inge's most autobiographical play. The Flood fam-

ily is closely modeled after Inge's own, and Sonny Flood is unquestionably based upon Inge's own boyhood. *The Dark at the Top of the Stairs*, the reworking of *Farther Off from Heaven*, offers Inge's most complex and compelling characterizations, his richest complement of plot and symbolic language, and his most sympathetic rendering of the themes that occupy almost all of his creative writing.

The Flood family resides in a small Oklahoma town during the 1920s. Rubin, the father, is frequently gone because he is a traveling salesman who has an increasingly difficult time finding buyers for harness. Cora, his wife of seventeen years, often argues with him to take a job in the town to help her raise the children and to keep him from having the affairs she suspects he has on the road. Reenie, their teenage daughter, is a shy wallflower, and Sonny is clearly in need of a strong male presence. All the Floods are afraid. Rubin fears the changing times, losing his job, and settling down to Cora and his children. Cora simultaneously fears losing and keeping Rubin; she depends on him but frequently deplores his behavior, which she con-

siders coarse. She also fears that she has overpro-
tected her children, drawing them too close to her
to compensate for Rubin's absence. The darkness
at the top of their stairs, which, fittingly, lead to
the Floods' bedrooms, is the pervasive symbol of
their fears, profoundly rooted in sex. Rubin and
Cora had a whirlwind courtship, and Inge implies
that their marriage was hurried because of Rubin's
sexual insistence. Cora considers sex "animal" and
is somewhat embarrassed by her enjoyment of it.
Rubin and Cora are unable to confront and discuss
their fears. The central action of the play involves
a series of events that enable them to come to a
better understanding and acceptance of each other.

This series of events begins with a spirited
argument. Cora has bought Reenie an expensive
dress for the country club dance, and Rubin, who
has just lost his job without telling Cora, insists it
must be returned. Soon, Rubin and Cora are arguing about Rubin's absences and his behavior
while gone. Cora dares Rubin to hit her, and, for
the first time in their marriage, he does. Then he
stalks out of the house, his loss of job still a secret,
swearing not to return. While Rubin is gone, Cora
must contemplate survival without him. At first she
turns her emotions even more directly to Sonny.
After he is taunted by other boys, Cora soothes him
and says, "I love you, Sonny. More than anything
else in the world." Elsewhere, Inge shows even
more directly the oedipal bond between the two
when he writes, "For a moment, mother and son
lie together in each other's arms. Then Cora stands,
as though fearing her own indulgence."

Cora invites her sister and brother-in-law,
Lottie and Morris Lacey, to come from Oklahoma
City for a visit. She hopes that Lottie and Morris
will allow her and the children to live with them,
but Lottie refuses. Lottie and Cora have a serious
discussion in which Lottie confesses that although
she and Morris are outwardly very happy, their
marriage is joyless and sexless. Lottie, one of Inge's
most memorable characters, admits that her parents made her fearful of sex and that she has never
been able to enjoy it. Lottie's remarks surprise
Cora, for Lottie has always seemed worldly and
knowledgeable. Her vulnerability is masked by an
amusing bluster. Lottie eventually relents and tells
Cora that she and the children can come to Oklahoma City, but Cora has begun to reevaluate her
situation and declines.

Inge shows the extreme prejudices of the
town in connection with Reenie's date for the
dance. Reenie is petrified at the prospect of a blind
date, aware that such dates are arranged for people

too unpopular to make their own. Her date is
Sammy Goldenbaum, the son of a bit-part Hollywood actress who ignores him, shuttling him from
one boarding school to another. Sammy is lonely
and rejected, but when he arrives for Reenie he is
courteously patient while Reenie hides in her room.
Cora finally persuades Reenie to go to the dance
but shortly after arriving, Reenie, mortified that no
one cuts in, introduces Sammy to the hostess and
hides in the ladies' room. When the inebriated hostess learns that Sammy is Jewish, she tells him he
must leave. Sammy, unable to find Reenie, departs
from the country club, takes a train to Oklahoma
City, and commits suicide there.

Sammy's character is not well drawn and his
suicide is overdramatic, but Inge uses it to develop
Reenie's character. After Sammy's death, Cora admonishes Reenie that she could have prevented
Sammy's tragedy if she had overcome her ridiculous shyness. Cora tells Reenie it is time for her to
stop "being so shy and sensitive and afraid of people," and Reenie begins to understand that her
mother is correct. Events have jarred Cora into
realizing that she also must recognize her fears and
try to overcome them.

Finally, Rubin returns, apologetic. He tells
Cora he has lost his previous job but found a new
one selling oil-field equipment. Cora begins to complain that it is another traveling job; at first Rubin
is angry, and their old argument seems imminent.
However, Rubin expresses fears about the new job
and the changing times, and Cora, who had never
heard him admit fear before, softens. For the first
time, they talk freely about their fears and their
need for each other. The family is reunited when
Sonny and Reenie appear. To console Reenie,
Sonny offers to take her to the movies. Cora is
touched by Sonny's generosity, but he avoids her
embrace before he and Reenie leave. Rubin, who
has gone upstairs, calls Cora, and she starts up the
steps, stopping for "one final look at her departing
son." Sonny "stops for one final look at his mother,
his face full of confused understanding." The symbolic ending is complete when Cora climbs the steps
"like a shy maiden" while "we see Rubin's naked
feet standing in the warm light at the top."

Rubin Flood is one of Inge's most believable
and sympathetic male characters, surpassed only
by Doc Delaney. Cora has the frustrations of many
of Inge's other female characters but also displays
an admirable resilience and growth. Although *The
Dark at the Top of the Stairs* is not as well structured
as *Come Back, Little Sheba*, the range of characters
and the consistency of action and theme make it

the best of his popular plays. Inge brought his awareness of Freudian analysis to the nostalgic memories that inspired *The Dark at the Top of the Stairs,* which he called his "belated attempt to come to terms with the past," and the result is, with the exception of the character Sammy Goldenbaum, a very fine play. Inge was not again so explicitly autobiographical until he wrote his memoir-novel, *My Son Is a Splendid Driver* (1971), published shortly before his death. But his interest in portraying oedipal conflict continued in the two unsuccessful plays that followed *The Dark at the Top of the Stairs* on Broadway.

A Loss of Roses, Inge's fifth New York play, is primarily concerned with the resolution of an Oedipus complex. In a little Kansas town during the Depression, Kenny Baird, twenty-one, lives with his widowed mother, Helen, showing no interest in young women his own age. Helen, a nurse, encourages Kenny to leave home, for she fears she has held him too close after the death of her husband; Kenny, however, wants her to quit working and let him support her. Lila Green, a voluptuous unemployed actress, comes to stay with them while her boyfriend looks for work in Kansas City. Lila was once a neighbor girl who helped Helen take care of Kenny when he was a baby, and Inge quickly establishes Lila as a surrogate mother. Lila is emotionally weak, having walked a narrow line between being a performer and a prostitute. Kenny has been kept at a distance by Helen, but Lila fusses over him, returning some of his romantic interests.

After a scene in which Helen rejects an expensive watch Kenny tries to give her to replace an old one given to her by her husband, Kenny is angered and hurt and turns to Lila for comfort. Lila, who has learned that the only work available to her is posing for lewd photographs in Kansas City, is desperate for genuine affection. Swearing that he loves her and wants to marry her despite their age difference, Kenny sleeps with Lila. However, the next day he changes his mind. "It's like I wanted something my whole life that now I don't want any more," he tells Lila. Lila is crushed by Kenny's reversal and makes a poor attempt to slash her wrists. After recovering, she leaves for Kansas City and an uncertain fate. Kenny decides he will leave for Wichita and a better job, and Helen is left, as she says, to "deal with loneliness for myself." *A Loss of Roses* suffers from a very obvious handling of plot and from characters too much like psychological case studies. The action of the play implies that Kenny's twenty-one-year attachment to his mother and his assumption of his father's role are suddenly and drastically altered by one night of sex with Lila. The resolution of this conflict derives from the necessities of melodramatic plot construction, not from an authentic change in Kenny's character.

Inge's next Broadway play, *Natural Affection,* is better written and portrays resolution of an Oedipus complex not by sex with a substitute but by killing a substitute. It contains the strongest language Inge put into a Broadway play, and it is also his most violent drama. Unlike his previous works, the play is set in the present in Chicago and contains criticism of contemporary times. Inge claimed to have read stories of teenage violence which gave him the idea of dramatizing the rejection, resentment, and erupting violence of Donnie Barker, the Oedipus figure in this play. Donnie's mother, Sue, put him in an orphanage shortly after he was born because his father abandoned her. Sue has kept seeing Donnie over the years but has always felt guilty about deserting him because he became a juvenile delinquent and eventually was incarcerated at a reformatory. An oedipal bond exists between Sue and Donnie despite their frequent separation. Sue now has a good job and is living with Bernie Slovenk, a younger man who works very little and whom she largely supports. Sue wants Bernie to marry her, admitting to him that "at my age, a woman gets to feeling kind of desperate," but he is not interested.

The action intensifies when Donnie comes from the reformatory for a Christmas visit. He does not have to return to the reformatory if Sue consents to keep him. Donnie's alternatives are made clear by Inge: stay with Sue and have a chance to "go straight," or return to the reformatory and his rough existence. Soon, Donnie and Bernie are at odds, each clearly jealous of the other, and it becomes inevitable that Sue must make a choice. Donnie tells Sue he will be the man in her life, pointing out that Bernie does not really provide—and also that Bernie cheats on Sue with Claire, a woman who lives across the hall. When Sue confronts Bernie, he admits seeing Claire but reminds Sue that he is also Sue's lover, which Donnie could never be. Calculatedly, Bernie tells Sue he was thinking of marrying her until Donnie came. In a powerful scene, after Bernie has walked out, Sue makes her choice over Donnie's desperate pleas. She screams, "I'm not going to give up the rest of my life for a worthless kid I never wanted in the first place," then chases after Bernie, leaving the door open. Donnie flings himself on the couch in anguish as a drunk woman from a next-door party wanders in through the door. The woman tries to romance Donnie, who savagely orders her out. When she does not go, he hits her, and she screams. In a shaking rage, Donnie grabs a knife from the kitchen and stabs her several times. Suddenly calmed, he drinks from a container of milk, then "walks out of the apartment forever" at the curtain.

Donnie's angry killing of a substitute for Sue is consistent with his character of a street-tough delinquent who has already experienced much sordidness before lashing out at losing his last hope. Sue's desperate decision is also well motivated, and in Sue and Donnie, Inge has created a more convincing, if shocking, oedipal bond than in the Helen-Kenny relationship of *A Loss of Roses*. *Natural Affection*'s violent ending, however, drew sharp criticism for what seemed a gratuitous shock effect. The often profane dialogue was also criticized strongly. John McCarten wrote that Inge was a "junior-varsity Tennessee Williams," writing only to shock his audience. Still, *Natural Affection* is the best of the plays which were unsuccessful on Broadway, with structure, conflict, characterization, and theme carefully crafted together. Inge was not an experimenter or innovator with dramatic form but a very able architect of the conventional. His final Broadway play, however, is his most poorly written.

Where's Daddy? is a domestic comedy that is primarily a vehicle for Inge's affirmation of traditional family roles and criticism of a variety of matters including psychoanalysis, race relations, and absurdist theater. The central problem involves Tom and Teena Keen, who aspire to acting careers and live a bohemian life in Manhattan. Teena has become pregnant. Tom is an orphan and has been a boy-lover to an aging homosexual; he does not want to accept parental responsibility. Tom's psychoanalyst has convinced him that he is maladjusted and immature, and therefore excused from the burdens of being a husband and father. Teena, a dropout from an affluent family, parrots Tom's rationalizations, convinced that their plan to separate and put the baby up for adoption is sensible because they both have a nearly religious faith in psychoanalysis. Teena's mother, however, confronts her by acknowledging her love for Teena and admitting errors in raising her. On Tom's side, his former lover-provider, Pinky, a professor, refuses to accept Tom back "temporarily" when he leaves Teena, because Pinky believes Tom should stop avoiding responsibility.

Tom vacillates constantly; he thinks he ought to leave Teena, but he is so afraid that he keeps running back to his analyst. This indecisiveness is counterpointed with numerous broadsides from Pinky about psychoanalytic mumbo jumbo, the irresponsibility of Tom and Teena's generation, method acting, and absurdist theater. Pinky serves as a father figure who helps Tom overcome his fears, but Pinky is also Inge's critic of a society and a theater which baffle him and in which he finds no real place for himself. As might be expected, the birth of the baby resolves the play. Teena realizes all she ever really wanted was motherhood, and Tom eventually decides to stay with her and the baby.

Where's Daddy?, although amusing in spots, is not a good play because its overall tone is one of whining complaint. Its setting and characters, excepting Pinky, are atypical of Inge. Wilfrid Sheed aptly said that Inge "used to be writing about cornpone themes he seemed to know," but knew little about "New York hippies." After the failure of *Where's Daddy?*, Inge returned to characters and themes in "cornpone" settings, but in the more personal medium of the novel, avoiding the producers and critics of Broadway.

The only other plays he put forward for wide public scrutiny were the one-act plays he had published in 1962 with *Summer Brave*, most of which were written in the 1950s. One of them, *People in the Wind*, and another, *Glory in the Flower*, were reworked into *Bus Stop* and the screenplay *Splendor in the Grass* respectively. Most of his one-act plays present familiar themes and character types of Inge's major plays but also contain more overt portrayals of sexual deviancy—including homosexuality, transvestism, and necrophilia—than can be found in his better-known works. Inge was always particular about the printed versions of his works, considering them the truest representation of his intent. His publication of these one-act plays with *Summer Brave* when he was riding the last crest of popularity in his career shows a desire to print plays that either set the record of his creative intent straight (*Summer Brave*) or reveal deviant dimensions of characters that were closer to his creative vision but unacceptable in the restricted atmosphere of commercial theater in the late 1950s. Many of the one-act plays seem only character or plot sketches, such as *Memory of Summer* and *The Tiny Closet;* but *The Mall*, a contrastive portrayal of different types of love, and *The Boy in the Basement*, about a small-town homosexual mortician dominated by his mother, are excellent.

Inge's other published writing includes a screenplay, *Splendor in the Grass*, and two novels, *Good Luck, Miss Wyckoff* and *My Son Is a Splendid*

Driver. All are set in small-town Kansas, and all are typical of his other works. *Splendor in the Grass* is about the unfulfilled love of Bud Stamper and Deanie Loomis, raised in a gossiping community by overprotective parents. Their repressions radically alter their lives, and the prevailing theme is that they must accept and cope with life's changes—as suggested by the passage of William Wordsworth's "Intimations Ode," from which Inge took the title: "Though nothing can bring back the hour/ Of splendor in the grass, glory in the flower,/We will grieve not, rather find/Strength in what remains behind."

Evelyn Wyckoff, the protagonist of Inge's first novel, is an unmarried virgin schoolteacher in tiny Freedom, Kansas, who eventually has a blatant sexual affair in her classroom with a Negro janitor. Discovery of her indiscretion costs her her job, but she leaves Freedom strengthened by the experience. Inge writes well in passages of this novel, but his attempts at erotic description are strained.

A lonely teacher is also the central character in Inge's second novel, *My Son Is a Splendid Driver*. It presents a first-person memoir of Joey Hansen, a sad writer/teacher who details the places and people of his life in a nostalgic tone of faint regret. *My Son Is a Splendid Driver* is much better than the previous novel and extremely revealing because Joey Hansen is clearly William Inge. The novel is the autobiography of an artist's sensibility, showing that the themes of loneliness, frustration, complex love, and the need for acceptance of life, so prevalent in Inge's work, were the themes of his life as well. Characters, events, and details, both major and minor, echo those that appear in Inge's earlier works. The small town in which it is set, again ironically called Freedom, is unquestionably Independence, Kansas. The memoir concludes with Joey's remembrance of visiting the ocean and seeing it as "something eternal" that "human efforts and affairs would never change." *My Son Is a Splendid Driver* focuses on the past to explain that Joey's life and vision are a search for a transcendent sublimity. The novel's epigraph from Thomas à Kempis's *Imitation of Christ* makes Inge's suicide shortly after the novel's appearance especially poignant: "Woe to those who do not know their own misery and woe to those who love this wretched and corruptible life."

William Inge's achievements are properly not regarded as equal to those of Eugene O'Neill, Tennessee Williams, and Arthur Miller. At his worst, Inge is overly dependent upon simplistic Freudian concepts. He was not interested in experimenting

with the theatrical form or convention; unlike his predecessors, he contributed little to the techniques of staging. What Inge did accomplish, however, was a significant widening of subject matter for Broadway. He was the dramatist of men and women struggling inwardly against outwardly dull lives in small midwestern towns. Before *Come Back, Little Sheba* and its successors, traditional Broadway theater focused primarily upon urban characters situated in the Northeast or upon Tennessee Williams's vibrant southerners. Inge depicted his world with a passionate sincerity and gave commercial theater a new area to develop. The humane intelligence which infuses his best plays makes his contribution to American drama permanent.

Interviews:
Naomi Barko, "William Inge Talks About *Picnic*," *Theatre Arts*, 37 (July 1953): 66-67;
Digby Diehl, "Interview with William Inge," in *Behind the Scenes: Theatre and Film Interviews from the Transatlantic Review*, edited by Joseph McCrindle (New York: Holt, Rinehart & Winston, 1971), pp. 108-115;
Lloyd Steele, "William Inge: the Last Interview," *Los Angeles Free Press*, 22 June 1973, pp. 18-22.

Bibliography:
Arthur F. McClure, *William Inge: A Bibliography* (New York: Garland Publishing, 1982);
The most thorough bibliography to date of Inge's works and works written about Inge.

Biographies:
Roy Newquist, "William Inge," in his *Counterpoint* (New York: Rand McNally, 1964), pp. 356-363;
Inge discusses his background, experiences, and ideas about his art and contemporary theater.

Robert B. Shuman, *William Inge* (New York: Twayne, 1965);
Out-of-date but useful biography covering Inge's life and work up to 1965.

Jean Gould, "William Inge," in her *Modern American Playwrights* (New York: Dodd, Mead, 1966), pp. 264-272;
Useful but brief account of Inge's life and career up to 1966.

References:

Robert Alan Aurthur, "Hanging Out," *Esquire,* 80 (November 1973): 42, 44, 48, 52;
A touching and revealing tribute written after Inge's death.

Robert Brustein, "The Men-Taming Women of William Inge," *Harpers,* 217 (November 1958): 53-57;
A perceptive but very negative assessment of Inge's four major plays of the 1950s that irreparably hurt Inge's self-image.

Gilbert Millstein, "The Dark at the Top of William Inge," *Esquire,* 50 (August 1958): 60-63;
A revealing biographical piece in a popular magazine.

Wieder David Sievers, *Freud on Broadway: A History of Psychoanalysis and the American Drama* (New York: Hermitage House, 1955);
Sievers explores Inge's use of Freudian psychology in his plays prior to 1955.

Ralph F. Voss, "The Art of William Inge," Ph.D. dissertation, University of Texas, Austin, 1975;
A thorough study of Inge's life and published works.

Papers:

There are collections of Inge's papers at the Humanities Research Center, University of Texas; Independence Community College in Independence, Kansas; and the University of Kansas. The Billy Rose Collection in the Lincoln Center for the Performing Arts in New York City has clippings on the New York productions, manuscripts, playbills, photographs, and correspondence.

Shirley Jackson

This entry was updated from the entry by Martha Ragland (Virginia Commonwealth University) in DLB 6, American Novelists Since World War II.

Places	Vermont	Syracuse	Bennington College
Influences and Relationships	Sir James G. Frazer (*The Golden Bough*)	Howard Nemerov Stanley Edgar Hyman	Leonard Brown
Literary Movements and Forms	Horror Fiction		
Major Themes	Mob Reactions Isolation Evil in Human Nature	Moral Bankruptcy Superstition Psychological Abnormality	Ritual Social Prejudice
Cultural and Artistic Influences			
Social and Economic Influences			

BIRTH: San Francisco, California, 14 December 1919, to Leslie Hardie and Geraldine Bugbee Jackson.

EDUCATION: University of Rochester, 1934-1936; B.A., Syracuse University, 1940.

MARRIAGE: 3 June 1940 to Stanley Edgar Hyman; children: Laurence Jackson, Joanne Leslie, Sarah Geraldine, Barry Edgar.

AWARDS AND HONORS: Edgar Allan Poe Award for "Louisa Please," 1961; Syracuse University Arents Pioneer Medal for Outstanding Achievement, 1965.

DEATH: North Bennington, Vermont, 8 August 1965.

SELECTED BOOKS: *The Road Through the Wall* (New York: Farrar, Straus, 1948);
The Lottery; or, The Adventures of James Harris (New York: Farrar, Straus, 1949; London: Gollancz, 1950);
Hangsaman (New York: Farrar, Straus & Young, 1951; London: Gollancz, 1951);
Life Among the Savages (New York: Farrar, Straus & Young, 1953; London: Joseph, 1954);
The Bird's Nest (New York: Farrar, Straus & Young, 1954; London: Joseph, 1955);
The Witchcraft of Salem Village (New York: Random House, 1956);
Raising Demons (New York: Farrar, Straus & Cudahy, 1957; London: Joseph, 1957);
The Sundial (New York: Farrar, Straus & Cudahy, 1958; London: Joseph, 1958);
The Haunting of Hill House (New York: Viking, 1959; London: Joseph, 1960);
We Have Always Lived in the Castle (New York: Viking, 1962);
The Magic of Shirley Jackson, edited by Stanley Edgar Hyman (New York: Farrar, Straus & Giroux, 1966);
Come Along With Me, edited by Hyman (New York: Viking, 1968).

Shirley Jackson's name is most often associated in readers' minds with the haunting short story "The Lottery," which was originally published in 1948 and has since become a frequently anthologized American classic. To those familiar with the rest of Jackson's fiction, her stories and novels have earned her a reputation as a "literary sorceress," a

Shirley Jackson (photo by Erich Hartmann)

writer with a peculiar talent for the bizarre, a creator of psychological thrillers, an adroit master of effect and suspense. In spite of her popularity, however, her work has received little critical attention. Jackson's remarkable versatility may account partly for the silence. In her lifetime she published novels, short stories, plays, children's books, television scripts, and humorous sketches of domestic life—all of which prevented her easy classification.

Above all Jackson is a storyteller; her stories aim to entertain. Yet the entertainment value of her fiction masks a pessimistic view of human nature; social criticism, overt or implicit, is central to every one of her works. Humankind is more evil than good. The mass of men is profoundly misguided, seemingly incapable of enlightenment. Lacking either the capacity to reason or the strength to act upon moral convictions, their lives are dictated by habit and convention. They often behave with callous disregard of those around them. Set against this backdrop are the victimized protagonists. They may be victims of society, of family or friends, or victims of their own fragmented and disintegrating personalities. Yet even in the novels and stories that deal almost exclusively with the private worlds of individuals, the isolation of these lonely figures is intensified by the sense that the world surrounding them is cruel—peopled with weak or malignant characters. Emotional warmth and closeness are rare in Jackson's fictional universe; there is little to sustain a healthy personality.

The origin and development of Jackson's vision of society and mankind necessarily remain speculative, since she was reluctant to discuss either her fiction or her life before the public. The daughter of Leslie Hardie Jackson and Geraldine Bugbee Jackson, she was born into a family of successful San Francisco professionals. She seemed to have wanted to be a writer from an early age. She wrote poems and kept journals throughout her childhood. These journals reveal an interest in superstition and the supernatural, and one entry (a 1933 New Year's resolution) is interesting and perhaps revealing: "seek out the good in others rather than explore for the evil."

When Jackson was fourteen, the family moved from California to New York. After one unhappy year at the University of Rochester, she dropped out of school to spend the next year (1936 to 1937) at home, pursuing a career as a writer. She set herself a quota of at least a thousand words a day and established a disciplined routine that she was to follow the rest of her life. The following year she entered Syracuse University, where she made her first acquaintance with the texts of anthropology, including James G. Frazer's *The Golden Bough* (1890), which were to influence her later work. She also published both fiction and nonfiction regularly in campus magazines. Her editorials championed the underdog and denounced prejudice on campus, particularly against blacks and Jews.

Upon graduation in 1940 she married fellow student Stanley Edgar Hyman and moved to New York City. A clerical job she held there became the subject of her first nationally published short story, "My Life With R. H. Macy." Over the next few years she continued to publish short fiction regularly, despite the birth of her first child, Laurence, in 1942. In 1945 a daughter, Joanne, was born, and in that same year she and her growing family moved to North Bennington, Vermont, where she was to remain, apart from brief absences, "comfortably far from city life" for the rest of her writing career. The Hymans had two more children: Sarah in 1948 and Barry in 1951.

The first few years in Vermont were outwardly less productive ones, but in 1948 *The Road*

Through the Wall, her only novel set in suburban California, was published. Several households on the same block form the subject of the novel, and the rather spiteful interactions between individuals and between families become the basis for the plot. The characters' lives reflect a certain moral bankruptcy, which is passed from parents to children. The novel was received with moderate acclaim and demonstrated that Jackson could sustain reader interest through the novel form. On 28 June of that year the *New Yorker* printed "The Lottery." The story occasioned so much public outcry that Jackson's reputation—and notoriety—were assured from then on.

"The Lottery" is about the reenactment in contemporary society of an ancient scapegoat ritual. Its genius lies in the juxtaposition of the savage and the modern. A public stoning performed in the town square of an otherwise peaceful community communicates a powerful shock to the reader, an effect heightened by Jackson's unemotional narrative style. A modern fable, "The Lottery" reveals men and women to be timid, conformist, callous, and cruel. Although Jackson published dozens of short stories during her lifetime, she never again produced such a satire of the evil in human nature. She turned instead to studies of individuals, exploring the private worlds of lonely, often mentally ill, characters. Her short stories contain a diversity of themes and employ a variety of techniques, including what may well be her hallmark, a deliberate blurring of the lines between reality and fantasy. Some of these techniques were reproduced to even greater effect in the novels, yet the short fiction is striking in its own right.

"The Lottery" was included in *Prize Stories of 1949: The O. Henry Awards.* Appearing in *Best American Short Stories* were "The Summer People" in 1951; "One Ordinary Day With Peanuts" in 1956; and "Birthday Party" in 1965. Jackson received the Edgar Allan Poe Award for "Louisa Please" in 1961. She was honored by Syracuse University in 1965 with the Arents Pioneer Medal for Outstanding Achievement.

In her second novel, *Hangsaman* (1951), Jackson writes about a young woman who is perilously close to mental disintegration. Natalie is seventeen, highly intelligent, and under the shadow of her father's dominating personality. She enrolls in an exclusive women's college (her father's choice) and, from the first, experiences the sensation of being an outsider. Her keen mind and reserved nature seem to act as a barrier between herself and others, and the passing months only increase her sense of estrangement. Correspondence with her father becomes more strained; her journal entries reveal at least a tendency toward schizoid patterns of thinking. A brief infatuation with her literature professor is quashed when she sees his insensitive treatment of his wife. At this point she meets Tony, a young woman who appears on the campus at unexpected times and places, a seeming loner like herself. Friendship with Tony is at first satisfying and seems to promise relief from Natalie's acute loneliness and rejection by the other girls. The two friends study together, tell each other's fortunes, even sleep side by side. But is Tony real, or a creation of Natalie's disturbed mind? As in the shorter works of fiction, it is difficult to establish her existence for certain.

The novel's final scene has puzzled critics. It is nighttime, and Tony and Natalie have taken a bus to a lonely wooded area outside of town. The bus is making its last route; when it departs the girls will be stranded. Natalie is frightened and wants to return to the college, but Tony, laughing at her fears, leads her deeper into the woods. Natalie loses sight of her in the dark. She calls out. When Tony refuses to answer, the uneasiness which she has always subconsciously felt with Tony surfaces, and Natalie succumbs to pure panic. Tony reappears then and coaxes her into an embrace. Surprised and bewildered, Natalie runs away. When she regains control of herself she finds her way back to town, and the novel ends on a hopeful note: "She was now alone, and grown-up, and powerful, and not at all afraid."

Interpretations of *Hangsaman* vary, depending upon whether the reader accepts Tony as Natalie's real or imaginary companion. On a realistic level, the book has been regarded as a study of adolescence, a perceptive tale of a young girl's initiation into adulthood. In this context, a possible implication is that Natalie has rejected a homosexual liaison with Tony, and that this is part of her growing-up process. If, on the other hand, Tony is a figment of Natalie's imagination, then the book becomes an exploration of the private world of a schizophrenic. If the reader is meant to believe that Natalie has recovered her sanity at the end of the book, critics have noted that the return to normality is too abrupt, and her full recovery seems implausible. If her recovery at this point is implausible, the optimism in the last lines becomes extremely ambiguous.

Whatever Jackson intended in *Hangsaman*, she clearly set out to fictionalize a dissociated personality in *The Bird's Nest* (1954). This book was the

fruit of Jackson's extensive study of mental illness, and the multiple personality of Elizabeth-Beth-Betsy-Bess is based on an actual case history she turned up in the course of her research. The book is divided into six sections, each assuming the point of view of one of several characters, including Elizabeth's aunt and Elizabeth's attending psychiatrist, Dr. Wright.

The first section of the novel establishes the basic situation. Twenty-three-year-old Elizabeth works on the third floor of a museum which is in bad need of repair but nevertheless provides the perfect refuge for "cringing scholarly souls." Subject to severe headaches since her mother's death four years before, Elizabeth lives with her aunt and seems to do little besides eat, sleep, and work. Her life is vague and undirected. She has no friends.

Elizabeth begins to discover quasi-obscene letters in the carriage of her typewriter. Is she writing them to herself? This is the first indication to the reader that another personality is about to disturb the surface of Elizabeth's uneventful life. The second, then the third and the fourth personalities emerge. They wage a terrific struggle for dominance, distorting Elizabeth out of all recognition. She is now under the care of Dr. Wright, whose journals describing his process with his patient form the greater part of the book. The juxtaposition of his point of view with Betsy's is extremely effective; to plunge back into the point of view of the fragmented personality after dwelling in the saner world of Dr. Wright is disturbing and frightening.

Jackson's mastery of effect is evident in *The Bird's Nest*. She shapes what would in any event be a fascinating case study into a dramatic tale of psychological suspense. The story climaxes in a dreary New York hotel room, where Betsy, the most vicious of the personalities, attacks the passive Elizabeth. In other words, one of the inner selves actually destroys the other, and Elizabeth nearly loses her life in the process. She wakes up in a hospital, is rescued by her aunt and doctor, and returns home. Eventually she gets well. Aided by the basically kind, if erratic, attentions of her aunt and by two and a half years' therapy with Dr. Wright, Elizabeth's recovery is convincing, unlike Natalie's in the previous novel.

In spite of the harrowing subject matter, *The Bird's Nest* sparkles with wit and humor. The book was well received critically, even hailed as "a kind of twentieth-century morality play." In this novel the problems which plagued *Hangsaman* were less evident, in that there was less room for ambiguity in the interpretation of the central character. Metro-Goldwyn-Mayer purchased film rights and eventually made a movie, released in 1957 under the title *Lizzie*.

Jackson's fame received another boost when M-G-M purchased film rights to a novel published in 1959, *The Haunting of Hill House*. The movie, *The Haunting*, was released in 1963. In this book the themes of isolation, loneliness, and emotional deterioration are explored through the character of a young unmarried woman, Eleanor. A ghostly manor is the setting, and at first the novel seems to conform to the pattern of the formula Gothic. Thirty-two-year-old Eleanor, orphaned and drab, is on the threshold of an adventure. Because of an association with a poltergeist phenomenon in her childhood which led to some small stir of publicity in her hometown, she has been invited by Professor Montague to participate in a study of a supposedly haunted house in New England, some distance from her home. She, along with two or three others, will assist the professor in his investigation into the psychic spirits which he believes inhabit Hill House.

Eleanor is the first member of the group to arrive at Hill House. From the moment that she sees it, the looming manor fills her with foreboding. An inner voice warns her that she must get away at once, but she stays nevertheless, held by a sort of fascination for the place and, even more pathetic, a need to belong to someone, or to something. Dr. Montague, a young woman named Theo, and Luke, the nephew of Hill House's owner, arrive soon after. They make themselves ready for a stay of several weeks. With frightening promptness the spirits of Hill House manifest themselves. During the second night of their stay, Eleanor is awakened by a violent pounding down the hall. She creeps into Theo's adjoining bedroom and the two of them huddle against the sudden draft of supernatural cold, listening to the hammering on the wall, then to the "small seeking sounds" at their very door. This is no human agent, nor can natural explanations account for the words HELP ELEANOR PLEASE COME HOME she finds scrawled on the wall the next day.

The spirits continue to scrawl messages and hammer on walls and to despoil clothing, singling out Eleanor as the weakest, most vulnerable member of the group. The pleas to COME HOME ELEANOR may be playing upon Eleanor's guilt for her imagined neglect of her invalid mother prior to her death three months before, or the messages may be referring to Hill House. When she

first meets the other members of the group at Hill House she is happy—happier, one suspects, than she has ever been. She experiences a brief infatuation with Luke and appears to be making friends with Theo. But both attempts to bridge the lifelong isolation between herself and others are doomed to failure. Luke proves disappointingly weak; he is drawn to her primarily as a mother figure, and Theo turns out to be narcissistic and insensitive to the point of cruelty toward Eleanor. Furthermore, Luke and Theo begin to form a romantic attachment which conspicuously excludes her. Eleanor becomes more and more lonely and isolated. Her retreat unto a private world of fantasy is pathetic and as chilling as any of the more flamboyant supernatural effects in the novel.

At last Dr. Montague asks Eleanor to leave. Her mental disturbance is evident, but he believes she will be better when she gets away from the atmosphere at Hill House. Luke and Theo simply wish to be rid of her. Once again, as in other Jackson works, a thin veneer of sympathy and kindness hides a layer of human nature that is fundamentally uncaring. Eleanor, dazed and humiliated, is escorted to her car. Driving down the long driveway away from the house, convinced that at least the ghostly inhabitants of Hill House wish her to remain even if the human ones do not, she accelerates her car wildly and crashes into a tree. *"Why am I doing this?"* she thinks with terrifying lucidity as she dies. *"Why don't they stop me?"* That plea is a clue to what may well be a weakness in Jackson's fiction. There are few close, warm human ties in any of the stories or novels. The characters are nearly always seen in isolation from one another, and the predominating emotions are fear and anxiety. Nor is there a God in Jackson's fictional universe. Even in *The Sundial* (1958), a novel which comes closest to exploring metaphysical questions and the issue of belief and faith, no mature interpretations of the meaning of life are proffered by any of the characters.

In *The Sundial* the Hallorans and a few select associates are waiting for the end of the world. The spirit of Father Halloran has notified them, through the agent of eccentric Aunt Fanny, that on 31 August the world outside the walls of their estate will be consumed by storm and fire. Only those persons who take refuge in the Halloran house will survive the catastrophe. Father Halloran is the patriarchal founder of the family, and it is he who designed the estate, including the sundial from which the novel takes it name. This sundial

Claire Bloom, Russ Tamblyn, Julie Harris, and Richard Johnson in a publicity still from the 1963 M-G-M movie The Haunting, *based on Jackson's 1959 novel,* The Haunting of Hill House

is inscribed with the motto WHAT IS THIS WORLD?

With the aid of a few unexplained phenomena, such as the timely appearance of a brightly colored snake and the mysterious shattering of a plate glass window, the lunatic prophecy is accepted by the group as the truth. Curiously apathetic, they allow themselves to be dictated to by the strong-willed Mrs. Halloran, wife of Father Halloran's son Richard, who is confined to a wheelchair. They burn all the books in the library (except a *World Almanac* and a Boy Scout handbook) and cram the empty shelves with crates of canned olives, antihistamines, and plastic overshoes. The only one who seems to have doubts about any of it is Essex, a young man who was originally hired some months before to catalogue the library. But like other young men in Jackson's fiction, he proves ultimately weak and bows to Mrs. Halloran's more powerful personality.

With everything readied for the world's end, they have nothing to do but wait. They are a nasty, irritable bunch, riddled with small sins. To pass the time they play bridge and squabble about who is to do what in the next world. That this singularly unenlightened group of people is to replenish the earth is of course the final irony. But the statement the novel makes about the hollowness or sheer idiocy of human beings is a pessimistic one. Critics were not sure whether *The Sundial* was written primarily for entertainment or intended as a serious satire. Some reviewers said that the lack of counterbalancing qualities of strength or goodness in any of the characters weakened the novel. Most agreed that it was not one of Jackson's better books.

Jackson returns to the theme of mental pathology in her last completed novel, *We Have Always Lived in the Castle* (1962). Writing in the first person, a technique she rarely employed, she develops the central character of Mary Katherine Blackwood

(Merricat), a sociopathic girl who, at the age of twelve, poisoned four members of her family, including mother and father, with arsenic. The exploration of the mind of this queer and oddly pathetic character is considered by many to be Jackson's finest fictional achievement. Certainly the novel is more consistently successful than any of her previous works, sustaining a tone that can only be described as eerily poetic.

> My name is Mary Katherine Blackwood. I am eighteen years old, and I live with my sister Constance. I have often thought that with any luck at all I could have been born a werewolf, because the two middle fingers on both my hands are the same length, but I have had to be content with what I had. I dislike washing myself, and dogs, and noise. I like my sister Constance, and Richard Plantagenet, and *Amanita phalloides*, the death-cup mushroom. Everyone else in my family is dead.

The excellence of this opening passage has been justly remarked. With arresting precision the exact quality of Merricat's voice is established—disarmingly simple and childlike; clever, but crippled with queer logic. The last sentence twists like a knife. It hints at the unpredictable turns of thought which are the clue to Merricat's pathology and the source of the novel's suspense.

The setting is the Blackwood house, six years after the murders. Like the houses which are central to other Jackson novels, the Blackwood estate is at a distance from the nearest village and surrounded by a wall. Isolated and aloof, the Blackwood family has long been the object of community jealousy, which turned to outright persecution after the sensational scandal which attended the poisoning. Constance, the eldest daughter, was tried and acquitted of the deed, but the village is only too ready to believe her guilty. Merricat, Constance, and Uncle Julian now live as virtual recluses. Only Merricat goes into the village to shop. Merricat dwells in a highly imaginative world of her own making. The walk to town, for instance, becomes like a children's board game in which "there were always dangers"; and indeed, the villagers taunt her cruelly. Magic and superstition also play a role in her make-believe world. Events are omens of good luck or bad; to ward off evil she buries small objects—a doll or blue marbles—or nails them to trees. She cares only for her cat, Jonas, and for Constance, whom she loves with fierce possessiveness.

Constance is loyal to Merricat too, although she seems to know that her younger sister is guilty of the murder of their parents and siblings. At any rate, they live in undisturbed domestic harmony until Charles, a young male cousin, comes to visit. Infatuated with Constance, he nearly convinces her to leave her secure retreat and venture into the real world. But Merricat, instinctively fearing change, determines to drive him away by the force of her "magic." In the process she accidentally sets the house on fire. The blaze is put out before the entire house burns, but the villagers who have come to help extinguish the blaze, in a burst of pent-up hate toward the Blackwoods, vandalize the rest of the house. While the fire rages around him, Charles seems concerned only with preserving the family safe, which is too heavy to move. When the mob leaves he goes too. The Blackwood house is in ruins.

Alone, with only two or three cups and spoons, Merricat and Constance barricade themselves in the kitchen at the back of the house. A few villagers, apparently conscience stricken, begin to leave food on the doorstep. Yet these offerings are not likely to continue indefinitely, and at the end of the novel the sisters' fate is uncertain. Merricat, however, has what she has always wanted: Constance. The queer force of her personality triumphs over the potentially healthier personality of her sister. Without a moral sense, Merricat will never be tortured by guilt for the murders, nor aware of the sacrifices Constance has made for her. "We're on the moon at last," she announced to Constance in satisfaction. She has won.

During the writing of *We Have Always Lived in the Castle*, Jackson suffered from a number of health problems, including arthritis, colitis, asthma, and anxiety. Yet she worked with great care on this book and spent more time on it than on any other. Almost universally recognized as her finest novel, it was nominated for the National Book Award. It became a best-seller and was adapted for a Broadway production. The play had a short run at the Ethel Barrymore Theatre in 1966.

We Have Always Lived in the Castle was lauded especially for its imaginative treatment of Merricat, who is far removed from a text sociopath and made into a believable, even sympathetic, character. Though at the end of the novel the two sisters are sleeping on the floor and living behind boarded windows, their absolute dependence on one another is made to seem oddly appealing. Their narrow existence does not lack warmth, laughter, and kindness. The reader, though recoiling from a world which he logically knows to be grotesque, is brought to view the sisters with sympathy, even to share some of their happiness, which is no easy task for a writer.

But again, some readers may be left with the uneasy feeling that there are no choices for the characters. The world outside the Blackwood estate offers little to Constance and Merricat. That world is filled with the same weak or malignant characters who peopled "The Lottery." The reader has been entertained by the novel, even moved; but it is clear that Jackson's fictional world must be taken on its own terms.

In between the publication of her fiction, Jackson was writing humorous sketches of domestic life for publication in various women's magazines. These were later arranged chronologically and collected in two autobiographical works, *Life Among the Savages* (1953) and *Raising Demons* (1957). Together they form a domestic saga spanning from the time of her family's first house in Vermont until the year her youngest child enrolls in school. Ostensibly autobiographical, the anecdotal accounts of life in the Hyman household clearly have been embellished for the reader's entertainment. Lighter in tone than her fiction, they celebrate in an unsentimental way day-to-day life in a large and active family. They also reveal Jackson as a comic writer who at her best belongs in the ranks of the great American humorists.

At the age of forty-five Jackson died suddenly of heart failure. She had been active during her last years, delivering lectures at colleges and writers' conferences; three of the lectures are included in the same volume with the novel she was working on at the time of her death, *Come Along With Me* (1968). Two of these lectures, "Biography of a Story" and "Notes for a Young Writer," discuss the art of writing. Written for her daughter Sally, the latter imparts information and advice that should interest any writer or student of Jackson's fictional technique.

In Jackson's children's book, *The Witchcraft of Salem Village* (1956), she attempts to explain in necessarily simplified terms the "seeming madness" that swept seventeenth-century Salem. Men and women are susceptible to evil, Jackson seems to suggest. It surges up in society at certain times and in response to certain social conditions, then subsides again. But an elemental mystery also surrounds the presence of evil. There is no completely satisfactory cause for it, and no cure. It will spread until people "simply stop believing"; until, re-

morseful and repentant, they are "sick with the weariness of it all."

This children's book illuminates her fiction, touching upon many of her fundamental themes: superstition, community scapegoat rites, social prejudice, conformity, mass hysteria, violence. But development of themes is only part of Jackson's message. In "Notes for a Young Writer" she makes it very clear: the writer's only real job is to catch the reader's attention and hold it, to tell a good story. Some of her works have been aptly labeled "psychological thrillers," but others provide acute insights into the minds and hearts of her characters and have the magic power to move the reader as well as to entertain.

Bibliographies:

Robert S. Phillips, "Shirley Jackson: A Checklist," *Bibliographical Society of America Papers*, 56 (January 1962): 110-113;
A useful list which was prepared with the assistance of Jackson.

Phillips, "Shirley Jackson: A Chronology and a Supplementary Checklist," *Bibliographical Society of America Papers*, 60 (April 1966): 203-213;
A complete supplement which updates Phillips's previous checklist and was approved by Jackson before her death.

References:

Cleanth Brooks and Robert Penn Warren, "Interpretation," in their *Understanding Fiction* (New York: Appleton-Century-Crofts, 1959), pp. 72-76;
Studies "The Lottery" as an illustration of human inconsistency in the duality of humor and cruelty.

Chester E. Eisinger, *Fiction of the Forties* (Chicago: University of Chicago Press, 1963);
Examines Jackson's pessimism and her presentation of evil.

Lenemaja Friedman, *Shirley Jackson* (Boston: Twayne, 1975);
A thorough study of Jackson's life and work. Includes a selected bibliography.

Robert B. Heilman, *Modern Short Stories* (New York: Harcourt, Brace, 1950), pp. 384-385;
A study of "The Lottery" which contends that the ending is too unexpected to be realistic.

Stanley Edgar Hyman, *The Promised End* (New York: World, 1963), pp. 264, 349, 365;
Discusses Jackson's works briefly—specifically the James Harris ballads and the initiation rites of *Hangsaman.*

Seymour Lainoff, "Jackson's 'The Lottery,'" *Explicator,* 12 (March 1954);
Examines the savage tendencies in our supposedly civilized society.

John O. Lyons, *The College Novel in America* (Carbondale: Southern Illinois University Press, 1962);
A discussion of *Hangsaman* which contends that it is a representative college novel and presents Natalie's companion as a lesbian college student, rather than as a figment of the girl's imagination.

H. E. Nebeker, "'The Lottery': Symbolic Tour de Force," *American Literature,* 46 (March 1974): 100-107;
Thoroughly examines the symbols used in "The Lottery" and argues that man is a victim of his own unchanged traditions.

S. C. Woodruff, "The Real Horror Elsewhere: Shirley Jackson's Last Novel," *Southwest Review,* 52 (September 1967): 152-162;
Contends that the real madness of *We Have Always Lived in the Castle* lies in the brutality of the "so-called 'normal' world of ordinary people."

Papers:
The major collection of Jackson's papers is in the manuscript division of the Library of Congress.

Randall Jarrell

This entry was updated by Suzanne Ferguson (Wayne State University) from her entry in
DLB 48, American Poets, 1880-1945.

Places	1920s Hollywood Greensboro, North Carolina	Germany	Nashville
Influences and Relationships	John Crowe Ransom Robert Penn Warren Rainer Maria Rilke Anton Chekhov	Robert Lowell W. H. Auden J. W. von Goethe	Allen Tate Marcel Proust Peter Taylor
Literary Movements and Forms	Modernism	Post-Modernism	
Major Themes	Loneliness and Loss Childhood Art	Wishes and Dreams Transformation Women	Fairy Tales and Myth World War II Death
Cultural and Artistic Influences	19th and 20th Century Opera Freudianism	Myth and Fairy Tale Marxist History	European Renaissance Painting and Sculpture
Social and Economic Influences	World War II	Conspicuous Consumption	American Middle-Class Life

See also the Jarrell entry in DLB 52, American Writers for Children Since 1960: Fiction.

BIRTH: Nashville, Tennessee, 6 May 1914, to Owen and Anna Campbell Jarrell.

EDUCATION: B.A., 1936; M.A., 1939; Vanderbilt University.

MARRIAGES: 1 June 1940 to Mackie Langham (divorced). 8 November 1952 to Mary von Schrader.

AWARDS AND HONORS: *Southern Review* Poetry Contest prize, 1936; Jeannette Sewell Davis Prize, 1943; John Peale Bishop Memorial Prize for "The Märchen," 1946; Guggenheim Fellowship, 1946; Levinson Prize (*Poetry* magazine), 1948; National Institute and American Academy of Arts and Letters Award, 1951; Oscar Blumenthal Prize (*Poetry* magazine), 1951; National Book Award for *The Woman at the Washington Zoo*, 1961; elected to the National Institute of Arts and Letters, 1961; O. Max Gardner Award, 1962; D.H.L., Bard College, 1962; Ingram Merrill Literary Award, 1965.

Randall Jarrell in Greensboro, North Carolina, 1948 (courtesy of Mary Jarrell)

DEATH: Chapel Hill, North Carolina, 14 October 1965.

SELECTED BOOKS: *Blood for a Stranger* (New York: Harcourt, Brace, 1942);

Little Friend, Little Friend (New York: Dial Press, 1945);

Losses (New York: Harcourt, Brace, 1948);

The Seven-League Crutches (New York: Harcourt, Brace, 1951);

Poetry and the Age (New York: Knopf, 1953; London: Faber & Faber, 1955);

Pictures from an Institution (New York: Knopf, 1954; London: Faber & Faber, 1954);

Selected Poems (New York: Knopf, 1955; London: Faber & Faber, 1956);

The Woman at the Washington Zoo: Poems & Translations (New York: Atheneum, 1960);

A Sad Heart at the Supermarket: Essays and Fables (New York: Atheneum, 1962; London: Eyre & Spottiswoode, 1965);

The Bat-Poet (New York: Macmillan/London: Collier-Macmillan, 1964);

Selected Poems, including The Woman at the Washington Zoo (New York: Atheneum, 1964);

The Gingerbread Rabbit (New York: Macmillan/London: Collier-Macmillan, 1964);

The Animal Family (New York: Pantheon, 1965; London: Hart-Davis, 1967);

The Lost World (New York: Macmillan/London: Collier-Macmillan, 1965; London: Eyre & Spottiswoode, 1966);

The Complete Poems (New York: Farrar, Straus & Giroux, 1969; London: Faber & Faber, 1971);

The Third Book of Criticism (New York: Farrar, Straus & Giroux, 1969);

Jerome: The Biography of a Poem, edited by Mary von Schrader Jarrell (New York: Grossman, 1971);

Fly by Night (New York: Farrar, Straus & Giroux, 1976);

Kipling, Auden & Co.: Essays and Reviews, 1935-1964 (New York: Farrar, Straus & Giroux, 1980);

Randall Jarrell's Letters (Boston: Houghton Mifflin, 1985).

RECORDINGS: *Randall Jarrell Reads and Discusses His Poems Against War*, Caedmon (TC 1363), 1972;

The Gingerbread Rabbit, Caedmon (TC 1381), 1972;

The Bat-Poet, Caedmon (TC 1364), 1972.

OTHER: "The Rage for the Lost Penny," in *Five Young American Poets*, edited by James Laughlin (Norfolk, Conn.: New Directions, 1940), pp. 81-123.

TRANSLATIONS: Brothers Grimm, *The Golden Bird and Other Fairy Tales* (New York & London: Macmillan, 1962);
Ludwig Bechstein, *The Rabbit Catcher and Other Fairy Tales* (New York & London: Macmillan, 1962);
Anton Chekhov, *The Three Sisters* (New York: Macmillan/London: Collier-Macmillan, 1969);
Brothers Grimm, *Snow White and the Seven Dwarfs* (New York: Farrar, Straus & Giroux, 1972; Harmondsworth, U.K.: Kestrel, 1974);
Brothers Grimm, *The Juniper Tree and Other Tales*, 2 volumes, translated by Lore Segal, with four translations by Jarrell (New York: Farrar, Straus & Giroux, 1973; London: Bodley Head, 1974);
Goethe's Faust: Part I (New York: Farrar, Straus & Giroux, 1976);
The Fisherman and His Wife (New York: Farrar, Straus & Giroux, 1980).

Best known for his poetry of World War II and his incisive, memorably witty criticism, Randall Jarrell belonged to the second generation of American modernist poets. Like Robert Lowell and John Berryman—contemporaries and personal friends—he worked in his early years in the shadow of T. S. Eliot and W. H. Auden, gradually freeing his poetry from their influence in order to write his own characteristic work. Although educated in the South and a student in the early 1930s of Fugitive poets John Crowe Ransom, Donald Davidson, and Robert Penn Warren at Vanderbilt University—where he also associated with Allen Tate—Jarrell was a poet of midcentury American urban and suburban life, a confirmed Freudian in his view of personality and creativity, a Marxist in his interpretation of history, a liberal in politics. Though interested in modern theology, he was not religious; he wrote to Allen Tate in 1939, "I never had any certainties, religious or metaphysical, to lose, so I don't feel their lack. . . . I raised myself on Russell and Hume." An avid amateur tennis player, he was also an aficionado of sports cars, professional football, and opera (especially Richard Strauss).

A professor of creative writing and literature for virtually all his adult life, except for a stint in the U.S. Army Air Force during World War II and two years as Poetry Consultant at the Library of Congress in 1956-1958, Jarrell was a genuine man of letters, writing not only poetry but reviews and critical essays, introductions to anthologies, translations of poetry and plays, an unorthodox novel, and several children's books. In addition to creating the most poignant poetic representations of the ordinary American soldier or flyer of World War II (in such poems as "2nd Air Force," "A Pilot from the Carrier," "Siegfried," "Eighth Air Force," "Lines," "Absent with Official Leave," and "The Death of the Ball-Turret Gunner"), Jarrell also wrote striking poetic reworkings of traditional stories to show their underlying psychological significance (in "Cinderella," "A Quilt Pattern," "In the Ward: The Sacred Wood," "Sleeping Beauty: Variation of the Prince," "Jamestown," "The House in the Wood"); a superb evocation of childhood in early 1920s Hollywood—his own *Remembrance of Things Past*—(in "The Lost World" and "Thinking of the Lost World"); sympathetic dramatic monologues and narrative poems of middle-class loners, often women ("Burning the Letters," "Seele im Raum," "The Woman at the Washington Zoo," the 1961 poem titled "Hope," "Next Day," "Jerome"); and a number of poems engaging with works of visual art or sculpture ("The Knight, Death, and the Devil," "The Bronze David of Donatello," "The Old and the New Masters"). His shrewd and admiring assessments of Robert Frost, William Carlos Williams, Walt Whitman, and W. H. Auden set the tone for much subsequent criticism, and his critical witticisms are often quoted in present-day reviews and articles. Sensitive to and appreciative of the verbal gifts of other poets, he was more concerned in his own poems with moral understanding and feeling than virtuosic verbal display or sophisticated formal experimentation. "It is better to have the child in the chimney corner moved by what happens in the poem," Jarrell wrote, "in spite of his ignorance of its real meaning, than to have the poem a puzzle to which that meaning is the only key."

Randall Jarrell was the first of two sons born to Owen and Anna Campbell Jarrell. A daughter had died in infancy before he was born, and the motif of the lost sibling, particularly the sister, surfaced in Jarrell's work throughout his life (for example, "Orestes at Tauris," "The Black Swan," *The Animal Family*). On the other hand, the younger brother who lived is rarely an important figure. The working-class Jarrells came from rural Shelbyville, Tennessee, while Anna Campbell Jarrell was from a well-to-do Nashville business family.

She was, according to her second daughter-in-law, "an immaculate person" and "a costly wife . . . [but] a devoted mother." Her frequent spells of fainting are recorded in the 1961 poem called "Hope," and she seems to have had health problems most of her life. From 1915 to 1925 the family lived in California, mostly in Long Beach, where Owen Jarrell worked for a photographer. Other members of the Jarrell family had also settled in southern California. In 1925 Anna separated from her husband, taking her sons with her back to Nashville, where they were provided for by her candy-manufacturer brother, Howell Campbell.

During the spring of 1926, while his mother was in the hospital, Randall posed for the figure of Ganymede on the pediment of the concrete replica of the Parthenon in Nashville's Centennial Park. The sculptors, Belle Kinney and Leopold Scholz, were "enchanted with this child who told them myths of the gods while he posed," wrote Jarrell's widow in 1966. "Long afterwards his mother said the sculptors had asked to adopt him, but knowing how attached to them he was she hadn't dared tell him. 'She was right,' Randall said bitterly. 'I'd have gone with them like *that*.'"

In 1926 Randall went back to Hollywood to spend the summer and fall with his paternal grandparents, the couple called Mama and Pop in "The Lost World." The mingled happiness and pain of this time remained with Jarrell all his life, and he was able to write about it directly only in 1962, when his mother's returning to him of the letters he wrote her in 1926 stimulated a flood of magical memories. His affection for his grandparents (in addition to the great-grandmother, "Dandeen," and the Aunt Bettie who owned the M-G-M lion) was dashed when they let him go back to Nashville and his mother's family, and he never wrote to them or saw them again. His distress and feeling of guilt over this rupture are recorded in "A Story" (1939) and "The Lost World" (1962).

Although he was expected to help his mother—in straitened circumstances after the divorce—by delivering newspapers and doing odd jobs, he was active in writing, music, and dramatics during his school years. When he could not be persuaded to take an interest in his uncle Howell Campbell's candy business, Campbell generously sent him to Vanderbilt, where he completed work for a B.A. in 1935 (receiving the degree in 1936) and earned an M.A. in 1939. Although majoring in psychology, Jarrell studied with Ransom, Davidson, and Warren and edited an undergraduate humor magazine, the *Masquerader*. Ransom—Mr.

Ransom, Jarrell called him all his life—became his mentor. Tate, who lived in nearby Clarksville, helped and encouraged him with his poetry. Warren not only taught Jarrell at Vanderbilt but later published many of Jarrell's early poems and reviews after he went to teach at Louisiana State University and became an editor of the *Southern Review* in 1935 (Jarrell won the *Southern Review*'s poetry contest in 1936). Davidson directed Jarrell's master's thesis, "Implicit Generalization in Housman," after Ransom left Vanderbilt. Jarrell had wanted to write on Auden, who was then thirty—too "new" a poet for the conservative Vanderbilt English department. In 1937, when Ransom was offered a job at Kenyon College, Jarrell organized student efforts to get the Vanderbilt administration to make Ransom a counter offer, but Ransom left and Jarrell followed him to Kenyon, in Gambier, Ohio, where he held a part-time instructorship (and coached several sports, including tennis) until 1939. In later years Ransom was to recall Jarrell swooping down the Gambier hillsides on skis, arms outflung, calling "I feel just like an angel!" (to the disapproval of the Episcopal administration of the college). His first year there, Jarrell roomed in Ransom's house with an undergraduate student, Robert Lowell, who had transferred to Kenyon from Harvard to study with Ransom. During 1938-1939 the young men moved into college housing with Peter Taylor, who had followed Ransom to Kenyon from Vanderbilt that year. Taylor and Lowell became Jarrell's lifelong closest friends.

During his Vanderbilt years, Jarrell had formed an attachment to Amy Breyer, a medical student several years older than he and one of several children of a friendly Jewish family who welcomed Jarrell into their Nashville home. The relationship was deep but, in the end, troubled: Breyer felt unable to live up to Jarrell's intellectual and emotional expectations. While he was at Kenyon she broke off with him and soon married a young surgeon in Boston. A number of poems record the painful end of the relationship: "Che Faro Senza Euridice?," "The Christmas Roses" (whose medical imagery may have come from Breyer), "On the Railway Platform," "In Those Days," "The Bad Music" (which substitutes—no doubt significantly—Jarrell's mother's name, Anna, for that of the lost beloved), and "A Story" (which also closely parallels the loss of his father's family in his childhood).

In 1939 Jarrell took a teaching post at the University of Texas at Austin, where he met his first wife, Mackie Langham, who had just received her M.A. from that university. They were married on 1 June 1940, and Jarrell's first collection (of twenty poems), "The Rage for the Lost Penny," appeared in *Five Young American Poets* (1940). The other contributors were John Berryman, W. R. Moses, Mary Barnard, and George Marion O'Donnell. Ransom reviewed the volume for the *Kenyon Review* (1941), praising Jarrell's "angel's velocity and range with language, and . . . dazzling textures of meaning," but reproving the "phonetic raggedness so consistent that we know he must be nursing some infection of puritan principle." Jarrell excluded all but two of these poems, which were strongly influenced by Auden and Tate, from *Selected Poems* (1955). In most of these poems he takes a sociological approach to the human condition, generalizing in imagery that is concrete but not specific, as in "The Automaton," with its

> great shape . . .
> The slave and remnant of the slain,
> ....
> Unconquered, inexhaustible,
> The genius of a world's desire,
> And cast at that world's judgment
> Into the world-consuming fire—

The subject of many of the poems is the imminent and inevitable self-destruction of human civilization, the result of greed, lust for power, and self-centered indifference.

Jarrell's first independent volume, *Blood for a Stranger* (1942), contained all twenty poems from "The Rage for the Lost Penny" and two dozen others, including the more characteristic "90 North," with its theme of the child's confrontation with nothingness; "Children Selecting Books in a Library," the first of several "library" poems explaining the power of literature to "cure that short disease, myself " by allowing the child to live other lives by "trading another's sorrow for our own"; and "The Memoirs of Glückel of Hameln," in which the poet speaks to a historical figure, an eighteenth-century Jewish woman who, after she was widowed, ran the family business and wrote her memoirs for her children. Reviewing the volume for the *New York Herald-Tribune Book Review* (29 November 1942), Ruth Lechlitner criticized the impersonal international-modernist style of the poems (and was the first to point out the resemblance of "90 North" to Stephen Spender's "Polar Exploration"), but she identified Jarrell's "recurrent theme . . . that humanity walks in an inescapable maze of guilt."

The poems of *Blood for a Stranger* are not war poems (most were written before World War II) though many address the deteriorating international situation caused by the tendency of "States" to seek infinite power and of individuals to lose themselves in egotism. Besides poems in which the poet speaks directly to the reader, there are quasi-narrative or dramatic poems whose protagonists are often children, or adults looking back into childhood. The style of the poems, like that in *Five Young American Poets,* seems adapted from Tate (to whom the volume is dedicated) and Auden, with echoes of Thomas Hardy, A. E. Housman, and Ransom (especially in "The Blind Sheep"). However, in the speaker who addresses his characters, urging them to "change" their lives, and in the imagery drawn from fairy tale and traditional fantasy, a number of the poems foreshadow Jarrell's mature writing.

By 1941 Jarrell was already embroiled in literary controversy because of his biting reviews. Malcolm Cowley wrote to the *New Republic,* whose associate editor, Edmund Wilson, had hired Jarrell in 1940, complaining of "the technical skill and the attitude—the *dandysme*—of the reviewer" which become "more important than the subject matter" in Jarrell's negative review of Conrad Aiken's *And in the Human Heart* (1940). (Jarrell had, among other things, likened Aiken's rhetorical skills to "Merlin's pulling a quarter from a schoolboy's nose," and his poems to "finger exercises by Liszt.") Jarrell's response insisted that he praised poetry he admired and unrepentantly extended his objections to Aiken's book.

Early in 1942 Jarrell enlisted in the U.S. Army Air Force and was sent for aviation training to Sheppard Field in Wichita Falls, Texas. Not qualifying as a pilot, he was sent to Chanute Field, in Rantoul, Illinois, for training as a flight instructor. During the training period he wrote his wife many detailed letters describing life at the base. He turned some of this material into poems: "Lines," "Absent with Official Leave," "The Soldier," and "Soldier, T. P." An assignment in the mail room led to "Mail Call," and hospitalization for an illness produced "The Sick Nought." In a letter to one editor from this time, Jarrell said he wrote more about "the Army" than "the War"; the boredom, senselessness, and uncertainty of army life characterize these poems. At Chanute, too, he wrote a second "library" poem: "Carnegie Library, Juvenile Division," a considerably darker poem than "Children Selecting Books in a Library." Though the children go to books for vicarious experience, they can learn only "to understand but not to change."

From late 1943 until his discharge in 1946, Jarrell taught flight navigation in a celestial-navigation tower (a training dome similar to a planetarium) at Davis-Monthan Field near Tucson, Arizona. Reunited with his wife, who got a job with the Red Cross (and Kitten, a black Persian cat who appears in several poems and remained his adored pet until struck by a car in 1956), he wrote the rest of the poems of *Little Friend, Little Friend* (1945)—and some of those published in *Losses* (1948)—drawing upon his experiences with the flyers and planes and upon news dispatches by Ernie Pyle and others. The book was reviewed enthusiastically by Delmore Schwartz in the *Nation* (1 December 1945) for its advances over the earlier collections in theme and technique. The war gave the theme, but Jarrell's stance toward it was his own. He took "the particular part of the dead" who seek to understand the reasons for their deaths. Schwartz praised Jarrell's "justified repetition, hurried anapests, and a caesura fixed by alliteration" which give a "wonderfully expressive syncopation of movement" that enhances the obsessive questioning of the characters. Some of Jarrell's best-known poems appear in *Little Friend, Little Friend:* "2nd Air Force," "A Pilot from the Carrier," "Losses," "The Dream of Waking," "Siegfried," "The Metamorphoses," "The Wide Prospect," and "The Death of the Ball-Turret Gunner." The motif of the soldier as a child who barely learns the meaning of his life before he loses it, who lives and dies in a dream, estranged, anonymous, unable to see himself either as murderer or victim, is developed in one striking poem after another, as in these lines from "Siegfried":

> Under the leather and fur and wire, in the gunner's skull,
> It is a dream: and he, the watcher, guiltily
> Watches him, the actor, who is innocent.
> *It happens as it does because it does.*

Also in the volume is the haunting poem "The Snow-Leopard," that "heart of heartlessness" who looks indifferently at a caravan of humans suffering and dying in its mountain environment as they struggle to bring trade across the Himalayas: the leopard is for Jarrell a symbol of Spinozan Necessity, the working out of "Natural Law."

As a result of the reception of *Little Friend, Little Friend,* Jarrell was given a Guggenheim Fellowship after his discharge in 1946. He had recently taken over the "Verse Chronicle" reviewing column for the *Nation,* and while its literary editor

Margaret Marshall took a sabbatical he went to New York to assume her job as well from April 1946 to April 1947. The statement of interests that he thought qualified him for her job is instructive: "Gestalt psychology, ethnology and 'folk' literature, economics (especially Marxist), symbolic logic and modern epistemology and its origins." These interests lie behind the attitudes and subjects of many of Jarrell's poems from this period, though not obtrusively, for by this time Jarrell was careful to embody his ideas in characters and situations. Also in 1946-1947 he held a part-time teaching position at Sarah Lawrence College in Bronxville, New York, where he gathered much of the material for his long prose fiction *Pictures from an Institution* (1954). The then-president of Sarah Lawrence, Henry Taylor; his wife; and New York friends Jean Stafford, Hannah Arendt and her husband, Heinrich Bluecher, were among those who served as models for characters in the novel, as did Sara Starr, the daughter of long-time Jarrell friends from Nashville, Monroe and Zaro Starr; Mary McCarthy; and other "Lady Writers." The idyllic campus of Sarah Lawrence, its well-to-do, pretty girls, and its progressive educational philosophy were also portrayed in the book.

Jarrell came to dislike New York, and in the fall of 1947, encouraged by Peter Taylor, who was already teaching there, Jarrell went to Woman's College, later the University of North Carolina at Greensboro, as an associate professor. His wife, Mackie, had an instructorship. The couple bought a duplex with the Taylors and settled in.

Losses appeared in 1948. About two-thirds of its poems are related to the war and its aftermath. Jarrell's interest in modern theology (spurred by his attraction to Auden) emerges in several poems, such as "The Place of Death," a meditation in a cemetery; "Eighth Air Force," in which he examines the question of the guilt of bomber pilots; and "Burning the Letters," in which the widow of a flyer tries to come to terms with his death and her continuing life, unable to use the religion that once promised eternal life. A number of the poems in *Losses* deal with the war dead: victims of the concentration camps in "A Camp in the Prussian Forest" and "In the Camp There Was One Alive"; dead soldiers or flyers in "The Dead in Melanesia," "New Georgia," "The Subway from New Britain to the Bronx," "The Dead Wingman," and "The Range in the Desert"; the death of the old civilization in "1945: The Death of the Gods" and "The Rising Sun"—whose protagonist is a Japanese child left, like the widow of "Burning the Letters," to understand the death of a loved one and of a whole tradition. Prisoners are the subject of "Stalag Luft," "O My Name It Is Sam Hall," and "Jews at Haifa"; the sick and wounded of "A Field Hospital," "In the Ward: the Sacred Wood," and "A Ward in the States." The volume also contains Jarrell's "elegy" for the (presumably imaginary) little black girl, "Lady Bates"; his most extended, obscure poem about fairy tales and their significance, "The Märchen"; and a much earlier poem, very long and several times revised, "Orestes at Tauris."

This poem, first published in the *Kenyon Review* in 1943, had been among the poems which won the *Southern Review* poetry contest in 1936, but it was not published in the journal because it was so long. Like many Jarrell poems it is deeply personal but hides its intimacy beneath the surface of retold myth. Jarrell's own sense of loss and estrangement from his family seems to inform the feelings of the protagonist, who moves as if in a dream to his reunion with his sister Iphigenia—now a priestess of the fierce Taurian Artemis—which becomes his death. Orestes' resignation to being beheaded by his lost sister seems a projection of Jarrell's own complex attitude toward women (which would take a comic/ironic form in several later poems). "Orestes at Tauris" displays fear, love, desire for recognition and for union: emotions growing out of Jarrell's relations with his paternal grandmother—who beheaded chickens for her little grandson to eat—with his mother, and with Amy Breyer. Helen Hagenbüchle connects the threatening female figures of "Orestes at Tauris" and other poems with Jarrell's relationship not only to his mother but to his muse, explaining, "Orestes' quest in fact symbolizes the poet's quest, for, as Jungian psychology maintains, the artist's dependence on the Great Mother as a wellspring of inspiration is so strong that he is never capable of the matricide necessary for the liberation of the anima and its differentiation from the mother archetype." It is perhaps not coincidental that Jarrell's estrangement from his first wife coincides with periods in which he felt unable to write poems, periods brought to an end by new romantic attachments.

The dark strain of Jarrell's poetry has been pointed out by some critics as evidence that the poet had a terribly unhappy life. Jarrell's comment on the themes of "horror, loathing, morbidness, final evil" in the work of Robert Penn Warren (in a 1944 letter to Amy Breyer di Blasio) can apply very well to Jarrell's own: "to somebody who knows Red it's plain he manages his life by pushing all the evil in it out into the poems and novels. . . . All his theory says is that the world is nothing but evil, whereas the practice he lives by says exactly the opposite. . . . his poetry is a therapeutic device, the most wonderful one you could want. . . ." Jarrell shows his awareness of the problem with the therapeutic use of poetry when he continues, "the best poetry there is isn't that. There's a dialectical contradictory relationship between Red's life and his poetry, and either is to an extent falsified by the mere existence of the other." Jarrell's poetry is not, however, unrelievedly bleak; even in treating painful subjects Jarrell can find humor and beauty in human experience.

Losses was generally less favorably reviewed than *Little Friend, Little Friend,* with W. S. Graham attacking it in the September 1948 issue of *Poetry* (which nonetheless awarded the volume its Levinson Prize that year) as "a collection of poems which are mostly spun from what should be the involuntary incidentals of a poem, rather than the poem's being made first for the poetic action . . . little conversational phrases trailing off to dots which, as a device, have a loosening effect upon a poetic line which is, in the first place, conceived at too low-grade a tension. . . . the timbre of the prosodic voice is old-fashioned and laboriously clichéd." Many of these accusations were to return in other forms in criticism of later volumes; but the traits to which they attach were essential to Jarrell's poetic aims, announced as early as 1940 in a letter to Allen Tate: "I'd rather seem limp and prosaic than false or rhetorical, I want rather to be like speech." This is not to say, as some critics have, that Jarrell was indifferent or lazy about the aural qualities of his verse. The many pages of manuscript held by the University of North Carolina at Greensboro and by the Berg Collection of the New York Public Library (those to "Jerome" were published in 1971) show how Jarrell worked with his poetic lines, frequently scanning them to check out his metrical patterns, and keeping lists of words and images in his quest for the exact diction that would best convey his vision. He wrote, for John Ciardi's anthology *Mid-Century American Poets* (1950), "Rhyme . . . is attractive to me, but I like it best irregular, live, and heard." He delighted in coincidences between words and things, even when the effects, for others, proved crude ("the burlaps/lapping and lapping each stunned universe" of "The Snow Leopard," for example, offended James Dickey). Jarrell repeatedly championed both poetry and prose that took seriously as its subject "reality"—which to him meant daily life as expe-

Two drafts for a poem collected in Little Friend, Little Friend *(by permission of Mary Jarrell; courtesy of the Special Collections Division, Walter Clinton Jackson Library, University of North Carolina at Greensboro)*

SIEGFRIED

In the turret's great glass dome, the apparition, death,
Framed in the glass of the gunsight, a fighter's blinking wing,
Burns softly, ... engines; ... the flak's inked blurs,
Distributed, statistical... the vanished ...
Are death--... death under glass, a ... CHANCE
For some... yesterday, someone tomorrow; and the fire
That streams from the fighter which ... is ... there,
Does not warm ... not burn them, though they die.
Under the leather and ... and wire, in the gunner's skull.
It is ... dream: the he, the watcher, guiltily
Watches the him, ... actor, who is innocent

It is unnecessary to understand; if you are still
In this year of our warfare, indispensable
In general... in particular dispensable
As ... cartridge ...
It is only to... on so much machinery,
To enter ... miles so many feet.
... you tried to sight the guns were jerked from your ...
By the currents there in the ... of the wire

Do as they said; as they said, there is always a reason

             the unvalued facts
(In nature there is neither right, nor left, nor wrong).

rienced by people—in Walt Whitman, Robert Frost, William Carlos Williams, Marianne Moore, Christina Stead, Rudyard Kipling, and Anton Chekhov. To Moore he wrote, in 1954, "I'm particularly fond of poetry that doesn't remove itself from speech and prose and Life in Particular." The transformation of the commonplace into art was his ideal (hence his adoration of Rainer Maria Rilke), but it was a difficult quest, in which a misstep in one direction meant pretentiousness, in another, triviality.

It was "between books" and apparently somewhat disaffected from his wife that Jarrell went to teach at the Salzburg Seminar in American Civilization in the summer of 1948. Here he fell in love with Germanic Romantic civilization (to which he had already been attracted, though he was also repelled by its culmination in the two World Wars and the atrocities against the Jews) and formed a romantic attachment with one of its representatives, an Austrian woman named Elisabeth Eisler, herself a victim of Naziism and a creative person, a ceramist. The stimulation provided by the experience resulted in such poems as "Hohensalzburg: Variations on a Theme of Romantic Character," "A Soul," "Orient Express," "A Game at Salzburg," and "An English Garden in Austria." A number of letters from Jarrell to Eisler, annotated and published by Mary Jarrell in *American Poetry Review* in 1977, show Jarrell's characteristic way of working with phrases, images, or ideas drawn from his reading, his experiences, or his correspondence. The germs—even occasional phrases—of several of these poems in fact come from Eisler's letters to him.

The Seven-League Crutches (1951) contains the Salzburg poems and a number of poems based on fairy tales and literary works. It also includes some of Jarrell's first translations, from Tristan Corbière and Rilke, and his first extended treatment of a work of visual art, his "translation," as he liked to call it, of Albrecht Dürer's *The Knight, Death, and the Devil*. Several interesting longer poems also appear in the volume: "A Conversation with the Devil," in which the poet makes a mock-Faustian deal with Mephistopheles; "The Night Before the Night Before Christmas," which, despite its adolescent female protagonist, Mary Jarrell has called "semi-autobiographical"; and "A Girl in a Library." This poem is Jarrell's contemplation of the archetypal American college girl, so different from the fictional romantic heroine who is her foil in the poem, Pushkin's Tatyana Larina, but elementally human, and, in her own way, mythic:

Don't cry, little peasant. Sit and dream.
One comes, a finger's width beneath your skin,
To the braided maidens singing as they spin;
....
The firelight of a long, blind, dreaming story
Lingers upon your lips; and I have seen
Firm, fixed forever in your closing eyes,
The Corn King beckoning to his Spring Queen.

This poem was placed first in the 1955 *Selected Poems*. Its emotional opposite, the painful, memorable dramatic monologue "Seele im Raum," ends *The Seven-League Crutches*. The portrait of an individual who, amid her "normal" family life, nonetheless experiences a secret existence—symbolized by the imaginary eland which sits at her table and is a personification of her misery, her *elend*—"Seele im Raum" suggests Jarrell's projection of himself into his protagonist. *The Seven-League Crutches* received some strongly favorable reviews, including an ecstatic one from Robert Lowell in the *New York Times Book Review* (7 October 1951), and inspired the first substantial criticism of Jarrell's themes and techniques, Parker Tyler's long review essay in *Poetry* (March 1952), "The Dramatic Lyrism of Randall Jarrell."

In the summer of 1951 Jarrell taught at the University of Colorado School for Writers, where he met and encouraged a promising young poet, W. D. Snodgrass, and an aspiring novelist, the newly divorced, Germanic-named Mary von Schrader, who helped him read proof on *The Seven-League Crutches* and get over the feeling that it might be his last book of poetry. She was never to finish her novel, but Jarrell began writing some new poems. At the end of the summer, Jarrell arranged a formal separation from Mackie, who returned to the University of Texas for a Ph.D. in English and a career as a professor at Connecticut College. Jarrell went off to Princeton to teach creative writing and lecture in the Princeton Seminars in Literary Criticism. Here he associated with Berryman and Philip Rahv, wrote "The Lonely Man," and sent frequent, voluminous letters to Mary, who was back in California with her two daughters.

Not least among Mary's attractions was the fact that, born only days before him, she too had been brought up in Long Beach at exactly the same time, even patronizing the photographer for whom Jarrell's father worked and visiting her physician-father's office perhaps at the same time as Jarrell might have been waiting there for his mother, whose doctor shared the office. Mary von Schrader was, in a sense, the "sister" he had never had, as well as a new love. She shared his passion for sports cars (and owned, when they met, the same model and color Oldsmobile that he had), and when they were able to marry, on 8 November 1952, they spent part of their honeymoon at sports-car races at Madera, California. She was to write, "To be married to Randall was to be encapsulated with him. He wanted, and we had, a round-the-clock inseparability." His long poem "Woman," finished in the fall of 1952, suggests both his new happiness and his habitual wry self-consciousness about women.

In 1952 Jarrell had taught in a hot but convivial summer session as a fellow of the Indiana School of Letters, consolidating a long-lasting friendship with Robert Fitzgerald and coming to admire Leslie Fiedler (whom he had not expected to like). Fitzgerald later recalled days of swimming in a nearby quarry, where, "hanging on a floating log in the quarry pool, [Jarrell] began one day to quote aloud the poem, 'Provide, Provide,' and to his growing astonishment and delight succeeded in going straight through it from memory. 'Why, I didn't know I had memorized *that*!' Randall is one of the few men I have known who chortled. He really did. 'Baby doll' he would cry, and his voice simply rose and broke with joy." In his long, important essay on Frost, "To the Laodiceans," which appeared that autumn in the *Kenyon Review,* Jarrell praised "Provide, Provide" as "an immortal masterpiece . . . full of the deepest, and most touching moral wisdom—and it is full, too, of the life we have to try to be wise about and moral in. . . ."

His first book of criticism, *Poetry and the Age,* was published in the summer of 1953. In addition to two significant general essays on the state of poetry and criticism, "The Obscurity of the Poet" and "The Age of Criticism," the volume contained a number of Jarrell's most influential essays elevating or revaluating the work of important American poets: "Some Lines from Whitman," "Reflections on Wallace Stevens," two essays on Frost, two on Marianne Moore, his introduction to the *Selected Poems of William Carlos Williams* (1949), and a powerful review-essay on Lowell's *Lord Weary's Castle* (1948). The volume was well received, with rave reviews from Delmore Schwartz and John Berryman. Reviewing the book for the *New Republic* (11 February 1953), Berryman called it "the most original and best book on its subject since *The Double Agent* by R. P. Blackmur and *Primitivism and Decadence* by Yvor Winters." Jarrell was always somewhat resentful that he was able to place virtually

Mary and Randall Jarrell with her daughters, Alleyne and Beatrice, 1953 (courtesy of Mary Jarrell)

any of his prose pieces, while it was difficult to get his poems published. "The Obscurity of the Poet" and others of his more general essays both reflect this resentment and confirm it by being just the kind of witty, readable critiques of the writer's situation and public that editors loved to print.

Having taught for the spring semester of 1953 at the University of Illinois, Jarrell brought Mary and her daughters, Beatrice and Alleyne, to Greensboro in the fall. During this time, Jarrell was revising *Pictures from an Institution* and preparing his *Selected Poems* for publication. The novel, or "comedy," as he called it, is a collection of "portraits" juxtaposed to one another in a dialectical or "musical" arrangement, as the title, with its reference to Modest Musorgski's *Pictures at an Exhibition,* suggests. The pictures of faculty, students, and administration in a progressive women's college after World War II express Jarrell's frustration with and affection for such "education." Academic personality types are satirized, some gently—the pompous sociology professor, the accommodating but null "head" of a midwestern university English department, the sincere but dopey creative-writing student, the maiden-lady creative-writing teacher—and some more acerbically—the vapid, charming, young college president and his artificial, unpleasant wife, the waspish novelist who "smokes heads" for the novel she is writing about the college, and a pretentious teacher of painting whose students all imitate his work. Motifs of adoption by the ideal parents and of the quest for *good* art in a consumer-oriented culture are subsidiary themes, and many of Jarrell's enthusiasms and pet peeves surface in allusions. His own zest for life and art, as well as his at times superior, even ingenuously cruel, disdain for the shoddy or mediocre, are distributed among several of the book's characters and judged with both sympathy and severity. Robert Lowell called *Pictures from an Institution* "a unique and serious jokebook," and Eric Bentley wrote, "At the root of his writing is enjoyment and love; not misanthropy, envy or spiritual anemia. Jarrell is gay, defiant, and good for the soul." Other critics found the book fragmented and destructively funny at the expense of its characters and the people they presumably caricatured.

Though he enjoyed writing the novel and was apparently happy with his new wife's devotion (she even attended his classes), Jarrell was increasingly writing prose rather than poetry, and this situation worried him: "A bad fairy has turned me into a prose writer," he would sometimes complain. He was also doing more translating. A lover of Rilke's poetry from his first acquaintance with it in the 1940s, Jarrell translated more Rilke and undertook a translation of Goethe's *Faust*. Later he also translated several Grimms tales, some Eduard Mörike, Henrikas Radauskas, and Chekhov's *The Three Sisters*.

In the fall of 1956 Jarrell began a two-year appointment as Poetry Consultant at the Library of Congress. He found Washington living agreeable and made himself useful at the library, soliciting manuscripts from poets and arranging tapings of poets' reading. Two of his most touching later poems came from the Washington milieu: "The Woman at the Washington Zoo" (thought by some to be his best poem) and "Jerome." The essential loneliness of the middle and upper-middle classes in contemporary American society is mirrored in these poems, as in other poems of the 1950s that went into *The Woman at the Washington Zoo* (1960): "Nestus Gurley," "Over the Rainbow" (a long, "California" poem drawn partly on one of Mary's aunts), "Windows," and "The Lonely Man." The woman at the zoo speaks for all: "so/To my bed, so to my grave, with no/Complaints, no comment. . . ./The world goes by my cage and never sees me."

A summer trip to Italy in 1958 with Mary gave Jarrell the material for several poems on works of art, including the stunning sculpture poem, "The Bronze David of Donatello," with its sympathy for the defeated, bearded-like-Jarrell Goliath and its mixed attraction/repulsion for the androgynous, young, triumphant David. The poems and translations of *The Woman at the Washington Zoo* won Jarrell a National Book Award in 1961, and reviews were generally appreciative, though some found the number of translations—almost a third of the book—disquieting.

Jarrell kept up a full schedule of poetry readings, appearances at literary festivals, and academic assignments from the time of his return to Greensboro in 1958. There were frequent trips to New York to work with editors, visit the Arendts, and attend opera with and without friend and music critic B. H. Haggin. The Jarrells usually stayed at the Plaza Hotel, where Mary overheard the conversation that became "Three Bills" in *The Lost World*. Sometimes they took side trips to see the Warrens in Connecticut or other friends in the Northeast.

The *Faust* translation was taking most of Jarrell's creative energy in 1959, he wrote to his editor at Random House and later Atheneum, Hiram Haydn. He continued to work on *Faust*, but only part one and fragments of the second part were complete at the time of his death. During the summer of 1959 the Jarrells finally moved into a house of their own, built to their specifications in a wooded area on the edge of Greensboro near Guilford College.

In the summer of 1960 the family traveled in the western United States, staying for a time in Montecito, California, a suburb of Santa Barbara. There Jarrell completed the poem "In Montecito," with its expressionistic image of a death: "there visited me one night at midnight/A scream with breasts. As it hung there in the sweet air/That was always the right temperature, the contractors/Who had undertaken to dismantle it, stripped off/The lips, let the air out of the breasts." Its uncharacteristic violence jars against a more typical late Jarrell milieu: "Greenie has left her Bentley./They have thrown away her electric toothbrush, someone else slips/The key into the lock of her safety-deposit box/at the Crocker-Anglo Bank. . . ." In spring 1961 Jarrell was elected to the National Institute of Arts and Letters.

In that year Jarrell was able to complete several more poems for *The Lost World*—"Washing," "Well Water," and "The One Who Was Different"—as he continued teaching and working on various translating and editing projects, notably the preparation of *A Sad Heart at the Supermarket*, essays mostly from the 1950s, which was to be published in 1962 by Atheneum. The volume enhanced Jarrell's reputation as a critic of modern culture with such pieces as "The Intellectual in America," "The Taste of the Age," "The Schools of Yesteryear," and the title essay. Also included were his introductions to the selection of Kipling short stories he had made for Doubleday (1961) and to *The Anchor Book of Stories* (1958), and the essay he wrote for the 1960 revision of Brooks and Warren's textbook, *Understanding Poetry*, explaining the genesis of "The Woman at the Washington Zoo." It is his most revealing public statement about his composing process.

In 1962 several significant events occurred: first, Jarrell contracted hepatitis, which put him in the hospital and left him with intestinal and neuralgic disorders that were to plague him the rest of his life. While he was in the hospital, Michael di Capua, who was then children's book editor for Macmillan and later Jarrell's editor there and at Farrar, Straus and Giroux, proposed that Jarrell contribute a translation of several Grimms Brothers' fairy tales to an illustrated edition in a series including other well-known writers' translations and introductions. Di Capua was so pleased with Jarrell's work on "Snow-White" and "The Fisherman's Wife" that he invited the poet to write his first children's book. By the end of the year, not only *The Gingerbread Rabbit* but *The Bat-Poet* (both published in 1964) was finished.

Also in 1962 Jarrell's mother returned to him the letters he had written her from California during the summer and fall of 1926. These letters unlocked a torrent of memories, and like one of his favorite writers, Marcel Proust, he began to recover the past. He was encouraged in this effort by his wife, who had similar memories. In a burst of creativity, he wrote many of the poems that would appear in *The Lost World* (1965), reading some of them in September at the YMHA in New York. The book was essentially complete by April 1963. In the same creative period he had also written *Fly by Night* (1976), like *The Bat-Poet* a quasi-autobiographical children's story. During this time he formed his friendship with Maurice Sendak, who illustrated all but the first of the children's books.

When it first appeared in the spring of 1965, *The Lost World* was greeted with mixed reviews, some very negative indeed, but in retrospect it appears to be a significant volume. In it Jarrell continued to use the style and approach of the poems in *The Woman at the Washington Zoo* to write about aging middle-class women, in "Next Day" and "A

Well-to-Do Invalid"; about the dead, in "The One Who Was Different" and "In Montecito"; and about a baffled man's attempt to escape and/or embrace the "mothers" in his life, in "Hope" and "Woman." In "Woman," written in 1952 but not included in *The Woman at the Washington Zoo*, Jarrell had used more hexameter lines among his staple pentameters than in earlier poems, and many of the later poems maintain that freedom and sense of spaciousness. Several of the poems in *The Lost World* come from *The Bat-Poet* (the intrusion of so-called juvenile verse into an adult book was objectionable to some critics) and there are other brief, observation-based pieces such as "Well-Water" and "The X-Ray Waiting Room in the Hospital." The nightmarish folktalelike poems "A Hunt in the Black Forest"—a revision of a 1948 poem—and "The House in the Wood" recall earlier themes, while "In Galleries" and "The Old and the New Masters" belong to the group of responses to art works, again stimulated by a summer trip to Europe (in 1963). In "The Old and the New Masters" Jarrell disputes Auden's contention, in "Musée des Beaux Arts," that paintings by "the Old Masters" show humans' indifference to suffering and miracles, citing to the contrary Hugo van der Goes's *Nativity* (the *Portinari Altarpiece*) and Georges de la Tour's *St. Sebastian Mourned by St. Irene*. In a turn that reflects his attack on modernist painting in "The Age of the Chimpanzee" (a 1957 essay for *Art News*), Jarrell concludes in "The Old and the New Masters" that the indifference to spiritual values which characterizes modern art accurately foreshadows the end of civilization:

> in abstract
> Understanding, without adoration, the last master
> puts
> Colors on canvas, a picture of the universe
> In which a bright spot somewhere in the corner
> Is the small radioactive planet men called Earth.

Besides "Woman," "Next Day," and "The Lost Children," a poem based on Mary Jarrell's account of her dream about her then-grown daughter and a girl who died, the important poems of *The Lost World* are the title poem and its companion-piece, "Thinking of the Lost World." Especially in the title poem, autobiography is presented as an American child's myth. In the myth, problems are solved by wishes and by the daily miracles of life—visits to the aunt who owned the M-G-M lion, drives to the library in an electric car with "yellow roses/In the bud vases" and a friendly, decorous "Half wolf, half police-dog" on the back seat; the world is just as the child would have it if he could invent it himself. Fears of the radio "mad scientist" are soothed by the grandfather. The world portrayed is clearly artificial, made to conform to fantasies: on the way home from school the boy sees "dinosaur/And pterodactyl, with their immense pale/Papier mâché smiles" looking out over Melrose Avenue, and "a star/Stumbl[ing] to her igloo through the howling gale/Of the wind machines." The verse form of "The Lost World" is terza rima, though the tercets are run together, and the language is so colloquial that the rhymes become unobtrusive (like the couplets of Robert Browning's "My Last Duchess," a poem Jarrell particularly admired, alluding to it in "Hope").

While the memories Jarrell summoned up for the poem are presented nonchronologically, its psychological plot takes off from the boy's impressions of his weekend: playing, listening to his grandfather tell stories of *his* boyhood, eating dinner, driving to the library with Mrs. Mercer, "Floating by on Vine, on Sunset" in the electric car. This first section is titled "Children's Arms": the fantastic and real experiences arm the child for life. The second and third sections, "A Night with Lions" and "A Street off Sunset," are spoken by the man looking backward, imposing the perspective of later years upon the child's view. Now he can admit the sexual attractiveness of the aunt who kept the lion and who talked to him "Of *Jurgen* and Rupert Hughes, till in the end/I think as a child thinks: 'You're my real friend.'" Even now, "my breath comes fast/Whenever I see someone with [her] skin,/Hear someone with [her] voice." Only now can he confront the pain of having left these loving relatives. He feels "real remorse . . . : the little girl is crying/Because I didn't write. Because—/of course,/I *was* a child, I missed them so. . . ." He lives again through the horror of his grandmother's killing a chicken for dinner and his realization that the same thing could happen to a rabbit, his pet rabbit:

> The farm woman tries to persuade
> The little boy, her grandson, that she'd never
> Kill the boy's rabbit, never even think of it.
> He would like to believe her . . . And whenever
> I see her, there in that dark infinite,
> Standing like Judith, with the hen's head in her hand,
> I explain it away, in vain—a hypocrite,
> Like all who love.

After years of guilt and confusion, he can now look back with happiness, recovering the memories, which he calls, at the end of "Thinking of the Lost World," "the nothing for which there's no reward." Of this line John Crowe Ransom wrote, "I felt at first that this was a tragic ending. But I have studied it till I give up that notion. The NOTHING is the fiction, the transformation; to which both boy and man are given. That World is not Lost because it never existed; but it is as precious now as ever." Denis Donoghue compared Jarrell's position here to that of Wallace Stevens, who created a world out of nothingness through imagination. "Stevens thinks of it as a wonderful resilience of perception. It is what Jarrell comes to, at the end: winter, and then, 'in happiness,' the mind of winter. In his case I think of it as a resilience, equally wonderful, of love."

The children's books written during this period also tend to illuminate the mature Jarrell's reconciliation with the pangs of estrangement he felt as a gifted child in an ordinary environment. *The Bat-Poet* is a parable about the poet's development, as the young bat tries to look carefully at experience and translate it into language. Imitating his models (mockingbird, bluejay, chipmunk, owl), performing for his devoted fan, the chipmunk, and his mentor and critic, the mockingbird, the bat achieves several elegant poems about things he admires or fears by projecting himself into them. The task of knowing and writing about himself is harder, but in the end his poem about bats is his best. After writing it he goes back simply to being a bat, not with the anxiety that plagued Jarrell when he was "between" poems or books of poems, but peacefully.

Fly by Night is a more obviously Freudian portrayal of a child's dream life. Only in dreams has David, the protagonist, the power of flight; in sleep he floats out away from his dreaming family, his pets, and the farm animals into the wild world, where the animals seem to speak to him in verse. Meeting a mother owl—who like Mama in "The Lost World" kills to be a good mother—he goes home with her and hears her bedtime story to her children. In mother owl's verse story, a lonely baby owl finds an orphaned owlet who becomes his sister. The motifs of quest, adoption, and transcendence reverberate in *Fly by Night* as in the last children's story Jarrell wrote, *The Animal Family* (1965). Writing a review of *Fly by Night* for the *New York Times Book Review* (14 November 1976), John Updike remarked upon "the tact of his language and the depth at which his imagery seeks to touch

Randall Jarrell at the University of North Carolina at Greensboro, 1961 (courtesy of Mary Jarrell)

. . . the forbidden actual. All of Jarrell's children's tales have a sinister stir about them, the breath of true forlornness felt by children."

The idea for *The Animal Family*, of the man who brings home a mermaid and makes her his wife, had occurred to Jarrell in 1951 (soon after he met Mary von Schrader). The essential different-ness of women from men and their more "elemen-tal" quality is embedded in the mermaid image, as it is in other images of the poetry and *Pictures from an Institution*. Many objects the Jarrells had col-lected for the house they built on the wooded out-skirts of Greensboro turn up in the book: a hunting horn, a window-seat, and a ship's figurehead, de-scribed as "a woman with bare breasts and fair hair, who clasped her hands behind her head; she wore a necklace of tiny blue flowers, and had a garland of big flowers around her thighs. But her legs and feet weren't a woman's at all, but the furry, delicate, sharp-hooved legs of a deer or goat—and they were crossed at the ankles. . . ." Since the man and the mermaid have no children of their own, they adopt animals—a bear and a lynx, like the one the Jarrells fed at the Washington Zoo—then find a ship-wrecked, orphaned boy to bring up as their own.

As the boy grows, he refuses to believe he is a foundling, and in the end it seems to the man and mermaid that they have had him "always."

While Jarrell was writing this wish-fulfilling story, he was going through a difficult period. De-pressed in the spring and early summer of 1964, and still troubled by intestinal problems (see "The X-Ray Waiting Room in the Hospital"), Jarrell vis-ited a psychiatrist he had met socially in Cincinnati when he taught there for six weeks in 1958. The psychiatrist increased the dosage of a new mood-elevating drug (Elavil) earlier prescribed by Jar-rell's internist and sent him to a gastroenterologist who put him on a new diet. For a while he seemed to get better, but the drug unbalanced him in the opposite direction, so that he became continually elated and hyperactive. He slept little, felt inspired, wrote many poems and fragments—including his last finished poem, "The Player Piano"—ha-rangued his classes and colleagues, and quarreled with his wife and friends. When, in February 1965, he was taken against his will to North Carolina Me-morial Hospital in Chapel Hill, he was diagnosed as a manic-depressive. In the hospital, taken off Elavil and put on Thorazine, he became despondent, wrote to his agent of impending divorce from his wife, and in April cut his left wrist and arm in a suicide attempt. Afterward, off the Thorazine, he began a recovery that reconciled him with Mary by late spring and brought him home on the first of July. Although he wrote Robert Penn Warren in September that he was not yet writing any poems, he was happy to be at home and back to teaching. He was also planning trips (including one to Russia) and making notes for an essay on Emily Dickinson. In October, bothered by pain and impaired mobility and control in the wrist he had injured, he went back to Chapel Hill, to Memorial's Hand Rehabilitation Center, for physical therapy and possible corrective surgery. A few evenings later, while walking about a mile from the hospital along a country highway, he was struck by a car and killed. Although the circumstances were suspicious—the couple in the car said he "appeared to lunge" into the side of their vehicle—they were inconclusive and the death was ruled accidental.

After the poet's death, his literary executor, Mary Jarrell, and his editor, Michael di Capua, put together *The Complete Poems* (1969), which included, along with all the poems from his other volumes, drafts and fragments and early uncollected poems; and *The Third Book of Criticism* (1969), which contained, among other pieces, Jarrell's long essay on Christina Stead's *The Man Who Loved Children*—a novel he had long recommended to friends and students; two essays on Auden; long review essays on Stevens and Robert Graves (especially interesting for Jarrell's comments on the "Mother-Mistress-Muse" of *The White Goddess*, 1948, an archetype that appeared often in his own work); an extended explication of Frost's "Home Burial"; and his 1962 National Poetry Festival address, "Fifty Years of American Poetry." This lecture had not been especially well received at the time, Jarrell had felt, because it slighted many of the poets in the audience. Its ranking of the modern American poets of the first part of the twentieth century now seems remarkably just, with only a few eccentricities. *Fly by Night* and Jarrell's translation of *Goethe's Faust, Part I* were published in 1976, followed in 1980 by another volume of criticism, *Kipling, Auden & Co.*, which contains previously uncollected reviews, introductions, and some essays from the out-of-print *A Sad Heart at the Supermarket*. In 1973 Mary Jarrell began assembling, transcribing, and annotating Jarrell's letters. From a total of about 2,500 she selected about 400 for publication in *Randall Jarrell's Letters* (1985). The letters do not so much add a new dimension to the personality re-

vealed in the poems and public prose as they confirm and deepen what was already known. In addition to letters to his two wives and other family members and "official" letters written as an editor (mostly for the *Nation*) and as Library of Congress poetry consultant, there are interesting letters to his poet friends and to editors announcing his own principles, and, to Lowell and Adrienne Rich, long letters giving frank and detailed criticism of individual poems and entire volumes sent him for comment.

A memorial service was held for Jarrell at Yale in 1966, organized by Cleanth Brooks, Robert Penn Warren, Robert Lowell, and Peter Taylor. The memoirs and tributes read there, with others and with republished reviews of several of Jarrell's books, were collected in *Randall Jarrell, 1914-1965* (1967). Jarrell was lucky in always having had a few sympathetic, perceptive reviews for each volume, and the serious criticism of Jarrell began in reviews by such writers as Lowell, Karl Shapiro, Schwartz, Berryman, William Meredith, Updike, John Logan, Philip Booth, and such critics as Helen Vendler and John Lucas. The first extended essays about Jarrell were Parker Tyler's review-essay on *The Seven-League Crutches* (1952) and Sister M. Bernetta Quinn's "Randall Jarrell: His Metamorphoses," in her book *The Metamorphic Tradition in Modern Poetry* (1955). Walter Rideout's substantial essay " 'To Change, to Change!' the Poetry of Randall Jarrell" in *Poets in Progress* (1962) stimulated interest in Jarrell, and later surveys by M. L. Rosenthal (1972), Jerome Mazzaro (1971), and Frederick J. Hoffman (1970) helped place Jarrell in his generation. The first book-length study was *The Poetry of Randall Jarrell* (1971) by Suzanne Ferguson.

Assessments of Jarrell's significance vary. To his admirers—Lowell, Schwartz, Quinn, Rideout, Hoffman, and, more reservedly, Vendler, Mazzaro, and Rosenthal—his poetry does what he intended it should: it records distinctively the life of midcentury America. Jarrell's sense of what was missing from Theodore Roethke's poetry suggests what he thought was important to put in his own: "hydrogen bombs, world wars, Christianity, money, ordinary social observation, . . . everyday moral doubts." It is this sense of "life" which continually draws him readers. William Pritchard has written that "even though the number of fully achieved poems is small, and the amount of dross in the *[Complete] Poems* is substantial, he is, along with Lowell, the American poet from the later part of this century I return to most often, and with continuing rewards, new discoveries.... [Other poets] can be admired as creators of more finished, concentrated, even verbally distinctive poems; yet Jarrell has something more, and to be as embarrassing as possible I will claim that what he has more of in his poetry is life." James Dickey, who found the *Selected Poems* on the one hand "the most untalentedly sentimental, self-indulgent, and insensitive writings that I can remember" (see his amusing "dialogue" review in *Sewanee Review* in Spring 1956), and thought that Jarrell had not "the power, or the genius, or the talent, or the inclination, or whatever, to make experience rise to its own most intense, concentrated, and meaningful level" in language, turned back upon these strictures to argue that "the poems give you the feel of a time, our time, as no other poetry of our century does, or could, even. They put on your face ... the uncomprehending stare of the individual caught in the State's machinery: in an impersonal, invisible, man-made, and uncontrollable Force. They show in front of you a child's slow, horrified, magnificently un-understanding and growing loss of innocence in which we all share and can't help ...: He gives you, as all great or good writers do, a foothold in a realm where literature itself is inessential, where your own world is more yours than you could ever have thought, or even felt, but is one you have always known."

Jarrell's intellect was far-ranging, inquisitive, and continually testing, and his poems reveal his strong perception of the ironic incongruity between people's ideals and the way they live, as well as a sure feeling for the moral and psychological crises people have in common and a messianic vocation to show others what he learned and saw in the contemporary world. Consciously limiting himself to a poetry of everyday life (and its corollary dream or nightmare) recorded in a language at times too much like that of everyday life, accepting perhaps too uncritically the Freudian model of motivation and behavior, Jarrell reserved for himself a place not among the great poets of the century, but among the very good, very representative ones.

Jarrell's criticism is less controversial, in retrospect, than his poetry because so many of Jarrell's judgments have turned out to be premonitory of the reputations now held by the various poets on whom he wrote. Reviewing *Kipling, Auden & Co.* (1980) for the *Times Literary Supplement* (19 June 1981), John Lucas commented: "his critical judgments feel unerring and final.... It is almost impossible to catch him out." Jarrell's praise of Lowell and of Elizabeth Bishop, his criticism of Cummings,

Spender, Williams, and the later Auden are remarkably telling. It is not only the judgments but the metaphoric and witty style that distinguish the criticism, as Pritchard, Vendler, and Lucas (among others) have noted. Indeed, it is difficult to resist the reviewer who wrote, for example, of the Auden of *The Age of Anxiety*, "The man who, during the thirties, was one of the five or six best poets in the world has gradually turned into a rhetoric mill grinding away at the bottom of Limbo, into an automaton that keeps making little jokes, little plays on words, little rhetorical engines, as compulsively and unendingly and uneasily as a neurotic washes his hands."

Perhaps Vendler is right: Jarrell put his talent into his poetry and his genius into criticism. Although his work is not at present much taught in universities, Jarrell's poetry continues to find readers in the literate public—a situation that on the whole would have pleased him.

Letters:

Randall Jarrell's Letters: An Autobiographical and Literary Selection, edited by Mary von S. Jarrell (Boston: Houghton Mifflin, 1985).

Bibliographies:

Charles Adams, *Randall Jarrell: A Bibliography* (Chapel Hill: University of North Carolina Press, 1958);

Adams, "A Supplement to Randall Jarrell: A Bibliography," *Analects,* 1 (1961): 49-56;

Karl Shapiro, *Randall Jarrell* (Washington, D.C.: Library of Congress, 1967), pp. 25-47;

Stuart Wright, *Randall Jarrell: A Descriptive Bibliography, 1929-1983* (Charlottesville: University Press of Virginia, 1985);
Complete, meticulous, and informative, with works cross-referenced to letters, etc.

References:

Analects, special Jarrell issue, 1 (1961);
Literary magazine of Woman's College, U.N.C. Essays by five critics, an interview with RJ, and part of *Faust* translation.

Suzanne Ferguson, *The Poetry of Randall Jarrell* (Baton Rouge: Louisiana State University Press, 1971);
Survey of the poetry, volume by volume. Identifies major themes and techniques and

provides readings of the most significant poems.

Ferguson, ed., *Critical Essays on Randall Jarrell* (Boston: G. K. Hall, 1983);
Selections of reviews of each volume of poetry, fiction, and criticism; general essays on the themes and value of the work, essays focusing on the poetry, fiction, criticism, and translations, both reprinted and written especially for the volume. Introductory survey of Jarrell criticism.

Helen Hagenbüchle, *The Black Goddess: A Study of the Archetypal Feminine in the Poetry of Randall Jarrell*, Schweitzer Anglistische Arbeiten, volume 79 (Bern: Francke, 1975);
Jungian interpretation of the theme of woman as loving and devouring muse in Jarrell's poetry.

Frederick J. Hoffman, Introduction to *The Achievement of Randall Jarrell*, edited by Hoffman (Glenview, Ill.: Scott, Foresman, 1970);
Introductory survey to a selection of poems.

Robert Humphrey, "Randall Jarrell's Poetry," in *Themes and Directions in American Literature*, edited by Ray B. Browne and Donald Pizer (Lafayette: Purdue University Press, 1969), pp. 220-233;
Traces themes of necessity and pain, dreams and hope.

Mary von S. Jarrell, "The Group of Two," in *Randall Jarrell, 1914-1965*, edited by Robert Lowell, Peter Taylor, and Robert Penn Warren (New York: Farrar, Straus & Giroux, 1967), pp. 274-298;
Reminiscences of her marriage to Jarrell and comments on the composition of the later poetry.

Jarrell, "Ideas and Poems," *Parnassus*, 5 (Fall-Winter 1976): 213-230;
Discussion of how Jarrell got ideas for his poems and discussion of inspiration for poems about women, including "Three Bills" and "Money."

Jarrell, "Letters to Vienna," *American Poetry Review* (July/August 1977): 11-17;
Exchange of letters between Jarrell and Elis-

abeth Eisler in the late 1940s, plus poems growing out of these letters.

Jarrell, "Peter and Randall," *Shenandoah*, 28 (Winter 1977): 28-34;
Discussion of Jarrell's relationship with Peter Taylor, fiction writer and friend from the 1930s.

Jarrell, "Randall Jarrell at Work," *Columbia Forum*, 2 (Summer 1973): 24-30;
Discussion of Jarrell's *Faust* translation.

Jarrell, "Reflections on Jerome," in *Jerome: The Biography of a Poem* (New York: Grossman, 1971), pp. 11-18;
Describes the background of the poem, "Jerome," in Washington, D.C., discussing works of art and Freudian psychoanalytic theory.

Robert Lowell, Peter Taylor, and Robert Penn Warren, eds., *Randall Jarrell, 1914-1965* (New York: Farrar, Straus & Giroux, 1967);
Tributes from memorial service, plus reprints of essays and reviews by various critics and fellow writers. Reminiscences by friends such as Robert Penn Warren, John Crowe Ransom, Eleanor Ross Taylor, Robert Fitzgerald. Illustrated.

Jerome Mazzaro, "Between Two Worlds: The Postmodernism of Randall Jarrell," rpt. in his *Postmodern American Poetry* (Champaign: University of Illinois Press, 1980), pp. 32-58;
A penetrating consideration, first published in 1971, of the development of Jarrell's personal and poetic philosophy, his quest to remedy "ontological insecurity" through language.

Sister M. Bernetta Quinn, *Randall Jarrell* (Boston: Twayne, 1981);
Biographical information followed by a thematic treatment focusing on war poems, poems on art, poems on girls and women, and poems on children. Contains an annotated secondary bibliography.

Quinn, "Randall Jarrell: His Metamorphoses," in her *The Metamorphic Tradition in Modern Poetry* (New Brunswick: Rutgers University Press, 1955), pp. 168-206;
First important consideration of Jarrell's place in twentieth-century poetry; concen-

trates on the theme of metamorphosis in the early- and middle-period work.

Walter Rideout, " 'To Change, to Change!' the Poetry of Randall Jarrell," in *Poets in Progress: Critical Prefaces to Ten Contemporary Americans,* edited by Edward B. Hungerford (Evanston: Northwestern University Press, 1962), pp. 156-178;
First survey essay with emphasis on the war poetry.

M. L. Rosenthal, *Randall Jarrell* (Minneapolis: University of Minnesota Press, 1972);
Introductory survey in pamphlet form of Jarrell in context of his contemporaries.

South Carolina Review, special Jarrell issue, 17 (Fall 1984): 50-95;
Papers from a special session on Jarrell at the Philological Association of the Carolinas in April 1984, plus additional work on various aspects of the poetry, fiction, and criticism.

Parker Tyler, "The Dramatic Lyrism of Randall Jarrell," review of *The Seven-League Crutches, Poetry,* 79 (March 1952): 335-346;
First extended essay on Jarrell identifying major themes and techniques.

Papers:
The major collections of Jarrell's papers are at the library of the University of North Carolina at Greensboro and in the Berg Collection at the New York Public Library.

Jack Kerouac

This entry was updated by Ann Charters (University of Connecticut) from her entry in
DLB 2, American Novelists Since World War II.

Places	Lowell, Massachusetts
	San Francisco/
	    Berkeley
		American Countryside
		New York/
		    Greenwich Village
			St. Petersburg, Florida

Influences and Relationships	Allen Ginsberg Gary Snyder Sterling Lord	William Burroughs John Clellan Holmes Joyce Johnson	Neal Cassady Gregory Corso
Literary Movements and Forms	Beat Generation	Spontaneous Prose	American Bohemianism

Major Themes	Cultural and Artistic
	    Reform
	Spontaneity
	Community
		Innocence vs.
		    Corruption
		Death
			Social Hypocrisy
			    (Sex and Drugs)
			Ancestors

Cultural and Artistic Influences	Modern Art Modern Jazz	Zen Buddhism	Roman Catholicism
Social and Economic Influences	World War II	French-Canadian Background	

See also the Kerouac entries in DLB 16, The Beats: Literary Bohemians in Postwar America, *and* DLB Documentary Series, Volume 3.

BIRTH: Lowell, Massachusetts, 12 March 1922, to Leo Alcide and Gabrielle Levesque Kerouac.

EDUCATION: Columbia University, 1940-1942; New School for Social Research, 1948-1949.

MARRIAGES: 22 August 1944 to Frankie Edith Parker (annulled). 17 November 1950 to Joan Haverty (divorced); child: Janet. 19 November 1966 to Stella Sampas.

DEATH: St. Petersburg, Florida, 21 October 1969.

The Town & the City (New York: Harcourt, Brace, 1950; London: Eyre & Spottiswoode, 1951);
On the Road (New York: Viking, 1957; London: Deutsch, 1958);
The Subterraneans (New York: Grove, 1958; London: Deutsch, 1960);
The Dharma Bums (New York: Viking, 1958; London: Deutsch, 1959);
Doctor Sax: Faust Part Three (New York: Grove, 1959; London: Deutsch, 1977);
Maggie Cassidy (New York: Avon, 1959; London: Panther, 1960);
Mexico City Blues (New York: Grove, 1959);
Excerpts From Visions of Cody (New York: New Directions, 1960);
The Scripture of the Golden Eternity (New York: Totem Press/Corinth Books, 1960; London: Centaur, 1960);
Tristessa (New York: Avon, 1960; London: World, 1963);
Lonesome Traveler (New York: McGraw-Hill, 1960; London: Deutsch, 1962);
Book of Dreams (San Francisco: City Lights Books, 1961);
Pull My Daisy (New York: Grove, 1961; London: Evergreen, 1961);
Big Sur (New York: Farrar, Straus & Cudahy, 1962; London: Deutsch, 1963);
Visions of Gerard (New York: Farrar, Straus, 1963); republished as *Visions of Gerard & Tristessa* (London: Deutsch, 1964);
Desolation Angels (New York: Coward-McCann, 1965; London: Deutsch, 1966);
Satori in Paris (New York: Grove, 1966; London: Deutsch, 1967);

Jack Kerouac, winter 1951, at the home of Neal and Carolyn Cassady (courtesy of Carolyn Cassady)

Vanity of Duluoz: An Adventurous Education 1935-46 (New York: Coward-McCann, 1968; London: Deutsch, 1969);
Scattered Poems (San Francisco: City Lights Books, 1971);
Pic (New York: Grove, 1971); republished with *The Subterraneans* (London: Deutsch, 1973);
Visions of Cody (New York: McGraw-Hill, 1972; London: Deutsch, 1973);
Trip Trap: Haiku along the Road from San Francisco to New York, 1959, by Kerouac, Albert Saijo, and Lew Welch (Bolinas, Cal.: Grey Fox Press, 1973).

PERIODICAL PUBLICATIONS: "Essentials of Spontaneous Prose," *Black Mountain Review*, 7 (Autumn 1957): 226-228;
"Old Angel Midnight," *Big Table*, 1 (Spring 1959): 7-42;
"Belief and Technique For Modern Prose," *Evergreen Review*, 2 (Spring 1959): 57;
"The Origins of the Beat Generation," *Playboy*, 6 (June 1959): 31-32, 42, 79.

Jack Kerouac, regarded in modern American fiction as the authentic voice of the "beat generation," thought of himself as a storyteller in the innovative literary tradition of Proust and Joyce, creating an original style that he envisioned as "the prose of the future." He wrote with the same theme of idealism as Emerson, Thoreau, Melville, and Whitman, reasserting the American dream of romantic individualism in each of his eighteen published books, which he regarded as one vast autobiographical statement.

Kerouac (Jean-Louis Lebris De Kerouac) was born to French-Canadian parents in Lowell, Massachusetts on 12 March 1922. He attended local Catholic grammar schools and graduated from Lowell High School with an athletic scholarship to Columbia University (he starred in football and track) after a year at Horace Mann School in New York. During his sophomore year at Columbia, he left to join the U.S. Merchant Marine and Navy during World War II. He began a novel and continued writing after his return to New York City, where he was close friends with Allen Ginsberg and William Burroughs, Jr. His first published novel, *The Town & the City* (1950) was begun after his father's death in 1946. Kerouac later dismissed it as a fiction based on the model of Thomas Wolfe, written before he had found his own voice.

In April 1951, when he spent three weeks writing an autobiographical narrative on a 120-foot roll of teletype paper that was to be published nearly seven years later as *On the Road*, Kerouac found his style. He called it "spontaneous prose," and during the period between 1951 and 1956 he wrote several books which were considered too stylistically innovative to find publishers. During the long, disheartening wait before *On the Road* was accepted by Viking Press, Kerouac worked a series of jobs as a railroad brakeman and fire lookout, traveling between the East and West coasts, saving his money so he could live with his mother while he wrote what he conceived of as his life's work, "The Legend of Duluoz."

"The Legend of Duluoz," or "The Legend of Kerouac" (Duluoz was Kerouac's fictional name for himself in three of the novels), is a fictionalized autobiography, one of the most ambitious projects conceived by any modern American writer in its scope, depth, and variety. Kerouac intended in his old age to gather his books together in a uniform binding and insert the real names of his contemporaries into the narratives so that his larger design might be more apparent.

"The Legend of Duluoz" begins with the novel *Visions of Gerard* (1963), which describes the first years of Kerouac's childhood and the death of

his brother Gerard in 1926, when Jack was four years old. *Doctor Sax* (1959) is a fantasy of memories and dreams about his boyhood (1930-1936) in Lowell with an imaginary companion, Doctor Sax, like the pulp magazine hero The Shadow, the champion of Good in a mythic battle against the forces of Evil. *Maggie Cassidy* (1959) is a more realistic novel about his adolescence in high school and his first love (1938-1939). *Vanity of Duluoz* (1968) describes his years playing football at prep school and Columbia, and his experience in the merchant marine and navy during World War II. It was during these years (1939-1946) that Kerouac met Allen Ginsberg and William Burroughs, Jr., named "Irwin Garden" and "Will Hubbard" in the novel.

On the Road begins with Kerouac's meeting the legendary Neal Cassady, called "Dean Moriarty" in the narrative, who took Kerouac ("Sal Paradise") on the road between 1947 and 1950, hitchhiking and riding buses and cars across the United States on a search for joyful adventure. In this book Ginsberg is "Carlo Marx" and Burroughs is "Old Bull Lee." Neal Cassady was a strong personal and literary influence on Kerouac, and in *Visions of Cody* (1972) Kerouac attempted an "in-depth" description of this same period of his life with Cassady ("Cody Pomeray" here).

The Subterraneans (1958) continues the autobiography as an intense account of Kerouac's affair with a black girl in the summer of 1953; in this book he is "Leo Percepied," Ginsberg is "Adam Moorad," Burroughs is "Frank Carmody," and Gregory Corso is "Yuri Gligoric." In *Tristessa*, Kerouac describes a love affair in Mexico City during 1955 and 1956, the same time period as *The Dharma Bums* (1958). In *The Dharma Bums* Kerouac ("Ray Smith") adventures in California with Cassady ("Cody Pomeray") and Ginsberg ("Alvah Goldbook") and the West Coast poets Philip Whalen ("Warren Coughlin"), Michael McClure ("Ike O'Shay"), and Gary Snyder ("Japhy Ryder"), who taught Kerouac how to climb mountains, camp out with sleeping bags, and live as a Buddhist during the first year of the "Poetry Renaissance" in San Francisco.

Desolation Angels (1965) picks up the narrative in 1956, and continues until the fall, 1957, with the publication of *On the Road*, the best-selling novel that made Kerouac famous as the spokesman of the "beats." *Big Sur* (1962) and *Satori in Paris* (1966) are the last books in the narrative of "The Legend of Duluoz," chronicling 1960-1965 and Kerouac's final years of alcoholism and anger at the media's

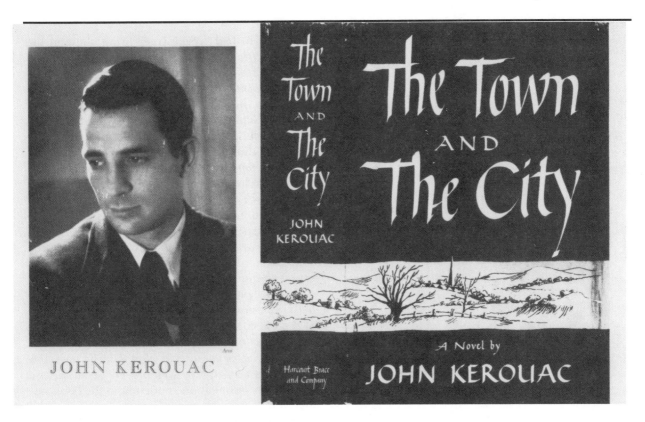

Kerouac later said he wrote his book "according to what they told me at Columbia University. Fiction. But . . . the novel's dead. Then I broke loose from all that and wrote picaresque narratives." Like almost everything Kerouac wrote, The Town & the City *is autobiographical.*

distortion of his work and refusal to regard him as a serious writer.

The larger design of Kerouac's "Legend of Duluoz" has been overshadowed by the popularity of three novels, *On the Road* (1957), *The Dharma Bums* (1958), and *The Subterraneans* (1958), that have been continuously in print since their first publication thirty years ago. In these novels Kerouac offered what a *Village Voice* reviewer saw as "a rallying point for the elusive spirit of the rebellion of these times." *On the Road* and *The Dharma Bums* are narrated in a direct prose style, telling the story of a search for a way of life in America that would fulfill an ideal of romantic individualism. In both novels Kerouac encounters "heroes" who appear to offer him alternatives to what he sees as the conformity of adult life in America after World War II.

In *On the Road* the hero is "Dean Moriarty" (actually Neal Cassady), a "young jailkid shrouded in mystery" whose energy and enthusiasm are so compelling that Kerouac follows him on a search for adventure, "because the only people for me are the mad ones, the ones who are mad to live, mad to talk, mad to be saved, desirous of everything at the same time. . . ." Dean Moriarty offers a life on the road as an alternative to settling down. As he explains, "You spend a whole life of non-interference with the wishes of others . . . and nobody bothers you and you cut along and make it your own way. . . . What's your road, man?—holyboy road, madman road, rainbow road, guppy road, any road. It's an anywhere road for anybody anyhow. Where body how?" Moriarty was "Beat—the root, the soul of Beatific," and he seemed to possess the secret of life, knowledge of the way to open the doors of experience to reveal the full richness and infinite possibilities of time itself.

Kerouac's portrait of Dean Moriarty was so compelling that most readers overlooked the conclusion of the novel, when the uncertainties and hardships of his way of life have overbalanced what he seemed to be offering Kerouac, who (as Sal Paradise) says goodbye to his friend at the end, a sad character in a ragged, moth-eaten overcoat. The vitality of Kerouac's descriptions of their trips together through America and Mexico, and the rushing optimism of their search for identity and

Jack Kerouac, 1952

fulfillment, are given depth by Kerouac's poignant sense of their shared mortality. *On the Road* is an American classic.

In *The Dharma Bums* the hero is "Japhy Ryder" (actually Gary Snyder), a young poet and student of Zen Buddhism whom Kerouac meets in Berkeley, "a great new hero of American culture." The description of the banality and repression of middle-class life is more specific in this novel, and the alternative is a way of life later to be defined as a "counterculture" to the American mainstream. It is basically Dean Moriarty's life of "non-interference" presented in *The Dharma Bums* in terms of oriental philosophy (dharma means truth) and the ecology movement. Japhy Ryder gives a political context to Kerouac's disaffiliation with his idea of a great "rucksack revolution" in American society, prophesying the hippies of the following decade.

Although the social context of Kerouac's rebellion is more clearly drawn in this novel, *The Dharma Bums* is not so substantial as *On the Road*. There is one memorable mountain-climbing episode, but there are dull scenes and mechanical passages. Kerouac later said that he wrote the book less on the strength of a genuine creative impulse than as an attempt to have another commercial success after *On the Road*. Its ending, when Kerouac

professed to feel "really free" living alone in the mountains, is contrived. In *Desolation Angels*, which closely followed the journals he kept at the time, he gave a much fuller account of his disillusionment with the experience. Kerouac was unable to live with Neal Cassady, and he also couldn't accept Gary Snyder's life-style for very long.

The third of Kerouac's most popular novels, *The Subterraneans*, is a confessional narrative, the story of his love affair with a black girl. It was written in "three full moon nights of October" on benzedrine in one of Kerouac's most astonishing creative bursts. He later said "the book is modelled after Dostoevsky's *Notes from Underground,* a full confession of one's most wretched and hidden agonies after an affair of any kind. The prose is what I believe to be the prose of the future, from both the conscious top and the unconscious bottom of the mind, limited only by the limitations of time flying by as our mind flies by with it."

The Subterraneans was closest in its narrative and its sexual detail to a Henry Miller novel, and later Miller wrote an introduction to the book saying that Kerouac's prose was as striking as his confession. There is no search for an alternative lifestyle in this novel. Here Kerouac confronted himself directly, and in his honesty about describing his failure to love the black girl "Mardou" he created one of his most dramatic illustrations of the basic theme in his work, his belief that "All life is suffering."

The explicit sexual description of *The Subterraneans*, the social anarchy suggested by the "rucksack revolution" in *The Dharma Bums*, the use of drugs and the hedonistic "joyriding" in *On the Road* angered many reviewers in the repressive McCarthy era, and Kerouac's books had a stormy critical reception. *On the Road* was so distinctive that it brought him immediate acclaim from Gilbert Millstein in the *New York Times* in September 1957, who wrote that Kerouac had produced "some of the most original work being done in this country," and that the novel marked "an historic occasion . . . the exposure of an authentic work of art."

But the controversy started immediately; the *Saturday Review* called the novel "a dizzy travelogue," and newspapers across America cried out against the "uncouth" characters, the "frantic fringe" that Kerouac celebrated in "the romantic novel's last whimper." The problem was that *On the Road* heralded a change of consciousness in American life. As Herbert Hill later wrote in *Anger and Beyond* (1966), the Beats succeeded in demonstrating in their life and work "that it was not necessary

Kerouac drew this comic strip, "Doctor Sax and the Deception of the Sea Shroud," for the Cassady children about 1952 (courtesy of Carolyn Cassady)

to sign up in the Establishment . . . that it was not necessary to buy all the cant that passed for serious thinking, the slop that passed for culture, the garbage that passed for statesmanship, and that even in the absence of radical political currents, it was possible to swim against the stream . . . and somehow to survive." In the uproar that followed *On the Road, The Dharma Bums,* and *The Subterraneans,* the originality of Kerouac's achievement as a writer was overlooked.

Even today, despite critics like John Tytell and Tony Tanner, who understand Kerouac's impact on American writing, the academic community continues to disregard him. There is finally an acceptance of the historical reality of the influence of the "beat generation" in American life; as Jess Ritter said in *The Vonnegut Statement,* "The great psychic migration of American youth since World War II can be charted by the novels they read and the novelists whose reputations they created. . . . Kerouac and the Beats represent the psychic revolt of the 1950's." However, the trend now is to give the credit to Allen Ginsberg or William Burroughs for originating the beat movement. In *Waiting for the End* Leslie Fiedler states that Ginsberg "invented the legend of Jack Kerouac . . . into a fantasy figure capable of moving the imagination of rebellious kids with educations and literary aspirations. . . . The legend of Kerouac is, to be sure,

much more interesting than any of his books, since it is the work of a more talented writer."

The fact is that both Ginsberg and Burroughs recognized Kerouac's originality and his contribution to their own work years before they became successful writers. It was Kerouac who titled both of their major works, *Howl* and *Naked Lunch,* and he also typed Burroughs's scraps of narrative and hallucination into the manuscript of *Naked Lunch.* Two years before *On the Road* was published, Ginsberg called Kerouac a "great prose Melville Jack," and in *Howl* Ginsberg's dedication to Kerouac credited him with "creating a spontaneous bop prosody and original classic literature. Several phrases and the title of *Howl* are taken from him."

Burroughs has said that when he first met Kerouac in 1944, Jack was "completely dedicated" to being a writer: "It was Kerouac who kept telling me I should write and call the book I wrote *Naked Lunch.* I had never written anything since high school and did not think of myself as a writer and I told him so." It was Herbert Huncke, a friend of Kerouac, Burroughs, and Ginsberg, who introduced them to the word "beat," as Kerouac described in *The Town & the City.* Kerouac himself coined the term "beat generation" in 1952, when John Clellon Holmes asked him to characterize the attitude of the young hipsters on Times Square. In 1959 the *American College Dictionary* published Ker-

Kerouac and Neal Cassady with Cassady's daughter, Cathy, 1953 (courtesy of Carolyn Cassady)

ouac's definition of the term: "*Beat Generation*—members of the generation that came of age after World War II who espouse mystical detachment and relaxation of social and sexual tensions, supposedly as a result of disillusionment stemming from the cold war."

The technical aspect of Kerouac's writing that influenced both Ginsberg and Burroughs was what Kerouac called "sketching," an unedited and unrevised spontaneity. After finishing *The Subterraneans* in 1953, Kerouac wrote down his major aesthetic statement for Ginsberg and Burroughs, who had asked him to describe the "Essentials of Spontaneous Prose." In nine paragraphs—Set-Up, Procedure, Method, Scoping, Lag in Procedure, Timing, Center of Interest, Structure of Work, Mental State—Kerouac outlined the process of free association within which he worked. "Blow as deep as you want, write as deeply, fish as far down as you want, satisfy yourself first, then reader cannot fail to receive telepathic shock and meaning-excitement by same laws operating in his own human mind."

Kerouac compared himself to a jazz musician improvising on a musical theme: "sketching lan-

guage is undisturbed flow from the mind of personal secret idea-words, blowing (as per jazz musician) on subject of image." There was to be no revision, except correcting obvious rational mistakes such as names. "Never afterthink to improve or defray impressions . . . tap from yourself the song of yourself, *blow!—now!—your* way is your only way—good—bad—always honest. . . ." The novel *The Subterraneans* and sketch "October in the Railroad Earth," a description of his work for the railroads in San Francisco included in *Lonesome Traveler*, are perhaps Kerouac's finest achievements with his technique of spontaneous prose.

Between 1959 and 1963, following the commercial success of *On the Road, The Dharma Bums,* and *The Subterraneans,* many of the books Kerouac had written between 1951 and 1957 were published (others still exist in manuscript): *Doctor Sax, Maggie Cassidy, Mexico City Blues* (a book of poetry where Kerouac considered himself "blowing a long blues in an afternoon jam session"), *Visions of Cody, Visions of Gerard, Book of Dreams* ("They were all written spontaneously, nonstop, just like dreams happen . . . and they continue the same story which is the one story that I always write about. The heroes of

318

On the Road and *The Subterraneans* reappear here
. . ."). Despite the fact that these titles included
some of his strongest and most original spontaneous extended narrative, especially *Doctor Sax* and
Visions of Gerard, the critics paid less and less attention to him as a serious writer in the furor over the
emergence of the Beat Generation.

Kerouac had shrugged off reviewers in *Time*
magazine who called him a "cut-rate Thomas
Wolfe" when he made the best-seller list, but he
was disheartened when *Doctor Sax* was panned as a
"largely psychopathic . . . pretentious and unreadable farrago of childhood fantasy-play." Kerouac
had hoped that *Mexico City Blues* would establish
him as a serious poet, but Kenneth Rexroth began
his review in the *New York Times* by stating, "The
naive effrontery of this book is more pitiful than
ridiculous." John Ciardi took him apart in the *Saturday Review;* Robert Brustein went after him in
"The Cult of Unthink" in *Horizon;* John Updike
parodied his style in a short story for the *New Yorker.*
Most memorably, Truman Capote attacked the
idea of spontaneous prose on David Susskind's television program in September 1959 by saying that
what Kerouac did wasn't writing: "it's typing."

Kerouac didn't have Allen Ginsberg's skill in
dealing with the mass media, but throughout the
1960s he continued to work on the "Legend of
Duluoz," publishing *Big Sur, Desolation Angels, Satori
in Paris* and *Vanity of Duluoz.* In 1966 he married
Stella Sampas, a childhood friend from Lowell, who
helped him take care of his invalid mother. In the
years before Kerouac's death on 21 October 1969
in St. Petersburg, Florida, he was, as his wife said,
"a very lonely man," disassociating himself from
his former friends, as well as the "beatniks" and
"hippies" who claimed descendancy from his
books. He was politically very conservative, a patriotic American who felt that the country had
given a good life to his French-Canadian ancestors,
and he was unable to understand why the vision of
America he had described so movingly in his books
had appealed to the counterculture of the 1960s.

Probably no famous American writer has
been so mishandled by the critics, who with few
exceptions ignored the larger design in Kerouac's
books, the integrity of his theme of individualism,
his romantic optimism and his reverence for life,
as well as the remarkable energy and humor of his
novels, the originality of his prose method and the
religious context of all of his writing. He was constantly attacked for being the spokesman for the
Beat movement, and only a few people listened

when he protested, "I'm king of the beats, but I'm
not a beatnik."

Allen Ginsberg tried to help by insisting that
Kerouac was a creative writer in his review of *The
Dharma Bums* for the *Village Voice* in 1958, and the
following year Warren Tallman was receptive to
"Kerouac's Sound" in his article for *Evergreen Review.* Although sympathetic, Tallman also understood the limitations of Kerouac's approach to
writing, which was "Kerouac's almost animal suspicion of the meaning values toward which words
tend. When his fictions converge toward meanings
something vital in him flinches back. His sound is
primarily a life sound, sensitive to the indwelling
qualities of things, the life they bear. To be Beat is
to be wary of moving such a sound into the meaning
clutter. It might become lost, the life. So Kerouac
draws back. Which is his limitation."

Since Kerouac's death in 1969 there has been
a little more sympathy for his work from the critics
and his influence has been noted on such writers
as Ken Kesey and Richard Brautigan. His life has
been taken as the subject of several biographies and
films. Kerouac is still widely read by young readers,
and *On the Road* was republished in 1972 by Penguin Books as a "Penguin Modern Classic." What
has been increasingly clear in the last twenty years
is that the fabric of American culture has never
been the same since "Sal Paradise" and "Dean Moriarty" went on the road. As Burroughs said, "Kerouac opened a million coffee bars and sold a trillion
Levis to both sexes. . . . Woodstock rises from his
pages." The "psychic revolt of the 1950's" represented a resurgence of the dominant thread of individualism that has been present in varying hues
in our history since its beginnings. Jack Kerouac
was as much an American idealist as Thoreau.
What he said he wanted was the same hut as Thoreau's, but in his hometown of Lowell, Massachusetts, not at Walden Pond. Something of a martyr—
like Thoreau—in his own time, Jack Kerouac was
a necessary hero who chronicled in his "Legend"
the rewards and hazards of romantic optimism in
mid-twentieth-century America.

Bibliographies:

Ann Charters, *A Bibliography of Works by Jack Kerouac 1939-1975* (New York: Phoenix Book
Shop, 1975);

J. Milewski, *Jack Kerouac: An Annotated Bibliography
of Secondary Sources, 1944-1979* (Metuchen,
N.J.: Scarecrow Press, 1981).

Kerouac's grave in Edson Cemetery, Lowell, on the tenth anniversary of his death (photo by Robert B. Perreault, courtesy of
Moody Street Irregulars)

Biographies:

Ann Charters, *Kerouac, A Biography* (San Francisco: Straight Arrow, 1973);
Earliest biography by Kerouac's bibliographer.

Charles E. Jarvis, *Visions of Kerouac* (Lowell, Mass.: Ithaca Press, 1973, 1974);
Biography by an early Lowell friend.

Barry Gifford and Lawrence Lee, *Jack's Book: An Oral Biography of Jack Kerouac* (New York: St. Martin's, 1978);
Interviews with Kerouac's friends and associates.

Dennis McNally, *Desolate Angel: Jack Kerouac, the Beat Generation, and America* (New York: McGraw-Hill, 1979);
General historical background.

Gerald Nicosia, *Memory Babe: A Critical Biography of Jack Kerouac* (New York: Grove, 1983);

Most comprehensive, detailed treatment of Kerouac's life.

References:

Ted Berrigan, "The Art of Fiction XLI," interview with Kerouac, *Paris Review,* 43 (Summer 1968): 60-105;
Long analysis of Kerouac's literary methods.

Bruce Cook, *The Beat Generation* (New York: Scribners, 1971), pp. 71-90;
Discussion of Beat literary and social issues.

Scott Donaldson, ed., *On the Road: Text and Criticism* (New York: Viking, 1979);
Annotated text and critical articles.

Frederick Feied, *No Pie in the Sky, The Hobo as American Culture Hero in the Works of Jack London, John Dos Passos, and Jack Kerouac* (New York: Citadel, 1964);

Academic analysis of Kerouac in literary context.

John Clellon Holmes, *Nothing More to Declare* (New York: Dutton, 1967), pp. 68-86;
Superb essays by one of Kerouac's closest friends.

Tim Hunt, *Kerouac's Crooked Road: Development of a Fiction* (Hamden, Conn.: Archon, 1981);
Detailed analysis of Kerouac's literary method of spontaneous prose.

Thomas Parkinson, ed., *A Casebook on the Beat* (New York: Crowell, 1961);

Poems, fiction, and essays by and about the Beats.

John Tytell, *Naked Angels: The Lives and Literature of the Beat Generation* (New York: McGraw-Hill, 1976), pp. 52-78, 140-211;
Excellent discussion of the work of Kerouac, Ginsberg, and Burroughs.

Papers:
Kerouac's letters to Allen Ginsberg are located at the Columbia University library.

Harper Lee

*This entry was updated by Laura M. Zaidman (University of South Carolina at Sumter)
from the entry by Dorothy Jewell Altman (Fort Wright College) in* DLB 6, American
Novelists Since World War II.

Places	Monroeville, Alabama		

Influences and Relationships	Truman Capote		

Literary Movements and Forms	Regionalism Romanticism	Contemporary Realism	Young Adult Literature

Major Themes	Ignorance vs.
	  Knowledge
	Prejudice vs.
	  Tolerance
	Race Relations
		Cowardice vs.
		  Heroism
		Persecution Vs.
		  Compassion
		Childhood Memories
			Guilt vs.
			  Innocence
			Traditions and
			  Superstitions

Cultural and Artistic Influences	Family Hometown	Studying Law	Southern Lifestyle

Social and Economic Influences	Small Town
	  Class System
		1950s Racial Situa-
		  tion in the South
			Judicial System

BIRTH: Monroeville, Alabama, 28 April 1926, to Amasa Coleman and Frances Finch Lee.

EDUCATION: Huntingdon College, 1944-1945; University of Alabama, 1945-1949.

AWARDS AND HONORS: Pulitzer Prize, 1961; Alabama Library Association Award, 1961; Brotherhood Award of National Conference of Christians and Jews, 1961; *Bestsellers*'s Paperback of the Year Award, 1962—all for *To Kill a Mockingbird*.

BOOK: *To Kill a Mockingbird* (Philadelphia: Lippincott, 1960; London: Heinemann, 1960).

PERIODICAL PUBLICATIONS: "Love—In Other Words," *Vogue*, 137 (15 April 1961): 64-65;
"Christmas to Me," *McCalls*, 89 (December 1961): 63.

Harper Lee's reputation as an author rests on her only novel, *To Kill a Mockingbird* (1960). An enormous popular success, the book was selected for distribution by the Literary Guild and the Book-of-the-Month Club and was published in a shortened version as a *Reader's Digest* condensed book. It was also made into an Academy Award-winning film in 1962. Moreover, the critically acclaimed novel won, among other awards, the Pulitzer Prize for fiction (1961), the Brotherhood Award of the National Conference of Christians and Jews (1961), and *Bestsellers*'s Paperback of the Year Award (1962).

Although Lee stresses that *To Kill a Mockingbird* is not autobiographical, she allows that a writer "should write about what he knows and write truthfully." The time period and setting of the novel obviously originate in the author's experience as the youngest of three children born to lawyer Amasa Coleman Lee (related to Robert E. Lee) and Frances Finch Lee. The family lived in the small town of Monroeville, Alabama. After graduating from Monroeville's public schools, Lee spent a year (1944-1945) at Huntingdon College in Montgomery, Alabama, and then attended the University of Alabama for four years (1945-1949), including a year as an exchange student at Oxford University. While she was a student at the University of Alabama, her satires, editorial columns, and reviews appeared in campus publications. She left the University of Alabama in 1950, six months short of a law

degree, to pursue a writing career in New York City.

Living in New York in the early 1950s and supporting herself by working as an airline reservations clerk, she approached a literary agent with the manuscripts of two essays and three short stories. The agent encouraged her to expand one of the stories into a novel which later became *To Kill a Mockingbird*. With the financial help of friends, she gave up her job and moved into a cold-water flat where she devoted herself to her writing. Although her father became ill and she was forced to divide her time between New York and Monroeville, she continued to work on her novel. She submitted a manuscript to Lippincott in 1957. While editors criticized the book's structure, suggesting it seemed to be a series of short stories strung together, they recognized the novel's promise and encouraged Lee to rewrite it. With the help of her editor, Tay Hohoff, Lee reworked the material, and *To Kill a Mockingbird* was finally published in July 1960.

To Kill a Mockingbird is narrated by Jean Louise "Scout" Finch, a woman recollecting her childhood years between six and nine. Scout lives with her brother, Jem, four years older than she, and her lawyer father, Atticus, in the small Alabama town of Maycomb during the 1930s. During the three years covered by the novel, Scout and Jem gain a better understanding of the adult world.

A key incident in their maturing is Atticus's legal defense of Tom Robinson, a black man falsely accused of raping a white girl named Mayella Ewell, daughter of evil Bob Ewell. In the months preceding the trial, Scout and Jem suffer the taunts of classmates and neighbors who object to Atticus's "lawing for niggers." As the trial nears, the situation intensifies, and a threatened lynching of Robinson is narrowly averted by the innocent intervention of Jem and Scout. In a climactic scene, the jury finds Robinson guilty even though Atticus has clearly proven him innocent. Maycomb's racial prejudice is so engrained that Atticus cannot influence the verdict of people reared to believe "that *all* Negroes lie, that *all* Negroes are basically immoral beings, that *all* Negro men are not to be trusted around . . . white women."

Another major interest in the novel is the unraveling of the mystery surrounding the neighborhood recluse, Arthur "Boo" Radley, who has remained secluded in the Radley house since he was arrested many years before for some teenage pranks and then released in his father's custody. Initially a victim of his father's uncompromising

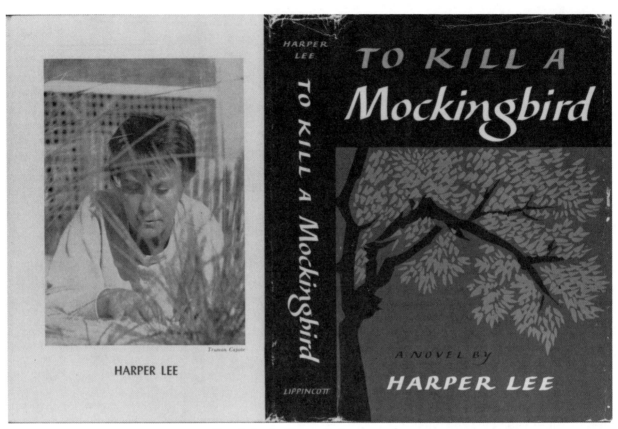

Dust jacket for Harper Lee's only novel

religion and family pride, Boo gradually becomes a victim of community prejudice, feared by adults and children alike. When Jem and Scout befriend Dill, a little boy who spends summers in Maycomb with his aunt, the three devote themselves to Dill's ideas for making Boo come out. At first the children imagine that the recluse dines on raw squirrels and roams the neighborhood by night. But finally they learn that Boo is truly a friend who has done a number of kind deeds for them. He hides gifts for the children in a hollow tree. He secretly mends Jem's torn pants, which were badly snagged on the Radleys' fence and abandoned there by the boy during an attempt to spy on Boo. Boo leaves them on the fence for Jem to retrieve. One cold winter night, while Scout stands shivering near the Radleys' steps as she watches a neighbor's house burn, Boo, unseen, covers her with a blanket. It is also Boo who rescues Scout and Jem from the murderous attack of drunken, vengeful Bob Ewell.

To Kill a Mockingbird contains a number of complex and opposing themes in a deceptively simple narrative—ignorance-knowledge, cowardice-heroism, guilt-innocence, and prejudice (persecution)-tolerance. The ignorance-knowledge theme is developed through characterization and action. Lee believes that children are born with an instinct for truth and justice. Their education, which is the result of observing the behavior of the adults around them, can nurture or destroy their intrinsic goodness. Fortunately, the Finch children have Atticus to provide the true education which the Maycomb school fails to provide. Structuring the action around the Boo Radley mystery and Robinson's trial gradually reveals the truth and further develops the ignorance-knowledge theme.

The character most central to the development of the cowardice-heroism theme is Atticus Finch; in counterpoint to Atticus's courage is the bullying cowardice of Bob Ewell. In part one of the novel, the children begin to think of their father as a hero when they see him shoot a rabid dog and learn for the first time that he was once "the deadest shot in Maycomb County." Atticus reforms the children's definition of courage when he has Jem read to Mrs. Dubose, a former drug addict, after school. The day after she dies, he tells Jem about her victory over morphine: "I wanted you to see what real courage is, instead of getting the idea that courage is a man with a gun in his hand. It's when you're licked before you begin but you begin anyway and you see it through no matter what." In part two of the novel, Atticus fulfills this definition of courage in defending Tom Robinson.

The themes of guilt-innocence and prejudice (persecution)-tolerance are closely related in the novel. The characters who are innocent—Tom Robinson and Boo Radley—are judged guilty by a prejudiced society. Tom is killed trying to escape from prison, but the novel expresses hope that prejudice will be overcome. Jem sheds tears at the end of the trial and vows to combat racial injustice. However, the climax of the trial is melodramatic, and the narrative flounders when characters mouth pious speeches against prejudice.

Lee's use of symbol is masterful. The mockingbird closely associated with Boo Radley and Tom Robinson represents joy and innocence. Both Atticus and Miss Maudie Atkinson, an optimistic neighbor, tell the children that it is a sin to kill a mockingbird, because "mockingbirds don't do one thing but make music for us to enjoy"; thus, Lee emphasizes how both Radley and Robinson are unjustly persecuted as innocent victims. When Maycomb has a light snowfall for the first time in years, Jem builds a snowman underlaid with mud to give it sufficient substance. The snowman melts when Miss Maudie's house burns. Thus, in a day the snowman's color goes from black to white and from white to black, showing how superficial skin color is.

When *To Kill a Mockingbird* appeared in 1960, its critical reception was mixed. R. W. Henderson called it "a compassionate, deeply moving novel, and a most persuasive plea for racial justice"; others praised Lee's "insight into Southern morés" and her "wit, grace, and skill." Negative comments were made about the novel's sermonizing and its melodramatic climax. Some critics found fault with the point of view. In *Atlantic* Phoebe Adams, missing the point that the action of the novel is recollected by Scout, found the story "frankly and completely impossible, being told in the first person by a six-year-old girl, with the prose style of a well-educated

adult." Granville Hicks noted in *Saturday Review* that "Miss Lee's problem has been to tell the story she wants to tell and yet to stay within the consciousness of a child, and she hasn't consistently solved it."

Scholarly articles in the 1970s praise the novel's technical excellence and recognize its place in literary tradition. R. A. Dave notes that in creating the small world of Maycomb, Lee has made "an epic canvas against which is enacted a movingly human drama of the jostling worlds—of children and adults, of innocence and experience, of kindness and cruelty, of love and hatred, of humor and pathos, and above all of appearance and reality—all taking the reader to the root of human behavior." Fred Erisman in "The Romantic Regionalism of Harper Lee" notes Lee's awareness of traditional southern romanticism and its pervasive influence on the South, but suggests that she sees the beginning of a new type of romanticism, "the more reasonable, pragmatic, and native romanticism of a Ralph Waldo Emerson."

With the novel's dramatic success, articles and interviews about Lee appeared in leading periodicals. The author of a 1961 *Newsweek* interview suggests that Lee "strongly calls to mind the impish tomboy who narrates her novel. There is a faint touch of gray in her Italian boy haircut and a heavy touch of Alabama in her accent." In interviews Lee's quick wit serves to protect her privacy. She describes herself as a Whig ("I believe in Catholic emancipation and repeal of the Corn Laws") and quotes as her favorite fan letter one which accuses her of playing down the serious problem of the rape of white women ("Why is it that you young Jewish authors seek to whitewash the situation?"); she fabricated a clever response signed "Harper Levy."

She does, however, speak seriously in interviews about her reading tastes and her work habits. She numbers among her favorite authors Charles Lamb, Robert Louis Stevenson ("the old gentlemen"), Jane Austen ("writing, cameo-like, in that little corner of the world of hers and making it universal"), and Thomas Love Peacock, as well as various religious memorialists of the nineteenth century. Describing herself as a "journeyman writer," she notes that "writing is the hardest thing in the world, . . . but writing is the only thing that has made me completely happy." Since 1961 she has lived in Monroeville, supposedly working on her second novel with a southern setting.

The reading public and the critics have eagerly awaited more of Lee's writing, but in the last twenty-five years no books have followed her best-seller, upon which her reputation rests. In 1961 two short articles, "Christmas to Me" and "Love—In Other Words," appeared in popular magazines. Although she travels extensively, Monroeville, where her sister Alice Lee practices law, remains home. Harper Lee's contribution to American literature is important, based on *To Kill a Mockingbird*, a regional novel with a universal message, for it combines popular appeal with literary excellence.

References:

Edwin Bruell, "Keen Scalpel on Racial Ills," *English Journal*, 53 (December 1964): 656-661;
Analysis, as an aid in teaching the novel, of Lee's use of irony. Shows how some of the townspeople are "myopic do-gooders" in their compassion for foreigners but show bigotry toward their native citizens.

Fred Erisman, "The Romantic Regionalism of Harper Lee," *Alabama Review*, 26 (April 1973): 123-136;
Article suggesting that while Lee is aware of traditional southern romanticism, this novel is more closely linked with a new type of romanticism—reasonable, pragmatic, and native as the nineteenth-century style of Emerson.

Nick Aaron Ford, "Battle of the Books: A Critical Survey of Significant Books By and About Negroes Published in 1960," *Phylon*, 22 (Summer 1961): 119-134;
Analysis of the novel's presentation of "living, convincing characters—neither saints nor devils," rather than stereotypes.

Edgar H. Schuster, "Discovering Theme and Structure in the Novel," *English Journal*, 52 (October 1963): 506-511;
A practical classroom approach to teaching the novel's theme and structure, pointing out that Lee's achievement is that she places racial prejudice in a larger perspective—the result of fear and lack of knowledge of people.

Bernard Malamud

This entry was updated by Jeffrey Helterman (University of South Carolina) from his entry in DLB 2, American Novelists Since World War II.

Places	New York City Russia	Vermont Israel	Oregon Italy
Influences and Relationships	Saul Bellow Fyodor Dostoyevski Henry James Nathaniel Hawthorne	Philip Roth D. H. Lawrence Robert Frost	I. B. Singer Anton Chekhov Martin Buber
Literary Movements and Forms	Symbolism Pastoral Romance	Yiddish Folk Literature	Mysticism
Major Themes	Anti-Semitism Spiritual Belief The Double Jewishness	Wise Folly Art Reflecting Life Moral Responsibility	Innocence The Outsider Seasonal Motifs
Cultural and Artistic Influences	Renaissance Art Impressionism Harlem Renaissance	Existentialism Biography Authurian Romance	New Testament Freudianism
Social and Economic Influences	The Depression Nuclear Destruction	The Holocaust Russian Revolution	Baseball Opening the Frontier

See also the Malamud entries in DLB 28, Twentieth-Century American-Jewish Fiction Writers, *and* DLB Yearbook: 1980.

BIRTH: Brooklyn, New York, 26 April 1914.

EDUCATION: B.A., City College of New York, 1936; M.A., Columbia University, 1942.

MARRIAGE: 6 November 1945 to Ann de Chiara; children: Paul, Janna.

AWARDS AND HONORS: *Partisan Review* Fellowship, 1956-1957; Rosenthal Award for *The Assistant,* 1958; Daroff Memorial Award for *The Assistant,* 1958; National Book Award for *The Magic Barrel,* 1959; Ford Foundation Fellowship, 1959; elected to National Institute of Arts and Letters, 1964; National Book Award for *The Fixer,* 1967; Pulitzer Prize for *The Fixer,* 1967; elected to American Academy of Arts and Sciences, 1967; Gold Medal for Fiction, American Academy and Institute of Arts and Letters.

DEATH: New York, New York, 18 March 1986.

BOOKS: *The Natural* (New York: Harcourt, Brace, 1952; London: Eyre & Spottiswoode, 1963);
The Assistant (New York: Farrar, Straus & Cudahy, 1957; London: Eyre & Spottiswoode, 1959);
The Magic Barrel (New York: Farrar, Straus & Cudahy, 1958; London: Eyre & Spottiswoode, 1960);
A New Life (New York: Farrar, Straus & Cudahy, 1961; London: Eyre & Spottiswoode, 1962);
Idiots First (New York: Farrar, Straus, 1963; London: Eyre & Spottiswoode, 1964);
The Fixer (New York: Farrar, Straus & Giroux, 1966; London: Eyre & Spottiswoode, 1967);
A Malamud Reader, edited by Philip Rahv (New York: Farrar, Straus & Giroux, 1967);
Pictures of Fidelman: An Exhibition (New York: Farrar, Straus & Giroux, 1969; London: Eyre & Spottiswoode, 1970);
The Tenants (New York: Farrar, Straus & Giroux, 1971; London: Eyre Methuen, 1972);
Rembrandt's Hat (New York: Farrar, Straus & Giroux, 1973; London: Eyre Methuen, 1973);
Dubin's Lives (New York: Farrar, Straus & Giroux, 1979; London: Chatto & Windus, 1979);
God's Grace (New York: Farrar, Straus & Giroux, 1982; London: Chatto & Windus, 1982);

photo by Janna Malamud

The Stories of Bernard Malamud (New York: Farrar, Straus & Giroux, 1983; London: Chatto & Windus, 1984).

In recent years, it has been impossible to discuss the career of Bernard Malamud without mentioning his place as the second partner, along with Bellow and Roth, in the ruling triumvirate of Jewish-American literature, which Bellow has called the Hart, Schaffner and Marx of American letters. Those who do not discuss the Jewishness of Malamud feel obligated to explain why they have avoided the issue. It is true that most of his protagonists are Jews (only *The Natural* among his novels has nothing to do with Jews), but their Jewishness seems part of Malamud's attempt to portray a most Christ-like figure, *homo patiens,* the man who suffers. Malamud sees this suffering for others as the ultimate test of humanity, and he is only half joking when he recasts the New Testament phrase about the lilies of the field, "consider the Jewish lily that toils and spins." Malamud's heroes rarely unloose the shackles of suffering and many, like Frank Alpine and Yakov Bok, deliberately ask for more, but they acquire a spiritual freedom when they learn how their suffering relates them to the rest of mankind.

Although many of the short stories (and *The Fixer*) are structured on the model of the Yiddish folktale, most of Malamud's longer fiction is based on non-Jewish archetypes: *The Natural* is the grail legend imposed upon the myths of baseball; *The Assistant* is a modern-day life of St. Francis of Assisi; *A New Life* is a travesty of the pastoral romance; and *Pictures of Fidelman* is a neo-Jamesian view of American innocence abroad. Seen from either the Jewish or the mythic perspective, the Malamudian hero, victimized to the end, learns to cast off the prison of self and reaches out to share the suffering of at least one other human being. While Malamud does not have the intellectual range of Bellow or command of Roth's verbal pyrotechnics, his moral vision reaches depths unprobed by either of his peers.

Malamud was born in Brooklyn, New York, of immigrant parents who, like Morris and Ida Bober of *The Assistant,* ran a small grocery store that stayed open late at night, leaving Malamud with little family life. His first writing was for the literary magazine at Erasmus Hall, from which he graduated in 1932. In the middle of the Depression, he spent four relatively unhappy years at the City College of New York where he obtained a B.A. His master's degree from Columbia University in English (with a thesis on the reception of Hardy's poetry in America) gave Malamud credentials similar to those of S. Levin in *A New Life,* and in the early 1940s he started writing short stories, while teaching night classes at Erasmus and later at Harlem High School. Formative influences from his reading included the Russians Chekhov, Dostoyevski, and Gogol, Yiddish writers Sholom Aleichem and I. L. Peretz, the short stories of Sherwood Anderson and Ernest Hemingway, and the novels of Thomas Mann and James Joyce.

In 1949 Malamud joined the faculty of Oregon State University, where he taught for twelve years while completing his first four books. Although he was relegated to teaching composition courses even after he had attained literary recognition and although much of his satiric academic novel, *A New Life,* is based on his experiences at Oregon State, Malamud was relatively content during these years. He felt, in particular, that the security of his position allowed him to write only what he wanted to write. In 1961 Malamud joined the faculty of Bennington College in Vermont where he taught full- or part-time until his death.

Although not secretive like J. D. Salinger or William Gaddis, Malamud never made himself into a writing personality and rarely submitted to interviews. His marriage to Ann de Chiara seems to have influenced his choice of Italian ancestry for Frank Alpine and things Italian generally. The Malamuds' year in Rome in 1956 provided the background for the stories which ultimately became *Pictures of Fidelman*. Malamud also traveled in Russia in 1965 researching *The Fixer*. He toured Italy in 1968 and returned a last time to Italy in 1983.

In his last years, Malamud spent part of the year in Bennington and part in his Gramercy Park apartment in New York City. He was comfortable in both the city and the country yet, like a number of his characters, always felt the pull from rural to urban environment and vice versa. In the early 1980s a stroke and subsequent bypass surgery weakened him, and on 18 March 1986 he died of heart failure. As always, he was at work on a novel about a man out of his element, this time a Jew in the Old West.

Malamud's fine eye for naturalistic detail, picked up both in his travels and in observing the life around him at home, seems missing only in his first novel, where realistic texture yields to symbolic imagery. Although Malamud has written symbolic novels throughout his career, nowhere is this so obvious as in his first novel, *The Natural* (1952), which superimposes the myth of the Wasteland upon the history of baseball. In the book, a composite of the classic lore of baseball—the Black Sox scandal, the shooting of Eddie Waitkus in a Chicago hotel, a number of events from the career of Babe Ruth, the poem "Casey at the Bat"—becomes the life of Roy Hobbs, the title character. These events are manipulated so they retell the story of the grail knight, Percival, and his attempt to heal the wounded Fisher-King which will restore plenty to the Fisher-King's land.

Roy is a "natural" in the baseball sense of having outstanding natural abilities for the game, but the title is also ironic since "natural" was the medieval term for a fool, particularly an unworldly innocent. His name carries on this duality. As Roy, he is the King (French, "roi") to restore the kingdom, but his last name suggests the country bumpkin (often called Hob in Renaissance drama) who is out of place in the sophisticated world of the city. Like Roy, Percival was also a country boy who came to the city to make good. The motif of the Wasteland as well as that of the outsider in an alien society reappears in almost all of Malamud's fiction.

At nineteen, Roy is on his way to Chicago for a tryout as a pitcher with the Cubs (the right team because he is still immature). He is shot and wounded by a young woman named Harriet Bird. The confrontation of the two, he with his lancelike bat and she with a gun in her grail hatbox, is a preliminary version of the hero's test. When Roy can explain his purpose no better than self-interest, Harriet Bird shoots him. Throughout the novel, birds symbolize the force of the destructive mother archetype. After a fourteen-year recovery, Roy returns to become a thirty-three-year-old rookie. He becomes the greatest batter in the annals of baseball and leads his team out of the cellar toward first place, but in the end, he sells out to gamblers. Roy's last-minute attempt to right this wrong fails because, like mighty Casey in the poem, he is struck out by the new Young Hero, named Youngberry. This repeats the cycle; as the novel opened, the nineteen-year-old Roy had struck out the old slugger, Whammer Wambold.

The handling of the grail legend is cleverly done but is by no means subtle. Roy's team, the New York Knights, is managed by Pop Fisher, who represents the Fisher-King whose land will remain barren until his wound is cured. In this case, the wound is athlete's foot of the hand, and the team's losing streak is reflected in the parched grass of the stadium. Roy literally knocks the cover off the ball with his handmade bat, Wonderboy, and, following a marvelous comic scene where the fielders try to play the unraveling string of the ball, rain comes and Pop's miraculous cure begins. Malamud uses the sexual overtones of the myth so blatantly that they work by comic overkill: Wonderboy is so obvious a phallic symbol that it sags when Roy is in a slump.

The grail legend, as Jessie Weston has shown in *From Ritual to Romance*, grew out of primitive fertility rites in which a new young hero replaced a dying one. The old hero in *The Natural* is the Knights' batting star, Bump Bailey, whom Roy taunts into a fatal crash into the outfield wall (patterned on Pete Reiser's crash into the outfield wall). Once Roy replaces Bump as baseball hero, he also tries to take his place as sexual hero by becoming the lover of Bump's girlfriend, Memo Paris. The death of Bump Bailey is more than a fertility ritual, however, because Roy never quite gets over his guilt in the matter. Furthermore, since he is ironically a middle-aged "young hero," he sees in Bump's fate his own.

Roy's tragic downfall grows out of his involvement with Memo Paris, whose name suggests Aphrodite, the goddess who tempted Paris with sexual love and the gift of Helen of Troy. Memo is the protégé of the Satanic figure, the gambler Gus Sands (the august Prince of the Barren Land), who dwells in the hellish nightclub, the Pot of Fire.

Memo is both temptress and the deceiver whose need for money leads Roy to sell out his team to the gambler. Although she is a beauty, Memo has a "sick breast" and is associated with death and corruption. Her first tryst with Roy takes place at a polluted stream, and when she drives away from the spot, Roy believes that their car has run down a boy walking in the road. This illusion, which Roy takes as real, signifies Roy's fear of his own death, and in Memo's presence he is always mindful of his mortality. Her first name may suggest the Latin motto of man's mortality, *memento mori*, "remember you are to die." As she promises Roy when their affair begins, "I'm strictly a dead man's girl."

Roy is offered a choice of women with the appearance of the earth mother figure, Iris Lemon (both flower and fruit suggest fertility and life), a thirty-three-year-old grandmother who first appears when Roy repeats Babe Ruth's feat of hitting a home run for a sick boy in the hospital. The boy recovers and Roy is cured of a batting slump which began after the night he and Memo "ran down" the boy on the road. Iris represents the life force and the ability to turn from self to others, but Roy, who can never forget his mortality, rejects her when he realizes that marrying her would make him a grandfather.

The two women stand for two different kinds of love, love as appetite and love as responsibility for another person. Roy is always hungry around Memo and eventually, coaxed by her, almost eats himself to death in a team party which is an ironic parody of communion and the grail feast. When Roy recovers from his eating orgy, he sells out to the gamblers (who are headed by Sands and the ironically named team owner, Judge Goodwill Banner). His wondrous homemade bat (in essence the living tree of the fertility rite and Percival's lance) splits in two when its owner is no longer worthy to possess it, and, reduced to the status of an ordinary mortal with a standard Louisville slugger, Roy strikes out, trying, too late, to undo his betrayal of the Knights and Pop Fisher.

The symbolism is far more subtle in Malamud's second novel, *The Assistant* (1957), where he combines the Wasteland motif with a life of St. Francis. Frank Alpine, the assistant in the grocery store of a poor Jew named Morris Bober, lives a modern version of the life of St. Francis of Assisi. The combination of the saint's life with the grail legend yields a double perspective on the two heroes. Under the influence of St. Francis, whose idea of the good life was perfect imitation of Christ, Frank learns goodness and moral strength from the Christ figure, Morris Bober, and Frank's circumcision becomes a sign similar to the appearance of the stigmata (the five wounds of Christ) on the body of the saint. At the same time that Morris exhibits Christ-like compassion for others, both friends and enemies, he himself has fallen into almost incurable despair, and Frank heals Morris, as Percival healed the wounded Fisher-King. Since the grocery represents the ruined grail castle which can no longer even feed its own inhabitants, Frank's restoration of the shop and the addition of restaurant service make possible the symbolic renewal of the grail feast.

Frank enters the novel as a wanderer looking for an identity. His latest self-image is that of a big-time mobster, but all he can manage is the robbery of fifteen dollars from Morris, who is wounded in the holdup. Morris's physical wound is less dangerous than the despair that has ruled his life since the death of his son, Ephraim. Frank, penitent over his part in the robbery, goes to the store, where he helps out Morris until he recovers from his wound and helps him as well to overcome his despair. Frank, an orphan, is looking for a father just as Morris is looking for a son. After a great deal of mutual misunderstanding, both men find what they are looking for. Their growing love is contrasted with the breakdown of the other father-son pairs in the novel: the landlord Karp, whose lazy son, Louis, gives up the family business he inherits; Sam Pearl, whose lawyer son forgets the traditional law of religion; and Detective Minogue, whose son is an incorrigible criminal.

A third medieval myth underlies the love story of Frank and Morris's daughter, Helen. In the French *Romance of the Rose*, the lover gets a kiss from a rose and then spends the rest of his life pursuing her but is thwarted by her *daunger* ("coldness"). In *The Assistant*, Frank gets a kiss from a carnival (etymologically, "farewell to the flesh") girl, but the girl dies before he can consummate the affair, and Helen replaces the girl as his ideal. Helen is made into the rose of the romance through flower and snow imagery associated with the winter in which most of the novel takes place. As with the Frank-Morris relationship, a Franciscan story is superimposed upon this myth. Francis built himself a snow-wife to show that he had forsaken the worldly life. At first Frank pursues Helen hungrily, but love replaces desire after he destroys his self-image as knight errant: he rescues Helen from being raped by Ward Minogue only to end up making love to her himself. After this, Frank devotes

himself to Helen with the same kind of selfless dedication that he has given Morris.

Although love in the novel means rising above selfish desires to something finer, it is also necessary for the characters to get rid of hollow romantic ideals. The reading habits of both Frank and Helen tell much about their ideals. Helen reads novels of tragic love affairs like *Anna Karenina* and *Madame Bovary*, while Frank reads biographies of great men. Frank yearns to be a hero while Helen's ideals are built around the dream of marriage to an extraordinary man. Even when she begins to fall in love with Frank, she dreams of a improved Frank, with straightened nose, better haircut, and a college education.

Morris's problem is not finding the right ideals, but rather putting off his despair long enough to carry out what he knows is right. The moral crises faced by Morris as he tries to give his family a future are similar to those faced by the

Dust jacket for Malamud's first story collection, winner of a 1959 National Book Award

poor shopkeepers who populate *The Magic Barrel.* Morris first tries to sell the store to a poor immigrant, but he cannot let another man take up his burden, and he tells the immigrant the truth about the shop's wretched business. Then Morris goes to an old friend who had once cheated him, but he cannot bring himself to call the friend to account. Finally, he deals with a demonic fire-setter who wants to burn the store for the insurance. Although Morris turns down the fire-setter, he then tries to burn the store himself by starting a fire with a photographic negative. He changes his mind but cannot put out the fire until Frank rescues him and the store. Morris's behavior is based always on the need for honesty in his dealings with others and, beyond this, a belief in the humanity of all men. Poor as he is, he always gives credit to those poorer than himself, knowing he will never be paid back.

Morris dies from a heart attack after shoveling snow. He believes that the store has been profitably sold to Karp, but this turns out not to be the case. At the funeral, Frank falls into Morris's grave, and when he emerges he becomes the new Morris. He takes over the store and the following Easter he becomes a convert to Judaism. The store survives and the reader is left with the impression that Helen finally understands Frank's true worth.

In *The Magic Barrel* (1958), his first collection of short stories, Malamud uses the form and rhythm of the Yiddish folktale to explore the terrible sacrifice in one's ideals that has to be paid for love. Many of his heroes are trapped in airless, past-tormented lives that open to a breath of life for those who dare to seize the moment, or else close with the terrifying stillness of death for those who do not. Except for three Italian stories, the settings are bleak ghetto shops, tenements, and stores where most human relationships depend on a humanistic notion of credit: "After all what was credit but the fact that people were human beings, and if you were really a human being you gave credit to somebody else and he gave credit to you."

The majority of the stories are of the same lyric-naturalistic mode as *The Assistant,* in which the grimy reality of poor city dwellers is made to glow with the Joycean light of epiphany while the characters learn the secrets of human love and despair. In "Take Pity," the reader is surprised to learn that the characters, a census-taker and a retired salesman, are in fact the Recording Angel and a dead man whose life is being evaluated, but Malamud handles the transition from naturalism to mystery so well that the revelation seems inevitable. The story shows how far a human being can go to offer charity to another human being and conversely how stubborn many human beings can be in refusing love which they interpret as pity. Two other stories, "The Bill" and "The Loan," show the guilt that accrues by accepting the credit of the heart when one refuses the responsibilities for repayment. In "The Loan," the wife of a baker refuses to lend money to an old friend of her husband, pleading that her escape from the Nazi incinerators has left her too insecure to give up the few hundred dollars for a headstone for the friend's wife. While she is refusing her husband's moral obligation, the bread burns, and when she opens the oven she sees the objective correlative of her niggardliness: "A cloud of smoke billowed out at her. The loaves in the trays were blackened bricks—charred corpses."

Several of the stories set ordinary humanity against the inhuman idealism of the protagonists. In "The First Seven Years," Feld, a shoemaker, wants the best for his daughter but finally discovers that the proper marriage for her is with his assistant, a balding refugee twice her age. The time span mentioned in the title is the medieval period of apprenticeship, and the assistant, Sobel, not only earns the right to replace his master in his craft, but has undergone, through his dedication, an apprenticeship in love. In a similar situation in the title story, a faithless rabbinical student named Finkle finds love through a marriage broker. The object of his desires, however, is not one of the broker's clients, but the man's daughter, whose picture has accidentally slipped into his folder. The girl, who brings love and love of God to Finkle, turns out to be a whore, and in the climactic last scene, Pinye, the broker, stands in the shadows chanting the prayer for the dead (signifying that Finkle has been lost to his faith) as Finkle goes to meet his daughter under a lamp post. The merchant of romantic dreams proves incapable of believing in the reality of his own product, while the student has staked the spirit of his law against its letter and has won.

In "Angel Levine," Malamud indulges in a fantasy in which an impoverished Jewish tailor, Manischevitz, is asked to believe the unlikely story that a Negro named Alexander Levine is his guardian angel. Manischevitz rejects the angel at first but then, impelled by love for his ailing wife, makes a surrealistic journey through Harlem to express his faith in the unbelievable. The pattern of faith triumphant is inverted in "The Lady of the Lake," a story set in Italy. The hero, a Jewish-American floorwalker in Macy's book department (this kind of existence on the margins of culture is almost always a sign of untested integrity in Malamud) falls in love with a beautiful Italian girl and denies his heritage and his identity so that she will marry him. His lie turns out to be his undoing when she proves to be a refugee from Buchenwald who treasures her suffering. She disappears into the mists that rise from the lake while he clutches vainly at the cold marble statuary of the place.

This story, like the two other Italian stories, "Behold the Key" and "The Last Mohican," shows the influence of Malamud's year in Rome while he held a Rockefeller grant and a *Partisan Review* Fellowship. "Behold the Key" is the story of a graduate student's frustrating search for an apartment in Rome, and "The Last Mohican" is the first of the Fidelman stories that were to be collected as *Pictures of Fidelman*.

Malamud's next novel, *A New Life* (1961), is based to some extent on his teaching career at Oregon State University, where, despite his growing literary reputation, he was never allowed to teach advanced literature courses because literature was for Ph.D.s. The hero's search for values is set against a satire on academic life in a "service-oriented" English department and a university that has long since gotten rid of its liberal arts program. Although the satire and the search for identity work well separately, the combination of the two undercuts the hero's dilemma because he finally has to choose between love and the academy. Since teaching at Cascadia College has already been proven worthless, his choice of love requires little moral strength.

The hero, Seymour Levin, like Roy Hobbs and Frank Alpine, is a *schlimazel*, a fool who gets into trouble by trying to improve things rather than a *schlemiel*, the passive victim of events. Levin's journey to Cascadia (Oregon) from New York reverses the paths of Frank Alpine, the westerner who comes east, and of Roy Hobbs, the country boy who goes to New York. Levin, a Jew with a master's degree in English, goes west to the wilds of Cascadia where he hopes to overcome a past of alcoholism in a setting that he expects to nurture bucolic freedom and humanistic study. In this dream of rural self-sufficiency he is like his namesake Levin in *Anna Karenina*, but unlike Tolstoy's hero, he finds no Kitty to support him in moments of inadequacy. His ideals are quickly shattered when he discovers that Cascadia has forsaken the humanities for the regimen of composition and that the local attitude toward nature has the predatory viciousness of sporting goods salesmen.

Levin's liberal ideas about McCarthyism, the Korean War, and Alger Hiss bewilder his dull students and dismay his arch-conservative colleagues. The only excitement he ever generates in the classroom occurs after he lectures on his ability to bring his students "a better understanding of who they were and what their lives might yield, education being revelation." The class seems to respond enthusiastically and then he looks down and discovers why his promise of revelation has brought looks of joy from his students: the classic nightmare of every professor has been realized—Levin has been lecturing with his fly open.

The Cascadia faculty does not even grant Levin the dignity of being an original enemy. Rather, they treat him as a reincarnation of the preceding resident radical, an Irishman named Leo Duffy. Hoping to discover his own identity, Levin pursues the history of Duffy only to find that his predecessor had committed suicide when he found that his life was pointless.

Levin's other colleagues give him even less hope. The chairman is a martinet whose only concern is that his text, *The Elements of Grammar*, will get into its fourteenth edition. Another faculty member spends his time cutting pictures out of *Life* magazine for a projected illustrated history of the United States; the product will be, therefore, a "new Life" of sorts. More dangerous to Levin are C. D. Fabrikant, a fellow liberal, who gives up his principles when his future is at stake, and, most importantly, the head of the composition program, Gerald Gilley, who becomes Levin's antagonist even before Levin seduces his wife. Gilley hates the humanities with a passion, although he still reserves the literature courses for the Ph.D.s in the department (he has a particular loathing for Thomas Hardy, the subject of Malamud's thesis). Gilley is an avid hunter and fisherman whose attitude toward his prey is one of savage antagonism, while his penchant for photography turns out to be a voyeuristic, secondhand approach to life. Symbolic of this antagonism to life, Gilley can produce no seed, and his children are both adopted.

While Levin halfheartedly copes with the endless paperwork and strict regimentation of the composition course, he attempts to fulfill himself through love. His sexual adventures are all comic disasters which play his literary idealism against the petty realities of life. He first attempts to seduce a waitress in a barn which he describes with idyllic lyricism that is lost on the waitress. Levin's pastoral romance is shattered when their clothes are stolen by his rival, a Syrian graduate student with a mania for cleaning bathrooms. Levin does consummate his affair with a student, after a slapstick car ride across the mountains to meet her at a distant motel near the Pacific. Levin thinks of himself as a new Balboa, but the glamor of the moment disappears when the girl comes to find out how much the assignation has raised her grade. Levin again suffers an interrupted seduction after he and another faculty member arouse each other by reading Keats and Tennyson. The woman, Avis Fliss, is an echo of Memo Paris of *The Natural.* With her birdlike name and an injured breast, Avis is symbolized as a life-denying character, and she eventually betrays Levin.

After so many tries at love, Levin comes close in his affair with Pauline Gilley, the wife of his immediate supervisor. The consummation of the affair takes place in a wooded setting on a spring-like day in January, but the idyll is short-lived, and the reader soon realizes that the setting is not a natural forest glade but a cultivated part of Cascadia's forestry school. Pauline is the Iris Lemon, earth mother figure, but she turns out to be flat chested. Levin wants to see his love for Pauline as an affirmation of life, but by the time he rides off with the pregnant Pauline and her two obnoxious children in his battered Hudson, he no longer loves her and he suspects that the feeling is mutual. Furthermore, he has bargained away his future as a teacher by getting custody of Gilley's children in exchange for a vow never to teach again. Levin's new life can be seen as real only as a kind of existential commitment which ignores the value of the thing committed to. Like Frank Alpine, his future depends upon a sense of duty, but Frank cared about Helen and the memory of Morris, while Levin acts only because he has found the strength to do what he has set out to do.

The stories in *Idiots First* (1963) deal with many of the same themes as those in *The Magic Barrel,* but Malamud casts a number of his characters in an allegorical framework which gives them clearer definition but less life. In "The German Refugee," the hero, Oskar Gassner is mired in despair because of his inability to set down roots in a new country and because he has left his Gentile wife behind in Germany. He is temporarily roused out of his gloom by the narrator, who coaches his English and helps him prepare a lecture on the influence of Whitman on German literature. The lecture, upon which most of the suspense is focused, is delivered successfully, but when Gassner discovers that his wife had converted to Judaism and was killed by the Nazis, he commits suicide.

The narrator's viewpoint adds to the shock value of Gassner's death because the young tutor's enthusiasm for the task of teaching English leads the reader to believe that Gassner's major problem is assimilation, while in fact it is isolation from the woman he loves. What distinguishes "The German Refugee" from similar tales in *The Magic Barrel* of one man trying to help another is Malamud's insistence on the similarity between the personal life of Oskar Gassner and political events in Europe. Through deft parallelism, the content of the lecture and the world political situation are epitomized in the life of one man. In *The Magic Barrel,* Malamud would have been content to tell Gassner's story without the historical overview.

The title story tells of the attempts of a dying man named Mendel to send his idiot son to an uncle in California. Mendel has made a compact with a bearded man named Ginzburg who gives him an evening to gather the money for a ticket. After being turned down by Fishbein, a wealthy man who gives charity only to institutions, Mendel gets the money in the form of the only warm coat of a sick rabbi. Mendel arrives at the station too late for the deadline, but after he struggles fiercely with Ginzburg, the latter lets the son go because of the ferocious courage love has given Mendel. Although the situation is similar to several in *The Magic Barrel,* particularly the confrontation between the dead Rosen and Davidoff, the cosmic census-taker in "Take Pity," this story has none of the well-textured humanity of the earlier collection. Instead, Malamud presents a morality play in which Mendel is abstracted to Mankind, Ginzburg to the Angel of Death, Fishbein to False Charity, and the rabbi to True Charity.

A similar demythologizing takes place in the collection's venture into fantasy. "The Jewbird" tells the adventures of a crow named Schwartz who tests the charity and wisdom of a successful Jew named Harry Cohen. Schwartz is a talking Jewish crow who moves in with the Cohens and becomes a surrogate father to Cohen's none-too-bright son, Maurie. Cohen cannot stand the bedraggled crow, whose poverty, thick accent, and old world habits remind him too much of his origins. He persecutes the bird and eventually throws him from the window to his death. Although the premise is more wildly fantastic than "Angel Levine" of the earlier collection, the story fails to capture the same mood of fantasy. Instead of focusing on the outrageous juxtaposition of man and bird, the story becomes an allegory of man's inhumanity to man, or more specifically Jews' anti-Semitism to Jews.

"Black Is My Favorite Color," a story that explores the black-Jewish relations that would become the primary concern of *The Tenants,* is entirely naturalistic in style, as a Jew recounts his relationships with blacks and particularly his love affair with a black woman. Despite his efforts to act without prejudice, the narrator can never penetrate into the alien culture, and, at the end of the story after the woman has rejected him, he tries to help a blind black man home only to discover that even a blind man can tell he is white.

Idiots First, which also contains a number of Italian stories which were to appear later as part of *Pictures of Fidelman,* is less even in quality than *The Magic Barrel,* and the stories, in general, strain too hard for their morals.

Malamud's finest novel, *The Fixer* (1966), won both the Pulitzer Prize and the National Book Award. The book is the account of a Jew in turn-of-the-century Russia who is arrested for the ritual

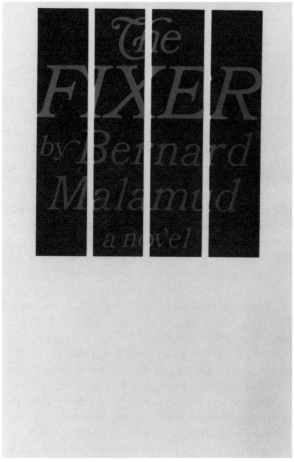

Dust jacket for Malamud's fourth novel, winner of both a Pulitzer Prize and a National Book Award

murder of a Christian child. Malamud based his novel on a historical event, the trial of Mendel Beiliss in 1913. Beiliss was acquitted after his trial in Kiev, but Malamud ends the novel at the moment his hero, Yakov Bok, leaves for the courtroom after his two-and-a-half-year pretrial confinement. The reader is thus left uncertain of Bok's fate.

The character of Bok (the name means "goat" and he is Malamud's ultimate scapegoat) is in many ways similar to that of Morris Bober in *The Assistant,* but the initial passive suffering of Bok is transformed into an active, deliberate suffering so that Bok adds Frank Alpine's commitment to Bober-like endurance. Unlike Bober's, Bok's prison is real, not metaphoric, and Malamud lets his readers know it. He grimly records the physical torment, mental suffering, and spiritual degradation Bok is put through in his cell. There is no relief from the insects, the pails of excrement, the beatings, and particularly the humiliating body searches in which each of Bok's orifices is probed, first two, and then six times a day. Through it all, Bok maintains his innocence, first from stubbornness, but later from a gradually emerging sense of principle. As with Bober, Bok's life is an endurance test whose only activity is suffering, but unlike Bober, Bok's actual imprisonment allows him to attain a spiritual freedom that eludes Bober. Bober finally learns to accept Frank Alpine's struggles in his behalf, but for Bok there is no one to carve some meaning out of the absolute absurdity of his existence except himself.

The technique of the novel is heavily influenced by the earthiness and mysticism of Isaac Bashevis Singer, Sholom Aleichem, and I. L. Peretz, who made the Yiddish folktale into an art form. The style validates the hero's philosophic musings, which are spoken in the simplest language possible, and also accommodates the dream visions, particularly the appearance to Bok of Czar Nicholas II, who tries to defend his realm's treatment of Jews. Although the style comes from the literate folktale, the philosophy itself comes from Dostoyevski, particularly *The Brothers Karamazov.*

Bok, a Jew who believes little of Jewishness, attempts to escape his unpromising future as well as his self-pitying condition by leaving the Russian ghetto in which he was born and going to Kiev. He passes for a Christian, gets a good job, and lives in a sector forbidden to Jews, all of which only makes him the likely scapegoat when the murdered child is found. While he is imprisoned, Bok learns that he cannot escape his fate or his history—that he is not only a Jew, but the symbol of all Russian Jews.

Although it is not clear whether or not Bok believes in God at the close of the novel, it is clear he understands that the possibility of retaining his human dignity requires belief in his Jewishness.

Like Frank Alpine, Bok must discover the meaning of the suffering that seems to be the central factor in the condition of being Jewish. When he can say, as Morris does to Frank Alpine, "I suffer for you," then he has understood his heritage and himself and has achieved freedom. In order to release himself from suffering, Bok is about to goad the guards into killing him. When he thinks of his father-in-law Shmuel, however, he realizes that his suicide scheme might be taken as a tacit admission of his guilt and the cause, therefore, of a wave of pogroms. Having understood that even isolated in his cell, he is part of the human race, he chooses to go on with his suffering: "He may even die for my death if they work up a pogrom in celebration of it. If so what do I get by dying, outside of release from pain? What have I earned if a single Jew dies because I did? Suffering I can gladly live without, I hate the taste of it, but if I must suffer let it be for something. Let it be for Shmuel."

Bok extends his commitment when his wife Raisl comes to ask him to give her illegitimate child his name. He accedes to her wishes, deliberately branding himself a willing cuckold, because he realizes that her unfaithfulness was caused largely by his self-centeredness and self-pity. In acknowledging his complicity in her actions he gives up part of the guiltless-victim persona which helps most martyrs face their torments. Far from undermining his strength, however, the act of legitimizing his wife's son makes him for the first time both father and husband.

Bok spends much of his imprisonment questioning the justice of his universe and the existence of a God who rules over it. Unlike Job, however, Bok finds no voice out of the whirlwind to give form to absurdity. "To win a lousy bet with the devil he killed off all the servants and innocent children of Job. For that alone I hate him, not to mention ten thousand pogroms. Ach, why do you make me talk fairy tales? Job is an invention and so is God. Let's let it go at that."

No matter what the state does, Bok will not admit to the trumped-up charge of ritual murder—that he has killed a Christian boy to use his blood in the manufacture of matzos. The reader, who is ready to suffer with the eternally victimized Bok, is unprepared for his heroism as his staunch courage (in Yiddish, *bok* means "a piece of iron" as well as "goat") begins to drive his prosecutors into a desperate frenzy. Bok is offered all kinds of deals up to a complete pardon and physical freedom itself, if he will just sign a confession, but he insists on coming to trial. When he is given a confession to sign, he writes instead the document giving his paternity to Raisl's son, Chaim, whose name means "life." Bok's heroism proves that human dignity can be maintained even at the most minimal levels of existence and among the most brutal examples of mankind.

Pictures of Fidelman (1969) is not precisely a novel, but rather a series of vignettes built around a single character, a Jewish-American art student, who later becomes a struggling artist and finally a successful artisan, named Arthur Fidelman. The book's title is meant to suggest Joyce's *Portrait of the Artist as a Young Man,* and, like that work, *Pictures of Fidelman* follows the moral growth of its hero. Fidelman seeks the meaning of life and art in Italy, making him an inversion of Frank Alpine, the Italian-American who searches for the meaning of life in a world of Jews. Most of the book had been published previously, both as separate short stories and in the earlier collection, and Fidelman is hardly a consistent character, even granting the necessary changes that occur in the growth and aging of a man.

Fidelman is another of Malamud's *schlemiels* whose search for the meaning of life is fraught with comic suffering. His first confrontation—with Shimon Susskind, a Jewish purveyor of Catholic religious objects—concerns itself with the nature of mutual responsibility. Although Susskind's relics are false, his deceptions of Fidelman are meant to show the young student the way to truth. Susskind pesters Fidelman to give him one of his two suits and then pilfers the art history manuscript that Fidelman has been working on. Fidelman rages at Susskind when he discovers that Susskind has burned his chapter, but he finally realizes that the act was kindness: the manuscript was as false as Susskind's relics. As Susskind says, "The words were there but the spirit was missing." As the chapter ends, Fidelman chases after his personal conscience, offering his suit.

Once Susskind has freed him from his sterile, secondhand relationship to art, Fidelman becomes a painter, but his life is complicated by his attempt at total commitment to both life and art. This leads to impossible dilemmas like having to send his mistress out into the streets so that he does not have to prostitute his talents. Fidelman is looking for love and finds that even approximations of it can be had only by compromising innumerable ideals.

The wild picaresque humor of the novel points out both the absurdities and complexities of human love.

Malamud cannot resist the endless play on appearance and reality possible in a book about artists. In one episode, Fidelman falls in love with his copy of Titian's *Venus,* which he has forged so that he can steal the original. In the end, he substitutes his own painting for the Titian, steals his copy, and runs away from his conspirators. In another story, Fidelman proves a terrible failure at seducing a young woman until he paints her as the Virgin. A series of typical *schlemiel* disasters temporarily cools her ardor, but when he dresses up as a priest for a self-portrait, her passion returns while she confesses to him, and then, as her penance, he makes love to her: "pumping slowly he nailed her to the cross."

Like S. Levin, Frank Alpine, and Yakov Bok, Fidelman is searching for a new life, and his change from second-rate artist begins in a ritual death and rebirth similar to Frank Alpine's fall into Bober's grave. Fidelman has been digging square holes in the ground and exhibiting them as works of pure form when he is pushed into one by a mysterious stranger who remarks that his work now has content as well as form.

Fidelman's ultimate salvation comes through perversion. He gives a private retrospective show of his life's work to Beppo, the husband of the woman he has been sleeping with. Beppo correctly sees it all as uninspired imitation of the techniques of others and destroys the whole lot. He argues that Fidelman should give up being an artist. "After twenty years if the rooster hasn't crowed she should know she's a hen. Your painting will never pay back the part of your life you've given up for it." The bisexuality is more than a metaphor—Beppo rapes Fidelman while Fidelman is making love to Beppo's wife. Beppo teaches him to create life instead of art and Fidelman returns at last to America, a craftsman (a glass-blower) who loves both men and women. In his Italian journey, the hero has changed from a dabbler (one who fiddles around) to a man of faith (*fidel)* in love and life.

Malamud's fifth novel, *The Tenants* (1971), is an evasive answer to the question, can a liberal Jewish novelist write the great American black novel? The response is a qualified no, because although the black novel never appears, there are enough tour-de-force fragments from it to suggest that Malamud half-seriously believes that he could do it. The story is also of a confrontation whose in-

tensity goes beyond anything that Malamud has yet written.

The protagonists, a Jew named Harry Lesser and a black named Willie Spearmint, are the last two inhabitants of an old apartment house that will be wrecked when Lesser gives up his lease. Willie is a squatter in the building; only Lesser is a tenant. Harry will not allow his landlord, Levenspiel, to tear down the building until he finishes the novel he has been working on for nine years. Lesser's dealings with the long-suffering landlord, which oppose the demands of art to those of everyday life, are familiar to readers of *Pictures of Fidelman,* but the focus of the novel, to the exclusion of everything else, is the struggle between Lesser and Spearmint.

Lesser is a writer concerned with perfect form to the point that content seems almost irrelevant. He is working on one of those reflective novels about a novelist writing a novel which he hopes can teach him how to live, life mirroring art: "Anyway, this writer sets out to write about someone he conceives to be not he yet himself. He thinks he can teach himself to love in a manner befitting an old ideal." Like his character, Lesser is trying to use his art to teach himself how to love, which means his novel, *The Promised End,* will never be finished and, more importantly, he will never learn to love.

Lesser, the author of two somewhat successful novels, encounters Willie, who is working on his first novel, a record of the black experience in America. Spearmint's work has its own paradoxes: the most realistic portions of Willie's novel, which Harry thinks are autobiographical, turn out to be pure invention, while Willie's short stories, whose events Harry finds too artificial, are not fiction, but fact. At first glance, the two men seem polar opposites—white and black, Jew and anti-Semite, polished professional and inspired amateur—but, in fact, both suffer the same failing; their concern with their writing cuts them off from life and loving. Both stalk each other warily, first mistrusting, then learning to respect the other's strengths—Willie's emotional power and Harry's craftsmanship. Each gradually invades the other's world, although there is a greater metamorphosis in Lesser as he enters Spearmint's Harlem.

Eventually their sparring turns to all-out war when Harry steals Willie's white girlfriend, Irene Bell (née Belinski). What Lesser fails to see is that Irene has left Willie because she cannot compete with his new mistress, art. Irene begins to turn toward Lesser when Willie tells her, "I can't lay up with you tonight. You know how hard that part I am now writing on my book has got. I need my strength and juice on my work tomorrow." Lesser, the kind of man who gets upset because he does not communicate as well as he writes, who feels he would like to revise his spoken words as well as his written ones, makes the same mistake, and eventually Irene leaves him as well. Her note sums up Malamud's philosophy: "No book is as important as me."

Another love story manifests itself below the growing hate of Lesser and Spearmint. Although Willie has burned Lesser's manuscript in revenge for the seduction of Irene, Lesser yearns to communicate with Spearmint, knowing that neither can write anymore unless he knows the other is also writing:

> Hey Bill, Lesser thought in the hallway, moved by the sight of a man writing, how's it going?
>
> You couldn't say that aloud to someone who had deliberately destroyed the almost completed manuscript of your most promising novel, product of ten years' labor. You understood his history and possibly yours, but you could say nothing to him.
>
> Lesser said nothing.

The two men do forgive each other for the stealing of the girl and the destruction of the manuscript, but it is too late. They can no longer write. Lesser has made Willie too concerned with form to write with any power, and Willie has freed Lesser from the well-loved burden of his endless manuscript. After Lesser destroys Spearmint's typewriter, the tension becomes unbearable, and Lesser caves in Spearmint's head with an axe, while Spearmint castrates Lesser with a razor.

Like most novels about the writing of novels, the book's central theme concerns the relative reality of life and art. Although Malamud wants to say "life," the answer is more paradoxical. Lesser's novel is about love, but his affair with Irene has more substance than the love he writes about. Nonetheless, he gives up the girl for the book in the end, and Malamud makes Lesser's passion for writing far more convincing than his passion for Irene. Neither man would kill the other for Irene, but both become bloodthirsty when their ability to write is destroyed. Malamud undercuts his thesis by demonstrating that while art may not be life, writing *is* living.

Malamud's third collection of stories, *Rembrandt's Hat* (1973), continues his concern with the

growth or collapse of the fine bond of compassion that binds two human beings together. The collection is populated with characters who live in the margin of their chosen discipline—biology teachers, art critics, hack writers, retired doctors—and so must prove themselves by relating not to their work, but to their fellow man; some succeed, others fail. The luminous otherworldliness of Malamud's earlier stories has almost disappeared. Only one story, "The Silver Crown," approximates the mystic world of Malamud's forte, the neo-Yiddish folktale. In the story, a young biology teacher named Albert Gans goes to a rabbi to buy a "miraculous" silver crown which is supposed to cure his dying father. Gans tries to bring the irrational world of the rabbi and his crown into his own rational sphere of competence. In the process of reducing mystery to science, Gans misses the point of the crown, that it is meant to remind him of his need to love his father. The rabbi tries to calm Gans's fears that the crown will not work if he has no faith in it: "Doubts we all got. We doubt God and God doubts us. This is natural on account of the nature of existence. Of this kind doubts I am not afraid so long as you love your father." Gans buys the crown for the wrong reasons: to assuage his guilt for ignoring his father and also as a scientific experiment in another kind of epistemology. But when he feels that he has become the victim of a con man, he admits his hatred for his father and old Gans dies. Malamud teases the reader about the reality of the crown, which is fair considering the allegorical conflict between love and reason in the story, but one wonders if Malamud has lost faith in his own ability to project the miraculous. In the stories of the 1950s, the reader takes the existence of such objects as a matter of faith validated by Malamud's prose.

Three other stories are about son-father (or father figure) betrayals. In one a student carries on an abortive seduction of his old teacher's young wife through the passing of rather childish notes; in another, the reader listens to the voices of a son and a father who alternately give their versions of the other's obnoxious characteristics; and in the third, a letter with nothing written on it becomes the symbol of two people's lack of communication.

A more ambitious story dealing with the nature of communication is "The Talking Horse," about a talking circus horse, Abramowitz, and his deaf-mute master, a clown named Goldberg. The story, told from the horse's point of view, is clearly an allegory about the nature of man. Abramowitz, with a human mind inside a horse's body, is a literal version of the way Gulliver felt among the

Houyhnhnms, a confused amalgam of beast and creature of reason. The trio, Abramowitz-man, Abramowitz-horse, and Goldberg, is an inversion of Freud's notion of the psyche. In this case, it is the intellect which is repressed: Abramowitz-man is the repressed intellect (the id that threatens to burst out of control) trapped inside and kept under control by Goldberg (the superego that tries to keep the intellect from disturbing the mores of the crowd-society). Abramowitz finally discovers that he is not a talking horse, but a centaur with an artificial horse head. Through this recognition of the worth of both mind and body, he is able to free himself from the restrictions of society and his doubt about his own nature.

This optimistic note is also sounded in the title story where Arkin, an art teacher, tries to compliment a colleague, Rubin, by telling him that his hat looks like one Rembrandt had painted in a self-portrait. Rubin, a failed sculptor, is insulted, and Arkin cannot understand why until he puts himself in Rubin's place and realizes that the second-rate sculptor cannot stand the implied comparison with a great artist. The compassion grows when Arkin also learns that even as a critic he has been off the mark: in reexamining the slide of the Rembrandt, he finds that he has been mistaken about what the hat looked like. This humbling experience and his ability to perceive nuances in human behavior break down the walls preventing communication between the two men.

The longest story in the collection, "Man in the Drawer," also concerns the need to reach out and put oneself in another's place. Like "The German Refugee" in *Idiots First*, which was also about one man reluctantly taking up the responsibility for another man's life, "Man in the Drawer" gives the reader a sense of historical place and time that is absent in most of the short stories. The story is set in cold-war Russia, and the hero's dilemma is based on that time and place. Harvitz, an American free-lance journalist and something of a coward, discovers a Russian taxicab driver, Levitansky (like himself a marginal Jew), who is a writer of fiction. Levitansky's politically heterodox work can be published only if Harvitz smuggles the stories out of the country. After a great deal of wrestling with his conscience and his fears, Harvitz takes up the burden of this near stranger and goes off to the airport with the manuscript hidden in his suitcase. The synopses of the stories to be smuggled, particularly one in which a gagged writer burns his work in the sink, show why he has changed his mind.

Always a patient craftsman, Bernard Malamud took five and a half years, two years longer than usual, to finish his novel *Dubin's Lives*. Never satisfied, he drove his publisher crazy revising even the final proofs, as he searched for the texture and substance of a man's life and surroundings. Malamud said of the writing process: "Working with words is working with water, trying to make something solid, to make something that never was before."

William Dubin, the hero of the novel, has a good deal of Malamud in him. Like his creator, Dubin is approaching his sixties, lives in relative isolation in rural Vermont, and earns his living as a free-lance writer, though of biography rather than fiction. Malamud saw his novel as a chance to sum up what he had learned about the experience of living. Although Dubin lives in the present, almost all his actions are filtered through what he knows of his own past and the pasts of others.

Dubin is another of Malamud's protagonists who live on the margins of either art or life and

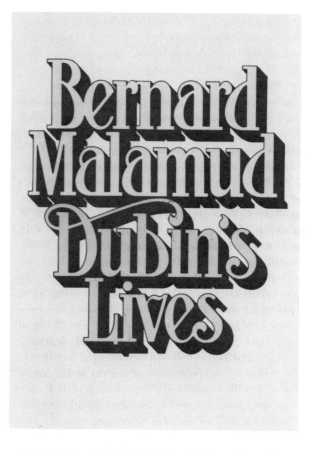

Dust jacket for Malamud's 1979 novel about a biographer. "I could use the stuff and material of biography for its many sources of harmony and counterpoint," the author stated.

whose stories depend on whether or not they can make a full commitment. William Dubin is a biographer who has gradually cut himself off from life, as he studies the lives of others. He had hoped that his work would give him new perspective on his own life, but as he approaches the end of middle age, his life seems without sufficient reward.

When the novel opens, Dubin has completed four books of biography: one each of Lincoln, Twain, and Thoreau, and *Short Lives,* a collection of lives of geniuses who died young. His current project is a biography of D. H. Lawrence. The Lincoln and Twain works do not weigh heavily in the novel, but the others tell us a good deal about Dubin. Malamud said of his subject matter, "I could use the stuff and material of biography for its many sources of harmony and counterpoint." What happens to Dubin is that he strives for harmony with the lives he writes and ends up at counterpoint, which often extends itself to pointed irony. The biographer of "Honest Abe" spends half of the novel lying to his wife about his sex life, and the Thoreau scholar never can quite make peace with nature. Dubin lives in a Thoreauvian setting in rural New England, and though he wants to love nature the way Thoreau did, he is never completely comfortable outside his study. After years in the country, he is still learning the names of much of the commoner flora and fauna. As he goes out into wintry weather to cure a state of depression, Dubin scoffs at Thoreau: "Thoreau was wrong in saying nature doesn't sympathize with sorrow." The winter assails him with a blizzard that almost kills him, until he is rescued by a mechanized version of a Saint Bernard—his wife driving the family car: "something . . . a truck, or car, its wheels churning in the slush, brights on, wipers flapping as it loomed up like a locomotive out of the raining snow." Dubin begins the novel by taking long walks through the countryside; he ends by taking his "walks" in the car. If Dubin cannot reach a feeling of oneness with nature, the same cannot be said of Malamud. His descriptions of rural New England in all seasons are wonderfully precise and evocative. He said of writing these passages: "If it is winter in the book, spring surprises me when I look up." For a novelist, who has been thought of as an urban poet, Malamud knew the country well—which is not really surprising since he spent the last third of his life in rural Oregon and Vermont.

Dubin offers a copy of his first work, *Short Lives,* in which no one lives to the age of forty, as a love gift to the woman who will become his mistress. From these lives of truncated genius, he had

originally gleaned a philosophy which saw the brilliance of their work as just compensation for the brevity of their lives. As he matures, however, the lesson he learns is reversed. "If you don't live life to the hilt, or haven't for whatever reason, you will regret it—especially as you grow older—every day that follows."

None of these earlier biographies influences Dubin as much as his work-in-progress, the life of D. H. Lawrence. Dubin begins to measure his life by Lawrence's theories of passion and finds it lacking. He has never known the kind of passion Lawrence writes about in his novels, and at this stage in his life he feels he has only one more chance at it, a chance which is offered to him by Fanny Bick, a girl young enough to be his daughter. Although the illicit courting of Fanny is filled with much of the comic misadventure found in both *A New Life* and *Pictures of Fidelman* and though Dubin does not consummate the affair until almost two-thirds through the novel, Dubin's problem is not so much how to get Fanny as, having gotten her, whether

Bernard Malamud, 1984 (photo by Layle Silbert)

to keep her in a perpetual Lawrentian fantasy or return to his long-suffering wife, Kitty. His decision in this matter depends in large measure on what he makes of Lawrence. Though it would seem that a biographer of Lawrence would choose the life of the body, the decision is complicated by the facts of Lawrence's own life. Lawrence, the advocate of absolute passion, was impotent by the time he was forty, so he could, in fact, not live the life of passion projected in his novels. Early in the book, Dubin warns himself, "one writes lives he cannot live." This stricture seems at first to apply solely to his own occupation, making it a vicarious parasitism on the lives of others, but it also applies to his subjects' lives. Lawrence was not the passionate man he creates in his novels. Thoreau likewise hungered for absolute communion with nature, but as Dubin notes, "the man went home often to see his mama." What happens then if the biographer tries to live the lives he writes? Which life does he live? The projected, pulse-pounding, lambent-loined fictive Lawrence, or the real, wife-dominated impotent Lawrence.

For William Dubin, the choice of two such lives comes down to the choice between the two women in his life. His wife, Kitty (a namesake perhaps of Levin's wife, Kitty, in *Anna Karenina,* an intelligently domestic counterweight to the passionate heroine of that novel), has carefully nurtured Dubin's talent, providing him with the domestic surroundings that allow him to write. Theirs is a marriage built on the modicum of love, but little passion. The marriage came relatively late in life for both partners (Kitty was a widow with a child) so that it is a merging of two already defined lives. Kitty's nurturing is enough for writing the lives of Lincoln, Twain, and Thoreau, but when Dubin comes up against Lawrence, he feels he cannot get to the core of his subject unless he understands passion.

It is from Fanny (who tells us she is named for a Jane Austen character, Fanny Price, but seems a more likely namesake of another eighteenth-century heroine, Fanny Hill) that Dubin learns about passion. Dubin is too controlled to respond to Fanny's first, unpremeditated, sexual offer, and thus dooms himself to a series of missed assignations that culminate in a comically humiliating week in Venice. The episode has the tone of a tale out of Boccaccio in which the jealous old husband is deceived by his randy, young wife. Dubin is the *jaloux* who is cuckolded by Fanny and a gondolier. Instead of ending Dubin's search for passion, however, the episode teaches him to desire and forces

him beyond the confines of his work, perhaps for the first time in his life. Eventually, Dubin does get Fanny and believes he has reached the Lawrentian ideal in which passion equals life. Fanny is passionate, but despite a large amount of sexual experience, she is relatively unformed. She is filled with potential, but has not finished school, has not embarked on a career, has not had a child. Though she is vitally alive, Fanny Bick has not yet lived.

Dubin, a careful observer of others' lives, is not insensitive about his own. He understands that much of his attraction to Fanny is part of the pursuit of fading youth, a pursuit that also takes the form of his regimen of exercise and diet. Like Thoreau, Dubin strives to keep off the specter of Death, in his case by clinging to things that are young—Fanny and what is left of his own still healthy body. His concern with his lost youth is not merely for what has once been but is also the yearning for what never was. "Middle age . . . is when you pay for what you didn't have or couldn't do when you were young."

What Dubin has to learn is perhaps Lawrence's greatest lesson: true passion does not fear the onslaught of death, but embraces it. Only through death can there be resurrection, and in a thematic pattern omnipresent in Malamud's earlier novels Dubin undergoes symbolic death and rebirth that correspond to the change of seasons.

Dubin's first winter after the botched Venetian affair is a spiritual dying with his creative juices drying up even as the sap freezes in the trees. He thinks of his writing as an act of procreation which he cannot perform: "Sentences breed sentences. But the notes tensed him." Eventually this creative impotence leads to sexual impotence with his wife so that ironically she shares the worst part of Lawrence's sexuality—*his* impotence with *his* wife. The winter's culmination is a death for Dubin as he loses his identity in the blinding blizzard. The biographer has tried to shape lives against the ravages of time, but finds that he has lost the battle. "I'm like a broken clock—works, time, mangled." Dubin, like Keats's woebegone knight (Keats is one of the subjects of *Short Lives*), has become the thrall of La Belle Dame sans Merci, so that he exists "alone and palely loitering."

With the spring, Fanny returns, now as a different aspect of the beautiful woman without pity. She becomes to Dubin what Fanny Brawne was to Keats, a "warm, white lucent, million-pleasured breast." As they make love for the first time among the springtime flowers, Dubin comes alive again, feeling "this evens it . . . for the cruel winter." His writing revives as well as he understands at last Lawrence's belief in the blood and the flesh.

Dubin discovers, however, that he is not the Lawrentian hero, partly out of his knowledge that Lawrence was not either. As he gets involved with Fanny, he brings Lawrence's impotence to his own marriage. The cause of his sexual failure with his wife is the growing number of lies he is forced to tell her. The duplicity necessary to maintain the affair cuts not only against all of Lawrence's dicta about honesty to the blood, but also against Dubin's own honesty that has served him well as a biographer. Dubin is enough of a man of principle to have refused Lyndon Johnson's request that he write the Texan's biography because he knew he couldn't please Johnson and tell the truth at the same time. When he deceives his wife, Dubin dreams that Richard Nixon comes to him and asks him to write a flattering biography, one liar to another, so to speak. The negative aspects of the affair are partly responsible for Dubin's turn away from the pure life of the flesh that he shares with Fanny. The other force is his nature and profession.

Dubin is a biographer who lives upon lives. He devours the lives of others. Fanny has no life yet, none of the complications and nuances that make biography interesting. Kitty, on the other hand, has both her own life and the life she has shared with Dubin. Two troubled children—one theirs, one hers—have become an integral part of his life. His dealings with these grown children, both Fanny's age, help convince him that his wife is a woman of his complexity with a life comparable to his own.

Fanny belongs in a Lawrence novel, not in Dubin's life. Only by being honest with himself and his wife can Dubin avoid the impotence that plagued Lawrence's last years. At the end of the novel, he makes a distinction which escapes Fanny as he explains why he will return to his wife:

> "But do you love her?"
> "I love her life."

Dubin loves Fanny, but it is not enough for the biographer. She doesn't yet have a life for him to share. Though the novel ends with Dubin about to return to his wife, a "bibliography" of Dubin's works tells us the move was the right one. Dubin completes the biography of Lawrence and goes on to write several other works.

Malamud's novel has an autumnal sense of completeness about it. He asks the same questions about Dubin that Dubin asks about all of his subjects: What does a man's life add up to? In *Dubin's Lives*, Malamud makes clear that even the most ordinary of lives is worth a biography.

In his last novel, *God's Grace* (1982), Malamud asks these questions on a larger scale as he returns to the allegorical mode of his first novel, *The Natural*. The hero of *God's Grace,* a paleontologist named Calvin Cohn, rises from scientific exploration of the ocean floor to discover that he is the last man on earth because the rest of mankind has wiped itself out in a nuclear holocaust. As a paleontologist, he had examined the past of life on earth through small fragments of bone, but now that the earth has no past, Cohn, without chart or compass, must contemplate the future and his place in it. From an egotistical, Noah-like position, he thinks the most important question is why he, of all humans, is allowed to survive?

Cohn finds that he does have a single companion—a chimp named Buz who has been taught by a colleague of Cohn's to speak. When the two discover an island populated by a few other apes and some baboons, Malamud produces an updated version of *Robinson Crusoe* with Buz playing Cohn's chimp Friday. Cohn is one of Malamud's most genial heroes, but his relentless humanity (a virtue outdated and even dangerous at this time and in this company) and his hopeful idealism are punctured by the chimp's matter-of-fact replies. Cohn's anthropo- and ego-centric attitudes will not allow him to leave things be, and he sets about civilizing his companions, even though civilizing has destroyed civilization. Though he preaches democracy, Cohn creates a near-totalitarian state in which the human way is always right. Typical of his self-centeredness, he first considers naming the island Chimpan Zee in honor of its majority population but then calls it Cohn's Island. He also insists on naming everything (with a strong human and Jewish bias) and on devising all laws, even though the apes are all intelligent and better aware of their nature than he is.

Like its antecedents, *Robinson Crusoe, Mysterious Island*, and *The Planet of the Apes*, the novel's initial concern is with the physical and moral structure of this new civilization: how things are built and how laws are made. In such stories, the civilizer tries to avoid the pitfalls of the world left behind, but always falls into new versions of the old traps. Cohn is no exception. Because he has seen mankind destroy itself, he sets out to create a society free of the faults that led to the holocaust. His answer is a safe and colorless humanism which fails miserably to take into account the nature of the new master race or even his own wretched lusts. Though he is a lapsed Jew, Cohn bridles at Buz's attempt to introduce Christianity, particularly the notion that God is Love, onto the island. Instead, he resurrects the forms of his old religion and inveigles the apes to a disastrous Passover Seder.

At one time in his past, Malamud's hero was a rabbi's son and his name was Seymour Cohn. In rechristening himself "Calvin Cohn," he has become a Designer Jew. At first this seems little more than an arch joke of Malamud's, a reminder that Cohn's Jewishness is as false and trendy as fortydollar jeans. As the novel proceeds, however, the Argument from Design, i.e., the idea that the world and all of its evil as well as good is part of God's design, becomes a central issue. Cohn tries to understand his fate and the future of the world by attributing different designs to God's universe. His alternatives come for the most part, not out of his scientific training, but out of his rabbinical heritage. He sees himself involved in one of three Old Testament myths: as Adam in the creation story of Adam and Eve, as Abel in the fratricidal war of Cain and Abel, or as Abraham willing to sacrifice his son, Isaac, to his God. In each case, Cohn refuses to recognize that it might be the other character, in this new world, an ape, who is the object of God's design.

When a beautiful and intelligent female chimpanzee falls in love with Cohn, he concludes that acting out a bizarre Adam and Eve story will insure the future of intelligent life on earth. As Calvin Cohn, he thinks that he has been kept alive so that his Designer Genes will assure that the race of Abraham, Isaac, and Jacob will go on. It never occurs to him that the beautiful chimp, named Mary Madelyn, is the proper bride of his Christian chimpanzee "son" Buz. As always in Malamud, the failure of intellect is not nearly so fatal as the failure of the heart. Though he teaches Mary Madelyn the story of Romeo and Juliet (hiding from her the tragic ending), he refuses to love her even when she is pregnant with his child. This failure leads to a series of catastrophes which upset the neat design Cohn has for the universe. In a powerful conclusion, Cohn discovers he has been wrong about which myth is operative in the postholocaust world, and even more wrong about which place he has in it. God's grace comes at a price much higher than Cohn can imagine.

Malamud has used medieval myths throughout this work, and two medieval voices may help define the distinctive quality of Malamud's heroes. Saint Augustine, after Paul the primary architect of Christian theology, divided all mankind into two races: that of Cain, which inhabited the City of Man, and that of Abel, which dwelt in the City of God. Three centuries later, the Beowulf Poet called his monster a *marc-stapa*, "one who walks along the borders," and Grendel is an outsider looking in, not only at the Danes, but at himself because he cannot understand how he can be both man and monster. The reason is found in his origins; he is of the race of Cain and as long as he believes in the watchword of his heritage, "I am not my brother's keeper," he must remain outside the pale of humanity.

All of Malamud's characters are "borderwalkers" in this sense. They are not merely outsiders in an alien culture like Roy Hobbs, country boy in the big city; Frank Alpine, Italian among Jews; Fidelman, Jew among Italians; Seymour Levin, easterner going west; but they also live on the borders of their own culture. If they are Jews, they are marginal Jews—Bober's eulogy must be delivered by a rabbi who has never met him; Finkle, the rabbinical student in "The Magic Barrel," doesn't believe in God; Bok leaves the *shtetl* to live like a Christian—and others are marginal artists—critics, historians, modish failures like Fidelman, novelists like Lesser who will never finish the big novel. Yet when these men commit themselves to another human being, they move from the margins of their world to the center. Bober becomes the Jew the rabbi says he is because of his commitment to Frank Alpine; Bok earns his place while denying the name of Judaism so he can save his fellow Jews from a pogrom. Lesser shows his faith in writing more when he commits himself to helping Spearmint than when he hacks away on his own endless novel, and Harvitz in "Man in the Drawer" proves himself as a writer when he rescues Levitansky's manuscript. In all cases, the question finally is not whether a man is a Jew or an artist, but whether he is a human being ready to take Abel's role rather than Cain's. It is this Augustinian duality that separates the moral failures from the successes in Malamud's fiction.

References:

John Allen, "The Promised End: Bernard Malamud's *The Tenants*," *Hollins Critic*, 8, no. 5 (1971): 1-15;
Discusses pairs of contrasting themes—racial hatred vs. brotherhood, art vs. life—as they are mutually destructive in this novel of doubles who share an identity even as they are diametrically opposed to each other.

Dust jacket for Malamud's 1983 collection for which he chose the twenty-five short stories he considered his best

Iska Alter, *The Good Man's Dilemma: Social Criticism in the Fiction of Bernard Malamud* (New York: AMS Press, 1981);
A thematic study which focuses on the way Malamud's characters struggle against the materialism of modern American life, on the relation of art to artist, and on the way he deals with minority problems of Jews, blacks, and women.

Robert Alter, "Malamud as Jewish Writer," *Commentary*, 42 (September 1966): 71-76;
Argues that Malamud writes about Jews without producing a sense of a Jewish community; instead Malamud's characters live in a world of Christian and natural archetypes.

Richard Astro and Jackson Benson, eds., *The Fiction of Bernard Malamud* (Corvallis: Oregon State University Press, 1977);
A collection of original essays written for a symposium at Oregon State University, where Malamud taught for a dozen years; a useful perspective on Malamud's achievement through 1976.

John A. Barsness, "*A New Life:* The Frontier Myth in Perspective," *Western American Literature*, 3 (Winter 1969): 297-203;
Discusses the way romantic legends of the West are shattered in *A New Life*.

Jonathan Baumbach, "The Economy of Love: The Novels of Bernard Malamud," *Kenyon Review*, 25 (Summer 1963): 438-457;
Analyzes the seasonal motifs in the novels and puts Malamud in the tradition of romance novelists like Cooper, Melville, and Hawthorne.

Samuel Bellman, "Women, Children, and Idiots First: The Transformational Psychology of Bernard Malamud," *Critique* (Winter 1972-1973): 123-138;
Argues that Malamud redeems his victims by transmuting their lives onto higher levels of meaning.

344

Sandy Cohen, *Bernard Malamud and The Trial by Love* (Amsterdam: Editions Rodopi, N.V., 1974);
  Measures Malamud's heroes on a scale extending from eros (selfish lust) to caritas (other-directed love of humanity).

John Desmond, "Malamud's Fixer: Jew, Christian or Modern?," *Renascence*, 27 (Winter 1975): 101-110;
  Discusses Bok as a Jew, and as an existential Christ figure.

Robert Ducharme, *Art and Idea in the Novels of Bernard Malamud* (The Hague: Mouton, 1974);
  Sees the theme of Malamud's novels as the tempering of idealism into realism.

Leslie A. Field and Joyce Field, eds., *Bernard Malamud and the Critics* (New York: New York University Press, 1970);
  A collection of essays embodying most of the important criticism to its date.

Field and Field, eds., *Bernard Malamud: A Collection of Critical Essays* (Englewood Cliffs, N.J.: Prentice-Hall, 1975);
  By the same editors as the preceding item, includes essays written from 1970 to 1975.

Maurice Friedberg, "History and Imagination: Two Views of the Beiliss Case," *Midstream*, 12 (November 1966): 72-76;
  Compares *The Fixer* to its source, the trial of Mendel Beiliss for the ritual murder of a Christian child in Kiev in 1913.

Mark Goldman, "Bernard Malamud's Comic Vision and the Theme of Identity," *Critique*, 7 (Winter 1964-1965): 92-109;
  Shows how comic irony undercuts the egotistical masks of many of Malamud's heroes.

Arnold Goldsmith, "Nature in Bernard Malamud's *The Assistant*," *Renascence*, 29 (Summer 1977): 211-223;
  Discusses images of the sea, the moon, flowers, and birds in their primarily negative aspect.

Rita Gollin, "Malamud's Dubin and the Morality of Desire," *Papers on Language and Literature*, 18 (Spring 1982): 198-207;
  Discusses the relation of romantic yearning to lust, showing how both are destructive as they become self-deceptive or possessive.

Giles B. Gunn, "Bernard Malamud and the High Cost of Living," in *Adversity and Grace: Studies in Recent American Literature*, edited by Nathan A. Scott (Chicago, 1968);
  Sees Malamud's heroes as American innocents in the tradition of *The Scarlet Letter*, *Billy Budd*, and *The Great Gatsby*.

Ihab Hassan, *Radical Innocence* (Princeton: Princeton University Press, 1961), pp. 161-168;
  Sees Malamud's heroes as never quite achieving their goals and argues that their half-success is Malamud's statement of the human condition.

Peter L. Hays, "The Complex Pattern of Redemption in *The Assistant*," *Centennial Review*, 13 (Spring 1959): 200-214;
  Shows how Morris's redemptive love, seen in the framework of Martin Buber's philosophy, leads Frank from despair to hope.

Jeffrey Helterman, *Understanding Bernard Malamud* (Columbia: University of South Carolina Press, 1985);
  A novel-by-novel analysis of the entire canon, emphasizing Malamud's symbolism and medieval backgrounds.

Sheldon Hershinow, *Bernard Malamud* (New York: Frederick Ungar, 1980);
  Stresses Malamud's importance as a humanistic moralist and discusses sources in the Old Testament.

Barbara Lefcowitz, "The *Hybris* of Neurosis: Malamud's *Pictures of Fidelman*," *Literature and Psychology*, 20, no. 3 (1970): 115-120;
  Presents Fidelman as a case study in obsessive-compulsive neurosis, and then shows how this neurosis is tested by the humanity of the characters he meets.

Brita Lindberg-Seyersted, "A Reading of Bernard Malamud's *The Tenants*," *Journal of American Studies*, 9 (April 1975): 85-102;
  Discusses the theme of the double in Malamud particularly as it comments on the relation of master to novice.

Irving Malin, "Portrait of the Artist in Slapstick: Malamud's *Pictures of Fidelman*," *Literary Review*, 24 (Fall 1980): 121-138;
Analyzes the different styles and techniques used by Fidelman as an artist.

Ruth Mandel, "Bernard Malamud's *The Assistant* and *A New Life:* Ironic Affirmation," *Critique*, 7 (Winter 1964-1965): 110-121;
Sees all sacrifice in these novels as selfish negation of apparent affirmation.

James Mellard, "Malamud's Novels: Four Versions of Pastoral," *Critique*, 9, no. 2 (1967): 5-19;
Relates Malamud's first four novels to the pastoral myth of Percival and the Wasteland.

S. V. Pradhan, "The Nature and Interpretation of Symbolism in Malamud's *The Assistant*," *Centennial Review*, 16 (Fall 1972): 394-407;
Argues that the symbolism used by Malamud does not have the cosmic intensity of pre-World War II novelists like Joyce and Faulkner.

Marc Ratner, "Style and Humanity in Malamud's Fiction," *Massachusetts Review*, 5, no. 4 (1964): 663-683;
Deals with the range of narrative styles in Malamud's fiction and shows how he uses contrasting styles to create point and counterpoint on the theme of humanity.

Sidney Richman, *Bernard Malamud* (New York: Twayne, 1966);
Shows the way Malamud balances ambiguities and ironies for a positive result; discusses influence of Dostoyevski and Martin Buber.

Earl Rovit, "Bernard Malamud and the Jewish Literary Tradition," *Critique*, 3 (1960);
Analyzes the influence of Yiddish folktales on Malamud's work.

Ben Siegel, "Victims in Motion: Bernard Malamud's Sad and Bitter Clowns," *Northwest Review*, 5 (Spring 1962): 69-80;
Finds Malamud, in his early novels, writing ideas rather than creating characters, describing motives rather than explaining them, and being ingenious rather than insightful.

Daniel Stern, "The Art of Fiction: Bernard Malamud" [interview], *Paris Review*, 16 (Spring 1975): 40-64;
Malamud discusses a number of influences (including Charlie Chaplin) on his writing and the importance of rewriting.

Earl R. Wasserman, "*The Natural:* Malamud's World Ceres," *Centennial Review*, 9 (Fall 1985): 438-460;
A sophisticated Jungian reading of *The Natural*, showing how the Percival story is built on even more primal archetypes, like that of the fertile Earth Mother.

Christof Wegelin, "The American Schlemiel Abroad: Malamud's Italian Stories and the End of American Innocence," *Twentieth Century Literature*, 19 (April 1973): 77-88;
Sees Malamud's handling of the theme of American innocence bowing to European worldliness as an inheritance from James and Hawthorne.

Papers:
The Library of Congress has manuscripts, typescripts, and proofs of *The Natural, The Assistant, A New Life, The Fixer, Pictures of Fidelman*, parts of *The Magic Barrel* and *Idiots First*, and various short stories.

Carson McCullers

This entry was updated by Robert F. Kiernan (Manhattan College) from his entry in DLB
2, American Novelists Since World War II.

Places	Columbus, Georgia
	Bachvillers, France
	Yaddo Artists' Colony,
	  Saratoga Springs
		Greenwich Village
		Nyack, New
		  York
			Brooklyn
			Fayetteville, North
			  Carolina

Influences and Relationships	Muriel Rukeyser	Tennessee Williams	
Literary Movements and Forms	Southern Grotesque	Lyrical Novel	Chekhovian Drama
Major Themes	Loneliness Love Sexual Confusion	Alienation Racial Injustice Adolescent Pain and Growth	Freaks Social Injustice
Cultural and Artistic Influences			
Social and Economic Influences			

See also the McCullers entry in DLB 7, *Twentieth-Century American Dramatists.*

BIRTH: Columbus, Georgia, 19 February 1917, to Lamar and Marguerite Waters Smith.

EDUCATION: Columbia University and New York University, 1935-1936.

MARRIAGES: 1937 to Reeves McCullers (divorced). 1945 remarried McCullers.

AWARDS AND HONORS: Guggenheim Fellowships, 1942, 1946; National Institute of Arts and Letters grant, 1943; New York Drama Critics' Circle Award, 1950; Donaldson Award, 1950; elected to American Academy of Arts and Letters, 1952.

DEATH: Nyack, New York, 29 September 1967.

BOOKS: *The Heart Is a Lonely Hunter* (Boston: Houghton Mifflin, 1940; London: Cresset, 1943);
Reflections in a Golden Eye (Boston: Houghton Mifflin, 1941; London: Cresset, 1942);
The Member of the Wedding (Boston: Houghton Mifflin, 1946; London: Cresset, 1947);
The Member of the Wedding: A Play (New York: New Directions, 1951);
The Ballad of the Sad Café: The Novels and Stories of Carson McCullers (Boston: Houghton Mifflin, 1951; London: Cresset, 1952);
The Square Root of Wonderful (Boston: Houghton Mifflin, 1958; London: Cresset, 1958);
Clock Without Hands (Boston: Houghton Mifflin, 1961; London: Cresset, 1961);
Sweet As a Pickle and Clean As a Pig (Boston: Houghton Mifflin, 1964; London: Cape, 1965);
The Mortgaged Heart (Boston: Houghton Mifflin, 1971; London: Barrie & Jenkins, 1972).

PERIODICAL PUBLICATIONS: "Wunderkind," *Story*, 9 (December 1936): 61-73;
"Madame Zilensky and the King of Finland," *New Yorker*, 17 (20 December 1941): 15-18;
"A Tree. A Rock. A Cloud.," *Harper's Bazaar*, 76 (November 1942): 50, 96-99;
"The Sojourner," *Mademoiselle*, 31 (May 1950): 90, 160-166;
"A Domestic Dilemma," *New York Post*, 16 September 1951 (magazine section), pp. 10 ff.;
"Sucker," *Saturday Evening Post*, 236 (28 September 1963): 69-71.

With Eudora Welty, Flannery O'Connor, and Katherine Anne Porter, Carson McCullers is an explorer of the southern grotesque, for the ambience of her fiction is always southern, whatever its geographic locale, and her characters are the solitary, the freakish, and the lonely. Her work is distinguished from her fellow regionalists' work in the grotesque genre, however, by a compassion for the disaffiliate so deep that she is his foremost spokesman in modern American literature. Indeed, she has transcended not only regionalism but Americanism as well and has become a spokesman for all the lonely and alienated people of the world. Her best work is tenderly lyrical rather than philosophical, but it merits a distinguished place in that eccentric, bleakly poetic body of southern fiction that takes as its subject the dark corners of the mind.

McCullers's mother, Marguerite Smith, was clearly the dominant influence in her life, for her consuming interest in persons who feel themselves vaguely freakish was prompted by Mrs. Smith's insistence that she was different from other children and destined to become famous. Certainly the thirteen-year-old McCullers's height of 5' 8 1/2" seemed to her to be freakish (as it was later to seem freakish to Frankie Addams in *The Member of the Wedding*) and the considerable freedom and the constant approval that her mother gave her produced an effect of aloofness and eccentricity in her behavior that

Carson McCullers, 1941 (photo by Louise Dahl-Wolfe)

was greeted by Columbus adolescents with catcalls of "Freak!"

Both McCullers and her mother thought that she was to have a career in music, for she was proficient at the piano at an early age and showed no concomitant talent for storytelling. Indeed, Marguerite Smith was herself the raconteur of the family, with a gift for storytelling so renowned that residents of Columbus refused for many years to believe that it was McCullers and not Mrs. Smith who wrote the early novels. Moreover, Mrs. Smith was famous for her technique of rearranging ordinary events into eccentric configurations that were the delight of her audiences—a technique not unlike McCullers's own, and that was probably its foundation. McCullers never acknowledged such an influence from her mother, but she liked often to say that her sense of form in literature derived from her early study of musical structure, a claim borne out by her novels.

McCullers left Columbus for New York City in 1934 at the age of seventeen, intending to study music at Juilliard and writing at Columbia, but she lost her tuition money for Juilliard on the New York subway and supported herself at such odd jobs as typing, clerking, and waiting on tables while she studied writing with Whit Burnett at Columbia and with Sylvia Chatfield Bates at New York University. These teachers have always been credited with doing much to foster her talent: it was for Bates's class that she wrote the story "Wunderkind," in fact, and she owed its publication in *Story* to Burnett.

Lula Carson Smith married Reeves McCullers, a fellow southerner, at the age of twenty. Her family encouraged the match, believing that they would mesh well, for Reeves seemed popular, personable, and steady, while Lula Carson was reclusive and mercurial. But Reeves had grown up in an unstable home, and he desperately needed to succeed in his own right. He unfortunately chose to be a writer and therefore to compete with his wife. The newlyweds thought they would take turns writing and working until they were both established, but Reeves was always to live in his wife's shadow and never to have his turn, and it is doubtful that he had much literary talent to begin with. He never ceased to love his wife, but their marriage was to destroy his sense of sexual identity and wreak havoc on his emotional life.

Marriage to Reeves afforded McCullers the leisure to complete her first novel, however, and less than two years after her wedding day, the manuscript of *The Heart Is a Lonely Hunter* was com-

plete. It was published in 1940 to a small number of reviews, but the critical reception was enthusiastic, and Louis Untermeyer even referred to the novel as "one of the most compelling, one of the most uncanny stories ever written in America."

The Heart Is a Lonely Hunter is the story of a deaf-mute named John Singer to whom heartfelt secrets are confided by a series of "grotesques": by Jake Blount, an embittered radical; by Benedict Mady Copeland, a disillusioned Negro doctor; by Biff Brannon, a sexually ambivalent restaurant owner; and by Mick Kelly, a twelve-year-old tomboy. The ironically named Singer is merely bewildered by these attentions, but he in turn confides in a feebleminded mute named Antonapoulos, completing the circle of desperate communication that goes nowhere. When Antonapoulos dies, Singer commits suicide, and his devotees are left to make what they can of him and to resume lives that no longer have a pressure valve. The organization of the book, as McCullers wrote to her publishers, is contrapuntal: "Like a voice in a fugue, each one of the main characters is an entity in himself—but his personality takes on a new richness when contrasted and woven in with the other characters in the book." But the book is most impressive for the maturity of its psychological understanding. Erotic and epistemological needs blend inextricably in the characters, and each character is dominated by a fixed set of ideas that makes it impossible for him to reach communion with others. Indeed, the characters are convinced they are doomed to solitude, and out of their frustration, they tend to make antisocial gestures that compound their isolation.

The novel is sometimes thought to center on Mick Kelly and her initiation into adulthood. Mick is certainly one of McCullers's most disarming characters, and certainly her story is the most representative of the five in the novel, but the plain, grave style, a pattern of ironic religious references, and the elaborate counterpoint of the novel suggest a broader range of implication than the initiation genre affords and render it more convincingly a fable about inescapable loneliness. In many ways, of course, Mick Kelly is the young Lula Carson Smith, for Mick, like McCullers, is preoccupied with music, and she learns the same truths about loneliness that McCullers abstracted from her experience at an early age and never substantially altered. Yet, in some ways, *The Heart Is a Lonely Hunter* is the least immediately autobiographical of any of McCullers's works, perhaps because her emotional life with Reeves was relatively stable and satisfying during the period of *Heart*'s writing.

Reeves McCullers was increasingly restive about his own lack of a career, however, and by 1939 both husband and wife found life in Fayetteville, North Carolina, where Reeves was then stationed, constraining. Under the pressure, their marriage began to disintegrate, and *Reflections in a Golden Eye* (1941) was McCullers's imaginative response to that disintegration. Written in two brief months during 1939, the novel seemed to McCullers to write itself, so this tale of bisexuality and estrangement might have had an emotional source in the McCullers marriage for both Carson and Reeves were developing bisexually and were shortly to take lovers of their own sex. Indeed, although she had not met her at the time of the novel's writing, McCullers dedicated the novel to Annemarie Clarac-Schwarzenbach, the first woman for whom she developed an uncontrolled passion, as if acknowledging the resonance of the book with her personal life.

McCullers and her husband, Reeves (photo by John Vincent Adams)

As *Reflections in a Golden Eye* bluntly proclaims, its cast of characters includes "two officers, a soldier, two women, a Filipino, and a horse." One officer is Captain Penderton, a bisexual, a sado-masochist, and a potential drug addict; the other is Major Langdon, a man who makes love to Penderton's wife, Leonora, in a blackberry patch two hours after meeting her. Leonora Penderton is a voluptuary who "could not have multiplied twelve by thirteen under threat of the rack," and Langdon's wife Alison is a recluse, so deranged by grief over the death of her deformed child that she has cut off her nipples with garden shears. Clearly these characters are antithetically poised one against the other, with Leonora and Major Langdon on the side of animal lust and Penderton and Alison on the side of repressed sexuality. Yet, ironically, the reader cares more for Penderton and for Alison than for their more vital spouses, simply because there is more to them and to their experiences. In the central action of the story, for instance, Penderton makes two attempts to break out of his nature: first, he attempts to ride his wife's spirited horse, Firebird, an emblem of sexual vitality; and second, he tries to break down the barriers of rank and nature between himself and Private Elgee Williams, a man who can ride Firebird bareback and who represents essential masculinity to Penderton (yet he takes his sexual pleasure with animals and spends his nights in Leonora's bedroom, voyeuristically watching her sleep: there is no such thing, we understand, as "essential masculinity"). At the end, Penderton, in an atavistic fit of jealousy, shoots Williams at his wife's bedside, all of his actions having confirmed the "queer coarse wrapper" that is his nature.

Once again, then, McCullers's themes are the utter alienation of individual natures and the absence of reciprocity in human relationships, but these themes are more insistent and more hopeless in *Reflections* than in almost any other of her novels, for her characters are given little humanity apart from their desperation and there is minimal lyricism to soften the reader's understanding of them. The critics liked the book no more than the staff at Fort Bragg (close by Fayetteville) and Fort Benning (where Reeves had earlier been stationed) or Mrs. George Patton, who denounced it in high dudgeon. Indeed, the critics charged the book with substituting caricatures for characters and adjectives for analysis, and many thought it gratuitously sensational. But the root problem of the novel is probably that McCullers attempted something beyond her—to philosophize about persons in a military world. She was always attracted by the easy, portentous abstraction, even when she did not fully understand it and when her story did not fully warrant it, and the easy abstractions of this novel are the typical failing of her work. Indeed, McCullers cared little for the literal reality of what she wrote about: she refused, for instance, to attend a convention of deaf-mutes with Reeves while writing *The Heart Is a Lonely Hunter* because she did not want her imaginative concept of a mute destroyed, and she resisted the confrontation with facts throughout her life, preferring her imaginative concept of what the facts should be.

In 1940 McCullers's editor at Houghton Mifflin secured her a fellowship to Bread Loaf Writers' Conference, an annual summer program of Middlebury College. She was gratified to receive the fellowship, not only for the honor, but because it meant leaving Reeves temporarily. Indeed, this was the first of many periods of living apart from Reeves: she was more and more to go her own way, almost unconscious of her rejection of Reeves and of the psychic and economic damage she did him. Reeves was a necessary presence in the background of her life, but his needs and wishes rarely shaped her life after the first years of marriage, and she maintained in general a love-hate relationship with him. Reeves himself was uncannily patient with her. He always understood her mercurial temperament and her single-minded passions.

In September of 1940, on her return from Bread Loaf, McCullers moved out of the Greenwich Village apartment she shared with Reeves and into an establishment in Brooklyn which was presided over by George Davis, the fiction editor at *Harper's Bazaar,* and which was shortly to include as residents W. H. Auden, Gypsy Rose Lee, Louis MacNeice, Benjamin Britten, Paul and Jane Bowles, and the Richard Wrights. The atmosphere of the house was almost surrealistic, and it crackled with the ideas of Marx, Freud, Kierkegaard, Jung, and Nietzsche. She could not have found a friendlier atmosphere for working on the manuscript of "The Ballad of the Sad Café," but in fact she was distracted by the ménage and did little writing.

In February 1941 during a vacation in Columbus, McCullers suffered her first cerebral stroke, although it was not properly diagnosed until years later. Reeves brought her back to the Greenwich Village apartment when she was ambulatory, and they resumed living together. Her closest friend during this period was the poet Muriel Rukeyser, and it was through Rukeyser that she met and fell in love with David Diamond, the composer

and musician. She also met Elizabeth Ames, the executive director of the Yaddo artists' colony in Saratoga Springs, New York, and Ames invited her to be a guest of Yaddo during the summer of 1941. Over the years, McCullers was to return to Yaddo many times, for it proved to be the place where she worked best, and Elizabeth Ames was to become one of her most trusted friends and advisers.

On her first visit to Yaddo, McCullers continued to work on the manuscript which was to become *The Member of the Wedding* but interrupted it in order to complete "The Ballad of the Sad Café," a work which is often regarded as her finest. "The Ballad of the Sad Café" is the story of a strange and tragic love triangle, the three members of which are Miss Amelia Evans, a brooding, hardfisted Amazon; Marvin Macy, her once-loving but unloved husband; and the hunchbacked Lymon, a sickly and self-indulgent confidence man. In the course of the story, Lymon transforms Amelia into a softer and more feminine person by insinuating himself into her affections under the pretense of being her cousin, and this change is externalized by the alteration of Amelia's feed store into a café— "the warm center point of the town." The café links the entire community to Amelia's fulfillment and gives them a share in it, but love is a perverse, fragile thing, and the café has only a brief existence. When Macy returns from prison to his estranged wife, Lymon falls passionately in love with him, and Macy, seizing his opportunity to avenge love's imbalance, defeats Amelia in a ceremonious wrestling match with Lymon's aid. Devastated, Amelia closes the café and withdraws behind closed blinds, and her eyes begin to cross "as though they sought each other out to exchange a little glance of grief and lonely recognition." In the most famous passage McCullers ever wrote (it brought tears to her eyes whenever she read it), the narrator insists that love is a private rather than a mutual experience, and that there is only an accidental relationship between the experience of love and the beloved person. In justification of its title, the story uses many traditional ballad motifs, such as natural and supernatural signs mirroring human events, characters who take their keynote from animals and birds, repeated stock phrases that approach incremental refrain, and, spectacularly, an envoi entitled "The Twelve Mortal Men" which recasts the events of the story in analogous terms.

"The Ballad of the Sad Café" is McCullers's most daring use of the grotesque: her characters are the most extreme she ever imagined, and their actions are so bizarre as seemingly to defy her control. Yet control them she does, and much of her success must be credited to her creation of a narrator, an anonymous but sensitive member of the community who bears the same weight of time and mutability as the characters, and who discovers the meaning of his own life as he talks. In a sense, the narrator is a recasting of the voyeur figure of *Reflections in a Golden Eye*, but he is more organically useful, for he mediates between the world of the grotesques and our familiar world. And, with his quaint, storytelling language, the narrator casts the aura of folklore over the tale: the characters become archetypes in his hands rather than grotesques, and their story becomes something elemental, mysterious, and suggestive. Indeed, the tension between the grotesquerie of the story and the narrator's placid rendering is one of the most vivid effects of the story, and one of its most haunting pleasures. The story was published first in *Harper's Bazaar* in 1943, and so it was not immediately reviewed, but in 1951 it was included in an omnibus volume entitled *The Ballad of the Sad Café: The Novels and Stories of Carson McCullers*. The omnibus volume received fine reviews and sold well, and "The Ballad of the Sad Café" was singled out for special praise by many of the reviewers.

The writing of "The Ballad of the Sad Café" came easily to McCullers, and the reason is probably that once again she was objectifying her immediate psychic experience. There are two possible sources of the story. Annemarie Clarac-Schwarzenbach had refused to vacation with McCullers a year earlier and had seemed to take Reeves's part against her; this vaguely triangular situation seemed to McCullers to prove once again that there is no reciprocity in love. More immediately, McCullers had recently discovered that her husband loved David Diamond as deeply as she did herself and that they were living together in Rochester while she was at Yaddo. She had no objection to Reeves taking a male lover, but she did fear exclusion from their relationship—the very exclusion that she fantasized Miss Amelia suffering from the union of Lymon and Macy.

When McCullers discovered in 1941 that Reeves had been forging her name to checks, she instituted divorce proceedings almost immediately. Always careless with money herself, she nevertheless demanded strict accounts from everyone else and tended increasingly to penuriousness. Reeves rejoined the army shortly after McCullers divorced him; yet their life apart was not markedly different from their married life, for they remained in close touch and seemed as emotionally dependent on

each other as ever. Indeed, McCullers stayed with Reeves at Fort Dix before his embarkation for Europe, and she had evidently no compunction about signing herself "A War Wife" in an open letter published in *Mademoiselle* in 1943. They toyed with the idea of remarriage as early as 1943 and finally remarried on 19 March 1945, after Reeves's discharge, but their marriage continued the on-again, off-again quality of their relationship.

After a bout with pleurisy, strep throat, and double pneumonia at the end of 1941, McCullers resumed work on *The Member of the Wedding*, occasionally interrupting the novel's slow progress to work on a short story. With the aid of a Guggenheim Fellowship, a National Institute of Arts and Letters grant, and summers at Yaddo between 1942 and 1945, the novel was finally completed, and upon its publication in 1946 the majority of critics (who had been offended by *Reflections in a Golden Eye*) took McCullers to their hearts a second time, quibbling somewhat that the novel was short of plot, but reveling in its characterizations, its honesty, and its seriousness.

The Member of the Wedding deals once again with the tortured world of adolescence. Frankie Addams is a gawky, motherless tomboy who feels herself "an unjoined person" and "a member of nothing in the world." Her only companions are the family cook, Berenice Sadie Brown, a stoical, God-respecting woman; and John Henry West, a six-year-old neighbor who dies of meningitis before the story is over and for whom the young Truman Capote is thought to have been the model. During this "green and crazy summer" Frankie decides to be a member of the wedding between her brother Jarvis and Janice Williams, and she rechristens herself F. Jasmine so that her name will alliterate properly with theirs. Berenice tries to tell her that "Me is me and you is you and he is he," but, in a famous phrase, Frankie declares that Jarvis and Janice are "the we of me" and maintains her illusion of accompanying the newlyweds until she is dragged from their honeymoon car. Then, as a more conventionally named "Frances," she begins the process of accommodation to the reality that Berenice has tried to teach her. But the more mature Frances is less attractive than young Frankie, and, as Lawrence Graver has observed, she is "just a bit too much like everybody else."

With the possible exception of "The Ballad of the Sad Café," *The Member of the Wedding* is McCullers's most perfect work and her most realistic. It has been criticized as a retreat from the broader social interests of *The Heart Is a Lonely Hunter* and

"The Ballad of the Sad Café," but the psychology of the characters is wholly under control in this novel as it is not in the earlier works, and there are none of the incoherent abstractions that so often mar McCullers's prose. Frankie's need to make connections is steadily and intricately elaborated, and allusions to music are used adroitly to bespeak the heart when words fail. The long, disjointed conversations between Berenice, Frankie, and John Henry are reminiscent of the monologues which the grotesques pour into the ear of John Singer in *The Heart Is a Lonely Hunter,* but whereas *The Heart Is a Lonely Hunter* is elaborately contrived to allow for those monologues, they emerge effortlessly in *The Member of the Wedding.* McCullers described herself as attempting in this novel to write "a lyric tragi-comedy in which the funniness and grief co-exist in the same line," an effect she really strove for in all of her fiction and which was central to her artistic aspirations, but which was never more completely realized than in this bittersweet novel of adolescence.

When McCullers joined Tennessee Williams at Nantucket for the summer of 1946, Williams proposed to her that she adapt *The Member of the Wedding* to the stage. McCullers had been annoyed by Edmund Wilson's contention that her novel lacked a sense of drama, so she responded to the challenge and completed a first draft of the play by the end of the year, before sailing with Reeves for Europe on her second Guggenheim Fellowship. A series of strokes cut short her intended stay in Europe and aborted her work on *The Member of the Wedding,* however, making it necessary for her to dictate revisions from her sickbed and leading to an unhappy attempt at collaboration with Greer Johnson. After considerable rewriting and many difficulties with casting and production, the play finally opened in New York on 5 January 1950 to glowing reviews, and it began a run of 501 performances. Harold Clurman directed Julie Harris, Ethel Waters, and Brandon de Wilde in the cast, and together they succeeded brilliantly with McCullers's fragile story and undramatic script. For Edmund Wilson was right about McCullers being no dramatist: she had seen only two Broadway plays in her life before attempting to dramatize *The Member of the Wedding,* and she was ignorant of all stagecraft. Still, miraculously, the dramatic version of *The Member of the Wedding* is one of the outstanding adaptations of a novel in the history of the American theater. Its weakness of structure seems Chekhovian plotlessness in a good production, and its reiteration of set speeches from

McCullers's original novel is pleasantly literary—a stiffening of the melodramatic story with eloquence. *The Member of the Wedding* won the New York Drama Critics' Circle Award for the best play of its season, and it was sold to Hollywood for $75,000, making McCullers financially secure for the first time in her life.

With increased financial security, McCullers indulged her wanderlust freely. Never one to stay long in a place, she had all her adult life varied her residence between Columbus and Nyack with her mother, New York with Reeves, Key West with Tennessee Williams, Yaddo with Elizabeth Ames, Brooklyn with George Davis, and wherever friends were living. But she had been unable to cross the ocean as often as she would have liked. Thus, in 1950 she visited Elizabeth Bowen in Ireland (quite uninvited), and in 1951 she traveled to England to visit with David Gascoyne and Dame Edith Sitwell, who became a much-loved friend. In 1952 she traveled with Reeves through Italy and France and then bought a home in Bachvillers, a village outside Paris, and tried to work on the manuscript of *Clock Without Hands* (1961). Neither McCullers nor her husband was well at this time: both had been drinking heavily for many years, and McCullers's health had progressively declined since the series of strokes in 1947. Walking was difficult for her, and a spastic arm made writing a laborious process. McCullers had in fact made a suicide attempt in 1948, but that attempt cured her forever of the impulse. Reeves, on the other hand, had become actively suicidal over his relationship with his wife and his lack of career since leaving the army, and he several times proposed a double suicide to Carson. Terrified for her life after one such proposal, McCullers fled to America, leaving Reeves to kill himself a few weeks later, alone in a Paris hotel. Apparently McCullers became so desperately afraid of her husband during their last weeks together that the emotional bond that had always survived her love-hate relationship to him snapped completely. She refused to bring Reeves's body home for burial and refused even to pay the cost of having his ashes sent to her. Many friends were alienated by her complete refusal to mourn him.

While in residence at Yaddo during the summer of 1954, McCullers wrote the first draft of her play *The Square Root of Wonderful* (1958) while continuing to work on the manuscript of *Clock Without Hands.* Arnold Saint Subber became interested in producing the play a year later, and soon he was collaborating with McCullers almost daily on the manuscript. McCullers was ill for almost the entirety of 1956, however, and she found revisions difficult, so progress was agonizingly slow. The play finally opened on 30 October 1956, with Anne Baxter in the lead, but a weak script had by that time been devastated by several changes of director, and the reviews were deservedly harsh. It closed in December after forty-five performances, when the advance ticket sales were exhausted.

The central character in the play, Molly Lovejoy, is based on Marguerite Smith. McCullers's mother had died suddenly in 1955, and she saw Molly as a memorial to her mother's "tranquil beauty and sense of joy in life." But Philip Lovejoy, the male lead in the play, is a failed novelist who is unable to come to terms with his failure and commits suicide as a final creative act: he is transparently modeled on Reeves. The action is worked out in terms of a life-death dialectic which is uncomfortably close to an apologia for the inconsistency between McCullers's callous treatment of her husband's remains and her ample grief over her mother's death. The play is a dramatic failure in almost every way—tenuously developed, blurred in theme, lifeless in characterization—but it offers fascinating insight into McCullers's need during this period to defend herself against the charge of callousness and to rationalize the values by which she had refused to grieve for her husband.

During the writing of *The Square Root of Wonderful,* McCullers had apparently envisioned herself as surpassing the work of her friend Tennessee Williams, and she suffered so acutely from depression after the closing of the play that her friends arranged for an interview with Dr. Mary Mercer, a psychiatrist who practiced in Nyack. Dr. Mercer concluded that McCullers did not need her professional care, but she did offer McCullers informal friendship and guidance, and she became the primary influence in McCullers's life after the death of her mother. She saw McCullers almost daily and brought a semblance of order to her very disordered life, arranging for the physical and psychic well-being of her friend until McCullers's death nine years later. Almost certainly, McCullers would not have lived as long as she did without Dr. Mercer's ministrations, and she would certainly have been unable to complete her last novel, *Clock Without Hands,* without Dr. Mercer's encouragement.

Clock Without Hands seems to have occupied McCullers's mind as early as 1941, although she did not seriously begin work on it until ten years later, and it was not completed until the end of 1960. It is the story of four men caught in the changing South of the 1950s: J. T. Malone, a small-town druggist who is dying of an incurable disease and who is distressed by the knowledge that he has never really lived; Judge Fox Clane, a senile former congressman who is indignant about the civil rights movement; Sherman Pew, the judge's black servant, who buys a home in a white neighborhood; and Jester Clane, the judge's grandson, who harbors vaguely erotic feelings for Pew. Each of these characters finds his identity challenged by the passage of time, but no one more vividly than Malone, the man who watches the clock that for him has no hands. Malone redeems his undistinguished life, however, by opposing Judge Clane's plan to bomb Pew's home. No such redemption is accorded the judge, who is a caricature of a southern redneck at his most ridiculous, and who refuses to acknowledge the passage of time. Sherman Pew and Jester Clane are parallel characters, both of whom try to set the clock of southern time ahead, Pew, too quickly, by buying the house in the white neighborhood and being lynched for his effrontery, and Clane, with presumable success, in resolving to be a civil rights lawyer.

Because the delicate state of McCullers's health and the physical difficulties she encountered in writing the novel were widely known, the critics were gentle in pointing out that *Clock Without Hands* fell far below the level of her earlier work. On a thematic basis it is her most ambitious novel, for all of her familiar concerns are there—the suffering of the freak, the horror of racial and social injustice, the traumas of adolescent loneliness and sexual confusion. But it is really her weakest novel, for it fails to relate its various concerns to one another. It needs a John Singer to pull the assorted grotesques together and to keep it from seeming a series of disjointed set pieces. It needs more sustained characterization, too, for Judge Clane, Sherman Pew, and Jester Clane become merely humorous for long stretches of the text, and the effect of such easy laughter is to undercut the basic seriousness of the novel. Only the portrait of J. T. Malone is really memorable, but even Malone is unfocused, and he tends to slip out of the novel's foreground.

The original inspiration for the character of J. T. Malone was apparently Annemarie Clarac-Schwarzenbach, for McCullers understood her to have faced the ruin of her tragic life and to have transcended despair in her Congo River poems, written shortly before her death in 1942. But as the prospect of death began to loom before McCullers herself, and as the completion of her last novel began to seem improbable, the story of the

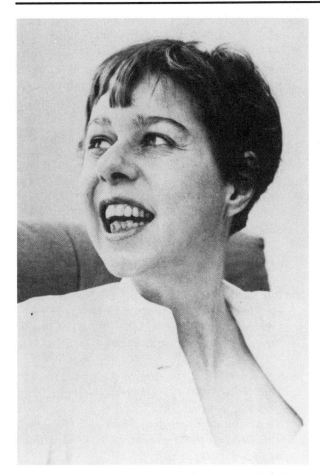

Carson McCullers, 1958 (photo by Werner J. Kuhn)

dying Malone became her own story as well, and it is fitting that Malone should transcend a novel otherwise forgettable.

The last years of McCullers's life were a physical agony. She was operated on twice in 1961 after the completion of her novel, and in 1962 she underwent surgery on her left hand and for the removal of her left breast. In 1963 her aching and crippled left leg was operated on, and in 1964 she was hospitalized still again for a broken hip and a shattered left elbow, sustained in a fall. In 1965 an exploratory operation discovered that a hip pin had worked itself loose, causing her discomfort that had been dismissed by her doctors as psychosomatic, and she was compelled to spend months on a flotation pad. She was almost never without pain, and there was increasingly little difference between her postoperative weakened condition and her normal condition. Nonetheless, she interested herself during these years in Edward Albee's dramatic adaptation of "The Ballad of the Sad Café," in John Huston's filming of *Reflections in a Golden Eye,* and

in Thomas Ryan's scripting of *The Heart Is a Lonely Hunter,* and she herself worked with Mary Rodgers on adapting *The Member of the Wedding* to a musical treatment that eventually came to nothing. Nor did she remain quietly at home in Nyack. During ambulatory periods she visited Edward Albee on Fire Island, she attended Dame Edith Sitwell's seventy-fifth birthday celebration in England, and she entertained Isak Dinesen, whom she had long admired, during the Danish writer's visit to America. Surrounded by elaborate medical precautions, she flew to Ireland to visit John Huston in April 1967, although she was unable to leave her bed for the entire visit. Four months later, on 15 August, she suffered a massive brain hemorrhage and lay comatose for forty-seven days, dying on 29 September in the Nyack Hospital at the age of fifty.

Although it was accepted at the time of her death that she had largely exhausted her imaginative resources, the reputation that McCullers had earned with *The Heart Is a Lonely Hunter,* "The Ballad of the Sad Café," and *The Member of the Wedding* was solidly established and in no way declining. Her fans were legion, both at home and abroad, and her place in modern American literature was assured. As the *New York Times* proclaimed editorially upon her death, she was "the vibrant voice of love and loneliness in the Southern novel."

Bibliographies:

Robert F. Kiernan, *Katherine Anne Porter and Carson McCullers: A Reference Guide* (Boston: G. K. Hall, 1976);
An annotated bibliography of secondary materials about McCullers and her writings, including reviews, critical articles, and dissertations.

Adrian M. Shapiro, Jackson R. Bryer, and Kathleen Field, *Carson McCullers: A Descriptive Listing and Annotated Bibliography of Criticism* (New York: Garland, 1980);
An annotated listing of McCullers criticism and a detailed physical description of the author's primary texts.

References:

Irving H. Buchen, "Divine Collusion: The Art of Carson McCullers," *Dalhousie Review,* 54 (1974): 529-541;
A study of McCullers's artist-children, who entangle their aesthetic impulses with childhood needs and dreams.

Virginia Spencer Carr, *The Lonely Hunter: A Biography of Carson McCullers* (Garden City: Doubleday, 1975);
An exhaustive biography incorporating the recollections of McCullers's family, friends, lovers, acquaintances, and enemies.

Harold Clurman, "Some Preliminary Notes for The Member of the Wedding," in *Directors on Directing: A Source Book of the Modern Theater,* edited by Toby Cole and Helen Krick Chinov, rev. ed. (Indianapolis: Bobbs-Merrill, 1963), pp. 380-389;
The Broadway director's notes for *The Member of the Wedding,* commenting on both the action of the play and its characters' motivations.

Richard M. Cook, *Carson McCullers* (New York: Ungar, 1975);
A readable study of McCullers's writing, text by text, together with a biographical chapter.

Frank Durham, "God and No God in The Heart Is a Lonely Hunter," *South Atlantic Quarterly,* 56 (1957): 494-499;
A reading of *The Heart Is a Lonely Hunter* as a religious allegory.

Oliver Evans, *The Ballad of Carson McCullers* (New York: Coward-McCann, 1966);
The development of McCullers's life and work, with emphasis on the biographical elements that shape her work.

Barbara Nauer Folk, "The Sad Sweet Music of Carson McCullers," *Georgia Review,* 16 (1962): 202-209;
The best of many studies of the musical allusions that permeate McCullers's fiction.

Lawrence Graver, *Carson McCullers* (St. Paul: University of Minnesota Press, 1969);
A pamphlet-length discussion that argues McCullers is more lyricist than philosopher in her fiction.

Ihab Hassan, "Carson McCullers: The Alchemy of Love and Aesthetics of Pain," *Modern Fiction Studies,* 5 (1959): 311-326;
An influential essay on the tension between the self and the world in McCullers's novels and on the tension between love and pain in her novelistic vision.

Cicely Palser Havely, "Two Women Novelists: Carson McCullers and Flannery O'Connor," in *The Uses of Fiction: Essays on the Modern Novel in Honour of Arnold Kettle,* edited by Douglas Jefferson (Milton Keynes, U.K.: Open University Press, 1982);
A consideration of the relationship between the inner lives and the public lives of McCullers and O'Connor.

Alfred Kazin, "We Who Sit in Darkness," in *The Inmost Leaf: A Selection of Essays* (New York: Harcourt, Brace, 1955), pp. 127-135;
By failing to absorb the audience in its action, *The Member of the Wedding* allows Ethel Waters (Berenice) a merely personal triumph.

Dayton Kohler, "Carson McCullers: Variations on a Theme," *College English,* 13 (1951): 1-8;
An influential essay on the themes of loneliness and longing in McCullers's fiction.

Joan S. Korenman, "Carson McCullers' 'Proletarian Novel,'" *Studies in the Humanities,* 5 (1975): 8-13;
An original reading of *The Heart Is a Lonely Hunter* as infused with McCullers's objections to capitalism.

David Madden, "The Paradox of the Need for Privacy and the Need for Understanding in Carson McCullers' *The Heart Is a Lonely Hunter,*" *Literature and Psychology,* 17 (1967): 128-140;
A study of the psychological vectors in *The Heart Is a Lonely Hunter;* avoids technical jargon.

Margaret B. McDowell, *Carson McCullers* (Boston: Twayne, 1980);
Survey of McCullers's oeuvre in the standard format of the Twayne United States Authors series.

John McNally, "The Introspective Narrator in 'The Ballad of the Sad Café,'" *South Atlantic Bulletin,* 38 (1973): 40-44;
A brief, careful analysis of how the narrator in "The Ballad of the Sad Café" discovers new meaning in his own existence.

John B. Vickery, "Carson McCullers: A Map of Love," *Wisconsin Studies in Contemporary Literature,* 1 (1960): 13-24;

An important study of McCullers's interest in lovers discovering their loneliness.

Papers:
The University of Texas has a major collection of McCullers's manuscripts.

Arthur Miller

Updated by Jeffrey Helterman (University of South Carolina) from his entry in DLB 7, Twentieth-Century American Dramatists.

Places	Brooklyn
	Salem, Massachusetts
	University of
	    Michigan
		Manhattan
		Auschwitz
		China
		Vichy
			Hollywood
			Connecticut
			Spoleto Festival,
			    South Carolina

Influences and Relationships	Henrik Ibsen Tennessee Williams	Bertolt Brecht Albert Camus	Jo Mielziner Ralph Waldo Emerson
Literary Movements and Forms	Expressionism	Realism	
Major Themes	American Dream Sibling Rivalry Blacklisting	Holocaust Anti-Semitism Marilyn Monroe	The Depression Witch Trials World War II

Cultural and Artistic Influences	Hebrew Mysticism
	Theory of
	    the Frontier
		Freudian Psychology
		Existentialism
		Radio Plays
			Theater of
			    Alienation

Social and Economic Influences	Psychiatry Italian Opera Great Depression	Communism Astrology	Judaism Sociology

BIRTH: New York, New York, 17 October 1915, to Isidore and Augusta Barnett Miller.

EDUCATION: A.B., University of Michigan, 1938.

MARRIAGES: 1940 to Mary Grace Slattery (divorced); children: Jane, Robert. 1956 to Marilyn Monroe (divorced). 1962 to Ingeborg Morath; children: Rebecca, Daniel.

AWARDS AND HONORS: Hopwood Award (University of Michigan) for *Honors at Dawn*, 1936; Hopwood Award for *No Villain*, 1937; Theatre Guild Award for *They Too Arise*, 1938; New York Drama Critics Circle Awards for *All My Sons*, 1947, and for *Death of a Salesman*, 1949; Pulitzer Prize for *Death of a Salesman*, 1949; Antoinette Perry (Tony) Award for *The Crucible*, 1953; Drama Critics Circle Award for *A View from the Bridge*, 1955; Honorary Doctor of Letters, University of Michigan, 1956; National Institute of Arts and Letters Gold Medal for Drama, 1959; President of P.E.N., 1965-1969; Brandeis University Creative Arts Medal, 1969-1970.

Arthur Miller, 1963

BOOKS: *Situation Normal* (New York: Reynal & Hitchcock, 1944);

Focus (New York: Reynal & Hitchcock, 1945; London: Gollancz, 1949);

All My Sons (New York: Reynal & Hitchcock, 1947; Harmondsworth, U.K.: Penguin, 1961);

Death of a Salesman (New York: Viking, 1949; London: Cresset, 1949);

An Enemy of the People, adapted from Ibsen's play (New York: Viking, 1951);

The Crucible (New York: Viking, 1953; London: Cresset, 1956);

A View from the Bridge: Two One-Act Plays (New York: Viking, 1955)—includes *A Memory of Two Mondays;* revised edition (New York: Dramatists Play Service, 1956);

A View from the Bridge: A Play in Two Acts, revised edition (New York: Dramatists Play Service, 1957; London: Cresset, 1957);

Collected Plays (New York: Viking, 1957; London: Cresset, 1958);

The Misfits (New York: Viking, 1961; London: Secker & Warburg, 1961);

Jane's Blanket (New York: Crowell-Collier, 1963; London: Collier-Macmillan, 1963);

After the Fall (New York: Viking, 1964; London: Secker & Warburg, 1965);

Incident at Vichy (New York: Viking, 1965; London: Secker & Warburg, 1966);

I Don't Need You Any More: Stories (New York: Viking, 1967; London: Secker & Warburg, 1967);

The Price (New York: Viking, 1968; London: Secker & Warburg, 1968);

Psychology and Arthur Miller, by Miller and Richard I. Evans (New York: Dutton, 1969);

In Russia, by Miller and Inge Morath (New York: Viking, 1969; London: Secker & Warburg, 1969);

The Portable Arthur Miller, edited by Harold Clurman (New York: Viking, 1971);

The Creation of the World and Other Business (New York: Viking, 1973);

In the Country, by Miller and Morath (New York: Viking, 1977);

The Theater Essays of Arthur Miller (New York: Viking, 1978);

Chinese Encounters, by Miller and Morath (New York: Farrar, Straus & Giroux, 1979);

The American Clock, adapted from Studs Terkel's *Hard Times* (New York: Viking, 1980; London: Methuen, 1983);

Playing for Time (New York: Bantam, 1981);
Collected Plays, Volume 2 (New York: Viking, 1981;
London: Secker & Warburg, 1981);
Salesman in Beijing, photographs by Morath (New
York: Viking, 1984).

SELECTED PLAY PRODUCTIONS: *The Man
Who Had All the Luck*, New York, Forest The-
atre, 23 November 1944, 4 [performances];
All My Sons, New York, Coronet Theatre, 29 Jan-
uary 1947, 328;
Death of a Salesman, New York, Morosco Theatre,
10 February 1949, 742;
An Enemy of the People, adapted from Ibsen's play,
New York, Broadhurst Theatre, 28 Decem-
ber 1950, 36;
The Crucible, New York, Martin Beck Theatre, 22
January 1953, 197;
A View from the Bridge (one-act version) and *A Mem-
ory of Two Mondays*, New York, Coronet The-
atre, 29 September 1955, 149;
A View from the Bridge (two-act version), London,
Comedy Theatre, 11 October 1956;
After the Fall, New York, ANTA Washington Square
Theatre, 23 January 1964, 208;
Incident at Vichy, New York, ANTA Washington
Square Theatre, 3 December 1964, 99;
The Price, New York, Morosco Theatre, 7 February
1968, 425;
The Creation of the World and Other Business, New
York, Shubert Theatre, 30 November 1972,
20; revised as *Up From Paradise*, Ann Arbor,
Mich., Power Center for the Performing Arts,
23 April 1974;
The Archbishop's Ceiling, Washington, D.C., Eisen-
hower Theatre, Kennedy Center for the Per-
forming Arts, 30 April 1977;
The American Clock, adapted from Studs Terkel's
Hard Times, Charleston, S.C., Spoleto Festival,
Spring 1980; New York, Biltmore Theatre,
21 November 1980.

SCREENPLAYS: *The Witches of Salem*, Kingsley-In-
ternational, 1958;
The Misfits, United Artists, 1961.

TELEVISION SCRIPTS: *Fame*, NBC, November
1978;
Playing for Time, CBS, September 1980.

OTHER: "The Man Who Had All the Luck," in
*Cross-section: A Collection of New American Writ-
ing*, edited by Edwin Seaver (New York:
Fischer, 1944), pp. 486-552.

PERIODICAL PUBLICATIONS: "The Plaster
Masks," *Encore*, 9 (April 1946): 424-432;
"Tragedy and the Common Man," *New York Times*,
27 February 1949, II: 1, 3;
"Arthur Miller on 'The Nature of Tragedy,'" *New
York Herald-Tribune*, 27 March 1949, V: 1, 2;
"The 'Salesman' Has a Birthday," *New York Times*,
5 February 1950, II: 1, 3;
"A Modest Proposal for the Pacification of the Pub-
lic Temper," *Nation*, 179 (3 July 1954): 5-8;
"The American Theatre," *Holiday*, 17 (January
1955): 90-98, 101-102, 104;
"A Boy Grew in Brooklyn," *Holiday*, 17 (March
1955): 54-55, 117, 119-120, 122-124;
"The Family in Modern Drama," *Atlantic Monthly*,
197 (April 1956): 35-41;
"The Shadows of the Gods," *Harper's*, 217 (August
1958): 35-43;
"Bridge to a Savage World," *Esquire*, 50 (October
1958): 185-190;
"The Bored and the Violent," *Harper's*, 225 (No-
vember 1962): 50-52, 55-56;
"On Recognition," *Michigan Quarterly Review*, 2
(Autumn 1963): 213-220;
"The Contemporary Theater," *Michigan Quarterly
Review*, 6 (Summer 1967): 153-163;
"The Limited Hang-Out: The dialogues of Richard
Nixon as a drama of the antihero," *Harper's*,
249 (September 1974): 13-14, 16, 18-20.

Arthur Miller was born in Manhattan, the son
of a middle-class ladies' coat manufacturer and a
schoolteacher mother. He has a brother who became a businessman and a sister who was an actress.
Although he went to grammar school in then fashionable Harlem, Miller was forced to move to
Brooklyn when his father suffered major losses
right before the Depression. Today, over half a
century after his move to Brooklyn, Miller lives the
life of a country squire on 400 acres of Connecticut
countryside, where he gardens, mows, plants ev-
ergreens, works as a carpenter, and writes four to
six hours every morning in an isolated studio.
There is both a real and metaphoric sense of planting new roots, but he remains haunted by the old.
The Depression still troubles him: "It seems easy
to tell how it was to live in those years, but I have
made several attempts to tell it and when I do try
I know I cannot quite touch that mysterious underwater thing."

In the Depression years, Miller lived on
Gravesend Avenue in the Midwood section of

Brooklyn and says that his house was constantly visited by salesmen uncles who filled the air with their boastful talk. He attended James Madison and Abraham Lincoln high schools in Brooklyn where he was an average student. Of his reading, Miller says that "until the age of seventeen I can safely say that I never read a book weightier than Tom Swift and the Rover Boys, and only verged on literature with some Dickens." When he graduated from Abraham Lincoln in 1932 in the depth of the Depression, his parents could not afford to send him to college, nor were his grades good enough to get him in. The University of Michigan turned him down because of his academic record, and years later, none of his high school teachers could remember having taught the Pulitzer Prize-winner.

During those days Miller was much more of an athlete like Biff Loman in *Death of a Salesman* (1949) than the man who would become America's "intellectual" playwright. He would, in fact, never become quite comfortable with that mantle. Miller has never been an intellectual playwright in the sense of Jean Genet in *The Balcony* (1960) or Edward Albee in *Tiny Alice* (1964): he is rarely concerned with the nature of being or reality, but rather with social issues. In the 1940s and 1950s, however, to be involved with social issues was to be an intellectual.

After his high school graduation, Miller worked for two and a half years at various jobs including a long stint at an auto supply warehouse, which becomes the setting for his one-act play, *A Memory of Two Mondays* (1955). Miller claims that, like Bert in that play, he saved thirteen dollars of his fifteen-dollar-a-week salary to pay for his college education. During this time, Miller was also a crooner for a small Brooklyn radio station, but his growing love for Dostoyevski led to a new and successful application to the University of Michigan.

At Michigan, Miller supplemented his income with various jobs: first as a mouse tender in a university laboratory and then as a night editor on the *Michigan Daily*. Miller began to write plays while he was at college and won two of the university's five-hundred-dollar Hopwood play writing awards for *Honors at Dawn* (1936) and *No Villain* (1937). *No Villain*, revised as *They Too Arise* (and revised again later as *The Grass Still Grows*), won the Theatre Guild Award for 1938, and the cash prize of $1250 encouraged Miller to become engaged to Mary Grace Slattery, whom he married in 1940. Miller was briefly associated with the Federal Theatre Project, which paid promising young playwrights a wage for working on plays. He expected to have

a play of his produced by the project, but the program was curtailed before production could begin. At this time, he also wrote half-hour radio scripts for such shows as "The Cavalcade of America" and the "Columbia Workshop." Miller found the radio plays useful for learning dialogue, but he also felt severely limited by the special demands of the shows. He complained that because of the producers' notion of what the audience could understand, there could be no subtlety of characterization, "every emotion in a radio script has to have a tag."

In 1944 Miller toured army camps as a researcher, gathering background material for the filming of Ernie Pyle's *Story of GI Joe* (1945). Miller turned his research into a wartime journal called *Situation Normal,* which was published that year. He worked hard to keep his journal free of the flag-waving patriotism that was the stuff of most Hollywood treatments of the war effort. As he toured such places as Fort Dix, Camp Croft, and Fort Benning, he became increasingly concerned with the soldiers' thinking about the aims of war. His description of a GI back from New Georgia in the southwest Pacific is a striking revelation of the new perceptions brought to the average American soldier by a life in combat.

Miller's first Broadway play, *The Man Who Had All the Luck,* opened in 1944 but ran for only four performances. The play was almost universally panned by the critics, who punned unmercifully on the title, though most saw promise in the young playwright if he could keep his characters from so much speech making. The play tells the story of a young garage mechanic, David Beeves (David Frieber in the published version), for whom everything always turns out right. Instead of rejoicing in his luck, however, David becomes more and more frightened because he cannot believe he deserves the gifts fate has handed him. He keeps hoping for small doses of trouble because he firmly believes in the notion of compensation—an idea put forth in Emerson's essay of the same name—according to which the good and the bad in life are ultimately doled out equally.

David's luck is not only incredible, but everything seems connected as if the fates could undo the string with one tug. His garage becomes a success when the state decides to put a highway next to it. His real test as a mechanic comes when he is brought a rare car, a Marmon, for repair. Although he does not know how to fix the Marmon, a Viennese refugee mechanic (and philosopher) happens along to give him instructions. The Marmon, in turn, helps David win the girl he loves when it accidentally runs over the girl's father as he is on his way to shoot David because the father opposes the couple's marriage. For a time David fears that his unborn child will be the gods' chance for revenge, but despite a nasty fall she has taken, his wife gives birth to the healthy boy he wished for. David then lets his luck ride on a decision to develop a mink ranch, seeing this as an operation that can be governed by no other force than luck. At this point, he is no longer trying to earn a living, but rather, deliberately tempting the gods.

In *The Man Who Had All the Luck* a basic Miller plot is established: the rivalry of two brothers for the affection of the father. The father has given all his love to David's brother in the hope of making the brother a baseball star and has kept the boy in the basement from age ten learning how to pitch. When the brother ascends from his cellar to the real world of baseball, he cannot cope with men on base and fails in his attempt to become a major leaguer. David cannot understand why he has succeeded while his brother, for all his effort, has failed.

In addition to his brother, David is confronted by a cynic in a wheelchair who argues that man is no more than a jellyfish unable to control his fate. This philosophy is countered by the Viennese mechanic who argues that man is free when he works. David seems to prove this point when for the first time he succeeds by dint of his own efforts and not by luck: he saves the minks by picking all the silk worms, poisonous to minks, off the fish the minks eat. The only problem with this treatment of the hard-work philosophy is that the baseball-playing brother works just as hard as David and yet he fails. With the hindsight gained from Miller's later plays, one would have to believe that the secret reason David succeeds is not because of hard work but because his father has favored his brother. This rivalry for the affection of a parent remains in force throughout Miller's work, down to *The Creation of the World and Other Business* (1972) where the ultimate fraternal rivals, Cain and Abel, struggle because Eve loves Abel best.

In 1945 Miller turned out *Focus*, a rather successful (90,000 copies) novel about anti-Semitism. The title refers to the metamorphosis the hero undergoes when he gets a new pair of glasses. Not only does he begin to see things more clearly, but everyone else sees him differently as well: Newman, a gentile, looks like a Jew with his glasses on, and people begin to suspect that his real name is Neumann. He is a basically timid man who is afraid of his colleagues at work, afraid of women, afraid of his neighbors. The novel opens when Newman ignores the cries of a rape victim because she has a foreign accent, and he rationalizes that a foreign woman out so late could only be a prostitute. He takes the same attitude to the office where he works in the personnel department identifying Jewish job applicants.

When his glasses make him look too Jewish, Newman is relegated to a clerical desk in a corner. He quits in outrage, but finds that he cannot find another job until he goes to a Jewish firm. While Newman is facing the pressures of anti-Semitism at work, his neighbors are forming a vigilante committee against the presence of Finklestein, a Jewish grocer in their community. Although he is involved in the passive phase of this anti-Semitism, Newman, spurred on by his own experiences with Jew-haters, acts to save Finklestein from night raiders. At the end of the novel, Newman redeems himself by taking up a baseball bat and coming to Finklestein's aid.

The novel is melodramatic with Newman's shifts in character overstated throughout, but two major themes of Miller's later plays surface here. The first, man's responsibility for all of his fellowmen, is clearly delineated in Miller's next play, *All My Sons* (1947), and a more specific aspect of that theme—all men are responsible for and have a share in the suffering of the Jews—becomes the central concern of *Incident at Vichy* and an important side issue in *After the Fall*, both produced in 1964.

Miller's first successful play, *All My Sons*, bears the stamp of Ibsen's influence in its style, its theme, and even its plot. Miller aimed the play's realism at a broad-based audience and deliberately excised all the bookishness of his early drafts. He changed, for example, the play's original title, "The Sign of the Archer" (a reference to Kate's interest in astrology), because it was too literary. He made the dialogue of *All My Sons* as plain as possible to fit both the blue-collar Keller household and nineteenth-century theories of realism. The play is "well-made" in the nineteenth-century sense of the term as well, with neatly articulated crises leading to an overwhelming crisis.

Miller notes that his treatment of chronology is modeled on Ibsen's method of having characters spend much of the present discussing the past. The closest parallel is Ibsen's *The Wild Duck* (1884) where every action in the present works toward a revelation of the past. Because Miller found this talky exposition of past events one of the most artificial devices of dramatic realism, he experi-

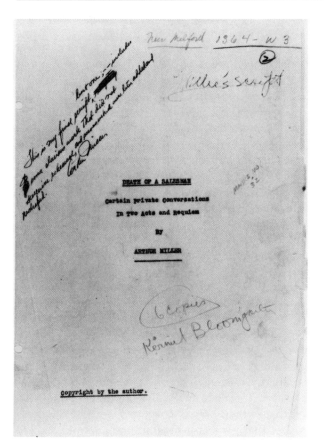

Title page of the penultimate typescript for Death of a Salesman *(Harry Ransom Humanities Research Center, University
of Texas at Austin)*

mented in his next play, *Death of a Salesman*, to work
out problems of exposition more fluidly.

The thematic concerns of *All My Sons* are also
Ibsen's. Like Gregers Werle in *The Wild Duck*, Chris
Keller is an idealist who insists on dredging up the
past so that the truth may set everyone free. As in
Ibsen's play, the revelation of the truth destroys
everyone it is supposed to cleanse. The secret hidden in the past is basically the same as that which
plagues Gregers's father in *The Wild Duck*. Chris's
father, Joe Keller, has sent the air force the defective engine parts which caused the deaths of
twenty-one flyers; then he left his partner to take
the blame. The father's guilt is magnified because
his eldest son, Larry, is a pilot who is missing and
presumed dead. Although Larry did not fly one of
the defective P-40s, his death becomes central to
the moral crisis of the story.

Although Ibsen is considered a dramatic realist, he continually imposed symbols on the realistic
surface of his plays, particularly by using commonplace details to make thematic statements about his

characters. So, for example, when Hjalmar Ekdal
in *The Wild Duck* is first seen at his occupation of
retouching photographs, Ibsen suggests that this is
a man who does not like the truth as it is. Miller
accomplishes the same task with the casual prop of
a newspaper. Joe Keller resolutely refuses to read
the news because he fears finding the truth. Instead, he reads the want ads because his life is based
on his belief that he is pursuing the life that every
American wants. Chris, on the other hand, reads
the book section, which hints that he is an intellectual until it is revealed that he reads the reviews
but never the books themselves: he is someone who
wants to appear knowledgeable about the finer
things in life, though he has no acquaintance with
their substance.

The most important symbol in *All My Sons* is
the apple tree planted as a memorial to Larry. A
storm has blown the tree down the night before
the action of the play begins, and everyone's ideal
memory of Larry will also be destroyed in the play.
When Chris, dressed in his best pants, is seen saw-
ing off the remains of the tree, it is clear that he is
trying to remove the dominant presence Larry still
has on his family. Chris's mother, Kate, warns him
that he will soil his good pants, and his attempt to
expunge Larry's memory does cast mud on Chris's
self-image.

At first, the play's theme seems to pit the relentless honesty of Chris Keller, who also is a World
War II veteran, against the crass pragmatism of his
father and the maudlin sentimentality of his
mother. This theme is echoed in the life of a neighbor, a doctor who dreams of doing selfless research
like Don Ameche in a Warner Brothers movie, but
yields instead to his wife's demands that he make
more money. The doctor's discomfort in Chris's
presence seems to reflect his own failure to live up
to his beliefs the way Chris has to his. As the action
progresses, however, the neatly opposed values
within the Keller household turn out to be more
complex than expected.

The first crack in Chris's idealistic armor appears when he refuses to let his father change the
company's name to Keller and Son. Although he
wants to believe his father is innocent, Chris knows
Joe is guilty. He also knows that his conscience will
force him to leave the company if he admits his
father's guilt to himself. Keeping his name off the
plant is Chris's halfhearted way of disassociating
himself from his father's act.

Kate, the mother, appears to use astrology
unrealistically to prove that her son Larry is not
dead. She reads the stars to prevent Chris from

marrying Larry's former girlfriend. Her argument is that allowing the marriage would be an admission of Larry's death. As it turns out, Kate is protecting the fiction of Larry's survival not for her own sentimental reasons but because she knows her husband would blame himself for Larry's death, even though the defective airplane part is not directly responsible. Kate realizes that the hope of Larry's survival is all that allows Joe to live with his guilt.

Chris's investigation of the past unearths more truth than anyone can bear. A letter from Larry to Ann, his former girlfriend and now Chris's fiancée, proves to be the key to the mystery, conveying more than anyone expects it to. Ann introduces it at first to prove to Kate that Larry is dead so that she will give the young people her blessing to marry. Chris doesn't know the contents of the letter except that, according to Ann, it establishes once and for all that Larry is dead. He reads it aloud to his father without having read it himself and then realizes that he has gone too far: in the letter Larry announces that he will commit suicide because he knows his father was responsible for the defective parts and therefore for the deaths of his brothers-in-arms. This direct blame for his son's death is too much for Joe Keller. While Chris, idealistic to the last, is insisting to Kate, "once and for all you can know there's a universe of people and you're responsible to it, and unless you know that you threw away your son because that's why he died," Joe goes into the house and shoots himself. Chris's last words recognize the enormity of his error in demanding the whole truth: "Mother, I didn't mean to—"

Earlier in the play, Chris, a war hero, speaks effusively about dying for one's fellowman in Europe when honor made a difference. Miller questions whether it is as easy to live for one's fellowman as it is to die for him. Also haunting Chris is the fact that he is still alive while others, including his brother, who fought in the war are dead. This theme of the guilt of those who escape is central in *The Man Who Had All the Luck,* and it reappears in *After the Fall* as well.

Although the men in the play seem tough-minded at first and the women merely dreamers, it turns out that Kate and Ann are the only ones willing to face reality in all its ugliness. They may try to shield their men from the truth, but they never hide it from themselves. Their great virtue lies not only in knowing the truth but also, like Regina Ekdal in *The Wild Duck,* in knowing how much of it ought to be suppressed. Linda in *Death*

of *a Salesman* and Beatrice in *A View from the Bridge* (1955) have much the same quality.

When *All My Sons* won the New York Drama Critics Circle Award in 1947, Miller was established as an important young playwright, particularly since the competition included Eugene O'Neill's *The Iceman Cometh.* In retrospect, the critics' choice seems somewhat off the mark; Miller's work is a solid piece and an important milestone in his career, but it is not a match for O'Neill's masterpiece.

The critics may just have been foresighted. Miller's next play, which won their award in 1949, was comparable to O'Neill at his best. *Death of a Salesman* was that wonder of wonders, a masterpiece that came easily. The play tells how its protagonist, Willy Loman, a middle-class salesman whose youth is but a memory, decides to end his life. He is loved by his wife, Linda, and he has two sons, Biff and Happy, whom he has tried to raise to become men of influence and power. Biff, the older son, now in his thirties, has not lived up to Willy's expectations, goals which were set when Biff was a high school football hero. When Biff's plans to borrow money to go into a sporting goods business fail, he confronts Willy with his version of the truth and then breaks down and weeps. Willy feels at last that his son loves him and commits suicide in the automobile so that Biff can have the life insurance money.

The basic script was turned out in six weeks when Miller went off to a small house that he had built with his own hands on some property in Connecticut. Miller's skill with tools is an ability he shares with his hero, but Willy Loman can never turn his mechanical ability into part of a positive self-concept. Almost everything he owns breaks down in the course of the play, but Willy is too busy being a salesman to fix anything. Though the writing of *Death of a Salesman* came easily, the same was not true of the backing. Angels shied away from the pessimistic title, the radical plans for staging, and the revolutionary set design of Joe Mielziner. Mielziner's set played a major part in making the journey into Willy's memory believable. After *The Man Who Had All the Luck* Miller became convinced that shifting scenery was one of the quickest ways to turn the audience's attention from the dramatic focus of the play. He wanted a set where characters could move through time and space without moving props. As he conceived of the play, exposition would become part of the action on stage and not a story told by one of the characters, Mielziner, who had just come from designing the set for *A Streetcar Named Desire,* where lighting had played an impor-

tant part in distinguishing the brutal Stanley Kowalski from the fragile Blanche Dubois,
constructed a set in which the skeleton of Willy's
house became all the places called for in the play—
not only the house itself, but also a business office,
a hotel room, a restaurant, and finally the cemetery.
An arbitrary convention neatly separated the present from the past: characters from the present observed the wall lines and used the doors to enter
the room, while characters from the past walked
through the "walls."

The lighting of the play, particularly the use
of various kinds of magic lantern shows, allowed
instant changes in time and place that would have
taken minutes in a conventional set. The return to
the glory days of Biff's youth, for example, was
signaled by projecting a springlike, leafy green pattern on walls and furniture. The apartment houses
that hem in Willy's home in his old age were produced by back lighting so they could be removed
to suggest the earlier, more hopeful days.

The set helped establish the dual quality of
the play, which is both a realistic study of the decline of one man, and at the same time, a symbolic
presentation of the pursuit of the American dream.
Miller set out to be nothing less than a modern
Sophocles of everyday man in this play. His essay
"Tragedy and the Common Man" suggests that
Willy, the "low man" on life's totem pole, is the
Oedipus for this generation: "I think the tragic
feeling is evoked in us when we are in the presence
of a character who is ready to lay down his life, if
need be, to secure one thing—his sense of personal
dignity." Critics have denied that Miller established
Willy's dignity on the grounds presented in the
essay and suggest that Willy's fate is perhaps pathetic. Miller, distinguishing a lesser form from
tragedy, argues that "pathos rules where . . . a character fought a battle he could not possibly have
won." Many critics do not believe that Willy could
have fulfilled his dream.

The American dream and its delusions are
everywhere. Though the present time of the play
takes place in Brooklyn, all parts of the United
States are continually invoked. Willy is the New
England man for his company, an explorer who
has opened up the territory for them, and his son
Biff has followed Horace Greeley's classic advice to
"go west, young man!," though with less sanguine
results than Greeley foresaw. Biff loves the outdoors and hates offices, and so his father's plans
for Biff's becoming a big shot are foiled when Biff
works on a ranch. Biff's trip west is a sure sign he
will never become a Southern gentleman and

scholar-athlete at Thomas Jefferson's University of
Virginia, a school he cannot enter because he failed
his senior math class. Willy's father, like Willy's
brother Ben more myth than man, is the archetypal
Yankee peddler peddling the products of his imagination across the land: "he'd drive the team right
across the country; through Ohio, and Indiana,
Michigan, Illinois . . . stop in the towns and sell the
flutes that he'd made on the way." This is the
dream; the reality is less inspiring: whipped American cheese—an adulteration of an already proc-
essed "food product," cars and appliances that
break down before they are paid for, and the tape-
recorded voice of Willy's boss's son naming the cap-
itals of all the states. Pathetically the boy's mechanical voice becomes the prelude to Willy's being
fired.

There are two incarnations of the successful
American dream in the play: Willy's brother Ben
and a salesman named Dave Singleman. Ben is the
man who succeeds without working; he has all the
luck. There is no sense that Ben is a real character,
but only a representation of the dream of instant
wealth and success: he heads for Alaska, but gets
his directions mixed up and accidentally ends up
in Africa where he stumbles on diamond mines. A
dream figure of Ben offers to take Willy on his
next venture to Alaska, but Willy refuses; he has
his own version of this ideal: "The whole wealth of
Alaska passes over the lunch table at the Com-
modore Hotel, and that's the wonder, the wonder
of this country, that a man can end up with diamonds here on the basis of being liked!"

Willy's dream of success then is to end up like
Ben, but not by any fanciful journeys to Darkest
Africa or frozen Alaska, but by selling himself. It
is significant that the audience is never told what
Willy sells because, as he makes clear, his real product is himself. This makes the need to sell far more
important and personal than would otherwise be
imagined. The inability to sell means there is something wrong, not with the product, but with the
salesman. Willy ties up both his self-image and his
manhood in his career. His standard of being well
liked is not a casual thing, but the basis of his identity. His memory of Dave Singleman is a description
of a life well lived: "What could be more satisfying
than to be able to go, at the age of eighty-four, into
twenty or thirty different cities, and pick up a
phone, and be remembered and loved by so many
different people? . . . when he died—and by the
way he died the death of a salesman, in his green
velvet slippers in the smoker of the New York, New
Haven and Hartford, going into Boston—when he

died, hundreds of salesmen and buyers were at his funeral." This funeral serves as a contrast to Willy's own at the end of the play, attended by no one except his immediate family and Willy's friend Charley. Instead of making the contrast merely ironical, Miller reminds us of the love Willy has inspired despite his faults. Charley insists: "He's a man way out there in the blue, riding on a smile and a shoeshine. . . . A salesman is got to dream, boy. It comes with the territory."

Most of Willy's frustrating encounters with the American dream occur before the present time of the play. In the present he is occupied with finding some legacy to pass on to his sons, Biff and Hap. This becomes nearly impossible when, at age sixty-two, Willy is fired. After years of wandering, Biff has returned and Willy dreams of his two boys going into business for themselves. In Mielziner's expressive set, which turned the boy's beds into secret elevators, the two boys are apparently sleeping in full view of the audience when they make an entrance dressed as teenagers. From this early point on, the audience accepts the rapid transitions in time as the play moves in and out of Willy's memories of his relationships with his sons, particularly with Biff.

Willy never stops selling himself, and selling means improving the product—making it sound better than it is. His reports of his selling trips, even on his best days, are always exaggerations. The step to outright lies is only a small one, and Hap inherits this trait from his father. Biff goes along with Willy's petty cheating until he discovers that Willy has cheated even on his own wife. From this point on, Biff uses petty thievery, not to get ahead, but to guarantee his own failure.

The more Willy's salesmanship falters, the more it becomes not merely a proof of his identity but a test of his masculinity as well. Willy continually asserts his manhood, both through Biff's athletic prowess and through his own ability to use tools. He continually denigrates his friend Charley, and Charley's son Bernard, for being unmanly. Charley cannot work with his hands, and Bernard is in short pants too long. The major crisis of the past time of the play turns on Willy's confusion of salesmanship and masculinity.

When Biff is unable to graduate from high school because he has failed a math test given by a teacher he had previously antagonized by mimicking him, he turns to Willy for help. Biff has been following in his father's path, looking for the easy way, so instead of preparing to go to summer school he goes to Boston hoping his father can talk the

teacher out of flunking him. Meanwhile, Willy, already losing his touch as a salesman, has seduced a buyer not so much for the seduction itself, but to prove he is still a man. When Biff finds the two of them together, suddenly all of the cheating that Willy has condoned—taking materials from construction sites, copying a classmate's homework, permanently borrowing basketballs from school—becomes reprehensible. For Biff the worst thing about Willy's affair in Boston is that he has given nylon stockings to the woman while Biff's long-suffering mother has had to repair her old stockings.

Since Biff now equates success with dishonesty, he refuses to succeed and wanders from job to job, always leaving when he has a chance to get ahead. As a way of insuring failure, he steals something from his employers. In the present time of the play, Biff steals a pen from a man who might back him and his brother, which dooms Willy's dream of the two boys becoming salesmen of athletic equipment.

Just as entrapped in his father's twisted ideals is Hap, the son who has remained at home. He has become a salesman like his father, but he has debased the notion of selling himself so that the dream behind it is gone—only the technique is left. Hap is almost a parody of his father, but like his brother Biff, he ruins everything he has a chance of completing. Instead of stealing things, Hap steals the women of the men he works for. Hap as "salesman" is seen at work when he picks up a girl in the restaurant. The pickup is an exchange of facades. Hap passes himself off as a champagne salesman and his has-been brother as a football star, while an obvious bar girl passes herself off as a model. The scene is a prelude to one of the cruelest pieces of business in modern stage history. The restaurant was to be the scene for the triumphant announcement that Biff has gotten backing for the boys' new career. Instead, when Willy arrives, Biff not only announces that he has failed, but then he and Hap go off with their girls when Willy goes off sick to the bathroom. Willy's horror is multiplied when—through Miller's use of surrealistic techniques—Willy's memory of events with the buyer in the Boston hotel room impinges upon his present distress.

The boys' desertion leads to a tremendous argument about the lies that have been told in the house, but finally the barriers that have been built up for so long between Willy and Biff are broken down, and father and son are reunited. This brings Willy back to his original problem of providing a legacy for his boys. He decides that only by suicide can he leave his boys anything. The suicide also appeals to him because he expects a grand funeral like Dave Singleman's. Such a funeral will prove to his boys that he was well liked: "All the old-timers with the strange license plates—that boy will be thunderstruck, Ben, because he never realized—I am known!"

The failure of the funeral to turn out like this suggests that Willy may also be wrong about the insurance paying off. The audience is never told whether or not it does, but the company would not pay the family if it could establish that Willy's death was a suicide. Furthermore it is not certain whether or not Willy paid the overdue premium on the insurance, though Miller makes his borrowing the money for it into an important scene. Despite the likelihood that Willy's plan to leave a cash legacy for his boys has failed, it seems proper to see his death as tragic rather than pathetic. Acting destructively because of misconceived ideals is the stuff of tragedy, particularly in Shakespeare and Ibsen. Brutus, Othello, and Hedda Gabler are no more

able to right things through their tragic deaths than is Willy Loman.

The critical and financial triumph of *Death of a Salesman* catapulted Miller into the front rank of American dramatists. The play won Miller's second Drama Critics Circle Award and a Pulitzer Prize in 1949. The royalties for *All My Sons* had paid for Miller's house in Brooklyn, but with Miller's characteristic disdain for props, it had remained half-furnished. The more than two-year run of *Death of a Salesman* furnished the house handsomely. In addition to the royalties for the Broadway production, there were two road companies that performed the play, soon to become a movie, and, perhaps most lucrative of all, a part of the repertory of almost every local theater in the country.

In 1950 Miller's adaptation of Ibsen's *An Enemy of the People* was produced on Broadway. The work strengthened Miller's already strong ties to Ibsen, but it also signaled his interest in a new type of hero. Up to this point Miller's heroes dissipated their energies in the pursuit of misguided ideals. For the most part, Ibsen's heroes are of this mold

Scene from the first production of Death of a Salesman, *starring Lee J. Cobb as Willie Loman (Billy Rose Theatre Collection, New York Public Library at Lincoln Center, Astor, Lenox and Tilden Foundations)*

as well, but Peter Stockmann's courage in the face of his town's moral cowardice needs no defensive explanation like that which Charley gives for Willy Loman at Willy's funeral. Stockmann is a doctor who refuses to permit the town to build a spa after he finds disease in the water supply. He becomes the town's enemy because his rectitude threatens its profits. The chief action of the play is the gradual turning of the entire town against a man who was once one of its most respected citizens.

A hero of this kind emerges in Miller's next play, *The Crucible* (1953). Although John Proctor has his weaknesses, they seem more like classical tragic flaws than the skewed idealism of Willy Loman or Chris Keller. At the end of the play, the audience has no sense at all that the hero's death has been an empty gesture.

The Crucible is set during the Salem witchcraft trials and the analogies with Senator Joseph McCarthy's "witch-hunts" for Communists were immediately perceived by the critics. Miller's comments on the play at this time encouraged such comparisons and the play's relevance becomes even more striking a few years later because Miller himself was called (in 1956) before the House Committee on Un-American Activities. In a classic case of life imitating art, Miller took the precise position Proctor took before his Puritan judges. Just as Proctor is willing to implicate himself but refuses to name other dabblers with witchcraft, so Miller named himself, but refused to identify any others involved in Communist-front activities.

Despite the contemporary relevance, the historic setting of the play brought about a change in the style of Miller's language. His first three plays are filled with the naturalistic dialogue of the American middle class, but the setting in Puritan New England allows Miller to use a much more formal pattern of speech. Miller sees his style in this play as more poetic than anything else he has done. Although at times the dialogue seems leaden, Miller for the most part makes exemplary use of this new style, its biblical echoes, its metaphorical richness, and its ethical basis. One could hardly imagine Proctor's speech denouncing his own lechery couched in modern English.

Like *An Enemy of the People*, *The Crucible* is about making moral choices in the face of community pressure and about the irrational basis of that pressure. In fact, for most of the play, the audience's emotion is more involved in the growing witch-hunt hysteria than in Proctor's taking a moral position against it. Miller promoted emphasis on the mass hysteria when he excised Proctor's con-

frontation with Abigail from the printed version of the play. In this scene, Abigail sees herself purified from sin by the purgatorial fire of their passion. Her unshakable faith in passionate love makes Proctor uncertain that she is acting out of hypocrisy. Since Proctor's sense of guilt and consequent moral uncertainty stem from his adulterous relations with Abigail, removal of the scene changes the play from Proctor's tragedy to the community's crime. Most productions since the 1958 off-Broadway run, most significantly Olivier's London production in 1965, have omitted the scene.

Since his concern is with the sources of the madness which was plaguing his own time as well as that of the Puritans, Miller explores the multifaceted causes for the growth of the witch-hunt. The first sources, social or economic, are rational. Reverend Parris, the village minister, finds it useful to explain his daughter's indecent behavior by attributing it to witchcraft rather than to his own inability to raise her properly, and Mr. Putnam, the town's richest man, finds great advantage in having his rival landowners charged with witchcraft. Because of her testimony, Abigail Williams, a serving girl and something of a slut, raises herself to a position of power in the town. As the fever grows, however, its sources lie more and more in the irrationality of the human psyche as both individual and mass hysteria take over the town. Paranoia surfaces: Mrs. Putnam's unfocused despair over the loss of her infants in childbirth turns to a more comforting hatred of Rebecca Nurse. Both Mrs. Putnam and Reverend Parris see a kind of inverse election in being tormented by the devil. Miller very convincingly describes the "positive" effects of paranoia. The "victims" of the witches begin to value themselves more highly than those who have been left alone, since it comforts them to know that someone, even Satan, is constantly watching out for them. The culmination of the mass hysteria occurs when the girls of Salem, egged on by the calculated deceptions of Abigail, truly believe that they see the devil in the form of a gigantic bird.

Miller also observes the tremendous force that mere accusation had at this time, something that was evident as well in the McCarthy witch-hunts. A man's career could be ruined if he were merely asked, "Are you now or have you ever been a member of the Communist party?" The power of accusation is seen in the town's reaction to the charges made by two servants, Abigail, who deliberately uses accusation for her own purposes, and Mary Warren, a timid girl who is overwhelmed by the great prominence she gains simply by accusing people of greater stature in the community. Mary's transformation is more interesting than Abigail's because she is a basically good, honest person who struggles against the power that the trials suddenly give her. In his revision of the play, Miller pays much more attention to Mary than Abigail, precisely because he wants to show how good men, even when wanting to do right, yield to the pressure of the group.

The growing corruption of much of the community is balanced by a number of characters who grow in self-understanding and courage as the excesses of the tribunal continue. The most radical change is in Reverend Hale, who comes to Salem as a certifier of witchcraft and finally realizes the horror he is helping to perpetrate. He loses his convictions when he confronts the twisted logic of the chief judge, Deputy Governor Danforth. Hale, once a cold man of principle, ends up by asserting: "Life is God's most precious gift; no principle however glorious, may justify the taking of it." A similar change occurs in Proctor's wife, Elizabeth, who comes to recognize how her denial of life has contributed to the disasters in the town and in her household. She has blamed her husband for his sexual misconduct and ultimately realizes that her own coldness is to a large extent responsible for his behavior. Both learn the strength they possess in the love they share, but in an ironic conclusion, Elizabeth, who has never lied in her life, lies for her husband when he needs her to tell the truth: Proctor can escape from the tribunal by proving Abigail is a harlot; Elizabeth, now reconciled with her husband, lies about his affair with Abigail because she believes that he is being charged with lechery.

In the topsy-turvy world created by the witch-hunts, lies and the truth cease to have their accustomed values. Giles Corey, whose farm Putnam covets, finds himself in an untenable position once accused of witchcraft. If he denies the charge he will be hanged, but if he accepts the charge he will lose all legal rights and therefore his property. Instead of answering the tribunal's indictment, Corey submits to the torture of pressing. He is crushed to death, but his silence protects his farm for his sons.

In a complex decision, Proctor decides to lie to save his life. His choice is not made out of cowardice but for two other reasons. First of all, because of his adultery and his failure to live an exemplary life, he finds himself unworthy of sharing the martyrdom of the others whose ideal behavior makes their refusal to confess saintly.

Second, he feels that he owes his wife the life of love they have not shared up to this point. She was willing to lie for him; now he will give up his honor for her. Proctor signs his confession, but refuses to confess that he knows of anyone else who has dealings with the devil. His judges grudgingly accept this limited confession, but when Proctor realizes the document will be used as propaganda to make other men confess, he tears the pardon and marks himself for the gallows.

Miller felt that both the audience and the critics were very uncomfortable with the theme of witch-hunting in the McCarthy era. *The Crucible* opened to polite, lukewarm reviews: "it got respectful notices, the kind that bury you decently," and after a run of a few months it closed. The play was very popular in Europe, however, and Miller was planning to attend the Brussels opening in 1954 when he was denied a passport by the State Department. The denial of the passport was just the beginning of Miller's troubles with the government over his alleged leftist sympathies. *The Crucible* was revived off Broadway in 1958 to glowing praise from the same critics who yawned over it five years earlier. This production ran for more than six hundred performances and established *The Crucible* as the second most popular play in the Miller canon.

In 1955 Miller brought two one-act plays, *A Memory of Two Mondays* and *A View from the Bridge*, to Broadway on the same bill. The plays were completely different in tone and theme. *A Memory of Two Mondays* is a nostalgic glance at Miller's teenage years about which he says that nothing "was written with greater love," while *A View from the Bridge* is a taut tragedy, like "some re-enactment of a Greek myth which was ringing a long-buried bell in my own subconscious mind." In 1956 Miller expanded *A View from the Bridge* into a two-act play that opened in London under the direction of Peter Brook.

A Memory of Two Mondays is an impressionistic view of Miller's days as a stock clerk in an auto supply house after he graduated from high school. The Miller figure, an eighteen-year-old boy named Bert, is different from the rest of the workers because he will get out of the petty microcosm that is the life of others. "It is a little world, a home to which, unbelievably perhaps, these people like to come every Monday morning, despite what they say." The play is made up of two scenes six months apart, one in summer, the other in winter. The events of the two days are similar, but the impression each day gives is very different. In the first scene, the small triumphs and tragedies of life seem rich. In the central business of the scene all of the workers combine to protect one of their number, a drunk, from being fired. In their charade, Bert courageously and cleverly outwits the boss. The characters seem imbued with a strength and dignity that go beyond their petty stations in life: the slightly lecherous advances of an old man seem to be the energy of life; a man with the ability to find a part for an antique auto seems almost the keeper of the racial memory; and Bert's determination to read Tolstoy's *War and Peace* on the subway appears to be the triumph of intellect over circumstance. All of the characters seem filled with hope about new cars, getting married, or even next weekend's date.

An important device for changing mood is the lighting, which shifts in the middle of the play from warm summery tones to cold wintry ones. All of the hopes of the first half of the play are quashed. The new car has proven too expensive to run; the old lecher has lost his wife and his energy; the weekend date has turned into a tawdry affair between a woman who is losing her youth and a married man. Although the drunk of the first scene is reformed, he has become joyless in his triumph over alcohol, while a poetry-spouting Irishman of the first scene has become the new alcoholic, with liquor-scrambled brains incapable of retaining the fourth line of a verse. Bert, whose departure for college should be the hope of the play, still has not finished reading his epic novel and there seems little chance that he ever will. More upsetting is the fact that no one seems to care about his departure and that in six months his existence will be forgotten altogether.

One of the notions Miller stressed is how the survival of this community even at a very minimal level depends upon its insularity. Bert and the poetic Irishman take it upon themselves to clean the filthy windows of the warehouse with the hope of brightening things up. Instead, the view of the world outside, including a run-down whorehouse, makes the workers less content with their lot. Like Gregers Werle in Ibsen's *The Wild Duck*, Bert's attempt to bring light only calls attention to the dirt.

In "Tragedy and the Common Man" Miller argues that it is possible to write tragedy in the classic Greek mode about the plight of modern man. Though the essay was written almost immediately after *Death of a Salesman*, it is in *A View from the Bridge* that Miller creates his contemporary classical tragedy. The tense conflict of loyalties in the play's protagonist, Eddie Carbone, reveals the same undiscovered passion and misconception of events in an essentially good man that is at the heart of *Oedipus Rex*. Eddie fits Miller's definition of the tragic hero in "his inherent unwillingness to remain passive in the face of what he conceives to be a challenge to his dignity, his image of his rightful status."

A View from the Bridge, set in the Italian-American community in Brooklyn, New York, presents Eddie's downfall coming about as the result of his incestuous longing for his young niece, Catherine, who lives with him and his wife Beatrice. Because he is so jealous of her, he cannot abide her growing interest in other men. When Catherine is attracted to an illegal alien, Rodolpho, Eddie, who is also Italian, betrays Rodolpho to the immigration authorities, precipitating his own fatal confrontation with Rodolpho's brother Marco.

The play is narrated by Eddie's lawyer Alfieri, a calm and reasonable man who perceives basic passions accurately. Alfieri functions like the chorus of a Greek play: he provides commentary on the action but is unable to stop its inevitable flow. Similarly the immigration officers are just as implacable as the Furies that hound Orestes. Furthermore the Italian-American community provides the necessarily rigid system of values which allows classical tragedy to take so precisely the measure of man: violating the laws of the community is just as dangerous to Eddie as Oedipus's trying to spurn the oracle at Delphi. The existence of the community and its code makes Eddie's betrayal of Marco and Rodolpho not merely a personal vendetta but a rupture in the order of things.

When *A View from the Bridge* was first produced on Broadway as a one-act play, it nearly foundered on Miller's insistence that Eddie's conflict with his world be presented as the spare collision of two forces. The telegraphic diction and nonnaturalistic style of acting left the audiences cold. Miller was trying to counter what he perceived to be the prevailing romanticism on Broadway, but he could not find a way to make Eddie's Brooklyn accent formal. The right style for the play was found, somewhat accidentally, when Peter Brook put it on in London with actors accustomed to playing Shakespeare. Their inability to capture the Brooklyn dialect combined with their training in playing larger-than-life roles to give the commonplace world of the community of Red Hook the stature of ancient Thebes. For the two-act London production, Miller expanded the role of Eddie's wife, Beatrice, adding a dimension of sympathy lacking in the one-act version.

Miller makes it clear that the Sicilian-American community in the shadow of the Brooklyn Bridge has grown up clinging to ancient codes of justice and revenge that are fully as exacting as those of Sophocles' Thebes. In the play the rules of the community are established early with the report of a disturbing incident: when a young boy betrays illegal immigrants ("submarines") staying in his father's house, he is beaten by his father and made an outcast by the community.

In Red Hook, there is no crime greater than treachery. As the play opens, the surface harmony of the Carbone household is about to be shattered by the arrival of Marco and Rodolpho, two other "submarines." The tension already in the house is seen in Eddie's relationship to his seventeen-year-old niece, Catherine. He has kept her from growing up—by keeping her in school, by not letting her go out with boys, by monitoring what she wears—ostensibly because he wants to do his best for his sister's child. Eddie is unwilling to face the real reason for his protectiveness: he has fallen in love with her. He refuses even to consider the possibility, though it is clear to Beatrice that Catherine's sexual maturity has destroyed their marriage. Since Eddie cannot admit to himself that he has betrayed his sister, he begins to project his guilt upon others, especially upon Rodolpho.

Marco, an ox of a man, has come to America to earn money for his family in Italy and plans to return, but Rodolpho has come to stay. Catherine falls in love with Rodolpho and Eddie begins to find fault with him. Like Othello, whose refusal to admit his own jealousy leads to incredible accusations, Eddie begins to see foulness everywhere because he will not see it in himself.

At first Eddie accuses Rodolpho of using Catherine as a "passport," marrying her so that he can stay in America because he is the husband of a citizen. When Catherine refuses to believe this allegation, Eddie raises a new specter: he suggests that Rodolpho, who likes to sing, sew, and cook, is a homosexual. With the issue of homosexuality, Miller shows how tragic events snowball from the protagonist's first mistake. The accusation is at first a logical maneuver on Eddie's part, much like Putnam and Parris's using accusations of witchcraft for their own advantage in *The Crucible*. Its purpose is to substantiate Eddie's claim that Rodolpho could be after Catherine only because he wants to stay in America. Little by little, Eddie's own manhood becomes tied up in the charge: the more he proves Rodolpho is not a man, the more Eddie can convince himself of his own manhood. Eddie is no longer a young man, and his sexual relations with his wife have deteriorated. For this reason, Rodolpho's youth threatens Eddie's virility and much of the last half of the play is a test of Eddie's manhood disguised as a test of Rodolpho's.

Miller begins to convert the verbal anger to physical conflict when Eddie teaches Rodolpho to box so that he can beat him up "fairly." Eddie stages the boxing lesson to parade his masculinity before Catherine, but it ends up differently from the way he expects. Marco picks up a heavy chair by one leg to demonstrate that he is strong enough to kill a man with his bare hands. The scene ends with Marco silently challenging Eddie to mock his brother a second time. Tension between the two fills the stage as the scene ends. In the inevitable flow of this tragedy, it is only a matter of time before Eddie will shame Rodolpho more brazenly and Marco will use his deadly hands.

In great tragedy, the smallest gesture can be earth shattering to the audience when they have been set up to make the tragic denouement unavoidable. For example, Othello's slapping Desdemona in front of her peers is perhaps more shocking than his murdering her in the privacy of their bedchamber. Miller sets up such a moment when, in rapid succession, Eddie kisses Catherine and then Rodolpho. The audience is astounded each time. When Eddie finds the two lovers coming from her bedroom, he kisses Catherine passionately. He cannot cope with this evidence of the lovers' intimacy, so he impugns Rodolphos's masculinity by offering Catherine a kiss meant to show her what a man's kiss is really like. Even at this point, Eddie will not admit that the kiss is an acknowledgment of his own passion rather than an object lesson for his niece. Eddie's self-deception is so great that he is genuinely shocked at the end of the play when Beatrice confronts him with the truth about his feelings for Catherine.

The implications of Eddie's second kiss are even more far reaching. Knowing how embarrassing such a kiss would be in the ultramasculine Sicilian community, Eddie kisses Rodolpho to shame him, perhaps hoping that Rodolpho will strike back and give Eddie an excuse to kill him. Eddie later tries to use the fact that Rodolpho cannot break out of his embrace as further proof of his homosexuality, arguing that he could have gotten free but that he did not want to. The kiss seems also to be the Sicilian kiss of death, Eddie's warning to Rodolpho that he means to destroy him, and finally, it is a Judas kiss, warning the audience that Eddie will betray Rodolpho.

Eddie's betrayal of Marco and Rodolpho must be bought at a terrible price. Like Creon in Sophocles' *Antigone,* Eddie calls on the law of the land to subvert a higher law. The difference is that Eddie's loyalties are with the law he rejects. The situation dictates that the tragic hero's crime extends far beyond the needs of his vengeance. Not merely does the betrayal ruin Rodolpho, but it also must destroy Marco, and therefore take the bread out of the mouths of Marco's children. Miller extends the crime against the community even further by planting two additional "submarines" in Eddie's building for the immigration authorities to find. Like Hamlet, who kills a half-dozen innocent people to carry out his revenge on Claudius, Eddie finds that fate can be pushed in a certain direction, but once started, its avalanche cannot be controlled. The price paid is, of course, not merely the unwitting destruction of others; Eddie is shamed before the community and inevitably killed by Marco. When Alfieri, Miller's narrator in the play, describes Eddie, he is also describing the quintessential Millerian hero—the man who may do things wrong but does them with every ounce of his being: "Most of the time now we settle for half and I like it better. But the truth is holy, and even as I know how wrong he was, and his death useless, I tremble, for I confess that something perversely pure calls to me from his memory—not purely good, but himself, purely, for he allowed himself to be wholly known and for that I think I will love him more than all my sensible clients."

A View from the Bridge won Miller his third Drama Critics Circle Award, and the production of the two one-act plays in 1955 marked the end of a fruitful eight-year period of play-writing. He was now to enter a nine-year period of personal and political problems that would keep him from finishing a new play until 1964.

In 1955 Miller was divorced from Mary Grace Slattery, and in the same year his troubles because of his leftist interests began in earnest. He had been working with the New York Youth Board on a film about juvenile delinquents when the American Legion and the Catholic War Veterans applied pressure to have the project dropped because of Miller's "Communist ties." He had, after all, been refused a passport the previous year as a "person believed to be supporting the Communist movement." The pressure by the two groups was successful and work on the film ceased.

Two years later, Miller was called before Representative Francis Walter's Committee on Un-American Activities. Miller chatted amiably with the committee members about his opinions on Ezra Pound, Elia Kazan, Howard Fast, Red China, and the repeal of the Smith Act, the 1940 law that made it a federal offense to advocate a violent overthrow of the government or to be a member of any group devoted to such advocacy. The committee was most cordial in discussing these matters with Miller, but then asked Miller about his attendance at a meeting of Communist writers in 1947. Miller refused to take the Fifth Amendment and freely admitted that he had been at the meeting, though he denied ever being a member of the Communist party. The committee then asked him to name other writers who were there. At this point, Miller, like Proctor in *The Crucible,* said that his conscience would not permit him to name any others. Since the committee already knew from other sources who had attended the meeting, it is clear that the questions were asked to see if Miller would implicate his colleagues. Proctor's judges too were not so much interested in knowing the names, but in having Proctor betray his fellows.

Because of his refusal to answer the committee's questions, Miller was put on trial for contempt of Congress. The judge decided that Miller's motives were commendable, but that his position was legally indefensible, and he found Miller guilty on two counts of contempt. Miller's sentencing was deferred pending an appeal. In the following year, 1958, Miller's conviction was overturned on a technicality by the U.S. Court of Appeals.

In 1956 Miller married Marilyn Monroe, sparking headlines of the "Pinko Playwright Weds Sex Goddess" variety. The marriage at first was more successful than the cynics predicted with Monroe almost reverent in the presence of her intellectual husband. She was tired of her "dumb blonde" roles and thought her marriage to Miller might end the typecasting: "If I was nothing but a dumb blonde, he wouldn't have married me." Despite her deference to his work habits, Miller soon fell into Monroe's orbit rather than vice versa. He became involved in her financial arrangements and her script choices, pushing her to make *Some Like It Hot,* her most successful movie. She was not particularly pleased, however, that Miller thought her perfect for the quintessential "dumb blonde" part of Sugar Kane. Miller also persuaded Yves Montand to star with her in *Let's Make Love.* Montand and his wife, Simone Signoret, had starred in a French production of *The Crucible,* and both were close friends of Miller's. The marriage began to founder as Monroe found herself unable to bear Miller's child. Though he seemed to be working constantly, Miller produced no new plays during their marriage. Eventually, he created a screenplay, *The Misfits*, as a vehicle for his wife. The screenplay is a revision of a short story he wrote soon after his divorce from Mary Grace Slattery. While in Nevada waiting for his divorce, Miller joined a group of cowboys who were rounding up mustangs to sell them for dog food. The mustangs, because they were too small to ride, were called "misfits." Miller was particularly impressed by the mechanization of the West as he watched the cowboys using trucks and light planes in their roundup. In his story, Miller tells of three such cowboys whose lives become as mechanized as the tools of their trade. Clearly they are as much misfits as the horses they pursue.

Marilyn Monroe's part of Roslyn, the dance hall girl, was grafted onto the original story. Roslyn identifies with the mustangs as fellow victims of life and ultimately convinces the cowboys to give up their work. Monroe was not happy with the part Miller wrote for her. She saw it as another "dumb blonde" role, with Roslyn using feminine rage instead of articulate logic to change the men's minds. "He was supposed to be writing this for me. He could have written me anything and he comes up with this. If that's what he thinks of me, well then I'm not for him and he's not for me," she complained. In addition to her quarreling with Miller over the roles he had created for her, she began to argue with him about whose picture it was. It had been written as a present for her after her last miscarriage, but Miller began to get angry with her for being late to the set of *his* picture. They left Hollywood separately and within the year (1961), they were divorced. The filming of *The Misfits* became even more traumatic for both of them when Clark Gable, who starred as Gay Langland, suffered a fatal heart attack on the last day of shooting. Miller attended the funeral, but Monroe did not.

When Miller rewrote his short story, he put some of his personal life into the part of Gay, who trades his freedom for married life with Roslyn. In the film the marriage marks the beginning of a new kind of responsible manhood. Miller says of Gay that he "has lived across the frontier all his life, but because he finally gets related to this woman, now he can choose something else—the gratification offered by their relationship." Perhaps Miller perceived this ideal in his relationship with Monroe, but the reality was something else. As she slid further and further into dependence on alcohol and drugs, he found himself unable to help her and frustrated by his inability to do so. Nonetheless

Miller had never worked harder on a project than on *The Misfits*, continually staying up after midnight, revising the script, trying to get Monroe's part right for the next day's shooting. Two months after the death of Gable, Monroe was in Mexico filing for divorce.

The Misfits would be Monroe's last film; after her divorce from Miller, she began to work on *Something's Got to Give*, a film for director George Cukor. The problems on the set escalated even beyond those on *The Misfits*, and Monroe left the set with her future in Hollywood up in the air. Two months later, on 4 August 1962, she was found dead from an overdose of sleeping pills. Joe DiMaggio arranged the funeral, barring all of Hollywood from the simple ceremony at Westwood Cemetery. Miller, who had recently married Ingeborg Morath, one of the photographers for *The Misfits*, did not attend the funeral.

In 1964 Miller finished *After the Fall*, his first play in nine years, for the Lincoln Center Repertory Company. The central theme of the play is how its protagonist, Quentin, can come to terms with his past. Dominated by Quentin's memory, the action of the play is expressionistic throughout, using an open space in which various people and events come and go, always confronting Quentin's judging mind. In this episodic structure the recurrent matter to be resolved is the nature of guilt, the limits of personal responsibility for the lives of others, and the means of expiation for crimes real or imagined. Three crises in Quentin's life are vividly presented: Nazi death camps, the suicide of Quentin's beautiful but neurotic wife, Maggie; and Quentin's confrontation with the anti-Communist House Committee on Un-American Activities.

When *After the Fall* opened most of the interest was in how closely the character of Maggie resembled Marilyn Monroe. Many of the critics saw Miller engaged in a tawdry game of marry-and-tell in which he used the central character, Quentin, as a mouthpiece to excuse his inability to keep Monroe from killing herself. Miller's denial of the autobiographical element only pitched the critical furor higher, and critics paraded the parallels between Miller's life and Quentin's. Like Quentin, Miller was the son of a wealthy man who went broke during the Depression; like Quentin, Miller had his share of troubles with the House Committee on Un-American Activities; like Quentin, Miller was greatly troubled by guilt for not having suffered in German concentration camps; but most important, like Quentin, Miller married a sensuous

From the rear, left to right: producer Frank Taylor beside Arthur Miller; Eli Wallach beside director John Huston; Montgomery Clift, Marilyn Monroe, and Clark Gable on location for The Misfits, *the movie Miller wrote as a gift for his wife Monroe*

woman for whom love was the only salvation, and he was not able to save her.

Despite the initial interest in the autobiographical elements, the play's greatest weakness is not that the characters are too lifelike but that they are too abstract: whomever they may be modeled upon, all the characters come to represent principles which Quentin is trying to sort out in his life. Since the play purports to take place in "the mind, thought, and memory of Quentin," one might say that Miller has succeeded in reducing human beings to attitudes, but this theoretical success does not produce satisfactory character interaction.

Characters from various points in Quentin's life emerge from the shadows of the nonrepresentational set to enact their lives. The voices overlap, and often characters from different plot lines will speak out of context on an incident to which they are not related. The effect of this multilevel chorus is not the deepening of understanding but rather the flattening of human experience as one event too neatly parallels another. It is ironic that Miller has Quentin voice the play's theme with the observation "We are killing one another with abstraction."

Although the play is mostly about Quentin's relationship with women, Quentin's emotional problem originates in the quintessential Miller plot: a failing father has two sons—one who goes off to seek ideals, the other who remains behind to help the father cope with the collapse. In *After the Fall* Miller focuses on the son who leaves home and never gets over his guilt for deserting his father. The father and the brother, Dan, are little more than shadows, but their voices are trumpets of guilt. Whenever Quentin does something he considers shameful, they remind him that despite his desertion his family is always behind him.

Quentin's mother provides one of the female role models in the play, and in many ways his life is a reaction against her manipulation of the family. Quentin's earliest memory is his mother's deserting him for a week while she goes to the beach with his older brother and then tries to buy back his love with a toy. His mother treats his father in the same way. She spends most of her time destroying his ego until the collapse of his business reduces him to misery and dependence. Then she takes great pleasure in being the comforter. Parallel to Quentin's mother is Elsie, the wife of Quentin's former law professor who treats her husband like a little boy by continually reminding him of his dependence on her. Elsie is completely contemptuous of her husband until he is crushed by antileftist investigations, at which point she becomes his protector.

In addition to the women who treat men like little boys so they can smother them with salvation, there are the martyrs who need to be saved. The martyrs include Felice, whom Quentin gives the courage to get a nose job; Holga, who needs reassurance that she is not guilty for escaping the ovens at Auschwitz; and finally Maggie, who wants to believe she has some value beyond her flesh. Basically Quentin's life is a flight from the first kind of woman to the second, but he never fully realizes that the second kind of woman creates a greater dependency in the man than the first. Like most of the women in Ibsen's *Hedda Gabler*, Quentin is so bent on saving people that he seems at a loss when there is no one to save. Significantly he first takes Maggie to bed after he has straightened out a legal problem of hers. "I can't even go to bed without a principle," he says. Once he has begun to save her, he can sleep with her. The play is set up as a *demande d'amour*, a request for the audience to decide an unresolved question about love. Quentin has had unsuccessful marriages with two women (Louise and Maggie) and asks if he should marry

a third, Holga. The women certainly parallel Miller's three wives: however, it seems likely that the self-centered Quentin will fail in his third marriage as well.

The play's title refers to the Fall from Eden and the loss of innocence. In the foreword to the play, Miller says, "through Quentin's agony in this play there runs the everlasting temptation of Innocence, that deep desire to return to when, it seems, he was in fact without blame. . . . But the closer he examines those seemingly unified years the clearer it becomes that his Paradise keeps slipping back and back." Like David Beeves in *The Man Who Had All the Luck*, Quentin feels he has never quite paid for his sins, and so he is wracked by guilt. Furthermore Quentin cannot possibly pay for his crimes because they are sins of omission. He has not stayed with his father; he has not communicated with Louise; he has not died at Auschwitz; he has not been forced to choose between his friend and his career as he expected. This last "crime" illustrates Miller's point and the absurdity of Quentin's obsession with guilt. Quentin has committed himself to defending Lou, his law professor, against the Committee on Un-American Activities, knowing that his law firm will fire him if he takes the case. Understandably Quentin has some qualms about his commitment. He is relieved when Lou releases him from his commitment by taking his own life, but then he feels guilty because he is relieved rather than upset. Miller's comment on the murder of Abel in reference to this play pinpoints Quentin's (and Miller's) own obsession with guilt: "The first 'real story' in the Bible is the murder of Abel. Before this drama there is only a featureless Paradise. But in that Eden there was peace because man had no consciousness of himself. . . . Presumably we are being told that the human being becomes 'himself' in the act of becoming aware of his sinfulness. He 'is' what he is ashamed of." Miller's parallel between the Old Testament's story of Cain and Abel and the events in *After the Fall* is, however, quite misleading. Murdering one's brother is one thing, but Quentin's sins of omission are something else. It is easy to discern one's own character from his sins; but one's concept of himself is necessarily more amorphous when it is determined by what one has not done. Shame over things which, in retrospect, one ought to have done but did not is radically different from shame over a positive transgression. Furthermore the list of one's responsibilities grows the more one is an idealist. For someone like Quentin with a salvation complex, everyone's misfortunes become his responsibility so his fund of guilt is endless.

The title's reference to Eden is also a reminder that Eve is the only woman who was literally an extension of her husband's self and not a separate personality. After the Fall, all lovers are separate individuals, but Quentin's relations with women founder on the question of how separate they should be. He leaves Louise because she has become a separate person, not dependent on him for emotional support nor existing to provide him with praise and comfort. On the contrary, he leaves Maggie because she is never a separate person. Maggie begins their relationship with adoration for Quentin and ends with blame, but her self-image is always based on him, not on herself. Quentin has an Adam's rib complex: he can deal with women only insofar as they are extensions of himself.

At the end of 1964, Miller wrote a second play for the Lincoln Repertory, *Incident at Vichy*. As the play opens, seven actors are seen frozen in "attitudes expressive of their personalities and functions." Even though the characters begin to move once the play starts, almost all of them remain locked in their own personalities for the rest of the play. *Incident at Vichy* tests those personalities to see whether anything, even the specter of the concentration camps, can stir them out of their rigidity. The seven men, all living in Vichy, France, have been rounded up by the Nazis, and it becomes increasingly clear that they have been caught in a racial purity dragnet. One by one, they are marched to the interrogation room, and as their circle grows smaller, those remaining argue about their fate and about the nature of humanity. What must be decided ultimately is whether or not the Nazis can strip them of every shred of human dignity.

Miller brilliantly shows the deepening of the moral crisis. At first all try to believe that the interrogation is routine—that they have been brought in for a simple check of credentials. As the situation worsens, each tries to separate himself from the rest of the group by finding a reason for the Nazis' wanting to destroy the others while leaving him alone: the other is a gypsy, a Communist, a Catholic, a Jew. Each wants to convince himself that he is better off not being one of *those*: "Each man has his Jew; it is the other . . . the man whose death leaves you relieved that you are not him, despite your decency." It becomes clear that for most men, real decency fails when the alternative is self-destruction.

As the Nazis continue to take away the survivors, those who deem themselves moral individ-

uals find their morality tested. Bayard, a Communist, finds a measure of courage in playing the role of spokesman of the people, even though he is alone. Miller suggests that role-playing is too fragile a response to stand up to such assaults on human dignity as the measuring of penises. As Bayard is taken he assumes "an artificial and almost absurd posture of confidence." No matter how great his bravery, he has not gotten out of his self, producing the irony of a Communist who has nothing in common with anyone else.

The final survivors, Leduc, a Jewish psychiatrist, and Von Berg, an Austrian Catholic aristocrat, debate the subject of personal responsibility in such matters. Leduc makes claims for responsibility while Von Berg notes the tendency of his own class to shirk its duty. Leduc's concern with responsibility finds a sensitive nerve in the Nazi major who is in charge of the investigation. The major, a regular army officer, is horrified by the business of racial policies, so Leduc pushes him to act, to stop the horror in some small way. The major undercuts Leduc's idealism when he tempts him with freedom: "If you were released and the others were kept . . . would you refuse?" When Leduc cannot deny he would take the pass to freedom, he loses his hold on the major's sympathies; the major returns to the work he loathes.

After his failure with the major, Leduc cross-examines Von Berg, whose beliefs make him an unlikely hero. Von Berg is able to make sense of the Nazis on aesthetic terms because they are, in a way, like him and his class in being beyond rationality. Like an aristocrat's maintaining the trappings of his rank even while destitute, the Nazis' destruction of the Jews is awesome because it does not make economic sense: "The fact that it costs money and uses up trains and personnel—this only guarantees the integrity, the purity, the existence of their feelings. . . . They are poets, they are striving for a new nobility, the nobility of the totally vulgar."

Although he vows that he hates the Nazis, Von Berg's logic would seem to leave him open to change his loyalty. Leduc argues that Von Berg had a chance to act on his loathing of the Nazis but failed to take it. Furthermore it is not enough that Von Berg feels guilty about this failure; it is his duty to act and take responsibility for his fellow human beings. It is here that Miller takes his characters a step beyond *After the Fall*. Quentin was overwhelmed by complicity of his fellow human beings—in fact, even in the deaths of concentration camp victims he had never seen—but his guilt never led him to being crushed so that another could survive. In *Incident at Vichy,* Von Berg takes this next step. When he comes out of the interrogation room, he holds a pass for freedom. He has been declared not guilty of brotherhood with his fellow prisoners: he is free. Von Berg understands, however, that no man can deny his bond with humanity and still remain a human being. He has learned that not only does rank have obligations but so does humanity. He hands the pass to Leduc and accepts fully his complicity in the human race. Quentin's problem seems to be that he has never had so neat a chance to pay the price of admission to the human race.

After Miller had two plays produced with the Lincoln Center Repertory (both performed at the company's temporary headquarters at the ANTA Washington Square Theatre), he broke with the theater's governing board over its repertory policy. Miller felt that the company was not trying to develop a true repertory theater like those in Europe. For this reason, he returned to Broadway with his next play, *The Price* (1968).

The Price is a most traditional piece of theater, harking back to *All My Sons,* not only in its theme of defining the price one pays for the choices in life but also in its technique of the characters uncovering the past by retelling events to reveal one incompletely understood motive after another in their present lives. The play has almost no present time; it is almost all recognition, as its setting soon makes clear. A policeman, at the brink of retirement, decides to sell his deceased father's furniture from the attic of a condemned brownstone. The play's title refers, first of all, to the price he can get for the furniture from a secondhand-furniture dealer. The play is set entirely in the attic and the claustrophobic set, which puts a whole houseful of furniture in one room, reinforces what Miller has been saying in all his plays: at some point in one's life everything important from the past will be set out and a price will have to be put on it.

The hero, Victor Frank, like Biff in *Death of a Salesman* or Chris in *All My Sons,* is an idealist whose refusal to compromise has cost him dearly. Like those other idealists of Miller's, however, there is something hollow at the core of his virtue. Victor sets out to bargain with the furniture appraiser, but he does not know how to bargain about either furniture or life.

The ninety-year-old furniture dealer, a marvelously comic creation named Gregory Solomon, is a shape-shifting con man, whose varied life contrasts brilliantly with Victor's dull lifetime on the force. In the course of their dealings, Solomon

claims he was a vaudeville acrobat, a sailor in the British navy, the husband of three or four wives (he loses count), and the president of the New York Furniture Dealers' Association. The audience is meant never to be certain how much of Solomon's stories are true: he exists as a foil for Victor. Victor, at fifty, is past the earliest retirement age for a policeman, and he feels that it is too late in life to make a new start. Solomon, the former acrobat, is far more flexible than Victor, a man forty years his junior. Victor is afraid to face the future, but Solomon comes out of retirement to face the challenge of selling Victor's once expensive, but now nearly worthless, furniture. Victor has dreams of doing "something in science," but he fears making a commitment because starting in science now will mean he has wasted his life to this point. The uncovering of the past will reveal he could have started thirty years earlier.

Victor's father, like Quentin's in *After the Fall* and Miller's own father, went bankrupt in the Depression, and Victor made the choice to stay with him rather than pursue his own dreams. He sees himself as the noble son who sacrificed his own future—he was always good in science—for his broken father, while his brother went off and became a success as a doctor. As a policeman, he can point to his life as one of public-spirited self-sacrifice. The linchpin of his sacrifice is his resentment of his brother, Walter, whom he has not seen in half a lifetime. The sale of the father's furniture brings them together for a bruising confrontation.

The audience has been prepared to dislike Walter as a selfish, money-hungry physician who not only deserted his father but also later refused to lend Victor the money he needed to go to college. The two men have not spoken since Walter turned down Victor's request. When Walter appears, the audience's suspicions seem to be confirmed. Walter is appalled at the low price that Victor has accepted for the furniture and offers a devious scheme for making a great deal of money out of it. Instead of selling the furniture, Walter will have Solomon overappraise it outrageously and then give it to charity, thereby reaping a huge profit in the form of a tax refund. When Walter offers to give the whole amount to Victor, it seems like blood money to pay off his guilt at having refused the loan years before. As the story unfolds, however, Victor's nobility loses much of its luster.

Both brothers' lives have been reactions to the father's failure. Walter has pursued money and success voraciously, hoping to insulate himself from his father's fate. The result has been a nervous breakdown and a divorce. He sees his life as a continual striving that has left no time for living, and he envies the full life he thinks Victor has lived.

Victor, on the other hand, has confused cause and effect in his sacrifice for his father. Victor's version of his life is as follows: his father was broke and broken in spirit so he had to sacrifice his future by taking a job he did not like to support his father; the job drifted into an unwanted career, and his life was wasted because he was caring for his father; his brother helped him ruin his life by refusing him a loan to pay for his education.

The long-hidden secret revealed at this time is that the father was not broke—though his millions were gone, he still had $4,000, a huge sum during the Depression and certainly enough to tide him over while his son finished school. Even more shocking is the revelation that Victor knew about the money, not to the penny, but he knew that his father was not destitute. This knowledge changes the meaning of his self-sacrifice: his father's poverty becomes his excuse for not succeeding rather than his reason. Like his brother, Victor does not want to repeat his father's fall, but he takes the opposite path to safety. Walter tries to get so high up nothing can reach him; Victor avoids a dangerous fall by not trying to scale the heights at all. It is also likely that Victor uses the excuse of his father's poverty to avoid direct competition with his brother. Victor had always been the smarter one in school, but at the time he was ready to go to college, Walter was already established as a doctor. As Walter points out, the loan was not necessary: if Victor did not want to take his father's money, he could have sold the family's harp, which even in the Depression was worth enough to pay for his tuition. Victor has kept the harp all these years, ironically symbolizing his desire to be an "angel" above the common wants of men.

As in all Miller plays, motivations remain complex even when they are explained, and here Walter's explanation is a little too facile: his father's weakness of character and refusal to admit he had any money do not really excuse Walter's neglect, and Walter's judgment that he should not have supported Victor's education because the money was there may be legally correct, but it is a judgment as harsh as Cain's about Abel—Walter has refused to be his brother's keeper.

As the revelations continue, Victor's staying with his father is seen to be more than cowardice: he had given his father, who trusted no one in the world, someone to believe in. It was not an act of love—for there was no love in the family's wealthy household—but an illusion of love to keep his father from falling apart. Victor's wife, Esther, sees that maintaining the illusion has generated its own love, and so the play ends on a note of muted optimism. Esther has just learned that she has reason to be bitter about her husband's wasted life, but in watching the brothers fight she realizes what is missing from their relationship: "It always seems to me that one little step more and some crazy kind of forgiveness will come and lift up everyone." She takes the step and walks out with her life and marriage intact.

With all Miller's concern with the loss of innocence and the conflict between two brothers, it was inevitable that he would return to the archetype in the book of Genesis. He had already written *After the Fall;* he moved to before the Fall in *The Creation of the World and Other Business* (1972). The play is a comic retelling of the Adam and Eve and Cain and Abel stories, but the "other business" in the title refers not only to these stories but also to the comic stage business or "shtick." The play is a light comedy that is also supposed to make a philosophic statement. In the program, each act is given a philosophic question to answer—"When Every Man Wants Justice, Why Does He Go On Creating Injustice?"—but it is unclear whether the questions are ironic counterpoints to the action or mere pretension.

Most of the humor of the play comes from anachronisms—God talking about Notre Dame, an angel playing Beethoven on a bassoon, Adam thinking about volleyball when he sees Eve's behind—and from the mixing of biblical language with modern slang. The comic aspect of Adam and Eve's attempt to learn about sex is embarrassingly heavy-handed. When Lucifer says "he's sticking it in her ear now," groans are the only possible response.

The play is a debate between God and Lucifer about the nature of good and evil with the Genesis stories used to illustrate their positions. For the most part, Lucifer is the more attractive of the pair, but his character seems confused, rather than paradoxical as in Milton or Shaw. At times he seems to be a Promethean liberator of mankind, at other times an earthly dictator looking for subjects to rule. The tree is the tree of sexual knowledge, and Lucifer urges Eve to eat its fruit so that God can have the grandchild he wants. Lucifer, for all his wit, does not seem to recognize the absurdity of God's behavior. God wants Adam and Eve to be fruitful and multiply, but they cannot because the tree holds the secret of how it is done; then, when they do eat from the tree, God is furious that they have disobeyed his prohibition.

In the Cain and Abel story, Miller seems to lose his sense of humor entirely. Lucifer, who is for the coexistence of good and evil because it equates him with God, tries to keep Cain from killing his brother, but even he cannot untangle the ultimate sibling rivalry. Like Quentin, Cain hates his brother because Abel was his mother's favorite. Miller has told his story one time too many.

The play was a bomb. It closed after twenty performances, with the critics attacking it unmercifully. Though some of the reviews were downright abusive, the worst were by the critics who condescended to Miller as the great man fallen on hard times. Miller angrily blasted the critics and stomped off to his home in Connecticut.

Miller was not yet finished with Eden, and the following year he turned *Creation of the World* into a musical for which he wrote the lyrics. He directed the performance of *Up from Paradise* at his alma mater, the University of Michigan.

Perhaps because he was so badly stung by the New York critics, Miller took his next play, *The Archbishop's Ceiling* (1977), to the Kennedy Center for the Performing Arts in Washington, D.C. The play is a response to Soviet treatment of dissident writers. It is set in some European Communist state where the hero, a renowned novelist named Sigmund, is pondering his fate. He has written an outspoken letter to the United Nations condemning conditions in his country and now he must choose between exile and trial for treason. Three other people are involved in his decision: Marcus, a rival novelist who was once a rebel like Sigmund but now has come to terms with the regime; Adrian, a best-selling American author who feels his success has come too easily; and Maya, an actress who was the lover of both European writers and the subject of novels by all three.

Sigmund's choice is the result of a four-cornered debate marked by shifting loyalties and the emergence of personal and professional jealousy and admiration. The play takes place in a room in what was once the archbishop's palace, and all of the characters believe that the ceiling is bugged, though none is certain that is the case. The fact that it is the archbishop's ceiling suggests that speaking in the room is like speaking under a heaven which may or may not be filled with a God, who may or may not be listening. Miller makes wonderful use of the uncertainty: everything said in the room is spoken for the benefit of both the ceiling and the other characters in the room. Only

by catching every nuance can a character pick up the others' real meanings, and even then there is uncertainty—the other characters may be untrustworthy, or all the others may be acting out an elaborate game set up by the government to manipulate Sigmund.

Though there are reminiscences of Jean Genet's *The Balcony* in the multiple possibilities of illusion (Maya's name can mean "the illusions that sustain man"), Miller allows himself his most optimistic conclusion since *The Man Who Had All the Luck*. Sigmund chooses to stay, gets Marcus to support his radical position, and convinces Adrian and Maya to smuggle out parts of his novel. Though it is likely they will be caught, their heroism is unlike anything in Miller's work except John Proctor's death in *The Crucible*.

The play's credo then reaffirms what Miller had said about human possibility twenty years earlier in the introduction to the *Collected Plays* (1957): "The past half century has created an almost overwhelming documentation of man as a nearly passive creation of environment and family-created psychological drives. If only from the dramatic point of view, this dictum cannot be accepted as final and 'realistic' any more than man's ultimate position can be accepted as his efficient use by state and corporate apparatus." Miller's commitment to this ideal both in his personal life and in his drama has made him one of the two or three most significant playwrights of his generation, both in this country and in Europe.

Since his 1962 marriage to Ingeborg Morath, Miller's life has become considerably less frenetic than it was throughout the 1950s and early 1960s. His Connecticut home is no longer a retreat from the attacks of the House Committee on Un-American Activities and the breakneck pace of Hollywood, but a place of calm where he can discuss literature with neighbors like William and Rose Styron. During this period he has successfully collaborated with his wife, writing the text for three books of photographs she has put together: two illustrate their travels in Russia and China respectively and the third portrays the pleasures of the Connecticut countryside.

Although his work of the last two decades has not matched the great creative surge of the late 1940s and early 1950s, Miller in his later plays continues to investigate complex moral decisions, where each man must weigh his individual conscience against the laws of the society in which he lives. That society may be made up of a nation, a community, or a family, and the hero may concur with its laws generally, yet his beliefs will be tested to a point where external verities no longer provide a useful absolute. At this point the hero must rely on his conscience. This is no easy decision and the choice made by conscience may be wrong, but Miller applauds the man who has the courage to make that choice. In his personal life as well as in his writings, Miller has never wavered from this belief.

Miller's latest plays, one for the theater and the other for television, are further investigations into the two subjects that trouble him most: the Depression and the Nazi terror. *The American Clock,* first produced at the 1980 American Spoleto Festival in Charleston, South Carolina, is a series of vignettes of life during the Depression and its effect on the American family. The play, based on Studs Terkel's *Hard Times,* reasserts Miller's belief in the moral strength of the family unit, an attitude supported by the appearance in the Charleston and New York productions of Miller's sister, Joan Copeland, in the role of the strong mother, Rose Baum. Though based loosely on Terkel's book, the central characters—Rose, her husband, Moe, and her son, Lee—are based on Miller's own Depression childhood with Lee experiencing a number of adventures that Miller had earlier told about himself.

The New York version of the play, rewritten after Spoleto, further emphasizes the role of the Baums, but was seen as less successful by most critics, who saw Miller's characters as stereotypes—the Wall Street financiers, the redneck sheriff, the poor blacks, and particularly the Miller family: depression-racked father, strong supportive mother, and sharp, observant son. The son's checkered career as menial laborer, WPA worker, Communist-party member, and sportswriter at Ohio State, roughly matches Miller's, but seems mostly a frame upon which to hang the vignettes of Depression life.

As in *The Price,* a treasured musical instrument, this time a piano, becomes the family's ticket to survival. In this case Rose finally sells her well-loved piano on which she had accompanied herself singing theatrical songs from the past. In essence, she is, sacrificing her past for her family's future. Miller, however, seems less willing to give up his own theatrical songs of the past. The Baums live at a lower intensity, but their lives are changes rung upon Willy, Biff, and Linda. In this version, we follow Lee up roads that Biff Loman took, although he did not elaborate on them the way this play does. Here we see the rest of America, an Iowa farm, a Mississippi steamboat, in the grip of the Depression, and yet, when all is said and done, Brooklyn

is home sweet home. The large cast of characters (forty roles played by about a third that many actors) and vast number of scenes, many projected with photographs on the stage, mark an unusual openness of conception for Miller, whose earlier large-cast play, *After the Fall,* took place in the hero's mind.

Miller has also written the screenplay for the 1980 television production of *Playing for Time,* Fania Fenelon's story of how she survived in Auschwitz by being part of the prison camp's female orchestra. The portrayal of individual courage in the face of brutal dehumanization is even more searing than in *Incident at Vichy.* The central character, Fania, has in her situation much that Miller looks for in his heroes. She is, at the start of the play, half-Jewish and uncommitted to her religion—so much so that the other girls in the orchestra permit her to remove half her star of David. When, through her music, through her need to survive, and through her understanding of her Jewishness, Fania fully enters the community of the orchestra, she sews back the rest of her star. Rather than being split by dual commitments, Fania grows into the multiple roles which allow her to survive. In contrast, the other characters become either fragmented or locked into limited identities. One, the niece of Gustave Mahler, becomes a rigid artist, who sacrifices her humanity for her music, another allows her beauty to become her entire personality, and a third gives up her integrity for her survival. That his heroine is able to unify multiple attitudes and that she has in fact survived to tell her story marks a decidedly positive conclusion to this most harrowing of scripts. Miller, despite much controversy, insisted on keeping Vanessa Redgrave, an outspoken supporter of Palestinian Arabs and opponent of Israel, in the starring role. He saw the case as one in which the banning of Redgrave for her political views would be no different than the blacklisting that he had undergone during his confrontations with House Committee on Un-American Activities. Redgrave's brilliant performance in the role confirmed Miller's refusal to bow to bias of any kind in the production.

Though Miller has continued to work at his craft, the most important productions of his plays in recent years have been revivals, with two of *Death of a Salesman* being particularly noteworthy. From March to May 1983, Miller went to Beijing (Peking) to direct a Chinese-language (though he did not speak it) version of *Death of a Salesman.* That he was able to motivate actors who had survived the cultural revolution and that a play so embedded in

American capitalism was able to reach the audience in the capital of communism is testimony that the play's true message is more personal and human than sociological. Miller's record of this forty-eight-day task—in diary form—has been published as *Salesman in Beijing* (1984, with photographs by his wife).

An American revival of the play in March of 1984, with Dustin Hoffman in the title role, showed that none of its impact has been lost in thirty-five years. Hoffman's Willy was less victimized and more feisty than Lee J. Cobb's original, and this energy changed the gloomy tragedy into a courageous but futile struggle against the emptiness of the American dream of success. The price Hoffman paid for this energy was to give the audience a smaller man, physically and emotionally, than Cobb did. The tragic grandeur was gone, replaced by a bantam-tough hope that seems, in its own way, true to Miller's conception of Willy as low man on the totem pole of life. As Hoffman's Willy drives off in his well-intentioned suicide to insure his son's future, he, at least, believes that this road trip will be a success. The very different tone and mood of the revival marks the true test of a classic—a performance that can change to fit the tenor of the times and still not lose its dramatic power or grip on the audience.

In February of 1983, the two-act version of *A View from the Bridge* which had been staged by Peter Brook in 1956 and ten years later by Ulu Grossbard Off-Broadway, finally reached Broadway. The production with Tony Lo Bianco in the central role of Eddie opened to mixed reviews with the naysayers finding Miller's Greek tragedy had turned to overacted melodrama. The production brought out the conflicting styles implicit in the structure of the play, those of classic tragedy and of realistic sociology. This combination, often present in Miller's plays, here turns into the stuff of Italian opera. Less successful was a shortened version of *After the Fall* with Frank Langella as Quentin. Though revised, this production failed to overcome the fragmentary structure of the original play so that the unity of events taking place in the hero's mind does not yet become dramatic unity.

Interviews:
Death of a Salesman: A Symposium," *Tulane Drama Review*, 2 (May 1958): 63-69;
    Discusses value system in *Death of a Salesman*, especially Willy's lack of "positive, viable, human values."

Philip Gelb, "Morality and Modern Drama," *Educational Theatre Journal*, 10 (October 1958): 190-202;
    Miller argues that to be moral, great drama must force the audience to make decisions about values rather than present a set of "answers" about morality.

Kenneth Allsop, "A Conversation with Arthur Miller," *Encounter*, 13 (July 1959): 58-60;
    Miller discusses a novel [*The Misfits*] he is writing and laments the post-World War II generation's waning sense of responsibility.

Allan Seager, "The Creative Agony of Arthur Miller," *Esquire*, 52 (October 1959): 123-126;
    Examines some fragments of Miller's works and shows how they are shaped into dramatic dialogue.

Henry Brandon, "The State of the Theatre," *Harper's*, 201 (November 1960): 63-69;
    Discusses the playwright's personal integrity and the relation of *The Crucible* to McCarthyism.

Alice T. McIntyre, "Making *The Misfits* or Waiting for Monroe or Notes from Olympus," *Esquire*, 55 (March 1961): 74-81;
    Miller discusses the characters in *The Misfits* and the difficulties of dealing with Marilyn Monroe on the set.

"Arthur Miller Talks," *Michigan Quarterly Review*, 6 (Summer 1967): 153-163;
    On the economics of the contemporary theater and the need for a subsidized repertory theater.

"Freedom in the Mass Media" [A Panel Discussion with Mike Wallace and Arnold Gingrinch], *Michigan Quarterly Review*, 6 (Summer 1967): 163-178;
    A harsh critique of *Time* magazine and an examination of the influence of the *New York Times*.

"Arthur Miller Talks Again: A Chat with a Class in Stage Direction," *Michigan Quarterly Review*, 6 (Summer 1967): 179-184;
    Discusses the playwright's relation to the director, particularly his to Elia Kazan.

Olga Carlisle and Rose Styron, "The Art of the Theatre II," *Paris Review*, 38 (Summer 1968): 61-98;
A wide-ranging interview in which Miller discusses the genesis of many of his plays as well as the influence of "method" acting on modern drama.

Robert A. Martin, "The Creative Experience of Arthur Miller," *Educational Theatre Journal*, 21 (October 1969): 310-317;
Miller discusses autobiographical elements and Jewish attitudes in his works.

Robert Corrigan, "Interview: Arthur Miller," *Michigan Quarterly Review*, 13 (Fall 1974): 401-405;
Discusses the shift from fate to character as the impelling force of tragedy.

Robert A. Martin and Richard D. Meyer, "Arthur Miller on Plays and Playwriting," *Modern Drama*, 19 (December 1976): 375-384;
Discusses the interaction of humanity and idealism in the plays.

Christian-Albrecht Gollub, "Interview with Arthur Miller," *Michigan Quarterly Review*, 16 (Spring 1977): 121-141;
Discusses the need for an American repertory theater and more support for regional theater in relation to the production of *The Creation of the World and Other Business.*

V. Rajakrishnan, "After Commitment: An Interview with Arthur Miller," *Theatre Journal*, 32 (May 1980): 196-204;
Discusses movement of his late plays from social to metaphysical issues.

Bibliographies:
Martha Eisenstadt, "Arthur Miller: A Bibliography," *Modern Drama*, 5 (May 1962): 93-106;
Useful to its date, includes a number of reviews and minor items.

Tetsumaro Hayashi, *An Index to Arthur Miller Criticism*, second edition (Metuchen, N.J.: Scarecrow Press, 1976);
This update contains many of the errors of the first edition; disorganized and hard to use.

George Jensen, *Arthur Miller: A Bibliographical Checklist* (Columbia, S.C.: Faust, 1976);
A reliable descriptive bibliography.

John Ferres, *Arthur Miller: A Reference Guide* (Boston: G. K. Hall, 1979);
Annotated bibliography of essays, reviews, and interviews.

References:
Henry Adler, "To Hell With Society," *Tulane Drama Review*, 4 (May 1960): 53-76;
Compares Miller unfavorably to Ibsen as a social playwright, seeing Miller's failure in his rationalism and his social consciousness.

Richard Barksdale, "Social Backgrounds in the Plays of Miller and Williams," *College Language Association Journal*, 6 (March 1963): 161-169;
Compares Miller to Ben Jonson as playwright for whom the backgrounds of social events are all-important.

Barclay Bates, "The Lost Past in *Death of a Salesman*," *Modern Drama*, 11 (1968): 164-172;
Discusses pastoral America as lost ideal in *Death of a Salesman.*

C. W. E. Bigsby, "The Fall and After: Arthur Miller's Confession," *Modern Drama*, 10 (1967): 124-136;
Discusses Miller's *After the Fall* in conjunction with Camus's *The Fall* in relation to the emptiness of "success."

Bigsby, "What Price Arthur Miller? An Analysis of *The Price*," *Twentieth Century Literature*, 16 (January 1970): 16-25;
Compares Miller with Peter Weiss as a Jew who had to come to terms with his guilt at having avoided the holocaust; sees *The Price* as existential play of responsibility where men are entirely answerable for their actions.

Guerin Bliquez, "Linda's Role in *Death of a Salesman*," *Modern Drama*, 10 (1968): 383-386;
Sees Linda as a negative force who supports Willy's hollow dreams rather than his life or reality.

Paul Blumberg, "Sociology and Social Literature: Work Alienation in the Plays of Arthur Miller," *American Quarterly*, 21 (1969): 291-310;
Argues that Miller's plays show the impact of social forces, particularly Marx's theory of

work alienation, on the psychology of his heroes.

Harold Clurman, "Director's Notes: *Incident at Vichy*," *Tulane Drama Review*, 9 (Summer 1965):
77-90;
Discusses the character types and "psychological gestures" used in directing this play.

Robert Corrigan, "The Achievement of Arthur
Miller," *Comparative Drama*, 2 (1968): 141-
160;
Studies Arthur Miller's career as achievement
of a man who successfully coped with being
a "monument after only his third play" (*Death
of a Salesman*).

William Dillingham, "Arthur Miller and the Loss
of Conscience," *Emory University Quarterly*, 16
(1960): 40-50;
Shows how the protagonist in many of Miller's
plays loses his conscience and then struggles
to regain it.

John Ditsky, "Stone Fire and Light: Approaches to
The Crucible," *North Dakota Quarterly*, 46
(1978): 65-72;
A thematic study of the play, analyzing various dualities of image patterns.

James Douglass, "Miller's *The Crucible:* Which Witch is
Which?," *Renascence*, 15 (1963): 145-151;
Argues that the witches are created by the
zealousness of the accusers.

Alan Downer, "Mr. Williams and Mr. Miller," *Furioso*, 4 (Summer 1949): 66-70;
Discusses poetic elements in Miller and Tennessee Williams.

Tom Driver, "Strength and Weakness in Arthur
Miller," *Tulane Drama Review*, 4 (May 1960):
45-52;
Sees Miller's strengths in his ability to handle
theatrical time and his desire to present life
realistically, finds his weakness in his attempt
to make psychological portraits of his heroes
fit the social fabric of the plays.

Arthur Epstein, "A Look at *A View from the Bridge*,"
Texas Studies in Literature and Language, 7
(1965): 109-122;
Discusses uneasy conflict between mythic set-

ting and realistic foreground in Miller's
Brooklyn-based drama.

Richard Evans, *Psychology and Arthur Miller* (New
York: Dutton, 1969);
A book-length series of interviews between
Miller and psychologist Evans which discusses
the psychology of Miller's characters and the
way in which they may be considered normal
or abnormal.

Alfred Ferguson, "The Tragedy of the American
Dream in *Death of a Salesman*," *Thought*, 53
(1978): 89-98;
Through his ancestry and own life, Willy re-
cords the life and death of the American
Dream of Innocence in a new world.

Barry Gross, "*All My Sons* and the Larger Context,"
Modern Drama, 18 (1976): 15-27;
Focuses on father/son conflict from son's side,
seeing ironies implicit in Chris's lost innocence.

Gross, "Peddler and Pioneer in *Death of a Salesman*,"
Modern Drama, 7 (1965): 405-410;
Discusses the peddler and pioneer as identities of American success that Willy apes without achieving.

Ina Rae Hark, "A Frontier Closes in Brooklyn:
Death of a Salesman and the Turner Thesis,"
Postscript, 3 (1986): 1-6;
Argues that Turner's Theory of the closing
of the American frontier applies to Willy (who
was born about the time the thesis was enunciated) and dooms him to tragic limitation.

Ronald Hayman, "Arthur Miller; Between Sartre
and Society," *Encounter*, 37 (November 1971):
73-79;
Emphasizes Miller's concern with historical
process—how things come about—and shows
that Miller's heroes, like Sartre's, accept responsibility for a world they never made.

Philip Hill, "*The Crucible:* A Structural View," *Modern Drama*, 10 (1967): 312-317;
By showing that *The Crucible* has all the elements of a "well-made play," Hill defends the
play against George Jean Nathan's charge that
it is badly structured.

Joseph Hynes, "Arthur Miller and the Impasse of Naturalism," *South Atlantic Quarterly*, 62 (1963): 327-334;
Sees Arthur Miller bogged down in naturalism so that *All My Sons, Death of a Salesman*, and *A View from the Bridge* become repetitive versions of the same play, in which common man seeks tragic dignity defined in his own terms.

Esther Jackson, "*Death of a Salesman:* Tragic Myth in the Modern Theatre," *College Language Association Journal*, 7 (September 1963): 63-76;
Discusses the way Miller re-invents tragic myth for twentieth-century American drama, using Willy's poetic vision as its source.

Irving Jacobson, "Family Dreams in *Death of a Salesman*," *American Literature*, 47 (1975): 247-258;
Shows how Willy yearns after images of success projected by Ben, Dave Singleman, and Biff, but fails to live by them because they were all men who made the world, rather than home, their home.

George Kernodle, "The Death of the Little Man," *Tulane Drama Review*, 1 (January 1956): 47-60;
Puts Willy in context of "little man" film clowns like Charlie Chaplin and Harold Lloyd.

Allen Koppenhaver, "*The Fall* and After: Albert Camus and Arthur Miller," *Modern Drama*, 9 (1966): 206-209;
Compares Miller's *After the Fall* to Camus's *The Fall*, showing each is about disgruntled lawyers who are forced back into caring for others after failing to prevent someone else's suicide.

Lawrence Lowenthal, "Arthur Miller's *Incident at Vichy:* a Sartrean Interpretation," *Modern Drama*, 18 (1975): 29-41;
Shows influence of Jean Paul Sartre's *Anti-Semite and Jew* and his notion of hopeless alienation on Miller's play.

Robert Martin, "Arthur Miller's *The Crucible:* Background and Sources," *Modern Drama*, 20 (1977): 279-292;
Analyzes Miller's use of the records of the witchcraft trials as a source of *The Crucible*.

Martin, ed., *Arthur Miller: New Perspectives* (Englewood Cliffs, N.J.: Prentice Hall, 1982);
A collection of critical essays on Arthur Miller, many original to this volume.

James J. Martine, ed., *Critical Essays on Arthur Miller* (Boston: G. K. Hall, 1979);
Critical essays and reviews of all the plays from *The Man Who Had All the Luck* to *The Creation of the World and Other Business*.

Emile McAnany, "The Tragic Commitment: Some Notes on Arthur Miller," *Modern Drama*, 5 (1962): 11-20;
Studies Miller's literary criticism which is then used as a tool for analyzing *Death of a Salesman*.

Leonard Moss, *Arthur Miller*, revised edition (New York: Twayne, 1980);
Discusses both thematic issues, especially the hero's struggle to assert himself against society, and stylistic issues, especially Miller's attempt to find a new form of drama to replace the realism of the late nineteenth and early twentieth century. Includes an interview with Miller.

Edward Murray, *Arthur Miller: Dramatist* (New York: Frederick Ungar, 1967);
A play-by-play analysis emphasizing psychology rather than sociology of Miller's work; rather mechanical in its approach.

Orm Overland, "The Action and Its Significance: Arthur Miller's Struggle with Dramatic Form," *Modern Drama*, 18 (1975): 1-14;
Discusses Miller's "distrust" of theater as useful medium for presenting his ideas and his consequent attempt to reformulate staging as narrative device.

Brian Parker, "Point of View in Arthur Miller's *Death of a Salesman*," *University of Toronto Quarterly*, 35 (January 1966): 144-157;
Argues that Miller, like Ibsen, deepens his realism through symbolism and also through expressionist memory scenes comparable to those of German writers of the 1920s.

Henry Popkin, "Arthur Miller's *The Crucible*," *College English*, 26 (1964): 139-146;
Examines *The Crucible* in relation to Senator Joseph McCarthy's "witchhunt" for un-Amer-

ican activities and to Bertolt Brecht's theory of dramatic "alienation."

Thomas Porter, *Myth and Modern American Drama* (Detroit: Wayne State University Press, 1969), pp. 127-152;
Discusses *Death of a Salesman* in relation to the mythos of the American business success story of the self-made man.

John Prudhoe, "Arthur Miller and the Tradition of Tragedy," *English Studies*, 43 (1962): 430-439;
Sets Miller's prosaic realism against Schiller's idealistic notion of free will in tragedy to argue the success of Miller's tragic mode.

Raymond Reno, "Arthur Miller and the Death of God," *Texas Studies in Literature and Language*, 11 (1969): 1069-1087;

Paul Siegel, "Willy Loman and King Lear," *College English*, 17 (1956): 341-345;
Compares *Death of a Salesman* and *King Lear* as examinations of relationships between fathers and children, particularly as the fathers learn painfully of themselves and the world they live in.

John Stinson, "Structure in *After the Fall:* The Relation of the Maggie Episodes to the Main Themes and Christian Symbolism," *Modern Drama*, 10 (1967): 233-240;
Sees both Quentin and Maggie as Christlike redeemers.

Clinton Trowbridge, "Arthur Miller: Between Pathos and Tragedy," *Modern Drama*, 10 (1967): 233-240;
Discusses the plays in relation to Miller's distinction between tragedy, a struggle that the hero might win, and pathos, a conflict where the hero has no possibility of victory.

Gerald Weales, "All About Talk: Arthur Miller's *The Price*," *Ohio Review*, 13, no. 2 (1972): 74-84;
Discusses the way language is used to inhibit, rather than further, communication in *The Price*.

Weales, "Arthur Miller: Man and his Image," *Tulane Drama Review*, 7 (September 1962): 165-180;
Shows how Miller's heroes struggle with a self-image that comes from social values and prejudices.

Dennis Welland, *Miller: The Playwright* (London: Methuen, 1979);
A comprehensive rewriting of his 1961 volume *Arthur Miller*, covering the canon through *The American Clock;* discusses family tensions as the central conflict in most of Miller's plays.

Sidney White, *Guide to Arthur Miller* (Columbus, Ohio: Merrill, 1970);
Discusses the "man of conscience" in Miller's plays; particularly insightful on Miller's dealings with the House Committee on Un-American Activities.

William Wiegand, "Arthur Miller and the Man Who Knows," *Western Review*, 21 (1956): 85-103;
Discusses Miller's college and radio plays as early essays into his major themes. Includes brief bibliography of unpublished plays and early radio plays which have since been published in collections.

Papers:
The University of Michigan at Ann Arbor, the University of Texas at Austin, and the New York Public Library have collections of Miller's papers.

Vladimir Nabokov

This entry was written by Charles Nicol (Indiana State University).

Places	St. Petersburg
	Cambridge
	   University
		Cornell University
		Cambridge,
		   Massachusetts
			Berlin
			Montreux,
			   Switzerland

Influences and Relationships	Aleksandr Pushkin Andrey Biely Edmund Wilson	Alexander Blok William Shakespeare Nladislav Khodasevich	Nikolay Gogol Lewis Carroll
Literary Movements and Forms	Symbolism Russian Formalism	Metafiction	Extraterritoriality
Major Themes	Memory Time as a Spiral Madness	Novelist as God The Double Recurrence of Patterns	Metamorphosis Denial of Death
Cultural and Artistic Influences	Lepidoptera Chess	Psychology	Cinema
Social and Economic Influences	Russian Revolution	Rise of Nazi Germany	

See also the Nabokov entries in DLB 2, American Novelists Since World War II, DLB Yearbook: 1980, *and* DLB Documentary Series, Volume Three.

BIRTH: St. Petersburg, Russia, 23 April 1899, to Vladimir Dmitrievich and Elena Ivanova Rukavishnikov Nabokov.

EDUCATION: B.A., Trinity College, Cambridge, 1922.

MARRIAGE: 15 April 1925 to Vera Evseevna Slonim; child: Dmitri.

AWARDS AND HONORS: Guggenheim Fellowships, 1943, 1952; National Institute of Arts and Letters grant, 1951; Brandeis University literary achievement prize, 1964.

DEATH: Montreux, Switzerland, 2 July 1977.

SELECTED BOOKS*: *Mashenka,* as V. Sirin (Berlin: Slovo, 1926); translated as *Mary* by Michael Glenny and Nabokov (New York: McGraw-Hill, 1970; London: Weidenfeld & Nicolson, 1971);

Korol, Dama, Valet, as V. Sirin (Berlin: Slovo, 1928); translated and revised as *King, Queen, Knave* by Dmitri and Vladimir Nabokov (New York: McGraw-Hill, 1968; London: Weidenfeld & Nicolson, 1968);

Zashchita Luzhina, as V. Sirin (Berlin: Slovo, 1930); translated as *The Defense* by Michael Scammell and Nabokov (New York: Putnam's, 1964; London: Weidenfeld & Nicolson, 1964);

Soglyadatay, as V. Sirin (Paris: Sovremennye Zapiski, 1930); translated as *The Eye* by Dmitri and Vladimir Nabokov (New York: Phaedra, 1965; London: Weidenfeld & Nicolson, 1966);

Podvig, as V. Sirin (Paris: Sovremennye Zapiski, 1932); translated as *Glory* by Dmitri and Vladimir Nabokov (New York: McGraw-Hill, 1971; London: Weidenfeld & Nicolson, 1972);

Kamera Obskura, as V. Sirin (Paris: Sovremennye Zapiski, 1932); translated as *Camera Obscura* by W. Roy (London: John Long, 1936); revised and retranslated as *Laughter in the Dark* by Nabokov (Indianapolis: Bobbs-Merrill, 1938; London: Weidenfeld & Nicolson, 1961);

Otchayanie, as V. Sirin (Berlin: Petropolis, 1936); translated as *Despair* by Nabokov (London: John Long, 1937; retranslated by Nabokov, New York: Putnam's, 1966; London: Weidenfeld & Nicolson, 1966);

Dar, as V. Sirin (Paris: Sovremennye Zapiski, 1937-1938); translated and supplemented as *The Gift* by Scammell and Nabokov (New York: Putnam's, 1963; London: Weidenfeld & Nicolson, 1963);

Priglashenie na Kazn, as V. Sirin (Paris: Dom Knigi, 1938); translated as *Invitation to a Beheading* by Dmitri and Vladimir Nabokov (New York: Putnam's, 1959; London: Weidenfeld & Nicolson, 1960);

The Real Life of Sebastian Knight (Norfolk, Conn.: New Directions, 1941; London: Editions Poetry, 1945);

Nikolai Gogol (Norfolk, Conn.: New Directions, 1944; London: Editions Poetry, 1947);

Bend Sinister (New York: Holt, 1947; London: Weidenfeld & Nicolson, 1960);

Conclusive Evidence (New York: Harper, 1951; London: Victor Gollancz, 1951); revised as *Speak, Memory: an Autobiography Revisited* (New York: Putnam's, 1966);

Lolita (Paris: Olympia, 1955; New York: Putnam's, 1958; London: Weidenfeld & Nicolson, 1959);

Pnin (Garden City: Doubleday, 1957; London: Heinemann, 1957);

Nabokov's Dozen (Garden City: Doubleday, 1958; London: Heinemann, 1959);

Poems (Garden City: Doubleday, 1959; London: Weidenfeld & Nicolson, 1961);

Pale Fire (New York: Putnam's, 1962; London: Weidenfeld & Nicolson, 1962);

Eugene Onegin by Pushkin, translated and annotated by Nabokov, 4 volumes, Bollingen Series (New York: Pantheon, 1964; London: Routledge, 1964);

Ada (New York: McGraw-Hill, 1969; London: Weidenfeld & Nicolson, 1969);

Poems and Problems (New York: McGraw-Hill, 1971; London: Weidenfeld & Nicolson, 1971);

Transparent Things (New York: McGraw-Hill, 1972; London: Weidenfeld & Nicolson, 1972);

A Russian Beauty and Other Stories (New York: McGraw-Hill, 1973; London: Weidenfeld & Nicolson, 1973);

Look at the Harlequins! (New York: McGraw-Hill, 1974; London: Weidenfeld & Nicolson, 1974);

Vladimir Nabokov (photo by T. Brauner)

Tyrants Destroyed and Other Stories (New York: McGraw-Hill, 1975; London: Weidenfeld & Nicolson, 1975);

Details of a Sunset and Other Stories (New York: McGraw-Hill, 1976; London: Weidenfeld & Nicolson, 1976);

Stikhi [Poems] (Ann Arbor: Ardis, 1979);

Lectures on Literature, edited by Fredson Bowers (New York: Harcourt Brace Jovanovich/Bruccoli Clark, 1980; London: Weidenfeld & Nicolson, 1980);

Lectures on Russian Literature, edited by Bowers (New York: Harcourt Brace Jovanovich/Bruccoli Clark, 1981; London: Weidenfeld & Nicolson, 1981);

Lectures on Don Quixote, edited by Bowers (New York: Harcourt Brace Jovanovich/Bruccoli Clark, 1983; London: Weidenfeld & Nicolson, 1983);

The Man from the U.S.S.R. and Other Plays, translated by Dmitri Nabokov (New York: Harcourt Brace Jovanovich/Bruccoli Clark, 1984; Lon-

don: Weidenfeld & Nicolson, 1984);

The Enchanter, translated by Dmitri Nabokov (New York: Putnam's, 1986).

* This list omits juvenilia, shorter works, scientific writings, and most translations by VN.

Vladimir Nabokov, one of the most important world novelists of the twentieth century, was almost unique in changing languages in mid career, from Russian to English. Not identified with either a particular location or a particular language, Nabokov seems to fit most closely into the group of international modernist authors that George Steiner identified as extraterritorial, whose use of language has a brilliance and playfulness not found in writers trapped within a single tongue and culture.

Vladimir Vladimirovich Nabokov was born in St. Petersburg, then the Russian capital, its "window on Europe," and its center of culture. His extremely wealthy family were aristocrats (although not members of the nobility) who had served for generations in important government posts. From the age of four, Nabokov studied English, French, and other subjects with private tutors. French was the usual language of the Russian aristocracy, but the family emphasis on English products, attitudes, language, and culture was unusual. Nabokov later claimed he had "an English childhood."

Nabokov's fondest memories, however, were not of the large family house in St. Petersburg, but of their summer house in the country. There Nabokov learned to play tennis and caught butterflies and moths, beginning a lifelong passion for the capture and classification of lepidoptera. Later it would be the location of his first love affair.

In 1913 Nabokov began attending the Tenishev School in St. Petersburg, probably the best preparatory school in Russia, where he was not entirely comfortable but where he played soccer and developed a deep appreciation for Russian poetry. After the beginning of World War I, Russia headed toward revolution, and in spite of Nabokov's stated indifference toward politics, his family was deeply involved in the history of the times. His father, Vladimir Dmitrievich Nabokov, was a professor of criminology, a member of the liberal Kadet party, and a member of parliament (the Duma);

The Nabokov family home in St. Petersburg, which they were forced to abandon in 1919, after the Bolshevik Revolution. The building now houses government offices (courtesy of Stephen Jan Parker and The Nabokovian).

at one time he had been imprisoned for protesting the actions of the Czar. When the Czar was overthrown, V. D. Nabokov became an important member of the democratic Kerensky government (July-November 1917), itself overthrown by Lenin and the Bolsheviks. In 1919 the Nabokov family fled to the Crimea, in the south of Russia, and after a few months fled again to Europe.

Nabokov attended Trinity College, Cambridge, from 1919 to 1922 and graduated with honors. His father was assassinated in Berlin in 1922, the victim of right-wing radicals; although Nabokov always guarded the privacy of his emotional life, his father's death seems to have had a very powerful impact on the young writer. Berlin had become a major center of Russian culture, where hundreds of thousands of émigrés had managed to preserve their own language and life-style, with their own newspapers and publishing houses. Nabokov spent the next fifteen years in Berlin; beginning with poems in newspapers and continuing with short stories and then novels (all written under the pen name of V. Sirin), Nabokov developed into a major writer, almost unknown outside of the Russian emigration. For most of this period, he supported himself by giving language and tennis lessons, supplemented by fees for publication and eventually by public readings.

In 1925 Nabokov married Vera Slonim, a Jewish Russian émigré. In 1926 Nabokov published his first novel, *Mashenka* (translated as *Mary*, 1970), whose title character had been the girlfriend of the protagonist Ganin in prerevolutionary days. Ganin lives in a boardinghouse in Berlin along with a comic collection of other Russian émigrés, all living in limbo—awaiting news, passports, or a change in the Russian government, all indifferent to the aimless drifting of their present existence. One of them turns out to be Mashenka's husband, anxiously awaiting her arrival from Russia. This news plunges Ganin into a deep reverie lasting several days, as he relives in his memory the highlights of his love affair. Although Ganin plots to meet Mashenka at the railroad station in place of her husband, he changes his mind abruptly, realizing that his vivid memories are the most valuable thing the past can offer and that he cannot relive his days with Mashenka. He leaves Berlin alone in order to break free from his stagnant inactivity.

Much of *Mashenka* is clearly autobiographical, and Ganin's memories of Mashenka are almost identical to Nabokov's memories of "Tamara" in *Speak, Memory*. Thus, Nabokov's first novel develops one of his main concerns, the reality and importance of memory. In most other respects, however, *Mashenka* does not resemble his later novels. It is a product of the Symbolist Movement, influenced by the Russian Symbolist poet Aleksandr Blok. Mashenka herself is both a fully realized character and a symbol of Russia. In consequence, this novel can be said to have a message: do not forget Russia, but do not wait for it to return; move on. In later life, Nabokov detested art with a message.

Nabokov's second novel, *Korol, Dama, Valet* (1928), is clumsy but much more experimental. The three main characters are all Germans, and Nabokov treats them much as cardboard figures might be treated; in fact, when the novel was eventually translated into English (*King, Queen, Knave,* 1968), he even changed the ending. The love triangle is the most overworked plot in fiction; Nabokov seems to have chosen it deliberately in order to see what changes he could ring on its basic theme. This plot concerns a love affair between a callow student and a businessman's shallow wife who decide to murder her husband but find that the planning of the murder is more complex than they anticipated. Of much more interest are the novel's references to films, its grotesque secondary characters (including a madman, an inventor, and a dog), the dazzling shifts of point of view, and the brief appearance of Nabokov and his wife.

In 1930 appeared Nabokov's first masterpiece, *Zashchita Luzhina* (translated as *The Defense,* 1964). The novel concerns a chess master's descent into madness and eventual suicide and is Nabokov's first major psychological study (he was a student of pre-Freudian case histories for many years). Although thoroughly convincing as a case study (resembling the breakdowns of several actual chess players), *The Defense* is even more impressive simply as a novel, in its language, viewpoint, characterization, and occasionally dizzying shifts of places and events. Luzhin, a very sympathetic character, is brilliant at chess but hopelessly confused by life; fat, asthmatic, absentminded, barely able to keep afloat in the complexities of ordering dinner or taking a walk, he manages to conduct a quaint romance and marry an understanding woman, but eventually he discerns in the events around him a pattern that repeats a disastrous series of events earlier in his life; suicide seems his only way to escape the repetition. Many of Nabokov's later novels would use the repetition of a pattern of events as a structural device.

A much shorter psychological work, *Soglyadatay* (1930, translated as *The Eye,* 1965), appeared soon after. It concerns a Russian émigré, Smurov, who attempts to commit suicide and then views himself from the outside, trying to redefine himself through integrating the extremely various attitudes toward Smurov of those people around him. Aside from demonstrating again Nabokov's strong interest in extreme mental states, this novella also marks his first use of the double as a theme.

Nabokov's next novel, *Podvig (The Exploit,* 1932, but translated as *Glory,* 1971), is generally agreed to be his weakest. The main character, Martin Edelweiss, lives through most of the scenes of Nabokov's young manhood (the Crimea, Cambridge, Berlin, southern France); after inventing a cruel imaginary country, Zoorland, to replace the reality of Soviet Russia, Martin is apparently killed while crossing the Russian border. The novel is a peculiar patchwork of Nabokov's earlier and later concerns: on the one hand it has the kind of autobiographical details and didactic features (Nabokov stated that it was "the only one of my novels with a message") of his first novel, *Mashenka;* on the other it creates the first of Nabokov's imaginary worlds, uses recurrent patterns as a structural device, and obliquely suggests, as do many later works, that the dead are possibly attempting to communicate with us. Although the text is straightforward, avoiding stylistic tricks, the overall impression of this novel is one of authorial confusion about its ultimate intentions.

The authorial indulgence of *Podvig* was in extreme contrast to *Kamera Obskura* (1932, considerably revised as *Laughter in the Dark,* 1938—even the main character's name is changed), a tightly plotted and somber story of a German who becomes infatuated with a vicious young woman, is betrayed, is blinded in an accident, and eventually is killed while attempting to murder the girl. The combination of German characters, the love triangle, attempted murder, and references to a film of the novel running throughout the novel itself all recall the earlier *King, Queen, Knave,* but this time the plot is compelling. The ending is written as a dramatic scene, and cinematic devices are used throughout the novel to great effect; indeed, it is probable that the work was originally intended as a screenplay for the German film industry. The novel is also notable for its third main character, a manipulative, cruel trickster who resembles Quilty of *Lolita* and other nightmarishly calculating figures in Nabokov's later works.

Between 1936 and 1938, as Nabokov's European career drew to a close, he finished three immensely different and interesting novels. The first, *Otchayanie* (1936, translated as *Despair*, 1937), was almost immediately translated into English by Nabokov, the earliest indication of his later decision to write in that language; he was probably encouraged by the 1936 publication of *Camera Obscura*, in an English translation by W. Roy. *Despair* is narrated by a madman, Hermann Karlovich, who kills someone he alone believes looks like his double in a plan to collect his own life insurance. His attempt to commit the perfect crime is flawed from the beginning, since the victim does not really resemble him, and it is further flawed in the execution. Both doubles and mentally deranged narrators had been particular features of Russian fiction, and Nabokov was soon to bring these features to American literature. But Nabokov not only draws on Russian literature for *Despair*, he parodies it, incorporating quotations from Gogol, Dostoyevski, and others in his text. Like Smurov of *The Eye*, Hermann is a half-Russian, half-German who views his own life as a series of actions which have meaning only if they are observed; perhaps his greatest satisfaction in committing a murder is confessing it. The very problem of having a madman tell his own tale is parodied, leading to a bizarre and confusing ending where the narrator writes out his actions at the same time he commits them.

In the shadow of the Nazi terror, Nabokov moved his family (his son Dmitri had been born in 1934) to Paris in 1937, where he completed his finest Russian novel, *Dar* (1937-1938, translated as *The Gift*, 1963), an elegy for both Russian literature and émigré life in Berlin. The protagonist, Godunov-Cherdyntsev, is a writer beginning his career. Each of the novel's five chapters is stylistically different and substantially self-contained. The early chapters are stylistically reminiscent of the classic Russian authors and include some of Godunov-Cherdyntsev's poems along with interpolated stories, imaginary conversations, and book reviews. The fourth chapter, ostensibly the main character's first major book, is a sarcastic biography of Chernyshevsky, a revered but clumsy and didactic Russian literary and political figure of the nineteenth century. (When the novel appeared in an émigré publication, this chapter was rejected by the editors as politically scandalous.) The last chapter details the protagonist's deepening involvement with his girlfriend, ending with the suggestion that he will eventually be the writer of the present novel. Throughout, the work has the calm brilliance of a masterpiece.

Almost as an afterthought, in 1938 Nabokov published one more short novel in Russian, *Prig-*

Nabokov and his son, Dmitri, 1936 (by permission of Vera Nabokov)

lashenie na Kazn (Invitation to a Beheading, 1959). The novel apparently came to him as an inspiration and was completed in a few weeks. Far in the future (apparently in Russia), Cincinnatus has been accused of "gnostic turpitude" (not being "transparent"), and is imprisoned, waiting his death. At the moment of his execution, however, the other characters reveal themselves to be two-dimensional figures on a collapsing stage-set as Cincinnatus goes to meet beings akin to himself. Probably influenced by Zamyatin's *We* and deliberately referring to Lewis Carroll in its ending (Nabokov had translated *Alice in Wonderland* into Russian as a young man), *Invitation to a Beheading* is Nabokov's most idealistic, airy, and fantastic work.

In May 1940 Nabokov left France with his family for the United States, bringing with him the manuscript for *The Real Life of Sebastian Knight*, his first novel written in English. In Russian, he had written not just the nine novels discussed here but a number of other works, including a few not especially successful plays. He had published hundred of poems, the earliest of which used religious imagery and were written in a rather archaic style. He had published over sixty stories, some of them small masterpieces, most of which he eventually translated into English. Yet he arrived in New York almost penniless, facing a new land with few prospects other than a teaching job at Stanford for the following summer.

Fortunately, he soon became close friends with Edmund Wilson, an important and influential critic, with whom he shared many traits and interests. Wilson helped Nabokov to place reviews in the *New Republic* and the *Nation,* to place stories in the *Atlantic* and later the *New Yorker,* to find publishers for *The Real Life of Sebastian Knight* and later novels, and to obtain a Guggenheim Fellowship in 1943.

If *The Gift* was Nabokov's farewell to Russian literature, then *The Real Life of Sebastian Knight* was his farewell to himself as a Russian writer. In this mock biography, V. attempts to find out the real character of his deceased half-brother Sebastian, who had written a number of novels in Russian that seem to echo Nabokov's own. Although V. never is able to pin down his brother's character or motives, he accidentally experiences situations similar to those that inspired Sebastian, and at the end of the novel, feeling that his movements have been directed by something beyond chance, he wonders whether his experiences have led him to a common identity with his brother, "or perhaps we both are someone whom neither of us knows."

In 1941 Nabokov began an uncertain lecturing position at Wellesley College, soon supplemented by another low-paying position as a fellow of the Museum of Comparative Zoology at Harvard, classifying lepidoptera. This fairly unproductive period ended with his appointment to a teaching post at Cornell University in 1948. In the course of these seven years Nabokov published several scientific papers on lepidoptera but only two major literary works: a brilliant and amusing biography of Nikolai Gogol (1944) and the novel *Bend Sinister* (1947).

The death of Nabokov's brother Sergey in a German concentration camp may have been the catalyst for *Bend Sinister,* which takes place in an imaginary but contemporary totalitarian state with obvious characteristics of both Stalin's Russia and Hitler's Germany. The country is ruled by Paduk, the Toad, a totally repellent character who had been a childhood enemy of Krug, a world-famous philosopher; Paduk is determined to get Krug to endorse the government, thus giving some international credibility to the regime. Krug (whose name means "circle" in Russian) believes that he is impervious to the dictator's demands, even when

his friends are sent to jail, but when his young son is kidnapped and killed, Krug goes insane. The actions of a totalitarian dictatorship are ridiculous in their stupidity, but when that stupidity reaches into the personal life of Krug (or of Nabokov), the result is too painful to endure. The brilliance of the novel's style is almost too much for its somber theme, but it is a dazzling combination of pain, horror, comedy, and tenderness.

During his ten years at Cornell (1948-1958), where his course on European fiction was legendary, Nabokov completed most of his best writing in English, possibly the best writing of his entire career, including *Speak, Memory* and the novels *Lolita* and *Pnin.* The history of *Speak, Memory* is convoluted, an extreme example of Nabokov's restless versatility: one chapter, "Mademoiselle O," about his French governess, was written in French ten years before the others and even in English appeared first in a collection of stories. Another chapter, "First Love," also appeared as a story and is frequently anthologized. The other chapters were also published separately, usually in the *New Yorker,* but not in the order they appear in the memoir itself, which initially appeared under the title *Conclusive Evidence* (1951). Even after publication under the present title, the book continued to evolve: a slightly different, longer version appeared in Russian under the title *Drugie Berega* (Other Shores), and then a further revised English language edition (1966) finished the publication cycle. *Speak, Memory* is a highly polished and very guarded memoir. Beautiful evocations of the Nabokov summer house south of St. Petersburg, sections devoted to riding trains, visiting southern France, designing chess problems, and collecting butterflies—all these lead the reader to forget how little Nabokov has actually revealed about his family or himself, and how carefully the devastations of history have been omitted from its pages. Nabokov's stated reason for writing his autobiography is not to reveal or explore his character but to analyze the patterns he sees in the external events of his life.

Although his position at Cornell was secure, Nabokov continued to live a seminomadic existence, continually moving with his family from one rented house to another; he also continued to take summer trips to collect moths and butterflies in the mountainous regions of the western United States. The discovery of a previously unnamed butterfly on a trip in 1949 may have been one of the events triggering the writing of *Lolita,* a shocking and brilliant novel about a middle-aged man's affair with a twelve-year-old girl, termed by the narrator a

Nabokov working on his lepidoptera (photo by Horst Tappe)

"nymphet"; but the novel had its inception in an earlier story in Russian (*The Enchanter,* 1986). *Lolita* is also a parody of the Freudian case-study, of confessional literature, and even of the Freudian version of the family relationship. It features Humbert Humbert, the most brilliant of Nabokov's madmen, as narrator; Lolita, a uniquely vivid portrait of a preadolescent girl; and Quilty, the most outrageous of Nabokov's tricksters. It is also Nabokov's most extended view of America, a loving and satiric tour of his adopted country. *Lolita* is not only Nabokov's best-known, it is arguably his finest, novel. Often his most complex, passionate, and inspired protagonists have isolated or protected themselves from the dangers of their world, so that his novels tend to focus narrowly on the relationship of an artist and his art. But Humbert's subject is Lolita, a character far too alive to be satirized, and she forces Humbert to confront a world—modern America—that he is unable to control.

The sexual theme of *Lolita* shocked many readers, not least because it suggested that children, while naive, are far from innocent; yet it is difficult today to realize that American publishers originally rejected the novel because they feared prosecution. Consequently, *Lolita* was first published in France in 1955, where it became controversial when the De Gaulle government attempted to have it banned and a number of literary figures defended it. After its American publication in 1958, Nabokov abruptly found himself rich, famous, and considerably misunderstood.

In the meantime, *Pnin* had been published in 1957. The gentle novel about Timofey Pnin, an émigré who teaches Russian in the United States, pronounces the English language in surprising ways, and is generally laughed at by his colleagues, is the most realistic and approachable of Nabokov's later works, perhaps because the tone, setting, and affectionate amusement of the campus novel are

*Front cover for the first edition of Nabokov's best-known work.
Because he was unable at first to find an American publisher,*
Lolita *was initially printed in Paris by a house known
for its erotica.*

so familiar that they tend to obscure Nabokov's originality. Only in one central chapter does the reader see Pnin with a group of his Russian friends and realize that what makes Pnin comic is America, and that he is an imposing figure when not stripped of his heritage, his language, and his scholarly dignity. One curious feature is that Pnin eventually loses his appointment to an old rival who is apparently Nabokov himself. While the surface of *Pnin* is clear and delightful, it is a complex novel; scholarship has revealed the novel's underlying patterns and indicated how the spirit of Pnin's youthful love, Nina Belochkin, seems to be protecting him from harm. A great sympathy pervades the book.

When *Lolita* became a best-seller, Nabokov found himself in a position of financial security he had not experienced since childhood. He retired from teaching and moved to Montreux, Switzerland (although retaining his American citizenship), where he stayed in a suite of rooms at the elegant Palace Hotel for the rest of his life. In Switzerland, Nabokov and his wife were close to relatives and old friends; moreover, the hotel staff protected him from unwelcome visitors, and the climate and terrain were excellent for collecting lepidoptera. Interviewers, scholars, and curious visitors arrived frequently. As articles about Nabokov appeared in various magazines, the world learned his controversial opinions about various literary figures and other matters; he became especially well known for his acerbic statements about Freud, whom Nabokov called the "Viennese witch doctor." The considerable public interest in Nabokov's works also gave him the opportunity, often in collaboration with his son Dmitri, to translate his earlier Russian works into English, an activity that continued for the rest of his life.

The first novel of this last period of Nabokov's life was *Pale Fire* (1962), an innovative work consisting of a long poem by John Shade and notes and commentary by Charles X. Kinbote, an émigré and madman who believes he is the exiled king of Zembla. John Shade's "Pale Fire" may even be a great meditative poem, one of the few since Johnson and Wordsworth, while Kinbote's commentary is the most outrageous parody of scholarship since Pope's *Dunciad.* The reader becomes involved in a compelling network of puzzles and cross-references that evokes the inspiration of scholarship even while satirizing it. This unlikely novel is a tour de force, one of literature's most surprising comic masterpieces.

Two years later, in 1964, it became clear what part of Nabokov's own career was satirized in *Pale Fire* when he published an immense work of scholarship on which he had labored for many years, his own translation of Pushkin's *Eugene Onegin* with extensive commentaries. Nabokov had already criticized the translations of other scholars; now he came under attack from his old friend Edmund Wilson for the peculiarities of his own work, with its deliberately archaic English vocabulary, its pedantry, and its attempt to be as literal a translation as possible; although Nabokov was generally agreed to have won the battle, a break with Wilson resulted, and he may have lost some other friends and admirers in the skirmishes. Nabokov's version of *Eugene Onegin* is brilliant beyond the bounds of scholarship; obsessive, outrageous, and inspired, it makes scholarship a separate art.

Vladimir Nabokov and his wife Vera (photo by M. Frank Wolfe, Globe Pictures)

In 1969 Nabokov published *Ada,* by far his longest and least approachable work. The novel is full of apparent digressions, while its language, saturated with multilingual puns and oblique references, may be an overabundance of riches. Although *Ada* is certainly not as difficult or obscure as James Joyce's *Finnegans Wake,* it has attracted the same kind of critical question as to whether it is a masterpiece or a self-indulgent failure. For Nabokov's own brand of reader, *Ada* is a heady work, and it has already been the sole subject of several books and dissertations. The main characters, Van and Ada, maintain an incestuous relationship for their whole lives, from adolescence through extreme old age; though the appended diagram of their family tree shows them as first cousins, in the reality they uncover they are brother and sister. They appear to live on the parallel planet of Antiterra where geography (Russia is a part of the United States) and history have been altered, where there are flying carpets and waterpowered telephones; however, because the novel is narrated by Van, who is extremely imaginative and forgetful,

it is likely that the events actually take place on our own planet but have been distorted by Van out of any easily recognizable context.

Nabokov's last two novels have not as yet attracted much interest. The first, *Transparent Things* (1972), concerns the shy and rather innocent Hugh Person, who strangles his unfaithful wife in his sleep and later dies in a hotel fire. The reader discovers only in the novel's last sentence that it has been narrated by the dead Mr. R., a novelist and friend of Person who greets him as he enters the afterlife. The device of throwing a new light on a novel at its very end, changing the reader's perception of the whole, is characteristic of several of Nabokov's works, while the metaphysical speculations of *Transparent Things* make it clearly akin to *Invitation to a Beheading* and *The Real Life of Sebastian Knight.* If not quite as compelling as some earlier works, this slight novel is undoubtedly attractive.

Look at the Harlequins! (1974) concerns Vadim Vadimovich, a writer whose name, novels, and biography parody those of his author. The narrative, which depends for much of its tension on the con-

First page of the 1926 Russian typescript for The Enchanter, *in which Nabokov first explored the themes developed in* Lolita

trasts of Vadim with Vladimir Vladimirovich Nabokov, may not be of great interest to those readers not already familiar with the rest of Nabokov's work.

At his death in 1977, Nabokov had been at work on a new novel, "The Original of Laura," but publication of the work in incomplete form was "expressly" forbidden; whether it will ever be available is an open question. Aside from the continuing translation of Nabokov's earlier Russian works, his classroom lectures have recently been edited for publication. He is survived by his wife and son, both of whom are intensely loyal to his memory, deeply involved in current translations of his works, and concerned for his enduring reputation.

Vladimir Nabokov was both a great and an influential novelist, and at least one generation of authors has been awed by his control over his materials, his ability to transform the novel into a self-referential, lucid maze, and his unbeatable, unique style. He was also a formidable critic. His passion for the classics of Russian literature has spurred American interest, while his vigorous

championing of some writers and denigration of others—Russian, European, American—have contributed to the continuing re-evaluation of which authors are indeed classics. Certainly his outspoken attacks on Freudian psychology have contributed significantly to the decline in interest in Freudian literary analysis. Nabokov's influence has been seen even inside the Soviet Union, where excerpts from his Russian works are now being published for the first time, and his reputation is secure for the foreseeable future.

Interviews and Letters:

Strong Opinions (New York: McGraw-Hill, 1973);
    A collection of Nabokov's carefully controlled and sharply worded interviews.

The Nabokov-Wilson Letters, edited by Simon Karlinsky (New York: Harper & Row, 1979; revised edition, New York: Harper Colophon, 1980);
    Interesting letters, primarily on literary matters, exchanged with the formidable critic Edmund Wilson.

Perepiska s sestroy (Ann Arbor, Mich.: Ardis, 1985);
    Correspondence with his sister, almost entirely in Russian.

Bibliographies:

Michael Juliar, *Vladimir Nabokov: A Descriptive Bibliography* (New York: Garland, 1986);
    An excellent and thorough inventory of primary works.

Samuel Schuman, *Vladimir Nabokov: A Reference Guide* (Boston: G. K. Hall, 1979);
    Annotated bibliography of articles on Nabokov through 1977.

References:

Alfred Appel, Jr., *Nabokov's Dark Cinema* (New York: Oxford University Press, 1970);
    A study of Nabokov's relationships to the cinema.

Appel, Jr., ed., *The Annotated Lolita* (New York: McGraw-Hill, 1970);
    An invaluable edition of *Lolita*, exhaustively thorough in its notes and annotations.

Appel and Charles Newman, eds., *Nabokov: Criticisms, Reminiscences, Translations, and Tributes* (Evanston, Ill.: Northwestern University Press, 1970);

Original articles by a number of well-known critics, together with some useful reminiscences.

L. S. Dembo, ed., *Nabokov: The Man and His Work* (Madison: University of Wisconsin Press, 1967);
The first collection of original articles on Nabokov and still useful.

Andrew Field, *Nabokov: His Life in Part* (Boston: Little, Brown, 1967);
The first study to consider Nabokov's Russian works in detail, as well as later writings, especially valuable for considering the early works.

Field, *VN: The Life and Art of Vladimir Nabokov* (New York: Crown, 1986);
The only major biography of Nabokov at this time, a controversial work that replaces Field's own earlier *Nabokov: His Life in Part.*

George Gibian and Stephen Jan Parker, eds., *The Achievements of Vladimir Nabokov* (Ithaca, N.Y.: Center for International Studies, Cornell University, 1984);
A recent collection of original materials, many of them related to Nabokov's ten years at Cornell.

Jane Grayson, *Nabokov Translated: A Comparison of Nabokov's Russian and English Prose* (London: Oxford University Press, 1976);
A clear view of Nabokov's methods in translating his own works, specialized but invaluable.

G. M. Hyde, *Vladimir Nabokov: America's Russian Novelist* (London: Marion Boyars, 1977);
The best single-author survey of Nabokov's major works and themes.

L. L. Lee, *Vladimir Nabokov* (Boston: Twayne, 1976);
A reliable survey in the Twayne format.

Bobbie Ann Mason, *Nabokov's Garden: A Guide to Ada* (Ann Arbor, Mich.: Ardis, 1974);
Devoted entirely to *Ada,* this book discusses the incest theme.

Modern Fiction Studies, special Nabokov issue, edited by Charles S. Ross, 25 (Autumn 1979);
A mixed group of original essays.

Donald E. Morton, *Vladimir Nabokov* (New York: Frederick Ungar, 1974);
Another reliable survey.

Julian Moynahan, *Vladimir Nabokov* (Minneapolis: University of Minnesota Press, 1971);
An extremely well-written long pamphlet, possibly the best introduction to Nabokov.

David Packman, *Vladimir Nabokov: The Structure of Literary Desire* (Columbia: University of Missouri Press, 1982);
A theoretical but stimulating description of several Nabokov novels in relationship to contemporary critical theories.

Stephen Jan Parker, ed., *The Nabokovian* (formerly *The Vladimir Nabokov Research Newsletter*) (Fall 1978-);
Article abstracts, notes, news, and bibliographical updates.

Ellen Pifer, *Nabokov and the Novel* (Cambridge, Mass.: Harvard University Press, 1980);
Demonstrates the depth of characterization in some of Nabokov's more "artificial" novels.

Carl Proffer, ed., *A Book of Things About Vladimir Nabokov* (Ann Arbor, Mich.: Ardis, 1973);
Another collection of original articles, especially focused on Russian backgrounds.

Peter Quennell, ed., *Vladimir Nabokov: A Tribute to His Life, His Work, His World* (London: Weidenfeld & Nicolson, 1979);
Another, more elegiac collection of original articles.

J. E. Rivers and Charles Nicol, eds., *Nabokov's Fifth Arc* (Austin: University of Texas Press, 1982);
Another collection of original articles, with valuable material on *Lolita* and *Ada.*

Phyllis Roth, ed., *Critical Essays on Vladimir Nabokov* (Boston: G. K. Hall, 1984);
A reprinting of many of the best articles on Nabokov from the last forty years.

W. W. Rowe, *Nabokov's Spectral Dimension* (Ann Arbor, Mich.: Ardis, 1981);
A controversial exploration of spiritualism in Nabokov's novels.

Dabney Stuart, *Nabokov: The Dimensions of Parody* (Baton Rouge: Louisiana State University Press, 1978);

Good essays on several novels, rather than a unified study.

Flannery O'Connor

This entry was updated by John R. May (Louisiana State University) from his entry in
DLB 2, American Novelists Since World War II.

Places	Savannah, Georgia Yaddo Artist's Colony	Milledgeville, Georgia Andalusia	University of Iowa

Influences and Relationships	Nathaniel Hawthorne
	Robert Giroux
	Sally and Robert
	    Fitzgerald
		Caroline Gordon
		Nathanael West
		Andrew Lytle
		Robert Lowell
			William Faulkner
			John Hawkes
			Pierre Teilhard
			    de Chardin

Literary Movements and Forms	Gospel Parables
	The Grotesque
	Apocalypse
		American Romance
		    Tradition
		Symbolism
			(Biblical) Prophetic
			    Tradition

Major Themes	The Demonic
	Mystery and
	    Manners
	Catastrophe as
	    Hierophany
	Kingdom of God
		The Word as
		    Revelation
		Sacramental View
		    of Life
		The Countryside and
		    the True Country
			Fall, Redemption,
			    and Judgment
			Displacement and
			    Homecoming

Cultural and Artistic Influences	Bible-Belt Funda- mentalism	Existentialism Backwoods Prophecy	Roman Catholicism

Social and Economic Influences	Southern Genteel
	    Tradition
	World War II's Dis-
	    placed Persons
		Racial and Social
		    Segregation
		Small Farm Life
			Good Country
			    Manners

399

See also the O'Connor entry in DLB Yearbook: 1980.

BIRTH: Savannah, Georgia, 25 March 1925, to Edward Francis and Regina Cline O'Connor.

EDUCATION: A.B., Women's College of Georgia (now Georgia College), 1945; M.F.A., State University of Iowa, 1947.

AWARDS AND HONORS: *Kenyon Review* fellowship, 1953; National Institute of Arts and Letters grant, 1957; O. Henry Memorial Awards first prize for "Greenleaf," 1957, and for other short stories, 1963, 1965; Ford Foundation grant, 1959; Litt.D., St. Mary's College, 1962; Litt.D., Smith College, 1963; Henry H. Bellamann Foundation special award, 1964; National Book Award for *The Complete Stories*, 1972; Board Award, National Book Critics Circle, for *The Habit of Being*, 1980.

DEATH: Milledgeville, Georgia, 3 August 1964.

BOOKS: *Wise Blood* (New York: Harcourt, Brace, 1952; London: Spearman, 1955);
A Good Man Is Hard to Find (New York: Harcourt, Brace, 1955); republished as *The Artificial Nigger and Other Tales* (London: Spearman, 1957);
The Violent Bear It Away (New York: Farrar, Straus & Cudahy, 1960; London: Longmans, 1960);
Everything That Rises Must Converge (New York: Farrar, Straus & Giroux, 1965; London: Faber & Faber, 1966);
Mystery and Manners (New York: Farrar, Straus & Giroux, 1969; London: Faber & Faber, 1972);
The Complete Stories of Flannery O'Connor (New York: Farrar, Straus & Giroux, 1971);
The Habit of Being: Letters, edited by Sally Fitzgerald (New York: Farrar, Straus & Giroux, 1979).

Flannery O'Connor's life is best summarized in Robert Fitzgerald's introduction to *Everything That Rises Must Converge*. As friend and literary executor, Fitzgerald writes of her with candor and love: "She was a girl who started with a gift for cartooning and satire, and found in herself a far greater gift, unique in her time and place, a marvel." That gift, of course, was story telling. She wrote two novels and thirty-one short stories and the critical response to her work has been extraordinary. Since her death in 1964, eighteen books of criticism have been published, as well as three collections of essays and five bibliographical studies.

In little more than three decades since her reputation began to develop in the mid 1950s, at least four hundred critical essays and reminiscences have appeared in journals.

One of the principal reasons for this overwhelming response to her fiction is undoubtedly the fact that in an age of existential angst and the eclipse of traditional belief, Flannery O'Connor wrote brilliant stories that brought the issue of religious faith into clear dramatic focus. She was a devout Roman Catholic living in predominantly Protestant rural Georgia. Her stories are far from pious; in fact, their mode is usually shocking and often bizarre. Yet the religious issues they raise are central to her work. As Robert Fitzgerald expresses it, "she kept going deeper . . . until making up stories became, for her, a way of testing and defining and conveying that superior knowledge that must be called religious."

O'Connor's fictional world as a Catholic writer is one founded on three basic theological truths: "the Fall, the Redemption, and the Judgment." But the "modern secular world," as she was accustomed to call it, is either unprepared or unwilling to accept that vision. The would-be existentialist prophet in *Wise Blood*, Hazel Motes, in preaching his "Church Without Christ," puts it this way: "I'm going to preach there was no Fall because there was nothing to fall from and no Redemption because there was no Fall and no Judgment because there wasn't the first two." "[The Catholic fiction writer] may have to resort," O'Connor believed, "to violent literary means to get his vision across to a hostile audience." The literary genre she chose was the grotesque— "grotesque with good reason," she would claim— because "to the hard of hearing you shout, and for the almost-blind you draw large and startling figures."

Because her talent was so great, her life seemed tragically short. Born in Savannah, Georgia, on 25 March 1925, Flannery O'Connor died when she was just thirty-nine on 3 August 1964, in Milledgeville, Georgia, where her family had moved in 1938. She succumbed to a disease, disseminated lupus, that first struck in December 1950. O'Connor completed her undergraduate work at Georgia State College for Women (now Georgia College, the location of the O'Connor Collection) and two years later, in 1947, earned a Master of Fine Arts degree from the University of Iowa. Her master's thesis, entitled *The Geranium: A Collection of Short Stories*, included six stories, the last of which, "The Train," reappeared in revised form

Flannery O'Connor with her self-portrait

as the beginning of her first novel, *Wise Blood* (1952).

O'Connor's modest bequest to American letters has been enough to assure her a permanent place among our greatest writers of fiction. She knew what held a good story together and expressed it this way, with characteristic reference to the element of mystery that she was convinced gave a story its worth: "I often ask myself what makes a story work, and what makes it hold up as a story," she told an audience at Hollins College in October 1963, "and I have decided that it is probably some action, some gesture of a character that is unlike any other in the story, one which indicates where the real heart of the story lies. This would have to be an action or a gesture which was both totally right and totally unexpected; it would have to be one that was both in character and beyond character; it would have to suggest both time and eternity." In terms of her Christian faith, this would be the literary analogue of the moment of grace.

It is almost invariably harder to expose the unifying structure of a novel than of a short story because the novel's greater elasticity of form diffuses its "dramatic center," yet the same pattern of

saving gesture or revealing word is found in O'Connor's novels. *Wise Blood,* a novel about the Fall of man (the title is O'Connor's facetious idiom for original sin), is framed by Hazel Motes's encounter with two "ordinary" women whose interest in him is perceptive beyond their realization. The first words spoken in the novel suggest its final meaning. On the train to Taulkinham, Mrs. Wally Bee Hitchcock says to Haze, "I guess you're going home," and follows it with, "Well . . . there's no place like home." Haze, of course, does not answer. Rather than going home, Haze, like Tarwater in the second novel, is running from "the bleeding, stinking mad shadow of Jesus." His flight from Jesus is a search for "place," but flight yields no place, only emptiness and despair, as Haze himself concludes: "Where you come from is gone, where you thought you were going to never was there, and where you are is no good unless you can get away from it. Where is there a place for you to be? No place." When, finally, his lifeless body is brought back to Mrs. Flood, her words connote far more than she realizes: "Well, Mr. Motes . . . I see you've come home." Haze has had, in the pattern of Oedipus, to blind himself in order to see. His act of atone-

Dust jacket for O'Connor's first book, about heretical preacher Hazel Motes, who taught in his "Church Without Christ" that "there was no Fall because there was nothing to fall from and no Redemption because there was no Fall and no Judgment because there wasn't the first two"

ment and the life of penance that leads to his death suggest that one must stop searching in order to find what one is looking for. The peace of place is within—and beyond.

In the title story of her first collection, *A Good Man Is Hard to Find* (1955), the saving gesture is the grandmother's recognition of The Misfit. This story, one of O'Connor's finest, reveals more clearly the dynamism of her fictional world in which unexpected events, usually tragic, yield genuine human insight and the possibility of Redemption. (If her audiences considered her situations alien and offensive, she was fond of asking them simply to read the daily newspaper to see how commonplace tragedy is.) The plot is simple enough: a family on

vacation is killed by an escaped convict. In preparing for and unfolding the dramatic conflict between the grandmother and The Misfit, O'Connor creates pure art out of the tragicomedy of life. She also discloses one of her characteristic signatures as a Christian writer: Good somehow is often wrenched from evil. The demonic figure of The Misfit serves as the agent of grace. O'Connor's "action of grace" is, typically, "in territory held largely by the devil."

The Misfit discloses the possibilities of existence to the grandmother when he reminds her how Jesus "thown everything off balance. If He did what He said," The Misfit claims, "then it's nothing for you to do but thow away everything and follow Him, and if He didn't, then it's nothing for you to do but enjoy the few minutes you got left the best way you can—by killing somebody or burning down his house, or doing some other meanness to him. No pleasure but meanness." His decision to kill the grandmother and her whole family is an apparent denial then that Jesus really had "raised the dead," yet he implies the very opposite when he concludes that "it's no real pleasure in life." The grandmother's response is the perfect ironic counterpart of The Misfit's. "Not knowing what she was saying," she mumbles a denial, "Maybe He didn't raise the dead," and then reaches out to The Misfit as if she actually believes in the Resurrection when she acknowledges her responsibility for his sin, "Why you're one of my babies. You're one of my own children!" To The Misfit, her touch is like the bite of a snake. The gesture of recognition and acceptance signals her death. The Misfit denies the Resurrection in deed yet seems finally to imply a desire for acceptance; the grandmother denies it in word, perhaps, but clearly accepts it in deed.

Demonic characters are the occasion of grace or at least of judgment in three other stories in the collection. Harry Ashfield in "The River" drowns while trying to escape from the hideous Mr. Paradise and is at last received by the river whose waters, he believes, will make him "count." In "A Circle in the Fire," it is not until three young delinquents from the city wantonly set fire to Mrs. Cope's woods that she comes to appreciate the misery of the world's dispossessed. Manley Pointer, the demonic Bible salesman in "Good Country People," demonstrates the power of the evil heart over the malignant mind when he strips Hulga of the symbols of her pride, her artificial leg and her glasses— her soul and its self-styled insight.

"A Stroke of Good Fortune" and "A Late Encounter with the Enemy" show how easily man can become his own worst enemy. Ruby Hill's sloth and selfishness will kill her faster than the unwanted child she comes to discover is growing within her. "General" Sash, on the other hand, has lived for so long off of history without any genuine sense of its meaning that it is nothing more than a final enemy he succumbs to when his granddaughter uses him to add prestige to her graduation. Two other stories illustrate perfectly O'Connor's use of the grotesque as an instrument of religious vision. In both "The Life You Save May Be Your Own" and "A Temple of the Holy Ghost," it is clear that the truly grotesque are not the physically handicapped but the spiritually deformed.

The remaining stories in the first collection, "The Artificial Nigger" and "The Displaced Person," rival the title story for a place among O'Connor's very best, and appropriately enough each displays her mastery of symbolism as art's way of joining time and eternity. The first is a modern variation on the *Inferno*, dramatizing descent into self-knowledge; the other, the last story in the collection, unveils the good man who is so hard to find, a latter-day Christ who brings salvation but is rejected. Confronted with the chipped statue of the Negro boy, Mr. Head confesses his awareness of personal sin by rejecting the artificiality of discrimination. "They ain't got enough real ones here," he tells his grandson, Nelson. "They got to have an artificial one." (The relationship between an old man and a young man becomes the heart of O'Connor's second novel.) The climactic dialogue between Mrs. McIntyre and Father Flynn in "The Displaced Person" is a masterpiece of misunderstood meaning and ignored revelation. Mrs. McIntyre shores up her decision to release Mr. Guizac, the displaced person who attempts to arrange his cousin's immigration to America by having her marry a black farmhand in the segregated South: "He didn't have to come in the first place," she tells the priest. But Father Flynn, contemplating the Transfiguration of Christ in the resplendence of the peacock (O'Connor's most successful use of natural symbolism), thinks she is referring to Christ's Advent and announces the good news of salvation: "He came to redeem us."

In subtlety of symbolism and obsession with the demonic, O'Connor's short stories are descendants of Nathaniel Hawthorne's tales; the starkness of her imagery and her use of the grotesque in both the short stories and *Wise Blood* are often related with reason to Nathanael West. When it comes to her second and decidedly superior novel, *The Violent Bear It Away* (1960), the literary indebtedness that can be discerned lies closer to home.

Dust jacket for O'Connor's second novel about a fundamentalist prophet seeking to impose Christian morality on his nephew's young son

Not only are the cadences of style suggestive of William Faulkner, but also some of the novel's major themes. Its preoccupation with the influence that the dead continue to exert on the living is clearly reminiscent of Addie Bundren's domination of her family in *As I Lay Dying* (Robert Fitzgerald reports that it was one of her favorite novels); there is also its pervasive concern about the relationship between words and deeds, a theme that has even deeper roots in the teaching of Jesus.

The novel abounds in images and symbols, but O'Connor is as successful here as in her richest stories in weaving them together into a harmonious whole. The principal ones are biblical in origin: fire, water, hunger, the bread of life, prophecy, the sower, and the Word. In the final analysis, though, it is not the symbolism that puts readers off, but the central character himself, Mason, a fundamentalist backwoods prophet for whom history begins with Eden and ends with the Day of the Lord. People find it hard to be objective in the presence of fanaticism, yet be objective one must if the novel is to be understood. Mason and his nephew Rayber are locked in mortal combat for the control of young Tarwater's education. Mason stands for faith in the supernatural, Rayber for disbelief. Yet in a fictional world in which the voice of reason turns out to be the dragon of seduction, the novel makes the eminently plausible point that only the enthusiast ("the violent") can gain the kingdom ("bear it away"). It is not until Tarwater has been violated in mind and body by the homosexual stranger and has thus for the first time experienced evil himself that he accepts the prophetic mission his great-uncle has given him. As he marches toward the city at the close of the novel, he hears Mason's command again: "GO WARN THE CHILDREN OF GOD OF THE TERRIBLE SPEED OF MERCY." "The words," we are told, "were as silent as seeds opening one at a time in his blood." One has to know evil before one can understand the need to preach redemption.

If the first collection of stories sketches a world that, for O'Connor, seems almost gracious in comparison with *Wise Blood* in its evocation of mercy for the fallen—there is no redemption, of course, without a fall—the world of the posthumous collection, *Everything That Rises Must Converge* (1965), is decidedly less so. Although the stories build toward a powerful climax suggesting an affirmative interpretation of the "convergence" of the title, it is the apocalyptic moment of Judgment for an unregenerate world that abounds here, as it does in *The Violent Bear It Away*.

In the title story, however limited Julian's mother's view of reality is, it is far superior to his mindless liberalism; and her single functioning eye, which rakes Julian's face for a final time and finds nothing, implies a judgment more scathing than words can achieve. The fierce, inflamed eye of a bird in the water stain on Asbury's ceiling is the instrument of judgment in "The Enduring Chill." Asbury's interracial communion in unpasteurized milk with Randall and Morgan is the cause of the undulant fever that will return periodically to chill his body as the icy image of the Holy Ghost chastens his mind and heart. As a historian, Thomas, in "The Comforts of Home," ought to have had sufficient insight to realize that his father, the figure "squatting" in his mind, had no rights over the sanctity of the human spirit. The peace that Thomas lies to protect ends in complex tragedy; one does not connive with evil in order to end it, as Haze learns in *Wise Blood*.

Mrs. May in "Greenleaf" is the victim of a bull's irresistible attraction to cars, but more precisely of her own refusal to allow anyone—even God—to alter her view of reality. In "A View of the Woods," Mr. Fortune hopes to make his granddaughter, Mary Fortune Pitts, into a Fortune, like himself a lover of progress—drive-ins, supermarkets, gas stations, and paved roads. She prefers to give up a fortune—and her life—rather than accept his sale of the land across the road that will destroy her view of the woods. The only quality of his that she has inherited is, ironically, his irascibility, and so they struggle to the death like two titans of pride. Rufus's cry "The lame shall enter first!" in the story with the same name sounds the evangelical note of the Beatitudes, condemning Sheppard for his scientific atheism and reminding us once again how Jesus has "thown everything off balance."

The title *Everything That Rises Must Converge* is borrowed from the evolutionary reflections of Pierre Teilhard de Chardin, the French paleontologist-theologian who was denied permission by Rome to publish his works. After his death in 1955, they were published by friends and colleagues; O'Connor read what was available with great interest, without apparently sharing fully Teilhard's optimistic view of man's rise in the evolutionary chain. The final three stories of O'Connor's second collection, nevertheless, sound an affirmative note about the human condition—and they too rank with her most highly acclaimed. Ruby Turpin in "Revelation" places herself close to the top of life's hierarchy of classes; Mary Grace pierces through to the heart of Ruby's discriminatory attitude and opens up for her a vision of the world in which God disregards human standards of judgment and sees through to the inner value of the person. O. E. Parker in "Parker's Back" suffers, but he grows through suffering; that sort of diminishment Teilhard de Chardin accepted as a necessary part of evolution. It is the stern eyes of the Byzantine Christ in the tattooer's book of religious pictures that speak the saving word of revelation to Parker—"GO BACK!" Parker goes back to his full name, Obadiah Elihue (which means "the servant of Yahweh, he is God"), *and* to his wife. To be rejected in an act of selfless love—the image on his back that Sarah Ruth cannot tolerate was after all for her alone—is to live unmistakably in the likeness of God's servant.

Although Flannery O'Connor undoubtedly had a great sense of the creative role of the writer, she was convinced that there were definite limits within which that creativity had to be exercised. In "The Church and the Fiction Writer," she speaks about the "what-is" that is the concrete material of the writer: "The writer learns, perhaps more quickly than the reader, to be humble in the face of what-is. What-is is all he has to do with; the concrete is his medium; and he will realize eventually that fiction can transcend its limitations only by staying within them." A writer creates by shaping reality to his purpose. "What he is rearranging *is* nature," she insisted.

The ultimate purpose of the artist's use of concrete reality is, as she saw it, to transcend it through vision. "The peculiar problem of the short-story writer," she asserts, "is how to make the action he describes reveal as much of the mystery of existence as possible. He has only a short space to do it in and he can't do it by statement. He has to do it by showing, not by saying, and by showing the concrete—so that his problem is really how to make the concrete work double time for him." For Flannery O'Connor, the mystery of existence discloses a transcendent world that is every bit as real as the visible world. On another occasion she wrote that the writer is "looking for one image that will connect or combine or embody two points; one is a point in the concrete, and the other is a point not visible to the naked eye, but believed in by him firmly, just as real to him, really, as the one that everybody sees." The writer must also have a strong sense of his own region. He leaves his region, she wrote, "at great peril to that balance between principle and fact, between judgment and observation, which is so necessary to maintain if fiction is to be true." For, "unless the novelist has gone utterly out of his mind, his aim is still communication, and communication suggests talking inside a community." She assumes, therefore, that the artist wishes to communicate. Aside from her assertion that communication works best within the community of those who share the same "manners," she speaks of the artist's communication of his prophetic vision as revelation to the reader, provided he sees the creative process as basically healthy. "Those who believe that art proceeds from a healthy, and not from a diseased, faculty of the mind," she writes, "will take what [the artist] shows them as a revelation, not of what we ought to be but of what we are at a given time and under given circumstances; that is, as a limited revelation but revelation nevertheless."

It is no surprise then that Sally and Robert Fitzgerald chose the title *Mystery and Manners* when they selected for publication and edited the collec-

tion of O'Connor's occasional prose five years after her death. The title encompasses briefly but accurately the dimensions of her art. While including a delightful piece that she wrote on peacocks and her introduction to *A Memoir of Mary Ann,* the work is principally a collection of her lectures and published essays related to the theory of fiction and to the call that she felt she had received to be, specifically, a Catholic writer.

The full legacy of O'Connor's short fiction was finally packaged in one volume and published in 1971 as *The Complete Stories.* There are thirty-one stories in the volume, twelve appearing for the first time in book form (although all twelve had been published before). The chronological sequence according to date of composition that the editor, Robert Giroux, follows provides the clearest possible index of O'Connor's growth as an artist. "Judgement Day," the last of *The Complete Stories* as well as the last in the second collection, is a revised and expanded version of the very first story O'Connor published, "The Geranium."

Both stories are concerned with exiles from their "true country," but whereas Old Dudley of "The Geranium" remains exiled from his Southern home because of his mistaken sense of place, it is perfectly clear (and confessionally appropriate) that in "Judgement Day" Old Tanner's imagined return to Corinth, Georgia, is a genuine victory over alienation—because he knows his place. O'Connor's last story is a truly distinguished American variation on the archetype of homecoming and perhaps our finest literary presentation of the significance of resurrection. Its evocation of spiritual triumph is a fitting crown for an illustrious, though regrettably short career. It is not at all strange that concern for an exile from home should be the alpha and omega of a writer whose faith was certainly as important as her art.

The publication in 1979 of *The Habit of Being,* a collection of O'Connor's letters, reinforces the notion that the dynamism of faith and region was every bit as much the substance of her life as it was of her fiction. In a 15 September 1955 letter to Andrew Lytle she wrote: "To my way of thinking, the only thing that keeps me from being a regional writer is being a Catholic and the only thing that keeps me from being a Catholic writer (in the narrow sense) is being a Southerner."

Sally Fitzgerald selected, edited, and wrote the introduction to this extraordinary collection of letters that spans Flannery O'Connor's productive years as a writer, from 1948 until her death in 1964. The letters provide indispensable clues to the

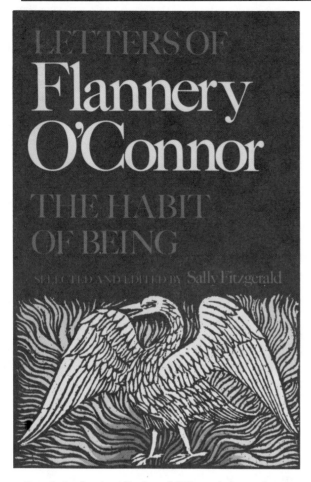

Dust jacket for the collection of O'Connor's letters that won a Special National Book Critics Circle Award, a Christopher Award, and a Bowdoin College Award in 1980

everyday source of her artistic material—events at Andalusia that found their way into fiction—and an essential confirmation of the soundness of her judgment about her own work. She voices repeated satisfaction, for example, with "The Artificial Nigger" and "Good Country People" and consistent regrets about "A Stroke of Good Fortune" and "The Partridge Festival." There is clarification of her intentions about the design of most of her stories, and an illuminating exchange with John Hawkes over his misunderstanding of the demonic in her fiction.

The release of major screen and television adaptations of two of O'Connor's works—*The Displaced Person* (1979) and *Wise Blood* (1980)—accompanied the appearance of *The Habit of Being*. *The Displaced Person*, adapted for Public Television's "American Short Story" series, had memorable performances by Shirley Stoler as Mrs. Shortley,

Irene Worth as Mrs. McIntyre, and John Houseman as Father Flynn. *Wise Blood*, the thirty-third feature film of director John Huston, is faithful both to the spirit of the novel and to the substance of its narrative, and is an exuberantly fine film in its own right. The excellence and success of both adaptations herald a new era of O'Connor's popularity as more of her fiction is brought to the screen.

Bibliographies:
Robert E. Golden and Mary C. Sullivan, *Flannery O'Connor and Caroline Gordon: A Reference Guide* (Boston: G. K. Hall, 1977);
An annotated bibliography of the criticism of O'Connor through 1976.

David Farmer, *Flannery O'Connor: A Descriptive Bibliography* (New York: Garland, 1981);
A complete listing of everything O'Connor published, fiction and nonfiction, as well as adaptations and translations of her works.

References:
Frederick Asals, *Flannery O'Connor: The Imagination of Extremity* (Athens: University of Georgia Press, 1982);
An excellent study of the growth of O'Connor's imagination, from a "Manichean" form of imagination into a fully realized sacramental and prophetic imagination.

Robert Coles, *Flannery O'Connor's South* (Baton Rouge: Louisiana State University Press, 1980);
A highly personal and very readable presentation of the segregated, fundamentalist southern setting of O'Connor's life and fiction.

M. Kathleen Feeley, S.S.N.D., *Flannery O'Connor: Voice of the Peacock* (New Brunswick, N.J.: Rutgers University Press, 1972);
Explores the relationship between O'Connor's readings, mostly of theological and biblical works, and "the ideas which one sees imaginatively expressed in her fiction."

Melvin J. Friedman and Beverly Lyon Clark, eds., *Critical Essays on Flannery O'Connor* (Boston: G. K. Hall, 1985);
Most recent and perhaps best of the three collections of critical essays: the full range of opinions about her work, including John

Hawkes's controversial "Flannery O'Connor's Devil."

James A. Grimshaw, Jr., *The Flannery O'Connor Companion* (Westport, Conn.: Greenwood, 1981);
A handsomely designed book with useful information and aids to reading O'Connor's works, for first-time readers.

Josephine Hendin, *The World of Flannery O'Connor* (Bloomington: Indiana University Press, 1970);
A psychological interpretation of O'Connor; claims her southern Irish-American womanhood and crippling disease affected her writing more than her Roman Catholic faith.

Carter W. Martin, *The True Country: Themes in the Fiction of Flannery O'Connor* (Nashville: Vanderbilt University Press, 1969);
Exploration of the theological themes in O'Connor, based in her sacramental view of reality.

John R. May, *The Pruning Word: The Parables of Flannery O'Connor* (Notre Dame: University of Notre Dame Press, 1976);
Offers analyses of all of *The Complete Stories* as well as the novels, as parables in the biblical tradition.

Dorothy Tuck McFarland, *Flannery O'Connor* (New York: Ungar, 1976);
Another treatment of themes in O'Connor's fiction.

Barbara McKenzie, *Flannery O'Connor's Georgia* (Athens: University of Georgia Press, 1980);
Excellent photographic study of O'Connor's rural Georgia—her Christ-haunted countryside.

Marion Montgomery, *Why Flannery O'Connor Stayed Home* (La Salle, Ill.: Sherwood Sugden, 1981);
Considers O'Connor's Catholic faith the greatest strength of her art, and O'Connor a "prophetic poet" in the tradition of Dante.

Gilbert H. Muller, *Nightmares and Visions: Flannery O'Connor and the Catholic Grotesque* (Athens: University of Georgia Press, 1972);
The fullest and most balanced treatment of the grotesque in O'Connor.

Miles Orvell, *Invisible Parade: The Fiction of Flannery O'Connor* (Philadelphia: Temple University Press, 1972);
Justifies O'Connor's world view in relation to the American "romance" tradition beginning with Hawthorne.

Robert E. Reiter, ed., *Flannery O'Connor* (St. Louis: Herder, 1968);
An early collection of critical views of O'Connor; somewhat dated now, but interesting nonetheless. Includes Robert Fitzgerald's "The Countryside and the True Country."

Dorothy Walters, *Flannery O'Connor* (New York: Twayne, 1973);
One of the Twayne United States Authors Series; a good, clear introduction to its subject.

Louise Westling, *Sacred Groves and Ravaged Gardens: The Fiction of Eudora Welty, Carson McCullers, and Flannery O'Connor* (Athens: University of Georgia Press, 1985);
A feminist reading of O'Connor's mother-daughter stories and her treatment of the Georgia landscape.

Papers:
The Flannery O'Connor Collection was donated to the Georgia College Library. It contains 328 folders of manuscript, 594 volumes from the author's personal library, audiotapes, 16 mm films, various editions and translations of the author's works, critical writings, newspaper clippings, and photographs.

Sylvia Plath

This entry was updated by Ellen Rosenberg (Columbia, South Carolina) from the entry by Thomas McClanahan (Idaho Department of Humanities) in DLB 5, American Poets Since World War II, and the entry by Nancy Duvall Hargrove (Mississippi State University) in DLB 6, American Novelists Since World War II.

Places	London Smith College Cambridge	Boston Wellesley	Devon New York City
Influences and Relationships	Anne Sexton	Robert Lowell	Ted Hughes
Literary Movements and Forms	Confessional Poetry		
Major Themes	The Double Initiation Family	Death Persecutor and Victim Roles of Women	Disembodiment Search for Identity
Cultural and Artistic Influences	Psychoanalysis		
Social and Economic Influences	World War II		

BIRTH: Jamaica Plain, Massachusetts, 27 October 1932, to Otto Emil and Aurelia Schober Plath.

EDUCATION: B.A., Smith College, 1955; Harvard University, summer 1954; M.A., Newnham College, Cambridge University, 1955-1957.

MARRIAGE: 16 June 1956 to Ted Hughes (separated); children: Frieda Rebecca, Nicholas Farrar.

AWARDS AND HONORS: *Mademoiselle* College Board contest fiction prize, 1953; Irene Glascock Poetry Prize, 1955; Fulbright fellowship, 1955-1957; Bess Hokin Award (*Poetry* magazine), 1957; first prize in Cheltenham Festival, 1961; Eugene F. Saxon fellowship, 1961.

DEATH: London, England, 11 February 1963.

SELECTED BOOKS: *A Winter Ship* (Edinburgh: Tragara Press, 1960);
The Colossus (London, Melbourne & Toronto: Heinemann, 1960; abridged edition, New York: Knopf, 1962);
The Bell Jar, as Victoria Lucas (London, Melbourne & Toronto: Heinemann, 1963; New York, Evanston, San Francisco & London: Harper & Row, 1971);
Ariel (London: Faber & Faber, 1965; New York: Harper & Row, 1966);
Uncollected Poems (London: Turret Books, 1965);
Three Women; A Monologue for Three Voices (London: Turret Books, 1968);
Wreath for a Bridal (Frensham, Surrey, U.K.: Sceptre Press, 1970);
Child (Exeter, U.K.: Rougemont Press, 1971);
Crossing the Water: Transitional Poems (London: Faber & Faber, 1971; New York, Evanston, San Francisco & London: Harper & Row, 1971);
Crystal Gazer and Other Poems (London: Rainbow Press, 1971);
Fiesta Melons (Exeter, U.K.: Rougemont Press, 1971);
Lyonesse Poems (London: Rainbow Press, 1971);
Million Dollar Month (Frensham, Surrey, U.K.: Sceptre Press, 1971);
Winter Trees (London: Faber & Faber, 1971; New York, Evanston, San Francisco & London: Harper & Row, 1972);
Pursuit (London: Rainbow Press, 1973);
The Bed Book (London: Faber & Faber/New York, Hagerstown, San Francisco & London: Harper & Row, 1976);

Sylvia Plath, 1954 (courtesy of Aurelia Schober Plath)

Johnny Panic and the Bible of Dreams, and Other Prose Writings (London: Faber & Faber, 1977); expanded as *Johnny Panic and the Bible of Dreams: Short Stories, Prose and Diary Excerpts* (New York, Hagerstown, San Francisco & London: Harper & Row, 1979);
Dialogue over a Ouija Board (Cambridge, U.K.: Rainbow Press, 1981);
The Journals of Sylvia Plath, edited by Ted Hughes and Frances McCullough (New York: Dial Press, 1982);
Stings (Northampton, Mass.: Smith College Library, 1983).
Collection: *Collected Poems*, edited by Ted Hughes (London: Faber & Faber, 1981).

OTHER: *American Poetry Now*, edited by Plath (London: Oxford University Press, 1963).

Now famous for her ritual flirtations with death, Sylvia Plath has emerged as a significant figure in contemporary American literature in the two and a half decades since her suicide on 11 February 1963. Her reputation as an accomplished and versatile author has developed as a response to the posthumous publication of the bulk of her work. A so-called modern confessional writer because of her open use of autobiographical material, Plath has been critically recognized for the intense focus of emotion in her art, especially in the crown jewel of her poetry collections *Ariel* (1965), written in the last six months of her life, and in her modern rite-of-passage novel *The Bell Jar* (as Victoria Lucas, 1963). In her relatively brief but highly productive career, she created—and is popularly remembered for—a complex, nearly mystical, and personal body of poetry that has struck a note of universality among contemporary readers. In her typically fastidious fashion, Plath had early set herself the task of mastering the techniques of poets of Western literature. Having completed that self-imposed apprenticeship through her disciplined experimentation with such forms as the villanelle and the Petrarchan sonnet in the period before 1956, she turned to a new exploration of her own voice. That effort culminated in the poems that comprise the bulk of her first published collection *The Colossus* (1960). Between the publication of that volume and her death, Plath wrote the mature work for which she is best known; at its best it is fiercely ironic, even comedic, intensely subjective, often ritualistic, and nearly always painful. Despite her efforts and successes as a poet, she herself once called poetry "an evasion from the real job of writing prose," and one of the professional tasks she set herself was to write clear "objective" narratives. It is not surprising, therefore, that the publication of works by Plath in the 1980s shows her to have been a prolific diarist, short story writer, and budding essayist who aspired to become a popular, highly paid, magazine-style short story writer and travel journalist.

Sylvia Plath was born on 27 October 1932 in Jamaica Plain, Massachusetts, to Aurelia Schober and Otto Emil Plath. Both were of German descent; her mother was a first-generation American, and her father came to the United States from Poland as a young man. In 1935 Plath's brother Warren was born, and two years later the family moved to Winthrop. Otto Plath, a professor of entomology specializing in the study of bees, suffered from diabetes mellitus and had had a leg amputated in consequence of that illness. He died in 1940, and his death became perhaps the central psychological event of Plath's life. Her writing is filled with allusions to her father's amputation and to what she

explicitly called her unresolved oedipal attachment to Otto Plath. From the title poem of *The Colossus*—"O father, all by yourself/You are pithy and historical as the Roman Forum"—to one of the last poems, "Daddy"—"Ghastly statue with one grey toe"—Plath's obsession with the loss of her father sounds a recurring, anguished note.

In 1942 Aurelia Plath took a job in Boston; and the family, including Plath's maternal grandparents, moved away from the coast, a place that Plath was always to associate with the innocence and happiness of youth. They settled in Wellesley, where Plath earned prizes for scholastic achievements, and her first short story was published in *Seventeen* just after her graduation from high school. Even this early, most of the issues, attitudes, and desires which were to dominate her life, especially her overriding desire for a perfection she felt she would never attain, were established, as evidenced by the following excerpts from a diary entry of 13 November 1949 (in *Letters Home,* 1975);

> Somehow I have to keep and hold the rapture of being seventeen. Every day is so precious I feel infinitely sad at the thought of all this time melting farther and farther away from me as I grow older. *Now, now* is the perfect time of my life. . . .
>
> I still do not know myself. Perhaps I never will. . . .
>
> I am afraid of getting older. I am afraid of getting married. Spare me from cooking three meals a day—spare me from the relentless cage of routine and rote. I want to be free—free to know people and their backgrounds—free to move to different parts of the world. . . .
>
> Never, never, never will I reach the perfection I long for with all my soul—my paintings, my poems, my stories. . . .
>
> There will come a time when I must face myself at last. Even now I dread the big choices which loom up in my life. . . . What do I want? I do not know.
>
> Oh, I love *now*, with all my fears and forebodings. . . .

By the time she entered Smith College in 1950, on an academic scholarship, she had already had prose and poetry accepted by the *Christian Science Monitor,* and while in school she continued to publish in *Seventeen* and served on the editorial board of the *Smith Review,* a student literary publication.

Plath excelled academically, was elected to various student offices, and received awards and

Excerpt from Sylvia Plath's high school diary (courtesy of Aurelia Schober Plath)

prizes for her short stories and poems. In the summer of 1953, she spent a month in New York as one of twenty guest editors for *Mademoiselle*'s college issue. Upon her return home, depressed by her failure to be admitted to a creative writing course at Harvard, by some of her experiences in New York, and by her personal sense of imperfection and lack of direction, she attempted suicide, crawling beneath the house and taking an overdose of sleeping pills. Found barely alive three days later, she then began the difficult road to recovery in a mental hospital. She later chronicled this period of her life in the autobiographical *The Bell Jar* published one month before her death. In many respects *The Bell Jar* forms the backdrop for recurring motifs in Plath's poetry.

Feeling herself strong enough to study again, Plath returned to Smith in January 1954 and graduated *summa cum laude* in June 1955. Not only had she received additional awards and written an honors thesis in English but she had also won a Fulbright fellowship for study at Cambridge University. There she met English poet Ted Hughes, who seemed to her a kind of ideal man, something she had never expected to find. Her wonder and joy were ecstatically expressed in letters to her mother: "I shall tell you now about something most miraculous and thundering and

terrifying. . . . It is this man, this poet, this Ted Hughes. I have never known anything like it." They were married on 16 June 1956, and Plath's letters reveal her happiness in having found what seemed a perfect relationship: "I love Teddy more and more each day and just can't imagine how I ever lived without him. Our lives fit together perfectly."

After a year in England, they came to America, spending the academic year 1957-1958 in Northampton, Massachusetts, where Plath taught freshman English at Smith, and the following year in Boston, where she wrote poems and attended Robert Lowell's poetry course at Boston University. During this period Plath worked on preliminary drafts of *The Bell Jar* and tried without success to have her first collection of poems published. In December 1959 Plath and Hughes returned to England and settled in London; soon afterwards *The Colossus* (1960) was accepted for publication by William Heinemann and in April a daughter, Frieda, was born.

The initial reception of her first full-length book of verse was unsatisfying for Plath. John Wain, writing in the London *Times Literary Supplement*, called it "clever, vivacious poetry, which will be enjoyed most by intelligent people capable of having fun with poetry and not just being holy about it." Other critics, notably P. S. Hurd and Thomas Blackburn, spoke respectively of "the adroit fashioning of metaphor and simile" and the "fine handling of language and vitality of observation," but no one praised the underlying passion of the poems. Plath wanted more than an affirmative nod toward her technical expertise with words and wit, and the lackluster reviews were hardly strong enough forces to pull her from the ensuing psychological trauma brought on by what she considered to be exhaustive efforts to write while raising a family.

During the next year, Hughes's career advanced steadily while Plath's seemed to her at a standstill. She was able to write little not only because of her responsibilities as wife and mother but also because of her poor health; apart from recurring sinusitis she had experienced a miscarriage and an appendectomy.

However, in the spring of 1961 she began working on *The Bell Jar* in earnest, confiding to a friend that she had "been wanting to do this for ten years but had a terrible block about Writing A Novel. Then suddenly . . . the dykes broke. . . ." She had become interested in novel writing because, as she said in an interview with Peter Orr, "you can get in toothbrushes and all the paraphernalia that one finds in daily life, and I find this more difficult in poetry." In May she applied for a Saxon fellowship in order to obtain money for a study and babysitters so that she could complete the novel. The Hugheses moved to a thatch-roofed house with an apple orchard and fields of daffodils in Devon on 1 September, and in November Plath was notified that she had received the Saxon fellowship. In her letter of acceptance, she noted: "I certainly do plan to go ahead with the novel and the award comes at a particularly helpful time to free me to do so." Although concentrating on *The Bell Jar* for most of the next year, she also wrote numerous poems. In February 1962 a son, Nicholas, was born.

The summer of 1962 was a very painful time in which the Hugheses' marriage broke up. Hughes, who was in love with someone else, moved to London, leaving a bitter and devastated Plath with the two children in Devon; she wrote to her mother in August that she wanted a legal separation because "I simply cannot go on living the degraded and agonized life I have been living, which has stopped my writing and just about ruined my sleep and my health. . . ." Battling her despair and disillusionment, she kept busy with beekeeping, took up horseback riding, and wrote intense and

often violent poems at top speed; in an October letter, she said that she "managed a poem a day before breakfast." She also completed *The Bell Jar*, which was accepted for publication by Heinemann, and began work on a second novel; to her brother Warren she confided, "[I] have had my first novel accepted (this is a secret; it is a pot-boiler and no one must read it!) and am ready to finish a second the minute I get a live-in nanny. . . ."

In December she left the isolation of Devon and moved to London, occupying a flat in a house where Yeats once lived. *The Bell Jar* was published in January and received relatively good reviews. Although her health was poor, her responsibilities for the children demanding, and her emotional state depressed, she continued to write and to struggle for a stable and meaningful life. Yet she seemed unable to throw off the effects of the past months, as she indicated in her last letter to her mother: "I have been feeling a bit grim—the upheaval over, I am seeing the finality of it all, and being catapulted from the cowlike happiness of maternity into loneliness and grim problems is no fun." In February she turned on the gas in her kitchen and ended her life.

In *Three Women; A Monologue for Three Voices* (1968), Plath speaks through a woman in a maternity ward. The words are an appropriate summation of Plath's movement toward annihilation in her art and in her life:

> A power is growing on me an old tenacity.
> I am breaking apart like the world.
>   There is this blackness,
> This ram of blackness. I fold my hands on a mountain.
> The air is thick. It is thick with this working.
> I am used. I am drummed into use.
> My eyes are squeezed by this blackness.
> I see nothing.

Plath expresses her anguish with her experiences as a writer, a wife, and a mother, coming to see her life dominated by forces beyond her control, by ungovernable and meaningless pain brought on, in many cases, by her own depression.

Plath's obsession with pain and annihilation results from a finely developed sense of self-importance; her poems are an outgrowth of an untiring egocentrism, much as Walt Whitman's stem from his conscious celebration of living. In an extensive passage published in Charles H. Newman's collection, *The Art of Sylvia Plath* (1970), Anne Sexton tells of Plath's obsession with talk of dying and suicide:

Suicide is, after all, the opposite of the poem. Sylvia and I often talked opposites. We talked death with burned up intensity, both of us drawn to it like moths to an electric light bulb. Sucking on it!. . . as if death made each of us a little more real at the moment. . . . We talked death and this was life for us, lasting in spite of us, or better, because of us, our intent eyes, our fingers clutching the glass. . . . I know that such fascination with death sounds strange (one does not argue that it isn't sick—one knows it *is*—there's no excuse), and that people cannot understand.

The "richness" to which Sexton alludes manifests itself in the poems of *The Colossus*. Plath recognizes the state of her existence and knows the "Colossus" will never be pieced together entirely:

> I shall never get you put together entirely,
> Pieced, glued, and properly jointed.
> Mule-bray, pig-grunt and bawdy cackles
> Proceed from your great lips.
> It's worse than a barnyard.

The poet's consciousness is totally fragmented in *The Colossus,* and recognizing the practical implications of such a state—insanity or death—she tries to piece together the figure that haunts her. But Plath seems to know intuitively that no glue is strong enough to hold the human mind forever in place, particularly when the psyche is forced to undergo the pain at the heart of the poet's writing. In many respects, Plath echoes French existentialists Jean-Paul Sartre and Albert Camus, as well as twentieth-century German philosopher Karl Jaspers in their attacks on the brutal nature of modern life. Each laments man's state in the "scheme of things" that makes individuals into pieced-together robots. The ego is shattered by technology and man is faced with nothingness, the void that informs him that meaning exists only in death. The last stanza of "The Colossus" might be read as an ironic mockery of T.S. Eliot's closing lines in *The Waste Land* (1922), where there remains at least the hope of redemption. For Eliot, man can shore up his ruins and begin to fish for some sort of meaning and order. Plath, however, entertains no such optimism:

> Counting the red stars and those of plum-color.
> The sun rises under the pillar of your tongue.
> My hours are married to shadow.
> No longer do I listen for the scrape of a keel

> On the blank stones of the landing.

Plath recognizes in man's condition a potential for destruction and pessimism that is not balanced by an alternative concept of hope. Her hours, "married to shadow," are measured by the bleakness of a meaningless landscape and the expressionless despair of "the blank stones of the landing."

In "All the Dead Dears," perhaps the darkest of the poems in *The Colossus*, Plath writes of a skeleton in the Cambridge museum. The poem illustrates her near obsession with death:

> How they grip us through thin and thick.
> Those barnacle dead!
> This lady here's no kin
> Of mine, yet kin she is; she'll suck
> Blood and whistle my marrow clean
> To prove it. As I think now of her head,
> From the mercury-backed glass
> Mother, grandmother, great grandmother
> Reach hag hands to haul me in,
> And an image looms under the fishpond surface
> Where the daft father went down
> With orange duck feet winnowing his hair—

The images of the family return to haunt the poet; the "barnacle-dead" reach out to pull her inside the "mercury-backed glass." Plath's theme revolves around the death of the poetic imagination, which is pictured as essentially female in nature. A conglomerate of images merges in the poem: the dead reaching out to haul the living into the grave with them, the women physically joined by blood and death, the father figure looming evil above the rest, the young poet mutilated and bled by some unnameable destructive force. Although the images and allusions are far-reaching, they are never dispersed. Each connects with another, and the effect is that of terror and blind power.

Plath's dominating concern for death, her own death in particular, ultimately surfaces as the controlling force of her poetry. Even in poems where death is not the stated theme, the implicit darkness of nonexistence hovers in the background. In "Watercolour of Grantchester Meadows," the setting is rimmed by an undertone of bleakness, and the pastoral landscape is interrupted by latent hysteria:

> Droll, vegetarian, the water rat
> Saws down a reed and swims from his limber grove,
> While the students stroll or sit,
> Hands laced, in a moony indolence of love—
> Black-gowned, but unaware

Marianne Moore being interviewed by Sylvia Plath for Mademoiselle, *1953 (courtesy of Aurelia Schober Plath)*

How in mild air
The owl shall swoop from his turret, the rat
cry out.

The "moony indolence of love" is disturbed by black gowns, gowns that reek of ritualistic unconcern. The vegetarian rat, about his constant business, is eclipsed by the carnivore. Only the poet hears the rat "cry out."

In *The Bell Jar* Plath's first courtship of death is chronicled in a narrative that treats the initiation themes of adolescence along with the more metaphysical concerns of disembodiment and annihilation.

The plot of *The Bell Jar* is neatly divided into three parts, covering a period of approximately eight months. In part one, the first nine chapters, the novel's narrator and major character, nineteen-year-old Esther Greenwood, describes her experiences during a one-month residence in New York City as a guest editor for the college issue of a fashion magazine. She remembers as well key episodes from her recent past in college. All the incidents reveal her slow but certain emotional and mental disintegration, as she fails to find an identity which satisfies her and as she becomes more and more disillusioned with the world in which she lives. A key scene takes place at the magazine office where Esther bursts into tears when asked what she wants to be. Several incidents, both past and present, show her unsatisfactory relationships with men: her date with Constantin, who disappoints her by making no attempt at seduction; her encounter with the brutal, woman-hating Marco, who beats her up; and various experiences with her college boyfriend Buddy Willard, who wants a conventional and ordinary marriage. On her last night in New York, she throws all her clothes off the roof

414

of her hotel in a bizarre, symbolic "ceremony" which clearly reveals her disillusionment and disorientation.

Part two (chapters 10-13) concentrates on her psychological deterioration upon her return home and ends with her suicide attempt. Dressed in a friend's clothes and with bloodstains still on her face from Marco's beating, she feels terrified at being trapped at home until the fall: "[The] white, shining, identical clap-board houses with their interstices of well-groomed green proceeded past, one bar after another in a large but escape-proof cage." In the following weeks she is unable to accomplish anything, cannot sleep, and refuses to wash her hair or change her clothes. Further depressed by visits to Dr. Gordon, an unsympathetic psychiatrist who gives her devastating shock treatments, she becomes obsessed by death and experiments with various methods of suicide. After an anguished visit to her father's grave, she crawls beneath the house and takes sleeping pills until she loses consciousness.

In the last seven chapters she describes her painful return to normalcy after surviving her suicide attempt. First placed in the psychiatric ward of a city hospital, she resists all efforts to help her, being uncooperative and even destructive. However, when she is moved to a private mental hospital, she makes great progress under the care of a sympathetic woman psychiatrist, Dr. Nolan. Allowed to leave the hospital for short excursions into Boston, she obtains a diaphragm and has her first sexual encounter, an unpleasant experience with disastrous consequences. Surviving that disillusionment as well as the subsequent suicide of her friend Joan, she awaits her imminent release from the asylum and prepares to return to life—"patched, retreaded and approved for the road." Yet her future is unsure, and the ominous threat of another breakdown later in her life haunts her: "How did I know that someday—at college, in Europe, somewhere, anywhere—the bell jar, with its stifling distortions, wouldn't descend again?"

Two major themes of the novel, the search for identity and rebellion against conventional female roles and attitudes, are closely linked. The multitalented Esther is unable to decide who she wants to be: "I saw my life branching out before me like [a] green fig tree. . . . From the tip of every branch, like a fat purple fig, a wonderful future beckoned and winked. One fig was a husband and a happy home and children, and another fig was a famous poet and another fig was a brilliant professor, and another fig was Ee Gee, the amazing

editor, . . . and beyond and above these figs were many more figs I couldn't quite make out." While the identity she seems most drawn to is that of the poet, the one she rejects most strongly is that of the traditional wife and mother. She sees marriage as a prison of dull domestic duties, a wife as a subservient inferior to her husband, and a mother as a drudge with dirty, demanding children. What she does want as a woman is the freedom to have an interesting life: "I wanted change and excitement and to shoot off in all directions myself, like the colored arrows from a Fourth of July rocket."

The character of Esther, the major figure, is a brilliant study of a girl who has a talent for creative writing. Her inner directness and wry sense of humor make her a likable character, as do her determination to be independent and her rejection of stereotyped molds of all kinds. Both her greatest asset and her greatest liability is her compulsion to excel, which drives her to demand of herself an unattainable perfection. Thus she is constantly plagued with feelings of failure and frustration. Further, she lacks self-confidence in the social and sexual areas, and she affects an urbane sophistication as often as possible. She is touching, funny, annoying, surprising, but always a very human and very sympathetic character.

Most of the numerous female characters who revolve around her represent different identities that she might assume. Doreen with her devil-may-care attitude symbolizes social and sexual sophistication. Other characters Esther encounters in New York include Betsy, an all-American girl from Kansas, who placidly accepts the stereotypes for women. Jay Cee, the magazine editor and Esther's boss, is an intelligent and successful businesswoman whom Esther admires, and often emulates, imagining herself as "Ee Gee, the amazing editor." Yet Jay Cee is flawed by a lack of femininity, implied by her use of neutral initials rather than a female first name, her "plug-ugly looks," and her "strict office suit." Esther is drawn to but ultimately rejects each of these characters.

Three female figures who appall Esther dominate the home scene. Representing conventionality both in career and in standards, Esther's mother urges her to take shorthand in order to become a secretary, and to guard her virginity in order to marry a fine, clean-cut boy like Buddy Willard. Buddy's mother is a typical housewife in a conventional marriage, appearing to Esther as a drudge and an inferior. Dodo Conway, who has six small children and is very pregnant with the seventh, is to Esther a grotesque figure of woman as mother.

In the third part Joan Gilling, another mental patient and Esther's alter-ego, is a lesbian who ultimately hangs herself. She represents choices Esther might have made. The one female character who is not flawed, who is an understanding and open-minded human being who has achieved an integration of her womanhood and her career is Dr. Nolan, Esther's psychiatrist at the private hospital. Although it is not explicitly stated, this woman who is largely responsible for Esther's salvation seems the model that Esther will use to find her own true identity as a woman.

The male characters are presented even more negatively than the female ones. The most important is Buddy Willard, who from Esther's point of view is flawed in two ways. First, he is a hypocrite, having slept with a waitress but pretending to be chaste. Second, he wants a conventional marriage with Esther as a conventional wife. The other male characters pass in and out of her experience in a nightmarish parade of cruelty, stupidity, and coldness: Lenny, the brash, sexually aggressive boyfriend of Doreen; Marco, the violent woman-hater; Dr. Gordon, the remote and unsympathetic psychiatrist; Irwin, the indifferent, unattractive math professor to whom Esther loses her virginity. All the men are portrayed almost exclusively in terms of their relationships with women, relationships in which they are at worst brutal and at best thoughtless or uncaring. While they are presented in this highly negative light, it is clear that Esther demands perfection from men as much as she demands it from herself. Obviously, no man can measure up, as is evident from Esther's comment, "I would catch sight of some flawless man off in the distance, but as soon as he moved closer I immediately saw he wouldn't do at all."

The style of *The Bell Jar* is conversational and informal, at first glance belying its craftsmanship and careful attention to detail. The simple sentence structure, ordinary diction, and slang terms of the 1950s are appropriate to the narrator, and the numerous concrete details bring to life in a very tangible way the places, people, and experiences that make up Esther's story. Certain aspects of the style are skillfully differentiated in each of the three parts, subtly reflecting the changes in the narrator's mental and emotional condition. While in the first part the sentences and paragraphs are of medium length and are logically developed, in the second part, as Esther's condition deteriorates, they become short and choppy, with paragraphs often containing only one sentence. The thoughts are fragmented and do not flow smoothly and logically,

but jump abruptly from subject to subject. As Esther moves toward recovery in part three, the style shifts back toward longer sentences and paragraphs that are logically connected.

There is a subtle difference too in the use of humor in each section. In the New York period there are many humorous episodes, most of which are based on the juxtaposition of Esther's naiveté with her affected sophistication; a prime example is her attempt to cover her inexperience in ordering mixed drinks by asking for a plain vodka, explaining that "I always have it plain." Her inner directness and honesty as well as her unusual way of seeing things—as when Buddy's genitals remind her disappointingly of "turkey neck and turkey gizzards"—provide other instances of humor. However, in part two there is a reduction in the amount of humor as well as a shift in kind to the grim humor of black comedy; for example, with the silk cord of her mother's bathrobe "dangling from my neck like a yellow cat's tail," Esther wanders through her house but never finds a place from which to hang herself. The last part is practically humorless; even those episodes, such as the "seduction" by Irwin, which contains incongruity and earlier would have evoked some touch of the comic, are treated in an entirely serious manner. Plath means to suggest perhaps that the breakdown has destroyed Esther's sense of humor or that the effort to recover requires a plodding, humorless concentration.

Finally, the novel is full of brilliant and effective symbols, some of which recur consistently to form major groups or patterns, while others appear only once but with striking force. One of the most significant of the dominant symbols is the bell jar, a personal and highly original symbol, which represents the condition of mental breakdown. Esther imagines her illness as a gigantic bell jar that descends upon her, imprisoning her, suffocating her, isolating her from others, and distorting her view of the world. The colors of black and white appear on nearly every page, the former conveying despair and gloom and the latter emptiness and deadness. In a striking use of both colors, Esther describes her future as "stretching ahead like a series of bright, white boxes, and separating one box from another was sleep, like a black shade." Prison images symbolize her feeling of being trapped in various ways: her body is a "stupid cage," her mother's car is like a "prison van," and her face reflected in the mirror of her compact "seemed to be peering from the grating of a prison cell after a prolonged beating." Last, her obsession with annihilation is conveyed by numerous images, comparisons, allusions, and actual deaths, which fill the novel from the opening page with its reference to the execution of the Rosenbergs and its simile describing the cadaver's head that haunts Esther's memory to the final chapter with its account of Joan's suicide and funeral.

Although *The Bell Jar* is Plath's only published, complete novel, it is a significant one that joins such works as J. D. Salinger's *The Catcher in the Rye* and James Joyce's *A Portrait of the Artist as a Young Man* in presenting the painful experiences of adolescence—and also begins a new tradition of novels exploring the experience of women. While its value lies to a great extent in these contributions, in its portrayal of the 1950s, and in its intense study of mental breakdown, its reputation ultimately rests on its concern with the universal human problem of self-discovery.

During the five months preceding her suicide, Plath wrote almost the entire body of poems that were to be collected two years later and published as *Ariel*. The poems are personal testaments to the loneliness and insecurity that plagued her, and the desolate images suggest her apparent fixation with death. The violence of the *Colossus* poems is continued in *Ariel*, and the suicidal themes become frighteningly direct, as in "A Birthday Present": "And the knife not carve, but enter/Pure and clean as the cry of a baby,/And the universe slide from my side."

Toward the end of 1962 Plath organized the poetry that she intended to include in *Ariel*. Hughes comments in his introduction to *Collected Poems* (1981) that Plath's original table of contents for the volume "excluded almost everything she had written between *The Colossus* and July 1962—or two and a half year's work." Variously titled "The Rival," "A Birthday Present," and "Daddy" before she hit upon *Ariel*, the collection that was eventually published took a different shape from the one Plath intended. Hughes deleted many of what he calls her "more personally aggressive" poems.

In *Ariel* the everyday incidents of living are transformed into the horrifying psychological experiences of the poet. The domesticity of the situations serves as an ironic backdrop to the tragic elements of nearly every poem. "The Bee Meeting," for example, concerns some people who are watching a beekeeper move virgin bees away from the queen. It is a simple job, but one that, when viewed from Plath's unique poetic perspective, acts as a symbol for human isolation and suffering. Initially, the poet is "nude as a chicken neck" without the protective gear necessary to approach the hives. Until she dons her smock, hat, and veil, she is in danger of being stung. However, the physical danger is no more menacing than the isolation that begins to take shape in the poet's imagination. As the poem progresses, she begins to identify with the queen bee, who will undoubtedly die when the other bees are released the following year. Toward the close of the poem, she anticipates her own death and asks: "Whose is that long white box in the grove, what have they accomplished, why am I cold?"

The undercurrent of violence in "The Bee Meeting" surfaces in Plath's most famous poem, "Daddy." The death of Plath's father when she was a child is of considerable importance to her writing, but the "daddy" of the poem is by no means a representation of her own father. Images for mutilation recur throughout the poem, but whereas the persona of "The Colossus" attempts to piece together the inhuman figure that haunts her, in "Daddy" the poet's own image is dichotomized before it is pieced together "with glue":

> I was ten when they buried you.
> At twenty I tried to die
> And get back, back, back to you.
> I thought even the bones would do.
>
> But they pulled me out of the sack
> And they stuck me together with glue.

The power of "Daddy" supersedes human hope. When there is an attempt at redemption, the necessary method is savage violence:

> If I've killed one man, I've killed two—
> The vampire who said he was you
> And drank my blood for a year,
> Seven years, if you want to know.
> Daddy, you can lie back now.
>
> There's a stake in your fat black heart
> And the villagers never liked you.
> They are dancing and stamping on you.
> They always knew it was you.
> Daddy, daddy, you bastard, I'm through.

In this pivotal poem the violence is not dissolved but only transferred to the villagers, people whose fear has turned to hatred and inhuman brutality. The Poles and Jews and gypsy women turn on the Nazi "panzer-men," but there clearly is no redemption, only dominance replaced by revenge.

Sylvia Plath and her husband, Ted Hughes, 1958 (courtesy of Aurelia Schober Plath)

"Tulips," one of the few *Ariel* poems written more than two years before Plath's death, recalls the time she spent in a hospital recovering from an appendectomy. As in the great majority of her poems, the protagonist is isolated and despairing, but the tone of the poem is reflective. In contrast to the frenzied anxiety of the speaker in "Daddy," the voice in tulips reflects thoughtful acquiescence to the pain and fear of living. The speaker, a hospital patient, is intent on surrendering her individuality to the faceless world around her: "I have given my name and my day-clothes to the nurses/ And my history to the anaesthetist and my body

to/surgeons." The attending nurses are anonymous creatures likened to birds:

> The nurses pass and pass, they are no trouble,
> They pass the way gulls pass inland in their white caps
> Doing things with their hands, one just the same as another,
> So it is impossible to tell how many there are.

The poet apprehends herself as an inanimate object, content to let others control her: "My body is a pebble to them, they tend it as water/Tends to the pebble it must run over." In allowing the nurses to "run over" her, the poet rejects her individual ability to bring about her own convalescence, a decision that foreshadows Plath's decision to kill herself.

A brief, ironic respite from Plath's obsession with death occurs in "Black Rook in Rainy Weather," a moving poem in the tradition of Robert Frost's skeptical verse and central for understanding her posture in *Crossing the Water,* a second posthumous volume published in 1971, shaped with "post-*Colossus*" and "pre-*Ariel*" verse. In particular, the poem is clearly reminiscent of four Frost poems—"Design," "For Once, Then, Something," "Dust of Snow," and "The Most of It." The parallel images and the stance taken by the poet in Plath's poem point to the close proximity of the two poets' skeptical perspectives. Plath questions the feasibility of universal order, as Frost does in "Design." She employs the same questioning stance as the poet figure in "The Most of It." There is concern for the brief epiphany brought on by a commonplace occurrence, which is Frost's concern in "A Dust of Snow." And the poet of "Black Rook in Rainy Weather" becomes aware of the fleeting nature of truth, much like the poet figure of "For Once, Then, Something."

In Plath's "Black Rook in Rainy Weather," the poet figure watches a rook arranging its feathers in the rain, and her observation prompts speculation on the nature of poetic inspiration. She begins with her stated cynicism:

> I do not expect miracle
> Or an accident
>
> To set the sight on fire
> In my eye, nor seek
> Any more in the desultory weather some design,
> But let spotted leaves fall as they fall,
> Without ceremony, or portent.

The poet figure is alone, and as her honest musings begin to unfold, her cynicism is replaced by the innocent desire to receive "some backtalk from the mute sky," some primitive "original response" that will help her hallow "an internal/Otherwise inconsequent/By bestowing largesse, honour/One might say love." Here Plath is not speaking of the indolent love witnessed in "Watercolour of Grantchester Meadows"; instead, she is after a kind of primordial inspiration, a sign that will link her perception to some nameless and sympathetic deity. The rook offers an instant of belief in life, but the final ironic

lines undercut the hope that has momentarily lodged in the poet's mind:

> I only know that a rook
> Ordering its black feathers can so shine
> As to seize my senses, haul
> My eyelids up, and grant
>
> A brief respite from fear
> Of total neutrality....
> ....
> Miracles occur,
> If you care to call those spasmodic
> Tricks of radiance miracles. The wait's begun again,
> The long wait for the angel,
> For that rare, random descent.

As in "Daddy" and "The Colossus," Plath patches together "a content of sorts," a content much like Frost's attempt to achieve momentary stays against confusion. The kind of miracles that occur to Sylvia Plath are simple, fleeting epiphanies, ridden with nuance and uncertainty. They are little more than "spasmodic/Tricks of radiance," as brief as they are unpredictable.

The theme of annihilation operates again in *Winter Trees* (1971), a collection of eighteen late-period poems and *Three Women*, which had been written early in 1962. In "Brasilio," for instance, where the idea of sacrifice becomes a thematic focal point, Plath reacts to the conglomeration of mechanistic and spiritualistic power:

> O you who eat
>
> People like light rays, leave
> This one
> Mirror safe, unredeemed
>
> By the dove's annihilation,
> The glory,
> The power, the glory.

The poet's religious imagery suggests the theme of redemption, a redemption accompanied by death at the hands of a sadistic deity. There is no human glory, no salvation except death.

The desire *not* to be redeemed translates into Plath's obsession with individual purgation, at both the spiritual and intellectual levels. The man is not redeemed by "the dove's annihilation" because the redemptive power is not centered in a loving deity. Instead, each individual is subjected to dominance by pure power, amoral and staggering in its scope and intensity. In the face of such awesome strength, the poet appears incapable or unwilling to establish a stable viewpoint from which to study the situation. Such ambivalence stems from a perception of reality colored by fear, fear of something "other," something beyond comprehension in both its loving and its hating potential, akin perhaps to the malevolent force in E. E. Cummings's *The Enormous Room* (1922), the pervasive fear in the works of Franz Kafka, or the faceless angst of the existentialist writers.

Sylvia Plath's desperate need to "talk death" is the underlying power of her poetry. As Anne Sexton points out, death seemed to make her "a little more real at the moment," and this perception of reality translates itself into poem after poem. One discovers in Plath's work an indulgence in ego so pervasive as to warrant the ego's own destruction. She is a twentieth-century Emily Dickinson who has left the silent insanity of a New England home and ventured into a world of existential despair. More primitively vocal than her nineteenth-century counterpart, Plath reacts to violence and fear in bursts of guttural emotion, as in "Daddy":

> Ich, ich, ich, ich
> I could hardly speak.
> I thought every German was you.
> And the language obscene
>
> An engine, an engine
> Chuffing me off like a Jew.

Characteristically, as in "The Colossus," Plath sees her own mind as a "mouthpiece of the dead." At her most articulate, meditating on the nature of poetic inspiration, she is a controlled voice for cynicism, plainly delineating the boundaries of hope and reality. At her brutal best—and Plath is a brutal poet—she taps a source of power that transforms her poetic voice into a raving avenger of womanhood and innocence.

Plath's legacy is one of pain, fear, and traumatic depression, born of the need to destroy the imagistic materialization of "Daddy." The horrifying tone of her poetry underscores a depth of feeling that can be attributed to few other poets, and her near-suicidal attempt to communicate a frightening existential vision nearly overshadows all discussion of technique.

Apart from these major collections Plath's published works include her children's book *The Bed Book* (1976); a variety of high quality limited edition poems and collections, such as *Fiesta Melons* (1971), *Lyonesse Poems* (1971), *Pursuit* (1973), and *Dialogue over a Ouija Board* (1981); her journals,

Dust jacket for a posthumously published collection that includes poems written in the period immediately preceding Plath's suicide

edited by Ted Hughes and published in 1982; and a collection of Plath's prose that includes a mere handful of her short stories. *Johnny Panic and the Bible of Dreams*, first published in 1977 and expanded in 1979, is a sampler from Plath's fiction, diaries, and essay pieces. The stories are of particular interest not only because they reflect the themes of Plath's major work—self-annihilation, the proper role of a woman, the search for identity—but they reflect the tenacity of those themes, since most were written in the late 1950s. The stories represented for her a unique challenge that she believed she had failed to meet. Out of her desire to fashion an "objective," linear, magazine-style story that would make her a popular and financial success, Plath created a body of short fiction—nearly seventy finished stories and fragments of novels, including the largest "Stone Boy with a Dolphin"—that "had actually . . . tap[ped] the molten source of her poetry as none, of her poems up to then [1958] had," according to

Hughes. This judgment is certainly true of the collection's title story.

"Johnny Panic and the Bible of Dreams" is a Kafkaesque tale, told in the first person by a clerk— "Assistant to the Secretary in one of the Out-Patient Departments of the Clinics Building of the City Hospital." Committing to memory those patients' dreams she has not had time to copy into her notebook before her boss returns from lunch each day, the protagonist finally indulges in remaining after work one evening to read the back files and catch up. From the moment the clinic director "finds" her jammed between the files dozing, until she describes the onset of electric shock therapy, the reader is plunged into a schizophrenic reality and does not know whether to trust the narrator's version of events. The focus of the clerk's obsession with the dreams of others is "Panic with a dog-face, devil-face, whore-face, panic in capital letters with no face at all—it's the same Johnny Panic, awake or asleep." Exploring fear, death, pain at the very notion of existence, the protagonist searches for Johnny Panic's telltale "thumbprint in the corner" of the dreams of others. Of course, the narrator has a dream of her own, a "Lake Nightmare, Bog of Madness," where "sleeping people lie and toss together among the props of their worst dreams. . . ." Plath's woman describes the stinking surface of the lake in terms that only find analogy in a Bosch landscape of people twisted with fear and depravity. But the author of this reality— Johnny Panic—is the narrator's ally; the staff intent on "healing" the "sick" dreamers is the enemy. And it is Johnny Panic who retains power over the demented narrator; as the electric jolt courses through her brain, Johnny Panic becomes fused with a vision of God.

> At a moment when they think I am most lost the face of Johnny Panic appears in a nimbus of arc lights on the ceiling overhead. I am shaken like a leaf in the teeth of glory. His beard is lightning. Lightning is in his eye. His Word charges and illumines the universe.
>
> The air crackles with his blue-tongued lightning-haloed angels.
>
> His love is the twenty-story leap, the rope at the throat, the knife at the heart.
>
> He forgets not his own.

This terrible reality of the protagonist's love affair with death is, as Hughes noted, probably quite close to the "molten source" of Plath's own attraction to her private demons. And if she strove

to create a linear narrative of the psychological terrain of a schizophrenic-like experience and thought she failed, then she may have judged herself too harshly. That Sylvia Plath could coherently describe those private experiences in a public forum, and that she could do so with a language that is beautiful in its terribleness attests to her great gift as a writer.

Letters:

Letters Home, edited by Aurelia Schober Plath (New York: Harper & Row, 1975);
> Source of information about routines and chronology of Plath's life.

Bibliographies:

Cameron Northouse and Thomas P. Walsh, *Sylvia Plath and Anne Sexton: A Reference Guide* (Boston: G. K. Hall, 1974);
> Lists primary and secondary materials, including reviews of Plath's work and critical articles about her.

Gary Lane and Maria Stevens, *Sylvia Plath* (Metuchen, N.J.: Scarecrow Press, 1978);
> Bibliography of Plath's published work which also lists poetry, prose, and some juvenilia that was unpublished when this bibliography was compiled.

References:

Eileen Aird, *Sylvia Plath: Her Life and Work* (New York: Harper & Row, 1973);
> A brief introduction to Plath's first-published books, it is most useful for identifying imagery and symbols appearing in Plath's work.

Paul Alexander, ed., *Ariel Ascending: Writings About Sylvia Plath* (New York: Harper & Row, 1985);
> Excellent anthology of critical essays and letters by such authors as Elizabeth Hardwick and John Frederick Nims.

A. Alvarez, *The Savage God* (New York: Random House, 1971), pp. 3-42;
> An essay that examines Plath's suicide in the context of her work.

Caroline King Barnard, *Sylvia Plath* (Boston: Twayne, 1978);
> Introductory bibliographical and critical study. Includes annotated secondary bibliography.

Lynda K. Bundtzen, *Plath's Incarnations: Women and Creative Process* (Ann Arbor: University of Michigan Press, 1983);
Study of Plath's work from a psychoanalytic and feminist viewpoint.

Edward Butscher, *Sylvia Plath: Method and Madness* (New York: Seabury Press, 1975);
The first full critical biography of Plath, it tries to keep academic jargon minimal.

Butscher, ed., *Sylvia Plath: The Woman and the Work* (New York: Dodd, Mead, 1976);
A two-part anthology: interviews, poems, and reminiscences by people who knew Plath; and critical scholarship by such writers as Irving Howe and Joyce Carol Oates.

David Holbrook, *Sylvia Plath: Poetry and Existence* (Atlantic Highlands, N.J.: Humanities Press, 1976);
Psychoanalytic examination of Plath's life and work.

Judith Kroll, *Chapters in a Mythology: The Poetry of Sylvia Plath* (New York, Hagerstown, San Francisco & London: Harper & Row, 1976);
Excellent scholarly study that focuses on Plath's work as literature rather than autobiographical confession.

Ingrid Melander, *The Poetry of Sylvia Plath; A Study of Themes* (Stockholm: Almquist & Wiksell, 1972);
Introductory textual discussion.

Charles Newman, ed., *The Art of Sylvia Plath* (Bloomington: Indiana University Press, 1970);
The first, and possibly best, general overview to Plath's life and work, this collection of critiques, reviews, and memoirs includes articles by Ted Hughes, Hugh Kenner, Anne Sexton, as well as artwork and reproductions of manuscript drafts by Plath.

Jon Rosenblatt, *Sylvia Plath The Poetry of Initiation* (Chapel Hill: University of North Carolina Press, 1982);
Plath's poetic development is discussed through analyses of the individual poems.

Nancy Hunter Steiner, *A Close Look at Ariel* (New York: Popular Library, 1973);
Slim, chatty reminiscence of Plath after her first suicide attempt written by her college roommate of one and a half years.

Linda Wagner, ed., *Critical Essays on Sylvia Plath* (Boston: G. K. Hall, 1984);
An anthology of analytical discussions of Plath's work; includes a secondary bibliography.

Kenneth Rexroth

This entry was updated by Ann Charters (University of Connecticut) from the entry by Charters and by Brown Miller (San Francisco, California) in DLB 16, The Beats: Literary Bohemians in Postwar America.

Places	San Francisco	Montecito, California	
Influences and Relationships	James Laughlin Lawrence Ferlinghetti	Gary Snyder Allen Ginsberg	Dylan Thomas
Literary Movements and Forms	Oriental Literature and Philosophy	Experimental Poetry and Jazz	Poetry as a Performance Art
	San Francisco/Bay Area Poetry—Pacifica Foundation (San Francisco State College Poetry Center)		
Major Themes	The Unlived Life/ Moral Responsibility	Political Commitment to Marxism/Free Thought	Unified/Mystical World View
Cultural and Artistic Influences	Beat Generation		
Social and Economic Influences	Great Depression	World War II	

See also the Rexroth entry in DLB 48, American Poets, 1880-1945, *and* DLB Yearbook: 1982.

BIRTH: South Bend, Indiana, 22 December 1905, to Charles Marion and Delia Reed Rexroth.

EDUCATION: Attended the Chicago Art Institute, circa 1920.

MARRIAGES: 1927 to Andrée Dutcher (deceased 1940). 1940 to Marie Kass (divorced). 1949 to Marthe Larsen (divorced); children: Mary, Katharine. 1974 to Carol Tinker.

AWARDS AND HONORS: California Literature Silver Medal Award for *In What Hour,* 1941, for *The Phoenix and the Tortoise,* 1945, and for *The Morning Star,* 1980; Guggenheim Fellowships, 1948, 1949; Eunice Tietjens Award, 1957; Shelley Memorial Award, 1958; Amy Lowell Fellowship, 1958; National Institute of Arts and Letters grant, 1964; Rockefeller grant, 1967; Akademische Austausdienfp, 1967; Academy of American Poets' Copernicus Award, 1975.

DEATH: Montecito, California, 6 June 1982.

SELECTED BOOKS: *In What Hour* (New York: Macmillan, 1940);
The Phoenix and the Tortoise (Norfolk, Conn.: New Directions, 1944);
The Art of Worldly Wisdom (Prairie City, Ill.: Decker Press, 1949);
The Signature of All Things (New York: New Directions, 1950);
Beyond the Mountains (New York: New Directions, 1951; London: Routledge & Kegan Paul, 1951);
The Dragon and the Unicorn (Norfolk, Conn.: New Directions, 1952);
In Defense of the Earth (New York: New Directions, 1956; London: Hutchinson, 1959);
Bird in the Bush: Obvious Essays (New York: New Directions, 1959);
Assays (Norfolk, Conn.: New Directions, 1961);
Natural Numbers: New and Selected Poems (Norfolk, Conn.: New Directions, 1963);
The Homestead Called Damascus (New York: New Directions, 1963);
An Autobiographical Novel (Garden City: Doubleday, 1966; Weybridge, U.K.: Whittet Books, 1977);

Kenneth Rexroth (Gale International Portrait Gallery)

The Collected Shorter Poems (New York: New Directions, 1967);
Classics Revisited (Chicago: Quadrangle, 1968);
The Collected Longer Poems (New York: New Directions, 1968);
The Alternative Society: Essays from the Other World (New York: Herder & Herder, 1970);
With Eye and Ear (New York: Herder & Herder, 1970);
American Poetry in the Twentieth Century (New York: Herder & Herder, 1971);
Sky Sea Birds Trees Earth House Beasts Flowers (Santa Barbara: Unicorn Press, 1971);
The Elastic Report: Essays in Literature and Ideas (New York: Seabury Press, 1973);
Communalism: From its Origins to the Twentieth Century (New York: Seabury Press, 1974; London: Owen, 1975);
New Poems (New York: New Directions, 1974);
Communalism from Its Origins to the Twentieth Century (New York: Seabury Press, 1974; London: Owen, 1975);
On Flower Wreath Hill (Burnaby, B.C.: Blackfish Press, 1976);

The Silver Swan: Poems Written in Kyoto, 1974-75 (Port Townsend, Wash.: Copper Canyon Press, 1976);

The Morning Star (New York: New Directions, 1979);

Excerpts from a Life, edited by Ekbert Fass (Santa Barbara: Conjunctions Books, 1981);

Between Two Wars (Athens, Ohio: Labyrinth Editions/San Francisco: Iris Press, 1982);

Selected Poems (New York: New Directions, 1984).

RECORDINGS: *Poetry Readings in "The Cellar,"* Fantasy Records, 7002, 1957;

Kenneth Rexroth at the Black Hawk, Fantasy Records, 7008, 1960.

OTHER: *Selected Poems of D. H. Lawrence,* edited, with an introduction, by Rexroth (New York: New Directions, 1948);

The New British Poets: An Anthology, edited, with an introduction, by Rexroth (Norfolk, Conn.: New Directions, 1949);

The Buddhist Writings of Lafcadio Hearn, edited by Rexroth (Santa Barbara: Ross-Erikson, 1977);

Kazuko Shiraishi, *Seasons of Sacred Lust,* edited, with an introduction, by Rexroth, translated by Ikuto Atsumi (New York: New Directions, 1977).

TRANSLATIONS: *Fourteen Poems by O. V. de L. Milosz* (San Francisco: Peregrine Press, 1952);

One Hundred Poems from the Japanese (New York: New Directions, 1955);

One Hundred French Poems (Highlands, N.C.: Jargon, 1955);

Thirty Spanish Poems of Love and Exile (San Francisco: City Lights Books, 1955);

One Hundred Poems from the Chinese (New York: New Directions, 1956);

Poems from the Greek Anthology (Ann Arbor: University of Michigan Press, 1962);

Pierre Reverdy, Selected Poems (New York: New Directions, 1969);

Love in the Turning Year: One Hundred More Poems from the Chinese (New York: New Directions, 1970);

One Hundred Poems from the French (Cambridge, Mass.: Pym-Randall Press, 1971);

The Orchid Boat: The Women Poets of China, translated by Rexroth and Ling Chung (New York: McGraw-Hill, 1972);

One Hundred More Poems from the Japanese (New York: New Directions, 1975);

The Burning Heart, The Women Poets of Japan, translated by Rexroth and Ikuto Atsumi (New York: New Directions, 1976);

The Complete Poems of Li Ch'ing-Chao (New York: New Directions, 1979).

In *The Norton Anthology of Modern Poetry,* Richard Ellmann and Robert O'Clair described Kenneth Rexroth's place in modern poetry: "Like William Carlos Williams and Ezra Pound, Kenneth Rexroth is one of the veterans of American modernist poetry and, like them also, a natural father-figure. During the 1920s he made his contribution to the literary revolution taking place in Chicago; he then moved to San Francisco, at that time as far from the center of American letters as one could get without leaving the country, and was joined there during the 1940s by other anarchist poets who fomented the San Francisco Renaissance, and during the 1950s by the Beats who had fled from New York, all of whom found in Rexroth an open-minded and enthusiastic sponsor."

Rexroth's ancestors included German scholars, German-American radicals, and American Indians. He was born in South Bend, Indiana, but his family moved to Elkhart, Indiana, a few months after his birth. His father, Charles Marion Rexroth, a pharmacist and wholesale druggist, and his mother, Delia (or Della as she was called) Reed Rexroth, had a circle of literary and artistic friends.

When Rexroth was seven years old, the family returned from a European tour to live in Battle Creek, Michigan, where Charles Rexroth's business failed and Delia Rexroth contracted tuberculosis. A few years later they moved to Chicago and then back to Elkhart. There, when Kenneth was eleven years old, his mother died of gangrene of the lung. Soon after her death, his father, who had sustained further business failures, died of alcoholism. Rexroth lived with his paternal grandmother for a brief period and then with his aunt on Chicago's South Side. He attend Englewood High School and the Art Institute and audited classes at the University of Chicago. By the age of sixteen he had already produced a considerable body of painting and poetry, and he was active as an actor, director, journalist, and political radical. Rexroth described his early years in his *An Autobiographical Novel* (1966).

In 1921 he worked his way to the West Coast and back to Chicago. His first long philosophical poem, *The Homestead Called Damascus,* was completed in 1922 in the midst of a love affair with Leslie Smith, a social worker. The poem, however, was not published until 1957 when it appeared in the *Quarterly Review of Literature*. In 1926 Rexroth did more traveling, again working for his passage; his journey included Europe and Mexico.

He married Andrée Dutcher in 1927 and finished a second long poem, "Prolegomena to a Theodicy," which was later published in *The Art of Worldly Wisdom* (1949), along with many of his poems written during this period. In the 1920s Rexroth did a lot of painting, and his early poems are mainly experiments with literary cubism and applications of other avant-garde developments from the European art scene. In this respect he is often compared with Gertrude Stein and James Joyce, prime movers in what was called the Revolution of the Word.

In 1927 Rexroth and his wife Andrée, who was also a painter, moved to San Francisco, which at the time "was very much of a backwater town and there just wasn't anything happening," as he recalled in an interview with David Meltzer. During the 1930s he became extremely involved in leftist politics and tried to organize maritime labor unions, writing a mimeographed newsletter, "all of the goddamn thing, week after week," he told

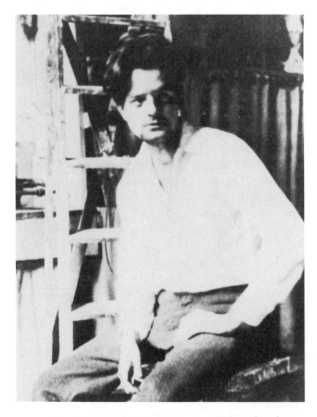

Kenneth Rexroth in San Francisco, 1935 (photo by John Ferren)

Meltzer. He also wrote many direct, polemical poems that deal with the decade's financial crisis; these are collected in his first published book, *In What Hour* (1940), which won the California Literature Silver Medal Award.

In 1940 Rexroth's wife died, and later that same year he married Marie Kass, a nurse. In 1941 he declared himself a conscientious objector. A long philosophical poem, *The Phoenix and the Tortoise* (1944), gives strong expression to the poet's belief in an anarchopacifist ethic, according to which each person must take total responsibility for his own actions. The terror of World War II is intensely felt in this book, which won for Rexroth his second California Literature Silver Medal Award.

In 1948 he was divorced from Marie Kass and traveled in Europe on a Guggenheim Fellowship. In 1949 he married Marthe Larsen, with whom he later had two daughters, Mary and Katharine. In 1950 *The Signature of All Things* was published, and it revealed another facet of the poet's work: intense love lyrics and visionary transcendence. It was soon after this that he began to have translations published. Eventually his translating included literature from a wide range of languages: Japanese, Chinese, French, Spanish, Greek, and Latin.

During this time Rexroth was also deeply involved in the California Bay Area avant-garde literary groups, starting as early as 1944 when his work appeared in George Leite's *Circle* magazine along with such Bay Area writers as Henry Miller, Robert Duncan, Brother Antoninus (William Everson), and Josephine Miles, a poet-professor at the University of California at Berkeley. As Morgan Gibson describes this artistic community in his book *Kenneth Rexroth*, the members included many people who had been, like Rexroth, conscientious objectors during World War II. The community was "anarchopacifist in politics, mystical-personalist in religions, and experimental in esthetic theory and practice." Weekly seminars were held in Rexroth's apartment debating political, philosophical, religious, and literary issues. In 1949 the members helped create the Pacifica Foundation and its first listener-sponsored radio station. Soon afterward, a Poetry Center, featuring poetry readings at San Francisco State College, was established by the poet Madeleine Gleason with the assistance of Robert Duncan and Rexroth.

By the mid 1950s many of the poets who were to become famous as Beat writers—Lawrence Ferlinghetti, Allen Ginsberg, Jack Kerouac, Michael McClure, Gary Snyder, Philip Whalen—had moved to San Francisco, attracted by the climate of radical poetry and politics, and they were soon part of Rexroth's circle. Ginsberg came to him with a letter of introduction from William Carlos Williams. When Ginsberg organized the historic reading at the Six Gallery in San Francisco in October of 1955, he asked Rexroth to preside as master of ceremonies. The invitation to this event, printed on a postcard, announced "Six Poets at the Six Gallery," with Rexroth considered one of the poets (although only the other five, the younger poets Ginsberg, McClure, Snyder, Whalen, and Philip Lamantia, read their works). At the censorship trial of Ginsberg's *Howl and Other Poems* beginning in August 1957, Rexroth appeared as witness for the defense, an eminent literary authority who praised *Howl* as serious prophetic literature and helped to convince the judge that it had redeeming social importance.

Considering the diverse aspects of Rexroth's interests in avant-garde art, radical politics, and Eastern philosophy, one can understand why he seemed the perfect mentor for the Beats. Their work also influenced his poetry for a short time. His most famous Beat poem was "Thou Shalt Not Kill," a memorial to Dylan Thomas, published in his book *In Defense of the Earth* (1956). This poem begins in a mood of regret for the wasted life of Dylan Thomas and all poet-seers in a capitalistic society:

> They are murdering all the young men.
> For half a century now, every day,
> They have hunted them down and killed them.

Then Rexroth calls the roll of modern poets who have died, sick or imprisoned or insane:

> What happened to Robinson,
> Who used to stagger down Eighth Street,
> Dizzy with solitary gin?
> Where is Masters, who crouched in
> His law office for ruinous decades?
> Where is Leonard who thought he was
> A locomotive? And Lindsay,
> Wise as a dove, innocent
> As a serpent, where is he?
> Timor mortis conturbat me.

As Rexroth catalogues the poets' deaths, the reader may be reminded of Ginsberg's *Howl*, although Rexroth's tone is far less angry and impassioned:

> All over the world
> The same disembodied hand
> Strikes us down.
> Here is a mountain of death.
> A hill of heads like the Khans piled up.
> The first-born of a century
> Slaughtered by Herod.
> Three generations of infants
> Stuffed down the maw of Moloch.

"Thou Shalt Not Kill" was most successful when Rexroth read it with jazz accompaniment at The Cellar, a jazz club in San Francisco that featured poetry readings. It became the centerpiece of his highly popular readings in the late 1950s. As jazz critic Ralph J. Gleason described the poetry readings to jazz in his liner notes to the record album *Poetry Readings in "The Cellar"*:

> During the Spring of 1957 a series of fascinating experiments took place in San Francisco.
>
> The scene was The Cellar, a downstairs nightclub that used to be a Chinese restaurant and has been converted into a jazz club by several musicians.
>
> The experiment was an attempt to meld the twin forms of modern expression—jazz and poetry.
>
> The participants were two San Francisco poets: Kenneth Rexroth, widely known for some years as a translator, poet, and commentator on the social scene, and Lawrence Ferlinghetti, a modern poet of considerable stature who operates a publishing house and a bookstore; and a group of jazz musicians....
>
> Rexroth was the prime mover in The Cellar series. He had experimented with jazz and poetry recitals in Chicago two decades ago but then put it aside.... Rexroth was motivated in his activity with jazz by an attempt to broaden the audience for modern poetry. "It is very important to get poetry out of the hands of the professors and out of the hands of the squares," he says. "If we can get poetry out into the life of the country it can be creative," he adds. "Homer, or the guy who recited Beowulf, was show business. We simply want to make poetry a part of show business...."

In addition to translating and writing poetry and reading it to jazz in these years, Rexroth also worked as a journalist. As the San Francisco correspondent for the *Nation*, he wrote articles publicizing the Beat writers when they were still

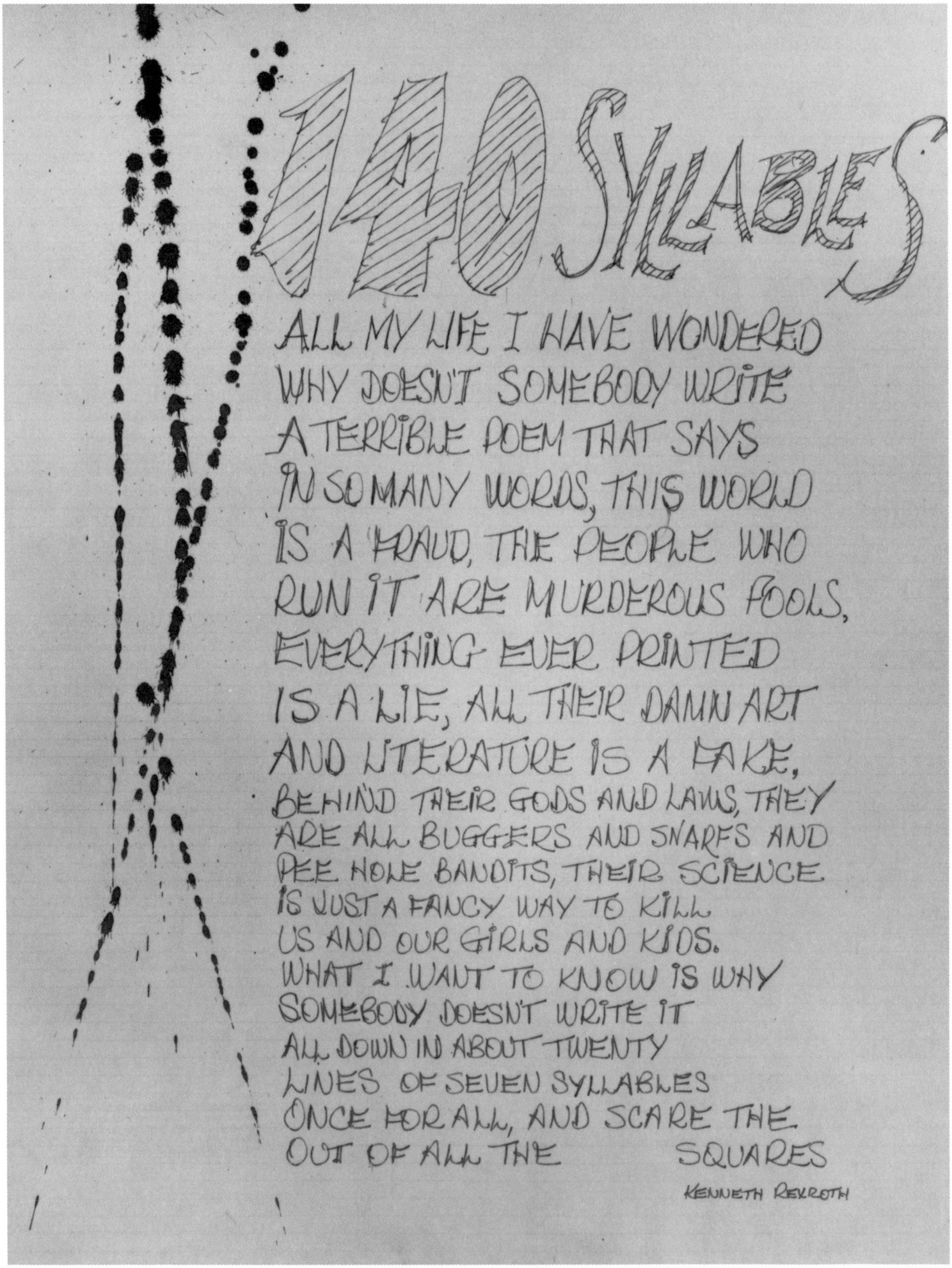

140 SYLLABLES

ALL MY LIFE I HAVE WONDERED
WHY DOESN'T SOMEBODY WRITE
A TERRIBLE POEM THAT SAYS
IN SO MANY WORDS, THIS WORLD
IS A FRAUD, THE PEOPLE WHO
RUN IT ARE MURDEROUS FOOLS,
EVERYTHING EVER PRINTED
IS A LIE, ALL THEIR DAMN ART
AND LITERATURE IS A FAKE,
BEHIND THEIR GODS AND LAWS, THEY
ARE ALL BUGGERS AND SNARFS AND
PEE HOLE BANDITS, THEIR SCIENCE
IS JUST A FANCY WAY TO KILL
US AND OUR GIRLS AND KIDS.
WHAT I WANT TO KNOW IS WHY
SOMEBODY DOESN'T WRITE IT
ALL DOWN IN ABOUT TWENTY
LINES OF SEVEN SYLLABLES
ONCE FOR ALL, AND SCARE THE
OUT OF ALL THE   SQUARES

KENNETH REXROTH

Broadside (by permission of Bradford Morrow for the Trustees of the Kenneth Rexroth Trust; courtesy of the Lilly Library, Indiana University) unknown, heralding them, as "San Francisco's Mature Bohemians" in an article on 23 February 1957. In that laudatory article he explained their connection with the radical tradition of protest literature on the West Coast. Thanks to Rexroth's journalistic efforts in the *Nation* and the *New York Times,* for which he was also a book reviewer and critic, American readers had the opportunity to learn about the poets involved in the San Francisco Poetry Renaissance in the early years of the Beat literary movement from a well-informed and (at first) sympathetic source. For example, in the second issue of the *Evergreen Review* (1957), a New York literary magazine that published a feature issue on the San Francisco Poetry Renaissance, Rexroth described the Beat poets as participating in an important movement of cultural "disaffiliation" from the ruling "convergence of interest—the Business community, military imperialism, political reaction, the hysterical, tear and mud drenched guilt of the ex-Stalinist, ex-Trotskyist American intellectuals." Later the critic Morgan Gibson pointed out that Rexroth's polemic was grounded in the fact that the Beat writers "did break through the widespread political cowardice and intellectual apathy of the Dwight Eisenhower years, following the Korean war."

In another important, widely read, and often discussed article titled "Disengagement: The Art of the Beat Generation," included in the 1957 *New World Writing Anthology,* Rexroth traced the contemporary styles of experimental poetry, jazz, and painting back to the work of two culture heroes, Dylan Thomas and Charlie Parker, who had recently died under pressure from what Rexroth described as a dehumanizing world. Rexroth felt that "Both of them did communicate one central theme: Against the ruin of the world, there is only one defense—the creative act." Rexroth extolled poetry that sought "clarity of image and simplicity of language," as opposed to the "metaphysical conceits which fascinate the Reactionary Generation still dominant in backwater American colleges." He believed in poetry as direct communication grounded in the spoken word, an easily understood "statement from one person to another," which was also part of the aesthetic of the Beat poets.

Soon Rexroth had a change of heart toward the Beat writers, however. He seemed to have become jealous of their success and widespread attention from the national press. He had fought for many years for his own recognition as a poet, and, as their popularity increased, his growing hostility toward the Beats was expressed in a series of ar-

ticles over the next several years. He said that he broke with the Beat writers because of what he regarded as their lack of artistic discipline, but his harshly critical reviews of important experimental books, like Kerouac's *Mexico City Blues* and *Doctor Sax,* which he judged childishly pretentious and self-indulgent when he reviewed them for the *New York Times* in 1959, alienated him from the writers whom he had helped a great deal at the beginning of their careers by his sympathy and support. Actually his championing of the writers went on for a rather brief time. As early as 16 February 1958, Rexroth was feeling superior to them as is evident in his article for the *San Francisco Chronicle,* "The Voice of the Beat Generation has some Square Delusions."

The Beat writers did not reply directly to his attack, although in 1958 Kerouac published his novel *The Dharma Bums,* in which Rexroth was humorously portrayed as Rheinhold Cacoethes and described as a "bowtied wild-haired old anarchist" presiding over poetry readings in San Francisco in 1955. In this novel Kerouac gave an accurate, vivid picture of Rexroth's conversation. " 'I guess the only real poets in the country, outside the orbit of this little backyard, are Doctor Musial, who's probably muttering behind his living-room curtains right now, and Dee Sampson, who's too rich. That leaves dear old Japhy here who's going away to Japan, and our wailing friend Goldbook and our Mr. Coughlin, who has a sharp tongue. By God, I'm the only good one here. At least I've got an honest anarchist background. At least I had frost on my nose, boots on my feet, and protest in my mouth.' He stroked his mustache."

The characters mentioned in this speech are poets William Carlos Williams ("Doctor Musial"), Gary Snyder ("Japhy"), Allen Ginsberg ("Goldbook"), and Philip Whalen ("Mr. Coughlin"). The way Cacoethes/Rexroth talks about them in *Dharma Bums* gives a good idea of the often condescending way Rexroth talked about other contemporary poets. Rexroth never forgave Kerouac for the less-than-flattering portrait of him in the novel. Of the Beat poets, he professed the most admiration for Gary Snyder at this time, since he regarded Snyder as a serious Buddhist scholar; Snyder also credits Rexroth for encouraging his early interest in Oriental poetry and philosophy. Snyder was influenced by the clarity and tone of Rexroth's nature poetry and translations, as in Rexroth's lines:

A hundred thousand birds
Warble in the Spring.

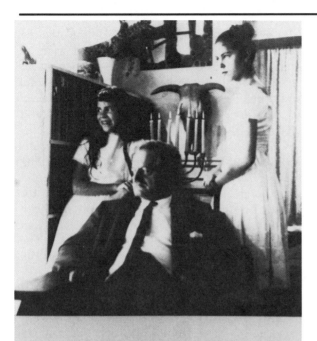

The Collected Shorter Poems of Kenneth Rexroth

Front cover for Rexroth's 1967 book: Rexroth is shown with his daughters, Katharine and Mary

> All things are made new.
> I alone
> Grow old and pass.

Years later Snyder's group of poems titled *The Back Country* (1968), his first book with Rexroth's publisher New Directions after nearly a decade of small-press publications, was dedicated to Rexroth.

Perhaps the most sympathetic description of Rexroth was made by his friend Lawrence Lipton in a 1957 piece for the *Quarterly Review of Literature:* "Think of him, first, as an 11th century figure of a man, scholar, poet, priest, a student from the Latin Quarter out on the town, a tramp scholar in the tradition of the goliards, unchurched, unfrocked, unschooled, from whom no book was safe if he needed it, no scholarly discipline too formidable to undertake, no language too arduous to study and master, no way of life too unconventional or too dangerous to sample. A restless experimenter, faithful and faithless by turns to every temp-

tation of the heart and mind, a terror to the Muse herself who is by turns mother, bitch, mistress, faithless whore. And today, in his middle years, a tall, greying figure in a ragged overcoat, with a knobbed walking stick and the look of a friendly uncaged lion who delights children and frightens their school teachers."

The changes in Rexroth's attitude toward the Beat literary movement can be followed by his essays. Before Kerouac's *On the Road* became a bestseller in the last months of 1957, Rexroth championed the Beat writers in his articles and reviews, but by 1959, with the collection of essays titled *Bird in the Bush,* he had repudiated the movement.

Rexroth's later book *American Poetry in the Twentieth Century* (1971) has a more balanced view of Beat writing, possibly because he conveniently ignored Kerouac's poetry and his dominant influence on Ginsberg's best work. In the last chapter of the book, Rexroth credits the Beats with what he calls the greatest change in American poetry since 1955, the "change of medium—poetry as voice not as printing. The climacteric was not the publication of a book, it was the famous Six Gallery reading, the culmination of twenty years of the oral presentation of poetry in San Francisco. . . . In the same year Kenneth Patchen, Lawrence Ferlinghetti and myself were doing poetry to jazz all over the country. It didn't really matter if the *Hudson Review* printed us or not, and it never would have occurred to us to try."

In this book Rexroth's list of those he considered the most important poets since 1955 was a roll call of the Beats and their friends, the Black Mountain College group, and the younger New York poets: Allen Ginsberg, Lawrence Ferlinghetti, Robert Duncan, Robert Creeley, Gregory Corso, Charles Olson, Philip Lamantia, Philip Whalen, Kenneth Koch, Frank O'Hara, John Ashbery, Denise Levertov, and "coming up as a slightly younger generation, Gary Snyder, Michael McClure, LeRoi Jones, and David Meltzer." Rexroth recognized that an outstanding characteristic of this group, which he called "the avant-garde of the Fifties and Sixties," is "its catholicity. They are more unlike each other than were T. S. Eliot and William Carlos Williams." Yet the poets of this generation, he understood, were united by their "quest for direct, interpersonal communication. Speech from one human to another."

In *American Poetry in the Twentieth Century,* Rexroth wrote most sympathetically about Ginsberg as a Beat poet, seeing his work as "an almost perfect fulfillment of the long, Whitman, Populist, social revolutionary tradition in American poetry." Rexroth awarded Ginsberg the highest marks, rating him even higher than his previous favorite poet, Dylan Thomas. Rexroth viewed Ginsberg as "a latter-day *nabi,* one of those Hebrew prophets who came down out of the hills and cried 'Woe! Woe!' to the bloody city of Jerusalem! in the streets. *Howl* resembles as much as anything the denunciatory poems of Jeremiah and Hosea." Ginsberg had, in Rexroth's opinion, single-handedly taken on the entire American cultural establishment and vanquished it, like David conquering Goliath: "After Ginsberg, the fundamental American tradition, which was also the most international and the least provincial, was no longer on the defensive but moved over to the attack, and soon, as far as youthful audiences were concerned, the literary Establishment simply ceased to exist. It's not that Ginsberg is the greatest poet of the generation of the Fifties, although he is a very good one, it's that he had the most charismatic personality. The only poet in my time to compare with him in effect on audiences was Dylan Thomas, and Dylan Thomas was essentially a performer, whereas Ginsberg meant something of the greatest importance and so his effects have endured and permeated the whole society, and Thomas's have not."

In the final analysis, of course, Rexroth rises above his role of "the *gad*father of the Beat generation," in Lawrence Ferlinghetti's phrase. Rexroth's books of poetry, essays, and translations were published steadily for thirty years, most of them by New Directions, and these books form a large, impressive body of work. His publisher James Laughlin says that "His translations of Japanese and Chinese poetry are perennial best-sellers on the New Directions list, different in their style but as fine as Pound's *Cathay.* He began them by working from Judith Gautier's French versions, but he was such a good linguist that he had soon mastered the basic Oriental characters and was working direct from them. He even 'translated' the work of a Japanese poet named Marichiko, whom I took to be completely authentic until he confessed, under pressure, that Marichiko was really KR. His translations from the French of Pierre Reverdy are first rate, and his version from the Italian of Leopardi's 'L'Infinito' is, in my opinion, as good as the original."

Biographer Morgan Gibson has summarized Rexroth's achievement:

Front cover for the collection that led one critic to call Rexroth "the American most capable of epic achievement"

The center of Rexroth's stormy life was quiet contemplation. He seemed to have done everything, to have met everyone of importance, to have read all of the great books and many minor ones, to have fought the good fights (nonviolently)—but all of this creative activity seemed to circulate around a calm center of light. Oceanic, ecstatic illuminations of the oneness of all beings had brought him an early sense of mission as philosophical artist and poet. These mystical experiences permeate his work, from *Homestead* (1920-1925, but not published as a whole long poem until 1957, concerning two brothers' quest for salvation) through *The Love Poems of Marichiko* (1978, a sequence of Tantric ecstasy written in Japan, his last great work). He told about early visionary experiences in *An Autobiographical Novel* (1966)— a work comparable to Yeats's *Autobiographies* in revealing the growth of a poet's mind: a sense of heavenly peace came over him when his mother died, and again when he nearly became a monk in an Anglo-Catholic monastery in New York state. Such experiences defy description or explanation, but he never stopped philosophizing about them and their meaning, and in doing so he absorbed and interpreted major religious, philosophical, and literary traditions, Asian and Western, for our own age. . . .

Rexroth published thirty-five books of poetry, of which thirteen are translations from Japanese and Chinese (including two volumes of women poets of Japan and China), Greek and Latin, French and Spanish. Virtually all of his poetry, excluding most of the translations and plays, can be found in *The Collected Shorter Poems* (1967), *The Collected Longer Poems* (including five of them, 1968), *New Poems* (1974), and *The Morning Star* (1979—containing three previously published sequences written in Japan: *The Silver Swan, On Flower Wreath Hill,* and *The Love Poems of Marichiko*). As for translations, he made the work of such poets as Pierre Reverdy, Martial, Sappho, Tu Fu, Li Ch'ing Chao, *Manyoshu* poets, Yosano Akiko, and Shiraishi Kazuko available in lively English versions. Japanese poets and critics have especially admired his translations, his comprehension of Japanese culture, and its absorption into his poetry and thought. His understanding of the cultures of both Japan and China seems more reliable than that of Pound or any other poet in English excepting Arthur Waley and Gary Snyder. His translations make the original poet seem vitally present in the poem—no doubt because of his practice of communing with dead poets in imaginary conversations. He called translation "an act of sympathy," rather than thinking of it as literal rendering. So translation was an essential activity in his vision of world community.

In his lifetime Rexroth espoused different creeds, but he never brought himself to the point of limiting himself to one or another. On 8 June 1982, two days after his death in his home in Mon-

tecito, California, the *New York Times* headline read "Kenneth Rexroth, 76, Author; Father Figure to Beat Poets." The *Times* obituary writer Wolfgang Saxon described Rexroth as being "a role model and father figure to the Beat generation that made its mark on the San Francisco literary scene of the late 50's." Rexroth would have been angered by the headline, because in his last years he again repudiated his connection with the Beat writers. From the 1920s to the 1960s, he was at the center of important radical artistic and political movements in the United States. Yet, characteristically, Rexroth even protested against his public image as a fiery radical. "I've never understood why I'm a member of the avant garde. I write like the great Greeks and Romans and the Chinese, and so forth. I try to say, as simply as I can, the simplest and most profound experiences of my life, and hope that out of this you will get exaltation."

Interview:

"Kenneth Rexroth," in *The San Francisco Poets*, edited by David Meltzer (New York: Ballantine, 1971);
Sympathetic, lengthy interview with Rexroth by a young Bay Area poet.

References:

Morgan Gibson, *Kenneth Rexroth* (New York: Twayne, 1972);
Fullest biographical and critical discussion to date.

Parkinson, "Phenomenon or Generation," in his *A Casebook on the Beat* (New York: Crowell, 1961);
Rexroth's essay reprinted in the context of controversy around Beat writers.

Theodore Roethke

*This entry was updated by Keen Butterworth (University of South Carolina) from his entry
in* DLB 5, American Poets Since World War II.

Places	Saginaw, Michigan Seattle, Washington	Lafayette College Bennington College	Pennsylvania State University
Influences and Relationships	Louise Bogan Rolfe Humphries Stanley Kunitz Kenneth Burke	Robert Lowell Dylan Thomas W. H. Auden	W. C. Williams W. B. Yeats T. S. Eliot
Literary Movements and Forms			

Major Themes	Literary Past
	The Abyss
	Sensibility of
	    Childhood
	Search for Identity
		Life as Journey
		Romantic Love
		Spiritual Transcen-
		    dence
			Natural World
			God as Metaphor
			The Unconscious
			    Mind

Cultural and Artistic Influences	Darwinism	Jungian Psychology	Freudian Psychology
Social and Economic Influences			

BIRTH: Saginaw, Michigan, 25 May 1908, to Otto and Helen Huebner Roethke.

EDUCATION: A.B., University of Michigan, 1929; M.A., University of Michigan, 1936; Harvard Graduate School, 1930-1931.

MARRIAGE: 3 January 1953 to Beatrice O'Connell.

AWARDS AND HONORS: Guggenheim Fellowships, 1945, 1950; Eunice Tietjens Memorial Prize (*Poetry* magazine), 1947; Levinson Prize (*Poetry* magazine), 1951; Ford Foundation grants, 1952, 1959; Pulitzer Prize for *The Waking*, 1954; Fulbright grant, 1955; Bollingen Prize, 1959; National Book Award for *Words for the Wind*, 1959; Shelley Memorial Award, 1962; Litt.D., University of Michigan, 1962; National Book Award for *The Far Field*, 1965.

DEATH: Bainbridge Island, Washington, 1 August 1963.

BOOKS: *Open House* (New York: Knopf, 1941);
The Lost Son and Other Poems (Garden City: Doubleday, 1948; London: Lehmann, 1949);
Praise to the End! (Garden City: Doubleday, 1951);
The Waking, Poems: 1933-1953 (Garden City: Doubleday, 1953);
Words for the Wind (London: Secker & Warburg, 1957; Garden City: Doubleday, 1958);
The Exorcism (San Francisco: Poems in Folio, 1957);
I Am! Says the Lamb (Garden City: Doubleday, 1961);
Party at the Zoo (New York: Crowell-Collier, 1963);
Sequence, Sometimes Metaphysical (Iowa City: Stonewall Press, 1963);
The Far Field (Garden City: Doubleday, 1964; London: Faber & Faber, 1965);
On the Poet and His Craft, edited by Ralph J. Mills, Jr. (Seattle & London: University of Washington Press, 1965);
The Collected Poems of Theodore Roethke (Garden City: Doubleday, 1966; London: Faber & Faber, 1968);
Theodore Roethke: Selected Poems, edited by Beatrice Roethke (London: Faber & Faber, 1969);
Straw for the Fire. From the Notebooks of Theodore Roethke, 1943-63, edited by David Wagoner (Garden City: Doubleday, 1972);
Dirty Dinkey and Other Creatures: Poems for Children,

Theodore Roethke (photo by Frank Murphy)

edited by Beatrice Roethke and Stephen Lushington (Garden City: Doubleday, 1973).

The motif of the journey is more crucial to the poetry of Theodore Roethke than to that of any other major American poet since Whitman. Perhaps it is more important to Roethke. Certainly it is more coherent. Whereas Whitman's journey, if it can be called that, is outward, in all directions, until the fragmented poet achieves reintegration by becoming the cosmos itself, Roethke's is a simple journey from beginning to destination. But to say that it is simple is not to imply that it is easy. The journey, as it is recorded in *The Collected Poems* (1966), is that of a modern-day *Pilgrim's Progress*, fraught with its own temptations of vanity and pride, its own sloughs of despond. But Roethke's journey is essentially more difficult. For Christian in *Pilgrim's Progress* there is a road, worn, and thus defined, by those who have gone before him, and always in the distance stand the Delectable Mountains to mark his destination and draw him onward. For Roethke there is no such well-defined path, nor are there signposts or prominences to indicate his destination. His journey is through a particularly American wilderness, and although the general direction of the journey is never in question, Roethke must make his groping way relying on his instincts or intuitions, "feeling" and learning by the very act of "going" itself, as he was to articulate the process in his poem "The Waking." Nevertheless, Roethke's quest is a religious one, just as Christian's is. In America, however, the order of European Christianity has given way to a pantheism, the structure of which is as uncertain as that of Nature itself. The American pilgrim makes his way westward through the wilderness toward discovery and self-realization: this is the movement of both Roethke's poetry and his life.

Roethke's journey is also an evolutionary one, essentially that described and speculated on by his contemporary Loren Eiseley in *The Immense Journey* (1957). In his second published book, *The Lost Son* (1948), Roethke returns to his evolutionary past, where he joins the worms, slugs, and snails in the slime of primordial existence. From that point, Roethke's poetry moves forward, through the realization of his kinship with the higher animals, through the realization of his own humanity (in *The Waking*, 1953, and *Words for the Wind*, 1957), and finally to the transcendence of spiritual man in *The Far Field* (1964). It is a movement from unconscious life, through various stages of intermediate consciousness, to the highest form of self-realization man is capable of.

These statements about the radical nature of Roethke's journey may seem to imply that he discarded tradition, particularly the old-world traditions, in his work. In a sense that is true: although *Open House* (1941) is certainly traditional, *The Lost Son, Praise to the End!* (1951), and parts of *The Waking* are an entirely new kind of poetry. Although in the later poetry, from *The Waking* through *The Far Field*, he adopts traditional poetic forms from both the Old World and American past, it appears as if Roethke were reinventing these forms rather than copying or imitating them. This is instructive, for in *Open House* Roethke is most definitely imitating tradition. As technically correct as these first poems are, Roethke himself understood their lack of distinction and vitality. Consequently, he rejected the tradition he felt was stultifying him in order to redefine poetry. Thus the development of his work is a journey also—this time a technical one, which parallels and reinforces the physical and spiritual journeys the poetry depicts.

Even when Roethke's poetry is most radical, as in *The Lost Son,* he never really escapes tradition. No poet of value ever does that; he cannot escape the poetic traditions any more than he can escape the traditions of the language in which he is writing. As Jenijoy La Belle has shown in *The Echoing Wood* (1976), Roethke's poetry is filled with echoes, paraphrases, and even direct borrowings from his poetic forebears. The lines of *The Lost Son* and *Praise to the End!* often suggest Wordsworth, Blake, Whitman, and others. Nonetheless, the radical readjustment and synthesis of traditional elements that Roethke effects in these poems give the impression of an entirely new kind of poetry that has broken with tradition. This is Roethke's genius. It is, in that way, much like the genius of Eliot, Picasso, and Stravinsky. A number of critics have praised this originality in *The Lost Son* and *Praise to the End!* Many feel that these books contain his best poetry and have criticized the later work (which calls attention to its relationships and debts to tradition), as imitative and unoriginal. But the later poetry is no less original for its formality. In fact, the originality of *The Lost Son* is only one step in the process that leads to *The Far Field:* it is a step that was necessary before Roethke could return to and revitalize those aspects of tradition he found still valid. The process is that of American history itself: in escaping old-world tradition Americans have been forced to invent new forms. Often they have found, however, that they merely reinvented old forms, readjusted perhaps, but essentially the old forms. Americans have revalidated those forms because they seemed appropriate, necessary to the conditions of a new existence. More important, in reinventing them, Americans have revitalized them. These principles are applicable to Roethke's poetry. Of all our major poets, Roethke—in his initial imitation of tradition, his subsequent departure from and final return to it—seems more representatively American, even, than Walt Whitman himself, who represents only the initial stages of the process.

Theodore Roethke was born in Saginaw, Michigan. His father, Otto Roethke, had immigrated to America from Germany as a child with his family in 1872. On arriving in Saginaw, the Roethkes bought twenty-two acres of land on which they established a market garden. Those were the days of the Michigan timber boom; consequently there was a great demand for fresh produce. The Roethkes prospered; and when Roethke's grandfather had made sufficient money, he built a greenhouse so that he could enter the florist business,

Dust jacket for the posthumously published collection of the poems Roethke wrote in his last years. This book won a National Book Award.

which also prospered. After the grandfather's death, Otto Roethke and Roethke's Uncle Karl took over the management of the business. In 1906 Otto married Helen Huebner, another German immigrant, and they took up residence in a house on Gratiot Avenue, where Roethke was born two years later. When Roethke was two years old, Otto built his own house just in front of the greenhouse, so that he would always be nearby to tend his flowers. As a child, Roethke followed his father about his work and was given small chores of his own. Thus, Roethke almost literally grew up among the plants of the greenhouse. His experience of this vegetable world affected him deeply: the greenhouse itself was to become the central image of *The Lost Son* and *Praise to the End!* Also on the property, beyond the greenhouse, was a large field, where Roethke often played as a child. This field, too, became an important image in his poetry.

The intense and painful introspection of his adulthood, which is so evident in his work, grew from a tendency established very early in his life. Roethke's playmates during these years seem to have been his cousins Violet and Bud, for June, Roethke's sister, was five years younger than he. Although Violet has recalled her relationship with Roethke fondly, she was two years older and had different interests. Bud was only six months older than Roethke, but he was much larger and seems to have bullied his younger cousin. Or, at least, Roethke found him threatening, for he developed an intense dislike for Bud that lasted most of his life. Also, Roethke was a frail and sickly child who had to spend a good deal of each winter indoors recovering from the effects of influenza and bronchitis. As a result he became retiring, shy, and he turned inward upon himself.

At five, Roethke was sent to the John Moore School, where he took the usual course of math, reading, composition, and, because of the large German population, an hour of that language each day. He was an intelligent child and appears to have gotten on well in school, although he retained almost none of the German he learned during these years.

In 1921 Roethke entered Arthur Hill High School in Saginaw. During his freshman year he distinguished himself by giving a speech on the Junior Red Cross, which was published and later translated into twenty-six languages for international distribution. Although filled with the usual platitudes and cliches, it was quite a good piece of writing for a thirteen-year-old boy. This recognition also whetted his ambition. He already knew that he wanted to become a writer, although he had not yet considered becoming a poet. At the time, he later recalled, he wanted to be a prose writer; so he began studying essayists, such as Walter Pater, Thoreau, and Emerson, and short story writers. But not all of his time during these high school years was devoted to reading, writing, and his other studies. He also joined a high school fraternity, most of whose members were athletes—with a reputation for drinking. To further his image of the all-around man, Roethke took up tennis. He had little natural ability and moved about the court awkwardly, flying into rages at himself whenever he made a mistake. Nevertheless, through hours of practice, he became a good enough player to enter several city and state tournaments—and later he would coach two college tennis teams.

During Roethke's second year at high school, his father died of cancer, a "kink in the bowels" as the doctors said. Outwardly, Roethke accepted the event calmly, probably because he had been prepared for it by the long illness that preceded Otto's death. However, as Roethke's mature poetry suggests, the loss had a deep and lasting effect on him. His attitude toward his father had been ambivalent. On the one hand, Otto had often been a hard taskmaster, demanding perfection from his son and belittling him when he failed to live up to standards. Consequently, Roethke resented his father as a threat to his own individuality and ego; at times this resentment seems to have been intense. On the other hand, Roethke could admire the life-giving quality in Otto, not just as his own progenitor, but as the gardener who could bring plant life from the soil, who devoted his life to the perpetuation of life. Also, even the young Roethke must have sensed that his father was responsible for the order of his world. In "The Lost Son," which is written from the point of view of the child, the father's arrival is associated with order (*ordnung*). In "My Papa's Waltz" Roethke captures the earthy vitality of Otto, and also something of his own joy, and bafflement, as the victim of his father's exuberant energy. Later, in "Otto," written forty years after his father's death, Roethke objectively records the vitality, order, and contradictions in his father's character.

But these poems represent the reflections of Roethke the mature poet. The adolescent Roethke adjusted quickly to his father's death. As the oldest child and the only male, he was now head of the family. He continued to work diligently at school, and even became something of a leader among the youths of the Presbyterian Church. During his senior year he announced to his mother that he wanted to go to Harvard, but she insisted that he go to the nearby University of Michigan at Ann Arbor. That summer, 1925, Roethke worked for the Heinz pickle factor in Saginaw (where he would work each summer during his undergraduate years), an experience that he used later in the poem "Pickle Belt." In the fall he entered the University of Michigan, the first member of his family to attend college.

Roethke did well in college and seems to have enjoyed his four years as an undergraduate (although he was to say later that he hated all the years of his schooling, high school through Harvard). Now at 6' 2 1/2", 190 pounds, he bought a gorgeous coonskin coat and sometimes walked about campus as if he were a great hulking bear, a self-image that he was to cultivate further in later years and use in some of his poetry. He also began

to develop the image of himself as a tough guy who had connections among the Chicago underworld. Indeed, he did go occasionally to a speakeasy near Detroit where gangsters and smugglers (it was the height of Prohibition) hung out. And though in later years Roethke bragged about his experiences with gangsters, this seems to have been the extent of his ventures into the underworld.

On campus, Roethke entered into the social life, joining Chi Phi fraternity and playing intramural tennis. His real interest, however, was in training himself to be a writer. He took a general course of study, but concentrated on literature and language. He had four courses in German, two in French, two in Polish, one in Sanskrit (in translation) and twelve in English composition and literature. He did well in all these courses, and was elected to Phi Beta Kappa during his senior year. In his study of Roethke's notebooks, Allan Seager discovered that it was also during the undergraduate years that Roethke began writing poetry, although he did not tell his friends and teachers about it.

After graduation in 1929, Roethke entered the University of Michigan law school. But his effort seems to have been half-hearted, for his mind was not suited to the study of law. In fact, Roethke enrolled in only one class, Criminal Law, and received a *D* in that. In February 1930 he withdrew from law school and entered the graduate school to pursue a master's degree in literature. Roethke did well in these studies, but his real interest had turned to writing poetry, rather than studying it as a scholar. He was serious about his poetry now and frequently talked about his favorites among the moderns: Elinor Wylie, for her lyricism, and E. E. Cummings, for his courage in experimentation. In June 1930 three of his poems appeared in the little magazine the *Harp.*

Roethke continued his studies at Michigan during the summer of 1930; in the fall, however, he entered Harvard Graduate School, where he would, as he said, study under "men he could respect." There he showed three of his poems to Robert Hillyer, who praised them and suggested that he submit them to reputable magazines. Two of them were accepted, "The Conqueror" by *Commonweal* and "Silence" by the *New Republic.* He also studied under the English critic I. A. Richards, who seems to have helped Roethke shape his own concept of his role as poet and gave him direction in pursuing his career. Probably, Roethke would have continued his graduate work at Harvard; perhaps he would have gone on to earn a Ph.D., as he had intended, but the Depression was affecting Roethke's family as it was the rest of America, and he was forced to withdraw from school and find a job. He sent out several applications for teaching positions and was accepted by Lafayette, a small Presbyterian college in Pennsylvania.

Roethke stayed at Lafayette for four years. There he got a reputation for his eccentricities and hard drinking, but his students found him informal and stimulating, a natural teacher. He was so well liked by his students that they petitioned the college to retain him when he was to be released in 1935. But he had been kept already two years beyond the normal tenure for an instructor, and was let go with excellent recommendations by his department head. He had been the college's tennis coach for two years and director of public relations: he was excellent at both jobs.

Socially this had been an important period in Roethke's life. He fell in love with Mary Kunkel, the daughter of a biology professor at Lafayette College. They talked of marriage, but Roethke was in no position to take on that kind of responsibility and they drifted apart. But other friendships formed during his years at Lafayette were to have a permanent influence on his career as poet. Poet Rolfe Humphries offered intellectual friendship, understanding criticism, and encouragement. Humphries also introduced Roethke to Louise Bogan, whom Roethke admired a great deal, and whose poetry he had studied seriously along with that of Elinor Wylie and Leonie Adams. In Stanley Kunitz, Roethke found a most sympathetic spirit. Roethke had studied and admired his poetry so much that he sought out Kunitz on his farm in Bucks County, Pennsylvania. Immediately, they struck up a friendship that was to last the rest of Roethke's life. Kunitz saw Roethke's potential as a poet and offered him helpful criticism. Despite Roethke's academic duties and social life he continued to devote a great deal of time to writing poetry. His colleagues remember that he always carried his notebook around, in order to jot down ideas and lines as they came to him. This was a habit Roethke started early and kept up all his life. (At his death he left behind 277 notebooks.) From these notes he built his poems. During 1932-1934 he published nineteen of them in such magazines as *Poetry, New Republic,* and *Saturday Review.*

From Lafayette, Roethke went to Michigan State College in Lansing. Again, students found him to be an exciting teacher. But Roethke was drinking very hard that fall, and he began to behave erratically. In November he had a mental breakdown, the first of a series that were to plague him the rest of his life. He was admitted to a local hospital for treatment and remained there until mid January 1936. Then he went home to Saginaw to recuperate, assuming that he would resume his teaching position in the fall. But later in the spring he learned that he had been replaced during his absence and would have to find another job.

During the spring Roethke resumed writing poetry (for he seems to have stopped during the turmoil of the previous fall) and applied for jobs at several colleges. He was accepted at Pennsylvania State. Here he fell in love again, this time with a librarian, Kitty Stokes, and began to live an active social life. He even took up cooking and fancied himself a gourmet, and again he became the college tennis coach. Roethke's life at Penn State seems to have been fulfilling. With Kitty Stokes's encouragement and help in typing his work, Roethke devoted much of his time and energy to his poetry. By 1939 he felt that he had enough poems for a book. Stanley Kunitz helped him arrange the poems and suggested the book's title. The manuscript went to several publishers before it was accepted by Alfred A. Knopf, who published it as *Open House* in March 1941. Always neurotic in his craving for approval, Roethke waited anxiously for the reviews. When they came, they were nearly all favorable, and by such people as W. H. Auden, Louise Bogan, Yvor Winters, Rolfe Humphries, Elizabeth Drew, and Babette Deutsch. Roethke's career as a poet was launched.

Open House is indeed a volume that shows poetic promise: the reader can see here a talented craftsman, a poet who knows well the tradition of his art; but it is obvious, in retrospect, that Roethke had not yet found his themes or his proper manner. Among the forty-seven poems there is a great variety of forms and tones. And there is the echo, sometimes an obvious imitation, of poets he had been reading and admired. For instance, "No Bird" and "Genesis" are obviously imitations of Emily Dickinson's short lyrics, and as Jenijoy La Belle has pointed out, "No Bird" seems to be Dickinson's epitaph. There are also echoes of and allusions to such poets as Donne, Blake, Hopkins, Robinson, Frost, Eliot, Auden, Wylie, and Bogan. There are several very good poems, such as "For an Amorous Lady," "Academic," and "The Bat," which foreshadow the humorous poems in *Words for the Wind* and the children's poems of *I Am! Says the Lamb* (1961). Several poems deal with his father's death, one of which, "The Premonition," suggests the manner he was to develop in *The Lost Son.* But if there is a recurring theme in *Open House* it is Roethke's expressed desire to shed the past and the poetic traditions he felt stultifying him. "Feud" states the case: "The spirit starves/Until the dead have been subdued." "Prognosis" puts it a different way: "Though the devouring mother cry, 'Escape me?/Never—'/And the honeymoon be spoiled by a father's ghost." In "The Auction" Roethke foresees success in escaping the past: "I left my home with unencumbered will/And all the rubbish of confusion sold." In "Sale" the strategy is to sell all the furniture and bric-a-brac inherited from past generations. Thus from this heterogeneous collection of poems, this confusion of styles, the reader hears Roethke's voice crying for release. He senses the need to escape his poetic forebears and create his own individual style. Significantly the volume ends with the poem "Night Journey." The train on which the narrator has embarked is heading west— away from tradition, toward purification and renewal.

After the publication of *Open House,* Roethke became dissatisfied with his job at Penn State, where, he said, his abilities and accomplishments went unrecognized. Although Roethke was still without a large reading public, he was now known by the literary community. Among his new acquaintances were Robert Frost, Bernard DeVoto, Morton Zabel, F. O. Matthiessen, and Henry S. Canby. He received further evidence of his recognition when he was invited to give one of the Morris Gray readings at Harvard in the spring of 1942. Always one to seize the main chance to further his career, Roethke set the wheels in motion to acquire a Guggenheim Fellowship, with the support of Canby, Stanley Kunitz, and Rolfe Humphries. Although Roethke's name was not on the list for 1943, he had contingency plans underway. The previous year he had applied for a position at Bennington College, where he thought the atmosphere would be much more congenial to his career as a poet and teacher. He was accepted, and in the spring of 1943, taking an indefinite leave of absence without pay from Penn State, moved to Bennington, Vermont.

Indeed, Bennington was a different kind of school. Although only thirteen years old, it had brought together a distinguished faculty, and it carefully screened the girls who were admitted. Moreover, the faculty was not hierarchical: all the members were considered equals, and the classes or seminars were run informally, as if the students were the intellectual equals of their teachers. This was a new challenge for Roethke. At first he ap-

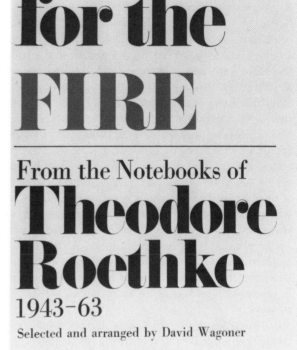

STRAW for the FIRE

From the Notebooks of

Theodore Roethke

1943-63

Selected and arranged by David Wagoner

Dust jacket for a selection from notebooks Roethke kept throughout his career

pears to have been intimidated by it, but that drove him on to perfect his teaching techniques. He developed courses on verse forms and the analysis of poetry that were thought by many to be the best literary courses in the school. Roethke drove himself, as well as his students. They were fascinated by his earnestness and vitality; many have said that Roethke made them believe poetry was the most important activity in life. Because of his magnetism a number of intimate relationships developed between Roethke and his students. In fact, one of his affairs was brought to the attention of the administration by the girl's parents, and nearly caused his dismissal: in all probability he would not have been rehired by the college in 1947, but he left of his own accord.

While at Bennington, Roethke established several important relationships with his colleagues. Mary Garrett, the dean of the school, assumed the motherly role that Mary Kunkel and Kitty Stokes

had played before her. Leonie Adams, whose poetry Roethke had admired for some time, was also
on the faculty. She helped in shaping his courses,
and they talked about poetry. But most important,
Roethke became friends with Kenneth Burke,
whose apartment was in the same cottage as his.
Burke was perhaps the most erudite man Roethke
had ever known and a discerning critic. Roethke
read him several of his new "greenhouse" poems:
Burke knew immediately that Roethke had struck
the right vein and told him so. With the encouragement of his new friends and colleagues,
Roethke threw himself into a fit of poetic creation
that was to produce the major poems of *The Lost
Son.* Unfortunately this frenzy of activity was the
result, or the cause, of another of Roethke's manic
states. A period of depression followed in the winter of 1945. He was taken to a hospital in Albany
where he underwent shock treatments. When he
was released from the hospital in January, he returned to Saginaw to recuperate under the care of
his mother and sister. Fortunately, Roethke had
applied for a Guggenheim Fellowship in 1945 and
this time had received it: thus he could remain in
Saginaw without having to worry about returning
to work.

Roethke resumed work on his poetry during
the spring while he was recovering his strength. He
had finished nearly all the poems he needed for a
second volume; he worked steadily through 1946.
By February 1947 the poems were completed, and
fearing that he would not be rehired at Bennington, he returned to Penn State to teach the spring
semester. That summer he went to Yaddo, where
he became friends with Robert Lowell. Also during
the summer he was accepted for a teaching position
at the University of Washington in Seattle. In September he went west.

Roethke had been disappointed in Knopf's
handling of *Open House;* they had not advertised
the book properly, he felt, and they had failed to
bring out a second printing, even when the first
small printing of 1000 copies had been sold out.
In the meantime he had established contacts at
Doubleday; consequently when the manuscript of
The Lost Son was completed in the spring of 1947,
he sent it to them, and it was accepted. Because of
delays caused by Roethke's stipulations about typography, binding, and publicity, however, publication was delayed until March 1948. Again
Roethke waited anxiously for the reviews; this time
they were even more laudatory than those for *Open
House.* This was original poetry, and the reviewers
recognized it as such.

Indeed, *The Lost Son* is *original* poetry in several senses of the word. First, it is original in the
sense that nothing like it had ever been written
before. Second, its rhythms, for the most part, are
of a primal nature: they suggest the unmeasured
rhythm and energy of unconscious life. And further, the poems are original in that they are about
a return to the very sources of life. Most of them
deal with plant life and animal life of a very low
order. The first section of the book contains a series
of poems about life in the greenhouse based on
Roethke's childhood memories. "Cuttings," "Root
Cellar," and "Forcing House" are concerned with
the first stirrings of life in the dank and dark underground. The other poems of this section deal
with activities and events in the greenhouse. The
second section contains contrasting poems of a
more traditional nature, such as the much anthologized "My Papa's Waltz" and "Dolor." The third
section returns to the world of unconscious life.
And the fourth section contains four long poems
all concerned with the evolution from the darkness
of the primitive vegetable and animal world toward
the light of the human world. The most important
poem in the book, the title poem, "The Lost Son,"
is found in this fourth and final section. In it the
themes and method of the book find their most
complete expression.

"The Lost Son" is a stream-of-consciousness
poem. Roethke is projecting himself back into his
own psyche as an adolescent at the time of his father's death. In the first section, "The Flight," the
trauma of the father's burial at Woodlawn Cemetery causes the boy to flee reality. His flight is into
the natural world looking for strength and answers
to his questions about existence; but nature is enigmatic; it offers only riddles without answers. As the
boy looks more desperately, he regresses into a
child's sensibility, represented by the nursery
rhyme stanzas at the end of the section. In the
second section, "The Pit," the regression continues.
The "Pit" is the dark fecund female principle: the
womb, in which life is unconscious and inchoate.
In the next section, "The Gibber," the boy re-
emerges from the pit, but still he is lost in the world.
The death wish then asserts itself as autoeroticism,
but he is called back into the rational human world
by material concerns, represented here by
"money." In "The Return" he makes his way
through the darkness toward light: the coming of
dawn and the rational order his father had imposed
upon his world, the world of the greenhouse. In
the final section, "It was the beginning of winter,"
the boy sees that although the answers have not

come to him yet (because it is an "in-between time"), the light, the "Lively understandable spirit," which in childhood was manifest in his father, will come again. He need only be patient and wait.

The poem has often been interpreted in terms of Freudian psychology; and certainly it has Freudian elements. But it is more comprehensible in terms of Jungian psychology. The patterns and movements of the poem are archetypal in nature: the death of the father; the descent into the depths (here into the evolutionary-genetic abyss of the self); the return to the world of light; the return of the father (here connected with the sun god); and the promise of renewal. These patterns are as old as myth itself, for they rise from the collective unconscious. The narrator is both Telemachus and Odysseus (for both are really two aspects of the same psyche).

There are two short poems in *The Lost Son* that help to explain one of the basic ideas or attitudes of the book: man's relationship to his evolutionary past. "Night Crow" suggests that certain images can conjure up analogical images from our collective unconscious, or even perhaps from a genetically transmitted memory. "River Incident" implies that our evolutionary past is present in our bodies; thus we can "feel" or intuit this past, since it is in our bones, flesh, and blood. It is precisely this past that Roethke explores in *The Lost Son*. This past also allows man to establish an intuitive rapport with the natural world. There has never been another Western poet who has achieved the same kind of feeling of oneness with nature in his poetry that Roethke has. Thoreau's, Whitman's, and their transcendentalist forebears' sense of communion with nature is spiritual, in that all partake of the Godhead, and quite different from Roethke's literal and concrete kinship. (Roethke once said that the trouble with all the "nature boys" like Wordsworth was that they didn't go far enough.) Before Darwin, Western man's belief in his superiority to the natural world would not allow him to feel that oneness. And even in the period after Darwin, evolution was only a novel idea for most people. But now many have had time to absorb the implications of evolution; they can feel, rather than merely understand, their relationship to the rest of nature. Roethke was the first poet to give intense expression to this new attitude.

Roethke had already moved to Seattle when *The Lost Son* was published. At first his feelings about the city were ambivalent. He liked the natural beauty of the area and especially the riot of plant life about him. He also liked the easy, informal campus life; there were none of the pretentions of dress and manners that he had endured in the East. On the other hand, Seattle was a provincial town— a bourgeois town run by matriarchs who had just stepped out from under the hairdryer, he said. But Roethke soon settled into a routine of life and was happier than he had been in any of his previous teaching positions. He was required to teach only two classes; he found the students good; and within his first year he was made a full professor. Again he was popular with his students. Among these students were several who were to become poets in their own right: Carolyn Kizer, David Wagoner, James Wright. Furthermore, Roethke got on well with the administration. Robert Heilman, who was made department head in 1948, became one of Roethke's most loyal supporters. Also, Roethke found almost upon arrival in Seattle a replacement for Mary Garrett and Kitty Stokes as a mother figure in Jerry Lee Willis, a widow, who was also a teacher in the English department.

Under these favorable conditions Roethke worked hard at both his teaching and his poetry. His serious work was on the poems that would make up *Praise to the End!*, but he was also writing a sequence of children's poems about animals that were published as *I Am! Says the Lamb* in 1961 (some of these poems appeared as early as 1950 in the magazine *Flair*). During the summer of 1949 Roethke went to Saginaw, where he could work uninterrupted. He concentrated intensely on his poetry throughout the vacation. When he returned to Washington in September, his friends saw that he was obviously in a highly agitated state. In October, he had to be taken to the local hospital, from which he was transferred in November to a sanitarium. Roethke remained there recuperating and working on his poetry until March 1950. Since he was on leave without pay from the university and his expenses were heavy, Roethke applied for another Guggenheim Fellowship, which was granted in the spring of 1950. That summer Roethke went east to Yaddo; in September he bought his first automobile and drove it cross-country to Seattle. Now recovered from his illness, he returned to teaching for the fall semester. Sometime during 1950 he finished the poems for *Praise to the End!* and sent the manuscript to Doubleday. They accepted the book and it was published in November 1951.

The title of the volume is taken from Wordsworth's *The Prelude* (I). It consists of thirteen long poems, nine of which were retained in *The Collected Poems*. Although reviews of the book were generally favorable, the reviewers expressed no sense of surprise, of discovery, as they had in reviews of *The Lost Son,* for *Praise to the End!* is really a continuation of the mode and themes of its predecessor. The volume explores further the child's sensibility, which has not been separated by self-consciousness from the world about it. In fact, it is a world in which there is a fluid movement between the conscious and the unconscious. It is a world of extraordinary immediacy—if the reader is willing to give himself over to it. But it is also a myopic and cloying world, especially the poems of the first section. Those of the second section, "Praise to the End!" and "I Cry, Love! Love!" in particular, open up the perspective a bit more. The narrator begins to indicate what he has learned in this immediate world of *things.* The "thingy spirit," a primitive spirit of energy and light that pervades primordial life, has revealed itself to him; and the reader senses that by the end of the volume the narrator is ready, and willing, to leave the world of plants and animals and inanimate things. He has absorbed all he can from it and is prepared to enter the conscious world of the adult. But, when at the end of "I Cry, Love! Love!" he says, "We never enter/Alone," the reader realizes the narrator will not leave that world behind: he will carry it with him as an integral part of his being.

Roethke now had three volumes of poetry and a reputation. In 1951 he received *Poetry* magazine's Levinson Prize. In 1952 he was awarded a Ford Foundation grant, which he had applied for so that he would have time to read in philosophy and theology, as well as work on his poetry. And in the spring of 1952 his friend Dylan Thomas visited the Seattle campus. There he stated that Roethke was the best poetry reader in America. (Roethke cherished this praise from the master reader himself and often repeated it.) Roethke was now at the height of his career and no longer had to worry about money as he had in the past. In June he went to Saginaw to see his family and work undisturbed, away from the distractions in Seattle. He remained in Saginaw most of the fall. In December he went to New York to give a poetry reading. There he ran into one of his former Bennington students, Beatrice O'Connell from Winchester, Virginia. She was now living in New York teaching art in a public school in Harlem. They began to see each other daily; their courtship was short: they married within a month, on 3 January 1953.

For their honeymoon, the Roethkes went to Europe, where W. H. Auden had lent them his villa at Ischia. They stayed at the villa from early March through May, living a relaxed if somewhat primitive existence. Here Roethke worked on poems that would go into *Words for the Wind.* From Ischia, they went on to Rome, to Geneva, then to Paris. In July they crossed the channel to England, where they remained until the first week in August. This was the first time Roethke had left the North American continent. He did not like the anxieties travel caused him and refused to do much sightseeing, but he enjoyed the social life, for he got to see many of his old acquaintances and make a number of new literary friends. In August they returned to America, visited Saginaw, and arrived in Seattle at the beginning of September. There they rented a house on the shore of Lake Washington and settled down to married life.

In September 1953 Doubleday brought out *The Waking,* a selection of Roethke's poems, written between 1933 and 1953. It also included eight new poems. The first of these—"O, Thou Opening, O," "A Light Breather," and "The Visitant"—continue in the mode of *The Lost Son* and *Praise to the End!* However, in "The Visitant" the form of a woman materializes briefly amidst the natural world: she seems to be the idealized female spirit who will lead the narrator out of his "thingy" world and into the social world where he can find his place in relationship to other human beings. And certainly the other new poems in the collection manifest an entirely different world from that of the first three. For instance, the often anthologized "Elegy for Jane," in which Roethke expresses his sense of loss at the death of a student, is quite conventional in its manner and sentiment. The two most successful poems in the collection, however, are "Four for Sir John Davies" and "The Waking"—two of the best poems Roethke ever wrote. In the first, a four-part poem, Roethke is having a good time with his jokes and wordplays, yet he still deals with serious metaphysical concepts. The initial idea for the poem was suggested by Davies's "Orchestra," but Roethke combines a number of other ideas and allusions here. (Particularly, Roethke pays his homage to Yeats, whom he had studied for some years and to whom he owed a great deal in developing his methods of composition.) The central concern of the poem is the relationship between the ideal and the material world. The "Dance" of the first section refers to the dance of life (done to the cadence of song). "The Partner" of the second section is the real woman who comes as a fulfillment of the female spirit of "The Visitant." She draws the narrator into a social context and lifts him above the animality of his baser nature. But she eventually does more than that, for in the Western tradition of romantic love she is an earthly embodiment of the ideal. Ultimately, like Dante's Beatrice, she leads the narrator into the realm of ideality. Thus, through love, the narrator transcends the material world and redeems his own fleshly nature. The whole poem builds in strong, even iambic cadences toward the final couplet—one of the most resounding in all poetry—"Who rise from flesh to spirit know the fall/The word outleaps the world, and light is all." It is the climactic expression of the theme that has been developed throughout the poem. But whatever one says about it seems totally inadequate to explain its precision and power. "The Waking" is an entirely different kind of poem. The theme is particularly modern: now that man can look back on the long evolution of life on earth and the development of human culture, he sees that the belief of the Enlightenment in his ability to control his destiny through the exercise of rational thought and will misses the mark considerably. Man has evolved through a long process of trial and error; his civilization has evolved in much the same way. And yet there seems to be an intuition, or spirit, that pervades the world; it, rather than rational thought, is the force that leads man's progress. In "The Waking" Roethke applies this idea to his own life. He "thinks by feeling" and "learns by going." He is not sure where he will end up, but he has faith that intuition will direct him to his proper destination. The tight, repetitious villanelle form reinforces the feeling that a purposeful fate is at work in his life.

In November 1953 Roethke had a minor mental breakdown, probably the result of the unsettling effect of travel during the past year, and of his intense emotional life with Beatrice. The precipitating event seems to have been the death of Dylan Thomas on 5 November. Roethke recovered quickly, however, and was home with his wife for Christmas. In February he suffered another bad shock when his mother died. It had been a bad fall and winter, but good news came several weeks later: he had won the Pulitzer Prize for *The Waking.*

During the next year the Roethkes remained in Seattle, moving their residence twice. Roethke continued his teaching and worked hard at his poetry. He had, however, in retrospect, decided that he liked to travel, particularly since it allowed him to escape from the routine of teaching. He applied for a Fulbright grant to go to Italy and was awarded one for the academic year 1955-1956. In September the Roethkes took passage to Gibraltar and

toured southern Spain. From there they went to Madrid, to Barcelona and then along the French Riviera to Italy, where Roethke was to teach at the Magistero in Florence. It was a teachers' college, and Roethke was unhappy with his students, because he could not get them to "hear" English poetry. But he liked being abroad well enough, for he tried to get his Fulbright extended for the next year to teach at Bedford College in London; his application, however, was turned down. In April Roethke delivered several lectures in Rome, and in the following month he gave two lecture-readings in Austria. In July, on their way home, the Roethkes stopped in Paris, where they met René Char. Roethke had admired his poetry, and now he found he liked the man as well. In August, before embarking for America, the Roethkes spent two weeks in England being entertained by old friends such as Stephen Spender, William Empson, and Dame Edith Sitwell. Roethke had enjoyed this European tour much more than the first. This time, he could travel without anxiety. And now he was sure that his work was respected and admired on both sides of the Atlantic.

In September 1956 Roethke resumed teaching at the University of Washington. The year went well, and during the summer the Roethkes purchased their first house—on the shore of Lake Washington where Roethke had lived when he first came to Seattle. In September 1957, however, he began to show symptoms of another mental breakdown. It was serious this time: he was hospitalized for three months. Nevertheless he recovered soon enough to return to his teaching duties in the spring. In the fall of 1958 Doubleday published *Words for the Wind* (forty-three new poems and a selection of the best work from his earlier volumes). The critical reception was overwhelmingly favorable, and for the volume he received a number of awards the following year; among them, the Bollingen Prize and the National Book Award. Roethke's ego, which always craved adulation, and had often felt slighted in the past, was elated by this well-earned recognition and praise: it was evident that he was a major poet—maybe *the* major poet.

The new poems of *Words for the Wind* are divided into five groups. The first contains several humorous pieces and children's verses. Roethke delighted in this kind of poetry all his life; only T. S. Eliot was his peer at writing it. The second is love poems. They continue and develop the theme of "Four for Sir John Davies": the relationship between the ideal and the real in the

Theodore Roethke (Gale International Portrait Gallery)

loved woman. As in *The Waking*, the woman appears first as an idealized vision (in "The Dream"). The vision then assumes material form in the lover. The first benefit the lover brings is to draw the narrator out of the abyss of himself and into the objective world, a world that gains completion by the conjunction of two opposites: the ideal descends to take palpable form in the woman as the animal nature of the man is drawn upward to meet it. The release in the narrator from the constrictions of self-love brings a great joy, which he shares with the lover: "I bear, but not alone,/The burden of this joy" ("Words for the Wind"). And finally, as in "The Swan," she redeems him through the transcendence of their love: "She sighs me white, a Socrates of snow."

One of the most famous of the love poems is "I Knew a Woman." Some critics have found its sentiment and exaggeration embarrassing. Certainly the poem is hyperbolic and sentimental. But the sentiment is beautifully balanced with humor: as the awkward lover moves about his primum mobile, the reader laughs but also senses the lover's earnestness and feels the power of love. It is one of the most successful love poems in the language.

"The Sensualists," from this section, is different in tone from the others. Here love has been degraded by the carnality of the lover, who has forgotten the ideal. Roethke seems to have included it, and placed it strategically, as a contrast and balance to the other love poems.

The third group of poems, "Voices and Creatures," represents a return to the natural world: both its ugliness and its grace are evoked. "The Beast" presents the narrator's desire to enter nature (or to be at one with his own animal nature), and his regrets about his inability to do so, for he is now part of the conscious, rational world of man.

The fourth division is a single poem, "Dying Man," written in memory of W. B. Yeats. It, like the love poems, represents an attempt to reconcile the life of the spirit with the life of the flesh, but in a much broader context—much like Yeats's "Sailing to Byzantium."

The final section, "Meditations of an Old Woman," is written in memory of Roethke's mother, and was begun shortly after her death in 1954. In actuality it seems to be an attempt to merge his and his mother's identities, to articulate for her those thoughts she could never have articulated herself. It carries forward the themes of the love poems and "Dying Man" to a pantheistic reconciliation to death. "Meditations" certainly is indebted to Yeats's Crazy Jane poems, but it owes a debt also to Wallace Stevens's "Sunday Morning."

In January 1959 Roethke had another mental breakdown and was admitted to Halcyon Sanitarium in Seattle. He continued to write poetry, and he was well enough to resume his teaching duties for the spring quarter. During the fall, however, he took leave without pay, having once again won a Ford Foundation grant. In the spring of 1960 the Roethkes went to New York, where Roethke gave several readings. In June they embarked for another trip to Europe. They went to Paris and Brittany, but Roethke's real object on this trip was to visit the country of Yeats and Joyce. In July they flew to Dublin. They toured the country and visited Yeats's widow. In November they went to London, where they stayed through the winter. There Roethke gave several readings and appeared on the BBC, as he had on his last visit in 1956. In March they flew back to America, in time for Roethke to teach for the spring quarter, and for the publication of his book of children's poems *I Am! Says the Lamb*.

Roethke remained in Seattle for the last years of his life, teaching, working on the poems that would appear posthumously as *The Far Field,* and making frequent trips to receive awards and give readings. In June 1962 he was presented an honorary Doctor of Letters degree from his alma mater, the University of Michigan. In October he gave a reading for the Seattle World's Fair. By the summer of 1963, he had completed the first draft of the manuscript for *The Far Field*. He intended to revise it further, but on 1 August, while swimming in a friend's pool, he had a coronary occlusion from which he could not be revived. He was buried beside his mother and father in Oakwood Cemetery in Saginaw. At the time of his death Roethke's reputation was high in both America and Europe. Many considered him the best American poet of his generation. Since his death, there has been a steadily increasing interest in his poetry both by critics and the reading public. Most have placed him in the top rank of all American poets. Had he lived another ten years, he might have received the Nobel Prize he so coveted during the later part of his life.

In 1964 Doubleday published *The Far Field* in the form Roethke had left it. The first, and best, section, "North American Sequence," contains six meditative poems. In tone and form they are indebted to Whitman, Eliot (of "Ash Wednesday" and *Four Quartets*), Stevens, and Robinson Jeffers. But no one save Roethke could have written them. Here the persona returns to the natural world; it is not, however, the same world of *The Lost Son* and *Praise to the End!* For between these two immersions, the poet has spent his time both in the social world and the philosophical and spiritual world of ideality. In the process the natural world has become objectified: it is no longer the subjective, internalized natural world of *The Lost Son*. Thus, when the poet of *The Far Field* reenters nature, he is not reentering himself. Rather his desire is to become one with all things. Although he has doubts, when the natural world seems to be a meaningless abyss, the prevailing image is one of nature redeemed by a pervasive spiritual light. This is particularly true of "Meditation at Oyster River" and "The Far Field." In the final poem of the sequence, "The Rose," he sees the world imbued with such spiritual significance that he feels no need for heaven.

The second section is a group of love poems. They are not nearly so good as those of *Words for the Wind*, but significantly Roethke projects himself into the mind of the loved girl in several of them. The following section is called "Mixed Sequence." The first poem, "The Abyss," is a continuation of the themes of "North American Sequence," but in a tighter form. It is followed by miscellaneous poems, including several about his childhood ("Elegy," "Otto," and "The Chums") and several written about his European experiences ("The Lizard" and "The Storm"). The final section is entitled "Sequence, Sometimes Metaphysical." It returns to the themes of the first section, but treats them in a more formal manner. The first poem, "In a Dark Time," is concerned with how one climbs out of the abyss of self to become one with God. The subsequent poems pursue this relationship between the man, the natural world, the loved woman, and the Godhead. The sequence reaches its conclusion in "Once More, the Round," which ends:

> Now I adore my life
> With the Bird, the abiding Leaf,
> With the Fish, the questing Snail,
> And the Eye altering all;
> And I dance with William Blake
> For love, for Love's sake;
>
> And Everything comes to One,
> As we dance on, dance on, dance on.

It is the fitting conclusion to the volume—and to Roethke's career: the poetic, emotional, and spiritual journey had come to its proper end. It is difficult to imagine where he could have gone from here.

Letters:

Selected Letters of Theodore Roethke, edited by Ralph J. Mills, Jr. (Seattle & London: University of Washington Press, 1968; London: Faber & Faber, 1970);
Reveals Roethke's personality, thought, artistic ideas and information about his public and private life.

Bibliographies:

James R. McLeod, *Theodore Roethke: A Manuscript Checklist* (Kent, Ohio: Kent State University Press, 1971);
A comprehensive listing of Roethke manuscripts and typescripts of books, individual poems and letters, and gives their locations.

McLeod, *Theodore Roethke: A Bibliography* (Kent, Ohio: Kent State University Press, 1973);
A descriptive bibliography of Roethke's books and periodical publications, including foreign appearances and translations, films and recordings, and musical settings; also lists original works and materials about Roethke.

Keith R. Moul, *Theodore Roethke's Career: An Annotated Bibliography* (Boston: G. K. Hall, 1977);
A list of Roethke's book and periodical publications, and an annotated list of writings about Roethke from 1922 to 1973.

Biography:

Allan Seager, *The Glass House: The Life of Theodore Roethke* (New York: McGraw-Hill, 1968);
The only complete biographical treatment of Roethke, written by a sympathetic fellow writer and friend.

References:

Richard Allen Blessing, *Theodore Roethke's Dynamic Vision* (Bloomington: Indiana University Press, 1974);
Discusses the techniques by which Roethke transformed the experiences of his life into a poetry of energy and motion.

Neal Bowers, *Theodore Roethke: The Journey from I to Otherwise* (Columbia: University of Missouri Press, 1982);
Deals with the spiritual movement of Roethke's poetry through an examination of his development of a creative anima spirit.

William Heyen, ed., *Profile of Theodore Roethke* (Columbus, Ohio: Merrill, 1971);
A collection of critical essays on Roethke's poetry, including articles by Delmore Schwartz, Stanley Kunitz, and Kenneth Burke's important study, "The Vegetal Radicalism of Theodore Roethke."

Jenijoy La Belle, *The Echoing Wood of Theodore Roethke* (Princeton: Princeton University Press, 1976);
A study of the literary influences on Roethke through allusions and references in his poetry.

Gary Lane, ed., *A Concordance to the Poems of Theodore Roethke* (Metuchen, N.J.: Scarecrow Press, 1972);
A computer concordance to *The Collected Poems of Theodore Roethke.*

Karl Malkoff, *Theodore Roethke: an Introduction to the Poetry* (New York: Columbia University Press, 1966);
A discussion of various influences on Roethke's thought and poetry: primarily Jung's psychoanalytic theory, Underhill's mysticism, and Buber's and Tillich's theology.

William J. Martz, *The Achievement of Theodore Roethke* (Glenview, Ill.: Scott, Foresman, 1966);
An argument for Roethke's status as a major writer, which sees him as both a "nature" and "meditative" poet.

Ralph J. Mills, Jr., *Theodore Roethke* (Minneapolis: University of Minnesota Press, 1963);
An early short but sensitive study of Roethke's career.

Jay Parrini, *Theodore Roethke: an American Romantic* (Amherst: University of Massachusetts Press, 1979);
An excellent, detailed study of the poetry with a Jungian slant.

Lynn Ross-Bryant, *Theodore Roethke: Poetry of the Earth, Poet of the Spirit* (Port Washington, N.Y.: Kennikat Press, 1981);
Concentrates on Roethke's vision of the spirit and how it relates to nature and life in general.

Arnold Stein, ed., *Theodore Roethke: Essays on the Poetry* (Seattle: University of Washington Press, 1965);
A collection of early essays on Roethke by such poets and critics as Louis Martz, John Wain, Stephen Spender, W. D. Snodgrass, and R. H. Pearce.

Rosemary Sullivan, *Theodore Roethke: The Garden Master* (Seattle: University of Washington Press, 1975);
A discussion of Roethke's search for identity from theological, philosophical and psychological points of view.

Harry Williams, *"The Edge Is What I Have"* (Lewisburg, Pa.: Bucknell University Press, 1977);
Discusses the Lost Son poems, "Meditations of an Old Woman" and "North American Sequence," as they relate to Roethke's search for identity, and includes a review of criticism to 1974.

George Wolff, *Theodore Roethke* (Boston: Twayne, 1981);

    A short format book which discusses the re-lationship of Roethke's life to his poetry and the evolution of his poetic techniques.

J. D. Salinger

This entry was updated by Warren French (Indiana University-Purdue University at Indianapolis) from his entry in DLB 2, American Novelists Since World War II.

Places	Manhattan ("Woody Allen Country") Yale University Hollywood	Cornish, New Hampshire Miami Beach	Fairfield County, Connecticut Nazi Germany
Influences and Relationships	Whit Burnett	F. Scott Fitzgerald	Rainer Maria Rilke
	"The Hapworth Recommendations"—Miguel de Cervantes, Jane Austen, Charles Dickens, John Bunyan, George Eliot, Leo Tolstoy, Swami Vivekananda, Marcel Proust, Alfred Erdonna		
Literary Movements and Forms	*New Yorker* School	The "Outsiders"	Zen Buddhist Mysticism
Major Themes	Adolescent Growing Pains Artistic Altruism The Jesus Prayer	Artistic Alienation Academic Pedantry The Search for the Poet-Seer	The Fall of Innocence Disaffiliation The Phony World
Cultural and Artistic Influences	1930s Hollywood Movies 1930s Radio Quiz Programs ("The Quiz Kids")	Classical Jazz The Meditation and Macrobiotic Food Movements	Zen Buddhism The Trend Toward Vanishing Celebrities
Social and Economic Influences	1950s "Rat Race" World War II (Fascism)	"Back to the Woods" Ecology Movement	"Silent Generation" of 1950s

BIRTH: New York, New York, 1 January 1919, to Sol and Miriam Jillich Salinger.

EDUCATION: Valley Forge Military Academy, 1934-1936; Ursinus College and New York University, 1937-1938; writing class at Columbia University, 1939.

MARRIAGE: 17 February 1955 to Claire Douglas (divorced); children: Margaret Ann, Matthew.

BOOKS: *The Catcher in the Rye* (Boston: Little, Brown, 1951; London: Hamish Hamilton, 1951);

Nine Stories (Boston: Little, Brown, 1953); republished as *For Esme—With Love and Squalor and Other Stories* (London: Hamish Hamilton, 1953);

Franny and Zooey (Boston: Little, Brown, 1961; London: Heinemann, 1962);

"Raise High the Roof Beam, Carpenters" and "Seymour: An Introduction" (Boston: Little, Brown, 1963; London: Heinemann, 1963).

PERIODICAL PUBLICATIONS: "The Young Folks," *Story*, 16 (March-April 1940): 26-30;

"Go See Eddie," *University of Kansas City Review*, 7 (December 1940): 121-124;

"The Hang of It," *Collier's*, 108 (12 July 1941): 22;

"The Heart of a Broken Story," *Esquire*, 16 (September 1941): 32, 131-133;

"The Long Debut of Lois Taggett," *Story*, 21 (September-October 1942): 28-34;

"Personal Notes of an Infantryman," *Collier's*, 110 (12 December 1942): 96;

"The Varioni Brothers," *Saturday Evening Post*, 216 (17 July 1943): 12-13, 76-77;

"Both Parties Concerned," *Saturday Evening Post*, 216 (20 February 1944): 14, 47-48;

"Soft-Boiled Sergeant," *Saturday Evening Post*, 216 (15 April 1944): 18, 82-85;

"Last Day of the Last Furlough," *Saturday Evening Post*, 217 (15 July 1944): 26-27, 61-64;

"Once a Week Won't Kill You," *Story*, 25 (November-December 1944): 23-27;

"A Boy in France," *Saturday Evening Post*, 217 (31 March 1945): 21, 92;

"Elaine," *Story*, 26 (March-April 1945): 38-47;

"This Sandwich Has No Mayonnaise," *Esquire*, 24 (October 1945): 54-56, 147-149;

"The Stranger," *Collier's*, 116 (1 December 1945): 18, 77;

"I'm Crazy," *Collier's*, 116 (22 December 1945): 36, 48, 51;

"Slight Rebellion Off Madison," *New Yorker*, 22 (21 December 1946): 76-79;

"A Young Girl in 1941 with No Waist at All," *Mademoiselle*, 25 (May 1947): 222-223, 292-302;

"The Inverted Forest," *Cosmopolitan*, 123 (December 1947): 73-109;

"A Girl I Knew," *Good Housekeeping*, 126 (February 1948): 37, 186-196;

"Blue Melody," *Cosmopolitan*, 125 (September 1948): 50-51, 112-119;

"Hapworth 16, 1924," *New Yorker*, 41 (19 June 1965): 32-40 ff.

The entire body of writing by which Jerome David Salinger wishes to be known is contained in four small books—one novel and thirteen short stories. All of these were published in the eleven and a half years between January 1948 and June 1959; and all but the novel and two of the stories originally appeared in the *New Yorker* magazine. Yet despite this limited body of work, Salinger remained for at least a dozen years, from 1951 to 1963, the most popular American fiction writer with serious high school and college students, as well as many adults, and his few publications elicited an enormous body of criticism. Few writers have developed such a major reputation for such a small body of work, largely from a single magazine noted for its rigid formulae and chic appeal to educated, upper-middle-class readers (especially since Salinger's fiction is notable for its unwavering attack on them). Only Salinger's last few published stories were notable for their controversial, anti-narrative structures; the novel and other stories are exemplary of the brisk, ironic "*New Yorker* style," used by other writers such as John O'Hara and John Cheever; but all Salinger's work is remarkable for his command of the brisk, nervous, defensive speech of young, upper-middle-class Manhattanites. His work is a unique phenomenon, important as the voice of a "silent generation" in revolt against a "phony world" and in search of mystical escapes from a deteriorating society rather than "causes" promising political revolution or reform.

Salinger was born and grew up in the fashionable apartment district of Manhattan, the son of a prosperous Jewish importer and his Scotch-Irish wife. In one of the few interviews he has granted, he said that his own childhood was much like that of the boy Holden Caulfield in his novel *The Catcher in the Rye*, though Salinger had only one sister. Like Holden, he was restless in fashionable prep schools, and he was finally sent to Valley Forge Military Academy, a model for Pencey Prep in his novel. Here and at nearby Ursinus College, which he attended briefly, he worked for literary magazines and wrote movie reviews. Subsequently a class in short story writing at Columbia University under Whit Burnett, founder-editor of the influential *Story Magazine,* in which many mid-century fiction writers were first published, led to his own earliest commercial publications in this magazine. He quickly graduated to the well-paying "slick" magazines of the period—*Collier's, Saturday Evening Post, Esquire, Good Housekeeping, Cosmopolitan,* and, at last, the *New Yorker.* To the first five of these and some other publications, Salinger contributed between 1941 and 1948 twenty stories that he has since 1954 refused to allow to be republished. (There does exist a pirated edition of them: *The Complete Uncollected Stories of J. D. Salinger,* 2 vols., 1974.) Most of these are very short, highly colloquial, sentimental, yet heavily ironic tales in the manner made popular by O. Henry. Many of them are the very popular "short, short stories" with a surprise ending, although one, "The Inverted Forest," is a novelette of considerable complexity with an ambiguous ending. Several of these stories are about draftees in the army during World War II and reflect Salinger's own service between 1942 and 1945 in the Army Signal Corps and the Counter-Intelligence Corps.

After the war, Salinger published in the *New Yorker* a short story, "Slight Rebellion Off Madison," subsequently revised for inclusion in *The Catcher in the Rye;* the work by which he wishes to be known began, however, with his second contribution to the magazine, "A Perfect Day for Bananafish," an enormously popular story about the suicide of Seymour Glass, who first appears in this story.

Salinger perhaps wishes his early stories hidden away because they are apprentice work; he may be embarrassed by their slickness. A few are interesting because they introduce an earlier conception of Holden Caulfield as a rebellious young soldier who is killed in World War II; but only "The Inverted Forest" really adds anything to Salinger's stature. This is the story of a writer who "can't stand any kind of inventiveness" and his pathetic difficulties in dealing with doting and exploitative women—mother, patron, wife, and mistress. Salinger never again so specifically allegorizes the view that the artist has no obligations to society as in this caustic story of a sorely pressed individual who withdraws from a meretricious world to live entirely within "the inverted forest" of his own imagination—an outlook that Salinger rejects in his later stories. Only some early chapters of *The Catcher in the Rye* and the short story "Pretty Mouth and Green My Eyes" among his collected works picture people without spiritual moorings in a plastic, materialistic world.

The major reason for Salinger's rejecting these early stories is that they do not reflect the Hindu-Buddhist influences that begin to color his work in "A Perfect Day for Bananafish," in which Salinger begins to depict escape from the "phony"

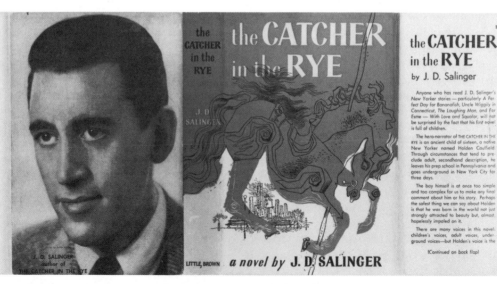

First dust jacket for The Catcher in the Rye. *Salinger requested that his photo not appear on later printings of the jacket.*

world as not defeat, but triumph for the sensitive individual. His work thereafter can most rewardingly be perceived as colloquial, contemporary American versions of the koans (cryptic object lessons) of the Zen Buddhist tradition.

By narrowing attention, then, to the novel and thirteen chosen stories, this whole body of work can be seen—like such other American classics as Whitman's *Leaves of Grass* and Thomas Wolfe's Eugene Gant/George Webber novel-cycle—as parts of a single statement, the theme of which is announced in the climactic moment in the last of these stories as Buddy Glass explains his older brother Seymour's suicide: "I say that the true artist-seer, the heavenly fool who can and does produce beauty, is mainly dazzled to death by his own scruples, the blinding shapes and colors of his own sacred human conscience."

Salinger's epic of the journey of the human spirit through the illusions of the material world to the transcendent spiritual Oneness beyond, which might be called "The Caulfield/Glass Saga," begins, chronologically, with a still controversial description of Seymour Glass's activities on the day of his suicide amidst the unparalleled vulgarities of Miami Beach, Florida, and ends with his disciple-brother's explanation of this action and of the unique importance of the "artist-seer." The rambling, seemingly structureless "Seymour: An Introduction" that still bothers plot-oriented readers can most satisfactorily be appreciated as Buddy Glass's petition for the sainthood of his brother by some unworldly body of right-thinking people. Seymour is indeed "a fool"—not only in the eyes of conventional, money-grubbing people, but in his own because of his romantic susceptibilities—but he does create and inspire beauty, and he does end this mortal life rather than compromise his integrity.

Using Buddy's pronouncement to make a division, a distinction can be made among Salinger's works between the stories of those who refuse to betray their sacred consciences and those who do compromise reluctantly in order to fulfill what they regard as their obligations in a conscienceless world. On the one side may be placed "A Perfect Day for Bananafish," "De Daumier-Smith's Blue Period," "Teddy," "Raise High the Roof Beam, Carpenters," and "Seymour: An Introduction." On the other there are "Uncle Wiggily in Connecticut," "Just Before the War with the Eskimos," "The Laughing Man," "Pretty Mouth and Green My Eyes," and *The Catcher in the Rye*. In the middle—and in the middle of Salinger's career—is the smallest body of what has generally proved his most

admired works, "Down at the Dinghy," "For Esme—With Love and Squalor," and *Franny and Zooey*—souvenirs of a fleeting time when Salinger apparently hoped that those not "seers" themselves might learn enough from these mentors to survive in the "waste land" without becoming contaminated.

As far as the published record goes, this saga began with some trial sketches for *The Catcher in the Rye*, "I'm Crazy," and "Slight Rebellion Off Madison." Comparison between the latter story and the final version of Holden Caulfield's disastrous date with Sally Hayes provides the only available opportunity for studying the development in Salinger's writing. Although it has often been observed—even by Salinger himself—that there are autobiographical elements in the novel, they are finally not so important as the fact that *The Catcher in the Rye* is a story of an urban American boy who at the adolescent crisis of his life—the point at which in a communally ordered society he would undergo traditional rites of initiation into manhood—chooses, on his own and unguided, an adulterated life in the "real" world rather than an escape from it.

Holden is aware of the options, because his younger brother Allie, who wrote Emily Dickinson's poems on his baseball mitt, has escaped (though through disease not choice), and his older brother, an artist but no seer, has prostituted himself to Hollywood. When Holden fears that he may "disappear" himself, he prays to his personal saint Allie to preserve him. Holden persists in living because, despite his frustrations in the "phony" world, he still has a naive sense of mission: in the famous passage that gives the novel its title he tells his little sister Phoebe, "I keep picturing all these little kids playing some game in this big field of rye and all. . . . And I'm standing by on the edge of some crazy cliff. What I have to do, I have to catch everybody if they start to go over the cliff." Holden learns that his dream can never be realized. Watching his little sister ride the carousel in Central Park and grab for the golden ring, he observes, "The thing with kids is, if they want to grab for the gold ring, you have to let them do it, and not say anything. If they fall off, they fall off, but it's bad if you say anything to them."

Even before acquiescing in his inability to arrest the life cycle and hold youth forever innocent, Holden has suffered another disillusionment. He has dreamed of escaping the city and going west where he could build "a little cabin somewhere . . . and live there for the rest of my life . . . near the woods, but not right *in* them, because I'd want it as sunny as hell all the time." (This description uncannily foreshadows exactly the kind of place in which Salinger has himself lived for thirty years now, not in the West, but in New England.) After he finds obscenities scratched, however, even on the walls of Phoebe's elementary school, he sadly concedes, "You can't ever find a place that's nice and peaceful, because there isn't any."

Rather than being driven out of this world by such disenchantments, Holden assures readers that he did go home after he felt "so damn happy . . . the way old Phoebe kept going around and around" while the carousel played "Smoke Gets in Your Eyes." He has made this choice after Phoebe pleads to run away with him; he must forego his own escape to do what he can for her. After this he begins "missing everybody," even those who have hurt him. He is a self-made martyr; but martyrdom in the "waste land" society means continuing to live, not accepting death. Holden chooses to live in a decadent society in order to help others live as they wish to live rather than to withdraw in order to preserve his own scruples or force his own brand of salvation on others. *The Catcher in the Rye* is a genuine initiation tale, even though it is only the candidate undergoing the ordeal who is conscious of what his final decision means; the real evidence of the decadence of his world is that the initiators who impose the ordeals upon him are too much wrapped up in themselves even to understand the meaning of their actions.

The collected *Nine Stories* (1953), by way of contrast, ultimately climaxes in not the acceptance but the transcendence of this world. Although the stories involve different characters, they may also be read collectively as the dramatization of a progressive action, so that they exemplify what Forest Ingram calls a "short-story cycle": "a book of short stories so linked to each other by their author that the reader's successive experience on various levels of the pattern of the whole significantly modifies his experience of each of its component parts." The links between the stories in this cycle, however, do not result in the kind of narrative progression based on physical growth that we find in James Joyce's *Dubliners,* John Steinbeck's *The Red Pony,* or Dylan Thomas's *Portrait of the Artist as a Young Dog,* but rather a progression based upon spiritual enlightenment, something like the believer experiences in the Christian ritual of the Stations of the Cross or, more appropriately, the stages that the neophyte passes through in his apprehension of Zen. What is represented through this group of stories that were published—and apparently written—in the order of their presentation is the purification of the ego by the passage of the soul through an intensifying series of the torments of the hell of this mortal world to the ego-free state in which one has at last achieved total unity with the infinite so that the individual life-form no longer matters—the one has been absorbed into *the* One.

The clue that has long been needed to make possible a fully coherent experience of this story-cycle in the perception that, despite the meaning of Seymour Glass's example and teachings to his sibling/disciples, Seymour is—from the Hindu view—a false guru (teacher), because he has not been able to transcend the temptations of mortal flesh. He is like the person that Teddy McArdle (title character of the final one of the nine stories) was in his previous incarnation. This person "fell from Grace before final illumination" when he met a lady and "sort of stopped meditating." Teddy in his final incarnation, Mirza demonstrates, is a true guru.

The story-cycle thus moves from the portrayal of the dichotomized saint-in-spirit/satyr-in-the-flesh who must destroy himself to liberate his tortured consciousness to the portrayal of a person whose unified mind/body is ready for the final illumination that will result in his disappearance from the material world through no action of his own, since he has become too etherealized to persist in it.

"A Perfect Day for Bananafish" is thus misread as a moral tale, a satirical attack on our bourgeois culture, or a study of alienation. It is rather what John Steinbeck might call a "non-teleological" work, a story of what *happens* to the partially illuminated person torn between the lustings of his instincts and the dictates of his conscience. The important thing is that this story *starts* rather than *ends* the cycle. Seymour is actually not too advanced for his society, but too primitive for it. He has the purity of vision of an Old Testament prophet without the sacred purification of Jesus or Buddha. He is even less sophisticated than Holden Caulfield; he is not able to adjust to his society, but neither can he transcend it without violence.

The successive stories through "Pretty Mouth and Green My Eyes," then, represent the successive stages in the adjustment to this society that Seymour cannot make. The central characters of these stories also progressively lose their purity of vision—the innocence that Wordsworth in "Ode: Intimations of Immortality" describes the child as

This filth is being recommended to your children for extra-curricular reading in the DADE COUNTY SCHOOL SYSTEM and elsewhere. (Palmetto High School, by English Teacher WARREN, who was defended by Principal CRABTREE and sanctioned by Supt. of Schools, Joe Hall) Jack Gordon, School Board member said of "Catcher in the Rye" that anyone calling it "obscene" had misread it. Is this the kind of book that should be recommended reading by teachers in our public schools?

The Catcher in the Rye 25

"No reason. Boy, I can't stand that sonuvabitch. He's one sonuvabitch I really can't stand."

"He's crazy about *you.* He told me he thinks you're a goddam prince," I said. I call people a "prince" quite often when I'm horsing around. It keeps me from getting bored or something.

"He's got this superior *at*titude all the time," Ackley said. "I just can't stand the sonuvabitch. You'd think he—"

"Do you mind cutting your nails over the *table,* hey?" I said. "I've asked you about fifty—"

"He's got this goddam superior attitude all the time," Ackley said. "I don't even think the sonuvabitch is intelligent. He *thinks* he is. He thinks he's about the most—"

"*Ack*ley! For Chrissake. Willya *please* cut your crumby nails over the table? I've asked you fifty times."

36 *The Catcher in the Rye*

It was only about a quarter to nine when we got back to the dorm. Old Brossard was a bridge fiend, and he started looking around the dorm for a game. Old Ackley parked himself in my room, just for a change. Only, instead of sitting on the arm of Stradlater's chair, he laid down on my bed, with his face right on my pillow and all. He started talking in this very monotonous voice, and picking at all his pimples. I dropped about a thousand hints, but I couldn't get rid of him. All he did was keep talking in this very monotonous voice about some babe he was supposed to have had sexual intercourse with the summer before. He'd already told me about it about a hundred times. Every time he told it, it was different. One minute he'd be giving it to her in his cousin's Buick, the next minute he'd be giving it to her under some boardwalk. It was all a lot of crap, naturally. He was a virgin if ever I saw one. I doubt if he ever even gave anybody a feel. Anyway, finally I had

46 *The Catcher in the Rye*

I didn't turn it off right away, though. I just kept laying there on Ely's bed, thinking about Jane and all. It just drove me stark staring mad when I thought about her and Stradlater parked somewhere in that fat-assed Ed Banky's car. Every time I thought about it, I felt like jumping out the window. The thing is, you didn't know Stradlater. I knew him. Most guys at Pencey just *talked* about having sexual intercourse with girls all the time—like Ackley, for instance—but old Stradlater really *did* it. I was personally acquainted with at least two girls he gave the time to. That's the truth.

"Tell me the story of your fascinating life, Ackley kid," I said.

134 *The Catcher in the Rye*

"Maybe I'll go to China. My sex life is lousy," I said.

"Naturally. Your mind is immature."

"It is. It really is. I know it," I said. "You know what the trouble with me is? I can never get really sexy—I mean *really* sexy—with a girl I don't like a lot. I mean I have to *like* her a lot. If I don't, I sort of lose my goddam desire for her and all. Boy, it really screws up my sex life something awful. My sex life stinks."

"Naturally it does, for God's sake. I told you the last time I saw you what you need."

"You mean to go to a psychoanalyst and all?" I said. That's what he'd told me I ought to do. His father was a psychoanalyst and all.

84 *The Catcher in the Rye*

"How do you mean?" I said. I didn't know what he was driving at or anything.

"Innarested in a little tail t'night?"

"Me?" I said. Which was a very dumb answer, but it's quite embarrassing when somebody comes right up and asks you a question like that.

'How old are you, chief?" the elevator guy said.

"Why?" I said. "Twenty-two."

"Uh huh. Well, how 'bout it? Y'innarested? Five bucks a throw. Fifteen bucks the whole night." He looked at his wrist watch. "Till noon. Five bucks a throw, fifteen bucks till noon."

"Okay," I said. It was against my principles and all, but I was feeling so depressed I didn't even *think.* That's the whole trouble. When you're feeling very depressed, you can't even think.

"Okay *what?* A throw, or till noon? I gotta know."

"Just a throw."

85

women out. He said, in this one part, that a woman's body is like a violin and all, and that it takes a terrific musician to play it right. It was a very corny book—I realize that— but I couldn't get that violin stuff out of my mind anyway. In a way, that's why I sort of wanted to get some practice in, in case I ever get married. Caulfield and his Magic Violin, boy. It's corny, I realize, but it isn't *too* corny. I wouldn't mind being pretty good at that stuff. Half the time, if you really want to know the truth, when I'm hors-

86 *The Catcher in the Rye*

ing around with a girl, I have a helluva lot of trouble just *finding* what I'm looking for, for God's sake, if you know what I mean. Take this girl that I just missed having sexual intercourse with, that I told you about. It took me about an *hour* to just get her goddam brassière off. By the time I did get it off, she was about ready to spit in my eye.

Anyway, I kept walking around the room, waiting for this prostitute to show up. I kept hoping she'd be good-looking. I didn't care too much, though. I sort of just wanted to get it over with. Finally, somebody knocked on the door, and when I went to open it, I had my suitcase right in the way and I fell over it and damn near broke my knee. I always pick a gorgeous time to fall over a suitcase or something.

When I opened the door, this prostitute was standing there. She had a polo coat on, and no hat. She was sort of a blonde, but you could tell she dyed her hair. She wasn't any old bag, though. "How do you do," I said. Suave as hell, boy.

"You the guy Maurice said?" she asked me. She didn't

Pages 182-184

reveal passages even more vulgar than those reprinted here, but postal regulations would not permit the mailing of this pamphlet if they were reprinted here.

From "Are Your Children Being Brainwashed?" (Miami: Committee to Oppose the Canonization of Karl Marx, n.d.)

bringing with him as he enters this world "trailing clouds of glory."

The next story in the cycle, "Uncle Wiggily in Connecticut," offers in a few pages the most clearly contrasting views of the "nice" and "phony" worlds that we find anywhere in Salinger's writing. Eloise, the principal character, has glimpses of the sacred world in which Seymour Glass yearns to live, but she is too mired in the phony world of Connecticut to free herself; she can only break out finally in the Wordsworthian cry, "I was a nice girl . . . wasn't I?" She is in much the same state that Holden Caulfield appears to be at the end of *The Catcher in the Rye*, although Holden has "grown up" enough to resemble more closely the sentimental Ginnie Maddox of the third story of the cycle, "Just Before the War with the Eskimos," who has become enough at home in the "phony world" to be able to make the generous gestures that elude the still embittered Eloise.

"The Laughing Man" presents a central figure another step removed from Seymour's neurotic perfectionism, another step closer to being able to make practical gestures to comfort others even in the midst of his own despair. When this "Chief" terrifies his young listeners/acolytes by letting the legendary laughing man of his seemingly endless episodic tale tear off his poppy-petal mask and die, he seems to be spitefully taking out his rage at a frustrated love affair on his helpless charges; but, paradoxically, his action is in their best interests, for the immediate pain of disillusionment is better than prolonged existence in a fantasy world that the Chief now knows must some day be dispelled painfully. But he is not yet a master of reconciliation; his technique is crude and abrupt.

The master is Boo-Boo Tannenbaum, one of Seymour Glass's two sisters. In "Down at the Dinghy," her son Lionel has cruelly had his illusions shattered at an even earlier age than the Chief's charges in "The Laughing Man." (Just what ails Lionel remains obscure; the story focuses on Boo-Boo's techniques.) Tactfully and with utmost patience rather than even well-intended harshness, Boo-Boo ends her son's attempt to withdraw from an intolerable adult world by making him accept its imperfect realities.

The master of reconciliation, the maker of as much happiness as we can ever know in the "phony world," is that proper young British girl who lends her name to the title of a great modern epithalamium, "For Esme—With Love and Squalor." Esme is able to readjust not just a young relative, but a grown man who much resembles Seymour

Glass. When Sergeant X, as this character is mysteriously identified, is in Germany on the verge of a nervous breakdown after observing squalid examples of the behavior of both Hitler's Nazi minions and his boorish American fellows-in-arms, he regains his "faculties" as he receives Esme's gift of her father's wristwatch with the crystal broken and the news that she is teaching her affectionate little brother to read and write. Esme's spontaneous generosity is as much communion as we can expect to experience in this hellish life; but it is important to contemplate the nature of her gift—a *time*piece with the transparent crystal smashed. The attempted gift of time, like the unequivocal gift of letters to her little brother, shows that Esme, for all her radiance, is completely of this linear world. Her jobs are family and marriage; she has no perception of the timeless realm of Teddy McArdle.

The temporal equilibrium that Esme achieves cannot endure. This is just what happens in the plunge from the ecstatic highs of "For Esme" into the depths of Salinger's darkest, most cynical story, "Pretty Mouth and Green My Eyes," in which a naive young man desperate for success is driven to lie about his wife's behavior to the very senior member of his law firm who is in fact cuckolding him. His spiritual death is signaled by his recognition that the wife's eyes are not actually as he had fancied "green," emblematic of youth and vitality, but "like goddam *sea* shells." No single recent story better demonstrates the line from T. S. Eliot's poem "Gerontion," "What is kept must be adulterated."

Many modern short-story cycles might have ended here, as James Joyce's *Dubliners* does, for example, with the completion of a movement from life-in-death to death-in-life. "Pretty Mouth and Green My Eyes" reaches the lowest pit of modern urban hell; there is no exit from here except into the extinguishing darkness of Samuel Beckett's *Endgame*—or upward by a surge of spirit into an entirely other world. One of Salinger's least comprehended stories, the genuinely mystical "De Daumier-Smith's Blue Period," makes this leap, and in so doing most conspicuously calls attention to the architectonics of *Nine Stories*. De Daumier-Smith is the first, actually the only, character in Salinger's work to experience—before the reader's eyes (Teddy's illumination has preceded our acquaintance with him)—a "liminal moment," an illumination on the threshold between the sensible and supersensible.

This vain artist from a decadent background has become a teacher in a correspondence-course art school and begins to try to manage his students' lives, especially that of a talented but unself-conscious nun. He lives above an orthopedic appliances shop; gazing in its window, he recognizes that "no matter how coolly or sensibly or gracefully" he might learn to live, he "would always at best be a visitor in a garden of enamel urinals and bedpans. . . ." One day, however, as he makes a friendly gesture to an attendant in the window, "Suddenly . . . the sun came up and sped toward the bridge of [his] nose at the rate of ninety-three million miles a second." He is blinded, and when his sight returns the girl is gone, "leaving behind her a shimmering field of exquisite, twice-blessed, enamel flowers." He goes home and notes in his diary, "I am giving Sister Irma her freedom to follow her own destiny. Everybody is a nun."

Scarcely another scene in literature makes so explicit the "dazzling" experience that Buddy Glass attributes to the "artist-seer." For De Daumier-Smith, however, this is only a transient experience; he returns to the great American sport of girl watching. He is not ready to make the final, permanent move into the enamel world that Teddy does in the last story in the collection.

"Teddy" is Salinger's one story whose reception he has commented upon through the medium of Buddy Glass. In "Seymour: An Introduction," Buddy, who has spoken of what are unmistakably other of Salinger's earlier stories as his own, mentions "an exceptionally Haunting, Memorable, unpleasantly controversial, and thoroughly unsuccessful short story about a 'gifted' little boy aboard a transatlantic liner." The story has indeed proved controversial, for critics still quarrel over whether Teddy at the end jumps into an empty swimming pool or is pushed in by his spiteful little sister. Salinger has never explained why the story was "unsuccessful," but it is probably largely because readers failed to comprehend that Teddy was but a passive agent in his fate. The clue to the conclusion is his suggestion to his parents at the beginning of the story that "after I get out this door, I may only exist in the minds of all my acquaintances." When an inquisitive schoolteacher asks Teddy if he has any emotions, the boy replies, "If I do, I don't remember when I ever used them. . . . I don't see what they're *good* for." He has become detached from both the feelings of frustration that most of Salinger's other characters feel and even the feelings of joy that Esme induces and that De Daumier-Smith discovers. Teddy is no longer a part of this neurotic world, so that he is ready to depart from it—but his departure is no tragedy. Rather, since he has attained spiritual truth, his is

a divine comedy. If he did not resist "dematerialization," however, neither would he—free of emotions—have taken any action of the kind that Seymour Glass did to destroy himself.

Nine Stories thus carries us through a series of emblematic tableaux of human spiritual evolution—from an opening portrait of a seer whose spiritual insight has completely outstripped his physical discipline, through the stages as one loses internal vision to gain external control of his body and emotions and then is projected suddenly into a spiritual development that provides momentary insights of timelessness, until one is absorbed altogether into the infinite. These stories should not be read, however, as models for behavior, but as what James Joyce called "epiphanies" or manifestations of behavior at typical stages in the human fall from glory and reascension back into it.

Franny and Zooey (1961) marks a movement beyond the creation of this static portrait gallery, perhaps even a presumptuous one. In the first of these two linked stories, Seymour Glass's youngest sibling, Franny, has grown—like Holden Caulfield—impatient and disgusted with the meretriciousness of life in the success-seeking world and yearns to move toward spiritual purification by repeating the "Jesus Prayer" continually. She succeeds only in driving herself into a nervous breakdown. In the sequel, her brother Zooey attempts to enlighten her by making her see that she is reacting against the egotism she despises with what is only another form of egotism: "You can say the Jesus prayer from now till doomsday, but if you don't realize that the only thing that counts in the religious life is de*tach*ment, I don't see how you'll ever even move an inch." She has been protesting the "unskilled laughter" of the audience; but Zooey, in his summoning up of a grotesque "Fat Lady," who is actually "Christ himself," tells her that depressing as the audience's reaction may be, it's none of her business: "An artist's only concern is to shoot for some kind of perfection, and *on his own terms*, not anyone else's." Zooey thus does advocate living humbly in this world, as Holden Caulfield had apparently determined to do; and by masquerading as Seymour during a phone call to Franny, he apparently succeeds in tranquilizing her into this acceptance too.

Actually one of the last two stories collected, "Raise High the Roof Beam, Carpenters" had originally appeared between the separate publications of "Franny" and "Zooey," but it belongs with the final story, "Seymour: An Introduction," as part of Salinger's evocation through the medium of Buddy

Glass of the artist whose only concern indeed is "to shoot for some kind of perfection," *on his own terms.*

That Salinger's vision of Seymour had changed from 1948 to 1959 is suggested by Buddy's observation in "Seymour: An Introduction" that the "Seymour" of the earlier story "was not Seymour at all but, oddly, someone with a striking resemblance to—alley oop, I'm afraid—myself." Coupled with the comments about the unsuccessfulness of "Teddy," this concession—following Salinger's own successful withdrawal from the "phony world" of *The Catcher in the Rye*—suggests that Salinger had begun to have a much more favorable impression of Seymour than when he wrote "A Perfect Day for Bananafish." Since Teddy's emotionless purity seemed beyond readers' comprehensions, they might identify more closely with a spiritually superior person who shares their own fleshly frailties. In "Raise High the Roof Beam, Carpenters," Buddy begins by saying of Seymour that, since his death, "I haven't been able to think of anybody whom I'd care to send out to look for horses in his stead," and in "Seymour: An Introduction," he goes on to say, "We have had only three or four *very* nearly non-expendable poets, and I think Seymour will eventually stand with those few." The curious form of the latter story, in which Buddy seeks to form an alliance with the reader against "the middle-aged hot-rodders who insist on zooming us to the moon, the Dharma Bums, the makers of cigarette filters for thinking men, the Beat and the Sloppy and the Petulant, the chosen cultists . . ." also suggests that these later Glass stories are attempts to convert readers through an embryonic saint's legend. (Buddy describes Seymour as "the only person I've habitually consorted with . . . who more frequently than not tallied with the classical conception, as I saw it, of a *mukta*, a ringding enlightened man, a God-Knower.") The detachment of *Nine Stories* has been supplanted by a skillfully manipulated conversion technique. As a result, perhaps, of his own successful retreat from the world, Salinger had achieved a kind of peace that made him feel that the artist did have something more *timely* to do than point to Teddy McArdle's merger with the infinite as the culmination of man's incarnations.

He may have changed his mind again, if one can trust the limited evidence of his most recent uncollected story, "Hapworth 16, 1924," which consists mostly of a letter that Seymour writes home from summer camp at the age of seven. This letter testifies to the prodigious learning that would make Seymour the star of a 1930s children's quiz pro-

gram, but it evidences also a prodigious sexuality that reinforces the early picture in "A Perfect Day for Bananafish" of the failed guru. If Salinger has swung back to a heightened appreciation of the timeless, egoless state achieved by Teddy McArdle, he has not chosen to let us know. In the one interview that he has granted in recent years (in a telephone call to San Francisco, primarily to protest the unauthorized publishing of his early stories in a collected edition), he reported that he was still writing furiously, but that he views publication as a "terrible invasion" of his privacy. He chooses to live isolated in New Hampshire, perhaps sustained by his view of the solitary splendor of neighboring Mount Ascutney.

Salinger was little known when *The Catcher in the Rye* was published; and the novel was not outstandingly acclaimed by reviewers, most of them sounding variations on the theme that, although the novel was "a case history of all of us," as one critic put it, it was "predictable and boring." Its reputation grew slowly by word of mouth, especially among college students and teachers; but little serious attention was paid to Salinger until after the publication of *Nine Stories* and "Franny." In 1956 and 1957 the first serious essays by respected scholars—Edgar M. Branch, Arthur Heiserman, James E. Miller, Jr., and Charles Kaplan—appeared, linking the novel to traditional quest myths and particularly to Mark Twain's *Adventures of Huckleberry Finn.* For the next six years the flood of articles rose constantly, until George Steiner denounced "The Salinger Industry" for promoting Salinger to greatness for his competent rendering of "the semi-literate maunderings of the adolescent mind."

There were other skeptics: John W. Aldridge included an influential misreading of *Catcher* in *In Search of Heresy;* Leslie Fiedler said that Salinger and Jack Kerouac echoed not "the tragic *Huckleberry Finn,* but the sentimental book with which it is interwined"; Frank Kermode supposed that Holden's attitudes pleased academics who shared these views that they could not openly express; Mary McCarthy belittled Salinger's obsessive affection for his own creations.

Many of Salinger's defenders, like Dan Wakefield and Christopher Parker, were sentimental and childishly hysterical; but a body of solid work began to appear with Donald Costello's study of Salinger's language, Carl Strauch's structural analysis of *Catcher,* and William Wiegand's sound analysis of the relationship of Salinger's art to modern Western philosophy. A landmark was Ihab Hassan's choice of Salinger as one of the four principal post-war fictionists in the pioneering study of the period, *Radical Innocence* (1961).

The peak came in 1962-1963, which saw the publication of six collections of essays about Salinger and the first book-length monograph about his work. This formidable array proved a turning point, however, coinciding, as it accidentally did, with the publication of what remains so far the last of his own books. Gradually at first, then dramatically, after 1963, new critical studies tapered off, while sales of the works themselves slowed.

Because of his lack of interest in political reforms and the passivity and escapism of his leading characters, Salinger did not appeal to young readers during the activist years of the late 1960s and early 1970s as he had earlier to members of the "silent generation" that identified with Holden Caulfield. It appears that what stands as the finest appreciation of this novelist by a distinguished American scholar, James E. Miller, Jr.'s pamphlet, *J. D. Salinger* (1965), might remain the last word on the man who possessed the singular ability to embody fictionally the alienated sensibility of the youth of a decade. Miller concludes that Salinger deserves "a place in the first rank, and even, perhaps, the preeminent position" in post-World War II American fiction.

Since then, however, there has been a rediscovery of Salinger as a writer of unique importance on different grounds. Lately arrived critics continue to rush into print with the news that Salinger is a spokesman for America's alienated adolescents. Although some mention of the influence of Asian thought upon his writings may be found in even early criticisms, only since 1966 have the influences of Zen Buddhism on Salinger's work been illustrated in detail.

Now that the early clamor over his works (including some censorious attacks upon its improprieties) has subsided, there seems little argument that Salinger, especially in *The Catcher in the Rye*, "Franny," and the more worldly of the *Nine Stories*, is unchallenged for having embedded in the amber of art the "bugs" of the depressingly paranoid McCarthy/Eisenhower years. But there is also growing evidence that his works are not just static museum pieces—like those that Holden Caulfield admires. Interest in oriental philosophies has been growing rapidly in America in recent years as we have achieved insights into their universality. Increasingly Salinger is winning recognition and acclaim as a writer thoroughly steeped in the manners and mannerisms of his own culture, who has deeply

enough absorbed this traditional wisdom from the East to be able to use it artfully in shaping legends that enable readers to appreciate through familiar icons the meaning of esoteric doctrines. Like the Phoenix of Eastern mythology, Salinger has risen from the ashes of his own *timely* reputation to assume what may prove a timeless one.

Perhaps the most remarkable thing about Salinger is that his presentation of adolescent angst has not been supplanted in the more than three decades since they appeared. Frequently since the high-water mark of the Salinger industry in 1963, heirs to Salinger's place in the affections of American readers have been proclaimed; but soon these pretenders have dropped out of print while Salinger's four thin paperbacks go right on selling and selling as he sits high on a New England hilltop, scribbling away but maintaining his silence—a writer who knew when he had said what he had to say, hoping that youth would keep on listening after he stopped talking, as indeed it did.

Bibliography:

Donald M. Fiene, "J. D. Salinger: A Bibliography," *Wisconsin Studies in Contemporary Literature,* 4 (Winter 1963): 109-149;
An exhaustive list, compiled at the height of Salinger's reputation, of Salinger's work and American and foreign criticism of his work. No adequate supplement is available.

References:

Eberhard Alsen, *Salinger's Glass Stories As a Composite Novel* (Troy, N.Y.: Whitston, 1983);
A thorough study of the interrelationships between Salinger's stories about the Glass family, demonstrating how they can be read as a single novel, which, in the order the stories were published, traces Buddy Glass's effort to understand his dead brother Seymour and how, in the order of the events they describe, "they focus on Seymour's quest of God."

Robert Coles, "Reconsideration: J. D. Salinger," *New Republic,* 28 April 1973, pp. 30-32;
The distinguished child psychologist explains reasons why readers continue to return to Salinger's work for "the wisdom he has offered us."

Warren French, *J. D. Salinger,* rev. ed. (Boston: Twayne, 1976);
The most detailed account of all Salinger's work, including the early stories that he has

not allowed to be reprinted, concentrating on the differences between his conceptions of the "nice" and "phony" worlds that were the key concerns of his work.

Henry A. Grunwald, ed., *Salinger: A Critical and Personal Portrait* (New York: Harper & Row, 1962);
Still the best collection of the scanty biographical material and the abundant criticism of Salinger that had appeared at the height of his fame.

Frederick L. Gwynn and Joseph L. Blotner, *The Fiction of J. D. Salinger* (Pittsburgh: University of Pittsburgh Press, 1958);
Although these two distinguished scholars' reading of Salinger is generally outdated, their brief book remains a unique record of the way he was received sympathetically before he became a cult hero.

Kenneth Hamilton, *J. D. Salinger: A Critical Essay* (Grand Rapids, Mich.: Eerdmans, 1967);
Part of a series on Contemporary Writers in a Christian Perspective, this pamphlet provides a sensitive appreciation of the writer's relationship to Christian and other religious traditions.

Marvin Laser and Norman Fruman, eds., *Studies in J. D. Salinger* (New York: Odyssey, 1963);
The most comprehensive of four "casebooks" on Salinger that appeared in the early 1960s, collecting biographical and critical material for research papers; though now out of print, it is well worth seeking out.

James Lundquist, *J. D. Salinger* (New York: Ungar, 1979);
This book brings together the materials which had been appearing throughout the 1970s in various commentaries about Salinger's knowledge of Zen Buddhism and his use of its mystical doctrines in his fiction and stresses also other autobiographical elements in his work.

James E. Miller, Jr., *J. D. Salinger* (Minneapolis: University of Minnesota Press, 1965);
The outstanding brief analysis of Salinger's alienation by one of the country's most distinguished humanists, who concludes that Salinger deserves "a place in the first rank, and even, perhaps the pre-eminent position" in post-World War II American fiction.

Gerald Rosen, "A Retrospective Look at *The Catcher in the Rye*," *American Quarterly*, 29 (Winter 1977): 547-562;
For a special collection of reassessments of important twentieth-century American documents, Rosen reviews after a quarter century the body of writing around Salinger's novel and finds that Holden's life, except for a "final conscious mature understanding," roughly parallels Buddha's and that the novel portrays "an attempt to create a counterculture."

George Steiner, "The Salinger Industry," *Nation*, 189 (14 November 1959): 360-363;
Still valuable as a bitter but well-informed attack on Salinger by an internationally acclaimed scholar attributing Salinger's phenomenal success to some of the things most seriously wrong with contemporary fiction.

Helen Weinberg, *The New Novel in America: The Kafkan Mode in Contemporary American Fiction* (Ithaca, N.Y.: Cornell University Press, 1970);
An attack on psychologically based criticism of Salinger's work, Weinberg defends his vision as one that shows "the potential of the spiritual self."

Anne Sexton

This entry was updated by David Cowart (University of South Carolina) from his entry
in DLB 5, American Poets Since World War II.

Places	Boston Area		
Influences and Relationships	Robert Lowell George Starbuck	Sylvia Plath John Holmes	Maxine Kumin W. D. Snodgrass
Literary Movements and Forms	Confessional Poetry		
Major Themes	Search for God Birth and Death Suicide	Craft of Poetry Personal Identification/ Sexuality as Love	Maternity Generations/ Family Relations
Cultural and Artistic Influences	Psychoanalysis		
Social and Economic Influences	Women's Movement		

BIRTH: Newton, Massachusetts, 9 November 1928, to Ralph Churchill and Mary Gray Staples Harvey.

EDUCATION: Garland Junior College, 1947-1948.

MARRIAGE: 16 August 1948 to Alfred M. Sexton II (divorced); children: Linda Gray, Joyce Ladd.

AWARDS AND HONORS: *Audience* Poetry Prize, 1958-1959; Robert Frost Fellowship at Bread Loaf Writers' Conference, 1959; Levinson Prize (*Poetry* magazine), 1962; American Academy of Arts and Letters traveling fellowship, 1963-1964; Ford Foundation grant, 1964-1965; Congress for Cultural Freedom literary magazine travel grant, 1965-1966; Shelley Memorial Award, 1967; Pulitzer Prize for *Live or Die*, 1967; Guggenheim Fellowship, 1969; Litt.D., Tufts University, 1970; Litt.D., Fairfield University, 1970; Litt.D., Regis College, 1973.

DEATH: Weston, Massachusetts, 4 October 1974.

BOOKS: *To Bedlam and Part Way Back* (Boston: Houghton Mifflin, 1960);
All My Pretty Ones (Boston: Houghton Mifflin, 1962);
Eggs of Things, by Sexton and Maxine Kumin (New York: Putnam's, 1963);
More Eggs of Things, by Sexton and Kumin (New York: Putnam's, 1964);
Selected Poems (London: Oxford University Press, 1964);
Live or Die (Boston: Houghton Mifflin, 1966; London: Oxford University Press, 1967);
Poems, by Sexton, Thomas Kinsella, and Douglas Livingstone (London: Oxford University Press, 1968);
Love Poems (Boston: Houghton Mifflin, 1969; London: Oxford University Press, 1969);
Joey and the Birthday Present, by Sexton and Kumin (New York: McGraw-Hill, 1971);
Transformations (Boston: Houghton Mifflin, 1971; London: Oxford University Press, 1972);
The Book of Folly (Boston: Houghton Mifflin, 1972; London: Chatto & Windus, 1974);
The Death Notebooks (Boston: Houghton Mifflin, 1974; London: Chatto & Windus, 1975);
The Awful Rowing Toward God (Boston: Houghton Mifflin, 1975; London: Chatto & Windus, 1977);

The Wizard's Tears, by Sexton and Kumin (New York: McGraw-Hill, 1975);
45 Mercy Street, edited by Linda Gray Sexton (Boston: Houghton Mifflin, 1976; London: Secker & Warburg, 1977);
Anne Sexton: A Self-Portrait in Letters, edited by Linda Gray Sexton and Lois Ames (Boston: Houghton Mifflin, 1977);
Words for Dr. Y. (Boston: Houghton Mifflin, 1978);
The Complete Poems (Boston: Houghton Mifflin, 1981).

OTHER: "Anne Sexton Some Foreign Letters," in *Poet's Choice,* edited by Paul Engle and Joseph Langland (New York: Dial Press, 1962), pp. 274-277.

PERIODICAL PUBLICATIONS: "The Barfly Ought to Sing," *Tri-Quarterly,* 7 (Fall 1966): 89-94;
"Anne Sexton: Worksheets" [ten drafts of "Wallflower," from *All My Pretty Ones*], *Malahat Review,* 6 (1968): 105-114;
"The Freak Show," *American Poetry Review,* 2 (May-June 1973): 38, 40;
"A Small Journal," *Ms.,* 2 (November 1973): 60-63, 107.

Anne Sexton, early 1960s (courtesy of Linda Gray Sexton)

Anne Sexton was a confessional poet; that is, she wrote poetry out of the most intimate and painful details of her life. To a certain extent every poet does this, but few have done so with the frankness and audacity of this one. Sexton presented the truth about herself, her experiences, and her psychic life in the starkest possible terms. She was strongly influenced by other confessional poets, including Robert Lowell and, in particular, W. D. Snodgrass; her friends Sylvia Plath, Maxine Kumin, and George Starbuck also played a part in her poetic development. Sexton's subject matter was often related to her mental therapy, for she was continuously under the care of a psychiatrist and was several times treated in mental institutions. Hence her poems—which in fact began as therapy—are often attempts to deal with the guilt, fear, and anxiety that were the legacy of her childhood. If the poems sometimes seem like one long psychiatric case history, they nevertheless document in a remarkable fashion the growth of a gifted and tortured sensibility, and readers undaunted by intimacy and intensity in poetry will find in Sexton's work an extraordinary aesthetic experience.

Sexton was born Anne Gray Harvey in Newton, Massachusetts. The daughter of Ralph Churchill Harvey and Mary Gray Staples Harvey, she attended the public schools of Wellesley, Massachusetts, from 1934 to 1945, the Rogers Hall preparatory school for girls in Lowell from 1945 to 1947, and Garland Junior College in Boston in 1947 and 1948. At the age of nineteen she eloped to North Carolina with Alfred Muller ("Kayo") Sexton II, whom she married 16 August 1948. In later years she lived with her husband in Baltimore and San Francisco, as well as in the Massachusetts towns of Cochituate, Lower Newton Falls, and Weston. A beautiful woman, she occasionally worked as a model, having studied modeling on a scholarship provided by the Hart Agency of Boston. Her first child, Linda Gray Sexton, was born 21 July 1953. The following year the young mother entered a mental institution after suffering a nervous breakdown. Out of the hospital, Sexton gave birth to a second daughter, Joyce Ladd Sexton, on 5 August 1955, but was again hospitalized for mental illness the following year. The first of several suicide attempts took place in 1956, but her life took a new course when her psychiatrist encouraged her to begin writing poetry. Actually Sexton was not a complete tyro, for she had as a schoolgirl written poetry, some of which appeared in the Rogers Hall school yearbook, but her mother made a slighting remark, and Sexton abandoned it. Out of her ex-

periences in the hospital and her anguish at seeing her children sent away to relatives would eventually come her first volume of poetry, *To Bedlam and Part Way Back* (1960).

In 1957 and 1958 Sexton participated in a poetry workshop with John Holmes at the Boston Center for Adult Education. This tentative beginning led to her attending the 1958 Antioch Writers' Conference, where she worked with W. D. Snodgrass, whose *Heart's Needle* (1959) she would always credit as a major inspiration and influence. Later that year she worked with Robert Lowell, taking his graduate poetry writing seminar at Boston University, and the following summer she attended the Bread Loaf Writers' Conference on a Robert Frost Fellowship in poetry. After the 1960 publication of *To Bedlam and Part Way Back*, the years brought increasing professional activity as she became recognized as an important new poet. She taught her craft not only at Harvard, Radcliffe, Oberlin, and Boston University, but also at high schools and mental institutions. She toured Europe and Africa, and read widely in England and in the United States. Continually under the care of psychiatrists, she was hospitalized twice more, in 1962 and 1973.

She quickly achieved international recognition. Poems from *To Bedlam and Part Way Back* and *All My Pretty Ones* (1962) were published in England as *Selected Poems* (1964), which was a Poetry Book Society selection; in 1965 she was elected a fellow of the Royal Society of Literature. The high point of her career was 1967, when she received the Poetry Society of America's Shelley Memorial Award, and her 1966 collection, *Live or Die*, received a Pulitzer Prize. In subsequent years she received honorary Phi Beta Kappa awards from Harvard (1968) and Radcliffe (1969), and honorary doctorates from Tufts University (1970), Fairfield University (1970), and Regis College (1973). Sexton's death came when her professional stature was at its height. She had attempted unsuccessfully to take her own life in 1956, 1966, and 1970. At 3:30 P.M. on 4 October 1974 she succeeded in committing suicide by carbon monoxide poisoning in her garage.

Not counting *Selected Poems* and a collection entitled *Poems* (1968), which also includes the work of Thomas Kinsella and Douglas Livingstone, Sexton produced ten volumes of verse, of which four or five are first-rate and only one or two, the product of her last, unhappy years, are truly unexceptional. With Sexton, as with most writers, there seems to be a direct correlation between revision and quality. Her later, poorer works were often first or second drafts hurried into print, but the finely crafted poems in her first volumes reveal both discipline and an acute and intuitive sense of form. Preferring syllabics to formal meter, she would work at a poem for days until she came to "know" whether its lines should be long or short and what length its stanzas should be. Though she took particular pride in her images, her rhymes were perhaps the greater accomplishment. Of few poets can it be said that virtually every rhyme is significant, but the merely decorative rhyme is remarkably rare in Sexton.

Her first book, *To Bedlam and Part Way Back*, contains some of the best work she would ever produce, much of it the product of agonizing, months-long revision. Some of the poems in this collection concern the experience of madness and life in an asylum; others begin what would be a career-long therapeutic probing of familial relationships. In "You, Doctor Martin" the inmate of a mental hospital addresses the psychiatrist. Its opening lines— "You, Doctor Martin walk/from breakfast to madness"—have been criticized as facile, but they have the rare and surely great quality of being utterly memorable. As the poem continues, the asylum is described by the speaker as a place of regimentation, isolation, and despair. "I am queen of all my sins forgotten," she declares, echoing "all my sins remembered," the words of the allegedly mad Prince of Denmark. The progression of rhymes within individual stanzas conveys a whole picture of life in a mental hospital: *walk, talk, stalk; make, take, break; sky, eye, cry*. Each of the stanzas is run on to the next through the use of enjambment; only the last ends with a full stop and the suggestive rhyme—for a mental patient—of *self* and *shelf*.

Some of the best poems are elegies. "For Johnny Pole on the Forgotten Beach" describes a fictitious brother as a boy at the seaside and as a young man dying in a wartime beach assault. Its acceptance by the *Antioch Review* in 1959 marked in Sexton's mind a turning point; she felt that she was beginning to be published in important poetry periodicals. Even finer are two poems about the poet's spinster great-aunt, Anna Ladd Dingley, who had lived with the Harveys after retiring as a newspaper editor. "Elizabeth Gone" went through a large number of drafts before attaining its final form. It is in two parts of two stanzas each. In the first part "Elizabeth" dies; in the second she is "let go" by the grieving speaker of the poem. The rhymes, again, are particularly effective. The two stanzas of each half of the poem contain two rhymes apiece, one of which is shared, thus unify-

ing the stanzas and making more absolute the break between the poem's two parts, which is the break between Elizabeth dying and Elizabeth dead. Another poem about "Nana," as Sexton called her great-aunt, is "Some Foreign Letters," a work admired by Robert Lowell. The poem follows "Elizabeth Gone," which ends with the poet's sorting the dead woman's things. Now she reads through letters written home from Europe in 1890, pausing to consider, from time to time, the difference between the withered old maid she has known and the sprightly girl on her grand tour so long ago. The traveler's letters are a window on the past, through which the poet sees "London . . . on Lord Mayor's Day," German castles, and amorous noblemen. But "I loved you last,/a pleated old lady with a crooked hand." "Some Foreign Letters" anticipates the poems of motherhood, daughterhood, and generation that conclude this collection, for the great-aunt lives—for the length of the poem at least—as girl and as crone in the mind of the woman in her prime who is the poet.

Another anticipation of the later poems is "Unknown Girl in the Maternity Ward," in which an unwed mother speaks to her illegitimate child, whom she will give up: "You will not know me very long." The poem seems to be a straightforward and realistic monologue, but at the end the girl says, "Go child, who is my sin and nothing more," and one hears echoes of envois from Chaucer to Pound. This "child" is also a poem, "my sin." The connection between poetry and the confession of sins will recur in later works, like "With Mercy for the Greedy" in *All My Pretty Ones:* "I was born/doing reference work in sin, and born/confessing it. This is what poems are."

The most impressive piece of work in this collection is "The Double Image," a sequence of seven poems. The poet describes two portraits, herself and her mother, facing each other on opposite walls. The "double image" becomes a metaphor for the thirty-year-old poet's split between the older generation and the younger, between her mother and her daughter. Like Shakespeare in his first twenty sonnets, Sexton shows that painting, poetry, and procreation are all image-making, but Sexton's replicating images, unlike Shakespeare's, are made relevant exclusively to the question of the poet's own problematic identity. The sequence begins with *I* and ends with *me*, and the unity of the generational selves described in the poem is underscored in the identical rhyme in its conclusion, where *me* is rhymed with itself.

All My Pretty Ones, nominated for a National Book Award, shows the poet gaining mastery. As the title of this new collection implies, these poems are about loss—loss of parents, lovers, God, even parts of the body in operations. As *To Bedlam and Part Way Back* ends with "The Division of Parts," a poem about dividing up the possessions of the poet's recently deceased mother, so *All My Pretty Ones* begins with further attempts to sort out the tangled emotions left at that death and at the death, shortly after, of Sexton's father. "The Truth the Dead Know," revised some three hundred times, according to the poet, concerns a funeral and its numb emotional aftermath. "All My Pretty Ones," which follows, is ironically titled, for Sexton's emotions toward the family she has lost are decidedly more ambivalent than those of the character in *Macbeth* who suffers a similar loss and laments his "pretty ones." This poem is primarily about the father, an alcoholic, and like the contemporary Scottish poet George MacBeth's "The Drawer," it is devoted to an inventory of the effects of the dead. It ends with the recognition that perhaps the father was not, after all, one of the poet's pretty ones. But "Whether you are pretty or not, I outlive you,/bend down my strange face and forgive you." Though one reviewer complained that "to forgive the dead is the ultimate condescension of the living," these lines and their sanguine rhyme express something central in Sexton's poetry, the need both to forgive her parents and to be forgiven by them for some nameless fault she seems always to have been convinced that she had.

As would be increasingly typical of her work, the modalities of loss seem often to have religious aspects or dimensions. In "With Mercy for the Greedy," for example, the poet identifies herself as a confessional poet in a double sense when she describes her work not merely as self-revelation, but as sacramental confession. Yet she balks at identifying herself as a believer, because "Need is not quite belief." Another poem, "In the Deep Museum," resembles D. H. Lawrence's *The Man Who Died* (1927) in that it describes Christ's regaining consciousness in the tomb and admitting that he had "lied." But where Lawrence's Christ walks out and makes a new life, Sexton's is eaten alive by rats. Both leave an empty tomb. "We have kept the miracle," says Christ in the poem, "I will not be here." Part of the bizarre effect of the poem lies in Christ's behaving like a gentle Saint Francis with the rats as they consume him in a travesty of the Eucharist. "For three days, for love's sake,/I bless this other death." A far cry from the maudlin "rowing toward

God" of the later Sexton, the poem is brutally effective whether it be taken as calculated sacrilege or—as Sexton seems to have intended—as heteroclite piety. Its slyest touch, at any rate, is the hint that the voracious and unsaved scavengers are not rats at all but Christians: "Unto the bellies and jaws/ of rats I commit my prophesy and fear." As early as this poem, Sexton may have been identifying herself with those rats.

The humor is less grim in the charming "Letter Written on a Ferry While Crossing Long Island Sound," a poem that begins in concrete everydayness—"at 2 o'clock on a Tuesday/in August of 1969"—and ends in a whimsical fantasy in which four nuns take flight from the deck of the ferry. Again, loss is the subject, for the speaker of the poem has just separated, perhaps finally, from someone she loves. Her misery generates the need for some miraculous escape from the painful moment, and so the poem is replete with emblems of salvation (the life preserver, the lifeboat) and of wholeness (things circular, from the life preserver to the round mouths of the nuns). The poem ends hopefully, if fantastically, with the nuns calling back "from the gauzy edge of paradise,/*good news, good news.*"

The good news is still relatively remote in Sexton's Pulitzer Prize-winning *Live or Die,* the poems of which date from early 1962 to early 1966. The volume's subject is again implicit in the title, for the poems, arranged in the order in which they were written, constitute a logbook of the poet's continual hesitation between a responsibility to life and a need for death. Prominent among these poems are reflections on the contrasting experience of the poet's own childhood and motherhood. "In the Beach House"—in which parental lovemaking, "the royal strapping," is overheard—and "Cripples and Other Stories"—in which a child's warped psyche threatens to manifest itself in ways that cannot be hidden—describe the childhood traumas that would concern this poet throughout her career. "Lovely Girl, My Stringbean, My Lovely Woman" and "A Little Uncomplicated Hymn" describe the poet's daughters in terms proving that however warped Sexton's childhood, she was capable of the warmest feelings for her own children. But always now these familiar subjects are subordinated to the mighty clash of the responsibility to live and the hunger for death, an antinomy that led one reviewer to compare the book to a fugue, its themes announced and developed contrapuntally. Although the book ends with "Live" and the resolution that title implies, one hears a greater intensity

Anne Sexton, self-portrait, 1950s (by permission of Linda Gray Sexton and Harry Ransom Humanities Research Center, University of Texas at Austin)

There may be further hints in "To Lose the Earth," a somewhat obscure poem that seems to be describing death as a return to the womb, imaged as an Egyptian grotto in which a mysterious flutist plays. The flutist is a "midwife," and "At the moment of entry/your head will be below the gunwales,/your shoulders will rock and struggle/as you ship hogsheads of water." One enters in this fashion a state that is "close to being dead." But is it death or the little death that is being described in terms of this "entry"? The suggestive imagery allows both readings, and although the reviewer who described "To Lose the Earth" as "about as Freudian as a poem can get" sounded somewhat frustrated, the poem is to be praised for the evocative richness of its ambiguity.

More than one of the poems in *Live or Die* describes a kind of visceral yearning for death. "I know at the news of your death," the poet says in "Sylvia's Death," "a terrible taste for it, like salt." In "Wanting to Die" she refers to "the almost unnameable lust" for death, the "drug so sweet" that has "dazzled" her. At the same time, however, at least in this poem, death is an "enemy," its invidiousness in curious balance with life, which is an

in the more numerous poems about death, which include "Sylvia's Death" (about Sylvia Plath), "Wanting to Die," "Suicide Note," and "Somewhere in Africa."

In the last, an elegy for her first poetry writing teacher, John Holmes, the poet deplores the jejune and shallow obsequies for her friend, the forms dictated by a religion he apparently did not practice. She invokes a richer ceremony presided over by a god "hidden/from the missionary, the well-wisher and the glad hand." Imagining this savage god as a woman, a "tribal female who is known but forbidden," the poet conjures a vision of Holmes in transit down some great river in Africa in this deity's "shallow boat" and apostrophizes the dead man: "John Holmes . . . lie heavy in her hold/and go down that river with the ivory, the copra and the gold." The poem ends here, but the reader knows that if Holmes goes downriver in Africa he journeys out of darkness toward some radiant and mysterious sea. "Somewhere in Africa" is one of the few poems in which Sexton, a poet with a tropism for death, hints at just what there might be to that undiscovered country.

Sexton, late 1940s (courtesy of Linda Gray Sexton)

"old wound." The poem's bleakness is relieved only by the inchoate spirituality that dictates the image of "breath," the pneuma, incarcerated in sinful flesh: "Death waits for me, year after year,/to so delicately undo an old wound,/to empty my breath from its bad prison."

The imagery of incarceration is muted in "Flee on Your Donkey," in which the mental institution to which the poet returns, "the scene of the disordered senses," is referred to as a "sad hotel." Despite its references to attempted suicide, its details of previous visits to this place, and its account of the inadequate therapy of dream analysis and hypnotic trips into the past, the poem is ultimately positive, for it ends with the speaker's resolution to leave, to flee on her donkey. Sexton worked on this poem off and on for four years; consequently it can be related to much of her other work, early and late. Versions of the poem's refrain, "O my hunger! My hunger!," and its central conceit, riding the donkey, figure in a number of other poems, notably the later "Suicide Note," in which the poet declares: "Once upon a time/my hunger was for Jesus./ O my hunger! My hunger!/ Before he grew old/he rode calmly into Jerusalem/in search of death." But Sexton seems not so much to hunger for Jesus as to identify with Him. The donkey she rides out of the asylum in the earlier poem carries her toward death in the later one; the "toy donkey I rode all these years" ultimately figures in the panoply of a death wish compounded with some obscure Christ complex. Humble and absurd, each rider acquiesces in the death that waits.

The horrors of wanting to die, of the asylum, and even of the traumatic childhood are at some remove in Sexton's next collection, *Love Poems* (1969), whose sales of over 14,000 copies within eighteen months made it one of Sexton's most popular books. The turn from madness and death to love, the perennial subject of poetry, is consistent with the resolution to live at the end of *Live or Die*. The image of the carpenter, used as an analogue to the suicide in "Wanting to Die" ("suicides. . . . Like carpenters . . . want to know *which tools*./They never ask *why build*"), is now used in "The Touch" for the lover who builds and heals and overcomes isolation. Of course not all the poems are simple celebrations of love; some, like "The Ballad of the Lonely Masturbator," "You All Know the Story of the Other Woman," and "The Interrogation of the Man of Many Hearts," concern the unhappiness of love's often unsmooth course. Several, including "The Nude Swim" and "Loving the Killer," are addressed to the poet's husband, while others, such

as "Song for a Lady," which describes lesbian lovemaking, and "Eighteen Days Without You," about waiting for a lover away on duty with the air force reserve, seem to belie—as one baffled reviewer observed—the dust jacket description of the author as a suburban, middle-class housewife with a husband and two daughters. But if some of the loves described in these poems are imaginary, one ought not to carp at a poet's transmuting emotions into little dramas whose fictitiousness is superficial: the passion, one feels, is authentic, and the eroticism manages to be both convincing and elegant. In poems like "The Breast," "Barefoot," "Knee Song," and "That Day," the figures for the body and its sexual parts are far from reticent but never coarse. The center of woman is an "eye" or a "jewel"; the phallus is an etching of red and blue veins; an erection is a "monument" that comes "forth more sudden than some reconstructed city" ("That Day").

"The Break," one of the collection's best poems, is a subtle critique of sensuality. Consisting of twenty regularly rhymed quatrains, it describes a painful and crippling broken hip suffered by the poet on her fortieth birthday. Although not exactly accident-prone, Sexton had her share of mishaps and serious operations—many of which became poems. As a child she had put her arm into the wringer of a washing machine and had lived for some time with the prospect of permanent disablement. The recurrent idea in the poems about such accidents is that external crippling will make the internal psychic crippling impossible to conceal; "would the cripple inside me/be a cripple that would show?," she asks in "Cripples and Other Stories," one of the poems in *Live or Die*. Thus when, as an adult, the poet falls down a flight of stairs and breaks her hip in two places, "the post of it and also the cup," the physical injury is viewed as merely emblematic of an emotional one, and the poem about the experience begins, "It was also my violent heart that broke." The breaking of the heart, "old hunger motor," has little to do with conventional amorous distress. It seems rather linked to the ineluctable fate of age and infertility, a fate she describes in lines hinting that for even the most confirmed sensualist, fertility somehow validates sexuality. "My one dozen roses are dead," the speaker says from her hospital bed. "They have ceased to menstruate./ . . ./And the heart too, that cripple, how it sang once."

Various kinds of emotional crippling also figure in Sexton's most popular book, *Transformations* (1971), in which she returns in a new way to the world of childhood and its fears. The seventeen

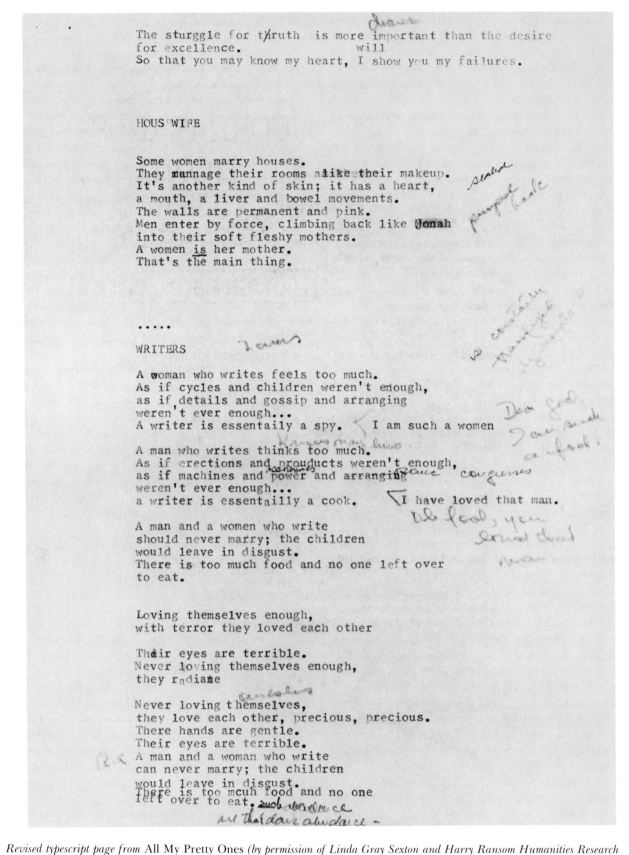

The sturggle for t/ruth is more important than the desire
for excellence.   will
So that you may know my heart, I show you my failures.

HOUS WIFE

Some women marry houses.
They munnage their rooms alike their makeup.
It's another kind of skin; it has a heart,
a mouth, a liver and bowel movements.
The walls are permanent and pink.
Men enter by force, climbing back like Jonah
into their soft fleshy mothers.
A women is her mother.
That's the main thing.

. . . . .

WRITERS

A woman who writes feels too much.
As if cycles and children weren't enough,
as if details and gossip and arranging
weren't ever enough...
A writer is essentaily a spy.   I am such a women

A man who writes thinks too much.
As if erections and prouducts weren't enough,
as if machines and power and arranging
weren't ever enough...
a writer is essentailly a cook.   I have loved that man.

A man and a women who write
should never marry; the children
would leave in disgust.
There is too much food and no one left over
to eat.

Loving themselves enough,
with terror they loved each other

Their eyes are terrible.
Never loving themselves enough,
they radiate

Never loving themselves,
they love each other, precious, precious.
There hands are gentle.
Their eyes are terrible.
A man and a woman who write
can never marry; the children
would leave in disgust.
There is too mcuh food and no one
left over to eat.

Revised typescript page from All My Pretty Ones *(by permission of Linda Gray Sexton and Harry Ransom Humanities Research Center, University of Texas at Austin)* poems in this collection are versions of fairy tales by the Brothers Grimm. Sexton's Ovidian title is a reminder that fairy tales often feature metamorphoses—of straw into gold and frogs into princes, if not maidens into laurel trees. It also points to Sexton's transforming of the idiom and moral of each tale so that it becomes a sardonic exposé rather than a cozy bedtime story. But the debunking of romantic clichés—the rescued maiden, the frog who proves to be a prince, the living happily ever after—is the simpler side of these deft pieces. The poems show the real genius of their creator in their frank treatment of what Freudians would call the "submerged fantasy content" of the original tales. Sexton converts stories normally thought of as a means of exorcising childish fears into a means of therapeutically revisiting—as she had so often done, on the couch and in verse—the childish origins of adult complexes. What is truly original and horrifying about these poems is their demonstration that the fears supposedly confined to childhood can intensify rather than disappear with maturation. Small wonder, then, as J. D. McClatchy has pointed out, that in his study of the psychological significance of fairy tales, *The Uses of Enchantment* (1976), Bruno Bettelheim has occasion to cite these poems.

Sexton tells her fairy stories in language that is colloquial and hip; each begins with a prologue, its tone varying from earnest to bitter, that introduces the poet's modern angle on her subject. Thus "Rumpelstiltskin" begins, "Inside many of us/is a small old man who wants to get out." The assertion that this horrid little man is something internal prepares the reader for the psychoanalytic treatment of the familiar tale that follows. Similarly the reader learns in the opening lines of "Rapunzel"—"A woman/who loves a woman/is forever young"—that the focus of this version of the story will be on the lesbian relationship between Rapunzel and Mother Gothel rather than on the relationship between Rapunzel and the prince.

The degree of the transformation into modern and personal relevance is heightened from poem to poem. Thus in one of the first poems, "Snow White and the Seven Dwarfs," the qualification of the original fantasy is subtle and understated. At the end, after the jealous stepmother has been disposed of, Snow White marries the prince and holds court—"sometimes referring to her mirror/as women do." The implication is that soon she will be asking it, "who is the fairest of us all?" The sly last words work perfectly to suggest the archetypal and cyclic relationship between the little Snow

Whites and all their jealous stepmothers. Later the satire becomes more intense, the fantasy content of the tales less ambiguous. The prologue to "The Frog Prince" seems to be addressed to a woman psychiatrist and contains a blunt observation about the symbolism of the frog: "Frog is my father's genitals." (Barbara Swan's drawing of the frog, which accompanies the poem, manages to suggest its phallic aspect with nice subtlety.) The fairy story then unfolds, from the princess "walking in her garden" to her retiring to bed with "the sinuous frog," who turns into a prince who has to be married. "After all he had compromised her."

"Cinderella" is one of the most successful of these redactions and is often anthologized. It begins with a modern analogue: "the plumber with twelve children/who wins the Irish Sweepstakes./ .../That story." The nursemaid, the milkman, and the charwoman all follow, each finding sudden wealth or love or happiness or all three. "That story" is the poet's repeated, sardonic comment on these fantastic wish fulfillments. And that is the story with Cinderella, who wins her prince in the familiar sequence of events. In Sexton's transformation of the story, the "happily ever after" cliché receives the full brunt of her sarcasm:

> Cinderella and the prince
> lived, they say, happily ever after,
> like two dolls in a museum case
> never bothered by diapers or dust,
> never arguing about the timing of an egg,
> never telling the same story twice,
> never getting a middle-aged spread,
> their darling smiles pasted on for eternity.
> Regular Bobbsey Twins.
> That story.

Transformations was Sexton's last good book. There are good poems in the later books, but fewer and fewer as the poet allowed herself to become facile or strident or incoherent. Of the later collections, only *The Book of Folly* (1972) contains much work of sustained quality. J. D. McClatchy, however, considers it significant in that it marks a return to the confessional mode, abandoned or adulterated since *Live or Die*. The subjects treated are for the most part familiar, but when the poet's relations with and feeling of guilt toward her parents undergo analysis yet again, the treatment of this Electral triangle begins to wear thin. Before Sexton's mother died of cancer in 1959, she accused her daughter of giving her the disease by attempting suicide. The charge was absurd, but it

Dust jacket for Sexton's 1971 collection comprising poetic revisions of Grimms' fairy tales

did much damage, and obsessive references to Mary Harvey's agonizing death recur in volume after volume. In this one they appear in appalling images of severed breasts and bloody lactation. The preoccupation with the baleful influence of the father also figures in this collection. Even Sleeping Beauty, in *Transformations,* had not been spared this obsession. At the end of her story, an insomniac as dependent on soporific drugs as Sexton herself, she speaks from bed: "It's not the prince at all,/but my father/drunkenly bent over the bed,/circling the abyss like a shark,/my father thick upon me/like some sleeping jellyfish." In *The Book of Folly* this nightmare receives further attention in the sequence entitled "The Death of the Fathers." These poems modulate from the merely suggestive "Oysters," in which the poet, a girl, consumes this reputed aphrodisiac in the company of her father and rises from the table a woman, to the explicit "How We Danced," in which, dancing with her father, the daughter discovers that he has an erection: "the serpent spoke as you held me close." But poems like this one must strike even the most committed Freudian as overdone. A good poet seems spoiled by excessive analysis. The problem, finally, is that the reader begins to feel more pity for the

maligned father than for the allegedly traumatized daughter. Yet "The Boat," another poem from the sequence, contains one of the finest moments in Sexton's poetry, a description of her family's near death when their speedboat is handled carelessly by her father. The boat goes through rather than over a wave, and the young passenger discovers that "Here in the green room/the dead are very close." Arresting the moment in the heart of the wave, Sexton makes it a moment out of time, and the effect is riveting.

Sexton's last years were apparently filled with hysteria, and the chronicle of these years is tremendously pathetic. According to Lois Ames and Linda Gray Sexton, editors of *Anne Sexton: A Self-Portrait in Letters* (1977), the poet came to demand more and more from her friends and became estranged from those who declined to give over their lives to keeping her company and soothing her fears. Late in 1973 she divorced her husband, expecting at the age of forty-five to commence a varied love life. She was disappointed and at one point even registered with a computer dating service. The poetry of these last, desperate years seems hurried; its "confessional" aspects seem a needless and ill-advised dragging of personal obsessions into the open. But the poems of her next collection, *The Death Notebooks*, which came out early in 1974 (to what Ames and Sexton call "universally poor" reviews), are not all from this period, for she had for some time been setting aside certain poems as unsuitable for publication during her lifetime. The source of her reticence is unclear, since nothing in the volume—which she decided to go ahead and publish—is as shocking as "The Death of the Fathers" in *The Book of Folly* or even certain of the less-inhibited poems in *Transformations*. The primary problem of *The Death Notebooks* is its lack of a center, its manifest desultoriness. Unlike every preceding volume, it has no central theme or dialectic. The title notwithstanding, meditations on death do not seem particularly important—though they are here, in "For Mr. Death Who Stands with His Door Open" (in which the poet becomes the reluctant bride of death who, unlike Emily Dickinson's courtly gentleman, is fat, "middle aged and lower-class") and in the six-poem sequence "The Death Baby." If any one mode dominates, it is the religious, seen in "Gods," "Mary's Song," "God's Backside," "Jesus Walking," and "O Ye Tongues." Some of these, notably "Jesus Walking" and "O Ye Tongues," seem genuinely pious; others reveal the religious uncertainty and ambivalence that Sexton was never able to shake completely. In "Gods" the gods of the world are sought far and wide but are finally found in the speaker's own bathroom, and the poem ends as she blithely locks the door, preparatory, one assumes, to dealing with them once and for all. In "God's Backside" the deity moons creation, and in "Hurry Up Please It's Time" the example is followed by the poet, who pulls down her pants and defecates in the face of both death and life. Of course any work of literature can be made to sound ridiculous in paraphrase, but these poems often skirt the ridiculous without ever approaching the sublime. Only occasionally is an observation couched in wit sufficient, as Dr. Johnson would say, to make it sweet: "Before there are words/do you dream!/In utero/do you dream?/Who taught you to suck?/And how come?" ("Hurry Up Please It's Time").

Even worse than the poems of *The Death Notebooks* are those of *The Awful Rowing Toward God* (1975), written for the most part in twenty days in January 1973, "with two days out for despair, and three days out in a mental hospital." She no longer revised extensively—sometimes she did not revise at all. Consequently the poems are formless, incoherent, and embarrassing, and one reads and reads without discovering anything redeeming or

memorable. The book contains only occasional images as good as "death looks on with a casual eye/and picks at the dirt under his fingernail" ("After Auschwitz") and only a few lines as rhythmic as "We must all stop dying in the little ways" ("Children"). The reviews, perhaps in deference to Sexton's passing, were not so uniformly bad as those of *The Death Notebooks*, but even well-disposed reviewers like Joyce Carol Oates, Robert Mazzocco, and Ben Howard (their reviews are collected in McClatchy's 1978 book) seem compulsively to devote their comments to other Sexton volumes, as if unwilling to trust themselves with the volume in hand.

Sexton had in her last months become somewhat obsessively religious, though the religiosity seems patently a desperate grasping for stability and comfort. The theme of *The Awful Rowing Toward God*, as the title implies, is the poet's quest for religious certainty. But while the most hardened atheist can respond to the religious poetry of John Donne or Gerard Manley Hopkins, neither he nor the believer will be anything but embarrassed by these poems, which seem genuinely unwholesome, even insincere, if insincerity be defined as professing without adequate conviction. The remarkable thing is that the poetry Sexton had written during periods of extreme mental instability before had been clear and honest. With the abandonment of discipline one perceives an abandonment of the will to fight for mental equilibrium and clarity. It is a sad dissolution.

Sexton's last books were posthumous collections edited by her daughter. The poems in *45 Mercy Street* (1976) are often somewhat difficult to make out, but again the reader shares a quest for value, love, stability, forgiveness, and sanity. The book is not particularly good, although it is less distressing than the volumes immediately preceding it. The work included dates from 1971 to 1974, and while these were Sexton's last, hardest years, the poems seem if anything less bleak than those of the previous volumes. The collection is divided into four sections, from "Beginning the Hegira" to "Eating the Leftovers." The hegira, of course, is never successfully completed—and leftovers are a sad note on which to end this ninth book, the last that Sexton herself had any hand in arranging. Another section is a sequence, "Bestiary U.S.A.," which contains poems describing various animals and reminds one of nothing so much as the grotesques and drolleries in the margins of medieval manuscripts. The centerpiece of the collection, the sequence entitled "The Divorce Papers," seems curiously restrained, almost elegiac; there is little violent emotion, only much ambivalence toward the man the poet had lived with for twenty-five years. It seems likely, though, that some of the poems excluded from the volume because of "the pain their publication would bring to individuals still living" come from this sequence.

Poems have also been excluded from *Words for Dr. Y.* (1978), "the first collection of Anne Sexton's poetry from which her editorial guidance was totally absent." This volume contains sequences and odd pieces discovered in the poet's files during the preparation of *Anne Sexton: A Self-Portrait in Letters*. One section, "Letters to Dr. Y.," was originally to have been part of *The Book of Folly* and dates from the 1960s. A number of the later works reveal a promising return to form. Especially noteworthy is "The Errand," dated 2 December 1972. For the most part artfully rhymed (though one winces at the rhyming of *folly* and *by golly*), it is in eight stanzas that develop the metaphor of life as an errand the single purpose of which is to visit the "one store" kept by shopkeeper Death. Like *The Book of Folly, Words for Dr. Y.* also contains prose. It concludes with three "horror tales," one of which is of particular relevance to Sexton's life and poetry. The title character and narrator of "The Ghost," although never actually identified, is obviously the poet's great-aunt, Anna Ladd Dingley, the subject of "Elizabeth Gone" and "Some Foreign Letters." Her influence, qua ghost, on the life of her grandniece is not as salubrious as one might expect, given the intimacy of the two in life.

"The Ghost" is one of the rare works in which Sexton looks at herself through the eyes of another person, and the effect is refreshing. The relationship between art and personal life is perforce an intimate one for a poet like Sexton, but ultimately the distinction must be preserved, as Patricia Meyer Spacks argues in an astute discussion of *45 Mercy Street* in the *New York Times Book Review* (30 May 1976).

In this review, which is reproduced in the McClatchy volume, Spacks applauds the honesty and precision of Sexton's early work but laments the narcissism, the obsession with the self and its misery, that spoils the later: "the verse implicitly argues that anguish is self-justifying, neither permitting nor demanding the further pain of balanced self-knowledge or the illuminations of controlled imagination and poetic technique. In life we forgive sufferers the necessities of their obsessions. In literature we must ask more: acknowledging the pain that produces such work as Anne

Sexton's later poems, yet remembering that art requires more than emotional indulgence, requires a saving respect for disciplines and realities beyond the crying needs, the unrelenting appetites, of the self."

When Sexton's *Complete Poems* appeared in 1981, the critical response was even less generous. This volume incorporates the earlier books, minus prose and illustrations, as well as six last poems written between March and late September of 1974. These concluding poems are for the most part valedictions, apparently to friends, family members, and lovers. Remarkably unhysterical, these leave-takings sound almost serene. But the critics, nonetheless, found little to praise. Although they noted the occasional gem in the collection, they deplored the unvarying voice and the tendency toward self-indulgence. There was general agreement regarding the distressing ratio of bad to good poems. Katha Pollitt, in *Nation* (21 November 1981), spoke for many reviewers: "There are beauties here—Sexton wrote as many tight, precise, brilliantly associative poems as any number of poets with more secure reputations. But she also wrote dozens and dozens of poems that are histrionic, verbose, mechanical, sentimental, mannered and very, very boring."

These remarks suggest the criteria by which all of Sexton's work must be evaluated. Yet one must not discount the magnitude of this poet's suffering or forget the heroism involved in producing much good poetry in spite of anguish and despair that must have been overwhelmingly debilitating. If she eventually crumbled under the weight of her manifold sorrows, she first set a formidable example of courage in the face of adversity. She was always capable of the kind of wan optimism manifested in the epitaph she chose for herself, a palindrome of which she was especially fond: "Rats live on no evil star." Glamorous and celebrated as she was, she often saw herself as humble and despised, but "the lowest of us all," as she observes in a poem on this palindrome in *The Death Notebooks,* "deserve to smile in eternity."

References:

Beverly Fields, "The Poetry of Anne Sexton," in *Poets in Progress,* edited by Edward Hungerford (Evanston, Ill.: Northwestern University Press, 1967), pp. 251-285;
An early discussion of Sexton's poetry that attempts to avoid the biographical approach, "to credit her with a degree of esthetic distance."

Suzanne Juhasz, "The Excitable Gift: The Poetry of Anne Sexton," in her *Naked and Fiery Forms: Modern Poetry by Women, A New Tradition* (New York: Harper, 1976), pp. 117-143;
A judicious survey of the verse, starting from the observation: "it is essential to observe that her 'confessionalism' grew out of the therapy situation, but that the therapy was occasioned by her womanhood itself, by the very real strains and conflicts that Sexton experienced while trying to exist in the world as a woman."

Juhasz, "Seeking the Exit or the Home: Poetry and Salvation in the Career of Anne Sexton," in *Shakespeare's Sisters: Feminist Essays on Woman Poets*, edited by Sandra M. Gilbert and Susan Gubar (Bloomington: Indiana University Press, 1979), pp. 261-268;
On Sexton's "vulnerability" as part of the price paid for her poems. Emphasis on the poet's disciplined approach to her craft and on the poetry's reflection of a widely recognized "secret domestic world and its pain." Interesting account of Sexton's conceit of the "gnawing, pestilential rat inside."

Maxine Kumin, "How It Was: Maxine Kumin on Anne Sexton," in *The Complete Poems* (Boston: Houghton Mifflin, 1981), pp. xix-xxxiv;
Touching recollections and incisive comments by Sexton's collaborator and close friend.

Estella Lauter, *Women as Mythmakers: Poetry and Visual Art by Twentieth-Century Women* (Bloomington: Indiana University Press, 1984);
The discussion of Sexton in this stimulating book concentrates on "the psychological and religious dynamics of her imaginative pilgrimage." Lauter concentrates on the later poetry "in the context of archetypal psychology and feminine theology."

J. D. McClatchy, ed., *Anne Sexton: The Poet and Her Critics* (Bloomington: Indiana University Press, 1978);
An extremely useful collection, with tributes and reminiscences by contemporaries, reviews, three interviews, and four worthwhile "overviews." Includes chronology and bibliography.

Katha Pollitt, Review of *The Complete Poems*, *Nation* (21 November 1981): 533-537;
A perspicacious and representative review of this volume.

M. L. Rosenthal, *The New Poets: American and British Poetry Since World War II* (New York: Oxford University Press, 1967), pp. 131-138;
Places Sexton among other confessional poets; discusses first two volumes of poetry.

Linda W. Wagner, "45 Mercy Street and Other Vacant Houses," in *American Literature: The New England Heritage*, edited by James Nagel and Richard Astro (New York: Garland, 1981), pp. 145-165.
Sympathetic readings of several poems in *45 Mercy Street*, comparing Sexton with Dickinson and Plath.

Papers:
The poet's "worksheets, private papers and letters" may be seen in the Anne Sexton Archive at Boston University.

Irwin Shaw

This entry was updated by Walter W. Ross (Columbia, South Carolina) from his entries in DLB 6, American Novelists Since World War II *and in* DLB Yearbook: 1984.

Places	Manhattan Paris	Brooklyn Klosters, Switzerland	Southampton, New York
Influences and Relationships	Ernest Hemingway		
Literary Movements and Forms	War Fiction	Novel of Manners	

Major Themes	Death
	International
	   Themes/America
	    vs. Europe
		Athletic Competition
		Anti-Nazism
		Rich and
		   Poor
			Communism vs.
			   Democracy
			Dedication to
			   Individual Work

Cultural and Artistic Influences	Theater		
Social and Economic Influences	World War II	Great Depression	

BIRTH: New York, New York, 27 February 1913, to William and Rose Tompkins Shaw.

EDUCATION: B.A., Brooklyn College (now Brooklyn College of the City University of New York), 1934.

MARRIAGE: 13 October 1939 to Marian Edwards; child: Adam.

AWARDS AND HONORS: O. Henry Memorial Award first prize for "Walking Wounded," 1944, second prize, 1945; National Institute of Arts and Letters grant, 1946.

DEATH: Davos, Switzerland, 16 May 1984.

Irwin Shaw, late 1940s (Culver Pictures)

BOOKS: *Bury the Dead* (New York: Random House, 1936);

The Gentle People (New York: Random House, 1939);

Sailor Off the Bremen (New York: Random House, 1939; London: Cape, 1940);

Welcome to the City (New York: Random House, 1942);

Sons and Soldiers (New York: Random House, 1944);

Act of Faith (New York: Random House, 1946);

The Assassin (New York: Random House, 1946);

The Survivors, by Shaw and Peter Viertel (New York: Dramatists Play Service, 1948);

The Young Lions (New York: Random House, 1948; London: Cape, 1949);

Mixed Company (New York: Random House, 1950; London: Cape, 1952);

Report on Israel, by Shaw and Robert Capa (New York: Simon & Schuster, 1950);

The Troubled Air (New York: Random House, 1951; London: Cape, 1951);

Lucy Crown (New York: Random House, 1956; London: Cape, 1956);

Tip on a Dead Jockey (New York: Random House, 1957; London: Cape, 1957);

Two Weeks in Another Town (New York: Random House, 1960; London: Cape, 1960);

Selected Short Stories (New York: Modern Library, 1961);

Children From Their Games (New York: French, 1962);

In the French Style (New York: MacFadden, 1963);

In the Company of Dolphins (New York: Random House, 1964);

Love on a Dark Street (New York: Delacorte, 1965; London: Cape, 1965);

Voices of a Summer Day (New York: Delacorte/Dial, 1965; London: Weidenfeld & Nicolson, 1965);

Short Stories (New York: Random House, 1966);

Retreat (London: New English Library, 1970);

Rich Man, Poor Man (New York: Delacorte, 1970; London: Weidenfeld & Nicolson, 1970);

Whispers in Bedlam (London: Weidenfeld & Nicolson, 1972);

Evening in Byzantium (New York: Delacorte, 1973; London: Weidenfeld & Nicolson, 1973);

God Was Here But He Left Early (New York: Arbor House, 1973; London: Pan, 1977);

Nightwork (New York: Delacorte, 1975; London: Weidenfeld & Nicolson, 1975);

Beggarman, Thief (New York: Delacorte, 1977; London: Weidenfeld & Nicolson, 1977);

Paris! Paris!, by Shaw and Ronald Searle (New York & London: Harcourt Brace Jovanovich, 1977; London: Weidenfeld & Nicolson, 1977);

Short Stories, Five Decades (New York: Delacorte, 1978; London: Cape, 1978);

The Top of the Hill (New York: Delacorte, 1979);

Bread Upon the Waters (New York: Delacorte, 1981; London: Weidenfeld & Nicolson, 1981);

Acceptable Losses (New York: Arbor House, 1982; London: New English Library, 1983).

PLAY PRODUCTIONS: *Bury the Dead,* New York, Ethel Barrymore Theatre, April 1936;

Siege, New York, Longacre Theatre, December 1937;

The Gentle People, New York, Belasco Theatre, January 1939;

Quiet City, New York, Belasco Theatre, March 1939;

Retreat to Pleasure, New York, Belasco Theatre, 1940;

Sons and Soldiers, New York, Morosco Theatre, May 1943;

The Assassin, New York, National Theatre, October 1945;

The Survivors, by Shaw and Peter Viertel, New York, Playhouse Theatre, January 1948;

Children From Their Games, New York, Morosco Theatre, April 1963;

A Choice of Wars, Glasgow, Scotland, Glasgow Citizens Theatre, 1967.

SCREENPLAYS: *The Big Game,* RKO, 1936;

Commandos Strike at Dawn, Columbia, 1942;

The Hard Way, by Shaw and Daniel Fuchs, Warner Bros., 1942;

Talk of the Town, by Shaw and Sidney Buchman, RKO, 1942;

Take One False Step, by Shaw and Chester Erskine, Universal, 1949;

I Want You, RKO, 1951;

Act of Love, United Artists, 1953;

Fire Down Below, Columbia, 1957;

Desire Under the Elms, Paramount, 1958;

This Angry Age, by Shaw and René Clément, Columbia, 1958;

The Big Gamble, Fox, 1961;

In the French Style, Columbia, 1963;

Survival, United Film, 1968.

TELEVISION SCRIPTS: "The Top of the Hill," WPIX, New York, 6-7 February 1980;

"The Girls in Their Summer Dresses," "The Man Who Married a French Wife," and "The Monument," adapted by Kenneth Cavender, WNET, New York, 1 June 1982.

OTHER: *Paris/Magnum: Photographs, 1935-1981,* text by Shaw (New York: Harper & Row, 1981).

PERIODICAL PUBLICATIONS: "Another Time, Another Village," *New York,* 14 (6-13 July 1981): 30-32;

"The Conscience of a Heavyweight," *Esquire,* 99 (June 1983): 272-274, 276;

"The Common Man," *Esquire,* 100 (December 1983): 591-595.

Irwin Shaw was born in New York City, the son of William Shaw, a salesman of hat trimmings, and Rose Tompkins Shaw. When he was very young the family moved to the Sheepshead Bay section of Brooklyn, where he attended local schools and developed a lifelong love of sports. Some of his best short stories, including "The Eighty-Yard Run" and "March, March on Down the Field," both about football, were drawn from his athletic experiences.

At the age of fifteen he graduated from James Madison High School and entered Brooklyn College. During his freshman year he failed calculus and Latin and was expelled from college. He worked at odd jobs for a year and then returned to obtain his B.A. degree. He continued his interest in sports by playing football for four years, contributed pieces to the school newspaper, and wrote plays that were staged by the school dramatic group. In a short autobiographical sketch, he recalled how he supported himself during his remaining years in college: "To make money when I got back into school I tutored children, worked in the school library, typed manuscripts, wrote theses in English for students in New York University." Years later Brooklyn College awarded him an honorary doctorate.

After graduating in 1934, Shaw began his career as a writer by writing serials for radio. Two shows, *Dick Tracy* and *The Gumps,* both based on comic strips, were successful. During this time he also wrote his first major play, *Bury the Dead,* which had an immediate impact when it opened at the Ethel Barrymore Theatre in 1936. Overnight Shaw was acclaimed as a promising young playwright.

The plot of *Bury the Dead* is simple. In "the second year of the war that is to begin tomorrow night," six dead soldiers refuse to be buried, arguing that society has never given them an opportunity to fulfill their lives. Despite appeals from members of their families and commands from their superior officers, the soldiers do not budge in their convictions. At the end of the play the soldiers and the gravediggers walk off the stage, dramatizing their hatred of war. Leslie Fiedler, writing in *Commentary,* said of the production: "I can remember with embarrassing clarity screaming in ecstasy as the soldiers walked portentously across the stage at the end of *Bury the Dead;* it seemed a play written for me and for my friends, *our* play." Shaw wrote many plays after this, including the moderately successful *The Gentle People* (1939), but none compared in popularity with *Bury the Dead.*

In the next few years Shaw wrote dozens of short stories for the *New Yorker, Collier's,* and *Esquire,* twenty of which were brought together in his first collection of short stories entitled *Sailor Off the Bremen* (1939). Until then he had been viewed primarily as a playwright, but this new collection confirmed his talent as a short story writer as well. Some of his most famous stories appeared here, including the title story, "The Girls in Their Summer Dresses," "The Boss," and "The Second Mortgage." Critics agreed that Shaw was at his best with stories dealing with characters and scenes from large cities, particularly New York.

A few stories reveal his strong social consciousness. In "Sailor Off the Bremen," Ernest, an American artist and an idealistic Communist, has lost an eye and had his face disfigured by a Nazi tough. Ernest's younger brother, a football hero, seeks revenge for what has happened to Ernest. Shaw's description of the bloody fight between Ernest's brother and the Nazi becomes a graphic dramatization on a small scale of the clash between the forces of Teutonic fascism and communism.

Most of these early stories, however, are simple tales with no higher message. Gould Cassal, writing in the *Saturday Review,* noted: "Shaw is chiefly interested in the henpecked Jewish tailor, the young wife who cannot control her jealousy, the bartender who values his professional integrity above money, the world-weary taxi drivers, and others who are part of New York City's seven million. You may read your own lessons into them. Sympathy, honesty, and lack of pretension in 'Sailor Off the Bremen' give this young playwright an auspicious debut as a short-story writer."

Shaw's new career was interrupted by World War II. He enlisted in the armed forces in 1942 and rose from private to warrant officer in the United States Army Signal Corps. He served in Africa, France, England, and Germany. When the war was over in 1945, he began working on his first and most famous novel, *The Young Lions* (1948). While working on this novel he served as drama critic for the *New Republic* in 1947-1948 and he taught creative writing at New York University in 1948-1949.

Months before the publication of *The Young Lions* critics were writing advance reviews, predicting it would be the best novel to come out of the war. The action covers the period from New Year's Eve 1938 until Hitler's war machine was crushed in 1945. It deals with the lives of three soldiers, two Americans and one German. They are Michael Whitacre, a stage manager who has grown disillusioned with the theater in Hollywood and New York; Noah Ackerman, a young introverted Jew who at the beginning of the war has found happiness in a recent marriage; and Christian Diestl, an Austrian ski instructor who has joined the Nazi party. The drama of their lives, their joys and sorrows, acts of cowardice, examples of bravery, are all played out against the backdrop of World War II. Finally in 1945, as the war draws to a close, the three men confront each other outside a concentration camp in Germany. There Michael finds meaning beyond all the bloodshed which has consumed his life for the last four years. He realizes if struggle and sacrifice will bring about the survival of a few men of decency, then all their hardships have been worth the cost.

In *The Young Lions* Shaw reveals again and again his eye for detail, especially in his descriptions of army life in the barracks and in war scenes such as Rommel's retreat, which one critic compared with Hemingway's sketch in *A Farewell to Arms* of the Italians' flight at Caporetto in World War I. Lee Rogow, writing in the *Saturday Review of Literature,* said: "Shaw has turned out a fine, full intelligent book, packed with wonderful talk and crackling writing. We have waited a long time for this novel of Irwin Shaw's. In *The Young Lions* he reveals in even greater stature the delicious wit, the dramatic sense of scene-making, and the full-hearted comparison of his short stories."

The idea for Shaw's second novel, *The Troubled Air* (1951), occurred when he learned that a radio producer had been advised to fire several people from his show because of their alleged leftist persuasions. In the novel the central character, Clement Archer, who runs the news program "University Town," is in a similar predicament. Five members of his panel have been labeled Communists by a right-wing newspaper and Archer must determine the truth of these accusations.

The Troubled Air focused on Archer as the well-intentioned seeker for truth. There are perceptive insights into the workings of the Communist mind and the tactics employed by right-of-center business groups. But Lionel Trilling found the book wanting as a novel: "whatever political satisfaction *The Troubled Air* may give, it gives but little pleasure as a work of fiction. What it tells us of the ordeal of its hero, Clement Archer, is adequate for a political morality but not for a novel."

Shortly after the publication of *The Troubled Air* Shaw decided to make his home in Europe, dividing his time between his apartment in Paris and his chalet in Klosters, Switzerland, a ski resort.

His stay outside of the United States had lasted so long that one critic suggested he no longer could write about America because he had lost touch with all the changes that had taken place in the last thirty years. In an interview in the *Paris Review*, Shaw answered that criticism: "The charge that I've become less American is ridiculous because I went back and forth all the time. I think I gained a whole lot of insight by living in Europe, and my books reflect it: *Lucy Crown*, for example, *Two Weeks in Another Town*, *Evening in Byzantium*, *Rich Man, Poor Man*, *Nightwork*, *Beggarman, Thief* would never have been written if it hadn't been for that European experience."

The first novel that Shaw wrote as an expatriate was *Lucy Crown* (1956). At the beginning of the narrative he sets forth a premise, which provides the underlying psychology of the book: "When we look back into the past, we recognize a moment in time which was decisive, at which the pattern of our lives changed, a moment at which we moved irrevocably off in a new direction." In *Lucy Crown*, this turning point occurred for Tony Crown when he witnessed his mother seducing his friend. As a result, Tony is sent to boarding school, and it is almost twenty years before a reconciliation takes place between mother and son.

Most of the critics found *Lucy Crown* too slick and contrived. More than once it was compared with daytime soap operas. But Charles Rolo, writing in the *New York Times Book Review*, thought otherwise: "Mr. Shaw's adventure into fresh territory, it is pleasant to report, has produced a continuously absorbing book—sharply drawn, highly charged and painfully moving."

During the 1960s Shaw wrote two novels, *Two Weeks in Another Town* (1960) and *Voices of a Summer Day* (1965). Generally neither book was well received by the critics. Shaw's novels were frequently compared unfavorably with his superb short stories of the 1930s and 1940s. He was called a facile novelist during this time, a writer who made no effort to create three-dimensional characters, while at his peak as a short story writer, some of his work could be compared with the best of Hemingway and Fitzgerald.

But with the publication of *Rich Man, Poor Man* (1970), the critics were more enthusiastic. This novel is large, even longer than *The Young Lions*, and covers the three decades from 1940 to 1970. The setting moves from Hollywood to New York to Paris. The central characters are the three children of Axel Jordache, a baker who resides near the Hudson River. He has two sons, Rudolph and Thomas, and a daughter, Gretchen. Rudolph is the hardworking, good, intellectual member of the family while his brother is belligerent, aggressive, and at times cruel. Gretchen is a cross between the two.

In the end, ironically, it is Thomas who achieves success and love in his life. Gretchen compromises her life through a series of cheap love affairs, and Rudolph is left unhappy by a wife who does not love him. W. G. Rogers, writing in the *New York Times*, said: "A wealth of know-how has gone into the fictional creation; even today, few of our younger technicians can beat Irwin Shaw's expertise. . . . Shaw whisks us off from a standing start to a velocity well beyond familiar limits. His pace doesn't slacken for chapter after chapter. Incidents lead to incidents—and they are uncommonly appealing."

During the 1970s Shaw wrote four novels—*Evening in Byzantium* (1973), *Nightwork* (1975), *Beggarman, Thief* (1977, a sequel to his *Rich Man, Poor Man*), *The Top of the Hill* (1979)—and several short stories. Of these four novels the best is *Evening in Byzantium*. It tells the story of a once-successful producer of plays and movies, Jesse Craig, who in the past few years has become unproductive. He travels to the Riviera at the time of the Cannes Film Festival in 1970, where he mixes with celebrities from all over the world. He arrives with more than his share of problems. He is separated from his wife, and the IRS is auditing his finances. While at the film festival, he meets a young journalist named Gail McKinnon and, with her help, explores his past. All of the novel takes place in the mind of Craig, and the reader soon finds himself concerned about the protagonist. Essentially *Evening in Byzantium* is the search for lost identity in the most unlikely setting of the lights and glitter of a film festival. Reviewer James R. Frakes noted: "There's something very reassuring about watching a really professional writer at work again, especially a veteran like Irwin Shaw, who knows his way around in many worlds—literature, publishing, movies, theater, international society, velvet robed restaurants and Third Avenue saloons—and who can handle the details of a business deal, an ulcer operation and a bedroom scene with equal aplomb and economical nonexploitation."

In the last five years of his life Shaw wrote a two-part television program, "The Top of the Hill," which was broadcast in February 1980. Three of his short stories, including the classic "The Girls in Their Summer Dresses," were shown on public television the following year. He also contributed the text for *Paris/Magnum: Photographs, 1935-1981* (1981), a collection of prints by world-famous photographers, and wrote his last two novels, *Bread Upon the Waters* (1981) and *Acceptable Losses* (1982).

Bread Upon the Waters is a novel about the breakdown of a family brought about largely by the unexpected intervention of an outsider. The Strand family appears in every way to be a close and happy one. Allen Strand, the father, has been teaching in the New York public school system for over twenty-seven years. His wife, Leslie, gives music lessons and paints watercolors. They have three children: Jimmy, an aspiring rock performer; Caroline, who is finishing up her senior year in high school; and the oldest, Eleanor, who at twenty-two has found a job in an advertising firm where she earns a larger salary than her father.

The harmony of the Strand family is dramatically and permanently disrupted by an unforeseen incident one late afternoon. After playing

Revised typescript page from Bread Upon the Waters

477

a few sets of tennis, Caroline starts to return home through Central Park. On the way she sees a man being attacked by three teenage boys. Immediately she enters the fight, giving one of the boys a nasty gash on the head with her metal tennis racket. Terrified, the boys release their victim and run away. Then Caroline manages to lead the injured man back to her apartment, where the whole family takes care of him.

The real action of the novel begins with the entrance of Russel Hazen, the victim of the mugging. After a while the Strands discover that Hazen is no ordinary person, but a prominent businessman and internationally known philanthropist. Overcome with gratitude for Caroline's help, Hazen is determined to repay her. Everyone in the Strand family is showered with an unending array of gifts beginning with tickets to a concert and followed by an invitation to Hazen's estate on Long Island. Hazen even manages to insinuate himself into the everyday life of the family. He finds a man who signs up rock performers and has Jimmy get in touch with him. Aware that Caroline has promise as a runner, he encourages her to practice daily so that she can win an athletic scholarship to college.

The suspense of Shaw's story rests on the reader's attempt to unravel the motives lying behind Hazen's good deeds. There is the strong feeling throughout that something awful will happen. The climax occurs in a small restaurant in the Loire Valley of France, where Hazen has invited his closest friends, including Leslie and Allen Strand, to a sumptuous dinner. While they are there an unexpected visitor arrives—Hazen's wife. Threatening to scream if anyone tries to leave, she holds the group spellbound while she describes her life with Hazen. He is responsible, she charges, for neglecting their marriage, spoiling their children, and engaging in dishonest business deals. When she finishes, she presents her husband with two options: either he will grant her a divorce with full possession of the Southampton estate, or she will commit suicide and ruin his reputation. Shaw describes the scene with painful clarity; the whole ugly episode is credible because of the earlier hints of impending disaster. The remainder of the story is anticlimactic. A series of unhappy events befalls Hazen and the Strands and explains Shaw's intended biblical quotation in the epigraph: "Cast thy bread upon the waters, for thou shall find it after many days."

Most critics praised Shaw's novel, arguing that it was of higher quality than the novels he had written earlier in the 1970s. Evan Hunter, writing

in the *New York Times Book Review* (23 August 1981), was especially enthusiastic: "The blending of a fast-paced story with thoughtful introspection . . . is executed with seeming effortlessness by the author—a sure sign that he has worked long and hard to master his craft. The prose is clean and spare, perfectly suited to the deceivingly plain tale he appears to be telling. The first chapter alone could be taught in creative writing courses across the land as a model of concise exposition."

There is at least one striking resemblance between *Bread Upon the Waters* and *Acceptable Losses*. In each, a single incident determines the course of the action. In the earlier novel it is Caroline's successful endeavor to save Hazen from injury. In *Acceptable Losses*, a phone call in the middle of the night is the starting point of Shaw's tale.

Roger Damon lives with his second wife, Sheila, in New York City. Now in his mid sixties, he has been working in a literary agency for over twenty years. Very late one Saturday evening when his wife is visiting her mother in Vermont, he is awakened by an ominous telephone call. At first he wonders if it might not be a practical joke played by an old friend visiting the city. It is soon made clear, however, that the call is no joke. Someone who identifies himself as Zalovsky insists that Roger meet him outside his apartment in fifteen minutes. Although Roger remains in his apartment and pretends the call is unimportant, it is obvious that he is deeply shaken.

For the next few weeks Roger's life abruptly changes. At first he tries to keep what has happened a secret. But after manuscripts go unread and arguments flare up with his wife, he finally tells her about the phone call. Now in earnest to find out who Zalovsky really is, Roger hires a private detective, who suggests his client draw up a list of possible personal and professional enemies. Much of the novel revolves around Roger's attempt to discover if anyone on his list is in fact out to get him. The story sustains high suspense until the identity of Zalovsky is uncovered.

The critics were not altogether friendly toward *Acceptable Losses*. The majority noted that Shaw seemed to devote an undue amount of attention to symbolism relating to death and disease, to the extent that it became a distraction. They also agreed that the central theme, Roger's search for the real Zalovsky, was often relegated to the background, leaving the reader wondering what the book was really about. John Jay Osborn, Jr., observed in the *New York Times:* "If the extraneous parts of this novel had been deleted by a crafty editor, 'Acceptable Losses' would have been a great short story." *Acceptable Losses* was Shaw's last work. He died of a heart attack at the age of seventy-one in Davos, Switzerland. Although his health had been poor during the past few years, he had continued to write to the end. He had always maintained that while most people retire, writers never do. From the window in his hospital room, he could see in the distance the mountains he used to ski down when he was younger. On his bedside table were Byron's *Poems* and Mann's *Buddenbrooks*.

At the time of Shaw's death, many mourned his passing and recalled his generosity to beginning writers. Gay Talese especially remembered the kindness and encouragement he got from Shaw: "He was so giving to young writers all over Europe and in the United States. . . . I met him in 1955, when I was in Paris and just a soldier, and he was as nice to me as he would have been to a John Steinbeck or to a Gary Cooper. I was obscure, unknown. He made you feel that you were on his level, even if you weren't. Generosity is the word. In his house in Switzerland, in his apartment in Paris, along the cafes of the Via Veneto in Rome, in the Hamptons, in the Ritz Hotel in New York, wherever he was, when you were with Irwin Shaw you felt that some of the energy and optimism of that man was infectious."

The consensus among authors concerning Shaw's place in American letters has not altered over the years. He is considered to have held great promise when he was starting out. Many believed that as a short story writer Shaw would one day be viewed as Hemingway's successor. But the publication of *The Young Lions* in 1948 was the great turning point in his writing career. That novel not only brought glowing reviews which compared his work with Norman Mailer's *The Naked and the Dead* and James Jones's *From Here to Eternity*, but it enabled Shaw to rise above a hand-to-mouth existence as a struggling author. The critics argue that Shaw then decided he could earn big money writing best-sellers and traded his integrity as a writer for slick novels and life among the beautiful people.

This remains the consensus today. Shaw did, for the most part, give up the short story and concentrate on the novel during the last forty years of his writing career. But he always worked hard at his craft. At some future date perhaps he will be remembered not as an author who early in life compromised his principles to make a fortune but as one of America's best storytellers—which he was.

Irwin Shaw (photo by Women's Wear Daily*)*

Interviews:
"The Art of Fiction, IV," *Paris Review,* 1 (1953): 27-49;
"The Art of Fiction, IV," *Paris Review,* 21 (Spring 1979): 248-262.

References:
John W. Aldridge, *After the Last Generation* (New York: McGraw-Hill, 1951);
　　Delivers a negative assessment of Shaw's first novel, *The Young Lions.*

Chester E. Eisinger, *Fiction of the Forties* (Chicago: University of Chicago Press, 1963), pp. 106-113;
　　A reassessment of Shaw's liberal stance in his early novels and short stories.

Bergen Evans, "Irwin Shaw," *English Journal,* 40 (November 1951): 485-491;
　　A study of Shaw's earlier plays and his first two novels, *The Young Lions* and *The Troubled Air.*

Leslie Fiedler, "Irwin Shaw: Adultery, The Last Politics," *Commentary,* 22 (July 1956): 71-74;
　　Fiedler regrets Shaw's betrayal of his high

principles of the 1930s and the lapse of his prose into sentimental jargon.

Herbert Mitgang, "Irwin Shaw, Near 70, Adds It Up and Feels 'Right,' " *New York Times,* 17 February 1983, III: 21;
At the age of seventy, Shaw reminisces over the highlights of his life from his school days to the present.

Mitgang, "Irwin Shaw, Writer, Is Dead; Acclaimed for Short Stories," *New York Times,* 17 May 1984, pp. 1, 47;
Obituary which lists the achievements of Shaw and furnishes a biographical sketch.

Roy Newquist, *Counterpoint* (New York: Rand McNally, 1964), pp. 543-551;
Interview with Shaw about his career as a writer. Shaw talks about his books and other writers and furnishes advice to young writers.

William Startt, "Irwin Shaw: An Extended Talent," *Midwest Quarterly,* 2 (1961): 325-337;
Argues that Shaw's real skill lies in the short story and not the novel.

Ross Wetzsteon, "Irwin Shaw: The Conflict Between Bucks and Good Books," *Saturday Review,* 8 (August 1981): 12, 14, 16, 17;
Challenges the myth that Shaw sacrificed his writing for big money; finds the author has been a literary craftsman all along.

Papers:
Collections of Shaw's papers can be found at Boston University, at Pierpont Morgan Library, and at Brooklyn College.

Isaac Bashevis Singer

This entry was updated from the entry by Barbara Frey Waxman (University of North Carolina at Wilmington) in DLB 28, Twentieth-Century American-Jewish Fiction Writers.

Places	New York City	Warsaw	Polish *Shtetls*
Influences and Relationships	Fyodor Dostoyevski Aaron Zeitlen	Israel Joshua Singer	Hans Christian Andersen
Literary Movements and Forms	Realism	Yiddish Literature	Jewish Folklore
Major Themes	Passions and Obsessions Sexual vs. Sacred Love	Perpetual Exile/ Rootlessness Doubt vs. Faith	Search for God Coincidence vs. Miracle
Cultural and Artistic Influences	Judaism	Mysticism	Hebrew Religious Texts
Social and Economic Influences	Jewish Immigration to the United States	Anti-Semitism	The Holocaust

See also the Singer entries in DLB 6, American Novelists Since World War II, *and* DLB 52, American Writers for Children Since 1960: Fiction.

BIRTH: Radzymin, Poland, 14 July 1904, to Pinchos Menachem and Bathsheba Zylberman Singer.

EDUCATION: Tachkemoni Rabbinical Seminary, 1920-1927.

MARRIAGES: Rachel (divorced; date and last name unknown); child: Israel. 14 February 1940, to Alma Haimann.

AWARDS AND HONORS: Louis Lamed Prizes for *The Family Moskat,* 1950, and for *Satan in Goray,* 1956; National Institute of Arts and Letters and American Academy Award in Literature, 1959; Harry and Ethel Daroff Memorial Fiction Award (Jewish Book Council of America) for *The Slave,* 1963; D.H.L., Hebrew Union College, 1963; National Council on the Arts Grant, 1966; National Endowment for the Arts Grant, 1966-1967; *Playboy* magazine award, 1967; Newbery Honor Book Awards for *Zlateh the Goat and Other Stories,* 1967, and for *The Fearsome Inn,* 1968; Bancarella Prize for Italian translation of *The Family Moskat,* 1968; Brandeis University Creative Arts Medal for Poetry-Fiction, 1970; National Book Awards for *A Day of Pleasure,* 1970, and for *A Crown of Feathers and Other Stories,* 1974; D.Litt., Texas Christian University, 1972; D.Litt., Colgate University, 1972; Ph.D., Hebrew University (Israel), 1973; Litt.D., Bard College, 1974; Agnon Gold Medal, 1975; Nobel Prize for Literature, 1978.

SELECTED BOOKS*: *The Family Moskat,* translated by A. H. Gross (New York: Knopf, 1950; London: Secker & Warburg, 1966);
Satan in Goray, translated by Jacob Sloan (New York: Noonday, 1955; London: Owen, 1958);
Gimpel the Fool and Other Stories, translated by Saul Bellow and others (New York: Noonday, 1957; London: Owen, 1958);
The Magician of Lublin, translated by Elaine Gottlieb and Joseph Singer (New York: Noonday, 1960; London: Secker & Warburg, 1961);
The Spinoza of Market Street, translated by Martha Glicklich, Cecil Hemley, and others (New York: Farrar, Straus & Cudahy, 1961; London: Secker & Warburg, 1962);

* This list includes only books published in English.

Isaac Bashevis Singer (photo by Layle Silbert)

The Slave, translated by Isaac Bashevis Singer and Hemley (New York: Farrar, Straus & Cudahy, 1962; London: Secker & Warburg, 1963);
Short Friday and Other Stories, translated by Joseph Singer and others (New York: Farrar, Straus & Giroux, 1964; London: Secker & Warburg, 1967);
In My Father's Court, translated by Channah Kleinerman-Goldstein, Gottlieb, and Joseph Singer (New York: Farrar, Straus & Giroux, 1966; London: Secker & Warburg, 1967);
Zlateh the Goat and Other Stories, translated by Elizabeth Shub and Isaac Bashevis Singer (New York: Harper & Row, 1966; London: Secker & Warburg, 1967);
Selected Short Stories of Isaac Bashevis Singer, edited by Irving Howe (New York: Modern Library, 1966);
Mazel and Shlimazel, Or the Milk of a Lioness, translated by Shub and Isaac Bashevis Singer (New

York: Farrar, Straus & Giroux, 1967; London: Cape, 1979);

The Manor, translated by Joseph Singer and Gottlieb (New York: Farrar, Straus & Giroux, 1967; London: Secker & Warburg, 1969);

The Fearsome Inn, translated by Shub and Isaac Bashevis Singer (New York: Scribners, 1967; London: Collins, 1970);

When Shlemiel Went to Warsaw & Other Stories, translated by Isaac Bashevis Singer and Shub (New York: Farrar, Straus & Giroux, 1968; London: Longman Young Books, 1974);

The Séance and Other Stories, translated by Roger H. Klein, Hemley, and others (New York: Farrar, Straus & Giroux, 1968; London: Cape, 1970);

A Day of Pleasure: Stories of a Boy Growing Up in Warsaw, translated by Kleinerman-Goldstein and others (New York: Farrar, Straus & Giroux, 1969; London: McRae, 1980);

The Estate, translated by Joseph Singer, Gottlieb, and Shub (New York: Farrar, Straus & Giroux, 1969; London: Cape, 1970);

Elijah the Slave, translated by Isaac Bashevis Singer and Shub (New York: Farrar, Straus & Giroux, 1970);

Joseph and Koza, Or the Sacrifice to the Vistula, translated by Isaac Bashevis Singer and Shub (New York: Farrar, Straus & Giroux, 1970);

A Friend of Kafka and Other Stories, translated by Isaac Bashevis Singer, Shub, and others (New York: Farrar, Straus & Giroux, 1970; London: Cape, 1972);

An Isaac Bashevis Singer Reader (New York: Farrar, Straus & Giroux, 1971);

Alone in the Wild Forest, translated by Isaac Bashevis Singer and Shub (New York: Farrar, Straus & Giroux, 1971);

The Topsy-Turvy Emperor of China, translated by Isaac Bashevis Singer and Shub (New York, Evanston, San Francisco & London: Harper & Row, 1971);

Enemies, A Love Story, translated by Aliza Shevrin and Shub (New York: Farrar, Straus & Giroux, 1972; London: Cape, 1972);

The Wicked City, translated by Isaac Bashevis Singer and Shub (New York: Farrar, Straus & Giroux, 1972);

A Crown of Feathers and Other Stories, translated by Isaac Bashevis Singer, Laurie Colwin, and others (New York: Farrar, Straus & Giroux, 1973; London: Cape, 1974);

The Hasidim, illustrations by Ira Moskowitz (New York: Crown, 1973);

The Fools of Chelm and Their History, translated by Isaac Bashevis Singer and Shub (New York: Farrar, Straus & Giroux, 1973; London: Abelard-Schuman, 1974);

Why Noah Chose the Dove, translated by Shub (New York: Farrar, Straus & Giroux, 1974);

Passions and Other Stories, translated by Isaac Bashevis Singer and others (New York: Farrar, Straus & Giroux, 1975; London: Cape, 1976);

A Tale of Three Wishes (New York: Farrar, Straus & Giroux, 1975);

A Little Boy in Search of God: Mysticism in a Personal Light, illustrations by Moskowitz (Garden City: Doubleday, 1976);

Naftali the Storyteller and His Horse, Sus, and Other Stories, translated by Joseph Singer, Isaac Bashevis Singer, and others (New York: Farrar, Straus & Giroux, 1976; Oxford: Oxford University Press, 1977);

Yentl, by Singer and Leah Napolin (New York, Hollywood, London & Toronto: French, 1977);

A Young Man in Search of Love, translated by Joseph Singer (Garden City: Doubleday, 1978);

Shosha, translated by Joseph Singer and Isaac Bashevis Singer (New York: Farrar, Straus & Giroux, 1978; London: Cape, 1979);

Old Love, translated by Joseph Singer, Isaac Bashevis Singer, and others (New York: Farrar, Straus & Giroux, 1979; London: Cape, 1980);

Nobel Lecture (New York: Farrar, Straus & Giroux, 1979; London: Cape, 1979);

The Power of Light; Eight Stories for Hanukkah (New York: Farrar, Straus & Giroux, 1980; London: Robson, 1983);

Reaches of Heaven: A Story of the Baal Shem Tov (New York: Farrar, Straus & Giroux, 1980);

Lost in America (Garden City: Doubleday, 1981);

The Meaning of Freedom (West Point, N.Y.: U.S. Military Academy, 1981);

The Collected Stories of Isaac Bashevis Singer (New York: Farrar, Straus & Giroux, 1982; London: Cape, 1982);

The Golem (New York: Farrar, Straus & Giroux, 1982; London: Deutsch, 1983);

My Personal Conception of Religion (Lafayette, La.: University of Southwestern Louisiana Press, 1982);

One Day of Happiness (New York: Red Ozier Press, 1982);

Isaac Bashevis Singer: Three Complete Novels (New York: Avenel Books, 1982)—includes *The Slave; Enemies, A Love Story;* and *Shosha;*

Love & Exile: A Memoir (Garden City: Doubleday, 1984);

Stories for Children (New York: Farrar, Straus & Giroux, 1984);

The Image and Other Stories (New York: Farrar, Straus & Giroux, 1985).

In his novels and short stories, Isaac Bashevis Singer has created a world of ghosts, dybbuks, witches, and demons, a world of eccentric people strongly rooted in the *shtetls* of Poland and of disoriented émigrés haunted by memories of the *shtetls* as they walk the streets of Manhattan or Miami Beach. Singer has created a world that reaches beyond the perimeters of traditional Yiddish literature, of people yearning for erotic love and of people possessed by perverse or even demonic kinds of love. His fictional universe has fascinated readers from America to Japan and has carved for Singer a permanent niche both in Yiddish literature and in the literary history of the world—a niche strengthened by his winning two National Book Awards and the 1978 Nobel Prize for Literature. Singer writes his works in Yiddish, often having them serialized in the Yiddish newspaper the *Jewish Daily Forward* before they are translated into English, often by him in collaboration with his editors. He not only writes fiction but for the past forty-five years he has also written free-lance articles, reviews, and essays for the *Jewish Daily Forward*. More recently he has also contributed to such magazines as *Commentary, Esquire, Midstream,* and the *New Yorker*.

Singer was born in Radzymin, Poland, the son and grandson of rabbis who intended for him to become a religious scholar. He and his family moved to Warsaw when Singer was four, and he grew up there except for spending three years in his grandfather's village of Bilgoray when he was an adolescent. Experiences in Bilgoray later became the subjects of many of Singer's tales of *shtetl* life. Influenced by his older brother Israel Joshua, who later achieved prominence as a Yiddish novelist, Singer dramatically shifted his interests from sacred to secular writing. He followed his brother to America in 1935, leaving behind him a wife and a son. He settled in New York City and launched his career by associating with the *Jewish Daily Forward*. In 1937 Singer met a German-Jewish immigrant woman named Alma Haimann, who became his wife three years later. He and Alma still live on New York City's Upper West Side. They also spend part of their time in their Surfside, Florida, condominium, and they travel several times a year to Israel, where his son by his first marriage, Israel Zamir (*zamir* is Hebrew for *singer*), lives with his

wife and Singer's four grandchildren. Zamir, a journalist for *Al Hamishmar,* frequently translates his father's works into Hebrew for publication in Israel. Besides still actively writing, Singer frequently lectures at such different places as Bard College in New York, Virginia Commonwealth University in Richmond, Washington Hebrew Congregation in Washington, D.C., and Hebrew University in Jerusalem.

Although Singer has most frequently written about Jewish folklore and life in the Polish *shtetls,* in recent years he has begun to set some of his tales in America. These American tales will be the main concern here, but to understand them properly, it is important to note the atmosphere and major themes of Singer's fictional works and memoirs rooted in the Polish *shtetls* and the Warsaw ghetto. These works range from his first serious novel, *Satan in Goray,* published in Poland in 1935 (and in English translation twenty years later), in which the protagonist, a cabalist, is possessed by Satan and by his own passion for the occult, while his village, Goray, is possessed by the "false messianism" rampant in seventeenth-century Poland, to *The Family Moskat* (1950), a realistic epic novel which, together with *The Manor* (1967) and *The Estate* (1969), forms a trilogy that Samuel H. Joseloff has described as "covering the Polish Jewish communities from the insurrections of 1863 until the Nazi conquest of 1939." These works, Singer's hundreds of short stories, and his memoirs of his boyhood, *In My Father's Court* (1966), enable us, says Joseloff, "to take . . . [a] journey into the past" of Jewish religious tradition, culture, and folklore. Other realistic novels, *The Magician of Lublin* (1960), set in nineteenth-century Poland, and *The Slave* (1962), set in seventeenth-century Poland, complete Singer's portrait of the Polish-Jewish past.

In many of these works, Singer's main characters struggle with intense, even pathological passions or obsessions which are frequently depicted as visitations by Satan or other demons and dybbuks, Singer's "spiritual stenography"—his own words—for his characters' psychological problems and often enigmatic behavior. Eroticism, "the weakness of the flesh," is also a prominent motif in these works; love and its transcendent power are treated with profound respect by Singer. In addition to the subject of passion, epistemological questions about truth and reality ("Is this life a dream?") also preoccupy Singer's characters, among them the protagonist-narrator of Singer's much admired short story "Gimpel the Fool" (collected in *Gimpel the Fool and Other Stories,* 1957). The "divine fool"

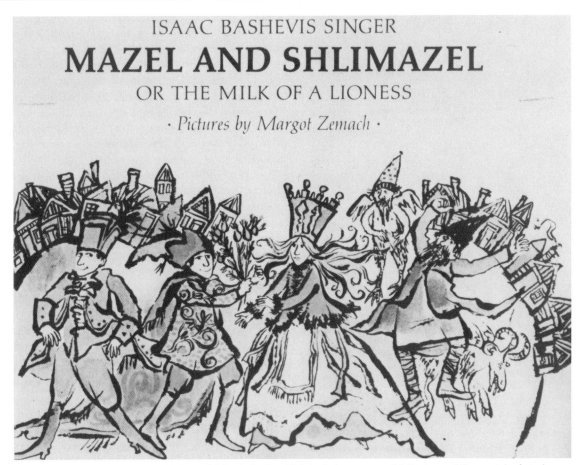

Cover for one of Singer's best-selling children's books which includes re-created folktales and three original stories
(Farrar, Straus & Giroux)

Gimpel, though apparently easily deceived by his wife and fellow townsmen of Frampol, apprehends some profound and touching truths about love, reality, evil in human beings, and spiritual faith. Other collections of stories, such as *The Spinoza of Market Street* (1961) and *Short Friday and Other Stories* (1964), embrace this wide range of topics and feature Singer's rich Jewish folk characterizations. They display a rootedness in the *shtetl*, in Jewish folklore, in Jewish religious ritual, in Jewish history, in the past.

Given the intense attachment of his protagonists to the past and to their European-Jewish roots, it is no wonder, then, that when Singer shifts the locus in some of his more recent stories to America, his European immigrant characters are usually depicted as suffering the torments of dislocation and deracination. Some twenty-five short stories and three novels take place in American settings, usually in New York City and its suburbs, Miami Beach, or the Catskill Mountains. Prominent

in these American tales is the theme of disorientation, or "lostness." Leslie Fiedler has said that Singer's Yiddish-speaking émigrés to America usually view themselves as being in perpetual exile; for these protagonists, America is a limbo and they are lost "semi-ghosts." Perhaps Singer's preoccupation with the themes of lostness and rootlessness reflects his own disorientation when he arrived in America as a young man. In an interview with Richard Burgin, which appeared in two installments in the *New York Times Magazine* just after Singer won the Nobel Prize, Singer described his emotional state as that of a "greenhorn": "I felt that I had been torn out of my roots and that I would never grow any roots in this country." This concern with roots is apparent in most of Singer's American stories. In the Burgin interview, Singer claims that a writer must acknowledge his roots, or he fails as a writer: "No assimilationist can be a great writer."

Singer's nonassimilated lost souls are often actively in search of God, while doubting His good-

Singer at Stockholm's Concert Hall receiving the Nobel Prize from King Carl XVI Gustaf (The Jewish Daily Forward)

ness. They are also frequently in quest of love, of union with a possessed, witchlike woman, a "metaphysical joining of male and female flesh," says Fiedler, "which goes beyond erotic mysticism of the *Zohar* into the realm of heresy." These American stories, like some of their European predecessors, are often preoccupied with forbidden passion, especially incest, and with the interrelationship between the sexual and the sacred. Are these stories of passion perhaps a tribute to his own passionate relationship with Alma, his wife of over four decades? Certainly there is a personal tone in these tales, since they are frequently narrated by a first-person narrator-protagonist, Singer's persona. The tone of this narrator is more often than not ironic, and the irony is occasionally aimed playfully against the narrator himself.

Most of all, Singer is concerned with being a spellbinding storyteller. In his Nobel Prize lecture, he declares that the masterful storyteller "must be an entertainer of the spirit . . . literally [must] intrigue the reader, uplift his spirit, give him the joy and escape that true art always grants." Although

Singer is often criticized for being a skeptic or a pessimist, he claims he is, rather, a truth seeker; in his Nobel lecture he says, "While the poet entertains he continues to search for eternal truths . . . he tries to solve the riddle of time and change, to find an answer to suffering, to reveal love in the very abyss of cruelty and injustice." Noting these words, it is no wonder that love's idealized, redemptive power is central among Singer's literary concerns.

Love, lostness, and a search for faith are all themes of *Enemies, A Love Story* (1972). The protagonist Herman Broder is the epitome of the alienated and disoriented émigré, the "semi-ghost." He is, appropriately, a ghostwriter, producing sermons and essays for a spiritually underdeveloped rabbi. Yet not only is he a ghostwriter but he is also, as Fiedler suggests, literally a "ghost who writes," vanishing at the end of the novel without a trace. His ghostliness seems to have something to do with his being a Holocaust survivor who is haunted by his past. Broder's Holocaust experiences are the main reason for his alienation from American-Jewish society. Edward Alexander notes that Broder's "unease in American Jewish society" may be due to American Jewry's failure to save East European Jews during World War II. Broder's contact with American Jews who have never been touched by the Holocaust inspires him only "with revulsion and a metaphysical disgust at worldly existence." American-Jewish life repels him with its vulgarity and materialism and its incomprehension of the Holocaust survivor's experiences and mentality.

Tormented by recurrent dreams of Nazi horrors, Broder seeks escape through reckless hedonism in an affair with another Holocaust survivor, Masha. His Gentile wife, Yadwiga, cannot be the object of his love. But he knows his empty pursuit of pleasure with Masha must be abandoned as he struggles to form a commitment to God, Torah, and the Talmud. However, his commitment to Judaism is never really affirmed, largely because it cannot be sustained in the insubstantial American-Jewish cultural environment, which, the novel claims, has as its "aim to ape the Gentile." As Alexander aptly surmises, "nothing remains to him [Broder] but a spiritually inconclusive petering out." Ironically, only the Gentile Yadwiga realizes the importance of the Jewish people's preservation. Her giving birth to Broder's child—although Broder does not know it—will be, Alexander points out, "an affirmation that no member of the family of nations shall be removed from the world to satisfy the blood-lust of another member." Fiedler has

486

Singer in Israel, 1970s

characterized *Enemies, A Love Story,* especially because of its ending, as an "eminently astonishing, terrifying and satisfactory book."

Most critics agree that it is in the short story form that Singer really excels. Remarking on Singer's "swift and dramatic" style, Irving Howe and Eliezer Greenberg say, "He is at his best in short forms, exciting bursts and flares of imagination." Singer himself acknowledges that for him the short story is more perfectible and controllable: "A short story is a lot easier to plan, and it can be more perfect, more accomplished, than a novel." Many critics, furthermore, consider his novels as traditional, while reading his short stories, as Alexander suggests, as "modernist excursions into diabolism, perversity, and apocalypse. . . ." Certainly some of these excursions are apparent in the stories which Singer sets in America. Stories selected from two of his collections, *Old Love* (1979) and *Passions and Other Stories* (1975), serve as examples.

As Singer explains in the author's note to *Old Love,* the title *Old Love* comes from a story collected in *Passions* but not republished here; love, Singer continues, is "the only hope of mankind"; the

source of all love is "love of life." Three stories in the collection, "A Party in Miami Beach," "There Are No Coincidences," and "The Psychic Journey," explore love among the aging, but the love seems to be perverse, disturbing, entrapping or absurd, hardly reassuring if it is the "only hope of mankind." The stories may, however, suggest the sense of dislocation of European Jews in American society.

"A Party in Miami Beach" is one of Singer's many tales about a Holocaust survivor, only this survivor, Max Flederbush, has become a multimillionaire in America. His wealth no longer brings him solace after he loses his family in an automobile accident. Like Herman Broder, Max wavers between faith and doubt, saying, "Well, but that's how man is—he believes and he doubts." Such an attitude toward religion reflects Singer's own: "Since there is no evidence attesting to what God is, I doubt all the time. Doubt is part of all religion."

The first-person narrator of the story is a much lionized writer, a vegetarian, Singer's persona. Flederbush, an admirer of his, gives a cocktail party in his honor and then treats him to dinner

Dust jacket for Singer's 1975 collection of twenty stories. In the author's note Singer describes his characters—"the Jews of East-ern Europe, specifically the Yiddish-speaking Jews who perished in Poland and those who emigrated to the U.S.A. The longer I live with them and write about them, the more I am baffled by the richness of their individuality and (since I am one of them) by my own whims and passions."

at an elegant restaurant. In the midst of this luxury, however, Flederbush extols the virtues of the con-centration camps: "in a certain sense, it's worse here than in the camps. There, at least, we all hoped." He contrasts the camp inmates' optimism to the hopelessness and purposelessness of the wealthy retired Miami Beach Jews, who sit around waiting to die.

Somehow Max Flederbush does not really live in Miami Beach. He dwells in the memories of his Holocaust experience, which he relates to the nar-rator: "three-quarters of a year behind a cellar wall . . . there were six of us men there and one woman." Flederbush says that the woman had sexual rela-tions during this time with her husband and with

him, "and she satisfied the others as best as she could," except for the two who turned to homo-sexuality. Despite his belief that "martyrdom and sex don't mix," Flederbush feels compelled to con-fess that the Jews of Poland "were people, not an-gels." While the love shared by the seven people may seem grotesque or even perverted, perhaps it saved their lives. It may have encouraged them to keep their hope, even while they experienced the "whole shame of being human." Flederbush, the narrator, and the narrator's friend who accompa-nies them to dinner, conclude that hope is what kept the Holocaust victims going; and hope will insure the survival of the "crazy" Jews for the next ten thousand years. With its atmosphere of futility, however, Miami Beach and its Jewish populace will be underwater by then. The futility of the Miami Beach Jews is what repels Max Flederbush and alienates him from their society.

A similarly unbearable futility invests the at-mosphere at a party set in a New York suburb in "There Are No Coincidences." At the party, one woman dominates the conversation with "senti-mental claptrap" about her study of living condi-tions in Sing Sing Prison. The protagonist, another first-person narrator, is bored—this is not a cause to which he can relate. Nor can another guest, a woman who leaves the party when the protagonist does. The two wind up stranded together in this suburb on a miserably stormy night, unable to find a taxi to take them back to Manhattan. They are inexorably drawn together, first by their common reaction to the party—alienation—and then, in a primal sense, by needing one another: "Every de-gree of warmth was now of utmost value. Like two stray animals, we pressed hard against one an-other." A sympathetic night watchman provides them with shelter in the cellar of his building, where the two spend the night. They talk of the "guardian angels" in their lives who have saved them from crises, they discuss the difference be-tween coincidences and miracles, and they question fate: "Why should fate continually play cat-and-mouse with a person? Why terrify and then make a last-minute rescue? It's simply that we explain every good coincidence as being a miracle and we blame all the adverse things on blind nature." Fi-nally, they embrace and kiss passionately once. The narrator concludes that they were meant to be drawn together on this lonely night, that there "are no coincidences." Fate had meant them to act like two "idiots," stirred by a passion as electrical as the lightning bolts flashing all around them.

XIV

already

my possessions I carried in this sack. As I told you I still car-

~~Jewish~~

ry the prayer book that the soldier gave me some-sixty-odd years

ago, as well as my parents' Chanukah lamp . Sometimes when I,m

on the road and I feel especially downhearted, I hide in a forest

and light Chanukah candles even though it is not Chanukah. At

night, the moment I close my eyes, Zeldele is with me. She is

young and she wears the white silken bridal gown which her parents

fantastic

had pepared in her trousseau. She pours oil into a ~~magnificent~~

~~her husband~~

Chanukah lamp and I light the candles with a long torch. Sometimes

the sky turns into an otherworldly Chanukah lamp with the stars

as its lights. I told my dreams to a rabbi and he said, "Love

comes from the soul and souls radiate light. I know that when

to die

my time comes, Zeldele, soul will wait for me in Heaven. Well,

its time to go to sleep. Good night, a happy Chanukah *to all*

of you

myself 98 years
ago.
JBS.

Revised typescript page, with an initialed self-portrait, of the conclusion to "Hanukkah in the Poorhouse," the final tale in Singer's
The Power of Light; Eight Stories for Hanukkah *(by permission of the author)*

489

"There Are No Coincidences" thus begins with a mood of isolation in the narrator and ends with the narrator at least temporarily not alone; he is less lonely at the end than Max Flederbush, though like Flederbush, he is still not comfortably a part of any larger group. Moreover, there is no indication at the story's end that the momentary passion between the two is anything more than momentary. The implied question is, why does "fate" bother with such slight feelings at all?

In "The Psychic Journey" the theme of alienation is again pursued, but the male-female relationship that develops in this story appears to be more destructive and frightening than is loneliness. The first-person narrator Morris's encounter, first in New York and then in Israel, with a psychic named Margaret Fugazy develops into a perverse kind of love—on Margaret's part. She claims that meeting him has saved her from "deep crises" in her life, from suicide even. The two become guides for a group tour to Israel. Margaret acts possessive, paranoid, and hysterical when Morris decides to leave the tour in Tel Aviv. She curses him, and he superstitiously fears she is "trying to bring the powers of evil down upon" him. Her hysterical reaction may be understood if Margaret, not the male protagonist, is considered as the figure of alienation and dislocation in this story: "her black eyes exuded the melancholy of those who estrange themselves from their own environment and can never be at home in another." The two part as the Yom Kippur War starts exploding around them—a fit emblem of the explosive and destructive nature of their relationship, and also of Margaret's tormented, "witch-like" personality. "Love" has ultimately done Margaret and the narrator very little good. It has, on the contrary, for its duration created havoc in their lives and alienated them from one another.

Two selected stories from *Passions* similarly treat of passions gone awry and of lost souls. As Singer says, "People are victims of their passions and this makes for a perilous world; but it's equally perilous to be without them." Harry Bendiner, protagonist of the short story "Old Love," is, at age eighty-two, "perilously without" passion in his life. An affluent widower waiting to die in Miami Beach, he has nothing to look forward to until a wealthy younger woman, a widow named Ethel Brokeles, moves into a nearby apartment. They spend a day together and discover that they both have roots in the same Polish *shtetl*—a familiar element of Singer's American writings. They speak freely, even intimately, contemplate marriage, and embrace once. That is the end of their "old love." In the middle of the night Ethel jumps out of a window—to be with her dead husband—and Harry is left to meditate over "why a man is born and why he must die." Harry, like the protagonist of "The Psychic Journey," is left feeling emptier than he did before the meeting. And Ethel's loneliness and despair evidently could not be assuaged by the promise of passion in old age.

In "The Admirer" a mentally unstable young woman suffering from, among other things, a miserable marriage, has become a passionate admirer of the protagonist, who is another first-person narrator, a writer by trade and Singer's persona. She is one of the "eccentrics—odd, lost souls" who often visit the narrator. Like many of Singer's lost souls, Elizabeth Abigail de Sollar is trying to find herself and claims the narrator's works have helped her in her search. Like Harry and Ethel, Elizabeth and the narrator talk familiarly and discover they are probably related, her mother and the narrator having come from a Polish town, Klendev, where Elizabeth's grandfather had been the rabbi; both she and the narrator are evidently descended from the Klendev rabbi and from Rabbi Moses Isserles. A complex series of events occurs during their afternoon together, including several alarming telephone calls from Elizabeth's family, Elizabeth's suffering some kind of fit, and a brief sexual interlude during which the narrator feels attracted to this sick, witchlike woman—another in Singer's long line of demonic females. The narrator seems to be the lover of Elizabeth's fantasies. We learn from the narrator that "every love is irrational" and that "no love of any kind is lost." Perhaps the love depicted in this story is redemptive, reflecting Singer's view of love in his Nobel lecture. Perhaps Elizabeth's love for the narrator has helped her briefly through some of her mental torment. Yet this does not seem the case for the narrator. Although the two never meet again, the narrator seems disturbed and haunted by this woman. She leaves behind in his apartment, and never reclaims, traces of her influence, tokens of their interaction: her umbrella and her grandfather's manuscript. Perhaps the only positive feature of this interaction is that a link has been forged between East European Jewry living in America and American-born Jewry. This link may ease the European Jew's sense of alienation.

This sampling from Singer's American oeuvre consistently reveals his preoccupation with the painful problems of readjustment into American culture experienced by European Jewish émigrés. Perhaps it is also Singer's own way of coping with his profoundly traumatic personal experience of entering American society in 1935. Singer's American tales emerge as a moving tribute to the human being's impulse to link in a meaningful way the precious, familiar, and timeless elements of his past to the dynamic, alien, and often threatening elements of his present and future.

Interviews:

Paul Rosenblatt and Gene Koppel, *A Certain Bridge: Isaac Bashevis Singer on Literature and Life* (Tucson: University of Arizona Press, 1971);

Richard Burgin, "Isaac Bashevis Singer Talks . . . About Everything" and "Isaac Bashevis Singer's Universe," *New York Times Magazine,* 26 November 1978, pp. 39-52.

References:

Edward Alexander, *Isaac Bashevis Singer* (Boston: Twayne, 1980);
A thorough study of Singer's career, which contains a glossary and a bibliography and discusses his life and works.

Irving Buchen, *Isaac Bashevis Singer and the Eternal Past* (New York: New York University Press, 1968);

A critical and scholarly work which extensively discusses Singer's work.

Leslie Fiedler, "Isaac Bashevis Singer, or the American-ness of the American Jewish Writer," *Studies in American Jewish Literature,* 1 (1981): 124-131;
Describes Singer's adjustment to his society and the feelings of exile which are present in his writing.

Irving Howe, Introduction to *Selected Short Stories of Isaac Bashevis Singer* (New York: Modern Library, 1966);
A detailed introduction to the author's short stories.

Samuel H. Joseloff, "Isaac Bashevis Singer," *Jewish Spectator* (November 1971): 14-16;
Frames the work of the author in his cultural background and provides insight into the Jewish tradition.

Irving Malin, *Isaac Bashevis Singer* (New York: Ungar, 1972);
Discusses Singer's works by explaining the author's biographical background.

Eudora Welty

This entry was updated by Ruth Vande Kieft (Queens College, City University of New York) from her entry in DLB 2, American Novelists Since World War II.

Places	West Virginia
	The Delta
	Small-Town Deep
	   South
		New York City
		Ohio River and
		   Farmland
			The Natchez Trace
			Appalachia
			Mississippi

Influences and Relationships	Elizabeth Bowen Virginia Woolf Anton Chekhov William Faulkner	W. B. Yeats Jane Austen Katherine Anne Porter	Reynolds Price Mark Twain Henry Green

Literary Movements and Forms	Myth and Symbolism
	Literary Impres-
	   sionism
	Experimentalism
	Fictional Lyricism
		Southern Renaissance
		Southern Oral
		   Tradition
		Comic Monologue
		Regionalism
			"Inside" and "Out-
			   side" Stories
			Psychological Novel
			   and Story

Major Themes	Music and Art
	Search for
	   Fulfillment
	Love and
	   Separateness
		Dream and Fantasy
		Chance, Accident,
		   and Death
		Teachers and
		   Schools
			Human Comedy
			Country People
			Family and Children
			Mystery of Identity

Cultural and Artistic Influences	Photography Painting Impressionism Southern History	The Grotesque Jazz Beethoven	Music Theater Romanticism
Social and Economic Influences	The Depression Race Relations The WPA Southern Protestantism	Plantation Life The "New South" Mississippi History	Popular Culture The Law Folkways

BIRTH: Jackson, Mississippi, 13 April 1909, to Christian Webb and Mary Chestina Welty.

EDUCATION: Mississippi State College for Women, 1925-1927; B.A., University of Wisconsin, 1929; Columbia School of Business, 1930-1931.

AWARDS AND HONORS: O. Henry Memorial Awards, 1942, 1943, 1968; Guggenheim Fellowship, 1942; elected to National Institute of Arts and Letters, 1952; William Dean Howells Medal of the American Academy of Arts and Letters for *The Ponder Heart*, 1955; Creative Arts Medal for Fiction from Brandeis University, 1966; Edward Mac-Dowell Medal, 1970; elected to American Academy of Arts and Letters, 1971; Gold Medal for Fiction of National Institute of Arts and Letters, 1972; appointment to National Council of the Arts, 1972; Pulitzer Prize for *The Optimist's Daughter*, 1973; National Medal of Literature and Medal of Freedom, 1973; Litt.D., Columbia University, 1982; William E. Massey lecture series, Harvard University, 1983; Modern Language Association Commonwealth Award, 1984; American Association of University Women Achievement Award, 1985; National Medal of Art, 1986.

BOOKS: *A Curtain of Green* (Garden City: Doubleday, Doran, 1941; London: Bodley Head, 1943);

The Robber Bridegroom (Garden City: Doubleday, Doran, 1942; London: Bodley Head, 1944);

The Wide Net and Other Stories (New York: Harcourt, Brace, 1943; London: Bodley Head, 1945);

Delta Wedding (New York: Harcourt, Brace, 1946; London: Bodley Head, 1947);

The Golden Apples (New York: Harcourt, Brace, 1949; London: Bodley Head, 1950);

Short Stories (New York: Harcourt, Brace, 1950);

The Ponder Heart (New York: Harcourt, Brace, 1954; London: Hamish Hamilton, 1954);

The Bride of the Innisfallen and Other Stories (New York: Harcourt, Brace, 1955; London: Hamish Hamilton, 1955);

Place in Fiction (New York: House of Books, 1957);

Three Papers on Fiction (Northampton, Mass.: Smith College, 1962);

The Shoe Bird (New York: Harcourt, Brace & World, 1964);

Losing Battles (New York: Random House, 1970; London: Virago Press, 1982);

Eudora Welty (copyright © by Jorge Gamio, courtesy of Capra Press)

One Time, One Place: Mississippi in the Depression, A Snapshot Album (New York: Random House, 1971);

The Optimist's Daughter (New York: Random House, 1972; London: Andrea Deutsch, 1973; London: Virago Press, 1984);

The Eye of the Story (New York: Random House, 1978);

The Collected Stories of Eudora Welty (New York: Harcourt Brace Jovanovich, 1980; London: Marion Boyars Ltd., 1981);

One Writer's Beginnings (Cambridge, Mass.: Harvard University Press, 1984; London: Faber & Faber, 1985).

PERIODICAL PUBLICATIONS: "The Reading and Writing of Short Stories," *Atlantic*, 183 (February, March 1949): 54-58, 66-69;

"How I Write," *Virginia Quarterly Review*, 31 (Spring 1955): 240-251;

"The Eye of the Story," *Yale Review,* 55 (1966): 265-
    274;

"Some Notes on Times in Fiction," *Mississippi Quar-
    terly,* 26 (1973): 483-492;

"Artists on Criticism of Their Art: 'Is Phoenix Jack-
    son's Grandson Really Dead?,'" *Critical In-
    quiry,* 1 (1974): 219-221.

Eudora Welty's importance lies in the fact that during the past four decades she has produced an original and enduring body of fiction. Independent of any specific literary group, clear even of the influence of her most illustrious fellow Mississippian, William Faulkner, she stands preeminent, with Robert Penn Warren, among living writers of the Southern Renascence, indeed, among all living American writers of fiction. Her best work is as difficult to describe or "place" as it is remarkable and secure in its excellence. If there is any key to her importance, it exists in the faithful exercise of a creative imagination which sees, hears, and celebrates the myriad life of humankind, suffers through a dilemma, probes a mystery, and fuses inner and outer reality, transmuting it into the language and forms of fiction. Her works are mostly short stories or novellas, though two are novels, one long (*Losing Battles,* 1970). These works are largely Mississippian in setting and atmosphere, for an important tenet of Eudora Welty's fictional theory is that attachment to place, or "regionalism," is not restrictive but becomes a means to universality in great literature, a way of getting to the roots of what is constant in human experience. She has produced a body of work which often seems more like a precious and alluring collection of smaller art objects than a great artistic oeuvre. Yet the whole is greater than the sum of its parts, much as they defy the process of summing up, and nothing could fairly be said of one work that might not be contradicted in another.

Eudora Welty has been full and generous in discussing her art, which she has done in several of the essays (subtitled "On Writing") included in her nonfiction collection *The Eye of the Story* (1978), as well as in response to the questions of interviewers. But for many years she backed off from the idea of her own biography. The prospect, she told an interviewer in 1972, made her "shy, and discouraged at the very thought, because to me a writer's work should be everything. A writer's whole feeling, the force of his whole life, can go into a story—but what he's worked for is to get an objective piece down on paper. That should be read instead of some account of his life." After the publication of *One Writer's Beginnings* (1984, originally three lectures given to an enthusiastic, largely student audience at Harvard University in spring of 1984), one can only urge that this autobiographical account of Eudora Welty's career be read *with,* if not before, her fiction, because she has made her beautiful, modest little book the best possible guide to her work. Throughout, the autobiography reveals the close relationship between her life and her development as a writer. The child is always prophetic of the woman writer, just as her parents, their heritage, and their places engendered and shaped the child.

Through her flexible narrative voice, which moves subtly and swiftly from factual to lyrical, understatement to exaggeration, comedy to satire to tragedy, Eudora Welty accomplishes much in a hundred pages. She takes an inward journey in search of herself as a writer, and she provides an acute commentary, often turning into meditation and wisdom, on her life's meaning. Equally valuable is her vivid re-creation, over more than a century of places, persons, and events remembered and tales told, of the settings, customs, values, and convictions of three independent American types who so fruitfully converged in the writer's life: the educated Appalachian pioneer, the midwestern farmer, and the small-town "New South" Mississippian. For the late-twentieth-century student, this remarkable evocation of late-nineteenth- and early-twentieth-century American character is invaluable as a way of getting into the look and "feel" of the period, the persons and the places of Eudora Welty's fiction, and a small album of family photographs included in the book is helpful to that end.

As private histories go, especially in these days of lurid self-disclosures and biographical hunts for the sensational, Eudora Welty's private history is refreshingly simple. Her "story" is that of a happy, free, nurturing childhood; a good education; early artistic promise and experiment; plenty of experience—personal and observed, both painful and joyful—for the making of stories; initial difficulties in getting published, but, with the proverbial "little help from friends," publication, and critical acclaim; a successful career, ordinary in having its ups and downs, yet full of surprises; a large number of honors and awards; generally harmonious relationships with the literary and home community; a continuing joy in creation—a life's raison d'être, deeply fulfilling and sustaining.

Eudora Alice Welty was the only daughter, with two brothers, of Mary Chestina Andrews and Christian Webb Welty. Her mother, the southern parent, a Virginian by descent, was of English, Irish, Scottish, and French Huguenot ancestry; she moved to Jackson from West Virginia soon after her marriage in 1904. Her father, the northern parent, was of German Swiss ancestry, though both families had come to America before the Revolutionary War. They were similar in being country people whose relatives often were schoolteachers, preachers, or country lawyers. Eudora Welty has presented these types, especially teachers, with great insight, not only in her autobiography but in her fiction—Miss Julia Mortimer, the dedicated mountain-country schoolteacher of *Losing Battles*, being an example. Many details of the life of Becky McKelva in *The Optimist's Daughter* (1972) also resemble those of her own mother, "Chessie," as a young woman in West Virginia. Like Miss Julia and Becky, her mother, a brave young teacher passionately devoted to books and learning, rode out on her horse every day to teach in a one-room school, "mountain children little and big alike," reciting poetry on the way to make the time pass more quickly. Life in West Virginia in those days was a rigorous but invigorating pioneer existence, both rough and tender. Strong independence of spirit, the capacity for risk-taking as a fiction writer, the love of tales told within the large mountain family which included five rambunctious and adoring uncles and an early-widowed grandmother—these were among the most important gifts Eudora Welty inherited from and through her mother.

From her father, a quiet and gentle man, motherless at a tender age and raised as an only child in a pious and sturdy Ohio farmer's household, she received less obvious but equally valuable gifts. He was a practical and protective man, yet visionary in his hope and confidence in the products of modern science and technology. A "Yankee" and a Republican, he built up a highly successful career in business, became president of the Lamar Life Insurance Company, and put up Jackson's first skyscraper (thirteen stories). He was a benign and indulgent father to his daughter and her two brothers, Edward and Walter, and provided the future writer with a "frame of regularity," helping to instill in her, as did her mother, a capacity for sacrifice and self-discipline which she needed to direct her "impressionable" nature. The supreme gift both her parents gave her, however, was that of their own love—for each other as well as for their children. Cherishing secrets, Eudora was in on that open secret of their love: it gave her, she rightly says, "the turn of mind, the nature of tempera-

ment, of a privileged observer" of "the loving kind."

Her mother in particular provided the energy and adventuresome spirit to encourage her daughter in her evolving artistic and educational pursuits. She was an avid reader and later described her early and continuing satisfaction of the appetite for books as "A Sweet Devouring." The legends, classical myths, fairy tales, tall tales, family tales, Mississippi and frontier history, as well as serious adult literature, were to become an influential part of her imaginative furnishings, summoned often to service in a tale of her own. So also were her love of gardening, nature study, music lessons, and her work as an amateur watercolorist.

After attending a public high school in Jackson, Eudora Welty went to Columbus to attend the Mississippi State College for Women, where she contributed drawings, prose, and poetry to student publications. From there she transferred to the University of Wisconsin, from which she graduated two years later as an English major. Her earlier interest in painting and sketching, later supplemented with photography, gave way to concentration on the writing she was bound for; however, she has always retained a painter's eye in her fiction, which excels in descriptive detail and visual effects. After college she studied advertising for a year at the Columbia School of Business, an attempt on her part, made at her father's urging, to find a means of practical employment. Coming onto the job market in 1931 at the height of the Depression, she returned to Jackson. In the same year her father died, a heavy loss to her and her family. She was able to find part-time work with radio and newspapers, and she put her father's typewriter to good use by writing stories. By 1933 she had found a job which was to prove more formative to her writing career than the techniques of advertising: as publicity agent for the State Office of the Works Progress Administration, she traveled for three years around the eighty-two counties of Mississippi doing feature stories on local projects, meeting and conversing with many different types of people, gathering impressions of the varied persons, groups, landscapes, and towns she visited. It was these impressions which were to feed her imagination for many years: pictures taken, literally and figuratively, set in "that time, that place" (Mississippi in the Depression), formed the basis of much of her fiction from her earliest stories to *Losing Battles*.

Often fascinated, troubled, or horrified by what she saw and photographed, she would de-

Eudora Welty in 1929, the year she received her bachelor's degree from the University of Wisconsin (courtesy of Eudora Welty)

velop her own prints in the kitchen at night and study them. These pictures seemed initially more successful than the stories she had started writing privately, some of the best of which met with dozens of rejection slips. Undiscouraged, she continued writing and trying to place her stories. Her first modest success came in 1936, not only in having a show of her unposed photographs of Mississippi blacks shown in a small New York camera shop, but more important, in the publication of "Death of a Traveling Salesman," in *Manuscript*. Soon her talent was discovered and her stories published by Robert Penn Warren and Cleanth Brooks, then editors of the *Southern Review;* the discriminating and

influential Diarmuid Russell became her literary agent and loyal supporter. In a couple of years the *Atlantic* was publishing her stories, Ford Madox Ford took up the cause of her fiction and pressed for its publication, and Katherine Anne Porter wrote an introduction to the first collection of Welty's stories, *A Curtain of Green* (1941). O. Henry Memorial short story awards for "A Worn Path" and "The Wide Net" helped to establish her reputation, and she soon had a national audience.

Her first three major publications—*A Curtain of Green, The Robber Bridegroom* (1942), and *The Wide Net and Other Stories* (1943), all of which appeared within a three-year period—established the most distinguishing marks of her fiction: the importance of place; the impulse to celebrate life; the exploration of human mystery; the theme of love and separateness; the sense of multiplicity in life; and an elusive, changing, and lyrical style.

The stories were set in and around the towns and countryside of Mississippi. "Place in fiction," she declared later in an essay by that title, "is the named, identified, concrete, exact and exacting, and therefore credible, gathering-spot of all that has been felt, is about to be experienced. . . ." Many of the stories take place, within a time spectrum of over a century, on or near the Natchez Trace. This was a path originally traced through the wilderness by animals, later followed by Indians, and then literally carved into the forest bed as it was traveled by river men on their way home after coming down the Mississippi, by traders, settlers, mail carriers, all heading northeast or southwest between Natchez and Nashville. It is on the Trace that the story "A Still Moment" takes place. In it Welty uses three actual historical characters from the early nineteenth century: Lorenzo Dow, circuit-riding evangelist; James Audubon, the naturalist and painter of birds; and James Murrell, an outlaw horse thief and murderer. In the story, which includes specific biographical details and even a few words from writings by and about Audubon and Dow, these three driven souls meet for a shared moment of private revelation centered on a snowy white heron. The Trace is also a setting for stories which take place in the twentieth century. Old Phoenix Jackson makes her journey on "The Worn Path" to fetch the "soothing medicine" for her little grandson, though Phoenix herself, the courageous old black woman born "before the Surrender" (at the close of the Civil War), seems as ancient and timeless as the Trace. It is on the Trace that dignified old Solomon carries his young wife to his "nice house" in the story named "Livvie." It is the

Trace that William Wallace and his large entourage follow on their way to the Pearl River in the title story of *The Wide Net*. These stories are mostly about country people, black and white, though others are placed in small towns and cities. Whatever the setting, Welty has been accurate in her depiction of the social structures that go with place and time.

Local customs of speech and language have also had a marked influence on her fiction. She has described the southern penchant for talking and listening as "a treasure I helped myself to." Southerners are "born reciters" and "great memory retainers. . . . Southern talk is on the narrative side." Welty has an impressive command of colloquial speech—apparent early in stories using dramatized narration, such as the conversational satire of "Petrified Man" and the monologues of "Why I Live at the P.O." and *The Ponder Heart* (1954). She has referred to these stories as having been written "by ear," her ears being like "magnets." She writes stories emphasizing speech from what she calls the "outside" point of view, dramatic in technique. They are usually comic in their effect, though rarely without serious implications.

Family continuity in southern life has also provided Welty with a natural basis for her fiction. She told an interviewer that "if you grew up in the South when things were relatively stable, when there was a lot of talk and so on, you got a great sense of the person's whole life. This is because you know all of the families. You know several generations because they all live together." Family histories lend themselves to novels more than to short stories, and in her novels, accordingly, they chiefly appear. Yet "Why I Live at the P.O." swiftly conveys the sense of family, and a kind of "extended family" of a rural community drags the river in "The Wide Net." In a later prizewinning story, "The Demonstrators," she conveys with remarkable economy the sense of a highly organized, subtly stratified, yet deeply interdependent community over a period of years. The clannishness of traditional southern society has provided her with ample material for fictionalizing community ceremonies. Though human foibles are often shown, the tone of this group comedy is usually tolerant, detached, amused, and occasionally even hilarious.

Not all of Welty's stories have southern settings. "Music from Spain" (from *The Golden Apples*, 1949), set in San Francisco, contains a splendid evocation of that exotically "foreign" American city. In the collection titled *The Bride of the Innisfallen and Other Stories* (1955) we find some of the fruits of what her "traveling self" discovered on ocean liners, trains, ferries, and cities among the Irish or Italian-Americans. It was in 1949 that Welty traveled to Europe and met, among others, the Anglo-Irish writer Elizabeth Bowen, who became a close friend. She shared an affinity of artistic aims and techniques with this writer, dedicated *The Bride of the Innisfallen* to her, and is said to have written the title story at Bowen's Court. The success of these stories shows how place has always sparked the imagination of Eudora Welty, whether or not that place has been her Mississippi home.

In "How I Write," she describes the emotional fuse to her imagination as the lyrical impulse of the mind, "the impulse to praise, to love, to call up, to prophesy"; it is "the outside signal that has startled or moved the creative mind to complicity and brought the story to active being: the irresistible, the magnetic, the alarming (pleasurable or disturbing), the overwhelming person, place, or thing." In the first two collections of her stories, the overwhelming person most impresses the casual reader. Powerhouse, the fantastic jazz musician, excites, outrages, terrifies, and delights both of his admiring audiences, the whites and the blacks, with the sheer energy of his talent and personality. She wrote that story one night after having been at a concert and dance where black jazz musician Fats Waller played, though the story is not especially about Fats Waller but rather any artist in an "alien world," whose life she had "tried to put . . . in the words and plot suggested by the music I'd been listening to." Phoenix Jackson of "A Worn Path" is overwhelming in her old age and fidelity, a solitary old black woman moving across the winter fields; she is a memorable figure Welty had once seen and then provided with incidental adventures and a mission of continuing, dedicated love. The three characters in "A Still Moment" are overwhelming in their urgent, single-minded pursuit of their disparate life goals and enigmas. Some of these early characters are overwhelming because they are grotesques or victims: the man-destroying women in the beauty parlor of "Petrified Man"; the little, clubfooted Negro snatched from home to become "Keela, the Outcast Indian Maiden" in a carnival show and made to bite off the heads of live chickens; the heroine of "Clytie," born in a gothic household, frustrated in her attempts to find love, ending upside down, drowned in a rain barrel; deaf-mutes in "The Key" and "First Love." Later Welty was to make less use of grotesque types, though at the time they served to point up the eloquent loneliness of their characters' inner lives. Yet many of the characters are ordinary, and no less remarkable for that; the ordinary is often turned into the fantastic or legendary in her fiction. There are the rootless protagonists of "Death of a Traveling Salesman" and "The Hitchhikers"; the romantic young country wife, Ruby Fisher, of "A Piece of News," fighting against her confined existence; and old Mr. Marblehall, leading a shocking double life in his fantasies. No "ordinary" person exists, once you get a look inside.

Inside is where all the mystery lies, and Welty's great pursuit has been to explore the mysteries of identity and meaning—of the essential self, which is inviolable. She gently probes the puzzles which human beings have about their thoughts and feelings as individuals, separated from others, resisting and rebelling against loneliness; needing love yet also needing the privacy and inner space to live as free, exploring individuals. Conveying these mysteries requires the capacity to "slip into" others, to find there the most elusive of human feelings. Welty has admitted the difficulty of conveying them. She believes that the peculiar, apparently perverse habit of the best artists is to be "obstructive"; they seem to "hold back their own best interests." This is because "beauty is not a . . . promiscuous or obvious quality—indeed, at her finest she is somehow associated with obstruction— with reticence of a number of kinds." The stories in which Welty deals most directly with these mysteries, written chiefly from the "inside" point of view (through the introspection of a central character), include some of the best known of her early stories: "Death of a Traveling Salesman," "A Still Moment," "A Curtain of Green," "First Love," "At the Landing." In the title story of *A Curtain of Green* a young woman whose husband is killed in a freakish accident when a tree falls and crushes him in his car tries to part the curtain of green, the veil of mystery cast over nature, by plunging herself into the wild fecundity of her garden. She learns only that the curtain cannot be lifted, that life and death seem to be capriciously interchangeable, that there is nothing a strong protective love can do but submit to the mystery of an unknowable and unaccountable universe.

Even when love seems to be fulfilled in marriage and family relationships, the mysteries remain; in several stories Welty shows that lovers and mates should not assume knowledge of each other, and members of a family must stand apart now and then to see others as inviolable, changing, growing, surprising. Families may be hard on outsiders, especially in-laws from another type of family or class structure; they may try to assimilate these outsiders into the family, devouring their identity in the process, even robbing them of their mates. This happens to the young wives in *Delta Wedding* (1946) and *Losing Battles*. The larger families of small towns and communities may be equally hostile to the independence of outsiders: a German music teacher, Miss Eckhart, suffers that fate in "June Recital." Provincial communities may also resist the efforts of a teacher, such as Miss Julia Mortimer in *Losing Battles*, to educate them and extend their hopes and visions.

In her fiction Welty shows how the most public things in life, love and death, are also the most mysterious and private, and must be kept so. Though privacy requires the risk of isolation and loneliness, it is a risk worth taking in order to achieve the proper balance between love and separateness. The failure to put a proper value on persons, places, and things, the violations of human privacy and dignity, is the essence of vulgarity in Eudora Welty's fiction and has drawn satire from her. The best known of her satirical stories is "Petrified Man," an account of a group of women in a cheap beauty parlor. They are crude; their tastes run to the freakish and sensational; and they reveal many perverted attitudes and practices relating to marriage, sex, and maternity. Most characteristically, her fiction is neither tragic, comic, nor satiric, but a blend of these elements. Though her earlier stories tended to concentrate on a single tonal effect, the mixtures and rapid shifts of human feeling and response have always been apparent in her fiction, making for a Chekhovian kind of realism in which the fluctuations of fiction are as rapid and subtle as they are in life, and the fact of mutability tempers any rapture or dream. Welty's own "double vision" is like that of one of her characters from *The Golden Apples*, Virgie Rainey, who "never saw it differently, never doubted that all the opposites on earth were close together, love close to hate, living to dying; but of them all, hope and despair were the closest blood—unrecognizable one from the other sometimes, making moments double upon themselves, and in the doubling double again, amending but never taking back."

The "double vision" has also given her a genial tolerance and humanity; her fiction is notably lacking in villainous characters and behavior, and in strong moral judgments. In her work she has never undertaken, as did Faulkner and Robert Penn Warren, the burden of southern history. To apply her own designations of "inside" and "outside" stories, the "inside" stories, sensitive and in-

6

"I won't do it harm coming on this excursion withyou," she said.
"I know I wouldn't do a thing like that."

"And your same old satchel over your shoulder! Are we marching
back to school!"

"Joe ~~hey~~, what I'm bringing with us is baby needs," ~~she said~~.

"Carry her too, for a while, if you want to," he offered, ~~ready
to go~~. "She's hotter than any stove."

~~"This tea is cold. Swap."~~
~~Could not give some to her?" "No, you don't know anything."~~
Among the standing trees could be seen, scattered, gray whole
naked fallen trees, ~~then the church, white as a table with a cloth
over it.~~

Joe ~~hey~~ and Willowdene, while she clasped the baby well, went
lightly running through the sweet high shade, and jumping back and
forth over the ~~long red creeks in the floor~~ that rayed down from
the top of the hill. They followed-the-leader around a grandfather
pine where a family of locust-shells went praying wide open up the
trunk.

"How much did you miss me, then?" he cried, as they ~~both walked
on their knees and~~ dipped side to side dodging each other and
balancing with arms spread. "How much?"

They touched shoulders. A long glittering dragonfly held.
dagger high, above Willowdene's forehead before a word was spoken.

"Remember when I ask you to marry and come on home with me?"
he cried then with his face behind hers. The noise of the river
swollen with rains came rushing to her ears where his ears were.
She could smell the gaseous fumes of the first daffodils in the
schoolyard, growing by the bunch, as if, just under the clay, red
fists kept tight hold on them. X

From typescript of Losing Battles

trospective, would link her with such modern writers as Katherine Mansfield, Chekhov, Virginia Woolf, and Elizabeth Bowen, from whom she probably learned more about the possibilities of fiction than from any southern writer. The "outside" stories, comic and brilliantly colloquial, seem more indigenous, less personal, and might link her with the Southwest humorists, Twain, Ring Lardner, the comic and colloquial Faulkner. ("Faulkner taught me," she said on one occasion, "that you can much better suggest the way we speak by cadences and punctuation than by any sort of spelling.") With equal justice, then, her style could be described as poetic, delicate, and intuitive, as robust, humorous, and tough. Her style can be as luminous and clear as a Vermeer and as impressionistic as a Turner painting. As surprise, chance, and experimentation play a thematic role in her fiction, so do they in her style and the whole body of her work. She has spoken of "the lure of *possibility,* all possibilities" in describing her experience of writing stories.

It was the lure of possibilities in form that led Eudora Welty to the writing of longer fictional works. Of her first novella, *The Robber Bridegroom* (1942), she said, "Everything in it is something I've liked as long as I can remember. . . ." It included "a lifetime of fairy-tale reading," folklore, tall tales, Southwest humor, legends of the Mississippi River during pioneer days, and a collection of indigenous character types. Among them were Natchez Indians; Mike Fink, champion keelboatman; the Harpe brothers, bandits noted for their cruelty; Clement Musgrove, an innocent and peaceful planter; the heroine, his beautiful daughter Rosamond, and her bandit lover Jamie; and New Orleans merchants. Time is compressed in this historical fantasy—Indians, bandits, and planters scarcely coexisted on the Southwest frontier—yet the novella manages to convey the sense of mutability as one culture displaces another, and the theme of "doubleness" is seriously explored. *The Robber Bridegroom* has been listed in an *Encyclopedia Americana* bibliography on the state of Mississippi, which attests to its historical fidelity. In the novella Welty also tapped some deep source of American folk art, as was evidenced by the popularity of a "country musical" based on the work which was first produced in 1974 and enjoyed a successful run on Broadway.

Delta Wedding (1946) was Eudora Welty's initial experiment with a full-length novel. She chose for its setting a Mississippi place not immediately familiar to her—the delta country. The events transpire in 1923, a year free of war, depression, or natural catastrophe, which gave her the opportu-

nity to explore both the potentials and limitations of love within a large southern family, the Fairchilds of Shellmound. Plot is tenuous in this novel; the central event is not, as the title suggests, the wedding of Dabney Fairchild to a plantation overseer named Troy, but rather an incident in which the bride's uncle, George Fairchild, saves a simpleminded cousin from being killed by a local train. His action sets off a complex of reactions, most important that of his young wife Robbie Reid in protest against the strong matriarchal family domination of her husband. In the novel Welty extends her technique of fusing internal and external reality, for the members of this burgeoning household are seen as a group of introverts, drawing toward and pushing away from each other as though in some balletic interplay of psyches. Amplitude is what the novel gives her: the opportunity to present, in the full panoply of aunts, cousins, and a dead soldier hero, the large southern legend-making family in all its formidable pride and solidarity; and within that family, to explore personal crises and relationships. Introspection predominates; clannishness is implicitly criticized, though not from the perspective of a social historian: rather from the point of view of an outsider who is also an insider, Ellen Fairchild, wife, sister, mother. A town-loving Virginian, a Fairchild only by marriage, Ellen is both clear-eyed and sympathetic, sensitive to individual needs but working for harmony—the sort of person in whose sensibility Eudora Welty has always seemed most familiar and effective as a writer. *Delta Wedding* was read by a larger audience than her earlier works had been—proving, perhaps, only that novels have always been more popular than collections of short stories.

In *The Golden Apples* (1949) experimentation is once more evident. It consists of stories written and published individually in various magazines and journals over a period of about two years, then revised by Welty, arranged in a loosely chronological order, extended with one major story and a cast of characters ("Main Families in Morgana"), and published as a short story cycle which may be read as though it were a novel. Covering a time span of forty years, it focuses on some leading characters and families in the delta town of Morgana, whose lives and destinies flow together and apart (for many of its inhabitants are wanderers who come and go) as each searches for the golden apples of fulfillment through love or the art of music. The stories are told from different narrative vantage points, variants of "inside" and "outside" narration: the first, "Shower of Gold," is a dramatic mono-

Dust jacket for Eudora Welty's longest novel, in which, she said, she tried "translating every thought and feeling into action and speech, speech being another form of action"

logue in which garrulous Katie Rainey plunges us into Morgana life by telling the story of King MacLain's amorous career, his wife Snowdie's patience, and the town's shocked but admiring response to it, and a Halloween trick played on him by his mischievous twin sons. "June Recital," as moving as it is technically brilliant, makes use of multiple points of view, playing various kinds of innocence against experience. It tells the story of a German music teacher, Miss Eckhart, and her tragic attempt to pass her musical passion and talent on to the one gifted student in Morgana, Kate's daughter Virgie, who rejects the gift and the discipline required to express it beautifully for the easier satisfactions of sex. Other stories deal with the frustrations in marriage of the MacLain twins; the experiences of Morgana girls in summer camp; and in the final story, "The Wanderers," we find Virgie Rainey, now a woman of forty, a detached participant in her mother's funeral rites. As an adult she finally *receives* the gift and meaning of Miss Eckhart's music through an evolved understanding of humanity in which heroic action, or hometown smugness, or even love may be seen as

victimizing, though the search for the golden apples, ideally caught in the music of Beethoven, continues so long as hope and joy persist.

In *The Golden Apples* Eudora Welty makes more use of classical myth and symbolism as unifying devices than in any of her other works. Behind King MacLain is the Zeus who took Danae, Leda, and other dazzled mortal women as sexual partners; behind Loch Morrison, youthful hero of "Moon Lake," and the Spanish guitarist in "Music from Spain," is Perseus; and behind all of these figures stand both the change and constancy of nature. Human beings are seen as stars and constellations in slow revolutions; they are like lost beasts, "terribly at large, roaming on the face of the earth," prehistoric and timeless. The perspective and wisdom achieved in this book, its technical virtuosity and mingled tragedy and comedy, its pervasive sense of time and mutability, make it one of Welty's greatest achievements, and one of her avowed favorites.

Another novella, *The Ponder Heart* (1954), was both a popular and critical success. It is the dramatic monologue of Edna Earle Ponder, small-town hotel manager and niece of her generous, fond, and foolish conveyor of love and money, Uncle Daniel Ponder. He literally tickles his silly little wife to death when a lightning fireball rolls into the room, and his trial turns into farce when he actually throws his money away in the courtroom. Because of its comic high spirits and adroit use of the southern colloquial idiom, the novella won Eudora Welty the William Dean Howells Medal of the American Academy for the most distinguished work of American fiction between 1950-1955. It also brought her work to the attention of the general public through the medium of theater, for in 1956 Jerome Chodorov and Joseph Fields made a play of *The Ponder Heart,* which had a successful run on Broadway and has since been revised and produced in Jackson and elsewhere.

During the next fifteen years Eudora Welty published no longer works, but there was in the making a fiction which grew in length and complexity as she worked on it. Originally conceived as a novella, it was finally completed and published as her longest novel, *Losing Battles* (1970), and her first to appear on the best-seller lists. In it she tried something new for her: "translating every thought and feeling into action and speech, speech being another form of action"; dropping introspection and extensive description, she tried to "make everything shown . . . without benefit of the author's telling any more about what was going on inside the characters' minds and hearts." It was, in short, her most extensive work of "outside" narrative. In the novel the Vaughn-Beecham-Renfro clan from the hill country of northwestern Mississippi meet for a reunion to celebrate the ninetieth birthday of Granny Vaughn and the homecoming (from prison) of the hero, Jack Renfro. The novel is a cornucopia of talk and action, much of it farcical; family stories are told in a rambling and contrapuntal manner by members of the clan, the history of which spans over six generations. The "losing battles" of the title are both comic and serious: they include Jack Renfro's attempt to save Judge Moody's Buick from plunging over "Lover's Leap"; the schoolteacher Miss Julia Mortimer's battle against ignorance and provincialism and her lonely death; the clan's struggle against the Depression which threatens their survival as farmers. Despite its length, Welty retains firm control of the themes and action of the novel, which takes place in a day and a half.

A long private ordeal, ending in her mother's death, led to a somewhat autobiographical novella, in that she made use of scenes and recollections from her mother's youth in West Virginia. Once again using the introspective form of narration, in *The Optimist's Daughter* (1972) Welty presents the painful inner journey of Laurel McKelva, the daughter of "optimist" Judge McKelva. For reasons Laurel finds difficult to imagine or accept, the judge married a vulgar, selfish younger woman, Fay Chisom, shortly after his wife's long illness and death. Since Fay has already violated her mother's memory, position, and home, Laurel faces the final ordeal of leaving that home to Fay, with all its treasures of memory and experience, after her father's death. This causes Laurel to review her parents' relationship and her own with her husband—brief and happy, perfected in time since his early death in World War II. She is forced to the conclusion that no one can be "saved" from others; that the more intense love is, the more it consumes what it seizes on. Even she and her parents had not been exempt from that destructive power of love. Yet Laurel proves herself transcendent over Fay, and an optimist in regaining her faith in the heart that "can empty but fill again, in the patterns restored by dreams."

The Optimist's Daughter, though relatively spare and clear in style, is a difficult work because of the emotional complexities presented, but that did not prevent it from appearing on the best-seller lists. It also won Eudora Welty a Pulitzer Prize—the prize some critics felt should have been awarded for *Losing Battles.* Of a fiction so various and steadily excellent in form and style, it is difficult to say whether her achievement has been greater in the "outside" or "inside" kind of narrative. Not only aesthetic but temperamental preferences are involved in such judgments. But probably the critics chose wisely.

As might be expected, an art so difficult to assess as Eudora Welty's had its effect on her reputation, the course of which has been traced by Victor Thompson in *Eudora Welty: A Reference Guide* (1976). Potential editors were initially reluctant to publish her work because, as one of them responded to Ford Madox Ford upon his effort to get a first collection published in 1939, "These highly developed, sensitive, elusive, tense and extremely beautiful stories will certainly appeal to discriminating readers but we haven't the hope that it would be possible to sell even the modest first edition of the book." When a collection did appear in 1941, it was to generally high critical acclaim, and though the audience was to become larger than predicted, it did remain, for many years, small and discriminating. One sector or another of that audience has always been critical of some facet, stage, or tendency of Eudora Welty's work. One objection was to southern "gothic" decadence in *A Curtain of Green.* Then, beginning with stories in *The Wide Net,* some critics raised objections to what seemed a needless obscurity, a portentous, dreamlike quality, a confusing blend of reality and fantasy. They complained that at its worst, the style seemed precious, suggestive of a rich meaning too tenuous to capture. These tendencies persisted in some of the stories of *The Golden Apples* and reached their peak in *The Bride of the Innisfallen.* Elaborateness, subtlety, sophistication of narrative technique, what Reynolds Price once called a "slow, dissolving impressionism," are distinguishing marks of those stories. Though some critics savored this style, others did not. Later the greater objectivity in narrative method of *Losing Battles* and *The Optimist's Daughter* met with wide approval, and many general readers and critics regarded either or both of these works as Welty's finest achievement. But to as many others or more, the earliest stories remained the best, and Welty's reputation to the end will rest on the perennial freshness and lyrical poignancy—or brilliant comedy—of a dozen or more stories from *The Curtain of Green, The Wide Net,* and *The Golden Apples.*

In the 1960s an objection flared up which had first been kindled among a few liberals with the publication of *Delta Wedding:* they found it a hopelessly regional exercise in nostalgia for the lost life of the southern plantation. Then as the issue of race relations pricked the national conscience, Welty was accused by such northern liberals as Diana Trilling and Isaac Rosenfeld of a lack of social consciousness. She was expected, as a notable and enlightened Mississippian, to employ her talents in the cause of civil rights. Her response to this attack was characteristically oblique. It came, at first, in an article titled "Must the Novelist Crusade?," which appeared in the *Atlantic Monthly* of October 1965. Her answer was that he must not, even granting the fact that "morality as shown through human relationships is the whole heart of fiction." Crusades spring from crisis; they must deal in arguments and speak in generalities; they must be clear; they must label. Writers of fiction, with an equal commitment to truth and morality, must deal with the interior life of particular, complex human beings, with all the confusions of actuality, where "people are not Right and Wrong, Good and Bad, Black and White personified." Crusades must be effected in public, while "fiction has, and must keep, a private address. For life is *lived* in a private

place; where it means anything is inside the mind and heart." The raw materials of fiction change rapidly, but the instruments of perceiving—the way the artist looks—stay the same. What is perceived, despite all the changes, is that "there is a relationship in progress between ourselves and other people; this was the case when the world seemed stable, too. There are relationships of the blood, of the passions and affections, of thought and spirit and deed. There is the relationship between the races. How can one kind of relationship be set apart from the others? Like the great root system of an old and long-established growing plant, they are all tangled up together; to separate them you would have to cleave the plant itself from top to bottom."

A story she wrote during the same general period, "The Demonstrators," was Welty's other, even more oblique response to those critics who required of her a crusading fiction. The story, also an O. Henry Memorial prizewinner, shows the intricate social structure of Holden, Mississippi. The enveloping action, the "issues" in the background suggested by the title, are very much those of the 1960s: racial tension, the "generation gap," a general challenging of all authority figures, and the clash of radical and conservative attitudes. Everyone in the story is a demonstrator, making a private claim to rights and privileges belonging to the self by reason of position, authority, or group membership. These demands are often made with hostility: the atmosphere is full of various kinds of social friction. And yet all of the people of Holden are linked together by society, tradition, common responsibility and service, personal and impersonal forms of love. Within this network of interdependence stands the inviolable personal self, "savage, death-defying, private." The story served for its author—perhaps unconsciously—both as a declaration of life and a declaration of independence: of the right to remain private as an artist, to choose her own subjects and treat them in her own way, which would be complex and truthful rather than tailored to any cause, however noble its aims.

It is interesting that this very private writer who has kept for years the same private address in the family home in Jackson, initially became more widely known to the general public through the medium of theater than she ever had through her early fiction. The Broadway production of *The Ponder Heart* helped to make Jacksonians aware of the celebrity who lived and worked among them. She had never been withdrawn or hostile to her home community: in fact, she has always been deeply involved in local southern life as, for example, a sustaining member of the Junior League, winner of the First National Bank Award (1964), sponsor of various public and private events. Yet within a decade (from 1957-1967) she passed from a state of relative local obscurity to being, as a *Jackson Daily News* reporter infelicitously described her, "one of Mississippi's better known products." By the time the governor of Mississippi proclaimed 2 May 1974 Eudora Welty Day, an event duly celebrated in the chamber of the House of Representatives of the old state capitol, at which she read from *Losing Battles*, Mississippians must have been sufficiently aware of her fame, and justifiably proud.

Eudora Welty has been the recipient of every major honor, award, and fellowship that the United States bestows upon its greatest authors, and countless other awards, including honorary degrees from many universities and colleges. The appearance on the best-seller lists of *Losing Battles, The Optimist's Daughter*, and *The Collected Stories* (1980), and particularly the immensely popular *One Writer's Beginnings*, brought her the kind of general fame she had not earlier experienced. She has been writer in residence at a variety of academic institutions, including Oxford and Cambridge University; her work has been the subject of a number of symposia, which she sometimes graces with her presence, contributing most often a reading and occasionally a lecture or appearance on a panel. She has frequently been honored by her state and city (Jackson has now named its library for her and Millsap College has an endowed chair in her name); she has appeared and read at a wide spectrum of occasions, from nationwide television programs to the scholarly Modern Language Association to small church and school groups in Jackson and elsewhere. Rarely has an American writer been so universally loved and admired wherever she goes, nor has praise been given an author so justly and joyfully and received so graciously and modestly.

Even though she has enjoyed personal friendships with several modern writers, including Katherine Anne Porter, Robert Penn Warren, Cleanth Brooks, Allen Tate, and others of younger generations, she sprang from no particular "school" of writers, nor has she established one. Reynolds Price, a close friend, has professed a general debt to her work, and a variety of writers, including V. S. Pritchett, Joyce Carol Oates, Toni Morrison, Walker Percy, and others, have expressed their admiration of it.

In her introduction to *One Time, One Place* (1971) Welty spoke of the "living relationship be-

tween what we see going on and ourselves," the necessity of both "exposure" to the outside world and "reflection" on it. Reflection is a slow process, demanding the gift of sympathy: both writer and reader need it. "We struggle through any pain or darkness in nothing but the hope that we may receive it, and through any term of work in the prayer to keep it." There has been no quick, easy way for her to perceive and communicate what people reveal of themselves, nor is there any shortcut for the reader of her stories. Any single approach to her work may be distorting; only by attentive reading and the exercise of a sympathetic imagination will the reader find the fiction of Welty slowly yielding its precious treasure of secrets and truths. As an eager and ignorant young photographer she learned something "away off one day up in Tishomingo County . . . that my wish, indeed my continuing passion, would be not to point a finger in judgment but to part a curtain, that invisible shadow that falls between people, the veil of indifference to each other's presence, each other's wonder, each other's human plight." If, as it seems likely, Eudora Welty's fiction will be read well into the future, it will be for the same reason that Faulkner's is read: for their mutual, though different, faithfulness to "the old verities and truths of the human heart."

Interviews:

Peggy W. Prenshaw, ed., *Conversations with Eudora Welty* (Jackson: University of Mississippi Press, 1984);
Invaluable collection of twenty-six interviews spanning forty years.

Bibliographies:

Victor H. Thompson, *Eudora Welty: A Reference Guide* (Boston: G. K. Hall, 1976);
A comprehensive listing of secondary material on Welty's fiction and biography, including reviews and newspaper clippings, from 1936-1975.

Peggy W. Prenshaw, "Eudora Welty," *American Women Writers: Bibliographical Essays*, edited by Maurice Duke, Jackson R. Bryer, and M. Thomas Inge (Westport, Conn.: Greenwood Press, 1983), pp. 233-267;
Excellent descriptive bibliography of Welty's works up to 1983, with discerning evaluations of all the important secondary sources on her work.

References:

J. A. Bryant, Jr., *Eudora Welty* (Minneapolis: University of Minnesota Press, 1968);

A brief introduction to Welty's fiction and criticism, stressing its perplexities, her visual imagination and use of place.

Albert J. Devlin, *Eudora Welty's Chronicle* (Jackson: University Press of Mississippi, 1983);

This study argues that Welty's work shows a structure of historical imagination, with a time span extending from the territorial era to the present.

Elizabeth Evans, *Eudora Welty* (New York: Ungar, 1981);

Sympathetic, reliable study of Welty's career, her fiction and nonfiction.

Michael Kreyling, *Eudora Welty's Achievement of Order* (Baton Rouge: Louisiana State University Press, 1980);

A sensitive and intelligent reading of Welty's fiction which traces a pattern of development in her control of fictional technique.

Peggy W. Prenshaw, ed., *Eudora Welty: Critical Essays* (Jackson: University Press of Mississippi, 1979);

Collection of twenty-five valuable essays by leading Welty critics, including general studies, special topics, and individual works. Selections from this volume appear in *Eudora Welty: Thirteen Essays*, edited by Peggy W. Prenshaw (Jackson: University Press of Mississippi, 1983).

Ruth M. Vande Kieft, *Eudora Welty* (New York: Twayne, 1962, 1973);

Valuable general introduction to and detailed explications of Eudora Welty's fiction up to 1955, placing it among southern and world writers. A revised and updated edition of this work will appear in 1987.

Papers:

A large collection of manuscripts, photographs, criticism, films, a newspaper clipping file, etc., are at the Department of Archives and History of the State of Mississippi in Jackson, Mississippi.

Tennessee Williams

This entry was updated from the entry by Sally Boyd (University of South Carolina) in DLB 7, Twentieth-Century American Dramatists.

Places	Saint Louis	New York City	Key West
Influences and Relationships	Carson McCullers Tallulah Bankhead	Gore Vidal	Donald Windham
Literary Movements and Forms	Naturalism Modern Romance	Confessional Literature	Symbolic Drama
Major Themes	Isolation Illusion vs. Reality	Spiritual Sterility Fear of Sensuality	The Awakening of Repressed Passion
Cultural and Artistic Influences	International Theater	Modern Art	
Social and Economic Influences	Drug Culture	The Depression	Homosexual Underground

See also the Williams entry in DLB Yearbook: 1983.

BIRTH: Columbus, Mississippi, 26 March 1911, to Cornelius Coffin and Edwina Dakin Williams.

EDUCATION: University of Missouri, 1929-1931; Washington University, St. Louis, 1936; B.A., University of Iowa, 1938.

AWARDS AND HONORS: Group Theatre Award for *American Blues*, 1939; Rockefeller Foundation Grant, 1940; American Academy of Arts and Letters Award, 1944; New York Drama Critics Circle Award, Sidney Howard Memorial Award, Donaldson Award, and *Sign* Magazine Annual Award for *The Glass Menagerie*, 1945; New York Drama Critics Circle Award, Donaldson Award, and Pulitzer Prize for *A Streetcar Named Desire*, 1948; elected to National Institute of Arts and Letters, 1952; New York Drama Critics Circle Award and Pulitzer Prize for *Cat on a Hot Tin Roof*, 1955; *London Evening Standard* Drama Award for *Cat on a Hot Tin Roof*, 1958; New York Drama Critics Circle Award for *The Night of the Iguana*, 1962; first place in London Critics' Poll for Best New Foreign Play for *The Night of the Iguana*, 1964-1965; Brandeis University Creative Arts Medal, 1964-1965; National Institute of Arts and Letters Gold Medal, 1969; first centennial medal of the Cathedral of St. John the Divine, 1973; elected to Theatre Hall of Fame, 1979; Kennedy Honors Award, 1979.

DEATH: New York, New York, 25 February 1983.

BOOKS: *The Summer Belvedere*, in *Five Young American Poets*, edited by James Laughlin, third series (New York: New Directions, 1944);
Battle of Angels (New York: New Directions, 1945);
The Glass Menagerie (New York: Random House, 1945; London: Lehmann, 1948);
27 Wagons Full of Cotton and Other One-Act Plays (Norfolk, Conn.: New Directions, 1946; London: Grey Walls Press, 1947)—includes *27 Wagons Full of Cotton, The Purification, The Lady of Larkspur Lotion, The Last of My Solid Gold Watches, Portrait of a Madonna, Auto-Da-Fé, Lord Byron's Love Letter, The Strangest Kind of Romance, The Long Goodbye, Hello from Bertha, This Property Is Condemned, Talk to Me Like the Rain and Let Me Listen*, and *Something Unspoken;*
You Touched Me!, by Williams and Donald Windham (New York: French, 1947);

Tennessee Williams, 1945

A Streetcar Named Desire (New York: New Directions, 1947; London: Lehmann, 1949);
Summer and Smoke (New York: New Directions, 1948; London: Lehmann, 1952);
American Blues: Five Short Plays (New York: Dramatists Play Service, 1948)—includes *Moony's Kid Don't Cry; The Dark Room; The Case of the Crushed Petunias; The Long Stay Cut Short, or, The Unsatisfactory Supper;* and *Ten Blocks on the Camino Real;*
One Arm and Other Stories (New York: New Directions, 1948);
The Roman Spring of Mrs. Stone (New York: New Directions, 1950; London: Lehmann, 1950);
The Rose Tattoo (New York: New Directions, 1951; London: Secker & Warburg, 1951);
I Rise in Flame, Cried the Phoenix (New York: New Directions, 1951);
Camino Real (Norfolk, Conn.: New Directions, 1953; London: Secker & Warburg, 1958);
Hard Candy: A Book of Stories (New York: New Directions, 1954);

Cat on a Hot Tin Roof (New York: New Directions, 1955; London: Secker & Warburg, 1956);

In the Winter of Cities (Norfolk, Conn.: New Directions, 1956; augmented, 1964);

Baby Doll (New York: New Directions, 1956; London: Secker & Warburg, 1957);

Orpheus Descending (London: Secker & Warburg, 1958); *Orpheus Descending with Battle of Angels* (New York: New Directions, 1958);

Suddenly Last Summer (New York: New Directions, 1958);

Garden District (London: Secker & Warburg, 1959);

Sweet Bird of Youth (New York: New Directions, 1959; London: Secker & Warburg, 1961);

Period of Adjustment (New York: New Directions, 1960; London: Secker & Warburg, 1961);

The Night of the Iguana (New York: New Directions, 1962; London: Secker & Warburg, 1963);

The Milk Train Doesn't Stop Here Anymore (Norfolk, Conn.: New Directions, 1964);

Eccentricities of a Nightingale and Summer and Smoke (New York: New Directions, 1964);

Grand (New York: House of Books, 1964);

The Knightly Quest: A Novella and Four Short Stories (New York: New Directions, 1966; revised and augmented, London: Secker & Warburg, 1968);

The Gnädiges Fräulein (New York: Dramatists Play Service, 1967);

The Mutilated (New York: Dramatists Play Service, 1967);

Kingdom of Earth (The Seven Descents of Myrtle) (New York: New Directions, 1968);

In the Bar of a Tokyo Hotel (New York: Dramatists Play Service, 1969);

The Two-Character Play (New York: New Directions, 1969);

Dragon Country (New York: New Directions, 1970)—includes *In the Bar of a Tokyo Hotel; I Rise in Flame, Cried the Phoenix; The Mutilated; I Can't Imagine Tomorrow; Confessional; The Frosted Glass Coffin; The Gnädiges Fräulein;* and *A Perfect Analysis Given by a Parrot;*

The Theatre of Tennessee Williams (New York: New Directions, 1971-   );

Small Craft Warnings (New York: New Directions, 1972; London: Secker & Warburg, 1973);

Out Cry (New York: New Directions, 1973);

Eight Mortal Ladies Possessed (New York: New Directions, 1974; London: Secker & Warburg, 1975);

Moise and the World of Reason (New York: Simon & Schuster, 1975; London: Allen, 1976);

Memoirs (Garden City: Doubleday, 1975; London: Allen, 1976);

Androgyne, Mon Amour (New York: New Directions, 1977);

Where I Live: Selected Essays, edited by C. Day and B. Woods (New York: New Directions, 1978);

Vieux Carré (New York: New Directions, 1979);

A Lovely Sunday for Crève Coeur (New York: New Directions, 1980);

Steps Must Be Gentle (New York: Targ, 1980);

Clothes for a Summer Hotel: A Ghost Play (New York: Dramatists Play Service, 1981).

PLAY PRODUCTIONS: *Cairo, Shanghai, Bombay,* by Williams and Bernice Dorothy Shapiro, Memphis, Garden Players, Rose Arbor Playhouse, 12 July 1935;

The Magic Tower, Webster Groves, Mo., Webster Groves Theatre Guild, 13 October 1936;

Headlines, Saint Louis, Mummers, Wednesday Club Auditorium, 11 November 1936;

Candles to the Sun, Saint Louis, Mummers, Wednesday Club Auditorium, 18 March 1937;

Fugitive Kind, Saint Louis, Mummers, Wednesday Club Auditorium, 30 November 1937;

The Long Goodbye, New York, New School for Social Research, February 1940;

Battle of Angels, Boston, Theatre Guild, Wilbur Theatre, 30 December 1940; revised as *Orpheus Descending,* New York, Producers Theatre, Martin Beck Theatre, 21 March 1957;

This Property Is Condemned, New York, New School for Social Research, May 1942; New York, Hudson Park Theatre, March 1946; in *Three Short Plays,* Dallas, Theatre '48, 1948; in *Three Premieres,* New York, Cherry Lane Theatre, 28 October 1956;

You Touched Me!, by Williams and Donald Windham, adapted from D. H. Lawrence's short story, Cleveland, Playhouse, 13 October 1943; Pasadena, Playbox, 29 November 1943; New York, Booth Theatre, 25 September 1945;

The Purification, Pasadena, Pasadena Laboratory Theatre, July 1944; Dallas, Theatre '54, May 1954; New York, ANTA Matinee Theatre Series, Theatre de Lys, 8 November 1959;

The Glass Menagerie, Chicago, Civic Theatre, 26 December 1944; New York, Playhouse Theatre, 31 March 1945;

Stairs to the Roof, Pasadena, Playbox, 25 March 1945; Pasadena, Pasadena Playhouse, 26 February 1947;

Moony's Kid Don't Cry, in *Two One-Act Plays,* Nantucket, Straight Wharf Theatre, 2 September

1946; Los Angeles, Actors' Laboratory Theatre, Las Palmas Theatre, 13 January 1947;

The Last of My Solid Gold Watches, Los Angeles, Actors' Laboratory Theatre, Las Palmas Theatre, 13 January 1947;

Portrait of a Madonna, Los Angeles, Actors' Laboratory Theatre, Las Palmas Theatre, 13 January 1947;

Summer and Smoke, Dallas, Theatre '47, Gulf Oil Playhouse, 11 July 1947; New York, Music Box Theatre, 6 October 1948; revised as *Eccentricities of a Nightingale,* Nyack, N.Y., Tappan Zee Playhouse, 25 June 1964; Washington, D.C., Theatre Club, 20 April 1966; Buffalo, Studio Arena Theatre, 8 October 1976; New York, Morosco Theatre, 23 November 1976;

A Streetcar Named Desire, New York, Ethel Barrymore Theatre, 3 December 1947;

The Rose Tattoo, New York, Martin Beck Theatre, 3 February 1951;

Camino Real, New York, National Theatre, 19 March 1953;

27 Wagons Full of Cotton, New Orleans, Tulane University, 17 January 1955; in *All in One,* New York, Playhouse Theatre, 19 April 1955;

Cat on a Hot Tin Roof, New York, Playwrights' Company, Morosco Theatre, 24 March 1955;

Something Unspoken, Lake Hopatcong, N.J., Lakeside Summer Theatre, 22 June 1955; in *Garden District,* New York, York Playhouse, 7 January 1958;

Three Players of a Summer Game, Westport, Conn., White Barn Theatre, 19 July 1955;

Sweet Bird of Youth, Coral Gables, Fla., Studio M Playhouse, 16 April 1956; New York, Martin Beck Theatre, 10 March 1959;

Suddenly Last Summer, in *Garden District,* New York, York Playhouse, 7 January 1958;

Talk to Me Like the Rain and Let Me Listen, Westport, Conn., White Barn Theatre, 26 July 1958;

Period of Adjustment, Miami, Coconut Grove Playhouse, 29 December 1958; New York, Helen Hayes Theatre, 10 November 1960;

I Rise in Flame, Cried the Phoenix, in *Two Short Plays,* Theatre de Lys, New York, 14 April 1959;

The Night of the Iguana, Spoleto, Italy, Festival of Two Worlds, 2 July 1959; Miami, Coconut Grove Playhouse, 1960; New York, Royal Theatre, 28 December 1961;

The Milk Train Doesn't Stop Here Anymore, Spoleto, Italy, Festival of Two Worlds, 11 July 1962; New York, Morosco Theatre, 16 January 1963;

The Gnädiges Fräulein, in *Slapstick Tragedy,* New York, Longacre Theatre, 22 February 1966; as *The Latter Days of a Celebrated Soubrette,* New York, Central Arts Cabaret Theatre, 16 May 1974;

The Mutilated, in *Slapstick Tragedy,* New York, Longacre Theatre, 22 February 1966;

The Two-Character Play, London, Hampstead Theatre Club, 12 December 1967; revised as *Out Cry,* Chicago, Ivanhoe Theatre, 8 July 1971; New York, Lyceum Theatre, 1 March 1973;

The Seven Descents of Myrtle, New York, Ethel Barrymore Theatre, 27 March 1968; revised as *Kingdom of Earth,* Princeton, N.J., McCarter Theatre Company, 6 March 1975;

In the Bar of a Tokyo Hotel, New York, Eastside Playhouse, 11 May 1969;

Confessional, Bar Harbor, Maine, Maine Theatre Arts Festival, Summer 1970; revised as *Small Craft Warnings,* New York, Truck and Warehouse Theatre, 2 April 1972;

I Can't Imagine Tomorrow, PBS-TV, 3 December 1970;

The Red Devil Battery Sign, Boston, Schubert Theatre, 18 June 1975;

This Is (An Entertainment), San Francisco, American Conservatory Theatre, Geary Theatre, 20 January 1976;

Vieux Carré, New York, St. James Theatre, 11 May 1977;

Tiger Tail, Atlanta, Alliance Theatre, 20 January 1978;

Crève Coeur, Charleston, S.C., Spoleto Festival U.S.A., 1 June 1978; as *A Lovely Sunday for Crève Coeur,* New York, Hudson Guild Theatre, 21 January 1979;

Will Mr. Merriwether Return from Memphis?, Key West, Fla., Tennessee Williams Fine Arts Center, 24 January 1980;

Clothes for a Summer Hotel, New York, Cort Theatre, 26 March 1980;

Some Problems for the Moose Lodge, in *Tennessee Laughs,* Chicago, Goodman Theatre, 11 November 1980; expanded as *A House Not Meant to Stand,* Chicago, Goodman Theatre, 1 April 1981; revised version, Chicago, Goodman Theatre, 27 April 1982;

Something Cloudy, Something Clear, New York, Jean Cocteau Repertory, 7 February 1982.

SCREENPLAYS: *The Glass Menagerie,* by Williams and Peter Berneis, Warner Bros., 1950;

A Streetcar Named Desire, by Williams and Oscar Saul, Warner Bros., 1951;

The Rose Tattoo, by Williams and Hal Kanter, Paramount, 1955;

Baby Doll, Warner Bros., 1956;

Suddenly Last Summer, by Williams and Gore Vidal, Columbia, 1959;

The Fugitive Kind, by Williams and Meade Roberts, United Artists, 1960;

Boom, Universal, 1968.

OTHER: Carson McCullers, *Reflections in a Golden Eye,* introduction by Williams (New York: New Directions, 1950).

PERIODICAL PUBLICATIONS: "Questions Without Answers," *New York Times,* 3 October 1948, II: 1;

"Tennessee Williams Presents His POV," *New York Times Magazine,* 12 June 1960, p. 19;

"Survival Notes: A Journal," *Esquire,* 78 (September 1972): 130-134, 166, 168;

"Let Me Hang It All Out," *New York Times,* 4 March 1973, II: 1.

Tennessee Williams's playwriting career spanned more than four decades and was marked by the highest acclaim, as well as the kind of critical controversy that is generated only by one whose achievements have been widely recognized and lauded. This recognition of achievement took many forms, most notably four New York Drama Critics Circle Awards and two Pulitzer Prizes. His choice to explore his basic themes through what have been labeled degenerate characters and sordid situations created controversy. Because of his southern roots, he was more closely tied in theme to twentieth-century southern fiction writers than to other dramatists of the period. His concern with isolation, the difficulty of communication, and the solitary search for values in a chaotic world—as well as the frequent use of southern settings and characters—links him to writers like William Faulkner and Carson McCullers. Though his work was preceded by the social protest of the 1930s, he focused on the individual rather than on the fabric of society as a whole; this artistic direction, along with his use of lyrical language, differentiates his work from that of Arthur Miller, his only contemporary to achieve the same major status.

He was born Thomas Lanier Williams on 26 March 1911 in Columbus, Mississippi, the second child of a Puritan-Cavalier marriage. His mother, Edwina Dakin Williams, prim daughter of the Episcopal minister, had been "swept off her feet" by robust salesman Cornelius Coffin Williams, descended from a line of East Tennessee frontiersmen and political officeholders. During Williams's early years his father was on the road a great deal, so he, his mother, and his older sister, Rose, lived in the rectory with his maternal grandparents. The family moved to Clarksdale, Mississippi, when young Williams entered school.

An early childhood plagued by illness—a near-fatal bout with diphtheria left him convinced that he had suffered irreparable heart damage—kept him from the company of other children. A weak physical condition, combined with the influence of his delicate and protective mother, earned him the ridicule of both other children and his boisterous, highly masculine father, who according to Williams nicknamed his son "Miss Nancy."

When Williams was eight years old, his father's promotion to a managerial position uprooted the family from the safe and serene world of small-town Mississippi. Negative effects of the move to industrialized Saint Louis were felt by Williams, his mother, and his sister. His brother, Dakin, was born soon after the relocation. A few years later, the unhappy young Williams turned to writing as a means of both escape and recognition. Through poetry and short stories, he won prizes from advertising contests, school publications, and women's clubs.

His first published work came in 1927: an essay answering the question "Can a Good Wife Be a Good Sport?" was awarded third prize in a contest sponsored by *Smart Set* magazine. The next year his short story "The Vengeance of Nitocris" was published in *Weird Tales;* he received thirty-five dollars.

In 1929 Williams entered the University of Missouri, where he won small prizes for poetry and prose, pledged a fraternity, and discovered alcohol as a cure for the extreme shyness that had thus far kept him in virtual isolation. When he failed ROTC during his third year, his father withdrew him from school and set him to work in the International Shoe Company warehouse. His days were spent in the monotony and drudgery of dusting shoes and typing order forms; during the nights he turned to writing. The tedium and repression of his job led to a nervous breakdown in 1935, from which he recovered by spending a year in Memphis with his sympathetic grandparents.

During the year in Memphis, Williams was introduced to drama. A farce about two sailors on shore leave, *Cairo, Shanghai, Bombay,* was his first produced play. The Memphis Garden Players' production on 12 July 1935 introduced him to the thrill of watching an audience react to his work. Returning to Saint Louis to enroll at Washington University, he had decided that writing would be his career.

While studying at Washington University, Williams wrote *Me, Vashya* as an entry in the school's annual playwriting competition; he was disappointed to win only honorable mention. During this period he also became involved with the Mummers, a small Saint Louis theatrical group headed by Willard Holland. Williams remembered the group as dynamic, nonconformist, and charged with electricity. He was invited to write a curtain raiser for their 1936 Armistice Day production of Irwin Shaw's *Bury the Dead.* The group subsequently produced two of Williams's longer early plays, *Candles to the Sun* (1937) and *Fugitive Kind* (1937) (a title later given to the film version of *Orpheus Descending*).

By 1937 his sister, Rose, who had since childhood become increasingly withdrawn and disturbed, was institutionalized as an incurable schizophrenic. She underwent one of the first prefrontal lobotomies performed in the United States. Williams had always felt an extreme closeness and fondness for his delicate sister, and the pain of watching her deterioration prompted his decision to leave Saint Louis. With his grandmother's financial assistance he entered the University of Iowa, where he studied with Professor E. C. Mabie, wrote two long plays (*Spring Storm* and *Not About Nightingales*), and in 1938 earned a B.A. degree.

Following his graduation from Iowa, Williams spent a year as an itinerant writer, wandering from Chicago (where he tried unsuccessfully to work with the WPA Writers' Project—his writing lacked "social content" and his family was not destitute) to Saint Louis, New Orleans, and California. During this period he concentrated on writing poetry and short fiction as well as one-act plays. He gathered valuable material which would appear later in the characters, settings, and situations of his short fiction and dramatic works. His short story "The Field of Blue Children" was published in the summer 1939 issue of *Story* magazine. This was his first work to appear under the name Tennessee Williams, the permanently adopted nickname replacing his given name, Tom.

About this time he was awarded a special prize of $100 in a play contest sponsored by the Group Theatre. His entry was the four long plays written up to that time, in addition to a group of one-acts called *American Blues.* While his full-length plays did not win the contest, the judges thought his one-acts merited attention, and they created a special award for the collection including five short works.

In *Moony's Kid Don't Cry,* the first of the group (produced in 1946), a young couple have awakened and are bickering in the middle of the night. As Moony complains about having left his job as a woodsman to work in a factory, his wife Jane frets that he will awaken their one-month-old son. Moony misses the freedom of the outdoors and resents being restrained by a dull, repetitive job and the responsibilities of a wife and child. They quarrel, and Moony announces that he is walking out. Jane brings the sleeping infant to him, telling him that if he is going, he can take his kid with him. Jane returns to bed as her husband becomes completely absorbed in his baby and croons to the child that he has no intention of leaving. The theme of the restless, unfulfilled dreamer battling against the restraints of practicality is repeated frequently in later plays.

In *The Dark Room* a prim social worker interviews an Italian woman ("an avalanche of female flesh") about her fifteen-year-old daughter. The mother is reluctant to answer questions, but gradually the social worker learns that the father is in the city sanatorium, the older sons have deserted the family, and the daughter has spent the past six months lying naked in bed in a darkened room. She is visited regularly by her married lover, who brings her food. Just before the curtain, the mother reveals to her already shocked inquisitor that the girl is pregnant.

The Case of the Crushed Petunias (dedicated to Helen Hayes in February 1941) is included in the published collection with a publisher's note. The author on rereading found the piece immature and requested that it be omitted but was persuaded to permit its inclusion. It is a didactic, unsubtle contest in which life wins over death (or death-in-life). Miss Simple of Primanproper, Massachusetts, is persuaded by a Young Man to forgive him for crushing the double row of petunias which serve to barricade her house and her heart from the world. She changes the name of her little shop from Simple Notions to Tremendous Inspirations and sets off to meet the Young Man on Highway No. 77 where she will exchange her spinsterish regimentation for thinking, feeling, experiencing, and living. The theme is handled much more effectively in later works.

The Long Stay Cut Short, or, The Unsatisfactory Supper is a three-character one-act which later served (with *27 Wagons Full of Cotton*) as the basis of the filmscript *Baby Doll* (1956). Archie Lee Bowman, a tooth-sucking rural southerner, and his large, indolent wife Baby Doll commiserate over Aunt Rose's cooking. Aunt Rose is a senile eighty-five-year-old relative with no home of her own who is passed from household to household; at present she is based with Archie Lee and Baby Doll, and they have grown weary of her forgetfulness and eccentricity. Despite his wife's protests, Archie Lee finally announces that it is time for Aunt Rose to move on. Sensing that despite all her efforts, she has become a burden, Aunt Rose wanders into the yard as a twister approaches. As the curtain falls, she struggles against the strong wind which is certain to blow her away. Though the conclusion smacks of deus ex machina, the play exhibits Williams's expertise at creating southern dialogue and sharply defined characterizations.

The longest of the volume's one-acts, *Ten Blocks on the Camino Real,* was later expanded into the full-length *Camino Real* (1953). The dreamlike fantasy contains characters from history, literature, and contemporary folklore placed in a Mexican setting. Kilroy, the all-American ex-boxer with a heart " as big as the head of a baby," has been dealt a losing hand—his naivete makes him an easy mark for swindlers—but he persists in seeking human goodness as he journeys down the hostile road known as Camino Real. When he dies, an autopsy reveals that his heart is solid gold. He comes back to life; attempts to win a gypsy's daughter with furs, jewels, and trinkets procured in exchange for his golden heart; and is rejected. At the end of the play he heads off with rusty-armored Don Quixote, who admonishes him to avoid self-pity.

Mollie Day Thatcher, one of the judges for the Group Theatre's award, was so impressed with this collection that she kindled the interest of Audrey Wood, a successful literary agent, who through a highly unusual procedure solicited Williams as a client, beginning a writer-agent relationship that would last for over two decades.

After exhausting the Group Theatre prize money, Williams returned to Saint Louis, where he worked on *Battle of Angels*. He soon received word that Audrey Wood had secured for him a $1000 Rockefeller Foundation grant, followed by a scholarship at the New School for Social Research in New York: There he worked with John Gassner

and Theresa Helburn on revisions of *Battle of Angels* and saw produced his one-act *The Long Goodbye* (1940). In the one-act play, Joe is a young would-be writer overseeing the move from the apartment where his family has lived for twenty-five years. As he packs and supervises movers, his reminiscences of a quarter of a century of family joys and sorrows, people now dead or gone, are played out in periodic flashbacks.

In December 1940 the Theatre Guild opened *Battle of Angels* in Boston, with plans for a New York production to follow. What Williams anticipated as a glorious beginning of his career proved to be a glorious disaster. The opening night audience—those few who remained until the onstage conflagration at the end of the play—were driven from the theater in a billow of smoke created by a stagehand overcompensating for his failure to produce more than a wisp during dress rehearsal. The critical response was negative, and the Boston City Council's reaction to the content of the play was even worse. Despite hasty revisions, the production was closed after its two-week Boston run.

The original story line follows the Lawrencian theme of repressed passion awakened by a wild and free poetic spirit. Disappointed in love and grieved over her father's death in a fire set by the town's leading citizens, Myra Torrance had years earlier consigned herself to a loveless marriage with a malicious, crotchety old storekeeper. At the beginning of the play, her husband's impending death from cancer has just been medically confirmed. Val Xavier, a vagabond poet dressed in a snakeskin jacket, is hired by Myra to do odd jobs in the dry goods store. Myra's repressed sexuality is awakened by the wild and mysterious Val, whose attractiveness creates quite a stir among the town's female population. Among those affected by his virility are Cassandra Whiteside, a fallen aristocrat who has given in to alcohol and promiscuity, and Vee Talbott, the sheriff's wife, whose sexuality is sublimated through primitive painting and religious fanaticism. Through her affair with Val, Myra blossoms, her former sharpness and tension replaced by a glowing softness. Both the townspeople and her dying husband are aware of the illicit relationship, and when on Good Friday Val is sought on a trumped-up rape charge, a lynch mob is ready. Jabe Torrance shoots his unfaithful wife, laying the blame on Val, who is carried off to the hanging tree by a hysterical posse armed with a blowtorch.

The production mounted by the Theatre Guild was the first version of Williams's perhaps most reworked play. Over the years it was to undergo numerous revisions and title changes. The original bears several of the Williams trademarks: it is set in a small southern town, it presents the romantic theme of repressed passion and spiritual sterility, and it contains several sharply drawn minor characters. Though Boston's city fathers objected to the playwright's mix of sex and religion, other critics generally agreed that offense to a puritanical sense of propriety and decorum is not the play's only problem. Its chief flaws are also typically Williams: too much plot makes it overly complicated and confusing, as well as lacking in unity; the characters tend toward morality-play symbols rather than real people; and the playwright's lyricism gets out of hand.

Dejected over the failure, Williams returned to the Vieux Carré in New Orleans. From there he moved to New York, where he worked as a theater usher, elevator operator, and waiter-entertainer. This bohemian period provided him with material for numerous short stories and one-acts. He also began collaboration with his friend Donald Windham on the comedy *You Touched Me!* (produced in 1945). In 1943, just when desperation over lack of funds was setting in, Audrey Wood secured for him a Metro-Goldwyn-Mayer scriptwriting contract in Hollywood at the incredible salary of $250 a week. He worked in Hollywood from May to November of that year. His first assignment was to write a Lana Turner vehicle (which he remembers as "The Celluloid Brassiere"); his script was rejected. With less than gracious comments about child actors, he refused his next assignment: a movie for Margaret O'Brien. He then presented an idea of his own for a film script, an outline of a work entitled "The Gentlemen Caller." This idea was also rejected, and shortly thereafter he was advised to continue to draw his paycheck but to stay away from the office. During the remainder of his contract he worked on his scenario, changing it to stage form and renaming it *The Glass Menagerie* (1944).

Agent Wood liked the play that had been rejected by Hollywood, and she found equal enthusiasm in Eddie Dowling, who agreed to direct as well as play the role of Tom. The production opened in Chicago in late December of 1944, bringing back to the stage the actress considered by many to be America's best, Laurette Taylor. Williams finally achieved the success that had eluded him four years earlier with *Battle of Angels.* Though audiences were sparse at first, a barrage of favorable newspaper criticism gradually generated interest, and after a few weeks people were flocking to see the play. By the time it opened in New York in

March 1945, eager audiences were awaiting it. Scarcely two weeks later, it was chosen after only fifteen minutes' deliberation for the New York Drama Critics Circle Award. Its Broadway run lasted almost two years.

The Glass Menagerie is Williams's gentlest play. By virtue of frequency of productions and publication in anthologies, it is probably his most popular. Because its focus is away from the "sex, decay, and violence" motifs so prevalent in most of his later works, it has appealed to audiences who have found his other plays distasteful in subject matter. Nonetheless, in both its mood and its concerns, the play is characteristic of Williams's mature and best work.

In contrast to the overly complicated *Battle of Angels,* it presents a story simply told through only four characters. Williams looked to his own family and experience in creating the Wingfields—Amanda and her grown children Tom and Laura—who live in a dingy Saint Louis apartment building during the Depression. The autobiographical character Tom serves as narrator, setting the scene at the beginning and periodically addressing the audience in poetic monologues; he also participates in the action, thus giving the audience a representational view of the events as he remembers them, as well as his retrospective comments. A poet trapped in a mundane existence, he works days in a shoe factory and spends his evenings writing or going to the movies. His sister, Laura, whose crippled leg is symbolic of her psychic deformity, is so painfully shy that she avoids reality almost altogether, creating her world through playing old phonograph records and tending a collection of glass animals. Their mother, Amanda, combines obsession with her romanticized southern debutante past and a fierce determination to survive a grim present. The husband/father of the family, referred to as "the telephone man who fell in love with long distances," deserted them years before. His prominent photograph is a constant reminder to Amanda of dreams gone sour; to Tom, the father with whom he is often bitterly compared represents escape.

The plot line is a simple one. Since high school, Laura has become more and more withdrawn. A business course proved a miserable failure; her shyness made her physically ill. Pinning all her hopes for the future on a marriage for her daughter, Amanda asks Tom to find a suitable young man among his friends at the warehouse. To pacify his mother—and missing the point of her grand design—he invites Jim O'Connor to din-

Anthony Ross, Laurette Taylor, Eddie Dowling, and Julie Hayden as Jim O'Connor, Amanda Wingfield, her son Tom, and her daughter Laura in a scene from the first Broadway production of The Glass Menagerie *(photo by Lucas-Pritchard, courtesy of the Museum of the City of New York)*

ner. Amanda is so excited over the prospect of a gentleman caller for her daughter that she practically redecorates the apartment in preparation. When Mr. O'Connor arrives, he proves to be everything Amanda could have desired: he is attractive, personable, and ambitious. He also turns out to be a former high school classmate of Laura's, someone she has quietly pined over for six years. After dinner, he and Laura talk, play music, and even dance. Their dancing is awkward, and they stumble into her animal collection, breaking the horn from a glass unicorn. The accident changes the mood from gaiety to tenderness, and what begins as Jim's attempt to build Laura's confidence becomes an expression of genuine admiration, ending in a kiss. Apologizing, Jim makes a clean breast by explaining that he cannot call Laura again because he is engaged to be married. His rather abrupt departure is followed by Amanda's railing at Tom for

the cruel joke he has played on his family. Frustrated and angry, Tom leaves the house. As narrator, he reveals in the final lyrical monologue that soon after the fateful dinner he left his mother and sister for good, and has since then tried unsuccessfully to blot out his guilt.

The play's major theme is illusion versus reality. Laura, patterned after the playwright's sister, Rose, is the first of a long series of Williams characters who exhibit a fragility that renders them incapable of coping with the harshness, cruelty, and insensitivity of reality. Williams maintains his sympathy for these tortured people, no matter in what direction their escape takes them. Unlike later sufferers who turn to drugs, alcohol, or sex, Laura creates her own fantasy world of romantic music and tiny, delicate glass ornaments. Like the animals of her collection, she is beautifully fragile—but easily broken. Amanda, faced with economic hardship, a son who she fears is unambitious and irresponsible, a daughter both physically and emotionally crippled, and rejection by the man who swept her off her feet, seeks solace in the past. She is a survivor—she has great depths of energy, pride, and even practicality—but scraping and clawing for survival rub against her grain. She retreats into numerous anecdotes of her days as the belle of the Delta, entertaining gentleman callers by the droves, and even demonstrates her charming technique (complete with a girlish frock resurrected from a trunk) when Jim O'Connor comes to dinner. Tom as narrator is of course able to recognize and comment on the variance between truth and illusion, and he admits his own penchant for airbrushing his memories of the past. The Tom who appears in the play's action is facing the poet's conflict between the practical and the ideal. He feels love and responsibility for his mother and sister, but he yearns for romance, adventure, experience, and escape from his stifling "two by four situation." Though narrator Tom calls Laura's gentleman caller "an emissary from a world of reality that we were somehow set apart from," Jim O'Connor also has created his own world of illusion. The former high school hero relies on self-improvement courses and cliché-ridden bravado to soften the jar of unfulfilled dreams and unrealized potential.

Though the play is effectively simple in plot, it is rich in symbolism as well as a blending of production elements to create a mood of strong yet controlled grief. Both music and lighting are employed to produce the effect of memory—gentle and poetic. The language is highly evocative, particularly in Tom's monologues; some critics have found fault with what they see as strained, overdone lyricism. Another element of the original script has also been widely criticized. Williams conceived of the use of a screen device which would bear legends or images underscoring the particular point of each scene. Eddie Dowling omitted the screen device from the original show, and except for rare experimental productions, it has not been used since.

In September following the highly successful opening of *The Glass Menagerie* came the opening of a much less successful play. Actually written before *The Glass Menagerie, You Touched Me!* was a collaboration between Williams and his friend Donald Windham. An adaptation of the D. H. Lawrence short story of the same title, the play is a lyrical comedy with symbolic characters and action. A dying old captain lives with his unmarried

daughter and sister. An adopted "charity boy," Hadrian, after an absence of several years returns in hopes of getting some of the old man's money. Hadrian is now a virile and attractive young man with romantic feelings toward the captain's hesitant daughter Matilda. Though she has been involved in a lengthy courtship with a clergyman, the captain's sister Emmie militantly disavows the flesh. Sex and freedom are pitted against reticence and frozen virginity, and a contrived ending leaves Matilda with Hadrian, Emmie with her clergyman, and the captain rejuvenated. The critics generally found the production disappointing: as a follow-up of *The Glass Menagerie*, Lewis Nicols termed it "a fall from grace."

The collection *27 Wagons Full of Cotton and Other One-Act Plays* was published in 1946. It includes *The Long Goodbye*, produced at the New School for Social Research in 1940, and a dozen other short works. Some in the collection later had New York productions; many contain characters and scenes that found their way into later longer works. The title work, for example, was later merged with *The Unsatisfactory Supper* to form the screenplay *Baby Doll. 27 Wagons Full of Cotton*, written circa 1941 and produced in 1955, is set on the front porch of Jake Meighan's doll-like Gothic cottage near Blue Mountain, Mississippi. As the curtain rises, Jake, a fat man of sixty, leaves the yard carrying a gallon can of coal oil. A moment later his wife, Flora, a large, slow-witted, babyish woman, comes out looking for her lost purse. Jake has set fire to the cotton gin of the neighboring Syndicate Plantation; through sadistic arm-twisting combined with kisses, he forces Flora to provide his alibi. The next day the owner of the burnt gin, Silva Vicarro, brings twenty-seven wagons full of cotton for Jake to gin in his mill. Telling the small Italian that his wife was a huge baby doll when he married her, Jake leaves for the mill, instructing Flora to keep Vicarro comfortable in his absence. Vicarro has little difficulty in trapping the simple-minded Flora into revealing that her husband is the arsonist. Determined to get revenge, he begins a rape/seduction that includes flicking the large woman with his riding crop, while at the same time confusing her with sweet talk. The scene ends as he forces her into the house and her despairing cry is heard above the sound of the gin pumping across the road. Flora emerges from the house a ravaged mess: clothing torn, skin bruised, and blood trickling from the corner of her mouth. The scene takes place in moonlight, and when Jake arrives home from his day of work he is too tired and preoccupied with outsmarting Vicarro to notice his wife's condition. As Flora vapidly and laughingly explains that Vicarro was so impressed with Jake's "good neighbor policy" that he will probably bring twenty-seven more wagons of cotton to be ginned tomorrow, her husband is totally absorbed in gloating. As Jake wanders into the house, Flora idiotically croons "Rock-a-Bye Baby" to her large kid purse which she has stuffed with Kleenex "to make it big—like a baby!"

The Purification is a verse drama interesting for its experimental nature. Set in the breathtaking country around Taos, New Mexico (where Williams visited D. H. Lawrence's widow, Frieda), it is a ritualistic trial involving incest, murder, retribution, and purification. Including guitar music, pageantry, pantomime, and dance, the play celebrates incestuous love between brother and sister as superior to the sister's barren, loveless marriage to a rancher who killed her. In style and structure it contrasts sharply with the other plays in the volume. Its first production was in December 1959.

The Lady of Larkspur Lotion depicts a dyed-blond woman of forty who lives in a rooming house in the French Quarter. Her crass landlady demands the rent and scorns her prostitute tenant's pretense of gentility. A derelict writer passionately defends the prostitute's right to live in a world of invention. As one who lives in his imagination, he pleads for compassion for the woman who awaits checks from the king of a mythical Brazilian rubber plantation. The prostitute who surrounds herself with dreams to compensate for life's brutality is a precursor of *A Streetcar Named Desire*'s Blanche DuBois.

The Last of My Solid Gold Watches (1947) presents a Willy Loman-type drummer at the end of the line. "Mistuh Charlie" Colton gets genuine respect from the old Negro porter who sets him up in his familiar hotel room, but the response from young salesman Bob Harper is only rudeness and impertinence. The contrast is sharp between "Mistuh Charlie," who takes pride in quality, craftsmanship, and strength of character, and the "young peckerwood" Harper, who represents the ignorance, bad manners, and cheap commercialism that have replaced the old values. "Mistuh Charlie" is an early version of *Cat on a Hot Tin Roof*'s Big Daddy. The sympathetic portrayal of the shoe salesman is indicative that Williams's feelings toward his own salesman father were by no means entirely negative.

The main character of *Portrait of a Madonna* (1947) is another preview of Blanche DuBois. Miss Collins is a middle-aged spinster who, without her knowledge, is being committed to the state asylum. While waiting for the authorities who will take her away, a sympathetic old porter and an impudent young elevator boy occupy her in conversation. Her illusionary role as hostess and coquette is reminiscent of Amanda and her gentlemen callers in *The Glass Menagerie*. Miss Collins is the epitome of repression. For the fifteen years since her mother's death, she has lived as a recluse in her apartment, surrounding herself with delusions and sexual fantasies. She imagines that she has been molested ("he indulged his senses with me") by the man who years before rejected her to marry a girl from Cincinnati, and that she is now pregnant with his child. She is led away by a dutiful doctor and his efficient nurse in a scene that anticipates the ending of *A Streetcar Named Desire*. The woman is obviously mad, but Williams draws her obsessive, overrefined character with a great deal of sympathy.

In *Auto-Da-Fé*, which the author calls "a tragedy in one act," a mama's boy in his late thirties bickers with his mother on the porch of their frame cottage in the Vieux Carré of New Orleans. Madame Duvenet, the frail mother, is a cleanliness fanatic; her son Eloi is a thinker of dirty thoughts. He reveals that by accident he has gained possession of a lewd photograph, and she orders him to burn it in her presence. Finding the corruption all around him inescapable, Eloi locks himself inside the house and sets it on fire in a lunatic mission of purification.

Lord Byron's Love Letter is set in the French Quarter during Mardi Gras. Two impoverished women attempt to cash in on the curiosity of the tourists by advertising that they possess a love letter written by Lord Byron to the grandmother of one of them. A matron from Milwaukee is intrigued with the story and persuades her husband to join her inside the women's parlor, but the sound of the parade draws them away without paying the dollar the two women request. The letter is a fake; it was written not by Lord Byron, but by the woman's grandfather—however, its lyrical romantic style is in ironically poignant contrast to the circumstances to which the pair have been reduced.

The Strangest Kind of Romance, a "lyric play in four scenes," is Williams's dramatization of his short story "The Malediction." In the first scene the Little Man moves into a furnished room in an industrialized midwestern city. The Landlady, an overbearing shrew, agrees to let him keep the cat that stayed in the room with the previous tenant. In the second scene she seduces the Little Man by arguing gently that "Nature says, 'Don't be lonesome.' " Three characters appear in the third scene: the Little Man, his cat to whom he lovingly feeds cream, and an Old Man who utters his malediction against corrupt industrialization. In the final scene the Little Man, who has been laid off at the plant because of his ineptitude with machinery, returns to find that his room has been rented to the Boxer and his beloved cat has been turned out. At the close, the Little Man has found his cat, the Boxer is slipping into the role of lover to the Landlady, and she gazes wonderingly out the window at "The funniest pair of lovers! The ghost of a man—and a cat named Nitchevo!" Though the social protest is a bit heavy-handed, the scenes between the Little Man and his cat are touchingly effective.

The main character of *Hello from Bertha* is another of Williams's prostitutes, but this one suffers no delusions of grandeur. She occasionally makes false claims of friends in high places, but she makes no attempt to deny her surroundings: she lies in a brass bed in a gaudy, disheveled bedroom in " 'the valley'—a notorious red-light section along the river flats of East St. Louis." What Bertha does deny is that she is close to death. As the landlady Goldie argues that she must see a doctor, Bertha maintains that she is fully capable of returning to work—she only needs rest. As her physical and mental deterioration become more and more apparent, she dictates a letter to a beau of bygone days who stood her up to marry "a little choir singer." The play is a grimly realistic, sympathetic but unsentimental view of the demise of a pathetic isolate.

The lead character of *This Property Is Condemned* is also a prostitute, a thirteen-year-old combination of childish innocence and worldly experience. As the girl Willie balances on a railroad track, she explains her delinquent life to a slightly older boy, Tom. Her mother "run off with a brakeman on the C. & E.I," her father disappeared, and her sister Alva (who was "The Main Attraction" with the railroad men) died two years before of "Lung affection." Since then Willie has worn her sister's clothes and makeup, inherited her beaux, and lived alone in a condemned house. She holds on to her doll, but speaks matter-of-factly about exchanging sexual favors for gifts from the railroad men, and dreams romantically of flowers, violin music, jewels, and going out with men who make good salaries. The play was produced in March 1946 at the Hudson Park Theatre in New York.

Talk to Me Like the Rain and Let Me Listen is a dramatic tone poem set in a furnished room in midtown Manhattan. As rain falls outside, the Man awakens from a drunken sleep and tells the Woman what he can remember of a days-long binge in various parts of the city. She then recites to him her fantasy of going away to a "little hotel on the coast" where she will live in quiet isolation for half a century, communing with no one except people in stories and dead poets. She imagines for herself a gentler version of Aunt Rose's demise in *The Unsatisfactory Supper:* she will grow thinner and thinner until she has no body at all, and the wind will "pick [her] up in its cool white arms forever, and [take her] away." Williams's stage directions at the beginning indicate that "the present scene between them is the repetition of one that has been repeated so often that its emotional contents, such as reproach and contrition, have been completely worn out and there is nothing left but acceptance of something hopelessly inalterable between them." The play was produced 26 July 1958 at the White Barn Theatre in Westport, Connecticut.

Something Unspoken reveals a love/hate relationship between two southern women. Miss Cornelia Scott is a snobbish, elderly spinster of some social prominence; Grace Lancaster has been her live-in secretary since she was widowed fifteen years before. Cornelia wants to be elected regent of the Daughters of the Confederacy, but, suspecting some opposition, has chosen to stay home from the meeting and periodically checks its progress through telephone conversations. A picture of the women's relationship emerges: there are hints of a lesbian relationship—perhaps unconsummated—between them. Cornelia dominates the weaker Grace, but the secretary is not totally overpowered. As Cornelia receives news that she has not been elected regent, Grace responds with "a slight equivocal smile . . . not quite malicious but not really sympathetic." The play was presented with *Suddenly Last Summer* on the double bill *Garden District* in January 1958.

The success of *The Glass Menagerie* led Williams into a period of isolation and depression which he chronicled in "On a Streetcar Named Success," a *New York Times* essay reprinted as the introduction to *A Streetcar Named Desire* (1947). Having been accustomed to struggling fiercely for survival, he found financial security and artistic recognition difficult to handle. An eternal hypochondriac, he also suffered physically. After undergoing the fourth in a series of cataract operations, he left New York in search of less civilized, therefore less complicated, surroundings. He found them in Mexico, where he stayed for a few months, working on "The Poker Night," a play that would become *A Streetcar Named Desire.* He returned to the States and spent the summer of 1946 on Nantucket Island with Carson McCullers. As the two began a long-term friendship and mutual admiration society (he had persisted in calling her the best American novelist of the twentieth century), they spent their mornings writing at opposite ends of a long table.

On 3 December 1947, *A Streetcar Named Desire* opened for a New York run that would last well over two years. The opening marked a culmination of drafts and revisions that had spread over a number of years. The play is set in the picturesque French Quarter, a section of New Orleans that Williams had come to know well through several extended stays scattered over almost a decade. The locale is described as a poor section with "a raffish charm," situated between the tracks and the river. It is inhabited by hardworking young couples—both black and white—who enjoy an easy contentment that remains undisturbed by outbreaks of passion. The sounds of a "Blue Piano," characterizing the "spirit of the life which goes on here," are heard intermittently throughout the play. It is against this backdrop that Williams sets his dra-

Marlon Brando and Jessica Tandy as Stanley Kowalski and Blanche DuBois in a scene from the first Broadway production of A Streetcar Named Desire *(Billy Rose Theatre Collection, New York Public Library at Lincoln Center, Astor, Lenox and Tilden Foundations)*

matic conflict between dying aristocracy and a cruder, but more vital, working class.

Blanche DuBois, dressed in white and looking as if she were going to a garden party, arrives at the home of her youngest sister, Stella. Stella is an aristocrat by birth, but as the family fortune dwindled, economic necessity forced her to seek a new life for herself. She has found happiness with her Polish husband, Stanley Kowalski, a sensual, attractive, high-tempered man who adores her. Her life with Stanley is a far cry from the plantation, Belle Reve, where the sisters grew up, but Stella accepts it with both honesty and pleasure. Stanley is unrefined—crude, even—but he has given her vitality and sexual passion. Sister Blanche's arrival on the scene disrupts Stanley and Stella's happy home; her presence threatens to destroy the contentment they have found.

The war that breaks out over the following months is one between gentility and commonness, illusion and truth, death and passion; and sex is the most frequently used weapon. Blanche is shocked by the coarseness of a life in which couples suddenly come to blows and equally as suddenly "kiss and make up," acting as though the violence had never occurred. She values the beauty that she associates with civilization: art, music, poetry, and refinement. Stanley is extremely threatened by this woman who does not hesitate to voice her dismay over the crudeness and coarseness she perceives. His love for Stella is genuine, and he fears that he is in danger of losing her, that Blanche's influence over her sister will take his wife away from him.

Blanche believes in illusion, while Stanley deals in hard reality. Recognizing that the world is not the beautiful ideal she would like, Blanche lives through creating illusions for herself and others. She claims to be on a leave of absence from her high school teaching job; in reality, she has been fired because of an involvement with a seventeen-year-old boy. She tells Stanley and Stella's friends that she is the younger of the sisters, when she is actually the older by five years. A paper shade hung over the bedroom light symbolizes her need to soften the glare of harsh reality. Stanley, on the other hand, has no patience with the kind of feminine wiles he perceives as hypocrisy and deception. After having his home disrupted and his marriage threatened, he is only too happy to expose Blanche as a fraud. Desperately needing to find security and peace, she has almost reached the point of marriage with Mitch, a large, awkward, gentle man who is devoted to his ailing mother. In a gesture motivated as much by retaliation toward Blanche as by masculine loyalty to his friend, Stanley reveals to Mitch that Blanche is not the virtuous lily with old-fashioned sexual ideals that she has pretended to be. Rather she has a past dotted with promiscuity: before coming to stay with Stanley and Stella, she had practically been thrown out of town for her numerous sexual escapades.

The conflict between Stanley and Blanche reaches physical culmination on the night that Stella is at the hospital giving birth to her first child. Distraught over the loss of Mitch, Blanche has retreated into alcohol and illusions of being rescued by an oil baron (reminiscent of the delusions of Miss Collins in *Portrait of a Madonna)*. Ecstatic over the impending birth of his child, Stanley returns home with a few celebratory drinks under his belt. His animalistic power has always frightened Blanche, but she also has been attracted by it. Her behavior toward him has often been flirtatious, even at times dangerously teasing. Her teasing has angered rather than aroused him, and, being a man who understands and respects power, he must retaliate for the threats to his manhood and self-esteem through an act of physical assertion. What begins as a conversation on a fairly even keel becomes a scene of violence. Feeling threatened physically, Blanche futilely attempts to use a broken bottle to fight off Stanley's advance. Announcing that, "We've had this date with each other from the beginning," he carries her inert figure to the bed for the rape that completely severs her tie with reality. In the final scene of the play, which takes place a few weeks later, a fragile, disoriented Blanche is led away to a state institution. As the curtain falls, Stanley "voluptuously, soothingly" comforts his sobbing wife, indicating that now that Blanche is gone, life for them will continue as before, that their relationship has weathered the enormous stress of her intrusion.

As attested by its tremendously popular and critical success, the play's strengths are many. Williams created a plot that is neither overly simplistic, nor burdened by the gratuitous complexities that marred the earlier *Battle of Angels*. With occasional expressionistic elements woven in to indicate Blanche's mental torment and deterioration, the action is for the most part straightforwardly representational, though heightened through the use of lighting, music, and details of set. The unique milieu of the French Quarter setting lends a vivid richness. The extensive use of symbols is less obtrusive and more intrinsic than in earlier plays. The excessive lyricism is confined for the most part to Blanche's speeches; given her character, they seem

not inappropriate. Williams also deals quite successfully with the conflicts of sexuality. He does not allow his characters to become representative types, diametrically pitted against each other as embodiments of good and evil. Stanley and Blanche are at irreconcilable odds, but Williams gives them both complexity and sympathetic treatment. Stanley is coarse and at times brutal, but he also embodies a vitality and an energy that the dying aristocracy lacks. Additionally he is a man under attack, and though his defensive counterattack is violent and destructive, it is mitigated somewhat by his devotion to Stella. Blanche, unequipped to deal with life's harshness and cruelty, hides in illusion and hypocrisy. Turning to promiscuity in search of warmth and comfort, she is unable to accept her own sexuality and creates a facade of virginal purity. However, her past is filled with traumas that justify psychological wounds—the suicide of her young husband, the prolonged illnesses and deaths of various relatives—and despite her hypocrisy, she exhibits genuine fragility, gentility, and compassion.

It is through the character of Stella that Williams best manages to avoid clear-cut dichotomy. Stanley is coarse and common, but he fully accepts, even revels in, his sexuality. Blanche, refined and aristocratic, denies hers. But Stella is proof that an overly simplified either/or choice is not necessary. Though she is by no means an easily derived combination of the two, she manages to maintain the gentility of her breeding while fully enjoying the sexual relationship that is central to her marriage.

The original production of *A Streetcar Named Desire* ran for 855 performances and won both the New York Drama Critics Circle Award and a Pulitzer Prize. It was followed by a highly successful film version, as well as London and Paris productions that drew unfavorable reviews but tremendous crowds. Thus Williams's reputation as a playwright was established internationally as well as in America.

His next New York production, *Summer and Smoke*, is a less successful treatment of some of the same themes. Completed before *A Streetcar Named Desire*, it was produced in Dallas in July 1947, five months before *A Streetcar Named Desire*'s opening. Its 102-performance New York run began 6 October 1948. It grew out of Williams's short story "The Yellow Bird" and is dedicated to Carson McCullers. Set in Glorious Hill, Mississippi, it focuses on the relationship between a minister's daughter and a young doctor. Again resorting to allegorical figures rather than well-drawn characters, Williams juxtaposes Miss Alma Winemiller with Dr. John Buchanan.

In the brief prologue, Alma and John as children meet in the town square in front of a statuary angel named Eternity. She has given him a box of handkerchiefs in a prim effort to improve his careless appearance. Calling her "Miss Priss," he refuses the gift, but gives her a rough kiss before jerking her hair ribbon and running away. The rest of the play takes place several years later; John and Alma are now in their twenties. Because her mother has slipped into senility and infantilism, Alma has assumed the duties of hostess of the rectory. With her overrefined manners and frequent heart palpitations, she is a clear image of repression. Young Dr. Buchanan, who has returned to live with his father (also a doctor) next door to the rectory, has shown great medical promise but has a penchant for "indulging his senses" with booze and women.

John and Miss Alma again meet in the park, and he is intrigued by the attractive young woman whose laughter is somewhat hysterical. Alma, likewise, is attracted by the vibrancy and charm of the man who diagnoses her as having a doppelgänger, an inner self-seeking release. Her invitation for him to attend a meeting of her literary club is a failure—he finds the members petty and dull—but a tenuous attraction-of-opposites rapport is established later that night when a hysterical attack sends her next door in search of the older doctor. Instead she finds John, who gives her sleeping pills, reveals that he is impressed with her sensitivity, and makes a date for the following Saturday.

On the date he takes her to Moon Lake Casino (Williams's ubiquitous romantic Mississippi night spot), a gambling, drinking, and gaming establishment "where anything goes." Alma explains her philosophy of life (man should reach beyond his grasp), chides him for his weak character and wasted talent, and confides that her unsatisfying relationships with men have been plagued by emotional distances, "wide stretches of uninhabitable ground." He kisses her, they discuss the various significances attached to sexual activity, he suggests going to a room above the casino, and Miss Alma, horribly offended, takes a taxi home.

A few weeks later John's house is the scene of a wild and noisy party in celebration of his engagement to Rosa Gonzales, a voluptuous Mexican girl seeking escape from poverty and deprivation. Goaded by a self-righteous neighbor, Alma calls John's father, who is working to eradicate a fever epidemic in a nearby town. Before his father's arrival, John is drawn from the party to the rectory,

where he finds comfort in the touch of Miss Alma's cool hands on his face. The party ends with a sudden gunshot; Rosa's drunken father mortally wounds the older Dr. Buchanan, who is outraged upon arriving to find his house the scene of raucous revelry.

A few months later Miss Alma is beginning to emerge from a period of psychologically induced illness and isolation. John has completed his father's work at the fever clinic and returned to town a hero. Miss Alma pays him a visit during which they discover that each has dramatically influenced the other. She has released her doppelgänger and, ready for life and experience, declares her love and offers herself to him. But, as Alma realizes, "The tables have turned with a vengeance." Taking to heart her pleadings that he strengthen his character and value spirituality, he has forsaken his wild ways and decided to settle down. He is now engaged to be married to Nellie Ewell, a young voice student of Miss Alma's who has flirted with him throughout the play. In the final scene, Miss Alma is again in the park near the stone angel. She strikes up a conversation with a young traveling salesman with whom she sets out for Moon Lake Casino, indicating that she is probably destined to become the town prostitute.

The culmination of the battle between the spirit and the senses seems to indicate that the flesh tempered by spirituality stands a better chance at survival than does its reverse. John has become respectable, but he has not sacrificed his vitality. Alma, however, too long locked in repressive physical denial, will know no limits once her bonds have been shaken. The battle between the mind and the flesh has excellent dramatic potential, but here Williams draws his symbols too sharply and distinctly for genuine flesh and blood characters to emerge. Miss Alma is too singular an embodiment of the spiritual, the "soul," which her name symbolizes. John's representation of physicality and science is blatant and heavy-handed. (He even lectures Alma on the essential centers of the human being, the brain, the belly, and the sex organs, using an anatomical chart as visual aid.) Williams allows symbols to take the place of characters, and the reversal of roles between these two symbols is unmotivated, therefore too neat. The play's minor characters do not rise above the level of stereotypes. Alma's puritanical father and peevish mother, the pseudo-intellectual members of the literary club, the giggling Nellie, and the hot-blooded Gonzaleses are either gratuitous cardboard figures or underdeveloped plot advancers.

The poorly received New York production did face the disadvantage of following the far superior *A Streetcar Named Desire,* to which it was inevitably—and unfavorably—compared. However, the earlier Dallas production was extremely well received, and a revival in 1952 was the off-Broadway hit of the season, even winning favorable reviews from some critics who had panned the Broadway debut. Both the Dallas and the Off-Broadway stagings were in small arena or thrust theaters. There is merit in the play's episodic structure which flows through lighting changes rather than scenery shifts, giving the piece an organic unity. Some critics believe that the less than subtle allegory and symbolism, which were so jarring in the larger-than-life emphasis of a large-scale production, dim somewhat in the more intimate setting of a small theater.

Two other notable events occurred during 1948: the publication of *American Blues: Five Short Plays* (the collection for which Williams had won the special Group Theatre Award in 1939) and *One Arm and Other Stories.* The short story collection includes "One Arm," "The Malediction" (dramatized as *The Strangest Kind of Romance*), "The Poet," "Chronicle of a Demise," "Desire and the Black Masseur," "Portrait of a Girl in Glass" (a germ of *The Glass Menagerie*), "The Important Thing," "The Angel in the Alcove," "The Field of Blue Children" (originally published in 1939; the first work published under the name Tennessee Williams), "The Night of the Iguana" (to be expanded into the later play of the same title), and "The Yellow Bird" (from which *Summer and Smoke* grew).

Williams's first attempt at longer fiction, the short novel *The Roman Spring of Mrs. Stone,* was published in 1950. His first visit to Rome in 1948 provided him material for the physical setting and social milieu. The title character is a recently widowed and recently retired actress who attempts to fill her life's emptiness by pursuing youth and sex. The portrayal is not sympathetic; her marriage to a rich "Easter bunny" businessman was a loveless one, and her acting career had depended on squashing others for her own self-advancement. As she seeks rebirth and rejuvenation in Italy, her predatory nature is no match for handsome gigolos who prey on rich, lonely women. The novel is much less successful than most of Williams's short fiction. The symbolism is too obvious, and, as in some of his drama, the characterizations are weak as a result of his concern with making them representatives of ideas or types. Some critics saw a descent into the pornographic (Mrs. Stone is followed around by an exhibitionist tramp with a penchant for urinating on walls). Donald Windham has unkindly suggested that Mrs. Stone is Williams's "first fictionalized self-portrait after his success."

Also significant during this period was the beginning of Williams's major intimate relationship. Though his sexual preference would not be officially announced to the world for several years, he had for a decade practiced homosexuality. His *Memoirs* (1975) chronicle his young and sincere (though unconsummated) love for Hazel Kramer; his only sexual experience with a female; and his discovery that his physical attraction was for his own sex. In the early 1940s his social circle became more and more homosexual, and according to his *Memoirs,* his own healthy-sized appetites were satisfied through almost constant sexual activity—often with pickups, sometimes with casual acquaintances, and occasionally with someone who would become a friend. The decade was dotted with a series of relationships, some of which Williams truly valued, but all of which were rather short-lived. In the fall of 1948, just before the opening of *Summer and Smoke,* he was reunited with a casual summer acquaintance, Frank Merlo, a young Sicilian from New Jersey. The two began living together, beginning a relationship that would continued until Merlo's death from lung cancer in 1963. They traveled together, and, though the relationship was not an exclusive one, their ties deepened so that *The Rose Tattoo,* which opened in 1951 after they had been together for two and a half years, was dedicated; "To Frank in return for Sicily."

Williams had found in the Mediterranean region a world that perfectly suited the anti-Puritan side of his nature. He was drawn to the warmth, cheerfulness, lustiness, and excitement he found in the Italian people. He began work on *The Rose Tattoo* in Rome and, after several revisions, completed it two years later in Key West, Florida. It is set in a Sicilian community on the Gulf Coast, thus combining the South of his origins and the Latin country for which he was developing a deep affection. The play is a warm celebration of sexual love.

Serafina delle Rose is a voluptuous woman whose total devotion to her husband Rosario is both cheerful and passionate. Rosario is a truck driver who hauls contraband under loads of bananas. Serafina, a seamstress, is pregnant; she claims that on the night of conception she awoke to find that her husband's tattoo of a rose had appeared for a few moments on her left breast, indicating that another "rose" was growing within her body. Fearing for

Rosario's safety, she anxiously awaits his return from his last haul in the employ of the Brothers Romano; tomorrow he will quit, pay for the ten-ton truck, and begin working for himself. As she waits, Estelle Hohengarten, a thin blond woman, promises to pay her an exorbitant price for the overnight construction of a rose silk shirt, an anniversary gift for a man she loves.

Serafina's worst fears are realized: Rosario is shot, his truck crashes, and he burns in the fire. A miscarriage results from her sudden grief. Three years pass; in the loss Serafina becomes slovenly and withdrawn. Having lost the husband with whom she made the marriage bed an altar, she now burns candles in front of the urn containing his ashes and worships the memories of her lost love. Her daughter, Rosa, grown into as passionate a female as her mother, has fallen in love with Jack, a young sailor, but Serafina, fearing impurity, shuts her daughter up in the house and locks away her clothes.

After a visit from Rosa's teacher, Serafina relents and allows her daughter to go to her high school graduation and picnic, but not before extracting from Jack a sacred promise that he will respect Rosa's innocence. Alvaro Mangiacavallo (Alvaro Eat-a-Horse) enters Serafina's house in pursuit of a novelty salesman who has bullied him on the highway; a violent argument ensues between the two strangers. The cheap salesman calls Alvaro names and knees him in the groin, leaving with threats to have him fired from his truck-driving job. In despair over his woes, Alvaro begins to cry, and Serafina joins him in his tears and then offers a bottle of wine. She is amazed to discover that this young truck driver who has a clown's face also has the body of her dead husband Rosario. As they drink the wine, they share past experiences and present troubles and begin to be drawn to each other. As she mends his torn clothing, Serafina gives him the unclaimed rose silk shirt to wear. They plan to meet for supper that evening, provided that young Rosa is not at home; Serafina insists that she must set a good example for her daughter.

When Alvaro comes that evening, Serafina has corseted and dressed herself to receive her caller. As they continue to exchange confidences, Alvaro's bumbling is more and more apparent, but the warmth between them grows. Gossip that her husband had not been faithful continues to nag Serafina, and Alvaro's phone call to Estelle Hohengarten confirms her fears that the man she worshiped had deceived her. She smashes the urn containing his ashes, gathers her strength, and makes plans for Alvaro to make a noisy pretense of leaving, but to return through the back door.

At daybreak Rosa and Jack return from the picnic. The wildly passionate Rosa wants to make love, but Jack is bound by his promise to her mother. As they argue, Serafina's cries can be heard from the house; Rosa assumes that her mother is dreaming of making love with Rosario. Jack leaves and Rosa goes inside, falling asleep crying on the couch. The next morning, obviously suffering from the wine of the night before, Alvaro stumbles out of the bedroom and in his stupor exclaims in amazement over the beauty of the sleeping Rosa. She awakens with a scream, arousing her mother, who violently chases Alvaro from the house. Rosa is angered by her mother's hypocritical inventions to explain Alvaro's presence in her bedroom. She defiantly leaves to meet Jack before he sails away, and at the last minute her mother gives her blessing. Then Serafina, realizing that her dead husband's ashes have blown away during the night, calls Alvaro back as she feels the burning of the rose tattoo on her breast, indicating that once again she has conceived.

The play suffers from some of the same flaws as *Battle of Angels* (one critic even called it a comic version of the earlier work). The plot is overly contrived and the ending is a simplistically happy wrap-up of a situation that has up to that point been developed through character complexity. Much of the symbolism is overdone. Among the dressmaker's dummies that fill the interior set are a widow and a bride "who face each other in violent attitudes, as though having a shrill argument." And Williams's excessive use of roses—from character names to tattoos to actual flowers—ultimately renders their effect almost comic. However, despite its weaknesses, the play does achieve a rich, robust, and warm effect. Its high-spirited earthiness, comic sequences, and convincing dialogue in some measure compensate for plot contrivance and excessive symbolism. As in *Battle of Angels*, there is a mixture of sex and religion, but in this case it is not an unhappy one: for Serafina, there is no conflict, for to her the one is the other. Thus when she discovers that the husband she had worshiped was not what she thought him to be, her reaction is to reevaluate and to continue her life, rather than to become embittered or to crumble. And though a particular man may prove faithless, she does not break faith with her belief in physical passion as the raison d'etre of her universe. Pleased with his celebration of the warmth of the Italian people, Williams reportedly dared the critics to mention "neurotic" in connection with this play. Though the production was met with mixed reviews, it enjoyed a successful run of 300 performances from early February through late October 1951.

Another significant event of 1951 was the publication of *I Rise in Flame, Cried the Phoenix,* Williams's dramatized tribute to D. H. Lawrence. The play finds Lawrence in the final moments before his death, seated before a banner of "the Phoenix in a nest of flames." Having seen most of his fiction banned, he is informed of the equivalent chaos created by his London exhibition of paintings. As he battles "like a tiger" in the face of death, his two companions are his German wife Frieda ("rather like a Valkyrie") and the soulful Englishwoman Bertha who reports the reaction to his exhibition. Lawrence recognizes rather ruefully that in his own unsuccessful search for God, he has himself become a god for many of his female admirers; his wife observes that he is jealous of Jesus Christ for having "beaten him to it," for having suffered "the *original* crucifixion." As the sun sets, he speaks metaphysically of the harlot darkness seducing the light, but triumphantly proclaims that "he'll climb out of her belly" and in the end there will be "great blinding, universal light." The brief play is suffused with Lawrencian notions and symbols that permeate many of Williams's works: the idealistic search for truth through art, the attaching of cosmic significance to sex, and the artist as Christ figure. The play's first professional production (of one performance) was on 14 April 1959.

Camino Real, an extended version of the earlier *Ten Blocks on the Camino Real,* was produced in March 1953. Though the ten "blocks," or scenes, were expanded to sixteen, the later play is in essence quite similar to its predecessor. It opens with rusty-armored Don Quixote and Sancho Panza arriving in the plaza of an unnamed tropical seaport bearing resemblance to "such widely scattered ports as Tangiers, Havana, Vera Cruz, Casablanca, Shanghai, New Orleans." On the left is the luxurious Siete Mares Hotel; across the street are a pawnshop, the gypsy's stall, and the flophouse "Ritz Men Only." A crumbling arch in the background leads to "Terra Incognita." In the foreground is a fountain (the source of water for the town's poor) that has gone dry. Recognizing the place as the end of the line, Sancho leaves his knight to return to La Mancha. Don Quixote announces that he will sleep, and from the figures of his dreams in this place, he will choose a new squire to accompany him on his journey.

What follows is Don Quixote's dream, "a pageant, a masque," set in the mythical seaport and populated with characters from history, literature, contemporary folklore, and the "dregs of humanity." The surrealistic action flows from scene to scene, with no lapse of time between. The scenes are announced by Gutman, the fat proprietor of the Siete Mares who represents the corruption of money. The other characters can be divided into two general types, the low-lifers and the romantics. In the first category are the streetcleaners, the loan shark, and other minor figures who suggest the dismal way of life on the plaza. Among the romantics is Lord Byron, a poet in search of freedom whose speeches include a particularly graphic description of the burning of Shelley's corpse. Another is Jacques Casanova, a proud gentleman fallen upon hard times who is ejected from the Siete Mares because of lack of funds. He finds some comfort in a relationship with Marguerite Gautier (Camille), whose advancing years force her to pay instead of being paid for the "love" she seeks. The hero of the piece is Kilroy, the cartoon character ex-boxer whose gullibility makes him easy prey for the vultures of the Camino Real, but whose blind optimism is unflagging.

The action within the frame of Don Quixote's dream is a surrealistic blend of carnival-type scenes and characters, lyrical and idealistic outpourings of hope, and mad chases which spill from the stage into the balconies and aisles of the theater. At the end Don Quixote awakens, water begins to flow from the fountain, and Kilroy accepts the old knight's invitation to travel with him into the Terra Incognita. The play closes with Don Quixote's optimistic and symbolic line "The violets in the mountains have broken the rocks."

A few reviewers criticized the play for both obscurity and overwhelming negativism. Many critics, however, found instead of obscurity a damaging lack of subtlety. And while many who populate the Camino Real have sunken into filth, sordidness, and vice, Williams clearly celebrates the notion that though life continuously deals dirty blows, it is only through maintaining hope and belief in the human spirit that the romantic may triumph in a cynical world. Stung by the negative response to the play, Williams suggested that audiences had perhaps become "a little domesticated in their theatrical tastes." However, experimentation with nonrealistic style is not the source of the play's lack of success. Rather the problems are the use of stock figures and types to replace characters, and the sentimentalizing of romantic idealism. The playwright attaches meaning and significance which do not legitimately grow out of the characters and situations. With his tendency to champion the underdog, Williams's fondness for the play (somewhat like his attachment for *Battle of Angels*) persisted; in a 1970 interview with David Frost, he stated that because it deals with the necessity of a romantic ideal, *Camino Real* is his favorite play. (It must be noted, however, that one of his purposes in the interview was to promote a current production of the play.) The theme is a valid one, though one which Williams deals with far more successfully in other works. The critics generally found it to be the least successful work of the earlier and most productive part of his career. The original production closed after only sixty performances.

In the following year, 1954, Williams's second collection of short stories was published. *Hard Candy: A Book of Stories* includes the title story; "Mysteries of the Joy Rio" (a variation on the same theme and setting as "Hard Candy," with different results); "Three Players of a Summer Game" (the germ of *Cat on a Hot Tin Roof*); "Two on a Party"; "The Resemblance Between a Violin Case and a Coffin"; "Rubio Y Moreno"; "The Mattress by the

Williams and his grandfather, the Reverend W. E. Dakin, December 1951 (reprinted by permission of the Memphis Commercial Appeal)

Tomato Patch"; "The Coming of Something to the Widow Holly"; and "The Vine." A major source of material was his experiences in New Orleans, but some characters and situations grew out of both his early years and his stint in California with M-G-M.

The tremendously successful *Cat on a Hot Tin Roof,* which opened 24 March 1955, satisfied audiences and critics that the author of *Camino Real* had not lost his touch. In this play he returns to a Southern setting, a realistic presentation, and a focus on crisis in one specific family. The universality of the play's situations and themes is unstated but rather allowed to grow naturally from its characters and events. Though various critics argue for one or another of the cast as *the* central figure, three emerge as major characters of the work. Brick Pollitt, a twenty-seven-year-old former athlete, has charm, good looks, and the possibility of inheriting a large Mississippi cotton plantation; but he has turned to alcohol and has formed a cool detachment from involvement of any sort. His wife Margaret, or Maggie, is a beautiful young woman intensely frustrated by her husband's rejection but fiercely determined not to walk away from the struggle. The third major figure is Brick's father, Big Daddy, a wealthy plantation owner by virtue of his own hard work, a man coarse of manner, but compelling in his vitality and decency.

The play is set in Brick and Maggie's bed sitting room of Big Daddy's plantation house. The occasion is Big Daddy's sixty-fifth birthday, but the party is planned as a double celebration: they have just received news that Big Daddy's suspected cancer has been diagnosed as only a spastic colon. However, all the family members except Big Daddy and his wife, Big Mama, have been told the truth; Big Daddy does in fact have terminal cancer. In a drunken escapade the night before, Brick has broken his ankle attempting to jump hurdles on the high-school athletic field. To include him in the party, the family is bringing the celebration upstairs to Brick and Maggie's room.

As Brick and Maggie dress for the party, their conversation provides both character development and exposition. The other houseguests are Brick's older brother, Gooper, his wife, Mae, and their five children (to whom Maggie refers as "no-neck monsters"). A long-term rivalry between brothers is apparent, though Brick has always maintained the favored position without exerting any effort at all. Gooper wants nothing more than he wants his father's approval, and he has doggedly followed all the rules in trying to win it. He has become an attorney, married a cotton carnival queen, and produced five grandchildren (with a sixth on the way) for his father. Brick, on the other hand, at present has little to recommend him. In his youth he was a football star, but an injury forced him out of his professional career, and he has given up a job as a sports announcer to do nothing but drink.

In addition to the obnoxiousness of the children, Mae's fertility is a sore point with Maggie, who is childless. Though Brick has no interest in taking over his father's plantation, Maggie urges her husband to fight for what is rightfully his. She knows, though, that their failure to produce children puts them at a disadvantage. However, she cannot admit to the rest of the family (though Mae's eavesdropping gathers the information) that her husband refuses to sleep with her.

Dialogue between Brick and Maggie reveals that the mysterious source of his discontent is somehow related to his relationship with Skipper, a college friend and football teammate who died of drugs and alcohol, the relationship between the two had been so strong that Maggie's jealousy had been aroused; after suggesting that their affection might be unnatural, she had forced Skipper into an unsuccessful attempt to prove her suspicions untrue. Taking Skipper's inability to perform in bed with her as proof, Maggie had concluded—and told Skipper—that the love he felt for her husband was indeed unacceptable in the world in which they were born and raised. Maggie assumes that it was her announcement of "truth" that led Skipper into a world of drugs, alcohol, and ultimately, death.

The second act begins with Big Daddy's birthday party, punctuated by simperings from Mae and Gooper and their children, the preacher's unsubtle suggestions that Big Daddy make a provision in his will for air-conditioning the church, and Big Mama's feeble attempts to ease the tension by making herself the butt of crass jokes. Big Daddy and Brick are left alone for the play's major confrontation scene, which begins with Big Daddy's demand to know why Brick drinks. His father's persistence results in Brick's expressing disgust with mendacity, to which Big Daddy replies that adjusting to lies and pretense is a necessity of life. After relentless probing, Brick reveals that Skipper's death came shortly after a phone call during which he made a drunken confession, and Brick hung up on him. Big Daddy announces his realization: Brick drinks because the disgust he feels is directed toward himself for his refusal to face the truth ("His truth, okay! But you wouldn't face it with him!"). As Big Daddy accuses Brick of being responsible for Skipper's death, of passing the buck, and of

refusing to face truth, Brick completes the exchange by telling his father that he has been lied to about the clinic reports; Bid Daddy is in fact dying of cancer: "Being friends is telling each other the truth. . . . You told *me*. I told *you!*" The act closes with Big Daddy's passionate curse against "ALL—LYING SONS OF—LYING BITCHES!"

The published play includes two versions of act three. The author's note explains that he wrote an altered ending at the request of director Elia Kazan. Three concerns of the director prompted the revision and mark the variation between the two versions. First Kazan "felt that Big Daddy was too vivid and important a character to disappear from the play except as an offstage cry after the second act curtain." Second he thought Brick's character should undergo some change as a result of the act two confrontation. Additionally he felt that the character of Maggie should be made more sympathetic. Williams disagreed with the first two of the three but deferred to Kazan and produced a third act incorporating all three suggestions. In his explanatory note he in no way acknowledges error in his original version, but indicates that the success of the playing script has more than justified the alterations made to satisfy Kazan. The Broadway version of act three is the one customarily used in production.

As Big Daddy exits cursing (there is no lapse of time between acts), Gooper and Mae gather the family members, the doctor, and the preacher to give Big Mama the truth about the cancer diagnosis. As the news is broken, Big Mama's evident partiality to Brick is agonizingly frustrating to Gooper and brings out all the nastiness in Mae. They have drawn up a dummy trusteeship which would give Gooper control over Big Daddy's holdings. In a sudden show of spunk Big Mama orders him to put away the papers, announcing that Big Daddy still lives, but even if he were to die, she might not be willing to let go of his rich land. When Big Daddy, disturbed by the stormy discussion, rejoins the family, Maggie announces that she is pregnant with Brick's child. As she and her husband are left alone, she admits the lie, but plans to make it true by locking up Brick's liquor until he makes love to her. As Brick expresses his admiration for her cunning and perseverance, Maggie speaks gently and determinedly of taking hold of him and handing his life back to him.

The play was one of Williams's most successful. The continuous action is tightly woven, and the themes of family conflict, lies and truth, spiritual paralysis, and literal decay and death are allowed to emerge naturally through character, dialogue, and situation. Neither the posturing, excessive lyricism, nor superimposed mythic proportions which mar so many other works exist in this play. Some of the minor characters (the mercenary Reverend Tooker, for instance) are no more than stereotypes. Mae is largely one-dimensional, and even Big Mama and Gooper provide challenges to actors to keep them from being flat. But Big Daddy, Maggie, and Brick are all vivid, complex, believable, and complete creations. The play ran for 694 performances and won for Williams his third New York Drama Critics Circle Award and second Pulitzer Prize.

In December of 1956 the film *Baby Doll*, directed by Elia Kazan, was released in New York. The plot line of Williams's script, a merging of the short plays *27 Wagons Full of Cotton* and The Unsatisfactory Supper, is essentially an interweaving of the two earlier plays; the major difference is that Baby Doll, instead of being middle-aged and fat, is a young and attractive blond. Archie Lee had married her two years previously, when her father died, agreeing that she would remain a virgin until her twentieth birthday (shortly approaching as the film opens). Long on physical appeal and short on intellect, she sleeps in a crib and sucks her thumb. The other characters from the two short plays—Archie Lee, Aunt Rose, and Silva Vacarro—remain virtually unchanged. As the story of arson in a Mississippi cotton town unfolds, Silva's seduction of Baby Doll varies from the original. He pursues the child-woman through her house, up into the rotting attic even, in a chase which frightens her at first, but gradually begins to excite her. When he finally gets what he wants—her signature on a statement that her husband burned Vacarro's gin—she is greatly disappointed. They spend the afternoon together (she sings a lullaby as he naps in her crib), but no consummation takes place. An attraction and rapport have been established, however, and he has awakened her sexually and given her a new awareness of her husband's meanness and brutality. Archie Lee returns, and in a drunken rage shoots Aunt Rose. As he is taken off by the police, Baby Doll and Silva (who have been hiding in a pecan tree) are free to celebrate her sexual awakening. Sensationally promoted, the film had tremendous popular appeal, but it elicited censorship battles and rousing critical condemnation. Thinking he had written only a funny story, Williams was mystified by critics who lambasted the film as "one of the most unhealthy and amoral pictures ever made in this country."

The volume of poetry *In the Winter of Cities* was published in 1956. It includes most of Williams's earlier poems (some revised) published in James Laughlin's *Five Young American Poets* (1944). Generally considered inferior to his drama, the poems express a range of ideas and themes which also appear in his plays: the artists as the "most destructible element in our society"; testimonials to D. H. Lawrence; sympathy for society's misfits; and the psychological merging of sex and religion.

In 1957 came the production of *Orpheus Descending,* a revision (according to Williams, seventy-five percent new writing) of the failed *Battle of Angels.* After the success of *A Streetcar Named Desire, The Rose Tattoo,* and *Cat on a Hot Tin Roof,* Williams thought audiences would be more ready than they had been in 1940 to accept the play's sexual and violent themes. He claims that despite its early failure, the work was never discarded, but remained "on the workbench" for the intervening seventeen years.

Orpheus Descending adheres closely to the story line of its predecessor. The revised play presents the downfall of a mysterious, charismatic wanderer, Val Xavier, as he kindles the affections of Lady Torrance, a middle-aged keeper of a dry goods store in a small Southern community. The title evokes comparison to the Greek myth of Orpheus, a skilled musician who goes into hell to retrieve his lost love Eurydice and is almost successful in shepherding her out. However, he is torn to pieces by the Furies when he gazes back at her before leaving the region of darkness. Val attempts to rescue Lady from the moribund psychological state she has entered as a result of being married to a tyrannical dying man, but he is eventually lynched by a vengeful and enraged mob.

A close reading of both *Battle of Angels* and *Orpheus Descending* reveals that Williams made significant alterations in characterization and events. For example, a frame device he had used in an earlier version of *Battle of Angels*—the play is opened and closed with brief scenes set a year following the horrible Easter weekend events—is eliminated. Myra's name is changed to Lady, intensifying her connection to the Holy Virgin, and Cassandra Whiteside becomes Carol Cutrere, sister of Lady's lost young lover. Instead of a fallen aristocrat, Carol is a burned-out humanitarian whose failed projects for social reform have led her to disillusionment, alcohol, and promiscuity. Val as Orpheus descends into the hell of the small Southern town choked by malevolent provincialism. In this version, the culprit becomes a vicious and degenerate society that destroys the nonconformist. The characters are more believable and the plot line is more plausible and less complex than in the earlier version.

Despite the improvements in the script, the production was a failure. Though there was little negative reaction to the play's "shocking" subject and theme, critics found it clumsily written. Their quarrel was not with the playwright's grim vision—he had written successful plays whose views were dark—but rather with a lack of artistry, as evidenced by "snarled symbolism" and unintentional self-parody. The production closed after only sixty-eight performances. Hollywood bought the play and with minor script assistance from Williams made of it a modestly successful film entitled *The Fugitive Kind* (1960). Then two and a half years after its Broadway failure, *Orpheus Descending* opened for an Off-Broadway run that received some critical acclaim and satisfied its author.

About the time of the failed Broadway production of *Orpheus Descending,* in 1957, Williams went into psychoanalysis. His friends had begun to comment that his plays were becoming more and more violent. The tensions of daily life that had always plagued him were becoming increasingly pronounced: he continued to suffer constant hypochondria, in addition to growing bouts with claustrophobia, fear of suffocation, and extreme dependency on alcohol. The death of his grandfather Dakin in 1955 and of his father in 1957 added to his depression. Seeking some relief from the growing anguish, he began a lengthy stint of expensive daily sessions with the Freudian analyst Dr. Lawrence Kubie. He also did extensive reading in related areas. Out of this period of his own life, as well as continued concern for his schizophrenic sister, Rose, who had been institutionalized after undergoing a prefrontal lobotomy, grew *Suddenly Last Summer,* considered by critics to be Williams's most shocking play. Coupled with the earlier one-act *Something Unspoken* in a package billed as *Garden District,* the play opened in early January of 1958.

Suddenly Last Summer takes place in the garden adjoining Violet Venable's Gothic mansion in New Orleans. The fantastic jungle-garden, filled with "massive tree-flowers that suggest organs of a body, torn out, still blistering with undried blood" and the cries and hisses of unidentified savage birds and beasts, had belonged to Mrs. Venable's late son Sebastian. As the play opens, she is reminiscing about her son with Dr. Curcrowicz (Polish for "sugar"), a handsome, white-clad young psychiatrist whom she has summoned to her home. According to Mrs.

Venable, her son was an accomplished poet (though publicly unrecognized—he "abhorred" false values that come from fame) who produced a single poem per year for twenty-five years. The two of them traveled extensively, universally recognized as "Violet and Sebastian" rather than as mother and son, as she nurtured his talent and sensitivity. "I was actually the only one in his life that satisfied the demands he made of people." She believes that he died chaste at the age of forty.

Mrs. Venable has devoted her life to what she considers the pure nurture of her poet son. She even joined him in his obsessive journey in search of "a clear image of God." Together they traveled to the Encantadas, where they watched the sea turtles lay their eggs in the sand of the beach. They returned at hatching time to witness thousands of baby turtles struggling to reach the sea before they were ripped apart by swarms of predatory birds that fed on the flesh of their soft undersides. Sebastian guessed that only one in a thousand survived to reach the sea. In this horrible natural occurrence he believed he had found a clear view of God.

Sebastian has died a violent death a few months before the time the play opens, and Mrs. Venable is seeking the doctor's assistance in preserving her reverent memory of her son and their relationship. The threat is Catharine Holly, her niece, who traveled with Sebastian on his last vacation and witnessed his death. Mrs. Venable promises a large endowment to his hospital if the doctor will agree to perform the prefrontal lobotomy that will silence Catharine. The niece is being brought to the Venable house to tell her story, and her recitation will serve two purposes: first it will afford the doctor an opportunity to observe the patient, and second it will allow Catharine a final opportunity to retract the "obscene" tale that her aunt cannot accept. In addition to having witnessed the awful death, lost the cousin she loved, and been confined in a psychiatric hospital, Catharine suffers the additional pressure of a mercenary brother and mother. Mrs. Venable has their inheritance from Sebastian tied up in probate, and unless Catharine changes her story, they stand little chance of gaining the tax-free fifty-thousand dollars each that he has left them.

Catharine, however, is compelled to tell the truth, no matter how hideous it is to her; an administration of truth serum assures that she cannot lie even if she was so inclined. Her lengthy monologue is punctuated with bird sounds from the jungle-garden and the doctor's calmly prodding questions.

Catharine implies that Sebastian was a homosexual, using his attractive mother to lure young men. When a stroke prevented her from accompanying him on his last vacation, he took along his younger and more attractive cousin as procuress. Catharine was unable to provide the support that his mother had given him, and Sebastian went to pieces. He was unable to write, and he drifted from the elegant life into association with the hungry urchins who frequented the public beach. One day while eating a late lunch in an open-air restaurant, the pair was surrounded by a band of naked black children begging for bread. As the beggars refused to leave, and began a bizarre serenade using instruments made of tin cans, Sebastian fled from the restaurant up a steep hill, the children in pursuit. As she saw them overtake and surround her cousin, Catharine ran in terror down the hill, calling for help. When she and the waiters and the police returned, they found Sebastian's naked body. "They had *devoured* parts of him. Torn or cut parts of him away with their hands or knives or maybe those jagged cans they made music with, they had torn bits of him away and stuffed them into those gobbling fierce little empty black mouths of theirs." What was left of Sebastian looked like "a big white-paper-wrapped bunch of red roses." As Catharine ends her recital, Mrs. Venable attempts to strike her, is stopped, and is led away. As the play ends, the doctor muses reflectively, "I think we ought at least to consider the possibility that the girl's story could be true. . . ."

Williams had expected to be crucified by the critics, to be "critically tarred and feathered and ridden on a fence rail out of the New York theatre." To his surprise, the critical response was not unfavorable, and the play was a box office success, running 216 performances. No doubt the sensationalism of the subject matter is responsible for attracting numbers of curious thrill seekers. However, some critics found in the play evidence of artistic control that had sometimes been lacking in earlier works. Though the ending may be a bit far-fetched, Catharine's use of evocative rather than explicit language—as well as the fact that the story is recounted rather than enacted—indicates the playwright's symbolic rather than literal intentions. All the jungle imagery, combined with the various direct and oblique references to cannibalism and predatoriness (Sebastian's jungle-garden even contains a Venus's flytrap), creates a dark view of man's survival chances as he struggles against nature and other men. Even the God that Sebastian discovers in the Encantadas only gives him an early vision of

his own death. Dialogue and character development, which are Williams's strongest points, are virtually absent from this play. Still the play is carefully structured for dramatic tension, and the setting, story, symbolism, and themes mesh to create an organically unified fable. The play is not easily staged, however. Williams provides almost an open invitation to both designers and performers to go overboard, to carry things too far. In performance the play can work only when handled with the utmost restraint.

Another play to grow out of the psychoanalysis period was *Sweet Bird of Youth*, which opened 10 March 1959 at the Martin Beck Theatre, the scene of the *Orpheus Descending* failure two years earlier. Dedicated to its producer, Cheryl Crawford, who had also produced *The Rose Tattoo* and *Camino Real*, the play deals with the theme of youth and innocence lost "to the enemy, time." It is set on Easter Sunday in St. Cloud, a small town along the Gulf Coast. Chance Wayne (symbolically named) at age twenty-nine has returned to the town of his boyhood with aging screen star Alexandra del Lago (the Princess Kosmonopolis). The first act, set in the bedroom they share in the Royal Palms Hotel, provides background for both characters while establishing the present situation. Chance was born in St. Cloud, a normal baby except for some kind of "quality 'X'" in his blood, "a wish or a need to be different." A would-be actor, he has never achieved the kind of success he desires, and though he says that stardom depends on luck and breaks, he is beginning to doubt his talent. He has found that he does have talent in the area of lovemaking, which he has turned to professionally. He has been able to give society matrons "a feeling of youth" and lonely debutantes an illusion of being wanted and appreciated. But he never gets back the satisfaction he gives; all of his desire is directed toward Heavenly Finley, his high-school sweetheart whom he cannot forget. The relationship has been disapproved by Heavenly's father, Boss Finley, a corrupt, racist small-town politician who claims divine inspiration. Chance hopes that his arrival in St. Cloud with the wealthy and glamorous screen star will be impressive enough to win Heavenly permanently.

Alexandra, who tries to "put to sleep the tiger raging in her" with pills, vodka, and hashish, is running away from fear of advancing years and a finished career. She had fled in terror from the premiere of her comeback film, certain that the picture was a failure. After meeting in Palm Beach, she and Chance have traveled together, he serving as caretaker/male prostitute as she attempts to obliterate her past. As Chance provides her with oxygen and narcotics, he turns on a tape recorder and prompts her to talk about the hashish she has smuggled into the country. He has hopes of advancing his acting career through blackmail. When his plan is revealed, Alexandra at first fears that she has been robbed, but when all her valuables are accounted for, she admits that she is somehow touched by his ploy. A business agreement is reached between them: she will cover all expenses and he will provide lovemaking on demand, never mentioning her past, her possible ill health, or death.

Chance has been drawn to St. Cloud by his desire for Heavenly, but he is immediately met with warnings to keep away from her. Unknowingly on a previous visit he had infected her with venereal disease, and she has undergone a hysterectomy ("a whore's operation," according to her father). Boss Finley has put out the word that if Chance reappears in town, he will have him castrated. Chance is threatened by the doctor who has been selected by Boss to marry Heavenly, and he is warned by Heavenly's Aunt Nonnie, a woman who likes Chance and fears for his safety. His compulsion is so strong that he ignores threats and friendly warnings alike.

Act two introduces the evil Boss Finley and his equally despicable son Tom. A political rally is planned for the evening, and Boss orders his daughter Heavenly to appear dressed in white to symbolize "the fair white virgin exposed to black lust in the South." Just prior to the rally, Chance appears in the hotel cocktail lounge, drinking and popping pills, again ignoring warnings that Boss has gathered support to carry out his castration threat. Through the loudspeaker Boss's supercharged political speech is heard; he garners support for the recent emasculation of a young black chosen at random to serve as an example that the whites mean business when it comes to protecting the purity of their blood. A heckler who raises questions about Boss's use of Heavenly to symbolize white virginity is brutally beaten by the crowd.

In act three Chance telephones a Hollywood columnist, instructing Alexandra to announce that she is returning to Hollywood with a new discovery, a young male actor. When Alexandra learns that her comeback film was not a failure, but instead a triumph, she makes no mention of Chance, but talks only of herself. She excitedly plans to return, fully realizing that the success of the film is only a temporary reprieve, but willing to accept it. She

recognizes the failure in Chance but offers to take him with her to Hollywood. He refuses, knowing that he would only be "part of her luggage." He also knows that what awaits him in St. Cloud is castration, but "That can't be done to me twice. You did that to me this morning, here on this bed." As Alexandra leaves and the members of the mob quietly begin to surround him, he steps to the forestage to deliver his curtain line: "I don't ask for your pity, but just for your understanding—not even that—no. Just for your recognition of me in you, and the enemy, time, in us all."

Though there was some incredulity over Chance's curtain speech addressed directly to the audience, the critical response was favorable. The financial success of the production was instantaneous; the play that was termed "affluent Bird" ran for 375 performances and became an equally successful film. However, the appeal of both play and film very likely resulted in large part from the popularity of the stars (Paul Newman and Geraldine Page) and the sensationalistic portrayal of the racist South. Alexandra emerges as a powerful character; she is a unique Williams heroine who, even though she recognizes truth, gathers her dignity and her resources to continue the struggle, refusing to allow herself to be defeated. Chance has charm, and his predicament elicits a certain degree of sympathy, but he does not have the substance necessary to justify strong reaction to his downfall. The other characters are either blatant caricatures (like Boss Finley) or ineffectually flat figures (like Heavenly). The play is structured to create dramatic tension, with the intense horror of the political rally sandwiched between Chance and Alexandra's scenes together, but the dialogue (particularly some of Chance's speeches) is some of Williams's most lyrically overwrought.

Period of Adjustment, subtitled *High Point over a Cavern* and labeled "A Serious Comedy," opened in New York in November 1960. It is set in a " 'cute' little Spanish-type suburban bungalow" near Memphis, Tennessee, on Christmas Eve. It deals with two rocky marriages, one of five years and the other only twenty-four-hours old. George and Isabel, on their honeymoon trip, drop in on George's old war buddy Ralph. George had met Isabel when he was a patient in a veteran's hospital—suffering from a case of inexplicable "shakes"—where she was a student nurse. Her sympathy turned to love, and they married before getting to know each other. She has been dismissed from her first job for fainting at the sight of blood, and George has quit his job because he found it boring. A long drive in an unheated car with radio blaring and husband drinking led to a honeymoon night which Isabel spent locked in the bathroom or faking sleep in a chair.

As they arrive at Ralph's house, "built over a great underground cavern and sinking into it gradually, an inch or two a year," George roars off in his secondhand funeral limousine, leaving his slightly hysterical bride alone with his old friend. As they share confidences about their marriages, Ralph reveals that his is less than ideal also. He has also quit his job (he was employed by his father-in-law), and his wife, Dorothea, left him when given the news. He had been talked into the marriage by her father when he cured in one night the psychic frigidity that a psychiatrist could not overcome at fifty dollars an hour. Ralph's gesture was not all magnanimous; he had designs on the old man's fortune. But his father-in-law, suffering from multiple ailments, has continued to "cheat the undertaker" and has given him only one raise in five years, on the occasion of his son's birth.

Ralph and Isabel talk, a maid dispatched by Ralph's in-laws to fetch his son's things is sent away, and George returns. The two men engage in typical "male talk," reminiscences that exclude Isabel. As the hostility between bride and groom becomes more and more pronounced, Ralph intermittently attempts to reassure them with his mundane comment that they are only "going through a little period of adjustment." Dorothea's parents arrive with a laundry basket to collect her belongings, and after an argument they leave, threatening a lawsuit. Dorothea herself returns, apologizing for her parents, and announcing that she intends to stay. The curtain falls with Ralph and Dorothea in their bedroom, George and Isabel on the sofa bed, implying that the "period of adjustment" has been weathered by both couples and everyone will live happily ever after—except that the house built over a cavern continues to tremble.

The critics found themselves at odds with Williams's apparent concept of comedy. Some of the dialogue rings true, and there are some entertaining stretches, but the extremely talky work is filled with the playwright's psychological posturings. There are endless discussions of virginity, inhibitions, impotence, and sexual insecurity. Ralph fears that his wife is turning their son into a sissy ("They'll do it ev'ry time, man"), Isabel's ties with her father are suspiciously strong, and the intensity of the camaraderie between the old war buddies makes Isabel uncomfortable. Isabel's blithe assessment—"The world's a big hospital, a big neurological ward

and I am a student nurse in it"—comes near the end of the play. The clichéd metaphor is indicative of the level of both Williams's view and his presentation of it. The production closed after 132 performances.

The Night of the Iguana, Williams's last major prizewinner, opened in late December 1961. Three divergent characters create a triangular tension in this drama of man, like the iguana tied under the veranda, "at the end of his tether." The setting is the Costa Verde Hotel, a run-down tourist spot on Mexico's rather wild and primitive west coast, in the summer of 1940. The lustiest and most sensual of the trio is Maxine Faulk, the recently widowed over-forty padrona of the establishment. T. Lawrence Shannon, a defrocked minister suffering from consuming cosmic guilt aggravated by his penchant for young girls, has arrived at the Costa Verde with his disgruntled charges: a busload of schoolteachers and an oversexed teenager on a Blake Tour. The third point of the triangle is Hannah Jelkes, a "New England spinster pushing forty" who travels with her "ninety-seven years young" poet grandfather, painting portraits of tourists to make a meager living.

Maxine, who has taken her young employee Pedro as a casual lover, is thrilled to see Shannon; she immediately begins to talk him into settling with her in an arrangement that would provide the two of them with comfort and security. Though Shannon resists Maxine, he has been drawn to the Costa Verde in hopes of getting rid of his "spook," a familiar unwelcome guest who has precipitated periodic emotional breakdowns in the past. His life at present is complicated by Charlotte, the sexy teenager who has thrown herself at him and now insists on marriage. Knowing fully the ludicrousness of her proposal and totally regretting his involvement, Shannon is threatened with rape charges by Miss Fellowes, Charlotte's caretaker and leader of the group of women. He is struggling not to drink, to extricate himself from Charlotte, to maintain control over his tour group who are beginning to mutiny because the ramshackle Costa Verde was not on their schedule, and to fight off the psychological demons that are beginning to engulf him.

As Shannon's torture increases, he draws some measure of comfort from the "fantastic" Hannah Jelkes. Though she in no way has designs on him as the jealous Maxine suspects, she does feel a kinship with the man whose psychic torment reminds her of similar past experiences of her own. An iron butterfly, the spiritual Hannah is by far the strongest of Williams's frail women. Her nature is totally gentle, yet she is shocked by nothing, and she has achieved a peace that allows her to accept gracefully that which she cannot improve. As Shannon rages—for a while Maxine even has him tied down in a hammock after he goes berserk when his tour bus leaves without him—Hannah offers him a sedative (poppyseed tea), observes that he finds some pleasure in his guilty suffering ("a *comfortable* crucifixion"), and offers the comfort of her philosophy: a full knowledge of grim reality, but a belief that demons can be withstood through endurance, and that occasional fleeting moments of human communication are possible.

As they talk, Shannon decides to "play God" and cut loose the iguana that the Mexican boys have tied under the veranda. The parallels between the panicky fettered creature and the situations of the play's characters are apparent. As Shannon frees the lizard, Hannah's grandfather Nonno excitedly announces that his last poem, after twenty years of work, is finally completed. As he recites, Hannah writes down his words, tears streaming down her face because she knows that anticipation of this last creative act is the only thing that has kept him alive. Shannon joins Maxine for a moonlight swim, knowing that he will accept her invitation to stay, and as the curtain falls, Hannah, after fighting momentary panic over Nonno's death, presses her head to her grandfather's crown in a tender, dignified tableau.

The play has flaws, not the least of which is a family of German tourists who cheer over news of the bombing of London, participate in clumsy and confused chase scenes, and generally add a discordant element of slapstick. The lusty, uncerebral Maxine is given less dialogue, therefore less development than Shannon and Hannah, but her character rings true. Shannon is such a mess of confused rage and guilt that he elicits an audience's interest and sympathy, but not much respect. The complex Hannah is the best drawn of the three characters. Even so, her recounting of two experiences—one innocuous and the other called by Shannon "a dirty little episode"—proves unsettling. Her recital is dramatically effective, but the fact that she labels them the sum total of her "lovelife" suggests an incongruity. This woman of delicate appearance has proven that she has looked life hard in the face and is nothing if not realistic toward what she sees. It is clear that Williams's interest in her two rather pathetic stories is in conveying her acceptance of humanity: "Nothing human disgusts me unless it's unkind, violent." The

acceptance is in keeping with Hannah's character, but her viewing these encounters as her "lovelife" is not. Still, through Hannah, Williams presents an altering view of the world. The cruelty and isolation are still there, but Hannah has learned to endure without impotently raging, escaping through sex, or sentimentally romanticizing. Both a critical and a popular success, the play ran 316 performances and won for its author his fourth Drama Critics Circle Award.

Though *The Night of the Iguana* was Williams's last major success, his productivity did not cease. In *The Milk Train Doesn't Stop Here Anymore* (1962) he extends the exploration of acceptance that was begun with Hannah in *The Night of the Iguana*. Here the comforter is Christopher Flanders, a thirty-five-year-old poet-Christ figure called the Angel of Death because of his frequent appearance with wealthy women about to die. In this case the woman is Flora Goforth, a rich widow who has survived four husbands, retreated to a guarded villa high on a peak of Italy's Divina Costiera, and begun to dictate her memoirs in a haze of drugs and alcohol as she fights against death. Chris appears to provide her with what she needs, rather than what she thinks she wants. As she rants and raves, alternately attempting to seduce him and accusing him of being a thief, he gives his message that is "vaguely Oriental with Occidental variations." He is gradually able to calm her, as her strength fades, into acceptance of death. The first version of the play was produced in 1962 at the Festival of Two Worlds in Spoleto, Italy. The first American production opened in mid January 1963. Criticism was generally favorable; though Williams's formerly unrelenting dark vision was beginning to be altered, critics began to note the rehashing of old material that was to mark so much of his work thereafter. There was also negative response to the complicated symbolism, particularly embodied in and expressed through the poet-Christ figure Chris. The New York premiere ran only sixty-nine performances, and a 1964 version closed after only four.

The play's lack of success was indicative of the remainder of the decade, which Williams refers to in his *Memoirs* as "my 'Stoned Age,' the sixties." His longtime lover and friend Frank Merlo died of lung cancer in 1963, precipitating a depression that ultimately led to even stronger drug and alcohol dependency than before. Williams continued to write, but with increased effort, and his plays continued to be produced. But (as he acknowledged) his "falling down state" made his preproduction involvement difficult, and the critics, as well as audiences,

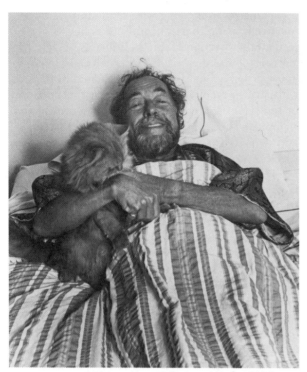

Tennessee Williams, late 1970s (copyright © 1980 by Mark Morrow)

protested his exposing his private psychoses through his plays. The period is characterized by first version openings, summer stock try-outs, and revisions—none of which had long runs.

Eccentricities of a Nightingale was tried out in stock and published in 1964. A 1948 revision of *Summer and Smoke*, it is a definite improvement over the earlier work. The story line is essentially unchanged, but complexity and motivation are added to the characters of Alma and John, resulting in greater believability. The addition to the story of Alma's Aunt Albertine, who disgraced the family by running off with the proprietor of the Musée Mechanique, serves both to define Alma's expectations and to foreshadow her destiny. A Public Broadcasting System presentation in 1976 gave the play its first major professional production and a national audience.

A double bill entitled *Slapstick Tragedy* opened in February 1966. Williams described the two one-acts as kin to "vaudeville, burlesque, and slapstick, with a dash of pop art thrown in." *The Mutilated* presents the perverse Christmas celebration of two old New Orleans whores, Celeste, a well-endowed shoplifter, and Trinket, a wino who has suffered a breast mutilation. The play is framed by carolers whose song asks pity for the wild, the mutilated,

the wanderers: "I think the strange, the crazed, the queer/Will have their holiday this year." *The Gnädiges Fräulein,* set in the Florida Keys, is a parable of the modern artist's struggle for success. The Fräulein, a one-time chanteuse (artist), must fight off the marauding Cocaloony birds (critics) for the fish which are her livelihood (success). Critic Harold Clurman, though he recognized the "effective mixture of gallows humor and Rabelaisian zest," could not bring himself to smile: "I was too conscious that the author was in pain." *Slapstick Tragedy* closed after only seven performances.

Also in 1966 came the publication of Williams's third volume of short fiction, *The Knightly Quest: A Novella and Four Short Stories.* Besides the title work, it includes "Mama's Old Stucco House"; "Man Bring This Up Road" (from which *The Milk Train Doesn't Stop Here Anymore* grew); "The Kingdom of Earth" (later dramatized, expanded, and retitled); and "Grand" (a moving reminiscence of his maternal grandmother Rose Dakin).

The short story "Kingdom of Earth" was dramatized as a one-act, then later expanded to full length and retitled. As *The Seven Descents of Myrtle,* it opened for a brief New York run on 27 March 1968. Lot Ravenstock, weak and tubercular, brings his new wife to his Mississippi Delta farmhouse. The third side of the triangle is Chicken, Lot's illegitimate half brother who is half Negro and who has a claim to Lot's property at his death. Scene locations alternate as Myrtle makes several descents from the upstairs bedroom of her dying husband to the crude kitchen below, which is the domain of the earthier, more virile Chicken. A flood approaches, Lot's adulation of his late mother culminates in his transvestite death scene, and Myrtle is won over by Chicken's crude philosophizing: "Ther's nothing in the world, in this whole kingdom of earth, that can compare with one thing, and that one thing is what's able to happen between a man and a woman." The critics generally found the play shabby; it closed after twenty-nine performances.

More than two years later, on 11 May 1969, *In the Bar of a Tokyo Hotel* opened for a short run Off-Broadway. The intensely personal play chronicles the panic, uncertainty, and isolation of an artist facing either new insight and achievement or the disintegration of his talent; he cannot be sure which. The characters are the painter, Mark, who is obsessed with his discovery about color; his unsympathetic wife, Miriam, who becomes impatient with her husband's antics and attempts to seduce the barman; and Leonard, the homosexual gallery director who is in sympathy with the tortures suffered by the artist. Most critics found the play too painfully personal for the stage; some even sounded the death knell for one of America's major playwright's. Shortly thereafter Williams went into a state of nervous collapse that resulted in hospitalization; his three-month stay enabled him to break his alcohol and drug dependency.

In 1970 *Dragon Country*, his third collection of short plays, was published. The volume includes the already produced *In the Bar of a Tokyo Hotel; I Rise in Flame, Cried the Phoenix; The Mutilated; The Gnädiges Fräulein*, as well as four then-unproduced works. *I Can't Imagine Tomorrow* deals with problems of communication: the man named Two cannot complete a sentence without help from the woman One. *Confessional*, exhibiting the patrons of the beachfront bar Monk's Place would be expanded into *Small Craft Warnings. The Frosted Glass Coffin* presents the geriatric inhabitants of a Miami retirement hotel. In *A Perfect Analysis Given by a Parrot*, two women in "the late afternoon of their youth" attending a convention in Saint Louis are out to have a good time.

Small Craft Warnings, Williams's only commercial success after *The Night of the Iguana*, opened Off-Off-Broadway on 2 April 1972. Set in a sleazy bar on the California coast, the play, according to its author, is "about communication and how we see people and how they show themselves to be what they really are." The bar is populated by a group of derelicts, each of whom has his moment of confessional monologue while spotlighted on the forestage. Among them are Leona, who persistently gropes for companionship in a life she recognizes as sordid and solitary; Violet, who gropes for male genitals under tables; a pair of young homosexuals, one a boy from Iowa who is excited over the Pacific Ocean and the other a Hollywood scriptwriter who is excited by nothing; Doc, a physician with a philosophical bent who has lost his license to practice medicine; and the proprietor Monk, who insists that his place will not become "a pad for vagrants" or a gay bar, but for whom the tavern and its patrons are home and family. In an attempt to boost the production's box-office appeal, Williams himself performed for a period in the role of Doc. While critics found in the play little more than seamier versions of past Williams characters, it was fairly successful with audiences, running a total of 194 performances.

First produced as *The Two-Character Play* in London in 1967, then revised, retitled, and produced in Chicago in 1971, *Out Cry* opened for a brief Broadway run in March 1973. Structured as a play-within-a-play, the work is set on the stage of a theater in an unspecified foreign country. Two actors, Felice and his sister Clare, have been declared insane and abandoned by the rest of their theatrical company. Nevertheless they decide to perform *The Two-Character Play*, a vehicle which may be the story of their own lives. In the play the two have retreated into the house where their father killed their mother and then committed suicide. Dreadfully afraid of the world outside, they even find almost impossible the simple task of going to the grocer's for food. Uncertain over its ending, they come out of the play to discover the house empty, the audience gone. After a discussion of the various options available to them—none of them appealing—they decide to complete the play. Though the play-within-a-play is unobscured, Clare and Felice seem to wander from one world to the other, suggesting a thin line between art and life, reality and illusion, sanity and insanity. Though critics generally treated this most personal work with sympathy, their respect was for the past achievements of its author and not for *Out Cry*. Its Broadway run closed after twelve performances.

Eight Mortal Ladies Possessed, published in 1974, is a collection of six short stories, five of which were written in the early 1970s. It includes "Happy August Tenth," "The Inventory of Fontana Bella," "Miss Coynte of Green," "Sabbatha and Solitude," "Completed," and "Oriflamme" (dated "January 1944, the month of my grandmother's death in St. Louis"). In 1975 came the publication of two more prose volumes. *Moise and the World of Reason* is supposedly the painter Moise's observations as told to the first-person narrator, but the narrator (who bears a striking resemblance to Williams himself) includes many of his own observations, experiences, and ideas.

Williams's *Memoirs* were also published in 1975. Written during the run of *Small Craft Warnings*, the volume is an unchronological, often stream-of-consciousness recollection of the playwright's childhood, friendships, professional associations, periods of mental distress, successes and failures, heavily laced with detailed accounts of his sexual experiences. The book is illustrated with a wealth of photographs of Williams, his family, his friends, and productions of his plays. The Tennessee Williams who emerges is an engaging and likable human being—witty, articulate, self-aware, and candid. (In drawing a comparison between old crocodiles and old playwrights, he observes, "Scratching the hide of the latter, you will discover that it can only be noticeably indented by the cutting edge of a diamond or by a bit of dandelion fluff in the atmosphere of a late summer afternoon.") The *Memoirs* are an excellent source for understanding the overall tapestry that is Williams, but they are frustrating to anyone seeking an orderly account of the weaving of the cloth. More interested in "truth" than fact, he admittedly has difficulty placing events in exact time and place, and therefore abandons any attempt at chronology. Furthermore his memories of many events have been colored by time and the artist's tendency to alter or embellish. As he wrote in a letter to Donald Windham, "Consistency, thy name is not Tennessee!"

Two plays produced in the mid 1970s were still considered "works in progress" and were not performed in New York. Both combine complicated plots with contemporary social and political concerns (the stronghold of big business, international conspiracy, revolution). *The Red Devil Battery Sign* was produced in Boston in 1975 and, in revised form, in Vienna the next year. *This Is (An Entertainment)* was given an American Conservatory Theatre production in San Francisco in early 1976.

Vieux Carré, which ran briefly in 1977, bears a strong resemblance to *The Glass Menagerie.* A young writer serves as both narrator and a participant in the action. Like Tom, this narrator faces the future with expectation, while others cling to the past, but *The Glass Menagerie*'s narrator does not abide in a house of ghosts. The boardinghouse in the French Quarter that provides the setting for *Vieux Carré* is inhabited by the dying—physically, spiritually, or both. The landlady who sleeps on a cot in the hall, armed with a flashlight against intruders, provides a home for a motley collection of down-and-outs: a homosexual painter, two penniless old women who scavenge for food, a would-be fashion designer from New York, and her junkie stud who works in a strip joint. Physical ailments abound in the boardinghouse: the painter is tubercular and the fashion designer is dying of leukemia. Critics were generally unreceptive; according to Clive Barnes, "It is, unquestionably, the murmurings of genius, not a major statement." The production ran only five performances.

A Lovely Sunday for Crève Coeur was first performed as *Crève Coeur* at the Spoleto Festival in Charleston, South Carolina, in May 1978. Essentially the same production—a relatively unaltered script and most of the same cast—opened off Broadway in January of the next year. Crève Coeur is a Saint Louis amusement park where Dorothea

Shirley Knight, Charlotte Moore, and Peg Murray in the New York production of A Lovely Sunday for Crève Coeur *(photo by Martha Swope). Knight and Moore played the roles they had created in the play's Spoleto premiere.*

and Bodey have planned to go for a Sunday outing. Not wanting to spoil the picnic, Bodey spends much of the day hiding from Dorothea the newspaper announcement of the high school principal's engagement. Dorothea, a civics teacher, has had a flirtation with the man; Bodey's plans are to be matchmaker for her roommate and her brother. They are visited by Helena, the chilly and refined art teacher who wants Dorothea to move with her into a very expensive apartment. The fourth character, a hysterical upstairs neighbor who speaks only German, occasionally adds confusion. Again critics noted the similarity to old material: the fading belle in the shabby Saint Louis apartment during the Depression. Some faulted the playwright for an unhappy mix of slapstick and pathos. The New York run lasted less than a month.

Clothes for a Summer Hotel, reuniting the playwright, director José Quintero, and Geraldine Page (who first worked together over a quarter of a century before on the Off-Broadway production of *Summer and Smoke*), opened 26 March 1980. Set outside the North Carolina asylum where she spent her last days and died in a fire, the play focuses on Zelda Fitzgerald, using flashbacks to include other stars of the Jazz Age: F. Scott Fitzgerald, Ernest Hemingway, and Gerald and Sarah Murphy. Some critics wondered at Williams's choice of material, noting that he offered no new insight into characters already thoroughly familiar to the American public. Walter Kerr complained that Williams's personal voice is absent from the play, an observation that is rather ironic in light of the decades of criticism decrying a playwright for speaking too directly and too personally. Acutely missing the author's "inimitable flair for language," Kerr concluded that *Clothes for a Summer Hotel* is Tennessee Williams holding his tongue." The critics were negative, and the play closed almost immediately.

In the last thirteen months of his life, Williams saw two of his plays produced, both of them provoking sympathetic responses from Williams's friends and harsh words from the critics. *A House Not Meant to Stand* was revised and tried out over a two-year period from a one-act play by Williams entitled *Some Problems for the Moose Lodge.* The final revision opened at the Goodman Theatre on 27 April 1982 and was Williams's last opening. Williams hoped for a New York production, but none was offered. Called by *Chicago Tribune* reviewer Richard Christiansen a "harsh, bitter, pain-filled shriek at the degenerative process of life," *A House Not Meant to Stand* is reminiscent of Williams's most successful works. The play concerns a troubled family at the edge of despair. Old age, faulty reminiscences about the past, the failure of hope, and despair over negligent children drive Bella McCorkle into madness at the play's end.

Williams's last New York play, *Something Cloudy, Something Clear,* was a frankly autobiographical "memory play," as Donald Spoto calls it, in which Williams's real-life homosexual lovers, Kip and Frank Merlo, as well as Tallulah Bankhead (who starred in *Battle of Angels, A Streetcar Named Desire, Sweet Bird of Youth,* and *The Milk Train Doesn't Stop Here Anymore*), appear as characters. Williams's own part is assigned to a playwright named August, who comes to the realization that his perceptions of his life are made up of "something cloudy and something clear." The play received negative reviews, though Donald Spoto calls it "possibly the best work of his last twenty years."

Williams did not enjoy a major success after *The Night of the Iguana* in 1961. Acknowledging just before his death that he seemed to have been in "a period of eclipse" in his last years, and that perhaps he was "too old to write," he insisted that he would

nevertheless continue, because writing was his life. Over the past two decades much ink has been spilled—and a great deal of it with some glee—over the question of whether Williams was "written out." The question is a specious one. What he put together over the past forty years is a richly checkered career marked by tremendous successes and colossal failures. In many ways his greatest strengths were also his greatest weaknesses. At times he was lambasted for parading across the American stage the products of his own psychosis; in recent years those of the "art grows from pain" school have wistfully concluded that in finding mental health Williams had lost his talent. His best work is lauded for its poetic language; his worst is marked by lush lyricism gone wild. His compassion for the tortured, the broken, the misfit, demonstrates his depth of feeling; but the line is thin between honest, compassionate portrayal of the unfortunate, and perverse fascination with sewer rats. Still his best work is characterized by masterful use of poetic language, realistic human confrontation, and empathy with victims of loneliness and isolation. As Walter Kerr noted in his review of *Vieux Carré,* Williams "has already given us such a substantial body of work that there is really no need to continue demanding that he live up to himself, that he produce more, more, more and all masterpieces." He produced no masterpieces in his later years; nonetheless Williams's place is securely established as a major figure in mid-twentieth-century American drama.

Letters:

Donald Windham, ed., *Tennessee Williams' Letters to Donald Windham, 1940-1965* (Verona: Sandy Campbell, 1976; New York: Holt, Rinehart & Winston, 1977).

Interviews:

Robert Rice, "A Man Named Tennessee," *New York Post,* 21 April-4 May 1958;

Arthur Gelb, "Williams and Kazan and the Big Walkout," *New York Times,* 1 May 1960, II: 1;

Lewis Funke and John E. Booth, "Williams on Williams," *Theatre Arts,* 46 (January 1962): 16-19, 72-73;

Tom Buckley, "Tennessee Williams Survives," *Atlantic Monthly,* 226 (November 1970): 98 ff;

"Playboy Interview: Tennessee Williams—A Candid Conversation," *Playboy,* 20 (April 1973): 69-84;

Mel Gussow, "Tennessee Williams on Art and Sex," *New York Times,* 3 November 1975, p. 49.

Bibliographies:

Delma E. Presley, "Tennessee Williams: Twenty-Five Years of Criticism," *Bulletin of Bibliography,* 30 (March 1973): 21-29;

S. Alan Chesler, "*A Streetcar Named Desire:* Twenty-Five Years of Criticism," *Notes on Mississippi Writers,* 7 (Fall 1974): 44-53;

Drewey Wayne Gunn, *Tennessee Williams: A Bibliography* (Metuchen, N.J.: Scarecrow Press, 1980).

Biographies:

Nancy M. Tischler, *Tennessee Williams: Rebellious Puritan* (New York: Citadel Press, 1961);

Edwina Dakin Williams (as told to Lucy Freeman), *Remember Me to Tom* (New York: Putnam's, 1963);

Catharine R. Hughes, *Tennessee Williams: A Biography* (Englewood Cliffs, N.J.: Prentice-Hall, 1978);

Dakin Williams and Shepherd Mead, *Tennessee Williams: An Intimate Biography* (New York: Arbor House, 1983).

References:

Harold Clurman, "Tennessee Williams: Poet and Puritan," *New York Times,* 29 March 1970, II: 5;
Discusses the conflict within Williams's characters and compares the author's "lost souls" theme with that of Eugene O'Neill's work.

Durante Da Ponte, "Tennessee Williams' Gallery of Feminine Characters," *Tennessee Studies in Literature,* 10 (1965): 7-26;
Competent discussion of the women represented in Williams's fiction.

Francis Donahue, *The Dramatic World of Tennessee Williams* (New York: Ungar, 1964);
Discusses the author's self-doubts and his main themes of sex, neuroticism, violence, and homosexuality.

Signi Lenea Falk, *Tennessee Williams* (New York: Twayne, 1961; revised edition, 1978);
Complete study of the author's life and work.

Norman J. Fedder, *The Influence of D. H. Lawrence on Tennessee Williams* (The Hague: Mouton, 1966);
Comparison between Lawrence and Williams. Claims that Williams simplifies experiences while Lawrence describes them accurately.

Esther Merle Jackson, *The Broken World of Tennessee Williams* (Madison: University of Wisconsin, 1965);
Discusses the myths and themes of Williams's works and focuses on *Camino Real.*

Robert Emmet Jones, "Tennessee Williams' Early Heroines," *Modern Drama,* 2 (December 1959): 211-219;
Describes the southern women who are portrayed in Williams's characters.

Francis L. Kunkel, "Tennessee Williams and the Death of God," *Commonweal,* 87 (23 February 1968): 614-617;
Criticizes Williams for his representation of God.

Richard F. Leavitt, *The World of Tennessee Williams* (New York: Putnam's, 1978);
A documented and pictorial history of Williams.

Marya Mannes, "Plea for Fair Ladies," *New York Times Magazine,* 29 May 1960, p. 16;
Discusses current theater in terms of violence and corruption.

Gilbert Maxwell, *Tennessee Williams and His Friends* (Cleveland: World, 1965);
A detailed account of Williams's personal life—the tension he felt, the friends he had, and the social life he led.

Benjamin Nelson, *Tennessee Williams: The Man and His Work* (New York: Obolensky, 1961);
Summarizes *Stairs to the Roof* and discusses the author's background and career.

Henry Popkin, "The Plays of Tennessee Williams," *Tulane Drama Review,* 4 (March 1960): 45-64;
Discusses the patterns, symbols, and "truths" of Williams's plays.

Mike Steen, *A Look at Tennessee Williams* (New York: Hawthorne, 1969);
Collection of interviews with the writer's friends. Includes stories about his work and personal relationships.

Kenneth Tynan, "Valentine to Tennessee Williams," *Mademoiselle,* 42 (February 1956):

130 ff;
Compares Williams with his own characters
and discusses his strengths and weaknesses as
a writer.

Gerald Weales, *Tennessee Williams* (Minneapolis:
University of Minnesota Press, 1965);

Discusses the characters Williams created and
the questions he asked about the world.

Papers:
A substantial collection of Williams's manuscripts
and letters is held by the Humanities Research Center, the University of Texas at Austin.

Contributors

Michael Adams .... *Louisiana State University*
Dorothy Jewell Altman .... *Fort Wright College*
Sally Boyd.. *University of South Carolina*
Robert E. Burkholder.. *Pennsylvania State University*
Keen Butterworth.. *University of South Carolina*
Steven R. Carter... *University of Puerto Rico*
Ann Charters .... *University of Connecticut*
Paul Christensen... *Texas A&M University*
David Cowart .... *University of South Carolina*
Leland H. Cox, Jr. .... *Columbia, South Carolina*
Leonard J. Deutsch .... *Marshall University*
Suzanne Ferguson.. *Wayne State University*
Fred M. Fetrow.. *United States Naval Academy*
Warren French .... *Indiana University-Purdue University at Indianapolis*
Craig Goad... *Northwest Missouri State University*
John Haffenden.. *University of Sheffield*
Nancy Duvall Hargrove.. *Mississippi State University*
Jeffrey Helterman.. *University of South Carolina*
Charles Israel .... *Columbia College*
Robert F. Kiernan.. *Manhattan College*
John MacNicholas.. *University of South Carolina*
James Mann.. *Columbia, South Carolina*
John R. May .... *Louisiana State University*
Thomas McClanahan .... *Idaho Department of Humanities*
Kenneth G. McCollum.. *Lisbonfalls, Maine*
Brown Miller.. *San Francisco, California*
James A. Miller.. *Trinity College*
Robert A. Morace .... *Daemen College*
Charles Nicol .... *Indiana State University*
Keith M. Opdahl .... *DePauw University*
John Ower .... *University of South Carolina*
Martha Ragland .... *Virginia Commonwealth University*
Joel Roache .... *University of Maryland, Eastern Shore*
John W. Roberts.. *University of Pennsylvania*
Ellen Rosenberg .... *Columbia, South Carolina*
Walter W. Ross .... *Columbia, South Carolina*
Larry Smith............................... *Bowling Green State University, Firelands College*
Fred L. Standley.. *Florida State University*
Stephen M. Vallillo.. *New York, New York*
Ruth Vande Kieft .... *Queens College*
Ralph F. Voss.. *University of Alabama*
Barbara Frey Waxman....................... *University of North Carolina at Wilmington*
Laura M. Zaidman .... *University of South Carolina at Sumter*

1: *The American Renaissance in New England,* edited by Joel Myerson (1978)

2: *American Novelists Since World War II,* edited by Jeffrey Helterman and Richard Layman (1978)

3: *Antebellum Writers in New York and the South,* edited by Joel Myerson (1979)

4: *American Writers in Paris, 1920-1939,* edited by Karen Lane Rood (1980)

5: *American Poets Since World War II,* 2 parts, edited by Donald J. Greiner (1980)

6: *American Novelists Since World War II,* Second Series, edited by James E. Kibler, Jr. (1980)

7: *Twentieth-Century American Dramatists,* 2 parts, edited by John MacNicholas (1981)

8: *Twentieth-Century American Science-Fiction Writers,* 2 parts, edited by David Cowart and Thomas L. Wymer (1981)

9: *American Novelists, 1910-1945,* 3 parts, edited by James J. Martine (1981)

10: *Modern British Dramatists, 1900-1945,* 2 parts, edited by Stanley Weintraub (1982)

11: *American Humorists, 1800-1950,* 2 parts, edited by Stanley Trachtenberg (1982)

12: *American Realists and Naturalists,* edited by Donald Pizer and Earl N. Harbert (1982)

13: *British Dramatists Since World War II,* 2 parts, edited by Stanley Weintraub (1982)

14: *British Novelists Since 1960,* 2 parts, edited by Jay L. Halio (1983)

15: *British Novelists, 1930-1959,* 2 parts, edited by Bernard Oldsey (1983)

16: *The Beats: Literary Bohemians in Postwar America,* 2 parts, edited by Ann Charters (1983)

17: *Twentieth-Century American Historians,* edited by Clyde N. Wilson (1983)

18: *Victorian Novelists After 1885,* edited by Ira B. Nadel and William E. Fredeman (1983)

19: *British Poets, 1880-1914,* edited by Donald E. Stanford (1983)

20: *British Poets, 1914-1945,* edited by Donald E. Stanford (1983)

21: *Victorian Novelists Before 1885,* edited by Ira B. Nadel and William E. Fredeman (1983)

22: *American Writers for Children, 1900-1960,* edited by John Cech (1983)

23: *American Newspaper Journalists, 1873-1900,* edited by Perry J. Ashley (1983)

24: *American Colonial Writers, 1606-1734,* edited by Emory Elliott (1984)

25: *American Newspaper Journalists, 1901-1925,* edited by Perry J. Ashley (1984)

26: *American Screenwriters,* edited by Robert E. Morsberger, Stephen O. Lesser, and Randall Clark (1984)

27: *Poets of Great Britain and Ireland, 1945-1960,* edited by Vincent B. Sherry, Jr. (1984)

28: *Twentieth-Century American-Jewish Fiction Writers,* edited by Daniel Walden (1984)

29: *American Newspaper Journalists, 1926-1950,* edited by Perry J. Ashley (1984)

30: *American Historians, 1607-1865,* edited by Clyde N. Wilson (1984)

31: *American Colonial Writers, 1735-1781,* edited by Emory Elliott (1984)

32: *Victorian Poets Before 1850,* edited by William E. Fredeman and Ira B. Nadel (1984)

33: *Afro-American Fiction Writers After 1955,* edited by Thadious M. Davis and Trudier Harris (1984)

34: *British Novelists, 1890-1929: Traditionalists,* edited by Thomas F. Staley (1985)

35: *Victorian Poets After 1850,* edited by William E. Fredeman and Ira B. Nadel (1985)

36: *British Novelists, 1890-1929: Modernists,* edited by Thomas F. Staley (1985)

37: *American Writers of the Early Republic,* edited by Emory Elliott (1985)

38: *Afro-American Writers After 1955: Dramatists and Prose Writers,* edited by Thadious M. Davis and Trudier Harris (1985)

39: *British Novelists, 1660-1800,* 2 parts, edited by Martin C. Battestin (1985)

40: *Poets of Great Britain and Ireland Since 1960,* 2 parts, edited by Vincent B. Sherry, Jr. (1985)

41: *Afro-American Poets Since 1955,* edited by Trudier Harris and Thadious M. Davis (1985)

42: *American Writers for Children Before 1900,* edited by Glenn E. Estes (1985)

43: *American Newspaper Journalists, 1690-1872,* edited by Perry J. Ashley (1986)

44: *American Screenwriters,* Second Series, edited by Randall Clark, Robert E. Morsberger, and Stephen O. Lesser (1986)

45: *American Poets, 1880-1945,* First Series, edited by Peter Quartermain (1986)

46: *American Literary Publishing Houses, 1900-1980: Trade and Paperback,* edited by Peter Dzwonkoski (1986)

47: *American Historians, 1866-1912,* edited by Clyde N. Wilson (1986)

ADVENTURE

OF

MODERN ART

Oto Bihalji-Merin

ADVENTURE OF MODERN ART

SIMILARITIES AND DIFFERENCES

IN ART IMAGES

PRIMITIVE, ANCIENT, AND MODERN

Harry N. Abrams, Inc., Publishers, New York

Milton S. Fox • *Editor-in-Chief*

Library of Congress Catalog Card Number: 66-13270

Printed and bound in Japan

CONTENTS

FOREWORD:

THE UNIFICATION OF THE WORLD IN ART

The present work is an attempt to examine modern art in its manifold conscious and unconscious aspects. The product of long years of study and daily contact with art and artists, it sets out not so much to judge as to present reality and dreams of reality as these are reflected in the arts.

As we know, art does not, any more than any other category of human activity, stand outside social existence. Art is subject to the laws of crisis and revolution, but these are portrayed according to special rules proper to art and are sometimes hard to read in the period of their formation. Artists are not only producers but also products of great change. The changes of the past may have developed successively and across great lapses of time. Modern metamorphoses have a dismaying tempo. Radical changes are completed in greater leaps and more dramatically than ever before. In a time of change, which we could also call a time of crisis, our many divergent directions and schools of art amount to a sort of polemic against custom and tradition. At the same time they are studies and preparations for a new world plan in the field of artistic vision.

The new formation of myths representing the abstract in a new concrete form is the rough draft of truths as yet hardly imaginable. Mythic thought belongs to the early epochs of humanity; it is the symbolic expression of the unmastered meaning of natural processes. In the second half of the twentieth century, mankind again stands, albeit on a higher plane of consciousness, before newly opened and still uncomprehended vistas. Echo and dream in the art of our day thus show analogies with the earliest epochs. In contrast to the spiritually unmastered macro- and microcosm, human vision is searching for a kind of mythical significance, even if it does so with the concepts of modern physics and the signs of modern art.

Despite Auschwitz and Hiroshima, the tragedy of existence in our epoch has in a certain sense canceled the existence of tragedy. A new humanism, which artists are creatively pondering, is manifested in the revised relationship between man and the cosmos. Man has become smaller and at the same time larger. The view of the universe has expanded, and at the same time the world has shrunk. A *rapprochement* is beginning among the world's cultures. The artists of this century create out of a total range of time and space.

In this book the flow of proximity and distance, place and time, into one another; the inclusion of all particulars and forms of whatever has been experienced; unhistorical eternity in the historical changes of modern art—these will be presented by the opposition of contrasting pairs of figures. A dialectical confrontation of things distant from one another in time yet visually related should help the viewer to recognize secret connections and the relationship between primordial anxieties and today's existential anxieties. Such connections are not to be taken directly and literally. They must not give the impression of mere imitation. Rather, they are creative correspondences of form, historically separated but unified in the mainstream of art.

We are beginning to identify as the style and handwriting of our age a common synthesis originating in the harmonies of stratified and opposing aspirations. Despite its differentiations and its profusion of aesthetic idioms, art in the second half of the twentieth century is approaching a certain unity of expressive form, growing out of the unity of the oppositions among many cultures, locales, periods.

This book places the fine arts at the center of consideration. But I also intend to focus some attention on related processes of development in the area of the other arts and the sciences. The chapters on literature, music, and architecture to some degree represent an attempt to examine their conformity with common laws. These problems, which expand beyond the scope of the narrower theme, could only be intimated. Strong emphasis has been placed on parallels between art and physics, technology and psychology. The breakthrough of a new conception of time and space and the revolutionary view of macroscopic and microscopic space have persistently expressed themselves in modern art.

With misgivings the artists have anticipated the still inexpressible connections in nature; with misgivings they have sighted in their work the developing unity of the world.

THE AWAKENING OF ARCHAIC AND PRIMITIVE CULTURES

The Unity of Early and Late

Our first task is to perceive, and to present to other people, the history of all the known civilizations, surviving and extinct, as a unity.

Arnold J. Toynbee

We decipher the way of man to the early cultural oases of his perception, to his tactile attempts at meaning and representation, from tattered documents of the vanished past and from toppled and buried monuments of early times. Preserved in the Bible, the fruit of the Tree of Knowledge (the Biblical ur-symbol of the Fall) has significance in the sublime fact of its emancipation from the still murky region of vegetative existence: it is the decisive step on the way to becoming man.

Cultures that developed separately on all continents, cultures determined by local characteristics and the availability of certain materials that left their mark on early forms of art, nevertheless show an astonishing unity in presenting death cults, the rite of the *magna mater*, totemism and mask forms, idols of fertility and symbols of taboo, the progress of the seasons—pictorial symbols of genesis, decay, and resurrection.

Even if one cannot readily localize in time and space the beginning of the universal historical processes of human culture, nevertheless a glance into the past gives us not only a view of an endless sequence of scattered cultural organisms, but also a synthetic perception of processes interrelated and unified by their nature.

Until our day the early cultures of mankind and the primitive cultures of today were studied very little. In the nineteenth century, world history was considered to have begun with Egypt and Mesopotamia. All else was considered folklore. Today a universal description of art chooses from the total process of development that which is unchanged throughout time; the bronze statues of Benin, the walls of the Lascaux caves, the works of Leonardo or Picasso—all are variations on a single current of creativity.

In another sense, too, the art of our time has achieved a global character. Experiments and discoveries of a single studio or by an important master are quickly imitated and, through print, film, and television, are disseminated throughout the world. Not only contemporary art but also that of past epochs preserved in collections or in museums at the site of its creation have become accessible through visual mass communication. Painters of the twentieth century create stimulation out of the

9

realms of the past and present. Their forms, colors, and conceptions are descended from the totality of artistic material. This comprehensiveness and simultaneity of the new and old, this proximity and distance side by side, are the ferments of a new, epic world picture.

As all national and parochial limitations become recognized as hindrances to development, a cultural neighborliness is established in this now easily surveyable world, a mutual influence of one people on another takes place, and a world climate becomes a possibility.

Between Myth and Utopia

The greatest works of art have always been myths of reconciliation. Can we recognize anywhere today the appearance of such images of reconciliation?

Herbert Read

The deeper man's recognition of Nature's conformity to certain laws, the paler become the mythic powers. As he cleared the jungles, sailed the seas, and climbed the heights man's myths and beliefs in the gods were changed to legend and fairy tale. In the language of fully developed consciousness, the unconscious conception of the archetype, the connection between meaning and its mythical background, became hardly expressible.

"Mythology is the original language of these psychic processes, and no intellectual formulation can come even close to the completeness and expressiveness of the mythical representation. It is a matter of prototypes which are therefore best and most strikingly reproduced through a pictorial language." (Carl Gustav Jung)

The acausal, instinctual, and prelogical elements in the mythical thought processes are transformed when they are identified and logically described. Thus the written formulations of the myths trans-

mitted from generation to generation in Mesopotamia and ancient Greece are the result of remote developments and changes and are far removed from the original essence of these myths.

Walter Abell pursues such an examination in his book about the collective dream in art: "What we are really dealing with is only an arrested moment of its evolutionary life: a moment comparable to the 'still' photograph that is sometimes extracted from a motion picture. To grasp the myth with anything like living reality, we must secure as many versions of it as possible, must note the transformations that take place as it goes through successive versions. . . ."

In modern art, related archaic-primitive pictorial compositions make their appearance in several areas of artistic creation. Abell sees in these categories of archaic visual conception manifestations of archetypal experience analogous to literary mythical themes. Many artists of our time who look for forms of expression that will break through individual boundaries of experience attempt to create art out of the source of man's collective life and the depths of time. In every nonartistic field it seems almost impossible to achieve the prototype of mythical expression. "None of the mythical derivations of humanity's latter years, neither philosophical-historical knowledge, nor historical accounts with their biographical varieties, nor historical fiction ever approached cosmogony. Yet thanks to their mythological heritage each of these strives, insofar as such striving really succeeds, to achieve a cosmogonologically ordered totality in order to become a 'creation,' a really new creation." (Hermann Broch)

The immersion in the area of the unconscious, the attempt to approach the mythological realm of collective experience, leads in modern paintings and sculpture to a self-renewal out of the ancient:

"In the horde pictures of Max Ernst, crowds of new mongrel types appear, and it is only the irony of the picture's title that prevents us from assuming that here a new nature mythology with Orphic characteristics breaks into the Occidental circle of figures. This, too, is a general precedent which has forcibly created its idols, in Picasso's magic sculptures or in Henry Moore's nature idols." (Werner Haftmann)

Clearly Picasso is the strongest witness for the experiments in creating latter-day myths. The irrational is for him the still unrecognized force in the universe. By the act of his entrance into it, the unknown becomes actuality. No one else has presented the tragic and shattering experiences of the twentieth century in so comprehensive a manner as Picasso in *Guernica, War and Peace,* and his many-layered metamorphoses of the image of man. Picasso raised the drama of Guernica from the level of occurrence in time and space to a symbol-like mythological event. It became not only a conscious picture of horror and annihilation but at the same time a picture of the irresistible strength of life, a symbol of reconciliation, a composition as lasting and deep as Homer's *Odyssey* and Joyce's *Ulysses.*

In *The Creative Nature of Humanism,* Herbert Read writes that from time to time the creation of a new symbol of reconciliation becomes acutely necessary. We are at present, he says, in such a critical moment of history. That is the reason we may hopefully speak of a new humanism.

Picasso's painting, Abell writes, is related to mythology. It differs from myth in that it derives from a very well differentiated mentality. The representational tension remains the basis of our rational capacity to judge and differentiate, and therefore the work does not reach full hallucinatory reality. Even if it is born of the deepest instincts, a modern work of art cannot be produced without intellectual conception. It symbolizes, it expresses, but it does not become identical with the original. "In this respect it corresponds, not to the true dream, but to the daydream . . . or, if we apply the analogy of the daydream, [it can be labeled] as day myth."

When our age becomes able to produce mythical forms, they will be of another order. Unconscious cosmogony, which manifested itself in a naïve, poetic representation of continuity, has become conscious. Humanity is no longer overcome by incomprehensible fate but rather becomes the accessory of creation. Wherever they arise, the new myths will be distinguished from those arising out of the instinctual, primordial representation of the world in that they will call this picture incomprehensible and recognize the ever continuing and changing nature of the present.

Man stands, infinitely diminished, on a higher step of perception, since he breaks through earthly law and planetary order. He stands anew before the seemingly chaotic relationships of cosmic space-time systems. And again his world view, schooled and founded on science, proves narrow, his conceptions dull. They do not suffice to grasp and give meaning to a view free of perspective. Again, the imagination of the artist and the poet is analogous to the mathematical formulas of the physicist; from the changed contacts between man and nature it forms myths and symbols of presentiment. Is there a secret relationship here too between humanity's early and late symbolic forms? Erich Neumann writes:

12

"The earliest symbols appearing among humanity are the simplest ones, which we tend to call 'abstract,' like the circle, and cross, and so forth. They are closest to the unperceptual nature of the 'archetypes in themselves' and are to be understood as preconcrete and prepictorial forms of the beginning, whose simplicity is elementary and not abstract. In the course of psychic development their schematic structure becomes increasingly filled with meaning, but in the further progress of the development of consciousness, these symbols are progressively de-emotionalized so that they may be finally experienced as abstract signs of the conscious mind. It is as though the spiritual aspect of the archetype embraced equally the primal depths and the ultimate heights of the human development of consciousness in that the same sign is used by man in the beginning as a symbol for a still inarticulate, yet unshaped multiplicity and finally for an abstracted and molded conception."

Archetype and Dream in Art

Shall we be able to put on like a new dress readymade symbols, grown in exotic earth, drenched with foreign blood, spoken in foreign tongues, nourished by foreign cultures, turned into foreign history?
Carl Gustav Jung

Jung's thesis of the collective unconscious attempts to restore the connection between the I-subject and the experience of humanity throughout the centuries and thus between the psychic contents of individuality and the collective contents of the buried past. Such a view allows art to appear as a sort of dream interpretation of the human race.

Beneath the superficial layer of the human psyche with its relatively individual contents of personal experience and acquisition, so Jung teaches, lies the nonpersonal, universal spiritual sphere of the collective unconscious.

Humanity has never lacked magic, protection-granting images against the sinister forms in the depths of the soul. The past exists without interruption. Ancient mysteries lived before Christian mythology, and these have been preserved from early neolithic days. They create a chain of similarity and simultaneous transformation. In certain periods of primarily rational civilization these images pale; humanity forgets what they have meant to it. The Byzantine and Reformation iconoclasm was an expression of social conflicts and collisions between awakening reason and the archetypal.

"The gods die from time to time because man suddenly discovers that they mean nothing, that they are useless things made by man's hand, formed of wood and stone. In reality man has only discovered thereby that he has never thought at all about his images." (Jung)

The spiritually latent, unconscious ur-images are a sort of mnemonic engram—engravings in the brain's structure preserving humanity's basic experience and collective events. Personal unconsciousness expands like a dream that can be regarded as the reflection of a motivating drive to create a spatial and temporal resonance between spiritual connections to the past and the mythic, archetypal collective symbols of mankind.

Jung says of the archetypes that they "exist preconsciously and presumably form the dominant structures of the psyche in general, comparable to the unperceptualized potential presence of the crystallizing lattice arising in the mother matrix." And Neumann adds:

"The 'archetype in itself' is a core phenomenon that transcends consciousness and whose 'eternal presence' is unperceptualized. But it not only directs the unconscious restraint of the personality like a magnetic field by way of the instincts as a pattern of behavior; it also appears in the consciousness as a pattern of vision in the arrangement of psychic material as symbolic pictures."

Mythical ur-symbols are the original language of the unconscious. Such original pictures can hardly be expressed in intellectual formulations. They seek imagistic expression:

"Above all, a linguistic simile asserts archetypal content. If it speaks of the sun and identifies it with the lion, the king, the golden treasure watched over by the dragon, and the life- and health-force of mankind, it is still neither the one nor the other but the unknown third element which may be expressed more or less accurately through all these similes, but which itself (though this remains annoying to the intellect) remains unknown and unformulable." (Jung)

In the second half of the nineteenth century, artists and poets, disgusted by the intellectual hypertrophy and civilizing activity, sought contact with primitive cultures and peoples motivated by instinct and living in the sphere of myth.

Later, not through a geographical bridging of the continents but through an immersion in the depths of the soul, came the attempt to return to origins and sources, to those archetypes that connect the individual experience of the soul with the collective dream of humanity. Miró says of the main characteristics of his art:

"My painting has to do with the unconscious. We are tired of civilization and experience a deep longing for the simple and free life. I feel myself strongly rooted in the soil and thus also in the subconscious that rests within me. I find the subconscious embodied above all in the art of ancient times, because the life forms descended from such art have grown more unconsciously, more undifferentiated, freer in the biological as well as in the spiritual sense. Thus the art forms of earlier epochs are purer than the later ones; that is why they attract me. . . ."

The Resurrection of the Red and Black Gods

*Oho! Congo asleep in thy bed of forests, queen of
     subjected Africa*
Let the mountain's phallus raise high thy banner
*For thou art woman by my head, by my tongue, for
     thou art woman by my belly*

*Mother of all things with nostrils, crocodiles
     hippopotamuses*
Manatees iguanas fish birds,
Mother of rising waters nurse of harvests. . . .
                              Léopold Sédar Senghor

The gaze of modern man seeks archaic memory signs—the paleolithic and neolithic idols, the petrified myths of Egypt, the pre-Columbian images of gods. If one looks to Greece, one looks to the Mycenean prelude or Doric beginnings; if to Rome, then to the Etruscan age. Byzantine wall mosaics and Romanesque devotional images affect the artistic sensibilities of our time more strongly than the harmony of the Renaissance or the virtuosity of the Baroque.

The artist's backward look toward the store of images of ancient times and to the archaic world of forms conforms to his weariness with the completeness and harmony of classical art and its reiterations, which limited themselves to representing the external aspects of life, "the unsecret, epidermal organism visible to all." (Ernst Bloch)

Paul Gauguin's trip to the Antilles in 1887 was the prelude to a turning point in aesthetics. What had been till then regarded as folklore now became news of the beauty and intensity of primitive art.

In his essay "Primitive Art and Modern Man," Herbert Read asks in his dialectic, sensitive mannner why the artists of this age found the art of the primitives particularly beautiful and meaningful: "I think there is little doubt that the answer to this question lies in the artist's revolt, conscious or unconscious, against the industrial civilization which, by the third quarter of the nineteenth century, had become such a hideous reality. In the case of Van Gogh and Gauguin, European civilization was a 'dismal swamp,' corrupt beyond redemption. Gauguin deliberately turned his back on it, and went to Tahiti to seek the primitive reality. To a certain extent he found it, and this is how he describes it: 'A delight distilled from some indescribable sacred horror which I glimpse of far off things. The odor of an antique joy which I am breathing in the present. Animal shapes of a statuesque rigidity: indescribably antique, august, and religious in the rhythm of their gesture, in their singular immobility. In the dreaming eyes is the overcast surface of an unfathomable enigma.' "

The Expressionists, the Cubists, and later the Surrealists followed this procession to the prelogical and primitive. But the protest against technology and the weariness of civilization do not suffice to explain this sudden awakening interest. Certain commonly held psychological assumptions acted more deeply than anything else. Herbert Read speaks of the spiritual, social, and metaphysical uncertainty of humanity today, and its relationship to the state of being of certain primitive religions of dread, atonement, and recompense. "When the existentialist begins to talk about the anguish or uneasiness which overcomes him when he faces up to the problem of man's cosmic predicament, he is merely using elaborate linguistic signs to describe the same feelings which overcome primitive men, but which they can only express in emotive symbols."

There is no change in the world that has not been reflected in an artistic vision of this change. The opening realms of knowledge show frightening chasms, mathematical dreams, and unnamable visions of the micro- and macrocosm. A new developmental process begins on the higher level of the space-time plane. In the broadened sphere of events that man does not yet comprehend, of energies that he is just beginning to measure, he is living through a new period of creativity; imagistic forms become the signs and symbols of a comprehensive, planetary, scientifically defined so-called primitivism of the twentieth century.

Archaic arts prove themselves to the modern eye to be spiritual relatives, and art in a technological age makes a pilgrimage to their spheres. The *haniwa* idols of early Japanese art (1), clay figures with masklike, round eyes and mouth holes and the secretive gesture of raised arms in ritual dance, awaken an echo in modern artists' feeling for form.

An elongated ivory figure (8) unearthed in Beersheba in the south of today's state of Israel, belonging to a culture that was blotted out before the beginning of historical reckoning, is not dissimilar to the towering, magical shadow figures of Alberto Giacometti (9).

In order to assert finality and an opposition to death, the art of Egypt expressed itself in the heaviness and durability of chiseled stone. Henry Moore's *King and Queen* (13) possesses something of the frontal sternness of the straight face and the elementary simplicity of the early Greek or Egyptian seated figures (12). It invokes dream and the ultimate loneliness of creatures. Proximity to nature, imaginative form, and myth are the ultimate materials of which Moore builds his figures. He comments: "The *King and Queen* group has nothing to do with present-day Kings and Queens but is more connected with the archaic or primitive idea of a King. The 'clue' to the group is perhaps the head of the King which is a head and crown, face and beard combined into one form and in my mind has some slight Pan-like suggestion, almost animal, and yet I think, something Kingly."

One of the five casts of Moore's royal couple stands on the bald hill of Scotland's Shawhead as though it belonged to the prehistory of the land. In their unity with their natural surroundings these figures remind one of the mighty forms seated before the rocky temples of Egypt and looking out on the endless desert.

Nevertheless, the young Moore loved the stylized art of the late dynasties and the colossi of Egypt less than the magical clarity of ancient Mexican sculpture. He writes: "Mexican sculpture, as soon as I found it, seemed to me true and right, perhaps because I at once hit on similarities in it with some eleventh-century carvings I had seen as a boy on Yorkshire churches. Its 'stoniness,' by which I mean its truth to material, its tremendous power without loss of sensitiveness, its astonishing variety and fertility of form-invention and its approach to a full three-dimensional conception of form, make it unsurpassed in my opinion by any other period of stone sculpture."

The depth of this impression became evident in Moore's work in the positive way in which only the greatest artists may adopt and conquer the past. The architectonic severity, the Cubistic strength of form, the magical intensity of Chac Mool (14) from Chichen Itza can be felt outside the mysterious rituals which it served and which have remained unknown to us. The head of the sun-god, turned to the right of his body, gazes with masklike immobility. With both hands the god grasps the dish intended to hold the offering. These figures of the Toltec and early Mayan cultures find their parallel in the variations of Moore's reclining female figures (15). In her quiet composure, her elemental female massiveness, and the beauty of her fold-draped figure, transforming architectural and natural space by her presence, she is perhaps a late messenger of the Great Mother in primordial-modern form.

The helmet head is somewhat totemlike in its threatening and demonic starkness (19). Werner Hofmann writes:

"It is probably not by chance that the two eyeholes behind the eye slits look like gun muzzles. . . . This helmet belongs to the age of earth satellites; it is a symbol of humanity which enters the prison of the rocket cabin in order to experience the freedom of outer space."

An analogy with Aztec skulls made of black obsidian should not be taken too literally. Nevertheless, such a comparison indicates the connection between the modes of existence. One could also compare Moore's helmet head with one of the Chac Mool gods. Modern man in this abstruse magic hood of nuclear death is more frightful and demonic than the sacrificing priests in their bloody rituals among the Mayan pyramids.

The reclining figure (17) by the Austrian sculptor Fritz Wotruba is intrinsically related to the Chac Mool stone god from Ihuatzio (16). Not only does the stark heaviness of the substance of the Wotruba testify to this; even more, it is the sense of a conscious homecoming to the climate of an original speech. These roughly sculpted cubelike forms, anatomically defined only in their basic lines, perhaps push even further into the past than the sculpture of Mexico. Their plain strength takes over the language of megaliths, dolmens, and menhirs:

"Thus something originates which man can denote as full material realization; the stone gradually attains a consciousness of its own existence. On the other hand, man, whose work it is to witness for the stone, is changed back into the subject." (Werner Hofmann)

One of the masters of modern art who fled to the United States to escape the barbarity of the Third Reich and brought with them their valuable luggage of creative inspiration was Jacques Lipchitz. He had gone beyond Cubism, but he retained its regularity, its simplified architectural imagery, and its ordered rhythms. Some of his figures carry something of a vegetative fantasy and the primitive forms of African sculpture. His *Large Figure,* 1926–30 (11), is a synthetic marriage of abstract, symmetrical Negro idols with South Pacific sculpture: "a hieratic, awe-inspiring power such as one might expect but rarely finds in primitive cult images." (Alfred H. Barr, Jr.)

Surrealism knew the isolation of anatomical fragments jolted into a magic light by their displacement in an unfamiliar milieu. The stark eyes make the Lipchitz *Figure* appear totemlike and mythical. It is not the medieval "eye of God" that governs space, and not the universal eye of Odilon Redon that soars into the firmament, but rather the fascinating and hypnotic double eye of the totemic eagle (10). The eyes that gaze from the scaffold of hard line in Hans Uhlmann's steel *Fetish* (44) are notable for a rare mixture of technique and magic. The totem-like *Rites in Sal Sefaeni* (45) by the American sculptor Dorothy Dehner; *Idol* by the Swiss Arnold

d'Altri, who forms an abstract god with strong gestures out of a rhomboid skeleton; *Figure* by the Italian Mirko Basaldella (35), whose fragmented limbs are set up as a memory symbol—these are all variations of modern totem figures.

Jean Arp's *Idol* (46) is closer in its lapidary sign quality to the appearance of a prototype than to a statue belonging to a primitive cult. Like Paul Klee, Arp wants to realize not the external form of nature's appearance, but her organic growth process. Harboring invisible and at the same time significant matters, his forms are loaded with secret power; in them one occasionally sees a consonance with the signs and symbols of primitive art.

A synthesis of creative originality and intensely purified form occurs in Brancusi's sculptures. The Romanian artist took a rustic, native heritage of form with him to Paris, where he unified the vision of Cubism with the instinctual art of the primitives. Some of his expressive, simplified figures originate in a magical-mythical sphere and in their impenetrable restraint remind one of the Cycladic idols (2, 3). It is as though this sculptor-poet had united the poles of time with his careful, creative hand. It is as though he wished to create myths of reconciliation for our times through formal creations that exist between life and matter.

In Picasso's works the greatness and danger of the adventure that the artists of our century have undertaken become particularly apparent. Through his refined senses Picasso has newly awakened our ancient heritage. He has broken through the tyranny of European forms and has made all cultures accessible to the modern desire for formal expression: Iberian-archaic and pre-Romanic forms, the demonic myths of the minotaur and the forms on Attic vases, Mediterranean light, the demonology of the pre-Columbian gods, and the dark idol world of Africa (24, 25).

The optics of Cézanne and the demonology of Negro masks (26, 27) meet in the female nude studies for the painting *Les Demoiselles d'Avignon*. Picasso's inborn instinct and his alert intelligence serve to fill the spatial architecture of symbolic formulas with the tension and intensity of magic fetishes.

The broad formal simplification and demonic substance of these naked female figures are filled with a strange and only apparently subdued heterogenous spirit taken from archaic and magical confines. This picture, which is supposed to be based on his recollections of a brothel in Barcelona, ushered in the so-called Negro Period in Picasso's work, which simultaneously became the point of origin for Analytical Cubism.

For the first time in the history of modern art the African mask face is used here to revitalize the forms of civilized art, drained by virtuosity. An attempt is made to infuse these emptied forms with the sap of the creative instinct. This is not so much a matter of having the forms of folk art break into the aesthetic consciousness of this artist; rather, the endeavors and experiments of the modern artist converge with the art of the primitives.

"The European tradition, and especially the discovery made through the Cubists of the actual intention of Cézanne, allows us to understand the artistic tendencies which came to light in the *Demoiselles d'Avignon* of Picasso, 1907, and in Georges Braque's Estaque landscapes, 1908. If one wishes to lay any value on such causal explanations, the external characteristics of their appearance are revealed in the pictures, or even better the sculptures which Gauguin created during his stay in the South Seas and which bear witness to the impression made on him by his Polynesian milieu. It is not a matter of the influence of Negro art on the Cubists, but rather of a phenomenon which one often observes at the beginning of a break with existing tradition: one seeks a confirmation of new tendencies which one has found elsewhere in time and space." (Daniel-Henry Kahnweiler)

Only later did African art come to be of fundamental importance for the development of modern European and American sculpture. Primitive art spread the old and now renewed message that the artist must portray the world not as it appears to the eye but as the artist knows and perceives it. Abandoning imitation and leaving behind all illusory expedients meant a break with the trends of classical tradition. Kahnweiler speaks of the fact that the Cubist recognized the masks of the Ivory Coast as signs that imitated nothing but forced the viewer to create an internal conception of a face. This discovery made it possible for painting to find and invent signs and led sculpture to the kind of transparency which permits the representation of the underlying concepts behind the visible forms. Kahnweiler writes:

"In this manner emblematic sculpture made its entrance into European art in place of the discarded sculpture of imitation and cleared the way for everything that has been realized since then, for example 'drawing in space' sculpture, made of wire, iron bars, cord, and willow twigs; wood constructions, and so on."

Picasso's pictures and sculptures show the inclusion of this African experience even, perhaps, when the artist is not fully conscious of it. Picasso had also grasped the element of continuity in the flux of time. Thus he overcomes the continuum of yesterday, today, and tomorrow. In art everything exists simultaneously, visible from many points of view. Time and space are subsumed in the work as myth and dream.

Besides Picasso and after him, other artists were touched by the experience of primitive art. Derain's *Crouching Man* has the square weight of native stone sculpture; Vlaminck, Schmidt-Rottluff, and Pechstein were moved by the sudden impact and dazzling color of the primitives. Ernst Ludwig Kirchner and the painters of the *Brücke* were concerned with wood sculpture that in its rough, pointed primitiveness leans almost too much on the sculpture of the South Seas and Africa. Emil Nolde's *Masks* and *Wood Figure with Mask* have been taken over almost without translation directly from the sphere of primitive art. The dark glow and intensity of the primitive instinct permeates Nolde's painting even when he celebrates Christian myths with magical expression. "I paint and draw and attempt to capture something of basic existence. In the artistic production of primitive peoples we have the last remnants of primordial art."

Modigliani was very much moved by the strength of Negro sculpture (28, 29). His solemn, stylized female faces, taking off from Brancusi, remind one of the Congo dance masks of the Mukui, the secret societies of the Machango, Balumbo and other tribes, whose whitened, powdered, expressive forms represent the spirits of the dead. Modigliani's hieratic creations—which are, above all that is idol-like in them, animated by symbolic and painful spirituality—show a relationship to the long-necked heads and stylized eyes of Pangwe sculpture.

Max Ernst early formulated his goal of becoming a magician and creating the myths of his time. Much of his work, created of directed chance and a foreboding perception of the universe, confirms this. Since the thirties he has also been sculpting riddlelike archetypal forms that, despite their grotesque trimmings and disguising, ironic titles, are drawn out of deeply buried levels of consciousness. He decorated his country house in Sedona, Arizona, with katchinas, with masks and fetishes, and with his own fantastic reliefs. *Capricorn,* a strange family of human-animal forms, is one of these. In the garden of the house in Huismes, France, stands the bronze sculpture *The King Plays with the Queen* (33). The horned bust of the king, whose arm clasps the smaller figure, reminds one of the magic sculptures of Africa (32). Whether Ernst had the helmet-mask with bull and

bird of the Senufo tribe of western Sudan in mind when he created his sculpture is almost a matter of indifference. For Ernst the art forms of primitive cultures are finds from the realm of impulses and instincts, building blocks of the unconscious mind that, when united with superconscious depth experiences of a later epoch, become the images of a broadened optical reality.

But analogies with the sculpture of the primitives are also to be found in the processes that are considered to be the specific inventions of the European artists of the second half of the twentieth century. The grotesque, monstrous troubadours of a late Surrealism formed by Eduardo Paolozzi out of machine parts, wheels, and metal pegs are similar to the Bakongo nail fetishes (38, 39). Even the somewhat abstract sculptural solutions developed by Barbara Hepworth, in which the rhythm of material and space allows one only vaguely to recognize the organic point of origin, is astonishingly closely related to the formal stringency of the pierced dance masks of the Dogon tribe of western Sudan (42, 43).

Paul Klee's relationship with primitive and archaic art leads us to a change of scene. Nature and mankind in their visible materiality are stricken from the program of his art. Instead, he probes into what moves and floats behind it, the apparently incomprehensible shadow picture of dream, memory, origin, and beginning. If some of his pictures are similar to fetishes and totems (22, 23), this occurs as a result of his own creative, enigmatic powers, which are able to find and interpret the very being of hidden things.

"If a primitive impression is sometimes given by my works, this primitiveness is to be understood by my discipline, which is to reduce things to few steps. It is only economy, a final professional perception, and thus the opposite of real primitiveness."

Gauguin and those artists inspired by the external form of exotic and archaic art filtered the primitive picture through the fine sieve of consciousness refined by culture. Klee allows himself to be led by his inner perception, by the signs of the unconscious. The complicated mechanism of psychoanalysis and the presentiments of bygone ages, combined with childlike naïveté, help to trace the hermetic meaning of the forms of primitive experience. *Senecio* (1922), that circular face of a cosmic view, in its abstraction and intensity equates the magical reliquary figures of the Bakotas (Gabon) with the brass-plated face of the full moon (30, 31).

The richness of form, strength, and emotional tension of primitive art found a deep resonance in modern artists. Hindrances set up by conventional thought had to be cleared away, aesthetic prejudices overcome in order to make accessible the landscape of primitive and archaic cultures that lay beneath the American continent. The rediscovery of pre-Columbian gods, Indian totem poles, the plastic arts and music of the Negro worked in a most fruitful way on the spirit and vision of American and world art. Would it be going too far to suspect in the totem variations of modern artists a return to the banished and extinct gods and demons?

While the artists of Europe and America refresh their imaginations, refined by intellectual and technical progress, at the well of the archaic and primitive, borrowing instinct and vitality from the idol carvers, the people of Africa are awakening within their virgin forests and striving to free themselves from the powerful influence of both their magicians and the white imperialists. Above all, for its most immediate development Black Africa clearly needs enlightenment and a new social order. Through contact with the civilization of modern times, Africa's special and native art is losing its potency and intensity. Contact with technology is depriving its gods and demons of power.

II

SIGNS OF THE EAST

Out of the object, which now no longer depresses me, a tension urges forward which becomes ever brighter and which continues like an echo to the very limits of the given painting surface. The noble teaching of Turner and the spiritual message of Zen painting have reached me.

André Masson, 1953

What the great meeting of cultures has meant to the twentieth century will only be fully recognizable from the distance of several decades. The spirit and techniques of modern times have deeply penetrated extra-European societal and cultural formations. At the same time, and as important, if not as immediately apparent, the figures and forms of pre-Columbian, African, and Far Eastern peoples have worked on the art of Europe and America.

Such a meeting gains meaning from a synthetic enrichment, but it can also, especially in the aesthetic sphere, lead to crises and shocks released by the antitheses of revolution and tradition, connection and dissolution.

"As the artistic connections between the Occident and the Far East go through several phases they become deeper. One could say that Europe penetrates this culture with shoots of its own late Western experience and fructifies it to its own use.

In the eighteenth century the borrowings were primarily of motifs and were thus relatively external. In the nineteenth century, in contrast, the influence originates in a principle of organization and is intensively assimilated. Spiritual assumptions, however, were still matters of indifference to the European artists. Only in the twentieth century did penetration of the source of Far Eastern art occur. In the sign of the mortal threat which the Occident unleashed, the Orient gained new attractiveness." (Günther Aust)

Almost simultaneously, the technical, industrialized indications penetrated the Far East and especially Japan, while the forerunners of Asiatic art traveled to Europe. Through the colored woodcuts of Hokusai and the prints of Hiroshige the artists of Paris succeeded in reaching to the classical Japanese woodcuts of the eighteenth century and saw there what they themselves were seeking and had begun to develop.

Manet, Gauguin, and Van Gogh discovered the construction of a picture based on planes of color; Degas and Bonnard discovered asymmetry and tension-laden picture sectioning; Toulouse-Lautrec discovered the abbreviating, light, silhouettelike brush writing; Félix Vallotton penetrated beyond Japanism and English commercial style to a painterly symbolism; Albert Marquet found stimulation and self-

20

confirmation in the simplified austerity of the Far Eastern representation of nature.

This generously simplifying, modified conception of nature, leading to abstraction, worked on these artists and others less as an actual influence than as a strengthening of long-latent aims.

More deeply and persistently, the spirit, form, and technique of Far Eastern watercolors consciously penetrated the modern art of Europe and America in the 1920s. This occurred especially among those artists who started to turn away from external reality in order to erect signs and pictorial symbols of submersion and sensibility in place of imitation and appearance. What captured these artists was the ability of the Chinese and Japanese artists to express essences through written characters.

In China and Japan writing has always possessed overwhelming importance. It was not only a medium of expression but also an expression of the writer's being. Writing was art; in order to master it one had to know how to achieve a spiritual level, learn to move the brush with musical lightness, and develop compositional talents with economy, a feeling for form, and self-discipline.

The art of expressing material, objective concepts in pictograms led to the special aesthetics of Far Eastern calligraphy, in which writing means the production of pictures.

But this art, too, which rests upon strict ancient tradition, experienced a radical renewal and change of meaning in the fragmentation of Japanese society after World War II. Gakiu Osawa (58, 62) and the other modern calligraphers broke through the old rule of legibility in order to release writing from the dead sphere of signs paralyzed by convention and allow them to become a subjective expression of the artists' sensitivities. Based on the knowledge of the handwork and philosophy of Zen Buddhism, modern calligraphy in Japan thus became an abstract art; it ceased to maintain the social function of writing—that is, its objective legibility.

Despite all the variations and differences among individual schools of art in Japan, of which there are about twenty, modern Japanese art can be divided into two main streams: the Nihon-ga painters of Japan's traditional style, and the Yoh-ga styles, influenced by the oil paintings of Western artists.

Part of the basic tradition of the Japanese style is its connection with organic forms of nature. Painting meant their emotional-poetic interpretation. Painters belonging to the traditional schools painted on silk and paper with *sumi* watercolors and specially prepared colors whose soft values corresponded to the Japanese attitudes toward life. Even the entrance of modern elements of style into the Nihon-ga painting could only temporarily repress the specific Japanese tradition. These elements were assimilated and subordinated to the tradition's own laws of form and measurement. Despite their enrichment from outside, the tradition-bound forms could but poorly illustrate the full scale of newly recognized views and basic connections in life. Where this tradition was worn away, a new school, Yoh-ga painting, arose, which subsumed the tendencies of modern Occidental art. Insofar as it did this, something peculiar developed: using the most modern means, it simultaneously drew upon the sources of archaic tradition, although it did dissociate itself from the continuous development of the past centuries. But its surrealistic visions awakened associations with ancient Japanese ghost and demon painting, and its abstract realizations were linked with calligraphy in their feeling for form and direction. At the same time and in an opposing movement, while Japanese and modern European art were coming closer together, the influence of Far Eastern calligraphy was making itself felt on European and American painting.

The talented Belgian painter and calligrapher Pierre Alechinsky asks:

"It is not curious that such a refined culture as

the Japanese could have united externally with certain groping attempts on our part, developed from an unconscious spirit along certain lines in a deeper level of existence? Without any educational imperative, without the least direct cultural inheritance, it is nevertheless possible for us to find a common ground of intuitive understanding. If we have been able, almost automatically, thus to understand certain obvious aspects of Japanese expression, we can perhaps regard this as a sign of the hoped-for return to the shattered sources of the imaginary and wonderful."

For anyone brought up in the spirit of Eastern culture, the forms of letters have immediate associations with thought. To the Far Eastern artist the calligraphic forms are documents of an event that has been played in time and whose resonance continues. This process, and not only the beauty and harmony of the forms, has inspired many European and American artists. Without fully understanding the spiritual background, the strangers guess the inner meaning and experience it as the expression of an ideogram, as the echo of a language that one can feel and decipher through submergence in it. Insofar as they use the intensity of their talent and their spiritual concentration, the foreign artists can, like the Zen Buddhist archers, through spontaneous and unconscious actions find the signs of identity that unite their beings with the meaning of the universe.

For the younger generation of Far Eastern calligraphers the contact with Western art was revolutionary. Stimulated by modern movements, they began to contemplate the source of their subjective relation to the world and recalled the essential meaning of that relation as displayed in the context of writing-painting. Certain abstract elements have always been part of the Sho works of Far Eastern calligraphy. After having been influenced by Abstract Expressionism, modern Japanese calligraphers abandoned their last ties to the meaning of their ancient signs, in order to discover new events in form and structure. Consequently, they renounced one very essential element: the profound wisdom contained in these signs. They had exchanged them for private experience.

One must ask whether the written characters are capable of conveying anything besides their direct linguistic implications. The truth is that written signs represent a form of being, a vibrating power moving the universe. During the process of writing —a moment of profound concentration and collectedness—it inherits the rhythm of the writer's blood stream, breath, and thought. The reality of the written word is one of essence: its meaning reaches far beyond the meaning of spoken words.

The Far Eastern calligraphic symbols were never autonomous in their significance, but have always specifically referred to something. And modern calligraphic painting expresses individual, objectively indeterminable moments of experience. One can therefore discover in these writing symbols and in the pictogram a point of contact between Eastern and Western art.

Klee liked to include bits of poetry in his paintings. But he created no allegoric symbol paintings, as did the Mannerists of the seventeenth century. Through a mixture of writing and color, Klee created a harmonious relation between thought and form. Miró, too, includes in his paintings poetic fragments that serve as compositional elements. If the psychographic signs of Klee and Miró were not influenced by Far Eastern writing-painting, they were perhaps influenced by the teachings of Buddhism that underlie this writing.

Kandinsky's expressive abstraction is only distantly related to calligraphy. Arp's "automatic writing," however, which found its magical symbols about 1916 in the circle of the Dadaists, already possessed an inner connection with the spirit of Zen painting.

In his book, *Zen and Japanese Culture*, D. T.

Suzuki quotes Georges Duthuit: "He who deliberates and moves his brush intent on making a picture, misses to a still greater extent the art of painting. [This seems like a kind of automatic writing.]"

The intensive influence of calligraphy was realized externally in formal analogies, but it rooted itself deeper in the artists' endeavors to free themselves from industrial and technical civilization and in their full concentration on grasping and representing the being and meaning of things.

André Masson's sand pictures (57) portray in their excited directness and passionate stillness a sort of continuation of automatic writing.

In 1934 Mark Tobey went to China and Japan to learn from the source of calligraphy, in the Buddhist monasteries, the difference between volume and flowing line and to practice the essence of that form whose language would be comprehensible to all men (60).

The ideograms that have appeared in Willi Baumeister's painting (63) since 1938 are related to the India-ink drawing of Chinese calligraphy. While Tobey's "white writing," his light lines over a dark plane, evoke a picture of landscape and time, Baumeister's black painted formulas are the signs of an unconscious Tao. They are swaying forms, weighed out, simple, like Han pottery.

Alfred Alcopley's small drawinglike paintings lie somewhere between the Salon des Réalités Nouvelles and the monastaries of Zen Buddhism.

Robert Motherwell (48), Adolph Gottlieb, Mark Rothko (164), and Franz Kline unite Western expression with Eastern meditation. Some of the spontaneously graceful signs in their painting are Far Eastern writing symbols gigantically projected. Kline's heavy beams and gray-black signs remind one of Seiyo Nagai's calligraphy (51, 52). Bradley Walker Tomlin went from Cubism to calligraphy. His rhythmic encasings remind one of the Eineck style, the simplification and asymmetry of Japanese writing symbols. Jackson Pollock's thorny tracks, squirted or pressed pastelike out of the tubes, are an expression of his psychically unrestrained spontaneity (157).

Hans Hartung's "calligraphies," (65) sternly disciplined and executed with a tangible sense of inner security, remind one of Far Eastern bamboo pictures. Looking at his works, one is inclined to quote from the writings of the Zen tradition:

"To become bamboo and then to forget while one is painting that one is united with it, that is the Zen of bamboo; that is to move 'in the life and rhythm of its being' which breathes in the bamboo even as it breathes in the artist himself. What is required here is a certain catching hold of meaning and yet a consciousness of it. This is an infinitely difficult spiritual task which may be achieved after long spiritual practice." (Takuan, *On Motionless Understanding*)

The inner intensity and radiating power in the works of Wols (277), his surrender to fate, allow one to suspect a connection with Tao. This complete passivity of reception and admission and the scrawls which look as though they had been conceived almost in a trance give his art something impersonal and anonymous. And yet it also has a sensitive subjectivity.

Pierre Soulages's dark, beamlike scaffoldings in space (53) also remind one of Chinese brush writing. The calligraphy of Georges Mathieu (55) is indebted to Far Eastern writing-painting, despite its dramatic gesture and historical motivation. After all, even the modern Japanese calligraphers have added to the original Eastern contemplativeness an expressive activism that is the clearly unavoidable characteristic of the technical age.

Giuseppe Capogrossi paints chain sequences of signs that consist of claws and brackets forming meaningful ornaments; Gerhard Hoeme builds walls of thought through bars of writing and associational rhythms. Jasper Johns uses numbers and alphabetical combinations that remind one of the mysterious hieroglyphics of extinct cultures; the plates created by Joaquín Torres-García were inspired by signs from Mayan calendars. And although Janez Bernik's banners, which include some crumbled pieces of writing, are hardly readable, they nevertheless radiate something authentic, documentary, as well as a poetic understanding of the world. Vostell's paintings use torn pieces of posters, which are placed on top of one another; in this fashion the colors, words, and fragments of letters from different layers fuse and become signs of association within diverging forms of experience. Similar to Vostell's decollages are Larry Rivers' writing-paintings, which remind one of the Dada period. They contain legible and rather provocative conglomerates of letters and numbers, and here again the result is a combination of structural and reflective experience.

Letters have been used as compositional elements of form by Picasso as well as by Braque (130) since 1911, and Juan Gris started using them soon thereafter (137). Letters were stenciled on paper or clipped from newspapers and then put into collages. The letter lost its original meaning and became an abstract sign—or sometimes an allusion to hidden meanings. While the letters and words used by the Cubists had to conform to the unity of the entire picture, Kurt Schwitters made them into independent material (141). Such a freely invented calligraphy of signs, which only resembled actual writing but was objectively illegible, communicated in its expressive abstraction a feeling of life. Such visually expressed experience by way of written constructions, which originated in the Far East, was elaborated and became more significant in Europe and America through psychic improvisations.

Inspired by Tachism and Action Painting, some talented painters permitted themselves to be led by psychic improvisations and wrote their Informal paintings in accordance with subjective impulses. Jaroslav Serpan attempted to resolve the impene-

trable mysteries of the human instinct. He created a gradual change of spastic rhythms ecstatically developed into indecipherable fragments of texts. The writing symbols of K. R. H. Sonderborg sprang from the rapidly scanning gesture of soul stenography. The wall paintings of Antonio Tàpies look like the cuneiform characters of some unknown, extinct culture. Rolf-Gunther Dienst connects rhythmically vibrating improvisations, which vaguely resemble certain labels, with an indistinguishable ornament, such as the earth's surface as it appears to the eye from great height. Klaus-Peter Dienst does something that resembles certain aspects of modern sculpture: he uses and gives equal importance to both the negative and the positive forms of the letters, creating a textual image that is legible to a minimal degree and may be accepted as an autonomous composition.

Besides Willi Baumeister, Theodor Werner, Julius Bissier, Fritz Winter, and Ernst Wilhelm Nay also belonged to the German Zen group, which was founded in 1949 and took this name as a symbol for an inner-directed art based on concentration. The tensions and rhythmic accents in Werner's painting make us think of an inner dictate that produces ideogramlike forms. The experience of the world was formulated by Winter in dark, curved constructions behind which colorful accents shine out. Bissier's watercolor variations (64) of meditative submergence in nature could also have originated in China. His miniatures, of spider-web weightlessness, appear to be the result of an inner tension, a feeling of ambiguity and uncertainty. They are painted mostly in black and gray tones; but here and there, as a contrasting element, one discovers small, quiet, blinking islands in gold, or Burgundy-red, which convey a feeling of hope, no matter how remote. Such inner signs of inspiration have, since Klee, been part of a realm of profound artistic experience.

Under European influence, young Japanese calligraphers have transformed their conceptual signs into abstract forms. In contrast, European and American painters try to deepen their abstract images by the essential content of Far Eastern meditation.

"The same spirit moves all men. We are attracted by the same desires and inspired by the same wishes that exist beyond all cultural boundaries. We wish to find a symbol which will symbolize all our capabilities of thought and action. Our means of expression all seek the same end: a human sign which is at the same time mature." It may be that Alechinsky's thoughts outrun reality; still, they express a basic tendency of modern art.

Spontaneous and intuitive Tachism is indebted to the calligraphic vein of Far Eastern art, even if the coincidental return to instinctual painting contradicts the tradition of the East. For all artists generally take from foreign cultures, which have grown out of tradition, custom, and ritual, only the part that they themselves happen to be looking for. In a meeting of two cultures, each finds in the other what it needs and assumes those elements that most deeply confirm its own developmental tendencies.

Inasmuch as the Western world for the past few years has been experiencing a rejection of pure abstraction, one is not surprised to notice among the Japanese calligraphers a return to their ancient signs. However, such a return has been neither simple nor easy. Objective legibility is again added to their new freedom of subjective experience, to their extremely individual forms of expression. Nevertheless, the new calligraphy is no longer as clear and unequivocal as the texts written in the old standard characters. In order to decipher it one has to be intensely absorbed. What is required is the same intensity of concentration that every other work of art asks of the observer.

III

METAPHORS OF THE HUMAN IMAGE

Literature and Form

And God said, Let us make man in our own image, after our likeness. . . . So God created man in his own image, in the image of God created he him. . . .

The Bible

The world of primitive man, the primordial and early history of humanity now give man a new position in the world and the universe, show him the dark roots of his origins, and seem to destroy as illusory his resemblance to God and his central position in the universe.

Erich Neumann

The idea of man as the image of God has dissolved with the old concept of the gods. The basic question of man's being appears just as new as those of the concepts of time and space. In his book *The Dehumanization of Art,* Ortega y Gasset wrote in 1925 that the relationships between things and men have changed. The high position that the older, expressive art had given to human beings has through irony and a displacement of point of view been reduced to the level of all other things.

The Romantic period already recognized the night view of life, the closeness of death, and the attraction of the chthonian powers. Its art was a countermovement to Rationalism and as such was dedicated to the spiritual powers. Still more strongly did the neo-Romantics form the poetic antithesis to Positivism and Naturalism. Since all phenomena of the world appeared to be measurable, art sought correspondences with its spiritual existence in irrationality, death, and the primordial powers.

The man of the Romantic period confronted cosmic images alone. They could inspire him, their immensity could stimulate his vision, but the locked universe did not disturb the balance of his conscious mind. The cosmic view of an earthly existence that dreams itself out into mystical eternity was dissolved only in the twentieth century, and with it the spatial view of the universe. The ancient opposites, time and space, were united and began to dissolve other opposing pairs that had been points of origin for pictorial perceptions and poetic perspectives.

The revolution of time perception began with Impressionism. The image of things appeared to the plein-air painters to be a relationship of light and object; it appeared to be the viewer's retinal reflex, created of sun and time and retained in the reflection of the moment. The Impressionist painter anticipated the dissection of aesthetic material: Monet, Pissarro, Renoir, and their circle saw the universe as a moving image created of pigmentlike particles of light. Debussy liberated music from the hobbling forms of traditional harmony and invented the technical sound and spirit of Impressionism in music. Through the disintegration of action and the insertion of dream impressions and associations, Proust invented the fluid glide of light and shade characteristic of Impressionist literature. These are the forms of expression of the Bergsonian interpretation of time. Proust achieves the fulfillment of, and at the same time transcends, the psychological novel. But however deeply and completely human tendencies, talents, prejudices, illnesses, anxieties, desires, and dreams are made transparent, Proust remains, despite his renunciation of plot, within the existence of man. His world of memory supplies the material of which he builds his artistic production.

In Joyce, duration is extended beyond the individual, and the existence of other, more distant, more submerged and hidden categories of life is included; the manifold natures of an occurrence are stored one on top of the other, as in the layers of an archaeological find. Joyce forsakes not only plot but also the hero, the supporting figure of the action. Placed in unified time and space, man is mythically interwoven with the past and the return. He does not tell the story of the wanderer Ulysses but the story of all those like him. The immediate event is only a point of departure for the returning wanderer of another name and form. The story of the modern Ulysses, the Irish Jew Leopold Bloom, is a universal synthesis of the human wanderer through an ordinary weekday of universal significance. In their symbolic nature the individual acts appear as parts of a disappearing and always newly forming reality. The repetition and unity of events both present and timeless, of limitlessness and flux, create the mythical quality of Joyce's work.

Even in primitive life-functions there is a connection that transcends time. Allegory gains power in continuity and secret connection. In the Joycean internal monologues, by means of associations taken from the depths of time, the I lays itself bare, in the process transforming its individualistic-psychological personality into an abstract I. The fusion of today's motifs with primordial ones, the fusion of consciously educated thought with irrational subconsciousness, occurs here not only through dissolution and mingling of time and place, of figure and symbol; it occurs also, and herein lies its particular fascination, in a new linguistic-musical arrangement.

Joyce was working to bring the myth of daily life to a conscious level by means of newly formed words and chains of mental associations never before known. In a conversation he told the Polish poet Jan Parandovsky that he was trying to crush words, to extract their substance, to cram one on top of the other, to cross them and so create unknown inflections.

The physicist Werner Heisenberg spoke on "Language and Reality" at a meeting of the Bavarian Academy of Sciences in 1960. Our linguistic tools, he indicated, have become insufficient for the sphere of modern physics. Not only the concepts but also linguistic logic, derived from Aristotle, must be changed in order to overcome the divergence with reality which has developed. The classical picture of reality is dissolving, and a new form of thought must create new speech forms. "I can create a language that corresponds to quantum theory, but only by using a different logic. . . . The designation 'above' and 'below' have no more meaning in the universe."

The linguistic neologisms are expressed still more strongly in Joyce's last work, *Finnegans Wake*, than in *Ulysses*. The night of dreams of a Dublin innkeeper's family is contrasted with the day of the three Dubliners in *Ulysses*. The actionless story is interspersed with insertions from many live and dead languages; its course is ambiguous, grotesque, nonlogical and superlogical, automatic and planned, governed by the suggestions of sounds and obviously on the way to forming a meaningful language independent of time and space. The interior monologue breaks out of its confines and expands into a dream conversation that mingles with the murmur of the river, with the chatter of the washerwomen on the banks, with the bushes and rocks, washed by the ebbing murmur of the words, which have become water. The present hour and the long-distant past, living and dead matter, dissolve into dream and cosmic presentiment.

Did Joyce succeed in establishing a modern myth through this anthropomorphic fictional world of his poetry?

"Joyce approached his problem in two stages: the first, *Ulysses,* simply extended ancient myth over all of history and thus over the life of humanity. Despite internal monologue and internal architectonics, therefore, it made use of external means, while the second, *Finnegans Wake,* penetrates the actual birthplace of myth in dream. Thomas Mann, more bound by tradition and therefore, even if ironically, still conscious of the obligation to delight and to instruct, catches myth in its temporal essence, that is, with the problem of its eternal presence. In that he works this mythology in with human events, he not only sees simultaneity in the myth's existence but timelessness in itself; the prophetic becomes so strong that the work in which it occurs itself becomes timeless. It has its beginning in myth, but it is still thoroughly logical prophecy because (and this goes no less for Joyce) it has grown on polyhistorical ground." (Hermann Broch)

William Faulkner's method is not repetition. Dostoevski, Proust, and Joyce were educational stations for him, but the original source of his inspiration is the time background, the mythic aperspective view of Indian cosmogony and the tragic-demonic burden of black fate.

In the stream of Faulkner's narrative, times, names, sexes, and facts are blended. Occurrences remain undetermined in time; one does not know whether they lie far in the past or are being prepared and are still to take place. Some of the figures in these novels carry the same names, even if these belong to different people of different sexes, and the reader must take pains to determine who is speaking and about what. Only the author knows the internal region of true names and fates, and because he does not for a moment write for anyone but lives in his act of writing, he forces the reader to approach him closely until he can look at the event from the same standpoint and can, if not create, then experience the work with him. It may occasionally be difficult to find one's way through the architectural thicket of dense, lianalike, yet instinctively organized sentences. Faulkner uses the veiling twilight of similes and often puts substantial sections in the shadow of uncertainty. He does not follow his own story chronologically. He ignores clock time. Of what has happened, only that which is retained in the present is real, not what happens now. All stages are called to witness. They stand next to one another as equals, a chain reaction of associations, a flow to the place of the event. Events become real only when they complete themselves and thus prevail. Basically, everything has already existed. The present is devalued by the intensity of the origins that determine it, by the everlasting turning to the past, by the brotherhood of the dead with the living. The past overshadows and devours the present. But starting from the jungle of dream and memory, the poet uses a sober, surgical method of considered precision in order to represent life, accelerated and enlarged.

Figures that were in the background in one novel next step into the glaring light, secondary figures become connected with one another, families and groups are carried through from generation to generation with their family trees delineated from their origin to their extinction. The major theme is repeated with many variations based on a synthetic consciousness and establishing a precedent like that adopted in the use of the camera in Kurosawa's film *Rashomon*. The author circles the event from different points of view; he changes his standpoint and allows parallel themes to run next to one another, touch, separate, and penetrate each other in frightful dissonance. Methodical, precise structure and ancient subterranean currents give characters the fatefulness of antique myths of humanity.

In the imaginary, provincially bounded dream world of Yoknapatawpha County, which the author colonized with all the weaknesses of human life, he creates the totality of a world, good and evil, close and distant, bounded and endless. It is a tragedy that is brother to the drama cycle of Aeschylus.

If the excellent sociologist Arnold Hauser, in his *Social History of Art,* does not even mention the most important epic writer of this late age, William Faulkner, his definition of the newly developed conception of time could be applied to Faulkner's creative technique: "The accent is now on the simultaneity of the contents of consciousness, the immanence of the past in the present, the constant flowing together of the different periods of time, the amorphous fluidity of inner experience, the boundlessness of the stream of time by which the soul is borne along, the relativity of space and time, that is to say, the impossibility of differentiating and defining the media in which the mind moves. In this new conception of time almost all the strands of the texture which form the stuff of modern art converge: the abandonment of the plot, the elimination of the hero, the relinquishing of psychology, the automatic method of writing, and, above all, the montage technique and the intermingling of temporal and spatial forms of the film."

Proust, Joyce, Thomas Wolfe, Virginia Woolf, and T. S. Eliot experimented with the concept of time. Faulkner eliminated time. There is no longer anything experimental in this dense, instinct-laden prose. It is multilayered, subterranean, and as timeless as nature herself.

The inexplicability of the dreams and narratives of Franz Kafka, the impenetrability of the powers and laws that lie behind them, simultaneously veil and reveal an estranged world. The guilt feeling of an era, the hovering anxiety of the merciless, cold, technical world, ungracious in its precision, is presented from the perspective of the modest observer: ". . . the monstrous world that I have in my head. But how to free myself and free it without tearing. A thousand times rather tear apart than hold it back in me or bury it. . . ." So wrote Kafka in 1912. His stories *The Judgment* and *The Metamorphosis* and his novels *The Trial* and *The Castle* are reflections of this abyss. Without a sound, without clamor in the disturbing twilight of doubt and lack of answers, the essential becomes visible. As in the magical, naïve language of the tax collector Henri Rousseau, without any tricks of art man is portrayed here as he moves in a sphere between dream and waking. Everyday things happen, simple words are spoken. The rules of causality do not hold good, the relationships of time and space are canceled. The powers that are called upon remain inaccessible; the doors remain closed.

Kafka's reality encloses more than a shadow world of metaphysical allegories. In his work fate does not have a nonhuman face. The insurance man Kafka not only experiences the transformation of man into insect but also the frustration of documents that can't be located and have become dusty numbers, the degradation of the little man by the unfathomable and nameless power structure of the administration. He creates a demonically banal atmosphere of gray corridors, endless stairs, and the impenetrable objectification of officials and state.

Jean Prévert portrays a related state:

Do not go there.
Everything has been contrived;
The match is rigged.

And when He steps into the ring
Radiant with magnesium lightning,
Then they voice the TE DEUM, roaring,
And before Thou has raised Thyself from Thy chair,
They loudly ring out all the bells. . . .

A pathetic Kafka would be unthinkable. Nothing definite exists; nothing is assured. In the twilight of his thoughts one find unexpected abysses. One takes in the horrors of his pictures, the perils of his situations. An all-inclusive fear accompanies the wanderer through this precise, thoroughly organized, bureaucratized world, which runs away and dissolves at every attempt to grasp it.

Hermann Broch emphasizes the absolutely unfalsified stylistic naïveté in Kafka's writing that allows us to recognize great fiction:

"Figures like the Kafkas or Henri Rousseaus are unique, not only because of their genius, but much more because they represent a genius that was successful in maintaining itself almost completely free of tradition in the very center, so to say, of European artistic tradition and thus of the universal art of that time."

Even in Broch's novel *The Death of Virgil* external continuous action hardly exists. While Joyce follows a day in the life of a modern Ulysses, Broch is concerned with the last eighteen hours in the life of the dying Virgil, from his arrival in the harbor of Brindisium to his death in the palace of Augustus. Even though written in the third person, it is an endless interior monologue, in the hour beyond reality between no more and not yet. Perhaps this backward look means more than an examination of the road that the poet of Aeneas had to take and contains something of the tragic flux of society in the twentieth century: an intertwining of the melodies of life, an interweaving of thought structures, and behind these the presentiment of an incomprehensible, endless and boundless world. Broch pictures Virgil in his last hours as recognizing the inadequacy of his existence and his work. It is only because of his empathy for the emperor who has befriended him, and who loves his poetry, that the ancient author gives up his idea of destroying his *Aeneid*. Is this motif of self-destruction ancient, or did Broch, looking backward upon the road and creations of his own life, mean himself, like Kafka, whom he placed above all others and who had wished to burn the work that would become so meaningful to a coming generation?

Are Samuel Beckett's plays, too, attempts to create the myth of the age, or if not that, then the counter-myth? His *Waiting for Godot* already appears to be an extreme expression of a revelation; lunatics and clowns, dressed like normal people, play life. Their existence fulfills itself in purposeless waiting. For whom? For man? For God? For oneself? In contrast, Beckett's *Endgame* is a dull fantasy of fate; in its unarresting course the stars are extinguished, human beings destroy one another, must destroy one another because destruction is already contained in all creation. In *Endgame* not only is the bitter poetry lost but also the last glimmer of hope. Here one does not wait any more. Or if one does, it is only for self-annihilation and death.

Beckett did not invent the anti-illusionist theater. A world between the appearance and existence of existential unmasking moves constantly and hauntingly from Pirandello to Dürrenmatt. It is no longer in doubt about itself but certainly about the fateful legend of the annihilation of mankind.

What is new in Beckett's black works of hopelessness is the absolute renunciation of the palliatives of artistic requisites. Ascetic, concerned only with the deepest essence of the world's hidden cipher, he renounces the architecture of action, the invoice of dialogue, and refuses to provide the viewer with pleasure.

Perhaps Bertold Brecht attacked illusionism on

the stage even more than did his contemporaries. It was for this purpose that he set up his very controversial theory of epic theater.

With Pirandello the modern theater began to fight against the complete transformation of the actor. Using his "estrangement effect," Brecht was the first to transform a generally vague and instinctual delivery into a specific style suited to the age. The actor *is not* Oedipus, Hamlet, or Mack the Knife. He *is not* the hero. He represents him. In the tension between play and existence the actor becomes the embodiment of an individual character and at the same time an archetype of human-inhuman conditions raised to the level of an abstract universal.

In *The Story of a Novel: The Genesis of Doctor Faustus* Thomas Mann quotes Harry Levin, the biographer and critic of James Joyce: "Joyce's technique passes beyond the limits of English realistic fiction. Neither *A Portrait of the Artist* nor *Finnegans Wake* is a novel, strictly speaking, and *Ulysses* is a novel to end all novels." And Mann adds:

"This probably applies to *The Magic Mountain, The Joseph Story,* and equally well to *Doctor Faustus.* T. S. Eliot's question whether the novel had not outlived its function since Flaubert and James, and whether *Ulysses* should not be considered an epic paralleled my own question whether in the field of the novel the only thing that counted was what was no longer a novel."

Are we eyewitnesses of newly developing forms, and will it become possible for the artist consciously to enfold instinct-bound powers, to fuse the schemes of the intellect and the archaic imagination to create a mythical totality?

The multidimensionality of a new experience of nature has changed the viewpoint of literature: in this newly viewed, infinitely broadened view, the anthropocentric picture of personality becomes relativized, but at the same time a unity of the individual and the universal is presented. Man's uniqueness seems impaired by decomposition and dissolution. He is deformed by the absurd gesture of the absurd and by the consideration of his "night" side. But internal vistas are revealed, deep soundings of his collective existence are taken. The weakening of the individual's power in a realm of anonymity, mass movements, and social relationships gives rise to the vision of a higher order of man in the systematic relationships of new truths.

What is happening in literature is happening in all areas of art. For this is at once the effect and the cause of a new language and study of existence.

The Amorphous and the Archaic

Dawn. The horizon
Half opens its lashes
And begins to see. What? Names.
They exist on the patina
Of things. . . .

        Jorge Guillén

The idea that God's creation of the world is unique has perished in the dizzying number of recorded stars and star systems of the universe. Even the Renaissance tradition's idolatry of the anthropomorphic picture as the symbol of all existence has been robbed of its meaning. The thinking consciousness of man extends itself beyond the earthly confines that have hitherto bound it, and its interests are directed toward the universal. This does not imply abandonment of human plans and desires but a broadening of them. All facts and actions, all areas of study, all times and places become essential materials of recognition. The conception of man as the measure of all things now contradicts philosophical and scientific thought; the validity of all visible things is questioned:

"The questioning of appearance, begun in ancient times in astronomy, dares all. But it does not intend to sink into emptiness; rather it intends to gain a better and unexpected comprehension of just that appearance. Intimate acquaintance with the unimaginable in physics by means of unperceptualized mathematics is an example." (Karl Jaspers)

Art, which lives these developments beforehand, cannot content itself with picturing the old anthropocentric world with its human-hero-god inhabitants. Other events of life, other secrets of material and existential construction, claim its attention. Above and below, the external and internal, are relationships of a co-ordinating system and are changeable in time and place. Every occurrence and every thought, from the very beginning and in the widest extension of space-time recognition, fascinates the gaze.

The sociologist Alfred Weber calls our age a time of transition:

"We must take leave of history up to now, and we must meet everything that surrounds us with the question, what does it mean as a symptom of this leave-taking? And to what extent can we recognize in this the signs of a new, newly conceived, deeper humanity, corresponding more to our real beginning as a result of the melding of this new conception with our old one? . . . With and after Cézanne artists forsake the old picture of existence constructed according to the laws of perspective. Thus they discard the means of expression developed throughout the centuries, even through millennia, which picture man with reference to organized space and consciously seek new means of expression. This means no less than that they have and are trying to establish a new, different world view. From an internal point of view, the fact that they tie in with the primitives means that they no longer feel themselves to be the continuators of our past history."

Portraiture and figured composition as the image of the autonomous and rounded personality now belong to that history. From Jan van Eyck's pictures of burghers to Holbein's portraits of England's aristocracy, and on to the autobiographical soul-analyses of Rembrandt, the portrait picture was the spiritual reflection of personality. Since the middle of the nineteenth century, the painted picture has been replaced by the daguerreotype and photograph. The best-adjusted and in a certain sense most typical man of our times no longer seeks prestige in painted portraits and marble sculpture, as did the lords of the Renaissance and Baroque period, and not even like the educated burghers who wanted to preserve themselves in an aesthetic and unique conception. In the rapidly changing conceptions of reality, figured compositions and portraits are treated like still lifes and landscapes. The sensitivity and coloristic experience of the artist make face and form lose their meaning. The formal substance becomes brittle, dissolves in the figures of the Impressionists and Intimists, and in Van Gogh becomes, by painful, self-destructive interpretation, the showplace of spiritual expression. The clear-sighted, neurotic transcendence and the hallucinatory radiance in James Ensor's painting are witness to the self-estrangement of mankind. Emil Nolde's magical, expressive powers fill the human bearer of life with demonic, primitive instincts. The human faces that Oskar Kokoschka paints show in their graphology of the soul an inner tension and poetic agitation. In Matisse, man becomes the image of pure form. Man as a subject becomes the occasion for harmonic, dissonant arrangements of colorful planes. Marko Celebonović anthropomorphizes nature, making of it the objects of newly experienced space. Human faces and the fruits of the earth and of fantasy are defined as equally justifiable forms of reality.

Even the deepest break does not quite annul the continuity of developments up to this time, but it does change the aspects of this development. Historical substance is simultaneously included and annulled. The artist's gaze is fascinated by the archaic and the primitive; nevertheless, it seeks to penetrate through the thin layers of historical deposits to the deep region of primitive history. The spiritualized formal beauty and hieratically severe stylization of the human face in Amedeo Modigliani (29) are still dependent on the natural form. Even if the direction of the lines indicates his Tuscan origins, his vision is enriched by the experience of the primitives. His melancholy deformations are descended from sensitive musicality and a poetic feeling for form.

Naum Gabo's *Female Head* (1917–20), of celluloid and metal (66), is a structure built of cells of space and is like a mechanism that, opening, allows us to look into the secret of a *Mona Lisa* made of synthetics and metal. The fateful meeting of technology and poetry, the numb and the breathing, the mechanical and the growing occurs here.

Antoine Pevsner, too, builds his *Torso* (1924–26) of space cells and hollow forms (67), which he nevertheless groups about a central vertical axis, thus developing an idol-like construction. Picasso's *Weeping Woman* (68) is peripheral to his *Guernica* (1937). She represents an aspect of the experience of horror and shock and in the large composition is echoed by the image of the lamenting mother. Not only does her mouth cry in shrill distortion, the strands of her hair cry beneath the screaming hat. Tears flow out of her black-bordered, fright-filled eyes. This human face,

dissolved by grief, seen in the nonperspective simultaneity of internal and external movement, is not a specific portrait; rather, it is a symbol of maternal despair, a mythological cryptograph of weeping, expressed in a universal language.

While Picasso synthesizes the spirit and styles of many ages, Paul Klee penetrates the prehistory of the visible world and, forebodingly and dreamingly, forms the future. *Fool of the Depths* (1927) leads us into the realm of origins, children's drawings, and the prelogical, and reports beyond all the norms of reason the insane mirages of existence (69). Here, too, is the red-pearl tear, where laughter and weeping join.

The Catalonian Julio Gonzalez is the father of the "Iron Age" in sculpture. His cubic mask-heads, with squares set into one another and trimmed with bolts and curved clips, have a demonic power of expression (70). They are derived from man, but they are found beyond his existence.

The helmetlike, curved, pierced head by Jacques Lipchitz (72) leaves the world of visible occurrences. This domelike hollowed skull with its vistas, created in 1932, can be considered the forerunner of Henry Moore's helmet heads.

In Moore's stone form, *Abstraction* (73), the original starting point of the human head and face may only be guessed at. Alexej von Jawlensky had prepared such a dissolution in 1926. In his picture *Red Light* (71) the natural form has been transformed into an abstract conception. Only the basic organic idea remains, retained in a few geometrical signs. It is an abstract icon of the human face.

Alexander Archipenko, who, in 1912, continuing the experiments of the Cubists, created images made of crossing and contrasting concave and convex forms, had a far-reaching effect on the transformation of the human image with his *sculpto-peinture* and his sculptures. His *Médrano* figures (78), created in 1914, those mechanical dolls and homunculi, are preparations for the machine people of Fernand Léger, the mannequins of De Chirico (79), and the glass personages in the triadic ballet by Oskar Schlemmer.

In the twenties, Archipenko tried to rescue the classical notion of beauty in constructive, simplified, richly curved forms. A female torso (1920–23) (74) was possibly inspired by the torso of the *Aphrodite of Cnidos* or perhaps by the *Aphrodite of Cyrene*, thus by classical antiquity, which had already freed itself from its bonds with the mythical conception of fate. The harmonious, decorative elegance and the precious materials disguise, despite all Archipenko's mastery, the processes and powers that make up the spirit and vision of modern art.

Toni Stadler's sculptures, too, live in the memory of the antique world of forms, even though his restrained archaic simplicity guards itself against classic completeness. "Once the harmony between work and symbolic meaning has been attained, Greece and Italy could only understand art as providing an all-inclusive fiction." (André Malraux)

The sculptures of Ewald Mataré are also rooted in early forms. Man and animal, related to the abstract forms of Scythian art, equally become idol-like symbols of life.

Marino Marini, who, in a secretive, archaic simplification, raises the image of man to a picture of existence, has also, in his series of conjurers, dancers, and acrobats (75), jolted bodily representation into a new light. In the preclassical era of early Greece, in Etruscan art, and Chinese wood carvings he found inspiration that he developed into a mythical modern natural corporeality.

Unassisted, original physical loveliness finds its successor in the sad, sensual naturalness of the *Girls* that Reginald Butler creates (85). Somewhat like Degas, he represents these girls as latent, grotesque, graceful movement, tormenting and unresolved in their fleshly constancy.

Picasso has covered the stations of his creative transformations with convincing sculpture. He has tried every material; every experiment has seemed attractive to him, and he has changed banal basic conceptions and made unusual forms of them. At the end of the forties he created two symbol-like, compassionate sculptures—*Shepherd with Lamb,* a symbol of preservation and protection in a world of war massacre and destruction, and *Pregnant Woman,* the theme of the loving, pregnant receptacle, anti-illusionistic, brutal, and at the same time a fateful sign of continuity and further life.

The contrapuntal, lively mass of Henrí Laurens becomes a physical, rhythmical womanliness (76) Henry Moore's heavy, secretive, and prophetic female forms, naked and at the same time veiled with animated drapery, remind one of the myths of Greece. And they take one further still into the sphere of origins, of the archetype of motherhood.

Angeli Radovani's *Bather* (77) belongs to a cycle of elementary female forms originating in the dual climate of Mediterranean transfiguration and primitive African growth. The broad-hipped, short-legged women, prisoners of their flesh, are incarnations of fruitfulness and ripeness; they are descended from an oversensitized and intellectual sensibility.

Archipenko's *Médrano* figures (78) have been discussed above. A composition dating from 1915, it is formed of tin, glass, wood, and linen, and is an example of the Russian synthesis of sculpture and painting which derived from the experiments of the Suprematists and Constructivists. Archipenko had previously busied himself with creating figures in space out of a variety of materials.

It was Umberto Boccioni's intention in the spirit of Futurism to add movement to the constructed figure. The works in glass of Vladimir Tatlin and the reliefs of Naum Gabo, in the beginning still modeled on objects, were modifications on the road to moving sculpture. Perhaps the *Médrano* figures, those moonstruck Pierrot mechanisms, were influenced by the scenarios of Russian ballet poetically realized by Mikhail Larionov and his wife, Natalia Gontharova. Picasso's figures for the ballet *Parade* (1917) were also mechanisms awakened into life. The Cubistic dancers in the Schlemmer's triadic ballet are perhaps close relatives.

Giorgio de Chirico's *Troubadour* (1917) carried the magical melancholy of the alienation and estrangement of man in a technological world and contrasts exaltation in the beauty of the machine with the archaic, stone landscape of perspective rigidity (79). Placed in classical space, equipped with eternal, pathetic gestures, the troubadour is a rare demonic combination of jointed doll and spectral form; a singer of anxiety, of riddles, of the uncomprehended and sinister world. Finely tuned sensibility and the simplicity of impenetrability connect the vision of the *pittura metafisica* with the sphere of the poet Franz Kafka.

Fernand Léger's human forms (92) belong to the world of technology. Cézanne, Henri Rousseau, and Cubism were forerunners of his development. For Léger, machines are not demonic nor men robots. The painted figures, put together of metallic forms and Cubistic elements, are infinitely simplified, emblematically formulated bearers of an affirmation of technology and the working world. His figures belong to the genre of planning and acting men who are related to the apparatus which guides them. They contrast with De Chirico's mysterious, estranged chimeras.

Léger's thing-objects are not enigmatic and not threatening. They are governed by men and included artistically in the unsentimental counterpoint of a new realism:

"Marvelous, masculine, logical age! Each value is in place; there is a hierarchy of values and order; rays shine through the elements, and the microscope penetrates even deeper. Some men called artists, a few very rare ones, strive to present in their works the countervalue to this clear, pure, undemanding life." (Léger)

Fritz Wotruba's figures have something in them akin to natural geology (81). In comparison, Gilgamesh himself, his battles and invasion of the underworld, appear recent. Wotruba leads us further into primordial existence before the fruit of knowledge laid upon man the responsibility for existence. His figures are primary forms, their anatomical functions laid bare in tubelike limbs that have not yet found their stride. The round head is not yet illuminated by the windows of the eyes and the smile of the mouth (17). It is not petrified life but rather a life that has not yet been born out of the hardness of the material, out of the stone blocks of timelessness.

Rudolf Hoflehner (82) creates strongly expressive humanistic abstract forms in his simple, vertical metal blocks. Through their emotional intensity and technical uniqueness these figures carry their own note into the metal sculpture of our time. With the help of the welding torch, four-sided rounded blocks are put together into weighty figures that evoke cool, sparkling, archaically distant creativity preserved in time and space.

The psychologist Erich Neumann speaks of the processes of transformation and dissolution in literature and music as expressions of the decline of the ancient world order and aesthetic values: "In conformity with the universal occurrence, ugliness, dissonance, and evil penetrate art."

Germaine Richier's sculpture (84) is just such an avowal of ugliness. She is governed by a deeply poetic, tragic desire for "unmasking." The figures of her fantasy are stranded survivors. They bear in themselves the nightmare of fear, torment, death. The taloned man, the devil—chimerical, rotten, crumbling, decomposing—tightens the threads of fate.

Like Germaine Richier, Alberto Giacometti (9) also belongs to the sphere of Surrealism. Like hers, his figures also grow out of brittle, rough bronze. But the rigid elevation of his dematerialized human figures in their towering linearity, lost in the infinity of space, are freed from evil. Perhaps Etruscan burial statuary worked on Giacometti's human sculpture, possibly also the cephalomorphic human sculpture of the Mangbetu tribe in the Congo. Or are these phantom figures, astral bodies locked behind the *huis clos* of Existential nightmares, the messengers of another, unknown world?

While Wotruba creates his figures exclusively of stone, Kenneth Armitage's figures live in the metal prison of solidified bronze. His *Seated Woman with Square Head* (1955–57) is the kind of grotesque mixture of forms that the sculptor forms as a protest against the absurdity and finite limitations of existence (88). These are all phantoms, images of helplessness, yet they are effective by virtue of their expression and their deep meaning:

"Chadwick and Armitage create their images with the necessary creative passion; but they are indifferent to the irrationality of the world they create. It is not for the artist to make sense of the world's absurdity, but to be the authentic witness to its diversity. Art is not an instrument of understanding, but of consciousness. It is the presentation of the concrete, the sensuous, of the carnal. Armitage's later works are dramas of the flesh, conflicts of bone and flesh, of the skeletal and the visceral; and they signify nothing more than the absurdity of the body that the human spirit is condemned to occupy." (Herbert Read)

Lynn Chadwick's *Stranger* (1955) is perhaps a delegate from Albert Camus, born of his spirit and a late, dynamic Cubism. It is only a small step from Camus to *Figure of a Stranger III,* but over the swaying figure, instead of the beaked mask of the bird, a rectangular head appears. Chadwick himself was a flier in the war and knew the cruel glory and terror of the sky. The light plays with the triangular, pointed elements of the forged-iron structures. A bat-pilot, a fluttering being striving upward; streaming movement, caught and captured. The flow is made to congeal (89).

Eduardo Paolozzi's figures (90) are messengers of an unmastered existence that has grown sinister. *Icarus,* with its demonic, ironic gestures, already carries the fall within itself. *Black Devil* and *The Holy Man* are built of equal parts of decay and destruction. The *Greek Heroes* and *Robots,* fraternally bound with one another, are put together from machine parts that look as though they had been diseased in the flesh, used, and discarded.

Likewise, César (Baldaccini) uses old pieces of iron and forms abstract, fantastic figures that he calls *Naked* (91) or *Devil*. The picture in his imagination has dissolved and permeated the rhythmically formed hardness of the material.

Reginald Butler sculpted the peril facing mankind with materials of wire and iron (186). Inspired by Gonzalez' and Picasso's metal sculptures, Butler, who was an ironworker during the war, forms figures that seem to derive from Kafka's *The Metamorphosis*. His *Girl and Boy* (85) live an insect life. They stretch their limbs like flies' legs, and their bodies are related to the shells of grasshoppers. Butler's work is characteristic of a group of young English sculptors whose works, Sir Herbert Read says, are an iconography of despair and challenge: "images of flight, of ragged claws, 'scuttling across the floors of silent seas,' of excoriated flesh, frustrated sex, the geometry of fear."

Francis Bacon's tormented phantoms attempt to overcome the rigidity of death (86). This is the reason for the obliterated agitation of his contours. It is an attempt to follow the agitation of films, to evoke the "misprints" of outline in newspapers, the penetrating, laconic nature of the news itself. What he reports comes from the hidden depths of fallen, castoff man.

Dubuffet's human forms (87) emerge from formlessness; they come from the confines of the anti-aesthetic. This painter's Art Brut rises in protest against the established rituals of art, against the conventions of taste, against moral laws. The human being is only a scrawled, almost random sign on the edge of ruined walls, a shadow form hardly recognizable beneath the textured structure of the plaster.

Leonard Baskin's sculpture *Standing Laureate* is part of the genealogy of despair. The deformed wooden figure of alienation and the capitulation of the spirit before power and the body before age should be given the seat of honor in the academies of recognition.

Willem de Kooning's stormy, malevolent variations of female forms, created out of rage and pain, and Karel Appel's impulsive, expressive demons masquerading as men, belong to the realm of the amorphous figures. Should these series, determined by time and space, be connected with the despairing gesture of the man created by Ossip Zadkine, crying out in the destroyed city? Or with Karl Hartung's *Large Figure,* which changes itself into an empty throne? Or with Drago Tršar's dream of the collective formula of mass-established man (83)? Or with Willi Baumeister's picture *Figure with Yellow Circle* (93), in which the symbol of man becomes anonymous and returns to the material of origin, into the wall built of earth that only reminds one, as a geometric transcription and posthumous formula, that God created man in his own image?

There is no end to this gallery of the metamorphoses of human representation. The complexity of modern life, the vulnerability of modern men work directly and more abruptly than in earlier times. Are we witnessing a disintegration and annihilation of the human figure, of the equation with soulless mechanisms, machines, and automatons? Is this the reflection of a dehumanization in the age of atomic energy and cybernetics?

Some philosophers of cybernetics already see the rise of an era of thinking machines. Man will be replaced by electronic brains. L. Coufignal, director of the Blaise Pascal Institute in Paris, asserts that thinking machines are more powerful than human beings in that they are capable of constructing theories which the human imagination has not as yet constructed or cannot as yet even grasp.

Without electronic computers the orbits of artificial satellites and of the spaceships that escape the earth's gravity could not be calculated. But making absolutes of the machines takes us out of the realm of physical thought into a region of supermaterialistic metaphysics. This occurs not only because even the most perfect machines testify to the planning of the human brain but also because the material of human thought is contained even in the accomplishments that the human brain alone could not complete. For the origin of all the programed, directed machines remains the creative, perceptive substance of human thought. The deformation of the human image in modern art, its camouflage by the machine, Cubist dissection, Surrealist exposure of the unconscious, the transformation in symbolic forms, and the final dissolution of material forms—all are examples of a fundamental and probably creative crisis in the representation of man. It remains an open question whether forsaking the classical human image in art and converting it into abstraction occurs because the mythical, elemental meaning of its existence has been lost, and whether the conception of a new, broader, and more secure image of man will coincide with the building of a more human world.

IV

DREAM IMAGE AND THE LANDSCAPE OF THE UNCONSCIOUS

The Dark Background of Existence

I believe in the future resolution of the apparent contradiction between dream and reality in a sort of absolute Surrealist truth. . . .

André Breton

The connection between psychological perception and artistic procedure can be established more strongly in the program of Surrealism than in any other endeavors in modern art. This is so because Surrealism corresponds more to a literary-intellectual than to an aesthetic attitude toward life.

The great importance with which Sigmund Freud invested the subconscious mind, the key role of dream and sexual drive in the understanding of human behavior, appealed to the needs of every poet and artist who claimed the landscape of the subconscious mind as his own domain. In his manifesto on Surrealism, André Breton wrote:

". . . finally, supported by the discoveries of Freud, a current has been marked off; impelled by this the student of man will be able to continue his studies, in which he will no longer have to be bound to mere reality. With full justification Freud turned critically to dream. It is really incomprehensible that very little attention had been paid to this extended area of psychic activity, since from the birth of man to his death the sum total of his dream moments is not less than those of his waking consciousness."

The discovery of the subterranean subconscious and unconscious impulses as parts of psychic reality strengthened the latent endeavors of the artist to go beyond the traditional boundaries of rationality and logically discoverable reality and to draft a new "surreal" truth.

Surrealism developed as a countermovement against technology and the restless activity of the big city. Like Dadaism, to which it is related and whose attitudes of protest it adopts, it grew out of an "anti-artistic" theory that it systematized and developed. In order to express the pure and authentic voice of the unconscious mind, Surrealism makes use of automatic "*procédés.*"

Automatic writing and painting, which developed as an antithesis to the reproduction of external, rational, and conscious reality, made possible a broadening of the field of vision by representing subconsciousness and dream. Like traditional art, which only fragmentarily represents the visible image of existence, Surrealism, through automatic evocation and painfully accurate photographic faithfulness, reproduces the image of the subconscious mind, which for its part represents only a section of totality —its internal reflection.

The psychology of disclosure is one of the fundamental phenomena of the age. It is the expression of a social, scientific, and psychic crisis. Similar to Romanticism, it arises in the alienation of civilized men from their surroundings and to a certain extent indicates a denial of traditional values.

Of great importance is Freud's dynamic conception of the individual constantly driven by the sense of his ego's estrangement from the universe and circling about his own physical and psychic existence. The particular relevance of psychology to the understanding of art lies not in the biological foundation of artistic creation, but in its inclusion in the universal process of spiritual mechanisms in a system of interrelationships, of mutual dependencies and metamorphoses.

The psychoanalytic interpretation of human existence as a dialectical battle of drives and inhibitions, impulses and restraints, prohibitions and compensations, the division of the spiritual cosmos into conscious and subconscious zones, had a deep influence on scientific research and on art. Freud's scientific diagnoses and his interpretations of dream and reality met a need of modern art, which had lost faith in the traditional definition of reality and was prepared to abolish the boundaries between the external and internal worlds, waking and dream. The logical, naturalistic construction of the world had become questionable. Psychoanalysis helped create a new method of penetrating formerly sealed regions of the subconscious mind. The ambiguity, undecidedness, and superrealism in the artistic method of Surrealism possibly corresponds to the opposing impulses in neurotic tension and dream images as shown in psy-

choanalysis. Reactions of disguise and revelation, lack of clarity and super-sharp focus, and above all the dynamics of the *procédés* of Surrealist poetry and art found their analogues and confirmation in Freud's perceptions.

Although it is only since Freud that a complex method of thought has been adopted in psychology, it has advanced in depth and subtlety the knowledge of man that had been achieved in the psychological novel and has proceeded beyond to hardly dreamed-of levels of spiritual existence. But research in the area of social psychology and the sphere of man's collective fate is still fragmentary and insufficient:

"The question of the fate of mankind appears to me to be a question of whether and to what degree it will be possible in their cultural development to master the disturbances in community life arising from human drives of aggression and self-destruction." (Freud)

According to Freud the superego is nourished by the broad expanse of the collective past:

"With the help of the superego, in a manner still unclear to us, the ego creates out of the accumulated experiences of the past retained in the id." Freud recognized myth as a mass dream of earlier ages. "The dim recognition of psychic factors and relationships is reflected in the construction of a superrational reality which is to be retransformed by science into the psychology of the unconscious. One could venture to unravel the myths of paradise and the fall, of God, of good and evil, of immortality and similar things in such a way, transforming metaphysics into metapsychology."

According to Freud's skeptical, scientific method, the subconscious is rooted in individually acquired repressions, and the underlying, superindividual past is of only secondary significance for the modern individual. For Jung, in contrast, the few thousand years of man's conscious history are relatively unimportant. More decisive forces rest beneath the surface covering of experience in the resonating ground of deep, unconscious, primordial time. Against the destruction of instinct and the poverty of symbols that were the results of intellectualization and civilizational constraints, Jung set the primordial home of the unconscious, the world of myth. His psychosynthesis broadens perception in that it includes the collective unconscious—that is, myth—in what has become conscious. But he narrows this again by making absolutes of the instinctual powers, by recoupling them with magical forces and archaic systems of thought. Drawn into modern consciousness and seen with reference to the present, these become synthetic elements of the spirit and of art. Isolated and overvalued, they still signify an aversion to intellect, an abrogation of civilization, and collective regression.

The creative sensitivities of the artist are always viewed in psychoanalysis as sublimated libido. There is perhaps no stronger example than the consolation and vicarious contentment achieved by the great writer Marcel Proust when he called forth life from his sickbed.

The Unknown and Hidden

If the strangest things come together in one place, at one time, in a strange similarity, wonderful unities arise and singular connections—and one thing reminds us of all, becomes the sign of many.

Novalis

Romanticism had begun to see beauty and ugliness no longer as contrasting values but as opposing attractions. Ugliness became characteristic—that is, interesting. It met the artistic needs of the times.

In Baudelaire, who unified the elements of Romanticism with Symbolism, and even more in Rimbaud, ugliness, in contrasting operation, becomes beauty, the bearer of intensity and a new artistic expression. In the process of destruction and metamorphosis a new landscape of imperceptible word and form images is created out of a deformed reality and simultaneously substitutes for the unknown and the unseen. These thought metaphors remains always in the region of physical experience, but by combinations of fragments, by displacement of associations, they are raised to the level of the superreal. The act of a dominant imagination creates new images out of wornout components.

Dostoevski's *The Devils* and *The Brothers Karamazov* already carried in themselves the dissonant, agonized vision of hallucinatory situations. The subterranean depths of the human soul were illuminated here before Freud.

"The only way to avoid the abyss is to contemplate it, measure it, sound it, and descend into it," writes Cesare Pavese in his *The Trade of Life.*

Perhaps Goya's *Caprichos* had also sighted this subterranean, hidden, monstrous, and precipitous world: "The sleep of reason creates monsters." The horrifying elements of existence, their hallucinatory air, appear as demonic apparitions of reality. For the first time an artist consciously dared, without symbolic religious camouflage, to touch the abysses of man's soul; Goya showed us the sphere of the illogical, of subterranean dreams. He delineated a world possessed by hell, of horrifying and demonic existence. Hell is of this world, established in the consciousness of humanity. Therein lies its modernity.

Hieronymus Bosch and Pieter Bruegel painted the abysmal vision of hell with magical penetration. The hell that Goya paints grows out of despair with reality. The chain of associations of dehumanization and alienation from nature extends from Goya to Picasso and Salvador Dali. It is an apocalyptic, Spanish sequence, the background of which, perhaps, is haunted by the flaming faces of El Greco. The chimeras of Picasso arising from the Surrealistic underworld are decorated with evocative, folkloristic signs, which also enliven the Cubistic intellectualism of Garcia Lorca.

James Ensor anticipated the psychosis of modern civilization in his painting. He portrays universal experience as psychic danger, as the ego's fear of drowning in the mass, of losing its own face in the dress of convention and lies (94). Such is the autistic world of the isolated and estranged, raised to the level of pathological behavior and transposed into creativity. A deep panic grips the artist, an agoraphobia in the face of the swarm of veiled, gesturing, tittering demons of the present. His pictorial space is filled with the phantoms of a hallucinated, alienated big city. The boundaries between nightmare and reality are obliterated; the expressive, overrefined experience of ambiguity, concealment, and indefinability is raised to brilliant expression.

Before the turn of the twentieth century, Henri Rousseau, even though working unconsciously and naïvely, created magical, realistic, primitive forms, which detached and estranged men and objects from their trusted surroundings so that they obtained a glassy, sculptured hardness, a festive, secret, grotesque-poetic expressive force. Out of simple, profane objects, crippled and withered, out of petrified images of man looking as though they had been photographed with a slow-motion camera, Rousseau built a magical world in which the contact between man and object, lost in civilization, is restored.

About twenty years before Picasso's "Negro period" began, Rousseau demonstrated the richness and power of the original pictorial view of the primitives. The continent that Rousseau, the Columbus of naïve painting, had discovered, this paradise of primeval growth, of fabled beings and mysterious flora, arising from his poetic, simple soul, was simultaneously the anticipation of and overture to Surrealism. Rousseau's *Sleeping Gypsy* (1897) dreams under an ice-green sky in the loneliness of the desert and the boundlessness of existence (95). The great silence of sleep, the dream-deep experience of the safety of nature, takes place while fear hovers over man. Like an island the dark-faced woman lies in the interior monologue of her existence between the desert of the sky and the earth. A pitcher and a mandolin stand next to the sleeper. From now on they will inhabit the Surrealists' dreams and the Cubists' space.

Modern art has secularized death and hell. The pilgrimage to the edge of night led to Dadaism and Surrealism, to the magic of the primitives of the twentieth century, and to metaphysical painting.

Surrealism began at the borderline where Dadaism left off. The absolute *no* of Dadaism became insufficient. The sensitivity of the Surrealists revealed to the realm of the subconscious a new existence, an existence of myth and fantasy, hunting grounds of dream reality, of anxiety and the supernatural. Even if Surrealism did not regard itself as an aesthetic manifestation, its aspects still became the common property of modern art. In fact, time consciousness, where it turned against the programmatic absoluteness of Surrealism, nevertheless adopted and assimilated parts of its world view.

Giorgio de Chirico (96) presents new views and arouses secret relationships between objects and their surroundings. He has carried the concepts of metaphysics into art. His world has something strange and weird about it. In the rarefied air of his streets and squares appear figures of a mixed nature, both ancient statue and tailor's dummy, organic and mechanical, dream image and instruments of daily living. The heterogeneity of these juxtaposed objects and the dissimultaneity of modern architectural forms and objects burst historical time sequence. Over the glassy coldness of his ideal architecture lies the irregular rigidity of expectation; the drama of magical space asserts itself. Monuments put together out of the useless objects of a junk room stand in rigid expectation as signs of lifelessness and complete emptiness. These metaphysical still lifes and interiors suggest a feeling of disparity and nonlogicality: "In order for a work of art to be really immortal it must step completely out of the boundaries of humanity." (De Chirico, 1914)

Marc Chagall's work (97) signifies the meeting of medieval Eastern legends with the School of Paris. Baal Shem (the conceptualization of Jewish mysticism) is led through the twentieth century of Appollinaire on a colorful magic carpet of Russian folklore and the immediacy of Kafka. Chagall's fantasies are lyrical and soft; that is why they sometimes go unnoticed by the searchers for fantasy. They are as soft as the sleep of the ghetto inhabitants, as the arrival of the dybbuk, as the phantoms of the possessed who keep their mouths shut when they hear the step of the black centurions. These works convey the exorcism of Hasidic legends, the thousand-year-old melancholy of despair, and the sly hope of these oft-chosen people, the childlike quality of the very ancient. Chagall in Paris is Cubistic structure, Orphic arrangement of color. But he never gives up the naïve handwriting, the direct contact with God, the familiarity with the stars and eternity.

The associative connections of memory break through the barrier of logic. Before official Surrealism, Chagall opened the door to the subconscious world of dreams and imagination. Heaven and earth, above and below, are mingled; everything impossible becomes real, and everything real fantastic. As a matter of course people propel themselves through the air and play on the cello of their own bodies. Houses become great green eyes that look into the village of the future; red flames of destruction plunge down into the face of the crucified, while the clocks of the past are suspended above the horizon. The embryo becomes visible in the belly. The lovers' bouquet grows up over the rooftops of the village. For this is rapturous communion, bitter, childlike dream; these are ecstatic songs in the face of fear and the knowledge of millenniums.

Modern poetry is inspired by the impulses of dark, primordial visions. Dreams of the collective unconscious are its materials. Like automatic texts they express themselves in signs freed from the censure of reason.

Many different methods are developed in painting in order to set psychic automatism in motion. In collages made of coincidental and real waste products, in frottages that fix the grain of wood or the structure of material, imaginary images that exist in the unconscious are called up through thought associations.

Max Ernst (98) worked at such structural forms in the laboratory of the unconscious mind. The world of minerals and coral, of petrified materials, of proliferating crystals and vegetable deposits offers materials out of which he peoples an imaginary world with self-produced creatures. With an almost compulsive perseverance he attempts to escape the final boundaries of logic and substance. His pictorial images strive to comprehend taboo regions of existence. Ice-hardened dreams, filtered feelings, cosmic gestures—all these are brewed together with German mysticism, French irony, and cosmopolitan nihilism. The mosaic elements of photography—unreality, madness, dream, and the subconscious—whirl and tear in virtuoso, demonic play on the nerve strings of time. Ernst's Surrealistic conception contradicts the superstition of Western culture concerning conscious creativity in art.

"It was one of the first revolutionary acts of Surrealism to have attacked this myth objectively and most sharply and to have quite destroyed it, insisting most forcefully on the purely passive role of the 'author' in the mechanism of poetic inspiration and unmasking all 'active' rational moral or aesthetic control as inimical to inspiration. . . . The coincidental encounter of a sewing machine and an umbrella on a dissecting table (Lautréamont) is today a familiar, almost classic example of the phenomenon discovered by the Surrealists—that the proximity of two or more apparently unrelated objects on a plane unrelated to them provokes the strongest poetic inspiration. It is shown in the fact that the more freely the elements meet the more surely a fully or partially new interpretation of things must occur by virtue of the vaulting sparks of poetry." (Max Ernst)

The smooth, painstaking technique of Salvador Dali (99) attempts in importunate, penetrating plasticity to awaken the illusion that phantom objects really exist. His goal is to intensify the receptivity of man's spiritual powers to the limits of toleration. Neuroses, states of intoxication, hallucinations, delirium, and anxiety dreams are the engines of his fantasy. He calls his method "*activité paranoïque-critique.*" The photographically drawn hallucinations create a virtuoso scenario for veristic Surrealism. Dali's compositions are almost exclusively bravura pieces of technical accuracy but at the same time lead back to a perverted naturalism. "When the Surrealist carefully copies dream, insofar as he believes in his autonomous existence, in his creative powers, and neglects to discover them anew, he is no more and no less transcendent than the copy of any other reality." So writes Jean Bazaine, thus indicating that the existence of Surrealism is based on an old, rooted naturalism.

Joan Miró is the painter of the yet unborn, of childlike irrationality (101). He sets in motion a sort of ballet of radiolaria, amoebae, and larvae, microscopic organisms and forms that move on floating lines and spots, as though drawn by children. It is a comical, serene, wonderful, and simple poetic world of forms, often, however, penetrated by signs of fear, of danger, and of strange metaphors of dissonance, evil, shamelessness, and cruelty. His language is related to that of Paul Klee but projected into monumentality. Amusing, secretive, rebellious ghosts stand enlarged beside microscopic fantasies like the demons and gods of Tassili.

Yves Tanguy paints the hallucinatory world of Surrealism (100). His pictures are views of "extensive expeditions," as André Breton calls them, in enigmatic spaces of timelessness and eternity. He furnishes this secret-laden panorama of an unknown planet with the fantasy objects of dream—sculptural, yet giving the illusion of reality. Tanguy began to paint under the inspiration of a picture by De Chirico But he did not, like De Chirico, paint the estranged objects of this world. In the brilliant, slanting light stand the cartilaginous images of a contrived, absurd inventor, illusionistic, forcibly formulated—a dream scene that for its part inspired Dali and that he filled with grotesque, obscene figures.

The German veristic painters' unconditional insistence on foreground was insufficient for Max Beckmann's uncanny, ghostly vision, the crippling hallucination of threat, catastrophe, and death. Figures of depression and fear move in steep Gothic density; swords, masks, fish, knives, nets, and martyrs' stakes are the mythical supports of this night scenario. Anonymous towns, people from barracks, numbers in police registers, lives fettered in the restraint of convention, strangled in prejudices: dreams that begin with tears and end with the weeping of death (Klopstock, *Messias*). They are messengers from the chthonian world of our times. Like Joyce and O'Neill, Beckmann is concerned with the present myth. In his extensive oeuvre the triptychs are the principal items of his spiritual expression. The first, *Departure* was created in 1932–33. It is a symbolic representation and interpretation of his own dissolution. In Beckmann's unique, secretive, allegorical way, ferocity, torture, madness are represented on the side panels in gagged people, with their hands hacked off, a woman bound to the body of a slaughtered man, and the strangely clad drummer —summoner to protest or harbinger of terror? The bright central portion shows the sovereign, perhaps a great master of art, as he is led by the muffled ferryman into the land of the wide blue horizon.

The triptych *Experiment* (1937) shows the artist fettered to his easel. And the balancing act in the picture of acrobats made in the same year points toward the painter's own threatened emigrant existence. *Carnival* indicates a deeper masquerade— hiding and going underground not in fun but in the face of a growing danger. Of course Beckmann is not looking for direct actuality in mythical poetry. The classic simile is in no way intended as an Aesopian mask against censorship. Subterranean brutality continues to exist in man's soul and history.

Beckmann's expressive vitality and Surrealistic, brutally sensitive hearing portray the threat of man, suspiciously and prophetically. A very much transposed painting of ideas, related to the weird vision of Matthias Grünewald and the compassionate transparency of Georges Rouault, his works reveal the signs and myths of our century.

In the dream mirrors of the painter Mac Zimmerman the first childish steps of mankind are unified with atomic speeds. Radio antennas are attached to Stone Age log canoes; mammoth men are painted with tiny heads containing barely enough room to be the antechambers of the subconscious. They are veristic creatures in the expanse of unreality.

Gabrijel Stupica's fable of the fateful legend of human existence swings beyond reason and intellect (102). Facing the actuality of the world full of despair,

the separating wall between reality and appearance becomes uncertain for him. The fragmentary and dissonant, the impenetrably magical, become the expression of his inner direction. The liquid silver light of color evaporates and condenses into a dark covering for a phantomlike, suffering humanity. Women's faces framed with kerchiefs; pointed sharp, masklike men's faces; children's forms with indefinable toy ghosts—these arise from a solitary world in the nightmarish mother-of-pearl light that blinks out of the magical darkness. The rising isolation carries him deeper into an ascetic underworld of relationships that are hardly imaginable visually and hardly expressible. It is a shadow zone between the abstract and nonabstract. The pictures are collages that in reality are not collages but rather too clearly drawn banalities, irradiated by the aura of interior faces. Surreal abstraction here is final renunciation and secret exultation at an end game.

Miljenko Stančić affirms his human-extrahuman figures out of a dark dream background (103). With the coloristic intensity of the Delft master Vermeer he gives his fantastic beings a magical quality of reality. His art feels its way across the abyss and indicates an ominous and threatening landscape both before and after creation. In an atmosphere of mystical lasciviousness, live wax figures with wide-open, shadowy eyes wander through the imaginary landscape.

Paul Delvaux peopled his dream quarters of pillared cities with these naked, moonstruck odalisques (105). Despite their erotic gestures they are frigid, engaged to the skeleton that often steps out from behind the heavy, plush draperies and the secret arras doors of the fantasy architecture. It is a macabre world of nightmare, of repressed drives, of middle-class boredom, hopeless solitude, and hypnotic sleep, from which there is no awakening.

The world created by René Magritte is a labyrinth of the absurd (104). His paintings are metaphors of unreality, and every interpretation is a game with subterranean and inexplicable impulses. The over-accurate fixing of details, the pedantic optics of the material, mislead the viewer into drawing boundaries between appearances and reality. But the tightly closed door is only an apparent one, the red shoes in front of the precisely measured wooden partition are the hollowed-out, isolated feet of the absent man. The female body, stiffened into a torso, stands in empty space as though there were no longer any above or below, and as though it floated like the Montgolfière in the emptiness of the firmament. Emptiness dominates.

Leonor Fini left alchemistic landscape painting and formed the manneristic flowers of her comfort-less poetry. Dorothea Tanning's heavy, strengthless forms, too, live in the realm of fears and persecutions. The invocation of totemic demons by Matta Echaur-ren (107), and the symbolic, archaic powers in the pictures of Wifredo Lam (108), indicate the en-counter of the mature intellectuality of Paris with the pre-Columbian pantheon. Victor Brauner's hiero-glyphic pictorial signs (106) are a late mixture of Mayan culture and psychoanalysis. Wolfgang Paalen's symbioses of plants and humanoid creatures, which he calls *The Strange Ones,* are like shadowy travelers from another star (109).

In establishing a world beyond reality, the Surrealists enlarged hitherto consciously compre-hended reality. In penetrating the sphere of dream and the subconscious, they illuminated new realms of existence.

Paul Klee (112) stands beyond the interpretation of reality. He must himself discover and create the world that calls him: "I am not even comprehensible on this side. For I live just as much among the dead as among the unborn. Somewhat closer to the heart of creation than is usual—and still by far not close enough" (Klee). Using his intellect and knowledge, the viewer associates the spiritual miniatures of this artist with the naïveté of drawing or the original expression of early art. Time and space are simul-taneity and coexistence for him. He begins before logic and outside any causality. In the soft and pene-trating poetry of his art he comprehends and sur-mounts all schools and *procédés* of the age.

The great magician of the period is Picasso (111); he is the master and at the same time the creation of the phantoms he has created, like humanity in the face of cybernetic ghosts that attempt to emancipate themselves and rise up against their discoverers. He is the conjurer of art, not only because his universe is peopled with hybrids of horror and melancholy, of ghostlike form and demonic color, of hallucination and poetry, but above all because he forces us to see the world with his eyes.

Pablo Picasso dissected the human form into geometric elements, transformed them according to his will, and put them back together again. But not only man—everything he touches with his demonic fingers is changed and filled with unique tensions. With horrified and enchanted eyes we look at crea-tures as though we had never seen them before. His subjct is the drama of mankind. From the depths of unconsciousness and the strength of consciousness he forms amorphous, tragic, fantastic and secret-laden humanity, disguised in a thousand ways and eternally naked.

The contribution of Surrealism to modern times is more important the more it releases itself from dogma and sectarianism in order to reveal new aspects and wonders of existence.

Jean Dubuffet (110) takes as much from Surreal-ist art as he does from Abstract in order to create his pictures of rebellion against "art" and particularly against "taste." His human forms are realistic and imaginative, simultaneously naïve and very knowing, and perhaps they represent landscapes or mountain ranges. The flesh of monstrous female nudes also implies the earth's crust, a shell landscape, wooded valley's, and mountains. His animal world, his evening twilight, his botanical studies, his paths that lead into unknown places are like glasses with false bottoms and transform dried-up grass and old bits of wall into cosmic adventures in painting. It is not cynicism and mockery that create his attitude, but rather the desire to experience even ugliness without disguise, completely stripped, as part of the banquet of beauty. Each further step portends the transition from fantastic object to objectless fantasy. This direction brings the expected release from the Surrealist reliance on the intellect's literary background. At the same time, however, it brings about a definite dissociation from the optically comprehensible world of man's existence.

INDIVIDUALISM AND COLLECTIVISM

Creativity and the Masses

. . . Private ownership not only estranges the individuality of the human being, but also of things. . . .

Karl Marx, Holy Family

The great contemporary emancipation movements of peoples and races led to the inclusion in modern consciousness of millions formerly remaining in ignorance. Four hundred million Hindus, seven hundred million Chinese, Southeast Asia, and black and Islamic Africa are among those beginning to absorb modern Occidental civilization and technology. By means of modern developments, accelerating with avalanche force, these are uniting with the social revolutions among farmers and proletarians, with the social, economic and political revolutions of the age.

It could be that after this mutation period, in which ages and places, religions and social systems, ideologies and art forms penetrate one another, the physiognomy of civilization will have changed and that Toynbee's somewhat prophetically formulated thoughts will have come true: "And as, in the course of generations and centuries, a unified world gradually works its way toward an equilibrium between its diverse component cultures, the Western component will gradually be relegated to the modest place which is all that it can expect to retain in virtue of its intrinsic worth by comparison with those other cultures. . . ."

Even in the twenties Oswald Spengler spoke of the *Decline of the West.* The fiasco of Western civilization was to offer gloomy comfort for Germany's lost war. Such a philosophy of decline attempted to examine the expiration of cultures by organic-biological means and saw therein, as a parallel to the life cycle, a necessary aging and dying. Even if the decline of old cultures is less to be explained in its biological than in its social and historical connections, and no organic law necessitates the death of individual cultures, it does happen at certain periods that individual peoples and groups lose their towering and controlling significance.

Certain cultural philosophies since Le Bon's *Psychology of the Masses* and Ortega y Gasset's *Revolt of the Masses* have continued the message of the threat to individual personality residing in the mass. In the concept of "masses" there is for them apparently a pejorative quality.

Hans Weigert explains in his *Die Kunst am Ende der Neuzeit* ("Art at the End of the Modern Period") that with the rise of the masses to full social power

47

48

a soulless, mechanical age of surrogates begins. "Machine-made products take the place of genuine handicraft, mass production that of original art work, cinematic amusement that of the catharsis of tragedy. Leveling by increasing democratization takes the place of an organic gradation of things and people. . . ."

This criticism of the democratization of culture, which in reality is a criticism of the industrial age, can be contrasted with Karl Jaspers' thoughts as developed in his work *The Origin and Goal of History*:

"We can see the peaks of the past. It is then, as though from the broad foundation of existence, that the slight historical message pushes through to us that high spiritual creativity actually makes history. It is the life and work of individuals who call to one another through the continuity of time as friends and foes. Each individual, however, has his community which belongs to him and from which he hears, to which he is important; he has his circle of friends, his people in the context of language and intellectual transmission—his public.

But today this community is incompatible with the world, which is determined by the masses. Only that will remain which is adopted by the masses."

What is particularly worth pursuing in Jaspers' thought is the recognition that culture and art cannot flourish in the long run without contact with a broad and lively community. The gigantic trend of civilization in our age, just as in earlier revolutionary shifts, can by the action of leveling phenomena weaken the most sensitive cells of subjective art. Seen as a developmental process, however, these regroupings nevertheless bring a strengthening of the need for the experiences of art, a heightening of the desire for the deep, interpretative language of existence that the arts can offer.

In this sphere of social analysis and scientific revolution, art as a subtle reactor and finely vibrating sounding board for all metamorphoses is subject to a basic change. In increasing measure it renounces reproduction of till now visible reality in order, as it thinks, to be the intermediary of spiritual and poetic values. It undertakes to interpret connections between the individual and the soul of the universe, to symbolize the powers of cosmic rays, and, occasionally, to conquer the demands of all matter. Thus this art is served by an extremely subjective formal language comprehensible only to a small circle and inaccessible to the man not versed in art. The cleavage between the modern and the traditional becomes deeper the more eruptively and suddenly radical changes in the scientific and technical world picture are accomplished.

Such a contribution by modern art to the extra-human motifs of nonobjective and abstract forms is regarded from the standpoint of still undifferentiated mass culture as a flight from reality. Ernst Fischer writes: "This reality is so questionable, so unclear, and so estranged from men in the late capitalistic world, that poets, artists, writers increasingly do not consider it possible to master it artistically and resolve in despairing radicalism to deny its reality and recognizability and to abolish both. . . ."

It may be that the decomposition and dissolution of the reality visible up to now in art will result in a gnostic landscape. The bounding of reality, however, with the recognition of classical experience, the designation as "real" of that which can be counted on the ten fingers of ordinary understanding, the denial of every attempt to push forward into the uncontrollable or that which has hitherto been considered uncontrollable—all lead to a reduction of the comprehension of reality to its external, naturalistic aspects which were conquered in the second half of the nineteenth century. Spiral nebulae, crystals, the structural form of internal matter are not metaphysical backgrounds of the objective world but a newly glimpsed part of it. Also the concepts "objectivity" and "abstraction" have in a certain sense become obsolete. The abstract world of pictures is the concrete reflection of a widening picture, the necessary mastery of newly visualized space. Certainly crystalline structures, diagrammatic rhythms that tell of newly discovered force fields, and structural forms are no less concrete than anecdotes in genre style or the photographically accurate picture of a man with a painted tie. The exclusiveness, however, of an art that increasingly observes creatures beyond our scope and the structural processes of matter can lead to a seclusion from the totality of life. This is true not only because a canon of an inclination to academicism is noticeable in abstract-concrete art, but more, perhaps, because the dimensions of reality enclose, besides the newly discovered visibility, the old long-known and experienced one.

Clearly this esoteric language of forms leads to greater alienation and deepens the isolation of the arts. On the other hand, popularity has never been a criterion for the quality of art. Genre painting, scenes of family life, and historical painting were accessible and comprehensible to all in the nineteenth century without ever having reflected the great transformations in the art of that time. In the age of self-developing film, these subjects have been taken over by the camera. Waldemar George writes in an essay, "Paradoxes of Realism": "Socialist realism neither poses formal problems nor solves them. It is picture-painting in photographic style which misconstrues the values of painting and sacrifices form to content." Herbert Read, too, writes in *Art and Society:*

"In effect, then, socialist realism is but one more attempt to impose an intellectual or dogmatic purpose on art. It may be that the actual circumstances of the moment—the revolutionary urgencies to which most intellectuals and artists subscribe—demand a temporary supersession of the primary conditions of a great art: that art, like much else, must be sacrificed to the common good. If this is so, let it be clearly recognized, and do not let us deceive ourselves into imagining that a great art can be created under conditions which both the history of art and the psychology of the artist prove to be impossible." (117, 118)

Despite the certainty that art must evolve out of the laws of its own existence, it would be insufficient to explain the naturalistic academicism of our times solely as a socially determined manifestation. There is clearly a deeper harmony between this official aesthetic and the requirements of the broad mass of the people. The historical inconsistency as a result of which the socialist revolution was successful not in economically and culturally developed countries, but on the contrary in backward countries, which in the meantime have nevertheless managed to catch up in many things, explains better why the artistic horizons of the twentieth century's social reshufflings correspond to the taste of people in the middle of the nineteenth century.

The Conscience of Art in the Industrial Age

We know that the world changes and that man changes the world and the world man. . . .
                                                            Jean Paul Sartre

Will it be a different man? Or a different world? Perhaps only different gods? Or none?
                                                            Bertold Brecht

In an age of alienation from the object and increasing abstraction, the desire to attain a new relationship with an objective world that would at the same time be commonly understandable has led in many areas to attempts to comprehend the new facts in a sort of synthetic realism.

Diego Rivera and his circle connected the highly sophisticated form elements of Cubism with the naïve, archaic current of the Aztec-Toltec past. In order to be close to the masses and to serve the causes of social liberty, their frescoes in Mexico were composed as emblematic, simplified picture writing. These monumentally projected *biblia pauperum,* which achieved a pictorial bridge between the artist and the people by means of the simplicity of modern primitivism, had at the same time an archaic expressive power suitable to the educated aesthetic consciousness.

Rivera's childhood meeting with José Guadalupe Posada, the self-taught etcher and illustrator of the popular *corridas, ejemplas y calaveras,* left a lasting impression. The years of study in Paris followed, the influences of Cézanne, Delaunay, and Picasso. The confrontation with Cubism was joined to the experience of Giotto's frescoes and the compositions of Uccello, which he had become acquainted with in Italy.

The murals in the Palace of Labor in Mexico City and several of the ones in the entrance hall and the stairwell of the agricultural academy in Chapingo remind one of the frescoes of Giotto and Signorelli. The *Lament for a Revolutionary Hero* (113) is closely related in its ascetic, monumental simplicity and limitation to essentials to Giotto's lament over Christ in the Scrovegni Chapel in Padua. The quiet rhythm of the figures, the generous, naïve power of expression, the arrangement of the picture in its architectonic structure give Rivera's murals of this period the compactness and greatness of the classical model.

Despite all the virtuosity of the pictorial construction, the architectonic compactness is later sacrificed to exuberant delight in narration. The walls increasingly become the national picture book of enlightenment, of the proclamation and the critical representation of history and the present. The massing of content bursts the architectonic bounds. As from subterranean sources the grandiose picture writing streams and fascinates the educated and illiterate alike. Superlarge caricatured heads, imperious

giant hands, the symbols of political and ethical rituals accentuate the course of the painted story. An emphatically social, veristic symbolism, a superreal occurrence formulated in thousands of images, dissolves the classical, monumental pictorial plane and transforms it into a multicolored picture sheet not far removed from the popular *calaveras,* the melodramatic, tragic folk-songlike graphics of his Mexican teacher Posada. The entertaining, the macabre, the traditional Spanish-Indian mixture of "Mexicanidad" grows into a powerful, overflowing cantata capable of touching the emotions of the people.

It may be that the rationally conscious element in Rivera's painting often appears all too decorative, that he overestimates the carrying power of objectivity; still, moved by passionate sympathy, his art became the point of departure of a *peinture engagée* and led to the spontaneous renewal of a newly self-conscious Mexican culture.

José Orozco and David Alfaro Siqueiros belong with Rivera to the inner circle of the regenerators of Mexican monumental painting.

With inspired expressive impatience, Orozco forms his heroic, realistic epics against a fantastic background (114). He paints the tragic life of the people, not only the exterior, the noisy, colorful, vivid scenes, but the essence of man and things in the landscape of archaic reminder. If the gods and demons of ancient Mexico live in his art, they live covered over and buried in the depths of his interpretation of heaven, earth, and myth. His art is concerned with the basic social problems of Mexico, but in neither his frescoes nor his oil paintings is the scenic simplification decorative in the sense of the Mexican folk theater. Even this most direct social expression is overshadowed by the silence and demonic intensity of his intuition.

Siqueiros is the sculptor among painters. He builds heavy, compact volumes into large compositions. The classical structure is burst by an excess of temperament and is magically transformed by the intensity of a barbaric strength. The drawing of his frescoes in the Escuela Nacional Preparatoria shows the fast, bold, and pure line of his art. Elements of rhetoric and uneven vehemence may break through the compactness of the forms; still, expressive power and passionate dynamics are messengers of the truth and immediacy of his artistic experience. His book illustrations too, in which generally two or three everyday figures are raised to symbolic expression, show monumental strength. In these small pictures, action and poetry, didactic proclamation and universal humaneness are given expression.

Also among the regenerators of Mexican art are Xavier Guerero, Julio Castellanos, and above all Rufino Tamayo, who brought Surrealism's dreams and subterranean, analytic spiritual interpretation into the intellectual climate of Mexico. After an initial association he left the dictatorial and didactic program of the fresco painters. Tamayo wishes to spy out the secret and invisible greatness of things, the hidden sensuality, the disguised beauty of objects. Deep beneath his Cubistic, lyrical balancing act we feel a relationship with Picasso and the demons of Mexico. Tamayo and the generation that follows him no longer belong in the chapter on the social seekers for a new reality.

Perhaps the monumental style of the Brazilian painter Candido Portinari (115) is more closely connected with the works of Orozco and Rivera than with Tamayo's manic demonology. Portinari's paintings create a synthesis of archaic and modern inspiration. A humane and social sensitivity connects his work with the life of the Brazilian worker and peasant. A stormy, Fauvist line indicates the collective uncertainty of existence and overcomes it by symbolic stylization.

When Rivera went to New York in the thirties to execute the murals at Rockefeller Center, which later were covered because of their social emphasis, he was so stirred by Ben Shahn's Sacco and Vanzetti series that he invited him to join forces with him. In the later, independent frescoes that Shahn executed on commission from the Farm Security Administration in the town of Roosevelt, New Jersey, he painted America as a land of contrasts: Einstein leads the immigrants fleeing from Hitler's Germany past the coffins of the executed anarchists Sacco and Vanzetti in the land of their hope, America.

In contrast with the extremely individualistic and abstract direction of modern American art, Shahn defined his work as an expression of the fate of the masses: "Artists should recognize that there is no moral reason why art ought to go on if it has nothing further to express. Nor is there any moral or aesthetic reason why the public should bend the knee in reverence before the mere fact of art. We might assume instead that art is important only if it essays to be important.

If it adopts the manners and outlook and philosophy of a minor expression, then a minor expression it will be. If it aspires to an aesthetic of double-talk, just that will be its position, nothing more; and life itself will walk around it and let it alone."

In Paris, Shahn met the painters Rouault, Matisse, and Picasso; in New York he met Rivera. His talent assimilated everything that the times and the art of the times had to offer. In Shahn's work, the concept of "realism" can hardly be missed. But Shahn does not mean the external view of things. Realism is experience and discovery, sincerity and emotion. His art has the simplicity and purity of folk song. But behind an almost naïve fable, the inner story is told. Through the radiant power of his sensitivity the superindividual connection becomes tangible. The sharply simplifying drawing makes the motives of the action comprehensible. Accuser and accused become transparent. Sacco and Vanzetti, Tom Mooney, and other figures of the labor movement are real people and at the same time symbols of the drama of human and social development and sacrifice. His own unique power of expression lies in the magical marriage of the fertile industrial landscape of America with the Hasidic fable of his origins. The children's dreams of Kaunas and Brooklyn melt into one another, the landscape of factories and warehouses, playing fields and tenement houses carries an aroma of longing. Ben Shahn paints America, but the inner place of his existence is the world, the world of poverty and lonely life in the great cities filled with people.

In Marc Chagall, Slavic peasant naïveté was joined to the aesthetic of the Ecole de Paris. Ben Shahn took from Cubism, Fauvism, and even from Surrealism just what he needed to fill human existence with the intensity of accusing and hopeful love. By estrangement, common platitudes become dramatic occurrences; photographic records of the moment become poetic, human expressions. With considered precision and as though captured in speeded-up motion, the dullest things become indications of the essential: a boy in a forsaken street listening to a band—four men, in black Sunday best with the strident yellow slings of their trumpets, striding past the brick-red prison architecture of the factory. The lonely boy in the right-hand corner of the picture is the young Ben. It is the childhood of the artist with its fears and expectations, quartered in middle-class Brooklyn.

The lonely man among the masses, the loss of the human voice or human company in the era of the microphone, the broken communication in the bustle of the gigantic city. A man wanders through the fields on a Sunday, a workman resignedly plays his yearning song of longing on his harmonica. Red autumn leaves rain from the trees while the man in the heliotrope shirt dreams in color. It is the attempt of the city dweller to hold his dialogue with nature. This loneliness attains dramatic proportions in *Pacific Landscape* (125). Between the shore, the endlessly stretching mosaic of gray-yellow pebbles, and the liquid desert of the sea, as though washed up on the beach, is a figure, symbol of helpless humanity.

A one-legged man painfully mounts the ver-milion steps in a war-shattered landscape. It is the indigo hour of twilight. These two basic colors sound constantly through Shahn's work. They reappear in the melancholy and poetic picture of the little girl skipping rope in front of the broken red wall through which the carpet of many colored flowers shimmers like a metaphor of a life that can never be restored. How often the sad-faced girl, clothed in black and with lemon-colored hair, is drawn by Shahn with exaggerated foreshortening and thus, despite all perspective realism, is placed in magical space in which invisible tensions whirl. Next to the skipping girl but turned to the wall is the boy, separated from her and alone in his gaze.

Since Goya and Daumier there has not been a sharper and at the same time more human critic of social conditions. Now and then we may find an analogy in George Grosz. The sharply formed, psychoanalytic lines of the latter may be still more revealing and aggressive. He lacks not only the dissonant glare of the color dimension but still more the fervor and inner readiness of compassion.

No other political satirist of the twenties was Grosz's equal (121). His unshaded linear drawings look as though they had been done with the anatomist's dissecting knife. They penetrate decay and gloom like X rays and psychonalysis. There is no foreground and no background in his merciless black-and-white reports. Planes cut across one another, men walk through one another, their dress veiling their lust and greed. In the crowd of the city we recognize the individual people in their personal and social self-preoccupation.

Otto Dix covers the transparent framework of a superreal, ghostly actuality with the epidermis of his colors (122). An enlargement of convulsions and labor pains, a magically intensified precision in the fixing of existence, are his construction mediums for the ghostly, wretched, erotic dance halls, bargained love in dark corners or the harsh illumination of the bordello; for the bleakness of a Sunday family outing in a nature alienated from city people; for the festive idling of death; and above all for his trench pictures, scenes of organized mass death.

In Italy, too, painters sought to overcome their alienation from the object. Renato Guttuso attaches himself to the folkloristic vitality of Sicilian peasant painting and employs Cubist and Fauvist elements in order to deepen his pictorial language. The English critic John Berger, who did a study of Guttuso's paintings, feels that this painter has managed to avoid the fundamental errors that have limited the work of other socialist artists, who made use of the naturalistic style of the nineteenth century and merely changed the objects of representation—for example, representing factory workers instead of monks. Instead, Guttuso has studied the newer masters in order to find out how their discoveries could be adapted to the representational techniques of contemporary painting.

Guttuso values the experiment, however, not in itself but as a means. He wants to abolish the seclusion of the art laboratory and participate in humanity and the problems of his times. As Guttuso sees it, reality can be more deeply interpreted with broadened expedients. His *Flight from Aetna* (1938) was the first picture in Italy to express social tension and hidden protest against the Fascists; the natural catastrophe is an externally visible drama in which the subjugation of the people dares be expressed. Even if the sorrows of the Sicilian people provided the point of departure for the picture, nevertheless the artistic impetus certainly derives from Delacroix and Picasso. Like Elio Vittorini, who in his *Conversations in Sicily* made use of symbolic language in order to establish truth and formulate an accusation, Guttuso in his works indicates the progressive steps of his position. The *Crucifixion* painted in 1941 presents a Fauvist-Cubist stage in the development of his still eclectic style. It is an expression of protest against the war, suffering, and the martyrdom of mankind somewhat like Carlo Levi's *Christ Stopped at Eboli*.

The *Annexation of Uncultivated Fields* was produced in 1948 after much preliminary study. The rhythm and construction of this picture, created in passionate exaltation and crying out against the revolting poverty of Sicily's villages, originate in a rhetorical realism; Courbet's feeling for life and his sense of the materiality of existence, Van Gogh's dynamic power of experience, are sensible in Guttuso. At the same time, one sees the influence of Picasso's *Guernica,* a painting that radiated powerfully through the art of the resistance in Italy.

Through the character of his drawing and the metaphors of his color, Guttuso succeeds in illustrating the movement of the masses, in representing the dramatic tension of a heightened reality, and thus, by inclusion of certain experiences in modern art, in strengthening the capacity of realism (120).

Together with other Croatian painters, Krsto Hegedušić founded the group Zemlja in 1929. The name gives part of the program away: "Earth," but without romantic associations—rather as a sign of a close attachment to earthiness. Certain of the techniques of modern artistic representation were included, but the group aspired to an emancipation from the School of Paris. On the track of such a program Hegedušić roamed through the austere landscape of Prodavina, searching for himself and the essence of his art. In 1929 he met the peasant Ivan Generalić, then fifteen years old. It was a fruitful meeting, for in the years following it led to the establishment of an unusual community of peasant painters, which first revolved about Hegedušić and later, after World War II, found its master in Generalič. It was the school of the peasant painters of Hlebine.

The painting of the Zemlja period created in Hegedušić's works the basis for the observation and construction of objective existence. To these were added the invisible though no less real elements of the tensions of subterranean sensitivities to fear, brutality, and death in concentration camps.

Dead Waters (126), painted in 1956, is like a

mythical lament over mass death. Irrevocably distant, driven bodies, roots, and twigs float Ophelialike, with dead, glazed eyes and the wet chill of horror. The utmost accuracy of his apparently banal report on illness, decay, poverty, the refuse of the big city, the scraps of existence becomes the document of a poetic clairvoyance. In the twilight of the commonplace of ghostly ugliness, of mechanical and human remains, the pain of consciousness shimmers through: "The laurel has tired of being poetic," wrote Lorca.

In 1948, a group of young French painters appeared under the name "L'Homme Témoin." Claude Vénard, André Minaux, Bernard Buffet, and others interpreted the face and spirit of the time in their lyrical-existential paintings. Their work creates out of reality, interweaving emanations of isolation, alienation, and disappointment into a fabric of color and form. In Buffet, fish bones, dissected insects, plucked birds, and the lean fruits of the earth become still lifes of parsimony and symbols of privation. The emptiness of the world, the used, worn-out nature of everyday things, the petty stature of exiled man become poetic symbols. Especially the diagrammatically sterile ascetic forms, distilled in the white-yellow light of his palette, are symbols of a lost generation that tolerates reality by shaping it. For, says Buffet, every generation needs artists to represent it and thus preserve it for the future. Buffet's post-Expressionism turns step by step into the routine

clichés of tragedy; the human figure becomes a caricatured formula, and the existential sensitivity to loss becomes a posterlike assertion approximating the taste of the day.

In their social antagonism and conscientious protests, several angry young artists in England are trying, like John Osborne in his drama, to turn their artistic and lyrical intensity to the social spheres of more realistic and socially operative art. Among these are Derrick Graves, Edward Middleditch, Jack Smith, and John Bratby. These painters do not belong to a specific group; each by himself and in his own way searches for a way out of the self-imposed isolation of hermetic art forms. Bratby and Smith have included elements of abstract and analytical structural painting in their social and realistic works (119).

Realistic impulses are also expressed in the works of Graham Sutherland, especially in the strange gallery of his contemporary portraits. Because of its ecstatic nakedness of expression, his *Crucifixion*, painted for the church of Northhampton, was compared with Grünewald.

If a romantic, surrealistic sphere extends throughout Sutherland's work, man's uncertain relationships are characteristic of Francis Bacon's work (86). Man is turned upside down by fear, madness, and decay. Bacon paints him as persecuted, driven, dragged to the wall of unreality, forced into space, which crushes him and simultaneously stretches him into infinity.

Humanism and Myths of Reconciliation

Real men, for whom despair
nourishes the devouring flame of hope
together let us open the last bud of the future
                    Paul Eluard, "The Victory of Guernica"

Even though Vincent van Gogh died before the end of the nineteenth century, his expressive, hallucinatory vision continues its influence as though it had grown out of the spirit and experience of our times. His overwhelming love of people and things, his ecstatic abandonment to created nature, his social and religious ties with those living in darkness, and his alert penetration of all levels of existence have deepened modern art's consciousness of reality.

Georges Rouault portrayed the passion of man (116) in the Joblike lament of his art. Like Rembrandt, he interprets and brings to light the invisible legend of suffering in the mask of existence. Goya's demonism, Daumier's social protest, and Toulouse-Lautrec's critical, revelatory realism are related to Rouault. The religious and the profane unite in the dark visions of his devout, rebellious icons. The colors of his compositions shine like cathedral windows out of the austerely secured black of his outlines. Many of his graphic illustrations and especially the series *Misère et Guerre* are in their symbolic urgency the confession of art in the service of man.

His work has touched the conscience of the age in a different way from the equally tragic, human work of the graphic artist Käthe Kollwitz, whose work was rooted in the consciousness of the German realists. Her illustrations and drawings for Zola's *Germinal*, Gerhard Hauptmann's *The Weavers* and *Florian Geyer*, the representation of the peasant wars, of strikes and demonstrations, of war and revolution, starvation and unwanted pregnancies, all executed since the turn of the century, are related to the social indictments of Millet, Meunier, and Steinlen.

Like the Gothic masters of the Middle Ages who carved holy legends in wood for illiterate people, Frans Masereel carved the pictorial bible of the modern proletariat out of the sharpness of his conscience, the deep blackness of social criticism, and the glowing dream of his hope for the future. *The Book of Hours, Work, The Passion of Man,* and other books without words remind one of the masters of the scrolls. Van Gogh, Tolstoy, and Lenin influenced his symbols.

The graphic arts are particularly well suited to dissemination among the masses. Otto Pankok, too, wishes to stir the consciousness and feelings of simple men. In the internal agitation of the broad outline form, his black-and-white picture-writing creates an authentic witness: the great sermon of love for creatures and hidden and unseen things, which through the knowledge and humility of the artist gain luster and a cosmic beauty. In a humanized landscape, plants, animals, and people speak to one another in simple, fantastic brotherliness.

The work of the important German sculptor and poet Ernst Barlach has the elementary expressive power of Van Gogh. His roots perhaps reach all the way to Tilman Riemenschneider. With native truthfulness Barlach formalizes all creation. In his expressive Nordic consciousness are the power of brick Gothic and the bitter mischief of Eulenspiegel-like folk forms—sleepers, dreamers, shepherds, fishermen, tender girls, women, old men, driven by fears and seized with spiritual horror. One of his sculptures bears the foreboding name *Martyred Humanity*. The materiality of the figure suspended by its hands is dissolved by strictly linear simplicity; beneath the folds of the timeless robes the stiffening energies of the martyred body become visible. The pain-laden face, with its unique animation, is a self-portrait and also a portrait of suffering humanity (123).

Despite its tragic size, inner strength and fullness of experience, we recognize this suffering form only in a qualified way as a symbol of our times. It is as though the rationally conscious, scientifically conceived technique of our Golgotha required different signs and symbols in order to make the abyss and the extent of our horror visible. The actual tragedy seems to have overwhelmed the artistic one. What symbols of atonement can follow Auschwitz or Hiroshima?

In years of meditation, Iri Maruki and Toshiko Akamatsu, two Japanese artists, have created large picture cycles of the horror of Hiroshima: the explosion of the bomb, the burning earth, the ashes of death raining down beneath a colorful rainbow that does not indicate reconciliation. The death of Hiroshima attained a new dimension of horror. A cosmic material entered the service of destruction. The ancient Erinyes could not reach the conscience of the atomic pilot. The new dimensions of cosmic death are hardly to be mastered by the traditional *procédés* and symbols of art.

Perhaps Ossip Zadkine has come closer to the portrayal of amorphous fright in his memorial to the destroyed city of Rotterdam (124). Like a lighthouse the bronze figure stands on the site of the destruction. At the viewer's every step, the figure's form and face, being and expression seem to change. Clouds wander through the gaping body, which draws space and distance into itself. The bottomless sky shimmers between the masts of the hands calling for help. The bronze screaming figure towers like a totem pole. An original intention, not to portray but to be, has been recovered.

Another memorial of our age was created by the architect, smith, and sculptor Reginald Butler (186). In his conception of an insectlike gallows as a monument to an unknown political prisoner, he created a symbolic structure that projects a vision of brutality and tyranny out of technique and sensitivity. Beneath the ghostlike towers of mass annihilation stand three female figures, silent witnesses who preserve the secret of suffering for the future.

But man carries his fear beyond the boundaries of the earth. Butler's *Manipulator* stands with strange instruments in his hands, his defiant face directed upward. His demonic genius is clouded and dangerous. This figure, with the Janus face of the discoverer and destroyer, has mythic expressive power.

Fernand Léger built bridges of self-conscious hope out of the earthly material of a "new reality." His stereometrically simplified world of men and objects is like the conceptions of an engineer's blueprint. They are the symbols and motifs of modern civilization. He gives a new human and aesthetic formulation to the working world as an assembly point for collective effort. In Constant Permeke or Gustave de Smet, individual, strong, lively working figures are presented; in Marcel Gromaire these come closer to being the puristically schematized sign: man. It was Léger (127) who first discovered the emblematic simplification of human anonymity corresponding to the technical, rational, rhythmical, mechanical sphere of life and activity. He strips all expressive modes of existence. Human beings set into a gigantic landscape of machinery work with titanic strength, transforming heaven and earth. Antisentimental poetics and humanistic objectivity form the basic mood of his work.

Cézanne's geometric interpretation of things in nature and Rousseau's loving, magical concreteness led to transportations that Léger called "new realism." Léger's handwriting, filled with the harshness of the technical working world, is also full of vital warmth and humanistic life force. The machine as the representative symbol of our civilization—the strange object world of circles, cylinders, cubes, and spheres —loses the smell of accusation and alienation. The abstract and the concrete, man and machine, are unified here:

We have built houses
To preserve the light
So that night will not sunder our lives.

So writes Paul Eluard in celebration of Léger's picture cycle *The Builders*.

Picasso's dream bridges between an ever pending past and an imminent future are built of the texture of fantasy. They vault a time boundary that suspects the future, desires it, fears it, and suffers from the past. *Guernica* (128), kept in gray tones and built on the strict form of the triangle, tells this almost incomprehensible event of Spain's bleeding tragedy. Refugees hurry into the unknown, race through the night with a light in their hands, next to them the bull's immobility and secretiveness. A small lamp substitutes for the sun, illuminating horror, madness, fear.

Two things were necessary for this creation: darkness and the license to submerge in the bowels of the bull, in the nightmare world of *sueños* and bullfighting, in the ecstasy of Spain's heaven and hell, in the night of power madness, of funeral pyres, from the autos-da-fé to burning Guernica. And also the light of those who, challenging their courage, were the first to cross the oceans and discover the reality of new continents on the maps of their imagination. Picasso is the strongest witness for the carrying power of newly created myths of humanity.

Many artists and art lovers recognized in *Guernica* the visual projection of their own spiritual tension. Juan Larréa wrote:

"And if this *ecce mundus* at first was Guernica, soon thereafter it became Warsaw, Rotterdam, Nancy, Coventry—until one day when Europe was only a frightful material and moral ruin . . . On that terrible day it turned out that *Guernica* was the most European of all known paintings. . . ."

Herbert Read speaks of the fact that the culture of an age may not be confused and consolidated with its representative poets and artists. Before a Homer or a Dante can appear, a long period of crystallization and preparation for a new artistic truth must take place:

"To look for such points in our own cultural wilderness would be to miss them—who can say whether such a subtle fermentation is taking place at the present moment in China or Brazil, in Canada or Siberia. It is against historical probability that it would occur again in exhausted lands like Greece or Italy or England, but there is no law of causality in this realm of culture."

That careful, scientific attempt to widen the Europocentric standards that have been valid up to now reveals a new tendency. A break takes place here with the traditional conception of the necessary superiority of Occidental culture. An art that is becoming universal is beginning to erase racial and national boundaries. It is quite possible that old cultures that appear to be exhausted will finally gain an impulse of artistic renewal through contact with more vital people, and at the same time will abandon their imperialistic world position. When they renounced Spain's claim to world power and threw the key to the Cid's tomb into the ocean as a symbol of a vanquished myth, the generation of 1898 produced a renewal of the Spanish spirit and led to a new initiative for the Spanish peninsula and the world. This new initiative was felt from Pio Baroja, José de Larra, Unamuno, Ortega y Gasset, and Valle Inclan to the poems of Lorca and the visions of Picasso and Juan Gris.

In the Netherlands, paralleling and predicting the decline of the colonial empire, creative powers have been growing, blazing a trail in the realm of architecture and painting—J. J. P. Oud, Theo van Doesburg, Georges Vantongerloo, and above all Piet Mondrian.

In Great Britain, in the face of their crumbling world position, spiritual powers of unsuspected force have been moving and have produced James Joyce, T. S. Eliot, Henry Moore, and many others.

Perhaps one can conclude that future cultures are rooted in the old ones and that a crisis of social conditions includes both disappearance and origin.

But the gulf separating modern art from the masses, the self-destruction through isolation, can only be overcome by a long process of development, by the approximation of poetic and artistic works with the new self-consciousness of awakening peoples and masses. We are already experiencing the beginnings of a mutual influence of heterogeneous planes and spaces, a mutual penetration of times and cultures.

For art is the vision of a possible, comprehensive community.

VI

LIBERATION FROM THE OBJECT, RELEASE FROM FORM

Poetry and Reality

Dissonance is just as little a bearer of order as consonance is a guarantee of security.

Stravinsky

The young Rimbaud was searching for the fullness of the world, not for heaven. Reality was too narrow for him, transcendence too empty. The goal of his existential road was nothingness. Imaginatively, his poetry revealed the infinity of a new interpretation of the world through poetry.

This encounter with new realities made poetry sensitive to and aggressive toward all tradition. The alienating, the ugly, and the absurd all helped overcome the bleakness of the harmonies that had been handed down and the boredom and repetitiousness of traditional beauty.

For Rimbaud, the purpose of poetry was "to make visible the invisible, to hear the unheard." The poet attains the unknown, and even if he finally does

not comprehend his own vision, at least he has seen it "even if he is destroyed by his giant leap through unheard and unnamable things."

The immateriality and boundlessness of Rimbaud's prose poetry indicate a fusion of the visible with the audible and a transformation of the traditional speech forms in unexpected word associations. His words no longer serve comprehensibility, at least not exclusively; rather, they become the intermediaries of nonlogical landscapes that the poet may evoke by his spoken magic. Words follow musical configurations more than they serve the causal architecture of thought. Therefore, these poems are dissonant, twilight constellations, equivalent to music and precursors of abstract painting.

The intellectually controlled imagination of Stéphane Mallarmé operated with the impulse of language as today's Tachists operate with the impulse of color. Since Baudelaire, modern poetry has been determined by the concept that it does not portray reality but remodels it creatively. In Mallarmé's poems, things are metaphorically obscured and dematerialized. Their relationships to one another vibrate secretively in logically inconceivable word pictures. The key to this poetry cannot be found in emotional poetry. As Kandinsky paints with colors, so this poetry is painted with words freed from their actual objective meanings.

Mallarmé's words, therefore, were "Obliterate, abolish, be silent." For him the ideal of poetry was emptiness, the color white, and silence. The visible world is a distant point of departure. "The poet has only one thing to do—to work secretly with a view to the never attainable."

The transformed and transforming arts of poetry and painting no longer appear to be a matter of objective relationships, but rather of a way of viewing and penetrating these relationships. The natural life can only be a starting point in modern art; things and thoughts are taken apart, analyzed into their components, split, and estranged. Every hackneyed word association, every traditional thought association is considered painful. The process of disembodiment goes further and further until everything dissolves into a music of language or color. This is a basic law in the process of the dehumanization of poetry and painting. Even in his day Novalis was able to write: "The stones and matter are the most sublime things; man is the real chaos." Inorganic matter, metals, minerals, and crystals are in this phase all more strongly connected with reality and the objectivity of the soul than the perceptual, vegetative, creative elements.

Timelessness and nonobjectivism were artistically decisive in the work of the painter Kasimir Malevich too, down to the last reduced means, the pure poetry in which there is no declaration, only music, in which form changes to content.

The exhaustion of material objects is also expressed in the selection of those peripheral places that now only serve as a dumping ground for existential memories: the big city's garbage, fish bones, dried-up leaves, empty and nameless things transformed by the disposing power of art into the symbols of a questionable existence.

Pictures of refuse dumps and incinerators appear in Krsto Hegedušić's work; Leoncillo's plastic world rots in ruins and graves; Alberto Burri alludes to the vulnerability of all things in his pictures of sunken wood and torn linen. And the same is also found in Eugenio Montale's collection of poems *Cuttlebones*, and in Eliot's *Waste Land* in the lines "for you know only/A heap of broken images" and "These fragments I have shored against my ruins."

Rafael Alberti says in his *Dead Angels:*

> *In the sleeplessness of forgotten conduits*
> *In the brook's flow choked by the silence of*
> *   garbage*
> *Not far from the puddle which no longer reflects*
> *   the clouds,*
> *A pair of lost eyes,*
> *A broken ring*
> *Or a trodden star. . . .*

Here is the suspension of all concreteness, the devaluation of everything organic; metaphors of estrangement taken from every place and every time. "Always further away from the birthplace," says St. John Perse. The unknown is the goal. At the border waits the prohibition against taking the spirit and form of the past along. Language, color, and form appear to break down here. For the poet, sand, chalk, and ashes are the symbols of his internal experience. Even where his poetry is a forceful call to life, time and place remain untransparent, veiled in the imprecision of linguistic magic.

> *I have built upon the abyss,*
> *On the spray and the damp of the sand.*
> *I would sleep inside the cisterns*
> *And in the hollow spaced ships,*
> *In all the empty and stagnant places,*
> *Where the taste of greatness is.*

The Ligature and Freedom of Tonality

Painting and music have an ever growing tendency to create "absolute" works, that is, completely objective, independent organisms. These works stand closer to [purely and eternally artistic] art in abstracto. . . .

Kandinsky, 1913

In order not to wither in the artificial air of the age of technology, the arts are seeking renewal in myth and archaism. They tread the path of the extra-human, of dissolution, of abstraction, and seek new, nontraditional connections.

Decisive streams of contemporary painting have so closely approached the spirit of music that the laws of complete disintegration and of strictest connections, the concept of total freedom in total discipline, have gained acceptance for both arts alike.

Stravinsky writes:

"My freedom will be greater and more complete the more I define my field of action and the more impediments I set up around it. Whoever robs me of an opposition robs me of a strength. The more constraint one puts upon oneself the more one frees oneself from the chains that fetter the spirit."

In *The Rite of Spring*, a revolutionary creation of modern music, Stravinsky seizes on an archaic myth: primitive man and the unknown, fear of the almighty elemental power of nature and the instinctual, demonic breakthrough of magical possession, the mystic unity with primordial powers through sacrificial death.

Stravinsky's works of the Russian period—*The Firebird, Petrouchka, The Rite of Spring*—correspond more or less to Picasso's Negro period. Russian folk melodies offered Stravinsky an inexhaustible vitality and the archaic rhythms of the collective unconscious, which Picasso found in the magical realms of Negro sculpture.

One day, however, Stravinsky forsook the Russian folk sources and wrote the *Octet,* which deeply disquieted the public of 1923. What did this return to a new classicism mean? Why the "regressive" return to a scene that had already been passed? Picasso had already blazed this trail in 1920. Whoever had felt something faintly reminiscent of Pompeii in his pictures could only ascertain the presence in his *Maternité* and *Three Women at the Well* (1921) of an archaic, classic bearing penetrating the filter of the Cubist spirit. For his part, Stravinsky in his opera-oratorio *Oedipus Rex* (1927) and in his ballet *Apollon Musagète* (1927) displays the severe, renewed classicality in which all the emotional accents of romantic, folkloristic tonal experience are extinguished.

Arnold Schoenberg's emotionally exaggerated expressionism burst traditional aesthetics in the atonality of his twelve-tone system. "The work of the artist," said Schoenberg, "is instinctive." The conscious mind has little influence on it. Schoenberg said he felt that what he wrote was dictated to him. He was the implementer of a hidden will, of the unconscious, of instinct.

The decisive moment for Schoenberg, writes T. W. Adorno, is the functional interchange of the musical expression:

"Passions are no longer simulated; rather, loving impulses of the unconscious, shocks, traumas, are registered untransposed in the medium of music. They attack the taboos of form because form subjects such impulses to censorship; and because it rationalizes and transposes them into pictures. Schoenberg's formal innovations are kin to changes in the ingredients of expression. They serve to allow the truth of these ingredients to break through. The first atonal works are protocols in the sense of psychoanalytic dream protocols. In the first publications about Schoenberg, Kandinsky called his works "acts of the brain." But the scars of that revolution of expression are the stains which in painting as well as in music establish themselves as messengers of the indefinable IT—in opposition to a compositional will—destroying the surface and just as impossible to wipe away by later corrections as the blood stains in fairy tales."

The twelve-tone system, which Schoenberg invented and which exercises the widest influence on the music of the twentieth century, removes the relationship of melody and harmony to the basic note of a single key. The doctrine of the twelve interconnected halftones of the octave places a new, strict, responsible compositional order against the anarchic freedom resulting from the abolition of all tonal connections. Mathematical logic and expressive quickness of hearing are united here to form a unity of opposites.

Perhaps it is just these cool and inexorable tone rows that can express things surpassing the obligations of classicism. In Schoenberg's uncompleted opera *Moses and Aaron* and above all in his last great work, the cantata *A Survivor from Warsaw,* the powers of fate are called to account. In the latter, several thoughts of the survivor of the Warsaw ghetto are taken as the text:

"I can no longer remember everything; for a long time I was probably completely unconscious. I can only remember the grandiose moment when suddenly the old, forgotten prayer was sung. . . ."

From this simple material Schoenberg built his dramatic work. By means of the strictly structured, regular tone rows, the music attained a hallucinatory dimension that was able to communicate the invisible and inhuman in the awakening of the Jews in the predawn hours, the sergeant's muster, the counting of the dead, and the procession of the survivors into the gas chambers.

The introduction of the folklike closing song, the *cantus firmus,* signifies the twelve-tone system's necessary renunciation of all theoretical and polemic exclusivity. It is the last sacrifice to the martyrs and simultaneously opens the prospect of a future synthesis. This cantata, which lasts seventeen minutes, unites decisive form and contemporary means of expression. It is a humanistic work, analogous to Picasso's attempt to comprehend and represent mythically the destruction and horror of fascism in his painting *Guernica.*

In a manifesto that accompanied the publication in 1925 of Schoenberg's *Three Satires for Mixed Chorus,* we read: "First of all, I wanted to touch all those who seek their personal salvation in a middle road. But [my system] is used by those who nibble at dissonance, who wish to pass for modern but are too careful to draw the consequences."

Anton Webern was probably Schoenberg's most consistent follower. His stern and bald music, full of mathematical precision, crystal clarity, cosmic sound, and ascetic simplicity, reminds one of Mondrian's geometry. Just as Mondrian ruled out every symmetry, so in Webern's music there is no repetition in any area. The highest condensation of form, the decision to treat the musical material constructively and bind it in the strictest form, leads to the most consistent use of the twelve-tone technique.

The synthesis in Schoenberg's late work was wrung in bitterness from his own rules. In contrast, Arthur Honegger used certain aspects of atonality in order to enlarge his music's power of expression and message. His spiritual nobility and his bond with life guarded him against loss of direct contact with the public. "It was always my wish and my endeavor to write music which would be understandable to the large majority of listeners and which would yet be free of banality to such an extent that it would captivate the real music lovers." In his *Antigone* and his *Joan of Arc at the Stake* strangeness and popularity are closely connected. Proximity to the present and symbolic power, universal spirituality and simplicity lead one to think of Bertold Brecht's didactic works.

The work of Dmitri Shostakovich presents one of the most recent attempts to express the drama of man in the medium of the symphony. Deriving from Mahler, Bruckner, Tchaikovsky, and above all Beethoven, Shostakovich probably displays his creative powers best in symphonic form. Perhaps it may appear wrong that, more than a hundred years after Beethoven's death, a musician should formulate great dramatic experiences in the spirit and style of the classical master. But Shostakovich knows Hindemith, Stravinsky, and Schoenberg well enough to include in his work as much of the modern spirit as seems bearable in order to build into the transposed language of music the monumental epic compositions of the revolution that has occurred. In this sense his work should be counted among the most significant harbingers of a musical humanism.

"I want to try," says Shostakovich, "to approach the heart and spirit of the people." In his compositions, dramatic tension and a vital sense of immediacy and folk metaphor remind one from time to time of the canvases of Guttuso. Both artists burst the laboratory-experiment bounds of hermetic art.

Antoine Goléa writes in his book *Music of our Time:*

"Together with the Schoenberg of *A Survivor from Warsaw*, Dallapiccola is one of those musicians who are most closely bound up with the drama of contemporary humanity, one of those who have represented this drama in the most moving and expressive ways. Dallapiccola is a great representative of musical humanism not only because of the development of his tonal experiments, but just as much because of the attention he gives the basic problem which disturbs twentieth-century man with an insistence never before experienced — this problem of freedom and tyranny."

In his argument with the twelve-tone system and his blending with the song and musical sense of the Italian people, Luigi Dallapiccola created works of musical and human significance in the tragic years of fascism. Perhaps these are related to the literary efforts of Vittorini, whose *Conversations in Sicily* testify to the spirit's revolt against barbarism.

Goléa thinks that André Jolivet, Olivier Messiaen, and Dallapiccola in the course of their search for a new humanism aspire to a secure synthesis.

"Dallapiccola's *Incantations for Flute* itself is in a sense a new archetype of a music which seemed to have disappeared forever, lost in the interior of a part of Africa as yet unknown, of a music which rises anew from a thousand years of forgetfulness.

In Messiaen we find the wonderful constant contact with exotic but contemporary cultures; in Jolivet everything appears to arise from the depths of our times, and most surprising of all is perhaps the fact that this music, which stands in direct relationship with the cosmic systems. . . , appears, to those to listen to it without any idea of its deliberate and conscious production, to have sprung directly from the soul of the composer, a composer who is among the most progressive of his time. . . ."

Messiaen regards the exploration of rhythm as the basis of his music:

"The essence of my rhythmical system lies in the fact that it knows neither the measure of the bar nor of time. I studied the rhythms of the Hindus, Greeks, Romanians, and Hungarians and the rhythm in the motion of the stars, atoms, and the human body."

It is not only with respect to rhythm that Far Eastern music has influenced Messiaen; his variations and modes of harmony and melody also are determined by Indian and Chinese tonal scales. The enrichment of his musical language with respect to sound and rhythm is being further developed by his pupils.

Here too one may draw certain parallels with abstract calligraphic attempts on the part of certain painters who try through concentration and spiritual experience to formulate signs and the essential content of objects.

Béla Bartók connected Schoenberg's and Stravinsky's radical and antagonistic impulses with the elemental store of Magyar and Slavic musical folklore and combined them into an inspired and stylistically unified entity. Tonal, polytonal, and atonal elements are unified by a complicated creative process into a synthetic tonal picture. It is analogous to the cubistic, surrealistic poetry of Lorca, who used his Andalusian folk heritage for his creations.

Mikrokosmos, Bartók's 135 piano studies of progressive difficulty, shows the creative modification of an original melody into new spiritual sound through strict formal structure. Bartók's string quartets are among the most important achievements of modern music. They unite barbaric elementary musicality with the utmost auditory sensitivity and cultivated spirituality. Manfred Gräter characterizes Béla Bartók's work as follows:

"Intensified expression, a turning toward the primitive, primordial elements in music, radical linearity, and contrapuntal concentration, and finally the inclusion of traditional forms into the personal and clarified art of the late works—these are the stations of a new artistic development which Bartók saw as a pioneer and initiator of the new music."

In Manuel de Falla's works, Impressionist sounds had already been connected with Spanish folklore.

Carl Orff has returned to the elements of medieval Occidental music, and Ravel characterized jazz as "live wells of inspiration for all of today's composers."

Many contemporary musicians—Stravinsky, Milhaud, Honegger, Copland, Křenek, and others—have adopted the sounds of jazz instrumentation. The emotional musicality of the Afro-Americans in their spirituals, the collective plaint of a black community, the Negro ministrel songs, and above all the Negroes' passionate dance rhythms, carried throughout the American continent from the first Dixieland bands— all have influenced our contemporary ear.

Following the encounter of primordial African rhythms, transformed by Christian church music, with the artificial music of the machine age, percussion instruments came into their own, and music began to include rhythmical accumulations of big-city noises, the sound phenomena of a technological world.

Luigi Russolo, painter and musician of the Italian Futurist group, wrote in 1913 of the technical world of sounds in music:

"Today [music] becomes ever more complicated. It is seeking a combination of tones which strike the ear as very dissonant, strange, and rough. And so we come closer and closer to the technique of noise. . . . We Futurists have loved the music of the great masters. For years Beethoven and Wagner have deeply moved our hearts. But now we have had enough of them. We derive much greater pleasure from the ideal combination of the noises of streetcars, internal-combustion engines, automobiles, and the working masses than from hearing again, for example, the *Eroica* or the *Pastorale.* . . . We shall divert ourselves by orchestrating the noise of metal shutters being pulled down over windows, of slamming doors, the slurp and press of crowds, the mass restlessness of the train stations, steelworks, factories, printing presses, heavy industry, and subways. The new noises of war, too, must not be forgotten...."

The *musique concrète* developed by Pierre Schaeffer carried this idea further and to a certain extent actualized it. In Schaeffer's compositions, natural and technological sounds, elements of the spoken word and song, the tonal colors of exotic and traditional musical instruments are united. Such music is not devised or notated: it is fitted together on magnetic tape out of the reservoir of sounds found in reality. As in electronic music, the reproduction results from an electroacoustic process.

Until the twentieth century, European musical instruments were modeled on the human voice. The new phase, and this probably corresponds to the mechanization and increasing use of gadgetry in city life, develops instruments that are more like machines than instruments in the old sense. One does not "play" an electronic instrument; one operates it more or less as an engineer directs currents on an electrical panel. Modern technical thought has broken through into the world of music.

The tools of electronic music are similar to electrical generators, which prepare the raw material of sound. The composer creates or builds his work out of it and stores it in the information-storage battery. From there the compositions can be directed toward the listener by reproducing machines in electroacoustic processes. There are no interpreters any more. The composer has played once and for all.

This creative method may be used with all the conversion possibilities applicable to electronic waves: modulation, compression, expansion, inversion, and correlation. The composer is simultaneously musician and technician, creator and interpreter.

Are these endeavors of *musique concrète* and electronic music parallel to the visual expressions of painting that no longer describes its experiments as abstract but concrete art? This age has greatly enlarged the concept "reality," and the structure of matter, the diagrams of physical processes, micro- and macroscopic views appear more "real" than the immediate, everyday environment.

"This rigorous theoretical determination of permanent location is very significant for the new 'image of the artist' and the conception he has of himself and of his abilities. He sees himself as committed to creating pictorial reality on the basis of his contemporary existence, not recognizing the visible realities which he finds around him but evaluating them according to modern knowledge. His ability and its result, the work of art, are in the highest degree speculative phenomena. Intuition gives the first impulse of production which sets in motion the controlled and always verifiable issue of the formal mechanism; in this issue the intuitive impulse becomes visible as a fully formed image. This is a unique combination of surmising intuition and brightly alert speculation which is found also in modern poetry, in the work of Gottfried Benn, in modern music, in the work of A. Schoenberg, Webern, Messiaen, and even in modes of thought, as in Heidegger."

Thus the eminent critic of modern art Werner Haftmann formulates the developmental direction of art in the first half of the twentieth century. Benn, Schoenberg, and Webern have died; Messiaen and his pupils have in the process of their experiments indicated new tendencies.

One could conclude that Schoenberg's and Webern's work corresponds roughly to the painting of Kandinsky and Mondrian. In contrast, the works of the younger composers Pierre Boulez (piano sonatas and *Structures*) and Karlheinz Stockhausen (*Electronic Studies*) in a certain sense correspond to the instinctual paintings of artists such as Pollock, Wols, and Tàpies.

Are the engineers of music, the acousticians of unheard and earthly tonal phenomena, the interpreters of a tonality divorced from all conventions and traditions of music until now, or do the manipulations of the "sounding objects" imply extrahuman and extramusical tasks and procedures?

The Road to Abstraction

All art is a game with chaos; it moves in ever dangerous proximity to it and tears from it ever more extensive areas. If there is one improvement in the history of art, it is in the continual growth of these areas wrung from chaos.

Arnold Hauser

No form of creativity deserving the name "art" has ever exclusively served the world of appearance. Whenever form was presented, its essence—its intrinsic virtues—was also represented. Nevertheless, from the earliest times on one can follow two rather distinct artistic directions. One of them is in total harmony with nature and obtains its images and forms directly from empirical experience. The other direction emancipates itself from nature and transcends it; the latter no longer gives a direct representation of objects, but rather their conceptions and notions. Such an art will deal with mental processes expressed by way of geometric and abstract forms.

Realism and abstraction can be considered the two principal movements in the history of art. It is often difficult to find one free and exclusive of the other. Most of the time an artist caught in a particular phase will tend to try himself at one or the other direction, or will try to achieve a synthesis.

During the transition from the earlier to the later Stone Age, the first known change in artistic style occurred. Prompted by observation and experience, naturalism gave way to a geometrically composed world of forms. Prehistoric man began to leave behind the animal-like, instinctive existence of the hunter and collector. He changed the rhythm of such an existence by domesticating plants and animals and by systematically planning the breeding of cattle and the cultivation of soil. The pictures of animals on cave walls created at the inspiration of a direct life relation are left behind, and instead there begins a process of denaturalizing, reflected in abbreviations and pictographic signs—in an art aiming for abstraction. There are urnlike figures of the female body; on the islands of Paros and Amorgos we find mother idols resembling the forms of violins, and, on Cyprus, idols reduced to cubic forms (2). There exist simple geometric figures symbolizing fertility, such as the Venus of Lespugue; and in northern Japan we find the diagrammatic, abstract female figures of clay belonging to the Jamon period. These and many others are examples of a far-reaching distancing from the forms of nature, which, in final account, can only be analyzed as progressive spiritualization and translation into the abstract.

Egyptian art expressed its basic, archaic direction by way of a geometrically schematized transformation of figures and object (12). Sumeric and Acadic arts transformed the organic world into strictly composed monumental figures. An almost stiff geometrism distinguished the archaic figures of early Greece. Their symmetry and frontal emphasis remind one of early Egyptian sculpture.

In ancient American art everything structural appears in cubic forms and thus transcends the individual. Such closed masses of blocks are part of a pre-Columbian picture of reality. In its rigid stereometry the mythical concept becomes abstract, symbolic form (14, 16, 18).

The sculptures of primitive African peoples convey a belief in a world of spirits through a transformation of all natural forms into the geometric-abstract (26, 30, 32).

Islamic art consists of ornamental abstractions. The transcendentalism of the early Christian styles left behind earthly reality in order to discover the Divine in absolute space. Old Irish art, with its fascinating abstract ornamentation, changes nature into rhythmic, geometric symbols.

The tendency toward abstraction and an unreal construction of space is a fundamental characteristic of every mannerist style. Cézanne's paintings display a metamorphic process whereby visible nature is transformed into an autonomous world of artistic forms. The post-Impressionists, the divisionists—Seurat and Signac—manifested the fleeting movement of flooding light in technically legal principles of order. The Fauves and Expressionists deformed the outer image of the world in order to make visible its inner essence.

Analytical Cubism already displayed a decided detachment from appearances. Physical reality was decomposed and reorganized into a structure of geometrical facets. The portrait of Ambroise Vollard by Picasso (129) or the *Young Girl with a Guitar* by Braque (130) becomes recognizable through the crystal ceiling of spiritual experience. A synthesis is formed of nature, spirit, and geometry, and leads to abstraction.

The analytical experiments of the Cubists find a new constructive arrangement in the cool optics of Juan Gris (137). With contemplative spirituality and on the basis of geometrical forms, Gris builds a pictorial architecture, humanely classical, anticipating purism in painting.

Futurism set in motion the stereometrically decomposed pictorial reality of the Cubists. Umberto Boccioni's sculptural dynamism (132) and Gino Severini's kinetic multiplication of outlines sought the complete experience of a transparent reality in motion in which what has been seen, experienced, and recognized are simultaneously represented.

Robert Delaunay resolves his pointillistic, Cubistic pictures of cities into rhythm; he presents a dynamic orchestration of light and color that allows only a background of strong achitectonic surfaces to be recognized (131).

From this standpoint Lyonel Feininger's Gothic stained-glass-window world, seen through the crystal prism of a lyrical Cubism, becomes understandable. In strict, fuguelike rhythm he depicts nature and architecture as cosmic, geometric abstractions.

Franz Marc, too, abandoned the superficial view of things and beings and with increased sensitivity sought the inaccessible areas of existence:

"Today we take chaste and constantly deceptive nature apart and put it together again according to our own desires. We can see through matter, and the day is not far off when we shall be able to reach through its vibrating mass as we would through air. Matter is something that man at most tolerates but does not recognize."

In the search for essence, for the unexplained or not yet explainable origin of things, Marc, like St. Francis of Assisi, began a Cubistically disintegrating conversation with animals. About 1913 he crossed the borders of objectivity. He painted few abstract pictures before being killed in 1914 in World War I. With him one of the most daring turns in the development of modern art was broken off.

Fauvism, Cubism, and Orphism were the forerunners of abstraction. The Rayonism of Mikhail Larionov, who portrayed concrete abstractions in colorful parcels of rays, also prepared the way for the dissolution of matter.

The artists who consistently achieved full abstraction and whose attempts determined the two main directions of abstract art were Kandinsky, Malevich, and Mondrian. In all parts of the world, artists were trying to free themselves from the objective forms of visible nature and to achieve abstraction. It may, of course, be quite possible that here and there people painted abstract pictures even before Kandinsky. But these sporadic paintings were not always executed with a binding resolve as a necessary and definite formulation, as was the case with Kandinsky.

Kandinsky's first nonobjective pictures (133),

painted in 1910 and 1912, were attempts to test the sustaining capacity of abstraction. In a letter the artist wrote me in 1937 he explained:

"In *Composition*, 1911, the remains of objectivity are still evident. After this come the purely abstract pictures of the so-called 'dramatic' period—one of these with strongly defined lines—*Black Lines*, 1913, which at that time was considered an 'impermissible' use of the 'elements of painting.' Then come examples of the 'cold' and 'geometrical' period, the period of the circles—*Some Circles*, 1926 (in the State Gallery of Art, Dresden)—and so forth, up to the present period, which some call the 'synthetic,' or 'Paris period.' "

Kandinsky's expressive abstraction anticipated all the nonobjective pictorial expressions that were born after him out of feeling and instinct and which belong to the most recent forms of Tachism and Action Painting. The direction of constructive abstraction deriving from Cézanne and Cubism is the rational opposing pole of Kandinsky's emotional abstraction.

In eastern Europe, Malevich, Tatlin, Lissitzky, and other artists opposed overflowing soulfulness, muzhikdom, and Dostoevski's demonism with the cool weapons of mathematical tables and statistical analysis. Abstract art in Germany derived from Kandinsky and Moholy-Nagy. The German consciousness, it seemed, wanted above all not to miss the spiritual essence even in abstract endeavors. Even in final dissolution, basic philosophical ideas and ethical precepts must not be given up.

It could be that Malevich, too, who started from Cubism and Futurism and who as a final consequence achieved a black square on a white background, was influenced by a deeply emotional streak of nihilism (136). His pictures indicate a complete negation of traditional art—reduction, annihilation, the establishment of nothingness. This was the basic experience of nonobjectivism and made possible the undertaking of new, constructive attempts at absolute art.

Mondrian created his synthesis of objectivity out of metaphysical speculation and technical inspiration (135). This pictorial reality, created of balanced contrasts and achieved by abstraction and reduction, tending toward the basic geometrical elements of horizontal and vertical marks, seemed to embody for him the harmony of the universe.

Mondrian hid the harmonies of nature behind the screening pictures of his colored squares (255). Parallelism, meshed braces of bodies and planes, form and space, become in his work the outline of an abstract, scientifically interpreted world. His painting attempts to make connections visible, to create logical order in extraterrestrial spheres. His asymmetrical meditational pictures on black frames are intended as variations of the absolute. In them the sum of the world is to be stored, just as in medieval Masonic rites the letter G stands simultaneously for geometry and God. Thus Mondrian's pictures are abstract icons of a world plan, and behind the asceticism of their similes shimmers the idea of a cosmic urbanism. For Mondrian the urbane and organizational substance of all art has only representative meaning. In a self-organizing and harmonizing world such as he foresaw, art appeared superfluous as a special phenomenon, because the world itself in its harmonious complexity would develop into a work of art.

The new artistic direction leading to Paul Klee involves—in terms of theater—a change of scene: nature and man in their visible appearance become unimportant. Instead, we are told about what appearance disguises: the seemingly incomprehensible shadow image of dreams and primordial memory.

In Klee's world the substance of objects is often dissolved and at the same time retained, classified, and surpassed. In the many voices of his musicality, Cubism and Surrealism often sound together. His glance, directed inward, has never given up its reliance on nature, but he penetrates the superficial cloak in order to discover in the depths previously undiscovered and uninterpreted pictorial stores. The visible, concrete reality of the world is too small and too narrow, whereas the widening, transcendental world beyond seems too empty; Klee has succeeded in bridging the gulf between these two areas (269).

Abstract art develops an abundance of different forms of expression. Although these artists joined in groups and gave their movement a name, all classifications and generalizations are insufficient and should be regarded only as a helpful means of identification. Only the larger, polar possibilities of direction are determined within this newly opened cosmos of abstraction. We are presented on the one hand with expressions of psychic instincts emphasizing feeling—as in Tachism and Action Painting—and on the other hand there is Op art with its rational, pure forms and mathematical order.

The early wave of abstract art, which achieved its flood in the 1920s, could hardly find comprehension among critics and art lovers. Still, it made certain artists listen attentively. Did abstraction mean a narrowing or a broadening of reality in art? Did its language have the expressive power of previous formal elements, and would it be able with its new alphabet to express and interpret the internal and external manifestations of existence?

In 1912, Frantisek Kupka, at first a neo-Impressionist, exhibited paintings of pure abstraction—circles and ellipses—in the Salon d'Automne. The idea of creating a harmonious combination of color and form as musical elements originated with the aesthetic principles of the Nabis and finally inspired the art of Orphism.

The monumental compositions of Fernand Léger, who depicts actual objects or their parts, combine certain important elements of the reality found in simple, popular thinking with the geometric, abstract, fundamental forms of a spiritualized world of things (138).

The mature aesthetic of the purists, Ozenfant and Le Corbusier, which grew out of their Cubistic thinking, developed into a form of art answering in its pure and precise order to the demands of a technical civilization. Whereas in painting the purist program may or may not lead to a sort of artificial solidification, in architecture it is left free to realize itself creatively.

With his strict, hieratical, purist reliefs, Willi Baumeister stands close to Cubism and Constructivism (139). He is attracted by whatever is rational, planned, and scientific, but in the depths of his being instinctual powers probably stir, striving to make visible forgotten and forbidden worlds. Baumeister's creative discipline does not allow complete abandonment to the chthonian impulses of the blood. Even in spontaneous creation he links the psychic tension of the moment with the timeless, contemplative knowledge of the totality of the universe and existence. Some of the abstract painters outside and many within Germany received and digested Baumeister's work as both stimulus and directional indication.

The painter Kurt Schwitters, proceeding from Dadaism, created his sensitive, poetic collages out of actual waste products; these collages were the expression of a nihilistic frame of mind and at the same time led to abstract pictorial composition (141). Schwitters' significance however, is to be found elsewhere. Reference will again be made to it under the treatment of the Dada and neo-Dada movements.

Against the treatment of what is unconscious and instinctual stands a severe, cool, and rational art inspired by the technical spirit of the world of forms. Rhythmical order and mathematical-architectural counterpoint now develop into forms belonging exclusively to the realm of human reason. Nevertheless, whether consciously or not, these forms also represent reflections and transpositions of functional powers in a medium. Science, technology, and mind, the latest conditions of space and power, new intensity in motion, and the latest structural forms—all this sought and found new artistic expression.

One of the abstract movements of our time—geometric constructionism—will give in to and further its own fascination with the scientific picture of reality in which man participates. The mystery of numbers and measurements, of proportion and equation, and the beauty of geometry have become anti-picturesque elements in contemporary art. Shortly before his death in 1930, Theo van Doesburg wrote: "In the studio of the modern painter there should be the kind of climate found on snowy mountain ranges of three thousand meters; the cold air kills the germs. . . ."

Since Mondrian and Van Doesburg (142), the idea of harmony as a balance of contrasts has become the recognized basic principle of the abstract painting today known as "concrete." The cool figurations, the strict rhythms and formal relationships to a certain extent create a consonance with the Bauhaus attempts and the tendencies of the Abstraction-Création movement.

The time between the two wars was a mutation period for abstract art. The ideas of the Russian Constructivists, transmitted by Naum Gabo, Antoine Pevsner, and Lissitzky, the concrete pictures containing new forms and substances by Moholy-Nagy and Josef Albers, the aesthetic definition of space and the universe given by Max Bill (214), and other pictorial experiments and solutions should be named here in order to demonstrate the multiplicity and at the same time the unity of the influence and currents that form the abstract art of our times.

In Germany, the country in which Kandinsky's most consistent abstractions originate, abstract art at first achieved only slight success. It worked more on architecture and the graphic arts, which were especially fostered in the Bauhaus school.

A clear harmony fills the geometrical forms and lines of Friedrich Vordemberge-Gildewart (145), sounding poetically in the soft-pitched values of the balancing play. A bypath deriving from Kandinsky's theses led to the experiments of Viking Eggeling, who steps over the boundaries of painting with his symphony of diagonals and strives to organize form with lines, surfaces, and chiaroscuro—like Nicolas Schöffer, decades later, in his experiments with the luminoscope.

While the abstractions of Jean Arp and Joan Miró respond to elements of the soul and are therefore Surrealistic in style, we discover toward the end of the twenties the crystallization of ideas of Russian constructionists, of members of the Stijl group and the Bauhaus. This movement, which went under the name Abstraction-Création, was shaped as a response to the cool forms of scientific, industrial surroundings. The guiding idea was a detachment from everything objective. The artists attempted to express through the language of concrete abstraction, though sketched images and the rhythm of form and color, the plenitude of the world they lived in.

Georges Vantongerloo, who, with Auguste Herbin, can be considered one of the founders of Abstraction-Création, painted harmonious compositions inspired by the basic prescriptions of neo-Plasticism, and which were founded on mathematical calculations. Herbin, who was initially an Orphic Cubist, built strong, geometric surfaces with a vivid color contrast. His works are clearly meant to have a symbolic content.

With stubborn intensity, Sophie Täuber-Arp built her silent, logical, lyrical, geometrical constructions of rectangles and circles.

Ben Nicholson invents musical, architectonic compositions full of spatial harmony (144). His basic technical forms carry a muted intensity of color that evokes the permanence and preciousness of earlier icons. Classical proportion and restraint, together with emphatic formal precision, accompany this journey from objectivity to abstraction.

Victor Pasmore's constructive abstraction is indebted to Mondrian's vertical-horizontal style. On a clean background the lines are arranged into a balanced play of musical sensitivity.

Alberto Magnelli's geometrical, Constructivist world of form communicates something of the spirit of the Tuscan masters in its weighty rhythm and saturation of colors (143).

With Arp and Sophie Täuber, César Domela published the magazine *Plastique*. His rhythmically harmonized arrangements of lines attempted to awaken certain meditative moments. Jean Dewasne accentuates a musical, dramatic element by producing a chromatic construction of images and strong color sequences without any transition.

Victor Vasarely looks for absolute objectivity and tries to eliminate the last remnants of energies linked with feeling and instinct. In their place he puts logic and the conscious use of pure forms. Vasarely's compositions, with their transparent layers set one on top of the other, seem to achieve movement and perhaps pass beyond the dimensions of painting (240).

Abstract constructionism is practiced all over the world. The Brazilian Cicero Dias paints technically linear constructions of lyrical geometry with moderately toned colors. Richard Mortensen, from Denmark, builds large compositions showing a severe, leveled order and sensitively harmonized coloring. Richard Lohse, from Switzerland, constructs algebraically calculated, fugued rows of colors, thus constructing a theme. His rhythmical order of lines corresponds to certain tasks of town planning and of music. One perceives here the desire to prefabricate a moderate, rational order.

An inclination toward clarity and sharp intellectuality led Ivan Picelj to limiting formal means to their basic industrial, technical, and architectural elements. Silhouettelike combinations of elements—rectangles, curves, lines, and circles—combined with planelike, subdued colors, create a balance of harmony and dissonance (247).

After World War II arose Abstract Expressionism, a form of art with an emotional impulse which succeded in destroying the barriers of an objective world of forms and which flooded its time with the visual power of its expression. Certainly the interpretation of inner, spiritual attitudes through the spontaneous expression of pictorial forms is an echo of reality. Such art is like spiritual writing, and following its lead we may decipher internal areas of existence in the unconscious current of the self-representational faculties. This sort of art no longer has any analogy with the classical world of forms and visible reality. Neither by poetic transformation nor emotional associations does this art wish to remind one of the physical world.

Vieira da Silva's city pictures are products of the dissolution and transformation of technological and earthly space into dream and abstraction. She penetrates all earthly matter but still keeps the shores of earthly objectivity in misty but attainable sight.

In 1940, in Montreal, Jean-Paul Riopelle and Paul-Emile Borduas founded the Automatiste movement. The Surrealist principle of *écriture automatique* was resurrected here in a new variation as abstract art emphasizing instinct. Riopelle's painting is important because it signifies a fusion of guided instinct with refined vitality, and sounds vigorously, like Bartók's *Allegro Barbaro*.

Ernst Wilhelm Nay (149) made modulations of color sound together contrapuntally. His *Symphony in White, Instrumentation in Yellow, Rising Blue*, and all the shades of green, orange, and purple are nonrhythmical color constellations full of spiritual tension and abstract purity. These disk pictures are neither meant to represent the pure resonance of some great brightness, nor are they symbolic of perfection, nor do they designate the sketch of a fundamental world construction. They should be conceived of as spheres colliding with and penetrating one another. They become circles that open and close. They are world eye and genital eye: the cave of conception and the devouring grave; circles that look and perceive; eyes incapable of falling asleep, which then suddenly become opium capsules—which finally become geometric formulas of recognition.

Fritz Winter, a pupil of Klee's and Kandinsky's, freed himself from the object by internal argument. By means of sensitive optics he forms a transparent, islandlike, astral landscape, removed from time and space by curving black bars (152).

Antonio Zoran Musič's poetic, newly interpreted images of fishermen and shepherds surpass, and at the same time retain in themselves in abstract form, essential hieroglyphic elements of Dalmatian memory (281).

Serge Poliakoff's boldly simplified glowing forms are already self-created objects of the abstract gaze (259).

Internal, elementary natural powers inspire the painter Jean Bazaine; he is concerned not with the tree but with its blossoming and withering, not with the river but with its current and flow (146).

Using pure abstraction as his means of expression, Alfred Manessier attempts to return to the very sources of creation (147).

Hans Hartung (156) develops a means of expression that makes possible the process of construction, the improvisation of experience, and the direct translation of spiritual emotion into colorful forms. His sheaves of lines, placed in unbounded and dematerialized space, carry traces of spontaneity (65). The drama of creation becomes visible as the development of internal conditions.

Jean Fautrier (155) is also one of the discoverers of the new vision. On a flat, tinted surface, color is applied heavily, as though to a wall, with spatula strokes. Landscapes grow up, experienced from and transformed by excessive height. Maps of cosmic characteristics are outlined. In the aquarium of pictorial space, definitions of matter float, strongly formed, raw, and refined.

One of the early painters in whom instinctual art achieved explosive expression was Wols (154),

cofounder of Art Informal. In the flight from an infernal existence, the pictorial surface becomes the chronicle of his protests, an outcry against fate (277) in diagrams of nerves, arhythmical strokes of emotion, scrawls of coincidence, and spots of self-destruction in the trance of tensions, alcohol, and passion.

Emilio Vedova, too, detaches himself from the safeguard of convention and logic in order to conceive the picture as a passionately direct expression of spiritual conditions (153). The dynamic staccato of vehement dark rhythms and the glowing bright tones that shimmer behind them indicate the opposition of subconscious drives. The dominant darkness, a web of danger and menace, is irradiated by the shy searching lights of hope, by the half-tones of a sensitive affirmation of life.

Petar Lubarda reduces the visual experience of nature to its substance; formulas of fieldstone, sky, man, and animal are interwoven, dissolve, and become a vibrating radiance of color and light (151).

In his experiments, questions, and conclusions, in his variations and goals, Nicolas de Staël was of fateful importance to the young generation of painters who sought to fix their own attitudes to reality and abstraction. With their large surfaces, spatulated, rich in contrasts and luminous, his paintings are full of power, suggestiveness, and self-abandon (148).

The Italian Alberto Burri (160) makes use of simple burlap, wood, plastics, and corroded metals and thus achieves individual results. The concreteness of the raw substances seems to be canceled, the rough and banal materials transformed by his strict spatial compositions into reflections of a nonhuman, terrestrial landscape.

Several young Spanish painters have chosen pure painting as their area of investigation and construction. Antonio Tàpies (161) undertakes to discover the essence of primordial matter. With the divining rod of his special sensitivity he abandons himself to archaic impulse and with soft movement and unpretentious color modulations forms rugged, sandy expanses that evoke a sense of the past. It is as though the painter's poetic purity of vision had reawakened a past that now speaks to us.

Luis Feito's chromatic modulations in smoky gray and melting browns (162) produce an effect as though of a crater landscape seen through a thick fog and from a cosmic distance: "a surface which I love, which I make, which I cultivate. I burrow in its roots. I tear them up until I come upon my furrow. It grows, and I meet it. I beat it, I break it, I destroy it. . . ."

With rapid and sensitive instinct the Yugoslavian painter Edo Murtić conquers the dividing wall between the external and internal, above and below, time and distance, in order to define the now transparent substance and the musical optics of a new, universal experience.

The spiritual landscape of the Polish painter Tadeusz Kantor grows out of the substance of fluid, moving color. Following the eternal path of his instinct, he forms dynamic rhythms and spontaneous, independent, dissonant sounds (150).

Spontaneous expression and passionate impulsiveness give the painting of Bernhard Schultze its tension-laden dynamism. To him the creative process means submersion in uncontrolled and dangerous layers of existence, dramatic encounters with the essences of the ego and of matter.

Post-Tachist painting is now concentrated more on sculptural, spatial, and material expression. It strives to re-establish pictorial composition; it wants to get away from Abstract Expressionism but without accepting a rational geometrical conception.

K. R. H. Sonderborg's circling, diagonal brush strokes break through the static nature of his picture (272). Klaus Jürgen Fischer's monochrome relief paintings (245) remind one in their scratches and engravings of geological processes and powers.

In harmony with the discoveries of modern scholarship, artists attempt to express more or less consciously that which is unperceptualized. They do this by allowing themselves to be taken over without reservations by unconscious impulses.

Even though abstract art was born in Europe, it gained inspiration from the attitudes of Zen Buddhism, from Chinese ideograms and modern Japanese calligraphy. Such an influence can be strongly confirmed in the abstract painting of North America.

The art of America is not only the meeting of Europe and New York but also the contact and marriage of Occident and Orient. Mark Tobey's Eastern pilgrimage to Buddhism attests to this (60, 158). His painting is lyrically meditative, and his inner excitability becomes visible seismographically in the runic writing of his abstract symbols.

Some of the psychograms of the young American artists derive from the unification of Western expression with Oriental meditation. The spare textures and the screened and microscopic forms are portrayed in monumental dimensions. Perhaps this is a reflection of the size of the American continent.

The heavy beams, the gray-black, dynamic pictorial signs of Franz Kline (52) establish a presentiment of boundless and impenetrable spaces. The nervous handwriting of Jack Tworkov allows us to imagine the flooding color of a globe seen in distant flight. Bradley Walker Tomlin's rhythmical boxes give the painterly, organized, urbanist aspects of dream cities. The eruptions of Willem de Kooning, too, are dynamic; they give one a presentiment of the abysses of internal darkness (159). Mark Rothko's squares (164) shimmer in the aquarium of uncertainty like sunken portions of the earth.

In Adolph Gottlieb's pictorial world the graphical signs, the gradations and modulations of material are the reflection of an internal world. He is concerned with the problems of projecting pictorial forms that are difficult to grasp and fleeting, that possess an emotional value for him.

What thought connections do these floating parallelograms awaken in us: Barnett Newman's pictorial spaces divided by flaming stripes (236), and Clyfford Still's silent, macabre walls of matter?

All these seek a new relationship with space, not with objects, and not even the relationships of objects to one another, but rather their inclusiveness, their transformations in constantly changing, floating space; matter turned into motion, transformed into energy in infinite littleness and infinite expansion.

Sam Francis' proliferating, peacock-blue, glowing green, hyacinthlike amoebae creep like vines in the white depths of space. The spiny tracks of color rays in Jackson Pollock (157) seem to derive from nuclear impulses. They are moving streams of color discharging into one another, embracing the unconscious and the intentional, the coincidental and the optional. These canvases, with color applied by a spatula or squeezed out of a tube, or laid on the ground and then squirted with color through a box full of holes, deeply stimulated and influenced the younger generation. This is the purest instinctual painting, the direct gesture of color.

Among the young American sculptors there are some who employ and treat destroyed material, such as rusty metals and charred wood. Ashes become fertile here, and a dilapidated wall turns into an experience. The attempt to create existential symbols for or against deterioration, negation, destruction, and death has led to the production of shreds, things crumbling away, the patina, and the pure material.

For the first time in the history of modern art, there has come into existence in New York an indigenous school, which can easily be compared in rank with the Ecole de Paris, and which even influences European art: the art of psychic improvisation —Action Painting.

Led by instinct, by the sensitivity of the nervous system, American artists evoke the structural forms of matter, the dynamic principle of life. Not till Abstract Expressionism, the Informal variant of modern painting, was art able to abandon itself completely to subconscious powers. This method, which rejects any intellectual control, is like a trip through the darkness of the universe, without compass, purpose or map. Perhaps, however, some artist, if he re-enters the brightness of critical consciousness, will finally revise his creative output and, inspired by the course of guided coincidence, will correct his pictures with intellectual insight.

VII

ANTIART AND THE NEW REALITY

The Return to the Natural and the Unnatural

Today I visited that place where the garbage men dump their rubbish. God, how beautiful that was! Tomorrow they are sending me a few worthwhile objects collected from that heap—among others broken street lanterns to be looked at or to be used as model—if you wish. The whole thing was like an Andersen fairy tale. What a collection! All these old objects which have resigned their services—baskets, kettles, bowls, oil cans, metal wires, street lanterns, clap-pipes. . . .

Vincent van Gogh to Anthon van Rappard, 1883

During the final phases of a cultural period, when a civilization turns its back on the tortures of life, when a virtuoso refinement and polish take the place of pure instinct and intense living, one frequently notices radical changes in artistic activities.

Examples of such a striving for renewal and replenishing of vital strength can be found in artistic expressions from the beginning of recorded history: there is the love lyric stressing feeling in the sacerdotal elements of the late Egyptian dynasties; the idylls of Theocritus sung in a folkloric manner; the bucolic poesy of Hellenism; pastoral novels current among a feudalistic society living a life removed from nature; the crude dialect of François Villon's ballads; Rabelais's delight in exploring the most naïve elements of speech; the setting of secluded and sensitive simplicity we find in the art of Rococo; Jean Jacques Rousseau with his return to nature and simplicity; the gripping naturalism in Courbet's painting; and finally, Gauguin sailing to the islands of the primitive, and the simplistic vividness and clarity in the paintings of Henri Rousseau.

Dadaism, with its intended childishness, the paradise language of its sound poems, its noise-music, and its offenses and provocations, was nothing but an uprising. The Dadaists were revolting against man's alienation from nature, and more so against the monstrosities of the laws and conventions of their society.

Hugo Ball, one of the founders of Dadaism, defines this movement in his 1916 diary:

"The Dadaist fights against the agony and death frenzy of our time. Uninclined to show wisdom and reserve, he cultivates the curiosity of a person still capable of discovering an amusement and joy in the questionable forms of the Fronde. He knows that the world of systems has become shattered, and he is aware that his time has opened a grand rubbish sale of philosophers who lost their divine attributes and that there is a demand for hard cash. When the small shop owner experiences his first moment of fright and the beginning of a bad conscience, the Dadaist will already have his moment of laughter and appeasement. . . ."

An analogous turning point toward the primitive in our time is the movement called Pop art. This art can make no return to nature, for it is a reflection of our technological world of machines and of our civilizing diligence. No matter which way the Pop artist turns, he will always be surrounded by the primitive background of our industrial society. Part of the essence of Pop art comprises a resistance against the superiority of the human spirit. Its anti-intellectual and anti-European attitude reveals a nostalgia for simplicity, innocence, and possibly more a longing for the ordinary day-to-day living.

Jean Arp speaks about the origin of the word Dada:

"Tzara found this word on February 8, 1916, at six in the afternoon in the Café de la Terrasse [Zurich]. . . . Dada means 'yes, yes' in Romanian. In French it means 'gee-gee'—hobby horse! In German it designates a silly naïveté connected with baby talk. . . ."

The international meaning of this word points to the international character of the group of artists gathered in Zurich during World War I. There was the Romanian-French poet Tristan Tzara, the Alsatian sculptor Jean Arp, the Hungarian painter Marcel Janco, and the German writers Hugo Ball and Richard Hülsenbeck.

Preceding these activities in Zurich were other experiments and manifestations in art and antiart. Picasso and Braque had begun to include fragments of objects in their works. Boccioni built part of a window frame into several of his compositions. But above all, the Dadaists were influenced by Marcel Duchamp. By 1911 he had already succeeded in formulating through a system of heterogenous aspects—in the vein of Cubism—a definite mobility of mechanical equipment (140). One year later he created his *Nude Descending a Staircase,* which represented the kinetic procedure in fixed phases of images, moving in a filmlike manner. In 1914 he began his series of Ready-Mades. From broken pieces and parts taken from the technical world he created almost unexpected, magically estranged object compositions. Their meaning was a separation from all tradition and a complete emancipation of the aesthetic element in art. A result of provocation, irony, and play, these constructions of the absurd became a highly significant inspiration to the neo-Dadaist movement of today.

Duchamp did not translate the meaning of objects and equipment into the language of representation; rather, he restored the original reality of the thing. The very act of including certain meaningless objects of daily use within the unfamiliar sphere of art lent his Ready-Mades their fetish power of radiation. They are the masterworks of antiart.

Hans Richter, painter and film producer, who was connected with Dada since 1916 and who later produced abstract, avant-garde movies, presents an impressive analysis of his time in his book *Dada—Kunst und Antikunst.* Here he describes how and why a group of talented artists and writers, suffering from the destructions of World War I, came to regard art as superfluous and worthy only of disdain:

"Quite certainly, neither the bottle rack nor the toilet bowl is meant to be art. . . . With his Ready-Mades Duchamp demonstrated a reality which was to be placed face to face with the Laocoön and the Venus de Milo, as a purgative against a deceiving and self-deceiving world, and against a society so ruined that Duchamp managed to find a satisfactory expression for it in a Mona Lisa with mustache."

Such was the standpoint of negation of all ethical and aesthetic norms, a radical skepticism reacting against the dogma of a social existence, it also had to turn into a negation of art:

"Art has reached its end; it has dissolved into nothing. We are left with the nihil alone. Illusion has been removed with the help of logic. And what replaces the illusion? A vacuum of all moral or ethical elements. We live within a declaration of *nothing* which is neither cynical nor regretful. It is a statement of fact, and one has to acknowledge it."

The transposition of Dada from literature to art was accelerated when Francis Picabia arrived in Zurich. In the spirit of Duchamp and from the geometric humor of his own blueprints Picabia created surprisingly Dadaistic paintings (134). There was also Man Ray, who had begun with Cubism and come to Dadaism. His technical experiments, so full of fantasy, managed—almost half a century later—to influence the Pop artists.

Kurt Schwitters, that grotesquely naïve, friendly figure of Dadaism, never belonged to its original circle. A generally human weakness of these artists in Zurich, who were otherwise so totally unconventional and untraditional, may count as an explanation. When Schwitters asked Hans Richter in 1918 to join the Dada Club, the latter exerted every effort to obtain a membership, but in vain. The club considered itself too exclusive and judged Schwitters' harlequin naïveté as plebeian.

In his house in Hanover, Schwitters developed the kind of new realism that manipulated real objects. He elaborated the possibilities of Cubist collages; out of waste products, insignificant leftovers of reality —torn shoe soles, pieces of wire, rags, floor cloths, envelopes, cheese wrappings, trolley-car tickets—and

out of fantasy, he created poetic forms of expression that he called "Merz" pictures, ironically referring to *Kommerzbank* ("bank of commerce") (141). Schwitters died in exile in England, where he left behind many works of art that have strongly influenced the development of English Pop art.

Those men who gave birth to the Dada movement were in their own time classical representatives of nihilism and of antiart. Today, however, they all seem to claim and defend the status of art for their movement. A good number of them are protesting against the activities of some of the younger neo-Dadaists, who appear to them as parvenus. Raoul Hausmann, one of the founders of the Dada school in Berlin, writes the following: "What Dada presented in opposition to a universal corruption was a new form of being. Neo-Dadaism on the other hand wants to be something: a success on the market. . . ."

And here a few angry words by Hans Richter:

"Automobiles half wrecked—they just leave them that way . . . they merely put up a crushed fender. Or they dip a naked, shapely young girl into paint and roll her across the canvas. They are offering stuffed corpses of dolls in baby carriages and a music recital where the pianist sits in front of the piano for ten minutes without playing a single note. They offer a theatrical performance where nothing is performed. They feed stuffed teddybears with custard and attach a potato to the end of an old toilet cord. They present a pitch-black labyrinth in which visitors to the museum can break a leg. There are halls with music boxes, foam-rubber animals and an artificial beach; rooms where the furniture hangs from the ceiling and where the paintings, like galaxies à *la* Kiesler, lie around on the floor. We are offered shooting-galleries in which the visitor is allowed to shoot into a rotating bag containing colors and where after a hit he will have colored an enormous, white piece of sculpture entitled *My Contribution to a Work of Art,* etc., etc. This is a world of smoking mountains, shaking citadels and tingling phalli; the whole fair has been sold out. . . ."

Marcel Duchamp, who already in his youth had done some Pop art and is therefore highly respected as the prophet of this movement, writes in a tone of moral disdain in a letter to Richter:

"This Neo-Dada which now calls itself the New Realism, Pop art, Assemblage, etc., is nothing but a cheap amusement which nourishes itself from achievements of the original Dada. When I discovered the 'Ready-Mades' I had in mind to discourage the aesthetic hubbub. But the Neo-Dada people are trying to use the Ready-Mades in order to discover their 'aesthetic value'! When I threw into their face the bottle rack and the urinoir I meant it as a provocation. But instead, they are now admiring it as an aesthetic beauty. . . ." After having caused a scandal in 1913 at the Armory Show, Duchamp later on received an honorary doctorate from Wayne University in Detroit.

Richard Hülsenbeck, one of the founding

fathers of Dadaism, who is now living in New York as a practicing psychoanalyst, also criticizes the young generation of Pop artists. He sees their creations as wax figures, related to the ones in Madame Tussaud's: "This is no longer art. It is a frozen reality, paralyzed photography and murdered life. . . ."

In terms of their temporal origins Dada and Pop art may perhaps be regarded as contrasting. But when seen from a historical perspective, the lines of demarcation will disappear. Presumably, both movements will appear as expressions of the same apocalyptic world feeling. Whereas the original Dada group was intellectually highly conscious of their feeling of protest and of their bitter suffering, the Pop artists at times appear to see themselves as minstrels singing about the joy of life and the affirmation of their technical surroundings. Nevertheless, both groups have in common the same climate of fragmentation, of fractured mass consumption and of the abrasion of our industrial cities. Consciously or unconsciously, they formulate the very crisis that cries out for a new world design.

Dada and Neo-Dada

The latest Neo-Dadaism is an attempt to establish autonomy of the shock. They are trying to present the "antifetish" as possessing an artistic attribute. . . .
Hans Richter

The destructive élan that was present in the manifestations of the Futurists, Surrealists, and Dadaists is now, in the second half of the twentieth century, newly expressed through Pop art and happenings. One might ask, what is being opposed in these actions? There is a rebellion against the artifi-

ciality and isolation of art, and against the commercialism of the art scene—that is, against its moral and aesthetic selling aspect. Furthermore, what is found objectionable is the idea of art representing a professional exercise.

There were already conscious as well as unconscious elements of such an attitude present in the deformation that Expressionism developed. There were the collage compositions of the Cubists, which included real objects, and the aggressive announcements of the Futurists: "The racing car . . . is more beautiful than the Victory of Samothrace." There is a good deal of blasphemy in the provocations of the Dadaists, and there is paradox in the Surrealist automatism. And now Pop art has entered the scene of antiart movements. Pop is meant to represent a stumbling block and a provocation: it presents objects of everyday use: sanitary equipment, bicycles packed in cellophane, kitchen utensils put into a post office, and garbage exhibited in glass boxes. Pop artists are exponents of antiart and public amusement. Happenings, too, have become an expression of the desire to exhibit the creative, artistic act. Whoever wishes to experience such an art will have to perform it: these are happenings constructed out of actual events and improvisations. There is neither a claim for eternal validity nor for the possibility of repetition. These are Dadaist games of mystery without the presence of a god.

Picasso's movie demonstrations of his working process and, even more, Georges Mathieu's painting before an audience count as evolutionary steps toward these latest developments. Yves Klein's anthropometric images of naked women dipped into blue paint, who in front of a sensation-hungry audience print their bodies like seals onto broad canvases, are also part of this group. These are magic ceremonies that not only show the work of art but also strip bare some of the artist's most inner elements.

The production process is most fascinating to the Pop artist. Some of the real objects of industry and the market that they take over and group into compositions are things like captions from photographs, comic strips, movie advertisements, magazine ads, and advertising leaflets. These are some of the retail and consumer elements of our large cities. And there is very little else happening in this particular phase of art. Quite certainly, this act of creation could hardly be burdened by metaphysical inquiries into the primordial meaning of things. The Pop artist produces paintings and sculptures very much as an industrial worker will use parts to put together a car.

The success of Pop art can be explained through a popular industrial consciousness as well as through the fetish character of merchandise in general. We are living in an age of mass production that turns out commodities on an expansive scale and at a rapidly accelerating speed. We are witnessing a geometric increase of production calling for limited durability of its objects. Merchandise travels from the factory through the department store to the consumer and finally to the rubbish heap, the car cemetery, the scrap dump, where it will finally be picked up again for new production purposes.

The death of these objects is followed by their resurrection in Pop art—a resurrection of dilapidated, dead things. The Day of Judgment has come for garbage, scraps, and broken glass. And a new value is attributed to them as objects without a function, placed in the midst of the artistic scene.

One might want to ask whether a real Coca-Cola bottle placed in a frame can offer the same authentic imagery content as a painted bottle in a still life by Chardin or Morandi. Allan Kaprow feels that an advertisement is as capable of giving a perfect representation of a Buick as were the Christian works of art in their portrayal of God. He says in a treatment on the future of Pop art:

"For all its directness, apparent objectivity and detachment from personal emotions, most Pop Art evokes a romance for the era of twenty to thirty years ago, the time of the artists' childhood. It is very much like the mood we find in the novels of Jack Kerouac. Villeglé's (183), Hains' and Rotella's tattered posters, seeing America from afar, whose proclamations and has-been goddesses are beaten by weather and age, recall Walker Evans' photos of years ago; Lichtenstein's cartoons and products have an iconography and style of the forties; Rosenquist's dreamlike and sometimes bitter-sweet atmosphere reminds us of the old montages of Lowell Thomas and Movietone News; Oldenburg's objects and their unrefined treatment probe quaint and ugly memories of the immigrant American and his store; Robert Indiana's signs are not from Madison Avenue but the small-town drugstore pinball machine, flashing 'Tilt!', crying out 'America!', the word he prints on them so often, the America of Dillinger holdups and *Hellzapoppin!* When I saw Warhol's diagram of Arthur Murray's dance lesson, I immediately remembered that the song of my Junior High School days was 'Arthur Murray . . . taught me dancin' . . . in a hurry . . . I had some time to spare . . .' You see, Pop Art doesn't 'go' the way Action Painting 'goes'; it isn't usually an art of the moment."

In 1956, Ronald B. Kitaj, then living in England, wrote the word *POP* on one of his paintings. It is part of a colloquial beatnik vocabulary and designates the central blocking lever on an American slot machine. It was the critic Lawrence Alloway who gave the name "Pop art" to this artistic direction, which in

England had originated under the influence of Schwitters. Its American variation invoked the folklore art of the cities. Parallel to the widespread American folk-singing world, which expresses events in a simple, poetic style, one can observe the growth of this new artistic direction, which especially distinguishes itself through popular comprehension and adaptation to the entertainment industry. The idealized philosophy of life of the Socialist Realism in the East has thus found its opposite in the illusionistic interpretation of reality of a "capitalist realism."

The masses of people who as a result of an industrial upheaval have been herded into the large cities and whose mentality is being formed by a world of supermarket merchandise, by such visual phantoms as television, movies, and news publications, are able to experience through Pop art their very surroundings and their life's aroma.

A Change of Climate in Art

I don't want a picture to look like something it isn't. I want it to look like something it is. And I think a picture is more like the real world when it's made out of the real world.

Robert Rauschenberg

In the United States a process of modern myth making is taking place. This process is being sped up not so much through literature as through film and television. In recent times, one could observe art abandoning its esoteric spheres. The cowboy is a folklore hero who has entered the movie houses and television programs. The sentimental teenage cult around the movie star James Dean cannot simply be

explained away as juvenile fanaticism and hysteria; it should be understood, rather, as a desperate longing for an ideal—a hero—whom one wishes to resemble, and who towers high above one's rigidly standardized day-to-day living. Tarzan, the great conqueror of the Hollywood wilderness, has his counterpart in the symbolic figure of Melville's Ahab. The popular figure in bearskin is somewhat like Faulkner's totem character Old Ben, the bear. This myth reaches from the prospector legends of the Wild West as far as the unforgettable tragic comedy of Charlie Chaplin. And Walt Whitman's ideal characters and George Gershwin's *Porgy and Bess* are also projections of an unconscious universal dream. And hasn't Al Capone too become a public hero, a gladiator of the metropolis who deserves to be seen on the movie and television screen just as much as great boxers, baseball players, pin-up girls, and astronauts?

Bob Dylan, the popular folk singer of American students, is a belated descendant of the angry young men. He combines the social criticism of the beat generation with the cosmopolitical brotherhood of Walt Whitman. This kind of poetry will open the eyes of an image-hungry mass audience in the United States, so that they may appreciate a form of art so close to their conceptions and to their way of being: Pop art.

In the middle of the twentieth century, the young generation is beginning to portray the possessions of its era: all objects and utensils of the urban society, as well as parts of their technical surroundings and the mass media.

"To have and to eat," according to Hans Richter, is the subject of the new still lifes by the Pop artists. In Holland in the sevententh and eighteenth centuries, artists painted the fruits of the land and the ocean, the plunder and merchandise brought home from their overseas colonies. Such things were portrayed for the pleasure of Dutch burghers and gourmets. Our young Pop artists are led by similar motives: they make plaster representations of a half-eaten breakfast and hang it on the wall. The food paintings of the Pop artists that were shown at the Sidney Janis Gallery in New York represent the superabundance constantly produced by our industries; stove and cake-tin by Oldenburg; supermarket by Raysse; coffee cups by Rotella; salads, sandwiches, and dessert by Thiebaud; and Indiana's black diamond with the invitation: "Eat!" Then we have Wesselmann's still life with hamburgers, coffee, and catchup, and Segal's lunch table.

A change in spiritual climate is not an unknown historical factor. For example, in the case of the aging Rembrandt not only do personal intrigues carry the blame for the sharp criticism he encountered and for the loss of prestige; there was also a definite change in taste taking place among his audience and clients.

They began to embrace an "elegant" form of classicism that led them to regard Rembrandt's works as an insult to their social position.

Perhaps it was the same for De Kooning (159), the central figure of Abstract Expressionism. Lonely and misunderstood, he watched the younger generation, who moments ago still admired and celebrated him, giving this new junk culture, Pop art, their full enthusiasm and attention. If one struck an analogy with Rembrandt here, it would have to be reversed. While Rembrandt was accused of preferring plebeian, vulgar, and ugly scenes, today it is the commonplace, absurd, and grotesque that is driving out the subjective, aristocratic style of Abstract Expressionism.

Surely Robert Rauschenberg and Jasper Johns stand between the limits of Abstract Expressionism and Pop art. Nevertheless, they are regarded as pioneers of the new style. Rauschenberg's large paintings (166) represent a combining element between De Kooning's expressive painting-writing and the lyric kaleidoscopy of Schwitters' collages. Rauschenberg's banal subjects, his photo and print citations, his underlining and overpainting are all points of reference and information regarding a social reality. They may be understood as a critical and spiritual engagement. Part of Rauschenberg's creative method is influenced by elements of the worn-out and of the dissociated—a method developed by Alberto Burri and in use since the Merz paintings. Rauschenberg's conception of reality reminds us of the early Scholastics who saw the world as composed of empirically observable, singular parts. Recently, Rauschenberg has been using silk screens, a method that lends his works a fetishlike emphasis on the object and a poetically estranged power of expression.

During the middle fifties, Jasper Johns began painting his targets. Like the targets, maps and banners obtain new emphasis and significance through his methods and unexpected hints. His wax applications and the use of lettering and analytical symbols are capable of changing totally standardized objects into something else, never before encountered (165).

Roy Lichtenstein turned away from Abstract Expressionism and began composing works out of advertising material, films, and comic strips. Without adding any actual painting, he simply placed into the realm of art the stereotyped action and the frozen, conventional elements of advertising: Hawaiian girls with bleak, arrested smiles, men in uniform embracing doll-like women. His method of using enlarged halftone screens and plexiglass lends his compositions the clinical sterility of beauty contestants (184).

James Rosenquist's paintings are done on different surfaces and are composed of varied elements and conflicting image-content. He uses fragments of organic and inorganic materials and from them composes a totality. Men, objects, and landscapes are brought together suddenly and with intentional disregard of perspective. The theme is determined not by the objects, but rather by the relation between the different fragments and the metamorphosis of things through new groupings (182).

One of the first men who organized a happening in New York was Jim Dine. He manages in his compositions to obliterate the limiting boundaries between real and painted object. Real ax and the game of painted axes turn into an illusional, variable unity. Ax, hammer, saw, or scissors are mounted on the surface of the picture. Facsimile rows of colored shadows cover the canvas, integrate parts of the tools into the picture, and thereby make them seem unreal (167).

A good many of the Pop artists incorporate into their pictures real parts of the environment. Tom Wesselmann, for example, constructs his works by combining artistically imagined elements with real objects (177). There is a room, for example, with a table and a window looking out on a mounted town or a landscape. Or he will use parts of a real radiator or prints hanging on a wall, such as a nude by Matisse, all of which help to obliterate the distinction

between imagination and reality. While Schwitters constructs his collages from scraps, broken pieces, and shreds, Wesselmann employs parts or else whole objects for his plastic conceptions. The effect is to set up a reflection from one type of reality to another.

Such reverberations between two distinct realities already form an element in the works of the Italian Mannerists. Their concepts and imaginations have continued to produce their effect up to and including the illusionistic constructions of the Surrealists of our day.

First traces of such a mixture of relief sculpture and illusionistic painting are found in late Roman antiquity. The masters of Renaissance perspective, such as Mantegna and Uccello, were responsible for inspiring the Mannerists in their illusionistic daring, which culminates in the spatial explosions of the High Baroque style.

In Spanish and Italian churches and chapels of the sixteenth and seventeenth centuries one finds paintings and sculptures that are highly realistic in their reproduction of natural objects. A striking example (169) is *The Massacre of the Innocents* reproduced from a pilgrim's chapel (built between 1524 and 1620) on the Sacro Monte near the small town of Varallo in the Italian province of Vercelli. The terrible scene of the infants' murder becomes a decorative, splendid tale through an operatic, dramatic form of representation. The colorful, pompously dressed dolls blend perfectly with the figures painted on the walls. Beneath the magnificent stage set of Baroque porticoes, baldachins, furniture and carpets we witness the actions of heroes in their historical, exotic dress, one observes images similar to those created in the nineteenth century by the Viennese artist Makart, or presented in recent Hollywood films by Cecil B. de Mille.

Such a world of semblance and pretense, of pseudomythology and fetishism of materials, carries something frightful and intimidating with its euphoristic banalities and reminds one of Marisol's mannequins (174), George Segal's plaster robots (170), and the environments by Dine, Wesselmann (177) and the other Pop artists.

While the tragic event represented in the shrine of Sacro Monte, with its obtrusively precious material, was designed as faith-inducing propaganda, Pop artists are using by-products and cheap consumer goods to express their form of understatement. In this manner, a combination of illusionism and the world of objects expresses the paradoxes and the great void of feeling that haunt our modern civilization, and at the same time it ridicules the cult of ownership.

Andy Warhol was the person who took over the technique of the film and newspaper industry, introducing to art journalistic information in picture sequences. In the same way advertising slogans hammer consumer products into our minds, through constant repetition, Warhol presents us with the mechanical multiplication of movie stars and Coca-Cola bottles (172). So far, people like Marilyn Monroe or Elvis Presley have been considered unique individuals, never to reappear. In Warhol's sequences of pictures they turn into mass products. *Thirty is better than one* is the title of Warhol's 1963 oil on canvas of the Mona Lisa. The word "Mona" of course reminds of the Greek *monas*, "unity." Therefore, the use of Mona Lisa in the plural, presented as an article for mass consumers, seems quite absurd. Multiplicity and the blasphemy of its attitude makes this picture into something novel. There was already a form of sequence representation in Far Eastern Buddhism. Ever since the middle of the first millennium, China has had places with ninety-three carved Buddhas. Representations of one thousand Buddhas have existed in Japan since the later Heian period, 794–1185. And there is also a woodblock engraving showing the *Three Thousand Buddhas of Three Worlds*, 1278 (171). Warhol thus makes use of multiplicity to point to the mass age we live in, a time that has created the individual's exchangeability and mean-

inglessness. The original multiple representations of Buddha were intended to express the indestructibility of the One despite his multiplicity in incarnation: as the One, he becomes manifold, yet in his multiplicity continues to retain self-identity.

Such accumulative representations of a divinity testify to the decline of a great creed. Surely one cannot fail to notice here that institutionalization has reduced the private prayer to a purely mechanical action. These Buddhist prints, serving the use of this life and of the one hereafter, clearly indicate that number has taken the place of spirit.

It would be too simple, however, to reduce Warhol's intended meaning to the mass consumers' world of posters. His basic theme is the contemporary drama of civilization. The display window of his rather hypnotic repetitions offers us cruelty as well: racial persecutions, suicides, traffic accidents, catastrophes, and brutality. His multiplied throne of legal murder, the electric chair—in a twelve-time representation—reveals without disguise the icy-blue vacuum of horror. The effect of Warhol's compositions is to be found in the unequivocal quality of documentation: death without *pompes funèbres;* the life of literature undressed, as functional structure in the X-ray clarity of his vision.

Pop art has succeeded in calling into question the boundary between painting and sculpture. There are some sculptors who will treat their objects with paint, and there are painters who will build sculptural elements into their paintings. The sculpture-paintings by Claes Oldenburg are difficult to judge from an aesthetic standpoint. Forming and deforming them, he amasses consumer goods and foodstuffs of plaster (173), furniture and household equipment of intentionally chosen ugly materials painted in red. Oldenburg says:

"I am for the art of red and white gasoline pumps and blinking biscuit signs. I am for the art of old plaster and new enamel. I am for the art of slag

I am for the art of ... or the art of bending ... them and by pulling ... . I am for the art of ... t of underwear and ...

... n artistically created ... d to present it as a ... object—was initiated ... ture-collages go fur- ... between picture and ...

... mpositions fills en-

vironments with commodities, George Segal in his sculptures constructs their environments. Sculptures referring to real objects have natural dimensions: they are plaster casts of people, harmoniously fused with objects of their day-to-day living. A gas-station attendant holding a can of oil in his hand; a figure next to a Coca-Cola machine; a woman drinking a cup of coffee in a restaurant. These are arrested moments, life photography, frozen life (171). Segal's naturalistic figures remind one of the lava-preserved figures of Pompeii. His pieces are quite likely to bring about a feeling of indecision and dreamlike magic. At the same time they may arouse distrust with their suggestion of figures in a waxworks.

Pop Art and the New Realism

Pop art carries out a fusion between the iconic and formative elements of objects and prefabricated pictures. Only one danger lurks in the background with respect to these new "icons," namely, the mythicizing of their products.

Gillo Dorfles

A better model hardly exists for the transformation of Western man's attitude and world outlook during the twentieth century—and specifically the second half—than literature. It reflects the growing relativization of values, the collapse of moral norms, and the eruption of antihuman, primitive instincts.

The production of *Waiting for Godot* in 1955 in London brought respect and moral repute to the English theater. Beckett gave resonance to the angry voices of those young men who had begun open warfare against cultural phraseologies and social hypocrisy. Also after 1955, the young artists of the London

Royal College of Art began to mobilize elements of the banal, absurd, and cruel. They introduced kitsch and advertising to art in order to rid themselves of conventions of the abstract and in order to fight their battle against their time and society.

Ronald B. Kitaj, an American by birth, studied in New York, Vienna, and London. He adds a worldwide historic background to his paintings. He synthesizes parts of collage, writing, and picture. The event he portrays is not meant to be a genre image. Behind his theme one should be able to recognize an inner meaning.

Allen Jones is fascinated by the dialectic of polar structures and the harmonious play of rest and movement. His bus compositions, parachutists, and lovers have contours that flow into one another through movement (176). He effects a modulation of sharp and blurred images, very much like life photography, and very much like the method used by the Futurists several decades ago. Visible contours around individual objects are blurred or totally obliterated, so that above and below, front and back, have been reduced to mere relations of time and space.

Richard Hamilton's paintings are done in the spirit of social criticism. As he himself puts it, he attempts to create a new artistic image, seeking comprehension for man's perpetually changing condition and life's constantly altering direction. To Hamilton, banal objects and the bond between man and his daily life do not imply a negation of the aesthetic. The Pop message is as legitimate as any other form of artistic style. For the creation of the painting *Pin-Up* he took his inspiration from *Playboy* girls and *Beauty Parade* girls, but also from Renoir's nudes. Elements of reliefs, architectural drawings, advertising techniques, sex symbols, and irony find an elegant synthesis in his works.

Peter Blake, too, produces collage-constructions in which he combines pieces from sexy postcards with parts of reliefs. His arrangements represent a combination of glittering advertising and an obviously naïve longing for the neon paradise of a metropolitan youth. His paintings seem to grow out of the dream world of a new mass mythology (179).

Peter Phillips presents us with a sky of commercialism, where the stars become emblems of power, honorary badges, radiating the erotic by means of miniature nudes. Joe Tilson creates colorful, geometric relief constructions, using symbolic forms, words, and objects that have the effect of a Gestalt sign (181).

David Hockney's stylized, posterlike figures, with their lyric transformations, already seem to go beyond the unwritten, yet methodized, Pop program (180).

Eduardo Paolozzi's use of technical objects or worn-out parts of machinery tempts one to seek a relation between his sculptures and Pop art (90). His pieces of sculpture are machines without a function. They represent mixtures of mechanical and organic elements. Simultaneously, though, they are bearers

of the absurd—threatening symbols of something that man created and that then turned against him: technology. Paolozzi's sculptures, which have had their effect way beyond England's borders, succeed in paralyzing the human element and turning it into a mechanism, while allowing mechanism to grow into something aesthetic.

The neo-Dadaists of the United States and England incorporate the found object aesthetically into their compositions. The neo-Dadaists in Paris, who call their movement Nouveau Réalisme, can look at any object—even a totally unchanged one—and call it a potential work of art. It is simply choice and presentation that account for an object's transcending its vulgar and general sphere of reference to become a work of art. The theoretical framework of this movement has been expressed by the critic Pierre Restany:

"To give recognition to an autonomous expressiveness in objects of daily use does more than call into question the concept 'work of art.' Such a recognition elevates the poetic adventure to another level altogether. In New York one makes use of Ready-Mades in order to counteract the exploitation of Action Painting, while the New Realists in Paris express their disgust with the exaggerations of Tachism. They distrust the naturalistic humor of Art Brut, and they finally come to overthrow the ambiguity of the Informal. . . . The New Realists in Paris have discovered a new and modern sense for a metropolis-nature. They hail the fundamentalism of the real—in sharp opposition to Tachism's aesthetic combinations —and they are practicing a form of elementary hygiene. . . ."

This group of French neorealists was originally composed of twelve members: Tinguely, César, Hains, Arman, Christo, Dufrêne, Deschamps, Yves Klein, Villeglé, Rotella, Spoerri, and Niki de Saint Phalle.

Daniel Spoerri's "*tableaux-pièges*" are wooden

boards on which he has pasted everyday objects, such as tools, books, and food (168). Related to this idea are Arman's "*tableaux-robots*," which represent a collection of objects belonging to a specific person and capable of making a statement about that person. Both artists use scraps and leftovers, allowing their content of meaning to provoke literary-historic associations. These worn-out objects are employed not simply as aesthetic forms, but rather as a totality of relation to man. Arman's portrayal of Yves Klein consists of photos, tools, and wearing apparel placed in a glass case. They remind one of reliquaries and souvenirs, or objects such as Rembrandt's easel and palette or Beethoven's music stand and death mask. In opposition to these sentimental and memory-retaining assemblages there are some rather destructive, anarchic ones—for instance, Arman's violin of anger, one of the sequence of broken musical instruments. Violin, cello, horn, and guitar are beaten to pieces by the artist, and in the rhythm of his destructive ecstasy they will be placed together, ordered, and mounted into a picture. The idea of destruction becomes even clearer in the explosion pictures and objects, as well as in the piece of sculpture of the blasted sports car. Niki de Saint Phalle's destruction-sculptures done with shots into the art object are also part of this strange group. Are these chaotic acts of protest against the violence and death instinct that hide behind the mask of civilization? Or are they expressions of the hidden forces of sadism and the perverse joy of demolition, destruction, and extinction? Or do they perhaps express certain ambivalent potentialities and instinctive actions of youth and bravado?

Arman calls his 1960 household leftovers in a glass case *Poubelles*. They are cardboard boxes, tin cans, bottles, pieces of broken glass, strings, scraps of cloth, pieces of bread, plastic parts of toys, and different kinds of crumbled paper. This medium allows for a successful variation of everyday objects. Bottles are filled with various fluids, an alarm clock

is placed in a glass case; then comes the turn for gas-mask collections, *Home Sweet Home,* and the tragically grotesque assemblage *Little Hands*—doll hands of all sizes and colors, which in their rhythmic amassment look like chopped-off children's hands.

Hains, Rotella, Dufrêne, and Villeglé use torn posters and clippings from political writings, emphasizing their implicit meaning and thus making a statement about reality. César takes an old Buick and crushes it against the column of the ephemeral. He constructs a memorial to the death of a motor. Jean Tinguely, whose sculptures are pseudomachines, constructs his demonstration from wheels, iron scraps and wires (213).

A careful observation of the artistic movement of the past years will inevitably lead one to discover a close connection between the contrasting forms of this neonaturalism and certain elements of Dadaism, Surrealism, and Abstract Expressionism. The Italian Pistoletto uses silhouettes and figures on highly polished metal that draw the observer and his surroundings into the frame as a changing mirror image (175). Baj, from Milan, turns ready-made figures into monsters that remind one of the figures of Dubuffet and Paolozzi. They are heros of science fiction and mystery stories. His compatriot, Ceroli, creates figurelike wood carvings thematizing the grotesque and banal. The Germans H. P. Alvermann, Winfred Gaul, Konrad Lueg, and Gerd Richter have added their own variant to the Pop movement. Alvermann combines ready-mades, collages, and sculpture-painting into a construction, creating a polemic against conditions of power and spirit: art as "sociogram," a provocation implicit in the union of word and object, idea and form (178).

The possibility of introducing junk into art—that is, of using nonartistic media—leads to the mass media of a political, ideological language. Richter and Lueg organized an exhibition ironically titled Capitalistic Realism. Richter's paintings become a synthesis with life photography; Lueg's silhouettelike figures, mounted in front of a reflecting background, bear the dynamic character of advertising graphics. Because the art of this movement no longer insists on making visible that which is, but rather decides to choose and to represent the visible, it has become possible for photography and other reproduction techniques to function as a substitute for the artist's eye.

It seems that the entire wave of Pop art, which rolled across both the American and the European scene, has already reached its climax. Artistic styles are temporally conditioned. Ever since the middle of the nineteenth century, changes have greatly accelerated. And the twentieth century sees a change of cultural movements at the speed of news broadcasts and television reportage. Today it is already possible to observe a heightened awareness of the meaning of an object, as well as a stronger willingness to free art from its aristocratic isolation.

Seen from a historical perspective, the boundary between Dada and Pop art will undoubtedly disappear one day; both are bound to retain validity as variants of one basic idea in twentieth-century art. There will simply be a differentiation in nuances of expression, somewhat like the difference between father and son, inventor and administrator; nevertheless, a unity will be apparent in the execution of the adventurous revolt of modern art.

VIII

ART IN A TECHNOLOGICAL AGE

Invention of the Object

In essence, sculpture means occupancy of space, the construction of a thing with hollows and volumes, mass and void, variations and reciprocal tensions, and finally their equilibrium.

Henri Laurens

Placed in the dangerous and baffling conditions of nature, naked, unarmed, without specialized organs and instincts, man had to develop and use his intelligence to create substitute organs for himself through technology. From the earliest flint weapons and artifacts to atomic reactors, the development of the substitute organs has resulted in complete substitution for the organic.

All working mechanisms are first modeled on precedents taken from observed nature. The transition from the tool to the machine is quantitative. But the latest sources of energy no longer have any structural identity with organic life. Their technical form is nonmaterial and nonobjective.

In a time when technology has permeated the world, objects having no relationship to natural forms are invented out of a fascination with machinery and out of constructive consciousness. The object created by the spirit of this age—denatured, abstract, and autonomous—becomes for a time the central theme of the arts. The purely technical, the geometrical, the functional are considered "beautiful." "The

racing car whose body is packed with huge pipes, which seems to run on ball bearings, is more beautiful than the Victory of Samothrace," says the manifesto of the Futurist F. T. Marinetti. Thus technology, apart from its technical uses, becomes an absolute in art. Its functional form is seen as a gesture of existence, the artificial form of the machine as a mythical figure. It is a modern idol containing hidden substance.

While the poets and painters of Futurism prize the beauty of machines, the Dadaists and Surrealists demonstrate their demonic nature. Francis Picabia's blueprint objects and Max Ernst's coupling of implements and inventions all grew out of an enchantment with machines. Advertisements for typewriters and phonographs, mail-order catalogues became the dream books of poetic speculation. Marcel Duchamp's ready-made images are taken from the everyday world. They are isolated, profane objects that take on a fetishistic character through their alienation: a bicycle mounted on a chair, a corkscrew set on a marble pedestal. These are variants of the *objets trouvés* of the Surrealists and closely related to the Dadaists' montages motivated by irony and revolt.

In contrast to these antiaesthetic combinations, these objects derived from irony and intellect, the Russian modernists Tatlin, Rodchenko, Lissitzky, Pevsner, Gabo, and later the Dutch group De Stijl invented painted and plastic forms that derived their creative affirmation from the technical and scholarly climate as well as from the new materials.

The measuring, calculating, perceptive, and critical intellect stands in contrast to the spiritual, expressive, instinctual, and subterranean. Just as Cézanne and the Cubists analyzed the constructive backgrounds of things into crystalline forms, so the world, stripped of its secrets by the engineers, now appeared as a landscape of elementary geometrical forms.

Fernand Léger (138) created mechanical elements, transposed objects invented by the technicians.

"In the search for polish and intensity, I have used the machine as others use the nude or still-life; I have never enjoyed copying the machine. I invent mechanical pictures as others invent fantasy landscapes. The technical element is not a dogma that I have subsumed, not an attitude, but a means to make power and force visible."

The puristic experiments of Amédée Ozenfant and the painter-architect Jeanneret, known as Le Corbusier, in France and Willi Baumeister in Germany strive for a synthesis of technology and art.

In Malevich it was a square on a clean surface, in Mondrian a system of rectangular fields: a harmonious, architectural, pictorial simile that represents the functional clarity and the postulate of absolute painting. Puristic Constructivism led to the complete release from the models of nature. The aesthetic process was stimulated by a dictate of geometry, a catechism of the right angle or the circle.

The basic principles of Naum Gabo's sculptures are not destruction and decomposition, but construction and harmony. The compactness of mass is suspended; linear space constructions, artificial ribs stretched with nylon threads, kinetic and static forms indicate the new views and transhuman measurements of a cosmic, poetic vision (188, 197).

Antoine Pevsner's suggestive metal constructions are gloomy idols with secret and visionary powers. Their wavelike rhythms, their curving monumental forms are taken from the strict canon of scientific order—they are sacred symbols of the "godless dignity" of man (204).

In the search for sources, for the dormant beginning, for the first breath of form, Constantin Brancusi met the contemplative wisdom of the Far East. Many followed him: Isamu Noguchi's works demonstrate in elegant simplicity the penetration of modern spirituality and Zen Buddhist concentration.

Jean Arp (216) considered artistic creativity an organic process resulting in an imitation not of nature but of its essence. Alienation from the object was not enough for him. He strove for yet uncreated forms—images of existence, not of appearances, and as anonymous as creation itself.

Younger artists created in a similar mode. Alberto Viani created signs out of tension and balance (218); Vojin Bakić created spacious and self-enclosing volumes, in which human forms and objects flow into one another (219).

The internal and external unity that Henry Moore consciously attempts also lives where the last memories of human form and earthly objects have faded (80). Barbara Hepworth's ringing structures are strung like instruments; these abstract Orpheuses, technical menhirs covered with legendary spider webs, open silent substance and make it sound (207).

Sculptor technologists form their metallically welded and carved sculpture with the aggressive flame of the welding torch. Julio Gonzalez' idea of drawing in space with metal lines offered a generation of artists new possibilities for development.

David Smith's stern calligraphy drawn in the sky is an echo of the wrought-iron writing and the form symbols of Picasso and Gonzalez.

Pietro Consagra's figures are reliefs. They are wood, stone, and metal plates, irregularly scratched, hollowed and sawed out, covered with iron splinters —monumental writing tablets bearing the undecipherable runes of dreams. Berto Lardera's fantastic architecture of sharply bordered pierced metal disks creates an intensive impression of space by its suggestiveness and coolness. The expressive, Surrealistic sculptures of the American Theodore Roszak are baroque figural signs of fateful possession. The Swiss Robert Müller builds dematerialized forms of curves and domes out of sheet and rolled metal, developing surface tension and volume in space.

The intensified existence of imperceptible things is also the concern of Dušan Džamonja: lyrically tuned, suggestive pictures, cut, hammered, armored with a needle forest of spikes, covered by a silver-shimmering lead crust and sometimes radiating hidden things from glass intestines.

Harry Bertoia transforms plantlike tendrils into a pierced wall of shining bronze that becomes an element of architectural construction. The transposition of leafy twigs into the denatured flora of technological civilization displayed in one of the large New York banks shows the endeavor of sculpture to unite with architecture. Sculptural architecture and architectural sculpture strive toward one another.

For the architect and sculptor André Bloc, sculptural art, from the construction of a city to an individual object, means organization of space.

Max Bill (214) seeks to re-establish the unity of the pictorial arts of synthetically unifying sculptural and colorful graphic elements. Bill pursues the Bauhaus idea of intensified handicraft as the point of departure for the creation of an objective art.

His meeting with Mondrian inspired Alexander Calder (215) to the creation of his early puristic, technological forms. But it is not only nature that knows the dynamic principle: the spirit of technology, too, springs from this principle of motion. Calder succeeds in going from stark, geometric constructions to the moving images of his mobiles formed of light metals. Perhaps he was also inspired by the little gold disks decorating the eyebrows and lashes of ancient Peruvian gold mummy masks from Huarmey. These and the earrings and pendants shiver in the wind of one's breath. Calder's jingling, unfolding leaf stars,

these wind chimes of our time, have left the realm of geometry. The metallic plant metamorphoses, the blooming tree models moving in the wind and reminding us of flower arrangements in Japanese gardens, are also images that unite in themselves the opposing tendencies of time. Calder, it seems, has left the polemic phase of modernism behind. His technological bud forms do not grow only in the earth of understanding: they are forms and signs of spiritual concentration and intellectual alertness and are related to the concrete symbols of the Far East.

For the Espace group in Paris the work of art is not a matter of collections and museums but a part of urban life; the form and color of buildings, moving elements in paintings, colorful and mobile sculptures are essential parts of the total art work and identical with existence. Duchamp and Moholy-Nagy had been concerned with analogous problems. Calder's mobiles, Tinguely's painted mechanisms, and Schöffer's luminoscope are part of the family of dynamic spatial sculptural art.

Nicolas Schöffer (196) wanted to use the concrete walls of dams, the façades of modern cities, the crashing glass walls of waterfalls, and snow-covered peaks as the screen for the colored projections of his luminoscope. The natural and architectural planes are covered with moving and constantly changing pictures. The optic plan may be enriched by tonal chords that can be guided with the help of the photoelectric cell.

When the artist stands in his studio among his dynamic, imaginative sculptures, the vertically and horizontally harmonized constructions produce an effect as though he were surrounded by architectural models of skyscraper complexes. Despite their initially naïve results, Schöffer's dancing and sounding cybernetic sculptures and his projected storms of lively color open far-reaching possibilities.

The idolatry of the machine is expressed grotesquely and poetically in Tinguely's painted mechanisms. The artist displays a motor-driven machine that produces incalculable rhythmical colored modulations.

Certain variations of abstract artistic exercises seem to be parallels to technology and industry, as intellectual consonances with functional thought and form allow one to forget for a while that radio equipment, radar antennas, cybernetic machines, and space satellites are themselves creations of man's mind. Intended and created to serve man, technology appears to burst away from him. The machine fostered by man, the thought machine outfitted with an electronic brain, becomes in its phase of "intellectualization" a mechanical specter and a symbol of a phantom world.

Issuing from the modernist and functional teachings of the Bauhaus, this line of development found stimulus and confirmation in the functional construction of technical, scientific instruments. The pyramid of outstretched wire strings on a supporting frame of a radio transmission tower (185) reminds one of the early forerunners of the sculptural forms by Lissitzky, Gabo, and Moholy-Nagy. Reginald Butler's *The Unknown Political Prisoner* (186), too, fascinates one by the tension and ascetic strength of its poetic, technical construction.

The dynamically vaulting radar installations and telescopes have in their transparent metallic architecture something in common with the spatial modulations of the monumental elliptical sculpture Gabo created for Rotterdam (188).

The steering mechanisms of atomic technology and space travel have in their intellectually organized functionalism enlarged the consciousness of the artist and awakened new visual conceptions. The analogy of works of art with mechanical, technical forms is now weakened by the much more complicated energetic symbolic representation of the hardly visualizable structure of matter.

What is accomplished goes beyond the boundaries of what we have called "art" up to now. Discussing the "New Reality," Emil Praetorius writes:

"This modern work pushes inexorably beyond its boundaries, and it does so because it is fulfilled, carried, and driven by the extra- and superartistic tendencies of the latest common universal development, because it wishes to work together with all other means of expression to create a new meaning for life, a new value for life, because, in short, it wishes to be more than mere art and therefore certainly runs the risk of being less than art."

On the eve of World War I, Franz Marc wrote that future art would become the formal mold of our scientific convictions.

Seismographic sensitivity gives the art of our time the foreboding power of prophecy, the anticipation of the very origin of conceived realities, the visualization of processes that have not yet become conscious.

Sculptors, Architects, Engineers

An age of great problems, an age of analysis, of groping experiments, at the same time an age of great changes, an age that will work out a new aesthetic.
Le Corbusier

Modern architecture has an internal relationship with technology and science. The dematerialization of matter, the dynamification of space, the architectural experience as a space-time continuum find their analogies in the mathematical and physical abstractions of the age.

The spirit of technology has permeated architecture even more deeply than the fine arts. The boldest stimuli of architecture are indebted to the achievements of technology. The curved space of modern physics finds an ingenious correspondence here. S. Giedeon speaks of the pioneer significance of the great engineers E. Freysinnet and R. Maillart, who constructed eggshell vaults even in the twenties.

"Since then, principles that previously could be used only for the lightest materials, for hanging membranes like canopies, nets like hammocks, planes like tautly stretched drum surfaces, the principle of the soap bubble whose molecular tensions are in equilibrium with one another, all are translated into three-dimensional supporting structures that simultaneously support and enclose."

The mature architecture of the twentieth century appears as a fusion of technical and fine art, as a synthesis of technology, architecture, and sculpture.

For just that reason, industrial plants and geodesic architecture become the real monuments of our time, because they are perfect without being intended as artistic creations. Their beauty lies in the taming of their energies, in the arrangements of natural scenic complexes, in the harmonization of powerful installations. The span and soar of a bridge (208), the purity and monumental ordered capacity of a dam (209), the rhythmical functionalism of a traffic interchange, roads piled in stories one above the other (206) can be the crowning achievements of both construction and total aesthetic formation.

Around the turn of the century, Henry van de Velde wrote:

"There is a class of men whom we can no longer deny the title of artist. Their work is founded on the one hand on the utilization of materials whose uses were formerly unknown and on the other hand on such an extraordinary boldness that they even surpass the boldness of the cathedral builders. These artists, the creators of new architecture, are the engineers."

Strictly functional form dominated in the twenties. According to Mies van der Rohe, "form does not exist in itself; form is not the goal of our work but merely its outcome." The puristic phase in architecture was polemic: in contrast to the imitation of past decades, to eclectic mixtures of styles, it meant a definite return to objectivity and to functional, constructive modeling. Such a rationally based method saw in functionalism the essence of artistic quality.

Theo van Doesburg, founder of the Stijl group in Holland in 1917, eliminated consideration of all peripheral work in architecture in order to concentrate on its essential means of expression. Together with J. J. P. Oud and his friend the painter Mondrian, he attempted to call forth beauty in matter by the use of elementary harmonies.

Walter Gropius planned and influenced the direction of some of the most important architectural problems of our time. As the founder of the Bauhaus of Weimar in 1919, he laid the foundations of creative study in the area of industrial planning, which was to have effects far beyond Germany. One of the basic precepts of this new workshop went as follows: "The Bauhaus aspires to the collection of all artistic endeavors into a single entity, the reunification of all artistic disciplines into a new structural art as its indispensable constituent."

Gropius attracted important artists to the Bauhaus. With Kandinsky, Klee, Feininger, Schlemmer, and others, he developed a new consciousness for the artist who was willing to work in team to make a personal contribution to the common task. In closest contact with modern materials and means of production, a generation of architects and fine artists was to shape the common human environment in buildings, accommodations, and furniture.

The universality of Gropius' endeavors finds a parallel in the universal personality of Le Corbusier. As architect and city planner, sculptor and writer, theoretician and creator, Le Corbusier strongly influenced the architecture of our time.

Le Corbusier demands of an apartment that it function as well as a machine, of a house that it be logically formed, like an ocean-going ship or an airplane. The concept of functionalism was for a while seen by his contemporaries as a negation of the relationship between man and object, as mechanization and technification, as a despiritualization and bureaucratization of our existence.

If functionalism in architecture appears only as a realization of usefulness, an expression of strictly objective aspirations, it will not be able to satisfy a perceptual desire for transcendent perfection. The art of architecture has not given up its deeper meaning, even in the age of functionalism. The new instruments measuring stimulation no longer sound the heart but penetrate the cerebral cortex and the nervous system. The marvelous is thus not canceled but released from traditional realism.

The inspiration of the great technician Le Corbusier is not only logical, it is also visionary. His concern with the principles of the dwelling structure, which he was dedicated to remodeling as a contemporary instrument of life, derived from a social, humane conception that finally resulted in the unified complex of the planned city. For Le Corbusier, space is the unity of internal and external area. Interior and landscape create a unified form and together constitute the dwelling. For Mies van der Rohe, in contrast to this dynamic principle, a room must be quiet and harmonious and closed to the outside.

Ludwig Mies van der Rohe, the great architect of simplicity and proportion, teaches architecture as the ordering principle in the confusion of our time. The technically perfect constructions (198), with their structures made visible behind their glass skins, are consummate components of technically planned aesthetic material. Despite its programmatic preference for form as an end in itself, Mies van der Rohe's functionally conceived structures, through refinement of proportion and purity of structure, achieve the harmony and conclusiveness of great classical architecture. The functionalism of his structures, like all architecture, embraces in its vision and plan not only the practical welfare of external existence, but also the life essentials of psychic existence.

Frank Lloyd Wright had a unique attitude toward functional architecture: if he rejected the European followers of classical style, he also rejected the technical coolness of engineering art. According to his ideas, every structure should grow out of its own landscape and historical background. All his life Wright consistently advocated the line of "organic architecture" that he founded around the turn of the century in his country houses. The concept of the building as a spatially constructed organism, as a unity of landscape, vegetation, and climate, is fully realized in his famous house overhanging the waterfall (201). The overlapping, flaring rooms and terraces rest on reinforced concrete slabs over the tumbling water. They stand over the heart of the house in tension-laden relationship to the natural rock in which they are anchored.

The Guggenheim Museum (199, 200) in New York—Wright's last, posthumous work—was supposed to signal a return to the archaic, circular forms of America and Africa, freed from the hypnotic spell of the right angle in architecture. A round pyramid, rising from the broad foundation, a monumental, windowless space in which spiral ramps lead to a plexiglass dome, the building evokes intense memories of the round pyramids of the Aztecs in the Valley of Toluca (Mexico), called the Pyramids of Calixtlhuaca. This museum appears more like a temple in which the works of art are exhibited like fetishes or gods than a house of study and the intellectual discussion of art.

Inexhaustible imagination and fundamental subjectivity allowed Wright to solve every problem as a singular expression of his own existence. His bold, visionary conception, created on the basis of a relationship with nature, made Wright one of the most original and talented architects of the age, who yet managed to subordinate the functionalism of architecture to sculptural form.

Herbert Read calls architecture the "mother of sculpture." In its early form, architecture is in itself sculpture. The pyramids in Egypt and ancient Mexico, the palaces in Mesopotamia, the beehive tombs of Mycenae, the mosaic-decked Byzantine churches, and the medieval cloisters of Serbia and Macedonia, decorated with frescoes, were produced as the result of a unity with sculptural intent.

Later, middle-class individualism carried out a complete separation of the arts, dissolved the social connection of the artist with society or reduced it to a subjective communication of the artist with the narrowest circle of his own group. The separation of architecture, sculpture, and painting is equivalent to a cleavage of consciousness and dissolves the unity of sculptural aesthetics, which is a necessary assumption for the total work of art.

In Wright and the late works of Le Corbusier, the penetration of sculptural elements into architecture becomes apparent. This conception leads to a renewed synthesis of architecture and sculpture and thus, in a modern realization, connects with archaic principles.

But apparently Le Corbusier abandoned his theory of functionalism when he built the pilgrim's chapel of Ronchamp (203). With its mushroom roof soaring upward and the formal elements reminding one of technical structures, the window slits that allow the light to filter through as in a catacomb, this chapel has extended functionalism into a metaphysical realm. Like the pavilion for electronic music at the Brussels World's Fair in 1958, the chapel is a sculptural, architectural entity. The Philips Pavilion (202) is like an audible Pevsner sculpture, and the chapel of Ronchamp, which breaks with all tradi-

tional Christian church structure, is a sculpture of contemplation and inner composure.

The First Presbyterian Church in Stamford, Connecticut (190), built by the architectural firm of Harrison and Abramovitz and the engineers Sherwood, Nills, and Smith, is also part of the family of sculptural architecture. This building, in the form of a fish and made of glass and concrete ribs, unifies the metaphysical brilliance of Gothic cathedrals with the sober perfection of modern technology in luminous stained-glass windows.

Even if it was possible for Le Corbusier's imagination to unite the oldest with the newest—"an arch with the airplane"—sacred architecture still does not seem to us to be the main problem of building. One does not even have to go so far as Mies van der Rohe when in 1942 he said that all the endeavors of our age are secular. The attempts of the mystics will remain episodes, he insisted; despite a deepening of our concepts of life, we shall build no cathedrals.

In the architectonic work of Mies van der Rohe, Gropius, and Le Corbusier, the new principle of the unity of technology and architecture is realized.

After the skyscraper romanticism in the United States, Rockefeller Center in New York (195)—a collective undertaking of monumental proportions, whose main architect was Raymond Hood—appeared an extraordinarily grandiose composition of spatial architecture. The building complex cannot be comprehended with the eye from any point or perspective except an air view. The gigantic planes of the individual buildings in alternating, rhythmic, harmonious relationships, parallel or at right angles to one another, give the wandering gaze a spectacle of movement that can only be fully recognized in the alternating relationships. As in the time medium of the film, we experience the fugue of architecture in ever new aspects and never find the vantage point of quiet passivity that was a part of classical architecture.

In the past, the necessary framework for the

construction of a building was covered and made invisible by the external architecture. In the twentieth century, the construction has been divested of externals and made visible; it thus has become independent and in itself a means of artistic expression. In such broadened aesthetic consciousness, a scientific apparatus or technical construct itself operates creatively and completely as a work of art.

Max Bense says:

"Works of art are no longer exclusively the forms that exemplify aesthetic existence; the realm of functional objects, too, constantly breaks into this sphere. The process is as follows: aesthetic emancipation, the liberation of the means of artistic expression, destroyed the semantic, contentual, objective relationships of pictures, sculptures, and sometimes even prose and poetry. But what it achieved through the loss of that which is represented, that is, the really fictional objects, was the really beautiful object in itself—the product of the beautiful functional object. And the development proceeded in the same way from natural beauty, by way of artistic beauty, to technological beauty. The aesthetic world, which no longer requires the incentive of objects because it has objects itself as a goal, has become a world that has integrated technology in the kind of depth and volume we are otherwise used to only in physical things. It is visibly an art—and in it beauty has no substantial but rather structural, no objective but rather functional, meaning—in which the physical moments are embodied just as much as the technical. . . ."

Konrad Wachsmann's studies for the building of an airplane hangar (210, 211) offer interesting examples of the technical beauty of three-dimensional structures. The crystalline structure of the elements, carried through down to the last detail, no longer forms any center of gravity or fulcral point. Heaviness and starkness appear to have been overcome. A new category of spatial construction has been opened. Not a piling up of materials but perfect formation determines the logical and intuitive strength of the construct. Soaring potential and elasticity transform the static structure into a dynamic one. This scientifically calculated and technologically executed construction is full of poetic imagination in its pure economy and harmonious austerity and is related to the experiments of modern painting that seek the texture and the structural laws of matter, and also to Naum Gabo's linear space constructions, whose elasticity and sovereign tension breathe spiritual perfection.

Richard Buckminster Fuller's geodesic domes (194), too, those great expanses covered over with standard, structured, three-dimensional elements, are among the examples of the pure, planned contemporary engineering structures. His circular dynamic houses, which turn to follow the sun, and his geodesic-domed buildings are related in their regular harmony to the Lilliputian assemblages of circular, shimmering green primordial plankton families as revealed by the electron microscope (193). They also remind us of the organizational principle of the crystal lattice, the transparent, shimmering facets of inorganic nature.

Among the functional engineering structures also is the observatory at Mount Palomar in California (191), in whose shell the eminent astronomer George Ellery Hale built the largest reflecting telescope in the world. Unintentionally it shows an aesthetic relationship of cosmos and domes, more complicated than the richly referential sculpture Rudolf Belling (192) created in 1929. Belling's domed vault represents a more decorative soaring and virtuoso modification of cubistic forms than basic creative form and sculptural substance.

For Max Bill, sculpture and picture, architecture and implement, machine and object are equally justifiable forms of expression for the functional modeling of the world around us. He is part of the family of

Mondrian, Vantongerloo, and Van Doesburg, whose work cannot be understood as a parallel to the creations of organic nature. In its place these artists set symbols of expression and signs of a scientific, technological culture. New mathematical and physical conceptions, new aspects of the macro- and microcosmos are expressed in Bill's work in concrete, constructive, symbolic harmonies.

Architecture and communality are the basic problems of modern architecture. Not palaces and public buildings but dome architecture and housing projects are the main problem of our time, as are the humanization of the cities, harmonious city planning, new conceptions of space, a harmony of city and landscape. Modern man feels uneasy in the amorphous environment of a chaotic, random, and uncontrolled architecture. Modern city planning

wants to offer a secure life. City planning can only be realized in a social context.

In its visions, art at present undertakes to sketch the changing environment in which man himself changes. Constant's constructions are models of urban dreams (212). In his conception, life consists of a continuity of briefly creative and fleeting activities. In the fickleness and dynamism of our existence, artistic activity must comprehend communal life by transforming the environment and creating it anew, realizing itself in the process. Not the work of art itself but artistic activity is to be taken as the goal of the artist. All technological and material energies and forms, possibilities of sound, and principles of movement are invested in the superbuildings of the future city, the habitat of living poetry and images that the artist foresees.

Archaic and Technical Optics

In their search for absolute purity, artists were compelled to eliminate natural forms that conceal the purely constructive elements and to replace "natural form" by "art form." This is concrete rather than abstract painting, in the sense that nothing can be more concrete or more real than a line, a color, a plane. One might call this the "concretion" of the creative mind.

Theo van Doesburg, 1924

Toward the latter part of the fifties, one notices a waning of Tachism and Action Painting. Two antithetically related movements appear and begin to take shape, bringing to an end an artistic phase that

had been dedicated to decomposing all forms and order and that had left art completely at the mercy of instinct and coincidence: on the one hand so-called Pop art—influenced by Dadaism—which aimed at new configurations in art; and on the other hand Op art, which seizes the idea of pure form, which had been thought dead, and aligns itself with the aims of twentieth-century concrete art.

The growing unimportance of a natural, landscape background, the predominance of a mathematical-geometric order, the transformation of our visual world by technology and industry into a form pattern of artificiality—all these changes are bound to leave their mark on artistic creativity and cannot fail to uproot certain parts from the nourishing soil of naturalness. When this happens, the artist will begin more to resemble the engineer. He will be much closer to a builder than were his colleagues of past decades. Born into our civilization, the new generation of artists has no intention to illuminate, form, or represent the real; rather, they permit a liberation of the principles guiding their imagination. They follow their urge to free their intimate relation to numbers and their intricate rhythm from earthly principles of order, and thus come to experience events of cosmic extension. The implication of such a change is the denial of opposing geographic and national traditions of form. This is the moment when the creative personality expresses itself in nothing but intensity of vision, intelligence of thought, and the degree of refinement of hearing.

The first to formulate the concept "*art concret*" in its present meaning was Van Doesburg: the strict and absolute world of forms of the spirit that avoids all naturalness and embraces only órder, proportion, and structure.

While Pop art takes its point of departure from an elementary aesthetic of commonplace materials, Op art, influenced by the objectivity of physics, portrays, by means of mathematical-spiritual transpositions, the inner structure of substance and the abstract structure of the universe. Geometric forms in art can be thought of as a glorification of a pure, extrahuman form; they represent the embodiment of the idea of time, space and movement, freed from the barbarism of instinct and the fluctuations of feeling.

Visual patterns that represent no objects—or certainly no more than altered and transformed objects —have been in existence since the beginning of recorded art. The need to represent complex structures by means of few and simple elements was expressed as early as the Megalith culture, whose art was dominated by vertical and horizontal lines. The geometric ornament can originate from the urge to stylize the visual image of the real world as well as from the desire to express pure thought. The eastern European art of the later Stone Age was especially rich in it. For example, the mammoth-ivory plaques from Mezin, Ukraine, show surfaces that are completely spun over by zigzag and parallel lines. Such a pattern, which originally might have symbolized the flowing movement of water, could very well have been devised by today's Op artists (220, 221).

Certain Stone Age cultures from the eastern Mediterranean and from western Europe have created manifold variations of circular elements and spiral patterns. Examples can be found in the bronze ornamentation of Cretan-Mycenaean art.

Historians determine periods in art history according to the developmental stages of ornamentations. Although it may be difficult in many cases to recognize fully the original meaning of symbols, it is certain that the significance of the ornament goes beyond mere adornment and decor. Worringer sees the ornament as unmistakably pure expression of the will to create.

Ornamentation grows out of feeling and consciousness, but it also grows out of substances and the technical process of production. The events of man's world-cosmic experience—such as the movement of the sun, moon, and stars, the periodic changes of day and night, summer and winter, birth and death—determine his vision of reality just as much as his empirical experience of the materials and purposes of objects. The potter's wheel, for example, enabled man to produce round forms. Such circular movement then inspired the drawing of geometric lines. Finally, the circle—symbol of the one great roundness—is at the same time representative of procreation, of the male-female unity. In Egypt we find the snake biting its own tail; in China the circle embracing the great sign of 'Tao,' Yang and Yin—the creative light of masculinity, and receiving night, the principle of femininity. *Mandala* is the Sanskrit word for circle and symbolizes a mythic diagram of meditation in Buddhist and Taoist philosophy. The mandorla of Christianity, the almond-shaped halo embracing the Divine, originated from the halo. The circle as ring symbolizes permanent possession, and as crown and wreath symbolizes power and consecration. From the solar disk stems the wheel—the circling motif of roundness, the static nature of rosette and star.

From the period of the "Contending States" in China (481–221 B.C.), the spiral as image of the curling snake becomes the abstract symbol of the course of a life, a path of labyrinths that may end with either death or salvation (229). The graves of the Megalith culture, the sacral monuments of Egypt, early Far Eastern art, the archaic culture of Greece—all know this symbol of the limitless, the fateful, the eternal. In his dialogue *Philebos*, Plato develops his idea of the artistically beautiful:

"I am thinking of something straight and of something round; I am thinking of bodies which are brought into being by compass or square, according to a certain rule. For these are never beautiful in relation to some other thing, but always only in and for themselves."

Roman mosaics (223) and floor rosettes in Renaissance chapels show as an ornament the circle increasing in inner density (222). Michelangelo and Dürer created circular designs for floors of stone and parquet. The Gothic spirit of abstract thought mixed with the worldly spirit of the Renaissance becomes quite apparent when Dürer says: "The world will have to believe him who can prove his cause via geometry, and who can so thoroughly demonstrate truth." The dome, symbolizing the sky, originated in the Orient, was further developed in Rome, and reached its climax in Renaissance Europe.

The circle symbolizing sun and vulva, as sign for macro- and microcosm, has remained throughout all changes and sequences of style, and has in modern abstraction, with other elementary forms and geometric hieroglyphs, come to new life and strength.

The primitive and the cultured artist have found their point of contact: the geometric, elementary form that during the course of civilization became ornamentation for objects and utensils is now in the process of emancipation as secondary function—and finds an independent existence. There are the Orphic circles of Robert Delaunay; the color-radiating disks of Kenneth Noland (235) and Wojciech Fangor's twisting circles (249); the lacy crocheted rosettes of Ludwig Wilding; Miroslav Sutej's microstructure of light in screen pupils that in concentric layers achieve an increasing inner density (234); and the ball of circles representing the unity of a sensitized, molecular, positively and negatively ordered system by Vjenceslav Richter (225).

In his *Rundscheibe No. 5,* Ferdinand Kriwet's circle becomes a literary calligram, a round dance without beginning or end. A labyrinth of thought, this circle increases in inner density, thus leading the viewer inward, from association to association, until finally a drawing action will lead him to drown in the final space of depth (226). This lettered text of vision reminds one of the labyrinths of the masters of writing of the eighteenth century—or possibly more of the hieroglyphic disk from Phaestos, whose spiral form of writing remained impossible to decipher until recently (227).

Finally, the art inspired by a world of machines, by a spirit of technology, is intended to overcome the traditional procedures, in terms of method of creation as well as in the message it offers. The producer and the user of technical objects both must subject themselves to the discipline necessary for the employment of all mechanisms. Both the producer and the user form an integral part of the domain of the metropolis—which is where the act of co-operation plays such a dominating role.

In a sense, the main products of what is called Op art owe their existence to television. Those unintended variations of *moiré* patterns on the screen that disturb the audience's retina are optical SOS signals, which, fed from minute sources of light, appear as delicate, moving geometric figures. The kinetic principle, the movement and change of such an art form, can account partly for its popularity. The added construction and visual continuation of familiar designs belonging to an industrial milieu are what makes Op art so inspiring and popular.

The personal element of artistic creation has now been replaced by the anonymity of technical perfection: mass-produced art—sometimes the result of group work—marked by a collective signature. The individual artist steps into the background and thereby cancels the uniqueness of the work of art. The artist designs the work, and the experts complete the mass production. To a generation of artists growing up in an age of atomic energy and cybernetics, it hardly seems surprising or abnormal that works of art should be produced by means of machines.

Since the middle of the twentieth century, there has been a collision between these new ideas and traditional working methods. Revolutionary ideas are still being formulated within the framework of studio art; forms of art designed with scientific insight become reality in the form of easel pictures. Granted, Jackson Pollock stood on top of his painting, which he placed flat on the studio floor, so that he could work the canvas with a squeeze-bottle; yet his results do no more than enlarge quantitatively the framework of a subjective art of expression. Optic abstraction went from drawing to color, from painting to sculpture. It includes the hard-edge painting of the Mondrian followers, the polychrome geometry of Josef Albers (244), the monochrome planes of Barnett Newman's rhythmically arranged spatial experiences. Mark Rothko's meditative walls of prayer appear to be all renunciation and reduction. William Turnbull and Rupprecht Geiger push aside the concept of volume and express through colorful, elementary forms the experience of infinity. Kenneth Noland's shining disks have the effect of optical signals (235). The hypnotic language of Robert Indiana's rhythmic advertising metaphors, the advertising landscape filled with slogans and traffic signs by Winfred Gaul—both belong to the linguistic realm of this art.

Perhaps these artists have been inspired by Delaunay's Orphic circles. Frank Stella's chromatically ordered rhythms (241) and Morris Louis' color-streaked sheaves of lines point into unlimited space. Piero Dorazio's fence structures, and those by Jules Engel and Michael Kidner, lead from the painterly into the ascetic-graphic elements of optics. Vasarely's multidimensional condensation and control of visible space transform the observer from static viewer to dynamic participator (233). This type of event was predicted during the middle twenties by Henryk Berlewi with his experiments in "mechanofacture."

The art of compasses and screens requires discipline of the intellect, technical exactitude, and visual flexibility. Linear systems—one placed above the other, and shifted through circular movement—and condensations and resolutions of figuratively suggested zones produce in this cool world of geometric fantasy a spirit of functionless charts and disembodied filigrees of numbers: Bridget Riley, Richard Anuskiewicz, Larry Poons, Julian Stanczak, Mon Levinson, and others belong to this new optical wave, which will finally turn into anonymous groups of co-operative activity.

Op art, New Tendencies, Recherche Continuelle, Zero–O, Nieuwe Konceptie, Arte Programmata—all pursue goals parallel to the investigations of contemporary science. Neither the particular elements nor the results—the works of art—are at stake here. Emphasis is placed entirely on the act of investigation as such. The result may very well have already become obsolete during the act of formulation. But that is inessential. What interests the artists are processes of change in geometric configurations, the condition of movement and the progressive alteration of form.

One might ask, does this art deal with functionless structures become visible? Does it treat geometric forms and rhythms in empty space? Certain it is that the artists of this new movement start off with the intention of investigating and affecting the total structure of space, urban consciousness, the universal category of forms, which have become an integral part of modern man's awareness. Their aim is to overcome the abyss between individual creator and mass consumer. They seek to abolish the cult of artistic, personal creativity. For the element of uniqueness in a work of art, so they emphasize, is nothing more than a myth of the past.

In order to understand why so many artists cling to the natural sciences with their experiments, one has only to consider the importance of contemporary man's scientific achievements. Mathematical thinking and the laws of science exercise their power and influence on creativity and compel the artist to prac-tice the sort of disciplines and principles of order that necessarily contradict traditional art. Perhaps the basic geometric motive of Op art can be seen as an unconscious exercise aiming for the construction of a future epoch, founded on the control of instincts and the emancipation of pure reason. Simultaneously, though, these tactile elements of geometric precision may very well become fixed ideas, monomaniacal delusions, which with their mass-produced fence posts and screen structures will begin to encompass and suffocate man's heart and mind.

Whether these new geometric configurations simply reduce art to ornamentation or whether they are capable of revitalizing the meanings and tensions originally impicit in ornament and emblem can only be answered once this art has begun to occupy its proper place in the perspective of art history.

Light and Dynamics

Light is the primary condition of all visibility. Light is the sphere of color. Light is the element of life for man and image.

Otto Piene

The artist of the twentieth century looks at himself and the world from a totally different perspective than, for example, did the builders of pyramids, the artists and humanists of the Renaissance, or the painters of triumphant light and colorful shadows, the Impressionists.

Perception, having become a continuum of space and time, must with lightning speed transcend the world conception that presented itself to classical art. A dynamic contemporary art wants to design a visual realm capable of distinguishing itself from the kind of spatial concepts reached through the senses. To the three dimensions of art has been added a fourth: time. Crucial efforts in modern art are being made to treat movement as a new element of formation. Techniques of simultaneity have brought urban man to an accelerated mode of experiencing: picture, word, color, and movement have become linguistic elements of a synchronized mass communication.

Einstein's theory of relativity, formulated in 1905, not only effected a fundamental change in physics, but also left its significant mark on art. In 1907, Henri Bergson wrote his *Evolution Créatrice*, and in 1922 came *Durée et Simultanéité*, his contribution to Einstein's theory. The non-Euclidean world image designed by Hermann Minkowski, where "time and space enter into a union with the world," is constructed on the mathematical principle of a multidimensional concept of space. To the theory of nuclear physics is added the science of electronically operated machines, which Norbert Wiener called "cybernetics." The electronic brain finally seems to realize an old sculptor's wish, to animate his sculptures through kinetic steering.

Before the turn of the century, the temporal-spatially mixed form of the film, still rather primitive at the time yet perfectly aligned with the spirit of the epoch, began to develop. The animated photography of picture sequences produced with light; the simultaneity of events; the possibility of constructing alternating actions; the creation of fast and slow motion through slow-motion camera and quick-motion apparatus—these techniques influenced all the other arts.

In 1920 Antoine Pevsner and Naum Gabo proclaimed in their *Realist Manifesto* that kinetics had come to represent a new and vital element in art. Two years later, Moholy-Nagy and Zoltan Kemeny published in *Der Sturm* (Berlin) their *Manifesto of Kinetic Sculpture*. Calder's moving sculptures of wire introduced his Mobiles (215). Vasarely with his sliding screens produced studies of the motion of the infinitely small and the infinitely large, thus creating a mirror of the material universe. Bruno Munari, who cosigned the Futurist Manifesto of the Aeropittura, created wire figures set into motion by breath. Richard Mortensen's picture compositions of plane-geometric forms with electronic motion suggest a science-inspired, concrete form of painting. The metamorphic, polychrome pictures of Yaacov Agam, the *Peintures Cinétiques* by Jean Tinguely, and the electronically operated sculptures of Nicolas Schöffer are all exponents of an imaginary gallery of light painting and cybernetic sculpture.

Schöffer's approach to creating a work of art by means of cybernetics and light (196) is as natural as the traditional artists' approach to color, easel, and canvas. His "canvas" is the urban realm, the façades of squares and streets, which from his cybernetic tower he will illuminate, move, and transpose through changeable bundles of color and form. His cybernetic tower-sculpture, which was erected in Liège in 1961, emits light, form, color, and sounds in constantly altering variations. Schöffer's numino-dynamic *Spectacles;* Tinguely's colorful water games; Heinz Mack's cubes of light, reliefs of light (254), and machines of color play; Otto Piene's light ballets, light planets, and exotic fire flowers; Günther Uecker's gleaming forests of nails (252); Hermann Goepfert's light rotary; Le Parc's "light mobiles" (251)—all indicate an attempt to approximate art to the immediacy of life, to the busy multiplicity of the metropolis.

In this fashion artistic activities can enlarge the realm of the aesthetic, can reflect the world's substance through synchronized rhythms of motion, light, and sound, through harmonies of form and proportion. Or, working in favor of a cybernetic mannerism, they may serve modern *homo ludens'* desire for play and entertainment, by presenting as secularized mystery—with the help of regulated effects of curious automata and robots—the monumental drama of a machine folklore.

As early as the first manifesto of the Stijl group, in November, 1918, it was proclaimed that "there exists an old and a new awareness of time. The old directs itself toward individuality and the new toward universality." By placing the element of time within the framework of a composition, kinetic art creates a reflection of the movement of life. The artist-operator may on his own set his work into motion, somewhat like the conductor of an orchestra; or he may leave his work to the machines that will then distribute it among the consumers, more or less the way music is held and distributed on records and tapes.

In Informal art there was a subjective process that arose from instinct—from the unconscious—and became existential reality. The subjective process simultaneously became the point of departure and the end of the particular artistic event. The matter of fulfillment raised the problem of the impossibility of repeating a work of art. Realization meant sublimation and transcendence. Finally, the iconoclastic negation of the "informal trend" was meant to replace the subjective uniqueness of a work of art with the co-operative work of a collective investigation. Loneliness and isolation now have given way to a team of specialized technicians. Their guide lines are objective and scientific. Industrial civilization—modern man's real world—has in the light of these new tendencies changed from denatured, technical monstrosity to willfully accepted city nature. At this moment, one no longer sees brutal, destructive techniques but rather forces of a primitive order. Modern technology is young; its fascinating results are merely the beginning of a success, are merely hints at the possibility of a scientifically conceptualized world design.

IX

BREAKING THROUGH THE VISUAL BARRIER

The Reflection of the Scientific World Picture

A united front of all research and creativity—physics, philosophy, literature, art, and music—is at hand. If one sees scientific photographs, microphotographs, planned or sculptural diagrams, one notices a certain similarity with the forms in modern art—a relationship. The independent formal inventions of modern art thus equally construct the final. clarified forms in the sense of a higher order of everything visible—in the sense of an absolute vision.

Willi Baumeister

The transformation that scientific thought has undergone since the beginning of the twentieth century has many parallels with the metamorphoses of art. As the Renaissance broadened two-dimensional space in the classical teachings of perspective, so the theory of relativity bursts the perception and image of space and time conveyed by classical physics. Radio and X rays create a conception of the decay and regeneration of elements; their emanations penetrate matter and make it transparent. Psychoanalysis presses into heretofore unexplored spheres; it includes the area of the collective unconscious. Long shots and close-ups allow the membrane of artistic sensibility to soar into unsuspected ranges.

In physics, Albert Einstein sets the organic interrelation of time and space against their metaphysical separation. In his interpretation, our universe becomes a four-dimensional space-time continuum.

In previous conceptions, time was seen as a sort of historical sequence of past, present, and future. Today, not only does physics regard time as divided and discontinuous, but poets and artists do so too. Time is no longer isolated from space, no longer solely future-oriented. Modern literature, drama, sculpture, and painting portray the new space-time relationships.

"The stimulus of the new physical ideas on the artists' reflections may be accurately shown. If Boccioni notes in his diary in 1907 that to him art and artists seem in conflict with science and that scientific analysis and its view would have to reckon with the universe of art, he is expressing an attitude that later led in the development of Futurism to the introduction of the space-time concept. When in 1908 Hermann Minkowski conceived the fourth dimension as a unity of time and space, the Cubists were working to achieve a simultaneous view of things in art, their contemplation and reflection from several standpoints, and in this manner to replace the old static vanishing-point perspective with a novel and dynamic spatial conception that would comprehend the moment of time and movement together. Apollinaire had already recognized this consciously in 1911 and connected the aperspective spatial conceptions of Cubist and Futurist art with the scientific concept of the fourth dimension." (Werner Haftmann)

Even though the theory of relativity in no way denies that matter exists consciously independent of the space-time relationship, the fundamental physical relativity of all human conceptions of time and space has led to a theoretical acknowledgement of relativity, interpreting the appearance of reality as an intellectual construct or subjective observation. Such an interpretation of the universe and of reality appealed to the generation of artists who turned away from plein-airism and Impressionism in order to interpret and construct on the basis of their subjective and internal experience of the world.

The Expressionists' intensification of expression through deformity; the Fauves' use of the pure colors of a blazing palette, their vigorous brush strokes and radical simplification and pursuit of basic forms; the Cubists' analysis and baring of structure; the Orphists' exhaustion of the dynamic power of colors; the Futurists' new spatial conceptions and attempts at simultaneity; and the Surrealists' painting of dream and subconsciousness—all were stimulated by the new experimental spirit and the new subject-object relationship of modern science.

Nils Bohr writes:

"We see here in a new light the old truth that the purpose of our description of nature does not exist in ascertaining the real substance of appearances but only in tracing out as far as possible the relationships between varous aspects of our experience."

The Cubists did not begin with the deformation of reality. They conceived the object from a new point of view, independent of the visible world. Their form is a unique creation, no longer a variation of the objective world. An ascetic bent characterizes their polemic attitude to the Expressionists' emotional assertions and the Fauves' ecstatic color. Cézanne's order, philosophically and visually confirmed, served the Cubists as the basis of an intellectual principle. Guillaume Apollinaire said the task of the Cubists was "to organize chaos." The Cubists circle their objects, look at them from various points of view, from above and below, X-ray the objects, and dissect them into the elements of plane geometry. Their provocative, calm analytical constructions appear like diagrams of the new reality, which has become visible through an X-rayed dissection and reconstruction of forms.

Werner Heisenberg speaks of the fact that physics no longer deals with the universe as it is directly presented, but with a "dark background of the universe which we bring to light through our experiments." Knowledge in its present form and the traditional body of information are insufficient to grasp the newly captured realities. These newly glimpsed and formulated ideas are expressible, however, in physical and mathematical formulas. Precise physics rarely uses the formulation "It is thus"; more often we see "Thus it may be represented." In place of absolute explanations, many-sided, often opposing relationships and interrelated dialectical conclusions are indicated.

As physical processes are represented variously according to how they are observed, painters also do not accept an immovable point of view, an assured and unified position for contemplation. Rather, with respect to direction they accept various and often opposing points of view. This is also significant for the technique of a William Faulkner in his novels and for the director Kurosawa in the film *Rashomon*. Substance that has become transparent—

the cancellation of boundaries between internal and external appearance—is reflected in the books of Joyce and Kafka, in which the conscious incident simultaneously and consecutively runs parallel with the psychic and unconscious one.

Moholy-Nagy built models of a symbiosis of the artistic world of forms with the scientific elements. The experiments undertaken in the Bauhaus attempted to transform the reactions of matter, the rays of force fields, the dynamics of light, transparency, and simultaneity into pictorial conceptions.

As the expression of a technological and scientific revolution in art, Futurism denied a perspective conception of space and a static copy of reality. Stirred by the panicking speed of modern life, with its motorized rhythms, by the lively air views of the world, and by the film's dynamic image sequence, the Futurists proclaim an art of movement and activity. Optic and acoustic impressions are expressed in kinetic signs that characterize the dissonant polyphony of existence as phenomena of movement and simultaneity.

Perhaps film, Cinerama, and television, with the flashbacks and their ability to project simultaneous events and the fluctuating boundary of time and space, have realized the Futurists' wish projections. Silent film has learned to speak; black-and-white film has achieved color; two-dimensional film has attained three-dimensional effects. The public is now optically and acoustically included in the pictorial events. It sits before the illusion of an opened hand. The exaggerated dimensions of the curved screen and the directed sound effects coming from clusters of loudspeakers give the listener the illusion that he is included in the action. The shutter frees artistic reality from spatial and temporal causality; it encloses a sphere of fantasy: "An internal image is extinguished and a new one is disclosed. Between the opening and the closing of the shutter, fate is snatched up and leaps across time and space from one human being to another, from one mood to another, from reality to super-reality." *(Film, Rundfunk, Fernsehen,* ed. Dr. L. H. Eisner and H. Friedrich)

Up to now, no amount of imagination has been able to draft a model of atomic and subatomic events. The innermost reactions of matter suggest a universe bordering on imagelessness. Is there an analogy here with the development of art, which has lost the boundaries of that which heretofore served as a conception of pictorial form? The alienation of art from the reality recognizable by the naked eye is parallel to the direction of research in the physical sciences. Louis de Broglie writes:

"In order to satisfy the curiosity of the human spirit, it is just not sufficient for us to know how material bodies behave as units in their visible appearance, how the reactions between light and matter take place when one observes them in bulk. We must try to analyze the structure of matter and light, and define the elementary processes whose totality alone calls up the visible symptoms. In order to complete the examination we must first develop a very refined experimental technique. . . . We also require daring theories based on higher mathematics and enabling us to use completely new images and representations. . . ."

Inspired by the sensitive feelers of modern experimental equipment, by gigantic telescopes, microscopes, and X-ray films, painters have touched a heretofore hidden, secret, still uncatalogued but nevertheless existing world of forms. Paul Klee writes of this displacement of the dimensions of objectivity in the artist's conceptions:

"With a penetrating glance he observes things that nature presents already formed to his eyes. The deeper he looks, the more easily he can span points of view from today to yesterday, and the more the sole essential picture of creation as genesis is impressed on him in place of a completed picture of nature. And is it not true that even the relatively small step of a glance through a microscope presents the eye with pictures that we would all declare fantastic and exaggerated if without getting the point we were to see them somewhere, quite by accident?"

Classical imagery knew only how to project spatial constellations on one surface. Thus by perspective or parallel projections the three-dimensional form was fixed on a two-dimensional plane. The organs of sight were therefore responsible for transforming perceived impressions into perspective picture schemes. In the conscious process the two-dimensional projection was retransformed into a spatial object.

Our century's picture of reality has become more complex. X-ray pictures transmit images of internal structure. Microphotography opens galleries of hitherto unsounded areas. Macrophotography encloses a pictorial documentation of the universe. The electron microscope enables us to see into the world of metallic crystalline structure and also the structure of cellular substance and the fundamental basis of all life. The field electron microscope goes further. Even if it is not possible to portray atomic nuclei, one can nevertheless sight the paths of atomic reactions in so-called cloud chambers by letting them run through a layer of color on which a track may remain.

These illustrations are distinguished not only by their form as unseen but nevertheless real objects; above all they are distinguished by their reproduction in space-time models of two-dimensional projection. The illustration does not concentrate here on the elementary particle, which may be represented only as a point, but on the sum of its movements, the track of its path. Thus, as in moving film, the time sequence is also captured here in a static picture as a spatial sequence. However novel these conceptions are, they still may carry analogies with visual, human precedents. Those manifestations for which we lack imaginary conceptions are different. On the screen of the cathode-ray oscillograph, sounds are visually projected through a microphone in electrical impulses. The "visible-speech apparatus" can transmit language and music, organized in time and frequency, as surface signs on paper.

It is not an unreal world that the electron microscope communicates. What one sees here are extra-human but humanly established dimensions of existence, and it would be understandable if the sensitive eye of the artist, consciously or unconsciously, were stimulated by the structural forms of matter and the secrets of molecular construction.

The cellular structure of a bulrush stalk, micro-photographed by Carl Strüwe, is not unlike the reposeful picture that Piet Mondrian painted in 1918 and called *Lozenge with Gray Lines* (255, 256). Newly visualized nature and the new forms of art are related to one another, but the organization of the fibers within the bulrush is perhaps less systematic; they are grown, not devised. The linear construction of the artist appears stricter. In 1917, in the magazine *De Stijl*, Mondrian writes: "The rhythm of the color relationships and mass allows the absolute to become visible in the relativity of time and space." And elsewhere he says: "If we concentrate our attention upon calibrated relationships, the unity of nature and its objects will become visible albeit veiled."

The microscopic view of a piece of mud shows that nature can create—out of chalk or silica, cellulose or keratin—elastic, resilient, and functional constructions that are just as perfect as the structures of engineers and architects.

The relief window by the sculptor-architect François Stahly in the west nave of the church of Baccarat lets the light drip through, and the window panes, conceived irregularly according to an artistic law, create an analogy with the joisted structure of human bone. It is a natural construction of gracefully monumental limestone pillars that suggests the word "significant" to us (257, 258).

Ornamental structure, the surface of crystal and

stone, the reconstruction of the tiniest organism, and the construction of its texture have forecast endless possibilities for the human imagination. Under the microscope, sea animals and plants reveal a reality that the artist has felt without having seen. The micro-photograph of a sea louse is similar in its bold, simple, geometrical planes to the spare, intensive rhythms and muted color harmonies of Serge Poliakoff's paintings (259, 260).

Kandinsky's instinct led him to guess at a visual space before the overlapping and latticed bundles in the structure of bismuth could be electronically radioscoped in the laboratory. Kandinsky calls his picture *Deux etc.* Two surfaces appear, one light on a dark background, the other dark on a light back-ground, as though the artist had opened a secret book covered with various small lines, circles, and hooks which play with and about and around one another (261, 262).

The structure of corroded silver shown enlarged 1,200 times by an electron microscope is similar to the rhythmic structures in metal relief done by the sculptor Zoltan Kemeny (263, 264). The wave move-ment of the interference patterns on a piece of zinc is absolutely like the rhythmical reliefs created by Robert Delaunay, the founder of Orphism (265, 266).

The visual imagination of the artist is concerned not only with external and internal views as two sides of a dialectically comprehended unity but also with aerial views, the snapped pictures of cities that have become mere outlines, the global view of the earth, of spontaneous movement and of moving things.

Mondrian's *Victory Boogie-Woogie* appears to be an experience of the modern big city. In aerial photography too one can observe similar formations: the vertical photographs of the African city of Tetuán —with its squares, the cisterns and gardens on the roofs—a section of reality existing from time imme-morial but becoming visible in a new way repeats, so to speak, the artist's motifs (267, 268).

Air travel has altered the visual conception of the earth's surface. Large areas are drawn together, the long curves and diagonals of roads become fore-shortened, forests become shimmering green bou-quets, and high mountain peaks become wrinkles in the earth's skin. The cultivated fields and plains are colored patchwork quilts. Paul Klee, too, liked the long carpet strips representing gardens, countryside, fields, roads, and streets, all together. But these are not strictly geometrically ordered, because the artist's personality penetrates and transforms the subject (269, 270).

It is no longer the fast-frozen detail of single congealed moments, but rather things in motion, the opening, developing, moving pictures of the space-time plane, that fascinate the gaze. K. R. H. Sonder-borg's dynamic speed variations are formed from such conceptions of motion. Flat, energetic paths of supersonic speed are called forth by the generally diagonal brush strokes driven across the canvas. Sonderborg's "flying thought" combines lift, direc-tion, and power, while in an aerial photograph taken from a height of one hundred and twenty-five miles we see the Gulf of Mexico as though we were ob-serving the earth in its orbital motion and rotation (271, 272). The first stage of infinity has been reached. Satellites circle high above the atmospheric roof of the earth. They send us serial pictures of distant space,photographic views of the hitherto hidden side of the moon.

Max Ernst calls one of his pictures *The Sea*. Is it an eathly sea, or are these the dark regions of the moon's surface called "seas" (273, 274)? The artist is beckoned not only by the pictorial definition of the unconscious, but also by the voyages of discovery to the most remote regions of existence. His picture is like the dead world of the moon and perhaps also like the face of the earth as it may look millions of years from now. On astronomers' photographs we recognize moon mountains that throw shadows, sur-faces surrounded by craters. The extinguished star is circled by human planets. Perhaps there will soon follow a cosmic Columbus whose harbinger is the artist.

In 1925, when rockets to outer space seemed utopian, Kandinsky sent his steep rocket blitz diagonally to the suspended glowing circle of a heavenly body. This watercolor bears the name *Upward* and symbolizes a spiritual principle, a prophetic thought. But the Honest John rocket, which took its flight into space in 1959, carried together with the artist's dream the threat and danger of a technology not fully controlled by man (275, 276).

Wol's *Blue Phantom* reminds one of the mammoth mushroom cloud of an atomic explosion (277, 278). In his nuclear painting, the artist, who died young, captured the mood of the end of the world and the universal image of death created by the chain reaction of destruction and the extinction of life.

In their visions the artists now leave the galactic boundaries of this earth in order to grope their way to the interpretation of a new macrocosm. The Brazilian painter Danilo di Prete sees the fragments of the globe as though they had been photographed

from a rocket: a relief rising out of the darkness of space, a melancholy island structure in the cold light of the stars. The idyllic earthly landscape has been moved out into the cosmic footlights of invisible suns. Swimming in the misty light, the islands of the world are like the flare-illuminated archipelagoes of the Adriatic in a photograph taken in rapid flight, so that the islands glow phosphorescently out of the dark surface of the sea (279, 280).

In his painting *AX-100 F* (281), Antonio Zoran Musič has captured something of the new dimension of unbounded, not necessarily finite space. The dark spots on a grainy background are like a sunspot group or the washed-out mists of star clouds whose existence astronomers are beginning to sense with their powerful telescopes. They are portraits of universes that perhaps no longer exist because the light rays that bring the news have taken millions of years to reach us.

The task that the artist of today sets himself is not only to make conscious the unconscious but also to make audible the inaudible, visible the invisible.

The Opened Horizon

There is nothing in nature that is not in us.
Naum Gabo

In the early phases of civilization's development, technological inventions were modeled on earthly precedents. Complimentary techniques substituted for the lack of specialized human organs. The progress of technology brought relief and the elimination of physical labor through instruments and machines

whose forms and principles call up analogies with natural prototypes: planes are like huge birds, locomotives like horses, submarines like sharks. In its further expansion, technology carries the analogy out of animate into inanimate nature. There is no similarity between any biological forms and the rocket ships and satellites that sail in outer space.

Does this mean that man has broken off his relationship with nature and now produces his own mechanisms? Just as in science the boundary between organic and inorganic matter is in flux, so also technology passes from the organic forms to the structures and constructions of inorganic matter.

Modern art has not separated itself from reality any more than has technology. It creates its shapes out of the storehouse of reality, just as much as out of accessible things or, hurrying ahead of science, out of his own imagination. Dream and vision, too, are emanations of existence. The creative artistic imagination can anticipate the developmental direction of the conscious, inquiring mind. The conscious and unconscious actions of art are founded on the principles of nature:

"Like the concept 'number,' so the concept 'figure' is exclusively derived from the external world, not originating in the mind, in pure thought. There had to be things that had form and whose forms one compared before one could get to the idea of figure. Pure mathematics has as its object the spatial forms and quantitative relationships of the real world, thus very real substance. The fact that the substance appears in a highly abstract form can only superficially hide its origin in the external world. In order to be able to examine the forms and relationships in their pure states one must, however, completely separate them from their content and set these aside as matter of indifference." (Friedrich Engels)

The inadequacy of some abstract experiment in art thus lies not in an estrangement from nature but in a too strong subordination to the representation of the substance that has become transparent. Naum Gabo wrote:

"The new scientific vision of the world may affect and enhance the vision of the artist as a human being but from there on the artist goes his own way and his art remains independent from science; from there on he carries his own vision bringing forth visual images which react on the common human psychology and transfer his feelings to the feelings of men in general, including the scientists. It is in this field that the constructive contribution of art to human life lies."

As characteristic of the modern sciences, Karl Jaspers points to their basic "unreadiness," the radical nature of their questions, in which no phenomenon may be a matter of indifference and which, in their concentration on details, clarify all connections.

Most or almost all of these characteristics are valid for the endeavors of modern art too. It is universal, and in its spiritual process and transposition of all forms of time and space achieves its best work. It is less concerned with contrasts and creations than with connections and the relationships between objects and creatures.

Classical physics was based on the idea that matter was tangible, inert, and possessed of constant mass. The conviction persisted that energy was independent of mass and existed invisibly. In his theory of relativity, Einstein abolished the classical separation of matter and energy. He indicated the unity of mass and energy as different manifestations of the same substance. Werner Heisenberg and his co-workers undertook to formulate a unified-field equation replacing the theory that was valid only for single elementary particles, a hypothetical formula that would express the idea that all elementary particles can transform themselves into one another and that ultimately there is only one single substance, which is identical with energy.

A strong analogy with the aspirations of modern art can be demonstrated. To the art of today nothing seems too unimportant, nothing too incidental to be portrayed. A pebble is as worthy of portrayal as a Himalayan range, the structure of a drop of water as important as an ocean; the well-formed and the deformed are related aspects of the same thing. Externals and internals are views of the same thing; they all express the versatile relationships of the organism's unity under a multiplicity of appearances.

At the juncture between the two zones of art, the objective and the abstract, it becomes clear that as in the form world of the atom the boundaries are

conceived in flux. Beneath the visible layer of skin the innermost structure of existence becomes discernible as a unified principle.

Boundaries and Syntheses

—through metaphor to reconcile
the people and the stones.
Compose. (No ideas
but in things) Invent!
Saxifrage is my flower that splits
the rocks.

William Carlos Williams

The earth has shrunk, has become an island in the newly revealed infinity of the universe. The transcendental sphere beyond has revealed itself as a new cosmic reality. Man can no longer divide his world into the real here and the imaginary beyond. What he has just seen is more real than his consciousness of reality can grasp; at the same time, it is imaginary because his abstract mathematical conceptions are inadequate to define the new realities.

The disenchantment with an earthly heaven was not accomplished by man's conceptualization of a correspondingly monumental heaven with space-time deities, but by his beginning to articulate a language of the newly discovered relationships.

It is certainly not by accident that artistic intuition and the intellectual processes used in research invoke the same sources of the new interpretations of reality for their creations. Next to what, according to our traditional schooling, we regard as observable nature, there appears another nature that cannot be seen or expressed by our conscious complexes of

experience or by our physical organs of sense. More sensitive optics and newly created sense organs of a mathematical and physical nature attempt to create models that will be comprehensible by an earthly standard. Behind the islandlike reality of our universe, comprehended and organized according to classical dictates, realities are revealed that may be perceived only by mathematical equations and physical systems of thought. But the physical models and mathematical symbols, too, are expedients of analogy. These experimentally provable signs and symbols lead to a still unperceptualized and for the time being impenetrable but nevertheless existing reality.

All conceptions—in both cosmic relationships and the internal world of the atom—that derive from the perception of the terrestrial world lead to error. Man as a particle of the world can only think, interpret, and represent in terms of earthly conceptions, standards, and values, and only within the earthly system of references. In an informative essay, Will Grohmann writes:

"Together with the measure of what has been investigated the measure of what has not been investigated and also of that which cannot be investigated grows. Art remains a secret, and its symbols remain insoluble. Planck in a lecture named as only symbols the little-understood mathematical and physical formulas which are of importance to the contemporary world, symbols which he could not perceptualize. It is sometimes possible for art to look behind the veil and to make visible what could otherwise not be made visible."

As paleolithic man once stood before the chaos of natural occurrences, so man now finds himself standing on a "higher plane"; despite nuclear fission and the sending of rockets into space, he stands before the confusion of an expanded universe. His art, his pictorial symbols and images, transformed and transposed by the spirit of the twentieth century, resemble the paintings of Tassili, Lascaux, and Altamira.

In the early cultures, magic and faith, science and art portray a unity. In thousands of years of cultural development, a process of differentiation has occurred and has separated these categories from one another. Perhaps modern art is becoming adapted to something of the synthetic, many-sided unity of those early times, so that, forebodingly and at the same time playfully, it may symbolize the knowledge of the age and attempt to replace the spiritual powers lost to science and technology.

Certainly art is not merely an ersatz gratification for the soul, in place of the extinct gods dispensing consolation for the inadequacy of life. Still, it has taken over even these functions. At the moment it appears as a utopia of existence, as a dream and legend of a more complete and human life.

The substance of an objective and developmentally possible utopia consists in a not yet realizable, self-propelling and thus developing existence. The inclusion of the developing future in the present means working with its growth. Raising a utopia to consciousness means taking part in its actualization.

The utopia of art lies in the creative attempt to break up the contrast between seeming and being, between conception and reality, and to realize the unity of the ego and the universe, of dream and consciousness, of the human and the cosmic dimension.

LIST OF ILLUSTRATIONS

I THE AWAKENING OF ARCHAIC AND PRIMITIVE CULTURES

31. Paul Klee. *Senecio No. 1569* (1922). Öffentliche Kunstsammlung, Basel
32. Headdress with bull and bird. Senufo. Wood. Height 27⅝". Africa. Museum of Primitive Art, New York
33. Max Ernst. *The King Playing with the Queen* (1944). Bronze. Height 38½". Museum of Modern Art, New York. Gift of Mr. and Mrs. John de Menil
34. Figure. Gulf of Papua. Painted wood. New Guinea. Brooklyn Museum, New York (J. W. Vandercook Collection)
35. Mirko (Mirko Basaldella). *Figure* (1959). Iron
36. Ancestral figure. Dogon. 19th century. Wood. Sudan. Height 23⅝". Museum of Primitive Art, New York
37. Henri Laurens. *Woman with Bowl of Fruit* (1920). Stone
38. Nail-studded fetish. Bakongo, Mayombe region. Nails and wood. Central Africa. Height 26¾". Musée Royale du Congo Belge, Trevuren, Belgium
39. Eduardo Paolozzi. *St. Sebastian I* (1959). Bronze. Height 68⅛". Courtesy Hanover Gallery, London
40. Serbian tombstone. 14th–15th century. Lipenović, near Krupanj, Yugoslavia
41. Lazar Vujaklija. *Girl with Bird* (1959). Oil on canvas
42. *The White Monkey* (dancing mask). Dogon. Wood. Sudan. Height 14⅝". Musée de l'Homme, Paris
43. Barbara Hepworth. *Imprint* (1956). Bronze
44. Hans Uhlmann. *Fetish* (1958). Steel. Height 37¾"
45. Dorothy Dehner. *Rites at Sal Safaeni No. 2* (1957). Bronze. Height 26⅜". Peter A. Rubel collection, New York
46. Jean Arp. *Idol* (1950). Patinated bronze. Height 42⅞". B. Urvater collection, Brussels

II SIGNS OF THE EAST

47. Yuichi Inoue. *Buddha* (1957). Calligraphy: tusche on paper. Collection the artist
48. Robert Motherwell. *Elegy for the Spanish Republic XXXV* (1954–58). Oil on canvas. 79⅞ x 100". Courtesy Sidney Janis Gallery, New York
49. Jasutugu Morita. *In the Wind.* Calligraphy
50. Nicolas de Staël. From "Sketchbook 1945–48." Tusche
51. Selyo Nagai. *Phoenix* (1955). Calligraphy
52. Franz Kline. *Painting No. 7* (1952). Oil on canvas. 57½ x 81⅞". The Solomon R. Guggenheim Museum, New York
53. Pierre Soulages. *Painting* (May, 1955). Oil on canvas. 77⅛ x 55⅛". The Solomon R. Guggenheim Museum, New York
54. Toko Shinoda. *Inspired by the Character for "Fire."* Calligraphy
55. Georges Mathieu. *Blanche d'Escuadoeuvres* (1957). Oil on canvas. 38⅛ x 76¾". P. Dotremont collection, Brussels
56. Taiho Yamasaki. *Alone through Heaven and Earth* (1959). Calligraphy. 53¾ x 53¾"
57. André Masson. *Kabuki* (1955). Gouache
58. Gakiu Osawa. Page from a calligraphic sketchbook
59. Henri Michaux. *Chinese Brush Drawing No. 4* (1958)

60. Mark Tobey. *1951*. Tempera. 43¾ x 28". Joseph R. Schapiro collection, Oak Park, Illinois
61. Roger Bissière. *Painting 1958*. Oil on canvas. 15¾ x 19⅝". Dr. Gran collection, Oslo
62. Gakiu Osawa. Calligraphy

63. Willi Baumeister. *Ideogram* (1958). Oil on canvas. 39⅜ x 28¾". Private collection, Stuttgart
64. Julius Bissier. *Painting, April 8, 1958*
65. Hans Hartung. *Composition* (1950). Oil on cardboard. B. Urvater collection, Brussels

III METAPHORS OF THE HUMAN IMAGE

66. Naum Gabo. *Female Head* (1917–20). Celluloid and metal. 24½ x 19¼". Museum of Modern Art, New York
67. Antoine Pevsner. *Torso* (1924–26). Plastic and copper. Height 29¼". Museum of Modern Art, New York (Katherine S. Dreier Bequest)
68. Pablo Picasso. *Woman Crying* (1937). Oil on canvas 23⅛ x 18⅞". Roland Penrose collection, London
69. Paul Klee. *Fool from the Depths* (1927). Oil on canvas. 14⅝ x 16⅛". Curt Burgauer collection, Zurich
70. Julio Gonzalez. *Head Called Uncle Jean* (1930). Iron. Height 15". Courtesy Galerie de France, Paris
71. Alexej von Jawlensky. *Head: Red Light* (1926). Oil on canvas. 20⅞ x 18⅞". San Francisco Museum of Art
72. Jacques Lipchitz. *Head* (1932). Bronze. Height 9". Stedelijk Museum, Amsterdam
73. Henry Moore. *Abstraction*. Stone. 20⅞ x 16". Art Institute of Chicago (Edgar J. Kaufmann, Jr. Fund)
74. Alexander Archipenko. *Female Torso* (1920–23). Bronze. Height 14". Wilhelm Hack collection, Cologne
75. Marino Marini. *Acrobat*. Bronze. Art Institute of Chicago (Samuel Marx Collection)

76. Henri Laurens. *Woman with Grapes* (1953). Bronze. Height 22½". Courtesy Galerie Louise Leiris, Paris
77. Kosta Angeli Radovani. *Woman Bathing* (1950). Plaster. Height 74¾"
78. Alexander Archipenko. *Médrano* (1915). Painted tin, glass, wood, and oilcloth. Height 50". The Solomon R. Guggenheim Museum, New York
79. Giorgio de Chirico. *Troubadour* (1917). Oil on canvas
80. Henry Moore. *Reclining Figure* (1952–53). Bronze. Length 90½". J. Starrels collection, U.S.A.
81. Fritz Wotruba. *Brussels Relief* (1958), detail. Bronze. 116⅛ x 219¾". Bundesministerium, Vienna
82. Rudolf Hoflehner. *Achaea* (1959). Iron. Height 37". David Bright collection, Los Angeles
83. Drago Tršar. *Street Demonstration II* (1957). Bronze. 53⅞ x 66⅞"
84. Germaine Richier. *Devil with Claws* (1952). Bronze. Height 34⅝". Museum of Modern Art, New York
85. Reginald Butler. *Girl and Boy* (1950–51). Hammered and wrought iron. Height 65⅞". The Arts Council of Great Britain, London
86. Francis Bacon. *Reclining Figure* (1959). Oil on

canvas. 78 x 55¾". Courtesy Marlborough Fine Arts Gallery, London

87. Jean Dubuffet. *Female Body* (1950). Oil on canvas. 45⅝ x 35". Courtesy Pierre Matisse Gallery, New York

88. Kenneth Armitage. *Seated Woman with Square Head* (1955–57). Bronze. Height 24". Collection the Artist

89. Lynn Chadwick. *R 34 (Memorial for an Airplane)* (1959). Iron. 85⅞ x 104⅛"

90. Eduardo Paolozzi. *Greek Hero* (1957). Bronze. Height 68⅛". British Council, London

91. César (Baldaccini). *Naked* (1958). Iron. Height 37¾". Courtesy Galerie Claude Bernard, Paris

92. Fernand Léger. *King of Diamonds* (1927). Oil on canvas

93. Willi Baumeister. *Figure with Yellow Circle* (1920). Oil and sand on canvas. 31½ x 23⅝". Private collection, Germany

IV DREAM IMAGE AND THE LANDSCAPE OF THE UNCONSCIOUS

94. James Ensor. *Masks Confronting Death* (1888). Oil on canvas. 32 x 39½". Museum of Modern Art, New York

95. Henri Rousseau. *Sleeping Gypsy* (1897). Oil on canvas. 51 x 79". Museum of Modern Art, New York (Gift of Mrs. Simon Guggenheim)

96. Giorgio de Chirico. *The Disquieting Muses,* second version (1922). Oil on canvas. 37 x 24⅜". Henry Clifford collection, Philadelphia

97. Marc Chagall. *Motherhood* (1913). Oil on canvas. 76⅜ x 45¼". Stedelijk Museum, Amsterdam

98. Max Ernst. *The Dark Gods* (1957). Oil on canvas. 45⅝ x 35". Folkwang Museum, Essen

99. Salvador Dali. *The Temptation of St. Anthony* (1946). Oil on canvas. 35⅜ x 47¼". H. Robillart collection, Brussels

100. Yves Tanguy. *Slowly Toward the North* (1942). Oil on canvas. 42 x 36". Museum of Modern Art, New York

101. Joan Miró. *Rhythmic Shapes (1934).* Oil on canvas. 74¾ x 67¾". P. Dotremont collection, Brussels

102. Gabrijel Stupica. *Little Girl with Toys* (1956). Oil on canvas. Modern Gallery, Ljubljana

103. Miljenko Stančić. *The Dead Brother* (1954). Oil on canvas

104. René Magritte. *On the Threshold of Freedom* (1929). Oil on canvas. 44⅞ x 57½". Boymans-van Boyningnen Museum, Rotterdam

105. Paul Delvaux. *Hands (1941).* Oil on canvas. 43¼ x 51⅛". Claude Spaak collection, Paris

106. Victor Brauner. *Story of Poet from Sergemegetusa* (1946). B. Urvater collection, Brussels

107. Matta (Echaurren). *Give Light without Pain* (1955). Oil on canvas. 78¾ x 118⅛". B. Urvater collection, Brussels

108. Wifredo Lam. *Jungle* (1943). Gouache on paper mounted on canvas. 94¼ x 90". Museum of Modern Art, New York

109. Wolfgang Paalen. *The Aliens* (1937). Oil on canvas. B. Urvater collection, Brussels

110. Jean Dubuffet. *The Ejaculator* (1951). 36¼ x 28¾". Oil on canvas. Carlo Frua de Angeli collection, Milan

111. Pablo Picasso. *Night Fishing at Antibes* (1939). Oil on canvas. 6' 9" x 11' 4". Museum of Modern Art, New York (Mrs. Simon Guggenheim Fund)

112. Paul Klee. *Puppets* (1930). Oil on canvas

V INDIVIDUALISM AND COLLECTIVISM

113. Diego Rivera. *Lament for a Revolutionary Hero*. Wall painting. National Agricultural College, Chapingo, Mexico
114. José Clemente Orozco. *Peace* (1930). Oil on canvas. 30¼ x 48¼". Julio Serrano collection, Mexico
115. Candido Portinari. *Village Burial* (1944). Oil on canvas. 70⅞ x 86⅝". Museu de Arte, São Paulo
116. Georges Rouault. *Wounded Clown* (1930–35). Oil on canvas. 78¾ x 47¼". Private collection, Paris
117. Alexander A. Deineka. *The Defense of Petrograd* (1928). Oil on canvas. 85⅞ x 139⅜" Tretyakov Gallery, Moscow
118. I. I. Brodsky. *Lenin in the Smolny Institute* (1930). Oil on canvas. Tretyakov Gallery, Moscow
119. John Bratby. *Mother and Child* (1956). Oil on wood. 6½ x 4⅛". Beaux Arts Gallery, London
120. Renato Guttuso. *Discussion* (1959–60). Oil, tempera, and collage

121. George Grosz. *Funeral of the Poet Oskar Panizza* (1917–18). Oil on canvas. 55⅛ x 43¼". Staatsgalerie, Stuttgart
122. Otto Dix. *The Trenches in Flanders* (1920). Oil on canvas. Destroyed
123. Ernst Barlach. *Mankind's Martyrdom*. Wood
124. Ossip Zadkine. *City without a Heart* (monument commemorating the destruction of the city of Rotterdam) (1953–54). Bronze
125. Ben Shahn. *Pacific Landscape* (1945). Tempera on paper mounted on wood. 25¼ x 39". Museum of Modern Art, New York
126. Krsto Hegedušić. *Dead Water* (1956). Tempera and oil on canvas. Modern Gallery, Ljubljana, Yugoslavia
127. Fernand Léger. *Construction Workers*, final version (1950). Oil on canvas. Collection the artist
128. Pablo Picasso. *Guernica* (1937), detail. Oil on canvas. 11' 6" x 25' 8". Museum of Modern Art, New York (on extended loan from the artist)

VI LIBERATION FROM THE OBJECT, RELEASE FROM FORM

129. Pablo Picasso. *Portrait of Ambroise Vollard* (1909–10). Oil on canvas. 36¼ x 25⅝"
130. Georges Braque. *Girl with Guitar* (1913). Oil on canvas. 51⅛ x 29⅛". Musée National d'Art Moderne, Paris
131. Robert Delaunay. *The City* (1911). Oil on can-

vas. 57⅛ x 44⅛". The Solomon R. Guggenheim Museum, New York
132. Umberto Boccioni. *Fields of Force in the Street* (1911). Oil on canvas. 39⅜ x 31½". Private collection, Basel
133. Wassily Kandinsky. *Composition V* (1911). Oil

on canvas. 74¾ x 108¼". Dübi-Müller collection, Solothurn, Switzerland

134. Francis Picabia. *Edtaonisl* (1913). Oil on canvas. 116⅞ x 116⅞". The Art Institute of Chicago

135. Piet Mondrian. *Composition No. 6* (1914). Oil on canvas. 34⅝ x 24". S. B. Slijper collection, Blaricum, The Netherlands

136. Kasimir Malevich. *Suprematist Composition* (1915). Oil on canvas. 34⅝ x 27⅞". Stedlijk Museum, Amsterdam

137. Juan Gris. *Still Life* (1916). Oil on canvas. 18⅛ x15". The Solomon R. Guggenheim Museum, New York

138. Fernand Léger. *Tugboat* (1918). Oil on canvas. 25⅝ x 36¼". Wallraf-Richartz Museum, Cologne

139. Willi Baumeister. *Segmented Wall* (1921). Oil on canvas. 16½ x 19¾". Private collection, Germany

140. Marcel Duchamp. *Le Passage de la Vierge à la Mariée* (1912). Oil on canvas. 23⅜ x 21¼". Museum of Modern Art, New York

141. Kurt Schwitters. *Merzbild 25 A* (1920). Collage. Private collection

142. Theo van Doesburg. *Composition A 16* (1916)

143. Alberto Magnelli. *Diffused Light* (1950). Oil on canvas. 41⅜ x 56¾". Private collection, Wiesbaden

144. Ben Nicholson. *White Relief* (1938). Oil on wood. 47¼ x 72". Collection the artist

145. Friedrich Vordemberge-Gildewart. *Relief No. 8* (1924). 33½ x 25⅝"

146. Jean Bazaine. *Diver* (1949). Oil on canvas. 57½ x 45¼". P. Dotremont collection, Brussels

147. Alfred Manessier. *On the Meadow* (1954). Oil on canvas. 44⅞ x 63¾". P. Dotremont collection, Brussels

148. Nicolas de Staël. *Football Player* (1952). Oil on canvas. 44⅞ x 63¾". Jacques Dubourg collection, Paris

149. Ernst Wilhelm Nay. *With Poetic Blue* (1961). Oil on canvas. 94½ x 74¾"

150. Tadeusz Kantor. *Pas'akas* (1957). Oil on canvas. 66⅞ x 54⅜"

151. Petar Lubarda. *In Space (1960)*. Oil on canvas

152. Fritz Winter. *Black Paths* (1958). Oil on canvas. 53⅛ x 57⅛"

153. Emilio Vedova. *Road Block* (1951). Tempera. 66⅞ x 51⅛". Private collection

154. Wols (Alfred Otto Wolfgang Schulze). *Painting* (1944–45). Oil on canvas. 31⅞ x 32". Museum of Modern Art, New York (Mr. and Mrs. John de Menil Fund)

155. Jean Fautrier. *Magic Lantern,* four-sided painting (1957). Tusche and pastel on sized paper. 18⅛ x 13¾". Private collection, Paris

156. Hans Hartung. *Painting T. 56-13.* Oil. 70½ x 53⅞". Peter Adam collection, London

157. Jackson Pollock. *Number 12* (1952). Oil on canvas. 102 x 89". Private collection, New York

158. Mark Tobey. *Harvest* (1958). Tempera on paper. 36 x 24½". Mrs. Marian Willard Johnson collection, New York

159. Willem de Kooning. *February* (1957). Oil on canvas. 58¾ x 68⅞". Dr. and Mrs. Edgar Berman collection, Maryland

160. Alberto Burri. *Composition* (1953). Oil, gold leaf, and glue on canvas and burlap. 34⅛ x 39⅜". The Solomon R. Guggenheim Museum, New York

161. Antonio Tàpies. Painting (1955). Oil on canvas. 76⅜ x 66¼". P. Dotremont collection, Brussels

162. Luis Feito. *Number 110* (1959). Oil on canvas. 47¼ x 47¼". J. König collection, Paris

163. Jean-Paul Riopelle. *Forest* (1953). Oil on canvas. 51⅛ x 76¾"

164. Mark Rothko. *Black and White* (1956). Oil on canvas. 94⅛ x 54¾". Dr. and Mrs. Frank Stanton collection, New York

VII ANTIART AND THE NEW REALITY

165. Jasper Johns. *Device Circle* (1959). Encaustic on canvas and wood. 40 x 40". Mr. and Mrs. Burton Tremaine collection, Meriden, Connecticut

166. Robert Rauschenberg. *Canyon* (1959). Combine on canvas. 86½ x 70½ x 23". Courtesy Leo Castelli Gallery, New York

167. Jim Dine. *Hatchet with Two Palettes* (1963). Oil on canvas with wood and metal. 72 x 54 x 15". The Abrams Family collection, New York

168. Daniel Spoerri. *The Shower: Trompe-l'oeil in Reverse* (1961). Schwarz Gallery, Milan

169. Tanzio and Giovanni da Varallo. *The Massacre of the Innocents* (1616–28). Chapel XI, Sanctuary Sacro Monte, near Varallo, Italy

170. George Segal. *New Work* (1965). Courtesy Sidney Janis Gallery, New York

171. *Amida, the Thousand Buddhas.* Late Heian period (794–1185). Block print (height of figures 1⅝"). Joruri-ji Temple, Kyoto

172. Andy Warhol. *Coca-Cola Bottles* (1962). Oil on canvas. 82¼ x 105". The Abrams Family Collection, New York

173. Claes Oldenburg. *Pastry Case II* (1962). Plaster, glass, and enamel. Courtesy Sidney Janis Gallery, New York

174. Marisol (Marisol Escobar). *Baby Boy* (1963). Painted wood construction. 88 x 31". Mrs. Albert List collection, New York

175. Michelangelo Pistoletto. *Two People* (1963). Painted collage on polished stainless steel. 78¾ x 47¼". Courtesy Galerie Ileana Sonnabend, Paris

176. Allen Jones. *Man and Woman* (1963). Oil on canvas. 83⅞ x 71⅝". Private collection

177. Tom Wesselmann. *Great American Nude, No. 48.* Combine. 84 x 108". Mr. and Mrs. Frederick Weisman collection, Los Angeles

178. H. P. Alvermann. *Tribute to Düsseldorf* (1962). Assemblage of objects. 47¼ x 53⅛". Jährling collection, Wuppertal, Germany

179. Peter Blake. *Self-Portrait* (1961). 67¾ x 48". Courtesy Robert Fraser Gallery, London

180. David Hockney. *Marriage of Styles II* (1963). Mixed media. 71⅝ x 83⅞". Contemporary Art Society, London

181. Joe Tilson. *Nine Elements* (1963). Plastics and acrylic on wood relief

182. James Rosenquist. *For the American Negro* (1962–63). Oil on canvas. 80 x 210". Courtesy Leo Castelli Gallery, New York

183. Jacques de la Villéglé. *Posters Ripped off Wall on February 22, 1959, Porte Maillot.* Collage of posters on plywood panel. 22⅞ x 45⅝". Courtesy Galerie Jacqueline Ranson, Paris

184. Roy Lichtenstein. *Drowning Girl* (1963). Oil and magna on canvas. 68 x 68". Mr. and Mrs. C. B. Wright collection, Seattle

VIII ART IN A TECHNOLOGICAL AGE

185. Short-wave transmitter. Usingen, Germany
186. Reginald Butler. *The Unknown Political Pris-*

oner (project for a monument) (1951–53). Bronze with stone base. Height 17⅞". Museum of Modern Art, New York (Saidie A. May Fund)

187. Radio telescope built by Telefunken (1957). Bonn Observatory, Stockert in der Eifel, Germany

188. Naum Gabo. *Sculptured Construction*. Metal and plastic. In front of the De Beckendorf Department Store, Rotterdam

189. Launching pad for a Vanguard rocket

190. Wallace K. Harrison. Interior of the First Presbyterian Church, Stamford, Connecticut. 1958

191. Mount Palomar Observatory, San Diego, California

192. Rudolf Belling. Sculpture (1929). Height 3¾"

193. Microphoto of plankton, magnified 1,200 times

194. Richard Buckminster Fuller. Geodesic dome (1958). Union Tank Car Company. Baton Rouge, Louisiana

195. View of Rockefeller Center, New York

196. Nicolas Schöffer. *Statiodynamique* (1955). Steel

197. Naum Gabo. *Column* (1923). Plastic, wood, and metal. Height 41⅜"

198. Ludwig Mies van der Rohe and Philip C. Johnson. Seagram Building (1958), New York

199. Frank Lloyd Wright. Interior of the Solomon R. Guggenheim Museum (1959), New York

200. Frank Lloyd Wright. Exterior of the Solomon R. Guggenheim Museum (1959), New York

201. Frank Lloyd Wright. Kaufmann House, "Falling Water" (1936–39), Bear Run, Pennsylvania

202. Le Corbusier. Philips Pavilion for Electronic Music. 1958 Brussels World's Fair

203. Le Corbusier. Chapel of Notre Dame du Haut (1955), Ronchamp, France

204. Antoine Pevsner. *Developable Column* (1942). Brass and oxidized bronze. Height 20¾". Museum of Modern Art, New York

205. Frantisek Kupka. *Rhythms* (1912–13)

206. Four-level freeway intersection. Los Angeles

207. Barbara Hepworth. *Bent Form (Delphi)* (1955). Nigerian wood, white paint, and chestnut-brown strings. 42⅛ x 16⅛". Courtesy Galerie Gimpel Fils, London

208. Concrete bridge. Sandö River, Sweden

209. Reservoir and power plant. Parker Dam, Havasu Lake, California

210–11. Konrad Wachsmann. Model for an airplane hanger for Chicago. Plastics

212. Constant. Model for a future city (1958)

213. Jean Tinguely. *M K III* (1964). Iron machine. 62 x 82⅝". Museum of Fine Arts, Houston, Texas

214. Max Bill. *Construction with Thirty Identical Elements* (1938–39). Stainless steel. 60¼ x 180¾"

215. Alexander Calder. *Fins* (1954). Mobile. Courtesy Galerie Maeght, Paris

216. Jean Arp. *Metamorphosis* (1935). Bronze. Height 27⅛". Graindorge collection, Liège

217. Constantin Brancusi. *Bird in Space* (1926). Height 71⅝"

218. Alberto Viani. *Nude* (1954). Marble. Private collection, Venice

219. Vojin Bakić. *Head with Kerchief* (1954). Marble

220. Ornamental meander. Paleolithic. Incised mammoth tusk. Mezin, Ukraine

221. Reginald Neal. *Black and Yellow Squares* (1965). From the exhibition, "The Responsive Eye," Museum of Modern Art, New York

222. Inlaid marble floor (detail). c. 1225. Baptistry, Florence

223. Mosaic floor (detail). Roman, first century A.D. Terme Museum, Rome

224. Benjamin Frazier Cunningham. *Equivocation* (1964). Synthetic polymer paint on gesso panel. 26 x 26". Museum of Modern Art, New York (Larry Aldrich Foundation Fund)

225. Vjenceslav Richter. *Spherical Shape* (1956). Plastics

226. Ferdinand Kriwet. *Rundscheibe No. 5.* Example of Letterism
227. Disk with spiral hieroglyphics. Cretan, from Phaestos. Terracotta. Archaeological Museum, Heraklion, Crete
228. Zoran Radović. *Geometric Forms* (1966). Kinetic design created by a two-pendulum ornamentograph. Private collection, Belgrade
229. Spiral ornament. Period of the "Contending States," China. Bronze. Diameter 9¾". Musée Guimet, Paris
230. Tadasky. *A-101* (1964). Oil on canvas. 52 x 52" Museum of Modern Art, New York (Larry Aldrich Foundation Fund)
231. Incised shell. Late Mississippi (A.D. 1000–1600). Chickamuga Creek, Tennessee. Museum of Primitive Art, New York
232. Len Lye. *Loop* (1963). Steel. 60 x 72 x 6". Courtesy Howard Wise Gallery, New York
233. Victor de Vasarely. *Sir-Ris* (1965). Oil on canvas. 80 x 41". Courtesy Sidney Janis Gallery, New York
234. Miroslav Sutej. *Bombardment of the Optic Nerve II* (1963). Tempera and pencil on canvas. Diameter 79". Museum of Modern Art, New York (Larry Aldrich Foundation Fund)
235. Kenneth Noland. *Cycle* (1960). Oil on canvas. 69½ x 69½". Courtesy André Emmerich Gallery, New York
236. Barnett Newman. *Horizon Light* (1949). Oil on canvas. 30½ x 72½". Mr. and Mrs. Thomas Sills Collection, New York
237. Rolf Günther Dienst. *Moments-Diary* (1965). Oil on canvas. 31½ x 23⅝"
238. Bill Komodore. *Federal Pavilion* (1964). Liquitex on canvas. 60 x 60". Courtesy Howard Wise Gallery
239. Naum Gabo. *Linear Construction* (1942–43). Plastic and plastic thread. 13¾ x 13¾". Tate Gallery, London
240. Victor de Vasarely. *Black Vega* (1965). Tempera. 33½ x 33½". Courtesy Sidney Janis Gallery, New York
241. Frank Stella. *Nunca Pasa Nada* (1964). Metallic powder and polymer emulsion on canvas. 9 x 18". Lannon Foundation, Chicago
242. Benjamin Frazier Cunningham. *Six Dimensions of Orange* (1964–65). 81 x 114 x 57". Courtesy East Hampton Gallery, New York
243. Vault decoration. Byzantine, first half of the fifth century. Mosaic. Tomb of Galla Placidia, Ravenna
244. Josef Albers. *Frontward* (1957). Oil on composition board 40 x 40". Courtesy Sidney Janis Gallery, New York
245. Klaus Jürgen Fischer. *Yellow Square* (1964–65). Acrylic on canvas. 48⅜ x 48⅜"
246. Enzo Mari. *Structure No. 724* (1963). Anodized aluminum. 23⅝ x 23⅝ x 3⅞"
247. Ivan Picelj. *Candrai* (1965). Metal and wood. 39¼ x 39¼". Courtesy Howard Wise Gallery, New York
248. Vojin Bakić. *Light-bearing Forms V* (1963–64). Gallery of Contemporary Art, Zagreb, Yugoslavia
249. Wojciech Fangor. *No. 35* (1963). 51⅛ x 38⅛"
250. Len Lye. *Fountain* (1963). Stainless steel. 90 x 84". Courtesy Howard Wise Gallery, New York
251. Le Parc. *Light Continuum* (1963–65). Projected light on translucent screen. Courtesy Howard Wise Gallery, New York
252. Günther Uecker. *White Mill* (1964). Nails, canvas, wood, and white paint. Diameter 6½". Courtesy Howard Wise Gallery, New York
253. Yvaral. *Instability* (1962–65). Wood. 10 x 10". Courtesy Howard Wise Gallery, New York
254. Heinz Mack. *Rotor IV, "Silver Sun"* (1965). Glass, aluminum, and wood: motorized. 22⅝ x 22⅞". Courtesy Galerie Schmall, Düsseldorf

IX BREAKING THROUGH THE VISUAL BARRIER

255. Piet Mondrian. *Lozenge with Gray Lines* (1918). Oil on canvas, Diagonal 47⅝". Private collection, The Netherlands

256. Microphoto of the cell structure of a bulrush stalk magnified 120 times

257. François Stahly. Window in the west apse of the Church of Baccarat, France

258. Microphoto of human trabeculae magnified forty-five times

259. Serge Poliakoff. *Composition* (1956). Oil on burlap. 38⅛ x 51¼". Museum of Modern Art, New York (Gift of M. Knoedler & Company)

260. Microphoto of the shell of a sea louse (detail) magnified 1,200 times

261. Wassily Kandinsky. *Two, etc.* (1937). Oil on canvas. 35 x 45⅝". Courtesy Galerie Maeght, Paris

262. Model of the Brillouin Zone structure of bismuth. Franklin Institute, Philadelphia

263. Zoltan Kemeny. *Relief.* Metal

264. Microphoto of markings on silver magnified 12,000 times. Franklin Institute, Philadelphia

265. Robert Delaunay. *Rhythm* (1933). Painted plaster relief

266. Microphoto of markings on zinc, showing interference patterns, magnified 2,000 times. Franklin Institute, Philadelphia

267. Piet Mondrian. *Victory Boogie-Woogie* (1943–44). Oil on canvas. 50 x 50". Mr. and Mrs. Burton Tremaine collection, Meriden, Conn.

268. Aerial photograph of Tetuán, Morocco

269. Paul Klee. *Highways and Byways* (1929) Oil on canvas. 32⅝ x 26⅜". Wallraf-Richartz Museum, Cologne

270. Aerial photograph of farmland

271. The earth as seen from an altitude of 160 miles (showing the Gulf of Mexico). Satellite photo

272. K. R. H. Sonderborg. *Flying Thought* (1958) Tempera on paper. 42½ x 27⅝". Private collection, Paris

273. Max Ernst. *The Sea* (1928). Painted plaster on canvas. 22 x 18½". Museum of Modern Art, New York

274. The moon (north is to the right). Photographed through the reflecting telescope of the Hamburg Observatory

275. Wassily Kandinsky. *Upward* (1925). Watercolor

276. Honest John rocket

277. Wols (Alfred Otto Wolfgang Schulze). *Blue Ghost* (1951). Oil on canvas. 36¼ x 28¾". Dr. Riccardo Jucker collection, Milan

278. Detonation of an atomic bomb. British test of October, 1957

279. Danilo di Prete. *Cosmic Gesture II* (1960). Oil on canvas

280. Nighttime aerial photograph of the Kvarner Gulf in the Adriatic

281. Antonio Zoran Musič. *AX-100F* (1960). Oil on canvas

ILLUSTRATIONS

1   Japanese, Haniwa style

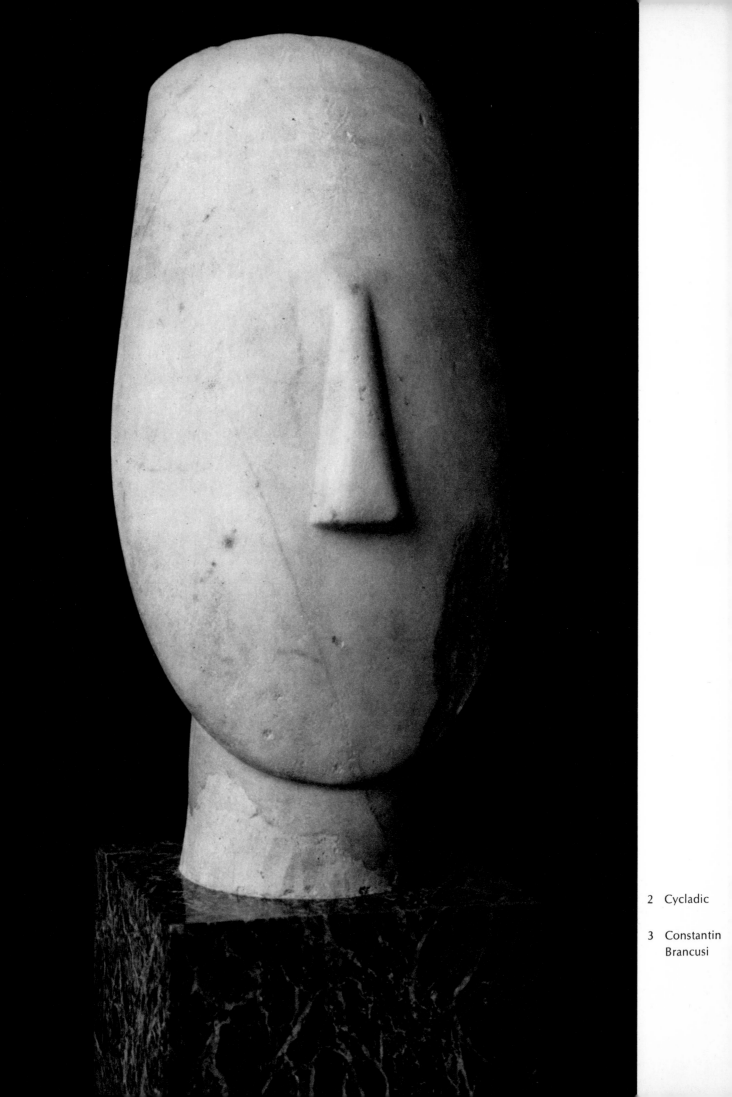

2 Cycladic

3 Constantin
  Brancusi

4 Easter Island

5 André Beaudin

6 Pre-Dynastic Egyptian

7 Bernhard Heiliger

8   Middle Eastern, 3500 B.C.

9   Alberto Giacometti

10 Haida Indian, British Columbia 11 Jacques Lipchitz

12 Egyptian, 18th Dynasty

13 Henry Moore

14 Mayan

15 Henry Moore

16 Mayan

17 Fritz Wotruba

18 Aztec

20 Pre-classical Mexican

19 Henry Moore

21 Olga Jančić

23 Paul Klee

22 Inca

24   Colombian, c. 1000–1300

25   Pablo Picasso

26 Itumba region, Africa

27 Pablo Picasso

28 Central Congo

29 Amedeo Modigliani

31 Paul Klee

30 Bakota tribe, Gabon, Africa

32 Senufo tribe, Africa

33 Max Ernst

34   New Guinea

35   Mirko (Mirko Basaldella)

36 Dogon tribe, Sudan   37 Henri Laurens

38   Bakongo tribe, Mayombe, Africa

39   Eduardo Paolozzi

41 Lazar Vujaklija

42 Dogon tribe, Sudan

43 Barbara Hepworth

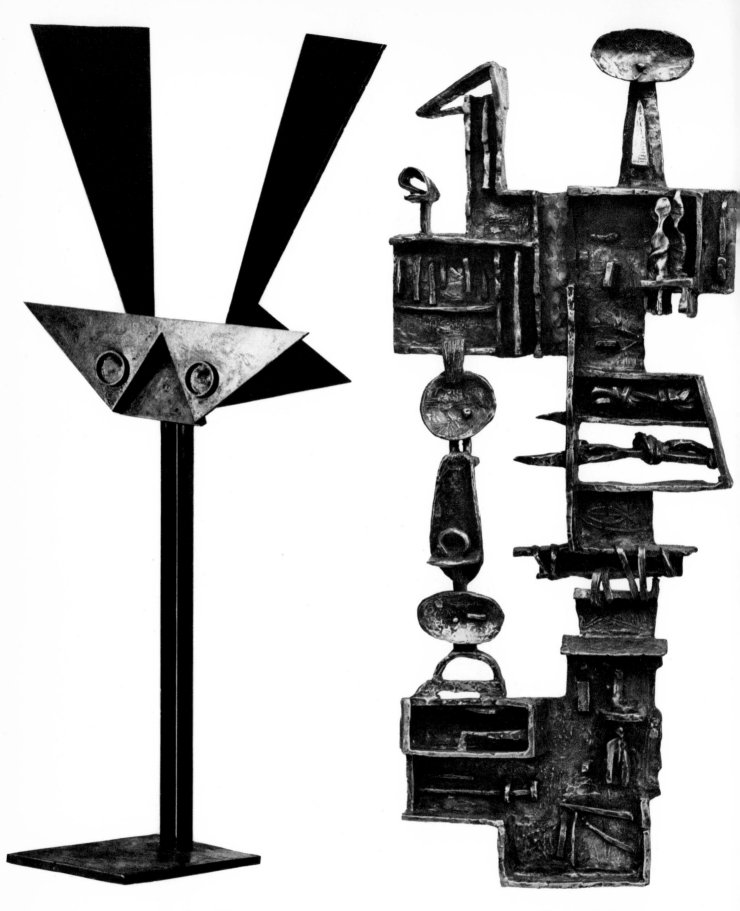

44 Hans Uhlmann

45 Dorothy Dehner

46 Jean Arp

47   Yuichi Inoue

48   Robert Motherwell

49   Jasutugu Morita

50   Nicolas de Staël

51 Seiyo Nagai

52 Franz Kline

53
Pierre
Soulages

54 Toko Shinoda

55 Georges Mathieu

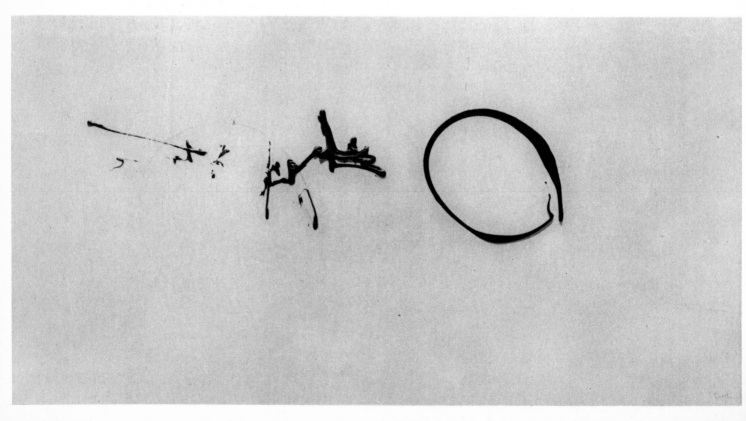

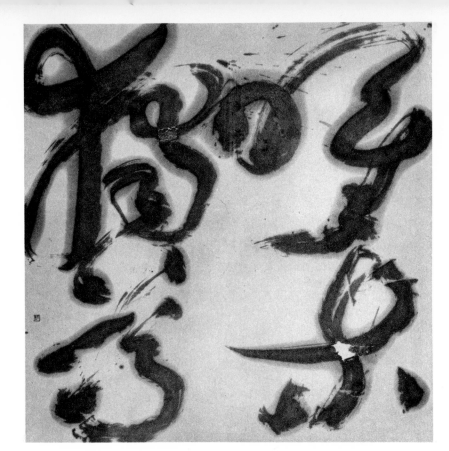

56 Taiho Yamasaki

57 André Masson

58 Gakiu Osawa

59 Henri Michaux

60 Mark Tobey

61 Roger Bissière

62 Gakiu Osawa

63 Willi Baumeister

64 Julius Bissie

65 Hans Hartun

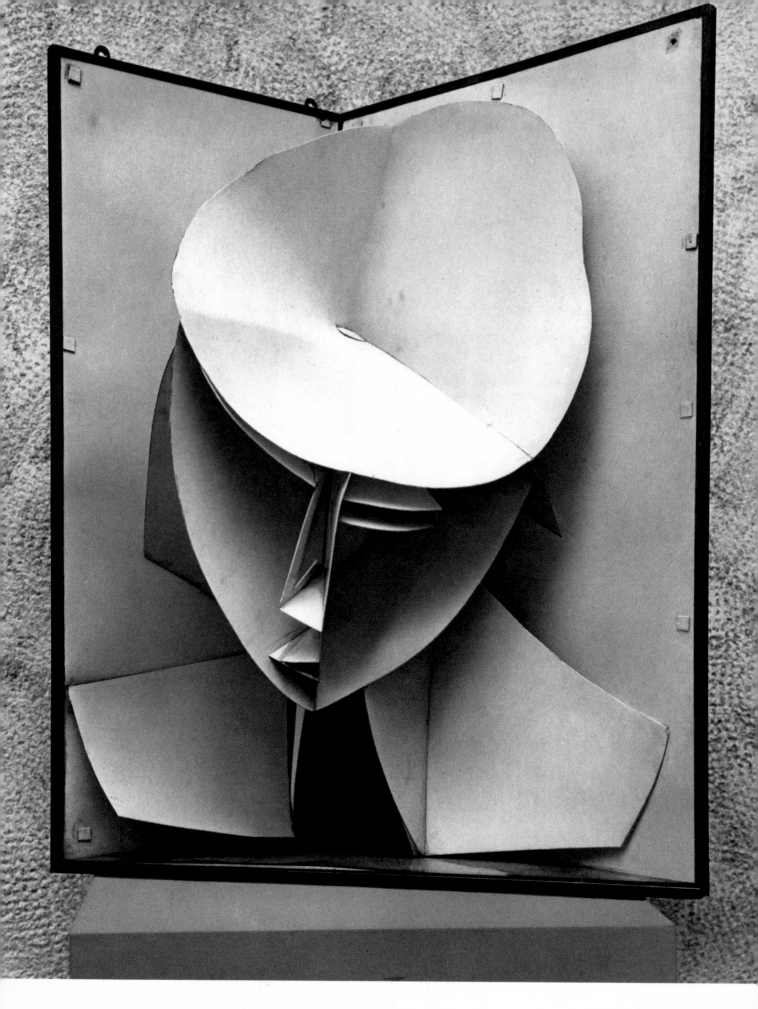

66 Naum Gabo

67   Antoine Pevsner

69 Paul Klee

70   Julio Gonzalez   71   Alexej von Jawlensky

74   Alexander Archipenko

75   Marino Marini

76 Henri Laurens

77 Kosta Angeli Radovani

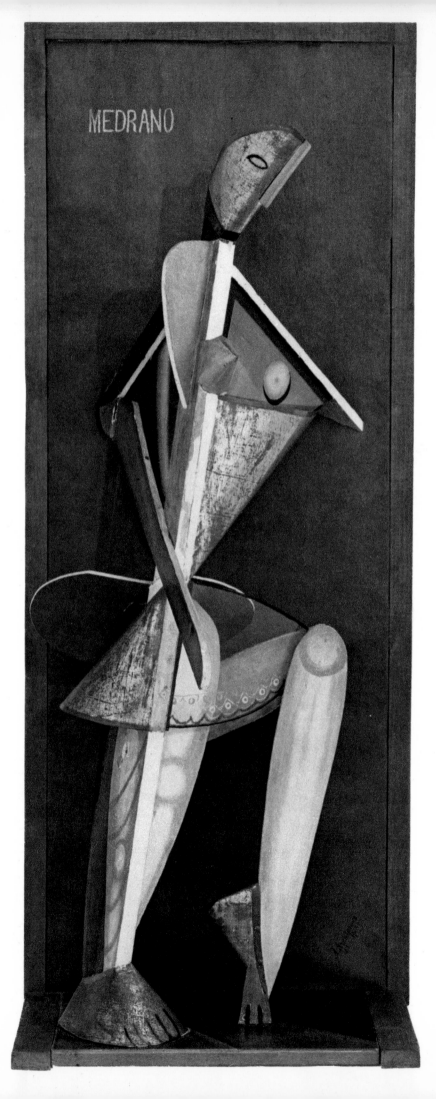

78 Alexander Archipenko

79   Giorgio de Chirico

80   Henry Moore

81   Fritz Wotruba

82   Rudolf Hoflehner

33   Drago Tršar

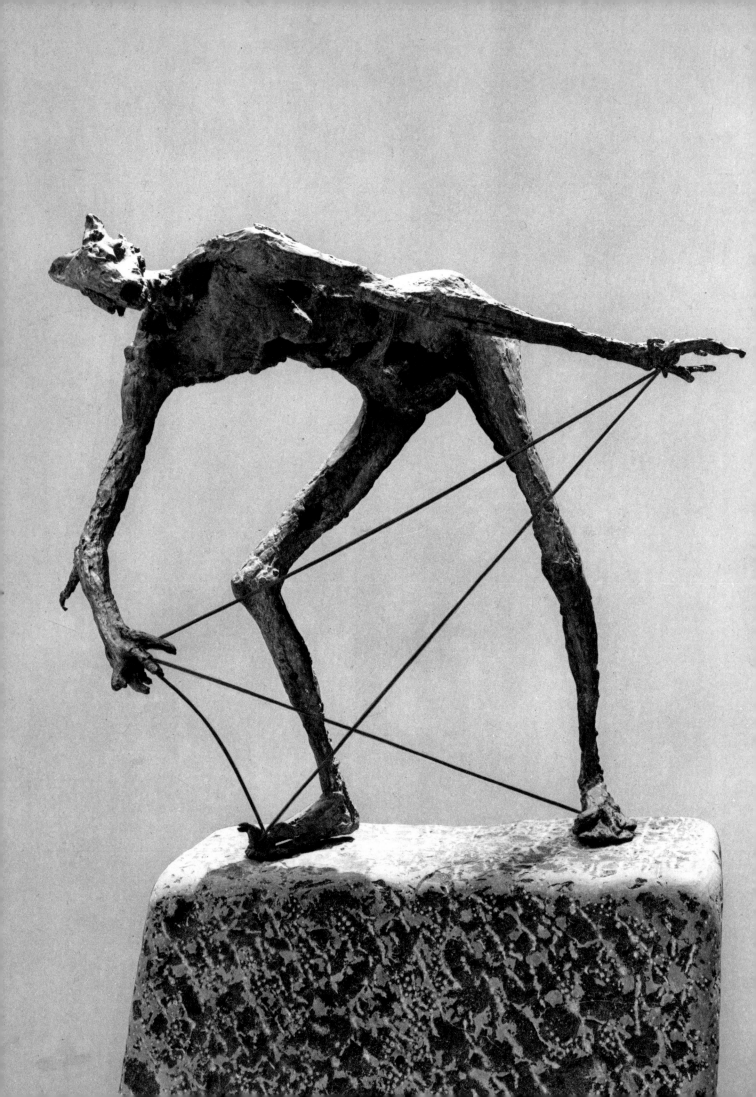

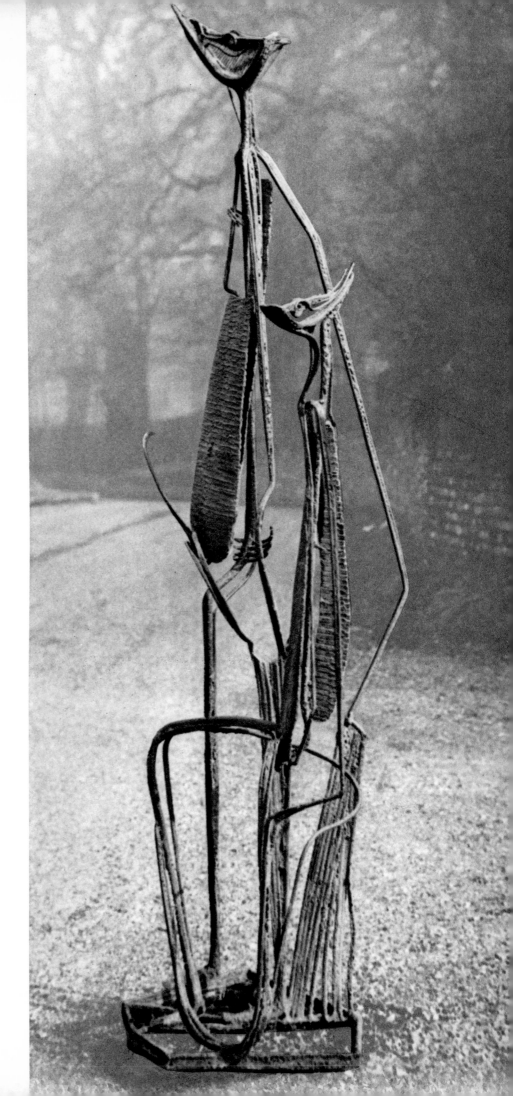

84 Germaine Richier

85 Reginald Butler

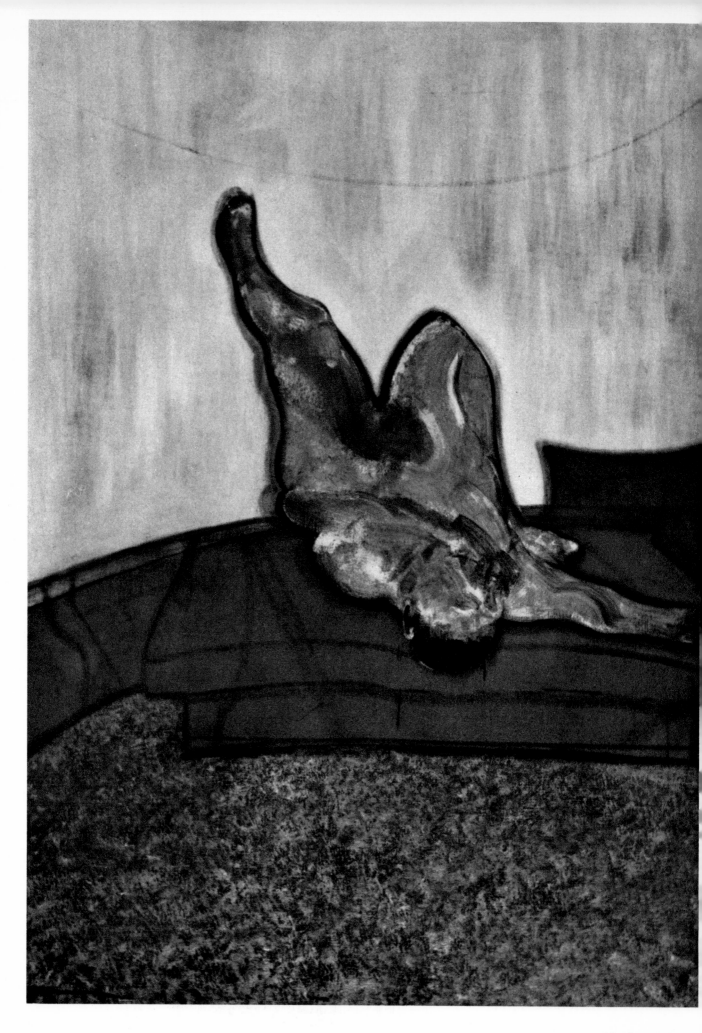

88   Kenneth Armitage

89   Lynn Chadwick

90   Eduardo Paolozzi

91 César (Baldaccini)

93　Willi Baumeister

94 James Ensor

95   Henri Rousseau

96 Giorgio
 de Chirico

97 Marc Chagall

98   Max Ernst

99   Salvador Dali

01   Joan Miró

102 Gabrijel Stupica

103 Miljenko Stančić

104   René Magritte

105   Paul Delvaux

108 Wifredo Lam

12   Paul Klee

114   José Clemente Orozco

113   Diego Rivera

115   Candido Portinari

117   Alexander A. Deinek

118   I. I. Brodsky

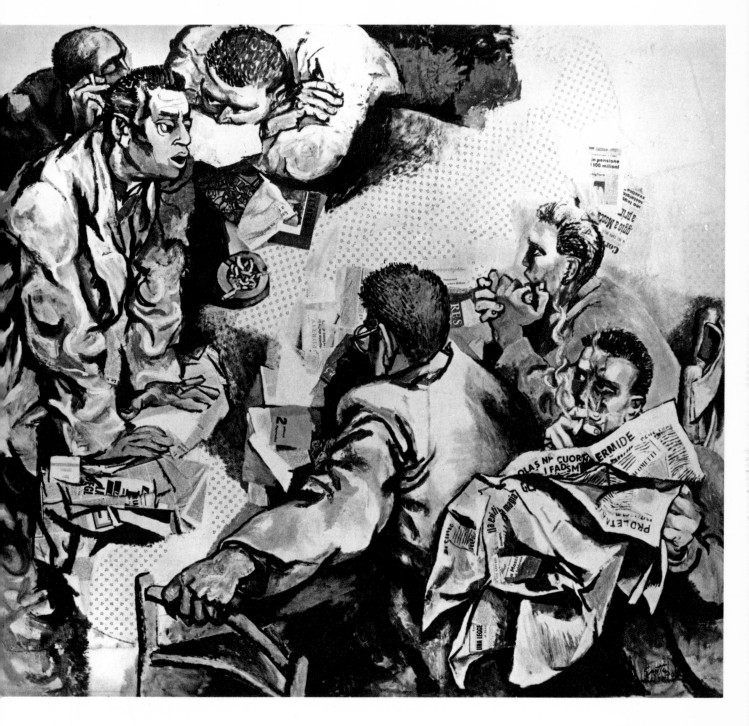

122   Otto Dix

123   Ernst Barlach

124   Ossip Zadkin

126   Krsto Hegedušić

127   Fernand Léger

29 Pablo Picasso

30 Georges Braque

La ville 1911 r.delaunay

133   Wassily Kandinsky

134   Francis Picabia

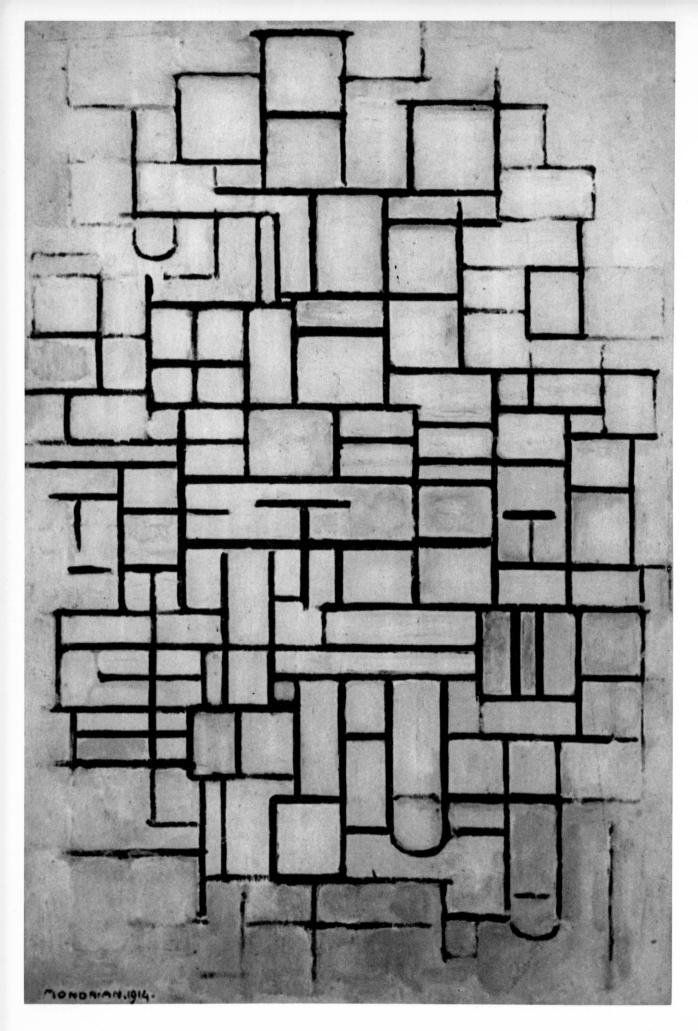

135 Piet Mondrian

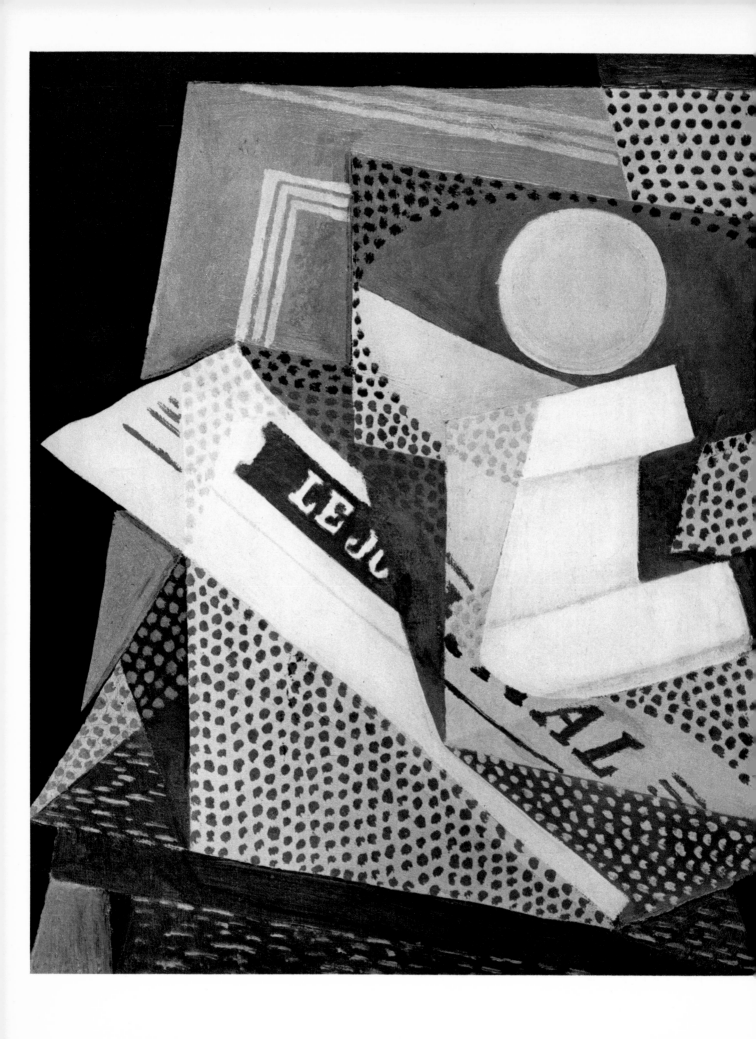

138 Fernand Léger

139 Willi Baumeister

LE PASSAGE de la vierge à la mariée

MARCEL DUCHAMP

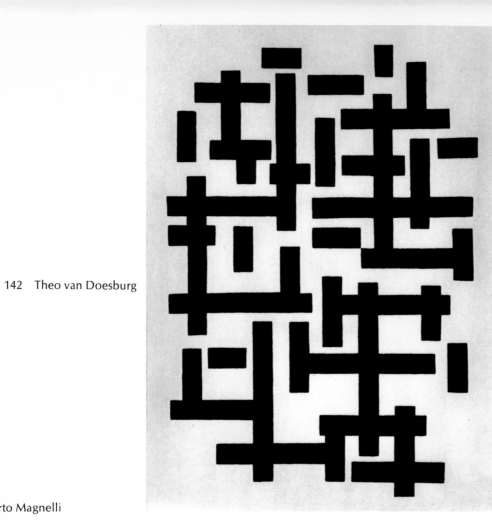

142 Theo van Doesburg

144 Ben Nicholso

143 Alberto Magnelli

14
Friedric
Vordemberge
Gildewar

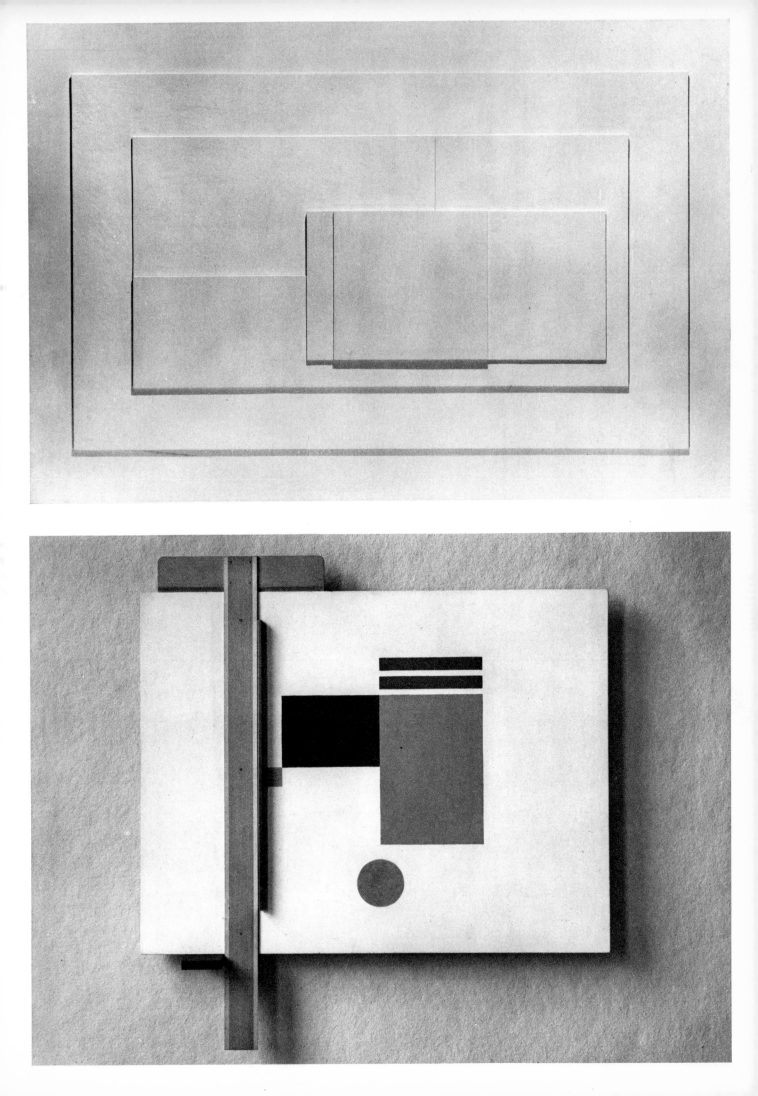

147 Alfred Manessier

146 Jean Bazaine

148 Nicolas de Staël

149   Ernst Wilhelm Nay

150   Tadeusz Kantor

151   Petar Lubarda

152   Fritz Winter

153   Emilio Vedova

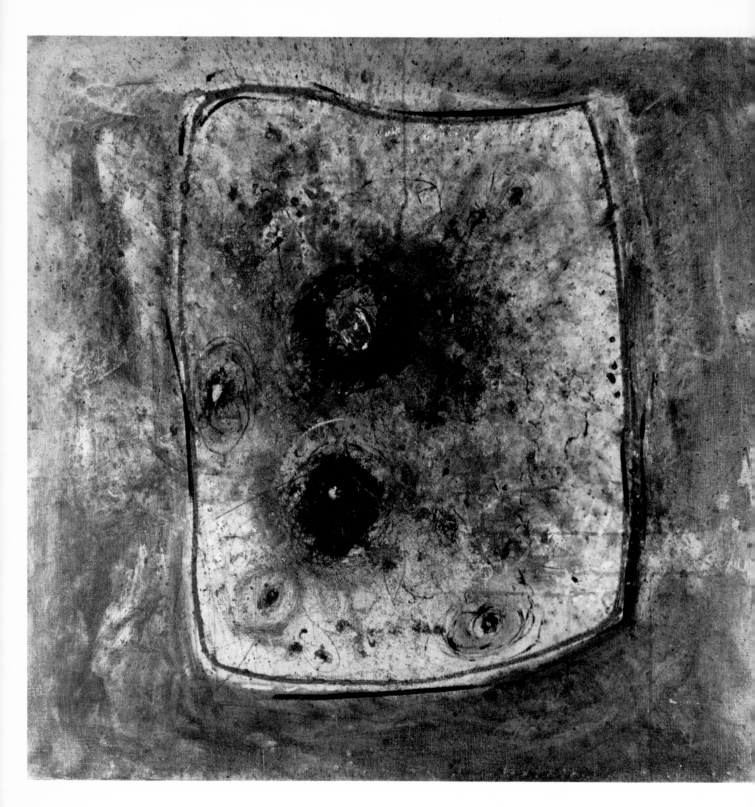

154   Wol

55   Jean Fautrier

157   Jackson Pollock

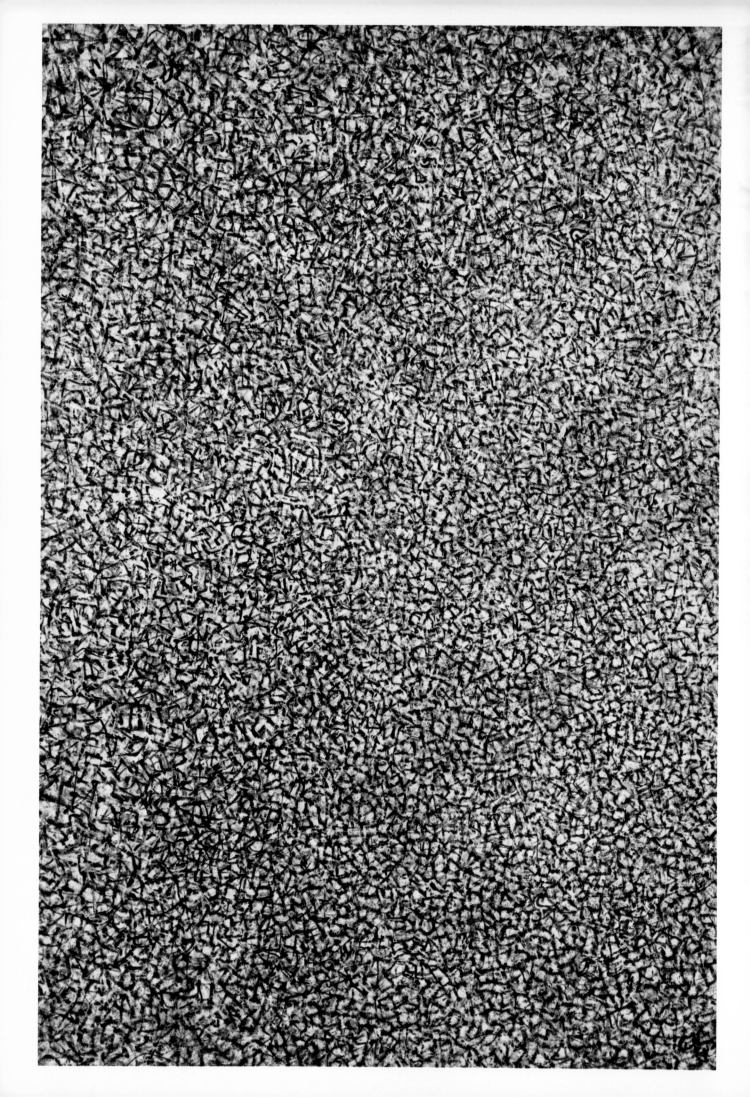

159   Willem de Kooning

160   Alberto Burr

161   Antonio Tàpies

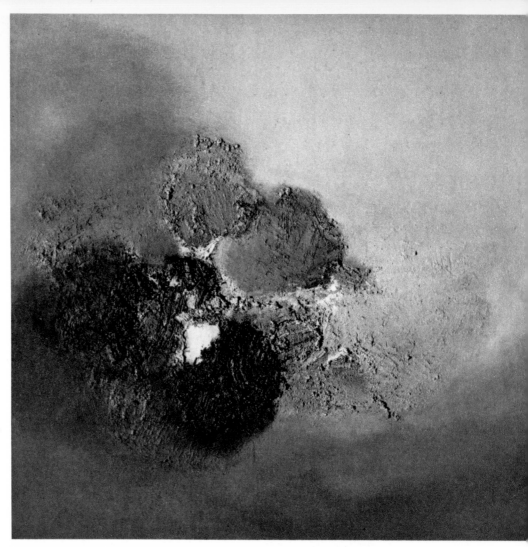

162 Luis Feito

163 Jean-Paul Riopelle

164   Mark Rothko

165   Jasper Johns

66   Robert Rauschenberg

168   Daniel Spoerri

167   Jim Dine

169   Tanzio and Giovanni da Varallo

170   George Segal

172 Andy Warhol

171 Japanese, c. 794–1185

173   Claes Oldenburg

174   Marisol

176 Allen Jones

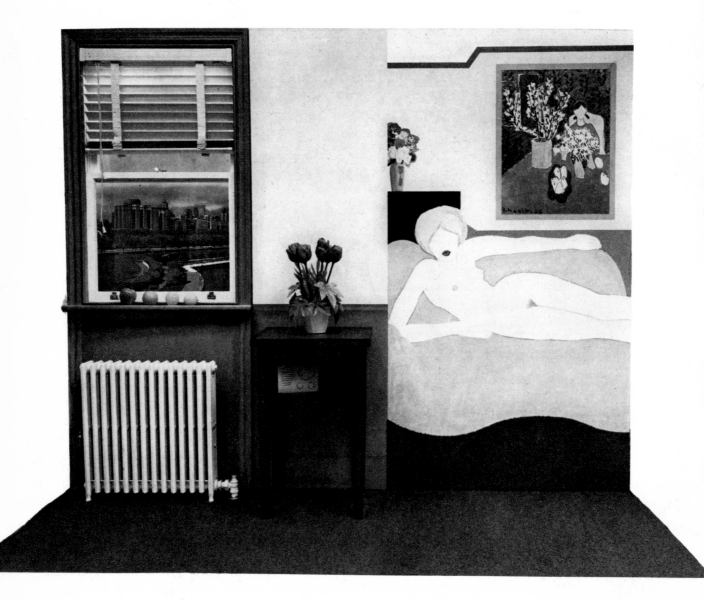

177 Tom Wesselmann

178   H. P. Alvermann

180   David Hockney

179   Peter Blake

181   Joe Tilson

182   James Rosenquist

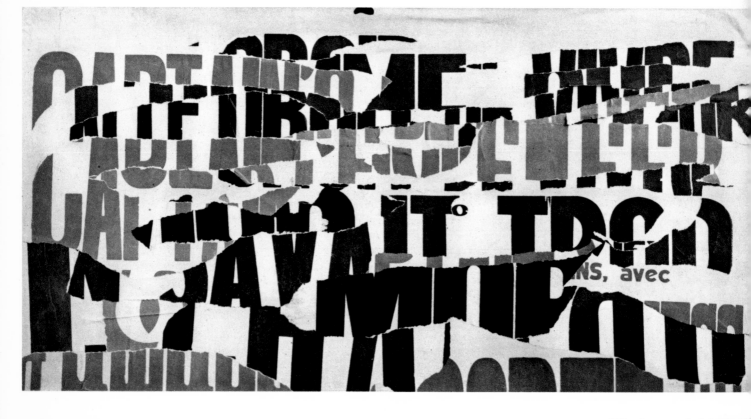

183   Jacques de la Villéglé

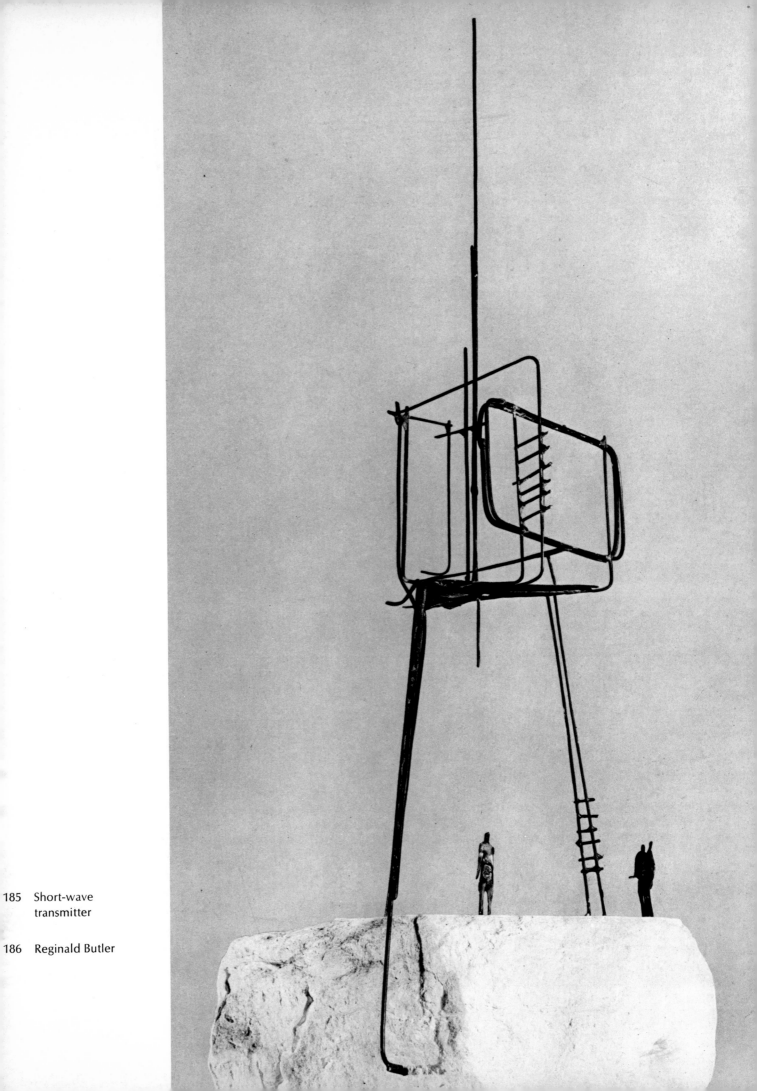

185 Short-wave
transmitter

186 Reginald Butler

187   Radio telescope

189   Rocket launching pad

190   Wallace K. Harrison

191 Mount Palomar Observatory

192 Rudolf Belling

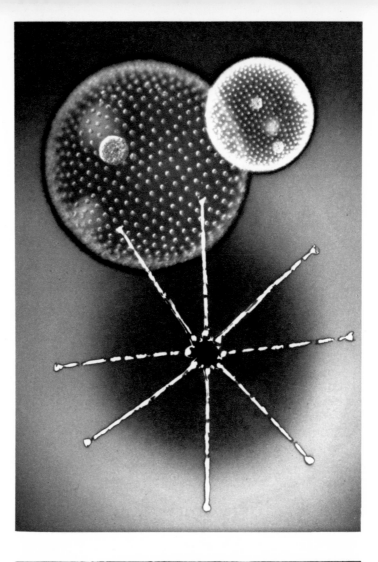

193   Microphoto of plankton

194   Richard Buckminster Fuller

196 Nicolas Schöffer

197   Naum Gabo   198   Ludwig Mies van der Rohe and Philip C. Johnson

202　Le Corbusier

203   Le Corbusier

204   Antoine Pevsner

205 Frantisek Kupka

206 Freeway intersection

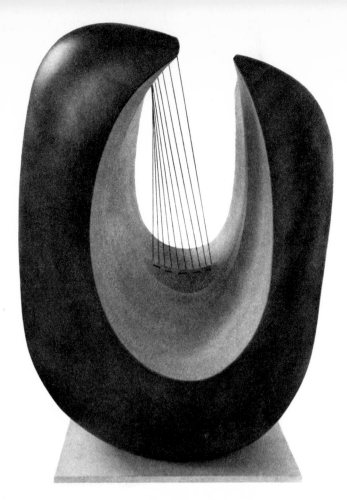

207 Barbara Hepworth

208 Concrete bridge

209   Parker Dam, Havasu
Lake, California

210-211   Konrad Wachsmann

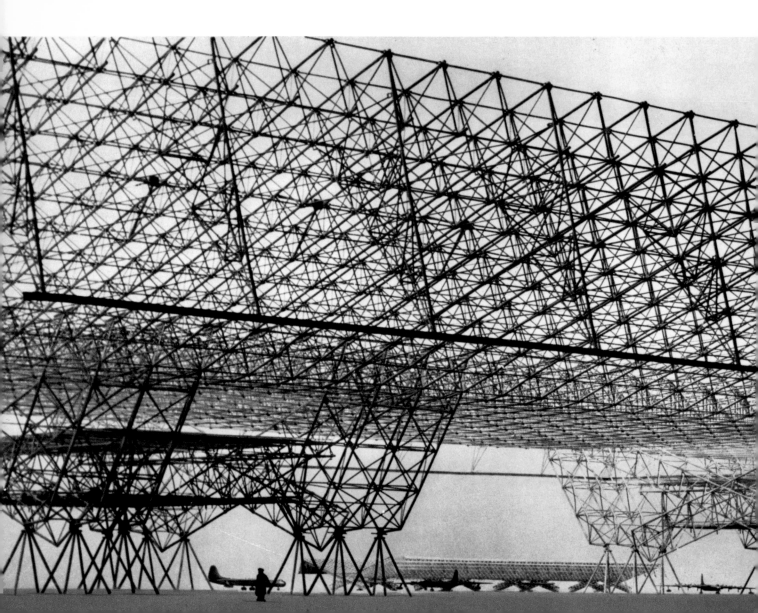

212 Constant

213 Jean Tinguely

214 Max Bill   215 Alexander Calder

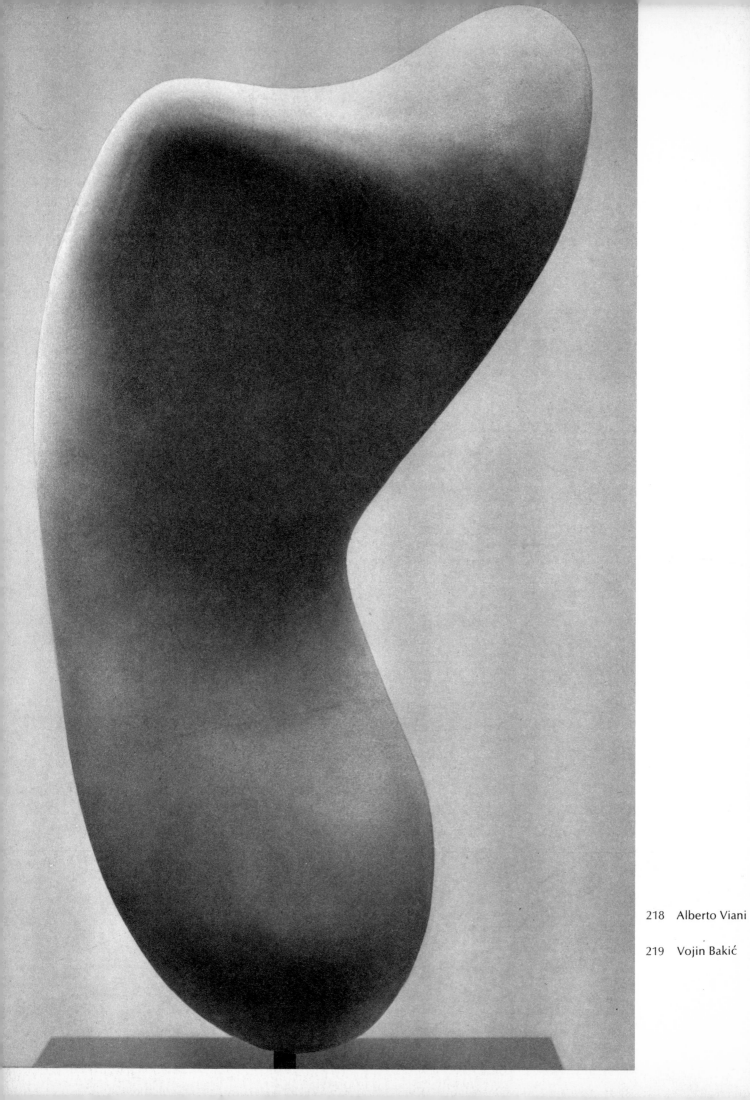

218 Alberto Viani

219 Vojin Bakić

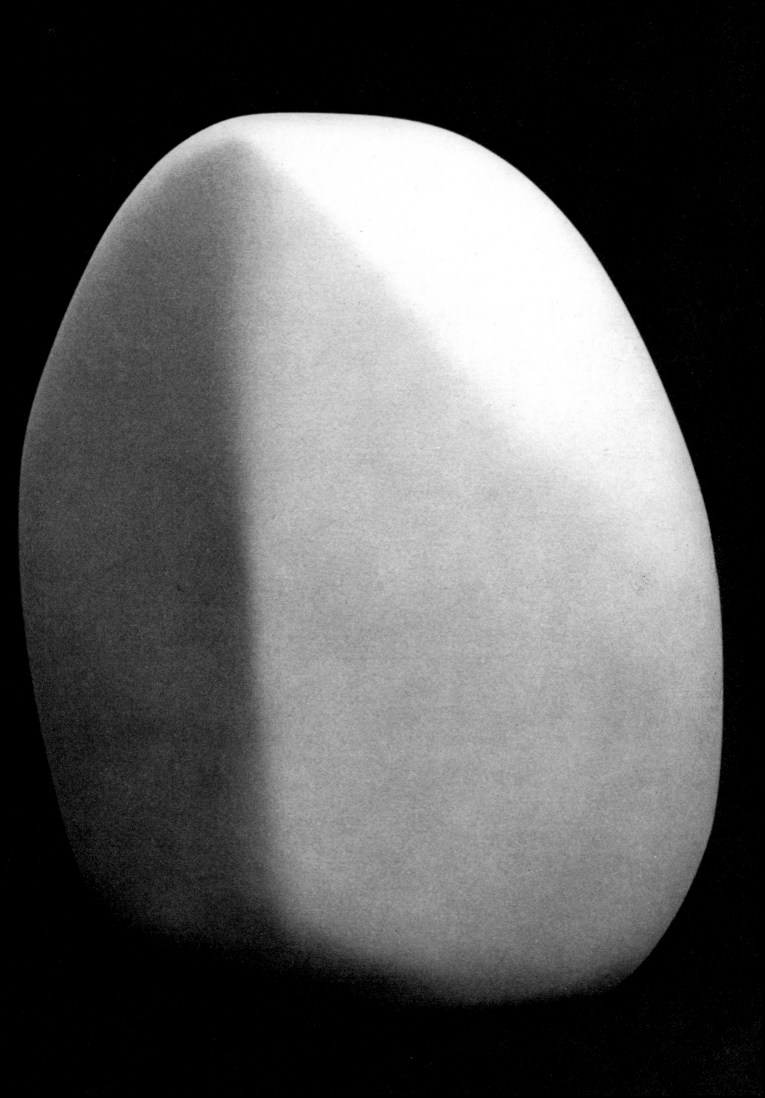

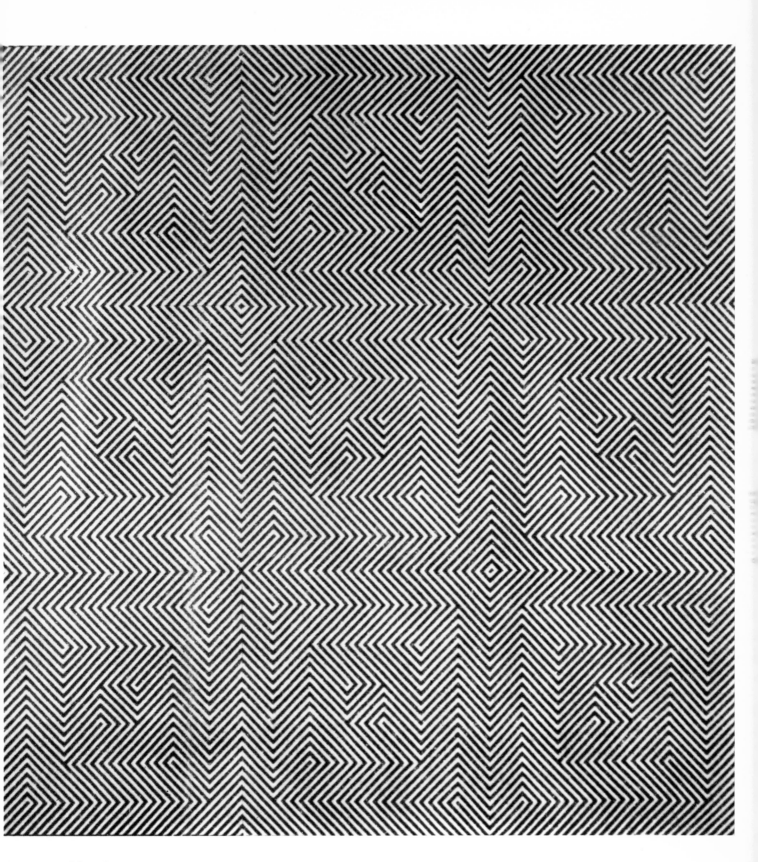

221   Reginald Neal

222 Italian, c. 1225

223 Roman, 1st
century A.D.

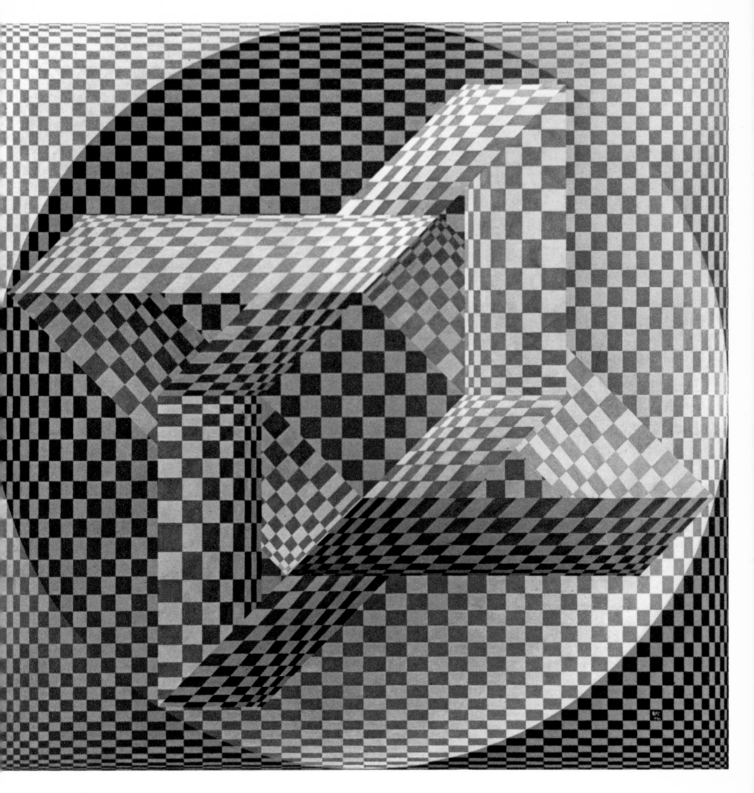

24   Benjamin Frazier Cunningham

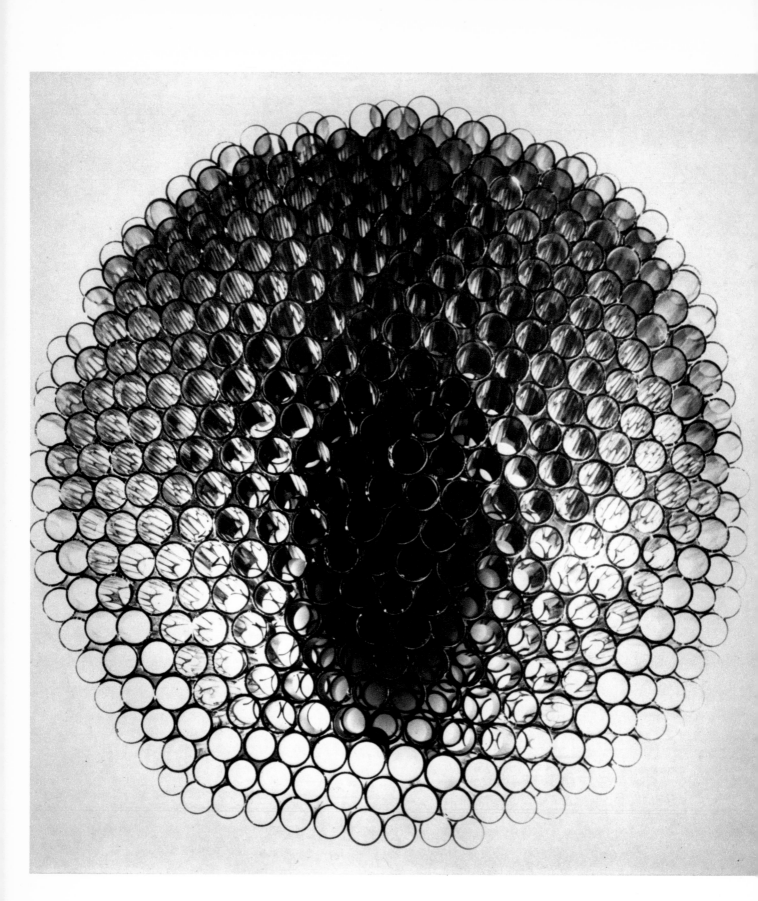

225   Vjenceslav Richter

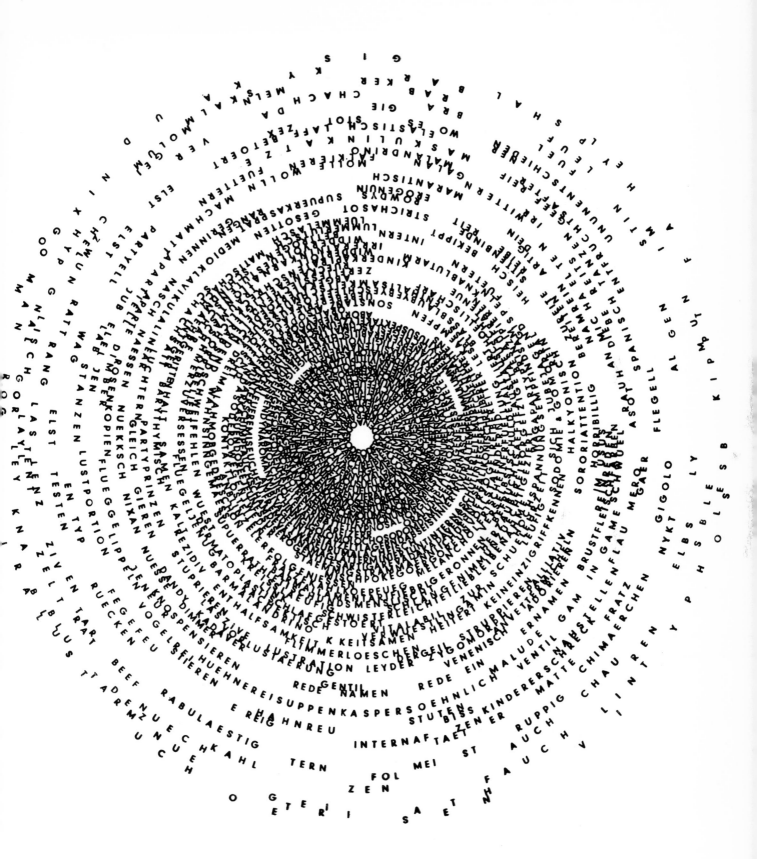

26   Ferdinand Kriwet

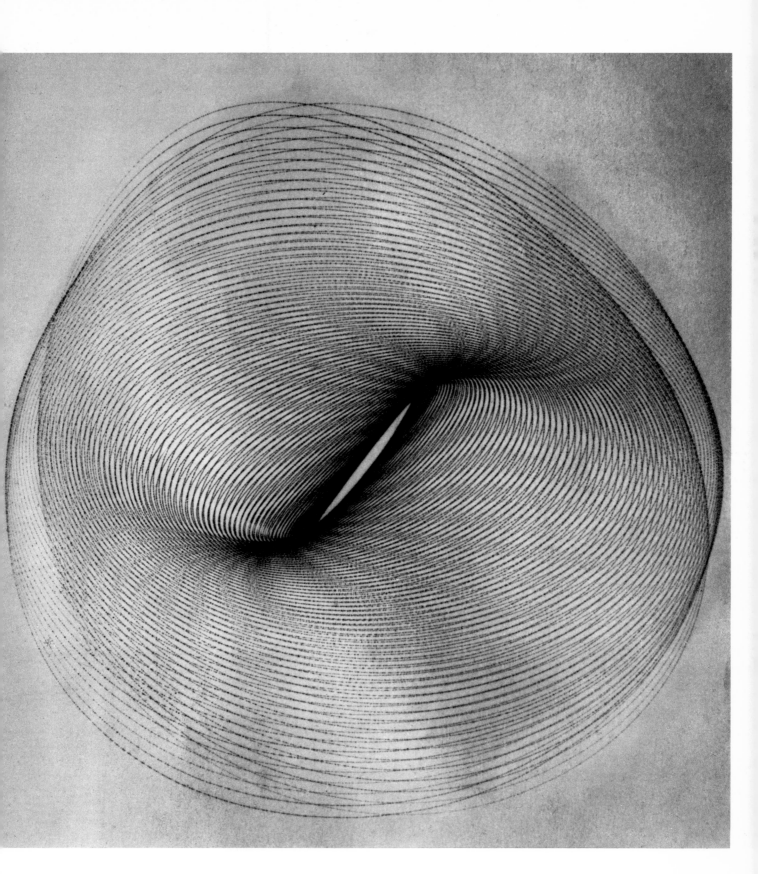

228   Zoran Radović

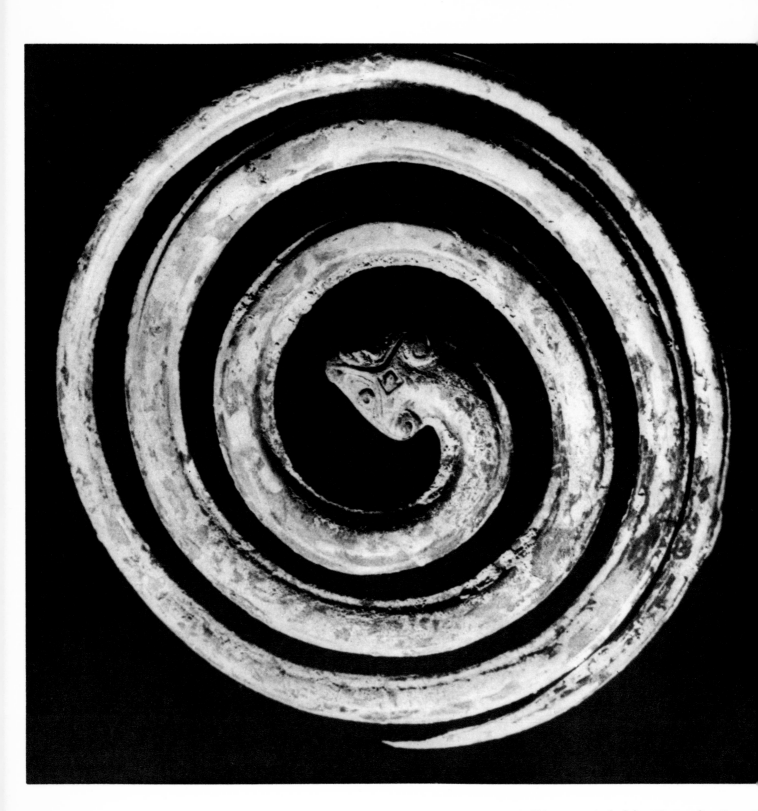

229   Chinese, period of the "Contending States"

230 Tadasky

234 Miroslav Sutej

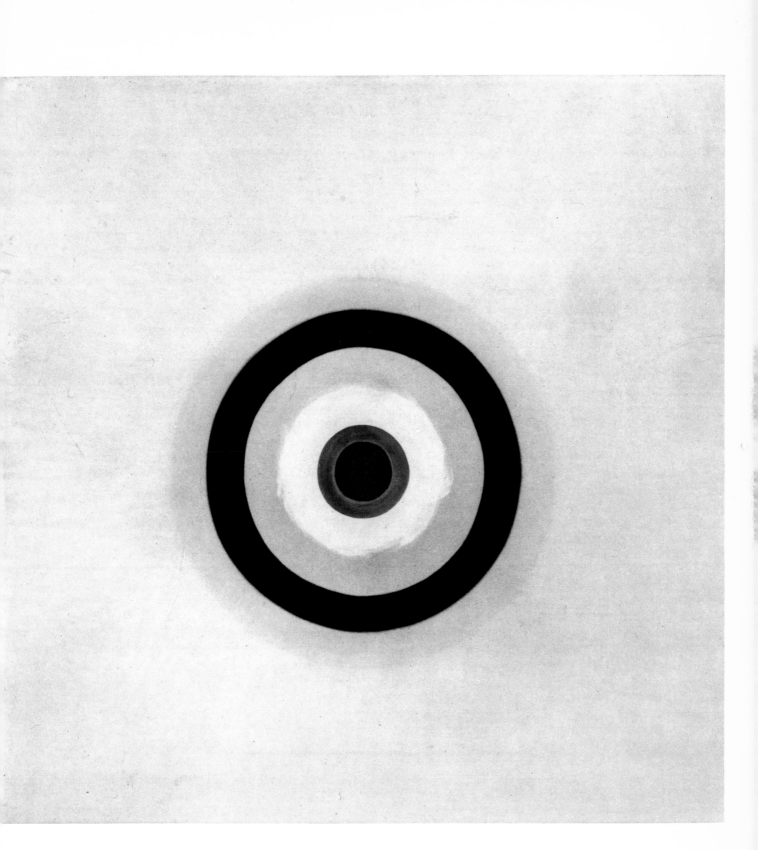

235   Kenneth Noland

236   Barnett Newman

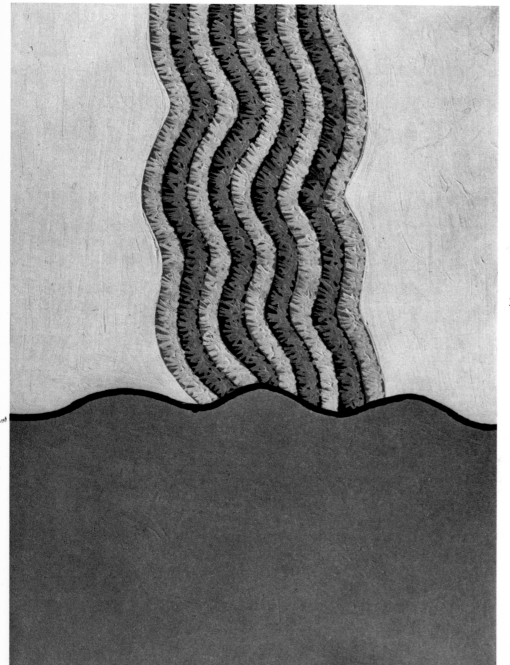

237   Rolf Günther Dienst

238   Bill Komodore

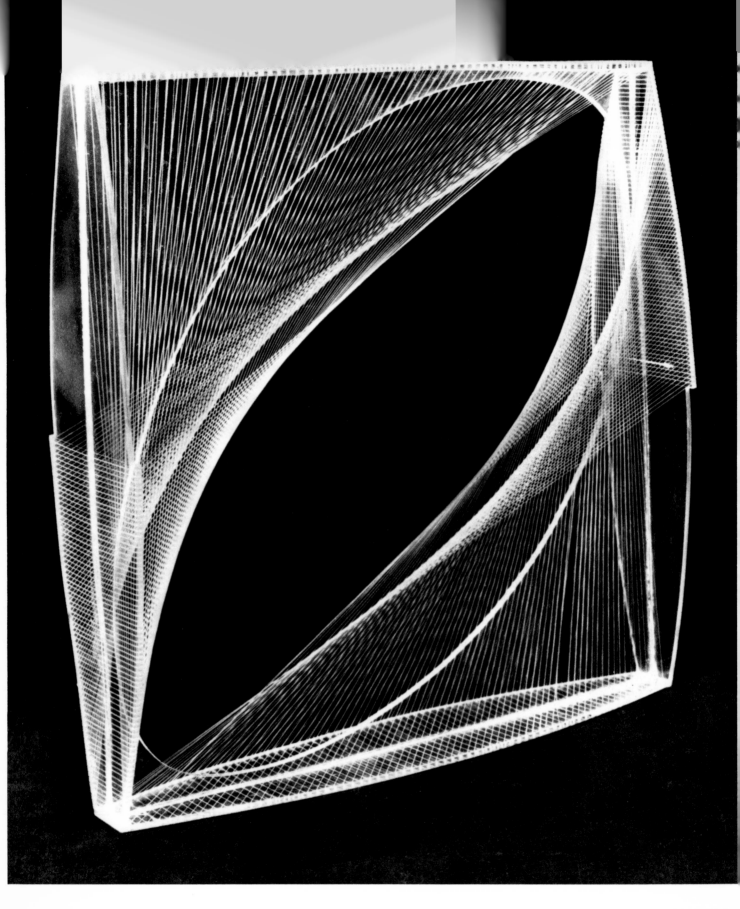

239   Naum Gabo

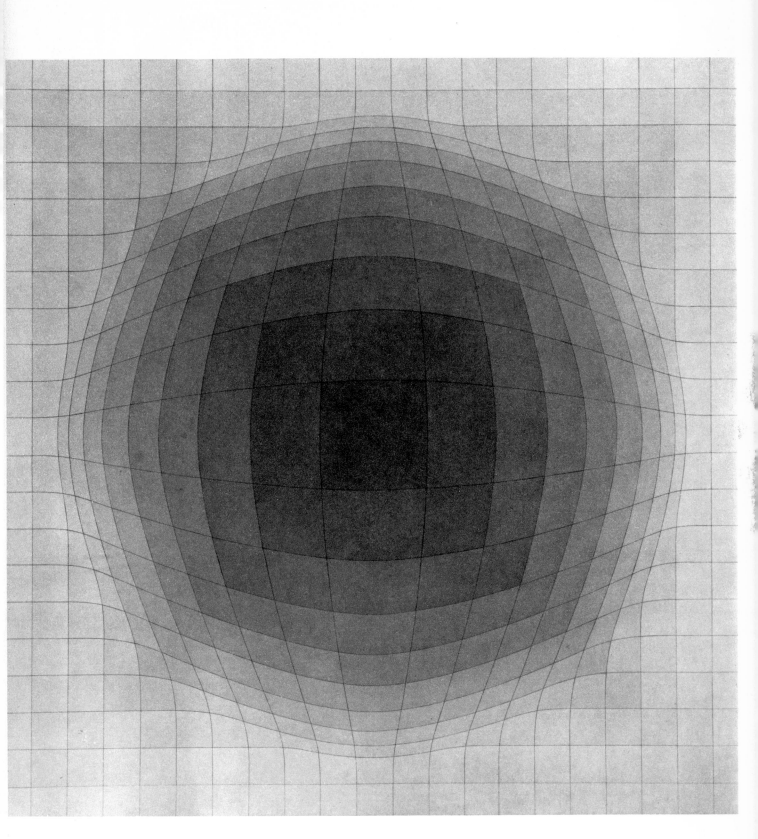

240   Victor de Vasarely

241 Frank Stella

242 Benjamin Frazier Cunningham

243 Byzantine

244   Josef Alber

ürgen Fischer

247   Ivan Picelj

248   Vojin Bakić

249   Wojciech Fangor

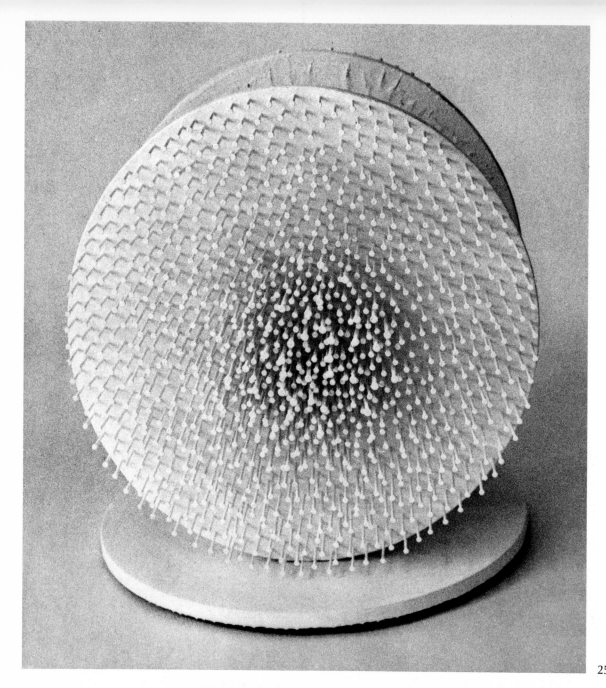

252 Günther Uecker

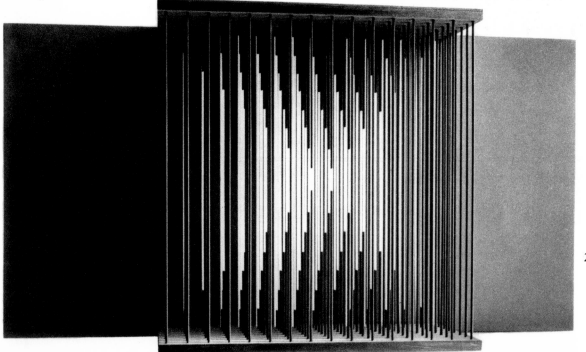

253 Yvaral

254   Heinz Mack

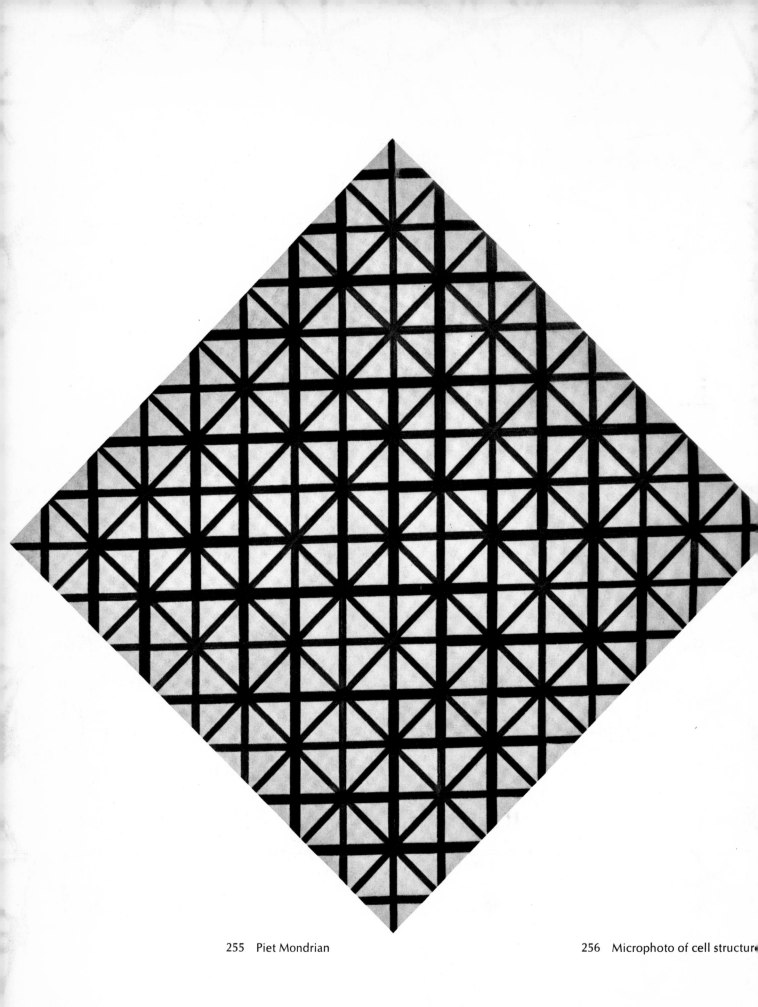

255   Piet Mondrian

256   Microphoto of cell structure

257   François Stahly

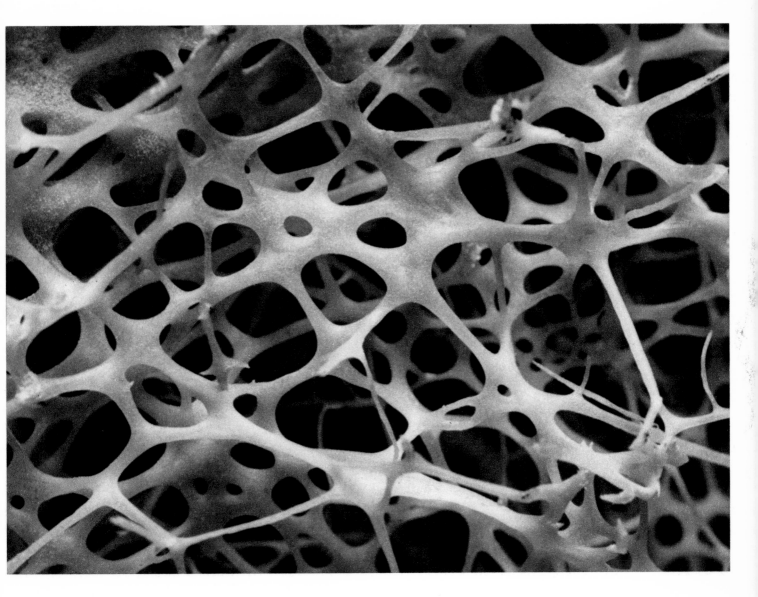

258   Microphoto of human trabeculae

259   Serge Poliakoff

260   Microphoto of a sea louse shell

261   Wassily Kandinsky

262   Brillauin Zone structure of bismuth

263 Zoltan Kemeny

264 Microphoto of the surface of silver

265 Robert Delaunay

266 Microphoto of the surface of zinc

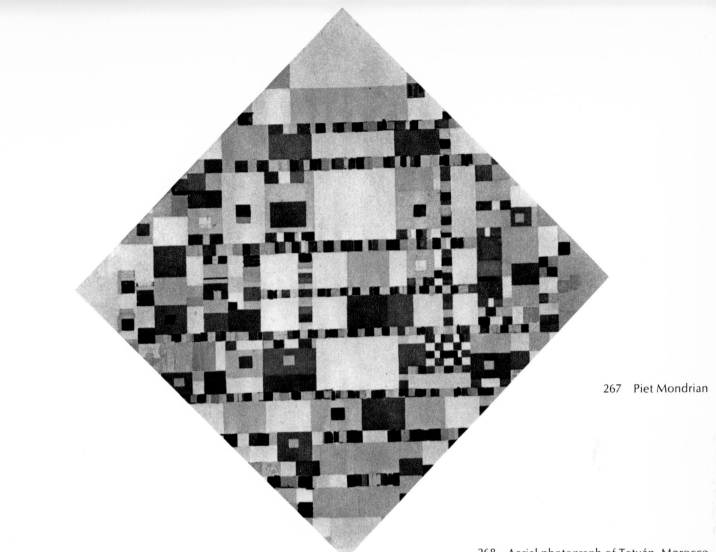

267 Piet Mondrian

268 Aerial photograph of Tetuán, Morocco

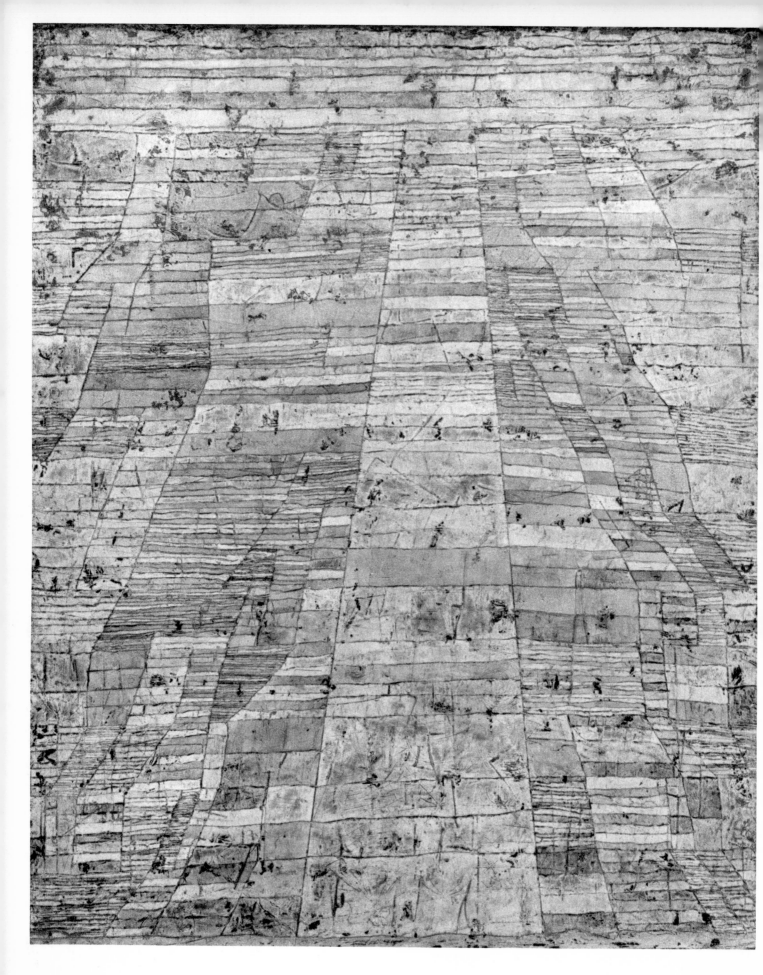

269 Paul Klee

270   Aerial photograph of farmland

271 Surface of the earth from 160 miles

272   K. R. H. Sonderborg

273 Max Ernst

274 The moon

275 Wassily Kandinsky

276 Honest John rocket

277   Wols

278   Detonation of an atom bomb

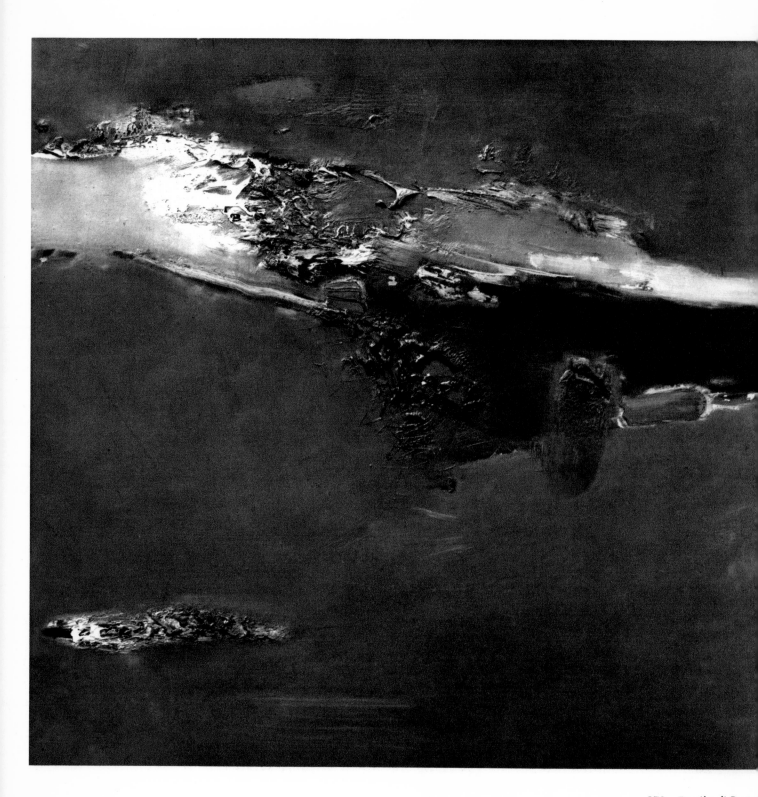

280   Nighttime aerial photograph

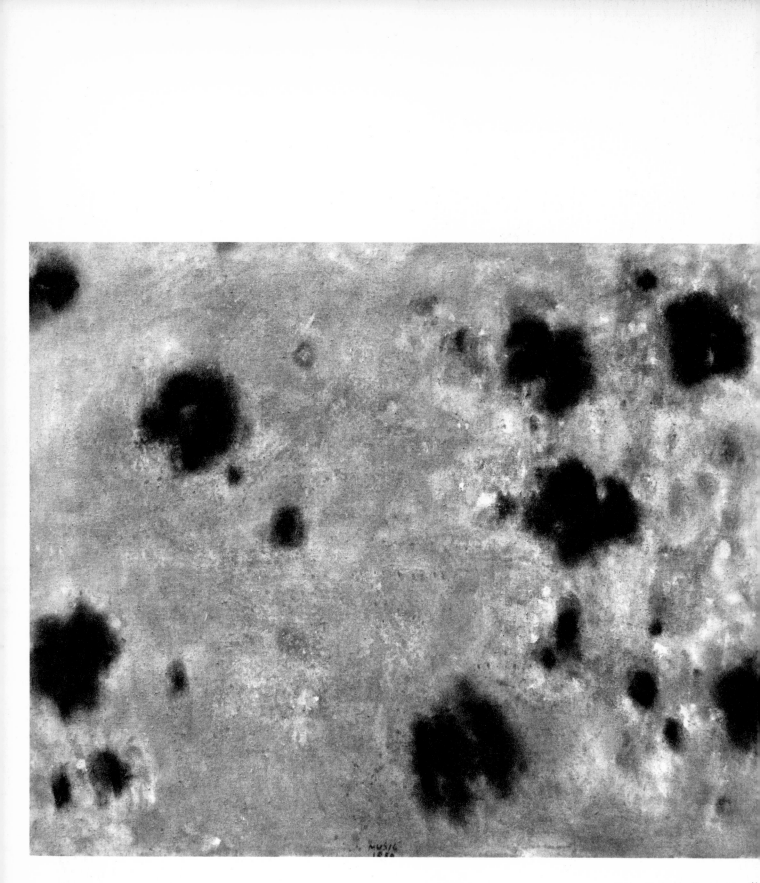

281 Antonio Zoran Musič

SELECTED BIBLIOGRAPHY

Abell, Walter. *The Collective Dream in Art*. Cambridge, Mass., 1957.

Adorno, Theodor W. *Philosophie der neuen Musik*. Tübingen, 1949.

    Prismen. Berlin, 1955.

Baumeister, Willi. *Das Unbekannte in der Kunst*. Cologne, 1960.

Bense, Max. *Ästhetik und Zivilisation*. Baden-Baden, 1958.

Berger, John. *Renato Guttuso*. Dresden, 1955.

Bloch, Ernst. *Das Prinzip Hoffnung*. 3 vols. Berlin, 1954–59.

Brion, Marcel. *Art abstrait*. Paris, 1958.

Broch, Hermann. *Essays*. Zurich, 1955.

Broglie, L. de. *Sens philosophique et portée pratique de la cybernétique*. Paris, 1956.

Cassou, Jean. *Situation de l'art moderne*. Paris, 1950.

Corbusier, Le. *La maison des hommes*. Paris, 1945.

Couffignal, Louis. *Les machines à penser*. Paris, 1952.

Fischer, Ernst. *Von der Notwendigkeit der Kunst*. Dresden, 1959.

Francastel, Pierre. *Art et technique aux XIXe et XXe siècles*. Paris, 1956.

Freud, Sigmund. *Civilization and Its Discontents*. Translated by J. Riviere. New York, 1958.

    Totem and Taboo. Translated by A. A. Brill. New York, 1960.

Giedion, Sigfried. *Architecture, You and Me*. Cambridge, Mass., 1958.

Giedion-Welcker, Carola. *Contemporary Sculpture*. Revised and enlarged ed. New York, 1961.

Goldwater, Robert J. *Primitivism in Modern Painting*. New York, 1958.

Goléa, Antoine. *Esthétique de la musique contemporaine*. Paris, 1954.

Grohmann, Will. *Bildende Kunst und Architektur*. Berlin, 1953.

    Wassily Kandinsky. New York, 1958.

Gropius, Walter. *Scope of Total Architecture*. London, 1956.

Haftmann, Werner. *Painting in the Twentieth Century*. Translated by R. Manheim. 2 vols. New York, 1961.

Hauser, Arnold. *The Philosophy of Art History*. New York, 1959.

    The Social History of Art. 4 vols. New York, 1957–58.

Hofmann, Werner. *Die Plastik des zwanzigsten Jahrhunderts*. Berlin, 1958.

Hollitscher, Walter. *Die Natur im Weltbild der Wissenschaft*. Vienna, 1960.

Jaspers, Karl. *The Origin and Goal of History*. Translated by M. Bullock. New Haven, 1953.

Jung, Carl Gustav. *The Archetypes and the Collective Unconscious*. Translated by R. F. C. Hull. New York, 1959.

    Bewusstes und Unbewusstes. Frankfurt, 1957.

—and Kerényi, K. *Essays on a Science of Mythology*. Translated by R. F. C. Hull. New York, 1949.

Neumann, Erich. *The Great Mother*. Translated by Ralph Manheim. 2nd ed. New York, 1964.

Neumann, J. von. *Mathematical Foundation of Quantum Mechanics*. Princeton, 1955.

Read, Herbert. *Art and Society,* 3d. ed. London, 1956.

    The Tenth Muse. New York, 1958.

Secker, Hans F. *Diego Rivera*. Dresden, 1957.

Seuphor, Michel. *Abstract Painting*. Translated by H. Chevalier. New York, 1961.

Stearns, Marshall W. *The Story of Jazz*. New York, 1956.

Suzuki, D. T. *Zen and Japanese Culture*. New York, 1959.

Toynbee, A. J. *Civilization on Trial*. New York, 1948.

Wiener, Norbert. *The Human Use of Human Beings; Cybernetics and Society*. Boston, 1950.

Winkel, F. and others. "Klangstruktur der Musik, Neue Erkenntnisse," in *Musikelektronischer Forschung*. Berlin, 1955.

INDEX OF PROPER NAMES

Numerals in **bold face type** refer to illustration numbers.